# The Top UK Pharmaceutical Wholesalers

Profiles of the leading 2800 companies

John D Blackburn

Editor

dp

First Edition

Summer 2019

ISBN-13: 978-1-912736-27-0

ISBN-10: 1-912736-27-6

All rights reserved. No part of this publication may be reproduced, distributed, or transmitted in any form or by any means, including photocopying, recording, or other electronic or mechanical methods, without our prior written permission, except in the case of brief quotations embodied in critical reviews and certain other non-commercial uses permitted by copyright law. For permission requests, please write to us.

Copyright © 2019 Dellam Publishing Limited

Printed in 8pt Nimbus Sans L

Designed by URW++ Design and Development GmbH

Dellam Publishing Limited

2 Heath Drive, Sutton, Surrey, SM2 5RP

Fax: 020 8770 7478    email: enquiries@dellam.com

SAN: 0177881    EAN/GLN: 5030670177882

## Table of Contents

1 Acknowledgements .................................................................. iv

2 Introduction .......................................................................... v

3 Total Assets League Table ........................................................ 1

- As a measure of size, total assets is preferable to turnover which is influenced by profit margins and whether companies are capital or labour intensive.

4 Age of Companies ................................................................. 19

- Each company is ranked by its date of incorporation. Newcomers are defined as those registered since 2017.

5 Geographic Distribution ......................................................... 35

- Each company is classed by county.

6 Company Profiles ................................................................. 51

- Full company name, date incorporated, net worth, total assets, registered office, activities, shareholders and parent company, directors (with date of birth, nationality and occupation) and number of employees (if available).

7 Index of Directorships .......................................................... 229

- Alphabetical list of directors showing their directorships. If several directors have identical names then their date of birth is shown.

8 Standard Industrial Classification ........................................... 293

- These codes are used to classify businesses by the type of economic activity in which they are engaged.

9 *finis* ............................................................................... 305

# Acknowledgements

This is a long and detailed publication containing thousands of facts and figures. It is only to be expected, despite continuous and repeated editing and checking, that errors may occur. In such cases, once we are aware of any, we publish a correction on our website.

**Readers are encouraged to check regularly at www.dellam.com/books for any corrections and updates.**

Although we take extreme care to ensure accuracy and being up-to-date, we cannot accept responsibility for any errors or omissions.

Contains public sector information licensed under Open Government Licence v3.0. from The Charity Commission (England and Wales) and The Charity Commission for Northern Ireland. © Crown Copyright and database right (2018).

Contains information from the Scottish Charity Register supplied by the Office of the Scottish Charity Regulator and licensed under the Open Government Licence v.2.0. © Crown Copyright and database right (2018).

Contains OS data © Crown copyright and database right (2018)

Contains Royal Mail data © Royal Mail copyright and database right (2018)

Contains National Statistics data © Crown copyright and database right (2018)

Contains Office for National Statistics © Crown copyright and database right (2018)

Maps based on those produced by the Office for National Statistics Geography GIS & Mapping Unit (2012 and 2018).

Contains HM Land Registry data © Crown copyright and database right (2018).

Contains Parliamentary information licensed under the Open Parliament Licence v3.0.

House of Commons Library Briefing Papers licensed under the Open Parliament Licence v3.0.

Contains Food Standards Agency data © Crown copyright and database right (2018).

Contains Eurostat data, 1995-2018, copyright European Commission by the Decision of 12 December 2011.

Maps based on produced by ONS Geography GIS & Mapping Unit.

Contains Companies House data supplied under section 47 and 50 of the Copyright, Designs and Patents Act 1988 and Schedule 1 of the Database Regulations (SI 1997/3032).

We appreciate your interest in our publications, and your comments and suggestions are always welcome. Please contact us at enquiries@dellam.com.

# Introduction

This study looks at all companies registered in the United Kingdom where they identify themselves as wholesalers of pharmaceutical goods.

This study includes companies that are dormant or non-trading some of which might be latent while others may operate under their owners' names but incorporate to protect the business name. In addition, all newly incorporated companies are included. The study will exclude those companies that do not specifically identify themselves as wholesalers of pharmaceutical goods.

The aim of this study is to provide an overview of the key movers and shakers in the UK pharmaceutical wholesale sector. Only key data has been isolated, particularly the company's net worth and total assets, but also its full name, date incorporated, registered office, other activities, shareholders, directors (with date of birth, occupation and nationality) and number of employees.

Two indicators of size are used: net worth and total assets. These are preferable to turnover which is influenced by profit margins and whether the companies are capital or labour intensive.

In the years 2016, 2017 and 2018, new company incorporations in the pharmaceutical wholesale sector were 188, 258 and 483 respectively.

In 1966, the National Association of Pharmaceutical Distributors (NAPD) was formed, which became from 1991, the British Association of Pharmaceutical Wholesalers or BAPW. In 2016, BAPW rebranded itself the Healthcare Distribution Association UK (HCA).

The HCA represents businesses who supply medicines, medical devices and healthcare services for patients, pharmacies, hospitals, dispensing doctors and the pharmaceutical industry. Their members distribute over 90% of NHS medicines.

GIRP, 'Groupement International de la Repartition Pharmaceutique' or 'European Association of Pharmaceutical Full-line Wholesalers', is the umbrella organisation of pharmaceutical full-line wholesalers in Europe.

The Pharmaceutical Services Negotiating Committee (PSNC) promotes and supports the interests of all NHS community pharmacies in England. Community pharmacists were known in the past as chemists.

The Commercial Medicines Unit (CMU) is part of the Medicine, Pharmacy and Industry Group of the Department of Health & Social Care which looks at supply and procurement in hospitals.

Pharmaceutical full-line wholesalers carry the full range of medicinal products and they own their stock. Nearly three-quarters of all medicines sold in Europe are distributed through pharmaceutical full-line wholesalers.

The market growth of the pharmaceutical wholesale sector has risen slowly. This is mainly due to the growing importance of alternative distribution systems such as Direct-to-Pharmacy (DTP) and Reduced Wholesale Agreements (RWA).

Standard cataloguing guidelines for company names in the profile section have been used, but there will be occurrences when the name may not be strictly alphabetical. A certain licence was adopted where it was felt that strictly alphabetical could lead to improper cataloguing. Some company names have been shortened in the league tables for aesthetic reasons.

John D Blackburn
Editor

*This page is intentionally left blank*

# Total Assets League Table

# The Top UK Pharmaceutical Wholesalers

| Company | Value |
|---|---|
| Astrazeneca PLC | £63,353,999,360 |
| CSL Behring Holdings Limited | £10,703,140,864 |
| ViiV Healthcare UK Limited | £7,015,779,840 |
| ViiV Healthcare Trading Services UK Limited | £3,306,328,064 |
| McKesson Global Procurement & Sourcing Limited | £3,192,374,272 |
| Pfizer Limited | £1,879,758,976 |
| Astellas Pharma Europe Ltd. | £1,343,135,104 |
| Alliance Healthcare (Distribution) Limited | £1,248,999,936 |
| AAH Pharmaceuticals Limited | £999,052,032 |
| Accord Healthcare Limited | £891,985,984 |
| Stada UK Holdings Ltd. | £861,665,920 |
| GlaxoSmithKline Consumer Trading Services Ltd | £781,051,008 |
| GlaxoSmithKline UK Limited | £723,723,008 |
| RB UK Commercial Limited | £689,331,008 |
| Clinigen Group PLC | £594,351,360 |
| Baxalta UK Investments Ltd. | £557,806,848 |
| Phoenix Healthcare Distribution Limited | £510,484,992 |
| Hoechst Marion Roussel Limited | £480,816,000 |
| Phoenix Medical Supplies Limited | £470,598,016 |
| GlaxoSmithKline Export Limited | £447,628,000 |
| Alloga UK Limited | £442,500,992 |
| Abbott Laboratories Limited | £428,572,000 |
| AbbVie Ltd | £398,508,992 |
| Aventis Pharma Limited | £373,788,000 |
| Bayer Public Limited Company | £350,952,992 |
| Napp Pharmaceutical Holdings Limited | £304,665,984 |
| Mundipharma Medical Company Limited | £298,486,304 |
| Piramal Critical Care Limited | £276,387,680 |
| Pfizer Consumer Healthcare Limited | £256,190,000 |
| Clinigen Healthcare Limited | £230,024,000 |
| McNeil Healthcare (UK) Limited | £210,890,000 |
| Celgene Limited | £190,243,632 |
| Servier IP UK Limited | £189,847,904 |
| National Veterinary Services Limited | £165,203,008 |
| Lloyds Pharmacy Clinical Homecare Limited | £155,136,992 |
| EUSA Pharma (UK) Limited | £152,351,008 |
| Astellas Pharma Ltd. | £133,302,000 |
| ViiV Healthcare Overseas Limited | £131,581,000 |
| Zimmer Biomet UK Limited | £127,072,000 |
| Eisai Limited | £126,478,576 |
| Barclay Pharmaceuticals Limited | £126,254,000 |
| Eco Animal Health Group PLC | £117,185,000 |
| Leadiant Biosciences Limited | £112,069,976 |
| OTC Direct Limited | £111,000,000 |
| McKesson Global Sourcing UK Limited | £110,886,528 |
| Lexon (UK) Limited | £110,045,000 |
| Laxmi BNS Holdings Limited | £109,609,696 |
| Gilead Sciences Ltd | £109,323,000 |
| Zoetis UK Limited | £106,904,000 |
| Novo Nordisk Limited | £106,459,000 |
| Beiersdorf UK Ltd. | £103,750,000 |
| Sigma Pharmaceuticals PLC | £101,851,080 |
| Genzyme Therapeutics Limited | £101,503,000 |
| Intercept Pharma Europe Ltd. | £98,879,544 |
| Allergan Limited | £98,128,000 |
| RB (China Trading) Limited | £96,318,000 |
| Leo Laboratories Limited | £95,717,000 |
| Mylan UK Healthcare Limited | £94,587,000 |
| Colgate-Palmolive (U.K.) Limited | £92,973,000 |
| Idis Group Holdings Limited | £92,804,000 |
| Movianto UK Limited | £92,244,000 |
| Takeda UK Limited | £91,023,712 |
| Day Lewis Medical Limited | £88,973,000 |
| Napp Pharmaceutical Group Limited | £87,942,000 |
| Idis Limited | £81,621,000 |
| Reckitt Benckiser Asia Pacific Limited | £80,899,000 |
| Mawdsley-Brooks & Company Limited | £80,231,000 |
| Euro Capital Management (ECM) Ltd | £80,000,000 |
| Galen Limited | £77,070,872 |
| Chiesi Limited | £76,823,000 |
| CooperVision Lens Care Limited | £75,802,000 |
| Shire Pharmaceuticals Limited | £75,774,000 |
| Testerworld Limited | £75,448,000 |
| Mundibiopharma Limited | £75,442,888 |
| Laxmico Limited | £75,175,608 |
| Boots International Limited | £74,912,000 |
| Glaxo Wellcome UK Limited | £71,871,000 |
| Bristol Laboratories Limited | £69,361,760 |
| Omega Pharma Limited | £67,744,000 |
| CSL Behring UK Limited | £60,219,000 |
| Merck Serono Limited | £60,114,000 |
| Britannia Pharmaceuticals Limited | £59,009,000 |
| Genus Pharmaceuticals Limited | £58,685,000 |
| Ethigen Limited | £53,002,624 |
| Alcura UK Limited | £52,400,000 |
| Glenmark Pharmaceuticals Europe Limited | £50,697,828 |
| Meda Pharmaceuticals Limited | £47,692,000 |
| Crescent Pharma Limited | £47,265,104 |
| Fittleworth Medical Limited | £45,724,332 |
| Waymade PLC | £44,720,000 |
| Genus Pharmaceuticals Holdings Limited | £44,398,000 |
| Chemidex Generics Limited | £42,801,256 |
| Munro Healthcare Group Limited | £42,710,328 |
| Abbott Healthcare Products Ltd | £42,670,000 |
| Prinwest Limited | £42,520,968 |
| Napp Pharmaceuticals Limited | £41,612,000 |
| Medreich PLC | £40,756,208 |
| Vygon (U.K.) Limited | £38,871,000 |
| Rayburn Trading Company Limited | £37,746,036 |
| GlaxoSmithKline Caribbean Limited | £37,655,000 |
| Galpharm International Limited | £37,058,000 |
| Smartway Pharmaceuticals Limited | £36,737,676 |
| Emcure Pharma UK Ltd | £36,279,172 |
| Gowrie Laxmico Limited | £35,392,188 |
| Bestway Pharmacy NDC Limited | £35,142,000 |
| Ontex Retail UK Limited | £35,052,964 |
| Drugsrus Limited | £34,788,344 |
| Orion Pharma (UK) Limited | £34,228,440 |

# The Top UK Pharmaceutical Wholesalers

| | | | |
|---|---|---|---|
| Bausch & Lomb U.K. Limited | £33,713,000 | Vifor Pharma UK Limited | £17,251,612 |
| Pharmaceuticals Direct Limited | £33,313,492 | Tillomed Laboratories Limited | £17,229,562 |
| Aspire Pharma Holdings Limited | £32,370,296 | Galderma (U.K.) Limited | £16,943,000 |
| C. S. T. Pharma Limited | £31,923,000 | Durbin PLC | £16,542,647 |
| Essential Pharma Limited | £30,423,222 | Recordati Pharmaceuticals Limited | £16,522,914 |
| Hospira UK Limited | £30,085,000 | Optima Consumer Health Limited | £16,419,000 |
| Sangers (Maidstone) Limited | £29,492,576 | Dr. Falk Pharma UK Limited | £16,351,891 |
| Ennogen Healthcare Ltd | £29,465,110 | Garusa Solutions U.K. Limited | £16,345,721 |
| Scientific Laboratory Supplies Group Ltd | £28,936,802 | Napp Laboratories Limited | £16,254,000 |
| Ranbaxy (U.K.) Limited | £28,360,372 | Norgine Pharmaceuticals Limited | £16,059,000 |
| Milpharm Limited | £27,974,948 | Nupharm Limited | £15,932,000 |
| Donald Wardle and Son Limited | £27,647,000 | BBI Healthcare Limited | £15,836,000 |
| Manor Drug Company (Nottingham) Limited (The) | £27,637,564 | Summit Pharmaceuticals Europe Limited | £15,805,989 |
| Livanova UK Limited | £27,514,002 | Medpro Healthcare Limited | £15,620,344 |
| Respond Healthcare Limited | £27,245,780 | Animalcare Ltd | £15,445,000 |
| Crosspharma Limited | £26,797,434 | BR Pharma International Limited | £15,056,712 |
| United Therapeutics Europe, Ltd. | £26,513,814 | Dechra Veterinary Products Limited | £14,944,000 |
| Nova Laboratories Limited | £26,162,616 | Almirall Limited | £14,548,521 |
| New Horizon Pharma (UK) Ltd. | £25,270,968 | Davis and Dann Limited | £14,469,876 |
| C.D. Medical Limited | £25,161,420 | Veterinary Surgeons Supply Company Limited | £14,182,157 |
| Ipsen Limited | £24,822,000 | Sunovion Pharmaceuticals Europe Ltd. | £14,098,638 |
| Biomarin (U.K.) Ltd. | £24,658,000 | Virbac Limited | £13,986,033 |
| Chemilines Group Holdings Limited | £24,584,000 | Hameln Pharmaceuticals Ltd | £13,764,480 |
| Ethypharm UK Limited | £24,475,888 | Unomedical Limited | £13,679,000 |
| Lundbeck Limited | £23,865,264 | L & R Medical UK Ltd. | £13,387,000 |
| Kanta Enterprises Limited | £23,451,408 | Creo Pharma Limited | £13,160,766 |
| Necessity Supplies Limited | £23,168,152 | Healthaid Holdings Limited | £12,840,210 |
| Pricecheck Toiletries Limited | £23,155,352 | Healthaid Limited | £12,840,210 |
| NSL (Holdings) Limited | £23,026,908 | Torrent Pharma (UK) Ltd | £12,814,323 |
| Sangers (Northern Ireland) Limited | £22,221,564 | Bracco UK Limited | £12,741,000 |
| P & A J Cattee (Wholesale) Ltd. | £22,205,096 | Mediwin Limited | £12,560,318 |
| Omnicell Limited | £22,200,000 | Genesis Pharmaceuticals Limited | £12,483,941 |
| M & A Pharmachem Limited | £21,316,352 | Pearl Chemist Group Limited | £12,396,708 |
| Servier Laboratories Limited | £21,261,000 | Delta Sales Ltd | £12,153,089 |
| Aspire Pharma Limited | £20,881,982 | Toiletry Sales Limited | £12,016,796 |
| Remedi Medical Holdings Limited | £20,844,708 | Cradlecrest Limited | £11,983,000 |
| Morningside Pharmaceuticals Limited | £20,841,896 | Crest Medical Limited | £11,901,093 |
| Strides Pharma Global (UK) Ltd | £20,348,244 | NSL Group Limited | £11,843,580 |
| A1 Pharmaceuticals Holdings Limited | £20,243,268 | SPL (2010) Limited | £11,813,111 |
| Strathclyde Pharmaceuticals Limited | £20,101,060 | NeilMed Holding Company Limited | £11,773,630 |
| Relonchem Limited | £19,773,460 | Allcures PLC | £11,338,690 |
| UK Pharma Impex Limited | £19,698,228 | Lumiradx International Ltd | £11,211,552 |
| Norbrook Laboratories (G.B.) Limited | £19,429,700 | Adelphi (Tubes) Limited | £11,198,076 |
| Bionical Limited | £18,866,000 | Amano Enzyme Europe Limited | £11,170,634 |
| Dexcel-Pharma Limited | £18,824,408 | Clarity Pharma Holdings Ltd | £11,139,000 |
| Veenak International Limited | £18,264,696 | Beachcourse Limited | £11,048,000 |
| Ferring Pharmaceuticals Limited | £18,245,226 | Interport Limited | £10,890,231 |
| Daiichi Sankyo UK Limited | £18,241,000 | U L Medicines Limited | £10,884,467 |
| Doncaster Pharmaceuticals Group Limited | £18,118,000 | SSCP Blink Bidco Limited | £10,881,720 |
| Disposable Medical Equipment Ltd | £18,083,790 | Clarity Pharma Ltd | £10,866,000 |
| Focus Pharmaceuticals Limited | £18,041,368 | L E West Ltd | £10,622,399 |
| A1 Pharmaceuticals Public Limited Company | £18,008,192 | Marlborough Pharmaceuticals Limited | £10,607,300 |
| Restate Management Ltd | £17,690,850 | Kays Medical Limited | £10,598,522 |
| Attends Limited | £17,365,974 | Clinimed Limited | £10,438,991 |

| | | | |
|---|---:|---|---:|
| Qdem Pharmaceuticals Limited | £10,346,000 | N.G. Limited | £7,209,579 |
| P.I.E. Pharma Limited | £10,276,358 | Pharmacosmos UK Limited | £7,102,583 |
| Kosei Pharma UK Ltd. | £10,155,097 | Chiesi Healthcare Limited | £7,054,000 |
| Chemilines Limited | £10,114,000 | Neilmed Limited | £6,988,272 |
| Agrihealth (N.I.) Limited | £10,024,094 | Kobayashi Healthcare Europe Limited | £6,985,520 |
| K. Waterhouse Limited | £9,957,925 | Stephar (U.K.) Limited | £6,978,415 |
| Guerbet Laboratories Limited | £9,877,870 | Ananta Medicare Ltd | £6,967,040 |
| Miller & Miller (Chemicals) Limited | £9,843,544 | S & D Pharma Limited | £6,941,872 |
| Masters Pharmaceuticals Limited | £9,841,748 | G. D. Cooper & Co Ltd | £6,912,176 |
| Nexcape Pharmaceuticals Ltd | £9,836,359 | Veriton Pharma Limited | £6,863,314 |
| Kinetic Enterprises Limited | £9,694,988 | Carbosynth Limited | £6,821,055 |
| Manichem Limited | £9,575,481 | Reliance Medical Ltd | £6,815,029 |
| Soho Flordis UK Limited | £9,538,450 | East Midlands Pharma Limited | £6,809,674 |
| Paul Hartmann Limited | £9,515,031 | Macks Ltd. | £6,780,867 |
| Ivor Shaw Limited | £9,485,436 | Pharmacy Supplies Limited | £6,674,295 |
| Pharm - Tex Limited | £9,446,986 | Healthpoint Limited | £6,661,664 |
| Dallas Burston Ashbourne Holdings Limited | £9,415,455 | Cellpath Limited | £6,661,234 |
| The Orange Square Company Ltd. | £9,386,181 | Shakespeare Pharma Ltd | £6,530,141 |
| Lupin Healthcare (UK) Limited | £9,375,929 | Medicare Products Limited | £6,449,164 |
| Beta Pharmaceuticals Limited | £9,334,672 | Alium Medical Limited | £6,375,887 |
| Manx Healthcare Limited | £9,309,355 | Farah Chemists Limited | £6,213,487 |
| A. Menarini Diagnostics Limited | £9,254,251 | Focus Pharma Holdings Limited | £6,046,418 |
| Nipro Diagnostics (UK) Limited | £9,189,512 | Servipharm Limited | £6,037,450 |
| New England Biolabs (U.K.) Limited | £9,168,252 | Discovery Pharmaceuticals Limited | £6,035,042 |
| Merz Pharma UK Limited | £9,142,150 | Prometheus Medical Ltd | £5,913,449 |
| Grunenthal Limited | £9,133,000 | Medartis Limited | £5,855,772 |
| Real Estate Alliance Ltd | £9,032,047 | Beechcroft Supplies Limited | £5,839,282 |
| Liam Bradley Ltd | £8,967,744 | Elite Pharma (Surrey) Limited | £5,760,431 |
| Vision Pharmaceuticals Ltd | £8,731,841 | Wilkinson Healthcare Limited | £5,712,483 |
| Pharmalab Limited | £8,720,000 | Arrowedge Limited | £5,676,449 |
| Hamilton Pharmaceuticals Ltd | £8,637,963 | Doncaster Pharmaceuticals Limited | £5,645,959 |
| Apollo Endosurgery UK Ltd | £8,624,000 | Medi-Gen Limited | £5,590,000 |
| Alissa Healthcare Research Limited | £8,606,352 | Healthcare 21 (UK) Limited | £5,497,000 |
| Abra Wholesales Ltd | £8,568,692 | M & N Traders Limited | £5,473,454 |
| Goldsmith Resources Limited | £8,482,515 | Acer Pharma Limited | £5,345,774 |
| Bioforce (U.K) Limited | £8,409,181 | C & P Medical Trading Limited | £5,296,407 |
| Thea Pharmaceuticals Limited | £8,378,239 | Omron Healthcare UK Limited | £5,192,664 |
| Countrywide Healthcare Supplies Holdings Limited | £8,314,353 | Santen UK Limited | £5,183,131 |
| Ypsomed Limited | £8,237,436 | Surgitrac Instruments UK Limited | £5,181,813 |
| Perricone MD Cosmeceuticals UK Limited | £8,062,350 | Steritech Limited | £5,168,218 |
| Uno Healthcare Limited | £8,004,642 | Galar Ireland Ltd | £5,149,057 |
| Lil-Lets UK Ltd | £7,884,000 | Pharmasure Limited | £5,113,464 |
| Masta Limited | £7,836,798 | R.A. Racey (Gt. Yarmouth) Limited | £5,105,723 |
| Scope Ophthalmics Limited | £7,732,882 | Richardson Healthcare Limited | £5,061,057 |
| Iam Finance Limited | £7,646,464 | Medimpex UK Limited | £5,038,348 |
| Eclipse Generics Limited | £7,610,000 | Pennine UK Procedure Packs Limited | £5,000,000 |
| Bowmed Ibisqus Limited | £7,604,834 | WE Pharma Ltd | £4,998,185 |
| Brancaster Pharma Limited | £7,555,798 | Periproducts Limited | £4,960,000 |
| Gedeon Richter (UK) Limited | £7,527,196 | Icone International Limited | £4,924,762 |
| Paul Murray PLC | £7,488,329 | Biotest (U.K.) Limited | £4,907,940 |
| Aegerion Pharmaceuticals Limited | £7,445,512 | Alston Garrard & Co Limited | £4,885,612 |
| Spatone Limited | £7,425,000 | Melyd Medical Limited | £4,883,980 |
| ACG Europe Limited | £7,396,577 | Sovereign House Properties Limited | £4,879,000 |
| Insight Health Limited | £7,233,995 | Greiner Bio-One Limited | £4,827,444 |

# The Top UK Pharmaceutical Wholesalers

| Company | Revenue | Company | Revenue |
|---|---|---|---|
| Medi UK Ltd | £4,797,893 | Boston Healthcare Limited | £3,345,252 |
| Zecare Limited | £4,738,532 | Nucare Limited | £3,335,000 |
| Otsuka Pharmaceuticals (U.K.) Ltd. | £4,729,414 | Coramandel Limited | £3,299,657 |
| Knox Pharmaceuticals Limited | £4,664,978 | Aver Generics Limited | £3,295,417 |
| Rayner Pharmaceuticals Limited | £4,651,000 | Atnahs Pharma US Limited | £3,258,626 |
| Nordic Pharma Limited | £4,628,868 | Prima Brands Limited | £3,227,410 |
| ET Browne (UK) Limited | £4,616,082 | Mediva Pharma Limited | £3,200,779 |
| SP Services (UK) Limited | £4,571,751 | Cadila Pharmaceuticals (Europe) Limited | £3,200,216 |
| Purple Surgical UK Limited | £4,487,534 | Specialty Pharma of London Ltd | £3,198,265 |
| Idea Medica Limited | £4,422,632 | Whyte International Limited | £3,185,288 |
| Opalbond Limited | £4,386,072 | IQ Pharma Ltd | £3,171,426 |
| Principle Healthcare Limited | £4,341,947 | 11 Health & Technologies Limited | £3,153,145 |
| Dakota Pharma Limited | £4,299,038 | Actipharm Limited | £3,133,726 |
| Inter Trade Pharma Limited | £4,239,008 | Wonder World Ltd | £3,084,576 |
| Coombe KP Limited | £4,177,647 | CIGA Healthcare Limited | £3,005,476 |
| Fagron UK Ltd | £4,149,983 | OPD Laboratories Limited | £2,976,591 |
| Alk-Abello Limited | £4,138,556 | Purple Surgical International Limited | £2,949,368 |
| Kinesis Limited | £4,107,392 | Chanelle Medical U.K. Limited | £2,945,904 |
| Linepharma International Limited | £4,059,916 | Excel Health Care Limited | £2,938,233 |
| Ascend Laboratories (UK) Limited | £3,994,757 | Meditec International England Limited | £2,931,821 |
| Curium Pharma UK Ltd. | £3,979,374 | Alan Spivack Limited | £2,902,353 |
| Mossvet Limited | £3,952,923 | MGC Pharma (UK) Ltd | £2,896,542 |
| Syner-Medica Limited | £3,932,237 | Dispensing Healthcare Ltd | £2,871,178 |
| R.B. Radley & Company Limited | £3,923,011 | EMT Healthcare Limited | £2,865,794 |
| Lifecell EMEA Limited | £3,918,294 | Orphan Europe (UK) Limited | £2,853,200 |
| Butt & Hobbs Limited | £3,914,678 | Europharma Scotland Ltd | £2,814,880 |
| Berkshire Wholesale Supplies (2002) Ltd | £3,897,672 | Swingward Limited | £2,808,811 |
| Islestone Limited | £3,879,988 | Neon Diagnostics Ltd | £2,805,368 |
| Flintlow Limited | £3,801,943 | World Medicine Limited | £2,779,074 |
| Teoxane UK Limited | £3,792,919 | Vetsonic (UK) Ltd | £2,764,781 |
| Devonshire Healthcare Services Limited | £3,783,673 | Septodont Limited | £2,737,567 |
| Cambridge Healthcare Supplies Limited | £3,763,750 | Astek Innovations Limited | £2,735,559 |
| Mirage Distribution Limited | £3,749,724 | Insight Biotechnology Limited | £2,713,836 |
| Star Pharmaceuticals Limited | £3,741,231 | Impact Health Limited | £2,691,067 |
| Abstragan Holding Limited | £3,735,916 | Hambleton (UK) Limited | £2,678,146 |
| HRA Pharma UK & Ireland Limited | £3,718,713 | Interchem Europe (UK) Limited | £2,650,726 |
| ACI Group Ltd | £3,646,276 | Bioplax Limited | £2,646,677 |
| IMS Euro Limited | £3,640,390 | Ascot Pharma Ltd | £2,642,415 |
| Fenton Pharmaceuticals Ltd | £3,639,380 | Rhodes Pharma Limited | £2,631,416 |
| Fairview Health Limited | £3,632,866 | Target Healthcare Limited | £2,610,823 |
| Supra Enterprises Limited | £3,588,197 | Chewton Ventures Limited | £2,607,844 |
| Astute Healthcare Limited | £3,570,354 | Amaxa Pharma Ltd | £2,581,091 |
| SQR Pharma Consulting Ltd | £3,556,039 | General Pharmaceuticals Limited | £2,575,490 |
| Blackbird Pharmacy Limited | £3,523,827 | Kaam Pharma Limited | £2,574,166 |
| Home Health (U.K.) Limited | £3,521,874 | Lansdales Pharmacy Limited | £2,488,749 |
| Miltonia Health Science Ltd | £3,493,729 | Ennogen Pharma Ltd | £2,487,233 |
| Charmant UK Co., Limited | £3,487,567 | DB & A Cooper (Suffolk) Limited | £2,478,444 |
| Pharmadose Limited | £3,458,054 | Distinctive Medical Products Ltd | £2,464,403 |
| Medihealth (Northern) Limited | £3,410,237 | Resource Medical (UK) Ltd | £2,453,462 |
| S.T.D. Pharmaceutical Products Limited | £3,406,634 | Riteaim Limited | £2,447,788 |
| International Ingredients and Chemicals (IIC) Ltd | £3,396,826 | Ego Pharmaceuticals (UK) Limited | £2,443,516 |
| M.E.D. Supplies Limited | £3,382,626 | Besins Healthcare (UK) Limited | £2,404,841 |
| Vet Direct Services Limited | £3,368,402 | Advanced Laboratory Technologies Europe Ltd | £2,396,120 |
| TSI Health Sciences (Europe) Limited | £3,352,161 | Geistlich Sons Limited | £2,377,402 |

| Company | Amount | Company | Amount |
|---|---|---|---|
| Prestige Brands (UK) Limited | £2,353,120 | Moreton Pharmacy Ltd. | £1,781,663 |
| Steven F Webster Limited | £2,350,000 | George Twist (Wholesale) Limited | £1,770,391 |
| Kelisdar Enterprises Limited | £2,343,785 | Eico Ltd | £1,766,414 |
| Cytoplan Limited | £2,340,104 | McQuilkin & Co Limited | £1,761,050 |
| Docsinnovent Limited | £2,331,274 | Rafarm UK Limited | £1,761,024 |
| Mirada Medical Limited | £2,317,553 | Valley Northern Limited | £1,758,301 |
| Pharco Ltd | £2,294,234 | Technical & General Limited | £1,756,937 |
| Danel Trading Limited | £2,290,762 | Dene Healthcare Limited | £1,756,854 |
| Malem Medical Limited | £2,270,496 | European Veterinary Supplies Limited | £1,749,941 |
| Qualiti (Burnley) Limited | £2,269,252 | Zina Chemist Limited | £1,747,159 |
| Timstar Laboratory Suppliers Limited | £2,233,000 | New Seasons Natural Products Limited | £1,738,782 |
| Albert Harrison & Co.Limited | £2,225,611 | Universal Marine Medical Limited | £1,724,482 |
| F D C International Limited | £2,215,405 | DWH Pharma Limited | £1,723,270 |
| Devicor Medical UK Limited | £2,213,476 | BTA Pharm Limited | £1,718,931 |
| DMS Plus Limited | £2,191,171 | Best Value America (UK) Ltd | £1,717,109 |
| Lucis Pharma Ltd | £2,184,054 | Profoot (UK) Ltd | £1,714,433 |
| Medicom Healthcare Limited | £2,179,262 | NPA Services Limited | £1,707,395 |
| Dixons Pharmaceuticals UK Limited | £2,170,558 | Europlus Pharma Ltd | £1,703,491 |
| Bright Polar Limited | £2,155,260 | Intercept Pharma UK & Ireland Ltd | £1,680,810 |
| Philip Chapper & Company Limited | £2,140,000 | Chemi-Call Ltd | £1,680,425 |
| Rowtech Limited | £2,138,389 | Grandbydale Limited | £1,661,058 |
| C T Dang Limited | £2,129,821 | Shard Speciality Pharma Limited | £1,651,094 |
| Medipharma Limited | £2,120,060 | Chanelle Vet U.K. Limited | £1,637,249 |
| Universal Procurement Services Ltd | £2,109,599 | Receptor Holdings Limited | £1,626,342 |
| Planehill Limited | £2,105,650 | Ideal Healthcare Limited | £1,626,000 |
| A.J. Cope & Son Limited | £2,081,016 | Exeter Health Limited | £1,625,733 |
| Zelens Limited | £2,072,717 | Plexiam Limited | £1,617,827 |
| Ultrasun (UK) Limited | £2,030,502 | John Preston & Co. (Belfast) Limited | £1,616,562 |
| Egroup (UK) Limited | £2,016,523 | Sure Health & Beauty Limited | £1,598,176 |
| Lime Pharmacy Limited | £2,015,730 | Mooncup Ltd | £1,594,668 |
| Pedalglass Limited | £2,001,166 | Shantys Limited | £1,580,453 |
| Stanex Limited | £1,992,370 | Euro Lifecare Ltd | £1,569,884 |
| N.I.P. Pharma Limited | £1,986,943 | Arena Pharmaceuticals Limited | £1,566,893 |
| Pharmac Limited | £1,972,733 | Cyan Trading Ltd | £1,548,241 |
| Intramed Limited | £1,957,231 | Cambridge Healthcare Supplies 2012 Limited | £1,546,776 |
| Lillidale Ltd. | £1,940,225 | Ray Pharm Limited | £1,527,449 |
| Sonik Products Limited | £1,935,199 | Seren Plus Limited | £1,521,734 |
| Allied Pharmacies Limited | £1,912,964 | A.K. Fletcher (Preston) Limited | £1,513,545 |
| Glenhazel Limited | £1,900,000 | Derma UK Limited | £1,511,083 |
| Tor Generics Limited | £1,889,992 | Parapharm Development Limited | £1,509,540 |
| YJBPort Limited | £1,868,543 | Crescent Pharma OTC Limited | £1,508,043 |
| Trotwood Pharma Limited | £1,855,266 | ANP Partners Ltd | £1,500,000 |
| Shizhen TCM (UK) Limited | £1,851,308 | Mansett Limited | £1,496,212 |
| Pharmnet Group Ltd | £1,847,126 | Pennamed Limited | £1,467,642 |
| Credenhill Limited | £1,841,219 | The Medicines Company UK Limited | £1,467,348 |
| Fox Group International Ltd | £1,831,570 | Medshires Limited | £1,464,664 |
| Chloraco Healthcare Limited | £1,825,370 | Matoke Holdings Limited | £1,449,433 |
| Par Laboratories Europe, Ltd. | £1,821,345 | Brenton Invest and Trade Limited | £1,445,991 |
| C G Clark Limited | £1,811,323 | B.R. Pharmaceuticals Limited | £1,444,146 |
| Intermedical (UK) Ltd | £1,811,313 | RSS Wholesaling Limited | £1,442,743 |
| PS Dent Limited | £1,793,386 | Cardio Pro Limited | £1,439,557 |
| Beauty Hair Products Limited | £1,792,539 | Meadow Laboratories Limited | £1,436,486 |
| Dejure Limited | £1,786,605 | Incyte Biosciences UK Ltd | £1,434,727 |
| Metro Pharmacy Limited | £1,785,006 | Greenheys - Weenytot Limited | £1,430,209 |

# The Top UK Pharmaceutical Wholesalers

| | | | |
|---|---|---|---|
| THD (UK) Limited | £1,424,958 | APC Pharmaceuticals & Chemicals (Europe) Ltd | £1,140,794 |
| A B International Limited | £1,420,556 | Novachem Limited | £1,139,353 |
| Corpus Nostrum Limited | £1,417,190 | Nationwide Healthcare Solutions Limited | £1,134,839 |
| The Bagnall Group (Europe) Ltd | £1,409,504 | Twinklers Limited | £1,128,086 |
| PB & T Project Ltd | £1,405,251 | Springbourne Management and Trading Ltd | £1,122,176 |
| TRB Chemedica (UK) Limited | £1,398,420 | Prayosha Healthcare Limited | £1,121,233 |
| Client-Pharma Ltd | £1,393,029 | Maplespring Limited | £1,114,493 |
| Hillcroft Surgery Supplies Ltd | £1,376,173 | Acme Pharma Ltd | £1,105,146 |
| R M Jones Limited | £1,336,606 | Agri-Bio Limited | £1,091,376 |
| Kestrel Ophthalmics Limited | £1,334,197 | Hampton Brands Limited | £1,090,000 |
| Norsworthy Limited | £1,325,578 | IPG Pharma Limited | £1,089,620 |
| ANP Pharma Ltd | £1,320,168 | A D Healthcare Limited | £1,089,480 |
| E-Pharm Limited | £1,315,210 | Akro Pharmaceutical Company Limited | £1,086,336 |
| Isra Limited | £1,306,915 | Logichem Ltd | £1,085,008 |
| Jackson Immunoresearch Europe Limited | £1,301,088 | Shoebury West Road Ltd | £1,077,000 |
| Spadeground Limited | £1,272,832 | Orion Medical Supplies Ltd | £1,074,220 |
| Cis Pharmassist Limited | £1,271,702 | Colour Distributors Limited | £1,072,852 |
| Athrodax Healthcare International Limited | £1,265,830 | Aclardian Limited | £1,068,691 |
| Total Medcare Limited | £1,265,759 | Durham Pharmaceuticals Limited | £1,061,726 |
| Heathrow.Net Limited | £1,265,074 | Moores Pharmacy Limited | £1,057,702 |
| Pharma Medico Limited | £1,265,051 | Kestrel Medical Limited | £1,052,516 |
| Pharma Modus Limited | £1,262,139 | Utech Products Limited | £1,052,142 |
| Mintheath Developments Limited | £1,258,357 | M D M Healthcare Ltd | £1,039,737 |
| HealthVillagePlus Limited | £1,256,913 | Dent.O.Care Limited | £1,039,257 |
| Midmeds Limited | £1,248,576 | TTS Pharma Limited | £1,032,797 |
| Primecrown Limited | £1,245,528 | Acre Pharma Limited | £1,029,758 |
| Currentmyth Limited | £1,245,263 | Sentinel Laboratories Limited | £1,026,658 |
| Flen Health UK Ltd | £1,241,229 | Oxford Nutrition Limited | £1,020,713 |
| Biovendor Ltd | £1,232,387 | Unit 10 Distribution Limited | £998,909 |
| Meditech Endoscopy Ltd | £1,223,828 | Eureka Health Limited | £985,401 |
| Dream Pharma Ltd | £1,222,486 | Greens Pharmacy Limited | £979,323 |
| Rotapharm Limited | £1,222,298 | Regent Pharmaceuticals Limited | £976,710 |
| Parkview Leicester Limited | £1,220,121 | Genesis Medical Limited | £974,059 |
| Mensana Pharma Ltd. | £1,216,830 | P R Pharma Limited | £973,597 |
| Chelmack Limited | £1,216,080 | Mistry Medical Supplies Limited | £971,699 |
| KRKA UK Ltd | £1,204,849 | Pharmahouse Limited | £965,892 |
| Garstang Medical Services Limited | £1,203,688 | Ayva Pharma Limited | £961,568 |
| Medik Ostomy Supplies Limited | £1,202,075 | Pleskarn Limited | £955,232 |
| P & D Pharmaceuticals Ltd. | £1,198,665 | Clinova Limited | £955,018 |
| Infohealth Limited | £1,198,344 | 1966 Health International Limited | £948,913 |
| MDX Healthcare Ltd | £1,193,625 | Rand Rocket Limited | £948,324 |
| Evolet Healthcare Limited | £1,189,536 | Surgical Devices Developers Ltd | £945,169 |
| Angelina SW Ltd | £1,186,964 | Tradewings Worldwide Ltd | £944,749 |
| Dasco Investment Corporation Limited | £1,185,509 | Hisamitsu UK Limited | £941,929 |
| M.R.S. Scientific Limited | £1,180,663 | Sabel Pharmacy Ltd | £941,839 |
| Nunataq Limited | £1,180,021 | Aroschem Limited | £936,193 |
| Arnolds Pharmacy Limited | £1,172,844 | Allkare Limited | £934,477 |
| Bioavexia Ltd | £1,170,247 | Nimrod Veterinary Products Limited | £931,814 |
| Lewis Healthcare Limited | £1,168,877 | Sylk Limited | £930,472 |
| Perush Ltd | £1,163,341 | Independence Products Ltd | £917,951 |
| American Biochemical and Pharmaceuticals Limited | £1,162,832 | Adallen Pharma Limited | £917,146 |
| Flamingo Pharma (UK) Ltd | £1,162,386 | HBS Healthcare Limited | £916,402 |
| iMedix Limited | £1,149,750 | Elkay Laboratory Products (U.K.) Limited | £913,712 |
| Telephone House Limited | £1,144,091 | Lantheus MI UK Limited | £909,374 |

| | | | |
|---|---|---|---|
| Kavia Tooling Limited | £906,632 | Timeocean Ltd | £707,131 |
| Bahati19 Limited | £900,397 | Optident Labline Limited | £705,913 |
| Innomedi Limited | £898,991 | Prestige Dental Products Ltd | £704,324 |
| Park Health Ltd | £897,662 | Myriad Medical Supplies Limited | £702,326 |
| I-Pharma Healthcare Ltd | £885,316 | Unipharm Limited | £701,842 |
| Targeter (UK) Limited | £872,668 | Bradley Stoke Bristol Limited | £698,308 |
| Merlin Vet Export Ltd | £871,214 | Sanochemia Diagnostics UK Limited | £696,863 |
| Generic Partners UK Ltd | £869,615 | Sunniside Healthcare Limited | £696,088 |
| Biogenic Health Europe Ltd | £868,949 | Devilbiss Healthcare Limited | £689,211 |
| Henley Laboratories Limited | £868,762 | GP Laboratories Limited | £686,860 |
| Harmonium Investments Limited | £866,537 | Pharma-Export Ltd | £681,939 |
| RSR Pharmacare Limited | £861,501 | Enteromed Limited | £677,721 |
| Purepharm Ltd | £860,798 | Instachem Limited | £676,327 |
| Harvey Pharma Ltd | £855,370 | Ongar Medical Limited | £673,937 |
| JLS Pharma Limited | £843,372 | Interchem (Chemist Wholesale) Limited | £673,485 |
| John Lloyd Dental Equipment Services Limited | £836,585 | Jolinda Medical Supplies Limited | £672,780 |
| Interpharm Limited | £830,093 | Barton Pharmacy Limited | £670,035 |
| Aidwell Limited | £822,784 | Insight Medical Products Limited | £667,847 |
| Oxford Medpharma Ltd | £820,666 | United Pharma Ltd | £665,115 |
| Sunstore Limited | £819,153 | Clinimarg Ltd | £663,795 |
| Healthcare Pharma Limited | £818,327 | RI Pharma Limited | £663,269 |
| Walter Lloyd & Son Limited | £817,765 | Oxford Biosystems Limited | £661,944 |
| Bio-Synergy Limited | £816,656 | Trent Dent Products Limited | £658,927 |
| Sebbin UK Ltd | £805,155 | Amryt Pharma (UK) Limited | £656,628 |
| Strandland Limited | £799,819 | Aposave Ltd | £655,621 |
| P Y Imports Limited | £798,455 | Mill Pharm Limited | £655,342 |
| Gemapharm Limited | £794,252 | Zista Pharma Limited | £655,031 |
| Curas Limited | £784,269 | Cubic Pharmaceuticals Limited | £644,620 |
| Optimal Pharma Ltd | £781,634 | Allcures.Com (2006) Limited | £644,586 |
| Fast Track Sourcing Limited | £778,557 | Leeds Industries (UK) Ltd | £644,510 |
| Guest Medical Limited | £777,648 | Dent.O.Care Distribution Limited | £643,689 |
| Pound International Ltd | £777,339 | Dispensing Direct Services Ltd | £642,404 |
| Pharma Plus Supplies Ltd | £775,190 | Eurostar Scientific Limited | £637,861 |
| Pharmat Limited | £771,817 | Applied Medical Technology Limited | £634,738 |
| Pharmagona Limited | £764,388 | Sabona Rheumatic Relief Company Limited | £634,599 |
| Afdos Pharmaceuticals Limited | £763,486 | Go Go Chemist Limited | £632,476 |
| Andrews Pharmacy Limited | £763,270 | Apollo Medical Technologies Ltd | £632,258 |
| Viking Court Limited | £759,275 | GB Pharma Limited | £629,798 |
| Xanton Limited | £755,494 | Totally Pharmacy Ltd | £627,885 |
| G & L Simpson Limited | £753,355 | Biosure (UK) Limited | £627,107 |
| Pharmeurope UK Limited | £748,936 | G.A.P. Research Company Limited | £625,907 |
| R. N. Europe Limited | £746,091 | Bioloka Ltd | £623,881 |
| Baymed Healthcare Ltd. | £743,998 | Diamond Pharma Limited | £616,703 |
| Pro Teeth Whitening Co Limited | £743,047 | Czech, Moravian and Slovak Chemicals Limited | £616,032 |
| Zanza Specials International Limited | £741,188 | Casmed International Limited | £611,734 |
| Global Pharmaceuticals Ltd | £739,518 | Stallergenes (UK) Ltd | £610,500 |
| HNS Pharma Limited | £737,826 | Ainsworths (London) Limited | £610,314 |
| G & C Pharma Limited | £735,326 | Oakways Healthcare Limited | £610,155 |
| Quramax Limited | £733,409 | G P Supplies Limited | £607,765 |
| Silkgrange Limited | £730,424 | T.K. Impex Limited | £607,199 |
| Treforest Pharmacy Limited | £727,592 | Hemodia UK Ltd | £600,778 |
| Vision Matrix Limited | £725,074 | RIC Chemicals Limited | £600,671 |
| John Carrington Limited | £723,495 | Eurotech Medical Ltd | £600,152 |
| London United Exports Limited | £719,077 | Ihsan Pharma Ltd | £598,441 |

# The Top UK Pharmaceutical Wholesalers

| | | | | | |
|---|---|---|---|---|---|
| Pharma Insight Ltd | £597,794 | Decahedron Ltd | £488,501 | | |
| Mycology Research Laboratories Limited | £595,553 | Sawa Trading & Shipping Limited | £487,344 | | |
| Crosskills (P.E.) Limited | £591,414 | Brookmed Limited | £487,096 | | |
| Rkonnect Limited | £591,208 | Tricodent Limited | £486,320 | | |
| Inov8 Medical Solutions Limited | £587,717 | Kingspeed Services Limited | £485,878 | | |
| D & M Enterprises (UK) Limited | £587,598 | Jon West Trading Limited | £478,492 | | |
| Pharmapal Limited | £585,218 | Protec Medical Limited | £473,231 | | |
| Gainland (International) Limited | £579,250 | Medicstar (UK) Limited | £472,815 | | |
| Hapharm Ltd | £578,723 | Clinicpharma Limited | £470,728 | | |
| Stanningley Pharma Limited | £577,892 | Human Reproduction Group Ltd | £466,492 | | |
| Palatina Ltd | £576,279 | Assencion Pharmaceuticals Limited | £464,388 | | |
| Medeuronet (UK) Limited | £575,808 | Pioneer Veterinary Products Limited | £464,241 | | |
| Meridian Bioscience UK Limited | £574,692 | Harben Medical Limited | £461,666 | | |
| Alcyon Corporation Ltd | £573,384 | R.I.S. Products Limited | £458,924 | | |
| Welfare Healthcare (UK) Ltd | £573,287 | Purple Orchid Pharma Limited | £456,823 | | |
| Seltfar Ltd | £570,900 | Dermatonics Ltd | £448,469 | | |
| Santhera (UK) Limited | £565,972 | Dompe UK Limited | £446,927 | | |
| Medikit Limited | £562,766 | Bio Pathica Limited | £446,138 | | |
| Wave Pharma Limited | £562,583 | E.S.Shaw & Sons Limited | £444,661 | | |
| Medi-Inn (UK) Ltd | £556,696 | DNB Pharma Limited | £444,462 | | |
| Gordon Davie Chemist Limited | £556,138 | John O'Donnell Limited | £444,118 | | |
| Gulfstream Equity & Development Ltd | £556,002 | Sasmar Limited | £437,921 | | |
| Baymed Group Ltd. | £549,517 | Nalchem Ltd | £434,829 | | |
| Medical Developments UK Limited | £547,617 | Roe Pharmacy Ltd | £431,932 | | |
| Dasapharm Limited | £542,526 | Active Export Ltd | £431,351 | | |
| Chefarma Limited | £542,071 | Ideal Medical Solutions Ltd | £428,256 | | |
| Amdeepcha Limited | £540,527 | Una Health Limited | £425,226 | | |
| Maplewood Investments Limited | £540,039 | Pharmartel Limited | £424,617 | | |
| Europharmacia Ltd | £540,031 | Carl Woolf Limited | £418,694 | | |
| Ross London Limited | £539,876 | Medicare Europe Ltd | £418,685 | | |
| Frezyderm UK Limited | £534,036 | Pergamon Ltd | £417,754 | | |
| N H Southeast Ltd | £533,309 | Salcura Limited | £417,175 | | |
| Stragen UK Limited | £531,932 | Ria Generics Limited | £415,742 | | |
| Jambo Supplies Limited | £531,080 | Novochem Limited | £413,280 | | |
| Fair Pharm Limited | £530,397 | Healthcare Procurement Services Ltd | £411,847 | | |
| Dasco (Wholesale) Limited | £525,935 | Farmedic (UK) Limited | £409,985 | | |
| Oxford Laboratories Limited | £522,123 | B D S I Limited | £408,052 | | |
| N & G Pharma Limited | £521,040 | Bial Pharma UK Limited | £401,801 | | |
| Clinical Services International Ltd | £519,290 | Tanner Pharma UK Limited | £400,996 | | |
| K Chem (North East) Ltd | £519,035 | Biomedical Reproductive Research Ltd | £399,773 | | |
| Al-Ghani Limited | £517,570 | Meridian Medical Technologies Limited | £391,372 | | |
| OL123 Limited | £516,809 | Newbridge Pharma Ltd. | £390,239 | | |
| Solana Trade Ltd | £516,257 | Saxonia Medical Ltd. | £386,101 | | |
| Hunter Urology Ltd | £514,777 | Wellbeing Products Limited | £381,992 | | |
| Campbell Medical Supplies Ltd | £514,183 | Selsdon Healthcare Limited | £380,363 | | |
| Emkado Ltd. | £512,823 | Mediport Limited | £379,068 | | |
| Niayara Global Limited | £510,186 | IPSA Pharmacy Limited | £378,000 | | |
| Genopharm Ltd | £506,001 | Academy Hair and Beauty (UK) Ltd | £376,876 | | |
| Nuview Ltd | £505,992 | Stegram Pharmaceuticals Limited | £375,203 | | |
| Accordia Investments Ltd | £505,711 | Medhub Limited | £374,307 | | |
| Medilain Marketing Ltd | £504,657 | Jana Healthcare Ltd | £373,390 | | |
| Altin Medical Ltd | £504,102 | Storepharm UK Ltd | £371,903 | | |
| Martal Cosmetics Limited | £503,632 | QED Scientific Ltd | £369,381 | | |
| Pharmacierge Limited | £491,880 | Juice Sauz Ltd | £366,669 | | |

| | | | |
|---|---|---|---|
| Smart Medical Limited | £365,048 | CG Pharma Ltd | £283,953 |
| Westland Pharmaceuticals Limited | £364,994 | Intercept Pharma Ltd | £283,096 |
| ETP (UK) Limited | £364,176 | Coates Agencies Ltd | £281,921 |
| Mychem Limited | £362,249 | Alchem PLC | £276,270 |
| Koasta Limited | £359,501 | MAF Pharma Limited | £275,351 |
| Invitech Ltd | £358,078 | Hughenden Valley Pharma Limited | £274,784 |
| Mobility2you Ltd | £357,872 | Allipharm (UK) Limited | £273,581 |
| Advanced Formulations (Europe) Ltd | £350,880 | Medisante Limited | £273,248 |
| Lambsmead Limited | £350,601 | Ambe Limited | £272,796 |
| Respro-M Limited | £347,948 | Ballymote Pharmacy Limited | £271,744 |
| Incline Therapeutics Europe Ltd. | £347,378 | Sood-UK Ltd | £270,736 |
| Parasure Limited | £341,700 | WTE Services Limited | £269,420 |
| Camurus Ltd | £341,690 | Medicia Ltd | £267,500 |
| Selective Supplies Limited | £341,054 | Infutech Limited | £265,816 |
| Zeal Products Limited | £339,953 | Paul Baratte International Limited | £265,000 |
| Numedex Limited | £336,707 | Aerona Clinical Limited | £264,353 |
| MDD Europe Limited | £335,993 | GBY (UK) Ltd | £264,204 |
| Hunger Control Limited | £335,209 | Venture Pharma Ltd | £261,668 |
| Raumedic U.K. Limited | £334,310 | Jenson Chemicals Limited | £260,871 |
| I-Dispense Limited | £332,363 | Britannia Medical Limited | £256,361 |
| New Health Supplies Limited | £331,850 | Janvit Ltd | £255,630 |
| Mercia Dental Equipment Limited | £331,010 | Appia Healthcare Limited | £252,649 |
| KGP Laboratories (UK) Limited | £328,665 | The Heatpack Company Ltd | £252,532 |
| Vital Supplies (UK) Limited | £328,273 | Mirage Eyewear (1993) Limited | £249,360 |
| JMD Enterprises UK Limited | £327,419 | Your Products Limited | £248,439 |
| GHC Global Limited | £327,231 | Kuramo (UK) Limited | £248,244 |
| Charlwood Pharma Limited | £327,201 | Cimex Lectularius Limited | £246,919 |
| Aum Pharms Limited | £326,773 | Kelpharma Ltd | £246,793 |
| Schebo Biotech UK Limited | £326,588 | EPE Global Limited | £246,365 |
| Ram Enterprises Bristol Limited | £326,317 | Acupuncture Direct Ltd | £241,988 |
| DDWS Limited | £325,626 | Global Medical Supply UK Ltd | £239,013 |
| Life on Healthcare Ltd | £324,916 | RD & Med Company Limited | £238,898 |
| Currie Marketing Limited | £323,191 | Qualitech Healthcare Ltd | £237,416 |
| Ruby Box Limited | £322,036 | Hurley Assets Limited | £234,656 |
| Panorama Healthcare Limited | £319,209 | Pharma Concept UK Limited | £232,675 |
| Stratlab Limited | £317,747 | Drugsdirect Limited | £232,546 |
| Alpco Ltd | £316,166 | June Medical Ltd | £232,497 |
| Unit Medic-Aids Limited | £315,570 | Penlan Pharmaceuticals Limited | £231,968 |
| Poseidon Pharmaceutical UK Limited | £313,908 | Glemsford Services Limited | £231,834 |
| Aver Healthcare Ltd | £312,263 | Ethicor Pharma Ltd | £228,755 |
| Aroschem UK Limited | £311,905 | Alfavet Animal Healthcare Limited | £228,303 |
| Beijing Tong Ren Tang (UK) Limited | £309,169 | Universal Biologicals (Cambridge) Limited | £227,948 |
| Brituswip Limited | £303,000 | Double Wing Medical Ltd | £227,761 |
| The Portobello Pharmacy Limited | £302,666 | Labmedical System Limited | £227,039 |
| H4 Medical Limited | £302,159 | Rothes Pharma Limited | £226,442 |
| Amdega Brands Limited | £299,403 | Coward Pharmacy Limited | £225,315 |
| Raman Pharma Limited | £297,145 | Druid Pharma Limited | £224,908 |
| Pharma 777 Limited | £295,520 | Cuttlefish Limited | £223,861 |
| Techdow Pharma England Limited | £294,657 | Cyto-Solutions Limited | £223,425 |
| The Medical Warehouse Limited | £293,897 | Duncan Inc Ltd | £223,245 |
| Espere Healthcare Limited | £292,611 | Orly Pharma Limited | £220,820 |
| Metropharm Limited | £291,258 | Habberpharm Limited | £220,756 |
| Axis Medical Limited | £287,020 | Pearl Services (Tooting) Limited | £220,628 |
| Pharmethicals Limited | £285,999 | British Association of European Pharmaceutical Distrs | £220,266 |

# The Top UK Pharmaceutical Wholesalers

| Company | Amount | Company | Amount |
|---|---|---|---|
| Saving Life Technologies Limited | £219,966 | Payal London Consolidated Limited | £175,441 |
| Autono-Med Limited | £216,872 | Tank Puffin (Wholesale) Limited | £173,913 |
| Prayosha Enterprises Limited | £216,569 | Fab Medical Limited | £172,873 |
| Six Ways Birmingham Ltd | £215,951 | Etab Health Limited | £172,468 |
| Lifecare Limited | £215,151 | Z Tahir Limited | £171,998 |
| Jay & Jay Limited | £214,931 | Dutscher Scientific UK Limited | £171,885 |
| Crosscare Export Limited | £213,707 | Connective Pharma Limited | £171,080 |
| Astra MCR Limited | £213,445 | Pharma Procurement Services Ltd | £170,091 |
| Bioquote Limited | £212,446 | Melo Labs UK Ltd | £169,787 |
| Seagrave Pharma Consultancy Ltd. | £212,152 | Probiotec (UK) Limited | £169,506 |
| Global 1st Ltd | £211,314 | Skindoc Formula Limited | £169,000 |
| Nutresco Ltd | £208,645 | Glucozen Limited | £168,687 |
| UK Eagle Ltd | £208,555 | Mitochondrial Therapy Ltd | £168,038 |
| Pispo Ltd | £207,170 | R & H Trading Limited | £167,942 |
| Damum UK Limited | £205,191 | St George's Medical Limited | £167,865 |
| Betpharma UK Limited | £205,032 | PharmXC Ltd | £167,291 |
| Matrix Healthcare Solutions Limited | £202,916 | Dental Warehouse Ltd | £165,788 |
| Biomedica Nutraceuticals (UK) Ltd | £201,520 | CM Healthcare Limited | £164,773 |
| T-Pharma Limited | £201,141 | Elleco Limited | £164,634 |
| Device Technologies UK Ltd. | £199,897 | Added Pharma Ltd | £163,708 |
| Trion Pharma Limited | £199,601 | NOD Europe Ltd. | £162,363 |
| Pharma Mar Limited | £199,478 | Lifeshield Limited | £161,652 |
| Nasila Pharma Limited | £199,135 | Speedx Limited | £161,624 |
| Inventive Medical Solutions Limited | £199,034 | Daleacre Wholesale Limited | £161,490 |
| Acle Medical Limited | £197,302 | Citco Chemicals Ltd. | £160,112 |
| Pharmaceutical Health Limited | £196,775 | Tim Lever Distribution Ltd. | £159,793 |
| Medica Finance UK Ltd | £196,476 | Ecco Healthcare Limited | £159,362 |
| Manx Pharma Ltd | £195,131 | Skingen UK Ltd | £158,563 |
| Molecule Healthcare Limited | £194,411 | Medstore Limited | £158,357 |
| Eye Guard Ltd | £194,329 | Suerte Pharma Limited | £157,405 |
| Simcro (UK) Limited | £193,344 | Hartwood & Brooks Limited | £157,351 |
| Panacea Health UK Limited | £193,245 | V.S. Limited | £156,381 |
| Doctors Dispensing Services Limited | £191,089 | BN Medical Ltd | £155,595 |
| Euromed Pharmaceuticals Ltd | £189,982 | Health Supplies Limited | £154,525 |
| Ocusoft UK Limited | £189,972 | Pramod Rajani Organisation Limited | £154,229 |
| Omega Surgical Instruments Ltd | £189,432 | Opus Pharmacy Services Limited | £154,146 |
| Active Global Ltd | £188,153 | Cambridge Diagnostics (UK) Limited | £154,063 |
| Maps Healthcare Limited | £187,548 | Prime Pharmacare Ltd | £152,963 |
| MH (Newry) Ltd | £186,642 | AC Intertrade Limited | £152,700 |
| The Homeopathic Supply Company Limited | £185,898 | Yiling Ltd | £152,348 |
| Vital Pharma Limited | £185,697 | Gammaservice Limited | £152,013 |
| MedRx Distribution Limited | £185,505 | Pharmapoint UK Ltd | £151,939 |
| Sintetica Limited | £183,928 | Blackstone Pharma Ltd | £151,864 |
| Hilotherapy UK Limited | £182,756 | Curans Care Limited | £151,112 |
| Sword Medical UK Limited | £181,773 | Moscow Flyer Limited | £149,291 |
| Kemsource Limited | £180,558 | Accendo Pharma Ltd | £149,003 |
| PMS Korea Ltd | £180,291 | Kamm Trading Limited | £148,673 |
| Edmond Finance Ltd | £179,185 | Zanoprima Holdings Limited | £148,557 |
| Remote Pharma Solutions Limited | £179,027 | Arena (Eyewear) Limited | £148,214 |
| Per-Medic Limited | £177,713 | Neolife International Ltd | £146,835 |
| GHC (UK) Ltd | £177,561 | Priory Pharma Ltd | £146,625 |
| Lighthouse Mercury Limited | £176,930 | Bestlon Limited | £146,027 |
| Manx Generics Limited | £176,726 | Sage Therapeutics Limited | £143,230 |
| Orpharma Limited | £176,466 | Gorton Trading Limited | £142,919 |

| Company | Amount | Company | Amount |
|---|---|---|---|
| Westmead International Limited | £142,662 | Newtons Medical Supplies Ltd | £104,213 |
| Passion Dental Design Studio (Laboratory) Limited | £140,083 | Poldark Limited | £103,321 |
| TNF (UK) Ltd | £139,927 | Essential-Healthcare Ltd | £103,234 |
| Pura Pharmaceuticals Ltd | £139,902 | Petersone Group Ltd | £101,597 |
| June Medical International Ltd | £139,357 | Dentanurse (U.K.) Limited | £100,359 |
| Macrobiotics Group Ltd | £139,151 | Ebbcourt Limited | £99,707 |
| Srigen Pharma Ltd | £138,827 | Ved Healthcare Limited | £99,010 |
| Precision Healthcare Limited | £138,593 | Pharmadynamics UK Limited | £98,490 |
| Hygamp Limited | £138,343 | Euromed (U.K) Limited | £96,245 |
| Drilltex GB Ltd | £137,768 | Naturelo Ltd | £95,134 |
| Knightsbridge Importers Limited | £137,736 | Healthcare Source Limited | £94,972 |
| KPB Healthcare Limited | £135,312 | Nutridrinks Limited | £94,661 |
| Vitachem Limited | £133,598 | East Midlands Infotech PVT Limited | £94,375 |
| Valentis Life Sciences Limited | £131,490 | Tabtime Limited | £93,733 |
| Zaitun Limited | £131,414 | LTT Pharma Limited | £93,343 |
| Propharma-UK Ltd | £128,670 | Asymchem Limited | £92,867 |
| Vog Limited | £128,361 | Greenliving Pharma Ltd | £92,731 |
| Shardman Healthcare Limited | £128,136 | Rembrook Developments Limited | £92,519 |
| ABC Healthcare Limited | £128,066 | Specialty Diagnostix Limited | £92,403 |
| Tauva Limited | £127,218 | Rovi Biotech Limited | £91,474 |
| Willgen Consulting Limited | £125,873 | Kisska International Limited | £91,358 |
| Sun Exim Ltd | £124,091 | Westbourne Medical Limited | £91,216 |
| Active Pharma Supplies Limited | £122,973 | BR Scientific Limited | £90,556 |
| Biomedoc Limited | £122,468 | Advanced Eyecare Research Limited | £89,414 |
| Anaiah Healthcare Ltd | £120,677 | Mera Pharma Limited | £89,313 |
| Medipro Pharma Limited | £120,062 | Excelsior Scientific Limited | £89,030 |
| Groves Marchant Limited | £119,827 | Munro Healthcare (Caucasus & Middle Asia) Limited | £88,714 |
| Hunter International Associates Limited | £119,729 | Nagarjun Healthcare Limited | £88,216 |
| Novalabb Limited | £119,693 | The Lens Factory (N.E) Ltd | £87,187 |
| Bipsco Ltd | £118,326 | Niche Pharma Limited | £86,619 |
| Fortissa Ltd | £118,165 | Rapid Sample Processing Limited | £86,182 |
| Entod Research Cell (UK) Limited | £117,596 | Leca Pharma Limited | £85,936 |
| Osteo-Ti UK Limited | £117,565 | AEV Consulting Ltd | £85,665 |
| Skarby Gai Ltd | £115,441 | Genevet Ltd | £85,543 |
| Alexpharm GmbH Ltd | £114,138 | J.J. Worldhealth Limited | £84,686 |
| Atlanta Biological Europe Ltd | £113,914 | Clinres UK Limited | £84,434 |
| View Pharm Limited | £113,531 | Salon Sales Limited | £83,845 |
| GCL Marketing Ltd | £112,647 | Biomedox International Ltd | £83,690 |
| P A M Medical Supplies Limited | £112,182 | Maxilabs Limited | £83,257 |
| Symbio Europe Limited | £111,793 | Ordinant Medical Solutions Limited | £82,698 |
| Indigo Diagnostics Limited | £110,380 | IPY Healthcare Ltd | £82,284 |
| Accutest Solutions Limited | £109,705 | Pioneer Medical Europe Limited | £81,793 |
| UK Branded Medicines Ltd | £107,808 | ASG Pharma Ltd | £81,351 |
| Chemys Limited | £107,202 | Advanced Medical Systems Ltd. | £81,235 |
| ATI Atlas Ltd. | £106,984 | Higherplateau Limited | £80,781 |
| MCL Healthcare Limited | £106,899 | Elm Healthcare Limited | £80,282 |
| Hambleden Herbs Limited | £106,634 | Medicines By Design Ltd | £80,147 |
| Astriza UK Ltd | £106,219 | Max Remedies Limited | £80,000 |
| Beegood Enterprises Limited | £105,829 | Ash Medical Limited | £79,205 |
| Allans Healthcare Limited | £105,649 | Alpharma Limited | £79,086 |
| Creative Supply Solutions Ltd | £105,530 | Maze Healthcare Ltd. | £78,947 |
| WPG Wholesale Trading Ltd | £105,437 | Celtis Healthcare Ltd | £77,488 |
| Max Healthcare Limited | £105,000 | Yaubag Limited | £76,606 |
| Anuva International Limited | £104,244 | CPX Solutions Limited | £76,416 |

# The Top UK Pharmaceutical Wholesalers

| Company | Amount | Company | Amount | Company | Amount |
|---|---|---|---|---|---|
| SAR Health Limited | £76,334 | Macacha Health Limited | £55,277 | | |
| Guardian Pharmaceuticals Co Ltd | £75,068 | Cygnus Pharma Ltd | £55,100 | | |
| E.U.K. Limited | £74,046 | B & B Wholesale Limited | £54,609 | | |
| Alice & Associates Limited | £73,910 | Easho Limited | £54,227 | | |
| Soothingproducts Ltd | £72,505 | Cripps Medical Limited | £54,113 | | |
| Bakhu Limited | £71,418 | Biostate Limited | £53,746 | | |
| Eptheca Global Limited | £70,802 | Pharmadreams Limited | £52,975 | | |
| SRS Pharma Limited | £70,310 | Aneid UK Limited | £52,943 | | |
| Crowncrest Services UK Limited | £70,210 | Nostrum Life Sciences Ltd | £52,819 | | |
| Hot Pharma Ltd | £70,050 | Absolute Brands Ltd | £52,530 | | |
| Core Environmental PLC | £70,039 | FPD Group Limited | £52,430 | | |
| UK Lites Ltd | £69,561 | Trutek Europe Ltd | £52,304 | | |
| Latam HQ Health Ltd | £68,770 | Saxon Pharmaceuticals Limited | £52,152 | | |
| Modern Aesthetic Solutions Ltd | £68,580 | MWK Healthcare Limited | £50,900 | | |
| Titan Med Limited | £68,571 | Medical Drug Supplies Limited | £50,543 | | |
| N N Pharma Ltd | £68,549 | Pan Globus Limited | £50,381 | | |
| Leptrex Ltd. | £68,222 | Brex Medical Supplies Limited | £50,312 | | |
| Concord Extra Limited | £67,860 | Despina Pharma Ltd | £49,836 | | |
| Aspect Pharma Limited | £67,852 | Biomed Limited | £49,714 | | |
| Contract QP Resource Limited | £67,363 | DC Surgical Supplies Limited | £48,650 | | |
| Cenote Pharma Limited | £67,267 | Black and White Health Care Limited | £48,612 | | |
| Stan-Pol Ltd | £66,921 | Gill Pharma Limited | £48,564 | | |
| Bio Nutrition Health Products Limited | £66,711 | Pharmacierge Group Limited | £48,555 | | |
| Shieldasset Limited | £66,281 | Safe Pharma Consulting Ltd. | £48,248 | | |
| Vision.Net Limited | £66,272 | Zefer Pharma Ltd. | £48,150 | | |
| MD-Reproductive Health Solutions Ltd | £65,882 | Crystal Healthcare Limited | £47,845 | | |
| Eurocare Impex Services Limited | £65,350 | A Wise World Limited | £47,414 | | |
| Cofad Ventures Ltd | £65,218 | Phytoceutical Limited | £46,953 | | |
| Arctic Medical Limited | £64,174 | Euro-Link Pharma Ltd | £46,589 | | |
| Medi Saha Limited | £63,886 | A K Worldwide Trading Limited | £44,812 | | |
| Pharmacierge Technology Limited | £63,341 | MDS Pharmaceuticals Ltd | £43,730 | | |
| Quatromed Limited | £63,118 | Oxbridge Pharma Limited | £42,607 | | |
| Barry Elman (Wholesale) Limited | £62,107 | Angulus Pharma Limited | £42,286 | | |
| Project & Communications Limited | £61,683 | ZS Solutions Limited | £42,109 | | |
| Youmed Limited | £61,520 | Here We Flo Ltd | £41,030 | | |
| Ted Medical Ltd | £61,331 | RDO Medical UK Limited | £40,826 | | |
| KM Consulting (Chesterfield) Limited | £60,862 | Mena Pharma UK Limited | £40,649 | | |
| BM Alliance Limited | £60,564 | Silicon Pharma Limited | £40,193 | | |
| Noru Pharma PVT Ltd. | £60,333 | Seedos Ltd. | £40,139 | | |
| Ragit Services Ltd | £60,206 | Micro Industries Limited | £40,063 | | |
| FreshBreathOnline Limited | £60,150 | G Pharma Limited | £40,000 | | |
| Acure Pharma Limited | £60,000 | Pharmhouse Ltd | £39,768 | | |
| Biotech International Limited | £59,688 | Pharmassist Locums Limited | £39,468 | | |
| S M Locum Consultants Ltd | £59,300 | Medilink Limited | £39,129 | | |
| United Med Ltd | £59,286 | Medicure Scientific Limited | £39,000 | | |
| MMP Marketing Limited | £58,674 | Aston-Med Limited | £38,437 | | |
| Veramic Limited | £57,765 | Oxford PCS Limited | £38,163 | | |
| Mayfair Export London Limited | £57,690 | Globegen Laboratories Limited | £38,004 | | |
| Standard Organics International (UK) Ltd | £57,042 | Labjoy Ltd | £37,796 | | |
| IMS Ultrasound (UK) Ltd | £56,633 | HEC Pharm UK Limited | £37,566 | | |
| Excip Limited | £56,287 | PKA Healthcare Ltd | £37,238 | | |
| Friends of Pyrethrum Ltd | £56,095 | KD Pharmacon Ltd | £37,213 | | |
| Cape Pharmaceuticals Ltd | £55,969 | Premax Europe Limited | £37,085 | | |
| Europa Health Limited | £55,955 | By Direct Limited | £37,075 | | |

| | | | | |
|---|---|---|---|---|
| Zena Cosmetics (U.K.) Limited | £36,536 | Rifaray Limited | | £27,147 |
| Vitgarden Ltd | £36,478 | Linderma Limited | | £27,107 |
| So'dran Ltd | £36,000 | Clymed Healthcare Ltd | | £27,020 |
| TFS Med UK Limited | £35,945 | Wescroft Limited | | £26,656 |
| Korlyns Therapeutics Limited | £35,565 | International Medical Supplies Limited | | £26,476 |
| Be and Are Sales Limited | £35,334 | Ihealthcare Genius Limited | | £26,416 |
| Avanzcare Limited | £35,101 | GHC Medical Ltd | | £26,093 |
| Euroworld Enterprises Limited | £34,997 | Vitafree Health Limited | | £25,962 |
| GBBC Ltd | £34,677 | Abstragan Limited | | £25,600 |
| Rak Pharma Ltd | £34,514 | Pembroke Healthcare Limited | | £25,571 |
| Field House Pharma Limited | £34,047 | A V Pharma Limited | | £25,514 |
| Solo Nutrition Limited | £33,920 | Dilcare Health Limited | | £25,503 |
| Atlantic Imaging Limited | £33,816 | G S Seehra Limited | | £25,412 |
| Nouveau Health Ltd | £33,746 | Global Pharma Direct Ltd | | £25,384 |
| Mammoth Dental Supplies Ltd | £33,364 | Sprint Moto UK Ltd | | £25,349 |
| EVC Compounding Ltd | £33,294 | Bionutricals UK Ltd | | £25,275 |
| Rawmmed Trading Company Limited | £33,215 | Abacus Medicine Ltd | | £24,773 |
| Ham+Med Company Ltd | £33,130 | Elmstone Healthcare Limited | | £24,236 |
| KDC-UK Ltd. | £33,103 | Celgene UK Distribution Limited | | £24,108 |
| Webstar Dixon Limited | £33,091 | Steritech UK Limited | | £24,104 |
| Stainweld Limited | £32,424 | Gagnon Direct Ltd | | £23,786 |
| CoAcS Trading Limited | £32,217 | Mediclock Devices Limited | | £23,720 |
| 1st Health Products Ltd | £31,961 | NMB Medical Limited | | £23,615 |
| Granules Europe Limited | £31,811 | Global Dispensing Limited | | £23,514 |
| RF Vapes Limited | £31,677 | Connected Healthcare Ltd | | £23,307 |
| Carun (UK) Limited | £31,406 | Zhpharma Ltd | | £23,293 |
| Go-Kyo Science Limited | £31,287 | R.F. Medical Supplies Limited | | £23,249 |
| Engelpharma UK Limited | £31,183 | Medison Pharma Limited | | £23,045 |
| HH Pharma Limited | £31,141 | Insuphar Laboratories Limited | | £22,952 |
| Vitamins To Buy Ltd | £30,996 | Dragonstone Group Limited | | £22,755 |
| Mosaic Pharma Limited | £30,890 | Medisca UK Limited | | £22,749 |
| Wycombe Locum Services Ltd | £30,558 | Steripharm (UK) Limited | | £22,748 |
| Akysha Limited | £30,492 | Infolight Limited | | £22,672 |
| Intro International (TRDG) Limited | £30,289 | Clinitech Medical Ltd | | £22,577 |
| Hedigen Limited | £29,718 | Imperial Medical Innovations Limited | | £22,502 |
| J L J Healthcare Limited | £29,638 | Molab Ltd | | £22,475 |
| Doksy Limited | £29,610 | Elim Springs Biotech Ltd | | £22,125 |
| Trical Pharm Ltd | £29,592 | Din Commerce Ltd | | £22,075 |
| Phonepimps Limited | £29,456 | Hennessy Mason Ltd | | £22,069 |
| Naturenetics UK Limited | £29,401 | Trinity Impex Limited | | £21,908 |
| Marigold Footcare Ltd. | £29,042 | Roberts McCarron Ltd | | £21,744 |
| Orange Healthcare Limited | £29,024 | RPG Medical Limited | | £21,502 |
| Pura (UK) Ltd | £28,954 | Campmed Limited | | £21,492 |
| Double Wing Pharma Development Ltd | £28,828 | Anfarm Generics UK Limited | | £21,481 |
| Ozonex Limited | £28,615 | NSK Global Ltd | | £21,302 |
| Davcaps Limited | £28,458 | Elias Med Limited | | £20,980 |
| Welfar Healthcare Limited | £28,458 | Angus Medical Supplies Ltd | | £20,945 |
| Uni Supply Ltd | £28,408 | Omapharm Limited | | £20,815 |
| Antwerp Brokering Enterprises (U.K.) Limited | £28,208 | A & E Healthcare Limited | | £20,691 |
| Ursus UK Limited | £28,138 | Sahu & Co Limited | | £20,630 |
| Kerita Ltd | £28,000 | Eye2eye Contact Ltd | | £20,266 |
| Showman's Surgical Ltd | £27,803 | Al Medicines Limited | | £19,973 |
| Clifton Organic Limited | £27,782 | Source Healthcare Ltd | | £19,872 |
| AF First Aid Ltd | £27,357 | Neubourg Pharma (UK) Limited | | £19,796 |

# The Top UK Pharmaceutical Wholesalers

| | | | |
|---|---|---|---|
| H C Healthcare Ltd | £19,320 | Sara Post Ltd | £12,790 |
| Concord Pharma Services (UK) Ltd | £19,248 | Odiham OH Products Limited | £12,737 |
| LBC Solutions Limited | £19,172 | WD Pharma (UK) Limited | £12,651 |
| RJE Agencies Limited | £19,160 | Salutem Supplements Ltd | £12,615 |
| Swerve Cycling Limited | £18,840 | Sarbec Cosmetics Limited | £12,397 |
| Scanmed (UK) Limited | £18,697 | Medicern Export Ltd | £12,327 |
| SERB Ltd | £18,657 | GK Locums Ltd | £12,290 |
| Langdales Limited | £18,646 | Lab.Tv Limited | £12,242 |
| Imperial Bioscience Ltd | £18,581 | Izida Pharma Ltd | £12,227 |
| Alp Trading Limited | £18,213 | Deltapharma Limited | £11,943 |
| Primrose Hudson Limited | £18,023 | Third Hand Healthcare Ltd | £11,671 |
| Perrington & Co Limited | £17,711 | OM Medical Limited | £11,320 |
| Soliphar Limited | £17,502 | Mesopotamia Surgical Ultima Vitality Ltd | £11,127 |
| Dermocore Ltd. | £17,362 | Aromanature Limited | £10,885 |
| Probar Services Limited | £17,275 | Truscreen Limited | £10,702 |
| Trafalgar Pharma Ltd | £17,242 | Pharmacina Ltd | £10,637 |
| Bioturm Limited | £17,151 | Medigroup Ltd | £10,621 |
| Biocare Supplies Limited | £16,822 | Medbase Systems Ltd | £10,592 |
| ME Healthy Living H & L Ltd | £16,817 | JLVET Ltd | £10,489 |
| Ozone Medical Supplies Ltd | £16,664 | UK Biopharma Ltd | £10,316 |
| Identimed Limited | £16,506 | Blue Bean Medical Ltd | £10,201 |
| Emkkay of London Limited | £16,457 | Kestrol International Limited | £10,193 |
| Blue Horizon Healthcare Consulting Limited | £16,444 | Kanish Ltd | £10,108 |
| Pharmatec Ltd | £16,409 | Epsilon Pharmaceuticals Limited | £10,017 |
| Purple Pharma Limited | £15,990 | SDM Healthcare Limited | £10,002 |
| Pacific Pharma UK Limited | £15,965 | Appleby Pharmacy Limited | £9,982 |
| Scandasystems Limited | £15,792 | Sipco Pharma UK Ltd | £9,937 |
| CKF Limited | £15,768 | Serp Sales (UK) Limited | £9,804 |
| 2M PH. Intl. Limited | £15,601 | Sterling London Ventures Limited | £9,784 |
| Leung Healthcare Limited | £15,600 | M & M Taste of Harmony Export Ltd | £9,769 |
| Maria-Cristina Culita Ltd | £15,520 | PB's Locum Services Limited | £9,733 |
| Rosefield Pharma Ltd | £15,508 | Valupharm UK Limited | £9,730 |
| J & G Equipment Limited | £15,429 | Go Medical UK Limited | £9,549 |
| GP Meds Direct Limited | £15,314 | Hayat Gostar Ltd | £9,490 |
| OT Masters Limited | £15,072 | SW Medical Solutions Limited | £9,452 |
| London Health Suppliers Limited | £14,902 | ZS Pharma Limited | £9,405 |
| Jessica Inc Limited | £14,511 | Gate2pharma Ltd | £9,227 |
| Ace First Aid Supplies Ltd | £14,460 | Sanarah Ltd | £8,562 |
| Morton Medical Limited | £14,458 | London Healthcare Limited | £8,560 |
| Sprint Pharma Limited | £14,292 | F Chaudry Limited | £8,460 |
| IM High Tech Limited | £14,260 | M.G. Dental Supplies Limited | £8,339 |
| K & K Pharmaceuticals Limited | £14,238 | Amin Locum Limited | £8,291 |
| Newville Trading Limited | £14,077 | Pharma-X Consultancy Ltd | £8,232 |
| Novamedi Limited | £14,028 | Trans Swiss Ltd | £8,001 |
| R & D Healthcare Ltd | £14,001 | Gester Invest Limited | £7,948 |
| The Private Pharma Health Company Ltd | £13,698 | TPC Pharma Limited | £7,942 |
| Jules Pharma Limited | £13,687 | Stiltec Global (UK) Ltd | £7,941 |
| Invicta Pharma Limited | £13,687 | Astra Pharma (UK) Limited | £7,900 |
| 21CEC PX Pharm Ltd | £13,583 | RJP Impex Ltd | £7,862 |
| AG Pharmahealth Ltd | £13,319 | Nebel Healthcare Limited | £7,772 |
| MKK Consulting Ltd | £13,276 | PF Consultancy Plus Ltd | £7,563 |
| NV Campbell Limited | £13,249 | Winelia Company Limited | £7,451 |
| Neutradvance Limited | £13,188 | TTC Medical GTS Limited | £7,237 |
| V Sales and Marketing Limited | £12,861 | Tannerlac UK Limited | £7,149 |

| Company | Amount | Company | Amount |
|---|---|---|---|
| Dosego Limited | £7,143 | La Lune Noire Ltd | £3,622 |
| Sunstik Ltd | £6,904 | Turtle Rouge Ltd | £3,604 |
| I L Locum Ltd | £6,882 | Mad Doctor Holdings Limited | £3,588 |
| Leap Pharma Ltd | £6,841 | Masa Pharma Ltd | £3,414 |
| Medisale Limited | £6,707 | Tagma Pharma (UK) Ltd | £3,276 |
| Accmede Pharmaceuticals Limited | £6,677 | LV Global Limited | £3,136 |
| English Herbal Medicines Limited | £6,552 | Health Medbio Ltd | £3,050 |
| Inspiragen Limited | £6,523 | Rabimed International Limited | £3,016 |
| Viemeds Limited | £6,509 | NC Trade UK Ltd | £3,011 |
| Padma Healthcare Limited | £6,452 | UK Medical Centre Ltd | £2,904 |
| Beautons Ventures Ltd | £6,447 | Vedic Medical Hall Limited | £2,844 |
| Celloxess (Europe) Limited | £6,301 | Pharmacare (London) Limited | £2,819 |
| Yawskin Limited | £6,267 | Belfast Drug Ltd | £2,804 |
| Enfield Nutrition Club Ltd | £6,218 | HS Pharma Limited | £2,752 |
| Y A Toner Limited | £6,161 | Evolve Healthcare Partners Ltd | £2,720 |
| Healtholozy UK Limited | £6,123 | Swiftpath Corporation Limited | £2,704 |
| Pharmed Health Care Organisation Limited | £5,985 | Fortune Industries Limited | £2,669 |
| Medaesthetics Limited | £5,826 | I-Crackedit Ltd | £2,636 |
| Birch & Beech Limited | £5,712 | Nurse Prescribers Limited | £2,633 |
| Novamed Pharma Ltd | £5,616 | Winchpharma (Consumer Healthcare) Ltd | £2,538 |
| Perfect Vascular Natural Limited | £5,604 | Globyz Pharma (UK) Ltd | £2,501 |
| Geopharma UK Ltd. | £5,600 | Entrust & UK Ltd | £2,484 |
| Gumsaver Limited | £5,582 | NSA Pharma Limited | £2,467 |
| Allied Warden Marketing Limited | £5,579 | NLR Exports Limited | £2,430 |
| Bigvits Limited | £5,559 | Centline Ltd | £2,387 |
| Stem Cellx Limited | £5,305 | Berryfarm Ltd | £2,383 |
| RAR Pharmaceutics Ltd | £5,239 | A.H.P. Medical Supplies Ltd | £2,361 |
| Sanay Ltd | £5,164 | Gos Pharma Limited | £2,342 |
| Eyepak Limited | £5,137 | Laboratoires Forte Pharma UK Ltd | £2,306 |
| MK Medicals (UK) Ltd | £5,130 | JSK PVT Limited | £2,220 |
| Shkar Enterprise Limited | £5,121 | I.T.T.I.D. (Trading) Ltd | £2,217 |
| Indrugco (UK) Limited | £5,065 | Pharmasky Ltd | £2,208 |
| SJ Enterprises Limited | £5,047 | RxPharma Limited | £2,162 |
| Flairpath Limited | £5,020 | Stockman (UK) Ltd | £2,132 |
| Pharma Trading Limited | £5,000 | KHM Global Ltd | £2,063 |
| Sutherland Health Group Limited | £4,935 | C & N Medical Ltd | £2,045 |
| Willbay Limited | £4,895 | De-Bulad & Co. Ltd. | £2,036 |
| Vital Life International Limited | £4,868 | Prodigy Healthcare Limited | £2,016 |
| Vitane Pharma Limited | £4,817 | Sotra Pharma Ltd. | £1,980 |
| Novus Medicare Ltd | £4,667 | Macratio Limited | £1,942 |
| LSP Bio Limited | £4,484 | Haoma Pharma Ltd | £1,922 |
| Patient Ready Products Limited | £4,467 | Akvion Limited | £1,872 |
| Diamate Biotechnologies Limited | £4,424 | One Pharm Limited | £1,866 |
| Lamb's Locum Services Ltd | £4,330 | Wesbee Ventures Limited | £1,828 |
| Aeglos Ltd | £4,306 | Essentialink Limited | £1,697 |
| Hashmats Health Ltd | £4,303 | Universal Supplies (International) Ltd | £1,697 |
| Bannersbridge Limited | £4,084 | Pharmex-UK Ltd | £1,680 |
| Artmedica Ltd | £4,005 | Mcall Consulting Ltd | £1,647 |
| Remedine Limited | £3,970 | Dizzo Consulting (UK) Limited | £1,600 |
| Bio-Sight Ltd | £3,948 | WHL Contracts Ltd | £1,570 |
| Qamar Limited | £3,894 | Conceio Consulting Ltd | £1,555 |
| Malcolm B. Fagleman Ltd | £3,865 | Zanoprima LifeSciences Limited | £1,508 |
| Britpharm Limited | £3,859 | Nissi Business Services Limited | £1,486 |
| Medbarn Limited | £3,649 | Dynamic Development Laboratories Co Ltd | £1,454 |

# The Top UK Pharmaceutical Wholesalers

dellam

| Company | Value | Company | Value |
|---|---|---|---|
| AMK & Associates Ltd | £1,428 | FTS Bio Limited | £280 |
| Centurion Park Pharmaceuticals Limited | £1,302 | TTO Ventures Ltd. | £273 |
| A1 Natural Ltd | £1,299 | United Kingdom Medica Ltd | £216 |
| Alpha Pharma Ltd | £1,290 | Mountrow Trading Limited | £209 |
| Arco Iris Limited | £1,238 | Liberty Pacific Limited | £200 |
| Sakar Healthcare UK Ltd. | £1,200 | Irasco Ltd | £151 |
| ATI Pharmaceuticals Limited | £1,189 | Propharma Consultancy Ltd | £150 |
| Natures Healthworks Limited | £1,177 | Chronicles Medical Consulting Ltd | £120 |
| HMD Europe Ltd | £1,142 | Concept Pharma UK Limited | £108 |
| Ultimate Health Products Limited | £1,077 | Euromed Technologie Limited | £104 |
| Chanelle Medical GB Limited | £1,001 | Megapharma Ltd | £100 |
| Newtexko Ltd. | £1,000 | Imex International Group Limited | £100 |
| Vertibax Limited | £1,000 | Irmaan Limited | £100 |
| O'Connell Pharma Ltd | £1,000 | Global 4 Care Ltd | £100 |
| Dion Trade Ltd. | £1,000 | Jorvik Pharma Ltd | £100 |
| Vestex Trade Ltd | £1,000 | Saint-Germain Pharma Ltd | £100 |
| SD Alliance Ltd. | £1,000 | A B Alliance Limited | £100 |
| Cosmestore Limited | £1,000 | Curelife Ltd | £100 |
| Flowonix Medical Ltd | £1,000 | Anrise Trading Limited | £100 |
| Evorin Pharma Limited | £1,000 | RX Pharma (Europe) Limited | £100 |
| Water-Jel International Ltd | £1,000 | Advanced Medical Products Limited | £100 |
| Vitaminka Ltd | £1,000 | Buduscheye Techniqa Ltd | £100 |
| AAR Pharma Ltd | £999 | Discount Healthcare Ltd | £100 |
| Prolife (UK) Limited | £928 | Flow Wealth Ltd | £100 |
| Ofege Pharm Ltd | £920 | Zota Healthcare Limited | £100 |
| GP Mediplus Ltd | £896 | UK Pharmacies Ltd | £100 |
| Peart Med Ltd | £883 | Munro Healthcare Pharma Limited | £100 |
| Imex Ltd | £879 | Tarus Laboratories Limited | £78 |
| Vitamineral Limited | £877 | Creo Pharma Holdings Limited | £73 |
| Lab-PCR Limited | £866 | Powerlung Ltd. | £31 |
| Sterling Bio-Pharma Ltd | £862 | ECommedical Limited | £20 |
| Alzirr Ltd | £851 | Sanos Healthcare Ltd | £15 |
| Proup Ltd | £835 | Trilogy Medical Systems Limited | £10 |
| Dermal Aesthetics Clinic Limited | £824 | Victoria Pharma London Ltd | £2 |
| The Bolton Pharmaceutical Company 100 Ltd | £823 | Shaz Logistics Limited | £2 |
| A.T. Medical Ltd | £812 | Peter & Guys Salon Professional Ltd | £2 |
| Goldshore (UK) Limited | £668 | Moka Pharmaceuticals Limited | £1 |
| Jagmed Limited | £663 | Salonpas UK Limited | £1 |
| Specialised Marketing Services Limited | £661 | Hisamitsu Pharmaceutical UK Limited | £1 |
| RX Farma Limited | £606 | Benident Limited | £1 |
| European Nutriceutical Products Limited | £598 | G Pharmaceuticals Ltd | £1 |
| Evideon Daily Ltd | £588 | Cellexa Limited | £1 |
| Art Pharma Oxford Ltd | £580 | Renata (UK) Limited | £1 |
| Nikopharm Ltd | £539 | PLA Medical Supplies Limited | £1 |
| ThriveExtreme Health Limited | £517 | Gate Pharma Ltd | £1 |
| Arkad Healthcare Limited | £508 | Pharmex International Ltd | £1 |
| Incimed Ltd | £443 | Raj Ghai Associates Limited | £1 |
| Rind Pharma Limited | £415 | Einoxy Limited | £1 |
| Pharma World Ltd | £361 | AZL Holdings Ltd | £1 |
| Ideal Medical Holdings Ltd | £352 | Avicenna Ltd | £1 |
| Vine Pharmaceuticals Limited | £326 | Star Freight Forwarding Limited | £1 |
| Haydn Healthcare UK Limited | £319 | EAM Wholesale Ltd | £1 |
| Northwise Services Limited | £292 | Ecosse Hospital Products Limited | £1 |
| Sustainable Ethical Enterprises Limited | £287 | Clinical Direct Ltd | £1 |

*This page is intentionally left blank*

# Age of Companies

## 1800s
Allen & Hanburys Limited
Mawdsley-Brooks & Co Ltd
Stanton Ocean Services Limited

## 1910-1919
AAH Pharmaceuticals Limited
Bausch & Lomb U.K. Limited
Pfizer Consumer Healthcare Ltd
Phoenix Healthcare Distribution Ltd

## 1920-1929
Colgate-Palmolive (U.K.) Ltd
Glaxo Laboratories Limited
Napp Laboratories Limited
L.Rowland & Co Ltd

## 1930-1939
Abbott Laboratories Limited
Gee Lawson Limited
NPA Services Limited

## 1940-1949
ATI Atlas Ltd.
Beiersdorf UK Ltd.
Ecosse Hospital Products Ltd
Albert Harrison & Co.Limited

## 1950-1959 [16]
A.J. Cope & Son Limited
Credenhill Limited
Durham Pharmaceuticals Limited
Glaxo Wellcome UK Limited
GlaxoSmithKline Caribbean Ltd
Lil-Lets UK Ltd
Medimpex UK Limited
Pfizer Limited
Pound International Ltd
Purple Surgical UK Limited
Rayburn Trading Co Ltd
E.S.Shaw & Sons Limited
Robert Smith & Co, (Derry) Ltd
Targeter (UK) Limited
Veterinary Surgeons Supply Co Ltd
L E West Ltd

## 1960-1969 [26]
Abbott Healthcare Products Ltd
Astellas Pharma Ltd.
Paul Baratte International Ltd
Bayer PLC
Bripharm Limited
P & A J Cattee (Wholesale) Ltd.
Davis and Dann Limited
Barry Elman (Wholesale) Ltd
Galderma (U.K.) Limited
Geistlich Sons Limited
Global Pharmaceuticals Ltd
Knightsbridge Importers Ltd
Leo Laboratories Limited
Manor Drug Company (Nottingham) Ltd
Martal Cosmetics Limited
Meda Pharmaceuticals Limited
Napp Pharmaceutical Group Ltd
Norchem Limited
Omega Pharma Limited
John Preston & Co. (Belfast) Ltd
R.B. Radley & Co Ltd
S.T.D. Pharmaceutical Products Ltd

Sabona Rheumatic Relief Co Ltd
Servier Laboratories Limited
Ivor Shaw Limited
Zimmer Biomet UK Limited

## 1970-1979 [55]
Adelphi (Tubes) Limited
Aidwell Limited
Ainsworths (London) Limited
Allergan Limited
Antwerp Brokering Enterprises (U.K.)
Barton Pharmacy Limited
Baymed Healthcare Ltd.
Bestway Pharmacy NDC Limited
Biotest (U.K.) Limited
Philip Chapper & Co Ltd
G. D. Cooper & Co Ltd
CooperVision Lens Care Limited
Cripps Medical Limited
Doncaster Pharmaceuticals Ltd
EMT Healthcare Limited
H.N. Espley & Sons Limited
Ferring Pharmaceuticals Ltd
Grandbydale Limited
Greenheys - Weenytot Limited
Hameln Pharmaceuticals Ltd
Kays Medical Limited
Lambsmead Limited
Lewis Healthcare Limited
Lundbeck Limited
M & A Pharmachem Limited
M.G. Dental Supplies Limited
Merck Serono Limited
Miller & Miller (Chemicals) Ltd
Movianto UK Limited
Paul Murray PLC
Newco Pharma Limited
Novo Nordisk Limited
John O'Donnell Limited
Per-Medic Limited
Pleskarn Limited
Pricecheck Toiletries Limited
Prima Brands Limited
R.I.S. Products Limited
R.A. Racey (Gt. Yarmouth) Ltd
Renfield Limited
Sangers (Maidstone) Limited
Scandasystems Limited
Shantys Limited
Spadeground Limited
Alan Spivack Limited
Swingward Limited
George Twist (Wholesale) Ltd
Unit Medic-Aids Limited
Unomedical Limited
Vascular Products Limited
Virbac Limited
Vygon (U.K.) Limited
K. Waterhouse Limited
Westland Pharmaceuticals Ltd
Zena Cosmetics (U.K.) Limited

## 1980-1989 [132]
Agri-Bio Limited
Agrihealth (N.I.) Limited
Alchem PLC
Amalgamated Technology Corporation
Animalcare Ltd
Arena (Eyewear) Limited
Arrowedge Limited
Athrodax Healthcare International

Aventis Pharma Limited
Bailey Instruments Ltd
Bannersbridge Limited
Beauty Hair Products Limited
Bio Nutrition Health Products Ltd
Bioforce (U.K) Limited
Bioquote Limited
Britannia Pharmaceuticals Ltd
British Association of European Pharmaceutical Distributors
CSL Behring UK Limited
Cellpath Limited
Chemilines Limited
Chiesi Limited
Clinimed Limited
Corpus Nostrum Limited
Cradlecrest Limited
Crosscare Export Limited
Crosskills (P.E.) Limited
Crosspharma Limited
Cytoplan Limited
Daiichi Sankyo UK Limited
Danel Trading Limited
Dasco (Wholesale) Limited
Dasco Investment Corporation Ltd
Day Lewis Medical Limited
Dentanurse (U.K.) Limited
Diana Royal Jelly Limited
Doncaster Pharmaceuticals Group Ltd
Dr. Falk Pharma UK Limited
Eco Animal Health Group PLC
Eisai Limited
Euromed (U.K) Limited
Fittleworth Medical Limited
A.K. Fletcher (Preston) Ltd
G.A.P. Research Co Ltd
Gainland (International) Ltd
Galpharm International Limited
Genesis Medical Limited
Genus Pharmaceuticals Limited
GlaxoSmithKline Export Limited
Global Pharmaceuticals (UK) Ltd
Guest Medical Limited
Paul Hartmann Limited
Healthaid Holdings Limited
Hospira UK Limited
I.T.T.I.D. (Trading) Ltd
Idis Limited
Interchem (Chemist Wholesale) Ltd
International Ingredients and Chemicals (IIC)
Interport Limited
Intro International (TRDG) Ltd
Jambo Supplies Limited
Jay & Jay Limited
Jenson Chemicals Limited
Kanta Enterprises Limited
Lam Cash and Carry Limited
Leverton & Co Ltd
B.R. Lewis Pharmaceuticals Ltd
London United Exports Limited
Malem Medical Limited
Mansett Limited
Maplespring Limited
Marigold Footcare Ltd.
Masta Limited
Masters Pharmaceuticals Ltd
Med-Col Limited
Medi UK Ltd
Medilink Limited
A. Menarini Diagnostics Ltd
Meridian Medical Technologies Ltd
N.G. Limited

Necessity Supplies Limited
Nelson & Russell Limited
Norbrook Laboratories (G.B.) Ltd
Nordic Pharma Limited
Ontex Retail UK Limited
Orion Pharma (UK) Limited
Oxford Nutrition Limited
Payal London Consolidated Ltd
Perrigo Pharma Limited
Pharm - Tex Limited
Pharmalab Limited
Precision Fluid Controls Ltd
Prestige Dental Products Ltd
Primecrown Limited
Probar Services Limited
Rand Rocket Limited
Ratiopharm (UK) Limited
Receptor Holdings Limited
Rembrook Developments Limited
Sandyvale Limited
Sangers (Northern Ireland) Ltd
Sarbec Cosmetics Limited
Sentinel Laboratories Limited
Septodont Limited
Servipharm Limited
Shire Pharmaceuticals Limited
Sigma Pharmaceuticals PLC
Silkgrange Limited
Spatone Limited
Specialised Marketing Services Ltd
Stainweld Limited
Stegram Pharmaceuticals Ltd
Stephar (U.K.) Limited
Steritech Limited
Stiefel Laboratories Limited
Strandland Limited
Supra Enterprises Limited
T.K. Impex Limited
Technical & General Limited
Testerworld Limited
Timstar Laboratory Suppliers Ltd
Toiletry Sales Limited
Tricodent Limited
Trimark International Limited
Universal Biologicals (Cambridge)
Value Generics Limited
Vision Pharmaceuticals Ltd
Waymade PLC
Wellbeing Products Limited
Westmead International Limited
Zeal Products Limited
Zentiva Pharma UK Limited
Zina Chemist Limited

**1990-1994** [86]
A B International Limited
A1 Pharmaceuticals PLC
Advanced Formulations (Europe) Ltd
Alcura UK Limited
Alice & Associates Limited
Allipharm (UK) Limited
Amano Enzyme Europe Limited
Animal Prescriptions Limited
Arctic Medical Limited
Astellas Pharma Europe Ltd.
Astrazeneca PLC
Aura-Soma Limited
B.P. Pharma Limited
Barclay Pharmaceuticals Ltd
Beijing Tong Ren Tang (UK) Ltd
Biostate Limited
ET Browne (UK) Limited

CKF Limited
Charmant UK Co., Limited
Colour Distributors Limited
Condomania (UK) Limited
DB & A Cooper (Suffolk) Ltd
Coramandel Limited
Crowncrest Services UK Limited
Czech, Moravian and Slovak Chemicals
Dent.O.Care Limited
Dexcel-Pharma Limited
Ebbcourt Limited
Elkay Laboratory Products (U.K.) Ltd
Euro Ceuticals Limited
Eurocare Impex Services Ltd
Excel Health Care Limited
Fenton Pharmaceuticals Ltd
Flintlow Limited
GB Pharma Limited
Gilead Sciences Ltd
Greiner Bio-One Limited
Guerbet Laboratories Limited
HMD Europe Ltd
Hermes Pharmaceutical Limited
Hoechst Marion Roussel Limited
Impexport Services Limited
Indrugco (UK) Limited
Interpharm Limited
R M Jones Limited
Kinetic Enterprises Limited
Kuramo (UK) Limited
Roy Lamb Limited
Lifecare Limited
Lillidale Ltd.
Lloyds Pharmacy Clinical Homecare
M.E.D. Supplies Limited
Manx Healthcare Limited
McNeil Healthcare (UK) Limited
Medikit Limited
Medipharma Limited
Meditec International England Ltd
Melyd Medical Limited
Metro Pharmacy Limited
Mirage Eyewear (1993) Limited
Morningside Pharmaceuticals Ltd
Mossvet Limited
NLR Exports Limited
Neolife International Ltd
New England Biolabs (U.K.) Ltd
Nova Laboratories Limited
Nucare Limited
Omron Healthcare UK Limited
Orange Square Co Ltd.
Ostomart Limited
P & D Pharmaceuticals Ltd.
Periproducts Limited
Pharmaceutical Identity Ltd
Ranbaxy (U.K.) Limited
Respond Plus Limited
Riteaim Limited
S & D Pharma Limited
SJ Enterprises Limited
Tillomed Laboratories Limited
Vedic Medical Hall Limited
Veenak International Limited
Viking Court Limited
Vitachem Limited
Vitamineral Limited
Donald Wardle and Son Limited
Peter John Wood Limited

**1995** [19]
American Biochemical and Pharmaceuticals

CSL Behring Holdings Limited
European Veterinary Supplies Ltd
Flairpath Limited
Insight Biotechnology Limited
Intramed Limited
Knox Pharmaceuticals Limited
Lexon (UK) Limited
Walter Lloyd & Son Limited
M & N Traders Limited
Medreich PLC
Moores Pharmacy Limited
OTC Direct Limited
Pharmacosmos UK Limited
RIC Chemicals Limited
Surgitrac Instruments UK Ltd
Ultimate Health Products Ltd
V.S. Limited
Vivus UK Limited

**1996** [30]
A D Healthcare Limited
Alloga UK Limited
Axis Medical Limited
B.R. Pharmaceuticals Limited
Bio Pathica Limited
Casmed International Limited
Chiesi Healthcare Limited
Dejure Limited
Derma UK Limited
F D C International Limited
Farah Chemists Limited
Healthcare Services Group Ltd
Healthpoint Limited
Home Health (U.K.) Limited
Langdales Limited
M.R.S. Scientific Limited
Manx Pharma Ltd
OPD Laboratories Limited
Ongar Medical Limited
Orphan Europe (UK) Limited
P.I.E. Pharma Limited
Pharmat Limited
RJE Agencies Limited
Scanmed (UK) Limited
Sonik Products Limited
Sylk Limited
Twinklers Limited
Vision Matrix Limited
Vision.Net Limited
ZTK Business Services Limited

**1997** [40]
Academy Hair and Beauty (UK) Ltd
Advanced Medical Systems Ltd.
Alliance Healthcare (Distribution)
Amdega Brands Limited
Autono-Med Limited
Beachcourse Limited
Beechcroft Supplies Limited
Bio-Synergy Limited
Biomed Limited
Bristol Laboratories Limited
Cambridge Healthcare Supplies Ltd
Currentmyth Limited
Design Masters (Sales) Limited
ETP (UK) Limited
Evees (UK) Limited
G Pharma Limited
Gowrie Laxmico Limited
Greens Pharmacy Limited
Healthcare Product Services Ltd

Ideal Healthcare Limited
Interchem Europe (UK) Limited
Intermedical (UK) Ltd
J.J. Worldhealth Limited
Kinesis Limited
Meadow Laboratories Limited
Medicare Products Limited
Medicines Company UK Limited
Medik Ostomy Supplies Limited
Milpharm Limited
Mycology Research Laboratories Ltd
Napp Pharmaceutical Holdings Ltd
Oxford Laboratories Limited
Ozonex Limited
Pharmeurope UK Limited
SP Services (UK) Limited
Sunovion Pharmaceuticals Europe Ltd.
Takeda UK Limited
Ultrasun (UK) Limited
Veriton Pharma Limited
W.B. Superdrug Ltd.

**1998** [37]
Akro Pharmaceutical Co Ltd
Allied Warden Marketing Ltd
Applied Medical Technology Ltd
BR Pharma International Ltd
C & P Medical Trading Limited
Clarity Pharma Ltd
Durbin PLC
Egroup (UK) Limited
Eurostar Scientific Limited
Gemapharm Limited
Genus Pharmaceuticals Holdings Ltd
Grunenthal Limited
Hunter Urology Ltd
Kisska International Limited
L & R Medical UK Ltd.
Lifeshield Limited
A. Menarini Pharmaceuticals U.K.
Moka Pharmaceuticals Limited
Multi Pharma Limited
Myriad Medical Supplies Ltd
Napp Pharmaceuticals Limited
Norgine Pharmaceuticals Ltd
Optident Labline Limited
Otsuka Pharmaceuticals (U.K.) Ltd.
Oxford PCS Limited
Perrington & Co Limited
Phoenix Medical Supplies Ltd
Phytoceutical Limited
Prinwest Limited
Qualiti (Burnley) Limited
Quramax Limited
Seedos Ltd.
Soliphar Limited
Sovereign House Properties Ltd
Sunstore Limited
Steven F Webster Limited
Whyte International Limited

**1999** [42]
Acupuncture Direct Ltd
Alk-Abello Limited
Allcures PLC
Ambe Limited
Attends Limited
Baymed Group Ltd.
Be and Are Sales Limited
Biocare Supplies Limited
Birch & Beech Limited

Blackstaff Pharmaceuticals Ltd
J. Bradbury (Surgical) Ltd
Liam Bradley Ltd
Chanelle Medical U.K. Limited
Chemidex Generics Limited
Crest Medical Limited
Crystal Healthcare Limited
Drugsdirect Limited
E-Pharm Limited
E.U.K. Limited
European Nutriceutical Products Ltd
Firstchem Limited
Genesis Pharmaceuticals Ltd
Hunter International Associates Ltd
Insight Health Limited
J L J Healthcare Limited
Janvit Ltd
Jolinda Medical Supplies Ltd
Lansdales Pharmacy Limited
Natural Science.Com Limited
One Pharm Limited
Opalbond Limited
Pharmaceuticals Direct Limited
Phoenix Pharma Ltd.
Respro-M Limited
Ria Generics Limited
Schebo Biotech UK Limited
Selective Supplies Limited
Solo Nutrition Limited
Specials Laboratory Limited
Steritech UK Limited
Tarus Group Limited
Total Body Care Limited

**2000** [51]
Acorus Therapeutics Limited
Allgenpharma Limited
Arco Iris Limited
Blackbird Pharmacy Limited
Boots International Limited
Bracco UK Limited
Cadila Pharmaceuticals (Europe) Ltd
C G Clark Limited
Condomania PLC
Coward Pharmacy Limited
Crescent Pharma OTC Limited
Discovery Pharmaceuticals Ltd
Ecosse Pharmaceuticals Limited
Ethigen Limited
G P Supplies Limited
Groves Marchant Limited
Heathrow.Net Limited
Hunger Control Limited
Infohealth Limited
Insight Medical Products Ltd
Kaam Pharma Limited
Kelisdar Enterprises Limited
Kestrel Medical Limited
Labwarehouse Limited
John Lloyd Dental Equipment Services
London Healthcare Limited
MGI Pharma Limited
Macks Ltd.
Medi-Gen Limited
Medical Warehouse Limited
Medicom Healthcare Limited
Mintheath Developments Limited
Nipro Diagnostics (UK) Limited
Nurse Prescribers Limited
PF Consultancy Plus Ltd
Pharmac Limited
Pharmacare Logistics Limited

Pharmadreams Limited
Pharmasure Limited
Pharmethicals Limited
Prestige Brands (UK) Limited
Purple Surgical International Ltd
RX Farma Limited
Ross London Limited
Rothschild Pharmacy Limited
Shieldasset Limited
Showman's Surgical Ltd
Simcro (UK) Limited
Star Pharmaceuticals Limited
United Therapeutics Europe, Ltd.
Zeroderma Limited

**2001** [54]
A.H.P. Medical Supplies Ltd
Accordia Investments Ltd
Adallen Pharma Limited
Aeglos Ltd
Alfavet Animal Healthcare Ltd
Alium Medical Limited
Andrews Pharmacy Limited
Arena Pharmaceuticals Limited
Aromanature Limited
Aroschem Limited
Astra Pharma (UK) Limited
Berkshire Wholesale Supplies (2002) Ltd
C. S. T. Pharma Limited
Chelmack Limited
Chemilines Group Holdings Ltd
DDWS Limited
Damum UK Limited
Davcaps Limited
De-Bulad & Co Ltd
Devonshire Healthcare Services Ltd
Diamate Biotechnologies Ltd
Disposable Medical Equipment Ltd
Distinctive Medical Products Ltd
Euroworld Enterprises Limited
FreshBreathOnline Limited
Genopharm Ltd
Genzyme Therapeutics Limited
GlaxoSmithKline UK Limited
Homeopathic Supply Co Ltd
IMS Euro Limited
Kestrel Ophthalmics Limited
Kobayashi Healthcare Europe Ltd
Linderma Limited
Mediport Limited
Mediwin Limited
Northwise Services Limited
Oxford Biosystems Limited
Pharmabuyer Limited
Pharmed Health Care Organisation Ltd
Powerlung Ltd.
Precision Healthcare Limited
Principle Healthcare Limited
Profoot (UK) Ltd
Protec Medical Limited
R & H Trading Limited
Richardson Healthcare Limited
Gedeon Richter (UK) Limited
Sanochemia Diagnostics UK Ltd
Selsdon Healthcare Limited
G & L Simpson Limited
Summit Pharmaceuticals Europe Ltd
Swiftpath Corporation Limited
TRB Chemedica (UK) Limited
Tabtime Limited

# The Top UK Pharmaceutical Wholesalers

**2002** [44]
Accord Healthcare Limited
Alp Trading Limited
Baxalta UK Investments Ltd.
Brex Medical Supplies Limited
Clarity Pharma Holdings Ltd
Curans Care Limited
Dallas Burston Ashbourne Holdings
Ego Pharmaceuticals (UK) Ltd
Euro Lifecare Ltd
Malcolm B. Fagleman Ltd
Fair Pharm Limited
Focus Pharmaceuticals Limited
Harley's (UK) Ltd
Healthcare (Wales) Ltd.
Hisamitsu Pharmaceutical UK Ltd
Hisamitsu UK Limited
In 2 Healthcare Limited
Jules Pharma Limited
Kemsource Limited
Lab.Tv Limited
Medartis Limited
Medimax (UK) Ltd
Medshires Limited
Minmar (1008) Limited
Mooncup Ltd
Morton Medical Limited
Omnicell Limited
Oxbridge Pharma Limited
P R Pharma Limited
Parkview Leicester Limited
Pharmacina Ltd
Pramod Rajani Organisation Ltd
Rabimed International Limited
RxPharma Limited
Salcura Limited
Salonpas UK Limited
Smart Medical Limited
Stratlab Limited
Surgery Supplies (UK) Limited
Syner-Medica Limited
Tor Generics Limited
Universal Procurement Services Ltd
Wesbee Ventures Limited
Y A Toner Limited

**2003** [53]
21CEC PX Pharm Ltd
ACG Europe Limited
AF First Aid Ltd
Abra Wholesales Ltd
Advanced Eyecare Research Ltd
Akvion Limited
Apretique Limited
Aum Pharms Limited
B D S I Limited
Beta Pharmaceuticals Limited
Bolton Pharmaceutical Company 100 Ltd
Bosville Limited
Cambridge Pharmaceuticals Ltd
Chemi-Call Ltd
Crescent Pharma Limited
Cyto-Solutions Limited
Dream Pharma Ltd
Drugsrus Limited
Eclipse Generics Limited
Friends of Pyrethrum Ltd
Alston Garrard & Co Limited
Hambleton (UK) Limited
Hamilton Pharmaceuticals Ltd
Healthaid Limited

Hughenden Valley Pharma Ltd
Icone International Limited
Inbamay Resources (UK) Ltd.
Infinity Pharmaceuticals Ltd
International Medical Supplies Ltd
J & G Equipment Limited
MDS Pharmaceuticals Ltd
MH (Newry) Ltd
Maplewood Investments Limited
Maxilabs Limited
Medbase Systems Ltd
Merz Pharma UK Limited
Mosaic Pharma Limited
New Seasons Natural Products Ltd
Newstar Healthcare Limited
Novochem Limited
Nupharm Limited
Nuview Ltd
Orange Healthcare Limited
P A M Medical Supplies Limited
Pharma-Export Ltd
Pharmartel Limited
Poseidon Pharmaceutical UK Ltd
Pura Pharmaceuticals Ltd
Rawmmed Trading Co Ltd
Relonchem Limited
Rowtech Limited
Tauva Limited
Turtle Rouge Ltd

**2004** [48]
Allkare Limited
Astek Innovations Limited
Bioplax Limited
Biotech International Limited
Britannia Medical Limited
Clinigen CTS Limited
Deltapharma Limited
Doctors Dispensing Services Ltd
Dutscher Scientific UK Limited
Eico Ltd
English Herbal Medicines Ltd
Espere Healthcare Limited
Essentialink Limited
GCL Marketing Ltd
Garstang Medical Services Ltd
General Pharmaceuticals Ltd
Genevet Ltd
Glenmark Pharmaceuticals Europe Ltd
Global Dispensing Limited
Goldsmith Resources Limited
Halo GB Ltd
Healthcare 21 (UK) Limited
Healthcare Procurement Services Ltd
Healthmed Supplies (HMS) Ltd
Jackson Immunoresearch Europe Ltd
KGP Laboratories (UK) Limited
Lighthouse Mercury Limited
Livanova UK Limited
Medihealth (Northern) Limited
Moscow Flyer Limited
New Roots Herbal Limited
OL123 Limited
Okle Systems Limited
Opus Pharmacy Services Limited
P Y Imports Limited
Piramal Critical Care Limited
Qamar Limited
Reckitt Benckiser Asia Pacific Ltd
Resource Medical (UK) Ltd
Salon Sales Limited
Sotra Pharma Ltd.

Stragen UK Limited
Strathclyde Pharmaceuticals Ltd
Sutherland Health Group Ltd
V Sales and Marketing Limited
Vet Direct Services Limited
WTE Services Limited
World Medicine Limited

**2005** [69]
ABC Healthcare Limited
APC Pharmaceuticals & Chemicals (Europe)
Advanced Laboratory Technologies Europe
Ash Medical Limited
Authentic Ayurveda Limited
BBI Healthcare Limited
Brightfield Associates Ltd
Butt & Hobbs Limited
CIGA Healthcare Limited
Celgene Limited
Celgene UK Distribution Ltd
Chikhurst Limited
Clinicpharma Limited
CoAcS Trading Limited
Collardam PLC
Curas Limited
Cuttlefish Limited
Dakota Pharma Limited
Dechra Veterinary Products Ltd
Dene Healthcare Limited
Dilcare Health Limited
Dixons Pharmaceuticals UK Ltd
East Midlands Pharma Limited
Enlon Limited
Eptheca Global Limited
First Aid Supplies Limited
Fluidx Limited
GP Laboratories Limited
Galen Limited
Gilsun Limited
Glenhazel Limited
Goldshore (UK) Limited
Healthcare Generics Limited
Idis Group Holdings Limited
JLS Pharma Limited
K P Pharma Limited
Kavia Tooling Limited
Kestrol International Limited
Koasta Limited
LBC Solutions Limited
Marlborough Pharmaceuticals Ltd
Max Healthcare Limited
Megapharma Ltd
Micro Industries Limited
Midmeds Limited
N.I.P. Pharma Limited
NHS Generics Limited
Newtexko Ltd.
Novachem Limited
Panacea Health UK Limited
Pharma Insight Ltd
Pharmacy Supplies Limited
Prometheus Medical Ltd
QED Scientific Ltd
Rapid Sample Processing Ltd
Recordati Pharmaceuticals Ltd
Rotapharm Limited
Shaz Logistics Limited
Shizhen TCM (UK) Limited
Steripharm (UK) Limited
Stockman (UK) Ltd
Sure Health & Beauty Limited
TSI Health Sciences (Europe) Ltd

Z Tahir Limited
Teoxane UK Limited
Universal Supplies (International) Ltd
Victoria Pharma London Ltd
Vital Supplies (UK) Limited
Zecare Limited

## 2006 [44]
8 Pharma Ltd
Alissa Healthcare Research Ltd
Anuva International Limited
Betpharma UK Limited
Bright Polar Limited
Brookmed Limited
Budget Pharma UK Limited
CM Healthcare Limited
Carbosynth Limited
John Carrington Limited
Citco Chemicals Ltd.
Clinova Limited
Concept Pharma UK Limited
Creative Supply Solutions Ltd
Engelpharma UK Limited
Eurotech Medical Ltd
Evolve Healthcare Partners Ltd
Gammaservice Limited
Ham+Med Co Ltd
Idea Medica Limited
Independence Products Ltd
Laboratoires Forte Pharma UK Ltd
Logichem Ltd
Maps Healthcare Limited
Mensana Pharma Ltd.
Mychem Limited
Neilmed Limited
Newbridge Pharma Ltd.
Norsworthy Limited
Pedalglass Limited
Pharma Concept UK Limited
Pharmagona Limited
Pharmaxis Pharmaceuticals Ltd
Project & Communications Ltd
Quatromed Limited
Reliance Medical Ltd
Servier IP UK Limited
Standard Organics International (UK) Ltd
Stanex Limited
TPC Pharma Limited
Tagma Pharma (UK) Ltd
Tanberg Limited
UK Medical Centre Ltd
Vertibax Limited

## 2007 [49]
AEV Consulting Ltd
ANP Pharma Ltd
Alcyon Corporation Ltd
Alexpharm GmbH Ltd
Allcures.Com (2006) Limited
Almirall Limited
Beauty Shopper Ltd.
Bowmed Ibisqus Limited
Chanelle Vet U.K. Limited
Clinigen Healthcare Limited
Coombe KP Limited
Creo Pharma Holdings Limited
Creo Pharma Limited
Elite Pharma (Surrey) Limited
Elleco Limited
Emkkay of London Limited
Europharma Scotland Ltd

FPD Group Limited
Fab Medical Limited
Fagron UK Ltd
Fire N Ice Ltd
Focus Pharma Holdings Limited
Glemsford Services Limited
IPG Pharma Limited
Infutech Limited
Korlyns Therapeutics Limited
Manichem Limited
Max Remedies Limited
Mera Pharma Limited
Mistry Medical Supplies Ltd
Munro Medical Limited
Niayara Global Limited
Nimrod Veterinary Products Ltd
O'Connell Pharma Ltd
Palatina Ltd
Patient Ready Products Limited
Pennamed Limited
Pharmatec Ltd
Qingdao Polychem (U.K.) Ltd
Ray Pharm Limited
Rhodes Pharma Limited
Roe Pharmacy Ltd
Rolling Stones Trading Ltd
St George's Medical Limited
Surgidoc Limited
U L Medicines Limited
Willbay Limited
YJBPort Limited
Zaitun Limited

## 2008 [66]
A & E Healthcare Limited
Aclardian Limited
Actipharm Limited
Amdeepcha Limited
Ananta Medicare Ltd
Bakhu Limited
Belfast Drug Ltd
Berryfarm Ltd
Best Value America (UK) Ltd
CM & D Pharma Limited
Clinigen Group PLC
Cotton Craft Limited
Cubic Pharmaceuticals Limited
Currie Marketing Limited
Cyan Trading Ltd
Dental Warehouse Ltd
Dermatonics Ltd
Dion Trade Ltd.
Ecogen Europe Ltd
Europlus Pharma Ltd
Guna Biotherapeutics Limited
Guna Limited
Hampton Brand Management Co Ltd
Hampton Brands Limited
Hartwood & Brooks Limited
Iam Finance Limited
Invitech Ltd
Ipsen Limited
Kamm Trading Limited
LM3 Business Ltd
LTT Pharma Limited
Lantheus MI UK Limited
Tim Lever Distribution Ltd.
Lime Pharmacy Limited
M D M Healthcare Ltd
Medeuronet (UK) Limited
Mercia Dental Equipment Ltd
Mesopotamia Surgical Ultima Vitality Ltd

Mill Pharm Limited
Mirada Medical Limited
N H Southeast Ltd
NSL Group Limited
PTGO Sever UK Limited
Perricone MD Cosmeceuticals UK Ltd
Pharco Ltd
Pharma 777 Limited
Pharmadynamics UK Limited
Poldark Limited
RI Pharma Limited
Raumedic U.K. Limited
G S Seehra Limited
Serp Sales (UK) Limited
Sigmasis UK Limited
Stallergenes (UK) Ltd
Stan-Pol Ltd
THD (UK) Limited
Thea Pharmaceuticals Limited
Tradewings Worldwide Ltd
Unit 10 Distribution Limited
Universal Marine Medical Ltd
Vifor Pharma UK Limited
Vital Life International Ltd
WE Pharma Ltd
Wellspring Pharmaceutical Services
Wellspring Pharmaceutical Services UK
Westbourne Medical Limited

## 2009 [76]
Angelina SW Ltd
Aroschem UK Limited
Aspire Pharma Limited
Bigvits Limited
Biofex Limited
Biomarin (U.K.) Ltd.
Biomedical Reproductive Research Ltd
Bionical Limited
Birmingham Management Centre (UK)
Carbotang Limited
F Chaudry Limited
Clarity DTP Ltd
Concord Extra Limited
Cosmestore Limited
Despina Pharma Ltd
Devilbiss Healthcare Limited
Docsinnovent Limited
Dunamis Pharmaceutical Services Ltd
E-Pharma Chemical Int. Limited
Elm Healthcare Limited
Entrust & UK Ltd
Euro Capital Management (ECM) Ltd
Fairview Health Limited
Fortissa Ltd
Go-Kyo Science Limited
Gorton Trading Limited
HRA Pharma UK & Ireland Ltd
Habberpharm Limited
IPSA Pharmacy Limited
Impact Health Limited
Instachem Limited
Intela Europa Ltd
Islestone Limited
JJ Nutrihealth Ltd
JMD Enterprises UK Limited
KM Consulting (Chesterfield) Ltd
LSP Bio Limited
Laxmico Limited
Life on Healthcare Ltd
Lupin Healthcare (UK) Limited
MAF Pharma Limited
ME Healthy Living H & L Ltd

# The Top UK Pharmaceutical Wholesalers

Medicia Ltd
Miltonia Health Science Ltd
Mirage Distribution Limited
Moreton Pharmacy Ltd.
Mountrow Trading Limited
Munro Wholesale Medical Supplies Ltd
Nissi Business Services Ltd
Novmedic Limited
Pan Globus Limited
Pergamon Ltd
Pharmacare (London) Limited
Portobello Pharmacy Limited
Priory Pharma Ltd
Probiotec (UK) Limited
RDO Medical UK Limited
Ros Nutrition UK Ltd.
SD Alliance Ltd.
Salon Professional Limited
Salon Professional.Com Limited
Sasmar Limited
Sprint Moto UK Ltd
Total Medcare Limited
Totally Pharmacy Ltd
Treforest Pharmacy Limited
Trutek Europe Ltd
Una Health Limited
Unipharm Limited
Venture Pharma Ltd
Vestex Trade Ltd
ViiV Healthcare Overseas Ltd
ViiV Healthcare Trading Services UK
ViiV Healthcare UK Limited
Vog Limited
Wowwax Ltd.

## January-June 2010 [50]

A Wise World Limited
A.T. Medical Ltd
AAR Pharma Ltd
Active Export Ltd
Apollo Medical Technologies Ltd
Ashtons Healthcare Limited
Ashtons Medical Limited
Ashtons Medical Supplies Ltd
Aspect Pharma Limited
Benident Limited
Bessacarr Ltd
Beximco Pharma UK Limited
Cis Pharmassist Limited
Devicor Medical UK Limited
Econo-Beauty Ltd
Econo-Care Ltd
Econo-Group Ltd
Fast Track Sourcing Limited
Galar Ireland Ltd
Go Go Chemist Limited
H4 Medical Limited
Hashmats Health Ltd
I-Pharma Healthcare Ltd
Inter Trade Pharma Limited
Kingspeed Services Limited
Kosei Pharma UK Ltd.
Laxmi BNS Holdings Limited
MDTI Pharma Retail Division Ltd
Matoke Holdings Limited
Medical Drug Supplies Limited
Medisante Limited
Melcare (Europe) Limited
Nationwide Healthcare Solutions Ltd
OM Medical Limited
PB's Locum Services Limited
Park Health Ltd

Pharma Plus Supplies Ltd
Pioneer Medical Europe Limited
Ram Enterprises Bristol Ltd
SPL (2010) Limited
Saxonia Medical Ltd.
Six Ways Birmingham Ltd
Stanningley Pharma Limited
TFS Med UK Limited
Torrent Pharma (UK) Ltd
Trent Dent Products Limited
Vitanutrition UK Ltd.
Carl Woolf Limited
Yaubag Limited
Ypsomed Limited

## July-December 2010 [32]

Allied Pharmacies Limited
Ascot Pharma Ltd
BM Alliance Limited
Bugband Europe Ltd
Campmed Limited
Clarity Commercial Ltd
Clarity at Home Ltd
Entod Research Cell (UK) Ltd
Europharmacia Ltd
Excip Limited
Fortune Industries Limited
Health Supplies Limited
Hedigen Limited
Hurley Assets Limited
Inov8 Medical Solutions Ltd
Jessica Inc Limited
Juvela Limited
MWK Healthcare Limited
Medicstar (UK) Limited
Medilife Ltd
Model Medics Limited
New Health Supplies Limited
Nostrum Life Sciences Ltd
Pharmaceutical Health Limited
Pharmadose Limited
Pharmasky Ltd
Rkonnect Limited
Sabel Pharmacy Ltd
Sahu & Co Limited
Skingen UK Ltd
Vitafree Health Limited
Yiling Ltd

## January-June 2011 [42]

A K Worldwide Trading Limited
AG Pharmahealth Ltd
Al-Ghani Limited
Anaiah Healthcare Ltd
Assencion Pharmaceuticals Ltd
BTA Pharm Limited
Bagnall Group (Europe) Ltd
Biomedi Technology Limited
Biomedoc Limited
Boston Healthcare Limited
Couch Rolls Limited
Couchrolls.Com Ltd
Couchrolls.co.uk Ltd
Diamond Pharma Limited
Dispensing Healthcare Ltd
Dizzo Consulting (UK) Limited
Essential Pharma Limited
Euromed Pharmaceuticals Ltd
G Pharmaceuticals Ltd
Global 1st Ltd
Gumsaver Limited

Insuphar Laboratories Limited
MKK Consulting Ltd
Mcall Consulting Ltd
MedRx Distribution Limited
Medicare Europe Ltd
Mediva Pharma Limited
NOD Europe Ltd.
Neon Diagnostics Ltd
Optima Consumer Health Limited
Pharma-X Consultancy Ltd
Planehill Limited
Prime Pharmacare Ltd
SW Medical Solutions Limited
Sidhupharm Limited
Sunniside Healthcare Limited
TTops Healthcare Limited
Thurgab Medicals Ltd
Vetsonic (UK) Ltd
Willgen Consulting Limited
Zefer Pharma Ltd.
Zelens Limited

## July-December 2011 [59]

Absolute Brands Ltd
Abstragan Holding Limited
Appia Healthcare Limited
Aptil Pharma Limited
BFN Limited
Bioactive T Pharma Limited
Biomedox International Ltd
Bionutricals UK Ltd
Biosure (UK) Limited
C & N Medical Ltd
Cellexa Limited
Clarity Markets Ltd
Conceio Consulting Ltd
Decahedron Ltd
Econo-Supplies Ltd
Ennogen Healthcare Ltd
Ennogen Pharma Ltd
Evolet Healthcare Limited
GBY (UK) Ltd
Global Additives Ltd
Heatpack Co Ltd
Higherplateau Limited
I-Crackedit Ltd
I-Dispense Limited
Ideal Medical Solutions Ltd
Inglasia Ltd
Isra Limited
Izida Pharma Group Limited
Kadmon International Ltd
Leptrex Ltd.
Leung Healthcare Limited
MDX Healthcare Ltd
Medi Saha Limited
Medicines By Design Ltd
Nutridrinks Limited
Omega Surgical Instruments Ltd
PB & T Project Ltd
Penlan Pharmaceuticals Limited
PharmXC Ltd
Pharma Modus Limited
Prominent Life Style Ltd
Purple Orchid Pharma Limited
Qdem Pharmaceuticals Limited
R.F. Medical Supplies Limited
RJP Impex Ltd
Real Estate Alliance Ltd
Rose Europe UK Ltd
Safe Pharma Consulting Ltd.
Sawa Trading & Shipping Ltd

Scope Ophthalmics Limited
Seren Plus Limited
Shakespeare Pharma Ltd
Soothingproducts Ltd
Tarus Laboratories Limited
View Pharm Limited
Vitane Pharma Limited
WPG Wholesale Trading Ltd
Webstar Dixon Limited
Jon West Trading Limited

### January-March 2012 [26]
20 20 Optical Services Ltd
AbbVie Ltd
Active Pharma Supplies Limited
Bahati19 Limited
Bipsco Ltd
Blue Bean Medical Ltd
Cape Pharmaceuticals Ltd
Creative Brand Concepts Ltd
Emkado Ltd.
Ethicor Pharma Ltd
Go Medical UK Limited
Harben Medical Limited
Humn Pharmaceuticals (UK) Ltd
Izida Pharma Ltd
MDD Europe Limited
Mitochondrial Therapy Ltd
Modern Aesthetic Solutions Ltd
Munro Healthcare Group Limited
Ordinant Medical Solutions Ltd
Pispo Ltd
Prayosha Healthcare Limited
RSS Wholesaling Limited
Rifaray Limited
Sanarah Ltd
Symbio Europe Limited
Thlala Kolo (UK) Ltd

### April-June 2012 [30]
1st Health Products Ltd
Aegerion Pharmaceuticals Ltd
Amaxa Pharma Ltd
Aston-Med Limited
Cofad Ventures Ltd
D & M Enterprises (UK) Limited
DNB Pharma Limited
Dermocore Ltd.
Etab Health Group Limited
Etab Health Limited
Etab Pharma Limited
GlaxoSmithKline Consumer Trading Services
Globegen Laboratories Limited
HNS Pharma Limited
Human Reproduction Group Ltd
Intergal Pharma Limited
Labmedical System Limited
Leap Pharma Ltd
Lifecell EMEA Limited
Medical Developments UK Ltd
Neutradvance Limited
Norlington Trading Ltd
Seagrave Pharma Consultancy Ltd.
Ultrasoundgel Ltd
Veramic Limited
Winelia Co Ltd
Yawskin Limited
Zanza Specials International Ltd
Zoetis UK Limited
iMedix Limited

### July-September 2012 [31]
ANP Partners Ltd
Aarkios Health PVT Limited
Ace First Aid Supplies Ltd
Alpharma Limited
Aneid UK Limited
Astute Healthcare Limited
B & B Wholesale Limited
Brancaster Pharma Limited
Device Technologies UK Ltd.
Excelsior Scientific Limited
GHC (UK) Ltd
Generic Partners UK Ltd
HBS Healthcare Limited
Incimed Ltd
Infolight Limited
Kerita Ltd
Mobility2you Ltd
Noroc Concepts Ltd
Numedex Limited
Orion Medical Supplies Ltd
Parasure Limited
Rind Pharma Limited
Specialty Diagnostix Limited
Swiss Pharma UK Limited
TNF (UK) Ltd
Target Healthcare Limited
Telephone House Limited
Tynatex Limited
UK Biopharma Ltd
Winchpharma (Consumer Healthcare) Ltd
Wonder World Ltd

### October-December 2012 [33]
Acre Pharma Limited
Bidaya UK Ltd.
Bioloka Ltd
Black and White Health Care Ltd
Cambridge Healthcare Supplies 2012
Centline Ltd
Connected Healthcare Ltd
DWH Pharma Limited
Gordon Davie Chemist Limited
Direct Care Homes Limited
Emcure Pharma UK Ltd
Eyepak Limited
Hambleden Herbs Limited
Hana Supplies Limited
Harmonium Investments Limited
Hilotherapy UK Limited
Incline Therapeutics Europe Ltd.
Incyte Biosciences UK Ltd
Inspiragen Limited
Invicta Pharma Limited
Jana Healthcare Ltd
Lucis Pharma Ltd
Medilain Marketing Ltd
Medirite Limited
NMB Medical Limited
Nexcape Pharmaceuticals Ltd
Rayner Pharmaceuticals Limited
SERB Ltd
Silicon Pharma Limited
TTS Pharma Limited
Trotwood Pharma Limited
Xanton Limited
ZS Solutions Limited

### January-March 2013 [33]
Arnolds Pharmacy Limited
Atlanta Biological Europe Ltd
Atlantic Imaging Limited
Aver Generics Limited
Ayva Pharma Limited
Beegood Enterprises Limited
Carun (UK) Limited
Chewton Ventures Limited
Cimex Lectularius Limited
Clinres UK Limited
Coates Agencies Ltd
East Midlands Infotech PVT Ltd
Eureka Health Limited
Eye2eye Contact Ltd
FTS Bio Limited
Fortis Egregius Limited
MK Medicals (UK) Ltd
Medigroup Ltd
Molab Ltd
Munro Healthcare (Caucasus & Middle Asia)
Ontyme Logistics and Healthcare Ltd
Pharma Medico Limited
Phonepimps Limited
RAR Pharmaceutics Ltd
Rogia Romini Limited
Sanay Ltd
Sipco Pharma UK Ltd
Springbourne Management and Trading Ltd
UK Pharma Impex Limited
Valupharm UK Limited
Vitamins To Buy Ltd
Vitgarden Ltd
Wave Pharma Limited

### April-June 2013 [37]
11 Health & Technologies Ltd
A1 Pharmaceuticals Holdings Ltd
AMK & Associates Ltd
Akysha Limited
Angus Medical Supplies Ltd
BN Medical Ltd
Clinimarg Ltd
Dosego Limited
Edmond Finance Ltd
Ethypharm UK Limited
Exeter Health Limited
GBBC Ltd
Gilsun Healthcare Ltd
HealthVillagePlus Limited
K & K Pharmaceuticals Limited
Lab-PCR Limited
Lamb's Locum Services Ltd
Linepharma International Ltd
Med Procure Ltd
Meditech Endoscopy Ltd
Medpro Healthcare Limited
Merlin Vet Export Ltd
National Veterinary Services Ltd
Nutresco Ltd
Pura (UK) Ltd
Randa Pharma Ltd
Rich Almond (UK) Limited
Sante Primaire Limited
Shardman Healthcare Limited
Smartway Pharmaceuticals Ltd
So'dran Ltd
Solana Trade Ltd
Sun Exim Ltd
TTO Ventures Ltd.
United Pharma Ltd
Uno Healthcare Limited
Vasmed Technologies Limited

# The Top UK Pharmaceutical Wholesalers

**July-September 2013** [34]
Added Pharma Ltd
Alzirr Ltd
Besins Healthcare (UK) Limited
Cambridge Diagnostics (UK) Ltd
Dermatonics Trading Limited
Drilltex GB Ltd
Eye Guard Ltd
Flowonix Medical Ltd
Henley Laboratories Limited
I Like Limited
Imex International Group Ltd
June Medical Ltd
KDC-UK Ltd.
Lucky Herbalife24 Limited
MMEU 20/20 Ltd
Mediclock Devices Limited
Niche Pharma Limited
Nunataq Limited
Osteo-Ti UK Limited
Pembroke Healthcare Limited
Pharma Procurement Services Ltd
Prayosha Enterprises Limited
Purple Pharma Limited
Qualitech Healthcare Ltd
RSR Pharmacare Limited
Renata (UK) Limited
Restate Management Ltd
Ruby Box Limited
Stada UK Holdings Ltd.
Trinity Impex Limited
Truscreen Limited
WD Pharma (UK) Limited
Welfare Healthcare (UK) Ltd
Zhpharma Ltd

**October-December 2013** [26]
Abacus Medicine Ltd
Aposave Ltd
Biogenic Health Europe Ltd
Biomedica Nutraceuticals (UK) Ltd
Blackstone Pharma Ltd
Client-Pharma Ltd
Countrywide Healthcare Supplies Holdings
C T Dang Limited
Dent.O.Care Distribution Ltd
GK Locums Ltd
Gester Invest Limited
HH Pharma Limited
Haoma Pharma Ltd
Haydn Healthcare UK Limited
Healthcare Source Limited
McKesson Global Procurement & Sourcing
Medison Pharma Limited
Naturenetics UK Limited
Neubourg Pharma (UK) Limited
Pharhealth Limited
RB UK Commercial Limited
Regent Pharmaceuticals Limited
Remedi Medical Holdings Ltd
Rosefield Pharma Ltd
Saxon Pharmaceuticals Limited
Sood-UK Ltd

**January-March 2014** [31]
Accendo Pharma Ltd
Accmede Pharmaceuticals Ltd
Angulus Pharma Limited
Astriza UK Ltd
Ballymote Pharmacy Limited
Biobos Limited

Campbell Medical Supplies Ltd
Centurion Park Pharmaceuticals Ltd
Condom Dot Com Ltd.
ECommedical Limited
Euro-Link Pharma Ltd
Evideon Daily Ltd
Evorin Pharma Limited
Gill Pharma Limited
Glector Limited
HS Pharma Limited
Hillcroft Surgery Supplies Ltd
Irmaan Limited
KRKA UK Ltd
Lens Factory (N.E) Ltd
Maria-Cristina Culita Ltd
NSL (Holdings) Limited
Nalchem Ltd
Nebel Healthcare Limited
Pharmaceutical Direct Limited
Plexiam Limited
R. N. Europe Limited
Ripple Pharma Limited
SQR Pharma Consulting Ltd
Shanghai Neopharm Co., Ltd
Tank Puffin (Wholesale) Ltd

**April-June 2014** [48]
Acme Pharma Ltd
Alpha Pharma Ltd
Apollo Endosurgery UK Ltd
Aver Healthcare Ltd
Bejaa Medical (UK) Limited
Brenton Invest and Trade Ltd
Britpharm Limited
Contract QP Resource Limited
EPE Global Limited
Ellis Pharma Limited
Enteromed Limited
Flamingo Pharma (UK) Ltd
Glucozen Limited
Greenliving Pharma Ltd
Harvey Pharma Ltd
Hot Pharma Ltd
Irasco Ltd
KPB Healthcare Limited
LV Global Limited
Labjoy Ltd
Liberty Pacific Limited
Lionmark Limited
M2 Healthcare Ltd
Macratio Limited
Medi-Inn (UK) Ltd
Meridian Bioscience UK Limited
N & G Pharma Limited
Naskalmik Limited
New Horizon Pharma (UK) Ltd.
Newville Trading Limited
Nouveau Health Ltd
Perfect Vascular Natural Ltd
Peter & Guys Salon Professional Ltd
Pharmacy4life Ltd
Pharmahouse Limited
Pharmapal Limited
R & D Healthcare Ltd
Raman Pharma Limited
Shard Speciality Pharma Ltd
Sunstik Ltd
Swerve Cycling Limited
UK Heluns Industry Co., Ltd
UK Lites Ltd
UK Vimin Industry Co., Limited
United Med Ltd

Utech Products Limited
Welfar Healthcare Limited
Zanoprima LifeSciences Limited

**July-September 2014** [40]
AC Intertrade Limited
Allans Healthcare Limited
Alpco Ltd
Ardant Pharmaceuticals Ltd.
Ascend Laboratories (UK) Ltd
Bioceutics UK Ltd
Bradley Stoke Bristol Limited
Chela Animal Health Limited
DMS Plus Limited
Din Commerce Ltd
Essential-Healthcare Ltd
GJB Pharma Limited
Gate2pharma Ltd
Gemi Pharma Limited
H C Healthcare Ltd
Hapharm Ltd
Heisenberg Technologie Ltd
Hemodia UK Ltd
Intercept Pharma Europe Ltd.
Jagmed Limited
Lab-Club Limited
Lumiradx International Ltd
Medical-Mac Ltd
Medicine Optimisation Limited
Mylan UK Healthcare Limited
NSK Global Ltd
Natures Healthworks Limited
PKA Healthcare Ltd
PLA Medical Supplies Limited
PS Dent Limited
Peart Med Ltd
Santen UK Limited
Skindoc Formula Limited
Sunrize Trade Limited
Sword Medical UK Limited
Third Hand Healthcare Ltd
Valley Northern Limited
Vine Pharmaceuticals Limited
Wigmore Laboratories Limited
Zanoprima Holdings Limited

**October-December 2014** [39]
Afdos Pharmaceuticals Limited
Al Medicines Limited
Aspire Pharma Holdings Limited
Atossa Genetics UK Ltd
Biovendor Ltd
Clear Eyes Pharma Limited
Clinitech Medical Ltd
Curium Pharma UK Ltd.
Dasapharm Limited
EUSA Pharma (UK) Limited
Elim Springs Biotech Ltd
Field House Pharma Limited
Generic Physics Limited
Globyz Pharma (UK) Ltd
Gulfstream Equity & Development Ltd
IM High Tech Limited
Innomedi Limited
KHM Global Ltd
Lufuma B2b Services Ltd
Mayfair Export London Limited
Medicure Scientific Limited
Mundibiopharma Limited
Mundipharma Medical Co Ltd
NSA Pharma Limited

Novelgenix Therapeutics Ltd
Novus Medicare Ltd
Orpharma Limited
Ozone Medical Supplies Ltd
Par Laboratories Europe, Ltd.
Payal Pharma UK Ltd
Respond Healthcare Scotland Ltd
Rovi Biotech Limited
Sanos Healthcare Ltd
Sivanta Resourcing Limited
Spodefell Pharma Chemicals Ltd
Swanson Trade Ltd
Trion Pharma Limited
Wilkinson Healthcare Limited
Your Products Limited

**January 2015** [12]
Bestlon Limited
Brituswip Limited
Ecco Healthcare Limited
London Health Suppliers Ltd
Macacha Health Limited
McQuilkin & Co Limited
Medbarn Limited
Medis Medical (UK) Limited
Medstore Limited
Molecule Healthcare Limited
Prolife (UK) Limited
Sintal Impex Limited

**February 2015** [13]
Active Global Ltd
Bio-Sight Ltd
Euromed Technologie Limited
GHC Global Limited
IQ Pharma Ltd
MMP Marketing Limited
Mena Pharma UK Limited
Sara Post Ltd
Respond Healthcare Limited
Ris Healthcare Limited
Sebbin UK Ltd
Vital Pharma Limited
Winsor Pharma UK Limited

**March 2015** [14]
ATI Pharmaceuticals Limited
Duncan Inc Ltd
Gate Pharma Ltd
Grey Traders Limited
Latam HQ Health Ltd
Lorteben Trading Co., Ltd
MD-Reproductive Health Solutions Ltd
Nigem International Limited
PI Herman Trading as Peter's Ltd
Perush Ltd
Relyer Health Limited
T-Pharma Limited
ThriveExtreme Health Limited
Ursus UK Limited

**April 2015** [17]
C.D. Medical Limited
NV Campbell Limited
Chemys Limited
Druid Pharma Limited
June Medical International Ltd
Leadiant Biosciences Limited
Medicalstore-24 Limited
N N Pharma Ltd

Odiham OH Products Limited
Pamy International Ltd
Pharmacierge Group Limited
Pharmacierge Limited
Pharmacierge Technology Ltd
Pharmnet Group Ltd
SSCP Blink Bidco Limited
Tanner Pharma UK Limited
Technoglobal Ltd

**May 2015**
Acle Medical Limited
Delta Sales Ltd
Galenus Biomedical Limited
Pharmapoint UK Ltd

**June 2015** [10]
Accutest Solutions Limited
Chefarma Limited
Dompe UK Limited
Epsilon Pharmaceuticals Ltd
GHC Medical Ltd
Global 4 Care Ltd
Morgan Steer Developments Ltd
Rose Gentec Ltd
SV Syon Med Ltd
Soho Flordis UK Limited

**July 2015** [23]
BR Scientific Limited
Cardio Pro Limited
Charlwood Pharma Limited
Clarity Woundcare Ltd
Dispensing Direct Services Ltd
Elmstone Healthcare Limited
Frezyderm UK Limited
Gos Pharma Limited
Halewood Health Limited
Leca Pharma Limited
Manx Generics Limited
Newtons Medical Supplies Ltd
Ofege Pharm Ltd
Pharma Mar Limited
Pharmassist Locums Limited
Pharmex International Ltd
Remote Pharma Solutions Ltd
Santhera (UK) Limited
Sprint Pharma Limited
Strides Pharma Global (UK) Ltd
Surgihoney Limited
Trans Swiss Ltd
Youmed Limited

**August 2015** [6]
Anfarm Generics UK Limited
Clymed Healthcare Ltd
Ideal Medical Holdings Ltd
JSK PVT Limited
MGC Pharma (UK) Ltd
Purepharm Ltd

**September 2015** [14]
AIG Unico Ltd
Abstragan Limited
All1 Limited
Art Pharma Oxford Ltd
Blue Horizon Healthcare Consulting
Excel Pharma Limited
Imex Ltd
Intercept Pharma UK & Ireland Ltd

Kernfarm UK Limited
Lamyra International Limited
Nagarjun Healthcare Limited
Oakways Healthcare Limited
Sterling Bio-Pharma Ltd
WR Mediservices Limited

**October 2015** [10]
2M PH. Intl. Limited
Cibus Animal Nutrition Ltd
Dentel Group Ltd
Farmachem Limited
Raj Ghai Associates Limited
Ihealthcare Genius Limited
Pharmhouse Ltd
Pro Teeth Whitening Co Limited
Rak Pharma Ltd
Rex Pharmaceuticals Ltd

**November 2015** [9]
Altin Medical Ltd
Dragonstone Group Limited
Juice Sauz Ltd
Kelpharma Ltd
NC Trade UK Ltd
Novamed Pharma Ltd
SRS Pharma Limited
UK Branded Medicines Ltd
Zymix Limited

**December 2015** [9]
Cenote Pharma Limited
Flen Health UK Ltd
Medhub Limited
Passion Dental Design Studio (Laboratory)
RB (China Trading) Limited
Rafarm UK Limited
Seltfar Ltd
Sterling London Ventures Ltd
Zista Pharma Limited

**January 2016** [20]
Astra MCR Limited
Atnahs Pharma US Limited
BritaniaMark Limited
Chloraco Healthcare Limited
Connective Pharma Limited
Daleacre Wholesale Limited
GP Mediplus Ltd
Guardian Pharmaceuticals Co Ltd
Hayat Gostar Ltd
Imperial Bioscience Ltd
Indigo Diagnostics Limited
Leeds Industries (UK) Ltd
Nasila Pharma Limited
Orly Pharma Limited
Parapharm Development Limited
Pioneer Veterinary Products Ltd
Sintetica Limited
Tannerlac UK Limited
UK Eagle Ltd
Viemeds Limited

# The Top UK Pharmaceutical Wholesalers

**February 2016** [9]
Client-Pharmacy UK Ltd
G & C Pharma Limited
Healthbest Limited
JLVET Ltd
M & M Taste of Harmony Export Ltd
Medica Finance UK Ltd
Nordic Generics Ltd
Oxford Medpharma Ltd
RD & Med Co Ltd

**March 2016** [22]
ATP Medical Limited
Acer Pharma Limited
Apricot Forest Ltd
Dermal Aesthetics Clinic Ltd
Directpharm Ltd
Double Wing Health & Beauty Ltd
Double Wing Medical Ltd
Double Wing Pharma Development Ltd
EVC Compounding Ltd
Europa Health Limited
Everypharma Co., Ltd.
Global Pharma Direct Ltd
HEC Pharm UK Limited
Interport Direct Limited
Jorvik Pharma Ltd
Legendbio Beauty Group Limited
Medicern Export Ltd
Morvigor (UK) Ltd
Novamedi Limited
Propharma Consultancy Ltd
SF Pharma Limited
TRT Global Ltd

**April 2016** [14]
Arex Pharma Ltd
Euanet Limited
Hennessy Mason Ltd
Intercept Pharma Ltd
Interport Direct (Europe) Ltd
Monarch Health Ltd
Nutravit Ltd.
Pearl Chemist Group Limited
Pearl Services (Tooting) Ltd
Propharma-UK Ltd
Ragit Services Ltd
Saving Life Technologies Ltd
Titan Med Limited
Wescroft Limited

**May 2016** [17]
ASG Pharma Ltd
Aerona Clinical Limited
Bial Pharma UK Limited
Chanelle Medical GB Limited
Cynosure Group Ltd
Enfield Nutrition Club Ltd
Fayroz Ltd
Macrobiotics Group Ltd
Medtech Trading Limited
Padma Healthcare Limited
Phaximed Limited
Specialty Pharma of London Ltd
Speedx Limited
Srigen Pharma Ltd
Suerte Pharma Limited
Vipharm Limited
Water-Jel International Ltd

**June 2016** [12]
2 Shy 2 Buy Limited
A B Alliance Limited
Bioavexia Ltd
Celtis Healthcare Ltd
NeilMed Holding Co Ltd
Prominer Limited
Rothes Pharma Limited
Saint-Germain Pharma Ltd
Salutem Supplements Ltd
Scientific Laboratory Supplies Group Ltd
Swiss-American CDMO International
Vitamed Int Ltd

**July 2016** [6]
Curelife Ltd
Fox Group International Ltd
MCL Healthcare Limited
Remedine Limited
Trical Pharm Ltd
Wellness Clinical Supplies Ltd

**August 2016** [19]
378 Co Ltd
Aayur Limited
Benatur Limited
Bone Support UK Ltd
By Direct Limited
Chesdeg Limited
Geopharma UK Ltd.
Ihsan Pharma Ltd
Ivee Group Ltd
LGS Pharma Limited
PMS Korea Ltd
Pennine UK Procedure Packs Ltd
Pharmaethics International Ltd
Prema Naturals Limited
Premax Europe Limited
Private Pharma Health Co Ltd
Private Pharmacy Group Limited
RP Pharma International Ltd
Safenet Direct Ltd

**September 2016** [16]
Anrise Trading Limited
CG Pharma Ltd
Celloxess (Europe) Limited
Concord Pharma Services (UK) Ltd
Direct Pharma Limited
Harley Dentist Limited
Inventive Medical Solutions Ltd
London Health Sciences Ltd
Melo Labs UK Ltd
Prodigy Healthcare Limited
Pure Light Vision Ltd
SDM Healthcare Limited
Treas Biotechnology UK Ltd
United Kingdom Medica Ltd
Ved Healthcare Limited
Vitopia Ltd

**October 2016** [21]
Artmedica Ltd
Biophage Therapeutics Ltd
Caragen (UK) Limited
Clinical Services International Ltd
Einoxy Limited
Farmedic (UK) Limited
Matrix Healthcare Solutions Ltd
Metropharm Limited
Overseas Merchandising Corporation Ltd
Panorama Healthcare Limited
Patient Care Holdings Ltd
Primrose Hudson Limited
Proup Ltd
RPG Medical Limited
RX Pharma (Europe) Limited
Sakar Healthcare UK Ltd.
Sharief Pharma Limited
Shoebury West Road Ltd
Surgical Devices Developers Ltd
Trilogy Medical Systems Ltd
Vegamed UK Limited

**November 2016** [17]
Acure Pharma Limited
Amryt Pharma (UK) Limited
Curist Health Limited
Dynamic Development Laboratories Co Ltd
Emra Consult Limited
Health Medbio Ltd
Here We Flo Ltd
MB Pharma Limited
Pacific Pharma UK Limited
Pharma World Ltd
Pure Products London Limited
SAR Health Limited
Stem Cellx Limited
Sustainable Ethical Enterprises Ltd
Uni Supply Ltd
Valentis Life Sciences Limited
Zerocann Ltd

**December 2016** [15]
1966 Health International Ltd
Advanced Medical Products Ltd
Bluesky Cosmetics Limited
Clifton Organic Limited
Cryotag Limited
Gagnon Direct Ltd
Granules Europe Limited
HQEM Pharma Limited
Novalabb Limited
Optimal Pharma Ltd
Orphic Limited
S M Locum Consultants Ltd
System Deep Clinic Limited
Techdow Pharma England Limited
Vitaminka Ltd

**January 2017** [24]
Appleby Pharmacy Limited
Biovate Limited
Buduscheye Techniqa Ltd
Camurus Ltd
Chameleon Planet Ltd
DC Surgical Supplies Limited
GP Meds Direct Limited
Global Medical Supply UK Ltd
Healthcare Pharma Limited
Hotteeze International Limited
Mad Doctor Holdings Limited
Mammoth Dental Supplies Ltd
Masa Pharma Ltd
Munro Healthcare Pharma Ltd
Noru Pharma PVT Ltd.
Pamx Enterprise Limited
Prescribe Direct Limited
Skarby Gai Ltd
Sophos Medical Limited
Source Healthcare Ltd

Symmetry Inc Ltd
Timeocean Ltd
Trafalgar Pharma Ltd
Vitapro Limited

**February 2017** [20]
A1 Natural Ltd
AZL Holdings Ltd
Asymchem Limited
Chronicles Medical Consulting Ltd
Connexon Global Networks Ltd
Core Environmental PLC
Discount Healthcare Ltd
Garusa Solutions U.K. Limited
Great British Bee Co Ltd
IPY Healthcare Ltd
Imperial Medical Innovations Ltd
K Chem (North East) Ltd
My Dental Store Limited
New Health Global Solutions Ltd
Spey Limited
Spey Pharma Limited
Tradebuffalo Ltd
Vet Store Trading Limited
WHL Contracts Ltd
ZMI Investments Limited

**March 2017** [23]
Active Prescription Limited
Athem Pharma Limited
Bacteflora Ltd
Bbeauty Lounge Limited
Bioturm Limited
Crossbridge Concepts Limited
Doksy Limited
Flow Wealth Ltd
Future Healthcare Ltd
I L Locum Ltd
KD Pharmacon Ltd
Luban & Murr Ltd
Medipro Pharma Limited
Medisca UK Limited
Neo Farma Ltd
Omapharm Limited
Sage Therapeutics Limited
Springs Healthcare Limited
Stiltec Global (UK) Ltd
Storepharm UK Ltd
T-In Medical Limited
Wholesale 2 U Ltd
Zota Healthcare Limited

**April 2017** [19]
AP Import Export Ltd
Areessco Ltd
Arisio Ltd
Clinical Direct Ltd
Evolve Generics Limited
Evolve Pharma Limited
HJ Wholesale Limited
Hitop Pharmaceuticals Limited
Johnlee Pharmaceuticals (UK) Ltd
La Lune Noire Ltd
Medisale Limited
Nikopharm Ltd
Onpharma Limited
Pharma Trading Limited
Pharmex-UK Ltd
Shkar Enterprise Limited
TTC Medical GTS Limited
UK Pharmacies Ltd
Wycombe Locum Services Ltd

**May 2017** [20]
Beautons Ventures Ltd
Bri Trade Solutions Limited
CPX Solutions Limited
Cambpharma Ltd
Chemx Ltd
Easho Limited
Eastern Lighthouse Ltd
G9UK Limited
Gelu Life Limited
Green Guru Enterprices Ltd.
Herbaleva Ltd
J & T World Trade (UK) Limited
Maze Healthcare Ltd.
Medaesthetics Limited
OT Masters Limited
Paragen Pharma Ltd
Petersone Group Ltd
Rexcel Trading Ltd
St Marks Medical Ltd
Welcome Health Pharmacies Ltd

**June 2017** [16]
A V Pharma Limited
Aadverv Sourcing Solutions Ltd
Avanzcare Limited
DCH Subco Ltd
Dentitreat Co Ltd
Exmed Worldwide Limited
Healtholozy UK Limited
Hygamp Limited
IMS Ultrasound (UK) Ltd
Kanish Ltd
MQS Group London Limited
RF Vapes Limited
Randall Allison Limited
Simba Pharmatech Limited
Thexo Pharma Limited
ZS Pharma Limited

**July 2017** [18]
ACL Medical Limited
Attentive Pharma Limited
Day Med Limited
Elias Med Limited
Ely Pharma Ltd
Fayroz Pharma Limited
H & S Beauty Care Limited
Health Source Limited
Healthcare 4life Ltd
LZ Pharma Ltd
Nasser Waziri Ltd
Natures Merchant Ltd
Neo Health UK Limited
Pharmacy Business Consultancy Ltd
Sharepool Limited
Tech Innovation Laser Limited
Usme Limited
Vitalit Trade Limited

**August 2017** [14]
8 Trading Limited
Alizcare Limited
Amin Locum Limited
Avicenna Ltd
Bhendriks Resale and Retale Ltd
Future Pharmacare Limited
Koln Pharma Ltd
McKesson Global Sourcing UK Ltd
Nevik Limited

Samax Pharma Ltd
Sfera Trading Limited
Star Freight Forwarding Ltd
Stockport Healthcare Limited
Windzor Pharma Limited

**September 2017** [26]
Arkad Healthcare Limited
Atra Corporation Ltd
Behsarel Trading Ltd
CEU Pharm Ltd
Coastal Core Ltd
Coriungo Limited
Crown Global Traders Limited
Ecomed UK Limited
Elektro Genesis Limited
Essex Medical Supplies Ltd
GQC Solutions Ltd
Horopito Limited
Identimed Limited
LB Pharma Limited
Lifenza UK Limited
Medbury Limited
Naturelo Ltd
Pavay Venture International Ltd
Pharmayas UK Limited
RND Pharma Limited
Royce Health Sciences Ltd
Sarepta International UK Ltd.
Symom Limited
Theramex HQ UK Limited
UK Beauty Cosmetics International Group
Vityz Nutrition Limited

**October 2017** [25]
Alturix Limited
Amarox Limited
Augmenix UK Limited
Balagrae Ltd
Chelsea Pharma Limited
Cosmedic Pharmacy Limited
DML Pharma Consultancy Limited
Day Pharma Limited
EVR Biosciences (UK) Ltd
Herbal Food Life Limited
Iophtha Limited
Leigh Jones & Associates Ltd
Manta Medical Limited
Medix Supply International Ltd
Nanocor World Holdings Limited
New Medical World Ltd
Nosher Pharma Private Ltd
Nisha Patel Ltd
Pharmazz Europe Limited
Ted Medical Ltd
Topcell Pharma Limited
United Pharma Group Limited
Vak Enterprise Limited
Christopher Wood IXRS Consulting Ltd
Zoono Holdings Limited

## The Top UK Pharmaceutical Wholesalers

**November 2017** [32]
Aria Vape Ltd
Aryahakim Medical Equipment Co Ltd.
Better Earth Limited
Bioconnections Ltd
Boost Hair Limited
Brent Medicare Limited
Dil More Remedies UK Ltd
Edi Beryl Ltd
Florence Health & Beauty Ltd
GM Biopharma Ltd
Global Supply (U.K.) Ltd
HCP Limited
Herbert and Herbert Pharmacy Ltd
Immortalis Distribution Ltd.
Key Nutrients 4 Life Ltd
Kora Healthcare UK Ltd
Larmed Limited
Lyshaug Enterprises Limited
Marvellous Pharma Ltd
Matter Drinks Trading Ltd
Morn View Chemicals (UK) Ltd
Neubria Limited
Paria Medical Aesthetics Ltd
Pharmargus Healthcare Ltd
Priors Pharma Limited
Quirky Vapes Ltd
Remedy JV Limited
Riviere Groupe (Europe) Ltd
Roberts McCarron Ltd
Rosalique Skincare Limited
Sonifar Pharma Expert Limited
Welcome Medical Group Ltd

**December 2017** [21]
A.J. Prime Ltd
Aptitud Pharma Ltd
Belinda Limited
Bristol Consumer Health Ltd
Click Solutions Ltd
Construct4lyfe Ltd
EAM Wholesale Ltd
Fitnatix International Ltd
Five Star International Consulting
Kamo Dental Products Limited
Kids Medicare Limited
Kohilam Limited
MM Medical Equipment UK Ltd
McKinley Pharma Limited
Nutrabizz Nutraceuticals Ltd
Ocusoft UK Limited
Paraxmed Limited
Tia Marie Ltd
Unifarco Ltd
Wep Group Holdings Limited
Zolex Global Limited

**January 2018** [33]
Apetamintko Limited
Apotheke San Biagio SRL Ltd
Ardent Pharmaceuticals Ltd
Barustore Limited
CBS Trade Limited
Cygnus Pharma Ltd
DGI Technologies Limited
Decibel Biopharm Limited
Eyecon Vision Limited
Frontrow International UK Ltd
Got Heart UK Ltd
Healthy Era Ltd
House of Filler Limited

Huayawei Biomedical Co Ltd
Kingsley Specials Limited
LDC International Limited
London Spirit for Trading Ltd
Lucid Wholesale Ltd
Medinox (London) Limited
N-Pen Ltd.
New Generation Business UK Ltd
Old Latchmerians Limited
Oswell Penda Pharmaceutical Ltd
Parker Trading Ltd
Prescribe International Ltd
Sigmatec Limited
Smoketrees Ltd
Solarius UK & Overseas Limited
South China Bio-Pharma Co Ltd.
St Georges Pharmaceuticals Ltd
Tuluh Solutions Ltd
UK Lab Supplies Ltd
Ultrascan Solutions Ltd

**February 2018** [32]
ACESO Global Ltd
Aariana Impex Limited
Acre Medical Limited
Adicam Pharmaceuticals Ltd
All Med Care Limited
Alumier Medical UK Limited
Arquella Ltd
Athenex Euro Limited
Atrimusrx Ltd
Bin'auf Limited
Biogenix Ltd
A & P Blickling Ltd
Canary Islands Marketing Board Ltd
Cellcosmo Suisse Limited
Dark Atom Limited
Dermapure Aesthetics Limited
Enjoy Marketing Limited
Fitness and Nutrition of Europe Ltd.
Fox Group Global Ltd
Hydro Tan Limited
Iberia Skin Brands Ltd
Lexon UK Holdings Limited
Medcare Life UK Ltd
Menar UK Biotech Ltd
Modor & Bearn Limited
NBS Scientific Limited
Nicholas LifeSciences Ltd.
Oscar & Louis Limited
Pharmaco Halesowen Limited
Pharmunity Limited
Pneumech Limited
Positive Pharma Ltd

**March 2018** [41]
11239338 Ltd
ABI Training Academy Limited
ACI Group Ltd
Alixport Ltd
Apple Pharma Limited
Aviva Health Solutions Limited
Blink Street Limited
Clinic Supply Ltd
Expedite Therapeutics Limited
Feel and Heal UK Limited
Flydonging Eletctronic Ltd
General Shop Ltd
Hanseco Ltd
Healthbiotics Ltd
Healthcaps Europe Ltd

Honilac Nutrition Limited
Infinity Biomedical Ltd
Kganesha Pharma Ltd
MD Salisbury Ltd
MSB Pharma Ltd
Myly Pharma Limited
Novalio Pharma Limited
Novelius Medical Limited
PPQUK Ltd
Pennine Pharmaceuticals Ltd
Pharma Products Limited
Pinklady International Ltd
RB UK Hygiene Home Commercial Ltd
RJT Pharma Services Ltd
RR Cosmeceuticals (UK) Ltd
Rah Pharma Ltd
Ruger Barber Limited
Sinduram Healthcare International Ltd
Star Powa Limited
Streamline Pharmaceuticals Ltd
Support To Perform Ltd
Taineng Medicine Ltd
Tulip Cup Limited
Virudist Ltd
World Trends Ltd
Zululan Pharma Ltd

**April 2018** [28]
Acehides Limited
Adedoyin Adebisi Ltd
Angel & Lockhart (Pharma) Ltd
BB Lifestyle UK Limited
Bioleys Care Ltd
CBD -Tec Limited
Care Healthcare Ltd
Daryeel Medicines International Ltd
Dentlaser Limited
Dilmaherbals Limited
Foreverbeyoung Ltd
Health Nutrient Products Ltd
Holistic Med Ltd
IMI Ventures Limited
Kaboodan Limited
Keziah Ltd
Max Motivation Limited
Medex Pharma Limited
N4 Biotech Limited
Noohra Limited
Omega Alpha Pharma Limited
RPH Pharma Ltd
Receptor Technologies Limited
Sipco Nutrition (UK) Ltd
Tudor Pharma Ltd
Unmaan Healthcare Limited
Veenak Sourcing Limited
Venture Four Ltd.

**May 2018** [47]
Aces Pharma Limited
Amaxa Ltd
Avail Group UK Limited
Blackpool Medicines Limited
Bray Pharma Limited
CBD Oil Direct Limited
Chitorhino Ltd
Citux Medical Limited
Clever Connect Ltd
Crispin Enterprises Limited
Elanco UK AH Limited
Ever Pharma UK Limited
Eyekonic Wellbeing Limited

First Choice Suppliments Ltd
GMM Sales Ltd
Health Remit Limited
Karczek Ltd
London Supplements Distribution Ltd
Mapaex Consumer Healthcare (UK) Private
Matt L Consultancy Ltd
Mayapharm Limited
Medi-Arch Ltd
Medics Direct Pharmacy Limited
Medivast Limited
Meta Innovation Nutrition Ltd
Nascot Natural Health Limited
Newmeds Wholesale Limited
Nex Pharma Limited
Pharma Oasis Ltd
Pharmasif Direct Limited
Plurafores Pharma Limited
Quantum Biomed Ltd
Ria Sales Corporation Ltd
J Sherlee Ltd
Skylark Services Limited
Skymedic UK Limited
Sonchat Limited
Surgicaide Medical Supplies UK Ltd
TA-65 (UK) Wholesale Limited
Trishool Pharma Ltd
Tuba Ltd
Unidus Limited
United Orphan Pharma Limited
Uvita Health Limited
Vise Services Ltd
Vitb12 Academy Ltd
Zaaz Limited

**June 2018** [39]
10x Rational Ambulance Yield Ltd
AF Healthcare Ltd
Ascent (Hartlepool) Limited
Aspen Pharmacare UK Limited
Beauty Boosters Ltd
Mark Birch Hair Ltd
Dr Ba Limited
Eden CBD Limited
Faith and Pharma Limited
Gateway for Africa Ltd
Genmed UK Limited
Genrx UK Lipperts Ltd.
Goldpharma Ltd
HB Sirius Ltd
Herbialis Limited
Hilotherm Ltd
Instant Test Ltd
JE Medical Associates Ltd.
K588 Limited
MKS Pharma Ltd
Medspero Pharma Ltd
Nema Pharma Trade Limited
Pharma Maiden Ltd
Pope Enterprises Ltd
Premium Pharma UK Limited
Prime Medical Equipment Ltd
Redlight Exchange Ltd
Riebeeckstad Limited
Roble Medical Ltd
SG Pharma UK Limited
Sanzenica Limited
Satio Pharma Ltd.
Suplan Ltd
Supplemax Ltd
Timpext (Trading-Import-Export) Ltd
Unimed Global Limited

Univape Global Ltd
Whiterose Supplements Limited
Wilkies International Ltd

**July 2018** [38]
ABC Pharmaceuticals Ltd
Ananda Trading Limited
BDCP Ltd
Better'er Limited
Botha Group Ltd
Bpharm Group Limited
Bulgarian Healthy Products Ltd
Cambridge Biotics Ltd
Derma Distribution Ltd
Dollano Trading Limited
Elcon Pharma Limited
Fresh Cache Holdings Limited
Gideotech Limited
Global Medical Supplies Ltd
Hapa Medical UK Ltd
Iniaso Ltd
Iniaso Pharma Ltd
Inmed Ltd
Innovius Life Drugs Ltd
Legacy Private Limited
Medical Need UK Ltd
Meds Global Limited
Nova Pharmacare Ltd
Oak Zone Biotech UK Ltd
P C LDN Ltd
Pharmaethical Ltd
Rashedeen Pharma Group Ltd
Simply Meds Pro Ltd
Sonal Pharma (UK) Ltd
Sports Star Distribution UK Ltd
Stop Ltd
THS Solutions Limited
Topnot Ltd
V2M Pharma Limited
Vita Nova International Ltd
Vitwell Limited
Vyom International Ltd.
Xenium International Limited

**August 2018** [49]
AB Pharma Logistics Ltd
Aesthetics Clinic Dot Limited
Al Razi Pharma UK Ltd
Apex Lab Scientific Ltd
Auramedicann Ltd
Ba-Inspire Limited
Best-Bio Ltd
Bio Global Limited
Bioxane Ltd
Britpharma UK Limited
Busky Limited
CHM Trading Limited
Cannabinoidmeds Limited
Cannapharm Limited
Dayonix Pharma Limited
Detafinas Limited
Elite Pharma UK Limited
Frontier Lab Scientific Ltd
GPM Pharma Limited
Hasting Pharma Ltd
Ideal Cleaning Systems Ltd
Ikatrad Ltd
Irls Yorkshire Limited
Kyo Ltd
Lad & Company Private Limited
Longevity Life Ltd

MRG Creations Ltd
Masir Ltd
Med-Link Limited
Medica Ltd
Medicines Extra Healthcare Ltd
Moriah Healthcare Distribution Ltd
OFC Molecular Ltd
Pharmaxone Limited
Premium Pharm Ltd
Pure Skincare Limited
Rivertime Distribution Ltd
Secret Line Ltd
Skinlab Medical Ltd
Sky Hemp Ltd
Southampton Medical Group Ltd
Spectrum Biomedical UK Limited
Tearfilm Therapeutics Ltd
UK Lemenic International Medical Group
Unimed Healthcare Supplies Ltd
Victoria Meds Mondial Ltd
Vitaempower Ltd
Vivaorganiclife Ltd
Vwin Lifestyle Limited

**September 2018** [40]
56 Flowers Ltd
Acer Agri Ltd
Acre Aesthetics Limited
Andrei & Maria Ltd
Britannic Pharma Ltd
Day International Limited
Dr Pradeep Reddy's Laboratories (UK & EU)
E.P.G Pharma Ltd
Esthetica Pure Ltd
Five Pharm Ltd
Fulbo Ltd
GlaxoSmithKline US Trading Ltd
Global SCS Limited
Greens Roads UK Ltd
HMS Wholesale Ltd
Imphatec Ltd
Irismed Pharma Ltd
Katvic Limited
Kent Pharma UK Limited
Laogong Laopo Limited
Luye Pharma Ltd
Mayomed Limited
Medpharm Global UK Limited
Medsupply Ltd
Microskin Cosmeceuticals UK Ltd
Moogle Meds Ltd
My-Kaya Ltd
Organic Iway Ltd
PH Medicare Ltd
Pharmazon Limited
Pharmdex UK Ltd
Semenalysis Limited
Sup-Up Ltd
TMZ Naturals Limited
Treatlines Limited
U A Ali Ltd
Unison Pharmaceuticals Ltd
Vise Services PVT Ltd
A.Vogel Limited
Wellacy Limited

**October 2018** [42]
Alhaddag Phrma Ltd
Ascot Treatments Ltd
Biotus Ltd
CBD Vape Ltd

Chirock Trading Ltd
Dermconcept Ltd
Farmako Limited
Fijez Ltd
Furn WW Lux Ltd
Graviti Healthcare Limited
Haq Pharm Ltd
Honest Health Limited
Internal Luxe Heights Ltd
International Pharma Co Ltd
Ironbridge Medical Services Ltd
Irving and Skinner Ltd
Kings Medical Supplies Limited
LS Pharma UK Limited
Leafxtracts Ltd
Life Science Healthcare UK Ltd
Martini International Ltd
Maxlott Ltd
Mulberry Pharma Ltd
Adam Myers Solutions Limited
Nativis Bio Ltd
Nino and Blue Spruce Ltd
Nordic Nutraceuticals UK Ltd
Nutrifast Ltd
Odyssey Healthcare Limited
Raw Medicus Ltd
Rightdose Solutions Limited
Simcare Global Premium Healthcare Ltd
Standford Ltd
Sunmed Pharma Ltd
Supphero Ltd
Tetra Hydro Cannabinoid Oils Global Ltd
Triaton Ltd
VLCare Limited
Veyda Pharma Ltd
Vivacy Laboratoires Ltd
Z T Locums Ltd
Zeymos Pharma Ltd

**November 2018** [55]
AAP Healthcare Ltd
AMG Pharmaceuticals Limited
Aesthetic & Wellness Pharmacy Ltd
Allpa Kallpa Ltd
Alverda Ltd
Aventa International Corporation Ltd
Biophos Labs Ltd
Cannamedical Pharma UK Limited
Celestial Pharma Ltd
Cellchem UK Limited
Celltrion Healthcare United Kingdom
Codix Pharma (UK) Limited
Cutman Ltd
DLG Partners Limited
DMG Trading Limited
Dong Hwa UK Ltd
Dr Sproglet Ltd
Farmsvet Ltd
Fivtique Limited
Fox Pharma Limited
GMP-Orphan United Kingdom Ltd
Gama Group Services Ltd
Genesis Pharma Limited
Green Sun Ltd
Hana Healthcare Ltd
Hyaluron Health Ltd
Iaso Ltd
Infinite Percent Limited
JP & A Pharma Ltd
KW Wholesale Ltd
LK Health Ltd
Lax Pharma Limited

Layan Pharma Ltd
MSP Pharm Ltd
Manek Healthcare Ltd
Mayfair Distributors Limited
Medintek Holdings Ltd
Millennium Global Limited
NKCell Plus PLC
Natchy Ltd
ORAA Ltd
PF OFG UK 3 Ltd
Pfizer OFG UK Limited
Pharmacohub Limited
Pharmavit (UK) Limited
Portland Ventures Inc Ltd
Pure Solace Ltd
Rocha Products Limited
SL Clinical Ltd
Sanhak Ltd
SkInOne UK Ltd
Style Global Trading FZE Ltd
TBD Wellness Limited
UK Pharma Direct Limited
Valugen Pharma Limited

**December 2018** [39]
1st Class Medical Ltd
AMH (N.I.) Ltd
Azurite Health Ltd
Biocon Pharma UK Limited
Biogenez Ltd
Biotek Diagnostics Limited
Cannerald Group Ltd
Comebro International Ltd
Comfylife Ltd
Dr Kool Ltd
Drugget Ltd
Elara Care Limited
Eton Pharma Ltd
Farmvet Limited
Fen Health Ltd
Full Spectrum Pharma Limited
Geoorganics Limited
Hemastem Ltd
IPS International Corporation Ltd
Instantly White Ltd
JAO Enterprises Ltd
Leems Solutions Limited
Livewell Naturals Limited
Mast - Art Group Limited
Maximed Ltd
Modern Innovations Limited Ltd
My Nutrition London Ltd
P.I.C. International Ltd
Pharm Med Ltd
Pharmacare International Ltd
Rapid Pharma Limited
Skinska Pharmaceutica Limited
Specials Pharma Ltd
Springwell Transport and Logistics Ltd
Symbiosis Biosciences Limited
Vicars Cross Healthcare Ltd
Worldtrition Ltd
Zarroug Limited
Zoop Pharma Ltd

**January 2019** [57]
Activated Smile Ltd
Anti Venom Ltd
Aqua Hydration Limited
Arya House Pharma Ltd
Axe Pharma Ltd

Baron Medicare UK Limited
Biosensors International UK Ltd
Bosses Onlinestore Ltd
CBD4You Limited
Candover UK Ltd
Cannaid Ltd
Castle Green (N.I.) Ltd
Clyde Valley Cannaceuticals Ltd
Corwhite Solutions Limited
Croma-Pharma Limited
DCMP 8E Cepac Limited
Dacre Skincare Limited
Deva Pharma Medical Ltd
Diaylaa Ltd
Everhealth Ltd
Hooben Distributors Limited
Imamcom Ltd
Initio Cell Limited
Josana Limited
K N B Services Ltd
Karo Pharma UK Ltd
Libertas Medical Ltd
Lyferoots Ltd
Matrix Healthcare Limited
Medi Test Pharma Ltd
Medica Pharma UK Ltd
Meds Online 247 Limited
My Premium Nutrition Limited
Nascot Health Ltd
Niv Ltd
Norpan Hymbre Ltd
Nutramax Ltd
Orkal Ltd
Oxford Supramolecular Biotechnology
Pericia Ltd
Pharmasol London Ltd
Pro Orbit Limited
R & R Post Op Box Ltd.
Reviv Pharma Ltd
Rising Sun Ventures Ltd
SHL Medical Limited
Sampsonstore.Com (UK) Ltd
Schulz Medical Supplies Ltd
Stellar Labs Ltd
Sufi Enterprise Wholesalers Ltd
Tiamat Agriculture Ltd
Tour N' Cure International Ltd.
Trinity VN Limited
Ukcann Ltd
Veda Biosciences Limited
Veepharm Limited
Zhongfu (UK) Limited

**February 2019** [46]
1LIFE Distribution Limited
ANXT Ltd
Archangel's Pharmaceutical Services
Asaya Cosmeceuticals Limited
Astral Health Ltd
Branded Healthcare Ltd
Bristol Buttr Ltd
CBD Labz Ltd
CBD Platinum Ltd
Canconc Ltd
Capella Medical Device Ltd
Cebrenex Limited
Ceracoat Ltd
Cured CBD Ltd
Deise Pharm Ltd
Eddohealthcare Ltd
Equimed Medical Supplies Ltd
Ezhonsi Ltd

Falama Services Group Limited
Gerot Lannach UK Limited
Global Pharma Care Ltd
HAPA Group Holdings Limited
Hemp Remedy Ltd
Instinct Health Ltd
Intellix (Holdings) Limited
Kingston Pharma Limited
Limes Pharma Ltd
Matt 6:33 Ltd

Chanelle McCoy CBD UK Ltd
Chanelle McCoy Pharma UK Ltd
Medicaleaf Limited
My Chu Limited
Nivja Healthcare Ltd
Omark Plus Ltd
Parallel Investments Limited
Perennial Pharma Ltd
Pharm Recon Ltd
Pharma 313 Limited

Pharmedics Ltd
SSPharma4You Limited
Synergetic Global Limited
Tytek UK Medical Co Ltd
Unique Health Co Ltd
Value Medical Limited
Vital Haven Ltd
Wenimed Ltd

# Geographic Distribution by County

**Co Antrim** [25]
AMH (N.I.) Ltd
Activated Smile Ltd
Alchem PLC
Alp Trading Limited
Alpco Ltd
BTA Pharm Limited
Belfast Drug Ltd
J. Bradbury (Surgical) Ltd
CIGA Healthcare Limited
Crosspharma Limited
Galar Ireland Ltd
JLVET Ltd
Larmed Limited
Mansett Limited
Meridian Medical Technologies Ltd
John Preston & Co. (Belfast) Ltd
Prima Brands Limited
Prodigy Healthcare Limited
Sangers (Northern Ireland) Ltd
G & L Simpson Limited
Robert Smith & Co, (Derry) Ltd
Support To Perform Ltd
Swiss-American CDMO International
Trilogy Medical Systems Ltd
Veterinary Surgeons Supply Co Ltd

**Co Armagh** [7]
Agrihealth (N.I.) Limited
Galen Limited
Intergal Pharma Limited
Mossvet Limited
Nalchem Ltd
Paragen Pharma Ltd
Purepharm Ltd

**Co Down** [9]
AEV Consulting Ltd
Ballymote Pharmacy Limited
Castle Green (N.I.) Ltd
Elm Healthcare Limited
Excip Limited
MH (Newry) Ltd
N.I.P. Pharma Limited
Remedy JV Limited
Respond Healthcare Limited

**Co Fermanagh**
Deise Pharm Ltd

**Co Londonderry**
Coastal Core Ltd
Roe Pharmacy Ltd

**Co Tyrone**
Liam Bradley Ltd
Medbarn Limited
Omapharm Limited

**Aberdeenshire**
Steven F Webster Limited

**Angus**
Angus Medical Supplies Ltd
Moogle Meds Ltd

**Ayrshire** [5]
Bioforce (U.K) Limited
Condom Dot Com Ltd.
Ecco Healthcare Limited
Gorton Trading Limited
A.Vogel Limited

**Berwickshire**
Merlin Vet Export Ltd

**Dumfries-shire**
Eurocare Impex Services Ltd
Smoketrees Ltd

**Dunbartonshire**
Europharma Scotland Ltd

**Fife**
MAF Pharma Limited
MB Pharma Limited

**Lanarkshire** [48]
Alverda Ltd
Apple Pharma Limited
Aver Generics Limited
BN Medical Ltd
Baymed Group Ltd.
Baymed Healthcare Ltd.
Branded Healthcare Ltd
CBD -Tec Limited
CBD Oil Direct Limited
Chemx Ltd
Clyde Valley Cannaceuticals Ltd
Doctors Dispensing Services Ltd
Duncan Inc Ltd
EVR Biosciences (UK) Ltd
Eclipse Generics Limited
Ecosse Hospital Products Ltd
Ecosse Pharmaceuticals Limited
Ethigen Limited
Eyecon Vision Limited
Eyekonic Wellbeing Limited
GQC Solutions Ltd
Global Dispensing Limited
Healthcare Pharma Limited
Katvic Limited
Leca Pharma Limited
Tim Lever Distribution Ltd.
McQuilkin & Co Limited
Med-Link Limited
Munro Healthcare (Caucasus & Middle Asia)
Munro Healthcare Group Limited
Munro Healthcare Pharma Ltd
Munro Medical Limited
Munro Wholesale Medical Supplies Ltd
My Premium Nutrition Limited
Natures Merchant Ltd
Newco Pharma Limited
Newmeds Wholesale Limited
ORAA Ltd
Odyssey Healthcare Limited
Old Latchmerians Limited
Pharmabuyer Limited
Rightdose Solutions Limited
SPL (2010) Limited
Strathclyde Pharmaceuticals Ltd
TPC Pharma Limited
Target Healthcare Limited
U A Ali Ltd
Zululan Pharma Ltd

**Moray**
Rothes Pharma Limited

**Perthshire**
Agri-Bio Limited
Irasco Ltd

**Renfrewshire**
Bhendriks Resale and Retale Ltd
Campbell Medical Supplies Ltd
Cynosure Group Ltd

**Stirlingshire**
A D Healthcare Limited
Panorama Healthcare Limited

**Bedfordshire** [38]
8 Pharma Ltd
8 Trading Limited
Aneid UK Limited
Bright Polar Limited
Cape Pharmaceuticals Ltd
Cyan Trading Ltd
Cygnus Pharma Ltd
DMG Trading Limited
Discount Healthcare Ltd
Dr Kool Ltd
Emcure Pharma UK Ltd
Euro-Link Pharma Ltd
Excel Pharma Limited
Fair Pharm Limited
Fortis Egregius Limited
Healthcare Product Services Ltd
Healthcare Services Group Ltd
Herbert and Herbert Pharmacy Ltd
Intellix (Holdings) Limited
LBC Solutions Limited
Lab-Club Limited
Leems Solutions Limited
Marvellous Pharma Ltd
Movianto UK Limited
Mycology Research Laboratories Ltd
Oxford Supramolecular Biotechnology
Pharmacare (London) Limited
Pharmacare Logistics Limited
Pharmazz Europe Limited
RJE Agencies Limited
Regent Pharmaceuticals Limited
SDM Healthcare Limited
Seedos Ltd.
Sintal Impex Limited
Suplan Ltd
Tillomed Laboratories Limited
V2M Pharma Limited
Vak Enterprise Limited

# The Top UK Pharmaceutical Wholesalers

**Berkshire** [86]
2M PH. Intl. Limited
ACI Group Ltd
AZL Holdings Ltd
AbbVie Ltd
Abbott Healthcare Products Ltd
Abbott Laboratories Limited
Aegerion Pharmaceuticals Ltd
Alhaddag Phrma Ltd
Alk-Abello Limited
Ascot Treatments Ltd
Aspen Pharmacare UK Limited
Bayer PLC
Berkshire Wholesale Supplies (2002) Ltd
Bial Pharma UK Limited
Biobos Limited
Britannia Pharmaceuticals Ltd
Brituswip Limited
Candover UK Ltd
Carbosynth Limited
Carbotang Limited
Celloxess (Europe) Limited
Cenote Pharma Limited
Chanelle Medical GB Limited
Chanelle Vet U.K. Limited
Condomania (UK) Limited
Condomania PLC
Corwhite Solutions Limited
Czech, Moravian and Slovak Chemicals
DC Surgical Supplies Limited
Diana Royal Jelly Limited
Direct Pharma Limited
Elias Med Limited
Euromed Pharmaceuticals Ltd
Eye Guard Ltd
GCL Marketing Ltd
GMM Sales Ltd
Goldpharma Ltd
Ham+Med Co Ltd
Health Remit Limited
Hospira UK Limited
Inspiragen Limited
Ipsen Limited
KHM Global Ltd
Kamo Dental Products Limited
Kosei Pharma UK Ltd.
Langdales Limited
Leafxtracts Ltd
Leo Laboratories Limited
Lupin Healthcare (UK) Limited
Chanelle McCoy CBD UK Ltd
Chanelle McCoy Pharma UK Ltd
McNeil Healthcare (UK) Limited
Medical Need UK Ltd
Medicern Export Ltd
A. Menarini Diagnostics Ltd
Nasila Pharma Limited
Nicholas LifeSciences Ltd.
Nissi Business Services Ltd
Nordic Pharma Limited
Orphan Europe (UK) Limited
Otsuka Pharmaceuticals (U.K.) Ltd.
Parapharm Development Limited
Periproducts Limited
Pharma Mar Limited
Pharmacosmos UK Limited
Pharmalab Limited
Pro Orbit Limited
Pro Teeth Whitening Co Limited
Purple Orchid Pharma Limited
Qualitech Healthcare Ltd
RB (China Trading) Limited

RB UK Commercial Limited
RB UK Hygiene Home Commercial Ltd
Reckitt Benckiser Asia Pacific Ltd
Recordati Pharmaceuticals Ltd
SW Medical Solutions Limited
Sebbin UK Ltd
Servier IP UK Limited
Servier Laboratories Limited
Shard Speciality Pharma Ltd
Simcro (UK) Limited
Stada UK Holdings Ltd.
Stiefel Laboratories Limited
Sutherland Health Group Ltd
Valentis Life Sciences Limited
Vivus UK Limited

**Buckinghamshire** [44]
Advanced Eyecare Research Ltd
Allergan Limited
Alturix Limited
Arena Pharmaceuticals Limited
BDCP Ltd
Biotech International Limited
Bracco UK Limited
Cambridge Diagnostics (UK) Ltd
Clinimed Limited
Construct4lyfe Ltd
Daiichi Sankyo UK Limited
Design Masters (Sales) Limited
Dompe UK Limited
Dr. Falk Pharma UK Limited
Ego Pharmaceuticals (UK) Ltd
Eptheca Global Limited
Friends of Pyrethrum Ltd
Gelu Life Limited
Green Sun Ltd
Holistic Med Ltd
Hot Pharma Ltd
Hughenden Valley Pharma Ltd
I-Crackedit Ltd
IMI Ventures Limited
Imperial Medical Innovations Ltd
Infolight Limited
June Medical International Ltd
June Medical Ltd
Lansdales Pharmacy Limited
Life Science Healthcare UK Ltd
Lifecell EMEA Limited
Mediva Pharma Limited
A. Menarini Pharmaceuticals U.K.
Pharmazon Limited
SSPharma4You Limited
Spectrum Biomedical UK Limited
Sylk Limited
Takeda UK Limited
Trical Pharm Ltd
Vitamins To Buy Ltd
WR Mediservices Limited
Winelia Co Ltd
Wycombe Locum Services Ltd
Youmed Limited

**Cambridgeshire** [54]
A Wise World Limited
Aclardian Limited
Adedoyin Adebisi Ltd
Applied Medical Technology Ltd
Apretique Limited
Astrazeneca PLC
BM Alliance Limited
Beauty Shopper Ltd.

Cambpharma Ltd
Cambridge Biotics Ltd
Camurus Ltd
Celltrion Healthcare United Kingdom
Cimex Lectularius Limited
Corpus Nostrum Limited
Couch Rolls Limited
Couchrolls.co.uk Ltd
DDWS Limited
Dermocore Ltd.
Econo-Beauty Ltd
Econo-Care Ltd
Econo-Group Ltd
Econo-Supplies Ltd
Expedite Therapeutics Limited
Hambleden Herbs Limited
Infutech Limited
Invitech Ltd
Jackson Immunoresearch Europe Ltd
Kinesis Limited
Macratio Limited
Mundibiopharma Limited
Mundipharma Medical Co Ltd
Napp Laboratories Limited
Napp Pharmaceutical Group Ltd
Napp Pharmaceutical Holdings Ltd
Napp Pharmaceuticals Limited
Nigem International Limited
Oak Zone Biotech UK Ltd
Opalbond Limited
Pharma Insight Ltd
Pharmadose Limited
Precision Fluid Controls Ltd
Qdem Pharmaceuticals Limited
Salon Professional Limited
Salon Professional.Com Limited
Stratlab Limited
Ultrasoundgel Ltd
United Therapeutics Europe, Ltd.
Universal Biologicals (Cambridge)
Vitb12 Academy Ltd
Wilkinson Healthcare Limited
Wowwax Ltd.
Yaubag Limited
ZTK Business Services Limited
Zecare Limited

**Cardiganshire**
Apricot Forest Ltd

**Carmarthenshire**
Healthcare (Wales) Ltd.

**Cheshire** [72]
ABI Training Academy Limited
Acer Agri Ltd
Acer Pharma Limited
Acorus Therapeutics Limited
Advanced Medical Products Ltd
Amryt Pharma (UK) Limited
Andrews Pharmacy Limited
Archangel's Pharmaceutical Services
Astek Innovations Limited
Biomedica Nutraceuticals (UK) Ltd
Bosses Onlinestore Ltd
Caragen (UK) Limited
Chronicles Medical Consulting Ltd
Creative Supply Solutions Ltd
Crest Medical Limited
Dechra Veterinary Products Ltd
Deva Pharma Medical Ltd

Distinctive Medical Products Ltd
Dizzo Consulting (UK) Limited
Dr Ba Limited
First Aid Supplies Limited
Fox Group Global Ltd
Fox Group International Ltd
Fox Pharma Limited
G Pharma Limited
G Pharmaceuticals Ltd
Gee Lawson Limited
Genmed UK Limited
Grandbydale Limited
Guardian Pharmaceuticals Co Ltd
HCP Limited
HH Pharma Limited
HJ Wholesale Limited
Hamilton Pharmaceuticals Ltd
IMS Euro Limited
Initio Cell Limited
KD Pharmacon Ltd
Karczek Ltd
Laogong Laopo Limited
Matrix Healthcare Limited
Matrix Healthcare Solutions Ltd
Med-Col Limited
Medicalstore-24 Limited
Medicstar (UK) Limited
Melcare (Europe) Limited
Mistry Medical Supplies Ltd
Mitochondrial Therapy Ltd
Moscow Flyer Limited
My Chu Limited
Neubria Limited
Novus Medicare Ltd
Nucare Limited
Nupharm Limited
Pharmaxone Limited
Phoenix Healthcare Distribution Ltd
Phoenix Medical Supplies Ltd
Probiotec (UK) Limited
Qingdao Polychem (U.K.) Ltd
Reviv Pharma Ltd
L.Rowland & Co Ltd
SSCP Blink Bidco Limited
Skingen UK Ltd
T-Pharma Limited
Ted Medical Ltd
Trinity VN Limited
Unique Health Co Ltd
Vicars Cross Healthcare Ltd
Vision Pharmaceuticals Ltd
Vita Nova International Ltd
Westbourne Medical Limited
Winchpharma (Consumer Healthcare) Ltd
World Trends Ltd

**Cleveland** [12]
378 Co Ltd
Advanced Formulations (Europe) Ltd
Allans Healthcare Limited
Durham Pharmaceuticals Limited
GBY (UK) Ltd
NMB Medical Limited
Shkar Enterprise Limited
Sipco Nutrition (UK) Ltd
Sipco Pharma UK Ltd
Storepharm UK Ltd
Sunniside Healthcare Limited
Willgen Consulting Limited

**Clwyd**
Alston Garrard & Co Limited

S M Locum Consultants Ltd

**Co Derry**
Pharmacy Supplies Limited

**Co Durham** [8]
Coward Pharmacy Limited
Crispin Enterprises Limited
Dentitreat Co Ltd
Lens Factory (N.E) Ltd
Medi-Inn (UK) Ltd
Rand Rocket Limited
U L Medicines Limited
Welcome Health Pharmacies Ltd

**Cornwall** [6]
Betpharma UK Limited
Farmsvet Ltd
Mediclock Devices Limited
Steripharm (UK) Limited
Vasmed Technologies Limited
Zena Cosmetics (U.K.) Limited

**Cumbria**
CPX Solutions Limited
Greenliving Pharma Ltd
Malem Medical Limited
Turtle Rouge Ltd

**Denbighshire**
1st Health Products Ltd
JP & A Pharma Ltd
Melyd Medical Limited

**Derbyshire** [36]
2 Shy 2 Buy Limited
A V Pharma Limited
Alloga UK Limited
Ayva Pharma Limited
Bionical Limited
Contract QP Resource Limited
Credenhill Limited
Currie Marketing Limited
Cutman Ltd
Daleacre Wholesale Limited
Ellis Pharma Limited
Raj Ghai Associates Limited
H C Healthcare Ltd
IPG Pharma Limited
IQ Pharma Ltd
Inov8 Medical Solutions Ltd
Intela Europa Ltd
Kent Pharma UK Limited
LS Pharma UK Limited
Mad Doctor Holdings Limited
Max Healthcare Limited
Max Remedies Limited
Medartis Limited
Meditech Endoscopy Ltd
Meta Innovation Nutrition Ltd
N4 Biotech Limited
Pharmaceutical Health Limited
Pharmadreams Limited
Pharmhouse Ltd
QED Scientific Ltd
Quirky Vapes Ltd
RJT Pharma Services Ltd
Shakespeare Pharma Ltd
Ivor Shaw Limited
Viking Court Limited
Welfare Healthcare (UK) Ltd

**Devon** [23]
11239338 Ltd
A & E Healthcare Limited
Aerona Clinical Limited
Arnolds Pharmacy Limited
Aromanature Limited
Barton Pharmacy Limited
Cellexa Limited
Colour Distributors Limited
Exeter Health Limited
FreshBreathOnline Limited
Galpharm International Limited
Hunter Urology Ltd
Laboratoires Forte Pharma UK Ltd
Moreton Pharmacy Ltd.
Newbridge Pharma Ltd.
Oxford Nutrition Limited
Perrigo Pharma Limited
Probar Services Limited
Randall Allison Limited
Seagrave Pharma Consultancy Ltd.
Solo Nutrition Limited
Tech Innovation Laser Limited
Vine Pharmaceuticals Limited

**Dorset** [11]
Cis Pharmassist Limited
DCH Subco Ltd
Global 4 Care Ltd
Instachem Limited
Kestrel Medical Limited
Kestrel Ophthalmics Limited
Lillidale Ltd.
Modern Aesthetic Solutions Ltd
Pharma Procurement Services Ltd
Pharma Trading Limited
Salutem Supplements Ltd

**Dyfed**
Walter Lloyd & Son Limited
Surgery Supplies (UK) Limited

**Essex** [122]
A K Worldwide Trading Limited
A1 Pharmaceuticals Holdings Ltd
A1 Pharmaceuticals PLC
AC Intertrade Limited
AIG Unico Ltd
ATI Atlas Ltd.
ATI Pharmaceuticals Limited
Adallen Pharma Limited
Akro Pharmaceutical Co Ltd
Alfavet Animal Healthcare Ltd
Alium Medical Limited
Allgenpharma Limited
Ananda Trading Limited
Antwerp Brokering Enterprises (U.K.)
Axe Pharma Ltd
BR Pharma International Ltd
Be and Are Sales Limited
Beta Pharmaceuticals Limited
Better Earth Limited
Biosure (UK) Limited
Birch & Beech Limited
Blackstone Pharma Ltd
British Association of European Pharmaceutical Distributors
Cibus Animal Nutrition Ltd
Clarity Commercial Ltd
Clarity DTP Ltd

# The Top UK Pharmaceutical Wholesalers

Clarity Markets Ltd
Clarity Woundcare Ltd
Clarity at Home Ltd
Client-Pharma Ltd
Client-Pharmacy UK Ltd
Concord Pharma Services (UK) Ltd
Coombe KP Limited
A.J. Cope & Son Limited
Cosmestore Limited
Creo Pharma Holdings Limited
Creo Pharma Limited
Crowncrest Services UK Limited
Dallas Burston Ashbourne Holdings
De-Bulad & Co Ltd
Detafinas Limited
Directpharm Ltd
Dunamis Pharmaceutical Services Ltd
EAM Wholesale Ltd
Essential-Healthcare Ltd
Essex Medical Supplies Ltd
Ethypharm UK Limited
Excel Health Care Limited
Future Pharmacare Limited
Groves Marchant Limited
Healthcare Procurement Services Ltd
I Like Limited
IPS International Corporation Ltd
Ikatrad Ltd
Imex International Group Ltd
Infinity Pharmaceuticals Ltd
Inter Trade Pharma Limited
LK Health Ltd
LM3 Business Ltd
Labwarehouse Limited
Liberty Pacific Limited
Lucky Herbalife24 Limited
M.R.S. Scientific Limited
MSP Pharm Ltd
Maplewood Investments Limited
Maze Healthcare Ltd.
Meadow Laboratories Limited
Medical Drug Supplies Limited
Medicines By Design Ltd
Medicure Scientific Limited
Medspero Pharma Ltd
Midmeds Limited
Miller & Miller (Chemicals) Ltd
Minmar (1008) Limited
Mychem Limited
NSA Pharma Limited
Naskalmik Limited
Neon Diagnostics Ltd
Neubourg Pharma (UK) Limited
Newtons Medical Supplies Ltd
Nikopharm Ltd
Novachem Limited
John O'Donnell Limited
PMS Korea Ltd
PS Dent Limited
Parasure Limited
Nisha Patel Ltd
Patient Care Holdings Ltd
Pedalglass Limited
Pharma World Ltd
Pharmaceuticals Direct Limited
Pharmacy4life Ltd
Prescribe Direct Limited
Priors Pharma Limited
Quatromed Limited
RIC Chemicals Limited
R.B. Radley & Co Ltd
Relyer Health Limited

Renata (UK) Limited
Rind Pharma Limited
Safe Pharma Consulting Ltd.
Sanarah Ltd
Sante Primaire Limited
Shantys Limited
Shoebury West Road Ltd
Simply Meds Pro Ltd
Sivanta Resourcing Limited
Skinlab Medical Ltd
Specialised Marketing Services Ltd
Specials Pharma Ltd
Sprint Moto UK Ltd
Star Powa Limited
Sustainable Ethical Enterprises Ltd
TA-65 (UK) Wholesale Limited
TTO Ventures Ltd.
Tank Puffin (Wholesale) Ltd
Tauva Limited
Trotwood Pharma Limited
Universal Supplies (International) Ltd
Veepharm Limited
Wenimed Ltd
iMedix Limited

**Flintshire**
Gainland (International) Ltd
Unomedical Limited

**Glamorgan** [24]
Ash Medical Limited
BBI Healthcare Limited
Bahati19 Limited
Dermapure Aesthetics Limited
Evolve Generics Limited
Evolve Healthcare Partners Ltd
Evolve Pharma Limited
Flydonging Eletctronic Ltd
G & C Pharma Limited
Lamyra International Limited
Med Procure Ltd
Novochem Limited
Optima Consumer Health Limited
Ostomart Limited
Plexiam Limited
RI Pharma Limited
R.A. Racey (Gt. Yarmouth) Ltd
Respond Plus Limited
Ros Nutrition UK Ltd.
Seren Plus Limited
Solarius UK & Overseas Limited
Stephar (U.K.) Limited
Treforest Pharmacy Limited
Ultrascan Solutions Ltd

**Gloucestershire** [24]
Afdos Pharmaceuticals Limited
Alumier Medical UK Limited
Athrodax Healthcare International
Biocare Supplies Limited
Davcaps Limited
Dosego Limited
Druid Pharma Limited
Greiner Bio-One Limited
Hameln Pharmaceuticals Ltd
Hitop Pharmaceuticals Limited
Insight Medical Products Ltd
Intro International (TRDG) Ltd
Livanova UK Limited
Lucis Pharma Ltd
Nimrod Veterinary Products Ltd

Nuview Ltd
Patient Ready Products Limited
Pavay Venture International Ltd
Phoenix Pharma Ltd.
Protec Medical Limited
Sahu & Co Limited
Scanmed (UK) Limited
Smart Medical Limited
Steritech UK Limited

**Gwent**
Unit 10 Distribution Limited

**Hampshire** [56]
A.T. Medical Ltd
AMK & Associates Ltd
Alissa Healthcare Research Ltd
Arrowedge Limited
NV Campbell Limited
Capella Medical Device Ltd
Charlwood Pharma Limited
Clinova Limited
CooperVision Lens Care Limited
Core Environmental PLC
Cosmedic Pharmacy Limited
Crescent Pharma Limited
Crescent Pharma OTC Limited
Crystal Healthcare Limited
Curium Pharma UK Ltd.
DMS Plus Limited
Elanco UK AH Limited
Elkay Laboratory Products (U.K.) Ltd
Emra Consult Limited
Engelpharma UK Limited
F D C International Limited
Fab Medical Limited
Future Healthcare Ltd
GBBC Ltd
Halo GB Ltd
Imphatec Ltd
KPB Healthcare Limited
Key Nutrients 4 Life Ltd
Latam HQ Health Ltd
MD Salisbury Ltd
Medicom Healthcare Limited
Medipharma Limited
Paul Murray PLC
Naturenetics UK Limited
Natures Healthworks Limited
Nipro Diagnostics (UK) Limited
Odiham OH Products Limited
Pembroke Healthcare Limited
Penlan Pharmaceuticals Limited
Pharmaethical Ltd
Pharmahouse Limited
Pharmnet Group Ltd
Raman Pharma Limited
SJ Enterprises Limited
Schebo Biotech UK Limited
Southampton Medical Group Ltd
Srigen Pharma Ltd
Sure Health & Beauty Limited
Telephone House Limited
Universal Marine Medical Ltd
Universal Procurement Services Ltd
Viemeds Limited
Vwin Lifestyle Limited
Peter John Wood Limited
Yiling Ltd
Zymix Limited

### Herefordshire [6]
Medi UK Ltd
Prometheus Medical Ltd
Raumedic U.K. Limited
S.T.D. Pharmaceutical Products Ltd
V.S. Limited
Vascular Products Limited

### Hertfordshire [81]
11 Health & Technologies Ltd
Ascot Pharma Ltd
Aspect Pharma Limited
Atrimusrx Ltd
Axis Medical Limited
Beauty Hair Products Limited
Bristol Laboratories Limited
CBD4You Limited
CG Pharma Ltd
Philip Chapper & Co Ltd
Clarity Pharma Holdings Ltd
Clarity Pharma Ltd
Clear Eyes Pharma Limited
Clinres UK Limited
DML Pharma Consultancy Limited
Docsinnovent Limited
EUSA Pharma (UK) Limited
Eisai Limited
Espere Healthcare Limited
Furn WW Lux Ltd
Galderma (U.K.) Limited
Gama Group Services Ltd
Generic Physics Limited
Global Pharma Care Ltd
Grey Traders Limited
Gulfstream Equity & Development Ltd
HealthVillagePlus Limited
Heisenberg Technologie Ltd
Hygamp Limited
Idea Medica Limited
Infinity Biomedical Ltd
Jolinda Medical Supplies Ltd
Lundbeck Limited
MDD Europe Limited
MDS Pharmaceuticals Ltd
ME Healthy Living H & L Ltd
MGI Pharma Limited
Masters Pharmaceuticals Ltd
Maxilabs Limited
McKinley Pharma Limited
Medical Developments UK Ltd
Merz Pharma UK Limited
Mylan UK Healthcare Limited
NPA Services Limited
Natchy Ltd
Nebel Healthcare Limited
New England Biolabs (U.K.) Ltd
Ontex Retail UK Limited
PI Herman Trading as Peter's Ltd
Per-Medic Limited
Pharma Modus Limited
Pharmasure Limited
Pneumech Limited
Poldark Limited
Prestige Brands (UK) Limited
Pure Products London Limited
Purple Surgical International Ltd
Purple Surgical UK Limited
R & D Healthcare Ltd
R.I.S. Products Limited
Ris Healthcare Limited
Rothschild Pharmacy Limited

S & D Pharma Limited
SL Clinical Ltd
Santen UK Limited
Semenalysis Limited
Specialty Diagnostix Limited
Spodefell Pharma Chemicals Ltd
Strides Pharma Global (UK) Ltd
Symbio Europe Limited
Tanner Pharma UK Limited
Tannerlac UK Limited
Trimark International Limited
United Orphan Pharma Limited
VLCare Limited
Vitaempower Ltd
Vitane Pharma Limited
Vitanutrition UK Ltd.
Water-Jel International Ltd
Whyte International Limited
Zoop Pharma Ltd

### Humberside
Altin Medical Ltd

### Kent [81]
Ambe Limited
Anti Venom Ltd
Arctic Medical Limited
Ardant Pharmaceuticals Ltd.
Ardent Pharmaceuticals Ltd
Aver Healthcare Ltd
Bio Pathica Limited
Centurion Park Pharmaceuticals Ltd
Conceio Consulting Ltd
Cubic Pharmaceuticals Limited
Cyto-Solutions Limited
Gordon Davie Chemist Limited
ECommedical Limited
Eddohealthcare Ltd
Elcon Pharma Limited
Ennogen Healthcare Ltd
Ennogen Pharma Ltd
Eureka Health Limited
Falama Services Group Limited
G.A.P. Research Co Ltd
Garusa Solutions U.K. Limited
Gerot Lannach UK Limited
Gideotech Limited
Guest Medical Limited
Guna Biotherapeutics Limited
Guna Limited
Healthcare 4life Ltd
Impact Health Limited
Infinite Percent Limited
Innomedi Limited
Intermedical (UK) Ltd
Invicta Pharma Limited
Irismed Pharma Ltd
JE Medical Associates Ltd.
Kingspeed Services Limited
Leptrex Ltd.
Lewis Healthcare Limited
Lyferoots Ltd
MK Medicals (UK) Ltd
MQS Group London Limited
Medical Warehouse Limited
Medicaleaf Limited
Medpro Healthcare Limited
Meds Online 247 Limited
New Generation Business UK Ltd
Noohra Limited
Nordic Generics Ltd

Northwise Services Limited
Nutresco Ltd
P R Pharma Limited
PB & T Project Ltd
PF OFG UK 3 Ltd
Padma Healthcare Limited
Pfizer Consumer Healthcare Ltd
Pfizer Limited
Pfizer OFG UK Limited
Pharmadynamics UK Limited
Pharmatec Ltd
Pharmeurope UK Limited
Pioneer Veterinary Products Ltd
Pispo Ltd
Prayosha Enterprises Limited
Prayosha Healthcare Limited
Purple Pharma Limited
Ragit Services Ltd
Rifaray Limited
Saint-Germain Pharma Ltd
Samax Pharma Ltd
Sangers (Maidstone) Limited
Septodont Limited
E.S.Shaw & Sons Limited
So'dran Ltd
Spadeground Limited
Springs Healthcare Limited
Star Freight Forwarding Ltd
Sunmed Pharma Ltd
TTops Healthcare Limited
Unifarco Ltd
Ursus UK Limited
Welfar Healthcare Limited
Y A Toner Limited

### Lancashire [135]
1LIFE Distribution Limited
AAP Healthcare Ltd
AF First Aid Ltd
Active Pharma Supplies Limited
Aria Vape Ltd
Ascent (Hartlepool) Limited
Bailey Instruments Ltd
Bestway Pharmacy NDC Limited
Bioceutics UK Ltd
Biofex Limited
Biomedoc Limited
Biomedox International Ltd
Blackpool Medicines Limited
Blue Bean Medical Ltd
Bolton Pharmaceutical Company 100 Ltd
Bowmed Ibisqus Limited
Bray Pharma Limited
C.D. Medical Limited
CBD Vape Ltd
Cannaid Ltd
P & A J Cattee (Wholesale) Ltd.
Ceracoat Ltd
F Chaudry Limited
Chiesi Healthcare Limited
Chiesi Limited
Chloraco Healthcare Limited
Comebro International Ltd
Currentmyth Limited
DGI Technologies Limited
Day Med Limited
Dermal Aesthetics Clinic Ltd
Eden CBD Limited
Equimed Medical Supplies Ltd
H.N. Espley & Sons Limited
Euanet Limited
Malcolm B. Fagleman Ltd

Fayroz Ltd
Fayroz Pharma Limited
First Choice Suppliments Ltd
Fitnatix International Ltd
A.K. Fletcher (Preston) Ltd
Fluidx Limited
Fortissa Ltd
Garstang Medical Services Ltd
Geistlich Sons Limited
General Shop Ltd
Greenheys - Weenytot Limited
HBS Healthcare Limited
Hambleton (UK) Limited
Hapa Medical UK Ltd
Harben Medical Limited
Albert Harrison & Co.Limited
Paul Hartmann Limited
Health Nutrient Products Ltd
Healthpoint Limited
Heatpack Co Ltd
Hedigen Limited
Henley Laboratories Limited
Ideal Healthcare Limited
Identimed Limited
Ihsan Pharma Ltd
International Medical Supplies Ltd
JLS Pharma Limited
KW Wholesale Ltd
Kamm Trading Limited
Kavia Tooling Limited
LZ Pharma Ltd
Roy Lamb Limited
Lamb's Locum Services Ltd
Lifenza UK Limited
Linderma Limited
London Healthcare Limited
M & A Pharmachem Limited
MSB Pharma Ltd
Manor Drug Company (Nottingham) Ltd
Masa Pharma Ltd
Mawdsley-Brooks & Co Ltd
Medbury Limited
Medihealth (Northern) Limited
Medis Medical (UK) Limited
Medivast Limited
Mesopotamia Surgical Ultima Vitality Ltd
Millennium Global Limited
Nationwide Healthcare Solutions Ltd
New Medical World Ltd
Newstar Healthcare Limited
Nex Pharma Limited
OT Masters Limited
Omnicell Limited
Ordinant Medical Solutions Ltd
Oscar & Louis Limited
PPQUK Ltd
Pericia Ltd
Pharma 313 Limited
Pharmacy Business Consultancy Ltd
Pharmagona Limited
Positive Pharma Ltd
Prinwest Limited
Priory Pharma Ltd
Pure Skincare Limited
Qualiti (Burnley) Limited
RD & Med Co Ltd
RF Vapes Limited
RND Pharma Limited
RPH Pharma Ltd
Rayburn Trading Co Ltd
Rhodes Pharma Limited
Rivertime Distribution Ltd

Ruby Box Limited
Ruger Barber Limited
RxPharma Limited
SRS Pharma Limited
Shizhen TCM (UK) Limited
Showman's Surgical Ltd
Sidhupharm Limited
Soho Flordis UK Limited
Sonifar Pharma Expert Limited
Sports Star Distribution UK Ltd
Strandland Limited
Surgitrac Instruments UK Ltd
Swingward Limited
TMZ Naturals Limited
TRT Global Ltd
TSI Health Sciences (Europe) Ltd
Z Tahir Limited
Tradebuffalo Ltd
George Twist (Wholesale) Ltd
UK Eagle Ltd
UK Medical Centre Ltd
UK Pharma Impex Limited
Donald Wardle and Son Limited
Wellspring Pharmaceutical Services
Wellspring Pharmaceutical Services UK
Westmead International Limited
ZMI Investments Limited

**Leicestershire** [51]
APC Pharmaceuticals & Chemicals (Europe)
ATP Medical Limited
Accordia Investments Ltd
Black and White Health Care Ltd
Blackbird Pharmacy Limited
Budget Pharma UK Limited
Chelmack Limited
Dixons Pharmaceuticals UK Ltd
Doksy Limited
East Midlands Pharma Limited
Ecogen Europe Ltd
Europa Health Limited
Fire N Ice Ltd
Fulbo Ltd
Full Spectrum Pharma Limited
Gemi Pharma Limited
H & S Beauty Care Limited
HMS Wholesale Ltd
HQEM Pharma Limited
HS Pharma Limited
In 2 Healthcare Limited
Kids Medicare Limited
Kingsley Specials Limited
Lax Pharma Limited
John Lloyd Dental Equipment Services
MKS Pharma Ltd
Medicine Optimisation Limited
Mercia Dental Equipment Ltd
Morgan Steer Developments Ltd
Mulberry Pharma Ltd
Nova Laboratories Limited
PF Consultancy Plus Ltd
Parkview Leicester Limited
Pharmasif Direct Limited
Pharmex-UK Ltd
Premium Pharm Ltd
Pura (UK) Ltd
Royce Health Sciences Ltd
Shardman Healthcare Limited
Smartway Pharmaceuticals Ltd
Stan-Pol Ltd
Supra Enterprises Limited
Tynatex Limited

Unimed Global Limited
Unimed Healthcare Supplies Ltd
Univape Global Ltd
Utech Products Limited
Vitapro Limited
Xanton Limited
ZS Pharma Limited
Zhpharma Ltd

**Lincolnshire** [18]
Arkad Healthcare Limited
Aura-Soma Limited
Bioactive T Pharma Limited
Boost Hair Limited
Device Technologies UK Ltd.
Ezhonsi Ltd
Global Pharma Direct Ltd
Juice Sauz Ltd
Lifecare Limited
Medicare Products Limited
Medikit Limited
PH Medicare Ltd
Pamx Enterprise Limited
Rosalique Skincare Limited
Salcura Limited
Trafalgar Pharma Ltd
Vision.Net Limited
WTE Services Limited

**London** [733]
10x Rational Ambulance Yield Ltd
1966 Health International Ltd
1st Class Medical Ltd
A B Alliance Limited
A.H.P. Medical Supplies Ltd
AAR Pharma Ltd
AB Pharma Logistics Ltd
ABC Pharmaceuticals Ltd
ACESO Global Ltd
ACL Medical Limited
ANP Pharma Ltd
AP Import Export Ltd
Abacus Medicine Ltd
Abra Wholesales Ltd
Absolute Brands Ltd
Abstragan Holding Limited
Abstragan Limited
Accmede Pharmaceuticals Ltd
Aces Pharma Limited
Actipharm Limited
Active Export Ltd
Active Global Ltd
Acure Pharma Limited
Added Pharma Ltd
Adicam Pharmaceuticals Ltd
Advanced Laboratory Technologies Europe
Aeglos Ltd
Aesthetic & Wellness Pharmacy Ltd
Aidwell Limited
Akvion Limited
Al Razi Pharma UK Ltd
Alcura UK Limited
Alcyon Corporation Ltd
Alexpharm GmbH Ltd
Alice & Associates Limited
All1 Limited
Allcures PLC
Allcures.Com (2006) Limited
Allied Warden Marketing Ltd
Allkare Limited
Allpa Kallpa Ltd

Alzirr Ltd
Amalgamated Technology Corporation
Amaxa Ltd
Amaxa Pharma Ltd
Amin Locum Limited
Anaiah Healthcare Ltd
Ananta Medicare Ltd
Anfarm Generics UK Limited
Angelina SW Ltd
Anrise Trading Limited
Aposave Ltd
Apotheke San Biagio SRL Ltd
Aptitud Pharma Ltd
Areessco Ltd
Arex Pharma Ltd
Arisio Ltd
Art Pharma Oxford Ltd
Asaya Cosmeceuticals Limited
Ascend Laboratories (UK) Ltd
Astra MCR Limited
Astral Health Ltd
Asymchem Limited
Athenex Euro Limited
Atnahs Pharma US Limited
Atossa Genetics UK Ltd
Atra Corporation Ltd
Attends Limited
Augmenix UK Limited
Auramedicann Ltd
Avanzcare Limited
Aventa International Corporation Ltd
Aviva Health Solutions Limited
BFN Limited
Ba-Inspire Limited
Bannersbridge Limited
Barustore Limited
Bausch & Lomb U.K. Limited
Baxalta UK Investments Ltd.
Beachcourse Limited
Beauty Boosters Ltd
Behsarel Trading Ltd
Beijing Tong Ren Tang (UK) Ltd
Bejaa Medical (UK) Limited
Belinda Limited
Benatur Limited
Besins Healthcare (UK) Limited
Bessacarr Ltd
Bestlon Limited
Bidaya UK Ltd.
Bin'auf Limited
Bio-Sight Ltd
Bio-Synergy Limited
Biocon Pharma UK Limited
Biogenic Health Europe Ltd
Bioleys Care Ltd
Bioloka Ltd
Biomarin (U.K.) Ltd.
Biomedi Technology Limited
Biomedical Reproductive Research Ltd
Biophage Therapeutics Ltd
Biophos Labs Ltd
Biosensors International UK Ltd
Biostate Limited
Biotek Diagnostics Limited
Biotus Ltd
Bioxane Ltd
A & P Blickling Ltd
Blink Street Limited
Bone Support UK Ltd
Bosville Limited
Botha Group Ltd
Bpharm Group Limited

Bradley Stoke Bristol Limited
Brenton Invest and Trade Ltd
Brightfield Associates Ltd
BritaniaMark Limited
Britannia Medical Limited
Britpharm Limited
Britpharma UK Limited
Brookmed Limited
ET Browne (UK) Limited
CBD Labz Ltd
CBD Platinum Ltd
CBS Trade Limited
CEU Pharm Ltd
CKF Limited
Cambridge Pharmaceuticals Ltd
Campmed Limited
Canconc Ltd
Cannamedical Pharma UK Limited
Cannapharm Limited
Cannerald Group Ltd
Carun (UK) Limited
Cebrenex Limited
Celgene UK Distribution Ltd
Cellcosmo Suisse Limited
Chameleon Planet Ltd
Charmant UK Co., Limited
Chefarma Limited
Chela Animal Health Limited
Chelsea Pharma Limited
Chemi-Call Ltd
Chewton Ventures Limited
Chirock Trading Ltd
Chitorhino Ltd
Citco Chemicals Ltd.
Citux Medical Limited
Clever Connect Ltd
Clifton Organic Limited
Clinic Supply Ltd
Clinical Services International Ltd
Clinitech Medical Ltd
Clymed Healthcare Ltd
Codix Pharma (UK) Limited
Comfylife Ltd
Concept Pharma UK Limited
Connected Healthcare Ltd
Connexon Global Networks Ltd
Coramandel Limited
Cotton Craft Limited
Croma-Pharma Limited
Crossbridge Concepts Limited
Crosscare Export Limited
Crown Global Traders Limited
Cured CBD Ltd
Curist Health Limited
DCMP 8E Cepac Limited
DLG Partners Limited
C T Dang Limited
Dark Atom Limited
Daryeel Medicines International Ltd
Dasapharm Limited
Day International Limited
Day Pharma Limited
Dayonix Pharma Limited
Delta Sales Ltd
Deltapharma Limited
Dent.O.Care Distribution Ltd
Dent.O.Care Limited
Dentel Group Ltd
Dentlaser Limited
Dermatonics Ltd
Dermatonics Trading Limited
Dermconcept Ltd

Despina Pharma Ltd
Devicor Medical UK Limited
Dion Trade Ltd.
Dispensing Direct Services Ltd
Dollano Trading Limited
Dong Hwa UK Ltd
Dr Pradeep Reddy's Laboratories (UK & EU)
Drugget Ltd
Dynamic Development Laboratories Co Ltd
E.U.K. Limited
Eastern Lighthouse Ltd
Edmond Finance Ltd
Einoxy Limited
Elara Care Limited
Elektro Genesis Limited
Elim Springs Biotech Ltd
Enfield Nutrition Club Ltd
Enteromed Limited
Entod Research Cell (UK) Ltd
Entrust & UK Ltd
Essentialink Limited
Ethicor Pharma Ltd
Euro Capital Management (ECM) Ltd
Euro Lifecare Ltd
Euromed (U.K) Limited
Euromed Technologie Limited
Europharmacia Ltd
Euroworld Enterprises Limited
Evees (UK) Limited
Ever Pharma UK Limited
Everhealth Ltd
Everypharma Co., Ltd.
Evideon Daily Ltd
Evolet Healthcare Limited
Evorin Pharma Limited
Eyepak Limited
Faith and Pharma Limited
Farmako Limited
Farmedic (UK) Limited
Feel and Heal UK Limited
Fenton Pharmaceuticals Ltd
Fijez Ltd
Fitness and Nutrition of Europe Ltd.
Fittleworth Medical Limited
Flen Health UK Ltd
Flow Wealth Ltd
Focus Pharma Holdings Limited
Focus Pharmaceuticals Limited
Fresh Cache Holdings Limited
Frezyderm UK Limited
Frontrow International UK Ltd
G P Supplies Limited
GM Biopharma Ltd
GMP-Orphan United Kingdom Ltd
GP Mediplus Ltd
GPM Pharma Limited
Gagnon Direct Ltd
Galenus Biomedical Limited
Gate2pharma Ltd
Gateway for Africa Ltd
Generic Partners UK Ltd
Genesis Pharma Limited
Genopharm Ltd
Geoorganics Limited
Geopharma UK Ltd.
Gester Invest Limited
Gilead Sciences Ltd
Gilsun Healthcare Ltd
Gilsun Limited
Glector Limited
Global Additives Ltd
Global Medical Supply UK Ltd

# The Top UK Pharmaceutical Wholesalers

Global Supply (U.K.) Ltd
Go Go Chemist Limited
Goldshore (UK) Limited
Goldsmith Resources Limited
Gos Pharma Limited
Got Heart UK Ltd
Greens Roads UK Ltd
Gumsaver Limited
HAPA Group Holdings Limited
HB Sirius Ltd
HEC Pharm UK Limited
HNS Pharma Limited
HRA Pharma UK & Ireland Ltd
Hapharm Ltd
Harley Dentist Limited
Harmonium Investments Limited
Hartwood & Brooks Limited
Hasting Pharma Ltd
Hayat Gostar Ltd
Health Medbio Ltd
Healthaid Holdings Limited
Healthaid Limited
Healthbest Limited
Heathrow.Net Limited
Hemastem Ltd
Hemodia UK Ltd
Hennessy Mason Ltd
Herbaleva Ltd
Herbialis Limited
Here We Flo Ltd
Hermes Pharmaceutical Limited
Hisamitsu Pharmaceutical UK Ltd
Hisamitsu UK Limited
Honest Health Limited
Honilac Nutrition Limited
Hooben Distributors Limited
Horopito Limited
Hotteeze International Limited
Human Reproduction Group Ltd
Hunger Control Limited
Hydro Tan Limited
IPSA Pharmacy Limited
Iam Finance Limited
Iaso Ltd
Iberia Skin Brands Ltd
Icone International Limited
Ideal Cleaning Systems Ltd
Imamcom Ltd
Immortalis Distribution Ltd.
Impexport Services Limited
Indrugco (UK) Limited
Inglasia Ltd
Iniaso Ltd
Iniaso Pharma Ltd
Inmed Ltd
Insight Biotechnology Limited
Insight Health Limited
Insuphar Laboratories Limited
Interchem Europe (UK) Limited
International Pharma Co Ltd
Interpharm Limited
Inventive Medical Solutions Ltd
Irmaan Limited
Izida Pharma Group Limited
J & G Equipment Limited
J & T World Trade (UK) Limited
JAO Enterprises Ltd
JSK PVT Limited
Jagmed Limited
Janvit Ltd
Jay & Jay Limited
Jenson Chemicals Limited

Johnlee Pharmaceuticals (UK) Ltd
Leigh Jones & Associates Ltd
Josana Limited
K N B Services Ltd
K588 Limited
KRKA UK Ltd
Kaboodan Limited
Kadmon International Ltd
Kanish Ltd
Karo Pharma UK Ltd
Kerita Ltd
Kganesha Pharma Ltd
Kinetic Enterprises Limited
Kings Medical Supplies Limited
Kobayashi Healthcare Europe Ltd
Kohilam Limited
Koln Pharma Ltd
Kuramo (UK) Limited
Kyo Ltd
LDC International Limited
LGS Pharma Limited
Lab-PCR Limited
Lam Cash and Carry Limited
Lambsmead Limited
Lantheus MI UK Limited
Layan Pharma Ltd
Leadiant Biosciences Limited
Legacy Private Limited
Legendbio Beauty Group Limited
Libertas Medical Ltd
Life on Healthcare Ltd
Limes Pharma Ltd
Linepharma International Ltd
Lionmark Limited
Logichem Ltd
London Health Sciences Ltd
London Supplements Distribution Ltd
Luban & Murr Ltd
Lucid Wholesale Ltd
Lufuma B2b Services Ltd
Lumiradx International Ltd
Luye Pharma Ltd
Lyshaug Enterprises Limited
M & N Traders Limited
MGC Pharma (UK) Ltd
MKK Consulting Ltd
MRG Creations Ltd
Macacha Health Limited
Macks Ltd.
Mammoth Dental Supplies Ltd
Manta Medical Limited
Mapaex Consumer Healthcare (UK) Private
Maplespring Limited
Marlborough Pharmaceuticals Ltd
Martal Cosmetics Limited
Masir Ltd
Mast - Art Group Limited
Matt 6:33 Ltd
Matter Drinks Trading Ltd
Maximed Ltd
Maxlott Ltd
Mayfair Distributors Limited
Mayfair Export London Limited
McKesson Global Procurement & Sourcing
McKesson Global Sourcing UK Ltd
Medeuronet (UK) Limited
Medex Pharma Limited
Medhub Limited
Medi Test Pharma Ltd
Medica Finance UK Ltd
Medical-Mac Ltd
Medicare Europe Ltd

Medicia Ltd
Medicines Extra Healthcare Ltd
Medics Direct Pharmacy Limited
Medilain Marketing Ltd
Medimpex UK Limited
Medinox (London) Limited
Medintek Holdings Ltd
Medisca UK Limited
Medison Pharma Limited
Medpharm Global UK Limited
Meds Global Limited
Medsupply Ltd
Medtech Trading Limited
Megapharma Ltd
Melo Labs UK Ltd
Mena Pharma UK Limited
Menar UK Biotech Ltd
Mensana Pharma Ltd.
Meridian Bioscience UK Limited
Miltonia Health Science Ltd
Mobility2you Ltd
Model Medics Limited
Molab Ltd
Moriah Healthcare Distribution Ltd
Morn View Chemicals (UK) Ltd
Morton Medical Limited
Morvigor (UK) Ltd
Mosaic Pharma Limited
My Nutrition London Ltd
My-Kaya Ltd
Myly Pharma Limited
Myriad Medical Supplies Ltd
NBS Scientific Limited
NC Trade UK Ltd
NKCell Plus PLC
NLR Exports Limited
Nagarjun Healthcare Limited
Nascot Health Ltd
Nasser Waziri Ltd
Nativis Bio Ltd
Natural Science.Com Limited
Naturelo Ltd
Nelson & Russell Limited
Nema Pharma Trade Limited
Neo Farma Ltd
Neo Health UK Limited
New Horizon Pharma (UK) Ltd.
Newtexko Ltd.
Newville Trading Limited
Nexcape Pharmaceuticals Ltd
Nino and Blue Spruce Ltd
Nordic Nutraceuticals UK Ltd
Norlington Trading Ltd
Noroc Concepts Ltd
Nosher Pharma Private Ltd
Nova Pharmacare Ltd
Novalabb Limited
Novalio Pharma Limited
Novamed Pharma Ltd
Novamedi Limited
Novelius Medical Limited
Novmedic Limited
Nunataq Limited
Nutrabizz Nutraceuticals Ltd
Nutravit Ltd.
OFC Molecular Ltd
OPD Laboratories Limited
Omega Alpha Pharma Limited
Omega Pharma Limited
Onpharma Limited
Optimal Pharma Ltd
Orange Healthcare Limited

Organic Iway Ltd
Orion Pharma (UK) Limited
Orly Pharma Limited
Orpharma Limited
Osteo-Ti UK Limited
Overseas Merchandising Corporation Ltd
Oxbridge Pharma Limited
Oxford Laboratories Limited
Ozonex Limited
P C LDN Ltd
PB's Locum Services Limited
PTGO Sever UK Limited
Pacific Pharma UK Limited
Palatina Ltd
Pamy International Ltd
Par Laboratories Europe, Ltd.
Parallel Investments Limited
Paraxmed Limited
Paria Medical Aesthetics Ltd
Park Health Ltd
Pearl Chemist Group Limited
Pearl Services (Tooting) Ltd
Perennial Pharma Ltd
Perricone MD Cosmeceuticals UK Ltd
Perush Ltd
Peter & Guys Salon Professional Ltd
Petersone Group Ltd
Pharco Ltd
Pharm - Tex Limited
Pharm Recon Ltd
Pharma Maiden Ltd
Pharma Oasis Ltd
Pharma Products Limited
Pharmacare International Ltd
Pharmacierge Group Limited
Pharmacierge Limited
Pharmacierge Technology Ltd
Pharmaethics International Ltd
Pharmapal Limited
Pharmargus Healthcare Ltd
Pharmasky Ltd
Pharmasol London Ltd
Pharmaxis Pharmaceuticals Ltd
Pharmayas UK Limited
Pharmed Health Care Organisation Ltd
Pharmedics Ltd
Pharmex International Ltd
Pinklady International Ltd
Planehill Limited
Plurafores Pharma Limited
Portland Ventures Inc Ltd
Portobello Pharmacy Limited
Pound International Ltd
Premax Europe Limited
Prescribe International Ltd
Prime Medical Equipment Ltd
Private Pharma Health Co Ltd
Private Pharmacy Group Limited
Profoot (UK) Ltd
Project & Communications Ltd
Prolife (UK) Limited
Prominent Life Style Ltd
Proup Ltd
Pura Pharmaceuticals Ltd
Pure Solace Ltd
Quantum Biomed Ltd
R & R Post Op Box Ltd.
R. N. Europe Limited
RJP Impex Ltd
RR Cosmeceuticals (UK) Ltd
RX Farma Limited
Rabimed International Limited

Rafarm UK Limited
Rak Pharma Ltd
Randa Pharma Ltd
Rashedeen Pharma Group Ltd
Raw Medicus Ltd
Rawmmed Trading Co Ltd
Ray Pharm Limited
Real Estate Alliance Ltd
Redlight Exchange Ltd
Relonchem Limited
Remedine Limited
Remote Pharma Solutions Ltd
Rex Pharmaceuticals Ltd
Rexcel Trading Ltd
Ria Sales Corporation Ltd
Rich Almond (UK) Limited
Richardson Healthcare Limited
Gedeon Richter (UK) Limited
Ripple Pharma Limited
Rising Sun Ventures Ltd
Riteaim Limited
Riviere Groupe (Europe) Ltd
Rocha Products Limited
Ross London Limited
Rotapharm Limited
Rowtech Limited
SD Alliance Ltd.
SHL Medical Limited
SQR Pharma Consulting Ltd
SV Syon Med Ltd
Sabel Pharmacy Ltd
Safenet Direct Ltd
Sage Therapeutics Limited
Salonpas UK Limited
Sanos Healthcare Ltd
Santhera (UK) Limited
Sanzenica Limited
Sarbec Cosmetics Limited
Sarepta International UK Ltd.
Sasmar Limited
Satio Pharma Ltd.
Sawa Trading & Shipping Ltd
Saxonia Medical Ltd.
Scandasystems Limited
Schulz Medical Supplies Ltd
Secret Line Ltd
Selective Supplies Limited
Seltfar Ltd
Shanghai Neopharm Co., Ltd
Sharepool Limited
Shaz Logistics Limited
Shire Pharmaceuticals Limited
Sigma Pharmaceuticals PLC
Sigmatec Limited
Silkgrange Limited
Sintetica Limited
SkInOne UK Ltd
Skarby Gai Ltd
Skindoc Formula Limited
Skymedic UK Limited
Solana Trade Ltd
Sood-UK Ltd
Sotra Pharma Ltd.
South China Bio-Pharma Co Ltd.
Sovereign House Properties Ltd
Spatone Limited
Specialty Pharma of London Ltd
Speedx Limited
Spey Limited
Spey Pharma Limited
Alan Spivack Limited
Springbourne Management and Trading Ltd

Sprint Pharma Limited
St George's Medical Limited
St Marks Medical Ltd
Stallergenes (UK) Ltd
Stanex Limited
Sterling Bio-Pharma Ltd
Stiltec Global (UK) Ltd
Stop Ltd
Style Global Trading FZE Ltd
Summit Pharmaceuticals Europe Ltd
Sunovion Pharmaceuticals Europe Ltd.
Sunrize Trade Limited
Sup-Up Ltd
Surgicaide Medical Supplies UK Ltd
Surgical Devices Developers Ltd
Swanson Trade Ltd
Swiftpath Corporation Limited
Symbiosis Biosciences Limited
Symmetry Inc Ltd
T.K. Impex Limited
TBD Wellness Limited
Taineng Medicine Ltd
Tanberg Limited
Targeter (UK) Limited
Tearfilm Therapeutics Ltd
Technical & General Limited
Technoglobal Ltd
Theramex HQ UK Limited
Thexo Pharma Limited
Third Hand Healthcare Ltd
Thlala Kolo (UK) Ltd
Thurgab Medicals Ltd
Tia Marie Ltd
Timeocean Ltd
Topnot Ltd
Tour N' Cure International Ltd.
Tradewings Worldwide Ltd
Trans Swiss Ltd
Treas Biotechnology UK Ltd
Treatlines Limited
Trent Dent Products Limited
Triaton Ltd
Truscreen Limited
Tuba Ltd
Tudor Pharma Ltd
Tulip Cup Limited
Twinklers Limited
UK Beauty Cosmetics International Group
UK Branded Medicines Ltd
UK Heluns Industry Co., Ltd
UK Lab Supplies Ltd
UK Lemenic International Medical Group
UK Pharmacies Ltd
UK Vimin Industry Co., Limited
Ultimate Health Products Ltd
Unidus Limited
Unipharm Limited
Unison Pharmaceuticals Ltd
United Kingdom Medica Ltd
United Pharma Group Limited
United Pharma Ltd
Unmaan Healthcare Limited
Usme Limited
Uvita Health Limited
Veda Biosciences Limited
Vedic Medical Hall Limited
Vegamed UK Limited
Venture Four Ltd.
Venture Pharma Ltd
Vestex Trade Ltd
Veyda Pharma Ltd
Victoria Pharma London Ltd

The Top UK Pharmaceutical Wholesalers     dellam

Vifor Pharma UK Limited
Vipharm Limited
Virudist Ltd
Vise Services Ltd
Vise Services PVT Ltd
Vitachem Limited
Vital Haven Ltd
Vital Life International Ltd
Vitalit Trade Limited
Vitamed Int Ltd
Vitaminka Ltd
Vitgarden Ltd
Vitopia Ltd
Vivacy Laboratoires Ltd
Vog Limited
Vyom International Ltd.
W.B. Superdrug Ltd.
WD Pharma (UK) Limited
WE Pharma Ltd
K. Waterhouse Limited
Waymade PLC
Webstar Dixon Limited
Wep Group Holdings Limited
Wesbee Ventures Limited
Wescroft Limited
L E West Ltd
Wholesale 2 U Ltd
Wigmore Laboratories Limited
Wilkies International Ltd
Willbay Limited
Wonder World Ltd
Carl Woolf Limited
World Medicine Limited
Your Products Limited
ZS Solutions Limited
Zaaz Limited
Zanoprima Holdings Limited
Zanoprima LifeSciences Limited
Zefer Pharma Ltd.
Zelens Limited
Zeymos Pharma Ltd
Zoetis UK Limited
Zolex Global Limited
Zota Healthcare Limited

**Lothian**
Clinical Direct Ltd
Ivee Group Ltd
Supphero Ltd
TTC Medical GTS Limited

**Merseyside** [27]
Acehides Limited
Allied Pharmacies Limited
Andrei & Maria Ltd
Bakhu Limited
Buduscheye Techniqa Ltd
John Carrington Limited
Barry Elman (Wholesale) Ltd
Epsilon Pharmaceuticals Ltd
Eurostar Scientific Limited
Exmed Worldwide Limited
Healthmed Supplies (HMS) Ltd
Iophtha Limited
Kays Medical Limited
M D M Healthcare Ltd
Mayapharm Limited
NOD Europe Ltd.
R.F. Medical Supplies Limited
RX Pharma (Europe) Limited
Salon Sales Limited

Sharief Pharma Limited
Standford Ltd
Stanton Ocean Services Limited
Stellar Labs Ltd
Stockport Healthcare Limited
TTS Pharma Limited
Westland Pharmaceuticals Ltd
Zanza Specials International Ltd

**Middlesex** [247]
56 Flowers Ltd
A1 Natural Ltd
Aadverv Sourcing Solutions Ltd
Accendo Pharma Ltd
Accord Healthcare Limited
Acme Pharma Ltd
Active Prescription Limited
Alixport Ltd
Allen & Hanburys Limited
Allipharm (UK) Limited
Almirall Limited
Alpha Pharma Ltd
Amarox Limited
American Biochemical and Pharmaceuticals
Anuva International Limited
Appleby Pharmacy Limited
Arco Iris Limited
Artmedica Ltd
Assencion Pharmaceuticals Ltd
Astra Pharma (UK) Limited
Astute Healthcare Limited
Athem Pharma Limited
Authentic Ayurveda Limited
Azurite Health Ltd
B & B Wholesale Limited
Bacteflora Ltd
Baron Medicare UK Limited
Benident Limited
Best Value America (UK) Ltd
Best-Bio Ltd
Beximco Pharma UK Limited
Bio Global Limited
Biogenez Ltd
Mark Birch Hair Ltd
Brent Medicare Limited
Brex Medical Supplies Limited
Bugband Europe Ltd
By Direct Limited
C & N Medical Ltd
CHM Trading Limited
Cadila Pharmaceuticals (Europe) Ltd
Care Healthcare Ltd
Celgene Limited
Cellchem UK Limited
Chemilines Group Holdings Ltd
Chemilines Limited
Chemys Limited
Click Solutions Ltd
Clinimarg Ltd
Dasco (Wholesale) Limited
Dasco Investment Corporation Ltd
Davis and Dann Limited
Decahedron Ltd
Devonshire Healthcare Services Ltd
Diamate Biotechnologies Ltd
Diaylaa Ltd
Dil More Remedies UK Ltd
Dilcare Health Limited
Drugsrus Limited
Durbin PLC
ETP (UK) Limited
Easho Limited

Ecomed UK Limited
Edi Beryl Ltd
Egroup (UK) Limited
Eico Ltd
Elmstone Healthcare Limited
Emkkay of London Limited
Eton Pharma Ltd
Euro Ceuticals Limited
Fairview Health Limited
Farmachem Limited
Ferring Pharmaceuticals Ltd
Five Pharm Ltd
Flamingo Pharma (UK) Ltd
Fortune Industries Limited
Genesis Pharmaceuticals Ltd
Glaxo Laboratories Limited
Glaxo Wellcome UK Limited
GlaxoSmithKline Caribbean Ltd
GlaxoSmithKline Consumer Trading Services
GlaxoSmithKline Export Limited
GlaxoSmithKline UK Limited
GlaxoSmithKline US Trading Ltd
Glenhazel Limited
Glenmark Pharmaceuticals Europe Ltd
Global 1st Ltd
Global Medical Supplies Ltd
Global Pharmaceuticals (UK) Ltd
Global Pharmaceuticals Ltd
Global SCS Limited
Globyz Pharma (UK) Ltd
Gowrie Laxmico Limited
Graviti Healthcare Limited
Grunenthal Limited
Halewood Health Limited
Hampton Brand Management Co Ltd
Hampton Brands Limited
Hana Healthcare Ltd
Hana Supplies Limited
Harley's (UK) Ltd
Hashmats Health Ltd
Health Supplies Limited
Healthcaps Europe Ltd
Healthy Era Ltd
Home Health (U.K.) Limited
Huayawei Biomedical Co Ltd
IM High Tech Limited
Infohealth Limited
Instinct Health Ltd
Intramed Limited
Ironbridge Medical Services Ltd
J.J. Worldhealth Limited
JJ Nutrihealth Ltd
JMD Enterprises UK Limited
Jambo Supplies Limited
Jana Healthcare Ltd
Jessica Inc Limited
KGP Laboratories (UK) Limited
Kaam Pharma Limited
Kanta Enterprises Limited
Kestrol International Limited
Keziah Ltd
Koasta Limited
LV Global Limited
Lad & Company Private Limited
Laxmi BNS Holdings Limited
Laxmico Limited
Leap Pharma Ltd
London United Exports Limited
MDX Healthcare Ltd
MM Medical Equipment UK Ltd
MMP Marketing Limited
Macrobiotics Group Ltd

Manichem Limited
Maps Healthcare Limited
Marigold Footcare Ltd.
Medcare Life UK Ltd
Medi-Gen Limited
Medigroup Ltd
Medik Ostomy Supplies Limited
Medimax (UK) Ltd
Medipro Pharma Limited
Meditec International England Ltd
Merck Serono Limited
Metro Pharmacy Limited
Micro Industries Limited
Milpharm Limited
Mintheath Developments Limited
Mirage Distribution Limited
Moka Pharmaceuticals Limited
Molecule Healthcare Limited
Moores Pharmacy Limited
NSL (Holdings) Limited
NSL Group Limited
Necessity Supplies Limited
NeilMed Holding Co Ltd
Neilmed Limited
Nevik Limited
New Health Global Solutions Ltd
New Health Supplies Limited
Niayara Global Limited
Norgine Pharmaceuticals Ltd
Nostrum Life Sciences Ltd
Novelgenix Therapeutics Ltd
Numedex Limited
Nutramax Ltd
Nutridrinks Limited
OM Medical Limited
One Pharm Limited
Ozone Medical Supplies Ltd
P.I.E. Pharma Limited
Panacea Health UK Limited
Pergamon Ltd
Pharma 777 Limited
Pharma Concept UK Limited
Pharma Plus Supplies Ltd
Pharma-Export Ltd
Pharmapoint UK Ltd
Pharmartel Limited
Pharmassist Locums Limited
Pharmunity Limited
Phaximed Limited
Piramal Critical Care Limited
Pramod Rajani Organisation Ltd
Prime Pharmacare Ltd
Primecrown Limited
Prominer Limited
RSR Pharmacare Limited
Rah Pharma Ltd
Ranbaxy (U.K.) Limited
Rapid Pharma Limited
Respro-M Limited
Restate Management Ltd
Rkonnect Limited
Roble Medical Ltd
Rolling Stones Trading Ltd
SERB Ltd
Sakar Healthcare UK Ltd.
Sanay Ltd
Servipharm Limited
J Sherlee Ltd
Silicon Pharma Limited
Simba Pharmatech Limited
Simcare Global Premium Healthcare Ltd
Sinduram Healthcare International Ltd

Sky Hemp Ltd
Sonal Pharma (UK) Ltd
Sonchat Limited
Sonik Products Limited
Springwell Transport and Logistics Ltd
St Georges Pharmaceuticals Ltd
Star Pharmaceuticals Limited
Sterling London Ventures Ltd
Streamline Pharmaceuticals Ltd
Suerte Pharma Limited
Sufi Enterprise Wholesalers Ltd
Sun Exim Ltd
Swiss Pharma UK Limited
Symom Limited
Tetra Hydro Cannabinoid Oils Global Ltd
Tor Generics Limited
Total Body Care Limited
Total Medcare Limited
Totally Pharmacy Ltd
Trishool Pharma Ltd
Trutek Europe Ltd
V Sales and Marketing Limited
Valugen Pharma Limited
Ved Healthcare Limited
Veramic Limited
View Pharm Limited
ViiV Healthcare Overseas Ltd
ViiV Healthcare Trading Services UK
ViiV Healthcare UK Limited
Vital Pharma Limited
Vital Supplies (UK) Limited
Vitwell Limited
Vityz Nutrition Limited
Vivaorganiclife Ltd
Wave Pharma Limited
Wellacy Limited
Wellness Clinical Supplies Ltd
Winsor Pharma UK Limited
Worldtrition Ltd
YJBPort Limited
Zista Pharma Limited

**Midlothian** [10]
ANP Partners Ltd
Aryahakim Medical Equipment Co Ltd.
Humn Pharmaceuticals (UK) Ltd
Irving and Skinner Ltd
Meda Pharmaceuticals Limited
OL123 Limited
Perrington & Co Limited
Respond Healthcare Scotland Ltd
Soliphar Limited
Synergetic Global Limited

**Monmouthshire**
BR Scientific Limited
Dentanurse (U.K.) Limited
Instant Test Ltd
Juvela Limited

**Norfolk** [12]
Acle Medical Limited
Amdeepcha Limited
Beechcroft Supplies Limited
Cambridge Healthcare Supplies 2012
Cambridge Healthcare Supplies Ltd
Crosskills (P.E.) Limited
Field House Pharma Limited
Genevet Ltd
Homeopathic Supply Co Ltd
Lime Pharmacy Limited

MD-Reproductive Health Solutions Ltd
Vet Direct Services Limited

**Northamptonshire** [15]
Bioturm Limited
Busky Limited
Cofad Ventures Ltd
Dacre Skincare Limited
Dexcel-Pharma Limited
Discovery Pharmaceuticals Ltd
Excelsior Scientific Limited
GP Laboratories Limited
Healtholozy UK Limited
Morningside Pharmaceuticals Ltd
Norbrook Laboratories (G.B.) Ltd
Quramax Limited
Remedi Medical Holdings Ltd
Topcell Pharma Limited
WHL Contracts Ltd

**Northumberland** [11]
Ace First Aid Supplies Ltd
Doncaster Pharmaceuticals Group Ltd
Doncaster Pharmaceuticals Ltd
Kernfarm UK Limited
B.R. Lewis Pharmaceuticals Ltd
Norpan Hymbre Ltd
Pharmaceutical Identity Ltd
Renfield Limited
Specials Laboratory Limited
Testerworld Limited
Value Generics Limited

**Nottinghamshire** [25]
Apollo Medical Technologies Ltd
Aqua Hydration Limited
Bagnall Group (Europe) Ltd
Balagrae Ltd
Blue Horizon Healthcare Consulting
Boots International Limited
Decibel Biopharm Limited
Dilmaherbals Limited
E.P.G Pharma Ltd
EMT Healthcare Limited
East Midlands Infotech PVT Ltd
Elite Pharma UK Limited
Foreverbeyoung Ltd
GHC Medical Ltd
Independence Products Ltd
Kelpharma Ltd
Martini International Ltd
N-Pen Ltd.
Noru Pharma PVT Ltd.
Orkal Ltd
P.I.C. International Ltd
Rogia Romini Limited
Stanningley Pharma Limited
Valupharm UK Limited
Christopher Wood IXRS Consulting Ltd

**Oxfordshire** [24]
ABC Healthcare Limited
Advanced Medical Systems Ltd.
Amano Enzyme Europe Limited
Atlanta Biological Europe Ltd
Atlantic Imaging Limited
Biovendor Ltd
Collardam PLC
Fen Health Ltd
Genzyme Therapeutics Limited

## The Top UK Pharmaceutical Wholesalers

HMD Europe Ltd
Isra Limited
Matoke Holdings Limited
Medicines Company UK Limited
Mirada Medical Limited
New Seasons Natural Products Ltd
Nutrifast Ltd
Orion Medical Supplies Ltd
Oxford Biosystems Limited
Prema Naturals Limited
Pure Light Vision Ltd
Rapid Sample Processing Ltd
Sunstik Ltd
Surgihoney Limited
Timpext (Trading-Import-Export) Ltd

**Powys** [5]
Cellpath Limited
Hunter International Associates Ltd
R M Jones Limited
M.E.D. Supplies Limited
System Deep Clinic Limited

**Rutland**
English Herbal Medicines Ltd

**Shropshire** [11]
Accutest Solutions Limited
Aesthetics Clinic Dot Limited
Amdega Brands Limited
Arena (Eyewear) Limited
Dental Warehouse Ltd
MWK Healthcare Limited
Medshires Limited
Mirage Eyewear (1993) Limited
Poseidon Pharmaceutical UK Ltd
SP Services (UK) Limited
Timstar Laboratory Suppliers Ltd

**Somerset** [46]
20 20 Optical Services Ltd
AF Healthcare Ltd
Animal Prescriptions Limited
Bipsco Ltd
Bristol Buttr Ltd
CoAcS Trading Limited
Coates Agencies Ltd
Concord Extra Limited
Couchrolls.Com Ltd
Curas Limited
Danel Trading Limited
Double Wing Health & Beauty Ltd
Double Wing Medical Ltd
Double Wing Pharma Development Ltd
Dr Sproglet Ltd
Drilltex GB Ltd
Drugsdirect Limited
Enjoy Marketing Limited
Eurotech Medical Ltd
Gemapharm Limited
Granules Europe Limited
Hillcroft Surgery Supplies Ltd
Imex Ltd
Incimed Ltd
Incline Therapeutics Europe Ltd.
Intercept Pharma Europe Ltd.
Intercept Pharma Limited
Intercept Pharma UK & Ireland Ltd
Izida Pharma Ltd
Lifeshield Limited

Maria-Cristina Culita Ltd
Medilink Limited
Medisale Limited
Medisante Limited
P Y Imports Limited
Pharma Medico Limited
Pharmacina Ltd
Pharmethicals Limited
Ram Enterprises Bristol Ltd
Riebeeckstad Limited
Rose Europe UK Ltd
Rose Gentec Ltd
Sanochemia Diagnostics UK Ltd
Sfera Trading Limited
Swerve Cycling Limited
Jon West Trading Limited

**Staffordshire** [23]
Clinigen CTS Limited
Clinigen Group PLC
Clinigen Healthcare Limited
DNB Pharma Limited
Etab Health Group Limited
Etab Health Limited
Etab Pharma Limited
Go Medical UK Limited
IPY Healthcare Ltd
Idis Group Holdings Limited
Idis Limited
L & R Medical UK Ltd.
LB Pharma Limited
Longevity Life Ltd
National Veterinary Services Ltd
Pleskarn Limited
Reliance Medical Ltd
Sunstore Limited
TRB Chemedica (UK) Limited
Thea Pharmaceuticals Limited
Una Health Limited
Uni Supply Ltd
Valley Northern Limited

**Suffolk** [12]
Paul Baratte International Ltd
DB & A Cooper (Suffolk) Ltd
Glemsford Services Limited
Knightsbridge Importers Ltd
Mill Pharm Limited
PKA Healthcare Ltd
Pennine UK Procedure Packs Ltd
Precision Healthcare Limited
Sabona Rheumatic Relief Co Ltd
Standard Organics International (UK) Ltd
Virbac Limited
Zoono Holdings Limited

**Surrey** [147]
A B International Limited
A.J. Prime Ltd
Aarkios Health PVT Limited
Academy Hair and Beauty (UK) Ltd
Acupuncture Direct Ltd
Ainsworths (London) Limited
Akysha Limited
Alliance Healthcare (Distribution)
Angel & Lockhart (Pharma) Ltd
Angulus Pharma Limited
Aspire Pharma Holdings Limited
Aspire Pharma Limited
Astellas Pharma Europe Ltd.
Astellas Pharma Ltd.

Aston-Med Limited
Astriza UK Ltd
Attentive Pharma Limited
Aum Pharms Limited
Aventis Pharma Limited
Avicenna Ltd
B.P. Pharma Limited
Beautons Ventures Ltd
Beegood Enterprises Limited
Biomed Limited
Bioplax Limited
Brancaster Pharma Limited
Bripharm Limited
Bulgarian Healthy Products Ltd
CM & D Pharma Limited
Cannabinoidmeds Limited
Cardio Pro Limited
Casmed International Limited
Celtis Healthcare Ltd
Centline Ltd
Chemidex Generics Limited
Chesdeg Limited
Colgate-Palmolive (U.K.) Ltd
Connective Pharma Limited
G. D. Cooper & Co Ltd
Coriungo Limited
Cradlecrest Limited
Curans Care Limited
Damum UK Limited
Day Lewis Medical Limited
Dejure Limited
Direct Care Homes Limited
Disposable Medical Equipment Ltd
Dragonstone Group Limited
Dream Pharma Ltd
E-Pharm Limited
E-Pharma Chemical Int. Limited
Eco Animal Health Group PLC
Elite Pharma (Surrey) Limited
Enlon Limited
Essential Pharma Limited
European Nutriceutical Products Ltd
Firstchem Limited
Five Star International Consulting
Flairpath Limited
G9UK Limited
GB Pharma Limited
Gammaservice Limited
General Pharmaceuticals Ltd
Hanseco Ltd
Haoma Pharma Ltd
Healthbiotics Ltd
Healthcare Generics Limited
Healthcare Source Limited
Hoechst Marion Roussel Limited
Hurley Assets Limited
IMS Ultrasound (UK) Ltd
Ideal Medical Holdings Ltd
Ideal Medical Solutions Ltd
Incyte Biosciences UK Ltd
Interport Direct (Europe) Ltd
Interport Direct Limited
Interport Limited
Jules Pharma Limited
K & K Pharmaceuticals Limited
K P Pharma Limited
Korlyns Therapeutics Limited
La Lune Noire Ltd
Labjoy Ltd
Leeds Industries (UK) Ltd
London Health Suppliers Ltd
Lorteben Trading Co., Ltd

M2 Healthcare Ltd
MCL Healthcare Limited
Manek Healthcare Ltd
Matt L Consultancy Ltd
Mcall Consulting Ltd
MedRx Distribution Limited
Medaesthetics Limited
Medreich PLC
Metropharm Limited
Modern Innovations Limited Ltd
Mountrow Trading Limited
Multi Pharma Limited
NHS Generics Limited
Neutradvance Limited
New Roots Herbal Limited
Niv Ltd
Nivja Healthcare Ltd
Nurse Prescribers Limited
OTC Direct Limited
Omega Surgical Instruments Ltd
Ongar Medical Limited
Opus Pharmacy Services Limited
Orange Square Co Ltd.
Oxford Medpharma Ltd
Oxford PCS Limited
P & D Pharmaceuticals Ltd.
Payal London Consolidated Ltd
Payal Pharma UK Ltd
Peart Med Ltd
Pharm Med Ltd
Pharmaceutical Direct Limited
Pharmat Limited
Pharmdex UK Ltd
Powerlung Ltd.
Primrose Hudson Limited
Propharma Consultancy Ltd
Propharma-UK Ltd
Ria Generics Limited
Rovi Biotech Limited
Saving Life Technologies Ltd
Selsdon Healthcare Limited
Shieldasset Limited
Stegram Pharmaceuticals Ltd
Steritech Limited
Syner-Medica Limited
THS Solutions Limited
TNF (UK) Ltd
Tarus Group Limited
Tarus Laboratories Limited
Techdow Pharma England Limited
Tiamat Agriculture Ltd
Trinity Impex Limited
Ultrasun (UK) Limited
United Med Ltd
Veriton Pharma Limited
Victoria Meds Mondial Ltd
Windzor Pharma Limited
Xenium International Limited
Zentiva Pharma UK Limited
Zerocann Ltd
Zina Chemist Limited

**Sussex** [57]
21CEC PX Pharm Ltd
ACG Europe Limited
Aariana Impex Limited
Adelphi (Tubes) Limited
Appia Healthcare Limited
Aptil Pharma Limited
Aroschem Limited
Aroschem UK Limited
Ashtons Healthcare Limited

Ashtons Medical Limited
Ashtons Medical Supplies Ltd
BB Lifestyle UK Limited
Bio Nutrition Health Products Ltd
CSL Behring Holdings Limited
CSL Behring UK Limited
Canary Islands Marketing Board Ltd
Chanelle Medical U.K. Limited
Cripps Medical Limited
Cryotag Limited
Cuttlefish Limited
D & M Enterprises (UK) Limited
Greens Pharmacy Limited
Haydn Healthcare UK Limited
Hyaluron Health Ltd
Imperial Bioscience Ltd
Indigo Diagnostics Limited
Lab.Tv Limited
Lighthouse Mercury Limited
M & M Taste of Harmony Export Ltd
Mayomed Limited
Medbase Systems Ltd
Mediport Limited
Medirite Limited
Mediwin Limited
Modor & Bearn Limited
Mooncup Ltd
N H Southeast Ltd
Nanocor World Holdings Limited
Novo Nordisk Limited
Omron Healthcare UK Limited
Pharma-X Consultancy Ltd
Pharmac Limited
Pharmacohub Limited
Phytoceutical Limited
Rayner Pharmaceuticals Limited
Scope Ophthalmics Limited
Sentinel Laboratories Limited
Serp Sales (UK) Limited
Stragen UK Limited
Surgidoc Limited
T-In Medical Limited
Tabtime Limited
Torrent Pharma (UK) Ltd
Tricodent Limited
Uno Healthcare Limited
Vitafree Health Limited
Vitamineral Limited

**Tyne & Wear** [13]
Derma UK Limited
FTS Bio Limited
Fagron UK Ltd
Farah Chemists Limited
Fast Track Sourcing Limited
H4 Medical Limited
Islestone Limited
K Chem (North East) Ltd
Medilife Ltd
Perfect Vascular Natural Ltd
RPG Medical Limited
Sanhak Ltd
Sophos Medical Limited

**Warwickshire** [32]
AAH Pharmaceuticals Limited
AG Pharmahealth Ltd
Avail Group UK Limited
Barclay Pharmaceuticals Ltd
Berryfarm Ltd
Blackstaff Pharmaceuticals Ltd

Bristol Consumer Health Ltd
Din Commerce Ltd
European Veterinary Supplies Ltd
Genesis Medical Limited
Herbal Food Life Limited
Hilotherapy UK Limited
Hilotherm Ltd
Kemsource Limited
Livewell Naturals Limited
Lloyds Pharmacy Clinical Homecare
Manx Generics Limited
Manx Healthcare Limited
Manx Pharma Ltd
Masta Limited
Monarch Health Ltd
Nouveau Health Ltd
Oakways Healthcare Limited
Pope Enterprises Ltd
RDO Medical UK Limited
RP Pharma International Ltd
Receptor Holdings Limited
Receptor Technologies Limited
SF Pharma Limited
Source Healthcare Ltd
Trion Pharma Limited
Value Medical Limited

**West Midlands** [102]
AMG Pharmaceuticals Limited
ANXT Ltd
ASG Pharma Ltd
Acre Aesthetics Limited
Acre Medical Limited
Acre Pharma Limited
Al Medicines Limited
Alizcare Limited
All Med Care Limited
Arya House Pharma Ltd
Bbeauty Lounge Limited
Beiersdorf UK Ltd.
Bioavexia Ltd
Biotest (U.K.) Limited
Birmingham Management Centre (UK)
Bluesky Cosmetics Limited
Bri Trade Solutions Limited
Britannic Pharma Ltd
C. S. T. Pharma Limited
Celestial Pharma Ltd
Chikhurst Limited
Clinicpharma Limited
DWH Pharma Limited
Devilbiss Healthcare Limited
Diamond Pharma Limited
EPE Global Limited
Esthetica Pure Ltd
Europlus Pharma Ltd
Eye2eye Contact Ltd
Flintlow Limited
GHC (UK) Ltd
GHC Global Limited
GJB Pharma Limited
GK Locums Ltd
GP Meds Direct Limited
Gate Pharma Ltd
Globegen Laboratories Limited
Glucozen Limited
Go-Kyo Science Limited
Guerbet Laboratories Limited
Health Source Limited
Hemp Remedy Ltd
House of Filler Limited
I-Dispense Limited

# The Top UK Pharmaceutical Wholesalers

I-Pharma Healthcare Ltd
Ihealthcare Genius Limited
Innovius Life Drugs Ltd
Interchem (Chemist Wholesale) Ltd
Internal Luxe Heights Ltd
J L J Healthcare Limited
KDC-UK Ltd.
Kingston Pharma Limited
LSP Bio Limited
Labmedical System Limited
Lil-Lets UK Ltd
MDTI Pharma Retail Division Ltd
Medi Saha Limited
Medica Pharma UK Ltd
Mera Pharma Limited
Microskin Cosmeceuticals UK Ltd
Adam Myers Solutions Limited
N & G Pharma Limited
N N Pharma Ltd
N.G. Limited
NSK Global Ltd
Neolife International Ltd
O'Connell Pharma Ltd
Ocusoft UK Limited
Ofege Pharm Ltd
Omark Plus Ltd
Orphic Limited
P A M Medical Supplies Limited
PLA Medical Supplies Limited
Passion Dental Design Studio (Laboratory)
Pharhealth Limited
PharmXC Ltd
Pharmaco Halesowen Limited
Pharmavit (UK) Limited
Sara Post Ltd
Premium Pharma UK Limited
RAR Pharmaceutics Ltd
RSS Wholesaling Limited
Rosefield Pharma Ltd
SAR Health Limited
Sandyvale Limited
G S Seehra Limited
Sigmasis UK Limited
Six Ways Birmingham Ltd
Skylark Services Limited
Stainweld Limited
Stockman (UK) Ltd
Sword Medical UK Limited
Tagma Pharma (UK) Ltd
Tytek UK Medical Co Ltd
UK Biopharma Ltd
UK Pharma Direct Limited
Ukcann Ltd
Unit Medic-Aids Limited
Veenak International Limited
Veenak Sourcing Limited
Welcome Medical Group Ltd
Wellbeing Products Limited

**Wiltshire** [9]
C & P Medical Trading Limited
Great British Bee Co Ltd
Pan Globus Limited
Phonepimps Limited
Rembrook Developments Limited
Sampsonstore.Com (UK) Ltd

Teoxane UK Limited
Vygon (U.K.) Limited
Zimmer Biomet UK Limited

**Worcestershire** [14]
Better'er Limited
Cytoplan Limited
Gill Pharma Limited
LTT Pharma Limited
Lexon (UK) Limited
Lexon UK Holdings Limited
Max Motivation Limited
Norchem Limited
Norsworthy Limited
Okle Systems Limited
Pioneer Medical Europe Limited
R & H Trading Limited
THD (UK) Limited
Zeal Products Limited

**Yorkshire** [112]
Aayur Limited
Al-Ghani Limited
Alpharma Limited
Animalcare Ltd
Apetamintko Limited
Apex Lab Scientific Ltd
Apollo Endosurgery UK Ltd
Arquella Ltd
Autono-Med Limited
B D S I Limited
B.R. Pharmaceuticals Limited
Bigvits Limited
Bioconnections Ltd
Biogenix Ltd
Bionutricals UK Ltd
Bioquote Limited
Biovate Limited
Boston Healthcare Limited
Butt & Hobbs Limited
CM Healthcare Limited
C G Clark Limited
Countrywide Healthcare Supplies Holdings
Creative Brand Concepts Ltd
Curelife Ltd
Dakota Pharma Limited
Dene Healthcare Limited
Derma Distribution Ltd
Dispensing Healthcare Ltd
Dutscher Scientific UK Limited
EVC Compounding Ltd
Ebbcourt Limited
Elleco Limited
Ely Pharma Ltd
Emkado Ltd.
FPD Group Limited
Farmvet Limited
Fivtique Limited
Florence Health & Beauty Ltd
Flowonix Medical Ltd
Frontier Lab Scientific Ltd
Genrx UK Lipperts Ltd.
Genus Pharmaceuticals Holdings Ltd
Genus Pharmaceuticals Limited
Green Guru Enterprices Ltd.
Habberpharm Limited

Haq Pharm Ltd
Harvey Pharma Ltd
Healthcare 21 (UK) Limited
Higherplateau Limited
I L Locum Ltd
I.T.T.I.D. (Trading) Ltd
Inbamay Resources (UK) Ltd.
Instantly White Ltd
International Ingredients and Chemicals (IIC)
Irls Yorkshire Limited
Jorvik Pharma Ltd
KM Consulting (Chesterfield) Ltd
Kelisdar Enterprises Limited
Kisska International Limited
Knox Pharmaceuticals Limited
Kora Healthcare UK Ltd
Leung Healthcare Limited
Leverton & Co Ltd
London Spirit for Trading Ltd
M.G. Dental Supplies Limited
MMEU 20/20 Ltd
Medi-Arch Ltd
Medica Ltd
Medix Supply International Ltd
Medstore Limited
My Dental Store Limited
Nascot Natural Health Limited
Niche Pharma Limited
Ontyme Logistics and Healthcare Ltd
Optident Labline Limited
Oswell Penda Pharmaceutical Ltd
Parker Trading Ltd
Pennamed Limited
Pennine Pharmaceuticals Ltd
Prestige Dental Products Ltd
Pricecheck Toiletries Limited
Principle Healthcare Limited
Qamar Limited
Ratiopharm (UK) Limited
Resource Medical (UK) Ltd
Roberts McCarron Ltd
SG Pharma UK Limited
Saxon Pharmaceuticals Limited
Scientific Laboratory Supplies Group Ltd
Skinska Pharmaceutica Limited
Soothingproducts Ltd
Stem Cellx Limited
Supplemax Ltd
TFS Med UK Limited
ThriveExtreme Health Limited
Titan Med Limited
Toiletry Sales Limited
Tuluh Solutions Ltd
UK Lites Ltd
Vertibax Limited
Vet Store Trading Limited
Vetsonic (UK) Ltd
Vision Matrix Limited
WPG Wholesale Trading Ltd
Whiterose Supplements Limited
Yawskin Limited
Ypsomed Limited
Z T Locums Ltd
Zaitun Limited
Zarroug Limited
Zeroderma Limited
Zhongfu (UK) Limited

*This page is intentionally left blank*

# Company Profiles

### 10x Rational Ambulance Yield Limited
*Incorporated:* 20 June 2018
*Registered Office:* 24 Holborn Viaduct, London, EC1A 2BN
*Shareholder:* Andy Newton Cloud Consulting Ltd
*Officers:* Kenneth Kronohage [1963] Director [Swedish]; Khalil Fawwaz Malaeb [1963] Director [Lebanese]; Professor Andrew John Newton [1957] Director

### 11 Health & Technologies Limited
*Incorporated:* 22 April 2013  *Employees:* 8
*Net Worth:* £2,755,010  *Total Assets:* £3,153,145
*Registered Office:* Kinetic Business Centre, The Kinetic Centre, Theobald Street, Borehamwood, Herts, WD6 4PJ
*Officers:* Adam Simon Bloom, Secretary; Angus Murray Davidson [1966] Director; Bernhard David Gilbey [1967] Director; Massi Joseph Kiani [1964] Director/Medical Technology [American]; Michael Joseph Seres [1969] Marketing and Sales Director; Charles Alexander Evan Spicer [1965] Director

### 11239338 Ltd
*Incorporated:* 7 March 2018
*Registered Office:* 48 Westminster Road, Exeter, EX4 2LS

### 1966 Health International Limited
*Incorporated:* 8 December 2016
*Net Worth Deficit:* £5,849,355  *Total Assets:* £948,913
*Registered Office:* 3 Berkeley Mews, London, W1H 7AT
*Major Shareholder:* Chris Flannery
*Officers:* Chris Flannery [1965] Director/Executive

### 1LIFE Distribution Limited
*Incorporated:* 22 February 2019
*Registered Office:* 86 Heywood Street, Manchester, M8 0TD
*Shareholders:* Alessia Burchkard; Robert Paul Rimmer
*Officers:* Alessia Burchkard [1991] Director/Manager; Robert Paul Rimmer [1973] Director/Manager

### 1st Class Medical Ltd
*Incorporated:* 3 December 2018
*Registered Office:* 27 Gladstone Avenue, London, N22 6JU
*Major Shareholder:* Ali Ismail Osman Adan
*Officers:* Ali Ismail Osman Adan [1981] Director/Businessman

### 1st Health Products Ltd
*Incorporated:* 30 May 2012
*Net Worth:* £21,257  *Total Assets:* £31,961
*Registered Office:* Optic Technology Centre, St Asaph Business Park, St Asaph, Denbighshire, LL17 0JD
*Officers:* Dr John Anthony Rees [1965] Director/Biologist

### 2 Shy 2 Buy Limited
*Incorporated:* 10 June 2016
*Registered Office:* Unit 1b Harrison Court, Hilton Business Park, Hilton, Derby, DE65 5UR
*Officers:* Simon Robert Shakespeare [1967] Director

### 20 20 Optical Services Ltd
*Incorporated:* 5 March 2012
*Registered Office:* 1 Cornhill, Ilminster, Somerset, TA19 0AD
*Major Shareholder:* Mark Patrick Truss
*Officers:* Mark Truss, Secretary; Francesca Truss [1968] Director/Carer; Mark Patrick Truss [1961] Director

### 21CEC PX Pharm Ltd
*Incorporated:* 2 June 2003
*Net Worth:* £12,834  *Total Assets:* £13,583
*Registered Office:* 45 Oaklands, Westham, Pevensey, E Sussex, BN24 5AW
*Major Shareholder:* Claire Chan Bleasdale
*Officers:* Dr Claire Chan Bleasdale [1957] Director

### 2M PH. Intl. Limited
*Incorporated:* 20 October 2015
*Net Worth:* £9,574  *Total Assets:* £15,601
*Registered Office:* Bridge House, 2 Bridge Avenue, Maidenhead, Berks, SL6 1RR
*Major Shareholder:* Massimiliano Melano
*Officers:* Massimiliano Melano, Secretary; Massimiliano Melano [1966] Director/Entrepreneur [Italian]

### 378 Company Limited
*Incorporated:* 8 August 2016
*Registered Office:* 378 Linthorpe Road, Middlesbrough, Cleveland, TS5 6HA
*Officers:* Dr Sarabjit Singh Chahal [1971] Director/Doctor; Dr Anya Heywood [1970] Director/Doctor; Dr Peter Heywood [1968] Director/Doctor; Dr Amy Micklethwaite [1981] Director/Doctor; Dr Rajendra Kumar Pandey [1957] Director/Doctor; Dr Katie Senior [1982] Director/Doctor

### 56 Flowers Ltd
*Incorporated:* 3 September 2018
*Registered Office:* Ashwells Associates Limited, 54 Church Road, Ashford, Middlesex, TW15 2TS
*Shareholders:* John James Carter; Craig Payne
*Officers:* John James Carter [1992] Director; Craig Payne [1987] Director

### 8 Pharma Ltd
*Incorporated:* 8 August 2006
*Net Worth Deficit:* £9,518
*Registered Office:* 8 Premier Business Park, Dencora Way, Luton, Beds, LU3 3HP
*Major Shareholder:* Kevin Patel
*Officers:* Kevin Patel [1975] Director

### 8 Trading Limited
*Incorporated:* 8 August 2017
*Registered Office:* 8 Premier Business Park, Dencora Way, Luton, Beds, LU3 3HP
*Major Shareholder:* Kevin Patel
*Officers:* Kevin Patel [1975] Director

### A & E Healthcare Limited
*Incorporated:* 3 November 2008
*Net Worth:* £7,375  *Total Assets:* £20,691
*Registered Office:* 18 Tamar Close, Bere Alston, Yelverton, Devon, PL20 7HF
*Major Shareholder:* Ashley Hunter
*Officers:* Ashley Hunter [1962] Director/Pharmacist

### A B Alliance Limited
*Incorporated:* 8 June 2016
*Net Worth:* £100  *Total Assets:* £100
*Registered Office:* Solar House, 282 Chase Road, Southgate, London, N14 6NZ
*Major Shareholder:* Anastasia Angelopoulou
*Officers:* Anastasia Angelopoulou [1979] Director [Greek]

## The Top UK Pharmaceutical Wholesalers

**A B International Limited**
*Incorporated:* 1 March 1991  *Employees:* 3
*Net Worth:* £1,321,637  *Total Assets:* £1,420,556
*Registered Office:* Almac House, Church Lane, Bisley, Surrey, GU24 9DR
*Shareholders:* Rebecca Brown; David Brown
*Officers:* Rebecca Brown, Secretary; David Paul Brown [1966] Director; Rebecca Brown [1969] Director

**A D Healthcare Limited**
*Incorporated:* 13 December 1996  *Employees:* 12
*Net Worth:* £603,050  *Total Assets:* £1,089,480
*Registered Office:* 94 Main Street, Larbert, Stirlingshire, FK5 3AS
*Major Shareholder:* Keiron David Paterson
*Officers:* Keiron David Paterson [1982] Director; Roger Paterson [1943] Director/Retired

**A K Worldwide Trading Limited**
*Incorporated:* 9 February 2011
*Net Worth Deficit:* £66,551  *Total Assets:* £44,812
*Registered Office:* Unit E3, Harlow Business Centre, Lovet Road, Harlow, Essex, CM19 5AF
*Shareholders:* Amanda Grover; Kathy Horne
*Officers:* Amanda Grover [1966] Director

**A V Pharma Limited**
*Incorporated:* 29 June 2017  *Employees:* 2
*Net Worth Deficit:* £67,744  *Total Assets:* £25,514
*Registered Office:* Unit 1b Harrison Court, Hilton Business Park, Hilton, Derby, DE65 5UR
*Major Shareholder:* Simon Robert Shakespeare
*Officers:* Paul James Keeton [1968] Commercial Director; Simon Robert Shakespeare [1967] Director

**A Wise World Limited**
*Incorporated:* 1 June 2010  *Employees:* 1
*Net Worth:* £20,853  *Total Assets:* £47,414
*Registered Office:* 3 Bower Close, Peterborough, Cambs, PE1 5LL
*Shareholders:* Sayed Afzal Mehdi; Kanize Fatima Mehdi
*Officers:* Sayed Afzal Mehdi [1969] Director/Accountant

**A.H.P. Medical Supplies Ltd**
*Incorporated:* 27 February 2001
*Net Worth Deficit:* £88,050  *Total Assets:* £2,361
*Registered Office:* 64 Borough High Street, London, SE1 1XF
*Shareholder:* Ala Towfiq Sharif
*Officers:* Julie Sharif, Secretary; Dr Ala Towfiq Sharif [1950] Director

**A.J. Prime Ltd**
*Incorporated:* 7 December 2017
*Registered Office:* Unit 14 Long Acres Park, Newchapel Road, Lingfield, Surrey, RH7 6LE
*Major Shareholder:* Judit Honti
*Officers:* Attila Kranyik, Secretary; Judit Honti [1972] Director [Hungarian]

**A.T. Medical Ltd**
*Incorporated:* 19 January 2010
*Net Worth Deficit:* £45,313  *Total Assets:* £812
*Registered Office:* 117 Queens Park Avenue, Bournemouth, BH8 9HA
*Major Shareholder:* Juan Sebastian Osorio
*Officers:* Juliana Kang, Secretary; Juan Sebastian Osorio Puentes [1983] Director [Colombian]

**A1 Natural Ltd**
*Incorporated:* 27 February 2017  *Employees:* 1
*Net Worth Deficit:* £14,926  *Total Assets:* £1,299
*Registered Office:* 21 Beechwood Avenue, Ruislip, Middlesex, HA4 6EG
*Major Shareholder:* Wesam El-Maksoud
*Officers:* Wesam El-Maksoud [1980] Director

**A1 Pharmaceuticals Holdings Limited**
*Incorporated:* 30 April 2013  *Employees:* 37
*Net Worth:* £14,493,644  *Total Assets:* £20,243,268
*Registered Office:* Unit 20 & 21 Easter Industrial Park, Ferry Lane South, Rainham, Essex, RM13 9BP
*Officers:* Carmen Lewis [1965] Director/Secretary Administrator; Gary Stephen Lewis [1960] Director/Pharmacist

**A1 Pharmaceuticals Public Limited Company**
*Incorporated:* 24 February 1992  *Employees:* 37
*Net Worth:* £14,392,724  *Total Assets:* £18,008,192
*Registered Office:* Unit 20 & 21 Easter Industrial Park, Ferry Lane South, Rainham, Essex, RM13 9BP
*Shareholders:* Gary Stephen Lewis; Carmen Lewis
*Officers:* Carmen Lewis, Secretary/Administrator; Carmen Lewis [1965] Director/Secretary Administrator; Gary Stephen Lewis [1960] Director/Pharmacist

**Aadverv Sourcing Solutions Limited**
*Incorporated:* 1 June 2017
*Registered Office:* 14 Crofts Road, Harrow, Middlesex, HA1 2PH
*Major Shareholder:* Haradri Vyas
*Officers:* Sagitha George [1981] Director/Consultant [Indian]; Haradri Vyas [1981] Director/Consultant [Indian]

**AAH Pharmaceuticals Limited**
*Incorporated:* 27 July 1912  *Employees:* 2,989
*Net Worth:* £203,798,000  *Total Assets:* £999,052,032
*Registered Office:* Sapphire Court, Walsgrave Triangle, Coventry, Warwicks, CV2 2TX
*Parent:* Admenta Holdings Limited
*Officers:* Nichola Louise Legg, Secretary; Toby Matthew Anderson [1973] Director; Marcus Hilger [1977] Finance Director [German]; Catherine McDermott [1968] Operations Director; Nigel Swift [1966] Marketing & Sales Director

**AAP Healthcare Ltd**
*Incorporated:* 16 November 2018
*Registered Office:* 1060 Stockport Road, Manchester, M19 2SX
*Shareholders:* Adal Bashir; Hassan Ibish
*Officers:* Adal Bashir [1991] Director/Chemist; Hassan Ibish [1985] Director/Chemist

**AAR Pharma Ltd**
*Incorporated:* 9 April 2010
*Net Worth Deficit:* £5,262  *Total Assets:* £999
*Registered Office:* 3rd Floor, 49 Farringdon Road, London, EC1M 3JP
*Major Shareholder:* Ashwini Kumar Shiwach
*Officers:* Mary Jane Hoareau [1977] Director/Accountant [Seychellois]; Ashwini Kumar Shiwach [1967] Director [Indian]

**Aariana Impex Limited**
*Incorporated:* 2 February 2018
*Registered Office:* 13 Hammingden Court, Forge Wood, Crawley, W Sussex, RH10 3FR
*Major Shareholder:* Roushanara Akter
*Officers:* Roushanara Akter [1986] Director and Company Secretary [Bangladeshi]

## Aarkios Health PVT Limited
*Incorporated:* 21 August 2012
*Registered Office:* 2 Peterwood Way, Croydon, Surrey, CR0 4UQ
*Major Shareholder:* Saumil Gandhi
*Officers:* Saumil Mahendra Gandhi [1982] Director [Indian]

## Aayur Limited
*Incorporated:* 24 August 2016
*Registered Office:* Unit 3 Inspire Business Park, Bradford, BD10 0JE
*Shareholder:* Nigel Patrick Silcox
*Officers:* Cheryll-Anne Patricia Silcox [1961] Director; Nigel Patrick Silcox [1955] Director

## AB Pharma Logistics Ltd
*Incorporated:* 10 August 2018
*Registered Office:* 71-75 Shelton Street, Covent Garden, London, WC2H 9JQ
*Major Shareholder:* Adam Bowden
*Officers:* Adam Bowden, Secretary; Adam Bowden [1990] Director

## Abacus Medicine Ltd
*Incorporated:* 11 December 2013
*Net Worth:* £19,182 *Total Assets:* £24,773
*Registered Office:* Floor 30, The Leadenhall Building, 122 Leadenhall Street, London, EC3V 4AB
*Parent:* Abacus Medicine A/S
*Officers:* Flemming Wagner [1964] Director/Consultant [Danish]

## Abbott Healthcare Products Ltd
*Incorporated:* 5 March 1969 *Employees:* 18
*Net Worth:* £40,318,000 *Total Assets:* £42,670,000
*Registered Office:* Abbott House, Vanwall Business Park, Vanwall Road, Maidenhead, Berks, SL6 4XE
*Shareholders:* Abbott Laboratories Inc.; Abbott Laboratories
*Officers:* Kevan Gogay, Secretary; Neil Harris [1974] Director/General Manager; Georgios Mountrichas [1977] Director/General Manager [Greek]; Brian Yoor [1969] Director/Business Executive [American]

## Abbott Laboratories Limited
*Incorporated:* 23 June 1937 *Employees:* 516
*Net Worth:* £224,132,000 *Total Assets:* £428,572,000
*Registered Office:* Abbott House, Vanwall Business Park, Vanwall Road, Maidenhead, Berks, SL6 4XE
*Parent:* Abbott UK Holdings Limited
*Officers:* Kevan Gogay, Secretary; Neil Harris [1974] Director/General Manager; Georgios Mountrichas [1977] Director/General Manager [Greek]; Karen Peterson [1965] Director/VP Treasurer [American]

## AbbVie Ltd
*Incorporated:* 23 March 2012 *Employees:* 647
*Net Worth:* £287,118,016 *Total Assets:* £398,508,992
*Registered Office:* AbbVie House, Vanwall Business Park, Vanwall Road, Maidenhead, Berks, SL6 4UB
*Parent:* AbbVie Inc.
*Officers:* Kyle Alexander Poots, Secretary; Jerome Stephane Bouyer [1969] Director/Business Executive [French]; William Joseph Chase [1967] Director [American]; Gwenan Mair White [1969] Director of Communications

## ABC Healthcare Limited
*Incorporated:* 1 June 2005 *Employees:* 1
*Net Worth:* £53,228 *Total Assets:* £128,066
*Registered Office:* 6 Newbury Street, Wantage, Oxon, OX12 8BS
*Major Shareholder:* Angela Susan Stevens
*Officers:* Angela Susan Stevens [1959] Director

## ABC Pharmaceuticals Ltd
*Incorporated:* 26 July 2018
*Registered Office:* Ground Floor, 2 Woodberry Grove, London, N12 0DR
*Major Shareholder:* Ewan Prince Airhiavbere
*Officers:* Ewan Prince Airhiavbere, Secretary; Ewan Prince Airhiavbere [1965] Director/Pharmacist

## ABI Training Academy Limited
*Incorporated:* 26 March 2018
*Registered Office:* 80 High Street, Golborne, Warrington, Cheshire, WA3 3DA
*Major Shareholder:* Dawn Bingham
*Officers:* Dawn Bingham [1979] Director/Aesthetics & Beauty

## Abra Wholesales Ltd
*Incorporated:* 24 February 2003 *Employees:* 74
*Net Worth:* £1,833,838 *Total Assets:* £8,568,692
*Registered Office:* 5 Picketts Lock Lane, Edmonton, London, N9 0AS
*Shareholders:* Thuraichamy Thayananthan; Bhavani Thayananthan
*Officers:* Bhavani Thayananthan, Secretary; Sabanathan Jeyapragash [1981] Director; Sothinagaratnam Sothimaheswaran [1959] Director/Chief Financial Officer; Bhavani Thayananthan [1972] Director/Wholesale; Thuraichamy Thayananthan [1972] Director/Wholesale

## Absolute Brands Ltd
*Incorporated:* 12 August 2011
*Net Worth Deficit:* £4,664 *Total Assets:* £52,530
*Registered Office:* 18 Waldegrave Road, London, W5 3HT
*Major Shareholder:* Ghazi Abdullah Alharbi
*Officers:* Abdulrazzaq Al-Maeedh [1974] Director [Yemeni]

## Abstragan Holding Limited
*Incorporated:* 7 October 2011
*Net Worth Deficit:* £10,931 *Total Assets:* £3,735,916
*Registered Office:* Astra House, Arklow Road, London, SE14 6EB
*Parent:* Abstragan Limited
*Officers:* Mirzoev Ilkhomzhon [1980] General Director, Closed Joint Stock Company [Tajikistani]

## Abstragan Limited
*Incorporated:* 22 September 2015
*Net Worth:* £100 *Total Assets:* £25,600
*Registered Office:* Astra House, Arklow Load, London, SE14 6EB
*Shareholder:* Mirzoev Zafarkhon
*Officers:* Ilkhomzhon Mirzoev [1980] Director/Pharmaceutical Business [Tajikistani]; Zafarkhon Mirzoev [1972] Director/Pharmaceutical Business [Tajikistani]

## AC Intertrade Limited
*Incorporated:* 1 August 2014 *Employees:* 2
*Net Worth Deficit:* £9,249 *Total Assets:* £152,700
*Registered Office:* Unit M, Oyo Business Units, Hindmans Way, Dagenham, Essex, RM9 6LN
*Major Shareholder:* Charinjit Singh Puaar
*Officers:* Charanjit Puaar, Secretary; Charanjit Singh Puaar [1980] Director/Trader

## Academy Hair and Beauty (UK) Ltd
*Incorporated:* 2 May 1997
*Net Worth:* £188,029 *Total Assets:* £376,876
*Registered Office:* Doshi Accountants Ltd, 6th Floor, Amp House, Dingwall Road, Croydon, Surrey, CR0 2LX
*Shareholders:* Mohsin Janmohamed; Fidahusein Gulamali Asharia
*Officers:* Fidahusein Gulamali Asharia, Secretary; Mohsin Janmohamed [1961] Director/Businessman

## The Top UK Pharmaceutical Wholesalers

**Accendo Pharma Ltd**
*Incorporated:* 6 January 2014
*Net Worth:* £27,086 *Total Assets:* £149,003
*Registered Office:* Unit F5, Phoenix Business Centre, Rosslyn Crescent, Harrow, Middlesex, HA1 2SP
*Major Shareholder:* Zohaib Shariff
*Officers:* Syeda Sofia Shah [1988] Director/Administrator; Zohaib Shariff [1983] Director/Self Employed

**Accmede Pharmaceuticals Limited**
*Incorporated:* 7 February 2014 *Employees:* 5
*Net Worth:* £105 *Total Assets:* £6,677
*Registered Office:* Media House, Kingsbury Works Estate, Kingsbury Road, London, NW9 8UP
*Shareholder:* Janaksinh Jhala
*Officers:* Arjunsinh Gohil [1986] Director [Indian]; Janaksinh Jhala [1984] Director [Indian]

**Accord Healthcare Limited**
*Incorporated:* 21 November 2002 *Employees:* 1,197
*Net Worth:* £7,378,000 *Total Assets:* £891,985,984
*Registered Office:* Sage House, 319 Pinner Road, North Harrow, Middlesex, HA1 4HF
*Officers:* Pradeep Bhagia, Secretary; Dr James Burt [1974] Director/Chemical Engineer; Binish Hasmukhbhai Chudgar [1963] Director/Businessman [Indian]; Anthony Leonard Cordrey [1961] Senior Director - EU Strategic Operations; Lord Jitesh Kishorekumar Gadhia [1970] Director; John Geoffrey Goddard [1951] Director; Roger Marquilles Escola [1975] Director/Head of Legal Affairs - Europe [Spanish]; Nilesh Parmar [1968] Director; Phillip Semmens [1971] Director/Vice President Hospitals - Europe

**Accordia Investments Ltd**
*Incorporated:* 31 July 2001 *Employees:* 8
*Net Worth:* £271,280 *Total Assets:* £505,711
*Registered Office:* 14 Phoenix Park, Telford Way, Coalville, Leics, LE67 3HB
*Shareholders:* Mohamed Rajabali Kanani; Julie Kanani
*Officers:* Julie Kanani, Secretary; Julie Kanani [1960] Director; Mohamed Rajabali Kanani [1965] Director/Pharmacist

**Accutest Solutions Limited**
*Incorporated:* 4 June 2015
*Net Worth Deficit:* £21,952 *Total Assets:* £109,705
*Registered Office:* Brooklands House, Yeomanry Road, Battlefield Enterprise Park, Shrewsbury, Salop, SY1 3EH
*Major Shareholder:* Richard William Taylor
*Officers:* Richard William Taylor [1972] Director

**Ace First Aid Supplies Ltd**
*Incorporated:* 20 September 2012
*Net Worth Deficit:* £12,038 *Total Assets:* £14,460
*Registered Office:* 3 York Grove, Bedlington, Northumberland, NE22 6NX
*Major Shareholder:* Kevin Michael Heath Spearman
*Officers:* Kevin Michael Heath Spearman [1960] Director

**Acehides Limited**
*Incorporated:* 25 April 2018
*Registered Office:* 255 Poulton Road, Wallasey, Wirral, Merseyside, CH44 4BT
*Shareholders:* David Lannen; William Wilson
*Officers:* David Lannen [1966] Director [Irish]; William Wilson [1960] Director/Commodity Trader

**Acer Agri Ltd**
*Incorporated:* 17 September 2018
*Registered Office:* Tishon House, Warrington Road, High Legh, Knutsford, Cheshire, WA16 0RT
*Major Shareholder:* Thomas William Garton
*Officers:* Dr Thomas William Garton [1990] Director/Veterinary Surgeon

**Acer Pharma Limited**
*Incorporated:* 7 March 2016
*Net Worth:* £2,991,105 *Total Assets:* £5,345,774
*Registered Office:* 137 Wistaston Road, Willaston, Nantwich, Cheshire, CW5 6QS
*Major Shareholder:* Jason Yates
*Officers:* Jason Derick Yates [1973] Director/Sales Consultant

**Aces Pharma Limited**
*Incorporated:* 9 May 2018
*Registered Office:* 130 Old Street, London, EC1V 9BD
*Officers:* Kamran Khan, Secretary; Kamran Khan [1972] Director/Self Employed

**ACESO Global Ltd**
*Incorporated:* 21 February 2018
*Registered Office:* 3 Castleacre, 15 Hyde Park Crescent, London, W2 2PT
*Major Shareholder:* Shaghayegh Khajoo
*Officers:* Shaghayegh Khajoo [1972] Director

**ACG Europe Limited**
*Incorporated:* 26 August 2003 *Employees:* 8
*Net Worth:* £2,530,860 *Total Assets:* £7,396,577
*Registered Office:* Hardham Mill Business Park, Mill Lane, Pulborough, W Sussex, RH20 1LA
*Shareholders:* Jasjit Daljit Singh; Ajit Daljit Singh
*Officers:* Rashmi Mishra, Secretary; Russell Beeching [1958] Director; Selwyn Mariano Jonas Noronha [1962] Director/CEO & President [Indian]

**ACI Group Ltd**
*Incorporated:* 19 March 2018 *Employees:* 17
*Net Worth:* £330,537 *Total Assets:* £3,646,276
*Registered Office:* 22-23 Progress Centre, Whittle Parkway, Slough, SL1 6DQ
*Major Shareholder:* Roland Werner Muller
*Officers:* Jagjeevan Lal Desorh [1968] Director

**ACL Medical Limited**
*Incorporated:* 7 July 2017
*Registered Office:* Charter House, 8-10 Station Road, London, E12 5BT
*Major Shareholder:* Pantelis Papageorgiou
*Officers:* Pantelis Papageorgiou [1965] Director/Doctor [Greek]

**Aclardian Limited**
*Incorporated:* 10 October 2008 *Employees:* 7
*Net Worth:* £248,521 *Total Assets:* £1,068,691
*Registered Office:* Highfield Court, Church Lane, Madingley, Cambridge, CB23 8AG
*Officers:* Alan Gilbert Goodman [1951] Director; Daniel James William Roach [1955] Director

### Acle Medical Limited
*Incorporated:* 5 May 2015
*Net Worth:* £5,356  *Total Assets:* £197,302
*Registered Office:* Devlukia Chemist, 192 Norwich Road, Norwich, NR5 0EX
*Shareholders:* Prabodh Nilkanth Devlukia; Meena Prabodhkumar Devlukia
*Officers:* Prabodh Nilkanth Devlukia, Secretary; Meena Prabodhkumar Devlukia [1963] Director; Prabodh Nilkanth Devlukia [1957] Director

### Acme Pharma Ltd
*Incorporated:* 16 April 2014  *Employees:* 4
*Net Worth:* £266,007  *Total Assets:* £1,105,146
*Registered Office:* 337 Athlon Road, Wembley, Middlesex, HA0 1EF
*Major Shareholder:* Rinkle Rameshkumar Buddhadev
*Officers:* Rinkle Rameshkumar Buddhadev [1987] Director [Indian]

### Acorus Therapeutics Limited
*Incorporated:* 19 April 2000
*Registered Office:* Eden House, Lakeside, Chester Business Park, Chester, CH4 9QT
*Parent:* IS Pharma Ltd
*Officers:* Jason Rodney Tate, Secretary; Jayne Katherine Burrell [1974] Director; Alan Musgrave Olby [1971] Director; Christopher Paul Spooner [1968] Director

### Acre Aesthetics Limited
*Incorporated:* 7 September 2018
*Registered Office:* Unit 5-7 Tintagel Way, Aldridge, Walsall, W Midlands, WS9 8ER
*Parent:* Acre Pharma Limited
*Officers:* Aiden Bayati [1992] Director/Pharmacist; Neil John Clarkson [1973] Director; Robert Arthur Melville [1969] Director; Daniel Mark O'Connor [1981] Finance Director

### Acre Medical Limited
*Incorporated:* 22 February 2018
*Registered Office:* 5-7 Tintagel Way, Aldridge, Walsall, W Midlands, WS9 8ER
*Shareholders:* Robert Arthur Melville; Dean Spotswood
*Officers:* Robert Arthur Melville [1969] Director; Daniel Mark O'Connor [1981] Finance Director; Dean Cameron Spotswood [1983] Director; Jason Derick Yates [1973] Managing Director

### Acre Pharma Limited
*Incorporated:* 31 October 2012  *Employees:* 2
*Net Worth:* £51,810  *Total Assets:* £1,029,758
*Registered Office:* Unit 5-7 Tintagel Way, Aldridge, Walsall, W Midlands, WS9 8ER
*Officers:* Robert Arthur Melville [1969] Director; Daniel Mark O'Connor [1981] Director; Dean Spotswood [1983] Director; Jason Derick Yates [1973] Managing Director

### Actipharm Limited
*Incorporated:* 25 April 2008
*Net Worth:* £426,495  *Total Assets:* £3,133,726
*Registered Office:* 93 Fore Street, London, N18 2TW
*Shareholders:* Jignesh Patel; Amit Patel; Rashmibala Patel
*Officers:* Jignesh Patel [1980] Director/Pharmacist

### Activated Smile Ltd
*Incorporated:* 15 January 2019
*Registered Office:* Suite 329, Scottish Provident Building, 7 Donegall Square West, Belfast, BT1 6JH
*Major Shareholder:* Patrick Gerard O'Reilly
*Officers:* Patrick Gerard O'Reilly [1982] Director [Irish]

### Active Export Ltd
*Incorporated:* 17 March 2010
*Net Worth:* £19,260  *Total Assets:* £431,351
*Registered Office:* 2nd Floor, 13 John Prince's Street, London, W1G 0JR
*Major Shareholder:* Ivan Tkachev
*Officers:* Maria Berdanis [1991] Director/Consultant [South African]

### Active Global Ltd
*Incorporated:* 9 February 2015
*Net Worth:* £1,700  *Total Assets:* £188,153
*Registered Office:* Office 16011, 5 Percy Street, London, W1T 1DG
*Major Shareholder:* Oleksandr Bortnyk
*Officers:* Robert Michael Friedberg [1959] Director/Manager

### Active Pharma Supplies Limited
*Incorporated:* 8 February 2012
*Net Worth Deficit:* £4,602  *Total Assets:* £122,973
*Registered Office:* Unit 2 Forward Industrial Estate, Talbot Road, Leyland, Lancs, PR25 2ZJ
*Officers:* Marc Borson [1978] Director

### The Active Prescription Limited
*Incorporated:* 23 March 2017
*Registered Office:* Ryefield Court, 81 Joel Street, Northwood Hills, Northwood, Middlesex, HA6 1LL
*Major Shareholder:* Nicola Jane Davies
*Officers:* Nicola Jane Davies [1964] Director/Graphic Designer

### Acupuncture Direct Ltd
*Incorporated:* 8 July 1999
*Net Worth:* £218,675  *Total Assets:* £241,988
*Registered Office:* 1 Parkshot, Richmond, Surrey, TW9 2RD
*Major Shareholder:* Gerard Fraux
*Officers:* Claire Fraux [1988] Director/Engineer [French]; Gerard Fraux [1954] Director/Manager [French]

### Acure Pharma Limited
*Incorporated:* 21 November 2016
*Net Worth:* £25,957  *Total Assets:* £60,000
*Registered Office:* Office 126 Regus UK, 239 High Street Kensington, London, W8 6SN
*Shareholders:* Thomas Jacobsen; Stijn Van Rompay
*Officers:* Thomas Jacobsen [1974] Director [Danish]; Stijn Van Rompay [1976] Director [Belgian]

### Adallen Pharma Limited
*Incorporated:* 3 May 2001  *Employees:* 9
*Net Worth:* £462,907  *Total Assets:* £917,146
*Registered Office:* Treviot House, 186-192 High Road, Ilford, Essex, IG1 1LR
*Major Shareholder:* Richard Oliver Allen
*Officers:* Lydia Rosemary Allen, Secretary; Alfred David Allen [1948] Director/Pharmacist; Richard Oliver Allen [1979] Finance Director

### Added Pharma Ltd
*Incorporated:* 12 August 2013  *Employees:* 1
*Net Worth:* £104,599  *Total Assets:* £163,708
*Registered Office:* Suite 7, 46 Manchester Street, London, W1U 7LS
*Major Shareholder:* Jacobus Franciscus Gerard Marie Hurkmans
*Officers:* Jacobus Franciscus Gerard Marie Hurkmans [1959] Director/Entrepreneur [Dutch]

**Adedoyin Adebisi Ltd**
*Incorporated:* 18 April 2018
*Registered Office:* Flat 44, New Priestgate House, 57 Priestgate, Peterborough, Cambs, PE1 1JX
*Major Shareholder:* Adedoyin Adebisi
*Officers:* Adedoyin Adebisi [1977] Director/Pharmacist [Nigerian]


**Adelphi (Tubes) Limited**
*Incorporated:* 24 July 1970  *Employees:* 22
*Net Worth:* £5,242,753  *Total Assets:* £11,198,076
*Registered Office:* Olympus House, Mill Green Road, Haywards Heath, W Sussex, RH16 1XQ
*Shareholders:* Timothy John Austin Sheldon; Stephen Barron Holroyd
*Officers:* Angela Christine Holroyd, Secretary; Gavin Charles Craufurd Taylor [1970] Sales Director; Angela Christine Holroyd [1947] Director; Stephen Barron Holroyd [1943] Director; Penelope Jane Lanham [1969] Operations Director; Timothy John Austin Sheldon [1965] Managing Director


**Adicam Pharmaceuticals Ltd**
*Incorporated:* 14 February 2018
*Registered Office:* Mae House, Marlborough Business Centre, 98 George Lane, South Woodford, London, E18 1AD
*Major Shareholder:* Bhartiben Vaghela
*Officers:* Kamalesh Halder, Secretary; Kamalesh Halder [1973] Director/Self Employed [Bangladeshi]


**Advanced Eyecare Research Limited**
*Incorporated:* 21 July 2003  *Employees:* 1
*Net Worth:* £36,962  *Total Assets:* £89,414
*Registered Office:* Unit A, Fleming Way, Coronation Road, Cressex Business Park, High Wycombe, Bucks, HP12 3RP
*Shareholders:* Pamela Edith Angela Jamieson; Sarah Deirdre Hill
*Officers:* Christopher James John Jamieson, Secretary; Sarah Deirdre Hill [1951] Director/Training Consultant; Stephen Charles Hill [1950] Director/Consultant; Christopher James John Jamieson [1954] Director; Pamela Edith Angela Jamieson [1957] Director


**Advanced Formulations (Europe) Ltd**
*Incorporated:* 22 October 1993
*Net Worth Deficit:* £128,326  *Total Assets:* £350,880
*Registered Office:* Syence House, Owens Road, Skippers Lane Industrial Estate, Middlesbrough, Cleveland, TS6 6HE
*Major Shareholder:* Sean Campbell
*Officers:* Rowan Campbell, Secretary; Sean-Robbie Campbell, Secretary; Sean-Robbie Campbell [1965] Sales Director


**Advanced Laboratory Technologies Europe Ltd**
*Incorporated:* 10 June 2005
*Net Worth Deficit:* £27,092  *Total Assets:* £2,396,120
*Registered Office:* 3rd Floor, 207 Regent Street, London, W1B 3HH
*Major Shareholder:* Martin John Wickens
*Officers:* Andrew Rodney Noel Dickson [1964] Director


**Advanced Medical Products Limited**
*Incorporated:* 6 December 2016
*Net Worth:* £100  *Total Assets:* £100
*Registered Office:* 12 Burlington Close, Stockport, Cheshire, SK4 3BA
*Major Shareholder:* Saeed Nekooie
*Officers:* Saeed Nekooie [1955] Director


**Advanced Medical Systems Ltd.**
*Incorporated:* 5 December 1997  *Employees:* 2
*Net Worth:* £11,003  *Total Assets:* £81,235
*Registered Office:* 10 Manor Park, Banbury, Oxon, OX16 3TB
*Major Shareholder:* Godfrey William Victor Boulton
*Officers:* Godfrey William Victor Boulton, Secretary/Sales Manager; Godfrey William Victor Boulton [1942] Director/Sales Manager; Marko Boulton [1988] Director


**Aegerion Pharmaceuticals Limited**
*Incorporated:* 21 June 2012  *Employees:* 8
*Net Worth:* £6,730,963  *Total Assets:* £7,445,512
*Registered Office:* Royal Albert House, Sheet Street, Windsor, Berks, SL4 1BE
*Parent:* Novelion Therapeutics Inc.
*Officers:* Barbara Chan [1963] Director/Chief Accounting Officer [American]; Benjamin Scott Harshbarger [1968] Director/Global General Counsel, Legal [American]


**Aeglos Ltd**
*Incorporated:* 20 July 2001  *Employees:* 2
*Net Worth Deficit:* £11,595  *Total Assets:* £4,306
*Registered Office:* 21a Russell Gardens, Golders Green, London, NW11 9NJ
*Major Shareholder:* Matthew Leslie Benjamin Cooper
*Officers:* Sarah Cooper, Secretary; Sarah Cooper [1974] Director/Translator


**Aerona Clinical Limited**
*Incorporated:* 21 May 2016  *Employees:* 2
*Net Worth:* £40,746  *Total Assets:* £264,353
*Registered Office:* 165 High Street, Honiton, Devon, EX14 1LQ
*Major Shareholder:* Yasmin Jayne Crawford
*Officers:* Yasmin Jayne Crawford [1961] Director/Consultant


**Aesthetic & Wellness Pharmacy Ltd**
*Incorporated:* 5 November 2018
*Registered Office:* 179 North End Road, London, W14 9NL
*Major Shareholder:* Omama Holmes
*Officers:* Omama Holmes [1984] Director/Pharmacist; Sura Latif [1961] Director/Doctor


**The Aesthetics Clinic Dot Limited**
*Incorporated:* 20 August 2018
*Registered Office:* 4 Woundale, Bridgnorth, Salop, WV15 5PR
*Shareholders:* Ranjit Singh Samra; Anita Kaur Samra
*Officers:* Ranjit Singh Samra [1986] Director/Pharmacist


**AEV Consulting Ltd**
*Incorporated:* 21 May 2007  *Employees:* 1
*Net Worth:* £20,551  *Total Assets:* £85,665
*Registered Office:* 20 Millers Lane, Newtownards, Co Down, BT23 7AR
*Shareholder:* Alison Vidamour
*Officers:* Alison Vidamour [1962] Marketing Director; Roger Vidamour [1966] Director


**AF First Aid Ltd**
*Incorporated:* 28 August 2003
*Net Worth:* £2,350  *Total Assets:* £27,357
*Registered Office:* Homestead, Holmeswood Road, Holmeswood, Ormskirk, Lancs, L40 1TZ
*Officers:* Justine Farley, Secretary; Richard Andrew Farley [1961] Director

**AF Healthcare Ltd**
*Incorporated:* 27 June 2018
*Registered Office:* Stoneleigh, Chapel Allerton, Axbridge, Somerset, BS26 2PH
*Major Shareholder:* Paul Leopold Steckler
*Officers:* Paul Leopold Steckler [1972] Director/Chief Executive

**Afdos Pharmaceuticals Limited**
*Incorporated:* 26 November 2014  *Employees:* 1
*Net Worth:* £263,815  *Total Assets:* £763,486
*Registered Office:* 6 Maida Vale Business Centre, Mead Road, Cheltenham, Glos, GL53 7ER
*Major Shareholder:* Peter Guy Hulett
*Officers:* Maurice John Edgington, Secretary; Peter Guy Hulett [1965] Commercial Director; Maria Poco [1960] Director/Pharmacist [Portuguese]

**AG Pharmahealth Ltd**
*Incorporated:* 15 April 2011  *Employees:* 1
*Net Worth Deficit:* £9,650  *Total Assets:* £13,319
*Registered Office:* Unit B2, Little Heath Industrial Estate, Old Church Road, Little Heath, Coventry, Warwicks, CV6 7NB
*Shareholders:* Anu Bala Tugnet; Ganesh Tukaram Kodag
*Officers:* Ganesh Kodag [1980] Director/Self Employed [Indian]; Anu Bala Tugnet [1970] Director

**Agri-Bio Limited**
*Incorporated:* 20 April 1989
*Net Worth:* £1,070,796  *Total Assets:* £1,091,376
*Registered Office:* 66 Tay Street, Perth, PH2 8RA
*Major Shareholder:* Angus Ewart Donkin
*Officers:* Rosemary Donkin, Secretary; Angus Ewart Donkin [1943] Director

**Agrihealth (N.I.) Limited**
*Incorporated:* 10 August 1984  *Employees:* 47
*Net Worth:* £6,894,849  *Total Assets:* £10,024,094
*Registered Office:* 9 Silverwood Industrial Area, Silverwood Road, Lurgan, Craigavon, Co Armagh, BT66 6LN
*Major Shareholder:* Robert Henry Patton
*Officers:* Ciaran Maguire, Secretary; Ciaran Cunningham [1977] Director/Veterinary Surgeon [Irish]; Sean Guinan [1964] Director/Sales Manager [Irish]; Ciaran Maguire [1968] Director/Accountant [Irish]; Michael Joseph McAllister [1963] Director; Robert Henry Patton [1949] Director [Irish]

**Aidwell Limited**
*Incorporated:* 16 August 1979  *Employees:* 4
*Net Worth:* £481,162  *Total Assets:* £822,784
*Registered Office:* 37 Warren Street, London, W1T 6AD
*Parent:* RP Healthcare Ltd
*Officers:* Ravi Ashwin Patel [1985] Director

**AIG Unico Ltd**
*Incorporated:* 30 September 2015
*Registered Office:* 114a Aldborough Road South, Seven Kings, Ilford, Essex, IG3 8EZ
*Major Shareholder:* Saira Murad Bhola
*Officers:* Saira Murad Bhola [1981] Director

**Ainsworths (London) Limited**
*Incorporated:* 3 April 1974  *Employees:* 47
*Net Worth:* £375,172  *Total Assets:* £610,314
*Registered Office:* Kings Parade, Lower Coombe Street, Croydon, Surrey, CR0 1AA
*Major Shareholder:* Anthony Stuart Pinkus
*Officers:* Anthony Stuart Pinkus, Secretary; Anthony Stuart Pinkus [1958] Director

**Akro Pharmaceutical Company Limited**
*Incorporated:* 28 September 1998  *Employees:* 4
*Net Worth:* £178,742  *Total Assets:* £1,086,336
*Registered Office:* Abacus House, 68a North Street, Romford, Essex, RM1 1DA
*Shareholder:* Karl Adjei
*Officers:* Felicia Gloria Adjei, Secretary/Sales Person; Felicia Gloria Adjei [1956] Director/Sales Person; Karl Adjei [1985] Finance Director; Samuel Tetteh Adjei [1948] Director/Pharmacist

**Akvion Limited**
*Incorporated:* 9 April 2003
*Net Worth Deficit:* £198,655  *Total Assets:* £1,872
*Registered Office:* Floor 6, Quadrant House, 4 Thomas More Square, London, E1W 1YW
*Shareholders:* Mikhail Lazarev; Dmitry Lazarev
*Officers:* Dmitry Lazarev [1974] Director [Russian]

**Akysha Limited**
*Incorporated:* 11 April 2013
*Net Worth:* £16,674  *Total Assets:* £30,492
*Registered Office:* Doshi Accountants Ltd, 6th Floor, Amp House, Dingwall Road, Croydon, Surrey, CR0 2LX
*Major Shareholder:* Akeel Sarwar
*Officers:* Akeel Sarwar [1983] Director/Pharmacist

**Al Medicines Limited**
*Incorporated:* 6 November 2014  *Employees:* 2
*Net Worth:* £13,273  *Total Assets:* £19,973
*Registered Office:* 47 Cape Hill, Smethwick, W Midlands, B66 4SF
*Major Shareholder:* Ishrat Mehboob
*Officers:* Ishrat Mehboob [1962] Director/Practice Manager

**Al Razi Pharma UK Ltd**
*Incorporated:* 9 August 2018
*Registered Office:* 41 Brent House, 50 Wandsworth Road, London, SW8 2FL
*Major Shareholder:* Talal Almeshal
*Officers:* Dr Talal Almeshal [1977] Director; Saeed Radad Alzahrani [1959] Director/Chairman [Saudi Arabian]

**Al-Ghani Limited**
*Incorporated:* 10 May 2011  *Employees:* 13
*Net Worth:* £71,313  *Total Assets:* £517,570
*Registered Office:* 195a Lumb Lane, Bradford, W Yorks, BD8 7SG
*Officers:* Mohammed Abid [1990] Director/Dispensary Assistant; Amjad Khan [1984] Director/Pharmacist; Mohammad Usman Khan [1986] Director/Superintendent Pharmacist; Muhammad Haaroon Khan [1997] Director/Accounts Manager

**Alchem PLC**
*Incorporated:* 10 February 1983
*Net Worth:* £267,548  *Total Assets:* £276,270
*Registered Office:* 2 Marshalls Road, Belfast, BT5 6SR
*Parent:* UDG Healthcare (UK) Holdings Limited
*Officers:* Damien Moynagh, Secretary; Grainne McAleese [1979] Director [Irish]; Louise Tallon [1979] Director [Irish]

**Alcura UK Limited**
*Incorporated:* 5 July 1994
*Net Worth:* £11,100,000  *Total Assets:* £52,400,000
*Registered Office:* 4th Floor, Sedley Place, 361 Oxford Street, London, W1C 2JL
*Parent:* Alliance Boots Holdings Limited
*Officers:* Lucie Charlotte Massart, Secretary; Alexandro Depau [1970] Director [American]; Julian David Mount [1965] Director; Pablo Cortes Rivas [1972] Director [Spanish]

# The Top UK Pharmaceutical Wholesalers

**Alcyon Corporation Ltd**
Incorporated: 6 August 2007
Net Worth: £349,583  Total Assets: £573,384
Registered Office: 1st Floor, 26 Fouberts Place, London, W1F 7PP
Officers: Edgar Gilbert Bornet [1957] Director [Swiss]

**Alexpharm GmbH Ltd**
Incorporated: 30 August 2007
Net Worth: £31,565  Total Assets: £114,138
Registered Office: 2nd Floor, 13 John Princes Street, London, W1G 0JR
Officers: Maria Berdanis [1991] Director/Consultant [South African]

**Alfavet Animal Healthcare Limited**
Incorporated: 4 September 2001
Net Worth: £13,982  Total Assets: £228,303
Registered Office: Suite 1, Excelsior House, 3-5 Balfour Road, Ilford, Essex, IG1 4HP
Shareholder: Farouk Shamsudin
Officers: Farouk Shamsudin, Secretary/Hotel Operation Manager; Farouk Shamsudin [1957] Director/Hotel Operation Manager

**Alhaddag Phrma Ltd**
Incorporated: 2 October 2018
Registered Office: Aramex House, Old Bath Road, Colnbrook, Slough, SL3 0NS
Shareholders: Abdullah Wahebi Alwahebi; Naif Wahebi Alwahebi
Officers: Abdullah Wahebi Alwahebi [1985] Director/President [Saudi Arabian]

**Alice & Associates Limited**
Incorporated: 29 May 1990
Net Worth: £66,488  Total Assets: £73,910
Registered Office: 1a Colin Parade, Colindale, London, NW9 6SG
Major Shareholder: Alice Woon Kuen Chiu
Officers: Alice Woon Kuen Chiu [1945] Director

**Alissa Healthcare Research Limited**
Incorporated: 16 June 2006  Employees: 7
Net Worth: £6,351,100  Total Assets: £8,606,352
Registered Office: Unit 5, Fulcrum 1, Solent Way, Whiteley, Fareham, Hants, PO15 7FE
Officers: Robin Davies [1957] Director

**Alium Medical Limited**
Incorporated: 12 June 2001  Employees: 33
Net Worth: £5,263,362  Total Assets: £6,375,887
Registered Office: Haslers, Old Station Road, Loughton, Essex, IG10 4PL
Shareholder: Bennie Rabin
Officers: Kyriacos Costas Kyriacou, Secretary; Kyriacos Costas Kyriacou [1958] Director/Accountant; Bennie Rabin [1942] Director/Pharmacist; Ruth Moira Rabin [1950] Director/Company Secretary

**Alixport Ltd**
Incorporated: 13 March 2018
Registered Office: 8 Netley Road, Brentford, Middlesex, TW8 0SF
Officers: Abdulrahman Ali [1992] Director

**Alizcare Limited**
Incorporated: 23 August 2017
Registered Office: 7 Chad Road, Birmingham, B15 3EN
Major Shareholder: Mussarat Khattah
Officers: Dr Mussarat Fawad Khattak [1971] Director/Doctor

**Alk-Abello Limited**
Incorporated: 4 August 1999
Net Worth: £2,911,828  Total Assets: £4,138,556
Registered Office: 1 Manor Park, Manor Farm Road, Reading, Berks, RG2 0NA
Officers: Christopher Sean Guthrie Connor, Secretary; Christopher Sean Guthrie Connor [1969] Managing Director; Soren Jelert [1972] Director/Executive Vice President [Danish]

**All Med Care Limited**
Incorporated: 28 February 2018
Registered Office: 31 Jerrys Lane, Birmingham, B23 5NX
Major Shareholder: Rajinder Singh Sangha
Officers: Rajinder Singh Sangha [1969] Director/Businessman

**All1 Limited**
Incorporated: 22 September 2015
Registered Office: 28 Mortimer Street, London, W1W 7RD
Major Shareholder: Shadi Jabra Sharbain
Officers: Shadi Jabra Sharbain, Secretary; Shadi Jabra Sharbain [1990] Managing Director [Jordanian]

**Allans Healthcare Limited**
Incorporated: 3 July 2014  Employees: 2
Net Worth Deficit: £22,418  Total Assets: £105,649
Registered Office: 64 Beamish Road, Billingham, Cleveland, TS23 3DU
Shareholder: Tojin Joseph
Officers: Tojin Joseph [1979] Director/Manager; Aswathy Tojin [1982] Director/Superintendent Pharmacist

**Allcures PLC**
Incorporated: 11 March 1999
Net Worth: £3,569,110  Total Assets: £11,338,690
Registered Office: 213 St John Street, London, EC1V 4LY
Parent: Zodiac Health Limited
Officers: Jaipal Singh Cheema [1956] Director; Kirandeep Singh Cheema [1985] Director

**Allcures.Com (2006) Limited**
Incorporated: 23 January 2007
Net Worth: £150,774  Total Assets: £644,586
Registered Office: 213 St John Street, London, EC1V 4LY
Parent: Knight Noise Limited
Officers: Jaipal Singh Cheema [1956] Director/Pharmacist

**Allen & Hanburys Limited**
Incorporated: 29 December 1893
Registered Office: 980 Great West Road, Brentford, Middlesex, TW8 9GS
Parent: Glaxo Wellcome UK Limited
Officers: Victoria Anne Whyte, Secretary; James Borger [1963] Director/VP, Group Financial Planning and Analysis [American]; Alan George Burns [1975] Director

**Allergan Limited**
Incorporated: 13 April 1972  Employees: 283
Net Worth: £35,379,000  Total Assets: £98,128,000
Registered Office: 1st Floor, Marlow International, The Parkway, Marlow, Bucks, SL7 1YL
Parent: Allergan Holdings Limited
Officers: Patricia Maria Haran, Secretary; Judith Tomkins, Secretary; Dr David Carruthers [1981] Director; Nancy Ghattas [1980] Director [Kuwaiti]; Laurent Grippon [1974] Director [Venezuelan]; Paul Johnson [1972] Director; Aaron Sibley [1977] Director

**Allgenpharma Limited**
*Incorporated:* 23 October 2000
*Registered Office:* The Old Post Office, 14-18 Heralds Way, South Woodham Ferrers, Essex, CM3 5TQ
*Shareholders:* Gurkipal Sing Cheema; Allcures PLC
*Officers:* Norman Alan Smith, Secretary; Jaipal Singh Cheema [1956] Director/Pharmacist

**Alliance Healthcare (Distribution) Limited**
*Incorporated:* 7 October 1997
*Net Worth:* £258,000,000  *Total Assets:* £1,248,999,936
*Registered Office:* 43 Cox Lane, Chessington, Surrey, KT9 1SN
*Parent:* Alliance Boots Holdings Limited
*Officers:* Lucie Charlotte Massart, Secretary; Alexandro Depau [1970] Director [American]; Julian David Mount [1965] Director; Pablo Cortes Rivas [1972] Director [Spanish]

**Allied Pharmacies Limited**
*Incorporated:* 12 October 2010  *Employees:* 21
*Net Worth:* £343,357  *Total Assets:* £1,912,964
*Registered Office:* Unit 18 Neills Road, Bold Industrial Park, Bold, St Helens, Merseyside, WA9 4TU
*Major Shareholder:* Mohamed Sharief
*Officers:* Mohamed Sharief [1954] Director

**Allied Warden Marketing Limited**
*Incorporated:* 3 December 1998
*Net Worth:* £4,891  *Total Assets:* £5,579
*Registered Office:* c/o Temples, Kemp House, 152-160 City Road, London, EC1V 2NX
*Major Shareholder:* Marc Alexander Rene Mackie
*Officers:* Dr Marc Alexander Rene Mackie [1964] Director/Pharmacist [French]

**Allipharm (UK) Limited**
*Incorporated:* 4 November 1994  *Employees:* 2
*Net Worth:* £17,888  *Total Assets:* £273,581
*Registered Office:* 300a Hoe Lane, Enfield, Middlesex, EN1 4JW
*Officers:* Magdalene Rosamund Karikari, Secretary; Magdalene Rosamund Karikari [1961] Director/Teacher; Patrick Kofi Karikari [1961] Director/Pharmacist [Ghanaian]

**Allkare Limited**
*Incorporated:* 18 March 2004  *Employees:* 12
*Net Worth:* £681,910  *Total Assets:* £934,477
*Registered Office:* 213 St John Street, London, EC1V 4LY
*Parent:* Knight Noise Limited
*Officers:* Jaipal Singh Cheema [1956] Director/Pharmacist

**Alloga UK Limited**
*Incorporated:* 7 March 1996
*Previous:* Unidrug Distribution Group Limited
*Net Worth:* £34,143,000  *Total Assets:* £442,500,992
*Registered Office:* Amber Park, Berristow Lane, South Normanton, Alfreton, Derbys, DE55 2FH
*Parent:* Alliance Boots Holdings Limited
*Officers:* Lucie Charlotte Massart, Secretary; John Kallend [1959] Director; Julian David Mount [1965] Director; Pablo Rivas Cortes [1972] Director [Spanish]

**Allpa Kallpa Ltd**
*Incorporated:* 7 November 2018
*Registered Office:* 20-22 Wenlock Road, London, N1 7GU
*Major Shareholder:* Yanike Palmer
*Officers:* Yanike Palmer [1982] Director/Health Care

**Almirall Limited**
*Incorporated:* 23 July 2007  *Employees:* 35
*Net Worth:* £8,029,066  *Total Assets:* £14,548,521
*Registered Office:* 1 George Street, Uxbridge, Middlesex, UB8 1QQ
*Parent:* Almirall S.A.
*Officers:* Alfredo Baron de Juan [1967] Senior Director [Spanish]

**Alp Trading Limited**
*Incorporated:* 30 August 2002
*Net Worth:* £14,055  *Total Assets:* £18,213
*Registered Office:* 3 High Street, Larne, Co Antrim, BT40 1JN
*Major Shareholder:* Robert Auld
*Officers:* Robert Auld, Secretary; Joyce Auld [1956] Director/Wholesale/Distribution; Robert Auld [1959] Director/Wholesale/Distribution

**Alpco Ltd**
*Incorporated:* 28 August 2014  *Employees:* 7
*Net Worth:* £93,882  *Total Assets:* £316,166
*Registered Office:* 3 High Street, Larne, Co Antrim, BT40 1JN
*Shareholders:* Robert Auld; Joyce Auld
*Officers:* Joyce Auld [1956] Director; Robert Auld [1959] Director

**Alpha Pharma Ltd**
*Incorporated:* 10 April 2014
*Net Worth Deficit:* £10,710  *Total Assets:* £1,290
*Registered Office:* 46 Station Road, North Harrow, Harrow, Middlesex, HA2 7SE
*Major Shareholder:* Sameh Georgi
*Officers:* Sameh Georgi [1963] Director

**Alpharma Limited**
*Incorporated:* 24 September 2012
*Net Worth:* £23,581  *Total Assets:* £79,086
*Registered Office:* 195-197 Otley Road, Bradford, W Yorks, BD3 0JF
*Shareholders:* Mohammed Adam Issat; Asif Mahmood; Mohammed Ikhlaq
*Officers:* Asif Mahmood, Secretary; Mohammed Adam Issat [1975] Director/Pharmacist

**Altin Medical Ltd**
*Incorporated:* 2 November 2015  *Employees:* 1
*Net Worth:* £360,726  *Total Assets:* £504,102
*Registered Office:* Westwood House, Annie Med Lane, South Cave, Brough, N Humbers, HU15 2HG
*Major Shareholder:* Alexandros Epifanis
*Officers:* Alexandros Epifanis [1988] Director [Greek]

**Alturix Limited**
*Incorporated:* 3 October 2017
*Registered Office:* Studio 1/B, Witan Studios, 287 Upper Fourth Street, Milton Keynes, Bucks, MK9 1EH
*Officers:* Dr Simon Christopher Clough [1967] Director; Simon Andrew Fisher [1989] Director; James Michael Kettleborough [1992] Director; Sara Jane Kettleborough [1989] Director; Lakhveer Singh Sahota [1974] Director

**Alumier Medical UK Limited**
*Incorporated:* 14 February 2018
*Registered Office:* Unit 5 Draycott Business Park, Draycott Industrial Estate, Draycott, Moreton in Marsh, Glos, GL56 9JY
*Parent:* Alumier Labs UK Limited
*Officers:* Don Wessel Maree [1977] Managing Director

**Alverda Ltd**
*Incorporated:* 20 November 2018
*Registered Office:* Flat 0-2, 82 Broad Street, Glasgow, G40 2QN
*Major Shareholder:* Amarildo Cocoli
*Officers:* Amarildo Cocoli [1986] Director [Greek]

**Alzirr Ltd**
*Incorporated:* 26 September 2013 *Employees:* 1
*Net Worth Deficit:* £14,332 *Total Assets:* £851
*Registered Office:* Regus, City Point, 1 Ropemaker Street, London, EC2Y 9HT
*Major Shareholder:* Sergio La Barbera
*Officers:* Sergio La Barbera [1975] Director/R&D Manager [Italian]

**Amalgamated Technology Corporation Limited**
*Incorporated:* 21 April 1987
*Registered Office:* 1 Chiswick Square, London, W4 2QG
*Major Shareholder:* Nurdin Kassam
*Officers:* Nina Kassam, Secretary; Nurdin Kassam [1948] Director/Biochemist

**Amano Enzyme Europe Limited**
*Incorporated:* 9 January 1992 *Employees:* 10
*Net Worth:* £4,351,070 *Total Assets:* £11,170,634
*Registered Office:* Roundway House, Cromwell Park, Chipping Norton, Oxon, OX7 5SR
*Major Shareholder:* Motoyuki Amano
*Officers:* Dr Mitsutaka Nishida, Secretary; Motoyuki Amano [1956] Director/Company Chairman [Japanese]; Kunio Hara [1959] Deputy Administration Director [Japanese]; Kazuhiko Horikawa [1972] Sales Director [Japanese]; Shigeki Kimura [1953] Marketing Director [Japanese]

**Amarox Limited**
*Incorporated:* 5 October 2017
*Registered Office:* Congress House, 14 Lyon Road, Harrow, Middlesex, HA1 2EN
*Officers:* Venkata Narasa Reddy Attunuri [1963] Director [Indian]; Raveendranatha Reddy Kambham [1960] Director [Indian]; Chandramani Panda [1974] Director [Indian]; Manoj Prakash [1963] Director

**Amaxa Ltd**
*Incorporated:* 14 May 2018
*Registered Office:* 31 John Islip Street, London, SW1P 4FE
*Major Shareholder:* Jane Tkachenko
*Officers:* Gabriella Wheeler [1996] Director

**Amaxa Pharma Ltd**
*Incorporated:* 12 June 2012 *Employees:* 1
*Net Worth:* £290,990 *Total Assets:* £2,581,091
*Registered Office:* Portland House, Bressenden Place, London, SW1E 5RS
*Major Shareholder:* Jane Tkachenko
*Officers:* Jane Tkachenko [1996] Director [Ukrainian]; Vladimir Tkachenko [1971] Director [Ukrainian]

**Ambe Limited**
*Incorporated:* 19 July 1999 *Employees:* 8
*Net Worth Deficit:* £59,011 *Total Assets:* £272,796
*Registered Office:* Ambe House, Commerce Way, Edenbridge, Kent, TN8 6ED
*Major Shareholder:* Sandeep Ashokbhai Patel
*Officers:* Sandeep Ashokbhai Patel, Secretary; Sandeep Ashokbhai Patel [1974] Director/Chairman

**Amdeepcha Limited**
*Incorporated:* 11 September 2008 *Employees:* 1
*Net Worth:* £282,348 *Total Assets:* £540,527
*Registered Office:* 85 Yarmouth Road, Blofield, Norwich, NR13 4LQ
*Major Shareholder:* Parveen Chandrakant Ondhia
*Officers:* Parveen Chandrakant Ondhia [1954] Director/Pharmacist

**Amdega Brands Limited**
*Incorporated:* 18 December 1997 *Employees:* 7
*Net Worth:* £65,411 *Total Assets:* £299,403
*Registered Office:* 6 Knights Park, Hussey Road, Battlefield Enterprise Park, Shrewsbury, Salop, SY1 3TE
*Major Shareholder:* Sonal Manchanda
*Officers:* Helen Reynolds [1949] Director/Manager

**American Biochemical and Pharmaceuticals Limited**
*Incorporated:* 23 June 1995 *Employees:* 3
*Net Worth:* £587,469 *Total Assets:* £1,162,832
*Registered Office:* College House, 17 King Edwards Road, Ruislip, Middlesex, HA4 7AE
*Officers:* Patrick Byrne [1941] Director/Sales Consultant; Martin Grzebellus [1950] Director/Consultant [German]; Fritz Hans See [1943] Director/Consultant [German]

**AMG Pharmaceuticals Limited**
*Incorporated:* 16 November 2018
*Registered Office:* Corner Oak, 1 Homer Road, Solihull, W Midlands, B91 3QG
*Major Shareholder:* Charanjit Singh Bhandal
*Officers:* Charnjit Singh Bhandal [1966] Director/Pharmacist

**AMH (N.I.) Ltd**
*Incorporated:* 19 December 2018
*Registered Office:* 23 Sheepshill, Ballymena, Co Antrim, BT42 1QW
*Major Shareholder:* Angela Hopkins
*Officers:* Angela Hopkins [1969] Director

**Amin Locum Limited**
*Incorporated:* 14 August 2017
*Net Worth:* £3,374 *Total Assets:* £8,291
*Registered Office:* 112 Windsor Road, London, E7 0RB
*Major Shareholder:* Mohammed Amin Bhurawala
*Officers:* Mohammed Amin Bhurawala [1992] Director

**AMK & Associates Ltd**
*Incorporated:* 28 May 2013
*Net Worth Deficit:* £8,347 *Total Assets:* £1,428
*Registered Office:* The Coach House, 39 Athoke Croft, Hook, Hants, RG27 9UE
*Officers:* Ann Margaret Kelly [1961] Director

**Amryt Pharma (UK) Limited**
*Incorporated:* 4 November 2016 *Employees:* 3
*Net Worth:* £57,021 *Total Assets:* £656,628
*Registered Office:* 3rd Floor, 1 Ashley Road, Altrincham, Cheshire, WA14 2DT
*Parent:* Amryt Pharma PLC
*Officers:* Rory Peter Nealon, Secretary; Rory Peter Nealon [1967] Director [Irish]; Joseph Wiley [1971] Director [Irish]

**Anaiah Healthcare Ltd**
Incorporated: 8 March 2011
Previous: Anaiah Healthcare PVT Ltd
Net Worth Deficit: £217,726  Total Assets: £120,677
Registered Office: Level 17, Dashwood House, 69 Broad Street, London, EC2M 1QS
Major Shareholder: Ryan Rodrigues
Officers: Elsa Rodrigues [1973] Director/Mathematician [Norwegian]; Ryan Rodrigues [1975] Director [Norwegian]

**Ananda Trading Limited**
Incorporated: 6 July 2018
Registered Office: Dickens House, Guithavon Street, Witham, Essex, CM8 1BJ
Major Shareholder: Tony Kwok Fai Law
Officers: Tony Kwok Fai Law [1957] Director

**Ananta Medicare Ltd**
Incorporated: 16 April 2008
Net Worth: £322,534  Total Assets: £6,967,040
Registered Office: Suite 1, 2 Station Court, Townmead Road, Fulham, London, SW6 2PY
Major Shareholder: Pradeep Kumar Jain
Officers: Sunil Kumar, Secretary; Pradeep Kumar Jain [1972] Director [Indian]

**Andrei & Maria Ltd**
Incorporated: 13 September 2018
Registered Office: 8 Lillian Road, Liverpool, L4 0ST
Major Shareholder: Ionut-Alexandru Zisu
Officers: Ionut-Alexandru Zisu [1990] Director [Romanian]

**Andrews Pharmacy Limited**
Incorporated: 13 December 2001
Net Worth: £303,547  Total Assets: £763,270
Registered Office: 71 Kennedy Avenue, Macclesfield, Cheshire, SK10 3DE
Major Shareholder: Andrew James Hodgson
Officers: Andrew James Hodgson [1960] Director/Pharmacist

**Aneid UK Limited**
Incorporated: 14 August 2012  Employees: 3
Net Worth: £239  Total Assets: £52,943
Registered Office: Suite 8, The Spires, Adelaide Street, Luton, Beds, LU1 5BB
Shareholders: William Ahern; Marjaneh Seifi
Officers: William Ahern [1957] Director [Irish]; Marjaneh Seifi [1964] Director [Portuguese]

**Anfarm Generics UK Limited**
Incorporated: 11 August 2015
Net Worth: £12,991  Total Assets: £21,481
Registered Office: Langley House, Park Road, East Finchley, London, N2 8EY
Parent: Anfarm Hellas SA
Officers: Michael Thomas Gordon [1954] Director

**Angel & Lockhart (Pharma) Ltd**
Incorporated: 16 April 2018
Registered Office: 69 Banstead Road, Carshalton, Surrey, SM5 3NP
Major Shareholder: Barry Davis
Officers: Barry Davis [1965] Director

**Angelina SW Ltd**
Incorporated: 26 August 2009
Net Worth Deficit: £5,268  Total Assets: £1,186,964
Registered Office: Suite 1, 2 Station Court, Townmead Road, Fulham, London, SW6 2PY
Major Shareholder: Pradeep Kumar Jain
Officers: Sunil Kumar, Secretary; Pradeep Kumar Jain [1972] Director [Indian]

**Angulus Pharma Limited**
Incorporated: 6 March 2014  Employees: 4
Net Worth Deficit: £339,936  Total Assets: £42,286
Registered Office: Chancery House, 30 St Johns Road, Woking, Surrey, GU21 7SA
Shareholder: Khoon Lim Ang
Officers: Dr Albert Weng Wah Chan [1966] Director [Malaysian]

**Angus Medical Supplies Ltd**
Incorporated: 28 May 2013  Employees: 2
Net Worth Deficit: £19,463  Total Assets: £20,945
Registered Office: 86 Brook Street, Broughty Ferry, Dundee, DD5 1DQ
Major Shareholder: Alison June Butchart
Officers: Alison June Ritchie [1957] Director

**Animal Prescriptions Limited**
Incorporated: 5 May 1994
Registered Office: Centaur House, Torbay Road, Castle Cary, Somerset, BA7 7EU
Parent: Centaur Services Ltd
Officers: Brian Topper, Secretary; John Gardner Chou [1956] Director/Business Executive [American]; James Francis Cleary Jr [1963] Director/Business Executive [American]; Mark Jeffrey Shaw [1962] Director/Business Executive [American]; Brian Topper [1973] Director/MD [American]

**Animalcare Ltd**
Incorporated: 10 June 1980  Employees: 62
Net Worth: £9,898,000  Total Assets: £15,445,000
Registered Office: Unit 7, 10 Great North Way, York Business Park, Nether Poppleton, York, YO26 6RB
Parent: Animalcare Group PLC
Officers: Christopher Brewster, Secretary; Christopher James Brewster [1976] Director/UK Country Manager; Lord Arthur Francis Nicholas Wills Marquess of Downshire [1959] Director; Jennifer Ann Julia Winter [1960] Director

**ANP Partners Ltd**
Incorporated: 21 September 2012
Net Worth: £1,500,000  Total Assets: £1,500,000
Registered Office: WTC 1E Conference House, 152 Morrison Street, The Exchange, Edinburgh, EH3 8EB
Major Shareholder: Pavlo Krotenko
Officers: Pavlo Krotenko [1965] Director [Ukrainian]

**ANP Pharma Ltd**
Incorporated: 16 February 2007  Employees: 8
Net Worth: £876,075  Total Assets: £1,320,168
Registered Office: 55 Hainault Road, London, E11 1EA
Major Shareholder: Amit Neil Patel
Officers: Sarmista Patel, Secretary; Christopher Curran [1976] Director; Amit Patel [1981] Director; Deepa Rajendrakumar Patel [1982] Director/Radiologist

**Anrise Trading Limited**
Incorporated: 1 September 2016
Net Worth Deficit: £200  Total Assets: £100
Registered Office: 203 Kilburn High Road, London, NW6 7HY
Major Shareholder: Raka Srivastava
Officers: Dr Raka Srivastava [1958] Director/Physician

**Anti Venom Ltd**
Incorporated: 16 January 2019
Registered Office: 93 Shalmsford Street, Chartham, Canterbury, Kent, CT4 7RN
Shareholders: James Marcus Humphris; Charlotte Valentina Thompson
Officers: James Marcus Humphris [1991] Director; Charlotte Valentina Thompson [1988] Marketing Director

**Antwerp Brokering Enterprises (U.K.) Limited**
Incorporated: 2 December 1975
Net Worth: £8,057  Total Assets: £28,208
Registered Office: Hunters House, 109 Snakes Lane West, Woodford Green, Essex, IG8 0DY
Major Shareholder: Tracey Sarah Poggio
Officers: Beverley Ann Black, Secretary; Tracey Sarah Poggio [1968] Director

**Anuva International Limited**
Incorporated: 24 November 2006  Employees: 1
Net Worth Deficit: £15,990  Total Assets: £104,244
Registered Office: Devonshire House, 582 Honeypot Lane, Stanmore, Middlesex, HA7 1JS
Major Shareholder: Manish Somchand Shah
Officers: Nitesh Panachand Shah, Secretary; Manish Somchand Shah [1966] Director/Trader

**ANXT Ltd**
Incorporated: 18 February 2019
Registered Office: Block 5, 96 Mint Drive, Hockley, Birmingham, B18 6EB
Major Shareholder: Alexander Lawrence Fielding
Officers: Alexander Lawrence Fielding [1993] Director

**AP Import Export Ltd**
Incorporated: 28 April 2017
Net Worth Deficit: £30,788
Registered Office: Flat A, 299 Hornsey Road, London, N19 4HN
Major Shareholder: Adrian Nicolae Pop
Officers: Adrian Nicolae Pop [1982] Director [Romanian]

**APC Pharmaceuticals & Chemicals (Europe) Ltd**
Incorporated: 7 January 2005
Net Worth Deficit: £524,410  Total Assets: £1,140,794
Registered Office: Harborough Innovation Centre, Wellington Way, Airfield Business Park, Market Harborough, Leics, LE16 7WB
Major Shareholder: Ravindra Narayan Menon
Officers: Ajay Ashish Jaymal, Secretary; Friedrich Josef Fuchs [1948] Director [Austrian]; Ravindra Narayan Menon [1950] Director/Chairman [Indian]; Tejus Ravindra Menon [1985] Director of Sales & Marketing [Indian]; Thiruthipalli Gopal Menon [1964] Director/Consultant [Indian]

**Apetamintko Limited**
Incorporated: 9 January 2018
Registered Office: 8 Parkway Avenue, Sheffield, S9 4WA
Major Shareholder: Carla Ann Dixon
Officers: Carla Ann Dixon [1994] Director [American]

**Apex Lab Scientific Ltd**
Incorporated: 24 August 2018
Registered Office: 63-65 Heworth Road, York, YO31 0AA
Shareholders: Jolanta Labutyte; Prafful Prakash
Officers: Jolanta Labutyte [1992] Director [Lithuanian]; Prafful Prakash [1988] Director [Indian]

**Apollo Endosurgery UK Ltd**
Incorporated: 16 April 2014  Employees: 31
Net Worth: £959,000  Total Assets: £8,624,000
Registered Office: Unit 10 St James Business Park, Grimbald Crag Court, Knaresborough, N Yorks, HG5 8QB
Parent: Apollo Endosurgery, Inc.
Officers: Stefanie LEA Cavanaugh, Secretary; Stefanie LEA Cavanaugh [1964] Director/Accountant [American]; Brian Szymczak [1972] Director [American]; Jane Wright [1969] Director/Accountant

**Apollo Medical Technologies Ltd**
Incorporated: 23 February 2010
Net Worth: £242,731  Total Assets: £632,258
Registered Office: Fox Briars, 14 Marlock Close, Fiskerton, Southwell, Notts, NG25 0UB
Major Shareholder: Frederick Lauder Attwood
Officers: Frederick Lauder Attwood [1960] Director

**Aposave Ltd**
Incorporated: 11 December 2013  Employees: 1
Net Worth Deficit: £1,774,758  Total Assets: £655,621
Registered Office: Floor 30, The Leadenhall Building, 122 Leadenhall Street, London, EC3V 4AB
Major Shareholder: Flemming Wagner
Officers: Simon Estcourt [1969] Director; Flemming Wagner [1964] Director/Consultant [Danish]

**Apotheke San Biagio SRL Limited**
Incorporated: 19 January 2018
Registered Office: 27 Old Gloucester Street, London, WC1N 3AX
Shareholder: Francesco Cavaliere
Officers: Francesco Cavaliere [1976] Director/Manager [Italian]

**Appia Healthcare Limited**
Incorporated: 7 September 2011
Net Worth: £130,920  Total Assets: £252,649
Registered Office: Willowbank, Hayes Lane, Slinfold, Horsham, W Sussex, RH13 0SA
Major Shareholder: Alexander James Hanbury Duggan
Officers: Peter Allen [1954] Finance Director; Alexander James Hanbury Duggan [1970] Managing Director; Marielle Virginie Isabelle Duggan [1971] Director [French]; Wendy Jane Faulkner [1965] Director

**Apple Pharma Limited**
Incorporated: 5 March 2018
Registered Office: 272 Bath Street, Glasgow, G2 4JR
Major Shareholder: Julie Wilson Smith Aitchison
Officers: Iain Allan Aitchison [1973] Director/Oil Engineer; Julie Wilson Smith Aitchison [1973] Managing Director

**Appleby Pharmacy Limited**
Incorporated: 4 January 2017
Net Worth Deficit: £5,378  Total Assets: £9,982
Registered Office: Unit 3 Belvue Industrial Estate, Belvue Road, Northolt, Middlesex, UB5 5HX
Major Shareholder: Mohammed Muthir
Officers: Bader Wasim Al-Kassar [1993] Director; Mohammed Muthir [1989] Director

**Applied Medical Technology Limited**
*Incorporated:* 12 May 1998  *Employees:* 8
*Net Worth:* £382,623  *Total Assets:* £634,738
*Registered Office:* 3960 Enterprise, Cambridge Research Park, Beach Drive, Waterbeach, Cambs, CB25 9PE
*Parent:* Cane SpA
*Officers:* Claudio Cane [1984] Director [Italian]; Paolo Cane [1984] Director [Italian]

**Apretique Limited**
*Incorporated:* 4 September 2003
*Registered Office:* Pinnacle House Business Centre, Newark Road, Peterborough, Cambs, PE1 5YD
*Major Shareholder:* Alistair Martin Ashworth
*Officers:* Alistair Martin Ashworth, Secretary/Engineer; Alistair Martin Ashworth [1963] Director/Engineer

**Apricot Forest Ltd**
*Incorporated:* 24 March 2016
*Registered Office:* The Old Covent, Llanbadarn Road, Aberystwyth, Ceredigion, SY23 1WX
*Major Shareholder:* Alex Kolaczynski
*Officers:* Alex Kolaczynski [1962] Director

**Aptil Pharma Limited**
*Incorporated:* 28 September 2011
*Registered Office:* 3rd Floor, 4 Gatwick Road, Crawley, W Sussex, RH10 9BG
*Parent:* Torrent Pharma (UK) Ltd
*Officers:* Amul Kamal Kumar Agrawal [1977] Service Director [German]; Jamie Lee Durbidge [1978] Director; Sanjay Gupta [1965] Service Director [Indian]; Sudhir Menon [1972] Service Director [Indian]

**Aptitud Pharma Ltd**
*Incorporated:* 28 December 2017
*Registered Office:* 35 White City Estate, London, W12 7NE
*Officers:* Edison Rodolfo Velastegui Suquillo [1985] Managing Director

**Aqua Hydration Limited**
*Incorporated:* 10 January 2019
*Registered Office:* 550 Valley Road, Nottingham, NG5 1JJ
*Shareholders:* Jennifer Hayes; John Samuel Jones
*Officers:* Jennifer Hayes [1981] Director; John Samuel Jones [1981] Director

**Archangel's Pharmaceutical Services Limited**
*Incorporated:* 28 February 2019
*Registered Office:* The Old Rectory, Rectory Lane, Winwick, Warrington, Cheshire, WA2 8LE
*Shareholders:* Peter Saad; St George Healthcare Group Limited
*Officers:* Dr Naser Michel Fouad [1964] Director; Peter Saad [1988] Director

**Arco Iris Limited**
*Incorporated:* 30 March 2000
*Net Worth Deficit:* £10,495  *Total Assets:* £1,238
*Registered Office:* Waters Meet, Willow Avenue, Denham, Uxbridge, Middlesex, UB9 4AF
*Major Shareholder:* Shashi Bhushan Saurabh
*Officers:* Anand Ramsaha, Secretary; Shashi Bhushan Saurabh [1965] Director [Indian]

**Arctic Medical Limited**
*Incorporated:* 7 June 1993  *Employees:* 1
*Net Worth:* £23,035  *Total Assets:* £64,174
*Registered Office:* Unit 49 Basepoint, Shearway Business Park, Shearway Road, Folkestone, Kent, CT19 4RH
*Major Shareholder:* John Hardie
*Officers:* Inna Vladimirovna Salko, Secretary; John Hardie [1947] Director/Manager; Inna Vladimirovna Salko [1953] Director/Manager [Russian]

**Ardant Pharmaceuticals Ltd.**
*Incorporated:* 11 July 2014
*Previous:* Pharmabroker EU Limited
*Registered Office:* Ambe House, Commerce Way, Edenbridge, Kent, TN8 6ED
*Major Shareholder:* James Anthony Aylott
*Officers:* James Anthony Aylott [1971] Director

**Ardent Pharmaceuticals Ltd**
*Incorporated:* 9 January 2018
*Registered Office:* Ambe House, Commerce Way, Edenbridge, Kent, TN8 6ED
*Major Shareholder:* James Anthony Aylott
*Officers:* James Anthony Aylott [1971] Director

**Areessco Ltd**
*Incorporated:* 8 April 2017
*Registered Office:* 118 Elmer Gardens, Isleworth, London, TW7 6HA
*Major Shareholder:* Amit Varma
*Officers:* Amit Varma, Secretary; Amit Varma [1978] Director; Baldev Varma [1948] Managing Director

**Arena (Eyewear) Limited**
*Incorporated:* 17 July 1989
*Net Worth:* £77,004  *Total Assets:* £148,214
*Registered Office:* Midgley Court, Salters Lane, Newport, Salop, TF10 7PD
*Shareholders:* Matthew Phillip Newton; Angela Mary Newton; Samantha Priest
*Officers:* Angela Mary Newton [1974] Director; Matthew Phillip Newton [1985] Director; Samantha Priest [1970] Director

**Arena Pharmaceuticals Limited**
*Incorporated:* 4 January 2001  *Employees:* 3
*Net Worth:* £596,340  *Total Assets:* £1,566,893
*Registered Office:* Unit 14 Apollo Office Court, Radclive Road, Gawcott, Buckingham, MK18 4DF
*Parent:* Pethel Marali Ltd
*Officers:* Martin Robert Evans, Secretary/Accountant; Helen Elizabeth Goss [1971] Sales Director; Peter Goss [1956] Director/Commercial Manager

**Arex Pharma Ltd**
*Incorporated:* 29 April 2016
*Registered Office:* 71-75 Shelton Street, Covent Garden, London, WC2H 9JQ
*Major Shareholder:* Jorg Knizek
*Officers:* Jorg Knizek [1971] Managing Director [German]

**Aria Vape Ltd**
*Incorporated:* 10 November 2017
*Registered Office:* 233 Wigan Road, Wigan, Lancs, WN4 9SL
*Major Shareholder:* Farshad Ferdowsian
*Officers:* Farshad Ferdowsian [1981] Director

**Arisio Ltd**
Incorporated: 10 April 2017
Registered Office: 118 Elmer Gardens, Isleworth, London, TW7 6HA
Major Shareholder: Amit Varma
Officers: Amit Varma, Secretary; Amit Varma [1978] Director


**Arkad Healthcare Limited**
Incorporated: 28 September 2017
Net Worth Deficit: £1,674  Total Assets: £508
Registered Office: 55 Barrowby Road, Grantham, Lincs, NG31 8AA
Shareholders: Ian James Baker; Michael John Burgess
Officers: Ian James Baker [1973] Director; Michael John Burgess [1964] Director [Australian]; David Michael Hill [1967] Director/Regulatory Affairs Specialist


**Arnolds Pharmacy Limited**
Incorporated: 25 January 2013  Employees: 8
Net Worth Deficit: £19,720  Total Assets: £1,172,844
Registered Office: 21 Nelson Road, Westward Ho, Bideford, Devon, EX39 1LF
Major Shareholder: Osman Naveed Hamid
Officers: Osman Naveed Hamid [1980] Director/Pharmacist


**Aromanature Limited**
Incorporated: 11 April 2001
Net Worth: £8,100  Total Assets: £10,885
Registered Office: Cary Chambers, 1 Palk Street, Torquay, Devon, TQ2 5EL
Shareholder: Anthony Goffart
Officers: Nathalie Goffart, Secretary [French]; Anthony Goffart [1980] Director [French]


**Aroschem Limited**
Incorporated: 9 August 2001  Employees: 12
Net Worth: £581,493  Total Assets: £936,193
Registered Office: Ndirande, Fontwell Avenue, Eastergate, Chichester, W Sussex, PO20 3RU
Parent: Ariscroft Limited
Officers: Jennifer Mary Buchanan, Secretary; Dr Andrew David Bridger [1963] Director; Dr Ian Yule Buchanan [1957] Director/Doctor; Dr Richard Graham Paterson [1965] Director; Dr Susan Louise Rose [1965] Director


**Aroschem UK Limited**
Incorporated: 25 August 2009  Employees: 5
Net Worth: £234,697  Total Assets: £311,905
Registered Office: Ndirande, Fontwell Avenue, Eastergate, Chichester, W Sussex, PO20 3RU
Shareholder: Jennifer Mary Buchanan
Officers: Jennifer Mary Buchanan, Secretary; Dr Ian Yule Buchanan [1957] Director/Doctor; Jennifer Mary Buchanan [1960] Director/Company Secretary


**Arquella Ltd**
Incorporated: 14 February 2018
Registered Office: Arquella, Momentum House, Church Lane, Dinnington, Sheffield, S25 2RG
Shareholders: Emillio Reuben Javan Timoney; Paige Devon O'Neal
Officers: Paul Valentine Howell [1965] Director; Paige Devon O'Neal [1995] Director; Emillio Reuben Javan Timoney [1991] Director


**Arrowedge Limited**
Incorporated: 6 August 1982  Employees: 26
Net Worth: £3,766,322  Total Assets: £5,676,449
Registered Office: 62 Poole Road, Westbourne, Bournemouth, BH4 9DZ
Major Shareholder: Ullas Mahendrakumar Patel
Officers: Manjula Patel, Secretary; Nainesh Mahendra Patel [1962] Director/Chemical Engineer; Ullas Mahendrakumar Patel [1956] Director; Yatin Mahendrakumar Patel [1962] Director/Businessman


**Art Pharma Oxford Ltd**
Incorporated: 10 September 2015
Net Worth Deficit: £29,420  Total Assets: £580
Registered Office: International House, 24 Holborn Viaduct, London, EC1A 2BN
Major Shareholder: Romana Dorota Konarska
Officers: Mariusz Andrzej Lozuk [1971] Director/Manager [Polish]


**Artmedica Ltd**
Incorporated: 27 October 2016  Employees: 1
Net Worth: £1,808  Total Assets: £4,005
Registered Office: 161 Lancaster Road, Enfield, Middlesex, EN2 0JN
Major Shareholder: Vasiliki Kappou
Officers: Vasiliki Kappou [1979] Director [Greek]


**Arya House Pharma Ltd**
Incorporated: 16 January 2019
Registered Office: Unit A, 98-104 Lombard Street, Birmingham, B12 0QR
Major Shareholder: Harmeet Singh Bharaj
Officers: Harmeet Singh Bharaj [1988] Director


**Aryahakim Medical Equipment Co Ltd.**
Incorporated: 16 November 2017
Registered Office: 22 Drumsheugh Gardens, Edinburgh, EH3 7RN
Major Shareholder: Homayoun Moradi
Officers: Homayoun Moradi [1954] Director [Iranian]


**Asaya Cosmeceuticals Limited**
Incorporated: 11 February 2019
Registered Office: First Floor, 85 Great Portland Street, London, W1W 7LT
Major Shareholder: Natalie Echeverria
Officers: Natalie Echeverria [1970] Director


**Ascend Laboratories (UK) Limited**
Incorporated: 6 August 2014  Employees: 6
Net Worth: £275,411  Total Assets: £3,994,757
Registered Office: 5th Floor, 89 New Bond Street, London, W1S 1DA
Officers: Amit Ghare [1971] Director [Indian]; Amit Kumar [1980] Director [Indian]; Manish Narang [1970] Director [Indian]; Sandeep Singh [1982] Director [Indian]; Alok Verma [1955] Director/Accountant


**Ascent (Hartlepool) Limited**
Incorporated: 1 June 2018
Registered Office: 2nd Floor, 9 Portland Street, Manchester, M1 3BE
Parent: Ascent Holding Group Limited
Officers: Ammar Nazir [1979] Director; Qammar Nazir [1984] Director

**Ascot Pharma Ltd**
Incorporated: 2 November 2010  Employees: 6
Net Worth: £1,073  Total Assets: £2,642,415
Registered Office: Unit 1 Olds Approach, Tolpits Lane, Watford, Herts, WD18 9TD
Officers: Deepak Anantrai Ghelani [1961] Director; Bhavesh Amratlal Radia [1965] Director

**Ascot Treatments Ltd**
Incorporated: 4 October 2018
Registered Office: 42 New Road, Ascot, Berks, SL5 8QQ
Shareholders: Andrew Michael Fielder; Mark Chan; Richard Ayres
Officers: Richard Ayres [1992] Commercial Director; Andrew Michael Fielder [1966] Commercial Director

**ASG Pharma Ltd**
Incorporated: 13 May 2016
Net Worth: £35,337  Total Assets: £81,351
Registered Office: 64 Victoria Park Road, Smethwick, W Midlands, B66 3QL
Major Shareholder: Amrik Singh Gill
Officers: Amrik Singh Gill [1986] Director/Pharmacist

**Ash Medical Limited**
Incorporated: 11 October 2005
Net Worth: £62,518  Total Assets: £79,205
Registered Office: Temple Court, 13a Cathedral Road, Cardiff, CF11 9HA
Shareholders: Michael Anthony Stubbs; Yvonne Stubbs
Officers: Yvonne Stubbs, Secretary; Michael Anthony Stubbs [1966] Director

**Ashtons Healthcare Limited**
Incorporated: 25 June 2010
Registered Office: 4 Dyke Road Mews, 74-76 Dyke Road, Seven Dials, Brighton, BN1 3JD
Major Shareholder: Laurence Simon Sprey
Officers: Keith Hersee [1970] Director; Laurence Simon Sprey [1953] Director

**Ashtons Medical Limited**
Incorporated: 25 June 2010
Registered Office: 4 Dyke Road Mews, 74-76 Dyke Road, Seven Dials, Brighton, BN1 3JD
Officers: Keith Hersee [1970] Director; Laurence Simon Sprey [1953] Director

**Ashtons Medical Supplies Limited**
Incorporated: 25 June 2010
Registered Office: 4 Dyke Road Mews, 74-76 Dyke Road, Seven Dials, Brighton, BN1 3JD
Officers: Keith Hersee [1970] Director; Laurence Simon Sprey [1953] Director

**Aspect Pharma Limited**
Incorporated: 8 June 2010
Net Worth: £58,918  Total Assets: £67,852
Registered Office: 28 Stratford Way, Watford, Herts, WD17 3DJ
Major Shareholder: Amandip Sidhu
Officers: Amandip Sidhu [1976] Owner Director

**Aspen Pharmacare UK Limited**
Incorporated: 12 June 2018
Registered Office: 6 Bell Street, Maidenhead, Berks, SL6 1BU
Officers: Derek Davies [1963] Finance Director; Dennis Dencher [1973] Director [Danish]; Nicholas Peter Scott [1968] Director/Pharmaceutical Marketing

**Aspire Pharma Holdings Limited**
Incorporated: 11 November 2014  Employees: 32
Net Worth: £5,940,265  Total Assets: £32,370,296
Registered Office: 102 High Street, Godalming, Surrey, GU7 1DS
Shareholders: Graham Julian Fraser-Pye; Juno Pharmaceuticals Luxembourg S.A.R.L
Officers: Jacqueline Elizabeth Fraser-Pye, Secretary; Debra Joy Roberts, Secretary; Graham Julian Fraser-Pye [1968] Director; Ian Jacobson [1960] Director/Chief Executive [Canadian]; Debra Joy Roberts [1962] Financial Director; Mark Derek Roberts [1967] Director

**Aspire Pharma Limited**
Incorporated: 24 February 2009  Employees: 32
Net Worth: £13,414,915  Total Assets: £20,881,982
Registered Office: 102 High Street, Godalming, Surrey, GU7 1DS
Parent: Aspire Pharma Holdings Limited
Officers: Debra Joy Roberts, Secretary; Graham Julian Fraser-Pye [1968] Director/Pharmaceuticals; Ian Jacobson [1960] Director/Chief Executive [Canadian]; Debra Joy Roberts [1962] Financial Director; Mark Derek Roberts [1967] Director

**Assencion Pharmaceuticals Limited**
Incorporated: 17 May 2011
Net Worth: £261,316  Total Assets: £464,388
Registered Office: Unit 4 Halls Business Centre, Pump Lane, Hayes, Middlesex, UB3 3NB
Major Shareholder: Darshakkumar Patel
Officers: Darshakkumar Patel [1983] Director

**Astek Innovations Limited**
Incorporated: 7 April 2004
Net Worth: £2,361,846  Total Assets: £2,735,559
Registered Office: Astek House, Atlantic Street, Broadheath, Altrincham, Cheshire, WA14 5DH
Parent: Y.I. Europe Limited
Officers: David Michael Butler [1965] Director/Investor [American]; Dave Sproat [1967] Director [American]; John Straus [1982] Director/Investor [American]

**Astellas Pharma Europe Ltd.**
Incorporated: 29 March 1990  Employees: 399
Net Worth: £870,882,368  Total Assets: £1,343,135,104
Registered Office: 2000 Hillswood Drive, Chertsey, Surrey, KT16 0RS
Parent: Astellas Pharma Inc.
Officers: Sally Anne Hinchliffe, Secretary; Jochen Norbert Bohner [1971] Director/SVP Finance, Procurement & IS EMEA [German]; Masaaki Hirano [1967] Director/Businessman [Japanese]; Dr Dirk Armin Kosche [1963] Director/President EMEA Operations [German]; Daniel Benjamin Matthias Schulze [1975] Director/Vice President and General Counsel [German]; Toru Yoshimitsu [1963] Director [Japanese]

**Astellas Pharma Ltd.**
Incorporated: 10 January 1964  Employees: 195
Net Worth: £49,799,000  Total Assets: £133,302,000
Registered Office: 2000 Hillswood Drive, Chertsey, Surrey, KT16 0RS
Parent: Astellas Pharma Inc.
Officers: Ian Michael Hall [1966] Director/Chartered Accountant; Dr Jose Maria Sanz [1972] Director/General Manager

**Aston-Med Limited**
Incorporated: 28 June 2012
Net Worth: £11,380  Total Assets: £38,437
Registered Office: 18 St James Road, Purley, Surrey, CR8 2DL
Major Shareholder: Muhammad Sajjad Bhatti
Officers: Muhammad Sajjad Bhatti [1981] Managing Director

**Astra MCR Limited**
*Incorporated:* 6 January 2016
*Net Worth:* £5,169  *Total Assets:* £213,445
*Registered Office:* 32 Linnet Court, 47 Westleigh Avenue, London, SW15 6RJ
*Major Shareholder:* Haidar Hussain
*Officers:* Haidar Mahmood Hussain Hussain [1969] Director [Iraqi]

**Astra Pharma (UK) Limited**
*Incorporated:* 9 March 2001
*Net Worth Deficit:* £60,573  *Total Assets:* £7,900
*Registered Office:* 9 North Parade, Mollison Way, Edgware, Middlesex, HA8 5QH
*Major Shareholder:* Shabbir Kassam
*Officers:* Fatima Kassam, Secretary; Aziz Bhaidani [1969] Director/Salesman [Indian]; Shabbir Kassam [1957] Director; Semina Lakhani [1975] Director/Secretary

**Astral Health Ltd**
*Incorporated:* 12 February 2019
*Registered Office:* Work.Life ECH Limited, 33 Foley Street, London, W1W 7TL
*Parent:* ECH Limited
*Officers:* Dean Leslie Friday [1979] Director

**Astrazeneca PLC**
*Incorporated:* 17 June 1992  *Employees:* 60,000
*Net Worth:* £14,960,000,000  *Total Assets:* £63,353,999,360
*Registered Office:* 1 Francis Crick Avenue, Cambridge Biomedical Campus, Cambridge, CB2 0AA
*Officers:* Adrian Charles Noel Kemp, Secretary/Company Official; Professor Genevieve Bernadette Berger [1955] Director/Chief Research and Development Officer [Swiss]; Philip Arthur John Broadley [1961] Director; Graham Chipchase [1963] Director/Chief Executive; Marc Pierre Jean Dunoyer [1952] Director/Chief Financial Officer [French]; Deborah Disanzo Eldracher [1960] Board Director [American]; Leif Valdemar Johansson [1951] Director/Chairman [Swedish]; Rudolph Harold Peter Markham [1946] Director; Sherilyn Dawn McCoy [1958] Director [American]; Tony Shu Kam Mok [1960] Director/Professor [Canadian]; Sabera Nazneen Rahman [1967] Director; Pascal Claude Roland Soriot [1959] Director/Chief Executive Officer [French]; Marcus Wallenberg [1956] Director [Swedish]

**Astriza UK Ltd**
*Incorporated:* 27 February 2014  *Employees:* 1
*Net Worth:* £2,239  *Total Assets:* £106,219
*Registered Office:* Unit 5 Progress Industrial Park, Progress Way, Croydon, Surrey, CR0 4XD
*Shareholder:* Nileshkumar Indubhai Patel
*Officers:* Nileshkumar Indubhai Patel [1974] Marketing Director [Indian]

**Astute Healthcare Limited**
*Incorporated:* 18 July 2012
*Net Worth:* £872,316  *Total Assets:* £3,570,354
*Registered Office:* 337 Athlon Road, Wembley, Middlesex, HA0 1EF
*Major Shareholder:* Hetasveeben Mahendrabhai Vanapariya
*Officers:* Hetasveeben Mahendrabhai Vanapariya [1991] Director

**Asymchem Limited**
*Incorporated:* 13 February 2017  *Employees:* 1
*Net Worth:* £10,813  *Total Assets:* £92,867
*Registered Office:* 5th Floor, One New Change, London, EC4M 9AF
*Shareholder:* Hao Hong
*Officers:* Elut Hsu [1971] Director/President of Asymchem, Inc [American]

**Athem Pharma Limited**
*Incorporated:* 31 March 2017
*Registered Office:* 3rd Floor, Scottish Provident House, 76-80 College Road, Harrow, Middlesex, HA1 1BQ
*Major Shareholder:* Nilesh Prataprai Mehta
*Officers:* Nilesh Prataprai Mehta [1962] Director/Executive

**Athenex Euro Limited**
*Incorporated:* 16 February 2018
*Registered Office:* 4th Floor, New Penderel House, 283-288 High Holborn, London, WC1V 7HP
*Parent:* Athenex, Inc.
*Officers:* Teresa Brophy Bair [1971] Director/Legal Affairs & Corporate Development [American]

**Athrodax Healthcare International Limited**
*Incorporated:* 13 June 1980  *Employees:* 19
*Net Worth:* £1,145,949  *Total Assets:* £1,265,830
*Registered Office:* Hawthorn Business Park, Drybrook, Glos, GL17 9HP
*Major Shareholder:* Jean Miller
*Officers:* Jean Rosemary Miller, Secretary; Jean Rosemary Miller [1939] Director/Company Secretary; Simon John Miller [1970] Director/Manager

**ATI Atlas Ltd.**
*Incorporated:* 26 January 1949  *Employees:* 3
*Net Worth:* £94,805  *Total Assets:* £106,984
*Registered Office:* Devine House, 1299-1301 London Road, Leigh on Sea, Essex, SS9 2AD
*Major Shareholder:* Nigel Bryan Chitty
*Officers:* Mavis Irene Chitty, Secretary; Mavis Irene Chitty [1940] Director; Nigel Bryan Chitty [1943] Director

**ATI Pharmaceuticals Limited**
*Incorporated:* 16 March 2015
*Net Worth Deficit:* £12,063  *Total Assets:* £1,189
*Registered Office:* 100b Third Avenue, Dagenham, Essex, RM10 9BA
*Shareholder:* Hasan Master
*Officers:* Ryan Adrian Charles Eversley-Robertson [1986] Director/Pharmacist; Hasan Master [1985] Director/Pharmacist

**Atlanta Biological Europe Ltd**
*Incorporated:* 2 January 2013  *Employees:* 1
*Net Worth Deficit:* £14,175  *Total Assets:* £113,914
*Registered Office:* 13 Fernham Road, Faringdon, Oxon, SN7 7JY
*Major Shareholder:* Keith James Thrower
*Officers:* Dr Keith James Thrower [1941] Director/Consultant

**Atlantic Imaging Limited**
*Incorporated:* 8 March 2013  *Employees:* 1
*Net Worth Deficit:* £16,235  *Total Assets:* £33,816
*Registered Office:* El Paso, Old Road, Shotover Hill, Headington, Oxford, OX3 8SZ
*Major Shareholder:* Alan Tilley
*Officers:* Alan Tilley [1964] Director

**Atnahs Pharma US Limited**
*Incorporated:* 26 January 2016
*Net Worth:* £2,583,085  *Total Assets:* £3,258,626
*Registered Office:* Suite 1, 3rd Floor, 11-12 St James's Square, London, SW1Y 4LB
*Parent:* Atnahs Pharma UK Limited
*Officers:* Mark John Cotterill [1965] Director; Amit Vijaykumar Patel [1978] Director; Bhikhu Chhotabhai Patel [1949] Director; Dipen Vijaykumar Patel [1979] Director/Accountant; Vijaykumar Chhotabhai Patel [1947] Director

**Atossa Genetics UK Ltd**
*Incorporated:* 28 October 2014
*Registered Office:* Suite 1, 3rd Floor, 11-12 St James's Square, London, SW1Y 4LB
*Officers:* Kyle Guse, Secretary; Kyle Guse [1963] Director/CFO and General Counsel [American]; Dr Steven Carl Quay [1950] Director/CEO and President [American]

**ATP Medical Limited**
*Incorporated:* 7 March 2016
*Registered Office:* 9 Soar Lane, The Old Mill, Leicester, LE3 5DE
*Shareholders:* Hitendra Patel; Kirti Patel
*Officers:* Hitendra Patel [1966] Director; Kirti Patel [1968] Director

**Atra Corporation Ltd**
*Incorporated:* 14 September 2017
*Registered Office:* The Greenhouse, 8 Mackintosh Lane, Homerton, London, E9 6AB
*Officers:* Gabriel Voll [1993] Director/Private Employee [Estonian]

**Atrimusrx Ltd**
*Incorporated:* 6 February 2018
*Registered Office:* 42 Lytton Road, Barnet, Herts, EN5 5BY
*Officers:* John Morell Frellsen [1967] Director [Danish]; Tracy Pettitt [1966] Director

**Attends Limited**
*Incorporated:* 18 February 1999  *Employees:* 34
*Net Worth:* £5,195,751  *Total Assets:* £17,365,974
*Registered Office:* c/o Norose Company Secretarial Serices Ltd, 3 More London Riverside, London, SE1 2AQ
*Parent:* Domtar Corporation
*Officers:* Josee Mireault, Secretary; Dr Michael Earl Fagan [1961] Director/Senior Vice President [American]; Hans Hjelm [1959] Director/Controller [Swedish]

**Attentive Pharma Limited**
*Incorporated:* 18 July 2017
*Registered Office:* 102 High Street, Godalming, Surrey, GU7 1DS
*Shareholders:* OH Investors Limited; Aspire Pharma Holdings Limited; Aspire Pharma Holdings Limited
*Officers:* Richard Baderin [1983] Director; Graham Julian Fraser-Pye [1968] Director; Debra Joy Roberts [1962] Financial Director; Mr David Alan Rowley [1962] Director

**Augmenix UK Limited**
*Incorporated:* 5 October 2017
*Registered Office:* 100 New Bridge Street, London, EC4V 6JA
*Parent:* Boston Scientific Corporation
*Officers:* Vance Ronald Brown, Secretary; Vance Ronald Brown [1969] Director/Corporate Attorney [Canadian]; Mark Robert Slicer [1970] Director/Business Executive [American]

**Aum Pharms Limited**
*Incorporated:* 23 September 2003
*Net Worth:* £233,947  *Total Assets:* £326,773
*Registered Office:* 91 Stanstead Road, Caterham, Surrey, CR3 6AG
*Major Shareholder:* Dinesh Bhanubhai Patel
*Officers:* Dineshkumar Bhanubhai Patel [1948] Director/Manager

**Aura-Soma Limited**
*Incorporated:* 2 March 1994
*Registered Office:* Tower House, Lucy Tower Street, Lincoln, LN1 1XW
*Parent:* Aura-Soma Products Ltd
*Officers:* Claudia Gwendoline Forster Booth, Secretary; John Michael Booth [1950] Director/Consultant

**Auramedicann Ltd**
*Incorporated:* 31 August 2018
*Registered Office:* 71-75 Shelton Street, London, WC2H 9JQ
*Officers:* Steven Davies [1973] Director

**Authentic Ayurveda Limited**
*Incorporated:* 14 January 2005
*Registered Office:* 54 Hillbury Avenue, Harrow, Middlesex, HA3 8EW
*Officers:* George Myrants, Secretary; Pranav Sharma [1983] Director [Indian]; Siddhesh Sharma [1985] Director [Indian]; Bharatbhushan Krishnakant Shrikhande [1958] Director [Indian]

**Autono-Med Limited**
*Incorporated:* 8 August 1997
*Net Worth:* £157,652  *Total Assets:* £216,872
*Registered Office:* Bowcliffe Hall, Bramham, Leeds, LS23 6LP
*Major Shareholder:* David Robertson Maxwell Watt
*Officers:* David Robertson Maxwell Watt, Secretary/Director; Geoffrey Grant [1946] Director; Michael Philip Lowe [1966] Operations Director; David Robertson Maxwell Watt [1952] Director

**Avail Group UK Limited**
*Incorporated:* 11 May 2018
*Registered Office:* Kenilworth Business Centre, Unit B Princes Drive, Kenilworth, Warwicks, CV8 2FD
*Major Shareholder:* Katie Gaughan
*Officers:* Katie Gaughan [1987] Director

**Avanzcare Limited**
*Incorporated:* 15 June 2017
*Net Worth Deficit:* £100,905  *Total Assets:* £35,101
*Registered Office:* c/o Riverbank House, 2 Swan Lane, London, EC4R 3TT
*Officers:* Mohamed Ahmed Shafiek Mohamed Ahmed [1966] Managing Director [Egyptian]; John Adel Youssef Tabdros Botros [1968] Director/General Manager [Egyptian]

**Aventa International Corporation Ltd**
*Incorporated:* 2 November 2018
*Registered Office:* 3 Gower Street, London, WC1E 6HA
*Shareholders:* Ahmed Hassan Ahmed Albahnasawy; Mohamed Hussein Mohamed Mohamed Soliman
*Officers:* Ahmed Hassan Ahmed Albahnasawy [1976] Director [Egyptian]

**Aventis Pharma Limited**
*Incorporated:* 18 December 1980  *Employees:* 685
*Net Worth:* £106,780,000  *Total Assets:* £373,788,000
*Registered Office:* One Onslow Street, Guildford, Surrey, GU1 4YS
*Parent:* Sanofi-Aventis UK Holdings Limited
*Officers:* Francois-Xavier Duhalde [1965] Director/Chief Financial Officer [French]; Hugo Rupert Alexander Fry [1970] Director/UK Country Chair

**Aver Generics Limited**
*Incorporated:* 25 January 2013  *Employees:* 40
*Net Worth:* £544,331  *Total Assets:* £3,295,417
*Registered Office:* 20 Singer Road, East Kilbride, G75 0XS
*Major Shareholder:* Gordon McDowall

**Aver Healthcare Ltd**
*Incorporated:* 29 April 2014
*Net Worth:* £78,477  *Total Assets:* £312,263
*Registered Office:* 3 Montpelier Avenue, Bexley, Kent, DA5 3AP
*Major Shareholder:* Kalvinder Singh Ruprai
*Officers:* Kalvinder Singh Ruprai [1969] Director

**Avicenna Ltd**
Incorporated: 7 August 2017
Net Worth: £1  Total Assets: £1
Registered Office: Selsdon House, 212-220 Addington Road, South Croydon, Surrey, CR2 8LD
Parent: Avicenna Holdings Ltd
Officers: Salim Kassamali Esmail Jetha [1953] Director

**Aviva Health Solutions Limited**
Incorporated: 16 March 2018
Registered Office: Kemp House, 160 City Road, London, EC1V 2NX
Major Shareholder: Ashley Crowne
Officers: Ashley Crowne [1968] Director

**Axe Pharma Ltd**
Incorporated: 14 January 2019
Registered Office: 85 Trotwood, Chigwell, Essex, IG7 5JP
Major Shareholder: Elena Daniella Teodor
Officers: Elena Daniella Teodor [1982] Director [Romanian]

**Axis Medical Limited**
Incorporated: 25 October 1996
Net Worth: £229,290  Total Assets: £287,020
Registered Office: Enterprise House, Beeson's Yard, Bury Lane, Rickmansworth, Herts, WD3 1DS
Shareholders: Jill Smith; Peter Jeffrey Smith
Officers: Jill Smith, Secretary; Peter Jeffrey Smith [1944] Director/Marketing Consultant

**Ayva Pharma Limited**
Incorporated: 20 March 2013  Employees: 7
Net Worth: £170,952  Total Assets: £961,568
Registered Office: Unit 1b Harrison Court, Hilton Business Park, Hilton, Derby, DE65 5UR
Shareholders: Simon Robert Shakespeare; Youssef William Matta
Officers: Youssef William Matta [1979] Director/Pharmacist [Egyptian]; Nazmy Nassief [1960] Director [Egyptian]; Simon Robert Shakespeare [1967] Director

**AZL Holdings Ltd**
Incorporated: 8 February 2017
Net Worth: £1  Total Assets: £1
Registered Office: 41 Addington Road, Reading, Berks, RG1 5PZ
Shareholders: Abdulmoez Laklouk; Ziad Laklouk
Officers: Abdulmoez Laklouk [1990] Director/Pharmacist; Ziad Laklouk [1988] Director/Pharmacist

**Azurite Health Ltd**
Incorporated: 11 December 2018
Registered Office: 2nd Floor, College House, 17 King Edwards Road, Ruislip, Middlesex, HA4 7AE
Major Shareholder: Richard Graham
Officers: Richard Graham, Secretary; Richard Graham [1973] Director/IT Professional

**B & B Wholesale Limited**
Incorporated: 23 July 2012
Net Worth: £1,709  Total Assets: £54,609
Registered Office: 18 The Crescent, Wembley, Middlesex, HA0 3JT
Major Shareholder: Vipulkumar Bhagavatiprasad Patel
Officers: Vipulkumar Patel [1980] Director [Indian]

**B D S I Limited**
Incorporated: 20 February 2003  Employees: 6
Net Worth: £210,361  Total Assets: £408,052
Registered Office: Unit 14 Claycliffe Business Park, Cannon Way, Barugh Green, Barnsley, S Yorks, S75 1JU
Major Shareholder: Colin Edward Pooley
Officers: Sharon Gail Pooley, Secretary/Office Manager; Colin Edward Pooley [1955] Director/Accountant; Sharon Gail Pooley [1961] Director/Office Manager

**B.P. Pharma Limited**
Incorporated: 7 April 1993
Registered Office: 16 South End, Croydon, Surrey, CR0 1DN
Shareholders: Essam Halim Dimetrios; Mariam Ibrahim Malty
Officers: Dr Essam Halim Dimetrios, Secretary; Dr Essam Halim Dimetrios [1945] Company Secretary Director [Egyptian]; Mariam Ibrahim Malty [1947] Director [Egyptian]

**B.R. Pharmaceuticals Limited**
Incorporated: 27 February 1996  Employees: 12
Net Worth: £988,368  Total Assets: £1,444,146
Registered Office: Clayton Wood Close, West Park, Ring Road, Leeds, LS16 6QE
Shareholder: Omar Mahmood Abu Sheikha
Officers: Omar Mahmood Abu Sheikha [1956] Director [Jordanian]; Ziad Mahmoud Mousa Abu Sheikha [1960] Director [Jordanian]; Taisir Abusheikha [1973] Director [Canadian]

**Ba-Inspire Limited**
Incorporated: 29 August 2018
Registered Office: 47 Otterden Street, Bellingham, London, SE6 3SI
Major Shareholder: Banjo Ayodeji Samuel Adebisi
Officers: Banjo Ayodeji Samuel Adebisi [1986] Director [Nigerian]

**Bacteflora Ltd**
Incorporated: 22 March 2017
Registered Office: 156a Burnt Oak Broadway, Edgware, Middlesex, HA8 0AX
Major Shareholder: Kyriakos Kyriakopoulos
Officers: Kyriakos Kyriakopoulos [1970] Director/Sales Manager [Greek]

**The Bagnall Group (Europe) Ltd**
Incorporated: 18 May 2011  Employees: 2
Net Worth: £754,834  Total Assets: £1,409,504
Registered Office: Regent House, Clinton Avenue, Nottingham, NG5 1AZ
Shareholders: Maxwell Bagnall; William Bagnall
Officers: William Bagnall, Secretary; Maxwell Bagnall [1979] Director; William Bagnall [1976] Director

**Bahati19 Limited**
Incorporated: 28 March 2012
Net Worth Deficit: £939  Total Assets: £900,397
Registered Office: 99 The Meadows, Marshfield, Cardiff, CF3 2DY
Major Shareholder: Hetal Praful Panchmatia
Officers: Hettal Panchmatia [1979] Director

**Bailey Instruments Ltd**
Incorporated: 3 January 1989
Registered Office: Unit 19 Guinness Road Trading Estate, Trafford Park, Manchester, M17 1SB
Officers: Gemma Bailey [1987] Director; Joseph Bailey [1990] Director; Sally Jane Bailey [1959] Director; Timothy Martin Bailey [1954] Director; Simon Edwin Charlesworth [1956] Director/Business Manager; Joan Mary Gem [1943] Director/Podiatrist; Christopher Stewart Hacking [1945] Director/Judge

**Bakhu Limited**
Incorporated: 27 February 2008  Employees: 1
Net Worth: £2,563  Total Assets: £71,418
Registered Office: 10 Gainsborough Road, Southport, Merseyside, PR8 2EY
Officers: Sarah Braithwaite, Secretary; Colin Andrew Leece [1961] Director; Dr Lee Proctor [1967] Director

**Balagrae Ltd**
Incorporated: 3 October 2017
Registered Office: C16, The Ingenuity Centre, Triumph Road, Jubilee Campus, Nottingham, NG7 2TU
Major Shareholder: Aljali Hamed
Officers: Dr. Aljali Hamed [1979] Director and Company Secretary [Libyan]

**Ballymote Pharmacy Limited**
Incorporated: 26 February 2014  Employees: 5
Net Worth: £145,713  Total Assets: £271,744
Registered Office: Unit 3 Ballymote Centre, 40 Killough Road, Downpatrick, Co Down, BT30 6PY
Major Shareholder: Barbara Lennon
Officers: Barbara Lennon, Secretary; Edward Ronald Lennon [1956] Director/First Aid Supplier [Irish]

**Bannersbridge Limited**
Incorporated: 16 May 1984
Net Worth Deficit: £14,248  Total Assets: £4,084
Registered Office: 87 Berkeley Road, London, NW9 9DH
Major Shareholder: Mohammed Hanif Motiwala
Officers: Naveed MoTIwala, Secretary; Mohammed Hanif MoTIwala [1937] Director/Businessman

**Paul Baratte International Limited**
Incorporated: 2 March 1964
Net Worth: £265,000  Total Assets: £265,000
Registered Office: 12 Carlton Park Industrial Estate, Saxmundham, Suffolk, IP17 2NL
Major Shareholder: Detmar Albert Hackman
Officers: Detmar Albert Hackman, Secretary; Detmar Albert Hackman [1934] Director; Eunhee Hackman [1964] Director

**Barclay Pharmaceuticals Limited**
Incorporated: 3 December 1992  Employees: 338
Net Worth: £95,268,000  Total Assets: £126,254,000
Registered Office: Sapphire Court, Walsgrave Triangle, Coventry, Warwicks, CV2 2TX
Parent: Admenta Holdings Limited
Officers: Nichola Louise Legg, Secretary; Toby Matthew Anderson [1973] Director; Marcus Hilger [1977] Finance Director [German]; Catherine McDermott [1968] Operations Director; Nigel Swift [1966] Marketing & Sales Director

**Baron Medicare UK Limited**
Incorporated: 29 January 2019
Registered Office: 1st Floor, Healthaid House, Marlborough Hill, Harrow, Middlesex, HA1 1UD
Shareholders: Pratikkumar Patel; Sharmistahbahen Patel
Officers: Pratikkumar Patel [1990] Director [Indian]; Sharmistahbahen Patel [1984] Director/Homemaker

**Barton Pharmacy Limited**
Incorporated: 4 November 1971  Employees: 1
Net Worth Deficit: £33,798  Total Assets: £670,035
Registered Office: Ground Floor, 3 West Road, Woolacombe, Devon, EX34 7BW
Parent: Arnolds Pharmacy Limited
Officers: Osman Naveed Hamid [1980] Director/Pharmacist

**Barustore Limited**
Incorporated: 15 January 2018
Registered Office: Kemp House, 160 City Road, London, EC1V 2NX
Major Shareholder: Harry Irawanto Utomo
Officers: Harry Irawanto Utomo, Secretary; Harry Irawanto Utomo [1977] Director [Indonesian]

**Bausch & Lomb U.K. Limited**
Incorporated: 28 April 1916  Employees: 139
Net Worth: £17,843,000  Total Assets: £33,713,000
Registered Office: One Fleet Place, London, EC4M 7WS
Parent: Bausch & Lomb UK Holdings Limited
Officers: Duncan William Dow [1972] Director/General Manager; Eberhard Karl Heinz Kuehne [1965] Director/Regional Finance Lead [German]; Janice Kathleen Mary More [1961] Director/Lawyer; William Norman Woodfield [1976] Director [American]

**Baxalta UK Investments Ltd.**
Incorporated: 23 July 2002
Previous: Baxter Healthcare Pharmaceutical Limited
Net Worth Deficit: £88,212,856  Total Assets: £557,806,848
Registered Office: 1 Kingdom Street, London, W2 6BD
Parent: Takeda Pharmaceutical Company Limited
Officers: Damien Rodolphe Edmond Bailly [1966] Commercial Director [French]; Mark Gibbons [1984] Director/Accountant [South African]; Nicholas Hugh Meryon Insall [1982] Director/Accountant; Jonathan Clark Neal [1971] Managing Director

**Bayer Public Limited Company**
Incorporated: 8 July 1968  Employees: 739
Net Worth: £57,264,000  Total Assets: £350,952,992
Registered Office: 400 South Oak Way, Reading, Berks, RG2 6AD
Parent: Bayer Global Investments B.V.
Officers: Colin Andrew Barker, Secretary; Lars Friedrich Bruening [1963] Director [German]; Vera Hahn [1967] Director/Manager [Austrian]; Sreeparna Arun Kurdikar [1969] Director/Chief Financial Officer [American]

**Baymed Group Ltd.**
Incorporated: 27 September 1999
Net Worth: £901  Total Assets: £549,517
Registered Office: 32 Milton Road, East Kilbride, S Lanarks, G74 5BU
Officers: Richard Martin Dover [1967] Director

**Baymed Healthcare Ltd.**
Incorporated: 7 July 1977
Net Worth Deficit: £172,945  Total Assets: £743,998
Registered Office: 32 Milton Road, East Kilbride, S Lanarks, G74 5BU
Parent: Baymed Group Ltd
Officers: Richard Martin Dover, Secretary; Scott Donegan [1972] Director/Medical Supplier; Richard Martin Dover [1967] Director; Mark Simpson [1983] Director/Medical Supplier

**BB Lifestyle UK Limited**
Incorporated: 18 April 2018
Registered Office: The Old Casino, 28 Fourth Avenue, Hove, E Sussex, BN3 2PJ
Major Shareholder: Ramina Badalbit
Officers: Ramina Kharileh [1965] Director

The Top UK Pharmaceutical Wholesalers                                                                          dellam

**Bbeauty Lounge Limited**
*Incorporated:* 30 March 2017
*Registered Office:* Trilogy Suite, 9 Church Street, Wednesfield, Wolverhampton, W Midlands, WV11 1SR
*Major Shareholder:* Chad William Burgin
*Officers:* Chad William Burgin [1987] Director

**BBI Healthcare Limited**
*Incorporated:* 15 November 2005  *Employees:* 49
*Net Worth:* £2,230,000  *Total Assets:* £15,836,000
*Registered Office:* Berry Smith LLP, Haywood House, Dumfries Place, Cardiff, CF10 3GA
*Parent:* BBI Diagnostics Group Limited
*Officers:* Richard George Armitt Couzens [1973] Director; Claus Egstrand [1961] Managing Director [Danish]; Mario Pietro Gualano [1969] Director; Alan Edward Peterson [1947] Director

**BDCP Ltd**
*Incorporated:* 11 July 2018
*Registered Office:* 88 Pattison Lane, Woolstone, Milton Keynes, Bucks, MK15 0AY
*Major Shareholder:* Talaat Talaat Abdelhamid Ahmed Aldib
*Officers:* Talaat Abdelhamid Ahmed Aldib [1966] Director/Pharmacist [Egyptian]

**Be and Are Sales Limited**
*Incorporated:* 24 June 1999  *Employees:* 2
*Net Worth:* £24,937  *Total Assets:* £35,334
*Registered Office:* 19-20 Bourne Court, Southend Road, Woodford Green, Essex, IG8 8HD
*Shareholders:* Rachel Davidoff; Chava Davidoff
*Officers:* Rahel Davidoff [1956] Director/Administrator

**Beachcourse Limited**
*Incorporated:* 7 April 1997
*Net Worth:* £2,848,000  *Total Assets:* £11,048,000
*Registered Office:* 4th Floor, Sedley Place, 361 Oxford Street, London, W1C 2JL
*Parent:* Alliance Boots Holdings Limited
*Officers:* Lucie Charlotte Massart, Secretary; Alexandro Depau [1970] Director [American]; Pablo Cortes Rivas [1972] Director [Spanish]; David Charles Tooby [1971] Director

**Beautons Ventures Ltd**
*Incorporated:* 5 May 2017
*Net Worth:* £740  *Total Assets:* £6,447
*Registered Office:* 115 London Road, Morden, Surrey, SM4 5HP
*Major Shareholder:* Sabeen Bushra
*Officers:* Sabeen Bushra [1987] Director/Entrepreneur

**Beauty Boosters Ltd**
*Incorporated:* 19 June 2018
*Registered Office:* 71-75 Shelton Street, Covent Garden, London, WC2H 9JQ
*Major Shareholder:* Katarzyna Agata Devraj
*Officers:* Katarzyna Agata Devraj, Secretary; Katarzyna Agata Devraj [1980] Director [Polish]

**Beauty Hair Products Limited**
*Incorporated:* 17 August 1988  *Employees:* 8
*Net Worth:* £41,173  *Total Assets:* £1,792,539
*Registered Office:* 1 Tower House, Tower Centre, Hoddesdon, Herts, EN11 8UR
*Shareholders:* Antonis Kyriacou; Christine Kyriacou; Michael Kyriacou
*Officers:* Christine Kyriacou, Secretary; Antonis Loizou Kyriacou [1944] Director; Michael Kyriacou [1975] Director

**Beauty Shopper Ltd.**
*Incorporated:* 10 May 2007
*Registered Office:* Pinnacle House Business Centre, Newark Road, Peterborough, Cambs, PE1 5YD
*Major Shareholder:* Alistair Martin Ashworth
*Officers:* Alistair Martin Ashworth, Secretary; Alistair Martin Ashworth [1963] Director

**Beechcroft Supplies Limited**
*Incorporated:* 30 June 1997
*Net Worth:* £1,661,897  *Total Assets:* £5,839,282
*Registered Office:* 192 Norwich Road, New Costessey, Norwich, NR5 0EX
*Shareholder:* Prabodh Nilkanth Devlukia
*Officers:* Meena Devlukia, Secretary; Prabodh Devlukia [1957] Director/Pharmacist

**Beegood Enterprises Limited**
*Incorporated:* 25 February 2013  *Employees:* 4
*Net Worth:* £42,178  *Total Assets:* £105,829
*Registered Office:* Ping CA, P O Box 1077, Camberley, Surrey, GU15 9QH
*Officers:* Hilary Ann Andrews [1961] Director; Simon Rafe Cavill [1960] Director; John Colin LooSeniore [1948] Director [Australian]; David John Parker [1965] Director

**Behsarel Trading Ltd**
*Incorporated:* 27 September 2017
*Registered Office:* Park House, 1 Russell Gardens, London, NW11 9NJ
*Major Shareholder:* Elisha Koppel
*Officers:* Elisha Koppel [1981] Director [Australian]

**Beiersdorf UK Ltd.**
*Incorporated:* 20 May 1949  *Employees:* 217
*Net Worth:* £40,264,000  *Total Assets:* £103,750,000
*Registered Office:* Trinity Central, Trinity Park, Bickenhill Lane, Birmingham, B37 7ES
*Parent:* Beiersdorf AG
*Officers:* Patrick Albrecht [1970] Marketing Director [German]; Lynette Amanda Brown [1977] HR Director; Thomas Ingelfinger [1960] Director/Member Executive Board [German]; James Edward Livesey [1976] Finance Director; Andreas Ostermayr [1970] Director/General Manager [German]; Paul Bryan Price [1964] Director; Andrew Thomas Rawle [1976] Pharmacy Director; Thomas Riedner [1976] Supply Chain Director [German]

**Beijing Tong Ren Tang (UK) Limited**
*Incorporated:* 14 December 1993
*Net Worth Deficit:* £952,625  *Total Assets:* £309,169
*Registered Office:* 124 Shaftesbury Avenue, London, W1D 5ES
*Major Shareholder:* Kin Sum Chan
*Officers:* Chin Yu Lo, Secretary; Kin Sum Chan [1935] Director/Business Consultant; Chin Yu Lo [1960] Director/Supervisor Manager

**Bejaa Medical (UK) Limited**
*Incorporated:* 11 April 2014
*Registered Office:* 135-137 Station Road, Chingford, London, E4 6AG
*Shareholders:* Terence Richard Scott; Germaine Mojikon
*Officers:* Germaine Mojikon [1952] Director/Retired; Terence Richard Scott [1961] Director/Salesman

**Belfast Drug Ltd**
Incorporated: 3 December 2008
Net Worth Deficit: £202,337  Total Assets: £2,804
Registered Office: 14c Adelaide Park, Belfast, BT9 6FX
Major Shareholder: William Neil Hutton
Officers: William Neil Hutton, Secretary; William Neil Hutton [1965] Director

**Belinda Limited**
Incorporated: 27 December 2017
Registered Office: Astra House, Arklow Road, London, SE14 6EB
Parent: Abstragan Limited
Officers: Akobir Zohidov [1984] Director [Tajikistani]

**Benatur Limited**
Incorporated: 25 August 2016
Registered Office: 1st Floor, 37 Panton Street, London, SW1Y 4EA
Major Shareholder: Bharat Bhusan
Officers: Bharat Bhusan [1970] Director [Indian]; Souleymane Soumahoro [1969] Director

**Benident Limited**
Incorporated: 6 April 2010
Net Worth: £1  Total Assets: £1
Registered Office: 2 Whiteheath Avenue, Ruislip, Middlesex, HA4 7PS
Shareholders: Harshil Shah; Denis Igorevich Olarou
Officers: Denis Olarou, Secretary; Dr Harshil Shah [1984] Director/Dental Surgeon

**Berkshire Wholesale Supplies (2002) Ltd**
Incorporated: 13 December 2001
Net Worth: £1,507,725  Total Assets: £3,897,672
Registered Office: 6 The Harrow Market, Langley, Slough, Berks, SL3 8HJ
Major Shareholder: Corrin McParland
Officers: Corrin McParland, Secretary; Corrin McParland [1973] Director/Pharmacist; Heather Audrey McParland [1943] Director/Pharmacist

**Berryfarm Ltd**
Incorporated: 25 July 2008
Net Worth Deficit: £137,152  Total Assets: £2,383
Registered Office: 1110 Elliott Court, Coventry Business Park, Herald Avenue, Coventry, Warwicks, CV5 6UB
Major Shareholder: Evangelos Paraskevas
Officers: Evangelos Paraskevas [1965] Director/Doctor [Greek]; Antoaneta Vasileva [1978] Director [Bulgarian]

**Besins Healthcare (UK) Limited**
Incorporated: 18 September 2013  Employees: 26
Net Worth Deficit: £9,356,255  Total Assets: £2,404,841
Registered Office: 28 Poland Street, London, W1F 8QN
Parent: Besins Healthcare SA
Officers: Paul Martin Barnes [1953] Director; Delbert Alva Cohen [1955] Director/Business Consultant; Leslie Eric Giles Grunfeld [1959] Director

**Bessacarr Ltd**
Incorporated: 11 March 2010
Registered Office: 20 Burnham Court, Moscow Road, London, W2 4SW
Officers: Andrew James McDermott, Secretary; Andrew James McDermott [1949] Director

**Best Value America (UK) Ltd**
Incorporated: 31 March 2008  Employees: 1
Net Worth: £976,991  Total Assets: £1,717,109
Registered Office: 6 Hamilton Parade, Feltham, Middlesex, TW13 4PJ
Major Shareholder: Ashfaq Hussain
Officers: Ashfaq Hussain [1958] Director Sales & Marketing [Indian]

**Best-Bio Ltd**
Incorporated: 20 August 2018
Registered Office: 3 Hornbeam Road, Hayes, Middlesex, UB4 9ED
Major Shareholder: Awad Kazem Abbas
Officers: Awad Kazem Abbas [1955] Director/Businessman

**Bestlon Limited**
Incorporated: 21 January 2015
Net Worth Deficit: £138,805  Total Assets: £146,027
Registered Office: Regent House, 316 Beulah Hill, London, SE19 3HF
Officers: Jan Harm Snyman [1968] Director/Importer/Exporter [South African]

**Bestway Pharmacy NDC Limited**
Incorporated: 17 April 1972
Net Worth Deficit: £45,447,000  Total Assets: £35,142,000
Registered Office: Merchants Warehouse, Castle Street, Manchester, M3 4LZ
Parent: Bestway Panacea Holdings Limited
Officers: Lynette Gillian Krige [1966] Director/Chief Finance Officer [South African]; John Branson Nuttall [1963] Director/General Manager Health Care Group

**Beta Pharmaceuticals Limited**
Incorporated: 23 October 2003  Employees: 80
Net Worth: £5,926,742  Total Assets: £9,334,672
Registered Office: Unit 7 & 8 Swanbridge Industrial Park, Black Croft Road, Witham, Essex, CM8 3YN
Major Shareholder: Naseen Mohamed Valji
Officers: Mohamed Raza Kanji, Secretary; Mohamed Raza Kanji [1971] Director/Pharmacist; Naseen Valji [1959] Director/Chemist

**Betpharma UK Limited**
Incorporated: 5 April 2006
Net Worth: £194,549  Total Assets: £205,032
Registered Office: 52 Fore Street, Callington, Cornwall, PL17 7AJ
Major Shareholder: Mark Palos
Officers: Christine Rose Ann Palos, Secretary; Mark Palos [1967] Sales Director [South African]

**Better Earth Limited**
Incorporated: 14 November 2017
Registered Office: 25 Cranley Drive, Ilford, Essex, IG2 6AH
Major Shareholder: Yousaf Khan
Officers: Mariam Gul [1987] Director; Yousaf Khan [1987] Director

**Better'er Limited**
Incorporated: 2 July 2018
Registered Office: 16 Centurion Drive, Kempsey, Worcester, WR5 3NR
Major Shareholder: Aaran Abdul-Razak Oladipo Arogundade
Officers: Aaran Abdul-Razak Oladipo Arogundade [1991] Director/General Manager

**Beximco Pharma UK Limited**
*Incorporated:* 23 March 2010
*Registered Office:* Ahmed & Co, 284 Station Road, Harrow, Middlesex, HA1 2EA
*Parent:* Beximco Pharma Gulf FZE
*Officers:* Mohammed Nayem Syed, Secretary; Nazmul Hassan [1961] Director [Bangladeshi]; Salman Rahman [1951] Director/Chairman [Bangladeshi]; Rabbur Reza [1968] Director [Australian]; Mohammed Nayem Syed [1967] Director


**BFN Limited**
*Incorporated:* 5 July 2011
*Registered Office:* 29 Greyhound Road, London, W6 8NH
*Officers:* Sheida Moussavi [1941] Director


**Bhendriks Resale and Retale Ltd**
*Incorporated:* 21 August 2017
*Registered Office:* Flat 2/2, 33 Causeyside Street, Paisley, Renfrewshire, PA1 1UL
*Major Shareholder:* Bram Hendriks
*Officers:* Bram Hendriks [1996] Director/Business Owner [Dutch]


**Bial Pharma UK Limited**
*Incorporated:* 31 May 2016  *Employees:* 15
*Net Worth:* £205,511  *Total Assets:* £401,801
*Registered Office:* St Stephens House, Arthur Road, Windsor, Berks, SL4 1RU
*Parent:* Bial-S.G.P.S.,SA
*Officers:* Gilbert Marius Julien [1964] Director/General Manager and Member of The Board [French]; Antonio Luis de Azevedo Portela [1975] Director/Chief Executive Officer [Portuguese]; Miguel Luis de Azevedo Portela [1978] Director/General Manager and Member of The Board [Portuguese]; Jose Augusto Fernandes Redondo [1960] Director/General Manager and Member of The Board [Portuguese]; Jason Vincent Stone [1963] Director/BU Head


**Bidaya UK Ltd.**
*Incorporated:* 18 October 2012
*Registered Office:* 32 Chatsworth Court, Pembroke Road, London, W8 6DH
*Major Shareholder:* Ehab Ahmed Hamdi Ahmed Abdellatif
*Officers:* Ehab Abdel Latif [1972] Director/Business Development Manager [Egyptian]


**Bigvits Limited**
*Incorporated:* 5 April 2009  *Employees:* 7
*Net Worth:* £711  *Total Assets:* £5,559
*Registered Office:* Unit 4 Argyle Street, Unit Factory Estate, Hull, HU3 1HD
*Parent:* Bigvits Group Limited
*Officers:* William Richard John Brennand [1982] Director; Catherine Mary Bristow [1979] Director


**Bin'auf Limited**
*Incorporated:* 1 February 2018
*Registered Office:* 20-22 Wenlock Road, London, N1 7GU
*Major Shareholder:* Muhammad Usman Shahid
*Officers:* Muhammad Usman Shahid [1984] Director [Pakistani]


**Bio Global Limited**
*Incorporated:* 8 August 2018
*Registered Office:* 3 Hornbeam Road, Hayes, Middlesex, UB4 9ED
*Major Shareholder:* Mohaned Awad Abbas
*Officers:* Mohaned Awad Abbas [1992] Director/Businessman; Ross Generald Wilkins [1990] Director/Self Employed


**Bio Nutrition Health Products Limited**
*Incorporated:* 15 June 1988
*Net Worth:* £60,734  *Total Assets:* £66,711
*Registered Office:* G1 Chaucer Business Park, Dittons Road, Polegate, E Sussex, BN26 6QH
*Officers:* Brian Edward Bandy, Secretary/Accountant; Brian Edward Bandy [1943] Director; Janet Frances Bandy [1943] Director


**Bio Pathica Limited**
*Incorporated:* 22 January 1996  *Employees:* 5
*Net Worth:* £208,045  *Total Assets:* £446,138
*Registered Office:* Unit 16 Willesborough Industrial Park, Willesborough, Ashford, Kent, TN24 0TD
*Shareholders:* Juliet Macaraya Wilson; Roger Keith Wilson
*Officers:* Juliet Macaraya Wilson, Secretary; Craig Stephen William Sadler [1973] Director/General Manager; Roger Keith Wilson [1940] Director


**Bio-Sight Ltd**
*Incorporated:* 13 February 2015
*Net Worth Deficit:* £4,277  *Total Assets:* £3,948
*Registered Office:* 1 College Yard, 56 Winchester Avenue, London, NW6 7UA
*Officers:* Emiliano Vigna [1974] Director [Italian]


**Bio-Synergy Limited**
*Incorporated:* 23 May 1997  *Employees:* 3
*Net Worth:* £445,578  *Total Assets:* £816,656
*Registered Office:* 529 Finchley Road, London, NW3 7BG
*Officers:* Daniel Andrew Richard Herman, Secretary/Director; Daniel Andrew Richard Herman [1973] Director/Manufacturer; Barry Michael Howard Shaw [1956] Director/Solicitor


**Bioactive T Pharma Limited**
*Incorporated:* 1 July 2011
*Registered Office:* Office 6a, Aura Skegness Business Centre, Heath Road, Skegness, Lincs, PE25 3SJ
*Major Shareholder:* Hussein Mahdi Mohammed Al-Bayat
*Officers:* Eylem Unal [1976] Director/Company Representative [Turkish]


**Bioavexia Ltd**
*Incorporated:* 1 June 2016  *Employees:* 1
*Net Worth:* £164,523  *Total Assets:* £1,170,247
*Registered Office:* Unit 20 Phoenix Business Park, Avenue Close, Birmingham, B7 4NU
*Officers:* Mohammed Abrar [1978] Director


**Biobos Limited**
*Incorporated:* 10 March 2014
*Registered Office:* 33 Heather Drive, Thatcham, Berks, RG18 4BU
*Parent:* Boston Healthcare Ltd
*Officers:* Hamish George Salmond, Secretary; Colin Pollock Darroch [1953] Managing Director; Hamish George Salmond [1957] Director/Accountant


**Biocare Supplies Limited**
*Incorporated:* 17 May 1999
*Net Worth Deficit:* £129  *Total Assets:* £16,822
*Registered Office:* Steepleton House, Shipton Oliffe, Cheltenham, Glos, GL54 4JL
*Shareholders:* Eileen Teresa Buck; Robert Stuart Buck
*Officers:* Eileen Teresa Buck, Secretary/Businesswoman; Eileen Teresa Buck [1957] Director/Businesswoman; Robert Stuart Buck [1960] Director/Businessman

**Bioceutics UK Ltd**
*Incorporated:* 26 September 2014
*Registered Office:* Advantage Business Centre, 132-134 Great Ancoats Street, Manchester, M4 6DE
*Officers:* Dr Mohamed Shawki El Morsy Yousef [1977] Director/Pharmacist [Egyptian]

**Biocon Pharma UK Limited**
*Incorporated:* 7 December 2018
*Registered Office:* 16 Great Queen Street, Covent Garden, London, WC2B 5AH
*Officers:* Kiran Mazumdar Shaw [1953] Director [Indian]; John McCallum Marshall Shaw [1949] Director; Abhijit Zutshi [1975] Director [American]

**Bioconnections Ltd**
*Incorporated:* 23 November 2017
*Registered Office:* 23 Market Place, Wetherby, W Yorks, LS22 6LQ
*Shareholders:* Kenneth Denton; Janet Denton
*Officers:* Janet Denton [1950] Director; Kenneth Denton [1948] Director; Andrew Douglas Wood [1969] Director; Dawn Sandra Wood [1965] Director

**Biofex Limited**
*Incorporated:* 21 December 2009
*Registered Office:* Gilchrist Road, Northbank Industrial Estate, Irlam, Manchester, M44 5AY
*Officers:* Jason Joseph [1970] Director [American]; David Francis Pietrantoni [1972] Director [American]; Lindon Robertson [1961] Director [American]

**Bioforce (U.K) Limited**
*Incorporated:* 27 August 1986  *Employees:* 70
*Net Worth:* £6,069,988  *Total Assets:* £8,409,181
*Registered Office:* 36 West Portland Street, Troon, S Ayrshire, KA10 6AE
*Officers:* Janny Elizabeth Tan, Secretary; Peter Gmunder [1966] Director [Swiss]; Dr Harriet Mei-Lin Tan [1993] Director/Doctor; Janyn Elizabeth Tan [1963] Director; Jen Wei Tan [1960] Director/Doctor of Medicine; Johannes Tan [1989] Director/Manager; Dr Li-Anna Elizabeth Tan [1987] Director/Doctor

**Biogenez Ltd**
*Incorporated:* 24 December 2018
*Registered Office:* 10 Colwyn Avenue, Perivale, Greenford, Middlesex, UB6 8JX
*Major Shareholder:* Mazin Julien Al-Janabi
*Officers:* Mazin Julien Al-Janabi [1972] Director/Consultant

**Biogenic Health Europe Ltd**
*Incorporated:* 1 November 2013
*Net Worth Deficit:* £454,051  *Total Assets:* £868,949
*Registered Office:* Suite A, 6 Honduras Street, London, EC1Y 0TH
*Major Shareholder:* Szabolcs Zoltan Ladi
*Officers:* Dr Szabolcs Zoltan Ladi [1973] Director/Doctor [Hungarian]

**Biogenix Ltd**
*Incorporated:* 19 February 2018
*Registered Office:* Unit 9 Alliance Business Park, York Street, Bradford, W Yorks, BD8 0HA
*Major Shareholder:* Habib Ebrahim Ullah Akudi
*Officers:* Habib Ebrahim Ullah Akudi [1972] Director

**Bioleys Care Ltd**
*Incorporated:* 20 April 2018
*Registered Office:* Kemp House, 160 City Road, London, EC1V 2NX
*Major Shareholder:* Rohan Mukul
*Officers:* Rohan Mukul [1994] Director/Marketer [Indian]

**Bioloka Ltd**
*Incorporated:* 12 November 2012
*Net Worth Deficit:* £36,390  *Total Assets:* £623,881
*Registered Office:* First Floor, 85 Great Portland Street, London, W1W 7LT
*Shareholder:* Alexis Mertens
*Officers:* Alexis Hadelin Regis Ludovic Ghislain Mertens [1982] Director/Manager [Belgian]

**Biomarin (U.K.) Ltd.**
*Incorporated:* 23 December 2009  *Employees:* 67
*Net Worth:* £4,227,000  *Total Assets:* £24,658,000
*Registered Office:* 10 Bloomsbury Way, London, WC1A 2SL
*Parent:* Biomarin Pharmaceutical Inc.
*Officers:* George Eric Davis, Secretary; Astrid Irmgard Elfriede Baumann [1961] Director [French]; George Eric Davis [1971] Director/Attorney [American]; Chay Bradwen Morgan [1968] Director/Pharmaceutical Regulatory Affairs; Richard Gideon Morris [1973] Director/Barrister; John Joseph Shanahan [1969] Director [Irish]

**Biomed Limited**
*Incorporated:* 16 September 1997  *Employees:* 4
*Net Worth Deficit:* £8,615  *Total Assets:* £49,714
*Registered Office:* Ibex House, Baker Street, Weybridge, Surrey, KT13 8AH
*Officers:* Elicca Anne de Souza, Secretary; Elicca Anne de Souza [1985] Director; Everyll de Souza [1989] Director; Keith Francis de Souza [1955] Director Pharmaceuticals [Indian]; Remmie Anne de Souza [1957] Director

**Biomedi Technology Limited**
*Incorporated:* 28 June 2011
*Registered Office:* Room 403, Intershore Suites, Dowgate Hill House, 14-16 Dowgate Hill, London, EC4R 2SU
*Major Shareholder:* Wa Wing Tsoi
*Officers:* Wa Wing Tsoi [1969] Director/Merchant [Chinese]

**Biomedica Nutraceuticals (UK) Ltd**
*Incorporated:* 21 November 2013  *Employees:* 1
*Net Worth:* £129,685  *Total Assets:* £201,520
*Registered Office:* 810 Mandarin Court, Centre Park, Warrington, Cheshire, WA1 1GG
*Major Shareholder:* Daniel Baden
*Officers:* Daniel Baden [1962] Director [Australian]

**Biomedical Reproductive Research Ltd**
*Incorporated:* 15 April 2009
*Net Worth:* £36,686  *Total Assets:* £399,773
*Registered Office:* 3rd Floor, 207 Regent Street, London, W1B 3HH
*Major Shareholder:* Kyrylo Alpatov
*Officers:* Robert Elliot [1982] Director

**Biomedoc Limited**
*Incorporated:* 30 June 2011
*Net Worth:* £1,618  *Total Assets:* £122,468
*Registered Office:* Rutherford House, 40 Pencroft Way, Manchester Science Park, Manchester, M15 6SZ
*Major Shareholder:* Hamid Bohloli
*Officers:* Dr Hamid Bohloli [1963] Director [Iranian]

**Biomedox International Ltd**
*Incorporated:* 20 December 2011
*Net Worth:* £1,894  *Total Assets:* £83,690
*Registered Office:* Rutherford House, 40 Pencroft Way, Manchester Science Park, Manchester, M15 6SZ
*Major Shareholder:* Hamid Bohloli
*Officers:* Dr Hamid Bohloli [1963] Director/Medical Doctor [Iranian]

**Bionical Limited**
*Incorporated:* 28 October 2009  *Employees:* 320
*Net Worth Deficit:* £6,716,000  *Total Assets:* £18,866,000
*Registered Office:* The Piazza, Mercia Marina, Findern Lane, Willington, Derby, DE65 6DW
*Major Shareholder:* Andrew Derrick Leaver
*Officers:* Andrew Thomas Borkowski [1962] Director/Solicitor; Andrew Derrick Leaver [1962] Director; Darren Leaver [1966] Director; Jonathan Waring-Hughes [1988] Director

**Bionutricals UK Ltd**
*Incorporated:* 19 December 2011
*Net Worth:* £3,487  *Total Assets:* £25,275
*Registered Office:* Unit 4 Tanshelf Industrial Estate, Colonels Walk, Pontefract, W Yorks, WF8 4PJ
*Major Shareholder:* Donna Marie Raynor
*Officers:* Donna Marie Raynor [1980] Director/Manager

**Biophage Therapeutics Ltd**
*Incorporated:* 11 October 2016
*Registered Office:* 1st Floor, 24-25 New Bond Street, Mayfair, London, W1S 2RR
*Major Shareholder:* Robert Jackson
*Officers:* Timothy Jonathon Charles Butler [1962] Managing Director; Robert Jackson [1956] Director; Timothy Martin Tickner [1967] Director

**Biophos Labs Ltd**
*Incorporated:* 21 November 2018
*Registered Office:* c/o Silk Route Legal Limited, 33 Bedford Row, London, WC1R 4JH
*Major Shareholder:* Ranjit Vishawambar Sail
*Officers:* Ranjit Vishawambar Sail [1985] Director

**Bioplax Limited**
*Incorporated:* 5 November 2004
*Net Worth:* £2,227,751  *Total Assets:* £2,646,677
*Registered Office:* Endeavour House, 78 Stafford Road, Wallington, Surrey, SM6 9AY
*Shareholders:* Andrea Antonio Macchi; Franco Macchi; Matteo Rinaldo Macchi
*Officers:* Andrea Artioli [1968] Director [Swiss]

**Bioquote Limited**
*Incorporated:* 9 December 1987
*Net Worth:* £158,924  *Total Assets:* £212,446
*Registered Office:* The Raylor Centre, James Street, York, YO10 3DW
*Major Shareholder:* David Michael Samson
*Officers:* Trevor Rogers, Secretary; David Michael Samson [1957] Director

**Biosensors International UK Ltd**
*Incorporated:* 23 January 2019
*Registered Office:* 12 New Fetter Lane, London, EC4A 1JP
*Officers:* Thomas Kenneth Graham [1965] Managing Director & VP Sales EMEA; Russell Hughes [1971] Sales Director

**Biostate Limited**
*Incorporated:* 10 August 1994
*Net Worth:* £15,621  *Total Assets:* £53,746
*Registered Office:* Acton Hill Mews, 9 Uxbridge Road, London, W3 9QN
*Major Shareholder:* Brian Donald Whitley
*Officers:* Lynn Shirley Whitley, Secretary; Brian Donald Whitley [1953] Former Director

**Biosure (UK) Limited**
*Incorporated:* 29 July 2011
*Net Worth:* £444,290  *Total Assets:* £627,107
*Registered Office:* Unit 59 Hillgrove Business Park, Nazeing Road, Nazeing, Waltham Abbey, Essex, EN9 2HB
*Major Shareholder:* Brigette Anne Bradford
*Officers:* Brigette Anne Bard [1972] Director; Daryl Bradford [1965] Finance Director; Gary Richard Carpenter [1966] Clinical Director; Sir Nigel Knowles [1956] Director/Solicitor; Mel Sims [1957] Director/Solicitor

**Biotech International Limited**
*Incorporated:* 5 March 2004  *Employees:* 4
*Net Worth Deficit:* £3,729,300  *Total Assets:* £59,688
*Registered Office:* Oakridge House, Wellington Road, High Wycombe, Bucks, HP12 3PR
*Parent:* Biocide International PLC
*Officers:* Christopher John Hounsell, Secretary; Robin Carr [1943] Director

**Biotek Diagnostics Limited**
*Incorporated:* 12 December 2018
*Registered Office:* First Floor, Studio 6, 32-38 Scrutton Street, London, EC2A 4RQ
*Shareholder:* Mohammed Iqbal Memon
*Officers:* Dr Mohammed Iqbal Memon [1949] Director; Abdul Qazi [1959] Director

**Biotest (U.K.) Limited**
*Incorporated:* 6 August 1973  *Employees:* 12
*Net Worth:* £3,218,257  *Total Assets:* £4,907,940
*Registered Office:* First Floor, Park Point, 17 High Street, Longbridge, Birmingham, B31 2UQ
*Parent:* Biotest AG
*Officers:* Patricia Morey, Secretary; Patricia Morey [1964] Marketing Director; Eric Thomas [1962] Director/Manager [German]

**Bioturm Limited**
*Incorporated:* 2 March 2017
*Net Worth Deficit:* £25,207  *Total Assets:* £17,151
*Registered Office:* 1 Coneywel Court, Northampton, NN3 9DP
*Shareholders:* Dhanya Jacob; Suphil Philipose
*Officers:* Peelipose Chirackal [1942] Director [Indian]; Dhanya Jacob [1976] Director; Suphil Philipose [1973] Director

**Biotus Ltd**
*Incorporated:* 26 October 2018
*Registered Office:* WTC 1CV, New London House, 6 London Street, City, London, EC3R 7LP
*Major Shareholder:* Dmytro Grekulov
*Officers:* Dmytro Grekulov [1982] Director [Ukrainian]

**Biovate Limited**
*Incorporated:* 4 January 2017
*Registered Office:* Fanshawe House, Pioneer Business Park, Amy Johnson Way, York, YO30 4TN
*Major Shareholder:* Sami Safadi
*Officers:* Sami Safadi [1975] Director [Jordanian]

**Biovendor Ltd**
*Incorporated:* 8 December 2014
*Net Worth:* £208,765   *Total Assets:* £1,232,387
*Registered Office:* 184b Park Drive, Milton Park, Milton, Abingdon, Oxon, OX14 4SE
*Parent:* Biovendor Laboratorni Medicina AS
*Officers:* Helen Elizabeth Church [1965] Director; Dr Viktor Ruzicka [1965] Director/Chief Executive Officer [Czech]

**Bioxane Ltd**
*Incorporated:* 21 August 2018
*Registered Office:* Kemp House, 160 City Road, London, EC1V 2NX
*Major Shareholder:* Ahmed Mahmoud
*Officers:* Dr Ahmed Mahmoud, Secretary; Dr Ahmed Mahmoud [1979] Director/Manager [Egyptian]

**Bipsco Ltd**
*Incorporated:* 10 February 2012
*Previous:* Red Sea Pharma UK Ltd
*Net Worth:* £21,580   *Total Assets:* £118,326
*Registered Office:* Unit 8 Easton Business Centre, Felix Road, Bristol, BS5 0HE
*Major Shareholder:* Abdullrazak Dahir
*Officers:* Abdul Razak Dahir [1969] Director

**Birch & Beech Limited**
*Incorporated:* 7 December 1999
*Net Worth Deficit:* £3,912   *Total Assets:* £5,712
*Registered Office:* Unit 7 Howard Business Park, 47 Howard Close, Waltham Abbey, Essex, EN9 1XE
*Major Shareholder:* Iordanis Christodoulou Nikodimou
*Officers:* Iordanis Christodoulou Nikodimou [1959] Director [Cypriot]

**Mark Birch Hair Ltd**
*Incorporated:* 25 June 2018
*Registered Office:* 12 Tulip Way, West Drayton, Middlesex, UB7 7ED
*Major Shareholder:* Mark William Birch
*Officers:* Tuija Maarit Anneli Lindstrom [1970] Director/Chief Executive [Finnish]

**Birmingham Management Centre (UK) Limited**
*Incorporated:* 12 October 2009
*Registered Office:* 43 Canterbury Tower, St Marks Street, Birmingham, B1 2UJ
*Officers:* Dr Isiaka Oladimeji Lawal [1956] Director/Professor

**Black and White Health Care Limited**
*Incorporated:* 5 October 2012
*Net Worth Deficit:* £736   *Total Assets:* £48,612
*Registered Office:* Advanced Technology Innovation Centre, Loughborough University Science and Enterprise Parks, 5 Oakwood Drive, Loughborough, Leics, LE11 3QF
*Parent:* NDM Technologies Limited
*Officers:* Dewan Fazlul Hoque Chowdhury [1973] Director/Scientist

**Blackbird Pharmacy Limited**
*Incorporated:* 21 March 2000   *Employees:* 7
*Net Worth:* £1,249,523   *Total Assets:* £3,523,827
*Registered Office:* 575 Melton Road, Thurmaston, Leicester, LE4 8EA
*Officers:* Preeti Pattni, Secretary; Pravin Pattani [1957] Director/Pharmacist

**Blackpool Medicines Limited**
*Incorporated:* 17 May 2018
*Registered Office:* Unit 2b Premier House, Cornford Road, Blackpool, Lancs, FY4 4QQ
*Officers:* Dr Daniel Thomas Bennett [1979] Director; Stephanie Louise Milne [1983] Director; Samir Vohra [1971] Director

**Blackstaff Pharmaceuticals Limited**
*Incorporated:* 16 April 1999
*Registered Office:* Sapphire Court, Walsgrave Triangle, Coventry, Warwicks, CV2 2TX
*Parent:* Sangers (Northern Ireland) Limited
*Officers:* Nichola Louise Legg, Secretary; Toby Matthew Anderson [1973] Director; Marcus Hilger [1977] Finance Director [German]; Catherine McDermott [1968] Operations Director; Nuala Meier [1959] Director/Accountant [Irish]; Nigel Swift [1966] Marketing & Sales Director

**Blackstone Pharma Ltd**
*Incorporated:* 21 November 2013
*Net Worth Deficit:* £926   *Total Assets:* £151,864
*Registered Office:* Unit E2, The Loughton Seedbed Centre, Langston Road, Loughton, Essex, IG10 3TQ
*Shareholders:* Ayisha Zafar; Adam Zafar
*Officers:* Adam Zafar [1982] Director

**A & P Blickling Ltd**
*Incorporated:* 22 February 2018
*Registered Office:* 27 Old Gloucester Street, London, WC1N 3AX
*Officers:* Patrik Blickling [1983] Director/Businessman [Slovak]; Ana Eugenia Calero de Blickling [1974] Director/Businesswoman [Nicaraguan]

**Blink Street Limited**
*Incorporated:* 16 March 2018
*Registered Office:* 24 Lime Kiln Wharf, 94 Three Colt Street, London, E14 8AP
*Officers:* Ira Blinkovskaja [1982] Sales Director [Swedish]

**Blue Bean Medical Ltd**
*Incorporated:* 1 February 2012
*Net Worth:* £1,009   *Total Assets:* £10,201
*Registered Office:* 277 Stockport Road, Ashton under Lyne, Lancs, OL7 0NT
*Shareholder:* Carl Walkden
*Officers:* Michael Stanley Atkinson [1961] Director; Carl Michael Walkden [1959] Director/Owner

**Blue Horizon Healthcare Consulting Limited**
*Incorporated:* 2 September 2015   *Employees:* 2
*Net Worth Deficit:* £1,041   *Total Assets:* £16,444
*Registered Office:* 86 Priory Road, West Bridgford, Nottingham, NG2 5HX
*Major Shareholder:* Helen Louise Hamilton
*Officers:* Alan James Hamilton [1974] Director/Pharmaceutical Marketing Manager; Helen Louise Hamilton [1974] Director/Pharmaceutical Sales Consultant

**Bluesky Cosmetics Limited**
*Incorporated:* 13 December 2016
*Registered Office:* Trilogy Suite, 9 Church Street, Wednesfield, Wolverhampton, W Midlands, WV11 1SR
*Major Shareholder:* Chad William Burgin
*Officers:* Chad William Burgin [1987] Director

**BM Alliance Limited**
*Incorporated:* 23 July 2010
*Net Worth:* £16,448  *Total Assets:* £60,564
*Registered Office:* 44 Chalklands, Linton, Cambridge, CB21 4JH
*Major Shareholder:* John Watkin
*Officers:* John Watkin [1970] Director/Manager

**BN Medical Ltd**
*Incorporated:* 22 April 2013  *Employees:* 4
*Net Worth:* £49,599  *Total Assets:* £155,595
*Registered Office:* 9-11 Palacecraig Street, Coatbridge, N Lanarks, ML5 4RY
*Major Shareholder:* Blake Baljit Singh Brad
*Officers:* Blake Baljit Singh Brad [1986] Sales Director

**The Bolton Pharmaceutical Company 100 Ltd**
*Incorporated:* 27 October 2003  *Employees:* 3
*Net Worth Deficit:* £3,506  *Total Assets:* £823
*Registered Office:* Allenby Laboratories, Wigan Road, Westhoughton, Bolton, Lancs, BL5 2AL
*Parent:* CD Medical Limited
*Officers:* Lee Fairbrother, Secretary; Elsie Maureen Armstrong [1951] Director; Michael Gatenby [1942] Director; Gerard Michael Dominic Pessagno [1952] Director

**Bone Support UK Ltd**
*Incorporated:* 31 August 2016
*Registered Office:* 1st Floor, 236 Gray's Inn Road, London, WC1X 8HB
*Officers:* Emil Anders Billback [1970] Director [Swedish]; Lars Hakan Johansson [1963] Director [Swedish]

**Boost Hair Limited**
*Incorporated:* 2 November 2017
*Registered Office:* 36 High Street, Cleethorpes, N E Lincs, DN35 8JN
*Parent:* Brandhaus Holdings Ltd
*Officers:* Martin John Schiele [1983] Director

**Boots International Limited**
*Incorporated:* 11 July 2000
*Net Worth:* £43,343,000  *Total Assets:* £74,912,000
*Registered Office:* 1 Thane Road West, Nottingham, NG2 3AA
*Parent:* Alliance Boots Holdings Limited
*Officers:* Andrew Richard Thompson, Secretary; Rosemary Frances Counsell [1963] Director/Chief Financial Officer; Anne Louise Murphy [1967] Director

**Bosses Onlinestore Ltd**
*Incorporated:* 4 January 2019
*Registered Office:* Carpenter Court, 1 Maple Road, Bramhall, Stockport, Cheshire, SK7 2DH
*Major Shareholder:* Stefan Larsson
*Officers:* Stefan Larsson [1985] Director [Swedish]

**Boston Healthcare Limited**
*Incorporated:* 18 April 2011  *Employees:* 6
*Net Worth:* £1,391,012  *Total Assets:* £3,345,252
*Registered Office:* 6 Navigation Court, Calder Park, Wakefield, W Yorks, WF2 7BJ
*Shareholders:* Finance Yorkshire Equity GP Limited; Viking Fund Managers Limited
*Officers:* Hamish George Salmond, Secretary; Ian David Brown [1959] Director; Colin Pollock Darroch [1953] Director; Nicholas John Jones [1968] Director; Hamish George Salmond [1957] Director/Accountant; Steven Stocks [1952] Director

**Bosville Limited**
*Incorporated:* 8 January 2003
*Registered Office:* Unit 7 Stan Kelly & Co, Claverings Business Park, 14 Centre Way, Edmonton, London, N9 0AH
*Shareholders:* Jacob Olusegun Olusanya; Bolajoko Olusanya
*Officers:* Emmanuel Oloke, Secretary/Chartered Certified Accountant; Dr Bolajoko Olusanya [1959] Director/Medical Practitioner [Nigerian]; Jacob Olusegun Olusanya [1956] Managing Director [Nigerian]

**Botha Group Ltd**
*Incorporated:* 24 July 2018
*Registered Office:* Kemp House, 160 City Road, London, EC1V 2NX
*Major Shareholder:* Stefan Botha
*Officers:* Stefan Botha, Secretary; Stefan Botha [1988] Director/Banker [South African]

**Bowmed Ibisqus Limited**
*Incorporated:* 4 April 2007  *Employees:* 8
*Net Worth:* £3,530,669  *Total Assets:* £7,604,834
*Registered Office:* 2 Jordan Street, Knott Mill, Manchester, M15 4PY
*Parent:* Istituto Biochimico Italiano Giovanni Lorenzini S.P.A
*Officers:* Johannes Khevenheuller [1956] Director/Chairman [Italian]; Susan Margaret Myerscough [1962] Director

**Bpharm Group Limited**
*Incorporated:* 9 July 2018
*Registered Office:* 85 Great Portland Street, London, W1W 7LT
*Shareholder:* Ramil Eyyubov
*Officers:* Vassilios Karavas [1971] Director

**BR Pharma International Limited**
*Incorporated:* 1 July 1998  *Employees:* 36
*Net Worth:* £12,410,152  *Total Assets:* £15,056,712
*Registered Office:* Haslers, Old Station Road, Loughton, Essex, IG10 4PL
*Shareholders:* Joel Rabin; Rebecca Eleanor Blinston-Jones; Fabienne Rabin
*Officers:* Fabienne Rabin, Secretary; Sheryl Anne Glanvill [1970] Operations Director [New Zealander]; Joel Rabin [1974] Director; Christina White [1967] Finance Director

**BR Scientific Limited**
*Incorporated:* 1 July 2015
*Net Worth:* £54,470  *Total Assets:* £90,556
*Registered Office:* 14 Thornhill Way, Rogerstone, Newport, NP10 9FT
*Major Shareholder:* Bethan Rhian Morgan
*Officers:* Bethan Rhian Morgan [1992] Director

**Bracco UK Limited**
*Incorporated:* 10 October 2000  *Employees:* 19
*Net Worth:* £10,088,000  *Total Assets:* £12,741,000
*Registered Office:* Unit 15 Valley Business Centre, Gordon Road, High Wycombe, Bucks, HP13 6EQ
*Shareholder:* Diana Bracco
*Officers:* Sauro Orlandi, Secretary; Luca di Palma [1971] Director of Bracco UK Ltd [Italian]; Steven Kennedy [1955] Director; Frederic Tridon [1971] Director [French]

**J. Bradbury (Surgical) Limited**
*Incorporated:* 3 March 1999
*Registered Office:* 2 Marshalls Road, Belfast, BT5 6SR
*Parent:* Sangers (Northern Ireland) Limited
*Officers:* Nichola Louise Legg, Secretary; Toby Matthew Anderson [1973] Director; Marcus Hilger [1977] Finance Director [German]; Catherine McDermott [1968] Operations Director; Nuala Meier [1959] Director/Accountant [Irish]; Nigel Swift [1966] Marketing and Sales Director

**Liam Bradley Ltd**
*Incorporated:* 22 July 1999  *Employees:* 192
*Net Worth Deficit:* £199,505  *Total Assets:* £8,967,744
*Registered Office:* Unit 11 Dromore Road Industrial Estate, Omagh, Co Tyrone, BT78 1RE
*Major Shareholder:* Liam Bradley
*Officers:* Jolene Catherine O'Kane, Secretary; Liam Martin Bradley [1967] Director/Pharmacist [Irish]

**Bradley Stoke Bristol Limited**
*Incorporated:* 30 August 2014  *Employees:* 13
*Net Worth:* £408,020  *Total Assets:* £698,308
*Registered Office:* 364-368 Cranbrook Rd, Gants Hill, London, IG2 6HY
*Shareholders:* Azam Khan; Hitesh Mehta
*Officers:* Sadaqat Azam [1971] Director; Azam Khan [1969] Director; Ashish Mehta [1978] Director

**Brancaster Pharma Limited**
*Incorporated:* 15 August 2012  *Employees:* 5
*Net Worth:* £6,760,862  *Total Assets:* £7,555,798
*Registered Office:* The Office, Heath View, Ray Lane, Blindley Heath, Lingfield, Surrey, RH7 6LH
*Shareholders:* Alexander James Duckworth; Kimberley Duckworth
*Officers:* Alexander James Duckworth [1970] Pharmaceutical Director

**Branded Healthcare Ltd**
*Incorporated:* 21 February 2019
*Registered Office:* 111-117 Bell Street, Glasgow, G4 0TQ
*Parent:* Dagda Holdings Limited
*Officers:* Navdeep Basi, Secretary; Navdeep Basi [1970] Director/Business Administrator

**Bray Pharma Limited**
*Incorporated:* 25 May 2018
*Registered Office:* Primrose Studios, Primrose Road, Clitheroe, Lancs, BB7 1BT
*Major Shareholder:* Jane Anne Sharples
*Officers:* Kevin James [1955] Director; Dr Jane Anne Sharples [1964] Director

**Brent Medicare Limited**
*Incorporated:* 23 November 2017
*Registered Office:* 214 High Street, Brentford, Middlesex, TW8 8AH
*Shareholders:* Matthew Shamoon; Zain Manhal Shamoon
*Officers:* Matthew Shamoon [1984] Director/Pharmacist; Dr Zain Manhal Shamoon [1985] Director/Dentist

**Brenton Invest and Trade Limited**
*Incorporated:* 10 April 2014
*Net Worth:* £5,255  *Total Assets:* £1,445,991
*Registered Office:* c/o St Ioan Rilsky Chudotworec Ltd, 6 Hamilton Road, London, NW11 9EJ
*Shareholders:* Krasimir Tsanev; Dobrinka Tsaneva
*Officers:* Dobrinka Tsaneva, Secretary; Krasimir Tsanev [1955] Director [Bulgarian]

**Brex Medical Supplies Limited**
*Incorporated:* 5 August 2002
*Net Worth:* £7,492  *Total Assets:* £50,312
*Registered Office:* Congress House, 14 Lyon Road, Harrow, Middlesex, HA1 2EN
*Parent:* Brand Russell Chemists Limited
*Officers:* Tabarak Sadik [1990] Director/Pharmacist

**Bri Trade Solutions Limited**
*Incorporated:* 23 May 2017
*Registered Office:* Innovation Campus, Faraday Wharf, Holt Street, Birmingham Science Park, Birmingham, B7 4BB
*Shareholder:* Khalid Aziz
*Officers:* Khalid Aziz [1972] Managing Director

**Bright Polar Limited**
*Incorporated:* 31 October 2006  *Employees:* 8
*Net Worth:* £1,097,313  *Total Assets:* £2,155,260
*Registered Office:* 164 Bedford Road, Kempston, Bedford, MK42 8BH
*Major Shareholder:* Kevin Francis O'Farrell
*Officers:* Sarvjit Singh Marok, Secretary; Kevin Francis O'Farrell [1966] Director/Administrator

**Brightfield Associates Ltd**
*Incorporated:* 16 March 2005
*Registered Office:* 126 Donaldson Road, London, SE18 3LB
*Officers:* Katharina Ilse Rist, Secretary; Gerhard Otto Friedrich Rossbach [1944] Director/Merchant [German]

**Bripharm Limited**
*Incorporated:* 28 June 1967
*Registered Office:* 2000 Hillswood Drive, Chertsey, Surrey, KT16 0RS
*Parent:* Astellas Pharma Inc.
*Officers:* Ian Michael Hall [1966] Director/Chartered Accountant; Dr Jose Maria Sanz [1972] Director/General Manager

**Bristol Buttr Ltd**
*Incorporated:* 13 February 2019
*Registered Office:* Unit 3 Lawrence Hill Industrial Estate, Russell Town Avenue, Bristol, BS5 9LT
*Shareholders:* Lucy Rowe; John William Whittington; Forever Pedalling Bristol Ltd
*Officers:* Lucy Rowe [1990] Director

**Bristol Consumer Health Ltd**
*Incorporated:* 7 December 2017
*Registered Office:* 2 Heath Green Way, Coventry, Warwicks, CV4 8GU
*Officers:* Magda Andrews, Secretary; Maged Andrawes [1970] Director [Egyptian]; Magda Andrews [1972] Director [Egyptian]

**Bristol Laboratories Limited**
*Incorporated:* 27 June 1997  *Employees:* 335
*Net Worth:* £44,480,316  *Total Assets:* £69,361,760
*Registered Office:* Unit 3 Canalside, North Bridge Road, Berkhamsted, Herts, HP4 1EG
*Parent:* Bristol Laboratories Group Limited
*Officers:* Sreekumar Nair Kodupurath, Secretary; Sanjay Shrikishan Pashine [1975] Director; Raju Puthenvilayil Mathaikutty [1956] Director; Priti Ramachandran [1982] Director; Thembalath Ramachandran [1949] Director

**BritaniaMark Limited**
*Incorporated:* 6 January 2016
*Registered Office:* 18 King William Street, London, EC4N 7BP
*Major Shareholder:* Paul Larke
*Officers:* Paul Larke [1979] Director

**Britannia Medical Limited**
Incorporated: 6 May 2004
Net Worth Deficit: £425,471  Total Assets: £256,361
Registered Office: Elscot House, Arcadia Avenue, London, N3 2JU
Shareholders: Taife Al-Allaq; Mowafak Ismail
Officers: Ibraheem Al Bajari [1958] Director [Iraqi]; Samir Al Bajary [1954] Director [Iraqi]; Taife Al-Allaq [1974] Director; Dr Salah Al-Ani [1972] Director [Iraqi]; Esam Al-Shelby [1960] Director [Iraqi]; Mowafak Ismail [1948] Director/Pharmacist [Iraqi]

**Britannia Pharmaceuticals Limited**
Incorporated: 21 April 1981  Employees: 80
Net Worth: £40,942,000  Total Assets: £59,009,000
Registered Office: 200 Longwater Avenue, Green Park, Reading, Berks, RG2 6GP
Parent: Genus Pharmaceuticals Holdings Limited
Officers: Elizabeth Robinson, Secretary; Christoph Dengler [1969] Director [German]; Robert Kenneth Wood [1976] Managing Director

**Britannic Pharma Ltd**
Incorporated: 19 September 2018
Registered Office: Unit 15 Lyndon Road, Stechford, Birmingham, B33 8BU
Shareholder: Nasir Mumtaz
Officers: Hamed Mohammed Ahmed Al Grou [1982] Director; Nasir Mumtaz [1979] Director

**The British Association of European Pharmaceutical Distributors**
Incorporated: 21 March 1984
Net Worth: £115,943  Total Assets: £220,266
Registered Office: 15a Station Road, Epping, Essex, CM16 4HG
Officers: Richard Emil Freudenberg, Secretary/Director; John Cochrane [1957] Director; Richard Emil Freudenberg [1953] Director; Julio Iglesias Jimenez [1972] Director [Spanish]; Pritesh Ramesh Sonpal [1969] Director; Ashwani Kumar Sudera [1965] Director

**Britpharm Limited**
Incorporated: 11 June 2014  Employees: 3
Net Worth: £3,087  Total Assets: £3,859
Registered Office: Unit 3, 2 Somerset Road, London, N17 9EJ
Major Shareholder: Mohamed Hashi
Officers: Mohamed Abdiaziz Hashi [1982] Director/Businessman [Dutch]

**Britpharma UK Limited**
Incorporated: 25 August 2018
Registered Office: 71-75 Shelton Street, London, WC2H 9JQ
Shareholders: Mamta Chachan; Prasanna Chachan
Officers: Mamta Chachan, Secretary; Mamta Chachan [1980] Director [Indian]; Prasanna Chachan [1978] Director [Indian]

**Brituswip Limited**
Incorporated: 27 January 2015
Net Worth: £151,000  Total Assets: £303,000
Registered Office: 200 Longwater Avenue, Reading, Berks, RG2 6GP
Shareholders: Paul Breckinridge Jones; Britannia Pharmaceuticals Limited
Officers: Elizabeth Robinson, Secretary; Henry Van Den Berg [1958] Director/Vice President Medical Affairs [American]; Herbert Lee Warren [1959] Director/Chief Operating Officer [American]; Robert Kenneth Wood [1976] Marketing Director

**Brookmed Limited**
Incorporated: 2 March 2006
Net Worth: £384,600  Total Assets: £487,096
Registered Office: Unit 26 Leyton Business Centre, Etloe Road, Leyton, London, E10 7BT
Major Shareholder: Kevin Kwesi Brookman
Officers: Kevin Kwesi Brookman [1973] Director/Pharmacist

**ET Browne (UK) Limited**
Incorporated: 27 October 1992
Net Worth: £1,012,765  Total Assets: £4,616,082
Registered Office: 35 Ballards Lane, London, N3 1XW
Major Shareholder: Robert Charles Neis
Officers: Arnold Hayward Neis, Secretary/Chairman [American]; Paul Robert Rees Johns [1957] Managing Director; Arnold Hayward Neis [1938] Director/Chairman [American]; Robert Charles Neis [1963] Director/President [American]

**BTA Pharm Limited**
Incorporated: 11 April 2011  Employees: 11
Net Worth: £464,741  Total Assets: £1,718,931
Registered Office: 405 Lisburn Road, Belfast, BT9 7EW
Officers: Brendan Anglin [1959] Director [Irish]; Melanie Anglin [1958] Director

**Budget Pharma UK Limited**
Incorporated: 28 January 2006
Registered Office: Unit 2a Old Dalby Trading Estate, Station Road, Old Dalby, Melton Mowbray, Leics, LE14 3NJ
Parent: East Midlands Pharma Limited
Officers: Kirit Chimanbhai Patel Junior, Secretary; Kirit Chimanbhai Tulsibhai Patel [1980] Executive Director; Jayanti Chimanbhai Patel Junior [1984] Director

**Buduscheye Techniqa Ltd**
Incorporated: 23 January 2017
Net Worth: £100  Total Assets: £100
Registered Office: 130 Damwood Road, Liverpool, L24 2SS
Major Shareholder: Manab Chetia
Officers: Manav Chetia [1985] Director/Engineer [Indian]

**Bugband Europe Ltd**
Incorporated: 13 December 2010
Registered Office: 52 High Street, Pinner, Middlesex, HA5 5PW
Officers: David John Irons, Secretary; David John Burton Irons [1952] Director; Daniel Everett Ritter [1950] Director [American]; Bjorn Tuvsjoen [1950] Director [Norwegian]

**Bulgarian Healthy Products Limited**
Incorporated: 4 July 2018
Registered Office: Flat 7, 145 Commonside East, Mitcham, Surrey, CR4 2QB
Officers: Vasil Stefanov [1987] Director [Bulgarian]

**Busky Limited**
Incorporated: 20 August 2018
Registered Office: 4 Leys Close, Corby, Northants, NN17 5FZ
Major Shareholder: Betrand Kachukwu Agaba
Officers: Ngozi Mary Agaba, Secretary; Betrand Kachukwu Agaba [1968] Director/Pharmacy Technician

**Butt & Hobbs Limited**
*Incorporated:* 9 February 2005
*Net Worth:* £1,218,605  *Total Assets:* £3,914,678
*Registered Office:* Taylor House, 55-57 Bradford Road, Dewsbury, Wakefield, W Yorks, WF13 2EG
*Shareholders:* Zaheer Younis-Butt; Mohammad Saeed Younis; Naheed Younis
*Officers:* Mohammad Saeed Younis, Secretary; Mohammad Saeed Younis [1960] Director; Naheed Younis [1969] Director/Administration; Zaheer Younis Butt [1967] Director/Sales

**By Direct Limited**
*Incorporated:* 3 August 2016
*Net Worth:* £2,275  *Total Assets:* £37,075
*Registered Office:* 24 Brooke Avenue, Harrow, Middlesex, HA2 0NF
*Major Shareholder:* Yati Mehta
*Officers:* Yati Mehta [1987] Director [Indian]

**C & N Medical Ltd**
*Incorporated:* 9 November 2011
*Net Worth Deficit:* £148,285  *Total Assets:* £2,045
*Registered Office:* 3rd Floor, Scottish Provident House, 76-80 College Road, Harrow, Middlesex, HA1 1BQ
*Shareholders:* Nikunj Shantilal Malde; Deepak Shantilal Malde
*Officers:* Nikunj Malde, Secretary; Deepakkumar Shantilal Malde [1960] Director/Pharmacist; Nikunj Shantilal Malde [1958] Director/Doctor

**C & P Medical Trading Limited**
*Incorporated:* 11 August 1998  *Employees:* 34
*Net Worth:* £514,168  *Total Assets:* £5,296,407
*Registered Office:* Unit 1 Avro Business Centre, Avro Way, Bowerhill Estate, Melksham, Wilts, SN12 6TP
*Major Shareholder:* Peter John Shaw
*Officers:* Julia Lauren Shaw, Secretary/Director; Julia Lauren Shaw [1968] Director; Peter John Shaw [1970] Managing Director

**C. S. T. Pharma Limited**
*Incorporated:* 9 May 2001  *Employees:* 82
*Net Worth:* £7,887,000  *Total Assets:* £31,923,000
*Registered Office:* Unit 5-7 Tintagel Way, Westgate Park Industrial Estate, Aldridge, Walsall, W Midlands, WS9 8ER
*Officers:* Carl Falzon [1977] Commercial Director; Daniel Mark O'Connor [1981] Director; Caroline Poynter [1964] Commercial Director; Jason Derick Yates [1973] Managing Director

**C.D. Medical Limited**
*Incorporated:* 30 April 2015  *Employees:* 170
*Net Worth:* £14,595,119  *Total Assets:* £25,161,420
*Registered Office:* Unit 2002 Elland Close, Wingates Industrial Estate, Westhoughton, Bolton, Lancs, BL5 3XE
*Shareholder:* Elsie Maureen Armstrong
*Officers:* Lee Fairbrother, Secretary; Elsie Maureen Armstrong [1951] Director; Michael Gatenby [1942] Sales & Marketing Director; Gerard Michael Dominic Pessagno [1952] Director

**Cadila Pharmaceuticals (Europe) Limited**
*Incorporated:* 23 November 2000
*Net Worth:* £2,204,796  *Total Assets:* £3,200,216
*Registered Office:* Kings Suite, 4th Floor, Amba House, 15 College Road, Harrow, Middlesex, HA1 1BA
*Officers:* Amitabha Banerjee [1954] Director [Indian]; Dr Rajiv Indravadan Modi [1960] Director [Indian]

**Cambpharma Ltd**
*Incorporated:* 23 May 2017
*Registered Office:* 2 Cabot House, Compass Point Business Park, St Ives, Cambs, PE27 5JL
*Major Shareholder:* Karen James
*Officers:* James Norman Dickens [1988] Director; Emily James [1994] Director; Karen James [1956] Director

**Cambridge Biotics Ltd**
*Incorporated:* 11 July 2018
*Registered Office:* St Johns Innovation Centre, Cowley Road, Cambridge, CB4 0WS
*Major Shareholder:* Edward Anderson
*Officers:* Edward Anderson [1973] Director [Dominican]

**Cambridge Diagnostics (UK) Limited**
*Incorporated:* 25 September 2013  *Employees:* 2
*Net Worth:* £130,125  *Total Assets:* £154,063
*Registered Office:* 2 Burton House, Repton Place, White Lion Road, Amersham, Bucks, HP7 9LP
*Shareholders:* Alicja Drewnowska; Stan Wajs
*Officers:* Alicja Drewnowska [1954] Director; Stanley Adam Wajs [1944] Director

**Cambridge Healthcare Supplies 2012 Limited**
*Incorporated:* 29 October 2012  *Employees:* 3
*Net Worth:* £1,545,746  *Total Assets:* £1,546,776
*Registered Office:* Unit 1-2 Wymondham Business Park, Chestnut Drive, Wymondham, Norfolk, NR18 9SB
*Major Shareholder:* Yashvantrai Vallabhji Ondhia
*Officers:* Aruna Yashvantrai Ondhia [1951] Director; Punam Ondhia [1980] Director; Yashvantrai Vallabhji Ondhia [1948] Director/Chartered Accountant

**Cambridge Healthcare Supplies Limited**
*Incorporated:* 11 November 1997  *Employees:* 9
*Net Worth:* £2,084,170  *Total Assets:* £3,763,750
*Registered Office:* Unit 1 Wymondham Business Park, Chestnut Drive, Wymondham, Norfolk, NR18 9SB
*Officers:* Yashvantrai Vallabhji Ondhia, Secretary/Chartered Accountant; Aruna Yashvantrai Ondhia [1951] Director; Punam Ondhia [1980] Director; Yashvantrai Vallabhji Ondhia [1948] Director/Chartered Accountant

**Cambridge Pharmaceuticals Limited**
*Incorporated:* 5 December 2003
*Registered Office:* 23 Wigmore Street, London, W1U 1PL
*Major Shareholder:* Bedros Loutfig Eghiayan
*Officers:* Bedros Loutfig Eghiayan, Secretary/Pharmacist; Bedros Loutfig Eghiayan [1949] Director/Pharmacist

**NV Campbell Limited**
*Incorporated:* 29 April 2015
*Net Worth:* £269  *Total Assets:* £13,249
*Registered Office:* 87 High Ridge Crescent, New Milton, Hants, BH25 5BU
*Officers:* Nicola Veronica Campbell [1955] Director

**Campbell Medical Supplies Ltd**
*Incorporated:* 19 February 2014
*Net Worth:* £133,021  *Total Assets:* £514,183
*Registered Office:* Unit 2 Victoria Estate, Violet Street, Paisley, Renfrewshire, PA1 1PA
*Major Shareholder:* James Paul Campbell
*Officers:* Esther Campbell [1946] Director; James Paul Campbell [1947] Director

**Campmed Limited**
*Incorporated:* 8 December 2010
*Net Worth:* £3,377  *Total Assets:* £21,492
*Registered Office:* 93 Forest Drive West, London, E11 1JZ
*Officers:* Jawad Ali Khan [1972] Director

**Camurus Ltd**
*Incorporated:* 18 January 2017
*Net Worth:* £79,209  *Total Assets:* £341,690
*Registered Office:* The Officers' Mess Business Centre, Royston Road, Duxford, Cambs, CB22 4QH
*Parent:* Camurus AB
*Officers:* Richard Major Jameson [1964] Director; Eva Pinotti-Lindqvist [1963] Director [Swedish]; Sven Fredrik Tiberg [1963] Director [Swedish]

**Canary Islands Marketing Board Ltd**
*Incorporated:* 22 February 2018
*Registered Office:* 33 Farren Court, Redgeland Rise, St Leonards on Sea, E Sussex, TN38 9JT
*Major Shareholder:* Antonio Henriquez-Ramirez
*Officers:* Antonio Henriquez-Ramirez, Secretary; Antonio Henriquez-Ramirez [1958] Director [Spanish]

**Canconc Ltd**
*Incorporated:* 26 February 2019
*Registered Office:* 65 Hatherley Grove, London, W2 5RE
*Major Shareholder:* Keir Fitz-Gibbon
*Officers:* Keir Fitz-Gibbon [1962] Director/Chief Executive [British/American]

**Candover UK Ltd**
*Incorporated:* 2 January 2019
*Registered Office:* 14 The Business Village, Wexham Road, Slough, Berks, SL2 5HF
*Major Shareholder:* David Boakye Ansah
*Officers:* David Boakye Ansah [1988] Director; Darroll Hornbuckle [1951] Director [South African]

**Cannabinoidmeds Limited**
*Incorporated:* 16 August 2018
*Registered Office:* 54a Church Road, Ashford, Surrey, TW15 2TS
*Major Shareholder:* Amit Kochhar
*Officers:* Amit Kochhar [1976] Director

**Cannaid Ltd**
*Incorporated:* 17 January 2019
*Registered Office:* Manchester Tech Incubator, Oxford Road, Manchester, M1 7ED
*Shareholders:* Katy Alice Rea; David Hohne
*Officers:* David Hohne [1985] Director/Project Manager [German]; Katy Alice Rea [1987] Managing Director

**Cannamedical Pharma UK Limited**
*Incorporated:* 8 November 2018
*Registered Office:* No 1 London Bridge, London, SE1 9BG
*Major Shareholder:* David Friedrich Wilhelm John Henn
*Officers:* David Friedrich Wilhelm John Henn [1990] Director [German]; Gianfranco Salerno [1975] Director/Chief Legal Officer [Canadian]

**Cannapharm Limited**
*Incorporated:* 6 August 2018
*Registered Office:* 34 34 Darlan Road, London, SW6 5BT
*Major Shareholder:* Gavin Scott Leslie
*Officers:* Gavin Scott Leslie [1996] Director/Chief Executive

**Cannerald Group Ltd**
*Incorporated:* 20 December 2018
*Registered Office:* Suite 41, Victoria House, 38 Surrey Quays Road, London, SE16 7DX
*Shareholders:* Maik Marcel Pietrowski; Sascha Adrian Waeschle; Levin Kim Amweg
*Officers:* Levin Kim Amweg [1994] Director/Entrepreneur [Swiss]; Maik Marcel Pietrowski [1993] Director/Entrepreneur [Polish]; Sascha Adrian Waeschle [1995] Director/Entrepreneur [German]

**Cape Pharmaceuticals Ltd**
*Incorporated:* 25 January 2012
*Net Worth:* £8,664  *Total Assets:* £55,969
*Registered Office:* Shawn Buildings, 72 Cardigan Street, Luton, Beds, LU1 1RR
*Major Shareholder:* Sharan Patel
*Officers:* Sharan Patel [1987] Director

**Capella Medical Device Ltd**
*Incorporated:* 4 February 2019
*Registered Office:* Flat 6, Banister Grange, Banister Road, Southampton, SO15 2JN
*Major Shareholder:* Mohammad Reza Barmaki
*Officers:* Mohammad Reza Barmaki [1952] Director/Businessman

**Caragen (UK) Limited**
*Incorporated:* 6 October 2016
*Registered Office:* c/o Distinctive Medical Limited, 3 Seymour Court, Tudor Road, Manor Park, Runcorn, Cheshire, WA7 1SY
*Major Shareholder:* Andrew O'Connell
*Officers:* Andrew O'Connell [1961] Director [Irish]

**Carbosynth Limited**
*Incorporated:* 6 April 2006  *Employees:* 68
*Net Worth:* £2,955,279  *Total Assets:* £6,821,055
*Registered Office:* 8 & 9 Old Station Business Park, Compton, Newbury, Berks, RG20 6NE
*Parent:* Carbosynth Holdings Limited
*Officers:* Philip Jonathan Dawes, Secretary; James Bryce [1947] Director/Consultant; Philip Jonathan Dawes [1963] Finance Director; Dr Vanessa Mary Eastwick-Field [1962] Director/Chemist; Dr Victoria Gibson [1971] Technical Director

**Carbotang Limited**
*Incorporated:* 8 September 2009
*Registered Office:* 8-9 Old Station Business Park, Compton, Berks, RG20 6NE
*Parent:* Healtang Biotech Co Ltd
*Officers:* Vanessa Mary Eastwick-Field, Secretary; Dr Vanessa Mary Eastwick-Field [1962] Director; Chengzhen Jiang [1962] Deputy Director [Chinese]; Yilin Tang [1954] Director [Chinese]

**Cardio Pro Limited**
*Incorporated:* 15 July 2015
*Previous:* 09687192 Limited
*Net Worth:* £28,078  *Total Assets:* £1,439,557
*Registered Office:* Wayman House, 141 Wickham Road, Shirley, Croydon, Surrey, CR0 8TE
*Major Shareholder:* Abestis Iroglidis
*Officers:* Jeffrey Allen Altman [1952] Director/Chartered Accountant

**Care Healthcare Ltd**
*Incorporated:* 6 April 2018
*Registered Office:* 81a Spencer Road, Harrow, Middlesex, HA3 7AN
*Major Shareholder:* Priyankaben Amin
*Officers:* Priyankaben Amin [1988] Director

**John Carrington Limited**
Incorporated: 20 October 2006  Employees: 8
Net Worth: £448,551  Total Assets: £723,495
Registered Office: Carringtons Pharmacy, 128 Rake Lane, Wallasey, Merseyside, CH45 5DL
Shareholders: John Carrington; Helen Carrington
Officers: Margaret Flower, Secretary; Helen Carrington [1958] Director; John Carrington [1957] Director

**Carun (UK) Limited**
Incorporated: 28 March 2013
Net Worth Deficit: £94,120  Total Assets: £31,406
Registered Office: Crown House, Old Gloucester Street, London, WC1N 3AX
Major Shareholder: Michal Takac
Officers: Michal Takac [1979] Director [Czech]

**Casmed International Limited**
Incorporated: 30 April 1996  Employees: 6
Net Worth: £434,204  Total Assets: £611,734
Registered Office: 5 Robin Hood Lane, Sutton, Surrey, SM1 2SW
Major Shareholder: Deborah Mary Castle
Officers: Caroline Elisabeth Woodward, Secretary; Deborah Mary Castle [1956] Director

**Castle Green (N.I.) Ltd**
Incorporated: 29 January 2019
Registered Office: 79 Mill Hill, Castlewellan, Co Down, BT31 9NB
Major Shareholder: Kevin Sweeney
Officers: Kevin Sweeney, Secretary; Kevin Sweeney [1965] Director/Salesman [Irish]

**P & A J Cattee (Wholesale) Ltd.**
Incorporated: 29 April 1964
Net Worth: £7,272,659  Total Assets: £22,205,096
Registered Office: 11 Manchester Road, Walkden, Manchester, M28 3NS
Shareholders: Peter Cattee; Angela Jane Cattee; PCT Healthcare (Holdings) Limited
Officers: Angela Jane Cattee, Secretary/Pharmacist; Angela Jane Cattee [1953] Director/Pharmacist; Peter Cattee [1952] Director; Geoffrey Alan Tims [1943] Director/Pharmacist

**CBD -Tec Limited**
Incorporated: 6 April 2018
Registered Office: Javid House, 115 Bath Street, Glasgow, G2 2SZ
Shareholders: Christopher Jamie MacKenzie; Charles Frederick Jones McCallum
Officers: Christopher Jamie MacKenzie [1989] Director; Charles Frederick Jones McCallum [1974] Director

**CBD Labz Ltd**
Incorporated: 26 February 2019
Registered Office: 20-22 Wenlock Road, London, N1 7GU
Major Shareholder: Robin Michael Howard
Officers: Robin Michael Howard [1987] Director/Sales

**CBD Oil Direct Limited**
Incorporated: 3 May 2018
Registered Office: 6 Silverbanks Road, Cambuslang, Glasgow, G72 7FJ
Officers: John Semple [1943] Director/Entrepreneur

**CBD Platinum Ltd**
Incorporated: 14 February 2019
Registered Office: Kemp House, 160 City Road, London, EC1V 2NX
Major Shareholder: Monica Foster
Officers: Monica Foster [1995] Director/Entrepreneur

**CBD Vape Ltd**
Incorporated: 24 October 2018
Registered Office: 37 Howden Road, Manchester, M9 0RQ
Major Shareholder: Daniel Jones
Officers: Daniel Jones [1983] Director

**CBD4You Limited**
Incorporated: 28 January 2019
Registered Office: Flat 5, 11 Warwick Road, Barnet, Herts, EN5 5EE
Major Shareholder: Lloyd Alexander James Wilkinson
Officers: Lloyd Alexander James Wilkinson [1992] Director

**CBS Trade Limited**
Incorporated: 16 January 2018
Registered Office: 27 Old Gloucester Street, London, WC1N 3AX
Major Shareholder: Aleksandr Petrunin
Officers: Aleksandr Petrunin [1974] Director/Entrepreneur [Russian]

**Cebrenex Limited**
Incorporated: 11 February 2019
Registered Office: 1a Crown Lane, London, SW16 3DJ
Officers: Megan Janke [1994] Director/Consultant [South African]

**Celestial Pharma Ltd**
Incorporated: 14 November 2018
Registered Office: 36 Oxford Drive, Acocks Green, Birmingham, B27 6SH
Shareholders: Abbas Ali Fazal; Shahbaz Baig Mirza
Officers: Abbas Ali Fazal [1986] Director/Pharmacist; Shahbaz Baig Mirza [1987] Director

**Celgene Limited**
Incorporated: 2 June 2005  Employees: 152
Net Worth: £83,576,944  Total Assets: £190,243,632
Registered Office: 1 Longwalk Road, Stockley Park, Uxbridge, Middlesex, UB11 1DB
Parent: Celgene UK Manufacturing (II) Limited
Officers: Patrick Eugene Flanigan III [1973] Director [American]; Remo Gujer [1973] Director [Swiss]; Tuomo Tapani Patsi [1964] Director [Finnish]; David Walter Pignolet [1963] Director [Swiss]; Nakisa Serry [1965] Director [American]

**Celgene UK Distribution Limited**
Incorporated: 6 May 2005
Net Worth: £15,107  Total Assets: £24,108
Registered Office: 7 Albemarle Street, London, W1S 4HQ
Parent: Celgene Corporation
Officers: David Walter Pignolet [1963] Director [Swiss]; Nakisa Serry [1965] Director [American]

**Cellchem UK Limited**
Incorporated: 9 November 2018
Registered Office: 1B, First Floor, 142 Johnson Street, Southall, Middlesex, UB2 5FD
Officers: Soumendranath Ghosh [1968] Director/Consultant [Indian]; Shashank Jain [1976] Director

**Cellcosmo Suisse Limited**
Incorporated: 13 February 2018
Registered Office: Chase Business Centre, 39-41 Chase Side, London, N14 5BP
Shareholders: Kuan-Ying Lee; Chen-Hsing Lee; Su-Li Chen
Officers: Chen-Hsing Lee [1982] Director [Taiwanese]

**Cellexa Limited**
*Incorporated:* 22 August 2011
*Net Worth:* £1  *Total Assets:* £1
*Registered Office:* 2 Marypole Walk, Exeter, EX4 7HB
*Officers:* Todor Todorov [1968] Director [Bulgarian]; Tsvetelina Yankova Todorova [1973] Director/Financial Adviser [Bulgarian]

**Celloxess (Europe) Limited**
*Incorporated:* 22 September 2016
*Net Worth Deficit:* £24,851  *Total Assets:* £6,301
*Registered Office:* Griffins Court, 24-32 London Road, Newbury, Berks, RG14 1JX
*Shareholders:* Michael Close; Parviz Gharagozloo
*Officers:* Michael Close, Secretary; Michael Close [1971] Director; Parviz Gharagozloo [1960] Director

**Cellpath Limited**
*Incorporated:* 9 July 1984  *Employees:* 90
*Net Worth:* £2,787,715  *Total Assets:* £6,661,234
*Registered Office:* Unit 80 Mochdre Industrial Estate, Mochdre, Newtown, Powys, SY16 4LE
*Parent:* Cellpath (Holdings) Limited
*Officers:* Paul James Hatton Webber, Secretary; Paul James Hatton Webber [1964] Director; Peter James Webber [1935] Director; Philip Leslie John Webber [1966] Director; Clement Trevor Wheatley [1943] Director

**Celltrion Healthcare United Kingdom Limited**
*Incorporated:* 19 November 2018
*Registered Office:* Regus Wellington House, East Road, Cambridge, CB1 1BH
*Shareholder:* Jungjin Seo
*Officers:* Hangi Lee [1977] Director [South Korean]

**Celtis Healthcare Ltd**
*Incorporated:* 21 June 2016
*Net Worth:* £7,119  *Total Assets:* £77,488
*Registered Office:* c/o Accounting Contact, Coltwood House, 2 Tongham Road, Farnham, Surrey, GU10 1PH
*Shareholders:* Vanitaben Pankajkumar Patel; PVPharma Healthcare Private Limited
*Officers:* Pankajkumar Vastaram Patel [1971] Managing Director [Indian]; Vanitaben Pankajkumar Patel [1974] Director [Indian]; Venin Pankajkumar Patel [1994] Executive Director [Indian]

**Cenote Pharma Limited**
*Incorporated:* 10 December 2015
*Net Worth Deficit:* £70,655  *Total Assets:* £67,267
*Registered Office:* Griffins Court, 24-32 London Road, Newbury, Berks, RG14 1JX
*Major Shareholder:* Paul Ranson
*Officers:* Paul Ranson [1953] Director

**Centline Ltd**
*Incorporated:* 15 October 2012  *Employees:* 1
*Net Worth:* £438  *Total Assets:* £2,387
*Registered Office:* 4 Pathfields, Shere, Guildford, Surrey, GU5 9HP
*Major Shareholder:* Ahmed Al-Hemyari
*Officers:* Ahmed Al-Hemyari [1969] Director/Businessman

**Centurion Park Pharmaceuticals Limited**
*Incorporated:* 30 January 2014
*Net Worth Deficit:* £64,331  *Total Assets:* £1,302
*Registered Office:* 98 Palmerston Road, Chatham, Kent, ME4 5SJ
*Major Shareholder:* Muhammad Taha Sohawon
*Officers:* Muhammad Taha Sohawon [1970] Director/Pharmacist

**Ceracoat Ltd**
*Incorporated:* 20 February 2019
*Registered Office:* Suite 33854, Advantage Business Centre, 132-134 Great Ancoats Street, Manchester, M4 6DE
*Shareholders:* Elio Keller; Carmen Keller
*Officers:* Carmen Keller, Secretary; Dr Elio Keller [1957] Director [Swiss]

**CEU Pharm Ltd**
*Incorporated:* 26 September 2017
*Registered Office:* 165 Praed Street, London, W2 1RH
*Major Shareholder:* Natalia Fecsuova
*Officers:* Natalia Fecsuova [1992] Director/Pharmacist [Slovak]

**CG Pharma Ltd**
*Incorporated:* 5 September 2016
*Net Worth:* £18,620  *Total Assets:* £283,953
*Registered Office:* 84 Gibbs Field, Bishop's Stortford, Herts, CM23 4EZ
*Major Shareholder:* Hannah Gillian Currey
*Officers:* Hannah Gillian Currey [1991] Director

**Chameleon Planet Ltd**
*Incorporated:* 17 January 2017
*Registered Office:* Kemp House, 152-160 City Road, London, EC1V 2NX
*Major Shareholder:* Michael Hamill
*Officers:* Michael Hamill, Secretary; Michael Hamill [1969] Director/Project Manager [Irish]

**Chanelle Medical GB Limited**
*Incorporated:* 5 May 2016
*Net Worth:* £1,001  *Total Assets:* £1,001
*Registered Office:* Lodge Down Stables, Lambourn Woodlands, Hungerford, Berks, RG17 7BJ
*Major Shareholder:* Michael Hilary Burke
*Officers:* Lady Chanelle McCoy, Secretary; Michael Burke [1947] Director [Irish]; Lady Chanelle McCoy [1976] Director [Irish]

**Chanelle Medical U.K. Limited**
*Incorporated:* 2 November 1999  *Employees:* 3
*Net Worth:* £1,216,029  *Total Assets:* £2,945,904
*Registered Office:* 5 Liverpool Terrace, Worthing, W Sussex, BN11 1TA
*Parent:* Healthcare Pharma Limited
*Officers:* John Cochrane [1957] Director; Stuart John Overend [1970] Director

**Chanelle Vet U.K. Limited**
*Incorporated:* 4 April 2007  *Employees:* 10
*Net Worth:* £30,706  *Total Assets:* £1,637,249
*Registered Office:* Lodge Down House, Lambourn Woodlands, Hungerford, Berks, RG17 7BJ
*Major Shareholder:* Michael Hilary Burke
*Officers:* Lady Chanelle McCoy, Secretary/Director [Irish]; Michael Hilary Burke [1947] Director [Irish]; Chanelle McCoy [1976] Director [Irish]

**Philip Chapper & Company Limited**
*Incorporated:* 1 February 1971
*Net Worth:* £1,190,000  *Total Assets:* £2,140,000
*Registered Office:* Unit 30 Orbital 25 Business Park, Tolpits Lane, Watford, Herts, WD18 9DA
*Shareholders:* Philip Chapper; Vera Chapper
*Officers:* Vera Chapper, Secretary; Jonathan Simon Chapper [1977] Director/Solicitor; Paul Anthony Chapper [1981] Director; Philip Chapper [1944] Director/Pharmacist; Vera Chapper [1948] Director/Company Secretary

**Charlwood Pharma Limited**
*Incorporated:* 17 July 2015
*Net Worth:* £260,979  *Total Assets:* £327,201
*Registered Office:* Trotwood The Firs, Odiham, Hook, Hants, RG29 1PP
*Shareholders:* William David Potter; Eleanor Margaret Craig Farrant
*Officers:* Andrew David Farrant [1965] Director; Eleanor Margaret Craig Farrant [1970] Director; Lisa Jane Potter [1968] Director; William David Potter [1968] Director

**Charmant UK Co., Limited**
*Incorporated:* 25 October 1994  *Employees:* 18
*Net Worth:* £2,915,511  *Total Assets:* £3,487,567
*Registered Office:* Hill House, 1 Little New Street, London, EC4A 3TR
*Officers:* Toshihiro Matsumiya [1961] Director/Chief Financial Officer [Japanese]; Masao Miyachi [1958] Managing Director [Japanese]; Satoshi Otsuki [1967] Director/Independent Consultant [Japanese]

**F Chaudry Limited**
*Incorporated:* 8 December 2009  *Employees:* 1
*Net Worth:* £534  *Total Assets:* £8,460
*Registered Office:* 32 Azalea Road, Blackburn, BB2 6JU
*Major Shareholder:* Faisal Ahmed Chaudry
*Officers:* Faisal Ahmed Chaudry [1984] Director

**Chefarma Limited**
*Incorporated:* 4 June 2015
*Net Worth:* £420,061  *Total Assets:* £542,071
*Registered Office:* 49 Green Lanes, London, N16 9BU
*Officers:* Sevasti Chatzipavli, Secretary; Ioannis Chatzipavlis [1976] Director/Businessman [Greek]

**Chela Animal Health Limited**
*Incorporated:* 21 July 2014
*Registered Office:* First Floor, Roxburghe House, 273-287 Regent Street, London, W1B 2HA
*Parent:* Orion Holdings (UK) Limited
*Officers:* Minal Shah [1984] Director; Rajiv Bharat Kumar Shah [1985] Director

**Chelmack Limited**
*Incorporated:* 31 August 2001  *Employees:* 14
*Net Worth Deficit:* £258,276  *Total Assets:* £1,216,080
*Registered Office:* The Old Mill, 9 Soar Lane, Leicester, LE3 5DE
*Parent:* Smartway PW Holdings Limited
*Officers:* Kirti Patel, Secretary/Pharmacist; Hitendra Patel [1966] Director/Pharmacist; Kirti Patel [1968] Director/Pharmacist

**Chelsea Pharma Limited**
*Incorporated:* 6 October 2017
*Registered Office:* Unit 1N Ground Floor Right, Gateway Trading Estate, Hythe Road, London, NW10 6RJ
*Major Shareholder:* Mohammed Dhaffer Aal-Oleiwi
*Officers:* Mohammed Dhaffer Aal-Oleiwi [1994] Director [Iraqi]

**Chemi-Call Ltd**
*Incorporated:* 13 January 2003  *Employees:* 16
*Net Worth:* £550,725  *Total Assets:* £1,680,425
*Registered Office:* 38 Woodberry Grove, North Finchley, London, N12 0DL
*Shareholder:* Alpesh Bhanuchandra Shah
*Officers:* Bhanuchandra Shah, Secretary; Alpesh Bhanuchandra Shah [1972] Director; Bhanuchandra Shah [1945] Director & Secretary

**Chemidex Generics Limited**
*Incorporated:* 23 July 1999  *Employees:* 1
*Net Worth:* £41,655,200  *Total Assets:* £42,801,256
*Registered Office:* Chemidex House, Unit 7 Egham Business Village, Crabtree Road, Egham, Surrey, TW20 8RB
*Shareholders:* Navinchandra Jamnadas; Varsha Navinchandas Engineer
*Officers:* Nikesh Engineer [1985] Director/Doctor

**Chemilines Group Holdings Limited**
*Incorporated:* 30 November 2001  *Employees:* 113
*Net Worth:* £18,482,000  *Total Assets:* £24,584,000
*Registered Office:* Chemilines House, Alperton Lane, Wembley, Middlesex, HA0 1DX
*Shareholders:* Ravindra Prabhudas Karia; Jagdish Prabhudas Karia
*Officers:* Ravindra Prabhudas Karia, Secretary; Jagdish Prabhudas Karia [1958] Director; Ravindra Prabhudas Karia [1953] Director

**Chemilines Limited**
*Incorporated:* 28 July 1987  *Employees:* 84
*Net Worth:* £6,462,000  *Total Assets:* £10,114,000
*Registered Office:* Chemilines House, Alperton Lane, Wembley, Middlesex, HA0 1DX
*Parent:* Chemilines Group Holdings Limited
*Officers:* Ravindra Prabhudas Karia, Secretary; Sadhana Ravindra Karia, Secretary; Jagdish Prabhudas Karia [1958] Director; Ravindra Prabhudas Karia [1953] Director

**Chemx Ltd**
*Incorporated:* 23 May 2017
*Registered Office:* 2-3 Block A, 350 Argyle Street, Glasgow, G2 8ND
*Major Shareholder:* Ranjit Vishawambar Sail
*Officers:* Ranjit Vishawambar Sail [1985] Director

**Chemys Limited**
*Incorporated:* 22 April 2015
*Net Worth Deficit:* £61,227  *Total Assets:* £107,202
*Registered Office:* 550 Uxbridge Road, Pinner, Middlesex, HA5 3LX
*Major Shareholder:* Venichand Ranmal Harania
*Officers:* Venichand Ranmal Harania [1942] Director/Pharmacist; Siddhit Shah [1976] Director

**Chesdeg Limited**
*Incorporated:* 18 August 2016
*Registered Office:* 64 Foss Avenue, Croydon, Surrey, CR0 4EU
*Major Shareholder:* Evelyn Bannor-Addae
*Officers:* Evelyn Bannor - Addae [1972] Director/Nurse; Ama Serwah Brenyah [1977] Director [Ghanaian]; Samuel Kwesi Brenyah [1977] Director [Ghanaian]

**Chewton Ventures Limited**
*Incorporated:* 28 February 2013
*Net Worth:* £22,307  *Total Assets:* £2,607,844
*Registered Office:* 483 Green Lane, Palmers Green, London, N13 4BS
*Officers:* Salil Shrivastava [1971] Director [Indian]

**Chiesi Healthcare Limited**
Incorporated: 30 December 1996
Net Worth: £6,364,000   Total Assets: £7,054,000
Registered Office: 333 Styal Road, Manchester, M22 5LG
Parent: Chiesi Farmaceutici SpA
Officers: Matthew Wiggetts, Secretary; Alberto Chiesi [1938] Director [Italian]; Alessandro Chiesi [1966] Director [Italian]; Paolo Chiesi [1940] Director [Italian]; Thomas Joseph Delahoyde [1958] Managing Director; Ugo di Francesco [1960] Director [Italian]; Andrew Philip Dickinson [1970] Director; Michael Jonathon Dixon [1965] Director; Danilo Piroli [1954] Director [Italian]; Marco Vecchia [1960] Director/Lawyer [Italian]

**Chiesi Limited**
Incorporated: 18 June 1987   Employees: 250
Net Worth: £20,020,000   Total Assets: £76,823,000
Registered Office: 333 Styal Road, Manchester, M22 5LG
Parent: Chiesi Healthcare Ltd
Officers: Matthew Wiggetts, Secretary; Alberto Chiesi [1938] Director [Italian]; Alessandro Chiesi [1966] Director [Italian]; Paolo Chiesi [1940] Director [Italian]; Thomas Joseph Delahoyde [1958] Managing Director; Ugo di Francesco [1960] Director [Italian]; Andrew Philip Dickinson [1970] Director; Michael Jonathon Dixon [1965] Director; Danilo Piroli [1954] Director [Italian]; Marco Vecchia [1960] Director/Lawyer [Italian]

**Chikhurst Limited**
Incorporated: 2 June 2005
Registered Office: 10 Tythe Barn Lane, Shirley, Solihull, W Midlands, B90 1RW
Major Shareholder: Chikwendu Onyemachi Uruakpa
Officers: Dr Chikwendu Onyemachi Uruakpa, Secretary/Medical Practitioner; Dr Chikwendu Onyemachi Uruakpa [1959] Director/Medical Doctor

**Chirock Trading Ltd**
Incorporated: 11 October 2018
Registered Office: 20-22 Wenlock Road, London, N1 7GU
Shareholders: Chisom Chika Onyechi; Peter Meszaros
Officers: Chisom Chika Onyechi [1994] Director [Nigerian]; Peter Meszaros [1981] Director [Hungarian]

**Chitorhino Ltd**
Incorporated: 24 May 2018
Registered Office: 71-75 Shelton Street, London, WC2H 9JQ
Major Shareholder: Patrick Melder
Officers: Dr Patrick Melder, Secretary; Dr Patrick Melder [1967] Director/Physician [American]

**Chloraco Healthcare Limited**
Incorporated: 19 January 2016   Employees: 18
Net Worth: £285,290   Total Assets: £1,825,370
Registered Office: Waters Edge, Potters Lane, Samlesbury, Preston, Lancs, PR5 0UE
Major Shareholder: Rachel Claire Cookson
Officers: Michael Derek Cookson, Secretary; Rachel Claire Cookson [1981] Director

**CHM Trading Limited**
Incorporated: 28 August 2018
Registered Office: 49 Mowbray Road, Edgware, Middlesex, HA8 8JL
Major Shareholder: Rivkah Loebenstein
Officers: Rivkah Loebenstein [1985] Director [German]

**Chronicles Medical Consulting Ltd**
Incorporated: 23 February 2017
Net Worth Deficit: £880   Total Assets: £120
Registered Office: c/o Pelican Pharmacy, 344 Manchester Road, West Timperley, Altrincham, Cheshire, WA14 5NH
Officers: Gary Kai Wai Chan, Secretary; Gary Kai Wai Chan [1979] Director

**Cibus Animal Nutrition Ltd**
Incorporated: 22 October 2015
Registered Office: Suite 1, Excelsior House, 3-5 Balfour Road, Ilford, Essex, IG1 4HP
Shareholder: Farhan Karim Shamshudin
Officers: Farhan Karim Shamshudin [1989] Director [Kenyan]

**CIGA Healthcare Limited**
Incorporated: 5 January 2005   Employees: 22
Net Worth: £304,584   Total Assets: £3,005,476
Registered Office: c/o Hill Vellacott, Chambre of Commerce House, 22 Great Victoria Street, Belfast, BT2 7BA
Major Shareholder: Irwin Armstrong
Officers: Allan Armstrong [1978] Director; George William Irwin Armstrong [1950] Director/Chief Executive Officer; Neill Armstrong [1975] Director; Michael Hamilton Irvine [1974] Director/Chartered Accountant

**Cimex Lectularius Limited**
Incorporated: 8 March 2013
Net Worth: £20,258   Total Assets: £246,919
Registered Office: Willowbrook House, 25 Church Street, Nassington, Peterborough, PE8 6QG
Shareholders: Gareth John Purnell; Colin Gordon Campbell
Officers: Gareth John Purnell [1965] Director/Sales Consultant

**Cis Pharmassist Limited**
Incorporated: 15 June 2010
Net Worth: £161,673   Total Assets: £1,271,702
Registered Office: 19b Willow Way, Christchurch, Dorset, BH23 1JJ
Major Shareholder: Tetiana Muratova
Officers: Julie Ferris [1968] Director

**Citco Chemicals Ltd.**
Incorporated: 5 September 2006
Net Worth: £31,856   Total Assets: £160,112
Registered Office: Regent House, 316 Beulah Hill, London, SE19 3HF
Officers: Anthony Graeme Peplar [1967] Director/Consultant [South African]

**Citux Medical Limited**
Incorporated: 24 May 2018
Registered Office: 130 Old Street, London, EC1V 9BD
Officers: Raymond Chanengeta [1979] Director [Zimbabwean]

**CKF Limited**
Incorporated: 16 June 1992
Net Worth Deficit: £17,202   Total Assets: £15,768
Registered Office: 72 Wardour Street, London, W1F 0TD
Shareholder: Chan Kwai Fong
Officers: Pui Yi Fong, Secretary; Chan Kwai Fong [1963] Director/Pharmacist

**Clarity at Home Ltd**
Incorporated: 22 July 2010
Registered Office: Endeavour House, Coopers End Road, London Stansted Airport, Stansted, Essex, CM24 1SJ
Parent: Clarity Pharma Holdings Ltd
Officers: Tanya Monteith [1973] Director

**Clarity Commercial Ltd**
*Incorporated:* 11 August 2010
*Registered Office:* Endeavour House, Coopers End Road, London Stansted Airport, Stansted, Essex, CM24 1SJ
*Parent:* Clarity Pharma Holdings Ltd
*Officers:* Andrew Green, Secretary; Tanya Monteith [1973] Director

**Clarity DTP Ltd**
*Incorporated:* 10 February 2009
*Registered Office:* Endeavour House, Coopers End Road, London Stansted Airport, Stansted, Essex, CM24 1SJ
*Major Shareholder:* Margo Scott
*Officers:* Andrew Green, Secretary; Tanya Monteith [1973] Director

**Clarity Markets Ltd**
*Incorporated:* 20 October 2011
*Registered Office:* Endeavour House, Coopers End Road, London Stansted Airport, Stansted, Essex, CM24 1SJ
*Parent:* Clarity Pharma Holdings Ltd
*Officers:* Tanya Monteith [1973] Director

**Clarity Pharma Holdings Ltd**
*Incorporated:* 13 March 2002  *Employees:* 17
*Net Worth:* £4,647,000  *Total Assets:* £11,139,000
*Registered Office:* Causeway House, Dane Street, Bishop's Stortford, Herts, CM23 3BT
*Parent:* Clarity Global Pharma Solutions S.L
*Officers:* Andrew Green, Secretary; Tanya Monteith [1973] Director

**Clarity Pharma Ltd**
*Incorporated:* 28 October 1998  *Employees:* 17
*Net Worth:* £4,374,000  *Total Assets:* £10,866,000
*Registered Office:* Causeway House, 1 Dane Street, Bishop's Stortford, Herts, CM23 3BT
*Parent:* Clarity Pharma Holdings Ltd
*Officers:* Andrew Green, Secretary; Tanya Monteith [1973] Director

**Clarity Woundcare Ltd**
*Incorporated:* 31 July 2015
*Registered Office:* Endeavour House, Coopers End Road, London Stansted Airport, Stansted, Essex, CM24 1SJ
*Parent:* Clarity Pharma Holdings Ltd
*Officers:* Tanya Monteith [1973] Director

**C G Clark Limited**
*Incorporated:* 5 April 2000
*Net Worth:* £1,219,330  *Total Assets:* £1,811,323
*Registered Office:* 8 The Courtyards, Victoria Road, Leeds, LS14 2LB
*Shareholders:* Marshall Anthony Glynn; Anthony Golombeck
*Officers:* Marshall Anthony Glynn, Secretary/Pharmacist; Marshall Anthony Glynn [1962] Director/Pharmacist; Anthony Golombeck [1955] Director

**Clear Eyes Pharma Limited**
*Incorporated:* 16 December 2014
*Registered Office:* Suite 5, Clockhouse Court, 5-7 London Road, St Albans, Herts, AL1 1LA
*Parent:* Prestige Brands Holdings, Inc.
*Officers:* Ronald Lombardi [1964] Director/Chief Executive Officer [American]; William P'pool [1965] Director/SVP, General Counsel and Corporate Secretary [American]; Christine Sacco [1975] Director/Chief Financial Officer [American]

**Clever Connect Ltd**
*Incorporated:* 8 May 2018
*Registered Office:* 52 Abbeville Road, London, SW4 9NF
*Major Shareholder:* Jonathan Charles Edmund Alexander Cuffe
*Officers:* Jonathan Charles Edmund Alexander Cuffe [1985] Director/Entrepreneur

**Click Solutions Ltd**
*Incorporated:* 14 December 2017
*Registered Office:* Maniland House, 12 Court Parade, East Lane, Wembley, Middlesex, HA0 3HU
*Major Shareholder:* Jayesh Kumar Manilal Patel
*Officers:* Jayesh Kumar Manilal Patel [1954] Director

**Client-Pharma Ltd**
*Incorporated:* 8 October 2013  *Employees:* 11
*Net Worth:* £435,161  *Total Assets:* £1,393,029
*Registered Office:* 10-12 Mulberry Green, Harlow, Essex, CM17 0ET
*Shareholder:* Gary Campbell
*Officers:* Gary Campbell [1970] Director; Jonathan Paul Kilham [1966] Director; Andrew John Scott Walton-Green [1963] Director; Colin Wood [1968] Director

**Client-Pharmacy UK Ltd**
*Incorporated:* 10 February 2016
*Registered Office:* 10-12 Mulberry Green, Harlow, Essex, CM17 0ET
*Parent:* Client-Pharma Ltd
*Officers:* Gary Campbell [1970] Director; Jonathan Paul Kilham [1966] Director; Andrew John Scott Walton-Green [1963] Director/Chartered Accountant; Colin Wood [1968] Director/Accountant

**Clifton Organic Limited**
*Incorporated:* 1 December 2016  *Employees:* 1
*Net Worth:* £8,982  *Total Assets:* £27,782
*Registered Office:* Devonshire House, 1 Devonshire Street, London, W1W 5DR
*Shareholders:* Maxim Ippolitov; Levan Merabishvili; Georgi Sulkhanishvili
*Officers:* Levan Merabishvili [1969] Director [Georgian]

**Clinic Supply Ltd**
*Incorporated:* 27 March 2018
*Registered Office:* 9 Aylmer Road, London, N2 0BS
*Major Shareholder:* Maryam Hassan Ghalyaie
*Officers:* Maryam Hassan Ghalyaie [1984] Director/Dentist [Iranian]

**Clinical Direct Ltd**
*Incorporated:* 3 April 2017
*Net Worth:* £1  *Total Assets:* £1
*Registered Office:* 15-16 Waverley Industrial Units, Waverley Street, Bathgate, W Lothian, EH48 4HY
*Parent:* Semtrad Limited
*Officers:* Steven Murray, Secretary; Steven Edward Murray [1969] Director

**Clinical Services International Ltd**
*Incorporated:* 20 October 2016
*Net Worth:* £39,183  *Total Assets:* £519,290
*Registered Office:* 64 Cathcart Road, London, SW10 9JQ
*Major Shareholder:* Evangelia Vanessa Dekou
*Officers:* Dr Evangelia Vanessa Dekou [1973] Managing Director

**Clinicpharma Limited**
Incorporated: 13 April 2005  Employees: 13
Net Worth: £249,222  Total Assets: £470,728
Registered Office: Old Bank Buildings, Upper High Street, Cradley Heath, W Midlands, B64 5HY
Shareholders: Gurnam Singh; Sukhwir Kaur Rai
Officers: Sukhwir Kaur Rai, Secretary; Gurnam Singh [1970] Director/Pharmacist

**Clinigen CTS Limited**
Incorporated: 15 January 2004
Registered Office: Pitcairn House, Crown Square, Centrum 100, Burton on Trent, Staffs, DE14 2WW
Parent: Clinigen Healthcare Limited
Officers: Amanda Miller, Secretary; Martin James Abell [1974] Director; Shaun Edward Chilton [1967] Director

**Clinigen Group PLC**
Incorporated: 12 December 2008  Employees: 727
Net Worth: £311,386,304  Total Assets: £594,351,360
Registered Office: Pitcairn House, Crown Square, Centrum 100, Burton on Trent, Staffs, DE14 2WW
Officers: Amanda Miller, Secretary; Martin James Abell [1974] Executive Director; Peter Vance Allen [1956] Director; Alan Keith Boyd [1954] Director; Shaun Edward Chilton [1967] Director/Chief Operating Officer; John Hartup [1951] Director; Anne Philomena Hyland [1960] Director; Ian James Nicholson [1960] Director

**Clinigen Healthcare Limited**
Incorporated: 18 May 2007  Employees: 32
Net Worth: £70,231,000  Total Assets: £230,024,000
Registered Office: Pitcairn House, Crown Square, Centrum 100, Burton on Trent, Staffs, DE14 2WW
Parent: Clinigen Holdings Limited
Officers: Amanda Miller, Secretary; Martin James Abell [1974] Director; Shaun Edward Chilton [1967] Director

**Clinimarg Ltd**
Incorporated: 13 June 2013  Employees: 3
Net Worth: £119,896  Total Assets: £663,795
Registered Office: 4th Floor, Kings Suite, 15 College Road, Harrow, Middlesex, HA1 1BA
Shareholders: Nimeshkumar Somabhai Patel; Niruben Nimeshkumar Patel
Officers: Nimeshkumar Somabhai Patel [1976] Director

**Clinimed Limited**
Incorporated: 28 June 1982  Employees: 115
Net Worth: £1,354,202  Total Assets: £10,438,991
Registered Office: Cavell House, Knaves Beech Way, Loudwater, High Wycombe, Bucks, HP10 9QY
Parent: Clinimed (Holdings) Limited
Officers: Suzanne Bryden, Secretary; Sean LEA Farbrother [1967] Director/Group Chief Executive

**Clinitech Medical Ltd**
Incorporated: 18 November 2014
Net Worth Deficit: £22,193  Total Assets: £22,577
Registered Office: Kemp House, 152-160 City Road, London, EC1V 2NX
Major Shareholder: Christopher Docking
Officers: Christopher Paul Docking [1980] Managing Director; Katie Mahoney [1984] Director

**Clinova Limited**
Incorporated: 23 May 2006  Employees: 9
Net Worth: £314,029  Total Assets: £955,018
Registered Office: International House, Southampton International Business Park, George Curl Way, Southampton, SO18 2RZ
Shareholders: Arsalan Karim; Charles Ebubedike
Officers: Charles Ebubedike, Secretary; Charles Ebubedike [1981] Director; Arsalan Karim [1980] Director

**Clinres UK Limited**
Incorporated: 14 February 2013  Employees: 1
Net Worth: £71,202  Total Assets: £84,434
Registered Office: Manufactory House, Bell Lane, Hertford, SG14 1BP
Major Shareholder: Mollie Davies
Officers: Mollie Davies [1946] Director

**Clyde Valley Cannaceuticals Ltd**
Incorporated: 16 January 2019
Registered Office: 54 Vulcan Street, Motherwell, N Lanarks, ML1 1HB
Major Shareholder: Mark Leaning
Officers: Mark Leaning [1977] Director and Company Secretary

**Clymed Healthcare Ltd**
Incorporated: 8 August 2015  Employees: 1
Net Worth Deficit: £98,750  Total Assets: £27,020
Registered Office: New Bridge Street House, 30-34 New Bridge Street, London, EC4V 6BJ
Major Shareholder: Kamlesh Phulwani
Officers: Dharmesh Gordadhanbhai Savalia [1975] Director

**CM & D Pharma Limited**
Incorporated: 7 August 2008
Registered Office: Elder House, St Georges Business Park, 207 Brooklands Road, Weybridge, Surrey, KT13 0TS
Officers: Luis Cantarell Rocamora [1952] Director/President and CEO, Nestle Health Science SA [Spanish]; Claudio Kuoni [1967] Director/General Counsel [Swiss]

**CM Healthcare Limited**
Incorporated: 25 May 2006
Net Worth: £9,380  Total Assets: £164,773
Registered Office: 6 Heather Gardens, Ling Lane, Scarcroft, Leeds, LS14 3HU
Major Shareholder: Leonard Korn
Officers: Leonard Korn, Secretary; Leonard Korn [1926] Director/Retired; Philip Ashley Korn [1958] Director/Sales Manager

**CoAcS Trading Limited**
Incorporated: 23 August 2005
Net Worth: £31,212  Total Assets: £32,217
Registered Office: Kimbolton House, Mount Beacon, Lansdown, Bath, BA1 5QP
Major Shareholder: Stephen Humphrey Moss
Officers: Dr Stephen Humphrey Moss, Secretary; Dr Abdel Rahman Ahmed [1952] Director; Dr Stephen Humphrey Moss [1947] Director/Pharmacist

**Coastal Core Ltd**
Incorporated: 22 September 2017
Registered Office: 32e Ballyquin Road, Limavady, Co Londonderry, BT49 9EY
Major Shareholder: Robert Wheeldon
Officers: Robert Wheeldon, Secretary; Robert Wheeldon [1983] Director/Pharmacist

**Coates Agencies Ltd**
*Incorporated:* 15 March 2013
*Net Worth:* £200,680  *Total Assets:* £281,921
*Registered Office:* 7 Soundwell Road, Staple Hill, Bristol, BS16 4QG
*Major Shareholder:* Barry Keith Dawe
*Officers:* Barry Keith Dawe [1958] Director

**Codix Pharma (UK) Limited**
*Incorporated:* 19 November 2018
*Registered Office:* The Elevation Point, Elevation House, Thames Wharf, Herringham Road, London, SE7 8NJ
*Major Shareholder:* Samson Ogunjimi
*Officers:* Samson Ogunjimi, Secretary; Olumide Olumuyiwa Adeyileka [1961] Director; Abiola Akinsanya [1968] Director; Samson Ogunjimi [1965] Director

**Cofad Ventures Ltd**
*Incorporated:* 21 June 2012
*Net Worth:* £284  *Total Assets:* £65,218
*Registered Office:* 18 Livingstone Road, Corby, Northants, NN18 8SP
*Shareholders:* Foluke Kolawole-Moradeyo; Adetunji Kolawole-Moradeyo
*Officers:* Adetunji Kolawole-Moradeyo [1953] Director/Marketing

**Colgate-Palmolive (U.K.) Limited**
*Incorporated:* 7 January 1922
*Net Worth:* £32,711,000  *Total Assets:* £92,973,000
*Registered Office:* Guildford Business Park, Middleton Road, Guildford, Surrey, GU2 8JZ
*Parent:* Colgate-Palmolive Company
*Officers:* Christopher Robert Burniston [1980] Associate Legal Director; Philip Durocher [1964] Managing Director [Canadian/American]; Charalabos Klados [1967] Director/Division General Counsel [German]; Dean Pratt [1965] Finance Director

**Collardam PLC**
*Incorporated:* 24 March 2005
*Net Worth Deficit:* £394,116
*Registered Office:* Network House, Station Yard, Thame, Oxon, OX9 3UH
*Shareholders:* Claudine Nicola Bloom; Rebecca Padayachy
*Officers:* George Victor Manolescue, Secretary; Claudine Nicola Bloom [1970] Director/Administrator; George Victor Manolescue [1953] Director/Accountant

**Colour Distributors Limited**
*Incorporated:* 24 June 1992
*Net Worth:* £1,010,165  *Total Assets:* £1,072,852
*Registered Office:* 15a Silver Street, Barnstaple, Devon, EX32 8HR
*Officers:* David William Crick, Secretary; Avril Mary Ashford [1949] Director

**Comebro International Ltd**
*Incorporated:* 11 December 2018
*Registered Office:* 33 Canterbury Road, Preston, Lancs, PR1 5PT
*Shareholder:* Mian Naveed Ahmed
*Officers:* Mian Naveed Ahmed [1973] Director [Pakistani]

**Comfylife Ltd**
*Incorporated:* 5 December 2018
*Registered Office:* Kemp House, 160 City Road, London, EC1V 2NX
*Shareholders:* Zuhail Aboobacker; Sajid Sulaiman Kunnil Sulaiman
*Officers:* Zuhail Aboobacker, Secretary; Sajid Sulaiman Kunnil Sulaiman, Secretary; Zuhail Aboobacker [1980] Director/Self Employed; Sajid Sulaiman Kunnil Sulaiman [1976] Director/Self Employed

**Conceio Consulting Ltd**
*Incorporated:* 3 August 2011
*Net Worth:* £545  *Total Assets:* £1,555
*Registered Office:* 60 Constitution Hill, Snodland, Kent, ME6 5DH
*Major Shareholder:* Christopher James Sale
*Officers:* Christopher James Sale [1987] Director/Pharmaceutical Wholesaler

**Concept Pharma UK Limited**
*Incorporated:* 8 August 2006
*Net Worth:* £108  *Total Assets:* £108
*Registered Office:* Dalton House, 60 Windsor Avenue, London, SW19 2RR
*Parent:* Merchantilia Limited
*Officers:* Chan Wai Yin [1954] Director [Chinese]

**Concord Extra Limited**
*Incorporated:* 21 May 2009  *Employees:* 10
*Net Worth Deficit:* £318,887  *Total Assets:* £67,860
*Registered Office:* 4 King Square, Bridgwater, Somerset, TA6 3YF
*Officers:* Robert Edward Robinson [1943] Director/Chief Executive Officer

**Concord Pharma Services (UK) Ltd**
*Incorporated:* 16 September 2016
*Net Worth:* £14,326  *Total Assets:* £19,248
*Registered Office:* 40 Tavistock Gardens, Ilford, Essex, IG3 9BE
*Major Shareholder:* Abdulmateen Bagwan
*Officers:* Abdulmateen Bagwan [1976] Director/Pharmacist

**Condom Dot Com Ltd.**
*Incorporated:* 3 March 2014
*Registered Office:* 19 Marina Road, Prestwick, Ayrshire, KA9 1QZ
*Major Shareholder:* Shona Gillian Longmuir
*Officers:* Shona Gillian Longmuir [1964] Director

**Condomania (UK) Limited**
*Incorporated:* 27 January 1993
*Registered Office:* Unit 1 Rivermead, Pipers Way, Thatcham, Berks, RG19 4EP
*Major Shareholder:* George Mitchell Sutherland
*Officers:* Stephen John Coke, Secretary/Chartered Accountant; Stephen John Coke [1961] Director/Chartered Accountant

**Condomania PLC**
*Incorporated:* 9 February 2000
*Registered Office:* Unit 1 Rivermead, Pipers Way, Thatcham, Berks, RG19 4EP
*Officers:* Stephen John Coke, Secretary/Chartered Accountant; Stephen John Coke [1961] Director/Chartered Accountant; Sheena Sukumaran [1971] Director

**Connected Healthcare Ltd**
*Incorporated:* 5 December 2012
*Net Worth:* £22,527  *Total Assets:* £23,307
*Registered Office:* 8e Europa Studios, Victoria Road, London, NW10 6ND
*Officers:* Mahammed Russell [1984] Director/Pharmacist

**Connective Pharma Limited**
*Incorporated:* 25 January 2016  *Employees:* 2
*Net Worth:* £30,136  *Total Assets:* £171,080
*Registered Office:* Unit 5 Progress Industrial Park, Progress Way, Croydon, Surrey, CR0 4XD
*Shareholder:* Nileshkumar Indubhai Patel
*Officers:* Nileshkumar Indubhai Patel [1974] Director [Indian]

**Connexon Global Networks Ltd**
*Incorporated:* 21 February 2017
*Registered Office:* 5 Grampian Gardens, Golders Green, London, NW2 1JH
*Major Shareholder:* Carlos German Nocera
*Officers:* Carlos German Nocera [1969] Director/Biomedical Scientist [Italian]

**Construct4lyfe Ltd**
*Incorporated:* 19 December 2017
*Registered Office:* 33 Kimbolton Court, Giffard Park, Milton Keynes, Bucks, MK14 5PS
*Officers:* Mary Nyamapfene [1959] Director

**Contract QP Resource Limited**
*Incorporated:* 2 May 2014  *Employees:* 1
*Net Worth:* £53,652  *Total Assets:* £67,363
*Registered Office:* 9 Briar Close, Blackfordby, Swadlincote, Derbys, DE11 8BW
*Major Shareholder:* Stephen Morris
*Officers:* Dr Stephen Morris [1952] Director/Pharmaceutical Chemist

**Coombe KP Limited**
*Incorporated:* 22 March 2007  *Employees:* 2
*Net Worth Deficit:* £397,120  *Total Assets:* £4,177,647
*Registered Office:* c/o Haslers, Old Station Road, Loughton, Essex, IG10 4PL
*Parent:* Pharmadent Holdings Limited
*Officers:* Hital Patel, Secretary; Bemal Patel [1973] Director/Pharmacist; Hital Patel [1974] Director/Company Secretary

**G. D. Cooper & Co Ltd**
*Incorporated:* 23 June 1978  *Employees:* 36
*Net Worth:* £5,025,521  *Total Assets:* £6,912,176
*Registered Office:* 20 Progress Way, Croydon, Surrey, CR0 4XD
*Parent:* GDC (Holdings) Ltd
*Officers:* Mahendra Meghji Shah, Secretary; Khilan Mahendra Shah [1973] Director; Mahendra Meghji Shah [1945] Director/Businessman; Rahul Mahendra Shah [1977] Director

**DB & A Cooper (Suffolk) Limited**
*Incorporated:* 15 December 1994  *Employees:* 31
*Net Worth:* £2,071,681  *Total Assets:* £2,478,444
*Registered Office:* The Flint House, Heath Farm Business Centre, Tut Hill, Bury St Edmunds, Suffolk, IP28 6LG
*Shareholders:* Angela Cooper; Douglas Barham Cooper
*Officers:* Angela Cooper, Secretary; Angela Cooper [1936] Company Secretary/Director; Nicholas Cooper [1962] Director/Pharmacist

**CooperVision Lens Care Limited**
*Incorporated:* 11 September 1972
*Previous:* Sauflon Pharmaceuticals Limited
*Net Worth:* £69,024,000  *Total Assets:* £75,802,000
*Registered Office:* Delta Park, Concorde Way, Segensworth North, Fareham, Hants, PO15 5RL
*Parent:* CooperVision (UK) Holdings Limited
*Officers:* Brian George Andrews [1978] Director/Corporate Executive [American]; Kevin Paul Barrett [1959] Director; Richard Michael Cheshire [1969] Finance Director; Randal Louis Golden [1961] Director/Corporate Executive [American]; Mark Stephen Harty [1962] Director/President, Europe; Stephen Mathieson [1967] Managing Director; Agostino Ricupati [1967] Director/Corporate Executive [American]; Michael Francis Wilkinson [1962] Director/General Manager - Ace Region

**A.J. Cope & Son Limited**
*Incorporated:* 27 March 1958  *Employees:* 16
*Net Worth:* £571,736  *Total Assets:* £2,081,016
*Registered Office:* Unit 10 Cliffside Trade Park, Motherwell Way, West Thurrock, Essex, RM20 3XD
*Officers:* Brian Lewis Cope, Secretary; Ellen Ackee [1965] Director/Office Manager; Brian Lewis Cope [1936] Director/Glass Technician; Claire Cope [1978] Director/Designer; Colin John Cope [1947] Director/Glass Technician; Nigel Henry Cope [1964] Director/Sales Manager; John Robert Hodgson [1961] Director/Catalogue Manager; Jonathan Stephen Thomas Williams [1974] Director/IT Manager

**Coramandel Limited**
*Incorporated:* 27 January 1992  *Employees:* 2
*Net Worth:* £17,015  *Total Assets:* £3,299,657
*Registered Office:* Coramandel, First Floor Office Suite, 240 Earls Court Road, London, SW5 9AA
*Major Shareholder:* Yogendrabhai Natvarlal Patel
*Officers:* Jyotindra Chimanlal Dave, Secretary; Yogendrabhai Natvarlal Patel [1946] Director/Businessman

**Core Environmental PLC**
*Incorporated:* 2 February 2017
*Net Worth:* £46,538  *Total Assets:* £70,039
*Registered Office:* HJS Accountants Ltd, 12-14 Carlton Place, Southampton, SO15 2EA
*Shareholder:* Stuart Wright
*Officers:* Allan Albert Miller [1966] Director; Stuart Martin Wright [1968] Director

**Coriungo Limited**
*Incorporated:* 15 September 2017
*Registered Office:* 1 Golden Court, Richmond, Surrey, TW9 1EU
*Officers:* Pieter-Jan Beyls [1987] Director [Belgian]

**Corpus Nostrum Limited**
*Incorporated:* 26 April 1989  *Employees:* 31
*Net Worth:* £38,794  *Total Assets:* £1,417,190
*Registered Office:* Unit 1 Cardinal Way, Godmanchester, Huntingdon, Cambs, PE29 2XN
*Major Shareholder:* Karol Pazik
*Officers:* David Thomas Brazier, Secretary; David Thomas Brazier [1967] Director/Business Manager; Karol Pazik [1964] Managing Director

**Corwhite Solutions Limited**
*Incorporated:* 21 January 2019
*Registered Office:* 66 Hazel Drive, Woodley, Berks, RG5 3SA
*Major Shareholder:* Preeti Joon
*Officers:* Preeti Joon [1986] Director/Businesswoman [Indian]

**Cosmedic Pharmacy Limited**
*Incorporated:* 20 October 2017
*Registered Office:* 3 Compass Point, Ensign Way, Hamble, Hants, SO31 4RA
*Shareholder:* Innomed Investments Limited
*Officers:* David Nicholas Gower [1950] Director; Dr Martin Ian King [1974] Director/Doctor; Sharon Lesley King [1966] Director/Business Consultant

**Cosmestore Limited**
*Incorporated:* 25 November 2009
*Net Worth:* £1,000  *Total Assets:* £1,000
*Registered Office:* The Pavilion, Josselin Road, Burnt Mills Industrial Estate, Basildon, Essex, SS13 1QB
*Parent:* Adonia Medical Group Ltd
*Officers:* Ronald Thomas Sullivan, Secretary; Ronald Thomas Sullivan [1953] Director; Paul William Wilkinson [1965] Director

**Cotton Craft Limited**
*Incorporated:* 13 February 2008
*Registered Office:* 25-Laurence Court, Shortlands Road, London, E10 7AU
*Major Shareholder:* Haseeb Kamal
*Officers:* Naeem Ashraf, Secretary; Haseeb Kamal [1974] Director [Pakistani]

**Couch Rolls Limited**
*Incorporated:* 14 February 2011
*Registered Office:* Pinnacle House Business Centre, Newark Road, Peterborough, Cambs, PE1 5YD
*Major Shareholder:* Alistair Martin Ashworth
*Officers:* Alistair Martin Ashworth [1963] Director/Beauty Wholesaler

**Couchrolls.co.uk Ltd**
*Incorporated:* 14 June 2011
*Registered Office:* Pinnacle House Business Centre, Newark Road, Peterborough, Cambs, PE1 5YD
*Major Shareholder:* Alistair Martin Ashworth
*Officers:* Alistair Martin Ashworth [1963] Director/Engineer

**Couchrolls.Com Ltd**
*Incorporated:* 14 June 2011
*Registered Office:* 2 Castle Street, Taunton, Somerset, TA1 4AS
*Major Shareholder:* Alistair Martin Ashworth
*Officers:* Alistair Martin Ashworth [1963] Director/Engineer

**Countrywide Healthcare Supplies Holdings Limited**
*Incorporated:* 31 October 2013  *Employees:* 99
*Net Worth:* £1,614,118  *Total Assets:* £8,314,353
*Registered Office:* Countrywide House, Springvale Road, Grimethorpe, Barnsley, S Yorks, S72 7BA
*Major Shareholder:* Alastair Richard Kitching
*Officers:* Jeremy David Gilson [1967] Director; Richard Anthony Hannah [1986] Finance Director; Edward Keelan [1981] Director; Alastair Richard Kitching [1967] Director; Sarah Louise Robinson [1974] Operations Director

**Coward Pharmacy Limited**
*Incorporated:* 21 January 2000  *Employees:* 11
*Net Worth:* £170,366  *Total Assets:* £225,315
*Registered Office:* 88 Fenwick Way, Berryedge, Consett, Co Durham, DH8 5FE
*Parent:* Sri Kanaparthy Limited
*Officers:* Sri Lakshmi Narasimha Vara Prasad Kanaparthy [1981] Director/Pharmacist; Vijaya Chaitanya Kanaparthy [1982] Director/Pharmacist

**CPX Solutions Limited**
*Incorporated:* 16 May 2017
*Net Worth:* £47,355  *Total Assets:* £76,416
*Registered Office:* Dalmar House, Barras Lane Estate, Dalston, Carlisle, CA5 7NY
*Major Shareholder:* Brian Peters
*Officers:* Brian Peters [1962] Director

**Cradlecrest Limited**
*Incorporated:* 9 February 1982  *Employees:* 12
*Net Worth:* £11,324,000  *Total Assets:* £11,983,000
*Registered Office:* 2 Peterwood Way, Croydon, Surrey, CR0 4UQ
*Parent:* Day Lewis PLC
*Officers:* Ameetkumar Ramananbhai Patel, Secretary; Jayantibhai Chimanbhai Patel, Secretary; Tayabali Mohamedbhai [1955] Director; Heena Patel [1963] Finance Director; Jayantibhai Chimanbhai Patel [1945] Director

**Creative Brand Concepts Limited**
*Incorporated:* 28 February 2012
*Registered Office:* 11 Park Place, Leeds, LS1 2RX
*Parent:* B.R. Pharmaceuticals Limited
*Officers:* Ziad Mahmoud Mousa Abu Sheikha [1960] Director [Jordanian]

**Creative Supply Solutions Ltd**
*Incorporated:* 2 November 2006
*Net Worth:* £52,802  *Total Assets:* £105,530
*Registered Office:* 3 Crewe Road, Sandbach, Cheshire, CW11 4NE
*Shareholders:* Philip Howard; Nigel Philip Oakes; Wa Thompson
*Officers:* William Andrew Thompson, Secretary; Philip Howard [1963] Director/Engineer; Nigel Philip Oakes [1949] Director; William Andrew Thompson [1948] Director/Manager

**Credenhill Limited**
*Incorporated:* 1 April 1955  *Employees:* 30
*Net Worth:* £963,821  *Total Assets:* £1,841,219
*Registered Office:* 10 Cossall Industrial Estate, Ilkeston, Derbys, DE7 5UG
*Shareholders:* Tessa Margaret Varndell; Paul Allen Grove
*Officers:* Sally Grove, Secretary; Paul Allen Grove [1955] Director; Tessa Margaret Varndell [1958] Director/Retired

**Creo Pharma Holdings Limited**
*Incorporated:* 12 February 2007
*Net Worth:* £10  *Total Assets:* £73
*Registered Office:* Felsted Business Centre, Cock Green, Felsted, Essex, CM6 3LY
*Parent:* Amneal Pharma UK Holdings Limited
*Officers:* Sharon Ingmire Hart, Secretary; Luke Ingmire Hart [1972] Director; Sharon Ingmire Hart [1967] Director; Chintu Patel [1971] Director/Business Executive [American]; Chirag Patel [1966] Director/Business Executive [American]; Gautam Patel [1972] Director/Advisor [American]

**Creo Pharma Limited**
*Incorporated:* 5 February 2007  *Employees:* 17
*Net Worth:* £7,760,969  *Total Assets:* £13,160,766
*Registered Office:* Felsted Business Centre, Cock Green, Felsted, Essex, CM6 3LY
*Parent:* Creo Pharma Holdings Limited
*Officers:* Sharon Ingmire Hart, Secretary; Luke Ingmire Hart [1972] Director/Executive; Sharon Ingmire Hart [1967] Director/Executive; Chintu Patel [1966] Director/Business Executive [American]; Chirag Patel [1966] Director/CEOA Chairman [American]; Gautam Patel [1972] Director/Investor [American]; Janos Vaczi [1967] Managing Director [Hungarian]

**Crescent Pharma Limited**
*Incorporated:* 1 May 2003  *Employees:* 42
*Net Worth:* £17,988,892  *Total Assets:* £47,265,104
*Registered Office:* Units 3-4 Quidhampton Business Units, Polhampton Lane, Overton, Basingstoke, Hants, RG25 3ED
*Officers:* Mohammed Al-Doori [1965] Director/Engineer

**Crescent Pharma OTC Limited**
*Incorporated:* 6 March 2000
*Net Worth:* £1,098,858  *Total Assets:* £1,508,043
*Registered Office:* Units 3-4 Quidhampton Business Units, Polhampton Lane, Overton, Basingstoke, Hants, RG25 3ED
*Officers:* Mohammed Al-Doori [1965] Director; Peter Generald Malone [1950] Director

**Crest Medical Limited**
Incorporated: 15 November 1999  Employees: 104
Net Worth: £1,233,453  Total Assets: £11,901,093
Registered Office: Blue Dot House, 3 Chesford Grange, Woolston, Warrington, Cheshire, WA1 4RQ
Parent: Crest Medical Holdings
Officers: Matthew George Courtney, Secretary; Matthew George Courtney [1975] Director; Barry Cunningham [1979] Director/Accountant; Peter John Mason [1969] Director; Alastair Generald Lees Maxwell [1970] Director

**Cripps Medical Limited**
Incorporated: 6 May 1977
Net Worth: £44,079  Total Assets: £54,113
Registered Office: The Barn, High Street, Upper Beeding, Steyning, W Sussex, BN44 3WN
Major Shareholder: Christopher Anthony Cripps
Officers: Caroline Jane Cripps, Secretary/Director; Caroline Jane Cripps [1943] Director; Christopher Anthony Cripps [1941] Director; Ann Margaret Hayward [1949] Director; Miles Timothy Hayward [1978] Director

**Crispin Enterprises Limited**
Incorporated: 15 May 2018
Registered Office: Oakmere, Belmont Business Park, Durham, DH1 1TW
Major Shareholder: Iain Phillips Crispin
Officers: Iain Phillips Crispin [1978] Director/Pharmacist

**Croma-Pharma Limited**
Incorporated: 25 January 2019
Registered Office: Suite 1, 3rd Floor, 11-12 St James's Square, London, SW1Y 4LB
Officers: Andreas Prinz [1975] Director [Austrian]; Gerhard Prinz [1940] Director [Austrian]; Martin Schoeller [1981] Director [Austrian]

**Crossbridge Concepts Limited**
Incorporated: 9 March 2017
Registered Office: Flat 13, Hurley Court, 953 High Road, Barnet, London, N12 8FA
Major Shareholder: Alli Moh Egwaikhide
Officers: Alli Moh Egwaikhide [1968] Business Development Director

**Crosscare Export Limited**
Incorporated: 17 November 1983
Previous: Myplan Limited
Net Worth: £24,791  Total Assets: £213,707
Registered Office: 54 Portland Place, London, W1B 1DY
Officers: Paul Brady, Group Company Secretary [Irish]; Paul Declan Brady [1967] Director [Irish]; Daniel Peter Nicholas Tierney [1936] Director [Irish]; Donal Thomas Martin Tierney [1965] Director [Irish]; Jonathan James Tierney [1971] Director [Irish]

**Crosskills (P.E.) Limited**
Incorporated: 11 July 1984  Employees: 4
Net Worth: £439,462  Total Assets: £591,414
Registered Office: Anglia House, 6 Central Avenue, St Andrews Business Park, Thorpe St Andrew, Norwich, NR7 0HR
Shareholders: Fiona Jane Banham; Michael Harry Arthur Banham
Officers: Sharon Daley, Secretary; Michael Harry Arthur Banham [1959] Director

**Crosspharma Limited**
Incorporated: 22 July 1987
Net Worth: £1,873,812  Total Assets: £26,797,434
Registered Office: Forsyth House, Cromac Square, Belfast, BT2 8LA
Parent: Clonmel Healthcare Ltd
Officers: Edwin Charles Blythe, Secretary; Edwin Charles Blythe [1968] Director/Chartered Accountant; James Hanlon [1956] Director/Chief Financial Officer [Irish]

**Crown Global Traders Limited**
Incorporated: 26 September 2017
Registered Office: Ground Floor, 3 Portnall Road, London, W9 3BA
Officers: Appuraj Sivasubramanian [1964] Director [Indian]

**Crowncrest Services UK Limited**
Incorporated: 20 December 1993  Employees: 2
Net Worth: £94  Total Assets: £70,210
Registered Office: 4 Hadleigh Business Centre, 351 London Road, Hadleigh, Essex, SS7 2BT
Shareholders: Christopher Keith Neil Grant; Deborah Mary Grant
Officers: Deborah Mary Grant, Secretary; Christopher Keith Neil Grant [1952] Director; Deborah Mary Grant [1954] Director/Administrator

**Cryotag Limited**
Incorporated: 14 December 2016
Registered Office: Willowbank, Hayes Lane, Slinfold, Horsham, W Sussex, RH13 0SA
Major Shareholder: Peter Allen
Officers: Peter Allen [1954] Director

**Crystal Healthcare Limited**
Incorporated: 3 November 1999
Net Worth: £44,661  Total Assets: £47,845
Registered Office: Unit 461 Andover House, George Yard, High Street, Andover, Hants, SP10 1PB
Shareholders: Peter John Shaw; Julia Lauren Shaw
Officers: Julia Lauren Shaw, Secretary/Director; Julia Lauren Shaw [1968] Director; Peter John Shaw [1970] Managing Director

**CSL Behring Holdings Limited**
Incorporated: 25 May 1995
Net Worth: £10,702,278,656  Total Assets: £10,703,140,864
Registered Office: 4 Milton Road, Haywards Heath, W Sussex, RH16 1AH
Officers: Paul Richard Fellingham, Secretary; Dr Lutz Guenter Bonacker [1965] Director/Vice President and General Manager, Western Europe [German]; John Andrew Goodman Levy [1959] Director/Group Financial Controller [Australian]; Edward Owens [1956] Director/General Manager; Val Gene Romberg [1958] Director/Chemist [American]

**CSL Behring UK Limited**
Incorporated: 16 March 1982  Employees: 41
Net Worth: £40,338,000  Total Assets: £60,219,000
Registered Office: 4 Milton Road, Haywards Heath, W Sussex, RH16 1AH
Officers: Paul Richard Fellingham, Secretary; Dr Lutz Guenter Bonacker [1965] Director/Vice President and General Manager, Western Europe [German]; John Andrew Goodman Levy [1959] Director/Group Financial Controller [Australian]; Edward Owens [1956] Director/General Manager

**Cubic Pharmaceuticals Limited**
*Incorporated:* 5 June 2008
*Net Worth:* £385,505  *Total Assets:* £644,620
*Registered Office:* Unit 3 Sextant Park, Neptune Close, Medway City Estate, Rochester, Kent, ME2 4LU
*Shareholders:* Anwar Ali; Saumil Kiritkumar Bhatt; Arun Jangra
*Officers:* Arun Jangra, Secretary/Pharmacist; Anwar Ali [1969] Director/Pharmacist; Saumil Kiritkumar Bhatt [1976] Director/Pharmaceutical

**Curans Care Limited**
*Incorporated:* 4 March 2002  *Employees:* 48
*Previous:* Laetus Lodge Limited
*Net Worth:* £102,030  *Total Assets:* £151,112
*Registered Office:* 113 Parchmore Road, Thornton Heath, Surrey, CR7 8LZ
*Shareholder:* Mark Peake
*Officers:* Mark Anthony Peake, Secretary; Mark Anthony Peake [1964] Director/Administration; Michele Peake [1965] Director

**Curas Limited**
*Incorporated:* 16 November 2005  *Employees:* 22
*Net Worth:* £227,966  *Total Assets:* £784,269
*Registered Office:* 30-31 St James Place, Mangotsfield, Bristol, BS16 9JB
*Major Shareholder:* Casper Lykkegaard Kobke
*Officers:* Britt Axelsen Kobke, Secretary; Casper Lykkegaard Kobke [1974] Director [Danish]

**Cured CBD Ltd**
*Incorporated:* 18 February 2019
*Registered Office:* 22 Hanover Square, Mayfair, London, W1S 1BN
*Major Shareholder:* James Hindmarsh
*Officers:* James Hindmarsh [1996] Director

**Curelife Ltd**
*Incorporated:* 20 July 2016
*Net Worth:* £100  *Total Assets:* £100
*Registered Office:* Unit 174, Avenue B, Thorp Arch Estate, Wetherby, W Yorks, LS23 7BJ
*Officers:* Mustafa Al-Shalechy [1988] Managing Director; Mohammed Ali Alshamari [1988] Director/Business Development Manager

**Curist Health Limited**
*Incorporated:* 1 November 2016
*Registered Office:* Collingham House, 6-12 Gladstone Road, Wimbledon, London, SW19 1QT
*Shareholders:* David Frempong Addo; Akintoye Adeoye Akindele
*Officers:* Abigail Amma Afriyie Abora [1987] Director/Entrepreneur [Ghanaian]; David Frempong Addo [1981] Director/Pharmacist [Ghanaian]; Akintoye Adeoye Akindele [1974] Director/Investment Banker [Nigerian]; Ayodele Olubunmi Arogbo [1968] Director/Investment Banker [Nigerian]; Sylvia Adjoa Lawson [1974] Director/Chief Financial Officer [Ghanaian]

**Curium Pharma UK Ltd.**
*Incorporated:* 9 December 2014  *Employees:* 24
*Previous:* Mallinckrodt RP UK Ltd
*Net Worth:* £624,679  *Total Assets:* £3,979,374
*Registered Office:* Ground Floor, Building 1000, Lakeside North Harbour, Western Road, Portsmouth, PO6 3EZ
*Officers:* Xavier Anne Jean-Louis Defourt [1968] Director/Group General Counsel [Belgian]; Renaud Albert Gaston Dehareng [1973] Director/Chief Executive Officer [Belgian]; Francois Paul Pierre Labarre [1963] Director/Vice President Northern Europe [French]

**Currentmyth Limited**
*Incorporated:* 10 March 1997  *Employees:* 4
*Net Worth:* £168,296  *Total Assets:* £1,245,263
*Registered Office:* Regency House, 45-51 Chorley New Road, Bolton, Lancs, BL1 4QR
*Shareholders:* Ian James Andrews; Lynn Andrews
*Officers:* Ian James Andrews, Secretary/Wholesaler; Ian James Andrews [1955] Director/Wholesaler; Lynn Andrews [1956] Director/Wholesaler

**Currie Marketing Limited**
*Incorporated:* 13 August 2008  *Employees:* 1
*Net Worth:* £94,586  *Total Assets:* £323,191
*Registered Office:* 6 Manchester Road, Buxton, Derbys, SK17 6SB
*Major Shareholder:* James Balfour Currie
*Officers:* Rosemarie Currie, Secretary; James Balfour Currie [1951] Director/Food Ingredients Trader

**Cutman Ltd**
*Incorporated:* 22 November 2018
*Registered Office:* Parwich Hall, Parwich, Ashbourne, Derbys, DE6 1QD
*Major Shareholder:* David AG Shields

**Cuttlefish Limited**
*Incorporated:* 14 January 2005  *Employees:* 3
*Net Worth:* £63,319  *Total Assets:* £223,861
*Registered Office:* Fircroft, Blackberry Road, Felcourt, East Grinstead, W Sussex, RH19 2LH
*Shareholders:* Graeme Parkinson; Teresa Parkinson
*Officers:* Teresa Parkinson, Secretary; Graeme Parkinson [1966] Director

**Cyan Trading Ltd**
*Incorporated:* 10 September 2008  *Employees:* 4
*Net Worth:* £917,354  *Total Assets:* £1,548,241
*Registered Office:* 164 Bedford Road, Kempston, Bedford, MK42 8BH
*Major Shareholder:* Frederic Richer
*Officers:* Niten Patel, Secretary; Stephen Martin David Hayward [1960] Director [Cambodian]

**Cygnus Pharma Ltd**
*Incorporated:* 18 January 2018
*Net Worth Deficit:* £10,650  *Total Assets:* £55,100
*Registered Office:* 72 Cardigan Street, Luton, Beds, LU1 1RR
*Officers:* Sharan Patel [1987] Director

**Cynosure Group Ltd**
*Incorporated:* 10 May 2016
*Registered Office:* 24 Low Parksail, Erskine, Renfrewshire, PA8 7HS
*Major Shareholder:* Sheroz Tahir
*Officers:* Sheroz Tahir [1991] Director/Accountant

**Cyto-Solutions Limited**
*Incorporated:* 11 February 2003  *Employees:* 4
*Net Worth:* £183,807  *Total Assets:* £223,425
*Registered Office:* Suite 1, Invicta Business Centre, Monument Way, Orbital Park, Ashford, Kent, TN24 0HB
*Shareholders:* Juliet Macaraya Wilson; Roger Keith Wilson
*Officers:* Juliet Macaraya Wilson, Secretary; Craig Stephen William Sadler [1973] Director; Juliet Macaraya Wilson [1948] Director; Roger Keith Wilson [1940] Director/Consultant

**Cytoplan Limited**
Incorporated: 24 April 1980  Employees: 35
Previous: Nature's Own Limited
Net Worth: £1,604,248  Total Assets: £2,340,104
Registered Office: Unit 8 Hanley Workshops, Hanley Road, Hanley Swan, Worcs, WR8 0DX
Parent: Aim Foundation
Officers: Timothy David Higginson, Secretary; Simon John Holdcroft [1963] Sales & Marketing Director; Caroline Daphne Marks [1960] Director; Nicolas John Marks [1964] Director; Jeremy Edwin Montague Pakenham [1948] Director; Peter Austin Wallace [1946] Director/Chairman; Amanda Williams [1956] Managing Director

**Czech, Moravian and Slovak Chemicals Limited**
Incorporated: 27 October 1992
Net Worth: £588,007  Total Assets: £616,032
Registered Office: 8 & 9 Old Station Business Park, Compton, Newbury, Berks, RG20 6NE
Parent: Carbosynth Limited
Officers: Philip Jonathan Dawes, Secretary; Dr Vanessa Mary Eastwick-Field [1962] Director; Dr Victoria Gibson [1971] Technical Director

**D & M Enterprises (UK) Limited**
Incorporated: 23 May 2012
Net Worth Deficit: £142,752  Total Assets: £587,598
Registered Office: Unit C, Commerce Way, Modern Moulds Business Centre, Lancing, W Sussex, BN15 8TA
Parent: Greens Pharmacy Limited
Officers: Mahindra Chauhan [1958] Director/Pharmacist

**Dacre Skincare Limited**
Incorporated: 9 January 2019
Registered Office: 63 Broad Green, Wellingborough, Northants, NN8 4LQ
Major Shareholder: Alexandra May Howard Roberts
Officers: Alexandra May Howard Roberts [1985] Director

**Daiichi Sankyo UK Limited**
Incorporated: 12 March 1986  Employees: 83
Net Worth: £9,787,000  Total Assets: £18,241,000
Registered Office: Building 1, Chalfont Park, Gerrards Cross, Bucks, SL9 0GA
Officers: Manuel Reiberg [1974] Managing Director [German]

**Dakota Pharma Limited**
Incorporated: 2 December 2005  Employees: 4
Net Worth: £1,438,938  Total Assets: £4,299,038
Registered Office: 8 The Courtyards, Victoria Road, Leeds, LS14 2LB
Shareholders: Marshall Anthony Glynn; Anthony Golombeck
Officers: Anthony Golombeck, Secretary; Marshall Anthony Glynn [1962] Director; Anthony Golombeck [1955] Director

**Daleacre Wholesale Limited**
Incorporated: 12 January 2016  Employees: 1
Net Worth: £32,157  Total Assets: £161,490
Registered Office: 11 Wilsthorpe Road, Breaston, Derby, DE72 3EA
Parent: Daleacre Holdings Limited
Officers: David Richard Evans [1965] Director

**Dallas Burston Ashbourne Holdings Limited**
Incorporated: 13 May 2002
Net Worth: £8,691,742  Total Assets: £9,415,455
Registered Office: Bampton Road, Harold Hill, Romford, Essex, RM3 8UG
Parent: Ethypharm Holdings UK Ltd
Officers: Roseline Georgette Joannesse [1959] Director/Vice President Legal Affairs [French]; Jean-Hugues Louis Marie Lecat [1956] Director [French]; Emmanuel Schmidt [1969] Director/Chief Finance Officer [French]

**Damum UK Limited**
Incorporated: 8 August 2001  Employees: 1
Net Worth Deficit: £147,372  Total Assets: £205,191
Registered Office: Silverthorn, Wellington Avenue, Virginia Water, Surrey, GU25 4QR
Shareholder: Ahmed Yusuf Ahmed
Officers: Ahmed Yusuf Ahmed, Secretary/Entrepreneur; Ahmed Yusuf Ahmed [1978] Director/Entrepreneur; Hamzat Yusuf Ahmed [1986] Director; Ibrahim Yusuf Ahmed [1982] Director; Nuradeen Yusuf Ahmed [1980] Director

**Danel Trading Limited**
Incorporated: 19 June 1986  Employees: 9
Net Worth: £1,362,000  Total Assets: £2,290,762
Registered Office: Nexia Smith & Williamson, Portwall Lane, Bristol, BS1 6NA
Shareholders: Rachel Freedman; David Freedman
Officers: Dalya Shear, Secretary; David Freedman [1942] Director/Qualified Chemist; Neil Ailon Freedman [1967] Director; Rachel Freedman [1943] Director; Dalya Shear [1969] Director

**C T Dang Limited**
Incorporated: 6 November 2013  Employees: 12
Net Worth Deficit: £59,971  Total Assets: £2,129,821
Registered Office: 37 Warren Street, London, W1T 6AD
Shareholders: Tony Dang; Colin Dang; Fiona Dang
Officers: Colin Dang [1985] Director; Fiona Dang [1977] Director/Pharmacist; Tony Dang [1981] Director

**Dark Atom Limited**
Incorporated: 20 February 2018
Registered Office: Crown House, 27 Old Gloucester Street, London, WC1N 3AX
Officers: Michael Gregor Brabetz [1970] Director [Austrian]; Steve Mark West [1965] Director (Sales)

**Daryeel Medicines International Ltd**
Incorporated: 9 April 2018
Registered Office: 15a Parsons House, Claybrook Road, London, W6 8NB
Shareholders: Ciise Sandhere Musse; Sadia Hassan
Officers: Sadia Hassan [1983] Director/Pharmacist [New Zealander]; Ciise Sandhere Musse [1984] Director/Associate Practitioner [Swedish]

**Dasapharm Limited**
Incorporated: 25 November 2014
Net Worth: £2,868  Total Assets: £542,526
Registered Office: 2nd Floor, 201 Haverstock Hill, London, NW3 4QG
Shareholders: Dan Spivak; Dinara Adilova; Alexander Katzman
Officers: Dimitri Mevzos [1972] Director/Business Consultant [Israeli]

### Dasco (Wholesale) Limited
*Incorporated:* 23 June 1986  *Employees:* 8
*Net Worth:* £250,180  *Total Assets:* £525,935
*Registered Office:* 10 Hall Farm Close, Stanmore, Middlesex, HA7 4JT
*Parent:* Dasco Investment Corporation Limited
*Officers:* Dilip Raichand Shah [1953] Director/Accountant

### Dasco Investment Corporation Limited
*Incorporated:* 26 June 1980  *Employees:* 1
*Net Worth:* £1,101,308  *Total Assets:* £1,185,509
*Registered Office:* 10 Hall Farm Close, Stanmore, Middlesex, HA7 4JT
*Officers:* Dilip Raichand Shah [1953] Director/Accountant

### Davcaps Limited
*Incorporated:* 30 January 2001
*Net Worth:* £10,802  *Total Assets:* £28,458
*Registered Office:* Unit 5 Tarlings Yard, Church Road, Bishops Cleeve, Cheltenham, Glos, GL52 8RN
*Shareholders:* Martyn Douglas Davis; Susan Joyce Davis
*Officers:* Andrew Riby, Secretary; Martyn Douglas Davis [1953] Director; Susan Joyce Davis [1959] Director

### Gordon Davie Chemist Limited
*Incorporated:* 17 December 2012
*Net Worth:* £334,422  *Total Assets:* £556,138
*Registered Office:* 195 Southborough Lane, Bromley, Kent, BR2 8AR
*Major Shareholder:* Rajesh Doshi
*Officers:* Rajesh Doshi [1972] Director/Pharmacist

### Davis and Dann Limited
*Incorporated:* 26 March 1965  *Employees:* 9
*Net Worth:* £5,725,378  *Total Assets:* £14,469,876
*Registered Office:* Kanta House, Victoria Road, South Ruislip, Middlesex, HA4 0JQ
*Officers:* Satish Jamnadas Chatwani, Secretary; Jawahar Jamnadas Chatwani [1948] Director; Rashmi Jamnadas Chatwani [1954] Director; Satish Jamnadas Chatwani [1953] Director

### Day International Limited
*Incorporated:* 7 September 2018
*Registered Office:* 19 Derwent Crescent, London, N20 0QH
*Major Shareholder:* Amirsaeed Malekshahi
*Officers:* Amirsaeed Malekshahi [1974] Director/Entrepreneur [Dominican]

### Day Lewis Medical Limited
*Incorporated:* 12 April 1985  *Employees:* 197
*Net Worth:* £54,927,000  *Total Assets:* £88,973,000
*Registered Office:* 2 Peterwood Way, Croydon, Surrey, CR0 4UQ
*Parent:* Day Lewis PLC
*Officers:* Ameetkumar Ramananbhai Patel, Secretary; Jayantibhai Chimanbhai Patel, Secretary; Tayabali Mohamedbhai [1955] Director; Heena Patel [1963] Finance Director; Jayantibhai Chimanbhai Patel [1945] Director

### Day Med Limited
*Incorporated:* 25 July 2017
*Registered Office:* 11 Woodford Avenue, Oldham, Lancs, OL2 8HJ
*Officers:* David Younie [1954] Director

### Day Pharma Limited
*Incorporated:* 13 October 2017
*Registered Office:* 239-241 Kennington Lane, London, SE11 5QU
*Major Shareholder:* Yeliz Erdil
*Officers:* Yeliz Erdil [1976] Director [Turkish]

### Dayonix Pharma Limited
*Incorporated:* 24 August 2018
*Registered Office:* 19 Derwent Crescent, London, N20 0QH
*Major Shareholder:* Amirsaeed Malekshahi
*Officers:* Amirsaeed Malekshahi [1974] Director/Entrepreneur [Dominican]

### DC Surgical Supplies Limited
*Incorporated:* 20 January 2017
*Net Worth:* £46,600  *Total Assets:* £48,650
*Registered Office:* Griffins Court, 24-32 London Road, Newbury, Berks, RG14 1JX
*Major Shareholder:* Terry Collette
*Officers:* Terry Collette [1956] Director

### DCH Subco Ltd
*Incorporated:* 6 June 2017
*Registered Office:* Dorset County Hospital, Williams Avenue, Dorchester, DT1 2JY
*Officers:* Nicholas James Johnson [1980] NHS Director; Rebecca Anne King [1966] Director/Accountant; Andrew Thomas Prowse [1974] Director/Pharmacist; Matthew George Rose [1969] Director/Accountant

### DCMP 8E Cepac Limited
*Incorporated:* 2 January 2019
*Registered Office:* 121 Silver Street, Edmonton, London, N18 1RG
*Major Shareholder:* Andree Exner
*Officers:* Andree Exner, Secretary; Andree Exner [1964] Director/Entrepreneur [Australian]

### DDWS Limited
*Incorporated:* 15 February 2001  *Employees:* 5
*Net Worth:* £41,045  *Total Assets:* £325,626
*Registered Office:* The Staploe Medical Centre, Brewhouse Lane, Soham, Cambs, CB7 5JD
*Officers:* Doctor James Edward Howard, Secretary; Dr Richard Brixey [1983] Director/Medical Practitioner; Dr Richard Peter Burnford [1960] Director/Doctor; Dr Alun Michael George [1962] Director/GP; Dr Anthony Edward Gunstone [1971] Director/Medical Practitioner; Dr James Edward Howard [1967] Director/Doctor; Dr Anne Heather Molyneux [1962] Director/GP

### De-Bulad & Co. Ltd.
*Incorporated:* 5 February 2001
*Net Worth:* £280  *Total Assets:* £2,036
*Registered Office:* 30 Arnold Road, Dagenham, Essex, RM10 9PA
*Officers:* George Ayodeji Lawal, Secretary; Bunmi Lawal [1981] Director; Lanre Lawal [1981] Director/Manager; Maryam Dupeola Lawal [1968] Director/Biomedical Scientist

### Decahedron Ltd
*Incorporated:* 8 August 2011  *Employees:* 2
*Net Worth Deficit:* £773,202  *Total Assets:* £488,501
*Registered Office:* 161 Lancaster Road, Enfield, Middlesex, EN2 0JN
*Parent:* Cosmos Holdings Inc
*Officers:* Nikolaos Lazarou [1979] Director [Greek]; Grigorios Siokas [1965] Director [Greek]

### Dechra Veterinary Products Limited
*Incorporated:* 8 March 2005  *Employees:* 80
*Net Worth:* £6,447,000  *Total Assets:* £14,944,000
*Registered Office:* 24 Cheshire Avenue, Lostock Gralam, Northwich, Cheshire, CW9 7UA
*Parent:* Dechra Pharmaceuticals PLC
*Officers:* Melanie Jane Hall, Secretary; Richard John Cotton [1961] Director; Anthony Gerard Griffin [1963] Director [Irish]; Ian David Page [1961] Director

**Decibel Biopharm Limited**
*Incorporated:* 26 January 2018
*Registered Office:* 49 Darrel Road, Retford, Notts, DN22 7DH
*Major Shareholder:* Daniel Mazhandu
*Officers:* Daniel Mazhandu [1977] Managing Director [Zimbabwean]

**Deise Pharm Ltd**
*Incorporated:* 21 February 2019
*Registered Office:* 10 Cloverbrae, Enniskillen, Co Fermanagh, BT74 4AB
*Major Shareholder:* Jamie Hallahan
*Officers:* Jamie Hallahan [1986] Director/Pharmacist [Irish]

**Dejure Limited**
*Incorporated:* 12 February 1996 *Employees:* 33
*Net Worth:* £764,954 *Total Assets:* £1,786,605
*Registered Office:* 7 Station Parade, Sanderstead Road, Sanderstead, Surrey, CR2 0PH
*Shareholders:* Chaitanyakumar Jayantilal Patel; Smita Chaitanya Patel
*Officers:* Chaitanyakumar Jayantilal Patel, Secretary/Pharmacist; Chaitanyakumar Jayantilal Patel [1959] Director/Pharmacist; Smita Chaitanya Patel [1960] Director/Pharmacist

**Delta Sales Ltd**
*Incorporated:* 20 May 2015 *Employees:* 1
*Net Worth:* £206,381 *Total Assets:* £12,153,089
*Registered Office:* 45 Pall Mall, London, SW1Y 5JG
*Shareholders:* A-Start 2000 Eood; Nastasia Olegovna Ivanova; Michael Mihaylov Minkov
*Officers:* Michael Mihaylov Minkov [1966] Director

**Deltapharma Limited**
*Incorporated:* 7 April 2004
*Net Worth Deficit:* £41,822 *Total Assets:* £11,943
*Registered Office:* 49 Green Lanes, London, N16 9BU
*Officers:* Faidra Theofanous, Secretary; Faidra Theofanous [1986] Director/Administrator [Cypriot]

**Dene Healthcare Limited**
*Incorporated:* 18 April 2005 *Employees:* 14
*Net Worth:* £1,073,653 *Total Assets:* £1,756,854
*Registered Office:* 4-7 Gate Way Drive, Yeadon, Leeds, LS19 7XY
*Major Shareholder:* Michael Drakard
*Officers:* Susan Drakard, Secretary; Stewart Craig Arnott [1980] Director; Michael Drakard [1962] Director; Brian Owen Grimes [1955] Business Development Director

**Dent.O.Care Distribution Limited**
*Incorporated:* 9 October 2013
*Net Worth:* £143,356 *Total Assets:* £643,689
*Registered Office:* 5 Technology Park, Colindeep Lane, Colindale, London, NW9 6BX
*Shareholders:* Adam Keller; Natalie Claire Keller
*Officers:* Adam Keller [1973] Director; Natalie Claire Keller [1976] Director

**Dent.O.Care Limited**
*Incorporated:* 4 July 1990 *Employees:* 20
*Net Worth:* £280,724 *Total Assets:* £1,039,257
*Registered Office:* 5 Technology Park, Colindeep Lane, Colindale, London, NW9 6BX
*Parent:* Zans Management Limited
*Officers:* Natalie Keller, Secretary; Adam Keller [1973] Director; Natalie Claire Keller [1976] Director

**Dental Warehouse Ltd**
*Incorporated:* 18 August 2008 *Employees:* 3
*Net Worth:* £675 *Total Assets:* £165,788
*Registered Office:* 10 Park Plaza, Battlefield Enterprise Park, Shrewsbury, Salop, SY1 3AF
*Shareholders:* Jacqeline Davis; Timothy John Davis
*Officers:* Jacqeline Davis [1957] Director/Secretary; Tim John Davis [1956] Director/Technical Sales

**Dentanurse (U.K.) Limited**
*Incorporated:* 5 March 1986
*Net Worth:* £81,595 *Total Assets:* £100,359
*Registered Office:* Singleton Court Business Park, Wonastow Road Industrial Estate West, Monmouth, NP25 5JA
*Major Shareholder:* Jennifer Dolores Lees
*Officers:* Jennifer Dolores Lees, Secretary; Jennifer Dolores Lees [1949] Director/Company Manager

**Dentel Group Ltd**
*Incorporated:* 30 October 2015
*Registered Office:* 483 Green Lanes, London, N13 4BS
*Major Shareholder:* Edmund Johannes Heinrich Thau
*Officers:* Edmund Johannes Heinrich Thau [1937] Director [German]

**Dentitreat Company Limited**
*Incorporated:* 20 June 2017
*Registered Office:* Netpark Incubator, Thomas Wright Way, Sedgefield, Co Durham, TS21 3FD
*Officers:* Giorgina Atkinson-Reed, Secretary; Giorgina Atkinson-Reed [1991] Director

**Dentlaser Limited**
*Incorporated:* 13 April 2018
*Registered Office:* 17 Savile Row, London, W1S 3PN
*Major Shareholder:* Emek Zubeyde Kulur
*Officers:* Emek Zubeyde Kulur [1971] Director/Dentist [Turkish]

**Derma Distribution Ltd**
*Incorporated:* 25 July 2018
*Registered Office:* 4 Poplar View, Pollington, Goole, E Yorks, DN14 0DH
*Officers:* Kristy Hopkins [1986] Director/Aesthetician; Suzanne Jobling [1962] Director/Retired

**Derma UK Limited**
*Incorporated:* 8 August 1996 *Employees:* 19
*Net Worth:* £747,594 *Total Assets:* £1,511,083
*Registered Office:* Toffee Factory, Unit S20 Lower Steenbergs Yard, Quayside, Ouseburn, Walker Road, Newcastle upon Tyne, NE1 2DF
*Parent:* Derma UK (Holdings) Limited
*Officers:* Nicholas Stephen Pass [1959] Director

**Dermal Aesthetics Clinic Limited**
*Incorporated:* 31 March 2016
*Net Worth Deficit:* £850 *Total Assets:* £824
*Registered Office:* 2 Shillingten Close, Worsley, Manchester, M28 0YF
*Major Shareholder:* Parisa Asadi
*Officers:* Parisa Asadi [1986] Director/Manager

**Dermapure Aesthetics Limited**
*Incorporated:* 8 February 2018
*Registered Office:* 17 Swanfield, Ystalyfera, Swansea, SA9 2JD
*Major Shareholder:* Thomas Benjamin Lewis
*Officers:* Thomas Benjamin Lewis [1987] Director/Pharmacist

**Dermatonics Ltd**
*Incorporated:* 14 January 2008  *Employees:* 4
*Net Worth:* £156,805  *Total Assets:* £448,469
*Registered Office:* 42-48 Charlbert Street, London, NW8 7BU
*Major Shareholder:* Gregory James Robert Andrell
*Officers:* John Page Lewis, Secretary; Gregory James Robert Andrell [1961] Director

**Dermatonics Trading Limited**
*Incorporated:* 29 August 2013
*Registered Office:* 42-48 Charlbert Street, London, NW8 7BU
*Shareholder:* Gregory James Robert Andrell
*Officers:* Gregory James Robert Andrell [1961] Director

**Dermconcept Ltd**
*Incorporated:* 5 October 2018
*Registered Office:* 1st Floor North, Devonshire House, 1 Devonshire Street, London, W1W 5DS
*Shareholders:* Theodora Mantzourani; Nikolaos Psathas
*Officers:* Dr Theodora Mantzourani [1968] Director/Doctor [Greek]; Nikolaos Psathas [1975] Director/Pharmacist [Greek]

**Dermocore Ltd.**
*Incorporated:* 30 May 2012
*Net Worth Deficit:* £10,243  *Total Assets:* £17,362
*Registered Office:* 6 Lynfield Lane, Cambridge, CB4 1DR
*Shareholders:* Jamal Baker; Innoderm SARL
*Officers:* Richard Andrew Snell, Secretary; Jamal Baker [1957] Director [Swiss]; Richard Andrew Snell [1971] Business Development Director

**Design Masters (Sales) Limited**
*Incorporated:* 16 December 1997
*Net Worth Deficit:* £21,133
*Registered Office:* Anglo House, Bell Lane Office Village, Bell Lane, Amersham, Bucks, HP6 6FA
*Major Shareholder:* Colin D'Souza
*Officers:* Colin D'Souza, Secretary; Colin D'Souza [1969] Director/Group Legal Counsel, Chief Financial Officer

**Despina Pharma Ltd**
*Incorporated:* 9 December 2009
*Previous:* Holmewood Park Limited
*Net Worth Deficit:* £49,164  *Total Assets:* £49,836
*Registered Office:* Dorandi, 1a Mortimer Road, Ealing, London, W13 8NG
*Officers:* Amanda Louise Magagnin, Secretary; Sarvesh Bhargava [1962] Director [Indian]

**Detafinas Limited**
*Incorporated:* 1 August 2018
*Registered Office:* 184 Danbury Crescent, South Ockendon, Essex, RM15 5XE
*Shareholders:* Samson Olufemi Famojuro; Kehinde Olufunke Famojuro
*Officers:* Kehinde Olufunke Famojuro [1980] Director [Nigerian]; Samson Olufemi Famojuro [1972] Director

**Deva Pharma Medical Ltd**
*Incorporated:* 10 January 2019
*Registered Office:* 33 Churchward Close, Chester, CH2 2BG
*Major Shareholder:* Vasif Baha Bakiler
*Officers:* Atiye Bakiler, Secretary; Vasif Baha Bakiler [1979] Director

**Device Technologies UK Ltd.**
*Incorporated:* 3 July 2012  *Employees:* 6
*Net Worth Deficit:* £89,130  *Total Assets:* £199,897
*Registered Office:* 15 Newland, Lincoln, LN1 1XG
*Parent:* Device Technologies Australia Pty Ltd
*Officers:* Ben James Arthur, Secretary; Emma Jane Cleary [1969] Director/Chief Operating Officer [Australian]; Michael Bernard Trevaskis [1972] Director [Australian]

**Devicor Medical UK Limited**
*Incorporated:* 26 February 2010  *Employees:* 2
*Net Worth:* £61,554  *Total Assets:* £2,213,476
*Registered Office:* Suite 1, 3rd Floor, 11-12 St James's Square, London, SW1Y 4LB
*Parent:* Danaher Corporation
*Officers:* Olaf Andrich [1970] Director [German]; Alain Humbert Marie Antoine Mathieu de Lambilly [1968] Director [French]; David George White Inman [1980] Director

**Devilbiss Healthcare Limited**
*Incorporated:* 7 December 2009  *Employees:* 19
*Net Worth:* £25,628  *Total Assets:* £689,211
*Registered Office:* Unit 3 Bloomfield Park, Bloomfield Road, Tipton, W Midlands, DY4 9AP
*Parent:* Devilbiss Healthcare LLC
*Officers:* Timothy FitzGenerald Walsh, Secretary; Oliver Herbert Niemann [1967] Managing Director [German]; Amy O'Keefe [1970] Director/Chief Financial Officer [American]; Timothy FitzGenerald Walsh [1964] Director/Accountant [American]

**Devonshire Healthcare Services Limited**
*Incorporated:* 5 January 2001  *Employees:* 12
*Net Worth:* £3,271,183  *Total Assets:* £3,783,673
*Registered Office:* 1 Maple Grove Business Centre, Lawrence Road, Hounslow, Middlesex, TW4 6DR
*Shareholders:* Mary Ellen Power; Timothy Peter Smith
*Officers:* Mary Ellen Power [1957] Director [Irish]; Timothy Peter Smith [1957] Director/Pharmacist

**Dexcel-Pharma Limited**
*Incorporated:* 31 August 1994  *Employees:* 32
*Net Worth:* £14,974,620  *Total Assets:* £18,824,408
*Registered Office:* 7 Sopwith Way, Drayton Fields Industrial Estate, Daventry, Northants, NN11 8PB
*Parent:* Dexcel Pharma Laboratories Ltd
*Officers:* Terry Kenneth Grigg, Secretary; Terry Grigg [1949] Managing Director; Anastasis Konstantinou [1984] Director [Cypriot]; Dan Oren [1941] Director/Company Manager [Israeli]

**DGI Technologies Limited**
*Incorporated:* 23 January 2018
*Registered Office:* Fairways House, George Street, Prestwich, Lancs, M25 9WS
*Major Shareholder:* Jeremy Michael Josephson
*Officers:* Jeremy Michael Josephson [1956] Director [American]

**Diamate Biotechnologies Limited**
*Incorporated:* 1 June 2001
*Net Worth Deficit:* £3,044  *Total Assets:* £4,424
*Registered Office:* 205 Pentax House, South Hill Avenue, South Harrow, Middlesex, HA2 0DU
*Officers:* Zulfiqar Hussain, Secretary/Accountant; Zulfiqar Hussain [1968] Director/Accountant

**Diamond Pharma Limited**
*Incorporated:* 16 June 2011
*Net Worth:* £4,501  *Total Assets:* £616,703
*Registered Office:* Unit M1, Anchor Brook Business Park, Aldridge, Walsall, W Midlands, WS9 8BZ
*Shareholders:* Mark Anthony Paul Blount; Bharat Jogia; Tina Marie Blount; Merisha Jade Jogia
*Officers:* Tina Marie Blount [1980] Director; Merisha Jade Jogia [1996] Director

**Diana Royal Jelly Limited**
*Incorporated:* 12 June 1989
*Registered Office:* 12 Brudenell, St Leonards Hill, Windsor, Berks, SL4 4UR
*Officers:* Anthony Adel Kseib [1981] Director; Antoinette Kseib [1956] Director

**Diaylaa Ltd**
*Incorporated:* 24 January 2019
*Registered Office:* United Business Centre, 1000 Great West Road, Brentford, Middlesex, TW8 9DW
*Major Shareholder:* Ali Hussein Mahmood Al Azawi
*Officers:* Ali Hussein Mahmood Al Azawi [1970] Director [Iraqi]

**Dil More Remedies UK Ltd**
*Incorporated:* 7 November 2017
*Registered Office:* 170 Draycott Avenue, Harrow, Middlesex, HA3 0BZ
*Major Shareholder:* Diliprao Pandurang More
*Officers:* Neeta Avinash Mavani [1958] Director; Dr Diliprao Pandurang More [1970] Director [Indian]

**Dilcare Health Limited**
*Incorporated:* 26 September 2005
*Net Worth:* £100  *Total Assets:* £25,503
*Registered Office:* 20 Hawthorn Drive, Harrow, Middlesex, HA2 7NX
*Shareholder:* Ajay Pattni
*Officers:* Ajay Pattni [1965] Director/Manager

**Dilmaherbals Limited**
*Incorporated:* 30 April 2018
*Registered Office:* 39 Belfry Way, Edwalton, Nottingham, NG12 4FA
*Major Shareholder:* Gaurav Gupta
*Officers:* Gaurav Gupta [1990] Director/Pharmacist

**Din Commerce Ltd**
*Incorporated:* 10 July 2014
*Net Worth:* £10,621  *Total Assets:* £22,075
*Registered Office:* 53 Whateleys Drive, Kenilworth, Warwicks, CV8 2GY
*Major Shareholder:* Mykola Godvan
*Officers:* Mykola Godvan [1970] Director/Financial Manager [Ukrainian]

**Dion Trade Ltd.**
*Incorporated:* 5 June 2008
*Net Worth:* £1,000  *Total Assets:* £1,000
*Registered Office:* 19 Kathleen Road, London, SW11 2JR
*Officers:* Izeth Del Carmen Samudio Tapia [1972] Director/Manager [Panamanian]

**Direct Care Homes Limited**
*Incorporated:* 21 November 2012
*Registered Office:* Bemin House, Cox Lane, Chessington Industrial Estate, Chessington, Surrey, KT9 1SG
*Major Shareholder:* Bemal Patel
*Officers:* Bemal Patel [1973] Director

**Direct Pharma Limited**
*Incorporated:* 26 September 2016
*Registered Office:* 2 La Roche Close, Slough, SL3 7RJ
*Officers:* Abdul Rehman Khan [1974] Director

**Directpharm Ltd**
*Incorporated:* 8 March 2016
*Registered Office:* c/o Haslers, Old Station Road, Loughton, Essex, IG10 4PL
*Major Shareholder:* Bemal Patel
*Officers:* Bemal Patel [1973] Director

**Discount Healthcare Ltd**
*Incorporated:* 10 February 2017  *Employees:* 2
*Net Worth Deficit:* £15,067  *Total Assets:* £100
*Registered Office:* Unit 4 Brewers Yard, Ivel Road, Shefford, Beds, SG17 5GY
*Shareholders:* Daniel Mark Yellop; Alexander James Coker
*Officers:* Alexander James Coker [1990] Director; Daniel Mark Yellop [1990] Director

**Discovery Pharmaceuticals Limited**
*Incorporated:* 21 July 2000  *Employees:* 2
*Previous:* Whatdrug Ltd
*Net Worth:* £1,983,500  *Total Assets:* £6,035,042
*Registered Office:* 7 Sopwith Way, Drayton Fields Industrial Estate, Daventry, Northants, NN11 8PB
*Parent:* Dexcel-Pharma Limited
*Officers:* Terry Grigg [1949] Managing Director; Anastasis Konstantinou [1984] Director [Cypriot]

**Dispensing Direct Services Ltd**
*Incorporated:* 1 July 2015
*Previous:* Euromed Consulting Ltd
*Net Worth:* £59,282  *Total Assets:* £642,404
*Registered Office:* 1st Floor, 314 Regents Park Road, Finchley, London, N3 2LT
*Major Shareholder:* Carl Daniel Woolf
*Officers:* Carl Daniel Woolf [1970] Director/Pharmacist

**Dispensing Healthcare Ltd**
*Incorporated:* 25 February 2011
*Net Worth:* £820,474  *Total Assets:* £2,871,178
*Registered Office:* 210b Wellgate, Rotherham, S Yorks, S60 2PD
*Officers:* Asad Ali [1983] Director; Shakeel Ahmed Bashir [1978] Director; Khizer Qureshi [1981] Director; Sajid Razaq [1981] Director

**Disposable Medical Equipment Ltd**
*Incorporated:* 4 May 2001  *Employees:* 22
*Net Worth:* £13,520,286  *Total Assets:* £18,083,790
*Registered Office:* Unit 4 Wintonlea, Monument Way West, Woking, Surrey, GU21 5EN
*Officers:* Parag Khiroya, Secretary/Accountant; Parag Khiroya [1963] Director/Accountant; Varsha Khiroya [1964] Director; Nilesh Nathwani [1961] Director/Pharmacist; Panna Nathwani [1964] Director

**Distinctive Medical Products Ltd**
*Incorporated:* 19 January 2001  *Employees:* 8
*Net Worth:* £1,215,995  *Total Assets:* £2,464,403
*Registered Office:* 3 Seymour Court, Tudor Road, Manor Park, Runcorn, Cheshire, WA7 1SY
*Shareholder:* Paul Douglas Critchlow
*Officers:* Jacqueline Helen Critchlow, Secretary; Paul Douglas Critchlow [1953] Director; Gary L Sharpe [1947] Director/Company President [American]

**Dixons Pharmaceuticals UK Limited**
*Incorporated:* 10 January 2005  *Employees:* 21
*Net Worth:* £1,195,844  *Total Assets:* £2,170,558
*Registered Office:* Unit F4, Tom Bill Way, Ivanhoe Business Park, Smisby Road, Ashby-De-La-Zouch, Leics, LE65 2UY
*Major Shareholder:* Amrut Prajapati
*Officers:* Amrut Prajapati, Secretary/Director; Amrut Prajapati [1955] Director

**Dizzo Consulting (UK) Limited**
*Incorporated:* 16 February 2011
*Net Worth:* £850  *Total Assets:* £1,600
*Registered Office:* 1 Heathfield Avenue, Crewe, Cheshire, CW1 3BA
*Officers:* Ifeoma Kanu, Secretary; Denis Kanu [1979] Director/Pharmacist

**DLG Partners Limited**
*Incorporated:* 6 November 2018
*Registered Office:* 71-75 Shelton Street, London, WC2H 9JQ
*Shareholder:* Charles Desmond Desforges
*Officers:* Edouard-Henri Olivier Desforges, Secretary; Dr Charles Desmond Desforges [1940] Director/Scientist; Edouard-Henri Olivier Desforges [1985] Research & Development Director; John Peregrine Lycett-Green [1978] Director/Botanist

**DMG Trading Limited**
*Incorporated:* 30 November 2018
*Registered Office:* 18 Albany Road, Bedford, MK40 3PH
*Major Shareholder:* Dale Mark Gibson
*Officers:* Dale Mark Gibson [1969] Director

**DML Pharma Consultancy Limited**
*Incorporated:* 30 October 2017
*Registered Office:* c/o Jinal Shah, 5 Theobald Court, Theobald Street, Borehamwood, Herts, WD6 4RN
*Shareholder:* Dhirajlal Ladva
*Officers:* Dhirajlal Mavji Daya Ladva [1969] Director/Commercial Pharmaceuticals

**DMS Plus Limited**
*Incorporated:* 10 September 2014  *Employees:* 9
*Net Worth:* £1,470,293  *Total Assets:* £2,191,171
*Registered Office:* Unit 2-3 Blacknest Business Park, Blacknest Road, nr Bentley, Alton, Hants, GU34 4PX
*Shareholders:* Charles Trevor Bolton; Penelope Anne Bolton
*Officers:* Charles Trevor John Bolton [1954] Director; Penelope Anne Bolton [1964] Director

**DNB Pharma Limited**
*Incorporated:* 16 April 2012
*Net Worth:* £175,416  *Total Assets:* £444,462
*Registered Office:* 29 Regency Drive, Stockton Brook, Stoke on Trent, Staffs, ST9 9LG
*Major Shareholder:* David Brookes
*Officers:* Anita Brookes [1969] Director/Secretary; David Norris Brookes [1973] Sales Director

**Docsinnovent Limited**
*Incorporated:* 16 April 2009  *Employees:* 8
*Net Worth:* £1,732,620  *Total Assets:* £2,331,274
*Registered Office:* Suite F, Ground Floor, Breakspear Way, Hemel Hempstead, Herts, HP2 4TZ
*Major Shareholder:* Muhammed Aslam Nasir
*Officers:* Surendra Kumar Sumaria-Shah, Secretary; Roger John Bennett [1952] Director; Dr Muhammed Aslam Nasir [1961] Director/Anaesthetist; Surendra Kumar Sumaria-Shah [1955] Director/Chartered Accountant

**Doctors Dispensing Services Limited**
*Incorporated:* 9 August 2004  *Employees:* 1
*Net Worth Deficit:* £124,742  *Total Assets:* £191,089
*Registered Office:* 3 Young Place, East Kilbride, G75 0TD
*Parent:* Munro Healthcare Group Limited
*Officers:* John Cochrane [1957] Director

**Doksy Limited**
*Incorporated:* 10 March 2017
*Net Worth Deficit:* £21,400  *Total Assets:* £29,610
*Registered Office:* 5 Barrington Road, Leicester, LE2 2RA
*Officers:* Dominique Patricia Corneillo [1963] Director [French]; Sylvain Luc Alexandre Forget [1966] Director [French]; Dr Kamlesh Sheth [1963] Director

**Dollano Trading Limited**
*Incorporated:* 2 July 2018
*Registered Office:* 71-75 Shelton Street, London, WC2H 9JQ
*Shareholders:* Lukas Kocfelda; Martin Sebesta; Dollano Care S.R.O.
*Officers:* Lukas Kocfelda [1981] Director [Czech]

**Dompe UK Limited**
*Incorporated:* 17 June 2015  *Employees:* 3
*Net Worth:* £73,883  *Total Assets:* £446,927
*Registered Office:* Jubilee House, Third Avenue, Marlow, Bucks, SL7 1EY
*Major Shareholder:* Sergio Gianfranco Luigi Maria Dompe
*Officers:* Giuseppe Andreano [1962] Director/Manager [Italian]

**Doncaster Pharmaceuticals Group Limited**
*Incorporated:* 21 January 1987  *Employees:* 102
*Net Worth:* £6,732,000  *Total Assets:* £18,118,000
*Registered Office:* 7 Regents Drive, Prudhoe, Northumberland, NE42 6PX
*Parent:* Doncaster Pharmaceuticals Limited
*Officers:* Mark James Gulliford [1969] Director; David Horry [1964] Director/Chairman; Haydn Peter Smith [1966] Group IT Director; Derek Andrew Wilson [1964] Director

**Doncaster Pharmaceuticals Limited**
*Incorporated:* 10 October 1977
*Net Worth:* £200  *Total Assets:* £5,645,959
*Registered Office:* 7 Regents Drive, Prudhoe, Northumberland, NE42 6PX
*Parent:* Converse Pharma Limited
*Officers:* Mark James Gulliford [1969] Director; Derek Andrew Wilson [1964] Director

**Dong Hwa UK Ltd**
*Incorporated:* 9 November 2018
*Registered Office:* Suite 31, Second Floor, 107 Cheapside, London, EC2V 6DN
*Major Shareholder:* Sung Eun Kim
*Officers:* Sung Eun Kim [1964] Representative Director [South Korean]

**Dosego Limited**
*Incorporated:* 28 June 2013
*Net Worth Deficit:* £101,995  *Total Assets:* £7,143
*Registered Office:* William Burford House, Lansdown Place Lane, Cheltenham, Glos, GL50 2LB
*Major Shareholder:* Robert Harland Games
*Officers:* Robert Harland Games [1971] Director/Patent Attorney; Adrian Niall Hocking [1972] Director/Mechanical Engineer

**Double Wing Health & Beauty Ltd**
Incorporated: 10 March 2016
Registered Office: Portwall Place, Portwall Lane, Bristol, BS1 6NA
Parent: Double Wing Pharma Ltd
Officers: Douglas Bruce Andrews [1951] Director [American]; Xiaoli Wang [1969] Director [Chinese]

**Double Wing Medical Ltd**
Incorporated: 10 March 2016  Employees: 5
Net Worth: £191,412  Total Assets: £227,761
Registered Office: Portwall Place, Portwall Lane, Bristol, BS1 6NA
Parent: Double Wing Pharma Ltd
Officers: Douglas Andrews [1951] Director [American]; Douglas Bruce Murdoch [1950] Director; Antony Twyford [1955] Sales Director; Xiaoli Wang [1969] Director [Chinese]

**Double Wing Pharma Development Ltd**
Incorporated: 10 March 2016  Employees: 3
Net Worth Deficit: £22,060  Total Assets: £28,828
Registered Office: Portwall Place, Portwall Lane, Bristol, BS1 6NA
Parent: Double Wing Pharma Ltd
Officers: Douglas Bruce Andrews [1951] Director [American]; Xiaoli Wang [1969] Director [Chinese]

**Dr Ba Limited**
Incorporated: 28 June 2018
Registered Office: 332 Norris Road, Sale, Cheshire, M33 2UG
Major Shareholder: Babak Amozandeh
Officers: Dr Babak Amozandeh [1964] Director [Swedish]

**Dr Kool Ltd**
Incorporated: 12 December 2018
Registered Office: 28 Limbury Road, Luton, Beds, LU3 2PL
Shareholder: Maria Angeles Silvia Gomez Fernandez
Officers: Moamen Abou-El-Wafa [1983] Director/Owner [Irish]; Maria Angeles Silvia Gomez Fernandez [1967] Company Secretary/Director [Spanish]; Ihab Kamal [1966] Director/Pharmacist

**Dr Pradeep Reddy's Laboratories (UK & EU) Limited**
Incorporated: 25 September 2018
Registered Office: Crown House, 27 Old Gloucester Street, London, WC1N 3AX
Shareholders: Bhavani Potlapadu; Pradeep Kumar Reddy Potlapadu
Officers: Bhavani Potlapadu [1981] Director/Finance Analyst; Dr Pradeep Kumar Reddy Potlapadu [1979] Director/Doctor

**Dr Sproglet Ltd**
Incorporated: 5 November 2018
Registered Office: 8 Lyndale Road, Bristol, BS5 7AA
Major Shareholder: Stuart Jenks
Officers: Stuart Jenks [1986] Director

**Dr. Falk Pharma UK Limited**
Incorporated: 20 October 1988  Employees: 23
Net Worth: £13,177,569  Total Assets: £16,351,891
Registered Office: Unit K, Bourne End Business Park, Cores End Road, Bourne End, Bucks, SL8 5AS
Officers: Anthony James McFadyen, Secretary; Anthony James McFadyen [1957] Director

**Dragonstone Group Limited**
Incorporated: 27 November 2015  Employees: 2
Net Worth Deficit: £12,412  Total Assets: £22,755
Registered Office: 40 Park Avenue, Egham, Surrey, TW20 8HJ
Shareholders: Liam Hickey; Philip Young
Officers: Liam Hickey [1987] Director/HM Forces; Philip Young [1988] Director/HM Forces

**Dream Pharma Ltd**
Incorporated: 15 January 2003
Net Worth: £1,221,461  Total Assets: £1,222,486
Registered Office: 4a Garside Close, Hampton, Surrey, TW12 3AN
Shareholder: Mehdi Alavi
Officers: Farizad Alavi, Secretary; Mehdi Alavi [1960] Director/Wholesale

**Drilltex GB Ltd**
Incorporated: 30 September 2013
Net Worth: £66,349  Total Assets: £137,768
Registered Office: 48 Dyrham Road, Kingswood, Bristol, BS15 4HP
Shareholders: Andrew Boulton; Imogen Ruth Boulton
Officers: Andrew Frederick Boulton [1962] Director/Engineer; Imogen Ruth Boulton [1972] Director/Secretary

**Drugget Ltd**
Incorporated: 4 December 2018
Registered Office: 71-75 Shelton Street, Covent Garden, London, WC2H 9JQ
Major Shareholder: Ham Mukama Yorachi
Officers: Juliet Namubiru, Secretary; Ham Mukama Yorachi [1991] Director

**Drugsdirect Limited**
Incorporated: 31 March 1999  Employees: 3
Net Worth: £333  Total Assets: £232,546
Registered Office: Unit 4, 12 Emery Road, Brislington, Bristol, BS4 5PF
Parent: Drugsdirect Global Limited
Officers: Larisa Atkinson, Secretary; Alona Courtney [1987] Director

**Drugsrus Limited**
Incorporated: 30 September 2003
Net Worth: £7,134,049  Total Assets: £34,788,344
Registered Office: 39a Joel Street, Northwood Hills, Northwood, Middlesex, HA6 1NZ
Major Shareholder: Anuj Somchand Shah
Officers: Anuj Somchand Shah [1966] Director

**Druid Pharma Limited**
Incorporated: 23 April 2015
Net Worth Deficit: £75,928  Total Assets: £224,908
Registered Office: 107 Arrowsmith Drive, Stonehouse, Glos, GL10 2QS
Major Shareholder: Madhana Sundaram Arumugam
Officers: Madhana Sundaram Arumugam [1967] Director

**Dunamis Pharmaceutical Services Limited**
Incorporated: 31 December 2009
Net Worth Deficit: £7,032
Registered Office: 28 Robinia Close, Hainault, Essex, IG6 3AJ
Major Shareholder: Abiola Odunlami
Officers: Abiola Folayemi Odunlami [1968] Director/Pharmacist

**Duncan Inc Ltd**
Incorporated: 31 March 2015  Employees: 1
Net Worth: £158,322  Total Assets: £223,245
Registered Office: Paxton House, 11 Woodside Crescent, Glasgow, G3 7UL
Major Shareholder: Stephen Peter Duncan
Officers: Rachel Duncan [1990] Director; Stephen Peter Duncan [1986] Director/Sales Executive

**Durbin PLC**
*Incorporated:* 4 September 1998 *Employees:* 121
*Net Worth:* £10,044,928 *Total Assets:* £16,542,647
*Registered Office:* Durbin House, Unit 5 Swallowfield Way, Hayes, Middlesex, UB3 1DQ
*Parent:* Durbin Group PLC
*Officers:* Carmen Gleen, Secretary/Director; Carmen Gleen [1947] Director; Leslie Morgan [1954] Director/Pharmacist

**Durham Pharmaceuticals Limited**
*Incorporated:* 15 February 1950 *Employees:* 19
*Net Worth:* £183,441 *Total Assets:* £1,061,726
*Registered Office:* St Aidans Terrace, Trimdon Station, Cleveland, TS29 6BT
*Major Shareholder:* Peter Robert Whitfield Grundy
*Officers:* Peter Robert Whitfield Grundy, Secretary; Peter Robert Whitfield Grundy [1951] Director

**Dutscher Scientific UK Limited**
*Incorporated:* 26 July 2004 *Employees:* 2
*Net Worth:* £142,875 *Total Assets:* £171,885
*Registered Office:* Orchard House, The Square, Hessle, E Yorks, HU13 0AE
*Parent:* Domique Dutscher SAS
*Officers:* Neil Bewell, Secretary; Robert Peter Chapman [1955] Director

**DWH Pharma Limited**
*Incorporated:* 28 November 2012
*Net Worth:* £361,886 *Total Assets:* £1,723,270
*Registered Office:* Corner Oak, 1 Homer Road, Solihull, W Midlands, B91 3QG
*Officers:* Simon Rodrick Webster, Secretary; Simon Rodrick Webster [1966] Director

**Dynamic Development Laboratories Co Ltd**
*Incorporated:* 16 November 2016
*Net Worth:* £293 *Total Assets:* £1,454
*Registered Office:* 316 Beulah Hill, Upper Norwood, London, SE19 3HF
*Officers:* Serhii Kucherenko [1974] Director [Ukrainian]

**E-Pharm Limited**
*Incorporated:* 3 March 1999
*Net Worth:* £726,086 *Total Assets:* £1,315,210
*Registered Office:* Aqua House, 24 Valley Walk, Shirley, Croydon, Surrey, CR0 8SR
*Shareholders:* Kalpesh Kumar Prabhudas Saglani; Hiten Patel
*Officers:* Mona Patel, Secretary; Hiten Patel [1966] Director/Pharmacist; Kalpesh Kumar Prabhudas Saglani [1978] Business Development Director

**E-Pharma Chemical Int. Limited**
*Incorporated:* 28 May 2009
*Net Worth Deficit:* £2,232
*Registered Office:* 19 Station Parade, Ockham Road South, East Horsley, Leatherhead, Surrey, KT24 6QN
*Major Shareholder:* Raja Sethupathy
*Officers:* Raja Sethupathy, Secretary; Raja Sethupathy [1957] Director [German]

**E.P.G Pharma Ltd**
*Incorporated:* 27 September 2018
*Registered Office:* Medicity Nottingham, D6 Building, Thane Road, Nottingham, NG90 6BH
*Major Shareholder:* Sherif Mohamed Aboelnaga Mohamed Elmasry
*Officers:* Sherif Mohamed Aboelnaga Mohamed Elmasry [1972] Director [Egyptian]

**E.U.K. Limited**
*Incorporated:* 16 July 1999 *Employees:* 1
*Net Worth Deficit:* £28,515 *Total Assets:* £74,046
*Registered Office:* Edelman House, 1238 High Road, London, N20 0LH
*Shareholders:* Jean-Pierre Cavin; Danielle Floret-Faure
*Officers:* Jean-Pierre Cavin [1951] Director/Export Manager [French]

**EAM Wholesale Ltd**
*Incorporated:* 19 December 2017
*Net Worth:* £1 *Total Assets:* £1
*Registered Office:* 13 Maypole Street, Newhall, Harlow, Essex, CM17 9JJ
*Major Shareholder:* Joost Muller
*Officers:* Joost Muller [1979] Wholesale Director [Dutch]

**Easho Limited**
*Incorporated:* 5 May 2017
*Net Worth Deficit:* £9,486 *Total Assets:* £54,227
*Registered Office:* Kanta House, Victoria Road, South Ruislip, Middlesex, HA4 0JQ
*Major Shareholder:* Sonya Chatwani
*Officers:* Sonya Chatwani [1989] Director

**East Midlands Infotech PVT Limited**
*Incorporated:* 24 January 2013
*Net Worth:* £2,476 *Total Assets:* £94,375
*Registered Office:* 509 Tamworth Road, Long Eaton, Nottingham, NG10 3GR
*Shareholder:* Bhasker Dhirendrabhai Parmar
*Officers:* Bhasker Dhirendrabhai Parmar [1975] Director [Indian]; Kaushal Pravinchandra Sheth [1978] Director [Indian]

**East Midlands Pharma Limited**
*Incorporated:* 15 February 2005 *Employees:* 78
*Net Worth:* £304,212 *Total Assets:* £6,809,674
*Registered Office:* Unit 2a Old Dalby Business Park, Station Road, Old Dalby, Leics, LE14 3NJ
*Parent:* Day Lewis PLC
*Officers:* Kirit Chimanbhai Patel Junior, Secretary; Ian Robert Adamson [1958] Director; Jayanti Chimanbhai Patel Junior [1984] Director

**Eastern Lighthouse Ltd**
*Incorporated:* 5 May 2017
*Registered Office:* 71-75 Shelton Street, Covent Garden, London, WC2H 9JQ
*Shareholder:* Hamada Ghith
*Officers:* Rafif Elbahy [1988] Director/MENA Region Representative [Egyptian]; Dr Hamada Ghith [1983] Director/General Manager [Egyptian]; Dr Fairouz Othman [1983] Director/Key Account Manager [Egyptian]

**Ebbcourt Limited**
*Incorporated:* 18 December 1992
*Net Worth:* £75,878 *Total Assets:* £99,707
*Registered Office:* Regents Court, Princess Street, Hull, HU2 8BA
*Shareholders:* Ann-Marie Keown; Nicholas Charles Lamson Keown
*Officers:* Fiona Frances Keown, Secretary; Nicholas Charles Lamson Keown [1954] Sales Director

**Ecco Healthcare Limited**
*Incorporated:* 30 January 2015
*Net Worth:* £48,084 *Total Assets:* £159,362
*Registered Office:* Block 1, Unit 3, 2 Watson Terrace, Drongan, Ayr, KA6 7AA
*Officers:* Christopher Robert Livingstone [1972] Managing Director; Joanne Elizabeth Livingstone [1976] Director

### Eclipse Generics Limited
*Incorporated:* 12 March 2003  *Employees:* 71
*Net Worth:* £2,940,000  *Total Assets:* £7,610,000
*Registered Office:* Unit 1 Langlands Place, Kelvin South Industrial Estate, East Kilbride, G75 0YF
*Parent:* Converse Pharma Limited
*Officers:* Mark James Gulliford [1969] Director; David Horry [1964] Director/Chairman; Haydn Peter Smith [1966] Group IT Director; Derek Andrew Wilson [1964] Director

### Eco Animal Health Group PLC
*Incorporated:* 22 May 1984  *Employees:* 207
*Net Worth:* £99,690,000  *Total Assets:* £117,185,000
*Registered Office:* 78 Coombe Road, New Malden, Surrey, KT3 4QS
*Officers:* Julia Trouse, Secretary; Brett Timothy Clemo [1962] Global Operations Director; Dr Andrew Alfred Jones [1960] Director/Management Consultant; Marc Denham Loomes [1961] Director; Anthony Paul Rawlinson [1957] Director/Chartered Accountant; Kevin Anthony Stockdale [1965] Finance Director; Julia Trouse [1966] Director; Richard Kenneth Wood [1944] Non-Executive Director Chairman

### Ecogen Europe Ltd
*Incorporated:* 1 February 2008
*Previous:* Ice Pharma Limited
*Registered Office:* Office 7, 5 Museum Square, Leicester, LE1 6UF
*Parent:* Redhawk Pharma UK Ltd
*Officers:* Gerard Darcy Klug [1951] Director/Executive [American]

### Ecomed UK Limited
*Incorporated:* 5 September 2017
*Registered Office:* College House, 17 King Edwards Road, Ruislip, Middlesex, HA4 7AE
*Major Shareholder:* Daniel Patrick Bennett
*Officers:* Daniel Patrick Bennett [1955] Director

### ECommedical Limited
*Incorporated:* 4 February 2014  *Employees:* 1
*Net Worth Deficit:* £8,093  *Total Assets:* £20
*Registered Office:* 33 Darnley Road, Gravesend, Kent, DA11 0SD
*Major Shareholder:* Cristina Racca
*Officers:* Cristina Racca [1978] Director [Italian]

### Econo-Beauty Ltd
*Incorporated:* 10 May 2010
*Registered Office:* Pinnacle House Business Centre, Newark Road, Peterborough, Cambs, PE1 5YD
*Major Shareholder:* Alistair Martin Ashworth
*Officers:* Alistair Ashworth [1963] Director/Engineer

### Econo-Care Ltd
*Incorporated:* 10 May 2010
*Registered Office:* Pinnacle House Business Centre, Newark Road, Peterborough, Cambs, PE1 5YD
*Major Shareholder:* Alistair Martin Ashworth
*Officers:* Alistair Ashworth [1963] Director/Engineer

### Econo-Group Ltd
*Incorporated:* 5 February 2010
*Registered Office:* Pinnacle House Business Centre, Newark Road, Peterborough, Cambs, PE1 5YD
*Major Shareholder:* Alistair Martin Ashworth
*Officers:* Alistair Ashworth [1963] Director/Engineer

### Econo-Supplies Ltd
*Incorporated:* 22 August 2011
*Registered Office:* Pinnacle House Business Centre, Newark Road, Peterborough, Cambs, PE1 5YD
*Major Shareholder:* Alistair Martin Ashworth
*Officers:* Alistair Martin Ashworth [1963] Director/Beauty Wholesaler; Hedley Edwin Cross [1954] Director/Accountant

### Ecosse Hospital Products Limited
*Incorporated:* 16 August 1944
*Net Worth:* £1  *Total Assets:* £1
*Registered Office:* 3 Young Place, Kelvin Industrial Estate, East Kilbride, G75 0TD
*Parent:* Munro Healthcare Group Limited
*Officers:* John Cochrane [1957] Director

### Ecosse Pharmaceuticals Limited
*Incorporated:* 12 September 2000
*Registered Office:* 3 Young Place, Kelvin Industrial Estate, East Kilbride, G75 0TD
*Parent:* Munro Healthcare Group Limited
*Officers:* John Cochrane [1957] Director; Shirley Agnes Gorrell [1967] Commercial Director

### Eddohealthcare Ltd
*Incorporated:* 7 February 2019
*Registered Office:* 5 Parkway, Erith, Kent, DA18 4HG
*Major Shareholder:* Olusola Olayinka Kujore
*Officers:* Olusola Olayinka Kujore [1968] Director/Pharmacist

### Eden CBD Limited
*Incorporated:* 14 June 2018
*Registered Office:* 9 Arkwright Court, Commercial Road, Darwen, Lancs, BB3 0FG
*Shareholders:* Matthew Moden; Abraham Spain
*Officers:* Matthew Moden [1973] Director; Abraham Spain [1977] Director

### Edi Beryl Ltd
*Incorporated:* 3 November 2017
*Registered Office:* 100a Long Elmes, Harrow, Middlesex, HA3 5JY
*Shareholders:* Pranav Jha; Pranav Jha
*Officers:* Vermeet Kaur Bambra [1989] Director [Indian]; Dr Pranav Jha [1986] Director [Indian]

### Edmond Finance Ltd
*Incorporated:* 28 June 2013
*Net Worth Deficit:* £1,810  *Total Assets:* £179,185
*Registered Office:* Premier, 40 Gracechurch Street, London, EC3V 0BT
*Major Shareholder:* Utpal Chowdhury
*Officers:* Utpal Chowdhury [1974] Director [Indian]

### Ego Pharmaceuticals (UK) Limited
*Incorporated:* 11 January 2002  *Employees:* 1
*Net Worth:* £279,198  *Total Assets:* £2,443,516
*Registered Office:* Abbey Place, 24-28 Easton Street, High Wycombe, Bucks, HP11 1NT
*Officers:* Alan Oppenheim, Secretary [Australian]; Alan Oppenheim [1957] Managing Director [Australian]; Victoria Marie Jane Oppenheim [1959] Scientific Director [Australian]

### Egroup (UK) Limited
*Incorporated:* 10 February 1998  *Employees:* 5
*Net Worth:* £1,651,409  *Total Assets:* £2,016,523
*Registered Office:* 505 Pinner Road, Harrow, Middlesex, HA2 6EH
*Shareholders:* Mustanseir Ebrahimjee; Safia Ebrahimjee
*Officers:* Safia Ebrahimjee, Secretary; Mustanseir Ebrahimjee [1957] Director/Import Exporter

**Eico Ltd**
Incorporated: 20 January 2004
Net Worth: £578,682  Total Assets: £1,766,414
Registered Office: 6 Becmead Avenue, Harrow, Middlesex, HA3 8EY
Major Shareholder: Seema Patel
Officers: Seema Patel, Secretary/Accountant; Kalpen Patel [1974] Director

**Einoxy Limited**
Incorporated: 11 October 2016
Net Worth: £1  Total Assets: £1
Registered Office: 27 Old Gloucester Street, London, WC1N 3AX
Major Shareholder: Subbiah Sugumaran
Officers: Subbiah Sugumaran, Secretary; Subbiah Sugumaran [1977] Director [Indian]

**Eisai Limited**
Incorporated: 11 April 1988  Employees: 182
Net Worth: £105,982,944  Total Assets: £126,478,576
Registered Office: European Knowledge Centre, Mosquito Way, Hatfield, Herts, AL10 9SN
Parent: Eisai Europe Limited
Officers: Simon Gerard Thomas, Secretary; Nicholas Conrad Burgin [1959] Director; Gary Bryan Hendler [1966] Director/President and CEO; Teiji Kimura [1963] Director [Japanese]; Kazuhiko Masano [1971] Director [Japanese]

**Elanco UK AH Limited**
Incorporated: 23 May 2018
Registered Office: Lilly House, Priestley Road, Basingstoke, Hants, RG24 9NL
Parent: Eli Lilly and Company Limited
Officers: Kristina Mary Hunt [1969] Director; Christopher Lewis [1978] Director/Finance Manager; Peter Troutt [1966] Director/General Manager

**Elara Care Limited**
Incorporated: 14 December 2018
Registered Office: 35 Kingsland Road, London, E2 8AA
Major Shareholder: Jasveer Matharu
Officers: Jasveer Matharu [1989] Director [Italian]

**Elcon Pharma Limited**
Incorporated: 13 July 2018
Registered Office: The Mount, Barrow Hill, Sellindge, Ashford, Kent, TN25 6JQ
Parent: Innomedi Limited
Officers: Andrius Daukantas [1979] Director [Lithuanian]

**Elektro Genesis Limited**
Incorporated: 4 September 2017
Registered Office: Flat 7, Glade Apartments, 24 Stebondale Street, London, E14 3NQ
Major Shareholder: Tarun Gupta
Officers: Monika Gupta [1978] Director/Wholesale Trade of Medical Equipment [Indian]; Tarun Gupta [1974] Director/Wholesale Trade Medical Equipment [Indian]

**Elias Med Limited**
Incorporated: 4 July 2017
Net Worth: £1,571  Total Assets: £20,980
Registered Office: 66 Eaton Avenue, Burnham, Slough, SL1 6EZ
Major Shareholder: Maher Khetyar
Officers: Catriona Khetyar, Secretary; Maher Khetyar [1972] Director

**Elim Springs Biotech Ltd**
Incorporated: 11 November 2014
Net Worth: £17,537  Total Assets: £22,125
Registered Office: 71-75 Shelton Street, Covent Garden, London, WC2H 9JQ
Major Shareholder: Jun Li
Officers: Mo Guan [1978] Director/Technical Support [Chinese]; Jun Li [1978] Director/Accountant [Chinese]

**Elite Pharma (Surrey) Limited**
Incorporated: 1 February 2007  Employees: 23
Net Worth: £1,623,269  Total Assets: £5,760,431
Registered Office: Unit 2 Molesey Business Centre, Central Avenue, West Molesey, Surrey, KT8 2QZ
Major Shareholder: Kiritkumar Meghji Shah
Officers: Ashokkumar Dahyabhai Patel, Secretary; Ashokkumar Dahyabhai Patel [1956] Director Secretary; Ramesh Vasudev Patel [1946] Director/Pharmacist; Kiritkumar Meghji Shah [1956] Director/Pharmacist

**Elite Pharma UK Limited**
Incorporated: 7 August 2018
Registered Office: 21 Sneinton Boulevard, Nottingham, NG2 4FD
Officers: Nihad Qader Bakr Harki [1987] Director [Iraqi]

**Elkay Laboratory Products (U.K.) Limited**
Incorporated: 6 January 1994  Employees: 15
Net Worth: £393,756  Total Assets: £913,712
Registered Office: Unit E, Lutyens Ind Centre, Bilton Road, Kingsland Business Park, Basingstoke, Hants, RG24 8LJ
Major Shareholder: Robin Conway
Officers: Jacqueline Helen Sleap, Secretary; Michelle Conway [1974] Marketing Director; Robin Conway [1955] Director

**Elleco Limited**
Incorporated: 18 October 2007  Employees: 2
Net Worth: £144,830  Total Assets: £164,634
Registered Office: 15a Laverock Crescent, Brighouse, W Yorks, HD6 2NR
Major Shareholder: Michelle Lesley Robinson
Officers: Michelle Lesley Robinson [1959] Director

**Ellis Pharma Limited**
Incorporated: 6 June 2014
Registered Office: The Piazza, Mercia Marina, Findern Lane, Willington, Derby, DE65 6DW
Parent: Bionical Limited
Officers: Andrew Thomas Borkowski [1962] Director/Solicitor

**Elm Healthcare Limited**
Incorporated: 19 May 2009
Previous: Aaron Homecare Limited
Net Worth Deficit: £5,529  Total Assets: £80,282
Registered Office: 1e Monaghan Street, Newry, Co Down, BT35 6BB
Shareholders: Talura Holdings Limited; Sally Murtagh
Officers: Sarah Murtagh, Secretary; Sarah Murtagh [1967] Director [Irish]

**Barry Elman (Wholesale) Limited**
Incorporated: 6 February 1964
Net Worth: £51,730  Total Assets: £62,107
Registered Office: 88 Venture Point West, Evans Road, Speke, Liverpool, L24 9PB
Major Shareholder: Barry Elman
Officers: Barry Elman [1936] Director

### Elmstone Healthcare Limited
*Incorporated:* 17 July 2015
*Net Worth:* £7,560  *Total Assets:* £24,236
*Registered Office:* Transport House, Uxbridge Road, Hillingdon, Middlesex, UB10 0LY
*Shareholder:* Anand Pankaj Amin
*Officers:* Anand Pankaj Amin [1980] Director; Bhaskar Jyoti Bora [1975] Director/Medical Doctor

### Ely Pharma Ltd
*Incorporated:* 19 July 2017
*Registered Office:* 14 Silverhill Drive, Bradford, BD3 7LD
*Shareholder:* Dara Karim Sharif
*Officers:* Dara Karim Sharif, Secretary; Dara Karim Sharif [1983] Director/Manager

### Emcure Pharma UK Ltd
*Incorporated:* 6 November 2012  *Employees:* 6
*Net Worth:* £8,047,284  *Total Assets:* £36,279,172
*Registered Office:* 220 Butterfield, Great Marlings, Luton, Beds, LU2 8DL
*Officers:* Zarir Jal Cama [1947] Director; William Steven Marth [1954] Director/Business Executive [American]; Samit Satish Mehta [1980] Director [Indian]; Tajuddin Shaikh [1974] Director/Accountant [Indian]; Ajit Chand Srimal [1958] Director/Chief Executive

### Emkado Ltd.
*Incorporated:* 1 March 2012  *Employees:* 4
*Net Worth:* £144,903  *Total Assets:* £512,823
*Registered Office:* First Floor Offices, County House, Dunswell Road, Cottingham, E Yorks, HU16 4JT
*Officers:* Karl Andrew Douglas [1972] Director

### Emkkay of London Limited
*Incorporated:* 6 November 2007
*Net Worth Deficit:* £6,826  *Total Assets:* £16,457
*Registered Office:* 40 Kenton Park Crescent, Kenton, Harrow, Middlesex, HA3 8UA
*Officers:* Sohesh Petel, Secretary; Keronn Patels [1949] Director

### Emra Consult Limited
*Incorporated:* 23 November 2016
*Registered Office:* 4 The Hundred, Waterlooville, Hants, PO7 6UR
*Shareholders:* Emmanuel Asiedu; Richmal Asante
*Officers:* Richmal Asante, Secretary; Emmanuel Asiedu [1979] Director/Pharmacist

### EMT Healthcare Limited
*Incorporated:* 7 January 1972  *Employees:* 42
*Net Worth:* £751,633  *Total Assets:* £2,865,794
*Registered Office:* Boulevard Industrial Park, Padge Road, Beeston, Nottingham, NG9 2JR
*Officers:* David Hemington, Secretary; Venichand Ranmal Harania [1942] Director; David Hemington [1955] Director/Chartered Accountant; Richard Gareth Muir [1989] Director/Sales Manager; Rodney David Muir [1977] Managing Director; Stephen Lindsay Muir [1950] Director; Amrik Singh Sagoo [1960] Director/Operations Manager

### Enfield Nutrition Club Ltd
*Incorporated:* 19 May 2016
*Net Worth:* £3,404  *Total Assets:* £6,218
*Registered Office:* 1 Kings Avenue, London, N21 3NA
*Major Shareholder:* Anthony Joseph Leonida
*Officers:* Anthony Joseph Leonida [1993] Director

### Engelpharma UK Limited
*Incorporated:* 15 December 2006  *Employees:* 1
*Net Worth:* £28,858  *Total Assets:* £31,183
*Registered Office:* 269 Farnborough Road, Farnborough, Hants, GU14 7LY
*Major Shareholder:* Zsolt Vas
*Officers:* Zsolt Vas [1970] Director [Hungarian]

### English Herbal Medicines Limited
*Incorporated:* 18 February 2004
*Net Worth:* £5,574  *Total Assets:* £6,552
*Registered Office:* Town Park Farm, Oakham Road, Brooke, Oakham, Rutland, LE15 8DG
*Major Shareholder:* Paul Nigel Chenery
*Officers:* Paul Nigel Chenery [1951] Director

### Enjoy Marketing Limited
*Incorporated:* 8 February 2018
*Registered Office:* 339 Two Mile Hill Road, Kingswood, Bristol, BS15 1AN
*Shareholders:* Rajesh Hariharan; Joanna Kill
*Officers:* Rajesh Hariharan [1968] Director

### Enlon Limited
*Incorporated:* 28 June 2005
*Registered Office:* D S House, 306 High Street, Croydon, Surrey, CR0 1NG
*Major Shareholder:* Gautum Patel
*Officers:* Manirhai Patel, Secretary; Gautam Patel [1953] Director/Trader

### Ennogen Healthcare Ltd
*Incorporated:* 14 October 2011  *Employees:* 10
*Net Worth:* £21,729,260  *Total Assets:* £29,465,110
*Registered Office:* Unit G4, Riverside Way, Dartford, Kent, DA1 5BS
*Major Shareholder:* Gurdev Singh Rurai
*Officers:* Gurdev Singh Ruprai [1960] Director/Pharmacist

### Ennogen Pharma Ltd
*Incorporated:* 24 August 2011  *Employees:* 9
*Net Worth:* £545,149  *Total Assets:* £2,487,233
*Registered Office:* Unit G4, Riverside Industrial Estate, Riverside Way, Dartford, Kent, DA1 5BS
*Major Shareholder:* Gurdev Singh Ruprai
*Officers:* Gurdev Singh Ruprai [1960] Director/Pharmacist

### Enteromed Limited
*Incorporated:* 23 May 2014
*Net Worth Deficit:* £25,689  *Total Assets:* £677,721
*Registered Office:* First Floor, 85 Great Portland Street, London, W1W 7LT
*Major Shareholder:* Elena Markaryan
*Officers:* Elena Markaryan [1975] General Director [Russian]

### Entod Research Cell (UK) Limited
*Incorporated:* 25 October 2010
*Net Worth:* £25,858  *Total Assets:* £117,596
*Registered Office:* 15 Tottenham Lane, Hornsey, London, N8 9DJ
*Officers:* Anjula Masurkar [1980] Director/Pharmacist; Nikhil Kishore Masurkar [1982] Director

### Entrust & UK Ltd
*Incorporated:* 3 April 2009
*Net Worth:* £2,484  *Total Assets:* £2,484
*Registered Office:* Flat 2, 251-253 Neasden Lane, London, NW10 1QG
*Major Shareholder:* Moamen Moustafa Abou-El-Wafa
*Officers:* Moamen Moustafa Abou-El-Wafa [1983] Director [Irish]

**EPE Global Limited**
*Incorporated:* 10 June 2014
*Net Worth:* £77,866  *Total Assets:* £246,365
*Registered Office:* 44-45 Calthorpe Road, Edgbaston, Birmingham, B15 1TH
*Major Shareholder:* Omair Javed
*Officers:* Omair Javed [1986] Director


**Epsilon Pharmaceuticals Limited**
*Incorporated:* 23 June 2015
*Net Worth Deficit:* £25,255  *Total Assets:* £10,017
*Registered Office:* Barnston House, Beacon Lane, Heswall, Wirral, Merseyside, CH60 0EE
*Shareholders:* William Michael Gould; Stephen Tickle
*Officers:* Annette Catherine Fearnley [1969] Director; Dr Caron Lynn Gould [1969] Director; William Michael Gould [1970] Director; Stephen Tickle [1962] Director


**Eptheca Global Limited**
*Incorporated:* 2 August 2005
*Net Worth:* £3,251  *Total Assets:* £70,802
*Registered Office:* 7 Shepherds Fold, Holmer Green, High Wycombe, Bucks, HP15 6XZ
*Major Shareholder:* Colin Jonathan Ward
*Officers:* Colin Jonathan Ward, Secretary; Michael Logan Rutt [1953] Director/Chartered Accountant; Colin Jonathan Ward [1957] Director/Businessman


**Equimed Medical Supplies Ltd**
*Incorporated:* 11 February 2019
*Registered Office:* 40 Walter Street, Blackburn, BB1 1RD
*Major Shareholder:* Almaan Masood
*Officers:* Almaan Masood, Secretary; Almaan Masood [1994] Director/Solicitor [Pakistani]


**Espere Healthcare Limited**
*Incorporated:* 3 February 2004  *Employees:* 6
*Net Worth Deficit:* £190,007  *Total Assets:* £292,611
*Registered Office:* Suite 3, Middlesex House, Rutherford Close, Stevenage, Herts, SG1 2EF
*Shareholders:* David Frederick Battershill; Christopher Keith Steeples
*Officers:* Joanna Ruth Fletcher, Secretary; David Frederick Battershill [1947] Director/Management Consultant; Joanna Ruth Fletcher [1974] Director/Medical Device Supplier; Dr Rupert Bernard Stuart Mason [1947] Director/Doctor; Christopher Keith Steeples [1960] Director


**H.N. Espley & Sons Limited**
*Incorporated:* 21 February 1978
*Registered Office:* P O Box 2076, Lynstock House, Lynstock Way, Lostock, Bolton, Lancs, BL6 4SA
*Parent:* Gorgemead Limited
*Officers:* Colin Caunce, Secretary; Andrew John Caunce [1974] Director/Accountant


**Essential Pharma Limited**
*Incorporated:* 2 February 2011  *Employees:* 1
*Net Worth:* £10,300,627  *Total Assets:* £30,423,222
*Registered Office:* 7 Egham Business Village, Crabtree Road, Egham, Surrey, TW20 8RB
*Shareholders:* Navinchandra Jamnadas; Varsha Navinchandra
*Officers:* Nikesh Engineer [1985] Director/Doctor


**Essential-Healthcare Ltd**
*Incorporated:* 24 July 2014
*Net Worth Deficit:* £51,790  *Total Assets:* £103,234
*Registered Office:* 249 Ongar Road, Brentwood, Essex, CM15 9DZ
*Major Shareholder:* Niketkumar Dipakkumar Shah
*Officers:* Niketkumar Dipakkumar Shah [1980] Director/Pharmacist


**Essentialink Limited**
*Incorporated:* 5 January 2004
*Net Worth Deficit:* £27,577  *Total Assets:* £1,697
*Registered Office:* 112 Morden Road, London, SW19 3BP
*Shareholder:* Hon Kan Kwan
*Officers:* Hon Kan Kwan [1951] Director/Engineer


**Essex Medical Supplies Ltd**
*Incorporated:* 12 September 2017
*Registered Office:* 44 Chudleigh Cresent, Ilford, Essex, IG3 9AS
*Major Shareholder:* Umar Faruq
*Officers:* Umar Faruq, Secretary; Umar Faruq [1976] Director


**Esthetica Pure Ltd**
*Incorporated:* 5 September 2018
*Registered Office:* 795 Chester Road, Erdington, Birmingham, B24 0BX
*Officers:* Syed Naseer Ahmed [1952] Director; Syed Salmaan Ahmed [1980] Director; Dr Mabroor Ahmed Bhatty [1958] Director/Plastic Surgeon; Nicola Susan Bhatty [1964] Director/Housewife


**Etab Health Group Limited**
*Incorporated:* 3 April 2012
*Registered Office:* 3 Manor Court, Dunstall Road, Barton under Needwood, Staffs, DE13 8AX
*Major Shareholder:* Christopher Wilson
*Officers:* Maxine Wilson, Secretary; Christopher Wilson [1960] Director


**Etab Health Limited**
*Incorporated:* 4 April 2012  *Employees:* 5
*Net Worth:* £137,706  *Total Assets:* £172,468
*Registered Office:* 3 Manor Court, Dunstall Road, Barton under Needwood, Staffs, DE13 8AX
*Parent:* ETAB Health Group Limited
*Officers:* Maxine Wilson, Secretary; Christopher Wilson [1960] Director


**Etab Pharma Limited**
*Incorporated:* 3 April 2012
*Registered Office:* 3 Manor Court, Barton under Needwood, Burton on Trent, Staffs, DE13 8AU
*Parent:* ETAB Health Group Limited
*Officers:* Maxine Wilson, Secretary; Christopher Wilson [1960] Director


**Ethicor Pharma Ltd**
*Incorporated:* 9 March 2012
*Net Worth Deficit:* £886,659  *Total Assets:* £228,755
*Registered Office:* First Floor, 24-25 New Bond Street, London, W1S 2RR
*Officers:* Richard Drury [1950] Director; Kelechi Chizoma Edomobi [1975] Director/Foreign Exchange Trader [Nigerian]; Dr Malvin Leonard Eutick [1949] Director [Australian]; Robert Ward Jackson [1956] Director; Sanford Robert Simon [1931] Director/Corporate Finance Advisor [American]; Timothy Martin Tickner [1967] Operations Director

**Ethigen Limited**
Incorporated: 6 July 2000  Employees: 268
Net Worth: £22,677,364  Total Assets: £53,002,624
Registered Office: 10-16 Colvilles Place, East Kilbride, G75 0SN
Shareholders: Nigel Joseph Kelly; Andrea Maria Kelly
Officers: Martin Kelly, Secretary; Nigel Joseph Kelly [1966] Director/Pharmacist

**Ethypharm UK Limited**
Incorporated: 11 June 2013  Employees: 17
Previous: DB Ashbourne Limited
Net Worth: £5,230,574  Total Assets: £24,475,888
Registered Office: Bampton Road, Harold Hill, Romford, Essex, RM3 8UG
Parent: Dallas Burston Ashbourne Holdings Limited
Officers: Paul Joseph Concannon [1959] Commercial Director; Jean-Hugues Louis Marie Lecat [1956] Director [French]; Philip Edward Parry [1965] Director/Quality Assurance Professional; Emmanuel Schmidt [1969] Director/Chief Finance Officer [French]

**Eton Pharma Ltd**
Incorporated: 11 December 2018
Registered Office: 98 Wembley Hill Road, Wembley, Middlesex, HA9 8DZ
Major Shareholder: Authman Al Mulla
Officers: Authman Al Mulla [1995] Director/Pharmacist

**ETP (UK) Limited**
Incorporated: 9 April 1997  Employees: 8
Net Worth: £141,451  Total Assets: £364,176
Registered Office: 9 Colman Parade, Southbury Road, Enfield, Middlesex, EN1 1YY
Major Shareholder: Hasan Turk
Officers: Ebru Turk [1987] Director; Hasan Turk [1960] Director

**Euanet Limited**
Incorporated: 2 April 2016
Registered Office: 11 Manchester Road, Walkden, Manchester, M28 3NS
Shareholders: Peter Cattee; Michael James Davis de Riz
Officers: Peter Cattee [1952] Director; Michael James Davis de Riz [1969] Director/Purchase Manager

**Eureka Health Limited**
Incorporated: 24 January 2013  Employees: 1
Net Worth: £11,250  Total Assets: £985,401
Registered Office: Globe House, Eclipse Park, Sittingbourne Road, Maidstone, Kent, ME14 3EN
Officers: Warren Lewis-Jagne [1987] Director/Company Manager

**Euro Capital Management (ECM) Ltd**
Incorporated: 30 September 2009
Net Worth: £80,000,000  Total Assets: £80,000,000
Registered Office: Apartment 615, 7 Baltimore Wharf, London, E14 9EY
Major Shareholder: Mukhaled Aziz Al-Dzhadir
Officers: Dr Mukhaled Al-Dzhadir [1961] General Director [Russian]

**Euro Ceuticals Limited**
Incorporated: 23 July 1992
Registered Office: Kanta House, Victoria Road, Ruislip, Middlesex, HA4 0JQ
Officers: Rakesh Tailor, Secretary; Bhasker Tailor [1955] Director/Chartered Accountant

**Euro Lifecare Ltd**
Incorporated: 11 January 2002  Employees: 4
Net Worth: £75,657  Total Assets: £1,569,884
Registered Office: 1st Floor, 26 Fouberts Place, London, W1F 7PP
Major Shareholder: Anil Nigam
Officers: Anil Nigam [1965] Director

**Euro-Link Pharma Ltd**
Incorporated: 24 March 2014
Net Worth: £11,567  Total Assets: £46,589
Registered Office: 72 Cardigan Street, Luton, Beds, LU1 1RR
Officers: Sharan Patel [1987] Director

**Eurocare Impex Services Limited**
Incorporated: 16 July 1992  Employees: 4
Net Worth Deficit: £48,746  Total Assets: £65,350
Registered Office: 166 Irish Street, Dumfries, DG1 2NJ
Shareholder: John David Murray
Officers: Linda Murray, Secretary; Dominique Claire Carr [1982] Director/Teacher; Darren Clarke Murray [1986] Director; John David Murray [1954] Director/Salesman; Jonathan Conrad Murray [1985] Director; Linda Murray [1952] Director/Teacher

**Euromed (U.K) Limited**
Incorporated: 18 May 1983
Net Worth Deficit: £123  Total Assets: £96,245
Registered Office: Palladium House, 1-4 Argyll Street, London, W1F 7LD
Major Shareholder: Charles Mendel Tannenbaum
Officers: Charles Mendel Tannenbaum, Secretary; Charles Mendel Tannenbaum [1948] Director; Fiona Tannenbaum [1951] Director

**Euromed Pharmaceuticals Ltd**
Incorporated: 17 January 2011
Net Worth Deficit: £23,655  Total Assets: £189,982
Registered Office: Unit 4 Progress Business Centre, Whittle Parkway, Slough, SL1 6DQ
Major Shareholder: Bhupinder Singh Dhaliwal
Officers: Bhupinder Singh Dhaliwal [1977] Director/Pharmacist

**Euromed Technologie Limited**
Incorporated: 5 February 2015
Net Worth Deficit: £487  Total Assets: £104
Registered Office: 55 Millbrook Road, London, SW9 7JD
Major Shareholder: Osman Farah Deiro
Officers: Osman Deiro, Secretary; Osman Farah Deiro [1969] Director/Sales Executive

**Europa Health Limited**
Incorporated: 18 March 2016
Net Worth: £54,875  Total Assets: £55,955
Registered Office: 109 Coleman Road, Leicester, LE5 4LE
Shareholders: Ravinder Malhi; Jaspal Malhi; Baljit Kaur Dhillon
Officers: Ravinder Malhi, Secretary; Ravinder Malhi [1976] Director/Businessman

**European Nutriceutical Products Limited**
Incorporated: 11 February 1999
Net Worth Deficit: £20,783  Total Assets: £598
Registered Office: Ibex House, Baker Street, Weybridge, Surrey, KT13 8AH
Parent: Equilibre Attitude
Officers: Dr Amine Achite, Secretary/CEO [French]; Dr Amine Achite [1963] Director [French]

**European Veterinary Supplies Limited**
*Incorporated:* 29 March 1995
*Net Worth:* £836,010  *Total Assets:* £1,749,941
*Registered Office:* Taylor Group House, Wedgnock Lane, Warwick, CV34 5YA
*Parent:* Richard's Pharma Limited
*Officers:* Laurence Dudley Taylor, Secretary; Malcolm Clive Ramsay [1964] Director; Simone Elizabeth Taylor [1958] Director

**Europharma Scotland Ltd**
*Incorporated:* 17 December 2007  *Employees:* 8
*Net Worth:* £354,288  *Total Assets:* £2,814,880
*Registered Office:* 5 Dunrobin Court, North Avenue, Clydebank Business Park, Clydebank, W Dunbartonshire, G81 2QP
*Officers:* Laura Elizabeth Crilly, Secretary; Dr Sunil Kadri [1965] Director; Paal Christian Kruger [1971] Director [Norwegian]

**Europharmacia Ltd**
*Incorporated:* 14 September 2010
*Net Worth:* £153,309  *Total Assets:* £540,031
*Registered Office:* 3rd Floor, 207 Regent Street, London, W1B 3HH
*Major Shareholder:* Nabeil Nasr
*Officers:* Nabeil Salah Al Dein El Sheshtawy Ali Nasr [1981] Director/Pharmacist

**Europlus Pharma Ltd**
*Incorporated:* 5 November 2008  *Employees:* 2
*Net Worth:* £1,450,775  *Total Assets:* £1,703,491
*Registered Office:* Unit 10 Cornwall Road Industrial Estate, Cornwall Road, Smethwick, W Midlands, B66 2JT
*Parent:* N.G Ltd
*Officers:* Vijay Sudera, Secretary; Ashwani Sudera [1965] Director; Vijay Kumar Sudera [1953] Director

**Eurostar Scientific Limited**
*Incorporated:* 6 November 1998  *Employees:* 6
*Net Worth:* £309,587  *Total Assets:* £637,861
*Registered Office:* 113 Century Building, Brunswick Business Park, Liverpool, L3 4BL
*Shareholder:* Paul James Rule
*Officers:* Susan Elizabeth Wilton Morgan, Secretary; Elisabeth Nest Anthony [1943] Director; Joanne Rule [1983] Sales Director; Paul James Rule [1953] Director; Timothy James Wilton Morgan [1952] Director

**Eurotech Medical Ltd**
*Incorporated:* 6 March 2006  *Employees:* 1
*Net Worth:* £379,381  *Total Assets:* £600,152
*Registered Office:* 1 Horstmann Close, Bath, BA1 3NX
*Officers:* Inese Rusina, Secretary; Nikolay Belousov [1974] Director/Entrepreneur [Russian]

**Euroworld Enterprises Limited**
*Incorporated:* 24 October 2001
*Net Worth:* £23,441  *Total Assets:* £34,997
*Registered Office:* 25 Balham High Road, London, SW12 9AL
*Officers:* Minaz Janmohamed, Secretary; Murtaza Janhohamed [1959] Director/Chemist

**EUSA Pharma (UK) Limited**
*Incorporated:* 26 November 2014  *Employees:* 51
*Net Worth:* £103,497,744  *Total Assets:* £152,351,008
*Registered Office:* Breakspear Park, Breakspear Way, Hemel Hempstead, Herts, HP2 4TZ
*Parent:* EUSA Pharma Holdco 2 (UK) Limited
*Officers:* Emma Jane Johnson [1981] Director; Dr. Dev Kumar [1974] Director/Head of Legal and Compliance; Lee Scot Morley [1970] Director; Bryan Geoffrey Morton [1955] Director

**EVC Compounding Ltd**
*Incorporated:* 10 March 2016
*Net Worth Deficit:* £1,293  *Total Assets:* £33,294
*Registered Office:* Big Picture House, Pontefract Road, Snaith, E Yorks, DN14 0DE
*Officers:* Damien Cain [1976] Director [Australian]; Richard Coppack [1961] Director; Angela Marie Lacey [1963] Director; Ann Walker [1969] Director

**Evees (UK) Limited**
*Incorporated:* 24 January 1997
*Net Worth Deficit:* £938
*Registered Office:* 511 Kingsbury Road, London, NW9 9EG
*Shareholder:* Sharif Mohamed Ebrahim
*Officers:* Nafisa Ebrahim, Secretary; Sharif Mohamed Ebrahim [1960] Director/Pharmacist

**Ever Pharma UK Limited**
*Incorporated:* 30 May 2018
*Registered Office:* 29-30 Fitzroy Square, London, W1T 6LQ
*Shareholder:* Friedrich Hillebrand
*Officers:* Dominic Michael Benning [1980] Director [German]; Robert Fletcher Cutting [1976] Director; Georges Kahwati [1972] Director [Austrian]

**Everhealth Ltd**
*Incorporated:* 7 January 2019
*Registered Office:* Flat 11, 66 Dalston Lane, London, E8 3AH
*Major Shareholder:* Thomas Mundy
*Officers:* Tom Mundy [1990] Director

**Everypharma Co., Ltd.**
*Incorporated:* 30 March 2016
*Registered Office:* Ground Floor, 2 Woodberry Grove, London, N12 0DR
*Major Shareholder:* Jun Shi
*Officers:* Jun Shi [1971] Director [Chinese]

**Evideon Daily Ltd**
*Incorporated:* 27 February 2014
*Net Worth:* £100  *Total Assets:* £588
*Registered Office:* 64 Southwark Bridge Road, London, SE1 0AS
*Shareholder:* Pietro Pelusi
*Officers:* Pietro Pelusi [1973] Director [Italian]

**Evolet Healthcare Limited**
*Incorporated:* 11 October 2011
*Net Worth Deficit:* £128,695  *Total Assets:* £1,189,536
*Registered Office:* Astra House, Arklow Road, London, SE14 6EB
*Parent:* Abstragan Holding Limited
*Officers:* Firuz Mirov [1983] Director/Chief Operations Officer West Asia and Europe [Russian]; Ilkhomzhon Mirzoev [1980] Director/Pharmaceutical Business [Tajikistani]; Zafarkhon Mirzoev [1972] Director/Businessman [Tajikistani]

**Evolve Generics Limited**
*Incorporated:* 12 April 2017
*Registered Office:* 1st Floor, 6 St Johns Court, Upper Fforest Way, Swansea, SA6 8QQ
*Major Shareholder:* Amin Farah
*Officers:* Amin Farah [1951] Director; Frank Michael Riebensahm [1967] Director [German]; Andrew David Thomas [1969] Director

**Evolve Healthcare Partners Ltd**
Incorporated: 3 January 2006
Net Worth Deficit: £73,094  Total Assets: £2,720
Registered Office: Institute of Life Sciences, ILS 2, Singleton Park, Swansea, SA2 8PP
Shareholders: Mohammed Shames; Amin Farah
Officers: Amin Farah [1951] Director

**Evolve Pharma Limited**
Incorporated: 12 April 2017
Registered Office: 1st Floor, 6 St Johns Court, Upper Fforest Way, Swansea, SA6 8QQ
Major Shareholder: Amin Farah
Officers: Amin Farah [1951] Director; Andrew David Thomas [1969] Director

**Evorin Pharma Limited**
Incorporated: 30 January 2014
Net Worth: £1,000  Total Assets: £1,000
Registered Office: 3 Gower Street, London, WC1E 6HA
Shareholders: Ibrahim Abdelrazik Albayoomi Fouda; Ahmed Sami
Officers: Ahmed Sami, Secretary; Ibrahim Abdelrazik Albayoomi Fouda [1978] Director [Egyptian]

**EVR Biosciences (UK) Ltd**
Incorporated: 3 October 2017
Registered Office: 103a Farmeloan Road, Rutherglen, Glasgow, G73 1EE
Major Shareholder: James Thomson Dalziel
Officers: Maria Cristina Pop, Secretary; James Thomson Dalziel [1955] Director/General Manager; Steven Brian Main [1965] Director [American]

**Excel Health Care Limited**
Incorporated: 19 August 1993  Employees: 25
Net Worth: £2,755,473  Total Assets: £2,938,233
Registered Office: Unit 5 Childerditch Industrial Park, Childerditch Hall Drive, Little Warley, Brentwood, Essex, CM13 3HD
Shareholder: Paul Edward Andrews
Officers: Amanda Grace Andrews, Secretary/College Librarian [Irish]; Amanda Grace Andrews [1970] Director [Irish]; Paul Edward Andrews [1957] Director/Engineer

**Excel Pharma Limited**
Incorporated: 8 September 2015
Registered Office: 43a Tithe Barn Road, Wootton, Bedford, MK43 9EZ
Major Shareholder: Arif Esmail
Officers: Anisha Karim Esmail [1962] Director/Accounts Officer; Arif Esmail [1963] Director/Pharmacist

**Excelsior Scientific Limited**
Incorporated: 20 August 2012
Net Worth Deficit: £17,110  Total Assets: £89,030
Registered Office: 15 High Street, Brackley, Northants, NN13 7DH
Major Shareholder: Jason Goodall
Officers: Jason Goodall [1980] Managing Director

**Excip Limited**
Incorporated: 19 October 2010
Net Worth: £56,287  Total Assets: £56,287
Registered Office: 8 Dallan Road, Warrenpoint, Co Down, BT34 3PJ
Major Shareholder: Gareth Robert James Maguire
Officers: Gareth Robert James Maguire [1977] Director/Chemical Engineer; Paul Oliver Maguire [1948] Director/Retired Senior Customs Officer

**Exeter Health Limited**
Incorporated: 15 April 2013  Employees: 2
Net Worth: £539,223  Total Assets: £1,625,733
Registered Office: Queensgate House, 48 Queen Street, Exeter, Devon, EX4 3SR
Officers: Julie Louise Bridge [1966] Director/Project Manager; Simon George Brundan [1964] Director/Business Executive; Ernest Bediako Sampong [1956] Director/Medical Wholesaler [Ghanaian]

**Exmed Worldwide Limited**
Incorporated: 23 June 2017
Registered Office: 130 Duke Street, St Helens, Merseyside, WA10 2JL
Shareholders: ASP Holdings Limited; JNP Holdings Limited
Officers: Carl Bamford [1992] Director; Jignesh Parekh [1984] Director; Sameer Patel [1987] Director

**Expedite Therapeutics Limited**
Incorporated: 28 March 2018
Registered Office: 1 Dorral Dean, Highfields Caldecote, Cambridge, CB23 7ZW
Major Shareholder: James Scott Clark
Officers: Dr James Scott Clark [1968] Director/Scientist

**Eye Guard Ltd**
Incorporated: 24 September 2013
Net Worth Deficit: £137,614  Total Assets: £194,329
Registered Office: Mayfield House, 14 Rochfords Gardens, Slough, Berks, SL2 5XJ
Major Shareholder: Samy Hasan
Officers: Ahmed El-Serafy, Secretary; Ahmed Ibrahim El-Serafy [1970] Director

**Eye2eye Contact Ltd**
Incorporated: 18 March 2013  Employees: 3
Net Worth Deficit: £9,941  Total Assets: £20,266
Registered Office: 24 Park View Road, Stourbridge, W Midlands, DY9 8XD
Shareholders: Nicholas Alan Nind; David William Carroll; Ian Michael Hardy
Officers: Norma Pinson, Secretary; Nicholas Alan Nind [1962] Director

**Eyecon Vision Limited**
Incorporated: 3 January 2018
Registered Office: 27 Pentland Road, East Kilbride, S Lanarks, G75 9GF
Major Shareholder: John Martin
Officers: John Martin [1964] Director

**Eyekonic Wellbeing Limited**
Incorporated: 4 May 2018
Registered Office: Flat 108, 10 Kings Drive, Newton Mearns, Glasgow, G77 5JA
Officers: Angela Konopate [1963] Managing Director; Paul Konopate [1995] Managing Director

**Eyepak Limited**
Incorporated: 21 November 2012
Net Worth Deficit: £36,804  Total Assets: £5,137
Registered Office: 50 Craven Park Road, South Tottenham, London, N15 6AB
Major Shareholder: Marcus Dresdner
Officers: Marcus Dresdner [1980] Director/Business Person [American]

**Ezhonsi Ltd**
Incorporated: 28 February 2019
Registered Office: Fields View, Church Lane, Tetney, Grimsby, N E Lincs, DN36 5JX
Shareholders: Isioma Charles Honnah; Ezinne Tochi Honnah
Officers: Ezinne Tochi Honnah [1985] Director/Pharmacist; Isioma Charles Honnah [1977] Director/Pharmacist; Ndubuisi Patrick Honnah [1981] Director/Businessman [Nigerian]

**F D C International Limited**
Incorporated: 13 June 1996  Employees: 2
Net Worth: £1,768,076  Total Assets: £2,215,405
Registered Office: Unit 6, Fulcrum 1, Solent Way, Whiteley, Fareham, Hants, PO15 7FE
Parent: FDC Limited
Officers: Pradeep Shah, Secretary; Ameya Ashok Chandavarkar [1978] Director [Indian]; Ashok Anand Chandavarkar [1941] Director [Indian]; Nandan Mohan Chandavarkar [1966] Director [Indian]

**Fab Medical Limited**
Incorporated: 22 January 2007
Net Worth Deficit: £57,756  Total Assets: £172,873
Registered Office: Unit 24a Romsey Industrial Estate, Greatbridge Road, Romsey, Hants, SO51 0HR
Shareholders: Paul David Slade; Fab Medical Acquisition LLC
Officers: Paul David Slade, Secretary/Director; Paul David Slade [1967] Director

**Malcolm B. Fagleman Ltd**
Incorporated: 15 July 2002
Net Worth: £253  Total Assets: £3,865
Registered Office: 25 Moorside Road, Kersal, Salford, M7 3PJ
Officers: Vivien Fagleman, Secretary; Alexander Fagleman [1999] Director/Full Time Student; Malcolm Bernard Fagleman [1955] Director; Vivien Fagleman [1963] Director/Secretary

**Fagron UK Ltd**
Incorporated: 15 August 2007  Employees: 8
Net Worth: £1,232,843  Total Assets: £4,149,983
Registered Office: Media Exchange, 4b Coquet Street, Newcastle upon Tyne, NE1 2QB
Officers: Karin de Jong, Secretary; Peter Batty [1966] Director/General Manager

**Fair Pharm Limited**
Incorporated: 20 March 2002
Net Worth: £261,032  Total Assets: £530,397
Registered Office: 103 Church Lane, Bedford, MK41 0PW
Major Shareholder: Hitesh Vanmali Patel
Officers: Bina Hitesh Patel, Secretary; Bina Hitesh Patel [1970] Director/Clerical; Hitesh Vanmali Patel [1962] Director/Pharmacist

**Fairview Health Limited**
Incorporated: 15 May 2009  Employees: 9
Net Worth: £2,102,242  Total Assets: £3,632,866
Registered Office: 2nd Floor, Congress House, Lyon Road, Harrow, Middlesex, HA1 2EN
Parent: The Fairview Group (UK) Ltd
Officers: Raziabai Esmail, Secretary; Riazali Esmail, Secretary/Pharmacist; Riazali Esmail [1957] Director/Pharmacist; Jawad Mohamed Merali [1981] Director/Chartered Accountant

**Faith and Pharma Limited**
Incorporated: 26 June 2018
Registered Office: 111 Compton House, 7 Victory Parade, London, SE18 6FT
Major Shareholder: Faith Mungwari
Officers: Faith Mungwari [1966] Director/Pharmacist [Zimbabwean]

**Falama Services Group Limited**
Incorporated: 5 February 2019
Registered Office: 6 Stanhope Road, Swanscombe, Kent, DA10 0AN
Shareholders: Alimatu Fatim Kabba; Mohamed Kamara
Officers: Alimatu Fatim Kabba [1984] Director/Support Worker [Dutch]; Mohamed Kamara [1969] Director/Employment Consultant

**Farah Chemists Limited**
Incorporated: 30 October 1996  Employees: 47
Net Worth: £1,370,727  Total Assets: £6,213,487
Registered Office: 44 Adelaide Terrace, Benwell, Newcastle upon Tyne, NE4 8BL
Parent: ISAA Holdings Limited
Officers: Mushtaq Ahmed, Secretary; Mushtaq Ahmed [1953] Director/Pharmacist; Nabeel Ahmed [1988] Director; Shakeel Ahmed [1979] Director/Manager; Shakeela Ahmed [1957] Director/Retailer

**Farmachem Limited**
Incorporated: 3 October 2015
Registered Office: 4 Saddlers Close, Pinner, Middlesex, HA5 4BA
Shareholders: Nyalchand Chandaria; Diple Chandaria
Officers: Nemu Chandaria [1939] Director; Nyalchand Chandaria [1941] Director

**Farmako Limited**
Incorporated: 17 October 2018
Registered Office: 6 Hays Lane, London, SE1 2HB
Officers: Niklas Alexander Kouparanis [1989] Director [German]

**Farmedic (UK) Limited**
Incorporated: 6 October 2016
Net Worth Deficit: £5,382  Total Assets: £409,985
Registered Office: BDO LLP, 55 Baker Street, London, W1U 7EU
Major Shareholder: Tomasz Dzitko
Officers: Tomasz Dzitko [1967] Director [Polish]

**Farmsvet Ltd**
Incorporated: 21 November 2018
Registered Office: 84 Mongleath Road, Falmouth, Cornwall, TR11 4PW
Shareholders: Alina Ligia Tatar; Gheorghe Betianu
Officers: Alina Ligia Tatar [1971] Director/Veterinary Surgeon [Romanian]

**Farmvet Limited**
Incorporated: 20 December 2018
Registered Office: Unit 3 Zenith Park Network Centre, Whaley Road, Barnsley, S Yorks, S75 1HT
Shareholder: Ian Carroll
Officers: Ian Carroll [1963] Director; Christopher Sparrow [1971] Director [Irish]; Ian Wilson [1964] Director

**Fast Track Sourcing Limited**
Incorporated: 15 March 2010
Net Worth: £142,910  Total Assets: £778,557
Registered Office: 5 Osborne Terrace, Jesmond, Newcastle upon Tyne, NE2 1SQ
Major Shareholder: William Alasdair Gray
Officers: William Alasdair Gray [1960] Director/General Manager; Andrew William McLeod Lowdon [1963] Director; Nicholas David Sutherland Owen [1963] Director/Businessman

**Fayroz Ltd**
Incorporated: 11 May 2016
Registered Office: The Pod, 141-143 Princess Road, Manchester, M14 4RE
Major Shareholder: Rashid Khalid Mohammed
Officers: Rashid Khalid Mohammed [1976] Director

**Fayroz Pharma Limited**
Incorporated: 19 July 2017
Registered Office: Flat 56, 20 Henderson Street, Manchester, M19 2GY
Major Shareholder: Fayroz Ali
Officers: Fayroz Ali [1974] Director [Sudanese]

**Feel and Heal UK Limited**
Incorporated: 22 March 2018
Registered Office: 71-75 Shelton Street, London, WC2H 9JQ
Officers: Thanveer Ahammed Puthyia Purayil [1978] Director [Indian]

**Fen Health Ltd**
Incorporated: 4 December 2018
Registered Office: Weir View, Wargrave Road, Henley on Thames, Oxon, RG9 3HX
Major Shareholder: Thomas Fennell
Officers: Thomas Fennell [1997] Managing Director

**Fenton Pharmaceuticals Ltd**
Incorporated: 8 April 1993  Employees: 6
Net Worth: £2,043,526  Total Assets: £3,639,380
Registered Office: Fenton House, 4 Hampstead Gate, 1a Frognal, London, NW3 6AL
Major Shareholder: Graham Alexander Fenton Hill
Officers: Judith Hill, Secretary; Graham Alexander Fenton Hill [1963] Director; Judith Hill [1938] Director

**Ferring Pharmaceuticals Limited**
Incorporated: 28 January 1975  Employees: 107
Net Worth: £3,635,637  Total Assets: £18,245,226
Registered Office: Drayton Hall, Church Road, West Drayton, Middlesex, UB7 7PS
Parent: Ferring Asset Management Limited
Officers: Raphael Cretegny, Secretary; Michel Lucien Pettigrew [1953] Director/Business Executive [Canadian]; Gilles Pluntz [1957] Director/Senior Vice President [French]

**Field House Pharma Limited**
Incorporated: 1 December 2014  Employees: 1
Net Worth: £21,704  Total Assets: £34,047
Registered Office: Field House, Aylsham Road, Swanton Abbott, Norwich, NR10 5DL
Shareholder: Antonia Jane McAnsh
Officers: Antonia Jane McAnsh [1961] Director; Dr Gordon Campbell McAnsh [1963] Director/Doctor

**Fijez Ltd**
Incorporated: 18 October 2018
Registered Office: First Floor, 172 Hoe Street, Walthamstow, London, E17 4QH
Major Shareholder: Rebecca Abena Boadu
Officers: Rebecca Abena Boadu [1975] Director/Pharmacist

**Fire N Ice Ltd**
Incorporated: 10 May 2007
Registered Office: 169 Brandon Street, Leicester, LE4 6AZ
Major Shareholder: Rajiv Devchand Patel
Officers: Rajiv Patel [1966] Director

**First Aid Supplies Limited**
Incorporated: 21 September 2005
Registered Office: Blue Dot House, 3 Chesford Grange, Woolston, Warrington, Cheshire, WA1 4RQ
Parent: First Aid Holdings Limited
Officers: Matthew George Courtney, Secretary; Matthew George Courtney [1975] Director/Marketing; Peter John Mason [1969] Sales Director; Alastair Generald Lees Maxwell [1970] Managing Director

**First Choice Suppliments Ltd**
Incorporated: 9 May 2018
Registered Office: 95 Meadow Street, Preston, Lancs, PR1 1TS
Major Shareholder: Louise Aanne Gillies
Officers: Louise Aanne Gillies, Secretary; Louise Aanne Gillies [1998] Director

**Firstchem Limited**
Incorporated: 23 July 1999
Registered Office: Chemidex House, Unit 7 Egham Business Village, Crabtree Road, Egham, Surrey, TW20 8RB
Shareholders: Navinchandas Jamnadas; Varsha Navinchandas Engineer
Officers: Dr Nikesh Engineer, Secretary; Nikesh Engineer [1985] Director/Doctor

**Fitnatix International Ltd**
Incorporated: 4 December 2017
Registered Office: 83 Henderson Street, Manchester, M19 2QR
Major Shareholder: Zahid Raja
Officers: Zahid Raja [1963] Director/Financial Broker

**Fitness and Nutrition of Europe Ltd.**
Incorporated: 13 February 2018
Registered Office: 21b Groombridge Road, London, E9 7DP
Major Shareholder: Francisco Javier Gomez Cortes
Officers: Francisco Javier Gomez Cortes [1968] Director/Entrepreneur [Spanish]

**Fittleworth Medical Limited**
Incorporated: 26 July 1984  Employees: 318
Net Worth: £27,367,340  Total Assets: £45,724,332
Registered Office: Hays Galleria, 1 Hays Lane, London, SE1 2RD
Parent: Hollister Europe Limited
Officers: Marvin Scott Holloway [1969] Director [American]; Robert Coleman Keeley [1954] Director/Businessman [American]; Adam Robert Smith [1972] Director/Assistant General Counsel Commercial Law [American]; Kenneth Alan Straup [1957] Director/Vice President and Treasurer of Hollister Incorporated [American]

**Five Pharm Ltd**
Incorporated: 5 September 2018
Registered Office: 7 Warwick Road, Southall, Middlesex, UB2 4NX
Major Shareholder: Jeet Singh
Officers: Jeet Singh, Secretary; Jeet Singh [1988] Director/Pharmacist

**Five Star International Consulting Limited**
Incorporated: 6 December 2017
Registered Office: Unit 97 Kingspark Business Centre, 152-178 Kingston Road, New Malden, Surrey, KT3 3ST
Major Shareholder: Paolo Urbano
Officers: Noella Soo Eom [1984] Director; Dr Paolo Urbano [1950] Director [Italian]

**Fivtique Limited**
*Incorporated:* 1 November 2018
*Registered Office:* Flat 3.06, Pennine House, Russell Street, Leeds, LS1 5RN
*Major Shareholder:* Tze Chuan Yii
*Officers:* Tze Chuan Yii [1988] Director [Malaysian]

**Flairpath Limited**
*Incorporated:* 31 March 1995
*Net Worth:* £4,205  *Total Assets:* £5,020
*Registered Office:* 9 Dunedin Drive, Caterham, Surrey, CR3 6BA
*Major Shareholder:* Mervyn Roderick Jones
*Officers:* Mervyn Roderick Jones [1946] Director/Retired Copywriter

**Flamingo Pharma (UK) Ltd**
*Incorporated:* 23 April 2014  *Employees:* 4
*Net Worth Deficit:* £988,000  *Total Assets:* £1,162,386
*Registered Office:* 1st Floor, Kirkland House, 11-15 Peterborough Road, Harrow, Middlesex, HA1 2AX
*Parent:* Flamingo Pharmaceuticals Limited
*Officers:* Richard Stuart Eggleston [1960] Director/Pharmacist; Ashwin Jethalal Thacker [1954] Director [Indian]; Pranay Ashwin Thacker [1986] Director [Indian]

**Flen Health UK Ltd**
*Incorporated:* 9 December 2015  *Employees:* 16
*Net Worth:* £118,946  *Total Assets:* £1,241,229
*Registered Office:* Suite 48, 88-90 Hatton Garden, London, EC1N 8PN
*Major Shareholder:* Phillippe Sollie
*Officers:* Philippe Sollie [1960] Director/Business Owner [Belgian]

**A.K. Fletcher (Preston) Limited**
*Incorporated:* 20 May 1982
*Net Worth:* £1,205,471  *Total Assets:* £1,513,545
*Registered Office:* 331 Garstang Road, Fulwood, Preston, Lancs, PR2 9UP
*Shareholder:* Anthony Keith Fletcher
*Officers:* Anthony Keith Fletcher, Secretary; Anthony Keith Fletcher [1940] Director/Chemist; Maureen Anne Fletcher [1944] Director/Chemists Manageress

**Flintlow Limited**
*Incorporated:* 17 January 1992  *Employees:* 36
*Net Worth:* £1,471,305  *Total Assets:* £3,801,943
*Registered Office:* 1406 Coventry Road, South Yardley, Birmingham, B25 8AE
*Major Shareholder:* Mohamed Gulamali Kanani
*Officers:* Abbas Mohamed Kanani, Secretary; Shan Abbas Hassam [1985] Director; Abbas Mohamed Kanani [1984] Director/Pharmacist

**Florence Health & Beauty Limited**
*Incorporated:* 21 November 2017
*Registered Office:* 3 Shining Bank, Sheffield, S13 9DJ
*Shareholders:* Muthana Obeed; Fatima Aloum
*Officers:* Fatima Aloum [1982] Director [Syrian]; Muthana Obeed [1976] Director [Iraqi]

**Flow Wealth Ltd**
*Incorporated:* 13 March 2017  *Employees:* 1
*Net Worth:* £100  *Total Assets:* £100
*Registered Office:* Room Q, 35a Astbury Road, London, SE15 2NL
*Major Shareholder:* Marian Benes
*Officers:* Marian Benes [1975] Director [Czech]

**Flowonix Medical Ltd**
*Incorporated:* 9 September 2013
*Net Worth:* £1,000  *Total Assets:* £1,000
*Registered Office:* Amp Technology Centre, Advanced Manufacturing Park, Brunel Way, Rotherham, S Yorks, S60 5WG
*Officers:* Dr. George Demetrios Boukouris, Secretary; George Demetrios Boukouris [1968] Director/Management Consultant

**Fluidx Limited**
*Incorporated:* 14 October 2005
*Registered Office:* Northbank Industrial Park, Gilchrist Road, Irlam, Manchester, M44 5AY
*Officers:* Jason Joseph [1970] Director [American]; David Francis Pietrantoni [1972] Director [American]; Lindon Robertson [1961] Director [American]

**Flydonging Eletctronic Ltd**
*Incorporated:* 21 March 2018
*Registered Office:* Companies House, Default Address, Cardiff, CF14 8LH
*Officers:* Guoqiang Hou [1971] Director [Chinese]

**Focus Pharma Holdings Limited**
*Incorporated:* 18 July 2007
*Net Worth:* £6,045,422  *Total Assets:* £6,046,418
*Registered Office:* Capital House, 85 King William Street, London, EC4N 7BL
*Parent:* Mercury Pharma Group Limited
*Officers:* Robert Sully, Secretary; Adeel Ahmad [1973] Director/Chief Financial Officer [Canadian]; Graeme Neville Duncan [1973] Director/Chief Executive Officer; Vikram Laxman Kamath [1977] Director/Vice President Finance and Group Controller [Indian]

**Focus Pharmaceuticals Limited**
*Incorporated:* 30 August 2002
*Net Worth:* £4,404,425  *Total Assets:* £18,041,368
*Registered Office:* Capital House, 85 King William Street, London, EC4N 7BL
*Parent:* Focus Pharma Holdings Limited
*Officers:* Robert Sully, Secretary; Adeel Ahmad [1973] Director/Chief Financial Officer [Canadian]; Graeme Neville Duncan [1973] Director/Chief Executive Officer; Vikram Laxman Kamath [1977] Director/Vice President Finance and Group Controller [Indian]

**Foreverbeyoung Ltd**
*Incorporated:* 16 April 2018
*Registered Office:* 172 Newgate Lane, Mansfield, Notts, NG18 2QA
*Officers:* Dan Zhao [1974] Director

**Fortis Egregius Limited**
*Incorporated:* 18 January 2013
*Registered Office:* c/o SJ Males & Co, Basepoint Business & Innovation Centre, 110 Butterfield, Great Marlings, Luton, Beds, LU2 8DL
*Shareholders:* William John Dowling; Richard Derek Sanderson
*Officers:* Janis Dowling [1953] Director; William John Dowling [1951] Director

**Fortissa Ltd**
*Incorporated:* 21 October 2009  *Employees:* 1
*Net Worth:* £58,778  *Total Assets:* £118,165
*Registered Office:* Centurion House, 129 Deansgate, Manchester, M3 3WR
*Shareholders:* Mark Donald Winterford; Richard Edward James Peter
*Officers:* Richard Peter [1973] Director; Mark Donald Winterford [1962] Director

# The Top UK Pharmaceutical Wholesalers

**Fortune Industries Limited**
*Incorporated:* 20 September 2010
*Net Worth Deficit:* £3,542 *Total Assets:* £2,669
*Registered Office:* Victoria House, 18 Dalston Gardens, Stanmore, Middlesex, HA7 1BU
*Shareholders:* Ravi Rajdev; Ronak Rajdev
*Officers:* Ravi Rajdev [1971] Director/Owner; Ronak Narottam Rajdev [1978] Director/Pharmaceuticals

**Fox Group Global Ltd**
*Incorporated:* 9 February 2018
*Registered Office:* 8a Cinnabar Court, Daresbury Park, Daresbury, Warrington, Cheshire, WA4 4GE
*Major Shareholder:* Michael Foxley
*Officers:* Michael Foxley, Secretary; Michael Foxley [1983] Director; Victoria Quinn [1986] Director

**Fox Group International Ltd**
*Incorporated:* 4 July 2016 *Employees:* 9
*Net Worth:* £829,140 *Total Assets:* £1,831,570
*Registered Office:* 8a Cinnabar Court, Daresbury Park, Daresbury, Warrington, Cheshire, WA4 4GE
*Shareholders:* Michael Foxley; Michael Foxley
*Officers:* Michael Foxley, Secretary; Michael Foxley [1983] Director; Victoria Quinn [1986] Director

**Fox Pharma Limited**
*Incorporated:* 1 November 2018
*Registered Office:* 8a Cinnabar Court, Daresbury Park, Daresbury, Warrington, Cheshire, WA4 4GE
*Parent:* Fox Group Global Limited
*Officers:* Michael Foxley [1983] Director; Victoria Quinn [1986] Director

**FPD Group Limited**
*Incorporated:* 20 July 2007
*Net Worth:* £169 *Total Assets:* £52,430
*Registered Office:* University Business Centre, Queen Square, Leeds, LS2 8AJ
*Shareholders:* Matthew McCartney; Andrew Hopkins
*Officers:* Andrew Hopkins, Secretary; Matthew McCartney [1977] Director

**Fresh Cache Holdings Limited**
*Incorporated:* 13 July 2018
*Registered Office:* 20-22 Wenlock Road, London, N1 7GU
*Major Shareholder:* Mark Anthony Paul Blount
*Officers:* Mark Anthony Paul Blount [1979] Director

**FreshBreathOnline Limited**
*Incorporated:* 16 January 2001
*Net Worth:* £8,980 *Total Assets:* £60,150
*Registered Office:* 1-5 Market Square, Ilfracombe, Devon, EX34 9AU
*Shareholders:* Joanne Alexandra Smith; Phillip John Smith
*Officers:* Joanne Alexandra Smith, Secretary/Administrator; Philip John Smith [1966] Director

**Frezyderm UK Limited**
*Incorporated:* 6 July 2015 *Employees:* 13
*Net Worth Deficit:* £405,393 *Total Assets:* £534,036
*Registered Office:* 1 Kings Avenue, London, N21 3NA
*Shareholders:* Ioannis Anastasiou; Efthymios Anastasiou
*Officers:* Ioannis Anastasiou [1969] Director [Greek]

**Friends of Pyrethrum Ltd**
*Incorporated:* 21 September 2003 *Employees:* 1
*Net Worth:* £32,565 *Total Assets:* £56,095
*Registered Office:* c/o APS Accountancy Limited, 4 Cromwell Court, New Street, Aylesbury, Bucks, HP20 2PB
*Officers:* Antonia Glynne-Jones, Secretary/Manager; Antonia Glynne-Jones [1957] Director/Manager

**Frontier Lab Scientific Limited**
*Incorporated:* 24 August 2018
*Registered Office:* c/o David Newton and Co Ltd. Harrogate Business Centre, Hookstone Avenue, Harrogate, N Yorks, HG2 8ER
*Shareholders:* Veera Venkata Pratap Davuluri; Anusha Kolli
*Officers:* Anusha Kolli [1986] Director [Indian]

**Frontrow International UK Ltd**
*Incorporated:* 29 January 2018
*Registered Office:* Basement Level, 137 Earls Court Road, London, SW5 9RH
*Major Shareholder:* Adielmofranches Fornoles
*Officers:* Adielmofranches Fornoles [1983] Director [Filipino]

**FTS Bio Limited**
*Incorporated:* 25 March 2013
*Net Worth:* £275 *Total Assets:* £280
*Registered Office:* 5 Osborne Terrace, Jesmond, Newcastle upon Tyne, NE2 1SQ
*Parent:* Fast Track Sourcing Limited
*Officers:* William Alasdair Gray [1960] Director; Andrew William McLeod Lowdon [1963] Director

**Fulbo Ltd**
*Incorporated:* 3 September 2018
*Registered Office:* 3 Judges Street, Loughborough, Leics, LE11 1RU
*Major Shareholder:* Gift Ogechi Wobo
*Officers:* Gift Ogechi Wobo [1991] Director/Pharmacist [Nigerian]

**Full Spectrum Pharma Limited**
*Incorporated:* 10 December 2018
*Registered Office:* 16 Leicester Road, Blaby, Leics, LE8 4GQ
*Shareholder:* Alex Spence
*Officers:* Alex Spence [1976] Director; Dean Tams [1979] Director

**Furn WW Lux Ltd**
*Incorporated:* 17 October 2018
*Registered Office:* 14 Holloways Lane, North Mymms, Hatfield, Herts, AL9 7NP
*Major Shareholder:* Michelle Wakefield
*Officers:* Michelle Wakefield [1992] Director

**Future Healthcare Ltd**
*Incorporated:* 15 March 2017
*Registered Office:* Unit D1, Railway Triangle, Walton Road, Portsmouth, PO6 1TH
*Major Shareholder:* Peter John Toon
*Officers:* Peter John Toon [1963] Director

**Future Pharmacare Limited**
*Incorporated:* 22 August 2017
*Registered Office:* Unit 3c, The Gattinetts, Hadleigh Road, East Bergholt, Colchester, Essex, CO7 6QT
*Major Shareholder:* Frazer James Rees
*Officers:* Frazer James Rees [1976] Director/IT Consultant

**G & C Pharma Limited**
Incorporated: 25 February 2016  Employees: 3
Net Worth: £29,996  Total Assets: £735,326
Registered Office: 32a St Cadoc Road, Cardiff, CF14 4NE
Shareholders: Gwawr Davies Jones; Claire Harris
Officers: Gwawr Davies Jones [1978] Director; Claire Harris [1978] Director

**G P Supplies Limited**
Incorporated: 19 September 2000  Employees: 15
Net Worth: £161,623  Total Assets: £607,765
Registered Office: Concept House, 6 McNicol Drive, London, NW10 7AW
Parent: Myriad Holdings Ltd
Officers: Shila Shah, Secretary/Administrator; Kamalkumar Shah [1955] Director/Pharmacist; Shila Shah [1955] Director/Administrator

**G Pharma Limited**
Incorporated: 29 July 1997
Net Worth Deficit: £2,163,000  Total Assets: £40,000
Registered Office: Rivington Road, Whitehouse Industrial Estate, Runcorn, Cheshire, WA7 3DJ
Parent: Phoenix Healthcare Distribution Limited
Officers: Stephen William Anderson [1966] Director; Kenneth John Black [1965] Director; Kevin Robert Hudson [1963] Director

**G Pharmaceuticals Ltd**
Incorporated: 27 June 2011
Net Worth: £1  Total Assets: £1
Registered Office: 286 Sealand Road, Chester, CH1 4LQ
Officers: Godwin Oduro [1974] Director/Pharmacist

**G.A.P. Research Company Limited**
Incorporated: 3 February 1987  Employees: 8
Net Worth: £159,274  Total Assets: £625,907
Registered Office: 2 Ebbsfleet Industrial Estate, Stoneridge Road, Northfleet, Gravesend, Kent, DA11 9DZ
Shareholders: Avtar Singh Photay; Gurnam Singh Photay
Officers: Gurnam Singh Photay, Secretary; Avtar Singh Photay [1960] Director/Chemist; Gurnam Singh Photay [1957] Director/Printer

**G9UK Limited**
Incorporated: 31 May 2017
Registered Office: 104 Oranmore Court, Regency Walk, Shirley, Croydon, Surrey, CR0 7UZ
Officers: Zehra Ambreen Ali, Secretary; Syed Mohammad Ali [1999] Director/Medical; Syed Mustafa Ali [1998] Director; Dr Syed Noor Uz Zia Ali [1967] Director; Zehra Ambreen Ali [1974] Director

**Gagnon Direct Ltd**
Incorporated: 9 December 2016
Net Worth: £18,678  Total Assets: £23,786
Registered Office: 4 Old Park Lane, London, W1K 1QW
Officers: Beth Gagnon [1951] Director [American]

**Gainland (International) Limited**
Incorporated: 31 October 1983
Net Worth: £509,152  Total Assets: £579,250
Registered Office: Building 11, Factory Road, Sandycroft, Deeside, Flintshire, CH5 2QJ
Major Shareholder: George Ball
Officers: Lynn Ball, Secretary; George Ball [1958] Director/International Trader

**Galar Ireland Ltd**
Incorporated: 26 February 2010  Employees: 48
Net Worth: £1,205,105  Total Assets: £5,149,057
Registered Office: 155 Andersonstown Road, Belfast, BT11 9EA
Parent: Galar Holdings Limited
Officers: Catherine Cooper [1982] Director [Irish]; Michael Cooper [1987] Director [Irish]; Paul Dominic Cooper [1956] Director/Pharmacist [Irish]; Sarah Cooper [1957] Director [Irish]

**Galderma (U.K.) Limited**
Incorporated: 14 February 1962  Employees: 81
Net Worth: £2,385,000  Total Assets: £16,943,000
Registered Office: Meridien House, 69-71 Clarendon Road, Watford, Herts, WD17 1DS
Officers: Jacques Bodevin [1961] Director/Chief Financial Officer Nestle Skin Health [Swiss]; Can Davut Ongen [1965] Director/Regional VP EMEA [Swiss]; Alexandra Tretyakova [1972] Director/General Manager [Russian]

**Galen Limited**
Incorporated: 16 September 2005  Employees: 23
Net Worth: £46,374,912  Total Assets: £77,070,872
Registered Office: Seagoe Industrial Estate, Craigavon, Co Armagh, BT63 5UA
Shareholders: Almac Trustees Limited; Almac Group Limited; Colin Hayburn
Officers: Colin Hayburn, Secretary; Alan David Armstrong [1958] Director; Dr Dennise Broderick [1975] Managing Director [Irish]; Stephen Campbell [1961] Director; Colin Hayburn [1969] Director/Solicitor; Kevin Stephens [1960] Director

**Galenus Biomedical Limited**
Incorporated: 18 May 2015
Registered Office: 45 Burnham Way, Ealing, London, W13 9YB
Shareholder: Wadih Toni Barbara
Officers: Wadih Toni Barbara [1974] Director/Architect

**Galpharm International Limited**
Incorporated: 24 February 1981  Employees: 70
Net Worth: £18,003,000  Total Assets: £37,058,000
Registered Office: Wrafton, Braunton, Devon, EX33 2DL
Parent: Galpharm Healthcare Limited
Officers: Annette Corcoran, Secretary; Neil Thomas Lister [1975] Director; Dominic James Rivers [1977] Director; Christopher Allan Rudd [1980] Director

**Gama Group Services Ltd**
Incorporated: 23 November 2018
Registered Office: 11 Melrose Avenue, Borehamwood, Herts, WD6 2BH
Major Shareholder: DI Octavian Goga
Officers: Octavian Goga [1970] Managing Director [Romanian]

**Gammaservice Limited**
Incorporated: 1 September 2006
Net Worth: £98,614  Total Assets: £152,013
Registered Office: The Old Rectory, Church Street, Weybridge, Surrey, KT13 8DE
Major Shareholder: Robert Andrew Schmid
Officers: Robert Andrew Schmid [1962] Director/Medical Service Engineer

**Alston Garrard & Co Limited**
Incorporated: 14 July 2003
Net Worth: £2,144,459  Total Assets: £4,885,612
Registered Office: 25 Grosvenor Road, Wrexham, Clwyd, LL11 1BT
Shareholders: Walter Robert Glenie; Saul Glenie
Officers: Robert Glenie, Secretary; Robert Glenie [1946] Director/Owner; Saul Glenie [1972] Director/Owner

# The Top UK Pharmaceutical Wholesalers

**Garstang Medical Services Limited**
*Incorporated:* 14 January 2004  *Employees:* 49
*Net Worth:* £14,808  *Total Assets:* £1,203,688
*Registered Office:* Garstang Medical Centre, Kepple Lane, Garstang, Preston, Lancs, PR3 1PB
*Officers:* Catherine Mary Thornton, Secretary; Dr Jonathan Timothy Williamson [1965] Director/Medical Practitioner

**Garusa Solutions U.K. Limited**
*Incorporated:* 28 February 2017
*Net Worth:* £16,343,964  *Total Assets:* £16,345,721
*Registered Office:* 3 Montpelier Avenue, Bexley, Kent, DA5 3AP
*Major Shareholder:* Kalvinder Singh Ruprai
*Officers:* Kalvinder Singh Ruprai [1969] Director

**Gate Pharma Ltd**
*Incorporated:* 31 March 2015
*Net Worth:* £1  *Total Assets:* £1
*Registered Office:* 52 Willingsworth Road, Wednesbury, W Midlands, WS10 7NJ
*Major Shareholder:* Zsolt Sebjan
*Officers:* Zsolt Sebjan [1986] Director [Hungarian]

**Gate2pharma Ltd**
*Incorporated:* 2 July 2014
*Net Worth Deficit:* £118,413  *Total Assets:* £9,227
*Registered Office:* 8B Accommodation Road, Golders Green, London, NW11 8ED
*Shareholders:* Rana Siadati; Rana Siadati
*Officers:* Rana Siadati [1966] Director

**Gateway for Africa Ltd**
*Incorporated:* 26 June 2018
*Registered Office:* 14 Alexandria Road, West Ealing, London, W13 0NR
*Major Shareholder:* Mohamed Yusuf
*Officers:* Dr Mohamed Yusuf [1968] Director/GP [Danish]

**GB Pharma Limited**
*Incorporated:* 5 March 1992  *Employees:* 3
*Net Worth:* £34,156  *Total Assets:* £629,798
*Registered Office:* Suite 9210, Access House, 141 Morden Road, Mitcham, Surrey, CR4 4DG
*Major Shareholder:* Pardeep Batra
*Officers:* Elzbieta Batra, Secretary; Pardeep Batra [1958] Director

**GBBC Ltd**
*Incorporated:* 31 May 2013
*Previous:* EBK Skincare Ltd
*Net Worth Deficit:* £6,237  *Total Assets:* £34,677
*Registered Office:* 80 High Street, Winchester, Hants, SO23 9AT
*Major Shareholder:* Benjamin Douglas Swift
*Officers:* Benjamin Swift [1979] Director

**GBY (UK) Ltd**
*Incorporated:* 4 July 2011
*Net Worth:* £125,462  *Total Assets:* £264,204
*Registered Office:* 6 Draycott Avenue, Middlesbrough, Cleveland, TS5 8EP
*Major Shareholder:* Sean Flanagan
*Officers:* Sean Francis Flanagan [1968] Director

**GCL Marketing Ltd**
*Incorporated:* 9 September 2004
*Net Worth:* £82,074  *Total Assets:* £112,647
*Registered Office:* 5 Jupiter House, Calleva Park, Aldermaston, Reading, Berks, RG7 8NN
*Major Shareholder:* Christian Guenter Latz
*Officers:* Christian Guenter Latz [1939] Director [German]

**Gee Lawson Limited**
*Incorporated:* 16 October 1939
*Registered Office:* Westminster House, 10 Westminster Road, Macclesfield, Cheshire, SK10 1BX
*Parent:* Gee Lawson Holdings Limited
*Officers:* Ivan Pennington [1972] Director

**Geistlich Sons Limited**
*Incorporated:* 1 March 1960  *Employees:* 16
*Net Worth:* £1,386,167  *Total Assets:* £2,377,402
*Registered Office:* 1st Floor, Thorley House, Bailey Lane, Manchester Airport, Manchester, M90 4AB
*Officers:* Julie Jones, Secretary; Matthias Peter Hermann Dunkel [1966] Director/Deputy Chief Operating Officer [Swiss]; Rolf Franz Jeger [1955] Director/Chief Financial Officer [Swiss]; Paul Druon Michael Note [1956] Director [French]; Frank Sellers [1963] Director

**Gelu Life Limited**
*Incorporated:* 22 May 2017
*Registered Office:* Thames House, Bourne End Business Park, Cores End Road, Bourne End, Bucks, SL8 5AS
*Shareholders:* George Michel Haddad; Luca Stefano Benati
*Officers:* Asmir Begovic [1987] Director; Luca Stefano Benati [1970] Director [Italian]; Dr George Michel Haddad [1968] Director

**Gemapharm Limited**
*Incorporated:* 8 July 1998  *Employees:* 1
*Net Worth:* £99,662  *Total Assets:* £794,252
*Registered Office:* 10 Saville Court, Saville Place, Clifton, Bristol, BS8 4EJ
*Major Shareholder:* Andrew Richard Lamb
*Officers:* Andrew Richard Lamb [1950] Director/Accountant; Bernard Jacques Schack [1945] Director [French]

**Gemi Pharma Limited**
*Incorporated:* 30 September 2014
*Registered Office:* Unit 2a Old Dalby Trading Estate, Old Dalby, Leics, LE14 3NJ
*Shareholders:* Ewa Nowakowska; Iwona Nowakowska
*Officers:* Ewa Nowakowska [1986] Director/Logistics Manager [Polish]; Iwona Nowakowska [1960] Director/Executive Board Member [Polish]; Katarzyna Nowakowska [1991] Director [Polish]

**General Pharmaceuticals Limited**
*Incorporated:* 19 January 2004  *Employees:* 2
*Net Worth:* £483,019  *Total Assets:* £2,575,490
*Registered Office:* Dixcart House, Addlestone Road, Bourne Business Park, Addlestone, Surrey, KT15 2LE
*Shareholders:* Gloria Tokatly; Ziad Tokatly
*Officers:* Gloria Tokatly [1979] Director/Chief Buyer; Ziad Tokatly [1974] Director

**General Shop Ltd**
*Incorporated:* 8 March 2018
*Registered Office:* Trafalgar Mill Business Exchange, Trafalgar Street, Burnley, Lancs, BB11 1TQ
*Officers:* John Green [1970] Director/Business Executive [Russian]

**Generic Partners UK Ltd**
*Incorporated:* 5 September 2012
*Net Worth:* £637,217  *Total Assets:* £869,615
*Registered Office:* 1 Doughty Street, London, WC1N 2PH
*Officers:* Krishnan Tirucherai Parthasarathy [1971] Director [Indian]; Mohana Kumar Pillai [1956] Director [Indian]

**Generic Physics Limited**
*Incorporated:* 31 December 2014
*Registered Office:* 17 Wenham Place, Hatfield, Herts, AL10 0DD
*Major Shareholder:* Hermann Yedoh
*Officers:* Dr Hermann Yedoh [1975] Director/Pharmacist [French]


**Genesis Medical Limited**
*Incorporated:* 24 September 1986
*Net Worth:* £227,668  *Total Assets:* £974,059
*Registered Office:* The Apex, 2 Sheriffs Orchard, Coventry, Warwicks, CV1 3PP
*Parent:* Genesis Medical Holdings Limited
*Officers:* Michael Frazzette [1962] Director [American]; Holger Christian Wilhelm Furstenberg [1965] Director [German]; Michael Rossi [1974] Director [American]


**Genesis Pharma Limited**
*Incorporated:* 9 November 2018
*Registered Office:* 84 Pembroke Road, London, W8 6NX
*Parent:* Genesis Pharmaceuticals Limited
*Officers:* Nilesh Prataprai Mehta, Secretary; Nilesh Prataprai Mehta [1962] Director; Dr David Louis Charles Solomon [1970] Director


**Genesis Pharmaceuticals Limited**
*Incorporated:* 29 September 1999  *Employees:* 10
*Net Worth:* £3,607,776  *Total Assets:* £12,483,941
*Registered Office:* 3rd Floor, Scottish Provident House, 76-80 College Road, Harrow, Middlesex, HA1 1BQ
*Parent:* Genethics Europe Limited
*Officers:* Nilesh Prataprai Mehta, Secretary/Director; Patrick Anthony Kingsford Chubb [1956] Commercial Director; Bharat Prataprai Mehta [1952] Director; Nilesh Prataprai Mehta [1962] Director; Dr David Louis Charles Solomon [1970] Director


**Genevet Ltd**
*Incorporated:* 3 September 2004
*Net Worth Deficit:* £397,515  *Total Assets:* £85,543
*Registered Office:* Cherry Tree Stables, Roydon Road, Diss, Norfolk, IP22 4LN
*Major Shareholder:* Marie Noelle Bouvet
*Officers:* Dr Marie Bouvet, Secretary [French]; Dr Marie Bouvet [1969] Director/Veterinary Surgeon [French]


**Genmed UK Limited**
*Incorporated:* 11 June 2018
*Registered Office:* 8 Tiverton Drive, Sale, Cheshire, M33 4RJ
*Major Shareholder:* Jiang Yu
*Officers:* Jiang Yu [1972] Managing Director [Chinese]


**Genopharm Ltd**
*Incorporated:* 17 July 2001
*Previous:* Novachem Industries Ltd
*Net Worth:* £31,545  *Total Assets:* £506,001
*Registered Office:* 3rd Floor, 207 Regent Street, London, W1B 3HH
*Major Shareholder:* Klavidia Dickson
*Officers:* Klavdiia Dickson [1982] Director [Ukrainian]


**Genrx UK Lipperts Ltd.**
*Incorporated:* 12 June 2018
*Registered Office:* Dept 302, 43 Owston Road, Carcroft, Doncaster, S Yorks, DN6 8DA
*Major Shareholder:* George Joseph Hubertus Lipperts
*Officers:* George Joseph Hubertus Lipperts [1952] Director/Entrepreneur [Dutch]


**Genus Pharmaceuticals Holdings Limited**
*Incorporated:* 21 August 1998
*Net Worth:* £10,109,000  *Total Assets:* £44,398,000
*Registered Office:* Manchester Road, Linthwaite, Huddersfield, W Yorks, HD7 5QH
*Parent:* Stada UK Holdings Ltd
*Officers:* Edwin Charles Blythe, Secretary; Charles Ashley Brierley [1963] Director


**Genus Pharmaceuticals Limited**
*Incorporated:* 6 February 1986
*Net Worth:* £44,653,000  *Total Assets:* £58,685,000
*Registered Office:* Manchester Road, Linthwaite, Huddersfield, W Yorks, HD7 5QH
*Parent:* Genus Pharmaceutical Holdings Ltd
*Officers:* Edwin Charles Blythe, Secretary; Charles Ashley Brierley [1963] Director


**Genzyme Therapeutics Limited**
*Incorporated:* 5 November 2001  *Employees:* 100
*Net Worth:* £42,235,000  *Total Assets:* £101,503,000
*Registered Office:* 4620 Kingsgate, Cascade Way, Oxford Business Park South, Oxford, OX4 2SU
*Parent:* Sanofi-Aventis UK Holdings Limited
*Officers:* Francois-Xavier Duhalde [1965] Director/Chief Finance Office UK [French]; Peter Sjoerd Kuiper [1960] Director/General Manager [Dutch]


**Geoorganics Limited**
*Incorporated:* 19 December 2018
*Registered Office:* 48 Gray's Inn Road, London, WC1X 8LT
*Major Shareholder:* George Kukhaleishvili
*Officers:* George Kukhaleishvili [1964] Director/Businessman


**Geopharma UK Ltd.**
*Incorporated:* 17 August 2016
*Net Worth:* £5,600  *Total Assets:* £5,600
*Registered Office:* Kemp House, 152 City Road, London, EC1V 2NX
*Officers:* Dr. Merab Lomia [1961] Director/Medical Doctor


**Gerot Lannach UK Limited**
*Incorporated:* 15 February 2019
*Registered Office:* Knockwood House, Ox Lane, St Michaels, Tenterden, Kent, TN30 6PE
*Parent:* GL Pharma GmbH
*Officers:* Dr Martin Bartenstein [1953] Director/Doctor [Austrian]; Andreas Gasser [1977] Director [Austrian]


**Gester Invest Limited**
*Incorporated:* 9 October 2013
*Net Worth:* £6,745  *Total Assets:* £7,948
*Registered Office:* 1a Crown Lane, London, SW16 3DJ
*Major Shareholder:* Alexey Egorov
*Officers:* Diederick Petrus Naude [1957] Director [South African]


**Raj Ghai Associates Limited**
*Incorporated:* 12 October 2015
*Net Worth:* £1  *Total Assets:* £1
*Registered Office:* 9 Tawny Way, Littleover, Derby, DE23 3XG
*Officers:* Rajesh Ghai [1967] Director

## GHC (UK) Ltd
*Incorporated:* 30 August 2012 *Employees:* 14
*Net Worth:* £66,320 *Total Assets:* £177,561
*Registered Office:* 59-61 Charlotte Street, St Pauls Square, Birmingham, B3 1PX
*Shareholders:* Sawern Singh Singh; Rajvinder Kaur
*Officers:* Rajvinder Kaur [1967] Director; Sawern Singh Singh [1963] Director

## GHC Global Limited
*Incorporated:* 19 February 2015 *Employees:* 4
*Net Worth:* £269,811 *Total Assets:* £327,231
*Registered Office:* 59-61 Charlotte Street, St Pauls Square, Birmingham, B3 1PX
*Shareholders:* Rajvinder Kaur; Sawern Singh Singh
*Officers:* Rajvinder Kaur [1967] Director; Sawern Singh Singh [1963] Director; Dr Amandeep Singh Suthi [1987] Director; Dr Govinder Singh Suthi [1991] Director; Dr Gurdeep Singh Suthi [1985] Director

## GHC Medical Ltd
*Incorporated:* 24 June 2015
*Net Worth:* £9,614 *Total Assets:* £26,093
*Registered Office:* Cawley House, 149-155 Canal Street, Nottingham, NG1 7HR
*Major Shareholder:* Gurdeep Singh Suthi
*Officers:* Harjit Kaur [1985] Director; Dr Gurdeep Singh Suthi [1985] Director/Doctor

## Gideotech Limited
*Incorporated:* 26 July 2018
*Registered Office:* 85 Galahad Road, Bromley, Kent, BR1 5DS
*Major Shareholder:* Morgan Ejiohuo
*Officers:* Morgan Ejiohuo [1967] Director/Mechanical Engineer

## Gilead Sciences Ltd
*Incorporated:* 27 September 1990 *Employees:* 132
*Net Worth:* £63,921,000 *Total Assets:* £109,323,000
*Registered Office:* 280 High Holborn, London, WC1V 7EE
*Parent:* Gilead Sciences, Inc.
*Officers:* Johanna Henry, Secretary; Rudolf Ertl [1960] Director [German]; Brett Pletcher [1968] Director [American]; Robin Washington [1962] Director [American]

## Gill Pharma Limited
*Incorporated:* 26 February 2014
*Net Worth:* £13 *Total Assets:* £48,564
*Registered Office:* 17 Silver Birches Business Park, Aston Road, Bromsgrove, Worcs, B60 3EU
*Major Shareholder:* Mohammed Munir Karim
*Officers:* Mohammed Munir Karim [1966] Director

## Gilsun Healthcare Ltd
*Incorporated:* 28 June 2013
*Registered Office:* 70 Brownpring Drive, London, SE9 3JX
*Major Shareholder:* Manjit Singh Gill
*Officers:* Manjit Singh Gill, Secretary; Manjit Singh Gill [1975] Director/Property Developer

## Gilsun Limited
*Incorporated:* 28 May 2005
*Registered Office:* 70 Brownspring Drive, London, SE9 3JX
*Major Shareholder:* Manjit Singh Gill
*Officers:* Manjit Singh Gill, Secretary; Manjit Singh Gill [1975] Director/Builder

## GJB Pharma Limited
*Incorporated:* 24 September 2014
*Registered Office:* Unit W5, Warwick House Industrial Estate, 18 Forge Lane, Minworth, Sutton Coldfield, W Midlands, B76 1AH
*Major Shareholder:* Gary John Birch
*Officers:* Garry John Birch [1963] Director

## GK Locums Ltd
*Incorporated:* 8 October 2013
*Net Worth:* £913 *Total Assets:* £12,290
*Registered Office:* 1192 Stratford Road, Hall Green, Birmingham, B28 8AB
*Major Shareholder:* Ghazanfar Karamat
*Officers:* Ghazanfar Karamat [1986] Director

## Glaxo Laboratories Limited
*Incorporated:* 28 May 1929
*Registered Office:* 980 Great West Road, Brentford, Middlesex, TW8 9GS
*Parent:* Glaxo Wellcome UK Limited
*Officers:* Victoria Anne Whyte, Secretary; James Borger [1963] Director/VP, Group Financial Planning and Analysis [American]; Alan George Burns [1975] Director

## Glaxo Wellcome UK Limited
*Incorporated:* 25 March 1950
*Net Worth:* £69,164,000 *Total Assets:* £71,871,000
*Registered Office:* 980 Great West Road, Brentford, Middlesex, TW8 9GS
*Parent:* Glaxo Group Limited
*Officers:* Victoria Anne Whyte, Secretary; James Borger [1963] Director/VP, Group Financial Planning and Analysis [American]; Alan George Burns [1975] Director; Charalampos Panagiotidis [1977] Director/Financial Controller, Corporate Entities [Greek]

## GlaxoSmithKline Caribbean Limited
*Incorporated:* 28 July 1953 *Employees:* 49
*Net Worth:* £34,652,000 *Total Assets:* £37,655,000
*Registered Office:* 980 Great West Road, Brentford, Middlesex, TW8 9GS
*Parent:* SmithKline Beecham Limited
*Officers:* Charalampos Panagiotidis [1977] Director/Financial Controller, Corporate Entities [Greek]; Adam Walker [1967] Director

## GlaxoSmithKline Consumer Trading Services Limited
*Incorporated:* 21 June 2012
*Net Worth:* £19,491,000 *Total Assets:* £781,051,008
*Registered Office:* 980 Great West Road, Brentford, Middlesex, TW8 9GS
*Parent:* GlaxoSmithKline Consumer Healthcare Holdings Limited
*Officers:* Victoria Anne Whyte, Secretary; Richard Green [1974] Director; Tobias Hestler [1972] Director [German/Swiss]; Neil O'Hara [1973] Director

## GlaxoSmithKline Export Limited
*Incorporated:* 18 October 1989 *Employees:* 1,214
*Net Worth:* £94,567,000 *Total Assets:* £447,628,000
*Registered Office:* 980 Great West Road, Brentford, Middlesex, TW8 9GS
*Parent:* Glaxo Group Limited
*Officers:* Victoria Anne Whyte, Secretary; Dylan Jackson [1972] Director/General Manager; Adam Walker [1967] Director; Jane Mary Whitmore [1968] Finance Director

**GlaxoSmithKline UK Limited**
*Incorporated:* 24 October 2001  *Employees:* 499
*Net Worth:* £617,320,000  *Total Assets:* £723,723,008
*Registered Office:* 980 Great West Road, Brentford, Middlesex, TW8 9GS
*Parent:* Glaxo Group Limited
*Officers:* Simon Paul Dingemans [1963] Director; Ville Kullervo Maukonen [1978] Finance Director [Finnish]

**GlaxoSmithKline US Trading Limited**
*Incorporated:* 12 September 2018
*Registered Office:* 980 Great West Road, Brentford, Middlesex, TW8 9GS
*Parent:* Glaxo Group Limited
*Officers:* Jonathan Box [1963] Director; Jay Wade Green [1972] Director [Canadian]; Mark Heathcote [1963] Director; Adam Walker [1978] Director

**Glector Limited**
*Incorporated:* 25 March 2014
*Registered Office:* 56 Leman Street, London, E1 8EU
*Shareholders:* Abhishek Singh Niranjan; Anurag Singh Niranjan
*Officers:* Abhishek Singh Niranjan [1988] Director [Indian]; Anurag Singh Niranjan [1987] Director [Indian]

**Glemsford Services Limited**
*Incorporated:* 1 March 2007  *Employees:* 7
*Net Worth:* £54,574  *Total Assets:* £231,834
*Registered Office:* The Surgery, Lion Road, Glemsford, Sudbury, Suffolk, CO10 7RF
*Shareholders:* Mary Emma Giblin; Matthew Thomas Piccaver
*Officers:* Dr Mary Emma Giblin [1969] Director/Doctor; Dr Matthew Thomas Piccaver [1978] Director/Doctor

**Glenhazel Limited**
*Incorporated:* 12 October 2005
*Net Worth:* £1,900,000  *Total Assets:* £1,900,000
*Registered Office:* Safedale House, 1 Aden Road, Enfield, Middlesex, EN3 7SE
*Officers:* Amit Balubhai Patel [1966] Director/Pharmacist; Balubhai Khushalbhai Patel [1942] Director/Pharmacist; Dr. Piyushbhai Khushalbhai Patel [1952] Director/Chemist

**Glenmark Pharmaceuticals Europe Limited**
*Incorporated:* 10 February 2004  *Employees:* 83
*Net Worth:* £12,932,667  *Total Assets:* £50,697,828
*Registered Office:* Laxmi House, 2B Draycott Avenue, Kenton, Harrow, Middlesex, HA3 0BU
*Shareholders:* Blanche Saldanha; Cherylann Pinto; Glenn Saldanha
*Officers:* Fiona Hill, Secretary; Oliver Henry Bourne [1980] Director; Achin Gupta [1976] Director [Indian]

**Global 1st Ltd**
*Incorporated:* 6 January 2011  *Employees:* 5
*Net Worth:* £3,074  *Total Assets:* £211,314
*Registered Office:* 32 Totternhoe Close, Harrow, Middlesex, HA3 0HS
*Parent:* Global 1st Holdings Limited
*Officers:* Anuj Ramniklal Shamji Shah [1969] Director; Shaili Anuj Shah [1974] Director

**Global 4 Care Ltd**
*Incorporated:* 1 June 2015
*Net Worth:* £100  *Total Assets:* £100
*Registered Office:* Suite 18, Equity Chambers, 249 High Street North, Poole, Dorset, BH15 1DX
*Officers:* Waldemar Florczyk [1978] Director [Polish]

**Global Additives Ltd**
*Incorporated:* 13 December 2011
*Previous:* Crystal Chemicals Limited
*Net Worth Deficit:* £383
*Registered Office:* 86-90 Paul Street, London, EC2A 4NE
*Shareholder:* Adnan Moien
*Officers:* Sobia Adnan [1981] Director/Trader [Pakistani]; Adnan Moin [1978] Director [Pakistani]

**Global Dispensing Limited**
*Incorporated:* 9 August 2004
*Net Worth:* £19,130  *Total Assets:* £23,514
*Registered Office:* 3 Young Place, East Kilbride, G75 0TD
*Parent:* Doctors Dispensing Services Limited
*Officers:* John Cochrane [1957] Director

**Global Medical Supplies Ltd**
*Incorporated:* 3 July 2018
*Registered Office:* 205 Pentax House, South Hill Avenue, Harrow, Middlesex, HA2 0DU
*Shareholders:* Zulfiqar Hussain; Colin Schauder
*Officers:* Zulfiqar Hussain [1968] Director; Dr Colin Schauder [1959] Director/Doctor

**Global Medical Supply UK Ltd**
*Incorporated:* 24 January 2017
*Net Worth Deficit:* £1,588  *Total Assets:* £239,013
*Registered Office:* Yahya Accountancy, 164 West Hendon Broadway, London, NW9 7AA
*Major Shareholder:* Abdullah Barakat
*Officers:* Abdullah Barakat [1971] Director/Executive Manager [Syrian]

**Global Pharma Care Ltd**
*Incorporated:* 7 February 2019
*Registered Office:* 15 Fullerton Close, Markyate, St Albans, Herts, AL3 8PL
*Major Shareholder:* Sarah Marcelle Banfield
*Officers:* Dr Sarah Marcelle Banfield [1983] Director and Company Secretary

**Global Pharma Direct Ltd**
*Incorporated:* 7 March 2016
*Net Worth Deficit:* £2,774  *Total Assets:* £25,384
*Registered Office:* Unit 9 Lyndon Business Park, Farrier Road, Lincoln, LN6 3RU
*Major Shareholder:* Peter Joyce
*Officers:* Salma Keshmiri, Secretary; Peter Joyce [1968] Director; Salma Keshmiri [1973] Director

**Global Pharmaceuticals (UK) Limited**
*Incorporated:* 1 February 1989
*Registered Office:* Global House, 653 River Gardens, North Feltham Trading Estate, Feltham, Middlesex, TW14 0RB
*Officers:* Bashir Sacranie, Secretary; Bashir Sacranie [1952] Director; Sir Iqbal Sacranie [1951] Director

**Global Pharmaceuticals Ltd**
*Incorporated:* 20 February 1967
*Net Worth:* £124,427  *Total Assets:* £739,518
*Registered Office:* Global House, 653 River Gardens, North Feltham Trading Estate, Feltham, Middlesex, TW14 0RB
*Officers:* Bashir Sacranie, Secretary; Bashir Sacranie [1952] Director

**Global SCS Limited**
*Incorporated:* 4 September 2018
*Registered Office:* 2nd Floor, College House, 17 King Edwards Road, Ruislip, Middlesex, HA4 7AE
*Major Shareholder:* Dip Thakkar
*Officers:* Dip Thakkar [1987] Director/Sales

**Global Supply (U.K.) Ltd**
*Incorporated:* 29 November 2017
*Registered Office:* 71-75 Shelton Street, Covent Garden, London, WC2H 9JR
*Officers:* Imdad Ullah [1968] Director

**Globegen Laboratories Limited**
*Incorporated:* 17 April 2012
*Net Worth Deficit:* £303,298 *Total Assets:* £38,004
*Registered Office:* 1406 Coventry Road, Yardley, Birmingham, B25 8AE
*Major Shareholder:* Mohamed Gulamali Kanani
*Officers:* Abbas Mohamed Kanani [1984] Director/Pharmacist; Mohamed Gulamali Kanani [1952] Director/Pharmacist

**Globyz Pharma (UK) Ltd**
*Incorporated:* 13 November 2014
*Net Worth:* £1 *Total Assets:* £2,501
*Registered Office:* 2 Pulborough Way, Hounslow, Middlesex, TW4 6DE
*Officers:* Muhammed Salman Pathan [1968] Director [Canadian]

**Glucozen Limited**
*Incorporated:* 11 June 2014
*Net Worth Deficit:* £77,008 *Total Assets:* £168,687
*Registered Office:* Corner Oak, 1 Homer Road, Solihull, W Midlands, B91 3QG
*Officers:* Onkar Singh [1970] Director/Pharmacist

**GM Biopharma Ltd**
*Incorporated:* 23 November 2017
*Registered Office:* 30-31 Furnival Street, London, EC4A 1JQ
*Major Shareholder:* Ashraf Uddin
*Officers:* Ashraf Uddin [1975] Director/Company Owner

**GMM Sales Ltd**
*Incorporated:* 14 May 2018
*Registered Office:* 7 Philbye Mews, Slough, Berks, SL1 5US
*Major Shareholder:* Grzegorz Michal Mruk
*Officers:* Grzegorz Michal Mruk [1986] Director [Polish]

**GMP-Orphan United Kingdom Ltd**
*Incorporated:* 6 November 2018
*Registered Office:* 55 Baker Street, London, W1U 7EU
*Officers:* Naseem Sajjid Amin [1961] Director; Mohamed Abdelkader Abdelhamid Mosa [1978] Director/General Manager

**Go Go Chemist Limited**
*Incorporated:* 21 January 2010 *Employees:* 14
*Net Worth:* £94,176 *Total Assets:* £632,476
*Registered Office:* 12 Pembridge Road, London, W11 3HL
*Shareholders:* Navid Masoud; Omid Masoud
*Officers:* Navid Masoud [1976] Director

**Go Medical UK Limited**
*Incorporated:* 13 March 2012
*Net Worth Deficit:* £16,264 *Total Assets:* £9,549
*Registered Office:* Deanfield House, 98 Lancaster Road, Newcastle-under-Lyme, Staffs, ST5 1DS
*Shareholders:* Alexander George Brian O'Neil; Christine O'Neil
*Officers:* Patsy Graieg, Secretary; Patsy Graieg [1957] Director/Chartered Accountant [Singaporean]

**Go-Kyo Science Limited**
*Incorporated:* 26 November 2009 *Employees:* 2
*Net Worth Deficit:* £5,179 *Total Assets:* £31,287
*Registered Office:* Kings House Business Centre, St Johns Square, Wolverhampton, W Midlands, WV2 4DT
*Shareholders:* Lakhveer Singh Sahota; Gurpreet Kaur Sahota
*Officers:* Gurpreet Kaur Sahota [1978] Director; Lakhveer Singh Sahota [1974] Director

**Goldpharma Ltd**
*Incorporated:* 7 June 2018
*Registered Office:* Office 1.01c, Regus Slough Town Centre, 18-24 Stoke Road, Slough, Berks, SL2 5AG
*Major Shareholder:* Gold Ifechikwadoro Ekeanyanwu
*Officers:* Gold Ifechikwadoro Ekeanyanwu [1993] Director/Pharmacist

**Goldshore (UK) Limited**
*Incorporated:* 24 June 2005
*Net Worth Deficit:* £5,693 *Total Assets:* £668
*Registered Office:* 8 Wimpole Street, London, W1G 9SP
*Major Shareholder:* Philippe Henri Prive
*Officers:* Gael Vanessa Prive [1980] Director [French]; Philippe Henri Prive [1954] Director [French]

**Goldsmith Resources Limited**
*Incorporated:* 11 August 2004
*Net Worth:* £174,936 *Total Assets:* £8,482,515
*Registered Office:* Floor 24-25, The Shard, 32 London Bridge Street, London, SE1 9SG
*Officers:* Mathew Peter Hart, Secretary; Andreas Aristeidou [1982] Director [Cypriot]

**Gorton Trading Limited**
*Incorporated:* 19 June 2009
*Previous:* SC361442 Limited
*Net Worth Deficit:* £173,666 *Total Assets:* £142,919
*Registered Office:* c/o Robert Gorton, 73e Westwood Avenue, Ayr, KA8 0RL
*Major Shareholder:* Robert Gorton
*Officers:* Robert Gorton [1970] Director

**Gos Pharma Limited**
*Incorporated:* 1 July 2015
*Net Worth Deficit:* £6,462 *Total Assets:* £2,342
*Registered Office:* Block B Unit 202.6, 100 Clements Road, London, SE16 4DG
*Shareholder:* Peng Hong Ooi
*Officers:* Peng Hong Ooi, Secretary; Sushil Waman Gaikwad [1979] Director/Solicitor

**Got Heart UK Ltd**
*Incorporated:* 29 January 2018
*Registered Office:* 17 Whiteadder Way, London, E14 9UR
*Shareholders:* Stephanie Limuaco; Melissa Yap
*Officers:* Lourdes Stephanie Limuaco [1983] Director/Businesswoman; Melissa Yap [1985] Director/Businesswoman [Filipino]

**Gowrie Laxmico Limited**
*Incorporated:* 8 October 1997  *Employees:* 297
*Previous:* Gowrie Limited
*Net Worth:* £17,930,260  *Total Assets:* £35,392,188
*Registered Office:* Unit 4 Bradfield Road, Ruislip, Middlesex, HA4 0NU
*Officers:* Govindji Thakershi Hathi, Secretary; Alpa Hathi [1968] Director/HR; Govindji Thakershi Hathi [1941] Director; Samit Hathi [1967] Director/Chief Executive


**GP Laboratories Limited**
*Incorporated:* 8 June 2005
*Net Worth:* £52,735  *Total Assets:* £686,860
*Registered Office:* 160 Cromwell Road, Rushden, Northants, NN10 0EF
*Shareholders:* Ashok Kumar; Debbie Kumar
*Officers:* Ashok Kumar, Secretary; Ashok Kumar [1958] Director/Biochemist; Debbie Kumar [1956] Director/Administrator


**GP Mediplus Ltd**
*Incorporated:* 11 January 2016
*Net Worth:* £897  *Total Assets:* £896
*Registered Office:* 20-22 Wenlock Road, London, N1 7GU
*Shareholders:* Georghios Petropoulakis; Goldman Capital Group Ltd
*Officers:* Michalakis Nestor Megas [1946] Director/Accountant [Cypriot]; Georghios Petropoulakis [1957] Director/Entrepreneur [Cypriot]


**GP Meds Direct Limited**
*Incorporated:* 20 January 2017
*Net Worth Deficit:* £4,191  *Total Assets:* £15,314
*Registered Office:* Unit 4c Seedbed Center, Avenue Road, Nechells, Birmingham, B7 4NT
*Major Shareholder:* Mohammed Ayaz
*Officers:* Mohammed Ayaz [1979] Director


**GPM Pharma Limited**
*Incorporated:* 6 August 2018
*Registered Office:* 495 Green Lanes, London, N13 4BS
*Shareholders:* George Menegas; Pantelis Papageorgiou
*Officers:* George Menegas [1972] Director [Greek]; Pantelis Papageorgiou [1965] Director/Doctor [Greek]


**GQC Solutions Ltd**
*Incorporated:* 13 September 2017
*Registered Office:* 33 Glen Lee, East Kilbride, S Lanarks, G74 3UU
*Major Shareholder:* Ross Gray
*Officers:* Ross Gray [1993] Director


**Grandbydale Limited**
*Incorporated:* 7 February 1979  *Employees:* 6
*Net Worth:* £1,229,808  *Total Assets:* £1,661,058
*Registered Office:* Onward Chambers, 34 Market Street, Hyde, Cheshire, SK14 1AH
*Shareholders:* Jitendra Kantibhal Patel; Hansa Jitendra Patel
*Officers:* Jitendra Kantibhal Patel, Secretary; Hansa Jitendra Patel [1951] Director/Sales Manager; Jitendra Kantibhal Patel [1948] Director/Pharmacist


**Granules Europe Limited**
*Incorporated:* 5 December 2016  *Employees:* 2
*Net Worth Deficit:* £167,261  *Total Assets:* £31,811
*Registered Office:* 11 Laura Place, Bath, BA2 4BL
*Officers:* Krishna Prasad Chigurupati [1954] Director [Indian]; Michael Frude [1958] Director/Manager [New Zealander]


**Graviti Healthcare Limited**
*Incorporated:* 1 October 2018
*Registered Office:* 209 The Heights, Northolt, Middlesex, UB5 4BX
*Major Shareholder:* Sridhar Rao Sampalli
*Officers:* Sridhar Rao Sampalli [1966] Director


**The Great British Bee Company Ltd**
*Incorporated:* 24 February 2017
*Registered Office:* 26 Victoria Road, Devizes, Wilts, SN10 1ET
*Officers:* Ben Swift [1979] Director


**Green Guru Enterprices Ltd.**
*Incorporated:* 9 May 2017
*Registered Office:* Dept 302, 43 Owston Road, Carcroft, Doncaster, S Yorks, DN6 8DA
*Shareholders:* Godwyn Joseph Orlando Roy Rollocks; Evert Charles Boom
*Officers:* Evert Charles Boom [1963] Director/Chief Operating Officer [Dutch]; Godwyn Joseph Orlando Roy Rollocks [1965] Director/Chief Executive Officer [Dutch]


**Green Sun Ltd**
*Incorporated:* 8 November 2018
*Registered Office:* 19 Diamond Court, Opal Drive, Fox Milne, Milton Keynes, Bucks, MK15 0DU
*Parent:* Simon One Limited
*Officers:* Antonio Simon Vumbaca [1971] Director [Italian]


**Greenheys - Weenytot Limited**
*Incorporated:* 23 March 1973  *Employees:* 19
*Net Worth:* £1,134,007  *Total Assets:* £1,430,209
*Registered Office:* Unit 6 Lane Ends Trading Estate, off Blackpool Road, Preston, Lancs, PR2 2DS
*Shareholders:* Michael Dean Fletcher; Maureen Anne Fletcher
*Officers:* Maureen Anne Fletcher, Secretary/Director; Maureen Anne Fletcher [1944] Director; Michael Dean Fletcher [1974] Director


**Greenliving Pharma Ltd**
*Incorporated:* 7 April 2014
*Previous:* Green Pharma Limited
*Net Worth Deficit:* £14,510  *Total Assets:* £92,731
*Registered Office:* Sprunston, Durdar, Carlisle, CA5 7AP
*Officers:* Islam Pearson [1974] Managing Director


**Greens Pharmacy Limited**
*Incorporated:* 10 February 1997
*Net Worth:* £786,636  *Total Assets:* £979,323
*Registered Office:* 1-3 St Marys Road, Shoreham by Sea, W Sussex, BN43 5ZA
*Major Shareholder:* Daksha Chauhan
*Officers:* Daksha Chauhan, Secretary; Daksha Chauhan [1963] Director/Manager


**Greens Roads UK Ltd**
*Incorporated:* 13 September 2018
*Registered Office:* Suite A, 6 Honduras Street, London, EC1Y 0TH
*Shareholders:* Arbelio Jose Barroso; Laura Michelle Fuentes; James Tundidor
*Officers:* Arbelio Jose Barroso [1970] Director/Chief Executive Officer [American]

# The Top UK Pharmaceutical Wholesalers

**Greiner Bio-One Limited**
*Incorporated:* 27 July 1992  *Employees:* 41
*Net Worth:* £2,690,405  *Total Assets:* £4,827,444
*Registered Office:* Unit 5 Stroudwater Business Park, Brunel Way, Stonehouse, Glos, GL10 3SX
*Parent:* Greiner Bio-One GmbH
*Officers:* Jonathan Frank Richard Pearson, Secretary; Noel Christopher Ennett [1958] Director/Operations Manager; Jonathan Frank Richard Pearson [1958] Director/Chartered Accountant; Thomas Milligan Woods [1958] Director/Salesman

**Grey Traders Limited**
*Incorporated:* 19 March 2015
*Registered Office:* Pellys Solicitors Limited, 18 The Causeway, Bishop's Stortford, Herts, CM23 2EJ
*Shareholders:* Michael John Frederick Sparrow; Olwyn Anne Sparrow
*Officers:* Michael John Frederick Sparrow [1948] Director/Consultant to The General Pharmaceutical Industry; Olwyn Anne Sparrow [1953] Director/Housewife

**Groves Marchant Limited**
*Incorporated:* 17 July 2000
*Net Worth:* £63,383  *Total Assets:* £119,827
*Registered Office:* Unit 7 Howard Business Park, 47 Howard Close, Waltham Abbey, Essex, EN9 1XE
*Major Shareholder:* Terry Neil Reid
*Officers:* Terry Neil Reid, Secretary; Terry Neil Reid [1960] Director/Pharmacist

**Grunenthal Limited**
*Incorporated:* 29 October 1998  *Employees:* 113
*Net Worth:* £3,298,000  *Total Assets:* £9,133,000
*Registered Office:* Regus, Lakeside House, 1 Furzeground Way, Stockley Park, Uxbridge, Middlesex, UB11 1BD
*Parent:* Grunenthal GmbH
*Officers:* Mark Fladrich [1959] Director/Pharmacist [Australian]; Amanda Flanagan [1971] Managing Director [Irish]; Thomas Spindler [1973] Finance Director [German]

**Guardian Pharmaceuticals Co Ltd**
*Incorporated:* 25 January 2016  *Employees:* 1
*Net Worth Deficit:* £118,762  *Total Assets:* £75,068
*Registered Office:* 4 Hawthorne Avenue, Nantwich, Cheshire, CW5 6HZ
*Officers:* Margarita Cholakyan Wistuba [1974] Director [Russian]

**Guerbet Laboratories Limited**
*Incorporated:* 20 June 1994  *Employees:* 20
*Net Worth:* £7,639,720  *Total Assets:* £9,877,870
*Registered Office:* Avon House, Stratford Road, Shirley, Solihull, W Midlands, B90 4AA
*Parent:* Guerbet SA
*Officers:* Charlotte Bamiere, Secretary; Harvey Lee Scott [1970] Director

**Guest Medical Limited**
*Incorporated:* 4 June 1987  *Employees:* 8
*Net Worth:* £405,683  *Total Assets:* £777,648
*Registered Office:* Unit A6, Larkfield Trading Estate, New Hythe Lane, Larkfield, Aylesford, Kent, ME20 6SW
*Officers:* Stephen Godfrey Mew, Secretary; Laure-Anne Cloutier [1990] Director/Chief Executive Officer [Canadian]; Stephen Godfrey Mew [1955] Commercial Director

**Gulfstream Equity & Development Ltd**
*Incorporated:* 21 November 2014
*Net Worth Deficit:* £35,723  *Total Assets:* £556,002
*Registered Office:* Ground Floor, Invision House, Wilbury Way, Hitchin, Herts, SG4 0TW
*Major Shareholder:* Iryna Dyachenko
*Officers:* Cristino Guevara Salazar [1964] Director [Panamanian]

**Gumsaver Limited**
*Incorporated:* 16 February 2011
*Net Worth Deficit:* £211,536  *Total Assets:* £5,582
*Registered Office:* 11 Playfield Crescent, London, SE22 8QR
*Major Shareholder:* Hani Mostafa Awadalla Mostafa
*Officers:* Dr Hani Mostafa Awadalla Mostafa [1974] Director/Dentist; Humayun Kabir Zaman [1971] Director/Sound Engineer

**Guna Biotherapeutics Limited**
*Incorporated:* 16 May 2008
*Registered Office:* Unit 16 Willesborough Industrial Park, Willesborough, Ashford, Kent, TN24 0TD
*Shareholders:* Juliet Macaraya Wilson; Roger Keith Wilson
*Officers:* Roger Keith Wilson, Secretary; Juliet Macaraya Wilson [1948] Managing Director; Roger Keith Wilson [1940] Managing Director

**Guna Limited**
*Incorporated:* 16 May 2008
*Registered Office:* Unit 16 Willesborough Industrial Park, Willesborough, Ashford, Kent, TN24 0TD
*Shareholders:* Juliet Macaraya Wilson; Roger Keith Wilson
*Officers:* Roger Keith Wilson, Secretary; Juliet Macaraya Wilson [1948] Managing Director; Roger Keith Wilson [1940] Managing Director

**H & S Beauty Care Limited**
*Incorporated:* 12 July 2017
*Registered Office:* 15 Borrowdale Way, Loughborough, Leics, LE11 3RG
*Major Shareholder:* Dandan Sun
*Officers:* Dandan Sun [1989] Director [Chinese]

**H C Healthcare Ltd**
*Incorporated:* 8 July 2014
*Net Worth Deficit:* £4,081  *Total Assets:* £19,320
*Registered Office:* Redhill Garage, Middle Lane, Tansley, Matlock, Derbys, DE4 5GD
*Shareholders:* David Michael Hill; Joanna Rachel Hill
*Officers:* David Michael Hill [1967] Director

**H4 Medical Limited**
*Incorporated:* 2 February 2010  *Employees:* 5
*Net Worth:* £183,868  *Total Assets:* £302,159
*Registered Office:* Suite 4, Earlshouse, Earlsway, Team Valley Trading Estate, Gateshead, Tyne & Wear, NE11 0RY
*Major Shareholder:* Mark Wayne Harris
*Officers:* Mark Wayne Harris [1962] Director/Consultant

**Habberpharm Limited**
*Incorporated:* 5 August 2009
*Net Worth:* £54,187  *Total Assets:* £220,756
*Registered Office:* 11 Keld Close, Barker Business Park, Melmerby Green Road, Melmerby, Ripon, N Yorks, HG4 5NB
*Major Shareholder:* Laura Ann Knox
*Officers:* Laura Ann Knox [1974] Director

**Halewood Health Limited**
Incorporated: 1 July 2015
Registered Office: The Mill, Horton Road, Staines upon Thames, Middlesex, TW19 6BJ
Major Shareholder: Susan Elizabeth de Zulueta
Officers: Robin Faber, Secretary; Susan Elizabeth de Zulueta [1957] Director

**Halo GB Ltd**
Incorporated: 26 November 2004
Registered Office: Hill House, 41 Richmond Hill, Bournemouth, BH2 6HS
Parent: Ceuta Healthcare Ltd
Officers: Edwin Charles Bessant [1953] Managing Director; Annette Zita D'Abreo [1962] Marketing Director

**Ham+Med Company Ltd**
Incorporated: 6 April 2006
Net Worth Deficit: £107,476  Total Assets: £33,130
Registered Office: 5 Jupiter House, Calleva Park, Aldermaston, Reading, Berks, RG7 8NN
Major Shareholder: Muso Rustemi
Officers: Muso Rustemi [1966] Director [German]

**Hambleden Herbs Limited**
Incorporated: 21 December 2012
Net Worth Deficit: £83,787  Total Assets: £106,634
Registered Office: Unit 6 Park Street Business Centre, Park Street, Chatteris, Cambs, PE16 6AE
Major Shareholder: David James Carter
Officers: David James Carter [1950] Director

**Hambleton (UK) Limited**
Incorporated: 26 March 2003  Employees: 3
Net Worth: £1,228,158  Total Assets: £2,678,146
Registered Office: Newlands House, 60 Chainhouse Lane, Whitestake, Preston, Lancs, PR4 4LG
Shareholders: Allison Jane Moosa; Iqbal Moosa
Officers: Iqbal Moosa [1963] Director

**Hameln Pharmaceuticals Ltd**
Incorporated: 14 December 1971  Employees: 22
Net Worth: £9,826,141  Total Assets: £13,764,480
Registered Office: Nexus, Hurricane Road, Gloucester Business Park, Gloucester, GL3 4AG
Major Shareholder: Christoph Kerstein
Officers: Stephen Allen Watkin, Secretary/Managing Director; Christoph Kerstein [1961] Director/Pharmacist [German]; Stephen Allen Watkin [1967] Managing Director

**Hamilton Pharmaceuticals Ltd**
Incorporated: 12 February 2003  Employees: 16
Net Worth: £5,669,142  Total Assets: £8,637,963
Registered Office: Falcon House, Unit 15 Lawnhurst Trading Estate, Oakhurst Drive, Cheadle Heath, Stockport, Cheshire, SK3 0XT
Parent: Healthcare Direct Holdings Limited
Officers: Piyush Ramniklal Mehta, Secretary; Manish Ramniklal Mehta [1971] Director

**Hampton Brand Management Company Limited**
Incorporated: 20 March 2008
Registered Office: 169 Waverley Avenue, Twickenham, Middlesex, TW2 6DJ
Shareholders: Sujith Nayanapriya Wijesena; Samangi Sudarshani Somapala
Officers: Samangi Sudarshani Somapala, Secretary; Sujith Nayanapriya Wijesena [1968] Director

**Hampton Brands Limited**
Incorporated: 19 March 2008
Net Worth: £230,000  Total Assets: £1,090,000
Registered Office: 169 Waverley Avenue, Twickenham, Middlesex, TW2 6DJ
Major Shareholder: Sujith Nayanapriya Wijesena
Officers: Samangi Sudarshani Somapala, Secretary; Sujith Nayanapriya Wijesena [1968] Director

**Hana Healthcare Ltd**
Incorporated: 28 November 2018
Registered Office: 89 Glebe Avenue, Ickenham, Uxbridge, Middlesex, UB10 8PF
Major Shareholder: Zac Hana
Officers: Zac Hana [1993] Director

**Hana Supplies Limited**
Incorporated: 13 December 2012
Registered Office: Sovereign House, Graham Road, Harrow, Middlesex, HA3 5RF
Officers: Jinan Shakir Shaban [1954] Director

**Hanseco Ltd**
Incorporated: 22 March 2018
Registered Office: The Courtyard, 14a Sydenham Road, Croydon, Surrey, CR0 2EE
Shareholders: Harindra Patel; Ashokkumar Naranbhai Patel
Officers: Ashokkumar Naranbhai Patel [1960] Director/Industrial Chemist; Harindra Patel [1995] Director/Undergraduate Pharmacist

**Haoma Pharma Ltd**
Incorporated: 11 November 2013
Net Worth: £1,666  Total Assets: £1,922
Registered Office: Adelphi Court, 1-3 East Street, Epsom, Surrey, KT17 1BB
Major Shareholder: Babak Gholamhosseini
Officers: Babak Gholamhosseini [1982] Director/Pharmacist

**HAPA Group Holdings Limited**
Incorporated: 21 February 2019
Registered Office: 165 Fleet Street, London, EC4A 2DY
Major Shareholder: Harry Karelis
Officers: Harry Karelis [1969] Director [Australian]; Tod McGrouther [1962] Director [Australian]

**Hapa Medical UK Ltd**
Incorporated: 23 July 2018
Registered Office: 88 Hollins Lane, Bury, Lancs, BL9 8AH
Major Shareholder: German Augusto Gonzalez
Officers: German Augusto Gonzalez [1962] Director/Business Executive [Swiss]

**Hapharm Ltd**
Incorporated: 3 September 2014
Net Worth: £150,466  Total Assets: £578,723
Registered Office: 590 Kingston Road, London, SW20 8DN
Major Shareholder: Artur Piotr Kurasinski
Officers: Artur Piotr Kurasinski [1989] Director [Polish]

**Haq Pharm Ltd**
Incorporated: 22 October 2018
Registered Office: Park Hill, Huddersfield, W Yorks, HD2 1QG
Major Shareholder: Hassan Haq
Officers: Hassan Haq [1991] Director/Locum Pharmacist

**Harben Medical Limited**
Incorporated: 10 January 2012  Employees: 2
Net Worth: £206,655  Total Assets: £461,666
Registered Office: Sterling House, 501 Middleton Road, Chadderton, Oldham, Lancs, OL9 9LY
Major Shareholder: Executors of Anne Craigie
Officers: Christopher John Rodger [1960] Director/Chartered Accountant; Simon Addison Smith [1956] Director/Pharmacist

**Harley Dentist Limited**
Incorporated: 27 September 2016
Registered Office: New Bond House, 124 New Bond Street, London, W1S 1DX
Major Shareholder: Ravi Gehlot
Officers: Ravi Gehlot [1982] Director

**Harley's (UK) Ltd**
Incorporated: 25 September 2002
Registered Office: 1 Bullescroft Road, Edgware, Middlesex, HA8 8RN
Officers: Premila Haria [1954] Director

**Harmonium Investments Limited**
Incorporated: 10 October 2012
Net Worth Deficit: £810,935  Total Assets: £866,537
Registered Office: 3rd Floor, Palladium House, 1-4 Argyll Street, London, W1F 7LD
Major Shareholder: Ugo Cosentino
Officers: Andrea Aimar [1983] Director [Italian]; Ugo Cosentino [1964] Director/Entrepreneur [Italian]

**Albert Harrison & Co.Limited**
Incorporated: 20 May 1940  Employees: 35
Net Worth: £1,385,092  Total Assets: £2,225,611
Registered Office: Unit 14a Mead Way, Shuttleworth Mead Business Park, Padiham, Burnley, Lancs, BB12 7NG
Parent: AH & Co Holdings Limited
Officers: Generald Richard Harrison [1938] Director; Graham Coupe Harrison [1957] Director; Cara McKenna [1976] Director; Paul Sanderson [1970] Director

**Paul Hartmann Limited**
Incorporated: 17 October 1980  Employees: 102
Net Worth: £4,057,003  Total Assets: £9,515,031
Registered Office: Unit P2, Parklands, Heywood Distribution Park, Pilsworth Road, Heywood, Lancs, OL10 2TT
Parent: Paul Hartmann AG
Officers: Trevor John Coupe, Secretary; Richard Cornwell [1972] Managing Director; Trevor John Coupe [1963] Director/Accountant; Marc Perez [1974] Director [Spanish]

**Hartwood & Brooks Limited**
Incorporated: 1 February 2008
Net Worth: £126,847  Total Assets: £157,351
Registered Office: 78 York Street, Marylebone, London, W1H 1DP
Major Shareholder: Andrew Rodney Noel Dickson
Officers: Andrew Rodney Noel Dickson [1964] Director and Company Secretary

**Harvey Pharma Ltd**
Incorporated: 10 June 2014
Net Worth: £496,890  Total Assets: £855,370
Registered Office: Unit 6 Carbrook Business Park, Dunlop Street, Sheffield, S9 2HR
Shareholders: Jeremiah Nguru Kiiru; Mercy Wambui Nguru
Officers: Mercy Wambui Nguru, Secretary; Jeremiah Nguru Kiiru [1972] Director/Pharmacist

**Hashmats Health Ltd**
Incorporated: 17 March 2010
Previous: Abagee Limited
Net Worth Deficit: £14,448  Total Assets: £4,303
Registered Office: Hashmats House, 123a-125a The Broadway, Southall, Middlesex, UB1 1LW
Officers: Akhtar Ali [1960] Director; Dilshad Ali [1996] Director; Fahid Ali [1987] Director

**Hasting Pharma Ltd**
Incorporated: 28 August 2018
Registered Office: Unit A29-31, Hastingwood Trading Estate, 35 Harbet Road, London, N18 3HT
Major Shareholder: Balambila Gloria Tenda
Officers: Balambila Gloria Tenda [1987] Director [French]

**Hayat Gostar Ltd**
Incorporated: 20 January 2016
Net Worth Deficit: £2,453  Total Assets: £9,490
Registered Office: 1st Floor, 2 Woodberry Grove, Finchley, London, N12 0DR
Major Shareholder: Mehdi Keshavarzi
Officers: Mehdi Keshavarzi [1967] Director

**Haydn Healthcare UK Limited**
Incorporated: 28 November 2013
Net Worth Deficit: £53,116  Total Assets: £319
Registered Office: Ground Floor, 19 New Road, Brighton, BN1 1UF
Shareholders: Carolyn Maria Thomas; Martin John Thomas
Officers: Carolyn Maria Thomas [1958] Director [American]; Martin John Thomas [1958] Director

**HB Sirius Ltd**
Incorporated: 5 June 2018
Registered Office: Flat 284, Fellows Court, Weymouth Terrace, London, E2 8LL
Shareholders: Ali Huseyin Yildirim; Burcu Cankiran
Officers: Burcu Cankiran [1992] Director; Ali Huseyin Yildirim [1992] Director

**HBS Healthcare Limited**
Incorporated: 17 July 2012
Net Worth Deficit: £185,296  Total Assets: £916,402
Registered Office: Former Preston College, Moor Park Avenue, Preston, Lancs, PR1 6AS
Shareholder: Salim Habib Patel
Officers: Salim Habib Patel [1978] Director

**HCP Limited**
Incorporated: 20 November 2017
Registered Office: Ailsa Craig, London Road, Northwich, Cheshire, CW9 8HN
Major Shareholder: Colin Kain-Duncan
Officers: Colin Kain-Duncan [1958] Director/Pharmaceutical Consultant

**Health Medbio Ltd**
Incorporated: 3 November 2016
Net Worth: £304  Total Assets: £3,050
Registered Office: 44 James Riley Point, Carpenters Road, Stratford, London, E15 2HY
Major Shareholder: James Obili
Officers: Ukah James Obili [1979] Director/Pharmacist

### Health Nutrient Products Limited
*Incorporated:* 20 April 2018
*Registered Office:* 13 Sherdley Road, Crumpsall, Manchester, M8 4GE
*Major Shareholder:* Amjad Hussain
*Officers:* Amjad Hussain [1972] Director

### Health Remit Limited
*Incorporated:* 8 May 2018
*Registered Office:* 33 Richards Way, Slough, SL1 5EU
*Officers:* Fawad Basheer, Secretary; Fawad Basheer [1970] Director/Accountant

### Health Source Limited
*Incorporated:* 17 July 2017
*Registered Office:* 179 West Bromwich Road, Walsall, W Midlands, WS1 3HL
*Major Shareholder:* Salman Saghir Ahmad
*Officers:* Salman Ahmad [1989] Director/Pharmacy

### Health Supplies Limited
*Incorporated:* 1 July 2010
*Net Worth:* £18,927 *Total Assets:* £154,525
*Registered Office:* 24 Brooke Avenue, Harrow, Middlesex, HA2 0NF
*Major Shareholder:* Brijesh Chachapura
*Officers:* Brijeshkumar Bhagvati Prasad Chachapura [1983] Director

### Healthaid Holdings Limited
*Incorporated:* 2 November 1988 *Employees:* 87
*Net Worth:* £11,455,930 *Total Assets:* £12,840,210
*Registered Office:* Galla House, 695 High Street, North Finchley, London, N12 0BT
*Shareholders:* Dilipkumar Patel; Rajendra Ambalal Patel
*Officers:* Rajendra Ambalal Patel, Secretary; Dilip Patel [1956] Director/Chairman; Rajendra Ambalal Patel [1960] Managing Director

### Healthaid Limited
*Incorporated:* 1 April 2003 *Employees:* 87
*Net Worth:* £11,455,930 *Total Assets:* £12,840,210
*Registered Office:* Galla House, 695 High Road, North Finchley, London, N12 0BT
*Parent:* Healthaid Holdings Ltd
*Officers:* Rajendra Ambalal Patel, Secretary/Director; Dilip Patel [1956] Director; Rajendra Ambalal Patel [1960] Director

### Healthbest Limited
*Incorporated:* 29 February 2016
*Registered Office:* International House, 24 Holborn Viaduct, London, EC1A 2BN
*Major Shareholder:* Naishadh Shah
*Officers:* Naishadh Shah [1986] Director [Indian]

### Healthbiotics Ltd
*Incorporated:* 19 March 2018
*Registered Office:* Unit 5 Progress Industrial Park, Progress Way, Croydon, Surrey, CR0 4XD
*Parent:* Nileshkumar Indubhai Patel
*Officers:* Nileshkumar Indubhai Patel [1974] Managing Director [Indian]

### Healthcaps Europe Ltd
*Incorporated:* 27 March 2018
*Registered Office:* 2nd Floor, College House, 17 King Edwards Road, Ruislip, Middlesex, HA4 7AE
*Major Shareholder:* Anuj Singh Gandhi
*Officers:* Anuj Singh Gandhi [1985] Director [Indian]

### Healthcare (Wales) Ltd.
*Incorporated:* 6 September 2002
*Registered Office:* 108a Lammas Street, Carmarthen, SA31 3AP
*Officers:* Christopher John James, Secretary/Chemist; Terry Baugh Griffiths [1946] Director

### Healthcare 21 (UK) Limited
*Incorporated:* 20 January 2004 *Employees:* 20
*Net Worth:* £1,754,000 *Total Assets:* £5,497,000
*Registered Office:* The Cuneiform, Maude Street, Leeds, LS2 7HB
*Officers:* Trevor Rodgers, Secretary; Owen Curtin [1954] Director [Irish]; David Charles Frederick [1966] Director; Tara Kearney [1974] Director [Irish]; Trevor Rodgers [1981] Director [Irish]

### Healthcare 4life Ltd
*Incorporated:* 20 July 2017
*Registered Office:* 4 Kings Row, Armstrong Road, Maidstone, Kent, ME15 6AQ
*Major Shareholder:* Nick Pullin
*Officers:* Maxine Brown, Secretary; Nick Pullin [1969] Director

### Healthcare Generics Limited
*Incorporated:* 22 June 2005
*Registered Office:* Chemidex House, Unit 7 Egham Business Village, Crabtree Road, Egham, Surrey, TW20 8RB
*Major Shareholder:* Navinchandra Jamnadas
*Officers:* Nikesh Engineer [1985] Director/Doctor

### Healthcare Pharma Limited
*Incorporated:* 16 January 2017
*Net Worth:* £1 *Total Assets:* £818,327
*Registered Office:* 3 Young Place, Kelvin Industrial Estate, East Kilbride, G75 0TD
*Parent:* Munro Healthcare Pharma Limited
*Officers:* John Cochrane [1957] Director; Stuart John Overend [1970] Director

### Healthcare Procurement Services Ltd
*Incorporated:* 20 May 2004 *Employees:* 1
*Net Worth:* £361,804 *Total Assets:* £411,847
*Registered Office:* Suite 310F, Sterling House, Langston Road, Loughton, Essex, IG10 3TS
*Major Shareholder:* David John Tipp
*Officers:* Christopher James Pace [1956] Director

### Healthcare Product Services Ltd
*Incorporated:* 10 December 1997
*Registered Office:* Progress Park, Bedford, MK42 9XE
*Parent:* Healthcare Services Group Limited
*Officers:* Kamaljit Singh Hunjan [1967] Director/Senior VP Movianto; Julia M. Munzinger [1968] Director/Accountant [American]; Nicholas Joseph Pace [1970] Director [American]; David John Tinsley [1977] Director

### Healthcare Services Group Limited
*Incorporated:* 12 December 1996
*Registered Office:* Progress Park, Bedford, MK42 9XE
*Parent:* O & M-Movianto UK Holdings Ltd.
*Officers:* Kamaljit Singh Hunjan [1967] Director/Senior VP Movianto; Julia M. Munzinger [1968] Director/Accountant [American]; Nicholas Joseph Pace [1970] Director [American]; David John Tinsley [1977] Director

# The Top UK Pharmaceutical Wholesalers

**Healthcare Source Limited**
*Incorporated:* 28 November 2013 *Employees:* 2
*Net Worth:* £52,922 *Total Assets:* £94,972
*Registered Office:* 11 Manor Way, Woking, Surrey, GU22 9JX
*Shareholders:* Samer Subhy Shamroukh; Suhad Ibrahim Al Fayoumi
*Officers:* Dr Suhad Alfayoumi [1970] Director/Pharmacist [Jordanian]; Samer Shamroukh [1968] Director [Jordanian]

**Healthmed Supplies (HMS) Limited**
*Incorporated:* 20 February 2004
*Registered Office:* Crosby Business Centre, Mersey View, Brighton-le-Sands, Liverpool, L22 6QA
*Major Shareholder:* Liz Hawksworth
*Officers:* Liz Hawksworth [1956] Director

**Healtholozy UK Limited**
*Incorporated:* 7 June 2017
*Net Worth Deficit:* £1,475 *Total Assets:* £6,123
*Registered Office:* 4 New Street, Daventry, Northants, NN11 4BU
*Major Shareholder:* Hafiz Ahmed
*Officers:* Hafiz Ahmed, Secretary; Hafiz Ahmed [1979] Director

**Healthpoint Limited**
*Incorporated:* 22 February 1996 *Employees:* 17
*Net Worth:* £3,472,170 *Total Assets:* £6,661,664
*Registered Office:* 11 Darwin Court, Blackpool Technology Park, Blackpool, Lancs, FY2 0JN
*Shareholder:* Robin Neil Womersley
*Officers:* Amanda Parkinson [1983] Director; Michael Ryan [1965] Finance Director; Robert William Waling [1956] Director; Robin Neil Womersley [1971] Director

**HealthVillagePlus Limited**
*Incorporated:* 13 June 2013 *Employees:* 3
*Net Worth Deficit:* £191,984 *Total Assets:* £1,256,913
*Registered Office:* 1 Beauchamp Court, 10 Victors Way, Barnet, Herts, EN5 5TZ
*Major Shareholder:* Mohammed Abrar
*Officers:* Mohammed Abrar [1978] Director

**Healthy Era Ltd**
*Incorporated:* 18 January 2018
*Registered Office:* 110 Denecroft Cresent, Uxbridge, Middlesex, UB10 9HZ
*Officers:* Sanyam Gandhi [1982] Director

**Heathrow.Net Limited**
*Incorporated:* 6 July 2000
*Net Worth:* £309,751 *Total Assets:* £1,265,074
*Registered Office:* c/o 49 West Ham Lane, London, E15 4PH
*Major Shareholder:* Augusto Montante
*Officers:* Augusto Montante [1942] Director/Entrepreneur [Italian]

**The Heatpack Company Ltd**
*Incorporated:* 17 October 2011 *Employees:* 10
*Net Worth:* £46,772 *Total Assets:* £252,532
*Registered Office:* 2nd Floor, 1 City Road East, Manchester, M15 4PN
*Shareholders:* Lauren Cohen; Jonathan Stuart Cohen
*Officers:* Lisa Simone Binder [1973] Director/Business Consultant; Dr Ben David Cohen [1948] Director/New Business Development; Howard David Cohen [1954] Director/Design Consultant; Jonathan Stuart Cohen [1978] Director; Valerie Ann Cohen [1957] Director/Administrator

**HEC Pharm UK Limited**
*Incorporated:* 25 March 2016 *Employees:* 1
*Net Worth:* £4,482 *Total Assets:* £37,566
*Registered Office:* 5 New Street Square, London, EC4A 3TW
*Officers:* Yijian Guo [1978] Director/Business Manager [Chinese]

**Hedigen Limited**
*Incorporated:* 26 October 2010
*Net Worth:* £16,862 *Total Assets:* £29,718
*Registered Office:* Unit 6 Millbrook Industrial Estate, Floats Road, Roundthorn Industrial Estate, Manchester, M23 9WT
*Major Shareholder:* Behrooz Ghasemi Firoozabadi
*Officers:* Dr Behrooz Ghasemi Firoozabadi [1966] Director

**Heisenberg Technologie Ltd**
*Incorporated:* 8 August 2014
*Registered Office:* rear Raydean House, Western Parade, Great North Road, New Barnet, Barnet, Herts, EN5 1AH
*Major Shareholder:* Jamie Ian Holoran
*Officers:* Jamie Ian Holoran [1972] Director

**Hemastem Ltd**
*Incorporated:* 7 December 2018
*Registered Office:* 20-22 Wenlock Road, London, N1 7GU
*Shareholders:* Aliya Zipporah Conway; Benjamin Joel Conway; Zahara Varda Conway
*Officers:* Richard Gary Conway [1955] Director

**Hemodia UK Ltd**
*Incorporated:* 11 August 2014 *Employees:* 4
*Net Worth:* £68,008 *Total Assets:* £600,778
*Registered Office:* c/o Pramex Int Ltd, 8th Floor South, 11 Old Jewry, London, EC2R 8DU
*Shareholder:* Pierre Montoriol
*Officers:* Pierre Montoriol [1945] Director [French]; Remi Teuliere [1971] Director [French]

**Hemp Remedy Ltd**
*Incorporated:* 5 February 2019
*Registered Office:* 34 Anchor Lane, Solihull, W Midlands, B91 2LA
*Major Shareholder:* Samira Alderwish
*Officers:* Samira Alderwish [1975] Director; Luke Thomas Hill [1983] Director

**Henley Laboratories Limited**
*Incorporated:* 23 September 2013 *Employees:* 1
*Net Worth Deficit:* £44,271 *Total Assets:* £868,762
*Registered Office:* Primrose Studios, Primrose Road, Clitheroe, Lancs, BB7 1BT
*Shareholders:* Robina Naz Shafiq; Jane Anne Sharples; Kevin James; Mohammed Choudhary Shafiq
*Officers:* Robina Naz Shafiq [1973] Director; Dr Jane Anne Sharples [1964] Director

**Hennessy Mason Ltd**
*Incorporated:* 29 April 2016 *Employees:* 1
*Net Worth Deficit:* £165,008 *Total Assets:* £22,069
*Registered Office:* c/o Oliver Phillips Ltd, 133 Whitechapel High Street, London, E1 7QA
*Shareholder:* Joseph Mason
*Officers:* Joseph Mason [1976] Managing Director

**Herbal Food Life Limited**
*Incorporated:* 17 October 2017
*Registered Office:* 87 Watersmeet Road, Coventry, Warwicks, CV2 3HT
*Shareholder:* Thangarajah Gunabalsinkam
*Officers:* Thangarajah Gunabalsinkam [1961] Director [German]

**Herbaleva Ltd**
*Incorporated:* 16 May 2017
*Registered Office:* Flat D, 290 Dollis Hill Lane, London, NW2 6HH
*Major Shareholder:* Abdelrahman Traboulssi Barake
*Officers:* Abdelrahman Traboulssi Barake, Secretary; Abdelrahman Traboulssi Barake [1968] Director [Swedish]

**Herbert and Herbert Pharmacy Limited**
*Incorporated:* 24 November 2017
*Registered Office:* 88 High Street, Clapham, Bedford, MK41 6BW
*Shareholders:* Inderpal Kaur Toor; Sarvjit Singh Toor
*Officers:* Sarvjit Singh Toor, Secretary; Inderpal Kaur Toor [1969] Director/Pharmacist; Sarvjit Singh Toor [1965] Director/Chartered Accountant

**Herbialis Limited**
*Incorporated:* 6 June 2018
*Registered Office:* 121 Silver Street, Edmonton, London, N18 1RG
*Major Shareholder:* Andree Exner
*Officers:* Andree Exner, Secretary; Andree Exner [1964] Director/Entrepreneur [Australian]

**Here We Flo Ltd**
*Incorporated:* 11 November 2016
*Net Worth Deficit:* £6,650  *Total Assets:* £41,030
*Registered Office:* 9 Perseverance Works, Kingsland Road, London, E2 8DD
*Parent:* Sustainable Ethical Enterprises Limited
*Officers:* Susan Charlene Allen [1985] Operations Director; Tara Chandra [1987] Managing Director [American]

**Hermes Pharmaceutical Limited**
*Incorporated:* 15 September 1994
*Registered Office:* c/o Laytons LLP, Level 5, More London Riverside, London, SE1 2AP
*Major Shareholder:* Johannes Franz Burges
*Officers:* Johannes Franz Burges [1939] Director [German]

**HH Pharma Limited**
*Incorporated:* 11 November 2013
*Net Worth:* £402  *Total Assets:* £31,141
*Registered Office:* M & S Transport, Unit A1 Appleton Industrial Park, Barleycastle Lane, Warrington, Cheshire, WA4 4RG
*Officers:* Trevor Caddick [1965] Director/Pharmaceutical Wholesaler; Pauline Carter [1965] Director/Pharmaceutical Wholesaler

**Higherplateau Limited**
*Incorporated:* 3 August 2011  *Employees:* 1
*Net Worth:* £76,229  *Total Assets:* £80,781
*Registered Office:* 8 Manor Road, Leeds, LS11 9AH
*Major Shareholder:* David Andrew Lestner
*Officers:* David Andrew Lestner [1962] Director

**Hillcroft Surgery Supplies Ltd**
*Incorporated:* 25 March 2014
*Net Worth:* £611,734  *Total Assets:* £1,376,173
*Registered Office:* 12 Oxford Road, Pen Mill Trading Estate, Yeovil, Somerset, BA21 5HR
*Officers:* Guy Howden [1982] Director/Salesman; Roger Alan Howden [1961] Director/Salesman

**Hilotherapy UK Limited**
*Incorporated:* 2 November 2012
*Net Worth Deficit:* £455,620  *Total Assets:* £182,756
*Registered Office:* Unit 3 The Venture Centre, University of Warwick Science Park, Sir William Lyons Road, Coventry, Warwicks, CV4 7EZ
*Shareholders:* Wallace George William Stein; Anthony Manfred Thomas Ley
*Officers:* Anthony Manfred Thomas Ley [1965] Director/Business Consultant; Wallace George William Stein [1952] Director/Business Adviser

**Hilotherm Ltd**
*Incorporated:* 11 June 2018
*Registered Office:* Unit 3 The Venture Centre, University of Warwick Science Park, Coventry, Warwicks, CV4 7EZ
*Major Shareholder:* Wallace George William Stein
*Officers:* Alexandra Margaret Murray Stein [1950] Director; Callum Wallace Alexander Stein [1990] Director; Katharine Elisabeth Derdre Stein [1976] Director; Wallace George William Stein [1952] Director

**Hisamitsu Pharmaceutical UK Limited**
*Incorporated:* 9 January 2002
*Net Worth:* £1  *Total Assets:* £1
*Registered Office:* 5 Chancery Lane, London, WC2A 1LG
*Parent:* Hisamitsu Pharmaceutical Co Inc
*Officers:* Yoshio Hiyama, Secretary; Yoshio Hiyama [1974] Director [Japanese]; Yuichi Isobe [1971] President and Managing Director [Japanese]

**Hisamitsu UK Limited**
*Incorporated:* 9 January 2002  *Employees:* 4
*Net Worth:* £835,534  *Total Assets:* £941,929
*Registered Office:* 5 Chancery Lane, London, WC2A 1LG
*Parent:* Hisamitsu Pharmaceutical Co., Inc.
*Officers:* Yoshio Hiyama, Secretary; Yoshio Hiyama [1974] Director [Japanese]; Yuichi Isobe [1971] President and Managing Director [Japanese]

**Hitop Pharmaceuticals Limited**
*Incorporated:* 28 April 2017
*Registered Office:* 6 Maida Vale Business Centre, Mead Road, Cheltenham, Glos, GL53 7ER
*Officers:* Qingxi Wang, Secretary; Tao Wang [1967] Director [Chinese]

**HJ Wholesale Limited**
*Incorporated:* 19 April 2017
*Registered Office:* Onward Chambers, 34 Market Street, Hyde, Cheshire, SK14 1AH
*Parent:* Grandbydale Limited
*Officers:* Hansa Jitendra Patel [1951] Director/Sales Manager; Jitendra Kantibhal Patel [1948] Director/Pharmacist

**HMD Europe Ltd**
*Incorporated:* 15 November 1991
*Net Worth:* £1,142  *Total Assets:* £1,142
*Registered Office:* 7-10 Station Road, Kingham, Chipping Norton, Oxon, OX7 6UP
*Parent:* Harmony Medical Distribution Ltd
*Officers:* Jim Alfred Belcher [1962] Director/Financial Consultant

**HMS Wholesale Ltd**
*Incorporated:* 14 September 2018
*Registered Office:* 17 Deane Street, Loughborough, Leics, LE11 5NQ
*Major Shareholder:* Bipinchandra Modi
*Officers:* Bipinchandra Modi [1957] Director/Pharmacist

**HNS Pharma Limited**
Incorporated: 17 April 2012
Net Worth: £3,851  Total Assets: £737,826
Registered Office: Unit 4 Forest Hill Industrial Estate, Perry Vale, Forest Hill, London, SE23 2LX
Major Shareholder: Hasmukh Manibhai Patel
Officers: Sangita Patel, Secretary; Hasmukh Manibhai Patel [1959] Director/Pharmacist; Nilen Patel [1987] Director

**Hoechst Marion Roussel Limited**
Incorporated: 29 June 1994  Employees: 2
Net Worth: £449,006,016  Total Assets: £480,816,000
Registered Office: One Onslow Street, Guildford, Surrey, GU1 4YS
Parent: Aventis Pharma Holdings Limited
Officers: Francois-Xavier Duhalde [1965] Director/Chief Financial Officer [French]; Hugo Rupert Alexander Fry [1970] Director/UK Country Chair

**Holistic Med Ltd**
Incorporated: 23 April 2018
Registered Office: 35 Pearl House, 10 Merivale Mews, The Vizion, Milton Keynes, Bucks, MK9 2FP
Major Shareholder: Anastasios Skiadopoulos Seimenis
Officers: Anastasios Skiadopoulos Seimenis, Secretary; Anastasios Skiadopoulos Seimenis [1979] Director/Dietician [Greek]

**Home Health (U.K.) Limited**
Incorporated: 21 March 1996  Employees: 32
Net Worth: £3,019,714  Total Assets: £3,521,874
Registered Office: Premier House, 45 Ealing Road, Wembley, Middlesex, HA0 4BA
Officers: John Peter Baxter, Secretary/Director; Jamie Richard Baxter [1983] Sales Director; John Peter Baxter [1949] Director; Emma Charlotte Hanson [1974] Financial Director; Mark Richard Hanson [1976] Operations Director

**The Homeopathic Supply Company Limited**
Incorporated: 1 March 2001  Employees: 7
Net Worth: £37,800  Total Assets: £185,898
Registered Office: The Street, Bodham, Holt, Norfolk, NR25 6AD
Shareholders: Alan Barker; Anne Barker; Robert Edward Barker
Officers: Anne Barker, Director/Secretary; Alan Barker [1982] Director; Anne Barker [1950] Director/Secretary; Robert Edward Barker [1953] Director

**Honest Health Limited**
Incorporated: 3 October 2018
Registered Office: Flat 11, 10 Baldwin Terrace, London, N1 7RU
Shareholders: Pavlo Maherovskyi; Samuel Julian Gluck
Officers: Samuel Julian Gluck [1985] Director/Co-Founder [Polish]; Pavlo Maherovskyi [1988] Director/Co-Founder

**Honilac Nutrition Limited**
Incorporated: 28 March 2018
Registered Office: Kemp House, 160 City Road, London, EC1V 2NX
Major Shareholder: Massoud Memari
Officers: Massoud Memari [1959] Director/Salesman [American]

**Hooben Distributors Limited**
Incorporated: 25 January 2019
Registered Office: 93 Evesham Road, London, N11 2RR
Shareholder: Nnaemeka Obumneke Eneli
Officers: Nnaemeka Obumneke Eneli [1980] Director; Obinna Eneli [1969] Director

**Horopito Limited**
Incorporated: 27 September 2017
Registered Office: 82 St John Street, London, EC1M 4JN
Major Shareholder: Adrian Hope
Officers: Adrian Hope [1958] Director

**Hospira UK Limited**
Incorporated: 18 June 1985  Employees: 70
Net Worth: £25,724,000  Total Assets: £30,085,000
Registered Office: Horizon, Honey Lane, Hurley, Maidenhead, Berks, SL6 6RJ
Parent: Pfizer Limited
Officers: Ian Eric Franklin [1965] Director/Accountant; Ben John Osborn [1977] Director; Edwin James Pearson [1974] Director/Solicitor

**Hot Pharma Ltd**
Incorporated: 30 April 2014  Employees: 2
Net Worth Deficit: £193,731  Total Assets: £70,050
Registered Office: 39 Carters Lane, Kiln Farm, Milton Keynes, Bucks, MK11 3HL
Shareholders: Jay Ranjit Savdas; Kalpesh Savdas
Officers: Jay Ranjit Savdas [1979] Director/Pharmacist; Kalpesh Savdas [1981] Sales Director

**Hotteeze International Limited**
Incorporated: 25 January 2017
Registered Office: 49 Nevil Road, Stoke Newington, London, N16 8SW
Officers: William James Benfield [1952] Director of Operations; Donna Margaret Burke [1964] Director [Australian]

**House of Filler Limited**
Incorporated: 8 January 2018
Registered Office: The Old Foundary, Bath Street, Walsall, W Midlands, WS1 3BZ
Officers: Hannah May Abbassi [1985] Director; Natasha Jackson [1990] Director

**HQEM Pharma Limited**
Incorporated: 8 December 2016
Registered Office: Unit 2a Old Dalby Trading Estate, Station Road, Old Dalby, Leics, LE14 3NJ
Shareholder: East Midlands Pharma Ltd
Officers: Jayanti Chimanbhai Patel [1984] Executive Director; Kirit Chimanbhai Tulsibhai Patel [1980] Executive Director

**HRA Pharma UK & Ireland Limited**
Incorporated: 4 March 2009  Employees: 8
Net Worth Deficit: £180,488  Total Assets: £3,718,713
Registered Office: Haines House, 21 John Street, Bloomsbury, London, WC1N 2BF
Officers: Richard Holme [1965] Director/General Manager; David John Wright [1964] Director

**HS Pharma Limited**
Incorporated: 30 January 2014  Employees: 2
Net Worth: £100  Total Assets: £2,752
Registered Office: 18 Foxton Road, North Hamilton, Leicester, LE5 1AY
Major Shareholder: Sarfraz Patel
Officers: Sarfraz Patel [1983] Director/Pharmacist

**Huayawei Biomedical Company Ltd**
Incorporated: 15 January 2018
Registered Office: c/o LL & Co, Office 201, 10 Courtenay Road, East Lane Business Park, Wembley, Middlesex, HA9 7ND
Major Shareholder: Xueli Wei
Officers: Xueli Wei [1980] Director

**Hughenden Valley Pharma Limited**
Incorporated: 2 June 2003  Employees: 2
Net Worth: £165,137  Total Assets: £274,784
Registered Office: Hughenden Surgery, Valley Road, Hughenden Valley, High Wycombe, Bucks, HP14 4LG
Officers: Dr Sara Lisa Gresham Cottam, Secretary; Dr Sara Lisa Gresham Cottam [1966] Director/General Medical Practitioner; Dr Mary Jane Mitchell [1959] Director/General Medical Practitioner

**Human Reproduction Group Ltd**
Incorporated: 18 May 2012
Previous: Alpha One Inc. Ltd
Net Worth: £12,053  Total Assets: £466,492
Registered Office: 2nd Floor, 13 John Prince's Street, London, W1G 0JR
Officers: Stephanus Janke [1964] Director/Manager [South African]

**Humn Pharmaceuticals (UK) Ltd**
Incorporated: 12 March 2012
Registered Office: 22 St Johns Road, Corstorphine, Edinburgh, EH12 6NZ
Officers: Brian Nigel Herron [1948] Director/Retired; Blair McInnes [1952] Director/Businessman [Canadian]; Adam Topp [1966] Director/COO Winnipeg Health Sciences Centre [Canadian]

**Hunger Control Limited**
Incorporated: 20 June 2000  Employees: 2
Net Worth: £248,013  Total Assets: £335,209
Registered Office: 104 Iffley Road, London, W6 0PF
Shareholder: Robert James Weir
Officers: Caroline Liddell, Secretary; Caroline Liddell [1948] Director; Robert James Weir [1937] Director

**Hunter International Associates Limited**
Incorporated: 10 November 1999
Net Worth Deficit: £22,892  Total Assets: £119,729
Registered Office: Windsor Business Centre, Pentre, Church Stoke, Montgomery, Powys, SY15 6SU
Major Shareholder: John Bryan Hunter
Officers: Elizabeth Hunter, Secretary; John Bryan Hunter [1947] Director

**Hunter Urology Ltd**
Incorporated: 16 September 1998  Employees: 5
Net Worth: £239,597  Total Assets: £514,777
Registered Office: 1 Skyways Business Park, Exeter Airport Industrial Estate, Clyst, Honiton, Exeter, Devon, EX5 2UL
Major Shareholder: Gary Francis Hunter
Officers: Gary Francis Hunter [1959] Sales/Marketing Director

**Hurley Assets Limited**
Incorporated: 15 October 2010  Employees: 5
Net Worth: £22,126  Total Assets: £234,656
Registered Office: Nightingale House, 46-48 East Street, Epsom, Surrey, KT17 3LX
Officers: Ashok Soni [1961] Director

**Hyaluron Health Ltd**
Incorporated: 9 November 2018
Registered Office: Unit 22 Bulrushes Business Park, Coombe Hill Road, East Grinstead, W Sussex, RH19 4LZ
Major Shareholder: Lajos Sipkovits
Officers: Dr Lajos Sipkovits [1971] Director [Hungarian]

**Hydro Tan Limited**
Incorporated: 5 February 2018
Registered Office: Kemp House, 160 City Road, London, EC1V 2NX
Officers: Robert Lannigan Russell [1975] Director

**Hygamp Limited**
Incorporated: 30 June 2017  Employees: 1
Net Worth: £95,920  Total Assets: £138,343
Registered Office: Manufactory House, Bell Lane, Hertford, SG14 1BP
Major Shareholder: Phillip Jeffrey
Officers: Beverley Jane Jeffrey [1957] Director; Dr Phillip Jeffrey [1958] Director

**I L Locum Ltd**
Incorporated: 27 March 2017
Net Worth: £2,960  Total Assets: £6,882
Registered Office: 9 Purlwell Hall Road, Batley, W Yorks, WF17 7NN
Major Shareholder: Ismail Loonat
Officers: Ismail Loonat [1970] Director

**I Like Limited**
Incorporated: 12 July 2013
Registered Office: 1 Station Court, Station Approach, Wickford, Essex, SS11 7AT
Officers: Ilya Baryshev, Secretary; Igor Samborskiy [1986] Director [Russian]

**I-Crackedit Ltd**
Incorporated: 20 December 2011
Previous: Lysis Medical Ltd
Net Worth Deficit: £3,042  Total Assets: £2,636
Registered Office: Aims, 36 Wattleton Road, Beaconsfield, Bucks, HP9 1SE
Major Shareholder: David Watson
Officers: David Watson [1969] Managing Director

**I-Dispense Limited**
Incorporated: 29 December 2011
Net Worth: £126,423  Total Assets: £332,363
Registered Office: Corner Oak, 1 Homer Road, Solihull, W Midlands, B91 3QG
Shareholder: Mohammed Hanif Patel
Officers: Amir Riaz [1981] Director/Pharmacist

**I-Pharma Healthcare Ltd**
Incorporated: 20 April 2010  Employees: 3
Net Worth: £474,611  Total Assets: £885,316
Registered Office: 39 Gravelly Industrial Park, Birmingham, B24 8TG
Major Shareholder: Khalid Hussain
Officers: Khalid Hussain [1981] Director

**I.T.T.I.D. (Trading) Ltd**
Incorporated: 3 March 1988
Net Worth Deficit: £2,220  Total Assets: £2,217
Registered Office: 809 Manchester Road, Bradford, W Yorks, BD5 8LN
Major Shareholder: Arif Mushtaq Ahmad
Officers: Sahar Ahmad, Secretary; Dr Arif Mushtaq Ahmad [1956] Director/Practitioner; Dr Sahar Ahmad [1968] Director/Housewife

**Iam Finance Limited**
Incorporated: 31 October 2008  Employees: 10
Net Worth: £2,821,666  Total Assets: £7,646,464
Registered Office: 24 Bedford Row, London, WC1R 4TQ
Major Shareholder: Lajwanti Lakhwani
Officers: Johnny Mohan Lakhwani [1981] Director/Manager [Danish]

## The Top UK Pharmaceutical Wholesalers

**Iaso Ltd**
*Incorporated:* 22 November 2018
*Registered Office:* Flat 8, 1 Shorrolds Road, London, SW6 7TR
*Shareholders:* Benjamin Marie Viaris de Lesegno; Eric Gustaf Bystrom
*Officers:* Eric Gustaf Bystrom [1982] Director/Chief Executive [Swedish]; Dr Benjamin Marie Viaris de Lesegno [1981] Director/Surgeon [French]

**Iberia Skin Brands Ltd**
*Incorporated:* 19 February 2018
*Registered Office:* 20-22 Wenlock Road, London, N1 7GU
*Major Shareholder:* Nitin Jain
*Officers:* Nitin Jain [1976] Director [Indian]; Agata Kieda [1990] Director [Polish]; Ridhima Sharma [1985] Director

**Icone International Limited**
*Incorporated:* 24 February 2003 *Employees:* 15
*Net Worth:* £3,292,879 *Total Assets:* £4,924,762
*Registered Office:* New Bridge Street House, 30-34 New Bridge Street, London, EC4V 6BJ
*Major Shareholder:* Hasu Shamir Shah
*Officers:* Usha Shah, Secretary; Hasmukh Lalji Shah [1943] Director; Hasu Shamir Shah [1979] Managing Director

**Idea Medica Limited**
*Incorporated:* 19 December 2006
*Net Worth:* £642,934 *Total Assets:* £4,422,632
*Registered Office:* 42 Lytton Road, Barnet, Herts, EN5 5BY
*Major Shareholder:* Tracy Pettitt
*Officers:* Tracy Pettitt [1966] Director/Wholesaler

**Ideal Cleaning Systems Ltd**
*Incorporated:* 16 August 2018
*Registered Office:* 112 Cumberland House, 80 Scrubs Lane, London, NW10 6RF
*Major Shareholder:* Falak Yussouf
*Officers:* Falak Yussouf [1958] Director

**Ideal Healthcare Limited**
*Incorporated:* 2 October 1997
*Net Worth:* £1,626,000 *Total Assets:* £1,626,000
*Registered Office:* Merchants Warehouse, Castle Street, Manchester, M3 4LZ
*Parent:* Bestway National Chemists Limited
*Officers:* John Branson Nuttall [1963] Managing Director

**Ideal Medical Holdings Ltd**
*Incorporated:* 6 August 2015
*Net Worth Deficit:* £719 *Total Assets:* £352
*Registered Office:* Hayles Bridge Offices, 228 Mulgrave Road, Cheam, Surrey, SM2 6JT
*Major Shareholder:* Andrew Wakeling
*Officers:* Andrew Wakeling [1973] Director

**Ideal Medical Solutions Ltd**
*Incorporated:* 19 September 2011 *Employees:* 12
*Net Worth Deficit:* £137,138 *Total Assets:* £428,256
*Registered Office:* Hayles Bridge Offices, 228 Mulgrave Road, Cheam, Surrey, SM2 6JT
*Major Shareholder:* Andrew Wakeling
*Officers:* Andrew Wakeling [1973] Managing Director

**Identimed Limited**
*Incorporated:* 7 September 2017 *Employees:* 1
*Net Worth:* £9,003 *Total Assets:* £16,506
*Registered Office:* Mentor House, Ainsworth Street, Blackburn, Lancs, BB1 6AY
*Shareholders:* Gary Calvert; Natalie Jayne Calvert
*Officers:* Gary Calvert [1977] Director

**Idis Group Holdings Limited**
*Incorporated:* 11 March 2005
*Net Worth:* £36,613,000 *Total Assets:* £92,804,000
*Registered Office:* Pitcairn House, Crown Square, First Avenue, Burton on Trent, Staffs, DE14 2WW
*Parent:* Clinigen Holdings Limited
*Officers:* Amanda Miller, Secretary; Martin James Abell [1974] Director; Shaun Edward Chilton [1967] Director

**Idis Limited**
*Incorporated:* 29 June 1987 *Employees:* 167
*Net Worth:* £17,865,000 *Total Assets:* £81,621,000
*Registered Office:* Pitcairn House, Crown Square, First Avenue, Burton on Trent, Staffs, DE14 2WW
*Parent:* Idis Group Limited
*Officers:* Amanda Miller, Secretary; Martin James Abell [1974] Director; Shaun Edward Chilton [1967] Director

**Ihealthcare Genius Limited**
*Incorporated:* 6 October 2015
*Net Worth:* £8,472 *Total Assets:* £26,416
*Registered Office:* 72 Sladefield Road, Birmingham, B8 3NX
*Major Shareholder:* Asad Shabir
*Officers:* Usman Shabir, Secretary; Asad Shabir [1986] Director/Pharmacist

**Ihsan Pharma Ltd**
*Incorporated:* 4 August 2016
*Net Worth:* £234,830 *Total Assets:* £598,441
*Registered Office:* AMS Medical Accountants, 2nd Floor, 9 Portland Street, Manchester, M1 3BE
*Major Shareholder:* Jawad Mehroof
*Officers:* Jawad Mehroof [1984] Director/Pharmacist

**Ikatrad Ltd**
*Incorporated:* 13 August 2018
*Registered Office:* 160a Greenstead Road, Colchester, Essex, CO1 2SN
*Shareholders:* Doha Mohamed Hassanin Yousif; Yousif Izzeldin Kamil Amin
*Officers:* Doha Mohamed Hassanin Yousif [1984] Director/General Manager

**IM High Tech Limited**
*Incorporated:* 8 October 2014
*Net Worth Deficit:* £8,126 *Total Assets:* £14,260
*Registered Office:* 45 Stanway Gardens, Edgware, Middlesex, HA8 9LN
*Shareholder:* Eng Teong Lim
*Officers:* Eng Teong Lim [1966] Director/Optician [Malaysian]; Sow Poh Tan [1957] Director

**Imamcom Ltd**
*Incorporated:* 24 January 2019
*Registered Office:* 3 Gower Street, London, WC1E 6HA
*Major Shareholder:* Mohamed Said Moustafa Ahmed Imam
*Officers:* Dr Mohamed Said Moustafa Ahmed Imam [1980] Director/Pharmacist [Egyptian]

**iMedix Limited**
Incorporated: 30 April 2012  Employees: 2
Net Worth: £232,031  Total Assets: £1,149,750
Registered Office: 2-4 Eastern Road, Romford, Essex, RM1 3PJ
Shareholders: Adam Zafar; Ayisha Zafar
Officers: Adam Zafar [1982] Director

**Imex International Group Limited**
Incorporated: 23 September 2013
Previous: Imex Autosport Limited
Net Worth: £100  Total Assets: £100
Registered Office: 2nd Floor, Finance House, 20-21 Aviation Way, Southend on Sea, Essex, SS2 6UN
Major Shareholder: Robert James
Officers: Robert James [1965] Director

**Imex Ltd**
Incorporated: 25 September 2015
Net Worth Deficit: £1,372  Total Assets: £879
Registered Office: 46a Westbury Hill, Westbury on Trym, Bristol, BS9 3AA
Officers: Marlo Moor [1977] Director/Bookkeeper

**IMI Ventures Limited**
Incorporated: 3 April 2018
Registered Office: 5 Bisham Court, Marlow, Bucks, SL7 1SD
Shareholders: Christopher Robin Brain; Karl Graham Goode; Mohammed Arif Waka
Officers: Christopher Robin Brain [1980] Director; Karl Graham Goode [1970] Director; Mohammed Arif Waka [1981] Director

**Immortalis Distribution Ltd.**
Incorporated: 15 November 2017
Registered Office: Office 32, 19-21 Crawford Street, London, W1H 1PJ
Shareholders: Anna Grochowalska; Wolfgang Knorr
Officers: Anna Krystyna Grochowalska, Secretary; Anna Krystyna Grochowalska [1976] Director [Polish]; Wolfgang Knorr [1965] Director [German]; Valerio Laghezza [1972] Director/Management Consultant [Italian]

**Impact Health Limited**
Incorporated: 20 August 2009  Employees: 8
Net Worth: £1,108,267  Total Assets: £2,691,067
Registered Office: 19 Montpelier Avenue, Bexley, Kent, DA5 3AP
Officers: Brian Robert Lewis, Secretary; Brian Robert Lewis [1939] Director/Chemist; Dipak Kumar Patel [1971] Director

**Imperial Bioscience Ltd**
Incorporated: 7 January 2016  Employees: 3
Net Worth Deficit: £59,870  Total Assets: £18,581
Registered Office: Mocatta House, Trafalgar Place, Brighton, BN1 4DU
Major Shareholder: Muhammet Avcil
Officers: Dr Muhammet Avcil [1984] Director

**Imperial Medical Innovations Limited**
Incorporated: 28 February 2017
Net Worth: £8,074  Total Assets: £22,502
Registered Office: 5 Bisham Court, Bisham, Marlow, Bucks, SL7 1SD
Shareholder: Christopher Robin Brain
Officers: Christopher Robin Brain [1980] Director; Mohammed Arif Waka [1981] Director

**Impexport Services Limited**
Incorporated: 30 January 1990
Registered Office: 1-5 Clerkenwell Road, London, EC1M 5PA
Major Shareholder: Noureddine Cherfi
Officers: Zoubida Kibboua, Secretary; Nour Eddine Cherfi [1958] Director/Engineer [Algerian]

**Imphatec Ltd**
Incorporated: 17 September 2018
Registered Office: Oak Cottage, Langley Bridge, Liss, Hants, GU33 7JP
Shareholders: James Peter Catt; Hassan Oliver James Morad
Officers: James Peter Catt [1991] Director/Assistant Underwriter; Hassan Oliver James Morad [1992] Director/PhD Student

**IMS Euro Limited**
Incorporated: 5 July 2001  Employees: 54
Net Worth: £2,592,831  Total Assets: £3,640,390
Registered Office: Europa Business Park, Bird Hall Lane, Cheadle Heath, Stockport, Cheshire, SK3 0XA
Parent: IMS Euro Holdings Limited
Officers: Omar Shamot, Secretary; Durgham Wasif Shamot [1965] Director

**IMS Ultrasound (UK) Ltd**
Incorporated: 21 June 2017
Net Worth: £46,156  Total Assets: £56,633
Registered Office: Hayles Bridge Offices, 228 Mulgrave Road, Cheam, Surrey, SM2 6JT
Shareholder: Andrew Wakeling
Officers: Andrew Wakeling [1973] Director

**In 2 Healthcare Limited**
Incorporated: 29 July 2002
Registered Office: SNK Investments LLP, Unit 3 Nursery Court, Kibworth Business Park, Kibworth, Leics, LE8 0EX
Parent: LL-Pharma Ltd
Officers: Ian David Waring, Secretary; Satnam Singh Butter [1961] Director; Shirazali Sharif Dharamshi [1949] Director; Amirali Sharif Tejani [1954] Director; Karim Sharif Dharamshi Tejani [1959] Director; Nazirali Sharif Dharamshi Tejani [1952] Director; Salim Sharif Dharamshi Tejani [1950] Director

**Inbamay Resources (UK) Ltd.**
Incorporated: 28 May 2003
Registered Office: 59 Brantwood Drive, Heaton, Bradford, W Yorks, BD9 6QR
Officers: Elizabeth Nnennaya Inwang, Secretary; Nse Bassey Inwang, Secretary; Dr Inwang Bassey Inwang [1954] Director/Chairman/Chief Executive [Nigerian]; Nse Bassey Inwang [1959] Director/Head of Personnel [Nigerian]

**Incimed Ltd**
Incorporated: 6 August 2012
Net Worth Deficit: £48,814  Total Assets: £443
Registered Office: 22 Billet Street, Taunton, Somerset, TA1 3NG
Major Shareholder: Elnur Orujov
Officers: Stephen John Dudley Hickson [1947] Director/Accountant; Stephen Martin Hubbard [1985] Director/Accountant

**Incline Therapeutics Europe Ltd.**
Incorporated: 17 October 2012  Employees: 1
Net Worth: £1,687  Total Assets: £347,378
Registered Office: First Floor, 10 Temple Back, Bristol, BS1 6FL
Parent: The Medicines Company
Officers: Andre Reinhold Heer [1970] Director/Head of Finance [German]

**Incyte Biosciences UK Ltd**
Incorporated: 10 October 2012  Employees: 11
Previous: Ariad Pharma (UK) Ltd
Net Worth: £174,508  Total Assets: £1,434,727
Registered Office: First Floor, Q1 The Square, Randalls Way, Leatherhead, Surrey, KT22 7TW
Officers: Thierry Stephane Bataillard [1969] Director/Head of Regulatory Affairs Europe [French]; Jonathan Elliott Dickinson [1967] Director; Mark Edwin Tanner [1962] Director

**Independence Products Ltd**
Incorporated: 8 September 2006  Employees: 10
Net Worth: £616,107  Total Assets: £917,951
Registered Office: Independence House, 30 Northern Court, Vernon Road, Basford, Nottingham, NG6 0BJ
Shareholders: Andrew Glyn Leese; Peter Darran Stockley
Officers: Andrew Glyn Leese, Secretary; Andrew Glyn Leese [1967] Director; Peter Darran Stockley [1965] Director

**Indigo Diagnostics Limited**
Incorporated: 14 January 2016
Net Worth: £84,738  Total Assets: £110,380
Registered Office: 168 Church Road, Hove, E Sussex, BN3 2DL
Officers: Dr Andrew Timothy Sweet [1964] Director; Dr Ruth Margaret Sweet [1962] Director

**Indrugco (UK) Limited**
Incorporated: 20 November 1991
Net Worth: £3,896  Total Assets: £5,065
Registered Office: 736 High Road, North Finchley, London, N12 9QD
Shareholders: Elaine Frances Chong; Anthony Kwang Aun Chong
Officers: Elaine Frances Chong, Secretary; Anthony Kwang Aun Chong [1954] Director/Pharmacist; Elaine Frances Chong [1957] Director

**Infinite Percent Limited**
Incorporated: 29 November 2018
Registered Office: CDL House, 1 Vestry Road, Sevenoaks, Kent, TN14 5EL
Shareholder: Cannon Services Limited
Officers: Neil Brown, Secretary; Richard Anthony Dillon [1965] Director; Simon John Hill [1961] Director; Steven Koskie [1969] Director [Canadian]; Michael Kenneth Shane [1955] Director [American]

**Infinity Biomedical Ltd**
Incorporated: 19 March 2018
Registered Office: 136D St Agnells Lane, Hemel Hempstead, Herts, HP2 6LQ
Major Shareholder: Benyamin Rahmani
Officers: Dr Benyamin Rahmani [1987] Director/Biomedical Scientist [Iranian]

**Infinity Pharmaceuticals Limited**
Incorporated: 13 May 2003
Registered Office: 100 High Street, Roydon, Harlow, Essex, CM19 5EE
Major Shareholder: Priti Vasani
Officers: Priti Vasani, Secretary; Priti Vasani [1965] Director/Pharmacy Assistant; Priyanka Vasani [1991] Director/Pharmacy Assistant

**Infohealth Limited**
Incorporated: 31 May 2000  Employees: 19
Net Worth: £251,094  Total Assets: £1,198,344
Registered Office: Samanvaya Cultural Centre, 1st Floor Office, Milton Road, Harrow, Middlesex, HA1 1ST
Parent: Infohealth Holdings Ltd
Officers: Amish Patel [1972] Director/Pharmacist; Rajive Patel [1973] Director/Pharmacist

**Infolight Limited**
Incorporated: 11 September 2012  Employees: 2
Net Worth: £12,698  Total Assets: £22,672
Registered Office: Dane House, 26 Taylor Road, Aylesbury, Bucks, HP21 8DR
Major Shareholder: Erica Wendy Revell
Officers: Erica Wendy Revell [1966] Director/Account Manager; Mark Revell [1965] Director

**Infutech Limited**
Incorporated: 28 March 2007  Employees: 1
Net Worth: £212,057  Total Assets: £265,816
Registered Office: 3 High Street, Milton, Cambridge, CB24 6AJ
Parent: Sona Management Services Ltd
Officers: Raymond Noel Morrissey [1947] Director/Engineer [Irish]

**Inglasia Ltd**
Incorporated: 16 November 2011
Registered Office: 3rd Floor, 14 Hanover Street, London, W1S 1YH
Officers: Anju Nadarajah, Secretary; Anju Nadarajah [1980] Director

**Iniaso Ltd**
Incorporated: 6 July 2018
Registered Office: 1st Floor, 24-25 New Bond Street, Mayfair, London, W1S 2RR
Major Shareholder: Brian McEwan
Officers: Brian McEwan [1956] Director

**Iniaso Pharma Ltd**
Incorporated: 6 July 2018
Registered Office: 1st Floor, 24-25 New Bond Street, Mayfair, London, W1S 2RR
Major Shareholder: Brian McEwan
Officers: Brian McEwan [1956] Director

**Initio Cell Limited**
Incorporated: 10 January 2019
Registered Office: Block 20 Mereside Alderley Park, Nether Alderley, Cheshire, SK10 4TG
Shareholders: Devrim Devrim Pesen Okvur; Aydin Aydin Oztunali
Officers: Devrim Devrim Pesen Okvur [1977] Director/Businesswoman [Turkish]

**Inmed Ltd**
Incorporated: 6 July 2018
Registered Office: 6 Woodman Parade, Woodman Street, London, E16 2LL
Major Shareholder: Florin-Benone Leau
Officers: Florin-Benone Leau [1975] Director [Romanian]

**Innomedi Limited**
Incorporated: 10 November 2014  Employees: 6
Net Worth: £117,391  Total Assets: £898,991
Registered Office: Folkestone Enterprise Centre, Shearway Business Park, Shearway Road, Folkestone, Kent, CT19 4RH
Shareholders: Andrius Daukantas; Audrunas Slepkovas
Officers: Andrius Daukantas [1979] Director/Pharmacist [Lithuanian]

**Innovius Life Drugs Ltd**
*Incorporated:* 6 July 2018
*Registered Office:* 11 Catches Drive, Bloxwich, Walsall, W Midlands, WS3 2LQ
*Major Shareholder:* Kalyanakumar Gurusamy
*Officers:* Dr Kalyanakumar Gurusamy [1971] Director

**Inov8 Medical Solutions Limited**
*Incorporated:* 7 October 2010 *Employees:* 6
*Net Worth Deficit:* £535,057 *Total Assets:* £587,717
*Registered Office:* c/o Smith Craven, Tapton Park Innovation Centre, Brimington Road, Chesterfield, Derbys, S41 0TZ
*Shareholders:* Peter John Ramsey; Daniel Andrew Markovitch
*Officers:* Daniel Andrew Markovitch [1973] Director; Peter John Ramsey [1969] Director

**Insight Biotechnology Limited**
*Incorporated:* 21 August 1995 *Employees:* 11
*Net Worth:* £2,200,383 *Total Assets:* £2,713,836
*Registered Office:* 110 Chandos Avenue, Whetstone, London, N20 9DZ
*Shareholders:* John Rawlinson; Alison Rawlinson
*Officers:* Alison Rawlinson, Secretary; Darren Croft [1969] Director; Alison Rawlinson [1961] Director/Administrator; John Rawlinson [1961] Director

**Insight Health Limited**
*Incorporated:* 11 November 1999
*Net Worth:* £4,387,722 *Total Assets:* £7,233,995
*Registered Office:* 110 Chandos Avenue, Whetstone, London, N20 9DZ
*Shareholders:* John Rawlinson; Alison Rawlinson
*Officers:* Alison Rawlinson, Secretary; Alison Rawlinson [1961] Director/Treasurer; John Rawlinson [1961] Director

**Insight Medical Products Limited**
*Incorporated:* 16 March 2000 *Employees:* 13
*Net Worth:* £375,209 *Total Assets:* £667,847
*Registered Office:* Unit 3 Priory Industrial Estate, Tetbury, Glos, GL8 8HZ
*Officers:* Florence Edith Hillman, Secretary; Florence Edith Hillman [1957] Director; Wayne Anthony Hillman [1954] Director

**Inspiragen Limited**
*Incorporated:* 7 November 2012
*Net Worth:* £868 *Total Assets:* £6,523
*Registered Office:* 635 Bath Road, Slough, Berks, SL1 6AE
*Shareholders:* Kamal Sandhu; Harinder Singh Sandhu
*Officers:* Kamal Sandhu [1984] Director/Pharmacy; Harinder Singh Saundh [1980] Director/Pharmacy

**Instachem Limited**
*Incorporated:* 16 February 2009 *Employees:* 17
*Net Worth Deficit:* £77,800 *Total Assets:* £676,327
*Registered Office:* Unit 55 Azura Close, Woolsbridge Industrial Estate, Three Legged Cross, Wimborne, Dorset, BH21 6SZ
*Officers:* Soonick Seow [1980] Director [Malaysian]

**Instant Test Ltd**
*Incorporated:* 18 June 2018
*Registered Office:* 4 Ivor's Street, Fleur-De-Lys, Caerphilly, NP12 3RF
*Shareholders:* Christine Jones; Lucy Catherine Spiller-Boulter
*Officers:* Christine Jones [1950] Director; Dr Lucy Catherine Spiller-Boulter [1974] Director

**Instantly White Ltd**
*Incorporated:* 10 December 2018
*Registered Office:* 59 Elphaborough Close, Mytholmroyd, Hebden Bridge, W Yorks, HX7 5JX
*Major Shareholder:* Timothy Weston Foulds
*Officers:* Timothy Weston Foulds [1961] Director

**Instinct Health Ltd**
*Incorporated:* 25 February 2019
*Registered Office:* 7 College Road, Isleworth, Middlesex, TW7 5DJ
*Major Shareholder:* Abbas Nadiadi
*Officers:* Abbas Nadiadi [1992] Director/Chemist

**Insuphar Laboratories Limited**
*Incorporated:* 7 March 2011
*Net Worth:* £22,652 *Total Assets:* £22,952
*Registered Office:* Ground Floor, Gadd House, Arcadia Avenue, Finchley, London, N3 2JU
*Major Shareholder:* Raushan Tahiyeu
*Officers:* Zafer Karaman, Secretary; Zafer Karaman [1958] Director/Account/Law

**Intela Europa Ltd**
*Incorporated:* 2 February 2009
*Previous:* IC Healthcare Limited
*Net Worth Deficit:* £5,673
*Registered Office:* The Old Police Station, Church Street, Swadlincote, Derbys, DE11 8LN
*Major Shareholder:* David Kenneth Bilton
*Officers:* Eileen Bilton, Secretary; David Kenneth Bilton [1954] Managing Director

**Intellix (Holdings) Limited**
*Incorporated:* 14 February 2019
*Registered Office:* 43a Tithe Barn Road, Wootton, Bedford, MK43 9EZ
*Officers:* Anisha Karim Esmail [1962] Director; Arif Esmail [1963] Director

**Inter Trade Pharma Limited**
*Incorporated:* 13 January 2010 *Employees:* 9
*Net Worth:* £2,388,030 *Total Assets:* £4,239,008
*Registered Office:* Unit 7 The Pinnacles, Harolds Close, Harlow, Essex, CM19 5TH
*Parent:* Intermedical Group
*Officers:* Sebastien Lovy [1975] Director [French]

**Intercept Pharma Europe Ltd.**
*Incorporated:* 18 September 2014 *Employees:* 47
*Net Worth Deficit:* £373,933,984 *Total Assets:* £98,879,544
*Registered Office:* One Glass Wharf, Bristol, BS2 0ZX
*Parent:* Intercept Pharmaceuticals, Inc.
*Officers:* Daniel Carey Cazel Hood, Secretary; Lisa Jane Bright [1967] Director/Business Person; Sandip Kapadia [1970] Director/Chief Financial Officer [Indian]; Dr Mark Pruzanski [1967] Director/CEO & President [Canadian]

**Intercept Pharma Ltd**
*Incorporated:* 28 April 2016 *Employees:* 2
*Net Worth:* £2 *Total Assets:* £283,096
*Registered Office:* One Glass Wharf, Bristol, BS2 0ZX
*Parent:* Intercept Pharmaceuticals, Inc.
*Officers:* Graham Charles Higson [1956] Director/Biologist; Daniel Carey Cazel Hood [1973] Director/Solicitor

**Intercept Pharma UK & Ireland Ltd**
*Incorporated:* 24 September 2015
*Net Worth Deficit:* £163,527  *Total Assets:* £1,680,810
*Registered Office:* One Glass Wharf, Bristol, BS2 0ZX
*Parent:* Intercept Pharmaceuticals, Inc.
*Officers:* Sandip Kapadia [1970] Director/Chief Financial Officer [Indian]; Giancarlo Notarianni [1973] Director/General Manager

**Interchem (Chemist Wholesale) Limited**
*Incorporated:* 19 October 1983  *Employees:* 3
*Net Worth:* £305,467  *Total Assets:* £673,485
*Registered Office:* Unit 1 Century Park, Garrison Lane, Birmingham, B9 4NZ
*Shareholders:* Hilal Mushtakali Fazal; Rubabbai Gulamabbas Fazal Rawji
*Officers:* Mohamed Gulamabbas Fazal, Secretary; Mohamed Gulamabbas Fazal [1953] Director/Pharmacist; Nassir Fazal [1957] Director/Pharmacist [Canadian]; Shaheed Fazal [1985] Director/Entrepreneur [Canadian]

**Interchem Europe (UK) Limited**
*Incorporated:* 17 April 1997  *Employees:* 3
*Net Worth:* £800,319  *Total Assets:* £2,650,726
*Registered Office:* Floor 6, Quadrant House, 4 Thomas More Square, London, E1W 1YW
*Shareholders:* Ronald Mannino; Joseph Pizza
*Officers:* Ronald Mannino, Secretary/Corporate Officer [American]; Ronald Mannino [1951] Director [American]; Joseph Pizza [1950] Director/Corporate Officer [American]

**Intergal Pharma Limited**
*Incorporated:* 8 May 2012
*Registered Office:* Seagoe Industrial Estate, Portadown, Craigavon, Co Armagh, BT63 5UA
*Parent:* Galen Limited
*Officers:* Colin Hayburn, Secretary; Alan David Armstrong [1958] Director; Dr Dennise Broderick [1975] Managing Director [Irish]; Stephen Campbell [1961] Director; Colin Hayburn [1969] Director; Kevin Stephens [1960] Director

**Intermedical (UK) Ltd**
*Incorporated:* 27 October 1997  *Employees:* 18
*Net Worth:* £1,426,306  *Total Assets:* £1,811,313
*Registered Office:* 2 Exeter House, Beaufort Court, Sir Thomas Longley Road, Rochester, Kent, ME2 4FE
*Shareholders:* Derek Alfred Curtis; Santina Curtis
*Officers:* Santina Curtis, Secretary; Derek Alfred Curtis [1945] Director; Santina Curtis [1951] Director/Company Secretary [Italian]; Livio Gagliardi [1979] Director/Operations Manager [Italian]

**Internal Luxe Heights Ltd**
*Incorporated:* 17 October 2018
*Registered Office:* 6 Mildenhall Road, Birmingham, B42 2PH
*Major Shareholder:* Jenna May Saymour
*Officers:* Jenna May Saymour [1996] Director

**International Ingredients and Chemicals (IIC) Ltd**
*Incorporated:* 20 May 1988  *Employees:* 18
*Previous:* ACI Group Ltd
*Net Worth:* £1,319,441  *Total Assets:* £3,396,826
*Registered Office:* The Old Library, 10 Leeds Road, Sheffield, S9 3TY
*Officers:* Franz Willi Gustav Smet [1947] Director/Consultant [German]

**International Medical Supplies Limited**
*Incorporated:* 10 July 2003
*Net Worth:* £24,323  *Total Assets:* £26,476
*Registered Office:* 39 West Street, Ince in Makerfield, Wigan, Lancs, WN2 2HF
*Major Shareholder:* Michael Haruwisi Mashingaidze
*Officers:* Adonia Mudeweti, Secretary/General Nurse [Zimbabwean]; Michael Haruwisi Mashingaidze [1956] Director/General Nurse [Zimbabwean]

**International Pharma Company Limited**
*Incorporated:* 4 October 2018
*Registered Office:* 121 Silver Street, Edmonton, London, N18 1RG
*Major Shareholder:* Andree Exner
*Officers:* Andree Exner, Secretary; Andree Exner [1964] Director/Entrepreneur [Australian]

**Interpharm Limited**
*Incorporated:* 25 June 1992  *Employees:* 2
*Net Worth:* £216,159  *Total Assets:* £830,093
*Registered Office:* First Floor, Roxburghe House, 273-287 Regent Street, London, W1B 2HA
*Shareholders:* Ashokkumar Naranbhai Patel; Michael Paul Davies
*Officers:* Jyotsna Ashokkumar Patel, Secretary; Michael Paul Davies [1964] Director/Chemist; Ashokkumar Naranbhai Patel [1960] Director/Chemist

**Interport Direct (Europe) Limited**
*Incorporated:* 7 April 2016
*Registered Office:* Bemin House, Cox Lane, Chessington Industrial Estate, Chessington, Surrey, KT9 1SG
*Major Shareholder:* Bemal Patel
*Officers:* Bemal Patel [1973] Director

**Interport Direct Limited**
*Incorporated:* 9 March 2016
*Registered Office:* Bemin House, Cox Lane, Chessington Industrial Estate, Chessington, Surrey, KT9 1SG
*Shareholders:* Interport Limited; Directpharm Limited
*Officers:* Bemal Patel [1973] Director

**Interport Limited**
*Incorporated:* 26 March 1981  *Employees:* 31
*Net Worth:* £7,303,536  *Total Assets:* £10,890,231
*Registered Office:* Brandon House, Marlowe Way, Croydon, Surrey, CR0 4XS
*Major Shareholder:* Harshadrai Ishwarbhai Ashabhai Patel
*Officers:* Snehlata Satish Patel, Secretary; Harshadrai Ishwarbhai Ashabhai Patel [1944] Director/Chemist; Dr Natasha Harshad Patel [1974] Director/Doctor/Consultant

**Intramed Limited**
*Incorporated:* 22 February 1995  *Employees:* 62
*Net Worth:* £932,661  *Total Assets:* £1,957,231
*Registered Office:* Fortuna Healthcare, Units 3-4 Northgate Business Centre, Crown Road, Enfield, Middlesex, EN1 1TG
*Shareholders:* Adrian Bavetta; Julian Bavetta; Sebastiano Bavetta
*Officers:* Julian Bavetta, Secretary; Adrian Bavetta [1968] Director/Importer and Distributor [Italian]; Julian Bavetta [1966] Director; Sebastiano Bavetta [1960] Director/Doctor of Medicine

**Intro International (TRDG) Limited**
*Incorporated:* 3 June 1980
*Net Worth:* £20,290  *Total Assets:* £30,289
*Registered Office:* Unit 3 Ambrose House, Meteor Court, Barnett Way, Barnwood, Gloucester, GL4 3GG
*Shareholders:* Terence James Maggs; Terence James Maggs
*Officers:* Philip John Taylor, Secretary; Terence James Maggs [1946] Marketing Director

**Inventive Medical Solutions Limited**
*Incorporated:* 17 September 2016
*Net Worth:* £124,353  *Total Assets:* £199,034
*Registered Office:* Kemp House, 160 City Road, London, EC1V 2NX
*Officers:* Adib Fallouh [1975] Director/Pharmacist [Syrian]

**Invicta Pharma Limited**
*Incorporated:* 22 October 2012  *Employees:* 2
*Net Worth Deficit:* £9,555  *Total Assets:* £13,687
*Registered Office:* 7 Clarendon Place, King Street, Maidstone, Kent, ME14 1BQ
*Major Shareholder:* William David Willis
*Officers:* Noleen Christine Willis, Secretary; William David Willis [1953] Director/Consultancy and Research

**Invitech Ltd**
*Incorporated:* 25 June 2008  *Employees:* 4
*Net Worth:* £220,978  *Total Assets:* £358,078
*Registered Office:* Unit 4 Molesworth Business Park, Molesworth, Huntingdon, Cambs, PE28 0QG
*Shareholders:* Suzanne Younghusband; Michael Younghusband
*Officers:* Suzanne Younghusband [1958] Director

**Iophtha Limited**
*Incorporated:* 19 October 2017
*Registered Office:* 255 Poulton Road, Wallasey, Wirral, Merseyside, CH44 4BT
*Shareholders:* Denise Claire Castell; Anthony Charles John
*Officers:* Denise Claire Castell [1957] Director; Anthony Charles John [1955] Director

**IPG Pharma Limited**
*Incorporated:* 17 December 2007  *Employees:* 9
*Net Worth:* £148,855  *Total Assets:* £1,089,620
*Registered Office:* The Old Police Station, Church Street, Swadlincote, Derbys, DE11 8LN
*Shareholders:* Gregory David Bilton; David Kenneth Bilton
*Officers:* Eileen Bilton, Secretary; David Kenneth Bilton [1954] Managing Director; Eileen Bilton [1959] Director/Corporate Services Manager; Gregory David Bilton [1992] Director

**IPS International Corporation Ltd**
*Incorporated:* 28 December 2018
*Registered Office:* c/o Talat Qazi Consulting, 58b Ilford Lane, Ilford, Essex, IG1 2JZ
*Major Shareholder:* Ahmed Ibrahim Fadel Abdelgalil
*Officers:* Ahmed Ibrahim Fadel Abdelgalil [1981] Director [Egyptian]

**IPSA Pharmacy Limited**
*Incorporated:* 8 September 2009
*Net Worth:* £313,004  *Total Assets:* £378,000
*Registered Office:* 7 Harben Parade, Finchley Road, London, NW3 6JP
*Major Shareholder:* Abdul Mustafa
*Officers:* Abdul Mustafa, Secretary; Abdul Mustafa [1976] Director; Ambia Rahman [1983] Director/Doctor

**Ipsen Limited**
*Incorporated:* 17 November 2008  *Employees:* 98
*Net Worth:* £7,730,000  *Total Assets:* £24,822,000
*Registered Office:* 190 Bath Road, Slough, Berks, SL1 3XE
*Parent:* Ipsen S.A.
*Officers:* Catherine Lamb, Secretary; Asad Mohsin Ali [1975] Director/GM; Isobel Louise Boyne [1969] Director/Accountant; Catherine Lamb [1978] Director/Solicitor

**IPY Healthcare Ltd**
*Incorporated:* 13 February 2017
*Net Worth:* £9,337  *Total Assets:* £82,284
*Registered Office:* Repton House, Bretby Business Park, Bretby, Burton on Trent, Staffs, DE15 0YZ
*Officers:* Joseph Mballa Nama, Secretary; Joseph Mballa Nama [1977] Director and Company Secretary

**IQ Pharma Ltd**
*Incorporated:* 26 February 2015
*Net Worth:* £463,214  *Total Assets:* £3,171,426
*Registered Office:* Westbourne, Gorse Bank Lane, Baslow, Bakewell, Derbys, DE45 1SG
*Major Shareholder:* Jonathan Tony Mottram
*Officers:* James Douglas Cousin [1949] Finance Director; Lesley Caroline Jarvis [1967] Commercial Director; Jonathan Tony Mottram [1969] Company Secretary/Director; Alan Pender [1971] Director

**Irasco Ltd**
*Incorporated:* 4 April 2014
*Net Worth Deficit:* £9,404  *Total Assets:* £151
*Registered Office:* 2 Coronation Avenue, Scone, Perth, PH2 6GA
*Major Shareholder:* Ahmed Alsaadi
*Officers:* Ahmed Al-Saadi [1978] Director [Iraqi]

**Irismed Pharma Ltd**
*Incorporated:* 3 September 2018
*Registered Office:* 3 Dunlin Drive, St Marys Island, Chatham, Kent, ME4 3JA
*Major Shareholder:* Julie Adedayo Olaniyi
*Officers:* Julie Adedayo Olaniyi [1982] Director

**Irls Yorkshire Limited**
*Incorporated:* 17 August 2018
*Registered Office:* West Hill House, Allerton Hill, Chapel Allerton, Leeds, LS7 3QB
*Major Shareholder:* Ian Howard Ainsworth
*Officers:* Ian Howard Ainsworth [1980] Director

**Irmaan Limited**
*Incorporated:* 27 February 2014
*Net Worth:* £100  *Total Assets:* £100
*Registered Office:* 29th Floor, 1 Canary Wharf, London, E14 5DY
*Shareholder:* Abdirahman Sheikh
*Officers:* Abdirahman Sheikh [1976] Director/MD; Mohamed Sheikh-Ahmed [1958] Director

**Ironbridge Medical Services Ltd**
*Incorporated:* 8 October 2018
*Registered Office:* Unit 3 Mill Farm Business Park, Millfield Road, Hounslow, Middlesex, TW4 5PY
*Major Shareholder:* Wei Guo
*Officers:* Wei Guo [1979] Managing Director

**Irving and Skinner Ltd**
*Incorporated:* 1 October 2018
*Registered Office:* Flat 1, 82 Harvesters Way, Edinburgh, EH14 3JJ
*Major Shareholder:* Stanley Udoka Okoro
*Officers:* Stanley Udoka Okoro [1990] Director/Businessman [Nigerian]

**Islestone Limited**
*Incorporated:* 16 July 2009  *Employees:* 17
*Net Worth:* £869,491  *Total Assets:* £3,879,988
*Registered Office:* 379 Princesway South, Team Valley Trading Estate, Gateshead, Tyne & Wear, NE11 0TU
*Shareholders:* David James Gulliford; Peter Gulliford
*Officers:* David James Gulliford [1988] Director; Dr Peter Gulliford [1949] Director

**Isra Limited**
*Incorporated:* 25 October 2011  *Employees:* 11
*Net Worth:* £267,205  *Total Assets:* £1,306,915
*Registered Office:* 59 Woodstock Road, Oxford, OX2 6HJ
*Shareholders:* Nusrat Bibi; Riaz Ahmed
*Officers:* Riaz Ahmed [1954] Director/Pharmacist

**Ivee Group Ltd**
*Incorporated:* 1 August 2016
*Registered Office:* P O Box 28143, 29 Badger Brook, Broxburn, W Lothian, EH52 5TB
*Shareholders:* Katarzyna Drywa; Michal Drywa
*Officers:* Katarzyna Drywa [1988] Managing Director [Polish]; Michal Drywa [1982] Managing Director [Polish]

**Izida Pharma Group Limited**
*Incorporated:* 8 September 2011
*Previous:* Meridius Commerce Limited
*Net Worth Deficit:* £1,912
*Registered Office:* 1a Crown Lane, London, SW16 3DJ
*Officers:* Willem Marthinus de Beer [1967] Director/Businessman [South African]

**Izida Pharma Ltd**
*Incorporated:* 11 January 2012
*Net Worth Deficit:* £23,517  *Total Assets:* £12,227
*Registered Office:* 1 Straits Parade, Bristol, BS16 2LA
*Officers:* Neil Young [1971] Director/Businessman

**J & G Equipment Limited**
*Incorporated:* 4 August 2003  *Employees:* 1
*Net Worth:* £4,154  *Total Assets:* £15,429
*Registered Office:* 47H Queen's Gate, London, SW7 5JN
*Major Shareholder:* Julia Freimane
*Officers:* Alexander Peschkoff, Secretary; Julia Freimane [1974] Director

**J & T World Trade (UK) Limited**
*Incorporated:* 16 May 2017
*Registered Office:* 3 Old Twelve Close, Hanwell, London, W7 1JA
*Major Shareholder:* John David Raby Jolley
*Officers:* Dr John David Raby Jolley [1945] Director/Doctor; Rahal Rahal [1963] Director [Australian]

**J L J Healthcare Limited**
*Incorporated:* 10 June 1999
*Net Worth Deficit:* £18,354  *Total Assets:* £29,638
*Registered Office:* 24 Tenterfields, Halesowen, W Midlands, B63 3LH
*Major Shareholder:* Jacqueline Lloyd-Jones
*Officers:* Adrian Bold, Secretary; Adrian Bold [1953] Director/Accountant; Jacqueline Lloyd-Jones [1958] Director/Nurse

**J.J. Worldhealth Limited**
*Incorporated:* 20 January 1997
*Net Worth Deficit:* £60,248  *Total Assets:* £84,686
*Registered Office:* 1 Weston Drive, Stanmore, Middlesex, HA7 2EX
*Officers:* Jagruti Jagdish Mehta, Secretary; Jagdish Vanichand Mehta [1955] Director; Jagruti Jagdish Mehta [1960] Director

**Jackson Immunoresearch Europe Limited**
*Incorporated:* 17 June 2004  *Employees:* 7
*Net Worth:* £564,581  *Total Assets:* £1,301,088
*Registered Office:* Cambridge House, St Thomas Place, Cambridgeshire Business Park, Ely, Cambs, CB7 4EX
*Shareholder:* Susan Caroline Hallett
*Officers:* Dr Leonard Charles Giunta [1941] Director/Physician Developer [American]; Susan Caroline Hallett [1949] Director/Biochemist; Ralph C. Hood Jr [1955] Director/VP Operations [American]; Ian James Nicholls [1968] Director; Lawrence Michael O'Donnell [1943] Director/Attorney [American]; William Jackson Stegeman [1942] Director/Biochemist [American]

**Jagmed Limited**
*Incorporated:* 11 September 2014
*Net Worth Deficit:* £91,612  *Total Assets:* £663
*Registered Office:* 8 Rodborough Road, London, NW11 8RY
*Shareholders:* Peter Ziman; Yosef Binyomin Gilbert
*Officers:* Yosef Binyomin Gilbert [1985] Director

**Jambo Supplies Limited**
*Incorporated:* 9 August 1989  *Employees:* 2
*Net Worth:* £140,287  *Total Assets:* £531,080
*Registered Office:* Unit 16 Silicone Centre, 28 Wadsworth Road, Perivale, Greenford, Middlesex, UB6 7JZ
*Shareholders:* Milankumar Lalji Shah; Bansri Shah
*Officers:* Bansri Shah, Secretary; Milankumar Shah [1960] Director/Businessman

**Jana Healthcare Ltd**
*Incorporated:* 11 October 2012
*Net Worth:* £6,634  *Total Assets:* £373,390
*Registered Office:* Brook House, 54a Cowley Mill Road, Uxbridge, Middlesex, UB8 2QE
*Officers:* Khaled Haj Mohamed [1964] Director/Doctor [Syrian]

**Janvit Ltd**
*Incorporated:* 18 November 1999  *Employees:* 2
*Net Worth:* £171,313  *Total Assets:* £255,630
*Registered Office:* 2 Helenslea Avenue, London, NW11 8ND
*Shareholder:* Kiritkumar Vaghjibhai Patel
*Officers:* Kirit Vaghjibhai Patel, Secretary; Jay Prakash Patel [1955] Director/Business Executive; Kirit Vaghjibhai Patel [1953] Director/Business Executive; Pravinkumar Vaghjibhai Patel [1946] Director/Business Executive

**JAO Enterprises Ltd**
*Incorporated:* 24 December 2018
*Registered Office:* 59 Ashbourne Road, London, W5 3DH
*Shareholders:* Vivek Behl; Amit Bir Singh Sra
*Officers:* Vivek Behl [1979] Director/Management Consultant; Dr Amit Bir Singh Sra [1981] Director/Management Consultant

**Jay & Jay Limited**
*Incorporated:* 11 October 1984
*Net Worth:* £145,119  *Total Assets:* £214,931
*Registered Office:* 6 Ritherdon Road, London, SW17 8QD
*Shareholders:* Mehboob Abid Jadawji; Shaina Mehboob Jadawji
*Officers:* Shaina Mehboob Jadawji, Secretary; Mehboob Abid Jadawji [1966] Director/Businessman; Shaina Mehboob Jadawji [1969] Director/Businesswoman

**JE Medical Associates Ltd.**
*Incorporated:* 11 June 2018
*Registered Office:* 6 Arundel Close, Bexley, Kent, DA5 1QQ
*Major Shareholder:* Osenadia Joseph-Ebare
*Officers:* Osenadia Joseph-Ebare [1995] Director/Entrepreneur

### Jenson Chemicals Limited
*Incorporated:* 30 May 1980  *Employees:* 1
*Net Worth:* £206,848  *Total Assets:* £260,871
*Registered Office:* Palladium House, 1-4 Argyll Street, London, W1F 7LD
*Parent:* Euromed (U.K) Limited
*Officers:* Charles Mendel Tannenbaum, Secretary; Charles Mendel Tannenbaum [1948] Director; Fiona Tannenbaum [1951] Director

### Jessica Inc Limited
*Incorporated:* 8 December 2010
*Net Worth:* £211  *Total Assets:* £14,511
*Registered Office:* First Floor, Healthaid House, Marlborough Hill, Harrow, Middlesex, HA1 1UD
*Shareholders:* Jessica Marie Frazier; Thomas Harwood Woods
*Officers:* Jessica Marie Frazier [1985] Director/Sales [American]; Thomas Harwood Woods [1978] Director/Senior Partner

### JJ Nutrihealth Ltd
*Incorporated:* 1 June 2009
*Registered Office:* 1 Weston Drive, Stanmore, Middlesex, HA7 2EX
*Shareholder:* Jagdish Vanichand Mehta
*Officers:* Jagdish Vanichand Mehta [1955] Director; Jagruti Jagdish Mehta [1960] Director

### JLS Pharma Limited
*Incorporated:* 8 August 2005  *Employees:* 1
*Net Worth:* £669,581  *Total Assets:* £843,372
*Registered Office:* Incom House, Waterside, Trafford Park, Manchester, M17 1WD
*Major Shareholder:* Natalie Gordon
*Officers:* Natalie Carol Gordon [1968] Director

### JLVET Ltd
*Incorporated:* 3 February 2016
*Net Worth Deficit:* £757  *Total Assets:* £10,489
*Registered Office:* 40 Railway Street, Lisburn, Co Antrim, BT28 1XP
*Shareholders:* Moss Veterinary Products Limited; Marte Investments Holdings Limited
*Officers:* Christopher William Sparrow [1971] Director/General Manager; Juliet Sparrow [1943] Director [Irish]

### JMD Enterprises UK Limited
*Incorporated:* 27 May 2009
*Net Worth:* £2,784  *Total Assets:* £327,419
*Registered Office:* c/o JMD House, 96 Western Road, Southall, Middlesex, UB2 5DZ
*Officers:* Varun Kumar Rishi [1985] Director

### Johnlee Pharmaceuticals (UK) Limited
*Incorporated:* 7 April 2017  *Employees:* 2
*Net Worth Deficit:* £1,734
*Registered Office:* 27 Old Gloucester Street, London, WC1N 3AX
*Shareholders:* Dilipkumar Kishanlal Jain; Girish Kishanlal Jain
*Officers:* Dilipkumar Kishanlal Jain [1980] Director/Businessman [Indian]; Girish Kishanlal Jain [1987] Director/Businessman [Indian]

### Jolinda Medical Supplies Limited
*Incorporated:* 4 January 1999  *Employees:* 3
*Net Worth:* £570,437  *Total Assets:* £672,780
*Registered Office:* 3a Chestnut House, Farm Close, Shenley, Herts, WD7 9AD
*Parent:* Jolinda Holdings Limited
*Officers:* Jacqueline Gertrude Mickler, Secretary; Barry Joseph Mickler [1937] Director

### Leigh Jones & Associates Ltd
*Incorporated:* 31 October 2017
*Registered Office:* Kemp House, 160 City Road, London, EC1V 2NX
*Major Shareholder:* David Jones
*Officers:* David Jones, Secretary; David Leigh Jones [1958] Director; Sonia Margaret Jones [1957] Director

### R M Jones Limited
*Incorporated:* 12 February 1993  *Employees:* 2
*Net Worth:* £1,311,598  *Total Assets:* £1,336,606
*Registered Office:* R M Jones Farmcentre, Oxford Road, Hay on Wye, Powys, HR3 5AJ
*Shareholders:* Roderick Edward Jones; R M Jones Funded Unappoved Benefit Scheme
*Officers:* Suzannah Jones, Secretary; Rebecca Frances Jones [1985] Director; Suzannah Jones [1958] Director

### Jorvik Pharma Ltd
*Incorporated:* 2 March 2016
*Net Worth:* £100  *Total Assets:* £100
*Registered Office:* St Oswald House, St Oswald Street, Castleford, W Yorks, WF10 1DH
*Major Shareholder:* Albert Edward Hills
*Officers:* Albert Edward Hills [1956] Business Development Director

### Josana Limited
*Incorporated:* 11 January 2019
*Registered Office:* A3 Broomsleigh Business Park, Worsley Bridge Road, London, SE26 5BN
*Shareholders:* Sarah Catherine Russell Lotzof; Natasha Eugenie Cherrett
*Officers:* Natasha Eugenie Cherrett [1979] Director/Business Manager; Dr Sarah Catherine Russell Lotzof [1963] Director/Doctor of Medicine

### JP & A Pharma Ltd
*Incorporated:* 20 November 2018
*Registered Office:* 4 Bryn Court, Prestatyn, Denbighshire, LL19 8BU
*Shareholders:* Jacek Bartosz Piasta; Agnieszka Maria Piasta
*Officers:* Agnieszka Maria Piasta [1981] Director/Manager [British/Polish]; Jacek Bartosz Piasta [1978] Director/Chemist [British/Polish]

### JSK PVT Limited
*Incorporated:* 11 August 2015
*Net Worth:* £1,966  *Total Assets:* £2,220
*Registered Office:* Flat 3, 349 Katherine Road, London, E7 8LT
*Major Shareholder:* Alpeshkumar Rambhai Patel
*Officers:* Maya Jasrajbhai Moghariya [1984] Director

### Juice Sauz Ltd
*Incorporated:* 30 November 2015  *Employees:* 15
*Net Worth:* £96,321  *Total Assets:* £366,669
*Registered Office:* 3 Pioneer Way, Doddington Road, Lincoln, LN6 3DH
*Shareholders:* Liam Chapman; Julie Chapman
*Officers:* Julie Chapman [1974] Director/Businesswoman; Liam Martin Chapman [1988] Finance Director

### Jules Pharma Limited
*Incorporated:* 14 January 2002  *Employees:* 1
*Net Worth:* £11,211  *Total Assets:* £13,687
*Registered Office:* 10 Lyndhurst Road, Coulsdon, Surrey, CR5 3HT
*Major Shareholder:* Andrew Nwachukwu Aghadiuno
*Officers:* Willa June Aghadiuno, Secretary; Andrew Nwachukwu Aghadiuno [1967] Director/Pharmacist

**June Medical International Ltd**
Incorporated: 7 April 2015
Net Worth Deficit: £25,543  Total Assets: £139,357
Registered Office: Innov8, Queen Alexandra Road, High Wycombe, Bucks, HP11 2GZ
Officers: Angela Spang, Secretary; Angela Helen Spang [1973] Director [Swedish]

**June Medical Ltd**
Incorporated: 16 July 2013  Employees: 9
Net Worth Deficit: £85,307  Total Assets: £232,497
Registered Office: Innov8, Queen Alexandra Road, High Wycombe, Bucks, HP11 2GZ
Major Shareholder: Lady Angela Helene Spang
Officers: Angela Helene Spang, Secretary; Lady Angela Helene Spang [1973] Director [Swedish]

**Juvela Limited**
Incorporated: 13 September 2010
Registered Office: Unit 3c Mamhilad Park Estate, Pontypool, Monmouthshire, NP4 0HZ
Shareholder: Arend Oetker
Officers: Stephen Lane, Secretary; Markus Lenke [1969] Director [German]; Claire Monks [1973] Marketing Director

**K & K Pharmaceuticals Limited**
Incorporated: 30 May 2013
Net Worth Deficit: £3,855  Total Assets: £14,238
Registered Office: Dawes Court House, Dawes Court, High Street, Esher, Surrey, KT10 9QD
Shareholder: Subhash Kantibhai Patel
Officers: Subhash Kantibhai Patel [1957] Director/Pharmacist

**K Chem (North East) Ltd**
Incorporated: 2 February 2017
Net Worth: £3,445  Total Assets: £519,035
Registered Office: 217 Coatsworth Road, Gateshead, Tyne & Wear, NE8 1SR
Officers: Omar Najeeb [1983] Director

**K N B Services Ltd**
Incorporated: 9 January 2019
Registered Office: 63 Aubrey Road, London, E17 4SL
Major Shareholder: Muhammad Kamran Saeed
Officers: Muhammad Kamran Saeed [1981] Director

**K P Pharma Limited**
Incorporated: 5 October 2005
Registered Office: Bemin House, Cox Lane, Chessington, Surrey, KT9 1SZ
Major Shareholder: Bemal Patel
Officers: Hital Patel, Secretary; Bemal Patel [1973] Director/Pharmacist; Hital Patel [1974] Director/Company Secretary

**K588 Limited**
Incorporated: 5 June 2018
Registered Office: 3rd Floor, Paternoster House, 65 St Paul's Churchyard, London, EC4M 8AB
Shareholders: Charles James Anthony Bradshaw; Robert Michael Calcraft
Officers: Charles James Anthony Bradshaw [1975] Director; Robert Michael Calcraft [1964] Director/Consultant

**Kaam Pharma Limited**
Incorporated: 28 November 2000  Employees: 8
Net Worth: £1,838,218  Total Assets: £2,574,166
Registered Office: 9 Westfield Drive, Kenton, Harrow, Middlesex, HA3 9EG
Officers: Arvind Makadia, Secretary; Arvind Makadia [1962] Director/Accountant; Mukund Kacharalal Patel [1964] Director/Sales Assistant

**Kaboodan Limited**
Incorporated: 5 April 2018
Registered Office: Flat 622, Craven Hill Gardens, London, W2 3ES
Major Shareholder: Amir Ali Manoocheheri
Officers: Amir Ali Manoocheheri [1998] Director/Student [Iranian/American]

**Kadmon International Ltd**
Incorporated: 14 October 2011
Registered Office: Suite A, 6 Honduras Street, London, EC1Y 0TH
Officers: Steven Gordon [1967] Director/Executive Vice-President, General Counsel [American]

**Kamm Trading Limited**
Incorporated: 12 November 2008  Employees: 13
Net Worth: £33,937  Total Assets: £148,673
Registered Office: Unit 10 Coppice Industrial Estate, Windsor Road, Oldham, Lancs, OL8 4AP
Shareholders: Muhammad Harun Anwar; Mohammed Azeem Azram Choudhry
Officers: Muhammad Harun Anwar [1991] Director; Mohammed Azeem Azram Choudhry [1985] Director

**Kamo Dental Products Limited**
Incorporated: 12 December 2017
Registered Office: 2 Temple Cottages, The Green, Datchet, Berks, SL3 9BJ
Officers: Dr Kameran Al-Naib [1950] Director/Dentist

**Kanish Ltd**
Incorporated: 21 June 2017
Net Worth: £2,040  Total Assets: £10,108
Registered Office: Alpha House, 646c Kingsbury Road, Kingsbury, London, NW9 9HN
Major Shareholder: Vishva Vijaychandra Purohit
Officers: Vishva Vijaychandra Purohit [1981] Director

**Kanta Enterprises Limited**
Incorporated: 26 January 1982  Employees: 34
Net Worth: £9,001,002  Total Assets: £23,451,408
Registered Office: Kanta House, Victoria Road, South Ruislip, Middlesex, HA4 0JQ
Officers: Satish Jamnadas Chatwani, Secretary; Jawahar Jamnadas Chatwani [1948] Director; Rashmi Jamnadas Chatwani [1954] Director; Satish Jamnadas Chatwani [1953] Director

**Karczek Ltd**
Incorporated: 23 May 2018
Registered Office: 15 Slackswood Close, Ellesmere Port, Cheshire, CH65 3AH
Officers: Rafal Gietka [1985] Director/Lawyer [Polish]

**Karo Pharma UK Ltd**
Incorporated: 23 January 2019
Registered Office: c/o Grant Thornton Company Secretarial Services, 30 Finsbury Square, London, EC2A 1AG
Parent: Karo Pharma Aktiebolag
Officers: Peter Blom [1961] Director [Swedish]

**Katvic Limited**
Incorporated: 19 September 2018
Registered Office: 202 Dalmellington Road, Glasgow, G53 7FY
Shareholders: Evarest Onwubiko; Mary Onwubiko
Officers: Dr Evarest Onwubiko [1979] Managing Director

**Kavia Tooling Limited**
Incorporated: 11 May 2005  Employees: 12
Net Worth: £185,794  Total Assets: £906,632
Registered Office: Unit 3 Bancroft Road, Burnley, Lancs, BB10 2RZ
Shareholders: Christopher Anthony Cole; Steven David Parker; Harvey Graeme Spence
Officers: Steven David Parker, Secretary/Director; Christopher Anthony Cole [1972] Director/Manager; Steven David Parker [1968] Director; Harvey Graeme Spence [1967] Director

**Kays Medical Limited**
Incorporated: 11 March 1976  Employees: 48
Net Worth: £3,566,427  Total Assets: £10,598,522
Registered Office: 1 Windward Drive, Speke, Liverpool, L24 8QR
Shareholders: David Henry Ludzker; Joyce Ludzker
Officers: Joyce Ludzker, Secretary; Benjamin Mathew Ludzker [1979] Director; David Henry Ludzker [1944] Director; Joyce Ludzker [1942] Director

**KD Pharmacon Ltd**
Incorporated: 2 March 2017
Net Worth: £26  Total Assets: £37,213
Registered Office: 405 London Road, Davenham, Cheshire, CW9 8HN
Major Shareholder: Colin Kain-Duncan
Officers: Colin Kain-Duncan [1958] Director/Pharmaceutical Consultant

**KDC-UK Ltd.**
Incorporated: 6 September 2013
Net Worth Deficit: £10,457  Total Assets: £33,103
Registered Office: 34 Waterloo Road, Wolverhampton, W Midlands, WV1 4DG
Major Shareholder: Kristiyan Krassimov Gotzev
Officers: Kristiyan Krassimirov Gotzev [1989] Director [Bulgarian]; Richard John Thorpe [1989] Director/Pharmacist

**Kelisdar Enterprises Limited**
Incorporated: 9 February 2000  Employees: 23
Net Worth: £1,863,213  Total Assets: £2,343,785
Registered Office: Suite 1, The Riverside Building, Livingstone Road, Hessle, E Yorks, HU13 0DZ
Officers: Lisa Kellett, Secretary; Darren Kellett [1967] Director/Pharmacist; Lisa Kellett [1971] Director/Pharmacist

**Kelpharma Ltd**
Incorporated: 12 November 2015  Employees: 5
Net Worth: £229,155  Total Assets: £246,793
Registered Office: Croylands, Church Lane, Averham, Newark, Notts, NG23 5RB
Shareholders: Keith Nickson; Emma Louise Nickson
Officers: Emma Louise Nickson [1977] Director; Keith Nickson [1973] Director; Margaret Rene Zeederberg [1958] Director [South African]

**Kemsource Limited**
Incorporated: 29 July 2002  Employees: 2
Net Worth: £16,090  Total Assets: £180,558
Registered Office: Unit 12 Hotchkiss Way, Binley Industrial Estate, Binley, Coventry, Warwicks, CV3 2RL
Officers: Keith William Maddaford, Secretary; Keith William Maddaford [1963] Director; Nicola Maddaford [1974] Director

**Kent Pharma UK Limited**
Incorporated: 18 September 2018
Registered Office: DCC Vital, Westminster Industrial Estate, Repton Road, Measham, Swadlincote, Derbys, DE12 7DT
Parent: Fannin (UK) Limited
Officers: Stephen Clifford O'Connor [1964] Director

**Kerita Ltd**
Incorporated: 26 September 2012
Net Worth: £21,810  Total Assets: £28,000
Registered Office: 41 Brinklow Crescent, Shooters Hill, London, SE18 3BS
Major Shareholder: Arvinder Singh Gill
Officers: Arvinder Singh Gill [1959] Director

**Kernfarm UK Limited**
Incorporated: 5 September 2015
Registered Office: The Estate Office, Hetton Steads, Lowick, Berwick upon Tweed, Northumberland, TD15 2UL
Shareholders: Tim Van Rijn; Diederik Van Rijn; Gijs Van Rijn
Officers: Diederik Van Rijn [1980] Director [Dutch]; Gijs Van Rijn [1982] Director [Dutch]; Tim Van Rijn [1979] Director [Dutch]

**Kestrel Medical Limited**
Incorporated: 12 December 2000  Employees: 6
Net Worth: £785,029  Total Assets: £1,052,516
Registered Office: Kestrel House, 7 Moor Road, Broadstone, Dorset, BH18 8AZ
Shareholders: Ian Arthur Ponsford; Meryl Julie Ponsford
Officers: Meryl Julie Ponsford, Secretary; Ian Arthur Ponsford [1945] Director; Meryl Julie Ponsford [1949] Director

**Kestrel Ophthalmics Limited**
Incorporated: 4 July 2001  Employees: 11
Net Worth: £652,963  Total Assets: £1,334,197
Registered Office: 9 Cabot Business Village, Holyrood Close, Poole, Dorset, BH17 7BA
Parent: Cutting Edge SAS
Officers: Lionel Claude Jean-Paul Jouet, Secretary; Jean-Pierre Boudet [1964] Director/General Manager [French]; Yves Brouquet-Laclaire [1958] Director/General Manager [French]

**Kestrol International Limited**
Incorporated: 19 October 2005
Net Worth: £110  Total Assets: £10,193
Registered Office: 4th Floor, Metroline House, 118-122 College Road, Harrow, Middlesex, HA1 1BQ
Major Shareholder: Nilesh Mamtora
Officers: Nilesh Mamtora, Secretary; Nilesh Mamtora [1962] Director/International Consultant

**Key Nutrients 4 Life Ltd**
Incorporated: 15 November 2017
Registered Office: 12 Salisbury Road, Cosham, Portsmouth, PO6 2PN
Major Shareholder: Gill Vigus
Officers: Gill Vigus [1960] Director

**Keziah Ltd**
Incorporated: 12 April 2018
Registered Office: 105 Easedale House, 71 Summerwood Road, Isleworth, Middlesex, TW7 7QF
Major Shareholder: Priscilla Adwoa Asamaniwa McKing
Officers: Priscilla Adwoa Asamaniwa McKing [1979] Director/Social Worker

**Kganesha Pharma Ltd**
*Incorporated:* 6 March 2018
*Registered Office:* 320 St John Street, London, EC1V 4NT
*Major Shareholder:* Jyoti Gupta
*Officers:* Jyoti Gupta [1976] Director

**KGP Laboratories (UK) Limited**
*Incorporated:* 13 February 2004
*Net Worth:* £179,962  *Total Assets:* £328,665
*Registered Office:* 6-9 The Square, Stockley Park, Uxbridge, Middlesex, UB11 1FW
*Major Shareholder:* Punitha Shanmugasundaram
*Officers:* Somendra Singh [1977] Director

**KHM Global Ltd**
*Incorporated:* 5 November 2014
*Net Worth Deficit:* £1,710  *Total Assets:* £2,063
*Registered Office:* 47 Edinburgh Gardens, Windsor, Berks, SL4 2AW
*Major Shareholder:* Kumbirai Makore
*Officers:* Kumbirai Makore [1981] Director

**Kids Medicare Limited**
*Incorporated:* 27 December 2017
*Registered Office:* 24 Bowley Avenue, Melton Mowbray, Leics, LE13 1RU
*Major Shareholder:* Siobhan Marie Scott
*Officers:* Siobhan Marie Scott [1971] Director/Administrator

**Kinesis Limited**
*Incorporated:* 29 April 1997  *Employees:* 53
*Net Worth:* £4,025,375  *Total Assets:* £4,107,392
*Registered Office:* 9 Orion Court, Ambuscade Road, Colmworth Business Park, Eaton Socon, St Neots, Cambs, PE19 8YX
*Parent:* Cole-Parmer Instrument Company Limited
*Officers:* Deborah Gallifant [1970] Finance Director; Jamie Ronald Gallifant [1968] Managing Director; Jon Salkin [1970] Director [American]

**Kinetic Enterprises Limited**
*Incorporated:* 5 December 1990  *Employees:* 53
*Net Worth:* £6,922,630  *Total Assets:* £9,694,988
*Registered Office:* 24 Bedford Row, London, WC1R 4TQ
*Major Shareholder:* Sunder Premchand Baharani
*Officers:* Sunder Premchand Baharani [1960] Director/Company Representative [Indian]

**Kings Medical Supplies Limited**
*Incorporated:* 11 October 2018
*Registered Office:* 33 Strutton Ground, St James Park, London, SW1P 2HY
*Major Shareholder:* Husainali Alidina
*Officers:* Husainali Alidina [1986] Director

**Kingsley Specials Limited**
*Incorporated:* 26 January 2018
*Registered Office:* 3 Foxpond Lane, Great Glen, Leicester, LE2 4RY
*Major Shareholder:* Gursharen Singh Sooch
*Officers:* Gursharen Singh Sooch [1983] Director

**Kingspeed Services Limited**
*Incorporated:* 27 May 2010  *Employees:* 5
*Net Worth:* £244,014  *Total Assets:* £485,878
*Registered Office:* Gwynfa House, 677 Princes Road, Dartford, Kent, DA2 6EF
*Major Shareholder:* David Stephen King
*Officers:* Andrew Spencer Jackson [1979] Director/Operations Manager; David Stephen King [1958] Director/Medical Supplies

**Kingston Pharma Limited**
*Incorporated:* 13 February 2019
*Registered Office:* Trilogy Suite, 9 Church Street, Wednesfield, Wolverhampton, W Midlands, WV11 1SR
*Major Shareholder:* Katie Georgina Kingston
*Officers:* Katie Georgina Kingston [1995] Director

**Kisska International Limited**
*Incorporated:* 21 January 1998
*Net Worth:* £51,118  *Total Assets:* £91,358
*Registered Office:* 63-65 High Street, Skipton, N Yorks, BD23 1DS
*Major Shareholder:* Katherine Mary Duxbury
*Officers:* Paul Thomas Duxbury, Secretary; Matthew Philip Duxbury [1982] Director; Paul Thomas Duxbury [1953] Director; Stephen Matthew Duxbury [1958] Director

**KM Consulting (Chesterfield) Limited**
*Incorporated:* 12 May 2009  *Employees:* 2
*Net Worth:* £16,803  *Total Assets:* £60,862
*Registered Office:* 2 Broomgrove Road, Sheffield, S10 2LR
*Shareholders:* Mark William Thorne; Kathryn Thorne
*Officers:* Mark William Thorne, Secretary; Kathryn Thorne [1965] Director/Retailer; Mark William Thorne [1965] Director

**Knightsbridge Importers Limited**
*Incorporated:* 15 March 1962
*Net Worth:* £123,049  *Total Assets:* £137,736
*Registered Office:* 4 Michaels Mount, Little Bealings, Woodbridge, Suffolk, IP13 6LS
*Major Shareholder:* Jennifer Bouffard
*Officers:* Jennifer Bouffard [1938] Director-Public Relations

**Knox Pharmaceuticals Limited**
*Incorporated:* 18 April 1995  *Employees:* 25
*Net Worth:* £2,865,312  *Total Assets:* £4,664,978
*Registered Office:* Unit 2 Barugh Way, Barker Business Park, Melmerby, Ripon, N Yorks, HG4 5NG
*Major Shareholder:* Branden William Knox
*Officers:* Branden Knox [1974] Director; Laura Knox [1974] Director

**Koasta Limited**
*Incorporated:* 22 August 2005
*Net Worth Deficit:* £49,122  *Total Assets:* £359,501
*Registered Office:* Banbury House, 121 Stonegrove, Edgware, Middlesex, HA8 7TJ
*Shareholder:* Olubukola Taofik Shodunke
*Officers:* Olubukola Taofik Shodunke [1971] Director

**Kobayashi Healthcare Europe Limited**
*Incorporated:* 14 March 2001  *Employees:* 7
*Net Worth:* £5,094,789  *Total Assets:* £6,985,520
*Registered Office:* 272 Gunnersbury Avenue, Chiswick, London, W4 5QB
*Parent:* Kobayashi Pharmaceutical Co., Ltd
*Officers:* Takaki Yagi, Secretary; Kazuhito Miyanishi [1962] Director [Japanese]; Takaki Yagi [1975] Director [Japanese]

**Kohilam Limited**
*Incorporated:* 4 December 2017
*Registered Office:* 105 Friern Barnet Lane, London, N20 0XZ
*Major Shareholder:* Kumar Kandasamy
*Officers:* Nigel Haniff [1963] Director/Sales Consultant; Kumar Kandasamy [1962] Director

**Koln Pharma Ltd**
*Incorporated:* 31 August 2017
*Registered Office:* 869 High Road, London, N12 8QA
*Major Shareholder:* Hamid Reza Tasbihgou
*Officers:* Hamid Reza Tasbihgou [1955] Director

**Kora Healthcare UK Ltd**
*Incorporated:* 28 November 2017
*Registered Office:* Bio Centre, Innovation Way, Heslington, York, YO10 5NY
*Major Shareholder:* James Patrick O'Daly
*Officers:* Conor James O'Daly [1985] Director/Chief Executive Officer [Irish]; James Patrick O'Daly [1939] Director and Businessman [Irish]; Aidan Joseph Ryan [1984] Director/Financial Controller [Irish]

**Korlyns Therapeutics Limited**
*Incorporated:* 17 April 2007  *Employees:* 4
*Net Worth:* £21,912  *Total Assets:* £35,565
*Registered Office:* 10 Linkfield Lane, Redhill, Surrey, RH1 1JL
*Shareholders:* Collins Iriajen; Evelyn Ivbagbha Iriajen
*Officers:* Evelyn Ivbagbha Iriajen, Secretary; Collins Iriajen [1969] Director/Salesman

**Kosei Pharma UK Ltd.**
*Incorporated:* 27 April 2010  *Employees:* 170
*Net Worth:* £2,060,003  *Total Assets:* £10,155,097
*Registered Office:* 956 Buckingham Avenue, Slough Trading Estate, Slough, SL1 4NL
*Major Shareholder:* Kohei Toda
*Officers:* Soumendranath Ghosh [1968] Director [Indian]; Kohei Toda [1976] Representative Director [Japanese]

**KPB Healthcare Limited**
*Incorporated:* 24 June 2014  *Employees:* 1
*Net Worth Deficit:* £8,357  *Total Assets:* £135,312
*Registered Office:* Rss Manor Way, Leigh Road, Eastleigh, Hants, SO50 9YA
*Major Shareholder:* Kevin Paul Bordley
*Officers:* Kevin Paul Bordley [1969] Director/Owner

**KRKA UK Ltd**
*Incorporated:* 18 February 2014  *Employees:* 8
*Net Worth Deficit:* £158,889  *Total Assets:* £1,204,849
*Registered Office:* Suite 1, 3rd Floor, 11-12 St James's Square, London, SW1Y 4LB
*Parent:* KRKA, D.D., Novo Mesto
*Officers:* Joze Arh [1967] Deputy Director of Animal Health [Slovenian]; Bostjan Korosec [1973] Sales Director [Slovenian]; Mojca Vidmar Berus [1969] Director of Corporate Performance Management [Slovenian]

**Kuramo (UK) Limited**
*Incorporated:* 14 March 1994  *Employees:* 3
*Net Worth Deficit:* £87,235  *Total Assets:* £248,244
*Registered Office:* 8B Accommodation Road, London, NW11 8ED
*Officers:* Rotimi Koyejo Odulate [1962] Director [Nigerian]

**KW Wholesale Ltd**
*Incorporated:* 1 November 2018
*Registered Office:* Suite 1, 177 Lees Road, Oldham, Lancs, OL4 1JP
*Shareholders:* Mohammed Khuram Shahzad; Amir Wahid Ikhlas
*Officers:* Amir Wahid Ikhlas [1985] Director; Mohammed Khuram Shahzad [1982] Director

**Kyo Ltd**
*Incorporated:* 14 August 2018
*Registered Office:* 39 Junction Road, London, N19 5QU
*Shareholders:* Ekta Patel; Ekta Patel; Ekta Patel
*Officers:* Ekta Patel [1989] Director/Pharmacist

**L & R Medical UK Ltd.**
*Incorporated:* 9 September 1998  *Employees:* 119
*Previous:* Activa Healthcare Limited
*Net Worth:* £10,248,000  *Total Assets:* £13,387,000
*Registered Office:* 1 Wellington Court, Newborough Road, Needwood, Burton on Trent, Staffs, DE13 9PS
*Parent:* Lohmann and Rauscher GmbH
*Officers:* Jane Elizabeth Doades [1974] Marketing Director; Simon Mangan [1971] Managing Director; Martin Johannes Ortwin Pohl [1976] Director [German]; Doctor Klemens Walter Schulz [1965] Director [German]; Wolfgang Suessle [1966] Director/Healthcare [German]

**La Lune Noire Ltd**
*Incorporated:* 7 April 2017
*Net Worth:* £3,622  *Total Assets:* £3,622
*Registered Office:* 41 Crutchfield Lane, Walton on Thames, Surrey, KT12 2QY
*Shareholders:* Georgina Louise Voysey; Gregory James Catmull
*Officers:* Gregory James Catmull [1990] Director; Georgina Louise Voysey [1996] Director/Accountant

**Lab-Club Limited**
*Incorporated:* 1 August 2014
*Registered Office:* 1 Doolittle Yard, Froghall Road, Ampthill, Beds, MK45 2NW
*Major Shareholder:* Susan Mary Burton
*Officers:* Dr Susan Mary Burton [1967] Director

**Lab-PCR Limited**
*Incorporated:* 23 April 2013
*Net Worth Deficit:* £100  *Total Assets:* £866
*Registered Office:* Ground Floor, Craven House, 40-44 Uxbridge Road, London, W5 2BS
*Major Shareholder:* Karol Wojciech Helowicz
*Officers:* Karol Helowicz [1977] Director [Polish]

**Lab.Tv Limited**
*Incorporated:* 10 December 2002
*Previous:* Labtech France Ltd
*Net Worth Deficit:* £202,847  *Total Assets:* £12,242
*Registered Office:* Mytogen House, 11 Browning Road, Heathfield, E Sussex, TN21 8DB
*Parent:* Labtech International Ltd
*Officers:* Attilia Natalia Page, Secretary; Dr Brian John Page [1950] Director

**Labjoy Ltd**
*Incorporated:* 16 May 2014
*Net Worth:* £8,788  *Total Assets:* £37,796
*Registered Office:* Unit 1 Heath Works, Beasleys Ait, Sunbury-on-Thames, Surrey, TW16 6AS
*Major Shareholder:* Justin Mooney
*Officers:* Justin Mooney [1994] Director

**Labmedical System Limited**
*Incorporated:* 28 June 2012
*Net Worth:* £3,082  *Total Assets:* £227,039
*Registered Office:* Suite 211, Cornwall Buildings, 45 Newhall Street, Birmingham, B3 3QR
*Officers:* Androniki Christodoulou [1978] Director [Cypriot]

**Laboratoires Forte Pharma UK Ltd**
*Incorporated:* 26 May 2006
*Net Worth Deficit:* £421,675  *Total Assets:* £2,306
*Registered Office:* Unit 9A Caddsdown Business Support Centre, Caddsdown Industrial Park, Bideford, Devon, EX39 3DX
*Parent:* Laboratoires Forte Pharma SAM
*Officers:* Gabriel Roig Zapatero [1972] Director [Spanish]

**The Labwarehouse Limited**
Incorporated: 9 February 2000
Registered Office: Unit 10 Cliffside Trade Park, Motherwell Way, Grays, Essex, RM20 3XD
Officers: Brian Lewis Cope, Secretary; Brian Lewis Cope [1936] Director/Glass Technician; Colin John Cope [1947] Director/Glass Technician

**Lad & Company Private Limited**
Incorporated: 28 August 2018
Registered Office: 247 Vicarage Farm Road, Hounslow, Middlesex, TW5 0AQ
Major Shareholder: Aida Brito
Officers: Aida Brito [1973] Company Secretary/Director [Portuguese]

**Lam Cash and Carry Limited**
Incorporated: 19 October 1981
Registered Office: 24 Bedford Row, London, WC1R 4TQ
Shareholders: Amir Tayebali Kapadia; Sukhminder Amir Kapadia
Officers: Amir Tayebali Kapadia, Secretary; Sukhminder Amir Kapadia, Company Secretary; Amir Tayebali Kapadia [1953] Director; Rafique Amir Kapadia [1980] Director/Hotel Manager

**Roy Lamb Limited**
Incorporated: 29 April 1992
Registered Office: 11 Manchester Road, Walkden, Manchester, M28 3NS
Parent: PCT Healthcare Ltd
Officers: Angela Jane Cattee, Secretary; Peter Cattee [1952] Director/Pharmacist; Geoffrey Alan Tims [1943] Director/Pharmacist

**Lamb's Locum Services Ltd**
Incorporated: 3 May 2013 Employees: 2
Net Worth Deficit: £855 Total Assets: £4,330
Registered Office: Beech House, 23 Ladies Lane, Hindley, Wigan, Lancs, WN2 2QA
Shareholders: Roy Lamb; Beverley Anne Lamb
Officers: Beverley Anne Lamb [1957] Director; Roy Lamb [1955] Director

**Lambsmead Limited**
Incorporated: 5 July 1976 Employees: 20
Net Worth: £257,433 Total Assets: £350,601
Registered Office: 222 Upper Richmond Road West, London, SW14 8AH
Officers: Ivor Deitsch, Secretary; Ivor Deitsch [1939] Director/Pharmacist; Lancelot Piers Duncan Deitsch [1971] Director; Sandra Estelle Deitsch [1942] Director; Sebastian Richard Oliver Deitsch [1969] Director

**Lamyra International Limited**
Incorporated: 15 September 2015
Registered Office: c/o DRP + Co Accountants Limited, 1st Floor, 6 St Johns Court, Upper Fforest Way, Swansea, SA6 8QQ
Major Shareholder: Amin Farah
Officers: Amin Farah [1951] Director; Andrew David Thomas [1969] Director

**Langdales Limited**
Incorporated: 3 September 1996
Net Worth: £10,417 Total Assets: £18,646
Registered Office: 1 High Street, Thatcham, Berks, RG19 3JG
Major Shareholder: George Mitchell Sutherland
Officers: Sheena Sukumaran [1971] Director

**Lansdales Pharmacy Limited**
Incorporated: 8 July 1999 Employees: 43
Net Worth: £950,121 Total Assets: £2,488,749
Registered Office: Stamford House, Short Street, High Wycombe, Bucks, HP11 2QH
Shareholders: Abdul Khaliq; Sakina Khaliq
Officers: Samina Hussain, Secretary; Khalil Ahmed Khaliq [1968] Director/Pharmacist; Saliya Halima Khaliq [1997] Director

**Lantheus MI UK Limited**
Incorporated: 24 April 2008
Net Worth Deficit: £9,638,295 Total Assets: £909,374
Registered Office: 61 Roehampton Lane, Putney, London, SW15 5NE
Parent: Lantheus Holdings, Inc
Officers: Michael Philip Duffy, Secretary/Vice President and General Counsel [American]; Michael Philip Duffy [1960] Director/Vice President and General Counsel [American]; Mary Anne Heino [1960] Director/President and CEO [American]; Robert J. Marshall Jr [1966] Director/Chief Financial Officer and Treasurer [American]

**Laogong Laopo Limited**
Incorporated: 19 September 2018
Registered Office: 95 Briony Avenue, Hale, Altrincham, Cheshire, WA15 8PZ
Major Shareholder: Fey Tsang
Officers: Fey Tsang [1989] Director

**Larmed Limited**
Incorporated: 29 November 2017
Registered Office: Forsyth House, Cromac Square, Belfast, BT2 8LA
Parent: Supraherbal Limited
Officers: Andrew Ross [1956] Director/Manager [American]

**Latam HQ Health Ltd**
Incorporated: 13 March 2015
Net Worth Deficit: £126,880 Total Assets: £68,770
Registered Office: 24 Howard Close, Fleet, Hants, GU51 3ER
Major Shareholder: Harold John Christopher Paul
Officers: Harold John Christopher Paul [1967] Director/Businessman; Simon John Christopher Paul [1941] Director/Consultant

**Lax Pharma Limited**
Incorporated: 26 November 2018
Registered Office: 3 Manor Close, Oadby, Leicester, LE2 4FE
Officers: Nikita Somaiya [1995] Director

**Laxmi BNS Holdings Limited**
Incorporated: 10 February 2010 Employees: 646
Net Worth: £22,051,180 Total Assets: £109,609,696
Registered Office: Unit 4 Bradfield Road, Ruislip, Middlesex, HA4 0NU
Officers: Govindji Hathi, Secretary; Alpa Hathi [1968] Director/HR; Govindji Thakershi Hathi [1941] Director; Samit Govindji Hathi [1967] Director

**Laxmico Limited**
Incorporated: 21 April 2009 Employees: 234
Net Worth: £3,491,584 Total Assets: £75,175,608
Registered Office: Unit 4 Bradfield Road, Ruislip, Middlesex, HA4 0NU
Major Shareholder: Samit Govindji Hathi
Officers: Govindji Hathi, Secretary; Alpa Hathi [1968] Director/HR; Govindji Thakershi Hathi [1941] Director; Samit Hathi [1967] Director/Pharmacist

**Layan Pharma Ltd**
*Incorporated:* 29 November 2018
*Registered Office:* 152-160 City Road, London, EC1V 2NX
*Shareholders:* Ahmed Badawy; Osama Abdelhamid
*Officers:* Abduallah Alradhi, Secretary; Mohammad Alrashdi, Secretary; Osama Abdelhamid [1984] Director/Chief Operations Officer (COO) [Egyptian]; Ahmed Badawy [1981] Director/Chief Executive Officer (CEO) [Egyptian]

**LB Pharma Limited**
*Incorporated:* 22 September 2017
*Registered Office:* 42 Holt Crescent, Cannock, Staffs, WS11 7ZA
*Officers:* Lorraine Lesley Gibbons, Secretary; Sally Gibbons [1984] Commercial Director

**LBC Solutions Limited**
*Incorporated:* 26 July 2005 *Employees:* 1
*Net Worth:* £80 *Total Assets:* £19,172
*Registered Office:* 35 Colworth House, Colworth Park, Sharnbrook, Bedford, MK44 1LQ
*Major Shareholder:* Ashok Kumar
*Officers:* Ashok Kumar [1958] Director

**LDC International Limited**
*Incorporated:* 19 January 2018
*Registered Office:* 1st Floor, Gallery Court, 28 Arcadia Avenue, London, N3 2FG
*Parent:* L.D. Collins & Co. Limited
*Officers:* Matthew Frank Philipps [1979] Managing Director

**Leadiant Biosciences Limited**
*Incorporated:* 15 April 2015 *Employees:* 15
*Net Worth:* £106,717,424 *Total Assets:* £112,069,976
*Registered Office:* 21 Holborn Viaduct, London, EC1A 2DY
*Officers:* Marco Maria Brughera [1955] Director [Italian]; Michael Ford [1946] Director/Chairman; Antonio Manuel Maia Devesa Gama Da Silva [1963] Director [Portuguese]

**Leafxtracts Ltd**
*Incorporated:* 18 October 2018
*Registered Office:* 26 Greenacres Avenue, Winnersh, Wokingham, Berks, RG41 5SX
*Shareholders:* Vijay Bedarkar; Rowland Gavin
*Officers:* Vijay Bedarkar [1987] Director/Manager; Rowland Gavin [1986] Director/Analyst

**Leap Pharma Ltd**
*Incorporated:* 30 May 2012
*Net Worth Deficit:* £188,895 *Total Assets:* £6,841
*Registered Office:* 13 The Causeway, Teddington, Middlesex, TW11 0JR
*Major Shareholder:* Francis Kwame Essuman
*Officers:* Francis Essuman, Secretary; Francis Kwame Essuman [1970] Director [Ghanaian]

**Leca Pharma Limited**
*Incorporated:* 14 July 2015
*Net Worth:* £22,462 *Total Assets:* £85,936
*Registered Office:* 8 Redwood Crescent, East Kilbride, S Lanarks, G74 5PA
*Major Shareholder:* Lewis Campbell
*Officers:* Lewis Campbell, Secretary; Lewis Campbell [1993] Director

**Leeds Industries (UK) Ltd**
*Incorporated:* 12 January 2016
*Net Worth:* £383 *Total Assets:* £644,510
*Registered Office:* 55a Palmerston Road, Sutton, Surrey, SM1 4QL
*Major Shareholder:* Abhijnan Mukherjee
*Officers:* Abhijnan Mukherjee [1985] Director

**Leems Solutions Limited**
*Incorporated:* 24 December 2018
*Registered Office:* Second Floor, 25 George Street, Luton, Beds, LU1 2AF
*Major Shareholder:* Mrudula Yalamareddy
*Officers:* Mrudula Yalamareddy [1990] Director [Indian]

**Legacy Private Limited**
*Incorporated:* 16 July 2018
*Registered Office:* 17 Blackberry Court, Woodmill Road, Hackney, London, E5 9GE
*Major Shareholder:* Nobantu Mukuruva
*Officers:* Nobantu Mukuruva, Secretary; Nobantu Mukuruva [1967] Director/Nurse

**Legendbio Beauty Group Limited**
*Incorporated:* 29 March 2016
*Registered Office:* 27 Old Gloucester Street, London, WC1N 3AX
*Major Shareholder:* Jianhua Liu
*Officers:* Jianhua Liu [1964] Business Director

**The Lens Factory (N.E) Ltd**
*Incorporated:* 13 February 2014 *Employees:* 3
*Net Worth Deficit:* £10,190 *Total Assets:* £87,187
*Registered Office:* Oakmere, Belmont Business Park, Durham, DH1 1TW
*Shareholders:* Adam Miles Gray; Paul Hepple
*Officers:* Adam Miles Gray [1993] Director; Paul Hepple [1969] Director

**Leo Laboratories Limited**
*Incorporated:* 14 June 1960 *Employees:* 141
*Net Worth:* £11,963,000 *Total Assets:* £95,717,000
*Registered Office:* Horizon, Honey Lane, Hurley, Maidenhead, Berks, SL6 6RJ
*Officers:* Philip Walker, Secretary; Gitte Pugholm Aabo [1967] Director/President, CEO [Danish]; Anders Kronborg [1964] Director [Danish]

**Leptrex Ltd.**
*Incorporated:* 28 September 2011
*Net Worth Deficit:* £24,353 *Total Assets:* £68,222
*Registered Office:* 135 Church Road, Folkestone, Kent, CT20 3ER
*Parent:* Allicin International Ltd
*Officers:* Carol Ann Coleman, Secretary; Norman John Bennett [1946] Director; Dr Edward Ramsey [1955] Director/Professor

**Leung Healthcare Limited**
*Incorporated:* 18 October 2011
*Net Worth:* £11,973 *Total Assets:* £15,600
*Registered Office:* Grafton House, Savile Road, Halifax, W Yorks, HX1 2BA
*Major Shareholder:* Kimberley Leung
*Officers:* Kimberley Leung [1988] Director

**Tim Lever Distribution Ltd.**
Incorporated: 17 June 2008
Net Worth: £128,239  Total Assets: £159,793
Registered Office: 38 Stonehouse Road, Sandford, Strathaven, S Lanarks, ML10 6PD
Shareholder: Timothy Matthew Lever
Officers: Timothy Matthew Lever [1966] Director/Distribution Agent; Julie Truman [1967] Director

**Leverton & Company Limited**
Incorporated: 18 December 1989
Registered Office: 1 Holly Street, Sheffield, S1 2GT
Officers: Ian Patrick Campbell [1955] Director/Chairman; Nathan James Smith [1976] Commercial Director; Leah Jane Styring [1978] Operations Director; Richard Ian Talbot [1978] Finance Director; Philip Neil Wood [1965] Production Director

**Lewis Healthcare Limited**
Incorporated: 21 December 1976
Net Worth: £1,041,576  Total Assets: £1,168,877
Registered Office: 19 Montpelier Avenue, Bexley, Kent, DA5 3AP
Shareholders: Brian Robert Lewis; Patricia Olivia Lewis
Officers: Patricia Olivia Lewis, Secretary; Brian Robert Lewis [1939] Director/Pharmacist; Patricia Olivia Lewis [1942] Director/Secretary

**B.R. Lewis Pharmaceuticals Limited**
Incorporated: 20 May 1987
Registered Office: 7 Regents Drive, Prudhoe, Northumberland, NE42 6PX
Shareholders: Doncaster Pharmaceuticals Group Limited; Amimed Direct Limited
Officers: David Balcombe [1966] Director; Derek Andrew Wilson [1964] Director

**Lexon (UK) Limited**
Incorporated: 6 July 1995  Employees: 636
Net Worth: £33,566,000  Total Assets: £110,045,000
Registered Office: 18 Oxleasow Road, Moons Moat East, Redditch, Worcs, B98 0RE
Parent: Lexon UK Holdings Limited
Officers: Timothy Paul Newman [1959] Director; Anup Sodha [1962] Director; Nitin Trembaklal Sodha [1955] Director/Pharmacist; Pankaj Sodha [1953] Director/Pharmacist; Pritesh Ramesh Sonpal [1969] Director/Buyer

**Lexon UK Holdings Limited**
Incorporated: 21 February 2018
Registered Office: 18 Oxleasow Road, Redditch, Worcs, B98 0RE
Officers: Anup Sodha [1962] Director; Nitin Trembaklal Sodha [1955] Director; Pankaj Sodha [1953] Director; Pritesh Ramesh Sonpal [1969] Director

**LGS Pharma Limited**
Incorporated: 9 August 2016
Registered Office: 2nd Floor, 151 Uxbridge Road, London, W13 9AU
Officers: Leeban Gulaid [1982] Director/Scientist

**Libertas Medical Ltd**
Incorporated: 30 January 2019
Registered Office: 2 Stamford Square, London, SW15 2BF
Major Shareholder: Richard Greatorex
Officers: Richard Greatorex [1964] Director/Self Employed - Healthcare Marketing Consultant

**Liberty Pacific Limited**
Incorporated: 15 April 2014
Previous: Medicare Products International Limited
Net Worth: £200  Total Assets: £200
Registered Office: The Gatehouse, 453 Cranbrook Road, Ilford, Essex, IG2 6EW
Officers: Michael Binder Bains [1963] Director/Salesperson

**Life on Healthcare Ltd**
Incorporated: 5 March 2009  Employees: 2
Net Worth: £78,586  Total Assets: £324,916
Registered Office: Unit C, Arlington Building, Bow Quarter, Fairfield Road, London, E3 2UB
Major Shareholder: Ganesh Krishna
Officers: Srinivas Gudipati [1976] Director/Businessman; Ganesh Krishna [1977] Director/Business Person

**Life Science Healthcare UK Limited**
Incorporated: 29 October 2018
Registered Office: 44 Douglas Place, Oldbrook, Milton Keynes, Bucks, MK6 2XG
Major Shareholder: Aroos Abdul Careem
Officers: Aroos Abdul Careem [1970] Director [Sri Lankan]; Husni Ahamed Mohamed Rafaudeen [1992] Director [Sri Lankan]

**Lifecare Limited**
Incorporated: 16 November 1994
Net Worth: £80,643  Total Assets: £215,151
Registered Office: The Surgery, Scotton Road, Scotter, Gainsborough, Lincs, DN21 3SB
Shareholder: Stacey Louise Jolly
Officers: Elaine Anderson, Secretary; Dr David Alan Jolly [1961] Director/Doctor; Dr Robert George Padley [1965] Director/Doctor (GP); Dr Satpal Singh Shekhawat [1979] Director/Doctor (GP) [Indian]

**Lifecell EMEA Limited**
Incorporated: 31 May 2012  Employees: 7
Net Worth Deficit: £20,012,432  Total Assets: £3,918,294
Registered Office: c/o Allergan, 1st Floor, Marlow International, The Parkway, Marlow, Bucks, SL7 1YL
Parent: Allergan Holdco UK Limited
Officers: Patricia Maria Haran, Secretary; Judith Tomkins, Secretary; Glen Curran [1973] Director; Nicholas Iain Hudson [1975] Director; Paul Johnson [1972] Director; Duncan James Reeves [1978] Director

**Lifenza UK Limited**
Incorporated: 26 September 2017
Registered Office: Unit 12/A Biz Space, Monsall Road, Manchester, M40 8WN
Shareholder: Prakash Badgujar
Officers: Prakash Badgujar, Secretary; Prakash Badgujar [1979] Director

**Lifeshield Limited**
Incorporated: 7 September 1998  Employees: 2
Net Worth: £21,374  Total Assets: £161,652
Registered Office: 3 Old Estate Yard, North Stoke Lane, Upton Cheyney, Bristol, BS30 6ND
Major Shareholder: Irina Ananina
Officers: Steven John Blackmore [1968] Director

**Lighthouse Mercury Limited**
Incorporated: 8 January 2004
Net Worth: £9,438  Total Assets: £176,930
Registered Office: Southlands, Cuckfield Lane, Warninglid, Haywards Heath, W Sussex, RH17 5SN
Officers: Dianne Janet Brough, Secretary; Miles Alan Brough [1951] Director

**Lil-Lets UK Ltd**
Incorporated: 11 May 1955  Employees: 25
Net Worth: £2,504,000  Total Assets: £7,884,000
Registered Office: Radcliffe House, Blenheim Court, Solihull, W Midlands, B91 2AA
Officers: Glen Kelly, Secretary; Jacobus Johannes Gertenbach [1971] Director/Chief Finance Officer [South African]; Daniel Wild [1976] Director/General Manager

**Lillidale Ltd.**
Incorporated: 26 May 1993  Employees: 10
Net Worth: £1,477,431  Total Assets: £1,940,225
Registered Office: Pig Oak Farm, Holt, Wimborne, Dorset, BH21 7DG
Shareholders: Melville Anthony Claremont; Michelle Anne Claremont
Officers: Michelle Anne Claremont, Secretary; Melville Anthony Claremont [1959] Director; Michelle Anne Claremont [1967] Director

**Lime Pharmacy Limited**
Incorporated: 23 December 2008
Net Worth: £569,173  Total Assets: £2,015,730
Registered Office: 192 Norwich Road, Norwich, NR5 0EX
Parent: Costessey (Norwich) Holdings Limited
Officers: Meena Devlukia [1963] Commercial Director; Prabodh Nilkanth Devlukia [1957] Director

**Limes Pharma Ltd**
Incorporated: 6 February 2019
Registered Office: Kemp House, 152-160 City Road, London, EC1V 2NX
Shareholders: Ahmed Hagisufi; Muhammad Habib; Dadir Habib Mohamed Mohamed
Officers: Muhammad Habib [1978] Director/Self Employed; Ahmed Hagisufi [1979] Director/Entrepreneur [American]; Dadir Habib Mohamed Mohamed [1971] Director/Self Employed

**Linderma Limited**
Incorporated: 17 December 2001  Employees: 2
Net Worth: £21,238  Total Assets: £27,107
Registered Office: Allenby Laboratories, Wigan Road, Westhoughton, Bolton, Lancs, BL5 2AL
Parent: C D Medical Limited
Officers: Lee Fairbrother, Secretary; Michael Gatenby [1942] Director; Gerard Michael Dominic Pessagno [1952] Director

**Linepharma International Limited**
Incorporated: 30 May 2013  Employees: 3
Net Worth: £3,147,673  Total Assets: £4,059,916
Registered Office: 16 Upper Woburn Place, London, WC1H 0BS
Officers: Jean Quinot [1956] Director [Swiss]; Thierry Sempere [1962] Director [French]; Marion Sophie Ulmann [1980] Director [French]

**Lionmark Limited**
Incorporated: 23 May 2014
Registered Office: 925 Finchley Road, London, NW11 7PE
Major Shareholder: Rajinder Singh Banga
Officers: Ramtin Siaghi, Secretary; Rajinder Singh Banga [1962] Director

**Livanova UK Limited**
Incorporated: 28 June 2004  Employees: 62
Previous: Sorin Group UK Limited
Net Worth: £4,077,083  Total Assets: £27,514,002
Registered Office: 1370 Montpellier Court, Gloucester Business Park, Gloucester, GL3 4AH
Parent: Livanova PLC
Officers: Alexander Hans-Josef Neumann [1969] Director/Vice President Corporate Legal Affairs [German]; Stefano Torelli [1961] Director [Italian]

**Livewell Naturals Limited**
Incorporated: 4 December 2018
Registered Office: 33 Mason Road, Coventry, Warwicks, CV6 7FF
Shareholders: Cristian Stefan Diaconescu; Pritesh Chandravaden Parekh; Dipak Chandravaden Parekh
Officers: Cristian Stefan Diaconescu [1988] Director/Fitness Instructor [Romanian]; Dipak Chandravaden Parekh [1981] Director; Pritesh Chandravaden Parekh [1980] Director/Health Club Manager

**LK Health Ltd**
Incorporated: 26 November 2018
Registered Office: 60 Legon Avenue, Romford, Essex, RM7 0UJ
Major Shareholder: Lansana Kailondo
Officers: Lansana Kailondo [1994] Director/Diagnostic Radiographer

**Walter Lloyd & Son Limited**
Incorporated: 5 July 1995  Employees: 17
Net Worth: £430,896  Total Assets: £817,765
Registered Office: 12 Lammas Street, Carmarthen, Dyfed, SA31 3AD
Shareholders: Megan Jayne Griffiths; Terry Baugh Griffiths; Christopher John James
Officers: Terry Baugh Griffiths, Secretary/Farmer; Megan Jayne Griffiths [1972] Director/Pharmacist; Terry Baugh Griffiths [1946] Director/Farmer; Christopher John James [1962] Director/Pharmacist

**John Lloyd Dental Equipment Services Limited**
Incorporated: 1 June 2000  Employees: 1
Net Worth: £780,437  Total Assets: £836,585
Registered Office: Prince William House, 10 Lower Church Street, Ashby De La Zouch, Leics, LE65 1AB
Major Shareholder: John Llewellyn Lloyd
Officers: Richard Lloyd, Secretary; John Llewellyn Lloyd [1957] Director/Service Technician

**Lloyds Pharmacy Clinical Homecare Limited**
Incorporated: 10 November 1992  Employees: 998
Previous: Bupa Home Healthcare Limited
Net Worth: £14,703,000  Total Assets: £155,136,992
Registered Office: Sapphire Court, Walsgrave Triangle, Coventry, Warwicks, CV2 2TX
Officers: Nichola Legg, Secretary; Toby Matthew Anderson [1973] Director; Marcus Hilger [1977] Finance Director [German]; Catherine McDermott [1968] Operations Director; Nigel Swift [1966] Director

**LM3 Business Ltd**
Incorporated: 4 September 2008
Registered Office: Office 59, Zebra Connections Business Centre, Southern Way, Harlow, Essex, CM18 7BL
Shareholders: Evelyn Allen; Samuel Adebambo Allen
Officers: Evelyn Allen, Secretary; Evelyn Allen [1973] Director/Pharmacist; Samuel Adebambo Allen [1967] Director/Lecturer

**Logichem Ltd**
*Incorporated:* 4 February 2006  *Employees:* 6
*Net Worth:* £350,517  *Total Assets:* £1,085,008
*Registered Office:* 869 High Road, London, N12 8QA
*Shareholders:* Massoud Nooshabadi; Hamid Reza Tasbihgou; Valerie Tasbihgou
*Officers:* Valerie Tasbihgou, Secretary; Massoud Nooshabadi [1959] Director/Business Development [Irish]; Hamid Reza Tasbihgou [1955] Director

**London Health Sciences Ltd**
*Incorporated:* 15 September 2016
*Net Worth Deficit:* £6,735
*Registered Office:* 20-22 Wenlock Road, London, N1 7GU
*Major Shareholder:* Kaya Duman
*Officers:* Kaya Duman [1977] Director [Turkish]

**London Health Suppliers Limited**
*Incorporated:* 26 January 2015
*Net Worth Deficit:* £3,983  *Total Assets:* £14,902
*Registered Office:* 122 Beddington Lane, Croydon, Surrey, CR0 4YZ
*Shareholder:* Mohammed Osman Uddin
*Officers:* Mohammed Naveed Ali [1967] Director; Amitkumar Chudasama [1975] Director [Portuguese]; Mehul Chudasama [1979] Director [Portuguese]; Mohammed Osman Uddin [1976] Director

**London Healthcare Limited**
*Incorporated:* 17 October 2000
*Net Worth Deficit:* £13,201  *Total Assets:* £8,560
*Registered Office:* Prince of Wales House, 18-19 Salmon Fields Business Village, Royton, Oldham, Lancs, OL2 6HT
*Major Shareholder:* Mohammed Abdul Hameed Taha
*Officers:* Mohammed Abdul Hameed Taha [1970] Director/Businessman [Emirati]

**London Spirit for Trading Limited**
*Incorporated:* 29 January 2018
*Registered Office:* 40 Fentonville Street, Sheffield, S11 8BB
*Major Shareholder:* Mootaz Salman
*Officers:* Dr Mootaz Mowfak Salman [1984] Director/Health and Wellbeing [Iraqi]

**London Supplements Distribution Ltd**
*Incorporated:* 18 May 2018
*Registered Office:* Kemp House, 160 City Road, London, EC1V 2NX
*Officers:* John Bradley Carless [1988] Director/IT Consultant

**London United Exports Limited**
*Incorporated:* 23 April 1987  *Employees:* 6
*Net Worth:* £586,188  *Total Assets:* £719,077
*Registered Office:* First Floor, Kirkland House, 11-15 Peterborough Road, Harrow, Middlesex, HA1 2AX
*Shareholders:* Karina Mohan Daryanani; Sunil Daryanani Mohan
*Officers:* Karina Mohan Daryanani, Secretary; Sunil Mohan Daryanani [1961] Director

**Longevity Life Ltd**
*Incorporated:* 13 August 2018
*Registered Office:* Jacksons Accountants Ltd, 98 Lancaster Road, Newcastle-under-Lyme, Staffs, ST5 1DS
*Shareholders:* Richard Francis Degg; Karen Sandra Darlington
*Officers:* Karen Sandra Darlington [1974] Director; Richard Francis Degg [1977] Director

**Lorteben Trading Co., Ltd**
*Incorporated:* 25 March 2015
*Registered Office:* Room 101, Maple House, 118 High Street, Purley, Surrey, CR8 2AD
*Major Shareholder:* Kejiang Li
*Officers:* Kejiang Li [1983] Director/Merchant [Chinese]

**LS Pharma UK Limited**
*Incorporated:* 3 October 2018
*Registered Office:* 117 Pear Tree Crescent, Derby, DE23 8RQ
*Major Shareholder:* Lubna Shaheen
*Officers:* Lubna Shaheen [1992] Director

**LSP Bio Limited**
*Incorporated:* 17 February 2009
*Net Worth Deficit:* £173,274  *Total Assets:* £4,484
*Registered Office:* 47 Sandhills Road, Barnt Green, Birmingham, B45 8NP
*Shareholders:* Stephen John Morgan; Mark Lewis
*Officers:* Stephen John Morgan, Secretary; Mark Lewis [1957] Director; Stephen John Morgan [1957] Director/Chartered Accountant

**LTT Pharma Limited**
*Incorporated:* 19 May 2008  *Employees:* 4
*Net Worth:* £73,343  *Total Assets:* £93,343
*Registered Office:* 18 Oxleasow Road, East Moons Moat, Redditch, Worcs, B98 0RE
*Parent:* Lexon UK Holdings Limited
*Officers:* Pritesh Ramesh Sonpal, Secretary/Buyer; Anup Sodha [1962] Director; Nitin Trembaklal Sodha [1955] Director/Pharmacist; Pankaj Sodha [1953] Director/Pharmacist; Pritesh Ramesh Sonpal [1969] Director

**Luban & Murr Ltd**
*Incorporated:* 28 March 2017
*Registered Office:* 20-22 Wenlock Road, London, N1 7GU
*Major Shareholder:* Saed Mohamed Jama
*Officers:* Saed Mohamed Jama [1975] Director/Entrepreneur

**Lucid Wholesale Ltd**
*Incorporated:* 15 January 2018
*Registered Office:* 20-22 Wenlock Road, London, N1 7GU
*Major Shareholder:* Robbie Colin Radford
*Officers:* Robbie Colin Radford [1975] Director

**Lucis Pharma Ltd**
*Incorporated:* 26 November 2012  *Employees:* 2
*Net Worth:* £1,608,028  *Total Assets:* £2,184,054
*Registered Office:* Aston Chase, 14 Aston Magna, Moreton in Marsh, Glos, GL56 9QQ
*Shareholders:* Kathryn Louise Diston-Hunter; Lucis Holdings Limited
*Officers:* Kathryn Louise Diston-Hunter, Secretary; Kathryn Louise Diston-Hunter [1976] Director/Business Development; Stuart Diston-Hunter [1973] Director/Administrator

**Lucky Herbalife24 Limited**
*Incorporated:* 9 September 2013
*Registered Office:* 3 Grosvenor Road, Westcliff on Sea, Essex, SS0 8ER
*Major Shareholder:* Adrian Nita
*Officers:* Adrian Nita [1977] Director/Marketing Manager [Italian]

**Lufuma B2b Services Ltd**
*Incorporated:* 10 October 2014
*Registered Office:* 30 Calverton Road, London, E6 2NT
*Major Shareholder:* Elie Mangayi Tsika
*Officers:* Elie Guy Hervais Mangayi Tsika [1974] Director/Public Relations/CEO [French]

**Lumiradx International Ltd**
*Incorporated:* 10 July 2014  *Employees:* 3
*Net Worth:* £1,637,221  *Total Assets:* £11,211,552
*Registered Office:* 3 More London Riverside, London, SE1 2AQ
*Parent:* Lumira Holdings Ltd
*Officers:* Dr Jerome Francis McAleer [1955] Director/Chief Scientific Officer; Dr David Scott [1956] Director/Chief Technology Officer; Ron Zwanziger [1954] Director/President & CEO

**Lundbeck Limited**
*Incorporated:* 1 February 1972  *Employees:* 54
*Net Worth:* £16,451,111  *Total Assets:* £23,865,264
*Registered Office:* 2nd Floor, Building 3, Abbey View, Everard Close, St Albans, Herts, AL1 2PS
*Parent:* Lundbeck Group Limited
*Officers:* Roberto Lapenna, Secretary; Thomas Bo Bjorn Klee [1971] Managing Director [Danish]; Joao Carlos Nunes Rocha [1958] Director/Chairman [Brazilian]

**Lupin Healthcare (UK) Limited**
*Incorporated:* 5 June 2009  *Employees:* 15
*Previous:* Lupin (Europe) Limited
*Net Worth Deficit:* £2,978,669  *Total Assets:* £9,375,929
*Registered Office:* Second Floor, The Urban Building, 3-9 Albert Street, Slough, Berks, SL1 2BE
*Parent:* Lupin Atlantis Holdings SA
*Officers:* Andrew Michael McDonald, Secretary; Benjamin James Ellis [1971] Director; Sunil Makharia [1959] Director/Executive VP - Finance [Indian]; Thierry Robert Andre Volle [1958] Director/President of EMEA [French]

**Luye Pharma Ltd**
*Incorporated:* 13 September 2018
*Registered Office:* Suite 1, 3rd Floor, 11-12 St James's Square, London, SW1Y 4LB
*Officers:* Bruno Delie [1963] Director/GM Luye Supply AG [French]; Hua Jiang [1977] Director/Vice President [Chinese]; Yehong Zhang [1963] Director/Business Executive [Chinese]

**LV Global Limited**
*Incorporated:* 9 June 2014
*Net Worth Deficit:* £6,000  *Total Assets:* £3,136
*Registered Office:* Unit 5a Wadsworth Business Centre, 21 Wadsworth Road, Perivale, Greenford, Middlesex, UB6 7LQ
*Major Shareholder:* Lakshmi Vuyala
*Officers:* Vinay Kumar Jaiswal [1977] Director; Lakshmi Vuyala [1965] Director

**Lyferoots Ltd**
*Incorporated:* 9 January 2019
*Registered Office:* Flat 3, Dewey Court, 7 St Marks Square, Bromley, Kent, BR2 9UZ
*Major Shareholder:* Egzona Makolli
*Officers:* Egzona Makolli [1991] Director

**Lyshaug Enterprises Limited**
*Incorporated:* 21 November 2017
*Registered Office:* Gibson House, 800 High Road, London, N17 0DH
*Shareholder:* David Flower
*Officers:* David Flower [1949] Director/Businessman [American]

**LZ Pharma Ltd**
*Incorporated:* 27 July 2017
*Registered Office:* 52 Warwick Close, Bury, Lancs, BL8 1RT
*Officers:* Lyndsay Pomfret [1984] Director

**M & A Pharmachem Limited**
*Incorporated:* 1 February 1977  *Employees:* 139
*Net Worth:* £9,661,144  *Total Assets:* £21,316,352
*Registered Office:* Allenby Laboratories, Wigan Road, Westhoughton, Bolton, Lancs, BL5 2AL
*Shareholder:* CD Medical Limited
*Officers:* Lee Fairbrother, Secretary; Elsie Maureen Armstrong [1951] Director; Michael Gatenby [1942] Sales & Marketing Director; Gerard Michael Dominic Pessagno [1952] Director

**M & M Taste of Harmony Export Ltd**
*Incorporated:* 3 February 2016  *Employees:* 2
*Previous:* Elsner System Ltd
*Net Worth Deficit:* £18,756  *Total Assets:* £9,769
*Registered Office:* 39 Withypitts, Turners Hill, Crawley, W Sussex, RH10 4PJ
*Shareholder:* Melinda Molnar
*Officers:* Melinda Molnar [1978] Director [Hungarian]

**M & N Traders Limited**
*Incorporated:* 20 November 1995  *Employees:* 14
*Net Worth:* £3,687,437  *Total Assets:* £5,473,454
*Registered Office:* 925 Finchley Road, London, NW11 7PE
*Shareholders:* Narinder Singh Kohli; Manjinder Kaur Kohli
*Officers:* Narinder Singh Kohli, Secretary [Indian]; Manjinder Kaur Kohli [1964] Director

**M D M Healthcare Ltd**
*Incorporated:* 18 April 2008  *Employees:* 2
*Net Worth:* £681,065  *Total Assets:* £1,039,737
*Registered Office:* Granite Building, 6 Stanley Street, Liverpool, L1 6AF
*Shareholders:* Daniel Bracey; Marcus Fritze; Marco Wolfgang Huelsbeck
*Officers:* Daniel Bracey [1974] Director; Marcus Fritze [1974] Director [German]; Marco Wolfgang Huelsbeck [1975] Director [German]

**M.E.D. Supplies Limited**
*Incorporated:* 12 November 1990
*Net Worth:* £3,291,916  *Total Assets:* £3,382,626
*Registered Office:* Tyr-Bryn, Church Street, Talgarth, Powys, LD3 0DW
*Shareholders:* Isobel Cathryn Atac; Murat Huseyin Atac
*Officers:* Isobel Cathryn Atac, Secretary; Huseyin Murat Atac [1949] Director/Pharmacist [Turkish]; Isobel Cathryn Atac [1956] Director/Pharmacist

**M.G. Dental Supplies Limited**
*Incorporated:* 14 June 1977
*Net Worth:* £2,634  *Total Assets:* £8,339
*Registered Office:* Vernon House, 40 New North Road, Huddersfield, W Yorks, HD1 5LS
*Officers:* Margaret Elizabeth Davies Gill, Secretary; Malcolm Gill [1944] Director/Dental Technician; Margaret Elizabeth Davies Gill [1946] Director/Company Secretary

**M.R.S. Scientific Limited**
Incorporated: 27 June 1996  Employees: 13
Net Worth: £546,040  Total Assets: £1,180,663
Registered Office: 5 Pilot Close, Fulmar Way, Wickford, Essex, SS11 8YW
Shareholders: Michael Robert Smith; Lesley Ann Smith
Officers: Lesley Ann Smith, Company Secretary/Director; Caroline Margaret Miles [1976] Director/Sales Manager; Anthony Craig Smith [1980] Director/Operations Manager; Brett Michael Smith [1986] Director/Purchasing Manager; Lesley Ann Smith [1952] Company Secretary/Director; Luke Andrew Smith [1988] Director/Logistics Manager; Michael Robert Smith [1953] Director

**M2 Healthcare Ltd**
Incorporated: 20 May 2014
Registered Office: 11 Church Road, Great Bookham, Leatherhead, Surrey, KT23 3PB
Major Shareholder: Jihad Masoud
Officers: Jihad Masoud [1980] Director/General Manager [Syrian]

**Macacha Health Limited**
Incorporated: 30 January 2015  Employees: 2
Net Worth Deficit: £199,210  Total Assets: £55,277
Registered Office: 7 Hatton Street, London, NW8 8PL
Major Shareholder: Ines Marcela Hermida
Officers: Ines Hermida, Secretary; Ines Hermida [1965] Director [Italian]

**Macks Ltd.**
Incorporated: 15 December 2000  Employees: 8
Net Worth: £4,627,030  Total Assets: £6,780,867
Registered Office: 24 Bedford Row, London, WC1R 4TQ
Officers: Kishore Kumar Mohan Lakhwani [1974] Director [Danish]

**Macratio Limited**
Incorporated: 25 June 2014  Employees: 1
Net Worth: £58  Total Assets: £1,942
Registered Office: 3 Wheatsheaf Way, Waterbeach, Cambridge, CB25 9GG
Major Shareholder: Ailsa Claire Liddle
Officers: Ailsa Claire Liddle [1977] Director/Pharmaceutical Consulting

**Macrobiotics Group Ltd**
Incorporated: 20 May 2016
Net Worth: £61,623  Total Assets: £139,151
Registered Office: 156a Burnt Oak Broadway, Edgware, Middlesex, HA8 0AX
Major Shareholder: Kyriakos Kyriakopoulos
Officers: Kyriakos Kyriakopoulos [1970] Director/Sales Manager [Greek]

**Mad Doctor Holdings Limited**
Incorporated: 26 January 2017
Net Worth Deficit: £3,929  Total Assets: £3,588
Registered Office: Unit 28 Graphite Way, Hadfield, Glossop, Derbys, SK13 1QH
Major Shareholder: Damian Savage
Officers: Damian Savage [1967] Director

**MAF Pharma Limited**
Incorporated: 12 June 2009  Employees: 4
Net Worth: £167,310  Total Assets: £275,351
Registered Office: 31 Townsend Place, Kirkcaldy, Fife, KY1 1HB
Officers: Mark Anthony Hedley, Secretary; Frederick Thomas Gourlay [1949] Director/Accountant; Mark Anthony Hedley [1968] Director

**Malem Medical Limited**
Incorporated: 9 June 1983  Employees: 2
Net Worth Deficit: £415,298  Total Assets: £2,270,496
Registered Office: Fairview House, Victoria Place, Carlisle, Cumbria, CA1 1HP
Shareholders: Hilal Malem; Valerie Joy Malem
Officers: Valerie Joy Malem, Secretary; Dr Hilal Malem [1949] Director; Valerie Joy Malem [1955] Director/Secretary

**Mammoth Dental Supplies Ltd**
Incorporated: 4 January 2017
Net Worth: £27,399  Total Assets: £33,364
Registered Office: Kemp House, 152 City Road, London, EC1V 2NX
Shareholders: Benjamin Lloyd; Sarah Lloyd
Officers: Benjamin Lloyd [1979] Director; Sarah Lloyd [1980] Director

**Manek Healthcare Ltd**
Incorporated: 21 November 2018
Registered Office: 73 High Street, Hampton Hill, Hampton, Surrey, TW12 1NH
Officers: Ajay Sharma [1978] Director/Chief Pharmacist

**Manichem Limited**
Incorporated: 2 January 2007  Employees: 188
Net Worth Deficit: £3,600,441  Total Assets: £9,575,481
Registered Office: 109-111 Field End Road, Pinner, Middlesex, HA5 1QG
Parent: Merrygood Ltd
Officers: Krishma Vikash Patel [1981] Director/Pharmacist; Niral Narendra Patel [1981] Director; Vikash Patel [1982] Director; Viresh Patel [1985] Director

**Manor Drug Company (Nottingham) Limited (The)**
Incorporated: 22 November 1967  Employees: 49
Net Worth: £21,460,402  Total Assets: £27,637,564
Registered Office: 11 Manchester Road, Walkden, Manchester, M28 3NS
Parent: W R Evans Healthcare Ltd
Officers: Angela Jane Cattee [1953] Director; Peter Cattee [1952] Director; Geoffrey Alan Tims [1943] Director

**Mansett Limited**
Incorporated: 4 December 1987
Net Worth: £1,496,212  Total Assets: £1,496,212
Registered Office: A & L Goodbody, 42-46 Fountain Street, Belfast, BT1 5EF
Parent: UDG Healthcare (UK) Holdings Limited
Officers: Damien Moynagh, Secretary; Grainne McAleese [1979] Director [Irish]; Louise Tallon [1979] Director [Irish]

**Manta Medical Limited**
Incorporated: 25 October 2017
Registered Office: 27 Old Gloucester Street, London, WC1N 3AX
Shareholder: Tomas Svoboda
Officers: Tomas Svoboda [1983] Director [Czech]

**Manx Generics Limited**
Incorporated: 22 July 2015
Net Worth Deficit: £1,616,633  Total Assets: £176,726
Registered Office: Taylor Group House, Wedgnock Lane, Warwick, CV34 5YA
Shareholders: Dudley Taylor Pharmacies Limited; Manx Healthcare Limited
Officers: Michael James Taylor [1957] Director; Richard Jeffery Taylor [1955] Director

**Manx Healthcare Limited**
*Incorporated:* 3 March 1994  *Employees:* 24
*Net Worth:* £2,401,544  *Total Assets:* £9,309,355
*Registered Office:* Taylor Group House, Wedgnock Lane, Warwick, CV34 5YA
*Parent:* Richard's Pharma Limited
*Officers:* Laurence Dudley Taylor, Secretary; Malcolm Clive Ramsay [1964] Director; Simone Elizabeth Taylor [1958] Director

**Manx Pharma Ltd**
*Incorporated:* 24 September 1996
*Net Worth Deficit:* £249,618  *Total Assets:* £195,131
*Registered Office:* Taylor Group House, Wedgnock Lane, Warwick, CV34 5YA
*Parent:* Richard's Pharma Limited
*Officers:* Laurence Dudley Taylor, Secretary; Malcolm Clive Ramsay [1964] Director; Simone Elizabeth Taylor [1958] Director

**Mapaex Consumer Healthcare (UK) Private Limited**
*Incorporated:* 25 May 2018
*Registered Office:* c/o Singhania & Co, 2nd Floor, 134 Buckingham Palace Road, London, SW1W 9SA
*Officers:* Rajendra Chandrakant Patel [1968] Director [Indian]

**Maplespring Limited**
*Incorporated:* 22 August 1983  *Employees:* 1
*Net Worth:* £1,104,358  *Total Assets:* £1,114,493
*Registered Office:* Accountancy House, 90 Walworth Road, London, SE1 6SW
*Shareholder:* Sailesh Manubhai Patel
*Officers:* Dr. Sailesh Manubhai Patel, Secretary; Daxa Sailesh Patel [1957] Director; Dr. Sailesh Manubhai Patel [1957] Director

**Maplewood Investments Limited**
*Incorporated:* 13 March 2003
*Net Worth Deficit:* £37,596  *Total Assets:* £540,039
*Registered Office:* 22 Gifford Road, Benfleet, Essex, SS7 5XU
*Officers:* Tinuola Sarah Anike Agbejule, Secretary; Adewale Olanrewaju Agbejule [1965] Director/Pharmacist; Irenitemi Michael Oluwatobiloba Agbejule [1999] Sales Director; Tinuola Sarah Anike Agbejule [1969] Director/Accountant

**Maps Healthcare Limited**
*Incorporated:* 2 March 2006  *Employees:* 3
*Net Worth:* £175,285  *Total Assets:* £187,548
*Registered Office:* 3rd Floor, Scottish Provident House, 76-80 College Road, Harrow, Middlesex, HA1 1BQ
*Shareholders:* Nilesh Prataprai Mehta; Sidharth Mehta
*Officers:* Sidharth Mehta, Secretary; Nilesh Prataprai Mehta [1962] Director; Sidharth Mehta [1980] Director

**Maria-Cristina Culita Ltd**
*Incorporated:* 17 March 2014
*Net Worth:* £2,487  *Total Assets:* £15,520
*Registered Office:* The Island House, Midsomer Norton, Radstock, Somerset, BA3 2DZ
*Major Shareholder:* Maria Cristina Culita
*Officers:* Maria Cristina Culita [1986] Director [Romanian]

**Marigold Footcare Ltd.**
*Incorporated:* 1 February 1984
*Net Worth Deficit:* £43,161  *Total Assets:* £29,042
*Registered Office:* 134 Montrose Avenue, Edgware, Middlesex, HA8 0DR
*Major Shareholder:* Shamim Fatima Khan
*Officers:* Rukshana Khan, Secretary; Shamim Fatima Khan [1945] Director

**Marlborough Pharmaceuticals Limited**
*Incorporated:* 24 January 2005
*Net Worth:* £3,675,708  *Total Assets:* £10,607,300
*Registered Office:* Suite 1, 3rd Floor, 11-12 St James's Square, London, SW1Y 4LB
*Parent:* Atnahs Pharma UK Limited
*Officers:* Mark John Cotterill [1965] Director; Amit Vijaykumar Patel [1978] Director; Bhikhu Chhotabhai Patel [1947] Director; Dipen Vijaykumar Patel [1979] Director; Vijay Kumar Chhotabhai Patel [1949] Director

**Martal Cosmetics Limited**
*Incorporated:* 25 January 1966
*Net Worth:* £463,782  *Total Assets:* £503,632
*Registered Office:* New Derwent House, 69-73 Theobalds Road, London, WC1X 8TA
*Shareholders:* Andrea Heather Sarner; Marcus Sarner
*Officers:* Andrea Heather Sarner, Secretary/Director; Marcus Sarner [1934] Director

**Martini International Ltd**
*Incorporated:* 5 October 2018
*Registered Office:* 7 Hillside Road, Radcliffe on Trent, Nottingham, NG12 2GZ
*Shareholders:* Flavia Martini; Valerio Martini; Alessandra Giannelli
*Officers:* Alessandra Giannelli [1964] Director/Nurse [Italian]; Flavia Martini [2001] Director/Student [Italian]; Valerio Martini [1970] Director/Businessman [Italian]

**Marvellous Pharma Ltd**
*Incorporated:* 20 November 2017
*Registered Office:* Abbey Gate Business Center, Unit B, 35 Hitchin Road, Luton, Beds, LU2 0ER
*Major Shareholder:* Medhat Mahmoud
*Officers:* Medhat Mahmoud [1973] Director/Pharmacist [Egyptian]

**Masa Pharma Ltd**
*Incorporated:* 3 January 2017
*Net Worth Deficit:* £11,523  *Total Assets:* £3,414
*Registered Office:* 9 Stocks Street, Manchester, M8 8GW
*Major Shareholder:* Ali Al-Hashimi
*Officers:* Ali Al-Hashimi [1985] Director/Pharmaceutical

**Masir Ltd**
*Incorporated:* 9 August 2018
*Registered Office:* Flat 14, 2 Vicarage Gate, London, W8 4HH
*Shareholders:* Sina Farshineh Adl; Mahsa Ranjbar
*Officers:* Sina Farshineh Adl [1984] Director/Businessman [Iranian]; Mahsa Ranjbar [1986] Director/Entrepreneur

**Mast - Art Group Limited**
*Incorporated:* 13 December 2018
*Registered Office:* 17 Green Lanes, London, N16 9BS
*Shareholder:* Umran Aysan
*Officers:* Umran Aysan [1976] Director [Turkish]

**Masta Limited**
*Incorporated:* 6 July 1984  *Employees:* 71
*Net Worth:* £4,440,303  *Total Assets:* £7,836,798
*Registered Office:* Sapphire Court, Walsgrave Triangle, Coventry, Warwicks, CV2 2TX
*Parent:* Medical Advisory Services for Travellers Abroad Limited
*Officers:* Nichola Louise Legg, Secretary; Toby Matthew Anderson [1973] Director; Marcus Hilger [1977] Finance Director [German]; Catherine McDermott [1968] Operations Director; Nigel Swift [1966] Marketing & Sales Director

**Masters Pharmaceuticals Limited**
*Incorporated:* 17 October 1984  *Employees:* 85
*Net Worth:* £485,273  *Total Assets:* £9,841,748
*Registered Office:* 380 Centennial Avenue, Centennial Park, Elstree, Herts, WD6 3TJ
*Officers:* Suzad Masters [1958] Director; Zulfikar Masters [1956] Director/Chairman

**Matoke Holdings Limited**
*Incorporated:* 4 February 2010
*Previous:* Healing Honey International Ltd
*Net Worth:* £1,030,079  *Total Assets:* £1,449,433
*Registered Office:* 2 Michaels Court, Hanney Road, Southmoor, Abingdon, Oxon, OX13 5HR
*Officers:* Ian David Pearson Jenkins, Secretary; Jonathan Cooke [1950] Director; James Andrew Currie [1967] Director; Matthew Scott Dryden [1958] Director; Michael Patrick Hoskins [1958] Director; Ian David Pearson Jenkins [1946] Director; Brian Dennis McGowan [1944] Director; Ian Lawrence Staples [1946] Director/Chief Executive; Stuart Michael Staples [1973] Sales Director; Alan Westwood [1951] Director

**Matrix Healthcare Limited**
*Incorporated:* 3 January 2019
*Registered Office:* 23S46, Mereside Alderley Park, Alderley Edge, Cheshire, SK10 4TG
*Parent:* Matrix Healthcare Solutions Limited
*Officers:* Charles Edward Toomey [1962] Director

**Matrix Healthcare Solutions Limited**
*Incorporated:* 19 October 2016  *Employees:* 3
*Net Worth Deficit:* £44,897  *Total Assets:* £202,916
*Registered Office:* 23S46 Mereside Alderley Park, Alderley Edge, Cheshire, SK10 4TG
*Major Shareholder:* Charles Edward Toomey
*Officers:* Charles Edward Toomey [1962] Director

**Matt 6:33 Ltd**
*Incorporated:* 5 February 2019
*Registered Office:* 20-22 Wenlock Road, London, N1 7GU
*Officers:* Ruth Seymour [1977] Director [Botswanan]

**Matt L Consultancy Ltd**
*Incorporated:* 17 May 2018
*Registered Office:* c/o Aanda Accounting Services, 2 Acorn Grove, Kingswood, Surrey, KT20 6QT
*Major Shareholder:* Matthew Lewis
*Officers:* Matthew Lewis [1974] Director

**Matter Drinks Trading Ltd**
*Incorporated:* 21 November 2017
*Registered Office:* Woodberry House, 2 Woodberry Grove, Finchley, London, N12 0DR
*Major Shareholder:* Austen David Merritt
*Officers:* Austen David Merritt [1952] Director

**Mawdsley-Brooks & Company Limited**
*Incorporated:* 24 July 1895  *Employees:* 480
*Net Worth:* £25,210,000  *Total Assets:* £80,231,000
*Registered Office:* P O Box 18, Number Three, South Langworthy Road, Salford, M50 2PW
*Parent:* Mawdsleys Group Investments Limited
*Officers:* Stephanie Joy Ellison, Secretary; Darren Robert Belcher [1966] Director; Ian Colin Brownlee [1948] Managing Director; Carol Currimjee [1946] Director; Stephanie Joy Ellison [1958] Director; Dr John Howard Mawdsley [1950] Director/Doctor of Medicine; William John Sanders [1966] Director; Gail Sanderson-Watts [1949] Director; Susan Penelope Westall [1944] Director

**Max Healthcare Limited**
*Incorporated:* 29 March 2005  *Employees:* 2
*Net Worth Deficit:* £71,000  *Total Assets:* £105,000
*Registered Office:* William Nadin Way, Swadlincote, Derbys, DE11 0BB
*Shareholder:* Liang Chang
*Officers:* James David Amery, Secretary; James David Amery [1975] Finance Director; Richard Henry Fielding [1968] Director; John Edward Hackett [1967] Managing Director

**Max Motivation Limited**
*Incorporated:* 6 April 2018
*Registered Office:* 43 Merstow Green, Evesham, Worcs, WR11 4BB
*Shareholders:* Hee Young Gee; Jun-Young Anthony Park
*Officers:* Hee Young Gee [1989] Director [South Korean]; Jun-Young Anthony Park [1990] Director [South Korean]

**Max Remedies Limited**
*Incorporated:* 5 March 2007
*Net Worth:* £15,000  *Total Assets:* £80,000
*Registered Office:* William Nadin Way, Swadlincote, Derbys, DE11 0BB
*Parent:* Max Healthcare Limited
*Officers:* James David Amery, Secretary; James David Amery [1975] Finance Director; Richard Henry Fielding [1968] Director; John Edward Hackett [1967] Managing Director

**Maxilabs Limited**
*Incorporated:* 22 September 2003
*Net Worth:* £67,083  *Total Assets:* £83,257
*Registered Office:* Hilltop House, Langley Hill, Kings Langley, Herts, WD4 9HQ
*Shareholder:* Frank Nellis Van Wyk
*Officers:* Lara Van Wyk, Secretary; Frank Nellis Van Wyk [1974] Director

**Maximed Ltd**
*Incorporated:* 31 December 2018
*Registered Office:* Kemp House, 160 City Road, London, EC1V 2NX
*Officers:* Malgorzata Grotowska [1963] Director/Businesswoman [Polish]

**Maxlott Ltd**
*Incorporated:* 22 October 2018
*Registered Office:* 6 Bemish Road, London, SW15 1DG
*Shareholders:* Thomas Woodman; Kathleen Woodman
*Officers:* Dr Thomas Woodman [1975] Director/Doctor

**Mayapharm Limited**
*Incorporated:* 23 May 2018
*Registered Office:* 130 Duke Street, St Helens, Merseyside, WA10 2JL
*Shareholders:* Sameer Patel; Chandrakant Patel
*Officers:* Chandrakant Patel [1960] Director; Sameer Patel [1987] Director

**Mayfair Distributors Limited**
*Incorporated:* 28 November 2018
*Registered Office:* 23 Stanley Road, London, E4 7DB
*Major Shareholder:* Madiha Hamid
*Officers:* Madiha Hamid [1988] Director [Pakistani]

**Mayfair Export London Limited**
*Incorporated:* 26 November 2014
*Net Worth:* £29,487  *Total Assets:* £57,690
*Registered Office:* 1008 Falcon Wharf, 34 Lombard Road, London, SW11 3RY
*Officers:* Hanna Dzhansyz [1974] Director

**Mayomed Limited**
*Incorporated:* 19 September 2018
*Registered Office:* 8b Kelvin House, Kelvin Way, Crawley, W Sussex, RH10 9WE
*Major Shareholder:* Junaid Nazir Choudhry
*Officers:* Junaid Nazir Choudhry [1976] Director [Pakistani]

**Maze Healthcare Ltd.**
*Incorporated:* 10 May 2017  *Employees:* 2
*Net Worth:* £6,547  *Total Assets:* £78,947
*Registered Office:* Unit E2, Seedbed Centre, Langston Road, Loughton, Essex, IG10 3TQ
*Officers:* Zeeshan Malik [1982] Director

**MB Pharma Limited**
*Incorporated:* 25 November 2016
*Registered Office:* 10 Abbey Park Place, Dunfermline, Fife, KY12 7NZ
*Major Shareholder:* Mark Buchan
*Officers:* Mark Buchan [1990] Director

**Mcall Consulting Ltd**
*Incorporated:* 17 May 2011
*Net Worth:* £149  *Total Assets:* £1,647
*Registered Office:* c/o Double Diamond Accountancy Services Ltd, Somers House, Linkfield Corner, Redhill, Surrey, RH1 1BB
*Major Shareholder:* Jane Mary Allen
*Officers:* Jane Mary Allen [1965] Director; Duncan Stuart Douglas McRobbie [1962] Director

**Chanelle McCoy CBD UK Ltd**
*Incorporated:* 15 February 2019
*Registered Office:* Lodge Down Stables, Lambourn Woodlands, Hungerford, Berks, RG17 7BJ
*Major Shareholder:* Chanelle Lady McCoy
*Officers:* Sir Anthony McCoy [1974] Director Jockey [Irish]; Chanelle Lady McCoy [1976] Director [Irish]

**Chanelle McCoy Pharma UK Ltd**
*Incorporated:* 15 February 2019
*Registered Office:* Lodge Down Stables, Lambourn Woodlands, Hungerford, Berks, RG17 7BJ
*Major Shareholder:* Chanelle Lady McCoy
*Officers:* Sir Anthony McCoy [1974] Director Jockey [Irish]; Chanelle Lady McCoy [1976] Director [Irish]

**McKesson Global Procurement & Sourcing Limited**
*Incorporated:* 2 October 2013  *Employees:* 13
*Net Worth:* £2,736,779,520  *Total Assets:* £3,192,374,272
*Registered Office:* TMF Corporate Administration Services Limited, 5th Floor, 6 St Andrew Street, London, EC4A 3AE
*Officers:* Stanton McComb [1970] Director/President, McKesson Medical-Surgical [American]; Jack Thomas Stephens III [1975] Director/Health Care [American]; Gareth Bryn Thomas [1964] Director/Chief Legal Counsel, Global Procurement & Sourcing

**McKesson Global Sourcing UK Limited**
*Incorporated:* 1 August 2017  *Employees:* 5
*Net Worth:* £16,817,168  *Total Assets:* £110,886,528
*Registered Office:* TMF Corporate Administration Services Limited, 5th Floor, 6 St Andrew Street, London, EC4A 3AE
*Officers:* Andrew Keith Birken [1964] Director/SVP, Global Sourcing-Medical [American]; Jack Thomas Stephens III [1975] Director/Health Care [American]; Gareth Bryn Thomas [1964] Director/Chief Legal Counsel, Global Procurement & Sourcing

**McKinley Pharma Limited**
*Incorporated:* 11 December 2017
*Registered Office:* 3 Churchgates, The Wilderness, Berkhamsted, Herts, HP4 2UB
*Major Shareholder:* Janet Margaret Hart
*Officers:* Janet Margaret Hart [1954] Director/Chartered Accountant

**MCL Healthcare Limited**
*Incorporated:* 15 July 2016
*Net Worth:* £16,162  *Total Assets:* £106,899
*Registered Office:* 9 St George's Yard, Castle Street, Farnham, Surrey, GU9 7LW
*Parent:* MedRx Pharmaceuticals Ltd
*Officers:* Clay William Linley Chaston [1981] Director

**McNeil Healthcare (UK) Limited**
*Incorporated:* 13 May 1994
*Net Worth:* £162,355,008  *Total Assets:* £210,890,000
*Registered Office:* c/o Johnson & Johnson Ltd, Roxborough Way, Maidenhead, Berks, SL6 3UG
*Parent:* McNeil Products Ltd.
*Officers:* Luc Huys [1967] Managing Director [Belgian]; Graham Rice [1968] Finance Director

**McQuilkin & Co Limited**
*Incorporated:* 9 January 2015  *Employees:* 11
*Net Worth:* £723,258  *Total Assets:* £1,761,050
*Registered Office:* 6-8 Rennie Place, East Kilbride, S Lanarks, G74 5HD
*Major Shareholder:* Walter Scott Kelso McQuilkin
*Officers:* Lindsay Reid McQuilkin [1947] Director; Walter Scott Kelso McQuilkin [1974] Director; Walter Gordon Campbell McQuilkin [1945] Director

**MD Salisbury Ltd**
*Incorporated:* 13 March 2018
*Registered Office:* Nightingale Pharmacy, Great Well Drive, Romsey, Hants, SO51 7QP
*Shareholders:* Danielle Dobson; Mark Dobson
*Officers:* Danielle Dobson [1977] Director/Pharmacist; Mark Dobson [1975] Director/Pharmacist

**MD-Reproductive Health Solutions Ltd**
*Incorporated:* 11 March 2015  *Employees:* 2
*Net Worth:* £22,543  *Total Assets:* £65,882
*Registered Office:* 10 Fairland Street, Wymondham, Norfolk, NR18 0AW
*Major Shareholder:* Peter Murray Stephenson
*Officers:* Deborah Anne Stephenson [1960] Director/Clinical Team Lead; Peter Murray Stephenson [1957] Director/National Sales Manager

**MDD Europe Limited**
Incorporated: 1 March 2012  Employees: 4
Net Worth: £11,197  Total Assets: £335,993
Registered Office: Five Ways, 57-59 Hatfield Road, Potters Bar, Herts, EN6 1HS
Shareholders: Mark Lait; Roger William John Lait; Peter Schroeder
Officers: Mark Lait [1961] Director; Peter Schroeder [1971] Director [German]

**MDS Pharmaceuticals Ltd**
Incorporated: 14 May 2003
Net Worth: £18,338  Total Assets: £43,730
Registered Office: 87a High Street, Hemel Hempstead, Herts, HP1 3AH
Major Shareholder: Divyesh Chokshi
Officers: Divyesh Chokshi [1968] Director

**MDTI Pharma Retail Division Ltd**
Incorporated: 10 March 2010
Registered Office: The Kace Building, Victoria Passage, Wolverhampton, W Midlands, WV1 4LG
Officers: Martin Leslie Levermore [1962] Director

**MDX Healthcare Ltd**
Incorporated: 20 October 2011  Employees: 11
Net Worth: £245,047  Total Assets: £1,193,625
Registered Office: 3rd Floor, The Heights, 59-65 Lowlands Road, Harrow, Middlesex, HA1 3AW
Major Shareholder: Daniel Chun Ying Cheung
Officers: Daniel Chun Ying Cheung [1980] Director; Fung Ha Sharan Chiu [1974] Director [Chinese]; Ho Ching Chung [1984] Director [Chinese]; Shuk Han Poon [1974] Director [Hong Kong]

**ME Healthy Living H & L Ltd**
Incorporated: 21 April 2009
Net Worth Deficit: £30,468  Total Assets: £16,817
Registered Office: Francis House, 2 Park Road, Barnet, Herts, EN5 5RN
Major Shareholder: Evangelia Menega
Officers: Evangelia Menega [1974] Director/Administrator [Greek]

**Meadow Laboratories Limited**
Incorporated: 2 October 1997  Employees: 2
Net Worth: £1,279,586  Total Assets: £1,436,486
Registered Office: Office T03, 103 Cranbrook Road, Ilford, Essex, IG1 4PU
Shareholders: Linda Jane Topping; Andrew Roberts
Officers: Linda Jane Topping, Secretary; Andrew Roberts [1970] Director; Linda Jane Topping [1968] Director/Accountant

**Med Procure Ltd**
Incorporated: 31 May 2013
Registered Office: 11 Calvert Terrace, Swansea, SA1 6AT
Major Shareholder: Peter Richard Martin Bodle
Officers: Linda Bodle [1956] Director; Peter Martin Bodle [1954] Director

**Med-Col Limited**
Incorporated: 1 October 1984
Registered Office: 41 Greek Street, Stockport, Cheshire, SK3 8AX
Shareholder: Colin Moss
Officers: Michael Harvey Moss, Secretary; Colin Moss [1938] Director/Pharmacist; Michael Harvey Moss [1947] Director/Consultant

**Med-Link Limited**
Incorporated: 1 August 2018
Registered Office: 116 Elderslie Street, Glasgow, G3 7AW
Officers: Ahmed Abdulrraziq Ali Laklouk [1985] Director [Libyan]

**Meda Pharmaceuticals Limited**
Incorporated: 16 March 1966  Employees: 76
Net Worth: £36,245,000  Total Assets: £47,692,000
Registered Office: Collins House, Rutland Square, Edinburgh, EH1 2AA
Parent: Ipex AB
Officers: Jean-Yves Brault [1967] Managing Director [Canadian]; Caroline Rebecca Louise Dixon [1968] Finance Director

**Medaesthetics Limited**
Incorporated: 4 May 2017  Employees: 2
Net Worth: £1,961  Total Assets: £5,826
Registered Office: 9 Sylverdale Road, Croydon, Surrey, CR0 4LD
Officers: Georgi Brankov [1971] Director; Maria Toncheva [1963] Director/Doctor [Bulgarian]

**Medartis Limited**
Incorporated: 29 November 2002  Employees: 11
Net Worth: £2,000,535  Total Assets: £5,855,772
Registered Office: 17a St Christophers Way, Pride Park, Derby, DE24 8JY
Major Shareholder: Thomas Straumann
Officers: Willi Miesch [1964] Director [Swiss]; Charles David Andrew Wilcher [1969] Director

**Medbarn Limited**
Incorporated: 13 January 2015
Net Worth Deficit: £9,473  Total Assets: £3,649
Registered Office: c/o 26 The Square, Moy, Co Tyrone, BT71 7SG
Major Shareholder: Richard William Barnes
Officers: Richard William Barnes [1971] Director/Pharmacist

**Medbase Systems Ltd**
Incorporated: 21 May 2003
Net Worth Deficit: £165  Total Assets: £10,592
Registered Office: 22 St Catherines Road, Crawley, W Sussex, RH10 3TA
Major Shareholder: Jaffar Ali Mirza
Officers: Jaffar Ali Mirza, Secretary; Jaffar Ali Mirza [1948] Director/Businessman

**Medbury Limited**
Incorporated: 12 September 2017
Registered Office: 14 Heywood Street, Bury, Lancs, BL9 7EA
Major Shareholder: Kharul Bashir
Officers: Kharul Bashir [1986] Director

**Medcare Life UK Ltd**
Incorporated: 6 February 2018
Registered Office: Nuchem Pharmacy, 24 Coldharbour Lane, Hayes, Middlesex, UB3 3EW
Officers: Talal Al Fadhli [1988] Director/Teacher; Hassan Mehdi Padhani [1988] Director/Lawyer; Shabir Hassanali Padhani [1958] Director/Pharmacist

**Medeuronet (UK) Limited**
Incorporated: 13 May 2008  Employees: 6
Net Worth: £33,892  Total Assets: £575,808
Registered Office: Unit LF2.7, The Leathermarket, Weston Street, Bermondsey, London, SE1 3ER
Officers: Kristine Ann Morrill, Secretary; Wilfrid Pierre Girard [1969] Director/Consultant [French]; Kristine Morrill [1961] Director/Partner [American]

**Medex Pharma Limited**
Incorporated: 18 April 2018
Registered Office: 16 Rosemount Road, London, W13 0HJ
Major Shareholder: Karam Almustafa
Officers: Karam Almustafa [1986] Director [Syrian]

**Medhub Limited**
Incorporated: 14 December 2015
Net Worth: £14,665  Total Assets: £374,307
Registered Office: 2nd Floor, 13 John Prince's Street, London, W1G 0JR
Officers: Nancy Bennett [1948] Director


**Medi Saha Limited**
Incorporated: 29 September 2011  Employees: 2
Net Worth: £45,641  Total Assets: £63,886
Registered Office: 314 Sutton Road, Walsall, W Midlands, WS5 3BD
Major Shareholder: Arjun Kumar Somabhai Desai
Officers: Arjun Kumar Somabhai Desai [1964] Director/Accountant


**Medi Test Pharma Ltd**
Incorporated: 25 January 2019
Registered Office: c/o Progress Advisory, 16 High Holborn, London, WC1V 6BX
Parent: Afin Holding Ltd
Officers: Dario Ruggieri [1963] Director [Italian]


**Medi UK Ltd**
Incorporated: 13 March 1987  Employees: 39
Net Worth: £1,141,506  Total Assets: £4,797,893
Registered Office: Plough Lane, Hereford, HR4 0EL
Parent: Medi Holding 2009 GmbH
Officers: Ian Austen Grant [1956] Director; Uwe Helmut Meyer [1959] Director [German]


**Medi-Arch Ltd**
Incorporated: 29 May 2018
Registered Office: 15 Ambleside Avenue, Bradford, BD9 5HX
Major Shareholder: Akeel Hussain
Officers: Akeel Hussain [1995] Director/Student


**Medi-Gen Limited**
Incorporated: 9 October 2000
Net Worth: £3,680,000  Total Assets: £5,590,000
Registered Office: 3rd Floor, Scottish Provident House, 76-80 College Road, Harrow, Middlesex, HA1 1BQ
Parent: Medi-Shop Limited
Officers: Nikunj Shantilal Malde, Secretary/Doctor; Deepakkumar Shantilal Malde [1960] Director/Pharmacist; Nikunj Shantilal Malde [1958] Director/Doctor


**Medi-Inn (UK) Ltd**
Incorporated: 9 April 2014
Net Worth Deficit: £230,778  Total Assets: £556,696
Registered Office: Kingfisher House, St Johns Road, Meadowfield Industrial Estate, Meadowfield, Co Durham, DH7 8TZ
Shareholders: HCS Hygiene Concept Solutions GmbH; Body Products Relax Pharma and Kosmetik GmbH
Officers: Mark Anthony Smith [1962] Director


**Medica Finance UK Ltd**
Incorporated: 26 February 2016
Net Worth Deficit: £2,126  Total Assets: £196,476
Registered Office: Lower Ground Floor, 40 Bloomsbury Way, London, WC1A 2SE
Officers: Agnieszka Grzymala [1981] Director [Polish]; Karolina Lassota [1979] Director [Polish]; Konrad Lassota [1979] Director [Polish]


**Medica Ltd**
Incorporated: 25 August 2018
Registered Office: 53 Sheepridge Road, Huddersfield, W Yorks, HD2 1HD
Shareholders: Riyadh Alallaq; Ahmed Alallaq
Officers: Dr Ahmed Alallaq [1975] Director/Financial Adviser [Iraqi]; Dr Riyadh Alallaq [1970] Director [Iraqi]


**Medica Pharma UK Ltd**
Incorporated: 8 January 2019
Registered Office: 205 Kings Road, Tyseley, Birmingham, B11 2AA
Major Shareholder: Rauhan Munir Aziz
Officers: Rauhan Munir Aziz [1996] Director/Student


**Medical Developments UK Limited**
Incorporated: 10 May 2012  Employees: 3
Net Worth Deficit: £87,513  Total Assets: £547,617
Registered Office: Causeway House, 1 Dane Street, Bishop's Stortford, Herts, CM23 3BT
Officers: Mark Robert Edwards, Secretary; John Stewart Sharman [1966] Director/Chief Executive Officer [Australian]; David John Williams [1953] Director/Investment Banker [Australian]


**Medical Drug Supplies Limited**
Incorporated: 26 January 2010
Net Worth Deficit: £21,016  Total Assets: £50,543
Registered Office: Unit 2 River Road Business Park, 33 River Road, Barking, Essex, IG11 0EA
Officers: Sameer Trivedi [1971] Director


**Medical Need UK Ltd**
Incorporated: 10 July 2018
Registered Office: Highlands House, Basingstoke Road, Spencers Wood, Reading, Berks, RG7 1NT
Officers: Carl Magnus Edlund [1979] Director [Swedish]; Peder Sven Walberg [1974] Director [Swedish]


**The Medical Warehouse Limited**
Incorporated: 4 August 2000  Employees: 7
Net Worth Deficit: £385,850  Total Assets: £293,897
Registered Office: 80 Churchill Square, Kings Hill, West Malling, Kent, ME19 4YU
Shareholders: Susan Joan Lee; Robert Frederick Grantham
Officers: Susan Joan Lee, Secretary; Robert Frederick Grantham [1958] Director/Ship Agent; Susan Leona Grantham [1949] Director/Artist; Susan Joan Lee [1957] Director


**Medical-Mac Ltd**
Incorporated: 28 August 2014
Net Worth Deficit: £14,954
Registered Office: Office 228, The Legacy Business Centre, 2a Ruckholt Road, London, E10 5NP
Major Shareholder: Pawel Walkiewicz
Officers: Pawel Walkiewicz [1962] Director/Company Owner [Polish]


**Medicaleaf Limited**
Incorporated: 4 February 2019
Registered Office: Suite 13, 23 Mount Pleasant Road, Tunbridge Wells, Kent, TN1 1NT
Shareholders: Anthony Ellis; Philip Mark Cox
Officers: Anthony Ellis [1948] Director/Business Consultant; Paul Anthony Ford [1964] Director

**Medicalstore-24 Limited**
*Incorporated:* 10 April 2015
*Registered Office:* Carpenter Court, 1 Maple Road, Bramhall, Stockport, Cheshire, SK7 2DH
*Major Shareholder:* Lothar Otto Hallay
*Officers:* Lothar Otto Hallay [1950] Director/Economist [German]

**Medicare Europe Ltd**
*Incorporated:* 11 May 2011  *Employees:* 2
*Net Worth:* £153,926  *Total Assets:* £418,685
*Registered Office:* 495 Green Lanes, London, N13 4BS
*Major Shareholder:* George Menegas
*Officers:* George Menegas [1972] Director/Salesman [Greek]

**Medicare Products Limited**
*Incorporated:* 19 March 1997  *Employees:* 8
*Net Worth:* £4,033,278  *Total Assets:* £6,449,164
*Registered Office:* Polyco Healthline, South Fen Road, Bourne, Lincs, PE10 0DN
*Parent:* PH Medical Holdings Ltd
*Officers:* Neil Wilson, Secretary; Jason Prichard [1969] Director; Gurcharan Singh Sira [1963] Director; James Anthony Hari Singh Sira [1989] Director; Neil Antony Wilson [1976] Director

**Medicern Export Ltd**
*Incorporated:* 7 March 2016
*Net Worth Deficit:* £1,393  *Total Assets:* £12,327
*Registered Office:* Market Chambers, 3-4 Market Place, Wokingham, Berks, RG40 1AL
*Major Shareholder:* Juan Cruz Ciocchini
*Officers:* Henrietta Ciocchini [1975] Director/Administrator [Hungarian]; Juan Cruz Ciocchini [1975] Director/International Manager [Italian]

**Medicia Ltd**
*Incorporated:* 27 October 2009  *Employees:* 1
*Net Worth Deficit:* £426,502  *Total Assets:* £267,500
*Registered Office:* Unit 4, 28-29 The Broadway, London, W5 2NP
*Major Shareholder:* Denys Fedyshyn
*Officers:* Denys Fedyshyn [1988] Director [Ukrainian]

**Medicine Optimisation Limited**
*Incorporated:* 1 August 2014
*Registered Office:* 4 Deeming Drive, Quorn, Loughborough, Leics, LE12 8NF
*Major Shareholder:* Kulsum Zulfikar Rajani
*Officers:* Kulsum Rajani, Secretary; Kulsum Rajani [1987] Director/Pharmacist

**Medicines By Design Ltd**
*Incorporated:* 5 December 2011
*Net Worth:* £67,002  *Total Assets:* £80,147
*Registered Office:* Suite E2, 2nd Floor, The Octagon, Middleborough, Colchester, Essex, CO1 1TG
*Parent:* Medicines By Design (Holdings) Limited
*Officers:* Benjamin James Gordon [1980] Director; Kerry Hinton [1971] Director/CEO of Medical Alliance Group Limited

**The Medicines Company UK Limited**
*Incorporated:* 16 December 1997  *Employees:* 4
*Net Worth:* £90,363  *Total Assets:* £1,467,348
*Registered Office:* 115l Milton Park, Milton, Abingdon, Oxon, OX14 4SA
*Parent:* The Medicines Company
*Officers:* Andre Heer, Secretary; Helmut Josef Giersiefen [1958] Director/SVP, Global Strategy, The Medicines Company [German]; Andre Heer [1970] Director/Vice President, EU Controller [German]; Arnout Sven Van Willigenburg [1949] Independent Director [Dutch]

**Medicines Extra Healthcare Ltd**
*Incorporated:* 7 August 2018
*Registered Office:* 37 Warren Street, London, W1T 6AD
*Shareholders:* Gbadebo Sunday Olaniyan; Janice Oluwagbemisoye Olaniyan
*Officers:* Gbadebo Sunday Olaniyan [1978] Director/Pharmacist; Dr Janice Oluwagbemisoye Olaniyan [1978] Director/Pharmacist

**Mediclock Devices Limited**
*Incorporated:* 26 July 2013  *Employees:* 2
*Net Worth Deficit:* £13,038  *Total Assets:* £23,720
*Registered Office:* 53 Richards Crescent, Truro, Cornwall, TR1 3RA
*Shareholders:* Craig John Pascoe; Tanya Jane Pascoe
*Officers:* Craig John Pascoe [1977] Director; Tanya Jane Pascoe [1976] Director

**Medicom Healthcare Limited**
*Incorporated:* 16 March 2000  *Employees:* 27
*Net Worth:* £545,861  *Total Assets:* £2,179,262
*Registered Office:* Office 1, 235 Hunts Pond Road, Titchfield Common, Fareham, Hants, PO14 4PJ
*Shareholders:* Simon Jonathan Martin; Atul Vijay Ajgaonkar; Madhurika Atul Ajgaonkar
*Officers:* Atul Vijay Ajgaonkar, Secretary; Atul Vijay Ajgaonkar [1965] Director; Simon Jonathan Martin [1960] Director

**Medics Direct Pharmacy Limited**
*Incorporated:* 30 May 2018
*Registered Office:* European Medical Aesthetics Ltd, 77 Harley Street, London, W1G 8QN
*Major Shareholder:* David Cumming
*Officers:* David Cumming [1955] Director

**Medicstar (UK) Limited**
*Incorporated:* 30 September 2010
*Net Worth:* £505  *Total Assets:* £472,815
*Registered Office:* 344 Manchester Road, West Timperley, Altrincham, Cheshire, WA14 5NH
*Parent:* Medicstar (HK) Limited
*Officers:* Gary Chan [1979] Director; Wai Fong Leung [1961] Director [Australian]

**Medicure Scientific Limited**
*Incorporated:* 13 October 2014
*Net Worth Deficit:* £6,000  *Total Assets:* £39,000
*Registered Office:* Unit 9-11 Charfleets Farm Way, Charfleets Farm Industrial Estate, Canvey Island, Essex, SS8 0PG
*Major Shareholder:* Baseer Ahmed
*Officers:* Baseer Ahmed [1985] Director

**Medigroup Ltd**
*Incorporated:* 11 January 2013
*Net Worth Deficit:* £262,284  *Total Assets:* £10,621
*Registered Office:* 28 Lindsay Drive, Harrow, Middlesex, HA3 0TD
*Shareholder:* Rohitkumar Babulal Mehta
*Officers:* Rohit Babulal Mehta [1953] Director

**Medihealth (Northern) Limited**
*Incorporated:* 30 January 2004  *Employees:* 21
*Net Worth:* £2,897,077  *Total Assets:* £3,410,237
*Registered Office:* P O Box 2076, Lynstock House, Lynstock Way, Lostock, Bolton, Lancs, BL6 4SA
*Shareholders:* Anwer Ibrahim Patel; Yakub Ibrahim Patel
*Officers:* Anwer Ibrahim Patel, Secretary/Director; Andrew John Caunce [1974] Director/Accountant; Adam Collins [1984] Director/Accountant; Anwer Ibrahim Patel [1954] Director

**Medik Ostomy Supplies Limited**
*Incorporated:* 29 December 1997  *Employees:* 3
*Net Worth:* £245,249  *Total Assets:* £1,202,075
*Registered Office:* Qualitas House, 100 Elmgrove Road, Harrow, Middlesex, HA1 2RW
*Major Shareholder:* Bhavini Badiani
*Officers:* Hemang Chhotalal Badiani, Secretary; Hemang Chhotalal Badiani [1960] Director/Pharmacist

**Medikit Limited**
*Incorporated:* 1 June 1990  *Employees:* 8
*Net Worth:* £405,822  *Total Assets:* £562,766
*Registered Office:* Unit 1 Newporte Business Park, Cardinal Close, Bishops Road, Lincoln, LN2 4SY
*Major Shareholder:* Geoffrey Philip Marchington
*Officers:* Geoffrey Philip Marchington, Secretary/Managing Director; Geoffrey Philip Marchington [1954] Managing Director; John Frederick Wilkinson [1952] Director/General Manager

**Medilain Marketing Ltd**
*Incorporated:* 16 October 2012
*Net Worth:* £132,764  *Total Assets:* £504,657
*Registered Office:* Suite 4, 10 Great Russell Street, London, WC1B 3BQ
*Major Shareholder:* Feliks Krichevskiy
*Officers:* Daniel Fraser John O'Donoghue [1983] Director/Writer

**Medilife Ltd**
*Incorporated:* 7 September 2010
*Registered Office:* 1 Jesmond Business Court, 217 Jesmond Road, Newcastle upon Tyne, NE2 1LA
*Shareholder:* Ian Humpish
*Officers:* Ian James Humpish [1955] Director

**Medilink Limited**
*Incorporated:* 16 February 1989
*Net Worth:* £31,134  *Total Assets:* £39,129
*Registered Office:* 217 Juniper Way, Bradley Stoke, Bristol, BS32 0DP
*Major Shareholder:* Allan John Molyneux
*Officers:* Emrys Williams, Secretary; Allan John Molyneux [1952] Director; Emrys Williams [1942] Director/Company Secretary

**Medimax (UK) Ltd**
*Incorporated:* 26 September 2002
*Registered Office:* 1 Bullescroft Road, Edgware, Middlesex, HA8 8RN
*Officers:* Premila Haria [1954] Director

**Medimpex UK Limited**
*Incorporated:* 27 January 1958  *Employees:* 5
*Net Worth:* £2,791,486  *Total Assets:* £5,038,348
*Registered Office:* 127 Shirland Road, London, W9 2EP
*Officers:* Michael Robert Firman, Secretary; Erik Attila Bogsch [1947] Director [Hungarian]; Dr Timea Halko [1980] Director [Hungarian]; Dr Kriszta Zolnay [1966] Director [Hungarian]

**Medinox (London) Limited**
*Incorporated:* 15 January 2018
*Registered Office:* Solar House, 282 Chase Road, Southgate, London, N14 6NZ
*Shareholders:* Kenneth Clifford Venn; Gordon John Matheson
*Officers:* Gordon John Matheson [1965] Director [South African]; Kenneth Clifford Venn [1956] Director [South African]

**Medintek Holdings Ltd**
*Incorporated:* 8 November 2018
*Registered Office:* 3rd Floor, 120 Baker Street, London, W1U 6TU
*Major Shareholder:* Farkhod Abdullaev
*Officers:* Farkhod Abdullaev [1980] Director/Businessman [Uzbek]

**Medipharma Limited**
*Incorporated:* 29 October 1991  *Employees:* 1
*Net Worth:* £1,491,700  *Total Assets:* £2,120,060
*Registered Office:* 21 & 22 Mayfield Avenue Industrial Park, Fyfield Road, Weyhill, Andover, Hants, SP11 8HU
*Parent:* Medipharma Group Limited
*Officers:* Debbie Matcham, Secretary; Feroze Issa Ismail Janmohamed [1946] Director

**Mediport Limited**
*Incorporated:* 18 June 2001
*Net Worth:* £361,250  *Total Assets:* £379,068
*Registered Office:* 13 Martello Enterprise Centre, Courtwick Lane, Littlehampton, W Sussex, BN17 7PA
*Major Shareholder:* Jean-Hugues Michel
*Officers:* Lisa Jane Cooke, Secretary; Lisa Jane Cooke [1969] Finance Director; Bertrand Michel [1975] Director [French]; Jean-Hugues Michel [1967] Director [French]

**Medipro Pharma Limited**
*Incorporated:* 23 March 2017  *Employees:* 3
*Net Worth Deficit:* £914  *Total Assets:* £120,062
*Registered Office:* c/o Saashiv & Co, Pentax House, South Hill Avenue, South Harrow, Middlesex, HA2 0DU
*Shareholders:* Anoop Shah; Rupeshkumar Dinubhai Patel; Tushar Vinodchandra Shah
*Officers:* Rupeshkumar Dinubhai Patel [1974] Director/Accountant; Anoop Shashikant Shah [1966] Director/Pharmacist; Tushar Vinodchandra Shah [1978] Director

**Medirite Limited**
*Incorporated:* 23 November 2012
*Registered Office:* Wightman & Parrish Limited, Station Road Industrial Estate, Hailsham, E Sussex, BN27 2QA
*Officers:* Nicholas Bryan Parrish [1964] Managing Director

**Medis Medical (UK) Limited**
*Incorporated:* 20 January 2015
*Registered Office:* 277 Stockport Road, Ashton under Lyne, Lancs, OL7 0NT
*Major Shareholder:* Dewei Zou
*Officers:* Dewei Zou [1962] Director [Chinese]

**Medisale Limited**
*Incorporated:* 4 April 2017
*Net Worth:* £110  *Total Assets:* £6,707
*Registered Office:* Elm House, 10 Fountain Court, New Leaze, Bradley Stoke, Bristol, BS32 4LA
*Major Shareholder:* Lydia Alexandra Telka
*Officers:* Lydia Alexandra Telka [1991] Director

**Medisante Limited**
*Incorporated:* 11 June 2010  *Employees:* 3
*Net Worth:* £121,403  *Total Assets:* £273,248
*Registered Office:* 37 Great Pulteney Street, Bath, BA2 4DA
*Major Shareholder:* Stephen William Riley
*Officers:* Stephen William Riley, Secretary; Stephen William Riley [1948] Director; Dr Christopher Smejkal [1976] Director/Regulatory Consultant

## The Top UK Pharmaceutical Wholesalers

**Medisca UK Limited**
*Incorporated:* 28 March 2017  *Employees:* 1
*Net Worth Deficit:* £104,095  *Total Assets:* £22,749
*Registered Office:* 33 St James's Square, London, SW1Y 4JS
*Major Shareholder:* Antonio Dos Santos
*Officers:* Noreen Mullane, Secretary; Antonio Dos Santos [1948] Director [Canadian]; Noreen Mullane [1978] Director/Accountant [Irish]; Andrew Rowe [1986] Director

**Medison Pharma Limited**
*Incorporated:* 3 October 2013
*Net Worth:* £5,422  *Total Assets:* £23,045
*Registered Office:* 1a Crown Lane, London, SW16 6AY
*Major Shareholder:* Alexey Egorov
*Officers:* Alexey Egorov [1961] Director [Russian]

**Meditec International England Limited**
*Incorporated:* 23 January 1991  *Employees:* 4
*Net Worth:* £1,648,670  *Total Assets:* £2,931,821
*Registered Office:* 8 Pinner View, Harrow, Middlesex, HA1 4QA
*Shareholders:* Akhil Kohli; Vinod Kohli
*Officers:* Akhil Kohli, Secretary/Student; Anil Kumar Jayantilal Shah, Secretary; Aditya Kohli [1980] Director/Medical Equipment Consultant [Indian]; Akhil Kohli [1978] Director/Medical Equipment Consultant; Anita Kohli [1950] Director/Housewife [Indian]; Vinod Kohli [1946] Director/Anaesthetist [Indian]

**Meditech Endoscopy Ltd**
*Incorporated:* 30 April 2013
*Net Worth:* £420,204  *Total Assets:* £1,223,828
*Registered Office:* c/o Smith Craven, Tapton Park Innovation Centre, Brimington Road, Tapton, Chesterfield, Derbys, S41 0TZ
*Shareholder:* Peter John Ramsey
*Officers:* Peter John Ramsey [1969] Director

**Mediva Pharma Limited**
*Incorporated:* 22 February 2011  *Employees:* 6
*Net Worth Deficit:* £289,286  *Total Assets:* £3,200,779
*Registered Office:* 66 Tanners Drive, Blakelands, Milton Keynes, Bucks, MK14 5BP
*Parent:* Solaris Holdings Limited
*Officers:* Alexander Fenech [1970] Director [Maltese]; Robert Spiteri [1970] Director [Maltese]

**Medivast Limited**
*Incorporated:* 24 May 2018
*Registered Office:* 53 Thornway Drive, Ashton under Lyne, Lancs, OL7 0AA
*Officers:* Anna Daniels [1981] Director

**Mediwin Limited**
*Incorporated:* 23 October 2001  *Employees:* 112
*Net Worth:* £3,353,078  *Total Assets:* £12,560,318
*Registered Office:* Unit 13 Martello Enterprise Centre, Courtwick Lane, Littlehampton, W Sussex, BN17 7PA
*Major Shareholder:* Jean-Hugues Michel
*Officers:* Lisa Jane Cooke, Secretary; Lisa Jane Cooke [1969] Finance Director; Delphine Kerhoas [1966] Director [French]; Bertrand Michel [1975] Director [French]; Jean-Hugues Michel [1967] Director [French]

**Medix Supply International Ltd**
*Incorporated:* 18 October 2017
*Registered Office:* 66 Meynell Heights, Meynell Approach, Leeds, LS11 9PY
*Major Shareholder:* Abdulqafar Mohamed Aden
*Officers:* Abdulqafar Mohamed Aden [1985] Director

**Medpharm Global UK Limited**
*Incorporated:* 10 September 2018
*Registered Office:* 7 Essex Court, Hammersmith Grove, London, W6 0NN
*Major Shareholder:* Abebaw Biru Ambaw
*Officers:* Abebaw Biru Ambaw [1979] Managing Director

**Medpro Healthcare Limited**
*Incorporated:* 22 April 2013  *Employees:* 1
*Net Worth:* £829,574  *Total Assets:* £15,620,344
*Registered Office:* 3 Montpelier Avenue, Bexley, Kent, DA5 3AP
*Major Shareholder:* Kalvinder Singh Ruprai
*Officers:* Kalvinder Singh Ruprai [1969] Director

**Medreich PLC**
*Incorporated:* 7 November 1995  *Employees:* 58
*Net Worth:* £20,507,924  *Total Assets:* £40,756,208
*Registered Office:* Ibex House, Baker Street, Weybridge, Surrey, KT13 8AH
*Officers:* Ashish Gupta, Secretary; Shinya Katafuchi [1960] Director [Japanese]; John McCullough [1970] Director; Yuji Sasaki [1958] Director [Japanese]; Hiromasa Takizawa [1964] Director [Japanese]

**MedRx Distribution Limited**
*Incorporated:* 15 April 2011
*Net Worth:* £175,082  *Total Assets:* £185,505
*Registered Office:* 9 St George's Yard, Castle Street, Farnham, Surrey, GU9 7LW
*Major Shareholder:* Clay Chaston
*Officers:* Clay William Linley Chaston [1981] Business Director

**Meds Global Limited**
*Incorporated:* 11 July 2018
*Registered Office:* Park Royal Road, London, NW10 7LQ
*Major Shareholder:* Lina Taher Albayati
*Officers:* Lina Taher Albayati [1980] Director

**Meds Online 247 Limited**
*Incorporated:* 14 January 2019
*Registered Office:* 11 Albion Place, Maidstone, Kent, ME14 5DY
*Major Shareholder:* David Robert Richardson
*Officers:* David Robert Richardson [1970] Director

**Medshires Limited**
*Incorporated:* 29 May 2002  *Employees:* 8
*Net Worth:* £679,342  *Total Assets:* £1,464,664
*Registered Office:* Unit 3 The Shops, Teagues Crescent, Trench, Telford, Salop, TF2 6RX
*Major Shareholder:* Kuldip Kaur Pahal
*Officers:* Kuldip Kaur Pahal [1970] Director/Pharmacist

**Medspero Pharma Ltd**
*Incorporated:* 18 June 2018
*Registered Office:* Flat 4 Henly Court, 265/267 Ilford Lane, Ilford, Essex, IG1 2SD
*Major Shareholder:* Krishnapriya Papisetty
*Officers:* Krishnapriya Papisetty [1988] Managing Director [Indian]

**Medstore Limited**
*Incorporated:* 13 January 2015
*Net Worth:* £100  *Total Assets:* £158,357
*Registered Office:* 202 Victoria Works, Calder Street, Brighouse, W Yorks, HD6 1NB
*Major Shareholder:* Shabana Siddique
*Officers:* Shabana Siddique [1981] Director

**Medsupply Ltd**
*Incorporated:* 26 September 2018
*Registered Office:* Flat 1, Catherine House, Thomas Fyre Drive, London, E3 2ZG
*Major Shareholder:* Ahmed Ahmed
*Officers:* Ahmed Ahmed [1990] Director/Administrator [Somali]


**Medtech Trading Limited**
*Incorporated:* 31 May 2016
*Registered Office:* Galla House, 695 High Road, North Finchley, London, N12 0BT
*Shareholders:* Aziza Shadibaeva; Aziza Shadibaeva
*Officers:* Aziza Shadibaeva [1977] Director [Uzbek]


**Megapharma Ltd**
*Incorporated:* 7 November 2005
*Previous:* Misterhandy.co.uk Limited
*Net Worth Deficit:* £3,040  *Total Assets:* £100
*Registered Office:* 407 Britannia House, 11 Glenthorne Road, London, W6 0LH
*Shareholders:* Sandor Papp; Laszlo Papp
*Officers:* Sandor Papp, Secretary; Laszlo Papp [1967] Director [Hungarian]; Sandor Papp [1957] Director [Hungarian]


**Melcare (Europe) Limited**
*Incorporated:* 4 January 2010
*Registered Office:* Carpenter Court, 1 Maple Road, Bramhall, Stockport, Cheshire, SK7 2DH
*Officers:* Anthony Peter Moloney [1960] Director [Australian]


**Melo Labs UK Ltd**
*Incorporated:* 21 September 2016
*Net Worth:* £143,442  *Total Assets:* £169,787
*Registered Office:* St Magnus House, Lower Thames Street, London, EC3R 6HD
*Shareholders:* Clive Diethelm; Francesco Porcu
*Officers:* Mara Pierantozzi [1974] Director/KYC Onboarding [Italian]


**Melyd Medical Limited**
*Incorporated:* 1 September 1994  *Employees:* 3
*Net Worth:* £4,794,926  *Total Assets:* £4,883,980
*Registered Office:* Unit 32 St Asaph Business Park, St Asaph, Denbighshire, LL17 0JA
*Major Shareholder:* Robb Hulson
*Officers:* Nicholas John Hulson, Secretary/Chartered Accountant; Robb Hulson [1962] Director/Business Administrator


**Mena Pharma UK Limited**
*Incorporated:* 12 February 2015  *Employees:* 2
*Net Worth Deficit:* £165,523  *Total Assets:* £40,649
*Registered Office:* Office 215, Mortlake Business Centre, 20 Mortlake High Street, Mortlake, London, SW14 8JN
*Shareholders:* Bashir Mohamed Gazla; Adel Taher Kallat
*Officers:* Dr Adel Taher Kallat [1966] Director/General Manager [Libyan]


**Menar UK Biotech Ltd**
*Incorporated:* 6 February 2018
*Registered Office:* 17 Green Lanes, London, N16 9BS
*Major Shareholder:* Adem Herdem
*Officers:* Adem Herdem [1972] Director [Turkish]


**A. Menarini Diagnostics Limited**
*Incorporated:* 7 April 1987  *Employees:* 75
*Net Worth:* £3,528,276  *Total Assets:* £9,254,251
*Registered Office:* 405 Wharfedale Road, Winnersh, Wokingham, Berks, RG41 5RA
*Officers:* Gianni Masselli, Secretary; Gianni Masselli [1965] Director/Controller [Italian]; Nico Noel Andre Samaille [1971] Director [Belgian]; Paul Tolan [1960] Director


**A. Menarini Pharmaceuticals U.K. Limited**
*Incorporated:* 25 November 1998
*Registered Office:* Menarini House, Mercury Park, Wooburn Green, High Wycombe, Bucks, HP10 0HH
*Parent:* Menarini International Operations Luxembourg S.A
*Officers:* Gianni Masselli, Secretary; Gianni Masselli [1965] Director/Controller [Italian]; Pio Mei [1954] Director/Vice Direttore Generale di Gruppo [Italian]


**Mensana Pharma Ltd.**
*Incorporated:* 16 November 2006  *Employees:* 2
*Net Worth:* £189,804  *Total Assets:* £1,216,830
*Registered Office:* Elscot House, Arcadia Avenue, London, N3 2JU
*Major Shareholder:* Molnar Lorant Janos
*Officers:* Lorant Molnar [1965] Director/Manager [Hungarian]; David Pearlman [1938] Director/Accountant


**Mera Pharma Limited**
*Incorporated:* 3 October 2007
*Net Worth Deficit:* £82,414  *Total Assets:* £89,313
*Registered Office:* 69 Great Hampton Street, Birmingham, B18 6EW
*Officers:* Khalid Saleh [1987] Director [Iraqi]; Muhamed Ismail Muhamed Seyan [1967] Director [Iraqi]


**Mercia Dental Equipment Limited**
*Incorporated:* 19 November 2008  *Employees:* 5
*Net Worth:* £150,969  *Total Assets:* £331,010
*Registered Office:* Prince William House, 10 Lower Church Street, Ashby-De-La-Zouch, Leics, LE65 1AB
*Shareholders:* Neil Stevenson; Laraine Stevenson
*Officers:* Laraine Stevenson, Secretary; Laraine Stevenson [1955] Director; Neil Stevenson [1954] Director


**Merck Serono Limited**
*Incorporated:* 2 October 1970  *Employees:* 173
*Net Worth:* £20,986,000  *Total Assets:* £60,114,000
*Registered Office:* Bedfont Cross, Stanwell Road, Feltham, Middlesex, TW14 8NX
*Parent:* Merck KGaA
*Officers:* Peter Biro [1967] Director/US Certified Public Accountant [Dutch]; Charles William Dring [1962] Director; Mary Elizabeth Henderson [1971] Managing Director [Irish]


**Meridian Bioscience UK Limited**
*Incorporated:* 23 June 2014
*Net Worth:* £262,689  *Total Assets:* £574,692
*Registered Office:* 16 The Edge Business Centre, Humber Road, London, NW2 6EW
*Parent:* Meridian Bioscience International Limited
*Officers:* Alan Michael Parker, Secretary; Charles Robert Caso [1962] Director/Vice President Commercial Operations [American]; John Patrick Kenny [1968] Director [American]; Alan Michael Parker [1959] Director/Chief Financial Officer; Eric Scott Rasmussen [1967] Director/Executive Vice President [American]

**Meridian Medical Technologies Limited**
*Incorporated:* 28 April 1987
*Net Worth Deficit:* £349,567  *Total Assets:* £391,372
*Registered Office:* Forsyth House, Cromac Square, Belfast, BT2 8LA
*Parent:* Pfizer Inc
*Officers:* Ian Eric Franklin [1965] Director; Thomas Handel [1964] Director [American]; Jacqueline Ann Mount [1963] Director; Paul Scott Muma [1960] Director [American]; Edwin James Pearson [1974] Director/Solicitor


**Merlin Vet Export Ltd**
*Incorporated:* 11 June 2013  *Employees:* 11
*Net Worth:* £497,284  *Total Assets:* £871,214
*Registered Office:* Unit 1 Turfford Park, Earlston, Berwickshire, TD4 6GZ
*Shareholder:* David Winston Taylor
*Officers:* Nicola Mary Kinghorn, Secretary; Robert Anderson [1957] Director/Veterinary Surgeon; Nicola Mary Kinghorn [1975] Director; David Winston Taylor [1963] Director/Veterinary Surgeon


**Merz Pharma UK Limited**
*Incorporated:* 19 March 2003  *Employees:* 54
*Net Worth:* £2,726,564  *Total Assets:* £9,142,150
*Registered Office:* 260 Centennial Park, Elstree Hill South, Elstree, Herts, WD6 3SR
*Parent:* Merz Pharmaceuticals GmbH
*Officers:* Stefan Brinkmann [1966] Managing Director [German]; Stuart Matthew Rose [1964] Pharmaceutical Managing Director


**Mesopotamia Surgical Ultima Vitality Ltd**
*Incorporated:* 16 May 2008  *Employees:* 1
*Net Worth:* £8,291  *Total Assets:* £11,127
*Registered Office:* 718a Wilmslow Road, Didsbury, Manchester, M20 2DW
*Officers:* Ahmed Beden [1969] Director/Doctor; Dr Anne Grace Beden [1973] Director


**Meta Innovation Nutrition Ltd**
*Incorporated:* 21 May 2018
*Registered Office:* Unit 6 Boarshead Industrial Estate, Clarke Street, Derby, DE1 2BU
*Major Shareholder:* Christopher Michael Francis McWilliams
*Officers:* Christopher Michael Francis McWilliams, Secretary; Christopher Michael Francis McWilliams [1985] Director/Businessman [South African]


**Metro Pharmacy Limited**
*Incorporated:* 15 November 1994  *Employees:* 16
*Net Worth:* £1,498,377  *Total Assets:* £1,785,006
*Registered Office:* The Pavilion, Rosslyn Crescent, Harrow, Middlesex, HA1 2SZ
*Major Shareholder:* Rajendra Shah
*Officers:* Alison Whitehead, Secretary; Rajendra Shah [1959] Director/Pharmacist


**Metropharm Limited**
*Incorporated:* 6 October 2016  *Employees:* 2
*Net Worth:* £26,655  *Total Assets:* £291,258
*Registered Office:* Unit 3 Valley Point Industrial Estate, Beddington Farm Road, Croydon, Surrey, CR0 4WP
*Major Shareholder:* Shailesh Amin
*Officers:* Shailesh Amin [1956] Director/Pharmacist


**MGC Pharma (UK) Ltd**
*Incorporated:* 26 August 2015  *Employees:* 4
*Net Worth:* £137,770  *Total Assets:* £2,896,542
*Registered Office:* Central Working, Ecclestone Yards, 25 Ecclestone Place, London, SW1W 9NF
*Officers:* Anthony Neville Chisholm Eastman [1974] Director/Chartered Accountant [Australian]; Brett Anthony Mitchell [1971] Director [Australian]; Nativ Segev [1978] Director [Israeli]; Roby Reuven Zomer [1980] Managing Director [Israeli]


**MGI Pharma Limited**
*Incorporated:* 16 November 2000
*Registered Office:* European Knowledge Centre, Mosquito Way, Hatfield, Herts, AL10 9SN
*Parent:* Eisal Co.,Ltd
*Officers:* Simon Gerard Thomas, Secretary; Nicholas Conrad Burgin [1959] Director; Gary Bryan Hendler [1966] Director/President and CEO; Shaji Mary Procida [1971] Director/President & COO [American]


**MH (Newry) Ltd**
*Incorporated:* 28 January 2003
*Net Worth Deficit:* £211,839  *Total Assets:* £186,642
*Registered Office:* Unit 14b Quays Shopping Centre, Newry, Co Down, BT35 8QS
*Officers:* Claire Garvey, Secretary; Richard Stephen Garvey [1977] Director/Pharmacist [Irish]


**Micro Industries Limited**
*Incorporated:* 21 April 2005
*Net Worth:* £20,000  *Total Assets:* £40,063
*Registered Office:* 6 Jardine House, Harrovian Business Village, Bessborough Road, Harrow, Middlesex, HA1 3EX
*Major Shareholder:* Thanaluxmy Ananthamohan
*Officers:* Thanaluxmy Ananthamohan, Secretary/Accountant [Sri Lankan]; Thanaluxmy Ananthamohan [1959] Director [Sri Lankan]


**Microskin Cosmeceuticals UK Ltd**
*Incorporated:* 5 September 2018
*Registered Office:* 795 Chester Road, Erdington, Birmingham, B24 0BX
*Officers:* Syed Naseer Ahmed [1952] Director; Syed Salmaan Ahmed [1980] Director; Dr Mabroor Ahmed Bhatty [1958] Director/Plastic Surgeon; Nicola Susan Bhatty [1964] Director/Housewife


**Midmeds Limited**
*Incorporated:* 29 April 2005  *Employees:* 20
*Net Worth:* £415,094  *Total Assets:* £1,248,576
*Registered Office:* Abacus House, 14-18 Forest Road, Loughton, Essex, IG10 1DX
*Shareholders:* David Jason Rones; Adam Jamie Rones
*Officers:* David Jason Rones, Secretary; Adam Jamie Rones [1984] Director/Sales Administration; David Jason Rones [1980] Managing Director; Rebecca Elisa Rones [1980] Director


**Mill Pharm Limited**
*Incorporated:* 16 June 2008  *Employees:* 31
*Net Worth:* £174,843  *Total Assets:* £655,342
*Registered Office:* The Mill Surgey, Church Street, Boxford, Sudbury, Suffolk, CO10 5DU
*Officers:* Dr Bryan Michael Anglim [1982] Director/Doctor; Dr Elizabeth Mary Cope [1961] Director/GP; Dr Gillian Mary Croot [1969] Director/GP; Dr Christopher Patrick Cullen [1962] Director/GP; Dr Caroline Rosalind Everitt [1966] Director/GP; Doctor John Nicholas Flather [1953] Director/GP; Dr Matthew Sean Lawrence Glason [1961] Director/GP; Dr Peter Thomas John Irwin [1961] Director/GP; Dr Ruth Mary Grace Nabarro [1964] Director/GP

**Millennium Global Limited**
*Incorporated:* 12 November 2018
*Registered Office:* 20 New Church Street, Radcliffe, Manchester, M26 2AJ
*Major Shareholder:* Ali Sylla
*Officers:* Ali Sylla [1977] Director [Guinean]


**Miller & Miller (Chemicals) Limited**
*Incorporated:* 4 November 1977  *Employees:* 18
*Net Worth:* £8,437,924  *Total Assets:* £9,843,544
*Registered Office:* Haslers, Old Station Road, Loughton, Essex, IG10 4PL
*Shareholder:* John Simon Miller
*Officers:* Natalie Laura Livingston, Secretary; Natalie Laura Livingston [1972] Director; David Miller [1974] Sales Director; John Simon Miller [1943] Director/Chemist


**Milpharm Limited**
*Incorporated:* 11 April 1997  *Employees:* 31
*Net Worth:* £12,127,246  *Total Assets:* £27,974,948
*Registered Office:* Ares Block, Odyssey Business Park, West End Road, South Ruislip, Middlesex, HA4 6QD
*Parent:* Agile Pharma B.V.
*Officers:* Thomas Broeer [1960] Director [German]; Venugopalan Muralidharan [1955] Director; Gorla Phaneemdra Prasad [1957] Finance Director [Indian]


**Miltonia Health Science Ltd**
*Incorporated:* 12 June 2009
*Net Worth Deficit:* £13,273  *Total Assets:* £3,493,729
*Registered Office:* 1st Floor, 14 Bowling Green Lane, London, EC1R 0BD
*Major Shareholder:* Raja Augustin
*Officers:* Mary Jane Hoareau [1977] Director/Accountant [Seychellois]


**Minmar (1008) Limited**
*Incorporated:* 11 July 2002
*Previous:* Skinbrands Limited
*Registered Office:* The Pavilion, Josselin Road, Burnt Mills Industrial Estate, Basildon, Essex, SS13 1QB
*Parent:* Adonia Medical Group Ltd
*Officers:* Paul William Wilkinson [1965] Director


**Mintheath Developments Limited**
*Incorporated:* 19 October 2000
*Net Worth Deficit:* £47,653  *Total Assets:* £1,258,357
*Registered Office:* Elm Park House, Elm Park Court, Pinner, Middlesex, HA5 3NN
*Major Shareholder:* Marino Lorenzo Castorina
*Officers:* Battista Pietro Ponti [1945] Director [Swiss]


**Mirada Medical Limited**
*Incorporated:* 27 February 2008  *Employees:* 52
*Net Worth Deficit:* £1,833,502  *Total Assets:* £2,317,553
*Registered Office:* Oxford Centre for Innovation, New Road, Oxford, OX1 1BY
*Officers:* Hugh Bettesworth [1966] Director; Sir John Michael Brady [1945] Director/University Professor; Samuel James Caiger Gray [1977] Director/Private Equity/Venture Capital Investor; David Gudgin [1972] Director/Investor; Eugene Saragnese [1956] Director/Chairman of The Board [American]


**Mirage Distribution Limited**
*Incorporated:* 18 November 2009
*Net Worth:* £2,501,451  *Total Assets:* £3,749,724
*Registered Office:* 12 Snaresbrook Drive, Stanmore, Middlesex, HA7 4QW
*Shareholders:* Ajaybhai Dilipkumar Patel; Dilipkumar Nathubhai Patel
*Officers:* Ajaybhai Dilipkumar Patel [1986] Director; Dilipkumar Nathubhai Patel [1957] Director


**Mirage Eyewear (1993) Limited**
*Incorporated:* 7 October 1992
*Net Worth:* £173,879  *Total Assets:* £249,360
*Registered Office:* Midgley Court, Salters Lane, Newport, Salop, TF10 7PD
*Shareholders:* Angela Mary Newton; Ronald Newton; Marjorie Diane Newton
*Officers:* Angela Mary Newton, Secretary/Accounts Manager; Angela Mary Newton [1974] Director/Accounts Manager; Marjorie Diane Newton [1946] Director; Ronald Newton [1951] Director


**Mistry Medical Supplies Limited**
*Incorporated:* 1 February 2007
*Net Worth Deficit:* £91,134  *Total Assets:* £971,699
*Registered Office:* Unit 2 Valley Court, Sanderson Way, Midpoint 18, Middlewich, Cheshire, CW10 0GF
*Shareholders:* Raman Ambaram Mistry; Kiran Mistry
*Officers:* Kiran Mistry, Secretary; Rajesh Mistry [1985] Director; Raman Ambaram Mistry [1958] Director/Pharmacist


**Mitochondrial Therapy Ltd**
*Incorporated:* 28 February 2012
*Previous:* Heartwise (UK) Limited
*Net Worth:* £123,741  *Total Assets:* £168,038
*Registered Office:* 12 Hibel Road, Macclesfield, Cheshire, SK10 2AB
*Major Shareholder:* Sheriden Dianne Dixon
*Officers:* Sheriden Dianne Dixon [1958] Director


**MK Medicals (UK) Ltd**
*Incorporated:* 13 March 2013
*Net Worth Deficit:* £60,959  *Total Assets:* £5,130
*Registered Office:* M K Medicals UK Limited, Unit 7 Capital Industrial Estate, Crabtree Manorway South, Belvedere, Kent, DA17 6BJ
*Major Shareholder:* Mohamed Khalil
*Officers:* Mohamed Khalil [1980] Director


**MKK Consulting Ltd**
*Incorporated:* 18 April 2011
*Net Worth:* £776  *Total Assets:* £13,276
*Registered Office:* Wisteria Grange Barn, Pikes End, Pinner, London, HA5 2EX
*Major Shareholder:* Mandeep Kaur Kalia
*Officers:* Mandeep Kalia [1979] Director/Consultant


**MKS Pharma Ltd**
*Incorporated:* 11 June 2018
*Registered Office:* Unit 20 Kingsley Court, Kingsley Street, Leicester, LE2 6DL
*Major Shareholder:* Gursheran Sooch
*Officers:* Gursheran Sooch [1983] Director

**MM Medical Equipment UK Ltd**
*Incorporated:* 20 December 2017
*Registered Office:* 205 Pentax House, South Hill Avenue, Harrow, Middlesex, HA2 0DU
*Shareholders:* Marwan Mohammed; Muthana Altaie
*Officers:* Muthana Altaie [1969] Director/Specialist Physician [Iraqi]; Marwan Mohammed [1976] Director/Specialist General Surgeon [Iraqi]

**MMEU 20/20 Ltd**
*Incorporated:* 4 July 2013
*Registered Office:* 2 Burns Drive, Rotherham, S Yorks, S65 2QH
*Shareholder:* Ravindra Dineshchandra Naik
*Officers:* Dr Ravindra Dineshchandra Naik [1961] Director

**MMP Marketing Limited**
*Incorporated:* 9 February 2015
*Net Worth:* £11,856 *Total Assets:* £58,674
*Registered Office:* 445 Kenton Road, Harrow, Middlesex, HA3 0XY
*Major Shareholder:* Stefan Frank
*Officers:* Kajsa Lena Elisabet Frank [1961] Director [Swedish]; Per Stefan Frank [1966] Director [Swedish]

**Mobility2you Ltd**
*Incorporated:* 16 July 2012 *Employees:* 5
*Net Worth Deficit:* £233,631 *Total Assets:* £357,872
*Registered Office:* 1 North Way, Claverings Industrial Estate, London, N9 0AD
*Shareholder:* Alpesh Bhanuchandra Shah
*Officers:* Alpesh Bhanuchandra Shah [1972] Director/Businessman; Bhanuchandra Shah [1945] Director/Businessman

**Model Medics Limited**
*Incorporated:* 14 July 2010
*Registered Office:* 5 Erskine House, Springfield Grove, Charlton, London, SE7 7TW
*Major Shareholder:* Adeniyi Adesanmi Adegbesan
*Officers:* Dr Adeniyi Adesanmi Adegbesan, Secretary; Dr Adeniyi Adesanmi Adegbesan [1968] Director/Medical Practice

**Modern Aesthetic Solutions Ltd**
*Incorporated:* 6 January 2012
*Net Worth:* £18,148 *Total Assets:* £68,580
*Registered Office:* 39 Steeple Close, West Canford Heath, Poole, Dorset, BH17 9BJ
*Major Shareholder:* Adam Marc Rubens
*Officers:* Stacey Louise Rubens, Secretary; Adam Marc Rubens [1967] Director

**Modern Innovations Limited Ltd**
*Incorporated:* 6 December 2018
*Registered Office:* 1 Purley Road, Croydon, Surrey, CR8 6EZ
*Major Shareholder:* Yasser Kamaleldin Ahmed Mostafa
*Officers:* Dalia Abdelhamid Husien Saleh, Secretary; Yasser Kamaleldin Ahmed Mostafa [1961] Director/GM [Egyptian]

**Modor & Bearn Limited**
*Incorporated:* 27 February 2018
*Registered Office:* Victoria House, Stanbridge Park, Staplefield Lane, Staplefield, W Sussex, RH17 6AS
*Major Shareholder:* Ashley Leitner-Murphy
*Officers:* Bryony Jane Johnson [1973] Director (Non-Executive); Ashley Leitner-Murphy [1990] Director; Simon Zussman [1958] Director (Non-Executive)

**Moka Pharmaceuticals Limited**
*Incorporated:* 23 January 1998
*Net Worth Deficit:* £379 *Total Assets:* £1
*Registered Office:* 1 Dorchester Mews, Twickenham, Middlesex, TW1 2LE
*Major Shareholder:* Nemanja Zrilic
*Officers:* Jelena Zrilic, Secretary; Nemanja Zrilic [1973] Director

**Molab Ltd**
*Incorporated:* 8 January 2013
*Net Worth:* £1,156 *Total Assets:* £22,475
*Registered Office:* Unit 8-10 Pembroke Building, Cumberland Park, Scrubs Lane, London, NW10 6RE
*Major Shareholder:* Daniel Goldberg
*Officers:* Daniel Goldberg [1988] Director

**Molecule Healthcare Limited**
*Incorporated:* 6 January 2015 *Employees:* 3
*Net Worth:* £104,622 *Total Assets:* £194,411
*Registered Office:* 264 High Road, Harrow, Middlesex, HA3 7BB
*Shareholder:* Aniruddhakumar Vora
*Officers:* Kaushik Kumar Bhagvanbhai Mangaroliya [1984] Director [Indian]; Aniruddhakumar Vora [1982] Director; Sanjaykumar Babubhai Zalawadiya [1982] Director

**Monarch Health Ltd**
*Incorporated:* 7 April 2016
*Registered Office:* 2 Bow House, Bushberry Avenue, Coventry, Warwicks, CV4 9NN
*Major Shareholder:* Joshua Calvin
*Officers:* Joshua Calvin [1983] Director

**Moogle Meds Ltd**
*Incorporated:* 10 September 2018
*Registered Office:* 70 Nolt Loan Road, Arbroath, Angus, DD11 2AH
*Shareholders:* Ross Milne; Hassan Alrahow
*Officers:* Hassan Alrahow [1993] Director/Pharmacist [Irish]; Ross Milne [1993] Director/Pharmacist

**Mooncup Ltd**
*Incorporated:* 18 April 2002 *Employees:* 17
*Net Worth:* £1,425,356 *Total Assets:* £1,594,668
*Registered Office:* The Old Casino, 28 Fourth Avenue, Hove, E Sussex, BN3 2PJ
*Parent:* Mooncup Employee Ownership Trustee Limited
*Officers:* Katherine Rhiannon Clements [1972] Director/Campaigns and Marketing Manager; Eileen Greene [1974] Director/International Trade Manager [Irish]; Rowan Helen Hobby [1980] Director/Operations Manager

**Moores Pharmacy Limited**
*Incorporated:* 20 June 1995
*Net Worth:* £766,417 *Total Assets:* £1,057,702
*Registered Office:* Laxmi House, 2B Draycott Avenue, Kenton, Harrow, Middlesex, HA3 0BU
*Shareholder:* Tushar Jayantilal Shah
*Officers:* Raksha Tushar Shah, Secretary; Tushar Jayantilal Shah [1960] Director/Pharmacist

**Moreton Pharmacy Ltd.**
*Incorporated:* 30 March 2009 *Employees:* 9
*Net Worth:* £274,202 *Total Assets:* £1,781,663
*Registered Office:* 14 New Street, Moretonhampstead, Devon, TQ13 8PE
*Shareholders:* David Hall Fulton; George Wickham Limited
*Officers:* Katherine Sarah Fulton, Secretary; David Hall Fulton [1967] Director/Pharmacist; George Simon Robert Wickham [1968] Director/Pharmacist

**Morgan Steer Developments Limited**
*Incorporated:* 1 June 2015
*Registered Office:* 9 Furnace House, Narborough Wood Business Park, Desford Road, Enderby, Leicester, LE19 4XT
*Shareholder:* Matthew James Jelley
*Officers:* Robert George Cradduck [1953] Director; Matthew James Jelley [1968] Director; Peter James Seddon [1951] Director

**Moriah Healthcare Distribution Limited**
*Incorporated:* 9 August 2018
*Registered Office:* 35 Wilcox Close, London, SW8 2UD
*Major Shareholder:* Amaniel Tesfai
*Officers:* Amaniel Tesfai [1987] Director

**Morn View Chemicals (UK) Limited**
*Incorporated:* 23 November 2017
*Registered Office:* 2nd Floor, 107 Charterhouse Street, Clerkenwell, London, EC1M 6HW
*Major Shareholder:* Wing Leung Chung
*Officers:* Wing Leung Chung [1961] Director

**Morningside Pharmaceuticals Limited**
*Incorporated:* 18 December 1991 *Employees:* 50
*Net Worth:* £6,005,035 *Total Assets:* £20,841,896
*Registered Office:* Nene House, 4 Rushmills, Northampton, NN4 7YB
*Parent:* Remedi Medical Holdings Limited
*Officers:* Monisha Nikesh Kotecha, Secretary; Monisha Nikesh Kotecha [1969] Director; Dr Nikesh Rasiklal Kotecha [1966] Director

**Morton Medical Limited**
*Incorporated:* 18 June 2002
*Net Worth Deficit:* £379,475 *Total Assets:* £14,458
*Registered Office:* International House, 142 Cromwell Road, London, SW7 4EF
*Shareholder:* Rene Carl David Herzfeld
*Officers:* Peter George Worsley Penny [1965] Director

**Morvigor (UK) Ltd**
*Incorporated:* 3 March 2016
*Registered Office:* 1417-1419 London Road, Norbury, London, SW16 4AH
*Shareholder:* Christopher Roberts
*Officers:* Eva Hanciles [1958] Director/Doctor [Irish]; Christopher Roberts [1942] Director/Scientist

**Mosaic Pharma Limited**
*Incorporated:* 21 May 2003 *Employees:* 1
*Net Worth:* £11,387 *Total Assets:* £30,890
*Registered Office:* 27 Mortimer Street, London, W1T 3BL
*Major Shareholder:* Philip Cockcroft
*Officers:* Philip Cockcroft [1951] Director

**Moscow Flyer Limited**
*Incorporated:* 6 December 2004 *Employees:* 9
*Net Worth:* £104,667 *Total Assets:* £149,291
*Registered Office:* 99 Wellington Road North, Stockport, Cheshire, SK4 2LP
*Shareholders:* Michael Joseph Gunning; Tajamal Hussain
*Officers:* Tania Maria Gunning, Secretary; Michael Joseph Gunning [1958] Director/Pharmacist

**Mossvet Limited**
*Incorporated:* 28 September 1994 *Employees:* 14
*Net Worth:* £2,823,336 *Total Assets:* £3,952,923
*Registered Office:* 34 Seagoe Industrial Estate, Portadown, Craigavon, Co Armagh, BT63 5QD
*Parent:* Moss Veterinary Products Ltd
*Officers:* Christopher William Sparrow, Secretary; Christopher William Sparrow [1971] Director/General Manager; Dermot S.H. Sparrow [1942] Director/Veterinary Surgeon; Juliet Rosalie Sparrow [1943] Director

**Mountrow Trading Limited**
*Incorporated:* 9 March 2009
*Previous:* High End Media Ltd
*Net Worth Deficit:* £156,595 *Total Assets:* £209
*Registered Office:* 83 Higher Drive, Purley, Surrey, CR8 2HN
*Major Shareholder:* Ajay Patel
*Officers:* Ajay Patel [1965] Director/Account Manager

**Movianto UK Limited**
*Incorporated:* 11 February 1976 *Employees:* 670
*Net Worth Deficit:* £510,000 *Total Assets:* £92,244,000
*Registered Office:* 1 Progress Park, Elstow, Bedford, MK42 9XE
*Parent:* Healthcare Services Group Limited
*Officers:* Kamaljit Singh Hunjan [1967] Director/Senior VP Movianto; Julia M. Munzinger [1968] Director/Accountant [American]; Nicholas Joseph Pace [1970] Director [American]; David John Tinsley [1977] Director

**MQS Group London Limited**
*Incorporated:* 30 June 2017
*Registered Office:* 72 Burch Road, Northfleet, Gravesend, Kent, DA11 9NE
*Officers:* Dr. Mahmood Qasim Majeed [1989] Director [Iraqi]

**MRG Creations Ltd**
*Incorporated:* 23 August 2018
*Registered Office:* 27 Old Gloucester Street, London, WC1N 3AX
*Major Shareholder:* Matthew Gallacher
*Officers:* Matthew Gallacher, Secretary; Matthew Gallacher [1982] Director

**MSB Pharma Ltd**
*Incorporated:* 26 March 2018
*Registered Office:* 4th Floor, Centenary House, 1 Centenary Way, Salford, M50 1RF
*Officers:* Mohammed Shabaz Basharat [1985] Pharmacist Director

**MSP Pharm Ltd**
*Incorporated:* 15 November 2018
*Registered Office:* 7a Central Parade, Ley Street, Ilford, Essex, IG2 7DE
*Shareholders:* Sobieslaw Arkadiusz Sopolinski; Mariusz Bedra
*Officers:* Mariusz Bedra [1981] Director [Polish]; Sobieslaw Arkadiusz Sopolinski [1978] Director [Polish]

**Mulberry Pharma Ltd**
*Incorporated:* 10 October 2018
*Registered Office:* 20 Kingsley Street, Leicester, LE2 6DL
*Shareholders:* Chhavi Mohley; Gursharen Singh Sooch
*Officers:* Chhavi Mohley [1984] Director [Indian]; Gursharen Sooch [1983] Director

**Multi Pharma Limited**
*Incorporated:* 25 February 1998
*Net Worth Deficit:* £2,719
*Registered Office:* 74 Heathside, Hinchley Wood, Esher, Surrey, KT10 9TF
*Officers:* Chiragni Amin, Secretary; Ketan Amin [1964] Director

**Mundibiopharma Limited**
*Incorporated:* 21 October 2014  *Employees:* 10
*Net Worth Deficit:* £19,397,526  *Total Assets:* £75,442,888
*Registered Office:* Unit 196 Cambridge Science Park, Milton Road, Cambridge, CB4 0AB
*Shareholders:* Hermance Bernadette Monique Schaepman; Jonathan David Sackler; Richard Stephen Sackler
*Officers:* Stuart David Baker [1935] Director/Lawyer [American]; Bryan George LEA [1961] Director/Lawyer; Alberto Martinez [1972] Director [Spanish]; David Alan Silver [1965] Director/Accountant; Ake Gunnar Wikstrom [1951] Director/Advisor [Swedish]

**Mundipharma Medical Company Limited**
*Incorporated:* 21 October 2014  *Employees:* 50
*Net Worth:* £42,364,160  *Total Assets:* £298,486,304
*Registered Office:* Unit 196 Cambridge Science Park, Milton Road, Cambridge, CB4 0AB
*Shareholders:* Hermance Bernadette Monique Schaepman; Leslie John Schreyer
*Officers:* Stuart David Baker [1935] Director/Lawyer [American]; Bryan George LEA [1961] Director/Lawyer; Alberto Martinez [1972] Director [Spanish]; David Alan Silver [1965] Director/Accountant; Ake Gunnar Wikstrom [1951] Director/Advisor [Swedish]

**Munro Healthcare (Caucasus & Middle Asia) Limited**
*Incorporated:* 17 January 2013  *Employees:* 1
*Net Worth Deficit:* £47,271  *Total Assets:* £88,714
*Registered Office:* 3 Young Place, East Kilbride, G75 0TD
*Parent:* Munro Healthcare Group Limited
*Officers:* John Cochrane [1957] Director

**Munro Healthcare Group Limited**
*Incorporated:* 14 February 2012  *Employees:* 197
*Net Worth:* £25,122,690  *Total Assets:* £42,710,328
*Registered Office:* 3 Young Place, East Kilbride, G75 0TD
*Shareholder:* John Cochrane
*Officers:* John Cochrane [1957] Director; Stuart John Overend [1970] Director

**Munro Healthcare Pharma Limited**
*Incorporated:* 16 January 2017
*Net Worth:* £100  *Total Assets:* £100
*Registered Office:* 3 Young Place, Kelvin Industrial Estate, East Kilbride, G75 0TD
*Parent:* Munro Healthcare Group Limited
*Officers:* John Cochrane [1957] Director; Stuart John Overend [1970] Director

**Munro Medical Limited**
*Incorporated:* 30 March 2007
*Registered Office:* 3 Young Place, Kelvin Industrial Estate, East Kilbride, G75 0TD
*Shareholders:* Kirsten Munro; Gail Munro
*Officers:* John Cochrane [1957] Director

**Munro Wholesale Medical Supplies Limited**
*Incorporated:* 3 November 2009
*Registered Office:* 3 Young Place, Kelvin Industrial Estate, East Kilbride, G75 0TD
*Parent:* Munro Healthcare Group Limited
*Officers:* John Cochrane [1957] Director; Shirley Agnes Gorrell [1967] Director

**Paul Murray PLC**
*Incorporated:* 5 June 1974  *Employees:* 80
*Net Worth:* £4,670,833  *Total Assets:* £7,488,329
*Registered Office:* Paul Murray PLC, Wide Lane, Southampton, SO18 2FA
*Parent:* Metro Gold Limited
*Officers:* Susan Claire Coatham, Finance Director; Susan Claire Coatham [1961] Finance Director; Mark Cox [1968] Operations Director; Charlotte Ann Eastwood [1985] Director; Thomas Eastwood [1981] Buying Director; Leigh Hadaway [1972] Buying Director; Nicholas Brian Hayton [1972] Sales Director; Karen Julia Murray [1954] Director; Maxwell John Murray [1979] Director/Hotelier; Paul Travis Murray [1948] Director; Gemma Louise Robertson [1981] Director

**MWK Healthcare Limited**
*Incorporated:* 18 August 2010  *Employees:* 2
*Net Worth Deficit:* £21,412  *Total Assets:* £50,900
*Registered Office:* F09 The Fort Offices, Artillery Business Park, Oswestry, Salop, SY11 4AD
*Major Shareholder:* Gareth Huw Jenkins
*Officers:* David Mark William Keeling, Secretary; David Mark William Keeling [1959] Managing Director

**My Chu Limited**
*Incorporated:* 15 February 2019
*Registered Office:* Egerton House, 55 Hoole Road, Chester, CH2 3NJ
*Major Shareholder:* Benjamin Parry
*Officers:* Benjamin Parry [1988] Director

**My Dental Store Limited**
*Incorporated:* 24 February 2017
*Registered Office:* 17 Great Russell Court, Fieldhead Business Centre, Bradford, BD7 1JZ
*Officers:* Amran Riaz, Secretary; Amran Riaz [1977] Director

**My Nutrition London Ltd**
*Incorporated:* 31 December 2018
*Registered Office:* Kemp House, 160 City Road, London, EC1V 2NX
*Officers:* Mohamed Elbawab [1986] Director [Egyptian]

**My Premium Nutrition Limited**
*Incorporated:* 29 January 2019
*Registered Office:* 272 Bath Street, Glasgow, G2 4JR
*Major Shareholder:* Viktoriya Dalton
*Officers:* Viktoriya Dalton [1978] Director

**My-Kaya Ltd**
*Incorporated:* 18 September 2018
*Registered Office:* Suite 5, Charan House, 18 Union Road, London, SW4 6JP
*Major Shareholder:* Cleves Valdo Lopes
*Officers:* Cleves Valdo Lopes [1975] Director [Brazilian]

**Mychem Limited**
*Incorporated:* 8 May 2006
*Net Worth:* £108,454  *Total Assets:* £362,249
*Registered Office:* 12a East Street, Tollesbury, Maldon, Essex, CM9 8QD
*Major Shareholder:* Gurvinder Singh Bhatia
*Officers:* Gurvinder Singh Bhatia [1974] Director

**Mycology Research Laboratories Limited**
*Incorporated:* 10 April 1997  *Employees:* 1
*Net Worth:* £369,006  *Total Assets:* £595,553
*Registered Office:* Suite 8, The Spires, Adelaide Street, Luton, Beds, LU1 5BB
*Shareholder:* William Ahern
*Officers:* Marjaneh Seifi, Secretary; William Ahern [1957] Director [Irish]; Malcolm Clark [1942] Director/Agri Business; David Law [1951] Director/Agri Business [American]

**Adam Myers Solutions Limited**
*Incorporated:* 2 October 2018
*Registered Office:* Corner Oak, 1 Homer Road, Solihull, W Midlands, B91 3QG
*Shareholders:* Ravinder Kaur Bhandal; Charanjit Singh Bhandal
*Officers:* Charnjit Singh Bhandal [1966] Director/Pharmacist; Ravinder Kaur Bhandal [1964] Director

**Mylan UK Healthcare Limited**
*Incorporated:* 28 August 2014  *Employees:* 29
*Previous:* BGP Products Ltd.
*Net Worth:* £18,299,000  *Total Assets:* £94,587,000
*Registered Office:* 20 Station Close, Potters Bar, Herts, EN6 1TL
*Parent:* Mylan Holdings Ltd
*Officers:* Falk Patrick Nuernberger, Secretary; Jean-Yves Brault [1967] Director/General Manager [Canadian]; Caroline Rebecca Louise Dixon [1968] Finance Director

**Myly Pharma Limited**
*Incorporated:* 21 March 2018
*Registered Office:* 167 Uxbridge Road, London, W7 3TH
*Officers:* Lakhvir Singh Gill [1962] Director

**Myriad Medical Supplies Limited**
*Incorporated:* 12 May 1998
*Net Worth:* £280,994  *Total Assets:* £702,326
*Registered Office:* Concept House, 6 McNicol Drive, London, NW10 7AW
*Parent:* Myriad Holdings Ltd
*Officers:* Shila Shah, Secretary/Administrator; Kamalkumar Shah [1955] Director/Pharmacist; Shila Shah [1955] Director/Administrator

**N & G Pharma Limited**
*Incorporated:* 24 June 2014
*Net Worth:* £3,822  *Total Assets:* £521,040
*Registered Office:* Corner Oak, 1 Homer Road, Solihull, W Midlands, B91 3QG
*Major Shareholder:* Charnjit Singh Bhandal
*Officers:* Charnjit Singh Bhandal [1966] Director; Peter Anthony Sidaway [1965] Director/IT Consultant

**N H Southeast Ltd**
*Incorporated:* 2 October 2008  *Employees:* 1
*Net Worth:* £531,354  *Total Assets:* £533,309
*Registered Office:* Charwood House, Oakhurst Business Park, Southwater, W Sussex, RH13 9RT
*Shareholders:* Global Consortium Limited; John Mark Andrews; James Christopher Andrews; Paul Anthony Andrews
*Officers:* John Mark Andrews [1960] Sales Director

**N N Pharma Ltd**
*Incorporated:* 15 April 2015
*Net Worth:* £40,461  *Total Assets:* £68,549
*Registered Office:* Trilogy Suite, 9 Church Street, Wednesfield, Wolverhampton, W Midlands, WV11 1SR
*Shareholders:* Nadeem Nasrullah; Ramzan Nasrullah
*Officers:* Nadeem Nasrullah [1991] Director/Pharmacist

**N-Pen Ltd.**
*Incorporated:* 11 January 2018
*Registered Office:* 12 Paddock Close, Nottingham, NG6 8RB
*Shareholders:* Immaculate Nwabuisi Ekpen; Immaculate Nwabuisi Ekpen
*Officers:* Immaculate Nwabuisi Ekpen [1988] Director/Pharmacist

**N.G. Limited**
*Incorporated:* 14 May 1986  *Employees:* 26
*Net Worth:* £2,776,895  *Total Assets:* £7,209,579
*Registered Office:* Unit 10 Cornwall Road Industrial Estate, Cornwall Road, Smethwick, W Midlands, B66 2JT
*Shareholder:* Vijay Kumar Sudera
*Officers:* Vijay Kumar Sudera, Secretary; Ashwani Sudera [1965] Director; Sudha Sudera [1962] Director; Vijay Kumar Sudera [1953] Director/Buyer

**N.I.P. Pharma Limited**
*Incorporated:* 21 July 2005  *Employees:* 8
*Net Worth:* £430,532  *Total Assets:* £1,986,943
*Registered Office:* Unit 8c Loughway Business Park, Newry, Co Down, BT34 2TH
*Parent:* PCO Manufacturing
*Officers:* Patrick Michael Wadding, Secretary; David Justin Brown [1973] Director/ICT Architect; Patrick Michael Wadding [1968] Director/MD [Irish]

**N4 Biotech Limited**
*Incorporated:* 18 April 2018
*Registered Office:* The Mills, Canal Street, Derby, DE1 2RJ
*Parent:* N4 Pharma PLC
*Officers:* Nigel James Theobald [1964] Director; Paul Charlton Titley [1952] Director

**Nagarjun Healthcare Limited**
*Incorporated:* 25 September 2015  *Employees:* 4
*Net Worth Deficit:* £33,025  *Total Assets:* £88,216
*Registered Office:* 101 B, Unit 1 Watling Gate, 297-303 Edgware Road, London, NW9 6NB
*Major Shareholder:* Atrey Aka Sharma Joshi
*Officers:* Atrey Satishkumar Joshi Aka Sharma [1982] Director [Indian]

**Nalchem Ltd**
*Incorporated:* 31 January 2014
*Net Worth:* £174,870  *Total Assets:* £434,829
*Registered Office:* 3a Bluestone Business Park, Moyraverty West Road, Moyraverty, Craigavon, Co Armagh, BT65 5HU
*Officers:* Martin McNally [1983] Director

**Nanocor World Holdings Limited**
*Incorporated:* 9 October 2017
*Registered Office:* Churchlands, Kirdford, Billingshurst, W Sussex, RH14 0LP
*Officers:* Samuel Andrew Skillman [1953] Director/Self Employed; Clinton Luke Smith [1977] Director/Self Employed [South African]

**Napp Laboratories Limited**
*Incorporated:* 26 September 1923  *Employees:* 3
*Net Worth:* £12,968,000  *Total Assets:* £16,254,000
*Registered Office:* Unit 196 Cambridge Science Park, Milton Road, Cambridge, CB4 0AB
*Parent:* Napp Pharmaceutical Group Limited
*Officers:* Stuart David Baker [1935] Director/Attorney [American]; Bryan George LEA [1961] Director/Solicitor; Ake Gunnar Wikstrom [1951] Director/Advisor [Swedish]

**Napp Pharmaceutical Group Limited**
*Incorporated:* 27 July 1966
*Net Worth:* £82,254,000  *Total Assets:* £87,942,000
*Registered Office:* Unit 196 Cambridge Science Park, Milton Road, Cambridge, CB4 0AB
*Parent:* Napp Pharmaceutical Holdings Limited
*Officers:* Stuart David Baker [1935] Director/Lawyer [American]; Ake Gunnar Wikstrom [1951] Director/Advisor [Swedish]

**Napp Pharmaceutical Holdings Limited**
*Incorporated:* 19 December 1997  *Employees:* 612
*Net Worth:* £191,744,000  *Total Assets:* £304,665,984
*Registered Office:* Unit 196 Cambridge Science Park, Milton Road, Cambridge, CB4 0AB
*Shareholder:* Stuart David Baker
*Officers:* Stuart David Baker [1935] Director/Lawyer [American]; Ake Gunnar Wikstrom [1951] Director/Advisor [Swedish]

**Napp Pharmaceuticals Limited**
*Incorporated:* 22 December 1998  *Employees:* 179
*Net Worth:* £6,491,000  *Total Assets:* £41,612,000
*Registered Office:* Unit 196 Cambridge Science Park, Milton Road, Cambridge, CB4 0AB
*Parent:* Napp Pharmaceutical Holdings Limited
*Officers:* Stuart David Baker [1935] Director/Attorney [American]; Hywel Rhys Day [1974] Managing Director; Bryan George LEA [1961] Director; Dr Julian Paul Schofield [1959] Medical Director; David Alan Silver [1965] Director/Accountant; Ake Gunnar Wikstrom [1951] Director/Advisor [Swedish]

**Nascot Health Ltd**
*Incorporated:* 2 January 2019
*Registered Office:* Tower 42, Old Broad Street, London, EC2N 1HQ
*Shareholders:* Tim Ambrose; Jon-Paul Doran
*Officers:* Tim Ambrose [1980] Director; Jon-Paul Doran [1987] Director

**Nascot Natural Health Limited**
*Incorporated:* 11 May 2018
*Registered Office:* 2 Elm Close, Darrington, Pontefract, W Yorks, WF8 3AF
*Major Shareholder:* James Gilbert McGrory
*Officers:* James Gilbert McGrory [1942] Director and Company Secretary

**Nasila Pharma Limited**
*Incorporated:* 21 January 2016  *Employees:* 2
*Net Worth Deficit:* £44,369  *Total Assets:* £199,135
*Registered Office:* Suite 2, Cedar Court, Grove Business Park, White Waltham, Maidenhead, Berks, SL6 3LW
*Shareholders:* Abdul Hamin Ali; Arif Esmail
*Officers:* Abdul Hamin Ali [1967] Director; Arif Esmail [1963] Director

**Naskalmik Limited**
*Incorporated:* 2 June 2014
*Registered Office:* 15 Joydon Drive, Romford, Essex, RM6 4ST
*Officers:* Firdowsa Abdulrahman [1973] Director/Wholesale Medicine

**Nasser Waziri Ltd**
*Incorporated:* 28 July 2017
*Registered Office:* 85 Great Portland Street, London, W1W 7LT
*Officers:* Waziri Nasser [1978] Director/Business Consultant [German]

**Natchy Ltd**
*Incorporated:* 6 November 2018
*Registered Office:* 20 Alban Avenue, St Albans, Herts, AL3 5SX
*Major Shareholder:* Osinachi Chinagozim Ajaegbu
*Officers:* Osinachi Chinagozim Ajaegbu [1971] Director

**National Veterinary Services Limited**
*Incorporated:* 16 April 2013  *Employees:* 564
*Net Worth:* £106,732,000  *Total Assets:* £165,203,008
*Registered Office:* Unit 4 Jamage Industrial Estate, Talke Pits, Stoke on Trent, Staffs, ST7 1XW
*Parent:* Patterson Companies, Inc
*Officers:* Glenn Aungles, Secretary; Leslie Brian Korsh [1969] Director/Vice President, General Counsel and Secretary [American]; Kevin Michael Pohlman [1962] Director [American]; Martin Holt Riley [1964] Director; Mark Steven Walchirk [1966] Director/President and CEO [American]

**Nationwide Healthcare Solutions Limited**
*Incorporated:* 9 June 2010  *Employees:* 9
*Net Worth:* £349,771  *Total Assets:* £1,134,839
*Registered Office:* 172 Willows Lane, Bolton, Lancs, BL3 4BU
*Officers:* Suleman Musa Darsot [1972] Director/Pharmacist; Enayat Iqbal Patel [1985] Director/Pharmacist; Naeem Aziz Patel [1984] Director/Pharmacist; Muhammad Awais Masood Rafiq [1983] Director/Pharmacist

**Nativis Bio Ltd**
*Incorporated:* 23 October 2018
*Registered Office:* 71-75 Shelton Street, London, WC2H 9JQ
*Shareholders:* Kian Tiak Lim; Kareen Siau Yen Lim
*Officers:* Trinh to Huynh [1978] Director/Pharmacist; Kareen Siau Yen Lim [1976] Director/Pharmacist [Malaysian]

**Natural Science.Com Limited**
*Incorporated:* 6 April 1999
*Registered Office:* Nelsons House, 83 Parkside, Wimbledon, London, SW19 5LP
*Officers:* Robert Nelson Wilson [1962] Director/Chairman

**Naturelo Ltd**
*Incorporated:* 20 September 2017  *Employees:* 1
*Net Worth:* £250  *Total Assets:* £95,134
*Registered Office:* 20-22 Wenlock Road, London, N1 7GU
*Major Shareholder:* Milan Yogesh Shah
*Officers:* Milan Yogesh Shah [1980] Director/MD

**Naturenetics UK Limited**
*Incorporated:* 20 November 2013
*Net Worth:* £14,233  *Total Assets:* £29,401
*Registered Office:* c/o Khan Morris Accountants Ltd, Empress Heights, College Street, Southampton, SO14 3LA
*Major Shareholder:* Graeme Potter
*Officers:* Graeme Potter [1977] Director

**Natures Healthworks Limited**
*Incorporated:* 9 September 2014
*Net Worth Deficit:* £16,008  *Total Assets:* £1,177
*Registered Office:* 12 Salisbury Road, Cosham, Portsmouth, PO6 2PN
*Shareholders:* Colin Potter; Gill Vigus
*Officers:* Colin Potter [1949] Director/Company Executive; Gill Vigus [1960] Director/Company Executive

**Natures Merchant Ltd**
*Incorporated:* 18 July 2017
*Registered Office:* 35 Dirleton Avenue, Cambuslang, Glasgow, G72 8ZB
*Major Shareholder:* Graeme Todd
*Officers:* Graeme Todd [1986] Director

**NBS Scientific Limited**
*Incorporated:* 15 February 2018
*Registered Office:* c/o Preiskel & Co LLP, 4 King's Bench Walk, Temple, London, EC4Y 7DL
*Officers:* Marjolein Van de Luitgaren [1974] Director/Manager [Dutch]

**NC Trade UK Ltd**
*Incorporated:* 9 November 2015  *Employees:* 1
*Net Worth Deficit:* £14,643  *Total Assets:* £3,011
*Registered Office:* 59 Worple Road, Isleworth, London, TW7 7BA
*Major Shareholder:* Evangelia Apergi
*Officers:* Evangelia Apergi [1972] Director [Greek]

**Nebel Healthcare Limited**
*Incorporated:* 6 February 2014
*Net Worth:* £533  *Total Assets:* £7,772
*Registered Office:* Wellington House, 273-275 High Street, London Colney, Herts, AL2 1HA
*Shareholders:* Chidi Emeka Okeke; Nneka Onwuachu
*Officers:* Nneka Onwuachu [1979] Director/Pharmacist

**Necessity Supplies Limited**
*Incorporated:* 15 April 1986  *Employees:* 20
*Net Worth:* £17,272,842  *Total Assets:* £23,168,152
*Registered Office:* Unit 4-5 Northolt Trading Estate, Belvue Road, Northolt, Middlesex, UB5 5QS
*Officers:* Vandana Wadhar, Secretary; Bharat Himatlal Mehta [1952] Director; Ketan Himatlal Mehta [1958] Director/Pharmacist

**NeilMed Holding Company Limited**
*Incorporated:* 23 June 2016  *Employees:* 18
*Net Worth:* £6,346,587  *Total Assets:* £11,773,630
*Registered Office:* 221 Kenton Lane, Kenton, Harrow, Middlesex, HA3 8RP
*Major Shareholder:* Ketan Chandrakant Mehta
*Officers:* Dr Ketan Chandrakant Mehta [1956] Director/Physician [American]; Nina Mehta [1961] Director [American]

**Neilmed Limited**
*Incorporated:* 30 June 2006  *Employees:* 8
*Net Worth:* £4,547,108  *Total Assets:* £6,988,272
*Registered Office:* 221 Kenton Lane, Kenton, Harrow, Middlesex, HA3 8RP
*Officers:* Dr Ketan Mehta [1956] Director/Physician [American]; Nina Mehta [1961] Director/Chairman [American]

**Nelson & Russell Limited**
*Incorporated:* 16 June 1989
*Registered Office:* Nelsons House, 83 Parkside, Wimbledon, London, SW19 5LP
*Parent:* A Nelson & Co Limited
*Officers:* Patrick Russell Wilson [1965] Director; Robert Nelson Wilson [1962] Director/Chairman

**Nema Pharma Trade Limited**
*Incorporated:* 13 June 2018
*Registered Office:* Flat 1, 43 Beak Street, London, W1F 9SB
*Officers:* Mark Wilfried Herold [1975] Managing Director [German]

**Neo Farma Ltd**
*Incorporated:* 8 March 2017
*Registered Office:* First Floor, Roxburghe House, 273-287 Regent Street, London, W1B 2HA
*Shareholder:* Bavaguthu Raghuram Shetty
*Officers:* Suresh Kumar Nandiraju [1969] Director [Indian]; Dr Bavaguthu Raghuram Shetty [1942] Director [Indian]

**Neo Health UK Limited**
*Incorporated:* 25 July 2017
*Registered Office:* 1 Doughty Street, London, WC1N 2PH
*Major Shareholder:* Sanjiv Puri
*Officers:* Aman Madan [1967] Director [Australian]

**Neolife International Ltd**
*Incorporated:* 18 March 1994  *Employees:* 1
*Previous:* GNLD International Ltd
*Net Worth:* £49,833  *Total Assets:* £146,835
*Registered Office:* Old Bank Chambers, 582-586 Kingsbury Road, Erdington, Birmingham, B24 9ND
*Officers:* Rok Podlesnik, Secretary; Hakan Bjorklund [1959] Director/Vice President of Operations Northern Europe [Swedish]

**Neon Diagnostics Ltd**
*Incorporated:* 28 April 2011
*Net Worth:* £1,911,377  *Total Assets:* £2,805,368
*Registered Office:* Unit 7 & 8 Swanbridge Industrial Park, Black Croft Road, Witham, Essex, CM8 3YN
*Shareholders:* Peter John Hope; Naseen Mohamed Valji
*Officers:* Peter John Hope [1963] Director; Naseen Valji [1959] Director

**Neubourg Pharma (UK) Limited**
*Incorporated:* 6 December 2013
*Net Worth Deficit:* £172,663  *Total Assets:* £19,796
*Registered Office:* 75 Springfield Road, Chelmsford, Essex, CM2 6JB
*Shareholders:* Gabriel Thomas McGlynn; Thomas Neubourg
*Officers:* Gabriel Thomas McGlynn [1947] Director/Pharmaceutical Consultant [Irish]; Dr Thomas Neubourg [1969] Director/Self Employed [German]

**Neubria Limited**
*Incorporated:* 1 November 2017
*Registered Office:* Hamilton House, Church Street, Altrincham, Cheshire, WA14 4DR
*Major Shareholder:* Brian George Kennedy
*Officers:* Timothy John Halpin [1981] Finance Director; Adrian Christopher Kirk [1961] Finance Director

**Neutradvance Limited**
*Incorporated:* 16 April 2012
*Net Worth:* £3,948  *Total Assets:* £13,188
*Registered Office:* Ibex House, Baker Street, Weybridge, Surrey, KT13 8AH
*Shareholders:* Elicca Anne Vazirani; Everyll de Souza
*Officers:* Elicca Anne de Souza, Secretary; Elicca Anne de Souza [1985] Director; David Freedman [1942] Director/Chief Operating Officer; Rachel Freedman [1943] Director

**Nevik Limited**
*Incorporated:* 30 August 2017
*Registered Office:* 3rd Floor, 166 College Road, Harrow, Middlesex, HA1 1BH
*Major Shareholder:* Neha Vishal Jain
*Officers:* Neha Vishal Jain [1982] Director

**New England Biolabs (U.K.) Limited**
Incorporated: 7 July 1993  Employees: 31
Net Worth: £6,325,422  Total Assets: £9,168,252
Registered Office: 75-77 Knowl Piece, Wilbury Way, Hitchin, Herts, SG4 0TY
Major Shareholder: Donald Comb
Officers: Peter Nathan, Secretary/Director; Dr Donald Comb [1927] Director [American]; James Ellard [1962] Director/Executive [American]; Peter Nathan [1956] Director

**New Generation Business UK Limited**
Incorporated: 16 January 2018
Registered Office: Flat 3, 10 Durham Road, Bromley, Kent, BR2 0SG
Shareholder: Kingsley Chidi Eze
Officers: Kingsley Eze, Secretary; Kingsley Chidi Eze [1972] Director/Public Servant

**New Health Global Solutions Ltd**
Incorporated: 1 February 2017
Registered Office: 40 Wood End Lane, Northolt, Middlesex, UB5 4JL
Shareholders: Fabrizio de Silvestri; Edoardo Romani
Officers: Fabrizio de Silvestri [1972] Director [Italian]

**New Health Supplies Limited**
Incorporated: 1 November 2010  Employees: 8
Net Worth: £81,704  Total Assets: £331,850
Registered Office: Unit 5 Archadale Business Centre, Brember Road, Harrow, Middlesex, HA2 8DJ
Officers: Pranav Hariprasad Patel [1976] Director; Pranav Hariprasad Patel [1976] Director; Prashant Hariprasad Patel [1976] Director

**New Horizon Pharma (UK) Ltd.**
Incorporated: 19 May 2014
Previous: 09046396 Ltd.
Net Worth: £760,434  Total Assets: £25,270,968
Registered Office: 49 Green Lanes, London, N16 9BU
Officers: Viktoria Gorenskaja [1985] Director/Private Employee [Estonian]

**New Medical World Ltd**
Incorporated: 26 October 2017
Registered Office: 55 Brighton Grove, Manchester, M14 5JT
Major Shareholder: Zli Mohamed Ramdan Omar
Officers: Zli Mohamed Ramdan Omar, Secretary; Zli Mohamed Ramdan Omar [1984] Director/Manager

**New Roots Herbal Limited**
Incorporated: 23 August 2004
Registered Office: Wey Court West, Union Road, Farnham, Surrey, GU9 7PT
Major Shareholder: Peter Frederick Wilkes
Officers: Peter Frederick Wilkes [1951] Director/Businessman [Canadian]

**New Seasons Natural Products Limited**
Incorporated: 13 February 2003  Employees: 6
Net Worth: £1,438,580  Total Assets: £1,738,782
Registered Office: 9 Worton Park, Cassington, Witney, Oxon, OX29 4SX
Officers: Antonia Anne Breakspear [1951] Director; Bill Nicholas George Breakspear [1978] Director; Jonathan Richard Breakspear [1950] Director; Jenna Catherine Jaaniste [1981] Sales Director

**Newbridge Pharma Ltd.**
Incorporated: 28 November 2006  Employees: 4
Net Worth: £256,662  Total Assets: £390,239
Registered Office: Unit 2 Brannam Crescent, Roundswell Business Park, Barnstaple, Devon, EX31 3TD
Major Shareholder: Andrew John Collier
Officers: Andrew John Collier, Secretary; Andrew John Collier [1960] Director; Lynne Collier [1961] Director/Sales Assistant

**Newco Pharma Limited**
Incorporated: 5 March 1975
Registered Office: 3 Young Place, Kelvin Industrial Estate, East Kilbride, G75 0TD
Parent: Strathclyde Pharmaceuticals Limited
Officers: John Cochrane [1957] Director; Shirley Agnes Gorrell [1967] Commercial Director

**Newmeds Wholesale Limited**
Incorporated: 16 May 2018
Registered Office: 4d Auchingramont Road, Hamilton, S Lanarks, ML3 6JT
Major Shareholder: Mohammed Ijaz
Officers: Mohammed Ijaz [1964] Director

**Newstar Healthcare Limited**
Incorporated: 13 May 2003
Previous: Newstar Imports Limited
Registered Office: Caxton House, Caxton Road, Fulwood, Preston, Lancs, PR2 9ZB
Parent: Newstar Group Ltd
Officers: Imran Bargit [1976] Director/Businessman

**Newtexko Ltd.**
Incorporated: 4 May 2005
Net Worth: £1,000  Total Assets: £1,000
Registered Office: 19 Kathleen Road, London, SW11 2JR
Officers: Nguyen Thanh Tung [1960] Director/Businessman [Vietnamese]

**Newtons Medical Supplies Ltd**
Incorporated: 14 July 2015
Net Worth: £40,360  Total Assets: £104,213
Registered Office: 11 Queens Road, Brentwood, Essex, CM14 4HE
Major Shareholder: Colin Francis Newton
Officers: Colin Francis Newton [1957] Director/Service Manager

**Newville Trading Limited**
Incorporated: 21 May 2014
Net Worth: £8,456  Total Assets: £14,077
Registered Office: 3rd Floor, 14 Hanover Street, London, W1S 1YH
Officers: Margaret Louise Janke [1969] Director/Consultant [South African]

**Nex Pharma Limited**
Incorporated: 18 May 2018
Registered Office: Mentor House, Ainsworth Street, Blackburn, BB1 6AY
Officers: Gary Calvert [1977] Director; Natalie Jayne Calvert [1975] Director; Krisjanis Ritovs [1989] Director [Latvian]; Martins Ritovs [1986] Director [Latvian]

**Nexcape Pharmaceuticals Ltd**
Incorporated: 12 November 2012  Employees: 9
Net Worth: £882,347  Total Assets: £9,836,359
Registered Office: 20-22 Wenlock Road, London, N1 7GU
Parent: Primanex Limited
Officers: Samir Haresh Parikh [1973] Director/W Planner

**NHS Generics Limited**
*Incorporated:* 20 May 2005
*Registered Office:* Chemidex House, Unit 7 Egham Business Village, Crabtree Road, Egham, Surrey, TW20 8RB
*Major Shareholder:* Navinchandra Jamnadas
*Officers:* Nikesh Engineer [1985] Director/Doctor

**Niayara Global Limited**
*Incorporated:* 25 June 2007
*Previous:* Autostyle Cars Limited
*Net Worth:* £354,877 *Total Assets:* £510,186
*Registered Office:* 4th Floor, Suite B, Congress House, Lyon Road, Harrow, Middlesex, HA1 2EN
*Major Shareholder:* Akeet Mukesh Patel
*Officers:* Mukesh Kanubhai Patel, Secretary; Akeet Mukesh Patel [1980] Director/Export Manager

**Niche Pharma Limited**
*Incorporated:* 16 August 2013 *Employees:* 1
*Net Worth:* £16,730 *Total Assets:* £86,619
*Registered Office:* 24a High Road, Balby, Doncaster, S Yorks, DN4 0PL
*Major Shareholder:* Jonathan Marcus McGill
*Officers:* Jonathan Marcus McGill [1965] Director/Pharmacist; Sarah-Jane McGill [1962] Director/Customer Service Manager

**Nicholas LifeSciences Ltd.**
*Incorporated:* 13 February 2018
*Registered Office:* 5 Jupiter House, Calleva Park, Aldermaston, Reading, Berks, RG7 8NN
*Officers:* Sanjeev Jain [1966] Director [Indian]

**Nigem International Limited**
*Incorporated:* 9 March 2015
*Registered Office:* 10 Bedstone Way, Stanground, Peterborough, Cambs, PE7 3DW
*Officers:* Germaine Asba [1971] Director/Owner

**Nikopharm Ltd**
*Incorporated:* 28 April 2017
*Net Worth:* £437 *Total Assets:* £539
*Registered Office:* 87 Cedar Road, Romford, Essex, RM7 7JS
*Major Shareholder:* Nikolay Atanasov Atanasov
*Officers:* Nikolay Atanasov Atanasov [1978] Director/Pharmacist [Bulgarian]

**Nimrod Veterinary Products Limited**
*Incorporated:* 12 December 2007 *Employees:* 9
*Net Worth:* £278,159 *Total Assets:* £931,814
*Registered Office:* Staverton Court, Staverton, Cheltenham, Glos, GL51 0UX
*Major Shareholder:* David John Renney
*Officers:* David John Renney, Secretary; David John Renney [1960] Director; Donna Theresa Renney [1959] Director

**Nino and Blue Spruce Ltd**
*Incorporated:* 26 October 2018
*Registered Office:* 27 Old Gloucester Street, London, WC1N 3AX
*Major Shareholder:* Nino Mamukashvili
*Officers:* Nino Mamukashvili, Secretary; Nino Mamukashvili [1980] Director [Georgian]

**Nipro Diagnostics (UK) Limited**
*Incorporated:* 29 February 2000 *Employees:* 18
*Net Worth:* £2,994,901 *Total Assets:* £9,189,512
*Registered Office:* Units 12-14 South Point, Ensign Way, Hamble, Hants, SO31 4RF
*Parent:* Nipro Europe NV
*Officers:* Serge Kemps [1971] Director/Chief Executive [Belgian]

**Nissi Business Services Limited**
*Incorporated:* 11 December 2009 *Employees:* 1
*Net Worth Deficit:* £129,103 *Total Assets:* £1,486
*Registered Office:* 25 St Luke's Road, Old Windsor, Windsor, Berks, SL4 2QL
*Shareholder:* Mojisola Adewunmi Okuwoga
*Officers:* Mojisola Adewunmi Okuwoga, Secretary; Dr Adeyinka Adebayo Okuwoga [1957] Director/Civil Servant [Nigerian]; Mojisola Adewunmi Okuwoga [1961] Director [Nigerian]

**Niv Ltd**
*Incorporated:* 21 January 2019
*Registered Office:* 65 Halesowen Road, Morden, Surrey, SM4 6NQ
*Shareholders:* Jetunkumar Ravajibhai Patel; Ritaben Gordhanbhai Ghatala
*Officers:* Ritaben Gordhanbhai Ghatala [1984] Director [Indian]; Jetunkumar Ravajibhai Patel [1985] Director [Indian]

**Nivja Healthcare Ltd**
*Incorporated:* 4 February 2019
*Registered Office:* 65 Halesowen Road, Morden, Surrey, SM4 6NQ
*Shareholders:* Jetunkumar Ravajibhai Patel; Ritaben Gordhanbhai Ghatala
*Officers:* Ritaben Gordhanbhai Ghatala [1984] Director [Indian]; Jetunkumar Ravajibhai Patel [1985] Director [Indian]

**NKCell Plus PLC**
*Incorporated:* 28 November 2018
*Registered Office:* 3rd Floor, 207 Regent Street, London, W1B 3HH
*Officers:* Lidell Page, Secretary; Malcolm Groat [1961] Director/Executive; Lidell Page [1971] Director/Attorney [American]

**NLR Exports Limited**
*Incorporated:* 11 October 1994 *Employees:* 2
*Net Worth Deficit:* £742,368 *Total Assets:* £2,430
*Registered Office:* c/o Moss Goodman Chartered Accountants, 24 Lyndhurst Gardens, Finchley Church End, London, N3 1TB
*Shareholders:* Janet Vivienne Gold; Peter Brian Gold
*Officers:* Nicola Alison Wood, Secretary; Janet Vivienne Gold [1947] Director

**NMB Medical Limited**
*Incorporated:* 5 October 2012
*Net Worth Deficit:* £41,313 *Total Assets:* £23,615
*Registered Office:* Exchange Building, 66 Church Street, Hartlepool, Cleveland, TS24 7DN
*Shareholders:* Mariam Naqesh-Bandi; Nazik Naqesh-Bandi
*Officers:* Mariam Naqesh-Bandi [1989] Director; Nazik Naqesh-Bandi [1987] Director

**NOD Europe Ltd.**
*Incorporated:* 13 May 2011
*Net Worth Deficit:* £198,143 *Total Assets:* £162,363
*Registered Office:* DWF LLP, 5 St Pauls Square, Old Hall Street, Liverpool, L3 9AE
*Officers:* David Brian Vanderdussen [1961] Director [Canadian]

**The Noohra Limited**
*Incorporated:* 27 April 2018
*Registered Office:* Innovation Centre Medway, Maidstone Road, Chatham, Kent, ME5 9FD
*Major Shareholder:* Ononuju Nkem Chukwumah
*Officers:* Ononuju Nkem Chukwumah [1976] Director/Pharmacist

**Norbrook Laboratories (G.B.) Limited**
*Incorporated:* 16 December 1983  *Employees:* 51
*Net Worth:* £10,635,163  *Total Assets:* £19,429,700
*Registered Office:* 1 Saxon Way East, Corby, Northants, NN18 9EY
*Shareholders:* Lady Ballyedmond; Robert William Roy McNulty; Philip Charles Cornwallis Trousdell
*Officers:* Martin Patrick Murdock, Secretary; John Paul McGrath [1972] Finance Director [Irish]; Martin Patrick Murdock [1962] Director/Accountant [Irish]; Liam Nagle [1962] Director [Irish]

**Norchem Limited**
*Incorporated:* 12 May 1960
*Registered Office:* 18 Oxleasow Road, Moon Moat East, Redditch, Worcs, B98 0RE
*Parent:* Lexon (UK) Ltd
*Officers:* Pritesh Ramesh Sonpal, Secretary; Anup Sodha [1962] Director; Nitin Trembaklal Sodha [1955] Director; Pankaj Sodha [1953] Director; Pritesh Ramesh Sonpal [1969] Director

**Nordic Generics Ltd**
*Incorporated:* 1 February 2016
*Registered Office:* 3 Montpelier Avenue, Bexley, Kent, DA5 3AP
*Major Shareholder:* Rakesh Vinodrai Patel
*Officers:* Rakesh Vinodrai Patel [1966] Director

**Nordic Nutraceuticals UK Ltd**
*Incorporated:* 16 October 2018
*Registered Office:* 71-75 Shelton Street, London, WC2H 9JQ
*Officers:* Kim Nielsen [1966] Director [Danish]

**Nordic Pharma Limited**
*Incorporated:* 2 April 1980  *Employees:* 19
*Net Worth:* £610,129  *Total Assets:* £4,628,868
*Registered Office:* St Stephens House, Arthur Road, Windsor, Berks, SL4 1RU
*Officers:* Anthony Brian Bratt, Secretary; Anthony Brian Bratt [1964] Director/General Manager; Veronique Marie Rebours-Mory [1963] Director/Vice President [French]; Drs Hans Schram [1953] Director/Chemist [Dutch]

**Norgine Pharmaceuticals Limited**
*Incorporated:* 13 March 1998  *Employees:* 63
*Net Worth:* £8,854,000  *Total Assets:* £16,059,000
*Registered Office:* Norgine House, Widewater Place, Moorhall Road, Harefield, Uxbridge, Middlesex, UB9 6NS
*Officers:* Alison Philamin Moses, Secretary; Christopher William Bath [1974] Director/Chief Financial Officer; Andy Crichton [1970] Director/General Manager UK & Ireland; Jeremy John Cuffe [1966] Director/General Manager UK; Peter Martin [1956] Director/Chief Operating Officer; Kenneth Eric Scrimgeour [1960] Director/Chief Commercial Officer

**Norlington Trading Ltd**
*Incorporated:* 29 May 2012
*Registered Office:* 3b Broadway Market, London, E8 4PH
*Major Shareholder:* David Ihenagwa
*Officers:* David Nkemdilim Ihenagwa [1979] Director/Pharmacist; Rita Gold Ihenagwa [1954] Director/Superintendent Pharmacist

**Noroc Concepts Ltd**
*Incorporated:* 14 September 2012
*Registered Office:* Flat 3, 97 Earls Court Road, London, W8 6QH
*Major Shareholder:* Augusto Montante
*Officers:* Augusto Montante [1942] Director/Entrepreneur [Italian]

**Norpan Hymbre Ltd**
*Incorporated:* 29 January 2019
*Registered Office:* 2 Beachway, Blyth, Northumberland, NE24 3PG
*Shareholders:* Neal Robert Wesley; Paul Guthrie Scott
*Officers:* Paul Guthrie Scott [1977] Director; Neal Robert Wesley [1974] Director

**Norsworthy Limited**
*Incorporated:* 21 July 2006  *Employees:* 19
*Net Worth:* £620,794  *Total Assets:* £1,325,578
*Registered Office:* The Business Centre, Edward Street, Redditch, Worcs, B97 6HA
*Parent:* J.A. Pharma Limited
*Officers:* Deborah Margaret Cox, Secretary; Deborah Margaret Cox [1970] Director/Pharmaceutical Consultant; Thomas George Walker [1949] Director/Pharmacist

**Northwise Services Limited**
*Incorporated:* 22 January 2001  *Employees:* 1
*Net Worth Deficit:* £2,427  *Total Assets:* £292
*Registered Office:* 39 Busheyfields Road, Herne Common, Herne Bay, Kent, CT6 7LJ
*Shareholders:* Philip Michael North; Jacqueline Caldwell
*Officers:* Jacqueline Caldwell, Secretary; Jacqueline Caldwell [1957] Director/Data Management; Dr Philip Michael North [1949] Director/Statistician

**Noru Pharma PVT Ltd.**
*Incorporated:* 6 January 2017
*Net Worth Deficit:* £75,457  *Total Assets:* £60,333
*Registered Office:* Medicity Nottingham, D6 Building, 1 Thane Road, Nottingham, NG90 6BH
*Major Shareholder:* Jaskirat Khara
*Officers:* Ian James Baker [1973] Director; Jaskirat Khara [1967] Director/Business Executive [Australian]

**Nosher Pharma Private Ltd**
*Incorporated:* 25 October 2017
*Registered Office:* 71-75 Shelton Street, London, WC2H 9JQ
*Major Shareholder:* Safiullah Nosher
*Officers:* Safiullah Nosher [1978] Director [Afghan]

**Nostrum Life Sciences Ltd**
*Incorporated:* 6 August 2010
*Net Worth:* £5,764  *Total Assets:* £52,819
*Registered Office:* 7 St John's Road, Harrow, Middlesex, HA1 2EY
*Shareholders:* Naresh Chudasama; Pankaj Madan
*Officers:* Naresh Chudasama, Secretary; Dr Pankaj Madan [1972] Director [Indian]

**Nouveau Health Ltd**
*Incorporated:* 7 April 2014
*Net Worth Deficit:* £81,945  *Total Assets:* £33,746
*Registered Office:* Unit 10S, 42 Bayton Road, Exhall, Coventry, Warwicks, CV7 9EJ
*Major Shareholder:* Dilkiran Singh Kular
*Officers:* Dilkiran Singh Kular [1990] Director

**Nova Laboratories Limited**
*Incorporated:* 25 November 1993  *Employees:* 217
*Net Worth:* £14,533,310  *Total Assets:* £26,162,616
*Registered Office:* Martin House, Gloucester Crescent, Wigston, Leics, LE18 4YL
*Parent:* Nova Bio-Pharma Holdings Limited
*Officers:* Clement Roger Staniforth, Secretary; Dr Peter John Pitt White [1948] Director/Pharmacist

**Nova Pharmacare Ltd**
*Incorporated:* 4 July 2018
*Registered Office:* Suite 6, 5 Percy Street, Fitzrovia, London, W1T 1DG
*Officers:* Maria Francina Joubert [1958] Director [South African]

**Novachem Limited**
*Incorporated:* 23 June 2005  *Employees:* 2
*Net Worth:* £1,092,477  *Total Assets:* £1,139,353
*Registered Office:* The Coach House, Powell Road, Buckhurst Hill, Essex, IG9 5RD
*Major Shareholder:* Abha Popatlal Panchal
*Officers:* Deepak Popatlal Panchal, Secretary; Abha Popatlal Panchal [1958] Director/Pharmacist

**Novalabb Limited**
*Incorporated:* 21 December 2016
*Net Worth Deficit:* £3,955  *Total Assets:* £119,693
*Registered Office:* c/o Preiskel & Co LLP, 4 King's Bench Walk, Inner Temple, London, EC4Y 7DL
*Shareholder:* Gijsbert van der Gaag
*Officers:* Gijsbert Van Der Gaag [1974] Director [Dutch]

**Novalio Pharma Limited**
*Incorporated:* 26 March 2018
*Registered Office:* First Floor, Thavies Inn House, 3-4 Holborn Circus, London, EC1N 2HA
*Major Shareholder:* Anuj Madhok
*Officers:* Dr Anuj Madhok [1975] Director/Chief Executive Officer [Danish]

**Novamed Pharma Ltd**
*Incorporated:* 4 November 2015
*Net Worth:* £4,866  *Total Assets:* £5,616
*Registered Office:* Suite 1, 5 Percy Street, Fitzrovia, London, W1T 1DG
*Officers:* Evaline Sophie Joubert [1981] Director/Manager [Seychellois]

**Novamedi Limited**
*Incorporated:* 3 March 2016
*Net Worth Deficit:* £85,863  *Total Assets:* £14,028
*Registered Office:* Sesame Apartment 301, 4 Holman Road, London, SW11 3PG
*Shareholders:* Ebru Ozgey; Murat Demirci; Vedat Demirci
*Officers:* Ebru Ozgey [1974] Director

**Novelgenix Therapeutics Limited**
*Incorporated:* 7 November 2014
*Net Worth Deficit:* £482
*Registered Office:* 79 College Road, Harrow, Middlesex, HA1 1BD
*Parent:* Novelgenix Therapeutics Private Limited
*Officers:* Dr. Shivprakash Rathnam [1965] Director/MD [Indian]

**Novelius Medical Limited**
*Incorporated:* 27 March 2018
*Registered Office:* 55 Princes Gate, Exhibition Road, London, SW7 2PN
*Major Shareholder:* Maja Lipovaca
*Officers:* Maja Lipovaca [1984] Director/Pharmaceutical Consultant [Slovenian]

**Novmedic Limited**
*Incorporated:* 17 December 2009
*Registered Office:* 42 Church Street, Edmonton, London, N9 9DU
*Officers:* Elias Demetroudi [1962] Director/Businessman

**Novo Nordisk Limited**
*Incorporated:* 18 June 1973  *Employees:* 367
*Net Worth:* £23,704,000  *Total Assets:* £106,459,000
*Registered Office:* 3 City Place, Beehive Ring Road, Gatwick, W Sussex, RH6 0PA
*Parent:* Novo Nordisk Holding Limited
*Officers:* Matthew O'Flynn, Secretary; Nicholas James Bailey [1973] Finance Director; Tomas Haagen [1966] Director [Danish]; Matt Joseph Regan [1971] Director/General Manager [Irish]; Pinder Sahota [1961] Director/General Manager and CVP UK

**Novochem Limited**
*Incorporated:* 2 December 2003
*Net Worth:* £38,934  *Total Assets:* £413,280
*Registered Office:* 2 Arfryn Terrace, Twynyrodyn, Merthyr Tydfil, CF47 0PP
*Major Shareholder:* Wendy Harris
*Officers:* Wendy Harris, Secretary; Wendy Harris [1957] Director

**Novus Medicare Ltd**
*Incorporated:* 10 December 2014
*Net Worth Deficit:* £57  *Total Assets:* £4,667
*Registered Office:* 3 Whitehall, Welsh Row, Nantwich, Cheshire, CW5 5HA
*Officers:* Martin Crowe, Secretary; Martin David Crowe [1959] Director/Accountant

**NPA Services Limited**
*Incorporated:* 3 August 1935  *Employees:* 35
*Net Worth Deficit:* £862,374  *Total Assets:* £1,707,395
*Registered Office:* Mallinson House, 40 42 St Peters Street, St Albans, Herts, AL1 3NP
*Parent:* National Pharmacy Association Ltd
*Officers:* Raj Kumar Aggarwal [1949] Director/Pharmacy; Michael Francis Guerin [1963] Director/Pharmacist [Irish]; Rajesh Ramniklal Patel [1964] Director/Pharmacist; Umesh Babubhai Patel Bsc Mrpharms [1950] Director/Pharmacist [Indian]; Ian Cameron Strachan [1965] Director/Pharmacist

**NSA Pharma Limited**
*Incorporated:* 18 November 2014
*Net Worth Deficit:* £25,865  *Total Assets:* £2,467
*Registered Office:* Unit 318 Fortis House, 160 London Road, Barking, Essex, IG11 8BB
*Shareholders:* Akindayo Habeeb Adegbesan; Nickesh Ravindra Gadhvi; Samuel Osunsanya
*Officers:* Akindayo Habeeb Adegbesan [1991] Director/Pharmacist; Nickesh Ravindra Gadhvi [1988] Director/Pharmacist; Samuel Osunsanya [1988] Director/Pharmacist

**NSK Global Ltd**
*Incorporated:* 30 September 2014  *Employees:* 2
*Net Worth Deficit:* £891  *Total Assets:* £21,302
*Registered Office:* 18-22 Stoney Lane, Yardley, Birmingham, B25 8YP
*Major Shareholder:* Mohamed Naveed Bashir
*Officers:* Mohamed Naveed Bashir [1981] Director

**NSL (Holdings) Limited**
*Incorporated:* 17 March 2014  *Employees:* 102
*Net Worth:* £16,892,672  *Total Assets:* £23,026,908
*Registered Office:* Unit 4-5 Northolt Trading Estate, Belvue Road, Northolt, Middlesex, UB5 5QS
*Shareholder:* Ketan Himatlal Mehta
*Officers:* Ketan Mehta, Secretary; Bharat Himatlal Mehta [1952] Director; Ketan Himatlal Mehta [1958] Director

**NSL Group Limited**
*Incorporated:* 7 March 2008  *Employees:* 2
*Net Worth:* £11,480,029  *Total Assets:* £11,843,580
*Registered Office:* Unit 4-5 Northolt Trading Estate, Belvue Road, Northolt, Middlesex, UB5 5QS
*Officers:* Ketan Himatlal Mehta, Secretary; Bharat Himatlal Mehta [1952] Director; Ketan Himatlal Mehta [1958] Director/Pharmacist

**Nucare Limited**
*Incorporated:* 25 May 1993  *Employees:* 27
*Net Worth Deficit:* £966,000  *Total Assets:* £3,335,000
*Registered Office:* Phoenix, Rivington Road, Preston Brook, Runcorn, Cheshire, WA7 3DJ
*Parent:* Phoenix Medical Supplies Limited
*Officers:* Stephen William Anderson [1966] Director; Kevin Robert Hudson [1963] Director

**Numedex Limited**
*Incorporated:* 13 August 2012  *Employees:* 2
*Net Worth:* £247,427  *Total Assets:* £336,707
*Registered Office:* Laxmi House, 2-B Draycott Avenue, Kenton, Middlesex, HA3 0BU
*Shareholder:* Sandhya Virendra Patel
*Officers:* Sandhya Virendra Patel [1964] Director

**Nunataq Limited**
*Incorporated:* 2 August 2013
*Net Worth:* £1,017,471  *Total Assets:* £1,180,021
*Registered Office:* Level 17, Dashwood House, 69 Old Broad Street, London, EC2M 1QS
*Major Shareholder:* Robert F Ryan
*Officers:* Dr. Robert Ryan, Secretary; Dr. Robert F Ryan [1960] Chairman, Director, President and CEO [American]

**Nupharm Limited**
*Incorporated:* 12 September 2003  *Employees:* 62
*Net Worth:* £5,104,000  *Total Assets:* £15,932,000
*Registered Office:* Rivington Road, Whitehouse Industrial Estate, Runcorn, Cheshire, WA7 3DJ
*Officers:* Stephen William Anderson [1966] Director; Kenneth John Black [1965] Director; Kevin Robert Hudson [1963] Director

**Nurse Prescribers Limited**
*Incorporated:* 29 December 2000
*Net Worth Deficit:* £375,853  *Total Assets:* £2,633
*Registered Office:* The White House, 2 Meadrow, Godalming, Surrey, GU7 3HN
*Major Shareholder:* James Martin Biggs
*Officers:* Antony Alastair John Biggs, Secretary; Dr James Martin Biggs [1944] Director

**Nutrabizz Nutraceuticals Limited**
*Incorporated:* 6 December 2017
*Registered Office:* Kemp House, 160 City Road, London, EC1V 2NX
*Officers:* Dr Mirza Azkar Ahmed Baig [1973] Director/Physician [Pakistani]

**Nutramax Ltd**
*Incorporated:* 2 January 2019
*Registered Office:* 2nd Floor, College House, 17 King Edwards Road, Ruislip, Middlesex, HA4 7AE
*Major Shareholder:* Dip Thakkar
*Officers:* Dip Thakkar, Secretary; Dip Thakkar [1987] Director/Sales

**Nutravit Ltd.**
*Incorporated:* 12 April 2016
*Registered Office:* Galla House, 695 High Road, North Finchley, London, N12 0BT
*Shareholders:* Mikesh Patel; Anish Patel
*Officers:* Anish Patel [1995] Director; Mikesh Patel [1990] Director

**Nutresco Ltd**
*Incorporated:* 27 June 2013
*Net Worth:* £122,726  *Total Assets:* £208,645
*Registered Office:* First Floor, Aspen House, West Terrace, Folkestone, Kent, CT20 1TH
*Officers:* Paul Davidson Pearson [1957] Director; Raymond Gerard Rohrbach [1961] Director

**Nutridrinks Limited**
*Incorporated:* 2 December 2011
*Net Worth:* £38,920  *Total Assets:* £94,661
*Registered Office:* 12 Snaresbrook Drive, Stanmore, Middlesex, HA7 4QW
*Major Shareholder:* Ajaybhai Dilipkumar Patel
*Officers:* Ajaybhai Dilipkumar Patel [1986] Director

**Nutrifast Ltd**
*Incorporated:* 17 October 2018
*Registered Office:* 7200 The Quorum, Alec Issigonis Way, Oxford Business Park North, Garsington, Oxford, OX4 2JZ
*Major Shareholder:* Khaled Mahmoud El-Sherbini
*Officers:* Dr Yasser Mahmoud El Sherbini [1976] Director/Consultant; Dr Khaled Mahmoud El-Sherbini [1978] Director/Sales Manager [Egyptian]

**Nuview Ltd**
*Incorporated:* 22 April 2003  *Employees:* 4
*Net Worth:* £182,867  *Total Assets:* £505,992
*Registered Office:* Vine House, Selsley Road, North Woodchester, Stroud, Glos, GL5 5NN
*Shareholder:* John Stephen Woods
*Officers:* Julia Margret Woods, Secretary; John Stephen Woods [1961] Sales and Marketing Director

**O'Connell Pharma Ltd**
*Incorporated:* 16 November 2007
*Net Worth:* £1,000  *Total Assets:* £1,000
*Registered Office:* 2 Wheeleys Road, Edgbaston, Birmingham, B15 2LD
*Shareholders:* Shafiq Choudhary; Robina Shafiq
*Officers:* Robina Shafiq, Secretary; Dr Mohammed Choudhary Shafiq [1964] Director

**John O'Donnell Limited**
*Incorporated:* 5 September 1973  *Employees:* 16
*Net Worth:* £242,474  *Total Assets:* £444,118
*Registered Office:* John O'Donnell Building, Victoria Road, Chelmsford, Essex, CM1 1NZ
*Major Shareholder:* John Michael O'Donnell
*Officers:* Margaret Betty Odonnell, Secretary; Julia Sian Kinninmonth [1972] Managing Director; Philip James O'Donnell [1970] Director/General Manager; John Michael Odonnell [1941] Director; Margaret Betty Odonnell [1945] Director

**Oak Zone Biotech UK Ltd**
*Incorporated:* 12 July 2018
*Registered Office:* The Bradfield Centre, 184 Cambridge Science Park, Milton Road, Cambridge, CB4 0GA
*Officers:* Young Sun Sonn [1974] Managing Director [South Korean]

**Oakways Healthcare Limited**
*Incorporated:* 29 September 2015  *Employees:* 4
*Net Worth Deficit:* £192,966  *Total Assets:* £610,155
*Registered Office:* Taylor Group House, Wedgnock Lane, Warwick, CV34 5YA
*Shareholders:* Donna Mary Gambrill; Richard Jeffery Taylor
*Officers:* Donna Mary Gambrill [1966] Director; Richard Jeffery Taylor [1955] Director

**Ocusoft UK Limited**
*Incorporated:* 15 December 2017
*Net Worth Deficit:* £74,225  *Total Assets:* £189,972
*Registered Office:* Blythe Valley Innovation Centre, Central Boulevard, Blythe Valley Park, Solihull, W Midlands, B90 8AJ
*Parent:* Ocusoft Inc
*Officers:* Nat G Jr Adkins [1949] Director [American]; Cynthia L Barratt [1953] Director [American]; Harold Stacy Foster [1954] Director [American]; Trevor Ronald McCormack [1963] Director [Irish]; Anne Elizabeth Prendergast [1966] Director [Irish]

**Odiham OH Products Limited**
*Incorporated:* 2 April 2015
*Net Worth:* £11,010  *Total Assets:* £12,737
*Registered Office:* Trotwood The Firs, Odiham, Hook, Hants, RG29 1PP
*Shareholders:* William David Potter; Lisa Jane Potter; Eleanor Margaret Craig Farrant
*Officers:* Eleanor Margaret Craig Farrant [1970] Director; William David Potter [1968] Director

**Odyssey Healthcare Limited**
*Incorporated:* 12 October 2018
*Registered Office:* 3 Raeside Avenue, Newton Mearns, Glasgow, G77 5AD
*Major Shareholder:* Nayl Ghaus Gilani
*Officers:* Nayl Ghaus Gilani [1994] Director/Pharmacist

**OFC Molecular Ltd**
*Incorporated:* 7 August 2018
*Registered Office:* 71-75 Shelton Street, London, WC2H 9JQ
*Shareholders:* Sorin-Mihai Popescu; Cristian Grigorescu-Popescu
*Officers:* Cristian Grigorescu-Popescu [1974] Director [Romanian]; Sorin-Mihai Popescu [1966] Director [Romanian]

**Ofege Pharm Ltd**
*Incorporated:* 16 July 2015
*Net Worth Deficit:* £8,154  *Total Assets:* £920
*Registered Office:* 28 Barrs Road, Cradley Heath, W Midlands, B64 7HG
*Major Shareholder:* Edith Ofege
*Officers:* Edith Ofege [1970] Director/Pharmacist [Cameroonian]

**Okle Systems Limited**
*Incorporated:* 21 January 2004
*Net Worth Deficit:* £2,024
*Registered Office:* 6 Shaw Street, Worcester, WR1 3QQ
*Shareholders:* Carmine D'Ambrosio; Massimo Di Nola
*Officers:* Carmine D'Ambrosio [1956] Finance Director [Italian]; Massimo di Nola [1972] Director/Architect [Italian]

**OL123 Limited**
*Incorporated:* 25 November 2004
*Previous:* Ortholink (Scotland) Ltd.
*Net Worth:* £385,467  *Total Assets:* £516,809
*Registered Office:* 1a Torphichen Street, Edinburgh, EH3 8HX
*Parent:* Link Orthopaedics UK Ltd
*Officers:* Helmut-Detlef Link [1946] Director/General Manager/CEO [German]; James Paxton Malcolm [1962] Director/Sales Manager; Peter Heinz Willenborg [1971] Director/Chief Financial Officer [German]

**Old Latchmerians Limited**
*Incorporated:* 17 January 2018
*Registered Office:* 178 Camp Street, Motherwell, N Lanarks, ML1 1UG
*Shareholders:* Robert Ernest Shipwright; Neil Martyn Underwood
*Officers:* Robert Ernest Shipwright [1949] Director; Neil Martyn Underwood [1949] Director

**OM Medical Limited**
*Incorporated:* 4 March 2010
*Net Worth:* £47  *Total Assets:* £11,320
*Registered Office:* 46 Yeading Fork, Hayes, Middlesex, UB4 9DQ
*Shareholder:* Vinay Mansukh
*Officers:* Kavita Mansukh, Secretary; Vinay Mansukh [1960] Director/Medical Representative

**Omapharm Limited**
*Incorporated:* 13 March 2017
*Net Worth Deficit:* £14,154  *Total Assets:* £20,815
*Registered Office:* Unit 11 Dromore Road Industrial Estate, Dromore Road, Omagh, Co Tyrone, BT78 1RE
*Officers:* Liam Bradley, Secretary; Liam Martin Bradley [1967] Director/Pharmacist [Irish]; Robert Gordon [1954] Director/Pharmacist; Michael Francis Guerin [1963] Director/Pharmacist [Irish]; Kevin Kelly [1964] Director/Pharmacist; Tom McGread [1968] Director/Pharmacist; Brendan Moore [1972] Director/Pharmacist [Irish]; Patrick Cyril Peter Slevin [1956] Director/Pharmacist [Irish]

**Omark Plus Ltd**
*Incorporated:* 19 February 2019
*Registered Office:* 98 Horseley Heath, Tipton, W Midlands, DY4 7AH
*Shareholders:* Oluwagbemileke Arikawe; Olutayo Arikawe
*Officers:* Olutayo Arikawe [1976] Director/Pharmacist; Oluwagbemileke Arikawe [1974] Director/Pharmacist

**Omega Alpha Pharma Limited**
*Incorporated:* 18 April 2018
*Registered Office:* Ground Floor, Bury House, 31 Bury Street, London, EC3A 5AR
*Major Shareholder:* Gordon Chang

**Omega Pharma Limited**
*Incorporated:* 14 November 1967  *Employees:* 135
*Net Worth:* £33,898,000  *Total Assets:* £67,744,000
*Registered Office:* First Floor, 32 Vauxhall Bridge Road, London, SW1V 2SA
*Parent:* Omega Pharma Holding (Nederland) BV
*Officers:* Annette Corcoran, Secretary; Neil Thomas Lister [1975] Managing Director; Dominic James Rivers [1977] Director; Christopher Allan Rudd [1980] Commercial Director

**Omega Surgical Instruments Ltd**
*Incorporated:* 20 December 2011  *Employees:* 1
*Net Worth:* £86,241  *Total Assets:* £189,432
*Registered Office:* Unit 1 Walton Lodge, Bridge Street, Walton on Thames, Surrey, KT12 1BT
*Shareholders:* Leonard Wilby; James Gordon Adam; Jeanie Adam
*Officers:* Jeanie Adam [1961] Director; Leonard Wilby [1960] Director

**Omnicell Limited**
*Incorporated:* 15 October 2002  *Employees:* 80
*Previous:* MTS Medication Technologies Limited
*Net Worth:* £16,429,000  *Total Assets:* £22,200,000
*Registered Office:* Two Omega Drive, River Bend Technology Centre, Irlam, Manchester, M44 5GR
*Parent:* Omnicell Inc
*Officers:* Alan Clark, Secretary; Mohit Bhatia [1975] Director [Indian]; Paul John O'Hanlon [1962] Director/Pharmacist; Joseph Brian Spears [1959] Director [American]

**Omron Healthcare UK Limited**
*Incorporated:* 2 May 1990  *Employees:* 15
*Net Worth:* £2,406,719  *Total Assets:* £5,192,664
*Registered Office:* 44 Grand Parade, Brighton, BN2 9QA
*Parent:* Omron Corporation
*Officers:* Graham Laurence Palmer [1963] Sales and Trade Marketing Director EMEA; Andre Louis Smit [1982] Director/Financial Controller [South African]

**One Pharm Limited**
*Incorporated:* 13 December 1999
*Net Worth Deficit:* £2,167  *Total Assets:* £1,866
*Registered Office:* 63 Holmstall Avenue, Edgware, Middlesex, HA8 5JQ
*Shareholders:* Sukhwant Singh Rai; Baldeesh Kaur Rai
*Officers:* Baldeesh Kaur Rai, Secretary/Business Executive; Baldeesh Kaur Rai [1961] Director/Business Executive; Sukhwant Singh Rai [1959] Director/Business Executive

**Ongar Medical Limited**
*Incorporated:* 11 March 1996  *Employees:* 3
*Net Worth:* £496,424  *Total Assets:* £673,937
*Registered Office:* 10 Bates Walk, Addlestone, Surrey, KT15 2DQ
*Shareholders:* Christopher Michael Harvey; Carol Ann Harvey
*Officers:* Carol Ann Harvey, Secretary; Carol Ann Harvey [1945] Director; Christopher Michael Harvey [1946] Director/Merchant

**Onpharma Limited**
*Incorporated:* 27 April 2017
*Registered Office:* Charter House, 8-10 Station Road, London, E12 5BT
*Major Shareholder:* Shreeya Ondhia
*Officers:* Harsh Kantilal Ondhia, Secretary; Harsh Kantilal Ondhia [1975] Director/Accountant; Shreeya Ondhia [1990] Director

**Ontex Retail UK Limited**
*Incorporated:* 12 February 1982  *Employees:* 18
*Net Worth:* £16,203,679  *Total Assets:* £35,052,964
*Registered Office:* 1st Floor, Unit 5 Grovelands Business Park, Boundary Way, Hemel Hempstead, Herts, HP2 7TE
*Parent:* Ontex Group NV
*Officers:* Thierry Navarre [1967] Director/Chief Operating Officer [French]; Steven Paul Jules Vandenbogaerde [1970] Finance Director [Belgian]

**Ontyme Logistics and Healthcare Limited**
*Incorporated:* 18 March 2013
*Previous:* Ontyme Logistics and Shipping Limited
*Registered Office:* 6 Victoria Avenue, Stepney Lane, Kingston upon Hull, HU5 1JH
*Major Shareholder:* Eric Kwaku Agyei
*Officers:* Justina Akua Agyei, Secretary; Eric Kwaku Agyei [1983] Director/Freight Forwarder

**Opalbond Limited**
*Incorporated:* 5 May 1999  *Employees:* 7
*Previous:* Opalbond Nutrition Limited
*Net Worth:* £2,651,195  *Total Assets:* £4,386,072
*Registered Office:* 10c Aspen House, Vantage Park, Washingley Road, Huntingdon, Cambs, PE29 6SR
*Major Shareholder:* Aran Douglas McNish
*Officers:* Dee Louise McNish, Secretary; Aran Douglas McNish [1964] Managing Director; Dee Louise McNish [1969] Director/Secretary

**OPD Laboratories Limited**
*Incorporated:* 2 April 1996  *Employees:* 75
*Net Worth Deficit:* £1,708,541  *Total Assets:* £2,976,591
*Registered Office:* First Floor, Roxburghe House, 273-287 Regent Street, London, W1B 2HA
*Parent:* Orion Holdings (UK) Limited
*Officers:* Manish Hansraj Shah, Secretary; Bharat Kumar Hansraj Devraj Shah [1949] Director/Pharmacist; Kamal Hansraj Shah [1959] Director; Manish Hansraj Shah [1955] Director/Accountant

**Optident Labline Limited**
*Incorporated:* 11 September 1998
*Net Worth:* £200,185  *Total Assets:* £705,913
*Registered Office:* International Development Centre, Valley Drive, Ilkley, W Yorks, LS29 8AL
*Parent:* Henry Schein UK Holdings Limited
*Officers:* Timothy Robert Butterfield, Secretary; Patrick Thompson Allen [1966] Director; Timothy Robert Butterfield [1968] Director; Adrian Spencer Martin [1969] Director/Accountant; Robert Nathan Minowitz [1958] Director/Business Executive [American]; Helen Louise Redding [1975] Director/Chief Financial Officer

**Optima Consumer Health Limited**
*Incorporated:* 24 January 2011  *Employees:* 30
*Net Worth:* £15,204,000  *Total Assets:* £16,419,000
*Registered Office:* Dr Organic Group Limited, Alberto Road, Valley Way, Swansea, SA6 8RG
*Parent:* Organic Group Ltd
*Officers:* Nicholas John Heywood Collins [1962] Director/Chief Strategy & Product Supply Officer International; Stephen Kelsey Ford [1968] Finance Director; Matthew James Richard Harvey [1980] Director/Chartered Accountant; Michael Henryk Lightowlers [1972] Managing Director; Stephen Ronald Price [1964] Group Export Director

**Optimal Pharma Ltd**
Incorporated: 28 December 2016
Net Worth: £496,756  Total Assets: £781,634
Registered Office: Kemp House, 160 City Road, London, EC1V 2NX
Major Shareholder: Sulochana Gautam Kadel
Officers: Sulochana Gautam Kadel [1984] Director


**Opus Pharmacy Services Limited**
Incorporated: 14 May 2004
Net Worth: £46,407  Total Assets: £154,146
Registered Office: Quatro House, Lyon Way, Frimley, Camberley, Surrey, GU16 7ER
Major Shareholder: Judith Manners
Officers: Judith Manners, Secretary; Rachel Elizabeth Charlick [1988] Director; Judith Manners [1960] Director/Pharmacist


**ORAA Ltd**
Incorporated: 20 November 2018
Registered Office: 42 Nithsdale Road, Glasgow, G41 2AN
Major Shareholder: Amar Ashraf
Officers: Amar Ashraf [1990] Director


**Orange Healthcare Limited**
Incorporated: 5 August 2003
Net Worth Deficit: £13,375  Total Assets: £29,024
Registered Office: Lower Ground Floor, 40 Bloomsbury Way, London, WC1A 2SE
Shareholder: Dmytro Manych
Officers: Kuldeep Jain [1969] Director/Marketing [Indian]


**The Orange Square Company Ltd.**
Incorporated: 20 March 1991  Employees: 181
Net Worth: £5,342,291  Total Assets: £9,386,181
Registered Office: Peregrine House, 26-28 Paradise Road, Richmond upon Thames, Surrey, TW9 1SE
Major Shareholder: Christopher Michael Hawksley
Officers: Jayne Elizabeth Fox [1958] Director; Christopher Michael Hawksley [1955] Managing Director


**Ordinant Medical Solutions Limited**
Incorporated: 23 January 2012  Employees: 6
Net Worth Deficit: £150,659  Total Assets: £82,698
Registered Office: Unit 2 Blackburn Technology Management Centre, Challenge Way, Blackburn, BB1 5QB
Shareholder: Shahid Mahmood
Officers: Shahid Mahmood [1977] Director; Tabassum Zabier [1978] Commercial Director


**Organic Iway Ltd**
Incorporated: 18 September 2018
Registered Office: 27 Old Gloucester Street, London, WC1N 3AX
Major Shareholder: Constantin Eduard Hristudor
Officers: Constantin Eduard Hristudor, Secretary; Constantin Eduard Hristudor [1985] Director/Engineer [Romanian]


**Orion Medical Supplies Ltd**
Incorporated: 16 August 2012  Employees: 14
Net Worth: £419,851  Total Assets: £1,074,220
Registered Office: E14 Telford Road, Bicester, Oxon, OX26 4LD
Shareholders: Salvatore Picillo; Shaun Kent Hazlett
Officers: Shaun Kent Hazlett [1959] Director; Salvatore Picillo [1971] Director


**Orion Pharma (UK) Limited**
Incorporated: 27 July 1988  Employees: 48
Net Worth: £31,527,732  Total Assets: £34,228,440
Registered Office: 5 Fleet Place, London, EC4M 7RD
Officers: Satu Maarit Ahomaki [1966] Director [Finnish]; Olli Heikki Houtari [1966] Director/Senior Vice President; Jari Ilmari Karlson [1961] Director/Chief Financial Officer


**Orkal Ltd**
Incorporated: 31 January 2019
Registered Office: 81 Melton Road, West Bridgford, Nottingham, NG2 6EN
Shareholders: Ben Abley; Kevan Abley; Gillian Lesley Abley
Officers: Gillian Lesley Abley, Secretary; Ben Abley [1996] Director; Gillian Lesley Abley [1959] Director; Kevan Abley [1963] Director


**Orly Pharma Limited**
Incorporated: 5 January 2016  Employees: 2
Net Worth Deficit: £81,022  Total Assets: £220,820
Registered Office: 1st Floor, Thavies Inn House, 3-4 Holburn Circus, London, EC1N 2HA
Shareholders: Melchior Catharina Martinus Jozef Scholten; Rob Heerema
Officers: Rob Heerema [1963] Director [Dutch]; Melchior Catharina Martinus Jozef Scholten [1965] Director [Dutch]


**Orphan Europe (UK) Limited**
Incorporated: 25 June 1996  Employees: 5
Net Worth: £2,100,757  Total Assets: £2,853,200
Registered Office: Chartam House, 16 College Avenue, Maidenhead, Berks, SL6 6AX
Parent: Orphan Europe SARL
Officers: Corrado Castellucci [1959] Director [Italian]


**Orpharma Limited**
Incorporated: 1 December 2014
Net Worth: £165,190  Total Assets: £176,466
Registered Office: Suite 102, Langdale House, 11 Marshalsea Road, London, SE1 1EN
Parent: Gledswood Limited
Officers: Paul Newman [1968] Director/Business Owner [Irish]


**Orphic Limited**
Incorporated: 12 December 2016
Registered Office: 74 Hales Crescent, Smethwick, W Midlands, B67 6QS
Shareholders: Shahista Sultana; Aysha Kousar
Officers: Zulaikha Faatima, Secretary; Aysha Kousar [1991] Director/Pharmacist; Ambreen Shahzad Mughal [1986] Director/Scientist; Shahista Sultana [1986] Director/Lawyer


**Oscar & Louis Limited**
Incorporated: 12 February 2018
Registered Office: Oscar & Louis, First Floor, Swan Buildings, Swan Street, Manchester, M4 5JW
Major Shareholder: Aaron Levin
Officers: Deborah Lester, Secretary; Aaron Levin [1990] Director


**Osteo-Ti UK Limited**
Incorporated: 7 August 2013
Net Worth Deficit: £35,209  Total Assets: £117,565
Registered Office: Unit 64, 54-56 Standard Road, London, NW10 6EU
Major Shareholder: Stewart Harding
Officers: Dorthe Brodersen Wiernicki, Secretary; Elisabeth Belly Suami Harding [1978] Marketing Director [French]

**Ostomart Limited**
*Incorporated:* 26 April 1994
*Registered Office:* Greypoint, Cardiff Business Park, Cardiff, CF14 5WF
*Parent:* Cliffe Medical Limited
*Officers:* Jeremy David Eakin [1967] Director; Paul Andrew Eakin [1962] Director; Paul MacQuillan [1958] Director/Chartered Accountant [Irish]

**Oswell Penda Pharmaceutical Ltd**
*Incorporated:* 11 January 2018
*Registered Office:* 106 Holme Lane, Hillsborough, Sheffield, S6 4JW
*Major Shareholder:* Clare Maria Chesworth
*Officers:* Clare Maria Chesworth [1973] Director; Marcus Lee Judd [1969] Director

**OT Masters Limited**
*Incorporated:* 2 May 2017
*Net Worth:* £100  *Total Assets:* £15,072
*Registered Office:* 43 Charlesworth Street, Beswick, Manchester, M11 3AG
*Major Shareholder:* Ibrahim Kreddan
*Officers:* Ibrahim Kreddan [1977] Director/Pharmacist

**OTC Direct Limited**
*Incorporated:* 27 October 1995
*Net Worth:* £59,200,000  *Total Assets:* £111,000,000
*Registered Office:* 43 Cox Lane, Chessington, Surrey, KT9 1SN
*Parent:* Alliance Boots Holdings Limited
*Officers:* Lucie Charlotte Massart, Secretary; Alexandro Depau [1970] Director [American]; Pablo Cortes Rivas [1972] Director [Spanish]

**Otsuka Pharmaceuticals (U.K.) Ltd.**
*Incorporated:* 14 August 1998  *Employees:* 45
*Net Worth:* £1,681,250  *Total Assets:* £4,729,414
*Registered Office:* Gallions, Wexham Springs, Framewood Road, Wexham, Slough, Berks, SL3 6PJ
*Parent:* Otsuka Pharmaceutical Europe Ltd.
*Officers:* Cheryl Charanjit Dhillon [1958] Director/Senior VP Supply Chain & Corp Project Management; Stewart Benjamin Pearce [1978] Managing Director (Pharmaceuticals)

**Overseas Merchandising Corporation Ltd**
*Incorporated:* 6 October 2016
*Registered Office:* Office 4, 219 Kensington High Street, London, W8 6BD
*Major Shareholder:* Hemant Kumar Pathak
*Officers:* Hemant Kumar Pathak [1962] Director [Indian]

**Oxbridge Pharma Limited**
*Incorporated:* 5 September 2002  *Employees:* 3
*Net Worth Deficit:* £396,884  *Total Assets:* £42,607
*Registered Office:* The St Botolph Building, 138 Houndsditch, London, EC3A 7AR
*Major Shareholder:* Jae-Young Ha
*Officers:* Dr Jai Jun Choung [1959] Director [South Korean]; Jae-Young Ha [1960] Director

**Oxford Biosystems Limited**
*Incorporated:* 14 February 2001  *Employees:* 8
*Net Worth:* £210,055  *Total Assets:* £661,944
*Registered Office:* 184b Park House, Milton Park, Milton, Abingdon, Oxon, OX14 4SR
*Parent:* Biovendor Limited
*Officers:* Helen Elizabeth Church, Secretary; Fiona Elizabeth Alcock [1966] Marketing Director; Michal Kostka [1973] Director [Czech]; Matej Milata [1983] Director [Czech]; Dr Viktor Ruzicka [1965] Director [Czech]; Mark Upton [1965] Director

**Oxford Laboratories Limited**
*Incorporated:* 15 December 1997
*Net Worth:* £2,735  *Total Assets:* £522,123
*Registered Office:* First Floor, Roxburghe House, 273-287 Regent Street, London, W1B 2HA
*Shareholders:* Andrei Medounitsyn; Satyajeet Sumant Khanolkar
*Officers:* Satyajeet Khanolkar, Secretary; Andrei Medounitsyn [1966] Director [Russian]

**Oxford Medpharma Ltd**
*Incorporated:* 3 February 2016  *Employees:* 2
*Net Worth:* £7,639  *Total Assets:* £820,666
*Registered Office:* St Marys Chambers, 59 Quarry Street, Guildford, Surrey, GU1 3UA
*Major Shareholder:* Ahmad Sarkaz
*Officers:* Sara Sarkaz, Secretary; Ahmad Sarkaz [1964] Director; Sara Jane Sarkaz [1969] Director

**Oxford Nutrition Limited**
*Incorporated:* 9 December 1983  *Employees:* 2
*Net Worth:* £1,011,412  *Total Assets:* £1,020,713
*Registered Office:* 5 Laurel Lane, Shaldon, Teignmouth, Devon, TQ14 0AL
*Shareholders:* Robert Hardy; Rachel Hardy
*Officers:* Rachel Hardy [1967] Director; Robert Hardy [1970] Managing Director

**Oxford PCS Limited**
*Incorporated:* 21 October 1998
*Net Worth:* £38,163  *Total Assets:* £38,163
*Registered Office:* Brook House, Mint Street, Godalming, Surrey, GU7 1HE
*Parent:* P & D Pharmaceuticals Ltd
*Officers:* Ian James Greenep [1944] Director/Pharmacist

**Oxford Supramolecular Biotechnology Limited**
*Incorporated:* 30 January 2019
*Registered Office:* Connaught House, 15-17 Upper George Street, Luton, Beds, LU1 2RD
*Shareholders:* Robert Tobias Steffen; Fangqian Wang
*Officers:* Robert Tobias Steffen [1973] Director [German]; Fangqian Wang [1976] Director [Chinese]

**Ozone Medical Supplies Ltd**
*Incorporated:* 13 November 2014
*Net Worth:* £5,772  *Total Assets:* £16,664
*Registered Office:* 2 Stanley Park Drive, Wembley, Middlesex, HA0 1SG
*Officers:* Hasmukhlal Dave [1984] Director/Trainee Accountant; Vijaykumar Bhikhabhai Patel [1979] Director/Wholesale of Pharmaceutical Goods

**Ozonex Limited**
Incorporated: 28 October 1997  Employees: 2
Net Worth: £3,392  Total Assets: £28,615
Registered Office: 66 Prescot Street, London, E1 8NN
Shareholders: Maria Luise Savitt; Jonathan Alan Savitt
Officers: Maria Luise Savitt, Secretary/Director; Jonathan Alan Savitt [1954] Director; Maria Luise Savitt [1947] Director

**P & D Pharmaceuticals Ltd.**
Incorporated: 27 March 1992
Net Worth: £516,343  Total Assets: £1,198,665
Registered Office: Brook House, Mint Street, Godalming, Surrey, GU7 1HE
Major Shareholder: Ian James Greenep
Officers: Susan Elizabeth Greenep, Secretary; Ian James Greenep [1944] Director/Pharmacist

**P A M Medical Supplies Limited**
Incorporated: 22 July 2003
Net Worth: £107,577  Total Assets: £112,182
Registered Office: Bay 4, Block D, Willenhall Trading Estate, Willenhall, W Midlands, WV13 2JP
Shareholders: Paul Alan Matthews; Cheryl Matthews
Officers: Paul Mathews, Secretary; Cheryl Mathews [1962] Director; Paul Mathews [1961] Director

**P C LDN Ltd**
Incorporated: 2 July 2018
Registered Office: 71-75 Shelton Street, London, WC2H 9JQ
Major Shareholder: Aaron Kris Lemon
Officers: Aaron Kris Lemon [1980] Director/Operations Manager

**P R Pharma Limited**
Incorporated: 20 August 2002  Employees: 2
Net Worth: £363,528  Total Assets: £973,597
Registered Office: 27 New Dover Road, Canterbury, Kent, CT1 3DN
Officers: Rajendra Chhotabhai Patel, Secretary; Prakash Patel [1955] Director; Rajendra Chhotabhai Patel [1958] Director/Pharmacy Owner

**P Y Imports Limited**
Incorporated: 14 January 2004  Employees: 1
Net Worth: £300,919  Total Assets: £798,455
Registered Office: 4 King Square, Bridgwater, Somerset, TA6 3YF
Major Shareholder: Malcolm Jordan
Officers: Stephen Vernon Patrick Maw [1953] Director

**P.I.C. International Ltd**
Incorporated: 17 December 2018
Registered Office: 13 Orchard Street, Long Eaton, Notts, NG10 1EW
Major Shareholder: Christopher Elliott
Officers: Christopher Elliott, Secretary; Christopher Elliott [1983] Director/Sales Person; Patrik Johansson [1983] Director/Software Consultant [Swedish]

**P.I.E. Pharma Limited**
Incorporated: 8 January 1996
Net Worth: £139,906  Total Assets: £10,276,358
Registered Office: 39a Joel Street, Northwood Hills, Northwood, Middlesex, HA6 1NZ
Major Shareholder: Anuj Somchand Shah
Officers: Anuj Somchand Shah [1966] Director/Actuary

**Pacific Pharma UK Limited**
Incorporated: 17 November 2016
Net Worth Deficit: £64,172  Total Assets: £15,965
Registered Office: Foframe House, 35-37 Brent Street, London, NW4 2EF
Major Shareholder: Irfan Omer
Officers: Irfan Omer [1957] Director [Pakistani]

**Padma Healthcare Limited**
Incorporated: 11 May 2016  Employees: 1
Net Worth Deficit: £69,548  Total Assets: £6,452
Registered Office: Lynwood House, Crofton Road, Orpington, Kent, BR6 8QE
Officers: Herbert Schwabl [1961] Director [Austrian]

**Palatina Ltd**
Incorporated: 15 November 2007
Net Worth: £17,425  Total Assets: £576,279
Registered Office: 64 Princes Court, 88 Brompton Road, Knightsbridge, London, SW3 1ET
Officers: Ioanna Vasilaki [1981] Director/Businesswoman

**Pamx Enterprise Limited**
Incorporated: 9 January 2017
Registered Office: 10 Florence Street, Lincoln, LN2 5LR
Major Shareholder: Austin Xavier
Officers: Austin Xavier [1974] Director/Office Staff [Indian]

**Pamy International Ltd**
Incorporated: 7 April 2015
Registered Office: 20-22 Wenlock Road, London, N1 7GU
Shareholders: Fabio Zanini; Bianca Cioffi
Officers: Fabio Zanini [1955] Director [Italian]

**Pan Globus Limited**
Incorporated: 12 October 2009
Net Worth Deficit: £8,575  Total Assets: £50,381
Registered Office: 103 Gloucester Road, Malmesbury, Wilts, SN16 0AJ
Officers: Richard Cole Millard, Secretary; Simeon Francis McKay Hopkins [1945] Director/Barrister (Retired); Richard Cole Millard [1948] Director/General Manager; Marc John Sheffner [1957] Director/University Professor

**Panacea Health UK Limited**
Incorporated: 11 March 2005
Net Worth Deficit: £400,489  Total Assets: £193,245
Registered Office: Unit 22 Hallmarks Trading Estate, Fourth Way, Wembley, Middlesex, HA9 0LH
Shareholder: Jawahar Shrimanker
Officers: Urshula Shrimanker, Secretary; Jawahar Shrimanker [1954] Director/Health Food Wholesalers and Retailers; Urshula Shrimanker [1962] Director/Health Food Wholesalers and Retailers

**Panorama Healthcare Limited**
Incorporated: 12 October 2016
Net Worth: £39,434  Total Assets: £319,209
Registered Office: 2a Bandeath Industrial Estate, Throsk, Stirling, FK7 7NP
Shareholders: Alexander Douglas Miller Cruickshank; Carmelo Stamato
Officers: Alexander Douglas Miller Cruickshank [1975] Director; Carmelo Stamato [1971] Director

**Par Laboratories Europe, Ltd.**
Incorporated: 12 November 2014  Employees: 8
Net Worth Deficit: £3,481,910  Total Assets: £1,821,345
Registered Office: 40 Bank Street, Canary Wharf, London, E14 5DS
Parent: Endo International PLC
Officers: Rahul Garella [1969] Director/Business Executive; Andrew Roy Marshall [1973] Director

**Paragen Pharma Ltd**
Incorporated: 24 May 2017
Registered Office: Room 1, 43a Summerisland Road, Loughgall, Co Armagh, BT61 8LG
Shareholders: Turlough Malachy Hamill; David Michael Hill
Officers: Dr Turlough Malachy Hamill [1981] Director/Pharmacist; David Michael Hill [1967] Director/Regulatory Consultant

**Parallel Investments Limited**
Incorporated: 1 February 2019
Registered Office: 1506 Fladgate House, 4 Circus Road West, Battersea Power Station, London, SW11 8EX
Major Shareholder: William Patrick O'Neill Ortiz
Officers: William Patrick O'Neill Ortiz [1984] Managing Director

**Parapharm Development Limited**
Incorporated: 13 January 2016  Employees: 4
Net Worth Deficit: £1,045,393  Total Assets: £1,509,540
Registered Office: St Stephens House, Arthur Road, Windsor, Berks, SL4 1RU
Officers: Benedict Stephens, Secretary; Sean Anthony Davis [1963] Managing Director; Jeffrey Hobbs [1942] Director; Charlotte Phelps [1964] Director/General Manager

**Parasure Limited**
Incorporated: 26 July 2012
Net Worth Deficit: £38,200  Total Assets: £341,700
Registered Office: 41 Blackwell Drive, Braintree Business Park, Braintree, Essex, CM7 2PU
Officers: Adrian Buckingham [1956] Director/Engineer; Tamoor Rafiq [1988] Director/Accountant [Pakistani]

**Paraxmed Limited**
Incorporated: 15 December 2017
Registered Office: 20-22 Wenlock Road, London, N1 7GU
Major Shareholder: Jahanshah Akhavan Zanjani
Officers: Jahanshah Akhavan Zanjani [1955] Director

**Paria Medical Aesthetics Ltd**
Incorporated: 27 November 2017
Registered Office: 20-22 Wenlock Road, London, N1 7GU
Shareholder: Pourya Shirali
Officers: Pourya Shirali [1987] Director/Pharmacist

**Park Health Ltd**
Incorporated: 8 April 2010  Employees: 8
Net Worth: £168,143  Total Assets: £897,662
Registered Office: 201 Haverstock Hill, London, NW3 4QG
Major Shareholder: Thoai Nguyen
Officers: Thoai Nguyen [1978] Director/Pharmacist

**Parker Trading Ltd**
Incorporated: 15 January 2018
Registered Office: 33 Denman Road, Wath upon Dearne, Rotherham, S Yorks, S63 3RL
Officers: Andy Parker, Secretary; Andy Parker [1968] Director

**Parkview Leicester Limited**
Incorporated: 28 February 2002  Employees: 9
Net Worth: £1,058,387  Total Assets: £1,220,121
Registered Office: 276 East Park Road, Leicester, LE5 5FD
Major Shareholder: Sureshchand Bharmal Shah
Officers: Bharti Sureshchand Shah, Secretary; Bharti Sureshchand Shah [1951] Director/Shop Assistant; Sureshchand Bharmal Shah [1946] Director/Pharmacist

**Passion Dental Design Studio (Laboratory) Limited**
Incorporated: 17 December 2015  Employees: 6
Net Worth: £49,650  Total Assets: £140,083
Registered Office: Studio 25, The Red House Glass Cone, High Street, Wordsley, Stourbridge, W Midlands, DY8 4AZ
Parent: G M Holdings (Stourbridge) Limited
Officers: George Oliver Morgan, Secretary; George Oliver Morgan [1979] Director/Dental Technician

**Nisha Patel Ltd**
Incorporated: 2 October 2017
Registered Office: 3 Hunter Road, Ilford, Essex, IG1 2NN
Major Shareholder: Nisha Patel
Officers: Nisha Patel [1992] Director

**Patient Care Holdings Ltd**
Incorporated: 31 October 2016
Registered Office: Riverside House, 1-5 Como Street, Romford, Essex, RM7 7DN
Officers: Ashok Joshi, Secretary; Shiv Kumar Bagga [1953] Director/Pharmacist; Arun James Neel Joshi [1987] Director/Pharmacist

**Patient Ready Products Limited**
Incorporated: 17 April 2007  Employees: 2
Net Worth: £4,467  Total Assets: £4,467
Registered Office: Nexus, Hurricane Road, Gloucester Business Park, Gloucester, GL3 4AG
Officers: Stephen Allen Watkin, Secretary/Director; Christoph Kerstein [1961] Director/Pharmacist [German]; Stephen Allen Watkin [1967] Director

**Pavay Venture International Limited**
Incorporated: 14 September 2017
Registered Office: 37a Market Place, Cirencester, Glos, GL7 2NX
Shareholder: Hongming Yang
Officers: Douglas Chi Shing Cheung [1959] Director; Qing Lin [1975] Director; Xue Li Wei [1980] Director

**Payal London Consolidated Limited**
Incorporated: 12 October 1983
Net Worth Deficit: £2,545  Total Assets: £175,441
Registered Office: Lynton House, 304 Bensham Lane, Thornton Heath, Surrey, CR7 7EQ
Major Shareholder: Bharatkumar Rajnikant Patel
Officers: Kalpana Bharat Patel, Secretary; Bharatkumar Rajnikant Patel [1959] Director & Pharmacist; Kalpana Bharat Patel [1962] Director/Accounts Clerk; Neel Bharat Patel [1988] Director

**Payal Pharma UK Ltd**
Incorporated: 16 December 2014
Registered Office: Lynton House, 304 Bensham Lane, Thornton Heath, Surrey, CR7 7EQ
Shareholders: Bharatkumar Rajnikant Patel; Kalpana Bharat Patel
Officers: Bharatkumar Rajnikant Patel, Secretary; Bharatkumar Rajnikant Patel [1959] Director; Kalpana Bharat Patel [1962] Director

**PB & T Project Ltd**
Incorporated: 25 November 2011
Net Worth: £1,681  Total Assets: £1,405,251
Registered Office: Cliffe House, Anthonys Way, Medway City Estate, Rochester, Kent, ME2 4DY
Shareholders: Andrius Bendoraitis; Raimondas Slepetys
Officers: Raimondas Slepetys [1969] Director [Lithuanian]

**PB's Locum Services Limited**
Incorporated: 25 May 2010
Net Worth: £2,978  Total Assets: £9,733
Registered Office: 36 Glebe Road, Finchley, London, N3 2AX
Major Shareholder: Pallavi Bhupesh Amin
Officers: Pallavi Bhupesh Amin [1983] Director

**Pearl Chemist Group Limited**
Incorporated: 25 April 2016  Employees: 73
Net Worth Deficit: £2,575,687  Total Assets: £12,396,708
Registered Office: New Bridge Street House, 30-34 New Bridge Street, London, EC4V 6BJ
Shareholders: Mayank Harendra Patel; Vijaykumar Harendra Patel
Officers: Mayank Harendra Patel [1975] Director; Vijaykumar Harendra Patel [1974] Director

**Pearl Services (Tooting) Limited**
Incorporated: 26 April 2016  Employees: 61
Net Worth: £8,679  Total Assets: £220,628
Registered Office: New Bridge Street House, 30-34 New Bridge Street, London, EC4V 6BJ
Parent: Pearl Chemist Group Limited
Officers: Mayank Harendra Patel [1975] Director; Vijaykumar Harendra Patel [1974] Director

**Peart Med Ltd**
Incorporated: 24 July 2014
Net Worth Deficit: £1,167  Total Assets: £883
Registered Office: The Hussar, 42 Burgh Heath Road, Epsom, Surrey, KT17 4LU
Major Shareholder: Balatheeban Balasubramaniam
Officers: Shyamala Ramajayam [1991] Director

**Pedalglass Limited**
Incorporated: 25 April 2006  Employees: 1
Net Worth: £646,582  Total Assets: £2,001,166
Registered Office: Haslers, Old Station Road, Loughton, Essex, IG10 4PL
Major Shareholder: Bemal Patel
Officers: Hital Patel, Secretary; Bemal Patel [1973] Director/Pharmacist

**Pembroke Healthcare Limited**
Incorporated: 15 July 2013
Net Worth Deficit: £58,040  Total Assets: £25,571
Registered Office: Unit 12 Farnborough Business Centre, Eelmoor Road, Farnborough, Hants, GU14 7XA
Major Shareholder: John Carroll
Officers: John Carroll [1980] Director/Pharmacist [Irish]

**Penlan Pharmaceuticals Limited**
Incorporated: 13 September 2011
Previous: Pharmasavings Limited
Net Worth Deficit: £831,821  Total Assets: £231,968
Registered Office: Chiltlee Manor, Haslemere Road, Liphook, Hants, GU30 7AZ
Parent: Penlan Healthcare Limited
Officers: Anthony Brian Bratt, Secretary; Stephen Jeremy Martin [1965] Director; Simon Paul Raynor [1966] Director

**Pennamed Limited**
Incorporated: 16 February 2007  Employees: 7
Net Worth: £1,045,537  Total Assets: £1,467,642
Registered Office: 30 Redcliff Road, Melton Industrial Park, Melton, E Yorks, HU14 3RS
Parent: IKP 2004 Limited
Officers: Kathryn Elizabeth Alison Penna, Secretary; Ignatius Dominic Penna [1972] Director/Medical Sales

**Pennine Pharmaceuticals Limited**
Incorporated: 16 March 2018
Registered Office: Office 15, The Elsie Whiteley Innovation Centre, Hopwood Lane, Halifax, W Yorks, HX1 5ER
Shareholders: Faheem Mukhtar; Maqsood Ahmed
Officers: Dr Maqsood Ahmed [1953] Director; Faheem Mukhtar [1978] Director

**Pennine UK Procedure Packs Limited**
Incorporated: 11 August 2016
Net Worth: £5,000,000  Total Assets: £5,000,000
Registered Office: Farboud Innovation Park, Formula Drive, Newmarket, Suffolk, CB8 0BF
Parent: Unisurge International Limited
Officers: Jahangir Farboud [1944] Director/Company Chairman; Terence Frederick Turner [1959] Director/Chief Operating Officer

**Per-Medic Limited**
Incorporated: 10 October 1977
Net Worth Deficit: £434,804  Total Assets: £177,713
Registered Office: Suite 44, Catalyst House, 720 Centennial Court, Centennial Park, Elstree, Borehamwood, Herts, WD6 3SY
Officers: Hasmukh Velji Shah, Secretary; Amratlal Velji Shah [1946] Director; Hasmukh Velji Shah [1950] Director; Mayurkumar Velji Shah [1961] Director

**Perennial Pharma Ltd**
Incorporated: 14 February 2019
Registered Office: Kemp House, 160 City Road, London, EC1V 2NX
Major Shareholder: Mark Roberts
Officers: Mark Roberts [1964] Service Director

**Perfect Vascular Natural Limited**
Incorporated: 1 May 2014
Net Worth Deficit: £2,780  Total Assets: £5,604
Registered Office: Collagen House, Duchess Street, Whitley Bay, Tyne & Wear, NE26 3PW
Shareholder: Kimberley Mack
Officers: Kimberley Mack [1958] Director; Stephen Maurice Mack [1955] Director; Robert Pongrac [1966] Director [American]

**Pergamon Ltd**
Incorporated: 3 November 2009  Employees: 2
Net Worth: £14,045  Total Assets: £417,754
Registered Office: Devonshire House, 582 Honeypot Lane, Stanmore, Middlesex, HA7 1JS
Parent: Aspire Trade Worldwide Limited
Officers: Nitinkumar Ramanlal Patel [1967] Director; Raxit Kirit Kumar Shah [1976] Director [Indian]

**Pericia Ltd**
Incorporated: 11 January 2019
Registered Office: 20 Bristol Avenue, Levenshulme, Manchester, M19 3NU
Major Shareholder: Mussarraf Hossain Khatun
Officers: Mussarraf Hossain Khatun [1976] Director/Taxi Driver [Spanish]

**Periproducts Limited**
Incorporated: 20 October 1993
Net Worth: £1,511,000  Total Assets: £4,960,000
Registered Office: Venture House, 2 Arlington Square, Bracknell, Berks, RG12 1WA
Parent: Venture Life Group PLC
Officers: Giuseppe Gioffre, Secretary; Sharon Mary Collins [1974] Commercial Director; Jeremy Anthony Phillip Randall [1964] Managing Director

**Perricone MD Cosmeceuticals UK Limited**
Incorporated: 14 January 2008  Employees: 20
Net Worth Deficit: £351,038  Total Assets: £8,062,350
Registered Office: rear Mezzanine, 16-18 Berners Street, London, W1T 3LN
Officers: Ronald Lee Fugate [1957] Director/Chief Executive Officer [American]; Tracey Mann [1966] Director/Chief International Officer; Susan Vandegrift [1964] Director [American]

**Perrigo Pharma Limited**
Incorporated: 16 March 1982
Registered Office: Wrafton, Braunton, Devon, EX33 2DL
Parent: Perrigo UK Acquisition Limited
Officers: Annette Corcoran, Secretary; Neil Thomas Lister [1975] Director; Dominic James Rivers [1977] Director; Christopher Allan Rudd [1980] Director

**Perrington & Co Limited**
Incorporated: 13 July 1998
Net Worth Deficit: £61,918  Total Assets: £17,711
Registered Office: Collins House, Rutland Square, Edinburgh, EH1 2AA
Major Shareholder: Rodolfo Wehe
Officers: Marta Irene Diaz de Saavedra, Secretary; Marta Irene Diaz de Saavedra [1955] Director [Panamanian]; Dianeth Isabel Matos de Ospino [1960] Director [Panamanian]; Jose Eugenio Silva Ritter [1963] Director [Panamanian]

**Perush Ltd**
Incorporated: 3 March 2015
Net Worth: £42,623  Total Assets: £1,163,341
Registered Office: 37 Warren Street, London, W1T 6AD
Shareholder: Shamir Kumar Sumantbhai Patel
Officers: Paaras Shamir Kumar Patel [1991] Director/Economist; Rushil Shamir Kumar Patel [1993] Director/Student; Shamir Kumar Sumantbhai Patel [1962] Director/Chemist

**Peter & Guys Salon Professional Ltd**
Incorporated: 28 May 2014
Net Worth Deficit: £774  Total Assets: £2
Registered Office: Herkes Courtney Wong Limited, 3rd Floor, 19 Gerrard Street, London, W1D 6JG
Shareholder: San Bing Seng
Officers: Sin Mon Seng, Secretary; San Bing Seng [1951] Director [Malaysian]; Sin Mon Seng [1985] Director [Malaysian]

**Petersone Group Ltd**
Incorporated: 31 May 2017
Net Worth: £632  Total Assets: £101,597
Registered Office: International House, 776-778 Barking Road, London, E13 9PJ
Major Shareholder: Angelika Petersone
Officers: Angelika Petersone [1988] Director/Manager [Latvian]

**PF Consultancy Plus Ltd**
Incorporated: 12 June 2000
Net Worth Deficit: £11,566  Total Assets: £7,563
Registered Office: Ostlers Barn, Park Farm, Willesley Woodside, Ashby De La Zouch, Leics, LE65 2UN
Shareholder: Michael Whitehead
Officers: Helen Joy Whitehead, Secretary; Helen Joy Whitehead [1965] Director/Operating Department Practitioner; Michael Harry Whitehead [1961] Director/Accountant

**PF OFG UK 3 Ltd**
Incorporated: 14 November 2018
Registered Office: Ramsgate Road, Sandwich, Kent, CT13 9NJ
Parent: Pharmacia Limited
Officers: Jacqui Mount, Secretary; Ian Eric Franklin [1965] Director; Hendrikus Hermannus Nordkamp [1969] Director [Dutch]; Edwin James Pearson [1974] Director/Solicitor

**Pfizer Consumer Healthcare Limited**
Incorporated: 6 November 1913
Net Worth: £221,754,000  Total Assets: £256,190,000
Registered Office: Pfizer, Ramsgate Road, Sandwich, Kent, CT13 9NJ
Parent: Pfizer Inc
Officers: Jacqueline Ann Mount, Secretary; Mark Wayne Davidson [1968] Director [Cypriot]; Ian Eric Franklin [1965] Director; Denise Jean Harnett [1964] Director; Jacqueline Ann Mount [1963] Director; Hendrikus Hermannus Nordkamp [1969] UK Managing Director, Pfizer [Dutch]; Edwin James Pearson [1974] Director/Solicitor; Paul Rose [1963] Director [Australian]

**Pfizer Limited**
Incorporated: 27 November 1953  Employees: 2,557
Net Worth: £777,881,984  Total Assets: £1,879,758,976
Registered Office: Pfizer Limited, Ramsgate Road, Sandwich, Kent, CT13 9NJ
Parent: Pfizer Inc
Officers: Jacqueline Ann Mount, Secretary; Ian Eric Franklin [1965] Director; Denise Jean Harnett [1964] Director; Hendrikus Hermannus Nordkamp [1969] UK Managing Director, Pfizer [Dutch]; Ben Osborn [1977] Director; Edwin James Pearson [1974] Director/Solicitor; Dr Berkeley Simon Phillips [1969] Director; Paul Rose [1963] Director [Australian]; Colin Malcolm Seller [1963] Director; Doctor Julian Keith Thompson [1960] Director/Doctor

**Pfizer OFG UK Limited**
Incorporated: 14 November 2018
Registered Office: Ramsgate Road, Sandwich, Kent, CT13 9NJ
Parent: Pfizer Limited
Officers: Jacqui Mount, Secretary; Ian Eric Franklin [1965] Director; Hendrikus Hermannus Nordkamp [1969] Director [Dutch]; Edwin James Pearson [1974] Director/Solicitor

**PH Medicare Ltd**
Incorporated: 24 September 2018
Registered Office: Polyco Healthline, South Fen Road, Bourne, Lincs, PE10 0DN
Shareholders: Polyco Healthline Limited; Sira Holdings Ltd
Officers: Neil Wilson, Secretary; Jason Prichard [1969] Director; Gurcharan Singh Sira [1963] Director; James Anthony Hari Singh Sira [1989] Director; Neil Antony Wilson [1976] Director

**Pharco Ltd**
Incorporated: 31 July 2008  Employees: 3
Previous: Tetra Med Home Health Care Co. Limited
Net Worth: £114,333  Total Assets: £2,294,234
Registered Office: 149 Cricklewood Lane, London, NW2 2EL
Major Shareholder: Mohammad Bashari
Officers: Maryam Khorramirouz, Secretary/Administration [Iranian]; Mohammad Bashari [1972] Director/Business Management

**Pharhealth Limited**
Incorporated: 2 October 2013
Registered Office: 3 Cofton Park Close, Rednal, Birmingham, B45 8DE
Shareholders: Chi Wai Tsang; Eric Kh Wong
Officers: Dr Chi Wai Tsang [1979] Director/Wholesale and Distribution [Danish]; Eric KH Wong [1982] Director/Wholesale and Distribution

**Pharm - Tex Limited**
Incorporated: 6 December 1988
Net Worth: £9,446,986  Total Assets: £9,446,986
Registered Office: SDC (2012) Ltd P/A Shah Dodhia & Co, 173 Cleveland Street, London, W1T 6QR
Officers: Vinay Lalji Shah, Secretary; Amritlal Lalji Shah [1941] Director; Anil Lalji Shah [1949] Director; Nalin Lalji Shah [1957] Director; Vinay Lalji Shah [1947] Director

**Pharm Med Ltd**
Incorporated: 28 December 2018
Registered Office: The Lansdowne Building, 2 Lansdowne Road, Croydon, Surrey, CR9 2ER
Shareholder: Silvia Maria Atanasoff
Officers: Silvia Maria Atanasoff [1992] Director/Analyst [Romanian]

**Pharm Recon Ltd**
Incorporated: 15 February 2019
Registered Office: 196 High Road, London, N22 8HH
Major Shareholder: Dmitrii Sharov
Officers: Dmitrii Sharov [1971] Director [Russian/Canadian]

**Pharma 313 Limited**
Incorporated: 11 February 2019
Registered Office: c/o Brierley Coleman & Co, 33 Turner Street, Manchester, M4 1DW
Shareholders: Mohammad Sarwar; Abdul Butt
Officers: Abdul Butt [1975] Quality Director; Mohammad Sarwar [1973] Director/Mortgage Advisor

**Pharma 777 Limited**
Incorporated: 3 December 2008
Net Worth Deficit: £329,190  Total Assets: £295,520
Registered Office: c/o George Little Sebire & Co, Oliver House, 23 Windmill Hill, Enfield, Middlesex, EN2 7AB
Major Shareholder: Robert Ralph Pietersen
Officers: Robert Ralph Pietersen [1950] Director [Australian]

**Pharma Concept UK Limited**
Incorporated: 2 October 2006
Net Worth: £71,703  Total Assets: £232,675
Registered Office: Scottish Provident House, 76-80 College Road, Harrow, Middlesex, HA1 1BQ
Major Shareholder: Shailesh Patel
Officers: Bharti Patel [1954] Director/Management; Shailesh Patel [1953] Director/Businessman

**Pharma Insight Ltd**
Incorporated: 20 November 2005  Employees: 2
Net Worth: £554,976  Total Assets: £597,794
Registered Office: Mill Road Farm, Mill Road, Little Wilbraham, Cambs, CB21 5LG
Shareholders: Anne Elizabeth Pass; Duncan Ian Pass
Officers: Anne Elizabeth Pass, Secretary; Anne Elizabeth Pass [1962] Director/Pharmacist; Duncan Ian Pass [1959] Director

**Pharma Maiden Ltd**
Incorporated: 14 June 2018
Registered Office: 152 Empress Avenue, London, E12 5HW
Major Shareholder: Doreen Bennett Cooke
Officers: Doreen Bennett Cooke [1979] Director/Pharmacist

**Pharma Mar Limited**
Incorporated: 1 July 2015  Employees: 7
Net Worth: £69,340  Total Assets: £199,478
Registered Office: Soane Point, 6-8 Market Place, Reading, Berks, RG1 2EG
Parent: Pharma Mar S.A.
Officers: Elena Calleja Crespo [1965] Finance Director [Spanish]; Luis Mora Capitan [1961] Managing Director [Spanish]

**Pharma Medico Limited**
Incorporated: 31 January 2013  Employees: 6
Net Worth Deficit: £55,704  Total Assets: £1,265,051
Registered Office: First Floor, 10 Temple Back, Bristol, BS1 6FL
Parent: Pharma Medico UK Limited
Officers: Geoffrey Stuart Cleall-Harding [1950] Director/Accountant; Christopher John Keeble [1961] Director

**Pharma Modus Limited**
Incorporated: 11 November 2011  Employees: 9
Net Worth: £593,753  Total Assets: £1,262,139
Registered Office: 18c Caxton Way, Watford, Herts, WD18 8UA
Shareholders: Brett Leigh Cantello; Diane Bowden
Officers: Diane Bowden [1960] Sales Director; Brett Leigh Cantello [1960] Director

**Pharma Oasis Ltd**
Incorporated: 18 May 2018
Registered Office: 20-22 Wenlock Road, London, N1 7GU
Major Shareholder: Ripudaman Singh
Officers: Ripudaman Singh [1987] Director/Purchasing Manager [Indian]

**Pharma Plus Supplies Ltd**
Incorporated: 28 January 2010  Employees: 1
Net Worth: £628,493  Total Assets: £775,190
Registered Office: Unit 3 Devonshire Court, Victoria Road, Feltham, Middlesex, TW13 7LU
Major Shareholder: Zhiying Yang
Officers: Zhiying Yang, Secretary; Zhiying Yang [1979] Director/Management

**Pharma Procurement Services Ltd**
Incorporated: 9 August 2013
Net Worth Deficit: £61,135  Total Assets: £170,091
Registered Office: 2a Pye Close, Corfe Mullen, Wimborne, Dorset, BH21 3NU
Officers: Gary Smart [1973] Director

**Pharma Products Limited**
Incorporated: 20 March 2018
Registered Office: 44 Theydon Road, London, E5 9NA
Major Shareholder: Moses Grossman
Officers: Moses Grossman [1990] Director

**Pharma Trading Limited**
Incorporated: 7 April 2017
Net Worth: £5,000  Total Assets: £5,000
Registered Office: 13 Freeland Park, Wareham Road, Poole, Dorset, BH16 6FH
Major Shareholder: Beau Caron
Officers: Beau Caron [1968] Director/President [Canadian]

# The Top UK Pharmaceutical Wholesalers

**Pharma World Ltd**
*Incorporated:* 16 November 2016
*Net Worth Deficit:* £179  *Total Assets:* £361
*Registered Office:* Flat 29 Pelly Court, Hemnall Street, Epping, Essex, CM16 4NA
*Major Shareholder:* Khabeb Mansha
*Officers:* Raymond Richard Burling [1949] Director

**Pharma-Export Ltd**
*Incorporated:* 28 April 2003
*Net Worth:* £46,056  *Total Assets:* £681,939
*Registered Office:* Office 12, Sigma Business Centre, 7 Havelock Place, Harrow, Middlesex, HA1 1LJ
*Officers:* Sonia Amrit, Secretary/IT Payroll Administrator; Benno Ranjitkumar Sabapathy [1968] Director

**Pharma-X Consultancy Ltd**
*Incorporated:* 19 April 2011
*Net Worth:* £1,088  *Total Assets:* £8,232
*Registered Office:* 29 Filsham Road, St Leonards on Sea, E Sussex, TN38 0PA
*Officers:* Harold Ian Dhanraj [1971] Director/Pharmacist

**Pharmabuyer Limited**
*Incorporated:* 12 January 2001
*Registered Office:* 3 Young Place, Kelvin Industrial Estate, East Kilbride, G75 0TD
*Parent:* Strathclyde Pharamceuticals Limited
*Officers:* John Cochrane [1957] Director

**Pharmac Limited**
*Incorporated:* 25 September 2000  *Employees:* 2
*Net Worth:* £1,634,309  *Total Assets:* £1,972,733
*Registered Office:* Suite 1, 1-3 Warren Court, Park Road, Crowborough, E Sussex, TN6 2QX
*Major Shareholder:* Mark Ayton
*Officers:* Sulaika Brobby Weihs, Secretary; Mark Ayton [1972] Sales Director

**Pharmacare (London) Limited**
*Incorporated:* 12 November 2009
*Net Worth Deficit:* £28,586  *Total Assets:* £2,819
*Registered Office:* 72 Cardigan Street, Luton, Beds, LU1 1RR
*Officers:* Kunal Saxena [1983] Director [Indian]; Dr Navin Satyapal Saxena [1953] Director [Indian]

**Pharmacare International Ltd**
*Incorporated:* 28 December 2018
*Registered Office:* 96-98 Baker Street, London, W1U 6TJ
*Major Shareholder:* Sanaa Al-Hadethee
*Officers:* Sanaa Al-Hadethee [1964] Director

**Pharmacare Logistics Limited**
*Incorporated:* 13 September 2000
*Registered Office:* Progress Park, Bedford, MK42 9XE
*Parent:* Movianto UK Limited
*Officers:* Kamaljit Singh Hunjan [1967] Director/Senior VP Movianto; Julia M. Munzinger [1968] Director/Accountant [American]; Nicholas Joseph Pace [1970] Director [American]; David John Tinsley [1971] Director

**Pharmaceutical Direct Limited**
*Incorporated:* 24 March 2014
*Registered Office:* Bemin House, Cox Lane, Chessington Industrial Estate, Chessington, Surrey, KT9 1SG
*Major Shareholder:* Bemal Patel
*Officers:* Hital Patel, Secretary; Bemal Patel [1973] Director

**Pharmaceutical Health Limited**
*Incorporated:* 15 September 2010  *Employees:* 1
*Net Worth:* £179,496  *Total Assets:* £196,775
*Registered Office:* 18 King Alfred Street, Derby, DE22 3QJ
*Major Shareholder:* Mandip Kaur Sidhu
*Officers:* Mandip Kaur Sidhu [1976] Director

**Pharmaceutical Identity Limited**
*Incorporated:* 29 April 1993
*Registered Office:* 7 Regents Drive, Prudhoe, Northumberland, NE42 6PX
*Shareholder:* Doncaster Pharmaceuticals Limited
*Officers:* Derek Andrew Wilson [1964] Director

**Pharmaceuticals Direct Limited**
*Incorporated:* 25 November 1999  *Employees:* 18
*Net Worth:* £18,600,224  *Total Assets:* £33,313,492
*Registered Office:* Old Station Road, Loughton, Essex, IG10 4PL
*Parent:* Pharmadent Holdings lmited
*Officers:* Hital Patel, Secretary; Bemal Patel [1973] Director; Hital Patel [1974] Director/Company Secretary

**Pharmacierge Group Limited**
*Incorporated:* 1 April 2015
*Net Worth Deficit:* £16,868  *Total Assets:* £48,555
*Registered Office:* 3rd Floor, Hathaway House, Popes Drive, London, N3 1QF
*Shareholders:* Stuart Charles Ungar; Robert David Lewis Ungar
*Officers:* Robert David Lewis Ungar, Secretary; Leon Alan Ungar [1936] Director; Robert David Lewis Ungar [1968] Director; Dr Stuart Charles Ungar [1943] Director

**Pharmacierge Limited**
*Incorporated:* 2 April 2015  *Employees:* 10
*Net Worth:* £121,951  *Total Assets:* £491,880
*Registered Office:* 3rd Floor, Hathaway House, Popes Drive, London, N3 1QF
*Parent:* Pharmacierge Group Limited
*Officers:* Robert David Lewis Ungar, Secretary; Leon Alan Ungar [1936] Director; Robert David Lewis Ungar [1968] Director

**Pharmacierge Technology Limited**
*Incorporated:* 2 April 2015
*Net Worth Deficit:* £140,666  *Total Assets:* £63,341
*Registered Office:* 3rd Floor, Hathaway House, Popes Drive, London, N3 1QF
*Parent:* Pharmacierge Group Limited
*Officers:* Leon Alan Ungar [1936] Director

**Pharmacina Ltd**
*Incorporated:* 23 May 2002
*Net Worth Deficit:* £38,603  *Total Assets:* £10,637
*Registered Office:* 8 Knightstone Place, High Street, Weston, Bath, BA1 4BY
*Major Shareholder:* Mohammed Rad-Niknam
*Officers:* Dr Mohammed Rad-Niknam, Secretary; Dr Mohammed Rad-Niknam [1955] Director/Medicinal Chemist

**Pharmaco Halesowen Limited**
*Incorporated:* 21 February 2018
*Registered Office:* 2 Wheeleys Road, Edgbaston, Birmingham, B15 2LD
*Parent:* Pharmaco 2000 Limited
*Officers:* Mushtaq Jafferali Ismail [1958] Director

**Pharmacohub Limited**
*Incorporated:* 21 November 2018
*Registered Office:* 30-34 North Street, Hailsham, E Sussex, BN27 1DW
*Shareholders:* Barbara Lumini Jean Erman; Dillan Marion Erman
*Officers:* Sianne Erman, Secretary; Tambimuttu Erman, Secretary; Barbara Lumini Jean Erman [1960] Director; Dr Dillan Marion Erman [1981] Director

**Pharmacosmos UK Limited**
*Incorporated:* 20 September 1995  *Employees:* 40
*Net Worth:* £379,971  *Total Assets:* £7,102,583
*Registered Office:* 6th Floor, The White Building, Kings Road, Reading, Berks, RG1 3AR
*Parent:* Pharmacosmos A/S
*Officers:* Robert Guglielmetti, Secretary; Lars Christensen [1943] Director/President and CEO [Danish]; Robert Gulielmetti [1964] Director/Executive Vice President CFO [Danish]

**Pharmacy Business Consultancy Limited**
*Incorporated:* 26 July 2017
*Registered Office:* 27 Montreal Road, Blackburn, BB2 7BY
*Officers:* Adam Esa, Secretary; Adam Esa [1992] Director/Pharmacist Business Consultant

**Pharmacy Supplies Limited**
*Incorporated:* 18 November 2005  *Employees:* 69
*Net Worth:* £2,355,446  *Total Assets:* £6,674,295
*Registered Office:* 5-7 Tobermore Road, Draperstown, Co Derry, BT45 7AG
*Major Shareholder:* Laurence O'Kane
*Officers:* Maura O'Kane, Secretary; Paul Robin Canning [1969] Sales Director; Louise Mary Donaghy [1983] Brand Director; John Paul McGuigan [1978] Purchasing Director; Catherine O'Connell [1979] Managing Director; Laurence Gregory O'Kane [1960] Director/Pharmacist; Maura O'Kane [1960] Director [Irish]

**Pharmacy4life Ltd**
*Incorporated:* 16 June 2014
*Registered Office:* 21 Easter Industrial Park, Ferry Lane, Rainham, Essex, RM13 9BP
*Officers:* Carmen Lewis, Secretary; Carmen Lewis [1965] Managing Director; Gary Stephen Lewis [1960] Director/Entrepreneur

**Pharmadose Limited**
*Incorporated:* 1 December 2010  *Employees:* 13
*Net Worth:* £254,573  *Total Assets:* £3,458,054
*Registered Office:* Unit 14 Dodson Way, Fen Gate, Peterborough, Cambs, PE1 5XJ
*Shareholders:* Svikrut Patel; Amita Patel; Divyeshkumar Patel
*Officers:* Divyesh Kumar Patel [1976] Director/Pharmacy Technician; Krishan Janak Patel [1989] Director/Financial Analyst; Svikrut Patel [1980] Director

**Pharmadreams Limited**
*Incorporated:* 7 March 2000
*Net Worth Deficit:* £5,656  *Total Assets:* £52,975
*Registered Office:* The Old Police Station, Church Street, Swadlincote, Derbys, DE11 8LN
*Shareholders:* Gregory David Bilton; David Kenneth Bilton
*Officers:* Eileen Bilton, Secretary; David Kenneth Bilton [1954] Director; Gregory David Bilton [1992] Director/Supply Chain Controller

**Pharmadynamics UK Limited**
*Incorporated:* 14 May 2008
*Net Worth:* £63,121  *Total Assets:* £98,490
*Registered Office:* Unit 36 Thomas Way, Lakesview International Business Park, Hersden, Canterbury, Kent, CT3 4JZ
*Major Shareholder:* Tony Irechukwu
*Officers:* Patricia Georgina Martha Black, Secretary; Leon Irechukwu [1996] Director/Bioscientist; Tony Irechukwu [1965] Director/Industrial Pharmacist

**Pharmaethical Ltd**
*Incorporated:* 19 July 2018
*Registered Office:* 9 Suttones Place, Southampton, SO15 2SJ
*Shareholders:* Mayuragoban Balasubramaniam; Siven Pillay Rungien
*Officers:* Dr Mayuragoban Balasubramaniam [1981] Director/Doctor; Dr Siven Pillay Rungien [1981] Director/Manager

**Pharmaethics International Limited**
*Incorporated:* 25 August 2016
*Registered Office:* 235 Old Brompton Road, London, SW5 0EA
*Major Shareholder:* Ijaz Khan
*Officers:* Ijaz Khan [1970] Director [Pakistani]

**Pharmagona Limited**
*Incorporated:* 20 September 2006  *Employees:* 7
*Net Worth:* £164,387  *Total Assets:* £764,388
*Registered Office:* Unit 6 Millbrook Industrial Estate, Floats Road, Roundthorn Industrial Estate, Manchester, M23 9WT
*Major Shareholder:* Behrooz Ghasemi Firoozabadi
*Officers:* Dr Behrooz Ghasemi Firoozabadi, Secretary/MD PhD Andrologist; Dr Behrooz Ghasemi Firoozabadi [1966] Director/MD PhD Andrologist

**Pharmahouse Limited**
*Incorporated:* 11 April 2014  *Employees:* 8
*Net Worth:* £311,929  *Total Assets:* £965,892
*Registered Office:* 1 Chancery Gate Way, Farnborough, Hants, GU14 8FF
*Parent:* Chris Scott Holdings Ltd
*Officers:* Christopher John Scott [1980] Director/Manager

**Pharmalab Limited**
*Incorporated:* 24 October 1986
*Net Worth:* £8,432,000  *Total Assets:* £8,720,000
*Registered Office:* 103-105 Bath Road, Slough, Berks, SL1 3UH
*Parent:* Sonet Investments Limited
*Officers:* Christine Anne-Marie Logan, Secretary; Richard Mark Greensmith [1973] Group Tax Director; Jonathan Timmis [1975] Finance Director

**Pharmapal Limited**
*Incorporated:* 15 April 2014  *Employees:* 3
*Net Worth:* £446,497  *Total Assets:* £585,218
*Registered Office:* 43 Overstone Road, London, W6 0AD
*Shareholders:* Raffi Kevork Palamoudian; Bared Palamoudian
*Officers:* Bared Palamoudian [1970] Director [Cypriot]; Raffi Kevork Palamoudian [1963] Director [Cypriot]

**Pharmapoint UK Ltd**
*Incorporated:* 8 May 2015
*Net Worth:* £3,634  *Total Assets:* £151,939
*Registered Office:* 227 Preston Road, Wembley, Middlesex, HA9 8NF
*Major Shareholder:* Bela Gnyanesh Gore
*Officers:* Shivani Gore Khanna [1990] Director/Pharmacist

**Pharmargus Healthcare Ltd**
Incorporated: 8 November 2017
Registered Office: 286b Chase Road, Southgate, London, N14 6HF
Major Shareholder: Sinan Cengiz Sofuoglu
Officers: Sinan Cengiz Sofuoglu [1976] Director

**Pharmartel Limited**
Incorporated: 4 November 2003   Employees: 7
Net Worth Deficit: £35,749   Total Assets: £424,617
Registered Office: Congress House, 14 Lyon Road, Harrow, Middlesex, HA1 2EN
Parent: Farsan Farma Limited
Officers: Ehsan Varavipour, Secretary; Fariba Mobara [1983] Director; Ehsan Varavipour [1983] Director

**Pharmasif Direct Limited**
Incorporated: 17 May 2018
Registered Office: 1 Wakerley Road, Leicester, LE5 6AR
Shareholders: Asif Patel; Shanaz Patel
Officers: Asif Patel [1982] Director/Pharmacist

**Pharmasky Ltd**
Incorporated: 11 November 2010
Net Worth: £1,228   Total Assets: £2,208
Registered Office: 11 Grove House, Queen Mary Avenue, London, E18 2FF
Major Shareholder: Said Abu Ammouneh
Officers: Said Abu-Ammouneh [1980] Director/Pharmacist

**Pharmasol London Ltd**
Incorporated: 28 January 2019
Registered Office: Office 1.02, Sky Gardens, 153 Wandsworth Road, Vauxhall, London, SW8 2GB
Major Shareholder: Khaled Mohammed Ali Omar
Officers: Khaled Mohammed Ali Omar [1975] Director [Egyptian]

**Pharmassist Locums Limited**
Incorporated: 23 July 2015   Employees: 1
Net Worth: £100   Total Assets: £39,468
Registered Office: 92 Ashford Avenue, Hayes, Middlesex, UB4 0NB
Major Shareholder: Anil Kumar Jhamat
Officers: Anil Kumar Jhamat [1987] Director/Locum Pharmacist

**Pharmasure Limited**
Incorporated: 21 February 2000   Employees: 35
Net Worth: £2,817,653   Total Assets: £5,113,464
Registered Office: Lentcroft, 10 Cassiobury Park Avenue, Watford, Herts, WD18 7LB
Shareholders: Terence Sullivan; Christine Olga Sullivan
Officers: Terence Sullivan, Secretary; Christine Olga Sullivan [1955] Director/Chairman; Terence Sullivan [1956] Managing Director

**Pharmat Limited**
Incorporated: 20 May 1996
Net Worth: £768,167   Total Assets: £771,817
Registered Office: Ground Floor, 16 Princeton Mews, 167-169 London Road, Kingston upon Thames, Surrey, KT2 6PT
Major Shareholder: Surud Hiwaizi
Officers: Ferial Jamil Ahmad, Secretary; Surud Hiwaizi [1967] Director/Pharmacist

**Pharmatec Ltd**
Incorporated: 21 December 2007   Employees: 1
Net Worth Deficit: £13,135   Total Assets: £16,409
Registered Office: 8 Crest View, Greenhithe, Kent, DA9 9QY
Major Shareholder: Satvinder Singh Rayat
Officers: Satvinder Singh Rayat [1967] Director

**Pharmavit (UK) Limited**
Incorporated: 7 November 2018
Registered Office: The Uplands, Oxhill Road, Birmingham, B21 8EU
Major Shareholder: Mohammed Jasim Salem
Officers: Mohammed Jasim Salem [1981] Director/Businessman

**Pharmaxis Pharmaceuticals Limited**
Incorporated: 3 February 2006
Registered Office: 25 Moorgate, London, EC2R 6AY
Parent: Pharmaxis Ltd
Officers: David Morris McGarvey, Secretary; David Morris McGarvey [1956] Director/Chief Financial Officer [Australian]; Gary Jonathan Phillips [1961] Director/Chief Executive [Australian]

**Pharmaxone Limited**
Incorporated: 20 August 2018
Registered Office: 90 Downs Drive, Timperley, Altrincham, Cheshire, WA14 5QU
Major Shareholder: Maek Sultan Trikam
Officers: Maek Sultan Trikam [1948] Director/Businesswoman [Kenyan]

**Pharmayas UK Limited**
Incorporated: 11 September 2017
Registered Office: Lower Ground Floor, One George Yard, London, EC3V 9DF
Major Shareholder: Ismaila Daou
Officers: Ismaila Daou [1963] Director [Malian]

**Pharmazon Limited**
Incorporated: 13 September 2018
Registered Office: 9 Lancaster Court, Coronation Road, Cressex Business Park, High Wycombe, Bucks, HP12 3TD
Parent: H Miller Trustees Ltd
Officers: Solange Tammy Hundal [1973] Director/Manager; Ali Miah [1975] Director/Chartered Accountant

**Pharmazz Europe Limited**
Incorporated: 26 October 2017
Registered Office: 25 Park Street West, Luton, Beds, LU1 3BE
Major Shareholder: Ajit Chand Srimal
Officers: Ajit Chand Srimal, Secretary; Ajit Chand Srimal [1958] Director and Company Secretary

**Pharmdex UK Ltd**
Incorporated: 25 September 2018
Registered Office: 14 Gainsborough Road, New Malden, Surrey, KT3 5NU
Major Shareholder: Geon Lee
Officers: Geon Lee [1982] Director [South Korean]

**Pharmed Health Care Organisation Limited**
Incorporated: 23 January 2001
Net Worth Deficit: £22,008   Total Assets: £5,985
Registered Office: 3rd Floor, 11-12 St James's Square, London, SW1Y 4LB
Major Shareholder: Marjan Farjam
Officers: Caterina Musgrave Juer [1983] Director/Senior Manager; David Rudge [1970] Director; Nishma Amit Sanghvi [1981] Director/Manager

**Pharmedics Ltd**
Incorporated: 13 February 2019
Registered Office: 71-75 Shelton Street, London, WC2H 9JQ
Major Shareholder: Adam Hersi
Officers: Adam Hersi [1964] Director

**Pharmethicals Limited**
Incorporated: 20 March 2000
Net Worth Deficit: £668,313  Total Assets: £285,999
Registered Office: Portwall Place, Portwall Lane, Bristol, BS1 6NA
Shareholder: David Freedman
Officers: Rachel Freedman, Secretary; David Freedman [1942] Director; Rachel Freedman [1943] Director; Elicca Anne Vazirani [1985] Director; Tushar Vazirani [1984] Director

**Pharmeurope UK Limited**
Incorporated: 3 September 1997
Net Worth: £740,459  Total Assets: £748,936
Registered Office: Bank Chambers, High Street, Cranbrook, Kent, TN17 3EG
Officers: Catherine Fournier, Secretary; Jean Claude Fournier [1953] Director [French]

**Pharmex International Ltd**
Incorporated: 30 July 2015
Previous: NGL459004 Limited
Net Worth: £1  Total Assets: £1
Registered Office: 461 Finchley Road, London, NW3 6HN
Major Shareholder: Abdul Kader Ali Saleh
Officers: Abdul Kader Ali Saleh [1968] Director [Lebanese]

**Pharmex-UK Ltd**
Incorporated: 11 April 2017
Net Worth Deficit: £3,832  Total Assets: £1,680
Registered Office: Unit 4C Cobden House, Cobden Street, Leicester, LE1 2LB
Shareholders: Ashwin Bebu; Dharmapal Virbhadrasinh Jadeja; Digvijaysinh Raysinh Gohil
Officers: Ashwin Bebu [1981] Director [Portuguese]

**Pharmhouse Ltd**
Incorporated: 8 October 2015
Net Worth: £17,108  Total Assets: £39,768
Registered Office: 20 Liversage Street, Derby, DE1 2LH
Officers: Yew Huey Thong [1989] Director [Malaysian]

**Pharmnet Group Ltd**
Incorporated: 29 April 2015  Employees: 2
Net Worth: £306,159  Total Assets: £1,847,126
Registered Office: Pharmacy Consulting Limited, Unit 12 Farnborough Business Centre, Eelmoor Road, Farnborough, Hants, GU14 7XA
Major Shareholder: Bogdan Pavel
Officers: Bogdan Nicolae Pavel [1974] Director/General Manager [Romanian]

**Pharmunity Limited**
Incorporated: 23 February 2018
Registered Office: 28 Shelley Gardens, Wembley, Middlesex, HA0 3QG
Shareholders: Alpesh Pindoria; Sima Jassal
Officers: Sima Jassal [1983] Director; Alpesh Pindoria [1984] Director and Company Secretary

**PharmXC Ltd**
Incorporated: 1 December 2011  Employees: 2
Net Worth: £45,651  Total Assets: £167,291
Registered Office: Unit 13 Wulfrun Trading Estate, Stafford Road, Wolverhampton, W Midlands, WV10 6HH
Shareholders: Rashpal Singh Dhaliwal; Kamaldeep Singh Bhogal
Officers: Kamaldeep Singh Bhogal [1984] Director/Web Developer; Rashpal Singh Dhaliwal [1984] Director/Procurement Manager

**Phaximed Limited**
Incorporated: 31 May 2016
Registered Office: 208 Horsenden Lane South, Perivale, Greenford, Middlesex, UB6 7NU
Shareholder: Olutobi Olusola Akindele
Officers: Temidayo Akenroye [1979] Director/Consultant (Procurement) [Nigerian]; Olutobi Olusola Akindele [1983] Director/Pharmacist; Olusola Olurotimi Arowojolu [1977] Director/Accountant [Nigerian]

**Phoenix Healthcare Distribution Limited**
Incorporated: 4 June 1913  Employees: 1,279
Net Worth: £214,886,000  Total Assets: £510,484,992
Registered Office: Rivington Road, Whitehouse Industrial Estate, Runcorn, Cheshire, WA7 3DJ
Officers: Stephen William Anderson [1966] Director; Kenneth John Black [1965] Director; Alan David Fairfield [1966] Director; Kevin Robert Hudson [1963] Finance Director; Stuart James Lucas [1970] Director; Jeremy David Meader [1966] Sales Director Pharmacy

**Phoenix Medical Supplies Limited**
Incorporated: 23 July 1998  Employees: 117
Net Worth: £88,456,000  Total Assets: £470,598,016
Registered Office: Rivington Road, Whitehouse, Runcorn, Cheshire, WA7 3DJ
Shareholders: Ludwig Merckle; Jutta Breu
Officers: Stephen William Anderson [1966] Director; Kenneth John Black [1965] Director; Helmut Karl Fisher [1970] Director [German]; Frank Grobe-Natrop [1961] Director [German]; Stefan Herfeld [1967] Director [German]; Kevin Robert Hudson [1963] Director; Oliver Thomas Windholz [1966] Director [German]

**Phoenix Pharma Ltd.**
Incorporated: 14 January 1999
Registered Office: Unit A4, Nexus Court, Gloucester Business Park, Brockworth, Gloucester, GL3 4AG
Major Shareholder: Christoph Kerstein
Officers: Stephen Allen Watkin, Secretary/Managing Director; Christoph Kerstein [1961] Director [German]; Stephen Allen Watkin [1967] Managing Director

**Phonepimps Limited**
Incorporated: 18 February 2013
Net Worth: £1,671  Total Assets: £29,456
Registered Office: 68 Windsor Road, Swindon, Wilts, SN3 1JX
Major Shareholder: Suresh Lakhman Vekaria
Officers: Seeta Patel, Secretary; Lakhman Patel [1958] Director/Carpenter

**Phytoceutical Limited**
Incorporated: 1 September 1998
Net Worth Deficit: £44,824  Total Assets: £46,953
Registered Office: The Harrow Cottage, North Street, Midhurst, W Sussex, GU29 9DJ
Major Shareholder: William Andrew Buchanan
Officers: William Andrew Buchanan [1957] Director Herbal Cosmetics

**PI Herman Trading as Peter's Limited**
Incorporated: 25 March 2015
Registered Office: Management House, 2 Sotheron Road, Watford, Herts, WD17 2QA
Major Shareholder: Peter Ian Herman
Officers: Peter Ian Herman [1945] Director

**Pinklady International Ltd**
Incorporated: 26 March 2018
Registered Office: Kemp House, 160 City Road, London, EC1V 2NX
Officers: Norzaidah Abdul Razak [1986] 2nd Director [Malaysian]; Heidi Shafiq Haidzir [1986] Director [Malaysian]

**Pioneer Medical Europe Limited**
Incorporated: 9 March 2010
Net Worth Deficit: £23,930 Total Assets: £81,793
Registered Office: 28 Green Sward Lane, Redditch, Worcs, B98 0EN
Shareholders: Susan Rosalyn Kowalski; John Joseph Alfons Kowalski
Officers: Jonathan Lindsay Holmes [1984] Director/Accountant; John Joseph Alfons Kowalski [1960] Director; Susan Rosalyn Kowalski [1958] Director

**Pioneer Veterinary Products Limited**
Incorporated: 21 January 2016 Employees: 4
Net Worth: £52,258 Total Assets: £464,241
Registered Office: Woolage Farm, Woolage Green, Canterbury, Kent, CT4 6SG
Major Shareholder: Adrian Clive Groombridge
Officers: Adrian Groombridge [1967] Director; Lucy Groombridge [1991] Director; Catherine Hibbert [1988] Director

**Piramal Critical Care Limited**
Incorporated: 22 June 2004 Employees: 16
Previous: Piramal Life Sciences (UK) Limited
Net Worth: £18,122,694 Total Assets: £276,387,680
Registered Office: Ground Floor, Suite 4, Heathrow Boulevard East Wing, 280 Bath Road, West Drayton, Middlesex, UB7 0DQ
Officers: Kaushik Upadhyay, Secretary; Peter Daniel Deyoung [1978] Director/Chief Executive Officer of Piramal Critical Care B [American]; William John Hargan [1958] Director/VP Sales and Marketing; Kaushik Upadhyay [1980] Director [Indian]

**Pispo Ltd**
Incorporated: 3 January 2012
Net Worth: £17,300 Total Assets: £207,170
Registered Office: Unit 9 London Road, West Kingsdown, Sevenoaks, Kent, TN15 6ES
Major Shareholder: Cristina Racca
Officers: Cristina Racca [1978] Director [Italian]

**PKA Healthcare Ltd**
Incorporated: 1 July 2014 Employees: 1
Net Worth Deficit: £16,804 Total Assets: £37,238
Registered Office: 28 Castle Street, Framlingham, Woodbridge, Suffolk, IP13 9BS
Shareholders: Patrick Jonathan Newton; Karl Legg; Antony Ailwyn Prendergast
Officers: Patrick Jonathan Newton, Secretary; Karl Legg [1964] Director/Pharmacist; Patrick Jonathan Newton [1961] Director/Pharmacist; Anthony Ailwyn Prendergast [1966] Director/Pharmacist

**PLA Medical Supplies Limited**
Incorporated: 24 July 2014
Net Worth Deficit: £8,885 Total Assets: £1
Registered Office: Nairn House, 1174 Stratford Road, Hall Green, Birmingham, B28 8AQ
Officers: Darren Lambert [1972] Director

**Planehill Limited**
Incorporated: 10 January 2011
Net Worth: £1,939,171 Total Assets: £2,105,650
Registered Office: Lower Ground Floor, One George Yard, London, EC3V 9DF
Parent: Tindrop Limited
Officers: Andrew Simon Davis [1963] Director

**Pleskarn Limited**
Incorporated: 17 October 1973 Employees: 23
Net Worth: £730,634 Total Assets: £955,232
Registered Office: c/o Reliance Medical Ltd, West Avenue, Kidsgrove, Stoke on Trent, Staffs, ST7 1TW
Parent: Reliance Medical Ltd
Officers: Andrew Mark Pear [1963] Director; Joshua Joseph Adam Pear [1991] Director

**Plexiam Limited**
Incorporated: 12 February 2014
Net Worth: £1,351,672 Total Assets: £1,617,827
Registered Office: Companies House, Default Address, Cardiff, CF14 8LH
Major Shareholder: Jon Weinburg
Officers: John Weinberg [1965] Director

**Plurafores Pharma Limited**
Incorporated: 15 May 2018
Registered Office: 93 Tabernacle Street, London, EC2A 4BA
Shareholders: John Anthony Evans; Ladislav Martiska
Officers: John Anthony Evans [1950] Director; Ladislav Martiska [1978] Director/Consultant [Slovak]

**PMS Korea Ltd**
Incorporated: 24 August 2016 Employees: 4
Net Worth Deficit: £72,823 Total Assets: £180,291
Registered Office: Central Chambers, 227 London Road, Hadleigh, Benfleet, Essex, SS7 2RF
Major Shareholder: Stephen John Hine
Officers: Stephen John Hine [1961] Director

**Pneumech Limited**
Incorporated: 22 February 2018
Registered Office: The Loft, Hill End Farm, Langley, Hitchin, Herts, SG4 7PT
Officers: Gareth Karl Woods [1987] Director

**Poldark Limited**
Incorporated: 5 March 2008
Net Worth Deficit: £27,693 Total Assets: £103,321
Registered Office: Broad House, 1 The Broadway, Old Hatfield, Herts, AL9 5BG
Shareholders: Guido Sarotto; Ross Mark Britten
Officers: Paul John Britten, Secretary; Ross Mark Britten [1979] Director/Property Developer

**Pope Enterprises Ltd**
Incorporated: 1 June 2018
Registered Office: 26 Canners Way, Stratford upon Avon, Warwicks, CV37 0BJ
Major Shareholder: Keiron Pope
Officers: Keiron Francis Geraint Pope [1991] Director

**Portland Ventures Inc Ltd**
Incorporated: 12 November 2018
Registered Office: SW9 Apartments, 4 St James's Crescent, London, SW9 7BY
Major Shareholder: Shane Lebert Heywood
Officers: Shane Lebert Heywood [1984] Director/Operations Manager [Canadian/Jamaican]

## The Portobello Pharmacy Limited
*Incorporated:* 14 May 2009  *Employees:* 2
*Net Worth:* £166,227  *Total Assets:* £302,666
*Registered Office:* 15 Elgin Crescent, London, W11 2JA
*Shareholder:* Christopher Soteriou
*Officers:* Dr Neil Duncan Haughton [1967] Director/GP; Sarah Catherine Anne Jordan [1965] Director/GP; Dr Martin John Scurr [1950] Director/Doctor of Medicine; Christopher Soteriou [1963] Director/Pharmacist

## Poseidon Pharmaceutical UK Limited
*Incorporated:* 8 December 2003  *Employees:* 6
*Previous:* Heightmarch Property Management Limited
*Net Worth Deficit:* £275,513  *Total Assets:* £313,908
*Registered Office:* Fernhill Estate Office, Fernhill Road, Sutton, Newport, Salop, TF10 8DJ
*Shareholders:* Darren Paul Mullinder; Samuel Cornes
*Officers:* Darren Paul Mullinder, Secretary; Samuel Cornes [1974] Director; Darren Paul Mullinder [1968] Finance Director

## Positive Pharma Ltd
*Incorporated:* 12 February 2018
*Registered Office:* Office 2, 149 Deane Road, Bolton, Lancs, BL3 5AH
*Major Shareholder:* Mohammed Bux
*Officers:* Mohammed Bux [1992] Director

## Sara Post Ltd
*Incorporated:* 27 February 2015
*Net Worth:* £1,520  *Total Assets:* £12,790
*Registered Office:* 10 Bissell Street, Birmingham, B5 7HP
*Major Shareholder:* Soran Rashid
*Officers:* Soran Rashid [1974] Director

## Pound International Ltd
*Incorporated:* 6 August 1958  *Employees:* 7
*Net Worth:* £523,692  *Total Assets:* £777,339
*Registered Office:* 1st Floor, Sackville House, 143-149 Fenchurch Street, London, EC3M 6BN
*Major Shareholder:* David Vaughan Racklin
*Officers:* Jacqueline Warin Racklin, Secretary; David Vaughan Racklin [1930] Director/Executive; Toni Rochelle Racklin [1952] Director/Executive; Nicole Deborah Racklin Asher [1961] Director/Writer

## Powerlung Ltd.
*Incorporated:* 11 September 2001
*Net Worth Deficit:* £7,496  *Total Assets:* £31
*Registered Office:* Alsyd, Taggs Island, Hampton, Surrey, TW12 2HA
*Major Shareholder:* Carolyn Morse
*Officers:* Carolyn Elice Morse, Secretary/Director; Carolyn Elice Morse [1947] Director; David John Wheeler [1931] Director/Accountant

## PPQUK Ltd
*Incorporated:* 7 March 2018
*Registered Office:* 82 Temperance Street, Manchester, M12 6HU
*Major Shareholder:* Abdussalam Elzawi
*Officers:* Abdussalam Elzawi [1965] Director/Manager [Libyan]

## Pramod Rajani Organisation Limited
*Incorporated:* 22 May 2002
*Net Worth:* £152,219  *Total Assets:* £154,229
*Registered Office:* 71 Reynolds Drive, Edgware, Middlesex, HA8 5PX
*Major Shareholder:* Pramod Tulsidas Rajani
*Officers:* Pramod Tulsidas Rajani [1959] Director

## Prayosha Enterprises Limited
*Incorporated:* 16 July 2013
*Net Worth Deficit:* £75,049  *Total Assets:* £216,569
*Registered Office:* 136 Windsor Drive, Orpington, Kent, BR6 6HQ
*Officers:* Dipakkumar Kumar Patel [1973] Director; Hiten Mukesh Patel [1991] Director; Parim Umakant Patel [1990] Director

## Prayosha Healthcare Limited
*Incorporated:* 6 February 2012
*Net Worth:* £192,036  *Total Assets:* £1,121,233
*Registered Office:* 136 Windsor Drive, Orpington, Kent, BR6 6HQ
*Shareholder:* Dipak Kumar Patel
*Officers:* Dipak Kumar Patel [1973] Director; Hinal Patel [1987] Director; Umakant Natubhai Patel [1961] Director

## Precision Fluid Controls Limited
*Incorporated:* 17 October 1989
*Registered Office:* Passhouse Farmhouse, Papworth St Agnes, Cambs, CB23 8QU
*Major Shareholder:* Kenneth Stanley Liddle
*Officers:* Janice Elizabeth Liddle, Secretary; Janice Elizabeth Liddle [1947] Director; Kenneth Stanley Liddle [1944] Director

## Precision Healthcare Limited
*Incorporated:* 23 November 2001
*Net Worth Deficit:* £391,384  *Total Assets:* £138,593
*Registered Office:* 89 High Street, Hadleigh, Ipswich, Suffolk, IP7 5EA
*Shareholders:* Gian Baptista Trepp; Matthew Caldwell-Nichols
*Officers:* Ying Li, Secretary; Matthew Caldwell-Nichols [1957] Director/Management Consultant; Gian Baptista Trepp [1968] Director [Swiss]

## Prema Naturals Limited
*Incorporated:* 31 August 2016
*Net Worth Deficit:* £2,752
*Registered Office:* 2 Hinksey Court, Church Way, Oxford, OX2 9SX
*Major Shareholder:* Dalia Monassebian
*Officers:* Bijan Monassebian [1939] Director/Entrepreneur [American]; Dalia Monassebian [1976] Director/Entrepreneur [American]

## Premax Europe Limited
*Incorporated:* 17 August 2016
*Net Worth Deficit:* £2,602  *Total Assets:* £37,085
*Registered Office:* 23 Ansdell Street, London, W8 5BN
*Shareholders:* Randall Lyall Cooper; Peter Damian Brucker
*Officers:* Peter Damian Brukner [1952] Director [Australian]; Randall Lyall Cooper [1974] Director [Australian]; Cameron John Tudor [1975] Director [Australian]

## Premium Pharm Ltd
*Incorporated:* 7 August 2018
*Registered Office:* 14 Hilders Road, Leicester, LE3 6HD
*Major Shareholder:* Artur Nowak
*Officers:* Artur Nowak [1988] Director/Financial Adviser [Polish]

## Premium Pharma UK Limited
*Incorporated:* 29 June 2018
*Registered Office:* Suite 308, Keys Court, 82-84 Moseley Street, Birmingham, B12 0RT
*Officers:* Ali Ahmed Mahmud [1980] Director

## Prescribe Direct Limited
*Incorporated:* 30 January 2017
*Registered Office:* Unit E2, The Seedbed Centre, Langston Road, Loughton, Essex, IG10 3TQ
*Officers:* Amjid Malik Khan [1975] Director; Ayisha Zafar [1985] Director [Pakistani]

**Prescribe International Limited**
*Incorporated:* 8 January 2018
*Registered Office:* Prescribe International Limited, c/o Quantum Capital Investors, 1st Floor, 99 Bishopsgate, London, EC2M 3XD
*Major Shareholder:* Hardeep Singh Gill
*Officers:* Hardeep Singh Gill [1973] Managing Director

**Prestige Brands (UK) Limited**
*Incorporated:* 9 March 2000  *Employees:* 3
*Net Worth:* £1,393,640  *Total Assets:* £2,353,120
*Registered Office:* Suite 5, Clockhouse Court, 5-7 London Road, St Albans, Herts, AL1 1LA
*Parent:* Prestige Brands Holdings, Inc.
*Officers:* Ronald Lombardi [1964] Director/Chief Executive Officer [American]; William P'pool [1965] Director/General Counsel [American]; Christine Sacco [1975] Director/Chief Financial Officer [American]

**Prestige Dental Products Ltd**
*Incorporated:* 2 June 1989
*Net Worth:* £1,994  *Total Assets:* £704,324
*Registered Office:* 7 Oxford Place, Bradford, W Yorks, BD3 0EF
*Shareholders:* Lucy Victoria Gabbitas; Paul Anthony Martin
*Officers:* Lucy Victoria Gabbitas, Secretary; Lucy Victoria Gabbitas [1969] Operations Director; Paul Anthony Martin [1958] Sales Director

**John Preston & Co. (Belfast) Limited**
*Incorporated:* 4 March 1964  *Employees:* 20
*Net Worth:* £839,877  *Total Assets:* £1,616,562
*Registered Office:* Unit 7a Altona Road, Lisburn, Co Antrim, BT27 5QB
*Parent:* John Preston & Co (Holdings)
*Officers:* Patricia Anne Cooke, Secretary; Christopher Alexander Cooke [1971] Director; Nicholas James Shelton Cooke [1975] Director/Salesman; Patricia Ann Cooke [1948] Director/Secretary

**Pricecheck Toiletries Limited**
*Incorporated:* 22 March 1978  *Employees:* 123
*Net Worth:* £12,630,976  *Total Assets:* £23,155,352
*Registered Office:* Pricecheck Toiletries Ltd, Old Colliery Way, Beighton, Sheffield, S20 1DJ
*Shareholders:* Mark Andrew Lythe; Deborah Harrison
*Officers:* Mark Andrew Lythe, Secretary; Barry John Corker [1972] Director; Deborah Harrison [1970] Sales Director; Jonathan Edward Harrison [1963] Director; Amanda Jane Lythe [1965] Director; Mark Andrew Lythe [1967] Director; Lee Philip Walker [1975] Finance Director

**Prima Brands Limited**
*Incorporated:* 2 July 1974  *Employees:* 3
*Net Worth:* £1,060,990  *Total Assets:* £3,227,410
*Registered Office:* 2 Marshalls Road, Belfast, BT5 6SR
*Parent:* Sangers (Northern Ireland) Limited
*Officers:* Nichola Louise Legg, Secretary; Toby Matthew Anderson [1973] Director; Marcus Hilger [1977] Finance Director [German]; David Jackson [1960] Director; Catherine McDermott [1968] Operations Director; Nigel Swift [1966] Marketing and Sales Director

**Prime Medical Equipment Ltd**
*Incorporated:* 20 June 2018
*Registered Office:* 71-75 Shelton Street, London, WC2H 9JQ
*Major Shareholder:* Mohamed Ali Mohamed Dermish
*Officers:* Mohamed Dermish, Secretary; Mohamed Ali Mohamed Dermish [1994] Director [Libyan]

**Prime Pharmacare Ltd**
*Incorporated:* 24 May 2011
*Net Worth:* £152,963  *Total Assets:* £152,963
*Registered Office:* Devonshire House, Honeypot Lane, Stanmore, Middlesex, HA7 1JS
*Major Shareholder:* Khyati Patel
*Officers:* Khyati Patel [1976] Director

**Primecrown Limited**
*Incorporated:* 31 October 1988  *Employees:* 84
*Net Worth:* £799  *Total Assets:* £1,245,528
*Registered Office:* Unit 4-5 Northolt Trading Estate, Belvue Road, Northolt, Middlesex, UB5 5QS
*Shareholder:* Ketan Himatlal Mehta
*Officers:* Ketan Himatlal Mehta, Secretary; Bharat Himatlal Mehta [1952] Director; Ketan Himatlal Mehta [1958] Director/Pharmacist

**Primrose Hudson Limited**
*Incorporated:* 18 October 2016
*Net Worth Deficit:* £15,286  *Total Assets:* £18,023
*Registered Office:* 7 Newbery Close, Caterham, Surrey, CR3 6GD
*Major Shareholder:* Nikin Tanna
*Officers:* Nikin Tanna [1983] Director/Finance

**Principle Healthcare Limited**
*Incorporated:* 7 September 2001  *Employees:* 23
*Net Worth:* £1,711,821  *Total Assets:* £4,341,947
*Registered Office:* Airedale Business Centre, Millennium Road, Skipton, N Yorks, BD23 2TZ
*Shareholders:* Principle Healthcare International; Principle Healthcare International Ltd
*Officers:* Richard Doyle, Secretary; Clare Campbell [1975] Director; Andrew Michael Davies [1982] Director; Michael John Davies [1951] Director; Philip Benjamin Davies [1977] Director

**Prinwest Limited**
*Incorporated:* 10 December 1998
*Net Worth:* £21,763,100  *Total Assets:* £42,520,968
*Registered Office:* 2076 Lynstock House, Lynstock Way, Lostock, Bolton, Lancs, BL6 4SA
*Shareholders:* Anwer Ibrahim Patel; Yakub Ibrahim Patel
*Officers:* Anwar Ibrahim Patel, Secretary; Anwer Ibrahim Patel [1954] Director; Yakub Ibrahim Patel [1953] Director

**Priors Pharma Limited**
*Incorporated:* 23 November 2017
*Registered Office:* 146 New London Road, Chelmsford, Essex, CM2 0AW
*Officers:* Munir Somji [1987] Medical Director

**Priory Pharma Ltd**
*Incorporated:* 7 April 2009  *Employees:* 1
*Net Worth:* £119,615  *Total Assets:* £146,625
*Registered Office:* 7 Priory Grove, Ormskirk, Lancs, L39 4XJ
*Major Shareholder:* Joanne Spencer
*Officers:* Joanne Spencer [1969] Director

**The Private Pharma Health Company Ltd**
*Incorporated:* 8 August 2016  *Employees:* 2
*Net Worth:* £1  *Total Assets:* £13,698
*Registered Office:* 62 Wilson Street, London, EC2A 2BU
*Parent:* The Private Pharma Group Ltd
*Officers:* Adam Simon Bloom [1973] Director; Daniel Anthony Gilbert [1976] Director

**The Private Pharmacy Group Limited**
*Incorporated:* 5 August 2016
*Registered Office:* 62 Wilson Street, London, EC2A 2BU
*Shareholders:* Adam Simon Bloom; Daniel Anthony Gilbert
*Officers:* Adam Simon Bloom [1973] Director; Daniel Anthony Gilbert [1976] Director

**Pro Orbit Limited**
*Incorporated:* 23 January 2019
*Registered Office:* 12 Worcestershire Lea, Warfield, Bracknell, Berks, RG42 3TQ
*Officers:* Marijana Vlahovic [1974] Director/Registered Nurse

**Pro Teeth Whitening Co Limited**
*Incorporated:* 7 October 2015 *Employees:* 3
*Net Worth:* £109,653 *Total Assets:* £743,047
*Registered Office:* Office 1, Bridgeview House, Ray Mead Road, Maidenhead, Berks, SL6 8NJ
*Parent:* Sylphar NV
*Officers:* Patrick Baeyens [1971] Director [Belgian]; Mathieu de Medeiros [1980] Investment Director [French]; Arash Peyami [1985] Director/Talent Consulting; Babak Peyami [1987] Director

**Probar Services Limited**
*Incorporated:* 16 January 1987 *Employees:* 1
*Net Worth:* £3,612 *Total Assets:* £17,275
*Registered Office:* Riversdale, Ashburton Road, Totnes, Devon, TQ9 5JU
*Major Shareholder:* Andrew Richard Paul Barons
*Officers:* Jenifer Rose Renfree-Barons, Secretary; Andrew Richard Paul Barons [1964] Managing Director

**Probiotec (UK) Limited**
*Incorporated:* 5 February 2009 *Employees:* 8
*Net Worth Deficit:* £1,233,502 *Total Assets:* £169,506
*Registered Office:* 2 Salmon Court, Rowton Lane, Chester, CH3 6AT
*Officers:* Jared Stringer, Secretary; Dustin Stringer [1981] Director/Sales Manager [Australian]; Wesley Stringer [1978] Director/Chief Operating Officer [Australian]

**Prodigy Healthcare Limited**
*Incorporated:* 21 September 2016
*Net Worth Deficit:* £6,720 *Total Assets:* £2,016
*Registered Office:* 14D Adelaide Park, Belfast, BT9 6FX
*Major Shareholder:* Frederick John Topping
*Officers:* Frederick John Topping [1970] Director/Sales Manager

**Profoot (UK) Ltd**
*Incorporated:* 8 June 2001 *Employees:* 12
*Net Worth:* £445,027 *Total Assets:* £1,714,433
*Registered Office:* Sterling House, Fulbourne Road, Walthamstow, London, E17 4EE
*Shareholders:* Simon Freeman; Lewis Andrew Freeman; Elliot Jamie Freeman
*Officers:* Simon Freeman, Secretary/Manager; Elliot Jamie Freeman [1976] Director/Manager; Lewis Andrew Freeman [1969] Director/Manager; Simon Freeman [1973] Director/Manager

**Project & Communications Limited**
*Incorporated:* 30 November 2006
*Net Worth:* £47,647 *Total Assets:* £61,683
*Registered Office:* 3rd Floor, 14 Hanover Street, Hanover Square, London, W1S 1YH
*Officers:* Giancarlo Carocci [1969] Director [Italian]

**Prolife (UK) Limited**
*Incorporated:* 28 January 2015
*Net Worth Deficit:* £1,368 *Total Assets:* £928
*Registered Office:* First Floor, Roxburghe House, 273-287 Regent Street, London, W1B 2HA
*Shareholders:* Ramachandran Venkataraman Iyer; Nandita Ramachandran Iyer
*Officers:* Nandita Ramachandran Iyer [1972] Director [Indian]; Ramachandran Venkataraman Iyer [1972] Director [Indian]

**Prometheus Medical Ltd**
*Incorporated:* 1 March 2005 *Employees:* 29
*Net Worth:* £4,372,444 *Total Assets:* £5,913,449
*Registered Office:* The Old Rectory, Hope-under-Dinmore, Hereford, HR6 0PW
*Major Shareholder:* Malcolm Russell
*Officers:* Kevin Gallagher, Secretary/Medical; Professor Charles David Seymour Deakin [1964] Director/Doctor; Kevin Gallagher [1964] Commercial Director; Dr Alastair McPherson Nicol [1965] Director/Medical Doctor; Dr Malcolm Quentin Russell [1969] Director/Doctor

**Prominent Life Style Ltd**
*Incorporated:* 30 August 2011
*Registered Office:* 27 Sussex Court, Spring Street, London, W2 1JF
*Officers:* Jean Hanna [1984] Director/Sales [Lebanese]

**Prominer Limited**
*Incorporated:* 29 June 2016
*Registered Office:* 6 Langham Court, Station Approach, Ruislip, Middlesex, HA4 6RX
*Officers:* Dipti Rajesh Shah [1966] Director [Indian]; Rajesh Ramanlal Shah [1962] Director [Indian]

**Propharma Consultancy Ltd**
*Incorporated:* 10 March 2016
*Net Worth:* £100 *Total Assets:* £150
*Registered Office:* 25 Meadow Hill, New Malden, Surrey, KT3 5RQ
*Major Shareholder:* Mina Vyas
*Officers:* Mina Vyas [1954] Director/Retired

**Propharma-UK Ltd**
*Incorporated:* 29 April 2016
*Net Worth:* £83,313 *Total Assets:* £128,670
*Registered Office:* 25 Meadow Hill, New Malden, Surrey, KT3 5RQ
*Officers:* Sunil Rameshchandra Patel [1960] Director/Pharmacist; Mina Vyas [1954] Director/Retired

**Protec Medical Limited**
*Incorporated:* 14 May 2001 *Employees:* 4
*Net Worth:* £398,674 *Total Assets:* £473,231
*Registered Office:* Kenton House, Oxford Street, Moreton in Marsh, Glos, GL56 0LA
*Shareholders:* Brian Collins; Phillip Michael Collins
*Officers:* Jennifer Ruth Noble, Secretary; Brian Collins [1948] Director; Phillip Michael Collins [1969] Director

**Proup Ltd**
*Incorporated:* 24 October 2016
*Net Worth:* £692 *Total Assets:* £835
*Registered Office:* First Floor, 85 Great Portland Street, London, W1W 7LT
*Shareholders:* Dominik Ciuchcinski; Aneta Grzmiel; Dominik Kacprzak
*Officers:* Dominik Ciuchcinski [1974] Director/Manager [Polish]

**PS Dent Limited**
Incorporated: 16 July 2014  Employees: 2
Net Worth: £1,404,460  Total Assets: £1,793,386
Registered Office: Haslers, Old Station Road, Loughton, Essex, IG10 4PL
Shareholders: Pedalglass Liimted; CP Dent Limited
Officers: Hital Patel [1974] Director; Meghna Chirag Patel [1979] Director

**PTGO Sever UK Limited**
Incorporated: 23 May 2008
Registered Office: 6 St David's Square, Westferry Road, London, E14 3WA
Major Shareholder: Dmitry Sokolov
Officers: Dmitry Sokolov [1965] Director [Russian]

**Pura (UK) Ltd**
Incorporated: 22 April 2013  Employees: 1
Net Worth: £615  Total Assets: £28,954
Registered Office: 4 Goscote Drive, Narborough, Leicester, LE19 3ES
Shareholders: Kavaljeet Singh Hundle; Randeep Singh Powar
Officers: Kavaljeet Singh Hundle [1981] Director/Pharmacist; Randeep Singh Powar [1983] Director/Accountant

**Pura Pharmaceuticals Ltd**
Incorporated: 27 August 2003
Net Worth: £17,366  Total Assets: £139,902
Registered Office: 41 Stroud Green Road, London, N4 3EF
Shareholder: Mohammad Reza Ashkan-Nejad
Officers: Mohammad Reza Ashkan Nejad [1966] Director/Pharmacist

**Pure Light Vision Ltd**
Incorporated: 28 September 2016
Registered Office: 8 Hydrangea Walk, Banbury, Oxon, OX16 1XX
Officers: Tomasz Andrzej Bilski [1990] Director/Online Health Store [Polish]

**Pure Products London Limited**
Incorporated: 14 November 2016
Registered Office: Unit 3 Stirling Court, Stirling Way, Borehamwood, Herts, WD6 2BT
Officers: Denise Chester, Secretary; Ray John Brilus [1973] Director

**Pure Skincare Limited**
Incorporated: 7 August 2018
Registered Office: Richmond House, 29 Parkfield Avenue, Ashton on Ribble, Preston, Lancs, PR2 1JB
Major Shareholder: Andrew Croft
Officers: Andrew Croft [1966] Director/Consultant

**Pure Solace Ltd**
Incorporated: 13 November 2018
Registered Office: 71-75 Shelton Street, Covent Garden, London, WC2H 9JQ
Major Shareholder: Elliott-Jay Anthony Munroop
Officers: Elliott-Jay Anthony Munroop [1997] Director/Operations

**Purepharm Ltd**
Incorporated: 28 August 2015  Employees: 6
Net Worth: £81,413  Total Assets: £860,798
Registered Office: 43a Summerisland Road, Loughgall, Co Armagh, BT61 8LG
Shareholder: Turlough Malachy Hamill
Officers: Dr Turlough Malachy Hamill, Secretary; Helen Louise Hamill [1981] Director/Pharmacy Staff; Dr Turlough Malachy Hamill [1981] Director/Pharmacist

**Purple Orchid Pharma Limited**
Incorporated: 5 December 2011
Net Worth Deficit: £253,222  Total Assets: £456,823
Registered Office: Albany House, 14 Shute End, Wokingham, Berks, RG40 1BJ
Parent: Orchis Mascula Ltd
Officers: Dr Karen Jane Gardiner [1968] Director

**Purple Pharma Limited**
Incorporated: 19 September 2013
Net Worth: £15,964  Total Assets: £15,990
Registered Office: Ambe House, Commerce Way, Edenbridge, Kent, TN8 6ED
Major Shareholder: Amit Gohil
Officers: Amit Gohil [1976] Director

**Purple Surgical International Limited**
Incorporated: 21 February 2000  Employees: 5
Net Worth: £1,710,515  Total Assets: £2,949,368
Registered Office: 2 Chestnut House, Farm Close, Shenley, Herts, WD7 9AD
Shareholders: Robert Sharpe; Purple Surgical Holdings Limited
Officers: Jane Eddy Sharpe, Secretary; Robert Sharpe [1963] Director

**Purple Surgical UK Limited**
Incorporated: 3 October 1953  Employees: 21
Net Worth: £2,601,963  Total Assets: £4,487,534
Registered Office: 2 Chestnut House, Farm Close, Shenley, Herts, WD7 9AD
Parent: Chartuseful Limited
Officers: Philip David Franklin, Secretary; Philip David Franklin [1960] Operations Director; Adam Millar Lusby [1957] Director; Mark Oldroyd [1971] Director; Robert Sharpe [1963] Director

**Qamar Limited**
Incorporated: 17 December 2004
Net Worth: £1,474  Total Assets: £3,894
Registered Office: 86 Mornington Street, Keighley, W Yorks, BD21 2EP
Major Shareholder: Mohammed Qamar
Officers: Raqiya Begum, Secretary; Mohammed Qamar [1972] Director/Pharmacist

**Qdem Pharmaceuticals Limited**
Incorporated: 9 November 2011
Net Worth: £643,000  Total Assets: £10,346,000
Registered Office: Unit 196 Cambridge Science Park, Milton Road, Cambridge, CB4 0AB
Parent: Napp Pharmaceutical Holdings Limited
Officers: Stuart David Baker [1935] Director/Attorney [American]; Hywel Rhys Day [1974] Managing Director; Bryan George LEA [1961] Director; Dr Julian Paul Schofield [1959] Medical Director; David Alan Silver [1965] Director/Accountant; Ake Gunnar Wikstrom [1951] Director/Advisor [Swedish]

**QED Scientific Ltd**
Incorporated: 28 June 2005  Employees: 8
Net Worth: £276,039  Total Assets: £369,381
Registered Office: Unit 21 Botany Business Park, Macclesfield Road, Whaley Bridge, High Peak, Derbys, SK23 7DQ
Shareholders: Iain Jaundrell Thompson; Gillian Margaret Jaundrell Thompson
Officers: Gillian Margaret Jaundrell Thompson, Secretary; Gillian Margaret Jaundrell Thompson [1956] Director; Ian Jaundrell Thompson [1952] Director

**Qingdao Polychem (U.K.) Limited**
*Incorporated:* 12 March 2007
*Registered Office:* 210 Greenwood Crescent, Warrington, Cheshire, WA2 0EG
*Major Shareholder:* Zhiwen Liu
*Officers:* Wen Han, Secretary; Zhiwen Liu [1969] Director/Businessman [Chinese]

**Qualitech Healthcare Ltd**
*Incorporated:* 11 September 2013 *Employees:* 8
*Net Worth Deficit:* £1,249,872 *Total Assets:* £237,416
*Registered Office:* 11 Castle Hill, Maidenhead, Berks, SL6 4AA
*Shareholders:* Peter William Clarke; Edgar Wallner
*Officers:* Peter Clarke, Secretary; Peter William Clarke [1941] Director/Retired; Nicola Ann Dill [1969] Director; Edgar Wallner [1937] Director

**Qualiti (Burnley) Limited**
*Incorporated:* 13 March 1998 *Employees:* 87
*Net Worth Deficit:* £1,392,322 *Total Assets:* £2,269,252
*Registered Office:* Walshaw Mill, Talbot Street, Briercliffe, Burnley, Lancs, BB10 2JY
*Officers:* Martin John Tedham [1960] Director

**Quantum Biomed Ltd**
*Incorporated:* 25 May 2018
*Registered Office:* 20-22 Wenlock Road, London, N1 7GU
*Major Shareholder:* John Tourette
*Officers:* Arnold Leonard Gustafson [1955] Director/Financial Consultant [Canadian]; John Tourette [1988] Foundation Managing Director [Greek]

**Quatromed Limited**
*Incorporated:* 23 May 2006
*Net Worth:* £57,854 *Total Assets:* £63,118
*Registered Office:* Unit 3-4 Coppen Road, Dagenham, Essex, RM8 1HH
*Major Shareholder:* Hiten Shantilal Pabari
*Officers:* Alpa Pabari, Secretary; Dr Hiten Shantilal Pabari [1980] Director

**Quirky Vapes Ltd**
*Incorporated:* 20 November 2017
*Registered Office:* 63a High Street, Chellaston, Derby, DE73 6TB
*Officers:* Martyn James Smith [1991] Director

**Quramax Limited**
*Incorporated:* 27 August 1998
*Net Worth Deficit:* £125,722 *Total Assets:* £733,409
*Registered Office:* Artisans' House, 7 Queensbridge, Northampton, NN4 7BF
*Officers:* Manitkumar Batuk Odedra, Secretary; Zachariah Abraham [1960] Director [Cypriot]; Devendra Kumar Belgotra [1971] Director [Indian]

**R & D Healthcare Ltd**
*Incorporated:* 16 April 2014
*Net Worth Deficit:* £3,741 *Total Assets:* £14,001
*Registered Office:* 6 Station Road, Harpenden, Herts, AL5 4SE
*Shareholder:* Bharat Gulabchand Shah
*Officers:* Chetna Shah, Secretary; Bharat Gulabchand Shah [1966] Director/Pharmacist; Chetna Shah [1969] Director

**R & H Trading Limited**
*Incorporated:* 13 November 2001
*Net Worth:* £159,558 *Total Assets:* £167,942
*Registered Office:* Unit 62 Sherwood Road, Aston Fields Industrial Estate, Bromsgrove, Worcs, B60 3DR
*Shareholders:* Robert William Hawker; Heather Hawker
*Officers:* Heather Hawker, Secretary; Heather Hawker [1959] Director; Robert William Hawker [1960] Director

**R & R Post Op Box Ltd.**
*Incorporated:* 7 January 2019
*Registered Office:* 305 Equiano House, 17 Lett Road, Stockwell, London, SW9 0AQ
*Shareholder:* Rosemary Anita Ramroop
*Officers:* Rosemary Anita Ramroop [1975] Director/Nurse

**R. N. Europe Limited**
*Incorporated:* 9 January 2014
*Net Worth:* £32,360 *Total Assets:* £746,091
*Registered Office:* First Floor, Roxburghe House, 273-287 Regent Street, London, W1B 2HA
*Shareholders:* Nitin Garg; Rohit Sham Garg
*Officers:* Nitin Sham Garg [1978] Director [Indian]; Rohit Sham Garg [1974] Director [Indian]

**R.F. Medical Supplies Limited**
*Incorporated:* 23 September 2011
*Net Worth:* £4,996 *Total Assets:* £23,249
*Registered Office:* Laburnum House, Crank Hill, Crank Rd, St Helens, Merseyside, WA11 7SF
*Major Shareholder:* Adelle Elizabeth Rasul
*Officers:* Adelle Elizabeth Rasul [1971] Director and Company Secretary

**R.I.S. Products Limited**
*Incorporated:* 19 June 1972 *Employees:* 7
*Net Worth Deficit:* £32,069 *Total Assets:* £458,924
*Registered Office:* 10 Prospect Place, Welwyn, Herts, AL6 9EW
*Major Shareholder:* Stephen Ronald Unwin
*Officers:* Brenda Unwin, Secretary; Charles Stephen Unwin [1978] Director/General Manager; Iris Dorothy Unwin [1930] Director; Stephen Ronald Unwin [1953] Director

**Rabimed International Limited**
*Incorporated:* 29 July 2002
*Net Worth Deficit:* £5,258 *Total Assets:* £3,016
*Registered Office:* Unit 61 Battersea Business Centre, 99-109 Lavender Hill, London, SW11 5QL
*Officers:* Dr Nolitha Mji [1965] Director/Gynaecologist [South African]

**R.A. Racey (Gt. Yarmouth) Limited**
*Incorporated:* 14 April 1975
*Net Worth Deficit:* £132,921 *Total Assets:* £5,105,723
*Registered Office:* Unit 4 Castell Close, Swansea Enterprise Park, Swansea, SA7 9FH
*Major Shareholder:* Jacqueline Mary Racey
*Officers:* Jacqueline Mary Racey, Secretary/Retail Manager; Christopher Stephen Racey [1958] Director; Jacqueline Mary Racey [1954] Director/Retail Manager

**R.B. Radley & Company Limited**
*Incorporated:* 18 October 1966
*Net Worth:* £3,117,015  *Total Assets:* £3,923,011
*Registered Office:* Shire Hill, Saffron Walden, Essex, CB11 3AZ
*Shareholders:* Russell Brian Radley; Iris Edith Radley; Russell Brian Radley; Iris Edith Radley
*Officers:* Iris Edith Radley [1936] Director; Mark David Radley [1966] Sales and Managing Director; Russell Brian Radley [1936] Director

**Rafarm UK Limited**
*Incorporated:* 1 December 2015  *Employees:* 3
*Net Worth Deficit:* £288,193  *Total Assets:* £1,761,024
*Registered Office:* 6th Floor, 2 Kingdom Street, London, W2 6BD
*Shareholders:* Eirini Rassia; Ioanna Rassia
*Officers:* Paolo Le Moli [1976] Managing Director [Italian]; Aristeidis Mitsopoulos [1973] Director [Greek]; Paul Norman Taylor [1967] Director

**Ragit Services Ltd**
*Incorporated:* 6 April 2016  *Employees:* 1
*Net Worth:* £34,924  *Total Assets:* £60,206
*Registered Office:* Flat 10, Hayne Court, 18 Hayne Road, Beckenham, Kent, BR3 4HY
*Major Shareholder:* Robert Aghadiuno
*Officers:* Robert Aghadiuno, Secretary; Robert Aghadiuno [1965] Director/IT Consultant

**Rah Pharma Ltd**
*Incorporated:* 7 March 2018
*Registered Office:* 173 Chaplin Road, Wembley, Middlesex, HA0 4UP
*Major Shareholder:* Nayer Rahnama

**Rak Pharma Ltd**
*Incorporated:* 20 October 2015
*Net Worth:* £2,916  *Total Assets:* £34,514
*Registered Office:* 7 Westmoreland House, Cumberland Park, Scrubs Lane, London, NW10 6RE
*Major Shareholder:* Raha Ahmadkhanbeigi
*Officers:* Raha Ahmadkhanbeigi [1987] Managing Director [Austrian]

**Ram Enterprises Bristol Limited**
*Incorporated:* 8 June 2010
*Net Worth:* £81,006  *Total Assets:* £326,317
*Registered Office:* 25 Badminton Road, Downend, Bristol, BS16 6BB
*Major Shareholder:* Robert Arthur Melville
*Officers:* Caron Jayne Melville [1967] Director/Manager; Robert Arthur Melville [1969] Director/Manager

**Raman Pharma Limited**
*Incorporated:* 19 June 2014
*Net Worth:* £11,312  *Total Assets:* £297,145
*Registered Office:* Unit 2 Fleet Business Park, Sandy Lane, Church Crookham, Fleet, Hants, GU52 8BF
*Major Shareholder:* Ritu Raheja
*Officers:* Ritu Raheja [1958] Director

**Ranbaxy (U.K.) Limited**
*Incorporated:* 21 November 1994  *Employees:* 19
*Net Worth:* £15,061,894  *Total Assets:* £28,360,372
*Registered Office:* 5th Floor, Hyde Park Hayes 3, 11 Millington Road, Hayes, Middlesex, UB3 4AZ
*Officers:* Hellen de Kloet [1965] Director/Business Executive [Dutch]; Prashant Savla [1974] Director [Dutch]; Neeraj Sharma [1972] Director [Indian]

**Rand Rocket Limited**
*Incorporated:* 31 December 1986  *Employees:* 12
*Net Worth:* £33,279  *Total Assets:* £948,324
*Registered Office:* AB Care House, Hownsgill Industrial Park, Consett, Co Durham, DH8 7NU
*Shareholder:* Randolph Vickers
*Officers:* Karen Lesley Vickers, Secretary; David Vickers [1962] Managing Director; Karen Lesley Vickers [1959] Director/Freelance Arts & Crafts Teacher

**Randa Pharma Ltd**
*Incorporated:* 30 May 2013
*Net Worth Deficit:* £13,408
*Registered Office:* 5 Greenwich Quay, Clarence Road, London, SE8 3EY
*Major Shareholder:* Robert Aghadiuno
*Officers:* Robert Aghadiuno [1965] Director/IT Consultant; Daniel Emeka Solomon [1996] Director/Project Manager

**Randall Allison Limited**
*Incorporated:* 1 June 2017
*Registered Office:* c/o HM HM Williams CCA, 5 Sandy Court, Ashleigh Way, Plymouth, PL7 5JX
*Shareholders:* Andrew Laurence Allison; Claire Randall
*Officers:* Mr Andrew Laurence Allison [1958] Director; Claire Randall [1979] Director

**Rapid Pharma Limited**
*Incorporated:* 5 December 2018
*Registered Office:* 1466 Greenford Road, Greenford, Middlesex, UB6 0HW
*Shareholders:* Mirag Patel; Priyan Patel
*Officers:* Mirag Patel [1982] Director; Priyan Patel [1986] Director

**Rapid Sample Processing Limited**
*Incorporated:* 23 December 2005  *Employees:* 2
*Net Worth:* £1,519  *Total Assets:* £86,182
*Registered Office:* 2 Minton Place, Victoria Road, Bicester, Oxon, OX26 6QB
*Officers:* Jean Marie Young, Secretary; Jean Marie Young [1959] Director

**RAR Pharmaceutics Ltd**
*Incorporated:* 28 January 2013
*Net Worth:* £165  *Total Assets:* £5,239
*Registered Office:* 14a Station Street, Darlaston, W Midlands, WS10 8BG
*Major Shareholder:* Rashid Ahmed Ravat
*Officers:* Rashid Ahmed Ravat [1988] Director/Pharmacist

**Rashedeen Pharma Group Ltd**
*Incorporated:* 31 July 2018
*Registered Office:* 254 Goldhawk Road, London, W12 9PE
*Major Shareholder:* Ahmed Aboelenin Mohamad Badawy
*Officers:* Ahmed Aboelenin Mohamad Badawy [1979] Director [Egyptian]

**Ratiopharm (UK) Limited**
*Incorporated:* 22 September 1988
*Registered Office:* Ridings Point, Whistler Drive, Castleford, W Yorks, WF10 5HX
*Parent:* Teva UK Holdings Limited
*Officers:* Dean Michael Cooper [1972] Director/Chartered Accountant; Kim Innes [1968] Director/General Manager

**Raumedic U.K. Limited**
*Incorporated:* 11 January 2008  *Employees:* 4
*Net Worth:* £309,270  *Total Assets:* £334,310
*Registered Office:* Hill Court, Walford, Ross on Wye, Herefords, HR9 5QN
*Officers:* Conor Brendan Ward, Secretary; Christoph Martin Bayer [1961] Director [German]; Thomas Knechtel [1975] Director Business Unit Assembly [German]; Conor Brendan Ward [1970] Director and Company Secretary

**Raw Medicus Ltd**
*Incorporated:* 25 October 2018
*Registered Office:* Office 3.11, 3rd Floor, NWMS Center, 31 Southampton Row, London, WC1B 5HJ
*Officers:* Jonathan Bibi [1984] Director [Seychellois]

**Rawmmed Trading Company Limited**
*Incorporated:* 29 July 2003
*Net Worth:* £31,254  *Total Assets:* £33,215
*Registered Office:* Lynton House, 7-12 Tavistock Square, London, WC1H 9LT
*Major Shareholder:* Effrosyni Economides
*Officers:* Marina Shimitra, Secretary; Androula Orphanidou Gavrielidou [1971] Director/Accountant [Cypriot]

**Ray Pharm Limited**
*Incorporated:* 28 August 2007
*Net Worth Deficit:* £161,219  *Total Assets:* £1,527,449
*Registered Office:* 7-11 Minerva Road, Park Royal, London, NW10 6HJ
*Officers:* Stylianos Stylianou [1979] Director [Cypriot]

**Rayburn Trading Company Limited**
*Incorporated:* 8 August 1957  *Employees:* 170
*Net Worth:* £20,589,942  *Total Assets:* £37,746,036
*Registered Office:* 2nd Floor, 1 City Road East, Manchester, M15 4PN
*Parent:* Jesem Holdings Limited
*Officers:* Tony Hobson, Secretary/Accountant; Howard Goldman [1978] Director; Michael David Goldman [1949] Director; Russell Stuart Goldman [1971] Director; Tony Hobson [1961] Director/Accountant; Simon Weiner [1956] Director

**Rayner Pharmaceuticals Limited**
*Incorporated:* 6 November 2012  *Employees:* 7
*Previous:* Rayner & Keeler Limited
*Net Worth:* £1,188,000  *Total Assets:* £4,651,000
*Registered Office:* The Ridley Innovation Centre, 10 Dominion Way, Worthing, W Sussex, BN14 8AQ
*Parent:* Rayner Surgical Group Limited
*Officers:* Cepta Kelly, Secretary; Darren Michael Millington [1976] Director

**RB (China Trading) Limited**
*Incorporated:* 22 December 2015  *Employees:* 5
*Net Worth:* £87,405,000  *Total Assets:* £96,318,000
*Registered Office:* 103-105 Bath Road, Slough, SL1 3UH
*Parent:* Reckitt Benckiser PLC
*Officers:* Christine Anne-Marie Logan, Secretary; John Dixon [1956] Director/SVP Tax; Adrian Nevil Hennah [1957] Director/Chief Financial Officer; Jonathan Timmis [1975] Director/SVP Corporate Controller; Lu Youming [1971] Director [Hong Kong]

**RB UK Commercial Limited**
*Incorporated:* 20 November 2013  *Employees:* 408
*Net Worth Deficit:* £134,646,000  *Total Assets:* £689,331,008
*Registered Office:* 103-105 Bath Road, Slough, Berks, SL1 3UH
*Parent:* Reckitt Benckiser PLC
*Officers:* Christine Anne-Marie Logan, Secretary; John Dixon [1956] Director/SVP Tax; Ariadna Granena Aracil [1974] Director/Lawyer [Spanish]; Bart Meermans [1972] Director/RD UK, Ireland, Turkey, Health [Belgian]; Harminder Singh Virdi [1978] Finance Director

**RB UK Hygiene Home Commercial Limited**
*Incorporated:* 29 March 2018
*Registered Office:* 103-105 Bath Road, Slough, Berks, SL1 3UH
*Parent:* Reckitt Benckiser (Hygiene Home) Holdings Limited
*Officers:* Christine Anne-Marie Logan, Secretary; Rohit Chandarana [1981] Finance Director; Eric Gilliot [1966] Regional Director, UK, Ireland, Hygiene Home [French]

**RD & Med Company Limited**
*Incorporated:* 5 February 2016
*Net Worth:* £6,730  *Total Assets:* £238,898
*Registered Office:* Flat 49 Royston Court, 30 Carlton Road, Manchester, M16 8LN
*Major Shareholder:* Tarek Taher
*Officers:* Tarek Taher [1962] Director/General Manager [Libyan]

**RDO Medical UK Limited**
*Incorporated:* 13 February 2009
*Net Worth Deficit:* £59,136  *Total Assets:* £40,826
*Registered Office:* The Techno Center, Puma Way, Coventry Technology Park, Coventry, Warwicks, CV1 2TT
*Shareholders:* Fuzil Anis Jamall; David Kubiak
*Officers:* Dr Fuzail Anis Jamall [1974] Director; David Kubiak [1975] Director

**Real Estate Alliance Ltd**
*Incorporated:* 28 September 2011
*Net Worth Deficit:* £160,311  *Total Assets:* £9,032,047
*Registered Office:* Suite 12, 2nd Floor, Queens House, 180 Tottenham Court Road, London, W1T 7PD
*Major Shareholder:* Alla Bielysheva
*Officers:* Fillip Krogh [1961] Director [Danish]

**Receptor Holdings Limited**
*Incorporated:* 4 October 1989  *Employees:* 3
*Previous:* Receptor Technologies Limited
*Net Worth:* £1,485,348  *Total Assets:* £1,626,342
*Registered Office:* Nelson House, 2 Hamilton Terrace, Leamington Spa, Warwicks, CV32 4LY
*Shareholders:* Steven William Summers; Janet Catherine Summers
*Officers:* Janet Catherine Summers, Secretary; Janet Catherine Summers [1949] Director/Administrator; Dr Steven William Summers [1949] Director

**Receptor Technologies Limited**
*Incorporated:* 13 April 2018
*Registered Office:* Nelson House, 2 Hamilton Terrace, Leamington Spa, Warwicks, CV32 4LY
*Major Shareholder:* Martin John Grant
*Officers:* Martin John Grant [1966] Director/Engineer

**Reckitt Benckiser Asia Pacific Limited**
*Incorporated:* 20 July 2004  *Employees:* 2
*Net Worth:* £34,452,000  *Total Assets:* £80,899,000
*Registered Office:* 103-105 Bath Road, Slough, Berks, SL1 3UH
*Parent:* Reckitt Benckiser PLC
*Officers:* Christine Anne-Marie Logan, Secretary; Richard Mark Greensmith [1973] Group Tax Director; Jonathan Timmis [1975] Finance Director

**Recordati Pharmaceuticals Limited**
Incorporated: 11 April 2005
Net Worth: £16,295,648  Total Assets: £16,522,914
Registered Office: 200 Brook Drive, Reading, Berks, RG2 6UB
Parent: Recordati S.P.A.
Officers: Miguel Isla Rodriguez [1962] Director [Spanish]; Nelson Ramiro Ferreira Pires [1972] Director [Portuguese]; Fritz Squindo [1956] Director [Italian]

**Redlight Exchange Ltd**
Incorporated: 5 June 2018
Registered Office: 42 Hampden Road, London, N17 0AY
Major Shareholder: Muhammad Abdul Qaiyum
Officers: Fatimah Begum, Secretary; Muhammad Abdul Qaiyum [1989] Director/Lawyer

**Regent Pharmaceuticals Limited**
Incorporated: 27 November 2013
Net Worth Deficit: £110,493  Total Assets: £976,710
Registered Office: 5 Darlington Close, Sandy, Beds, SG19 1RW
Officers: Samuel Akonwubel Atsu, Secretary; Faiz Juneja, Secretary; Rehan Ullah [1978] Commercial Director

**Reliance Medical Ltd**
Incorporated: 8 February 2006  Employees: 44
Net Worth: £2,149,388  Total Assets: £6,815,029
Registered Office: Reliance Medical, West Avenue, Talke, Stoke on Trent, Staffs, ST7 1TL
Major Shareholder: Andrew Mark Pear
Officers: Susan Dawn Pear, Secretary; Patricia Anne Clough [1954] Finance Director; Dr Paul Allan Knox [1981] Technical Director; Andrew Mark Pear [1963] Director; Joshua Joseph Adam Pear [1991] Director/Chartered Accountant; Thomas Andrew Pear [1988] National Accounts Director; Alan Anthony Smith [1972] Operations Director

**Relonchem Limited**
Incorporated: 21 May 2003  Employees: 9
Net Worth: £10,243,935  Total Assets: £19,773,460
Registered Office: 27 Old Gloucester Street, London, WC1 3XX
Parent: Marksans Pharma UK Limited
Officers: Gillian Jacks, Secretary; Sathish Kumar Konasagar Jayanna [1973] Managing Director; Mark Bosco Saldanha [1972] Director [Indian]; Sandra Saldanha [1971] Director [Indian]; Jitendra Mahavirprasad Sharma [1969] Director/Service [Indian]; Russell David Williams [1968] Director

**Relyer Health Limited**
Incorporated: 25 March 2015
Registered Office: 82 Caterham Avenue, Ilford, Essex, IG5 0QA
Major Shareholder: Krishnajeyam Rasu
Officers: Krishnajeyam Rasu [1961] Director/General Manager [Dutch]

**Rembrook Developments Limited**
Incorporated: 4 February 1988
Net Worth: £92,519  Total Assets: £92,519
Registered Office: 4 Merlin Way, Bowerhill Industrial Estate, Melksham, Wilts, SN12 6TJ
Parent: Genesis Manufacturing Limited
Officers: Mark Leroy Anderson [1951] Managing Director

**Remedi Medical Holdings Limited**
Incorporated: 16 October 2013  Employees: 50
Net Worth: £6,007,621  Total Assets: £20,844,708
Registered Office: Nene House, 4 Rushmills, Northampton, NN4 7YB
Shareholders: Monisha Nikesh Kotecha; Nikesh Rasiklal Kotecha; Blue Skies Investments Limited
Officers: Monisha Nikesh Kotecha, Secretary; Monisha Nikesh Kotecha [1969] Director; Dr Nikesh Rasiklal Kotecha [1966] Director

**Remedine Limited**
Incorporated: 20 July 2016
Net Worth: £170  Total Assets: £3,970
Registered Office: 64 Baker Street, London, W1U 7GB
Major Shareholder: Mitul Rach
Officers: Mitul Rach [1988] Director

**Remedy JV Limited**
Incorporated: 16 November 2017
Registered Office: 7 The Meadows, Kilmore, Crossgar, Co Down, BT30 9GT
Shareholders: Jeremy William Jonathan McCready; Viliam Krupa
Officers: Viliam Krupa [1981] Director [Slovak]; Jeremy William Jonathan McCready [1975] Director

**Remote Pharma Solutions Limited**
Incorporated: 28 July 2015
Net Worth: £126,061  Total Assets: £179,027
Registered Office: Unit 4, 3 Lever Street, London, EC1V 3QU
Major Shareholder: David Andrew Hatch
Officers: David Andrew Hatch [1971] Director/Pharmacist

**Renata (UK) Limited**
Incorporated: 26 September 2013
Net Worth: £1  Total Assets: £1
Registered Office: Greenway Business Centre, Harlow Business Park, Harlow, Essex, CM19 5QE
Parent: Renata Limited
Officers: Syed Kaiser Kabir [1963] Director [Bangladeshi]

**Renfield Limited**
Incorporated: 10 April 1975
Registered Office: 7 Regents Drive, Prudhoe, Northumberland, NE42 6PX
Parent: Doncaster Pharmaceuticals Limited
Officers: Mark James Gulliford [1969] Director; Derek Andrew Wilson [1964] Director

**Resource Medical (UK) Ltd**
Incorporated: 19 April 2004
Net Worth Deficit: £481,278  Total Assets: £2,453,462
Registered Office: 2 Carlton Avenue, Batley, W Yorks, WF17 7AQ
Major Shareholder: Zulfkar Akram
Officers: Zulfkar Akram [1954] Director/Businessman

**Respond Healthcare Limited**
Incorporated: 16 February 2015  Employees: 99
Net Worth: £21,620,268  Total Assets: £27,245,780
Registered Office: Kathleen Drive, 15 Ballystockart Road, Comber, Newtownards, Co Down, BT23 5QY
Shareholders: Paul Andrew Eakin; Jeremy David Eakin; Thomas George Eakin; Violet Pattison Eakin; Richard Gray
Officers: Jeremy David Eakin, Secretary; Jeremy David Eakin [1967] Director; Paul Andrew Eakin [1962] Director; Thomas George Eakin [1933] Director; Paul MacQuillan [1958] Director/Chartered Accountant [Irish]

### Respond Healthcare Scotland Limited
*Incorporated:* 30 October 2014
*Registered Office:* 4th Floor, 115 George Street, Edinburgh, EH2 4JN
*Parent:* Respond Healthcare Ltd
*Officers:* Jeremy David Eakin [1967] Director; Paul Andrew Eakin [1962] Director; Paul MacQuillan [1958] Director/Chartered Accountant [Irish]

### Respond Plus Limited
*Incorporated:* 27 August 1991
*Registered Office:* Greypoint, Cardiff Business Park, Cardiff, CF14 5WF
*Parent:* Cliffe Medical Limited
*Officers:* Jeremy David Eakin [1967] Director; Paul Andrew Eakin [1962] Director; Paul MacQuillan [1958] Director/Accountant [Irish]

### Respro-M Limited
*Incorporated:* 13 September 1999 *Employees:* 2
*Net Worth:* £110,651 *Total Assets:* £347,948
*Registered Office:* Chase Green House, 42 Chase Side, Enfield, Middlesex, EN2 6NF
*Shareholders:* Valery Uvarov; Irina Uvarova
*Officers:* Valery Uvarov, Secretary; Valery Uvarov [1954] Director/Company Secretary; Irina Uvarova [1960] Director

### Restate Management Ltd
*Incorporated:* 25 July 2013
*Net Worth Deficit:* £26,160 *Total Assets:* £17,690,850
*Registered Office:* 4 The Mews, Bridge Road, Twickenham, Middlesex, TW1 1RF
*Major Shareholder:* Valerii Los
*Officers:* Katherine Anne Hickson [1978] Director/Consultant

### Reviv Pharma Ltd
*Incorporated:* 16 January 2019
*Registered Office:* 8 King Street, Knutsford, Cheshire, WA16 6DL
*Parent:* Reviv Global Ltd
*Officers:* Sarah Lomas [1974] Director

### Rex Pharmaceuticals Ltd
*Incorporated:* 8 October 2015
*Registered Office:* 25a Orsett Terrace, Paddington, London, W2 6AJ
*Officers:* Dr Boyan Anastasov [1971] Director/Pharmaceuticals and Supplement [Bulgarian]

### Rexcel Trading Ltd
*Incorporated:* 31 May 2017
*Registered Office:* 71-75 Shelton Street, Covent Garden, London, WC2H 9JQ
*Major Shareholder:* Md Saiful Alam Bhuiyan
*Officers:* MD Saiful Alam Bhuiyan [1987] Director [Bangladeshi]

### RF Vapes Limited
*Incorporated:* 23 June 2017
*Net Worth Deficit:* £4,716 *Total Assets:* £31,677
*Registered Office:* 233 Wigan Road, Ashton in Makerfield, Wigan, Lancs, WN4 9SL
*Major Shareholder:* Farshad Ferdowsian
*Officers:* Farshad Ferdowsian [1981] Director

### Rhodes Pharma Limited
*Incorporated:* 14 March 2007 *Employees:* 5
*Net Worth:* £802,815 *Total Assets:* £2,631,416
*Registered Office:* Newlands House, 60 Chainhouse Lane, Whitestake, Preston, Lancs, PR4 4LG
*Shareholders:* Allison Jane Moosa; Iqbal Moosa
*Officers:* Riyaz Safri, Secretary; Tahera Bapu [1978] Director; Allison Jane Moosa [1965] Director; Riyaz Safri [1972] Director

### RI Pharma Limited
*Incorporated:* 21 August 2008
*Net Worth Deficit:* £520,016 *Total Assets:* £663,269
*Registered Office:* First Floor, 6 St John's Court, Upper Fforest Way, Swansea Enterprise Park, Swansea, SA6 8QQ
*Officers:* Amin Farah [1951] Director; Bassim Subhi Farah Khoury Nasr [1960] Director [Jordanian]

### Ria Generics Limited
*Incorporated:* 20 September 1999
*Net Worth:* £55,980 *Total Assets:* £415,742
*Registered Office:* 36 Ingleby Way, Wallington, Surrey, SM6 9LR
*Parent:* Kanchanlal Naginbhai Patel
*Officers:* Krishnamurthy Balasubramanian [1958] Director/Company Executive [Indian]; Kanchanlal Naginbhai Patel [1951] Director

### Ria Sales Corporation Ltd
*Incorporated:* 14 May 2018
*Registered Office:* 176 Franciscan Road, London, SW17 8HH
*Major Shareholder:* Manu Bhagwanlal Taunk
*Officers:* Manu Bhagwanlal Taunk [1976] Director/Administrator

### RIC Chemicals Limited
*Incorporated:* 15 August 1995 *Employees:* 3
*Net Worth:* £89,528 *Total Assets:* £600,671
*Registered Office:* Unit 1 Conqueror Court, Spilsby Road, Harold Hill, Romford, Essex, RM3 8SB
*Shareholders:* Kamlesh Kanubhai Patel; Kusumben Patel
*Officers:* Kamlesh Kanubhai Patel, Secretary/Chemist; Kamlesh Kanubhai Patel [1958] Director; Versha Kamlesh Patel [1959] Director

### Rich Almond (UK) Limited
*Incorporated:* 23 May 2013
*Registered Office:* Unit 16, 806 High Road Leyton, London, E10 6AE
*Major Shareholder:* Laurence Onwufuju
*Officers:* Laurence Onwufuju [1965] Director/Businessman

### Richardson Healthcare Limited
*Incorporated:* 30 March 2001 *Employees:* 17
*Net Worth:* £2,913,450 *Total Assets:* £5,061,057
*Registered Office:* 506 Kingsbury Road, London, NW9 9HE
*Major Shareholder:* Mayur Patel
*Officers:* Mayur Patel [1962] Managing Director

### Gedeon Richter (UK) Limited
*Incorporated:* 20 November 2001 *Employees:* 27
*Net Worth:* £613,214 *Total Assets:* £7,527,196
*Registered Office:* 127 Shirland Road, London, W9 2EP
*Officers:* Michael Robert Firman, Secretary; Erik Attila Bogsch [1947] Director [Hungarian]; Dr Timea Halko [1980] Director [Hungarian]; Dr Kriszta Zolnay [1966] Director [Hungarian]

### Riebeeckstad Limited
*Incorporated:* 8 June 2018
*Registered Office:* 23 Westfield Park, Redland, Bristol, BS6 6LT
*Major Shareholder:* Rogan Luke Auret
*Officers:* Rogan Luke Auret [1969] Director

**Rifaray Limited**
Incorporated: 4 January 2012  Employees: 1
Net Worth: £1,353  Total Assets: £27,147
Registered Office: Regus, Victory Way, Dartford Admirals Park, Dartford, Kent, DA2 6QD
Major Shareholder: Ganiat Folakemi Bose Adigun
Officers: Ganiat Folakemi Bose Adigun, Secretary; Ganiat Folakemi Bose Adigun [1976] Director/Pharmacist

**Rightdose Solutions Limited**
Incorporated: 12 October 2018
Registered Office: 1000 Cathcart Road, Glasgow, G42 9XL
Shareholder: Kasim Gulzar
Officers: Kasim Gulzar, Secretary; Kasim Gulzar [1983] Director/Pharmacist MD; Asim Sarwar [1982] Director/MD

**Rind Pharma Limited**
Incorporated: 12 July 2012
Previous: Ash Finished Limited
Net Worth Deficit: £23,096  Total Assets: £415
Registered Office: 42 Woolhampton Way, Chigwell, Essex, IG7 4QJ
Major Shareholder: Dr Richard Ndawula
Officers: Dr Richard Ndawula [1979] Director [Ugandan]

**Ripple Pharma Limited**
Incorporated: 19 February 2014
Registered Office: Unit 16, 806 High Road Leyton, London, E10 6AE
Major Shareholder: Laurence Onwufuju
Officers: Laurence Onwufuju [1965] Director

**Ris Healthcare Limited**
Incorporated: 5 February 2015
Registered Office: 10 Prospect Place, Welwyn, Herts, AL6 9EW
Shareholders: Charles Stephen Unwin; Stephen Ronald Unwin
Officers: Charles Stephen Unwin [1978] Director; Stephen Ronald Unwin [1953] Director

**Rising Sun Ventures Ltd**
Incorporated: 15 January 2019
Registered Office: 20-22 Wenlock Road, London, N1 7GU
Major Shareholder: Varun Kumar Rishi
Officers: Raj Kumari Rishi [1959] Director; Varun Kumar Rishi [1985] Director

**Riteaim Limited**
Incorporated: 31 March 1994  Employees: 4
Net Worth: £1,816,724  Total Assets: £2,447,788
Registered Office: c/o Amin Patel & Shah Accountants, 334-336 Goswell Road, London, EC1V 7RP
Major Shareholder: Mukesh Chhotabhai Patel
Officers: Jyotsana Mukesh Patel, Secretary; Mukesh Chhotabhai Patel [1959] Director/Pharmacist

**Rivertime Distribution Ltd**
Incorporated: 2 August 2018
Registered Office: 20 Finch Mill Avenue, Appley Bridge, Wigan, Lancs, WN6 9DF
Major Shareholder: Michael John Norris
Officers: Michael John Norris [1964] Director/Accountant

**Riviere Groupe (Europe) Limited**
Incorporated: 7 November 2017
Registered Office: 370 Neasden Lane North, London, NW10 0BT
Shareholders: Hing Yu Wong; Hiang Sim Chiu
Officers: Hiang Sim Chiu [1961] Director [Chinese]; Hing Yu Wong [1954] Director

**RJE Agencies Limited**
Incorporated: 13 March 1996
Net Worth Deficit: £100,582  Total Assets: £19,160
Registered Office: 36 Lower Hazeldines, Marston Moretaine, Beds, MK43 0TF
Major Shareholder: Richard James Edwards
Officers: Richard James Edwards [1950] Director/Importer

**RJP Impex Ltd**
Incorporated: 14 October 2011  Employees: 1
Net Worth Deficit: £16,279  Total Assets: £7,862
Registered Office: 925 Finchley Road, London, NW11 7PE
Major Shareholder: Rajiv Kumar Sarna
Officers: Rajiv Sarna [1959] Director

**RJT Pharma Services Ltd**
Incorporated: 23 March 2018
Registered Office: 89 Prince George Drive, Derby, DE22 3XA
Major Shareholder: Richard John Thorpe
Officers: Richard John Thorpe [1989] Director/Pharmacist

**Rkonnect Limited**
Incorporated: 7 December 2010  Employees: 5
Net Worth: £52,339  Total Assets: £591,208
Registered Office: 4 Rosecroft Walk, Crawford Avenue, Wembley, Middlesex, HA0 2JZ
Major Shareholder: Chirag Patel
Officers: Chiragkumar Patel, Secretary; Chiragkumar Ranchhodbhai Patel [1980] Director/Industrial Pharmacist

**RND Pharma Limited**
Incorporated: 8 September 2017
Registered Office: Flat 2, 270 Ryebank Road, Chorlton Cum Hardy, Manchester, M21 9LJ
Officers: Ali Moradi [1973] Director

**Roberts McCarron Ltd**
Incorporated: 1 November 2017
Net Worth: £175  Total Assets: £21,744
Registered Office: 78 Bence Lane, Darton, Barnsley, S Yorks, S75 5PE
Shareholder: Donald Andrew McCarron
Officers: Courtney Leigh McCarron [1994] Managing Director; Donald Andrew McCarron [1958] Managing Director; Allison Jane Roberts [1961] Managing Director

**Roble Medical Ltd**
Incorporated: 21 June 2018
Registered Office: 29 Pearce House, Brook Avenue, Wembley, Middlesex, HA9 8PH
Major Shareholder: Mohamed Haji Dahir
Officers: Mohamed Haji Dahir [1958] Director

**Rocha Products Limited**
Incorporated: 5 November 2018
Registered Office: 20-22 Wenlock Road, London, N1 7GU
Major Shareholder: Russell Francis Da Rocha
Officers: Russell Francis Da Rocha [1964] Director/Accountant

**Roe Pharmacy Ltd**
Incorporated: 24 May 2007
Net Worth Deficit: £280,645  Total Assets: £431,932
Registered Office: 11a Glenshane Road, Maghera, Co Londonderry, BT46 5JZ
Shareholders: Anne Gallagher; Rodney Gallagher
Officers: Anne Gallagher, Secretary; Anne Gallagher [1975] Director/Pharmacist [Irish]; Rodney Gallagher [1974] Director/Builder [Irish]

**Rolling Stones Trading Ltd**
*Incorporated:* 30 May 2007
*Registered Office:* Latif House, First Way, Wembley, Middlesex, HA9 0JD
*Shareholder:* Mehdi Shalviri
*Officers:* Mahmoud Rad [1960] Director Member [Iranian]; Vahid Saghatchi [1960] Director Member [Iranian]; Mehdi Shalviri [1966] Managing Director [American]

**Rogia Romini Limited**
*Incorporated:* 31 January 2013
*Previous:* Pharmajoint Limited
*Registered Office:* 23 Arnos Grove, Nuthall, Nottingham, NG16 1QA
*Major Shareholder:* Ramin Nooraldin Moosa
*Officers:* Ramin Nooraldin Moosa [1965] Director

**Ros Nutrition UK Ltd.**
*Incorporated:* 2 June 2009
*Registered Office:* Companies House, Default Address, Cardiff, CF14 8LH
*Major Shareholder:* Deepak Sharma
*Officers:* Sagina Taneja, Secretary; Deepak Sharma [1977] Director/Doctor of Medicine [Irish]; Sagina Taneja [1978] Director/Secretary [Indian]

**Rosalique Skincare Limited**
*Incorporated:* 2 November 2017
*Registered Office:* 36 High Street, Cleethorpes, N E Lincs, DN35 8JN
*Parent:* Bradhaus Holdings Ltd
*Officers:* Martin John Schiele [1983] Director; Claudia Talsma [1983] Director [Dutch]

**Rose Europe UK Ltd**
*Incorporated:* 7 October 2011
*Previous:* Rose Gentec Limited
*Registered Office:* Edinburgh House, 1-5 Bellevue Road, Clevedon, Somerset, BS21 7NP
*Major Shareholder:* Sibin You
*Officers:* Ying Kang [1966] Director [Chinese]; Sibin You [1991] Director [Chinese]

**Rose Gentec Ltd**
*Incorporated:* 4 June 2015
*Registered Office:* Badger House, Oldmixon Crescent, Weston-Super-Mare, Somerset, BS24 9AY
*Officers:* Ying Kang [1966] Director [Chinese]

**Rosefield Pharma Ltd**
*Incorporated:* 30 December 2013
*Net Worth:* £12,980 *Total Assets:* £15,508
*Registered Office:* 35 Fairway Avenue, Tividale, Oldbury, W Midlands, B69 1SU
*Major Shareholder:* Abbas Al Jabari
*Officers:* Abbas Al Jabari [1989] Director/Pharmacist [Dutch]

**Ross London Limited**
*Incorporated:* 14 July 2000
*Net Worth:* £69,031 *Total Assets:* £539,876
*Registered Office:* 2 St Georges Mews, 43 Westminster Bridge Road, London, SE1 7JB
*Major Shareholder:* Hasanain Kanji
*Officers:* Hasanain Giulamabbas Abdulla Kanji [1951] Director/Pharmacist

**Rotapharm Limited**
*Incorporated:* 19 October 2005 *Employees:* 1
*Net Worth:* £651,824 *Total Assets:* £1,222,298
*Registered Office:* Ground Floor, Gadd House, Arcadia Avenue, Finchley, London, N3 2JU
*Major Shareholder:* Raushan Tahiyeu
*Officers:* Tony Jack Douglas, Secretary; Tony Jack Douglas [1942] Director

**Rothes Pharma Limited**
*Incorporated:* 21 June 2016 *Employees:* 4
*Net Worth:* £67,915 *Total Assets:* £226,442
*Registered Office:* 26-28 High Street, Rothes, Aberlour, Moray, AB38 7AU
*Major Shareholder:* Kevin Douglas Herbert
*Officers:* Kevin Douglas Herbert [1979] Director

**Rothschild Pharmacy Limited**
*Incorporated:* 15 June 2000
*Registered Office:* Rothschild House, Chapel Street, Tring, Herts, HP23 6PU
*Shareholders:* Avinash Gupta; Panikos Sissou
*Officers:* Avinash Gupta, Secretary; Dr Panikos Sissou [1966] Director/General Practitioner

**Rovi Biotech Limited**
*Incorporated:* 3 December 2014 *Employees:* 2
*Net Worth Deficit:* £227,754 *Total Assets:* £91,474
*Registered Office:* Suite 425, 4th Floor, Davis House, Robert Street, Croydon, Surrey, CR0 1QQ
*Parent:* Laboratorios Farmaceuticos Rovi, S.A.
*Officers:* Ivan Lopez-Belmonte Encina [1971] Director/Entrepreneur [Spanish]

**L.Rowland & Company Limited**
*Incorporated:* 19 March 1928
*Registered Office:* Phoenix Medical Supplies Limited, Rivington Road, Whitehouse Industrial Estate, Preston Brook, Runcorn, Cheshire, WA7 3DJ
*Officers:* Stephen William Anderson [1966] Director; Kevin Robert Hudson [1963] Director

**Rowtech Limited**
*Incorporated:* 2 April 2003
*Net Worth:* £374,863 *Total Assets:* £2,138,389
*Registered Office:* 33 Alfred Place, Fitzrovia, London, WC1E 7DP
*Major Shareholder:* Sameer Shrivastava
*Officers:* Sameer Shrivastava [1971] Director [Indian]

**Royce Health Sciences Ltd**
*Incorporated:* 21 September 2017
*Registered Office:* 58 Aldfield Green, Hamilton, Leicester, LE5 1BP
*Shareholders:* Sinnan Fazwani; Rizwan Ladak
*Officers:* Sinnan Fazwani [1993] Director [Pakistani]; Rizwan Ladak [1982] Director

**RP Pharma International Limited**
*Incorporated:* 30 August 2016
*Registered Office:* Innovation Centre, Gallows Hill, Warwick, CV34 6UW
*Shareholders:* Pavels Telica; AS Recipe Plus
*Officers:* Pavels Telica [1995] Director [Latvian]

**RPG Medical Limited**
Incorporated: 13 October 2016
Net Worth Deficit: £58,318  Total Assets: £21,502
Registered Office: P O Box 268, Washington, Tyne & Wear, NE37 9BU
Shareholders: Philip Richard Winspear; Garry Gardner Burns; Robert John Bradshaw
Officers: Robert John Bradshaw [1953] Director; Garry Gardner Burns [1964] Director/Accountant; Philip Richard Winspear [1969] Director

**RPH Pharma Ltd**
Incorporated: 26 April 2018
Registered Office: Recipharm Ltd, Vale of Bardsley, Oldham Road, Ashton under Lyne, Lancs, OL7 9RR
Officers: Jean-Francois Hilaire [1964] Director/Executive Vice President [French]; Christopher Hirst [1977] Director

**RR Cosmeceuticals (UK) Ltd**
Incorporated: 7 March 2018
Registered Office: 925 Finchley Road, London, NW11 7PE
Major Shareholder: Mohd Rodzi Bin Abdul Rahman
Officers: Mohd Rodzi Bin Abdul Rahman [1972] Director [Malaysian]; Nor Faiz Bin Ahmad Helimi [1978] Director [Malaysian]

**RSR Pharmacare Limited**
Incorporated: 6 August 2013  Employees: 2
Net Worth: £97,850  Total Assets: £861,501
Registered Office: 41 Hillcroft Avenue, Pinner, Middlesex, HA5 5AL
Shareholders: Pritee Hitesh Panchmatia; Hitesh Kantilal Panchmatia
Officers: Hitesh Kantilal Panchmatia [1969] Director/IT Consultant; Pritee Hitesh Panchmatia [1970] Director/Pharmacist; Rakhee Patel [1972] Director/Pharmacist

**RSS Wholesaling Limited**
Incorporated: 26 January 2012
Net Worth: £31,905  Total Assets: £1,442,743
Registered Office: 274-276 Ladypool Road, Birmingham, B12 8LG
Shareholder: Rakesh Kumar Sirpal
Officers: Rohini Aggarwal [1986] Director; Rakesh Kumar Sirpal [1958] Director; Sonam Sirpal [1990] Director; Sudesh Bala Sirpal [1958] Director

**Ruby Box Limited**
Incorporated: 29 July 2013  Employees: 2
Net Worth: £215,954  Total Assets: £322,036
Registered Office: Carlyle House, 78 Chorley New Road, Bolton, Lancs, BL1 4BY
Shareholders: Vilochna Patel; Umesh Patel
Officers: Umesh Patel [1969] Director/Pharmacist; Vilochna Patel [1965] Director

**Ruger Barber Limited**
Incorporated: 10 March 2018
Registered Office: Balmoral House, Warwick Court, Park Road, Middleton, Manchester, M24 1AE
Shareholders: Alan Beak; Lindsey Beak
Officers: Lindsey Beak, Secretary; Alan Beak [1985] Director

**RX Farma Limited**
Incorporated: 15 December 2000
Net Worth Deficit: £161,578  Total Assets: £606
Registered Office: First Floor, Roxburghe House, 273-287 Regent Street, London, W1B 2HA
Parent: Orion Holdings (UK) Limited
Officers: Kamal Hansraj Shah, Secretary; Bharat Kumar Hansraj Devraj Shah [1949] Director/Pharmacist; Manish Hansraj Shah [1955] Director/Accountant

**RX Pharma (Europe) Limited**
Incorporated: 18 October 2016
Net Worth: £100  Total Assets: £100
Registered Office: 129 Leasowe Road, Wallasey, Merseyside, CH45 8PA
Officers: Dane Argomandkhah [1988] Director; Hassan Argomandkhah [1961] Director; Lynda Arnold [1967] Director; Javad Hosseini [1957] Director/Property Developer

**RxPharma Limited**
Incorporated: 7 June 2002
Net Worth Deficit: £47,336  Total Assets: £2,162
Registered Office: 3 Pall Mall, Billinge End Road, Pleasington, Blackburn, Lancs, BB2 6QD
Major Shareholder: Peter Alan Williams
Officers: Brian Whitfield, Secretary/Solicitor; Peter Alan Williams [1960] Director/Businessman

**S & D Pharma Limited**
Incorporated: 17 December 1990  Employees: 4
Net Worth: £6,273,521  Total Assets: £6,941,872
Registered Office: Unit 10 Delta Court, Manor Way, Borehamwood, Herts, WD6 1FJ
Parent: London Pharma & Chemicals Group Ltd
Officers: Andrea Nemcokova [1964] Director [Slovak]; Daniel Reuben Straus [1972] Director/Business Manager

**S M Locum Consultants Ltd**
Incorporated: 30 December 2016
Net Worth: £22,955  Total Assets: £59,300
Registered Office: 7 Llys Nantgarw, Wrexham, Clwyd, LL13 7SX
Major Shareholder: Sameer Al-Mashta
Officers: Dr Sameer Al-Mashta [1976] Director/Doctor

**S.T.D. Pharmaceutical Products Limited**
Incorporated: 8 May 1967
Net Worth: £2,772,302  Total Assets: £3,406,634
Registered Office: Plough Lane, Hereford, HR4 0EL
Major Shareholder: Bruce Montgomery Gardiner
Officers: Christopher Hugh Edwards Smith, Secretary; Bruce Montgomery Gardiner [1970] Director; Margaret Florence Gardiner [1945] Director/Farmer; Robert Norman Gardiner [1934] Director/Pharmacist; Anthony John Leach [1927] Director/Chartered Accountant; Nina Elizabeth Leach [1945] Director

**Sabel Pharmacy Ltd**
Incorporated: 21 December 2010  Employees: 6
Previous: R S Medical Supplies Limited
Net Worth Deficit: £18,994  Total Assets: £941,839
Registered Office: 116 Brent Street, London, NW4 2DT
Parent: Sabel Chemist Limited
Officers: Belinda Patel [1958] Director/Shop Manager; Rachael Louise Patel [1971] Director/Pharmacist; Samir Madhusudan Patel [1970] Director/Pharmacist

**Sabona Rheumatic Relief Company Limited**
Incorporated: 1 December 1960
Net Worth: £616,120  Total Assets: £634,599
Registered Office: 12 Carlton Park Industrial Estate, Saxmundham, Suffolk, IP17 2NL
Parent: Paul Baratte International Limited
Officers: Detmar Albert Hackman, Secretary; Detmar Albert Hackman [1934] Director; Eunhee Hackman [1964] Director; Robert Edward Hackman [1966] Director/Sales Manager [Australian]

**Safe Pharma Consulting Ltd.**
*Incorporated:* 17 October 2011
*Net Worth:* £11,362  *Total Assets:* £48,248
*Registered Office:* 10 Oxleys Road, Waltham Abbey, Essex, EN9 3PL
*Major Shareholder:* Sylvia Chinwendu Nwafornso
*Officers:* Osondu Osuji, Secretary; Sylvia Chinwendu Nwafornso [1981] Director/Scientist

**Safenet Direct Ltd**
*Incorporated:* 11 August 2016
*Registered Office:* 100 East Acton Lane, London, W3 7ER
*Major Shareholder:* Mansur Mijbel
*Officers:* Mansur Mijbel [1975] Director

**Sage Therapeutics Limited**
*Incorporated:* 1 March 2017  *Employees:* 4
*Net Worth:* £50,854  *Total Assets:* £143,230
*Registered Office:* 100 New Bridge Street, London, EC4V 6JA
*Parent:* Sage Therapeutics, Inc.
*Officers:* Anne Marie Cook [1961] Director/Business Executive [American]; Kimi Ellen Iguchi [1962] Director/Business Executive [American]

**Sahu & Co Limited**
*Incorporated:* 29 December 2010  *Employees:* 2
*Net Worth:* £16,096  *Total Assets:* £20,630
*Registered Office:* 17a Ermin Street, Brockworth, Gloucester, GL3 4EG
*Major Shareholder:* Muhammad Shahid Ali Sahu
*Officers:* Muhammad Sahu, Secretary; Muhammad Shahid Ali Sahu [1969] Director/Consultancy; Dr Dur-E-Shahwar Shahid [1970] Director/Medical Doctor

**Saint-Germain Pharma Ltd**
*Incorporated:* 7 June 2016
*Net Worth:* £100  *Total Assets:* £100
*Registered Office:* Linden House, Linden Close, Tunbridge Wells, Kent, TN4 8HH
*Parent:* Present Value Limited
*Officers:* Andrew Simon Michael Dean [1970] Director/Business Consultant

**Sakar Healthcare UK Ltd.**
*Incorporated:* 31 October 2016
*Net Worth:* £1,200  *Total Assets:* £1,200
*Registered Office:* 43 Cody Close, Harrow, Middlesex, HA3 9ES
*Major Shareholder:* Aarsh Shah
*Officers:* Aarsh Shah [1991] Director [Indian]; Viral Shah [1977] Director/Businessman

**Salcura Limited**
*Incorporated:* 25 April 2002  *Employees:* 6
*Net Worth:* £5,630  *Total Assets:* £417,175
*Registered Office:* 36 High Street, Cleethorpes, N E Lincs, DN35 8JN
*Parent:* Brandhaus Holdings Ltd
*Officers:* Martin John Schiele, Secretary/Student; Martin John Schiele [1983] Sales Director; Claudia Talsma [1983] Director [Dutch]

**Salon Professional Limited**
*Incorporated:* 9 February 2009
*Registered Office:* Pinnacle House Business Centre, Newark Road, Peterborough, Cambs, PE1 5YD
*Major Shareholder:* Alistair Martin Ashworth
*Officers:* Alistair Martin Ashworth, Secretary; Alistair Martin Ashworth [1963] Director

**Salon Professional.Com Limited**
*Incorporated:* 17 February 2009
*Registered Office:* Pinnacle House Business Centre, Newark Road, Peterborough, Cambs, PE1 5YD
*Major Shareholder:* Alistair Martin Ashworth
*Officers:* Alistair Martin Ashworth [1963] Director

**Salon Sales Limited**
*Incorporated:* 9 June 2004
*Net Worth:* £83,845  *Total Assets:* £83,845
*Registered Office:* 4 Howbeck Road, Prenton, Merseyside, CH43 6TG
*Major Shareholder:* Alan David Balsiger
*Officers:* Jacqueline Mona Taylor, Secretary; Alan David Balsiger [1949] Director

**Salonpas UK Limited**
*Incorporated:* 9 January 2002
*Net Worth:* £1  *Total Assets:* £1
*Registered Office:* 5 Chancery Lane, London, WC2A 1LG
*Parent:* Hisamitsu Pharmaceutical Co., Inc.
*Officers:* Yoshio Hiyama, Secretary; Yoshio Hiyama [1974] Director [Japanese]; Yuichi Isobe [1971] President and Managing Director [Japanese]

**Salutem Supplements Ltd**
*Incorporated:* 9 June 2016  *Employees:* 1
*Net Worth Deficit:* £21,153  *Total Assets:* £12,615
*Registered Office:* P J Molloy & Co Ltd, Nursery Cottage, Beckley, Hinton, Christchurch, Dorset, BH23 7ED
*Major Shareholder:* Simon John Lewis Meads
*Officers:* Andrew Paul Larwood [1959] Director; Simon John Lewis Meads [1965] Director

**Samax Pharma Ltd**
*Incorporated:* 14 August 2017
*Registered Office:* The Nucleus Business & Innovation Centre, Brunel Way, Dartford, Kent, DA1 5GA
*Major Shareholder:* Warren Anthony Crawford
*Officers:* Warren Anthony Crawford [1978] Managing Director

**Sampsonstore.Com (UK) Ltd**
*Incorporated:* 8 January 2019
*Registered Office:* Unit 3 Westbury Industrial Estate, Station Road, Westbury, Wilts, BA13 4HR
*Major Shareholder:* Sheung Wah Chow
*Officers:* Sheung Wah Chow [1983] Director [Hong Kong]

**Sanarah Ltd**
*Incorporated:* 22 March 2012  *Employees:* 1
*Net Worth:* £111  *Total Assets:* £8,562
*Registered Office:* 16 Lakeside Avenue, Redbridge, Ilford, Essex, IG4 5PJ
*Shareholders:* Mohammed Khalid Waseem; Yasmin Waseem
*Officers:* Mohammed Khalid Waseem [1968] Director

**Sanay Ltd**
*Incorporated:* 12 February 2013
*Net Worth:* £259  *Total Assets:* £5,164
*Registered Office:* Devonshire House, 582 Honeypot Lane, Stanmore, Middlesex, HA7 1JS
*Major Shareholder:* Neel Rameshchandra Shah
*Officers:* Neel Rameshchandra Shah [1974] Director

**Sandyvale Limited**
Incorporated: 30 July 1986
Registered Office: 1 Pottery Road, Oldbury, Warley, W Midlands, B68 9EX
Shareholders: Satish Kumar Jalota; Usha Kumari Jalota
Officers: Satish Kumar Jalota, Secretary; Sanjay Jalota [1979] Director; Usha Kumari Jalota [1950] Director/Pharmacy Technician

**Sangers (Maidstone) Limited**
Incorporated: 16 October 1979  Employees: 161
Net Worth: £23,646,672  Total Assets: £29,492,576
Registered Office: Parkwood, Sutton Road, Maidstone, Kent, ME15 9NE
Parent: Paydens Limited
Officers: John Patrick McConville [1959] Director; Alexander George Pay [1984] Managing Director; Dennis Charles Pay [1942] Director

**Sangers (Northern Ireland) Limited**
Incorporated: 16 May 1985  Employees: 84
Net Worth: £2,610,406  Total Assets: £22,221,564
Registered Office: 2 Marshalls Road, Belfast, BT5 6SR
Parent: AAH Pharmaceuticals Limited
Officers: Nichola Louise Legg, Secretary; Toby Matthew Anderson [1973] Director; Marcus Hilger [1977] Finance Director [German]; David Jackson [1960] Director; Peter George Lemon [1954] Director; Catherine McDermott [1968] Operations Director; Nuala Meier [1959] Director/Accountant [Irish]; Nigel Swift [1966] Marketing and Sales Director

**Sanhak Ltd**
Incorporated: 22 November 2018
Registered Office: 8 Rosslyn Mews, Sunderland, Tyne & Wear, SR4 7DA
Shareholders: Sudhakar Bathala; Sandhya Mohan Bathala
Officers: Sudhakar Bathala [1986] Director [Indian]

**Sanochemia Diagnostics UK Limited**
Incorporated: 20 April 2001  Employees: 4
Net Worth Deficit: £1,277,305  Total Assets: £696,863
Registered Office: 1 Friary, Temple Quay, Bristol, BS1 6EA
Parent: Sanochemia Pharmazeutica AG
Officers: Doctor Klaus Gerdes [1973] Director [German]; Dr Stefan Welzig [1970] Director [Austrian]

**Sanos Healthcare Ltd**
Incorporated: 9 December 2014
Net Worth Deficit: £6,753  Total Assets: £15
Registered Office: 552 Kingsbury Road, London, NW9 9HH
Shareholders: Ousameh Shallal; Sayed Arif Naziri
Officers: Sayed Arif Naziri [1982] Director; Ousameh Shallal [1986] Director

**Sante Primaire Limited**
Incorporated: 3 May 2013
Registered Office: 9 Mannering Gardens, Westcliff on Sea, Essex, SS0 0BG
Major Shareholder: Yuk-Ki (Jonathan) Tang
Officers: Yuk-Ki Tang [1967] Director/Pharmacist

**Santen UK Limited**
Incorporated: 29 August 2014  Employees: 10
Net Worth: £2,570,314  Total Assets: £5,183,131
Registered Office: Salisbury Hall, St Albans, Herts, AL2 1BU
Parent: Santen SA
Officers: Koki Kobayashi, Secretary; Luis Miguel Iglesias Fernandez [1961] Director [Spanish]; Christopher Paul Reindel [1966] Director/CFO of Stanten Europe; Kazuo Koshiji Takasu [1966] Director/Corporate Officer [Japanese]

**Santhera (UK) Limited**
Incorporated: 1 July 2015  Employees: 11
Net Worth: £188,940  Total Assets: £565,972
Registered Office: 26-28 Hammersmith Grove, London, W6 7HA
Parent: Santhera Pharmaceuticals Holding AG
Officers: Catherine Susanne Ammann [1973] Director/Head HR [Swiss]; Alain Frey [1975] Director/HR Manager [Swiss]; Christoph Andreas Rentsch [1959] Director [Swiss]; Oliver Strub [1963] SVP General Counsel/Director Human Resources & IT [Swiss]; Andrea Volk [1980] Director/Senior Legal Counsel [German]

**Sanzenica Limited**
Incorporated: 8 June 2018
Registered Office: 1a Dorset Street, London, W1U 4EE
Major Shareholder: Seyed Mahmoud Mostafavi
Officers: Seyed Mahmoud Mostafavi [1956] Director

**SAR Health Limited**
Incorporated: 14 November 2016  Employees: 2
Net Worth: £1,328  Total Assets: £76,334
Registered Office: 82-88 Sherlock Street, Digbeth, Birmingham, B5 6LT
Officers: Dazan Alyanai [1984] Director/Web Designer

**Sarbec Cosmetics Limited**
Incorporated: 20 April 1988
Net Worth Deficit: £460,052  Total Assets: £12,397
Registered Office: 50 Seymour Street, London, W1H 7JG
Major Shareholder: Rene Patrick Van Den Schrieck
Officers: Rene Patrick Van Den Schrieck [1943] Director [French]

**Sarepta International UK Ltd.**
Incorporated: 29 September 2017
Registered Office: Hill House, 1 Little New Street, London, EC4A 3TR
Parent: Sarepta Therapeutics, Inc
Officers: Joseph Bratica [1963] Director/Accountant [American]; Enrico Maria Dolfini [1970] Executive Director - International Legal Affairs [Italian]; Matthew Garrett Gall [1976] Director/Businessman [American]

**Sasmar Limited**
Incorporated: 20 July 2009
Net Worth: £384,968  Total Assets: £437,921
Registered Office: Level 17, Dashwood House, 69 Old Broad Street, London, EC2M 1QS
Officers: John-Michael Mancini, Secretary [Australian]; John-Michael Mancini [1979] Director/Chief Executive Officer [Australian]

**Satio Pharma Ltd.**
Incorporated: 11 June 2018
Registered Office: 5 City Garden Row, London, N1 8DW
Officers: Alessio Bruni [1988] Director [German]; Riccardo Bruni [1988] Director [German]; Nicholas Kasper Lory [1989] Director

**Saving Life Technologies Limited**
Incorporated: 11 April 2016
Net Worth: £50,261  Total Assets: £219,966
Registered Office: 16 Abbotsbury Road, Morden, Surrey, SM4 5LQ
Shareholder: Attaul-Haleem Ahmad
Officers: Attaul-Haleem Ahmad [1983] Director [German]; Jahanzeb Shaker [1982] Director [German]

**Sawa Trading & Shipping Limited**
Incorporated: 13 December 2011
Net Worth: £24,624  Total Assets: £487,344
Registered Office: 1a Crown Lane, London, SW16 3DJ
Officers: Nancy Bennett [1948] Director/Businesswoman

**Saxon Pharmaceuticals Limited**
*Incorporated:* 5 November 2013
*Net Worth Deficit:* £2,293  *Total Assets:* £52,152
*Registered Office:* St Oswald House, St Oswald Street, Castleford, W Yorks, WF10 1DH
*Major Shareholder:* Albert Hills
*Officers:* Albert Hills [1956] Director

**Saxonia Medical Ltd.**
*Incorporated:* 9 April 2010
*Net Worth:* £205,629  *Total Assets:* £386,101
*Registered Office:* Regent House, 316 Beulah Hill, London, SE19 3HF
*Major Shareholder:* Natasa Sos
*Officers:* Natasa Sos [1992] Director/Businesswoman [Hungarian]

**Scandasystems Limited**
*Incorporated:* 9 August 1979  *Employees:* 2
*Net Worth:* £13,849  *Total Assets:* £15,792
*Registered Office:* 93 Tabernacle Street, London, EC2A 4BA
*Shareholder:* Graham Brandon
*Officers:* Graham Brandon [1950] Director; Rosalyn Marsha Brandon [1952] Director

**Scanmed (UK) Limited**
*Incorporated:* 7 October 1996
*Net Worth Deficit:* £42,303  *Total Assets:* £18,697
*Registered Office:* Kenton House, Oxford Street, Moreton in Marsh, Glos, GL56 0LA
*Major Shareholder:* Brian Collins
*Officers:* Brian Collins [1948] Director

**Schebo Biotech UK Limited**
*Incorporated:* 8 April 1999
*Net Worth:* £190,292  *Total Assets:* £326,588
*Registered Office:* The Square, Fawley, Southampton, SO45 1DD
*Officers:* Johannes Scheefers [1946] Director/Biologist [German]; Dr Ursula Scheefers-Borchel [1950] Director/Biologist [German]; Ivor Randle Smith [1957] Director

**Schulz Medical Supplies Ltd**
*Incorporated:* 29 January 2019
*Registered Office:* 82 Adagio Point, 3 Laban Walk, London, SE8 3FJ
*Major Shareholder:* Bahram Fakouri
*Officers:* Bahram Fakouri [1967] Director/Surgeon [German]

**Scientific Laboratory Supplies Group Ltd**
*Incorporated:* 1 June 2016  *Employees:* 183
*Net Worth:* £16,201,027  *Total Assets:* £28,936,802
*Registered Office:* Orchard House, The Square, Hessle, E Yorks, HU13 0AE
*Parent:* Dominique Dutscher Distribution SAS
*Officers:* Kristen Jane Chapman, Secretary; Robert Peter Chapman [1955] Managing Director; Dominique Etienne Wencker [1959] Director/General Manager [French]; Younes Zemmouri [1974] Director/Partner [French]

**Scope Ophthalmics Limited**
*Incorporated:* 15 December 2011  *Employees:* 55
*Net Worth:* £411,966  *Total Assets:* £7,732,882
*Registered Office:* Unit 4 Amberley Court, County Oak Way, Crawley, W Sussex, RH11 7XL
*Officers:* John Freyne, Secretary; Laurence Michael Dunne [1968] Director/Accountant [Irish]; John Freyne [1974] Director [Irish]; Tom Freyne [1984] Director [Irish]

**SD Alliance Ltd.**
*Incorporated:* 28 April 2009
*Net Worth:* £1,000  *Total Assets:* £1,000
*Registered Office:* 19 Kathleen Road, London, SW11 2JR
*Officers:* Izeth Samudio Tapia [1972] Director/Manager [Panamanian]

**SDM Healthcare Limited**
*Incorporated:* 15 September 2016
*Net Worth:* £10,002  *Total Assets:* £10,002
*Registered Office:* 728 Capability Green, Luton, Beds, LU1 3LU
*Shareholders:* Edward James Martin; Tracey Anne Stockdale
*Officers:* Peter Ross Cox [1945] Director/Accountant; Edward James Martin [1973] Director; Tracy Anne Stockdale [1975] Director

**Seagrave Pharma Consultancy Ltd.**
*Incorporated:* 14 June 2012
*Net Worth:* £176,629  *Total Assets:* £212,152
*Registered Office:* Barton View, Lapford, Crediton, Devon, EX17 6PZ
*Shareholders:* David John Garton; Karen Lynn Garton
*Officers:* Karen Lynn Garton, Secretary; David John Garton [1964] Director/Pharmaceutical Consultant; Karen Lynn Garton [1970] Company Secretary/Director

**Sebbin UK Ltd**
*Incorporated:* 12 February 2015  *Employees:* 4
*Net Worth Deficit:* £1,103,302  *Total Assets:* £805,155
*Registered Office:* Unit 6 McKay Trading Estate, Blackthorne Road, Colnbrook, Slough, SL3 0AH
*Parent:* Groupe Sebbin SAS
*Officers:* Benoit Durand [1968] Director [French]

**Secret Line Ltd**
*Incorporated:* 16 August 2018
*Registered Office:* 27 Old Gloucester Street, London, WC1N 3AX
*Major Shareholder:* Walid Kenawy
*Officers:* Walid Kenawy, Secretary; Walid Kenawy [1972] Director [Egyptian]; Aneta Smolen-Kenawy [1976] Director [Polish]

**Seedos Ltd.**
*Incorporated:* 7 October 1998
*Net Worth:* £12,285  *Total Assets:* £40,139
*Registered Office:* ECL House, Lake Street, Leighton Buzzard, Beds, LU7 1RT
*Major Shareholder:* Colin Stewart Walters
*Officers:* Colin Stewart Walters, Secretary/Marketing Manager; Lynn Diana Jackson [1950] Director/Self Employed Consultant; Colin Stewart Walters [1949] Director/Marketing Manager

**G S Seehra Limited**
*Incorporated:* 25 November 2008  *Employees:* 2
*Net Worth:* £9,179  *Total Assets:* £25,412
*Registered Office:* Old Bank Buildings, Upper High Street, Cradley Heath, W Midlands, B64 5HY
*Shareholders:* Gurdeep Singh Seehra; Jaspreet Kaur Seehra
*Officers:* Gurdeep Singh Seehra [1983] Director/Pharmacist

**Selective Supplies Limited**
*Incorporated:* 23 June 1999
*Net Worth:* £229,931  *Total Assets:* £341,054
*Registered Office:* First Floor, Roxburghe House, 273-287 Regent Street, London, W1B 2HA
*Shareholder:* Philip Huw Thomas
*Officers:* Janette Denise Thomas, Secretary; Janette Denise Thomas [1958] Director; Phillip Huw Thomas [1958] Director

**Selsdon Healthcare Limited**
*Incorporated:* 12 December 2001  *Employees:* 2
*Previous:* Pallas Healthcare Limited
*Net Worth:* £209,335  *Total Assets:* £380,363
*Registered Office:* 1st Floor, Selsdon House, 212-220 Addington Road, South Croydon, Surrey, CR2 8LD
*Parent:* Avicenna Holdings Ltd
*Officers:* Salim Kassamali Esmail Jetha [1953] Director/Pharmacist


**Seltfar Ltd**
*Incorporated:* 17 December 2015  *Employees:* 2
*Net Worth:* £127,250  *Total Assets:* £570,900
*Registered Office:* 83 Baker Street, London, W1U 6AG
*Major Shareholder:* Zhanar Duisenova
*Officers:* Zhanar Duisenova [1964] Director [Kazakh]


**Semenalysis Limited**
*Incorporated:* 11 September 2018
*Registered Office:* Pendragon House, 65 London Road, St Albans, Herts, AL1 1LJ
*Officers:* Thomas Joseph O'Reilly [1958] Director; Vicrtoria Anne O'Reilly [1959] Director; David Philip Price [1952] Director; Margaret Mary Price [1951] Director


**Sentinel Laboratories Limited**
*Incorporated:* 17 March 1988  *Employees:* 5
*Net Worth:* £677,283  *Total Assets:* £1,026,658
*Registered Office:* Mitchell House, The Mardens, Ifield, Crawley, W Sussex, RH11 0AQ
*Shareholders:* Kirsty Ann Louise Browning; Victoria Gail Tamsinn Clare
*Officers:* Kirsty Ann Louise Browning [1977] Director/Sales Manager; Victoria Gail Tamsin Clare [1979] Marketing Director; Brian John Smith [1945] Director; Penelope Jane Smith [1948] Director/Secretary


**Septodont Limited**
*Incorporated:* 28 May 1986  *Employees:* 15
*Net Worth:* £1,841,812  *Total Assets:* £2,737,567
*Registered Office:* Units R & S, Orchard Business Centre, St Barnabas Close, Allington, Maidstone, Kent, ME16 0JZ
*Major Shareholder:* Olivier Nestor Schiller
*Officers:* Michael Graham Andre Cann [1965] Managing Director; Olivier Nestor Schiller [1960] Director [French]


**SERB Ltd**
*Incorporated:* 31 October 2012  *Employees:* 1
*Previous:* Laboratoires Serb UK Limited
*Net Worth Deficit:* £48,848  *Total Assets:* £18,657
*Registered Office:* Eagle Court, 9 Vine Street, Uxbridge, Middlesex, UB8 1QE
*Parent:* Charterhouse Capital Partners LLP
*Officers:* Jeremie Alexandre Urbain [1977] Director [French]


**Seren Plus Limited**
*Incorporated:* 8 September 2011  *Employees:* 16
*Net Worth:* £129,739  *Total Assets:* £1,521,734
*Registered Office:* Churchgate House, Church Road, Whitchurch, Cardiff, CF14 2DX
*Major Shareholder:* Abdul Rahman Kowsor
*Officers:* Nelufa Yasmin Kowsor, Secretary; Farida Ali [1984] Director/Dentist; Nelufa Yasmin Kowsor [1983] Director/Pharmacist


**Serp Sales (UK) Limited**
*Incorporated:* 1 February 2008
*Net Worth Deficit:* £1,144  *Total Assets:* £9,804
*Registered Office:* Fifth Floor, Intergen House, 65-67 Western Road, Hove, E Sussex, BN3 2JQ
*Major Shareholder:* Sossio Morra
*Officers:* Frederic Jaques Morra, Secretary; Sossio Morra [1948] Director [Dominican]


**Servier IP UK Limited**
*Incorporated:* 3 February 2006
*Previous:* Servier UK IP Limited
*Net Worth:* £182,211,152  *Total Assets:* £189,847,904
*Registered Office:* Sefton House, Sefton Park, Bells Hill, Stoke Poges, Slough, Berks, SL2 4JS
*Officers:* Charles Michael Brooks, Secretary; Claude Philippe Bertrand [1962] General Director of R&D [French]; Patricia Lafaix-Houser [1957] Director/Executive Assistant [French]


**Servier Laboratories Limited**
*Incorporated:* 2 December 1963  *Employees:* 81
*Net Worth:* £7,064,000  *Total Assets:* £21,261,000
*Registered Office:* Sefton House, Sefton Park, Bells Hill, Stoke Poges, Slough, Berks, SL2 4JS
*Officers:* Charles Michael Brooks, Secretary; Pierre Jean Bernard Andriot [1962] Director of Group Accounts Financial Balances [French]; Emeric Marc Bodineau [1968] Human Resources Director International Operations [French]; Hugues Constant Guillaume Renaut [1962] Managing Director - International Operation China [French]


**Servipharm Limited**
*Incorporated:* 22 May 1989  *Employees:* 28
*Net Worth:* £4,570,605  *Total Assets:* £6,037,450
*Registered Office:* 39a Joel Street, Northwood Hills, Northwood, Middlesex, HA6 1NZ
*Major Shareholder:* Vipul Shah
*Officers:* Vipul Shah [1963] Director/Businessman [Kenyan]


**SF Pharma Limited**
*Incorporated:* 2 March 2016
*Registered Office:* 7 Brick Kiln Lane, Atherstone, Warwicks, CV9 2LU
*Shareholder:* Fadel Takrouri
*Officers:* Fadel Takrouri, Secretary; Balraj Singh Chohan [1967] Director; Fadel Takrouri [1960] Director; Sireen Takrouri [1971] Director


**Sfera Trading Limited**
*Incorporated:* 30 August 2017
*Registered Office:* Office 16990, 51 Fishponds Road, Eastville, Bristol, BS5 6SF
*Major Shareholder:* Jurijs Toma
*Officers:* Jurijs Toma [1989] Director [Latvian]


**SG Pharma UK Limited**
*Incorporated:* 29 June 2018
*Registered Office:* 1 Lingfield Close, Rotherham, S Yorks, S66 1WS
*Officers:* Gowardhan Kotra [1977] Director; Sachin Tammewar [1976] Director/Pharmacist

**Shakespeare Pharma Ltd**
*Incorporated:* 12 December 2011  *Employees:* 23
*Net Worth:* £1,075,519  *Total Assets:* £6,530,141
*Registered Office:* Unit 1b Harrison Court, Hilton Business Park, Hilton, Derbys, DE65 5UR
*Major Shareholder:* Simon Shakespeare
*Officers:* Harvey Alan Shakespeare, Secretary; Paul Anthony Shakespeare [1969] Director of Regulatory Affairs; Simon Shakespeare [1967] Director; Stephen Wright [1971] Operations Director

**Shanghai Neopharm Co., Ltd**
*Incorporated:* 17 January 2014
*Registered Office:* 8 Standard Road, London, NW10 6EU
*Major Shareholder:* Lihua Zhu
*Officers:* Lihua Zhu, Secretary; Lihua Zhu [1982] Director [Chinese]

**Shantys Limited**
*Incorporated:* 29 November 1979  *Employees:* 9
*Net Worth:* £1,540,552  *Total Assets:* £1,580,453
*Registered Office:* Units 3-4 Coppen Road, Dagenham, Essex, RM8 1HH
*Shareholder:* Shantilal Laxmidas Pabari
*Officers:* Sarla Shantilal Pabari, Secretary; Sarla Shantilal Pabari [1948] Director/Secretary; Shantilal Laxmidas Pabari [1944] Director/Businessman

**Shard Speciality Pharma Limited**
*Incorporated:* 28 April 2014
*Net Worth Deficit:* £1,107,039  *Total Assets:* £1,651,094
*Registered Office:* c/o Logixx Pharma Solutions Limited, Abbey House, 1650 Arlington Business Park, Theale, Reading, Berks, RG7 4SA
*Officers:* Michael Stuart Close [1971] Director

**Shardman Healthcare Limited**
*Incorporated:* 17 April 2013
*Net Worth:* £22,082  *Total Assets:* £128,136
*Registered Office:* Unit 2 Charnwood Edge Business Park, Syston Road, Cossington, Leics, LE7 4UZ
*Major Shareholder:* Sudhir Mansukhlal Ruparelia
*Officers:* Rekha Sudhir Ruparelia [1964] Director; Sudhir Mansukhlal Ruparelia [1961] Director/Pharmacist

**Sharepool Limited**
*Incorporated:* 20 July 2017
*Registered Office:* Kemp House, 160 City Road, London, EC1V 2NX
*Shareholders:* Brown Okupa; Elyon Brown; Adebisi Brown
*Officers:* Brown Okupa [1977] Director/Student

**Sharief Pharma Limited**
*Incorporated:* 3 October 2016
*Registered Office:* Unit 18 Neills Road, Bold Industrial Park, Bold, St Helens, Merseyside, WA9 4TU
*Officers:* Suhail Sharief [1980] Director/Pharmacist

**E.S.Shaw & Sons Limited**
*Incorporated:* 23 December 1955  *Employees:* 13
*Net Worth:* £147,100  *Total Assets:* £444,661
*Registered Office:* 222-230 High Street, Sheerness, Kent, ME12 1UL
*Shareholder:* Keith Derek Shaw
*Officers:* Alan Norman Sidney Shaw, Secretary; Alan Norman Sidney Shaw [1945] Director/Company Secretary; Keith Derek Shaw [1948] Director

**Ivor Shaw Limited**
*Incorporated:* 29 March 1963  *Employees:* 265
*Net Worth:* £2,280,602  *Total Assets:* £9,485,436
*Registered Office:* City Gate, London Road, Derby, DE24 8WY
*Parent:* SP 225 Limited
*Officers:* Elizabeth Jane Fothergill [1953] Director; Luke Richard Fryer [1973] Director; David Nicholas Shaw [1960] Director; Ian Martin Shaw [1955] Director

**Shaz Logistics Limited**
*Incorporated:* 1 August 2005
*Net Worth:* £2  *Total Assets:* £2
*Registered Office:* Kemp House, 160 City Road, London, EC1V 2NX
*Major Shareholder:* John Gbolahan Joseph
*Officers:* John Gbolahan Joseph [1963] Director

**J Sherlee Ltd**
*Incorporated:* 16 May 2018
*Registered Office:* 368 Uxbridge Road, Hayes, Middlesex, UB4 0SE
*Major Shareholder:* Janali Sherali
*Officers:* Janali Sherali [1985] Director/Businessman

**Shieldasset Limited**
*Incorporated:* 26 April 2000
*Net Worth Deficit:* £27,059  *Total Assets:* £66,281
*Registered Office:* 34 Kenny Drive, Carshalton, Surrey, SM5 4PH
*Shareholders:* Ademola Eniola Adewakun; Anne Elvina Mausi Adewakun
*Officers:* Anne Elvina Mausi Adewakun, Secretary; Ademola Eniola Adewakun [1964] Director/Pharmacist; Anne Elvina Mausi Adewakun [1965] Director/Pharmacist

**Shire Pharmaceuticals Limited**
*Incorporated:* 26 June 1986  *Employees:* 102
*Net Worth:* £47,738,000  *Total Assets:* £75,774,000
*Registered Office:* 1 Kingdom Street, London, W2 6BD
*Parent:* Baxalta UK Limited
*Officers:* Damien Rodolphe Edmond Bailly [1966] Commercial Director [French]; Mark Gibbons [1984] Director/Accountant [South African]; Nicholas Hugh Meryon Insall [1982] Director/Accountant; Jonathan Clark Neal [1971] Managing Director

**Shizhen TCM (UK) Limited**
*Incorporated:* 5 January 2005  *Employees:* 9
*Net Worth:* £507,134  *Total Assets:* £1,851,308
*Registered Office:* 67 Ayres Road, Old Trafford, Manchester, M16 9NH
*Major Shareholder:* Yanzhong Xu
*Officers:* Yanzhong Xu [1959] Director

**Shkar Enterprise Limited**
*Incorporated:* 7 April 2017
*Net Worth Deficit:* £2,533  *Total Assets:* £5,121
*Registered Office:* 143 Saltwells Road, Middlesbrough, Cleveland, TS4 2DT
*Major Shareholder:* Huda Ali Mohammed
*Officers:* Huda Ali Mohammed [1990] Director/Businesswoman [Iraqi]

**SHL Medical Limited**
*Incorporated:* 11 January 2019
*Registered Office:* 31 Woodvale Way, London, NW11 8SF
*Major Shareholder:* Salma Eldamarawy
*Officers:* Salma Eldamarawy [1997] Director [Egyptian]; Mohamed Islam Ibrahim [1978] Director

**Shoebury West Road Ltd**
*Incorporated:* 12 October 2016  *Employees:* 7
*Previous:* SP3 (Essex) Ltd
*Net Worth Deficit:* £42,453  *Total Assets:* £1,077,000
*Registered Office:* 2 High Street, Shoeburyness, Southend on Sea, Essex, SS3 9AH
*Shareholders:* Shailendra Chandulal Shah; Sandhya Shailendra Shah
*Officers:* Sandhya Shailendra Shah [1951] Director/Businesswoman; Shailendra Chandulal Shah [1953] Director/Businessman

**Showman's Surgical Ltd**
*Incorporated:* 7 February 2000  *Employees:* 1
*Net Worth Deficit:* £5,135  *Total Assets:* £27,803
*Registered Office:* 27 Lower Turf Lane, Scouthead, Oldham, Lancs, OL4 4BG
*Major Shareholder:* June Harrison
*Officers:* June Harrison, Secretary/Manager; June Harrison [1945] Director/Manager

**Sidhupharm Limited**
*Incorporated:* 4 February 2011
*Registered Office:* 2 Heap Bridge, Bury, Lancs, BL9 7HR
*Major Shareholder:* Manjinder Singh Sidhu
*Officers:* Manjinder Singh Sidhu [1986] Director/Pharmacist

**Sigma Pharmaceuticals PLC**
*Incorporated:* 15 May 1981  *Employees:* 308
*Net Worth:* £31,049,618  *Total Assets:* £101,851,080
*Registered Office:* First Floor, Roxburghe House, 273-287 Regent Street, London, W1B 2HA
*Shareholder:* Orion Holdings (UK) Limited
*Officers:* Manish Hansraj Shah, Secretary/Chartered Accountant; Bharat Kumar Hansraj Devraj Shah [1949] Director/Pharmacist; Bhavin Manish Shah [1983] Director/Chartered Accountant; Hatul Bharat Kumar Shah [1978] Director/Pharmacist; Jayoti Bharat Shah [1952] Director/Credit Controller; Kalpana Manish Shah [1956] Director/Personnel Manageress; Kamal Hansraj Shah [1959] Director/Office Manager; Manish Hansraj Shah [1955] Director/Chartered Accountant; Nishal Kamal Shah [1991] Director/Doctor; Paras Kamal Shah [1987] Director; Rajiv Bharat Kumar Shah [1985] Director/Pharmacist; Sachin Manish Shah [1986] Director/Dentist

**Sigmasis UK Limited**
*Incorporated:* 3 September 2008
*Registered Office:* 129 Wells Green Road, Solihull, W Midlands, B92 7PQ
*Major Shareholder:* Sakina Ferdous Hossain
*Officers:* Khandakar Mohammad Tofazzal Hossain, Secretary; Sakina Ferdous Hossain [1985] Managing Director

**Sigmatec Limited**
*Incorporated:* 16 January 2018
*Registered Office:* Flat 1, Wellington House, Western Avenue, London, W5 1EX
*Major Shareholder:* Tarek Elsayed Abdelaziz Ismail
*Officers:* Tarek Elsayed Abdelaziz Ismail [1963] Director [Egyptian]

**Silicon Pharma Limited**
*Incorporated:* 29 November 2012
*Net Worth:* £30,800  *Total Assets:* £40,193
*Registered Office:* 4 Rosecroft Walk, Wembley, Middlesex, HA0 2JZ
*Shareholders:* Shilpa Patel; Chirag Patel
*Officers:* Chiragkumar Patel, Secretary; Chiragkumar Ranchhodbhai Patel [1980] Director/Industrial Pharmacist

**Silkgrange Limited**
*Incorporated:* 18 November 1980
*Net Worth:* £680,512  *Total Assets:* £730,424
*Registered Office:* Unit 3 Unicorn Works, 21-25 Garman Road, London, N17 0YU
*Major Shareholder:* Ramesh Chhaganbhai Patel
*Officers:* Ramesh Chhaganbhai Patel, Secretary/Director; Hitesh Ramesh Patel [1971] Director/Accountant; Ramesh Chhaganbhai Patel [1944] Director

**Simba Pharmatech Limited**
*Incorporated:* 14 June 2017
*Registered Office:* 52a Spring Grove Road, Hounslow, Middlesex, TW3 4BN
*Shareholder:* Harshad Kumar Raja
*Officers:* M Harshad Kumar Raja [1962] Director/Businessman

**Simcare Global Premium Healthcare Ltd**
*Incorporated:* 1 October 2018
*Registered Office:* Unit 7 Chailey Industrial Estate, Pump Lane, Hayes, Middlesex, UB3 3NB
*Major Shareholder:* Assif Mohammed
*Officers:* Al-Ameen Mohammed [1983] Director/Entrepreneur; Assif Mohammed [1953] Director/Doctor

**Simcro (UK) Limited**
*Incorporated:* 22 March 2000  *Employees:* 3
*Net Worth:* £87,107  *Total Assets:* £193,344
*Registered Office:* 11 Eastheath Avenue, Wokingham, Berks, RG41 2PP
*Officers:* Klaus Ackerstaff [1965] Director [German]; Daniele Della Libera [1969] Director [Swiss]

**Simply Meds Pro Ltd**
*Incorporated:* 18 July 2018
*Registered Office:* Imperial House, 1a Standen Avenue, Hornchurch, Essex, RM12 6AA
*Officers:* Avtar Singh Sagoo [1989] Director; Parvinder Singh Sagoo [1987] Director/Pharmacist; Dr Saranjit Singh Sihra [1977] Director/Dentist

**G & L Simpson Limited**
*Incorporated:* 28 February 2001
*Net Worth:* £360,476  *Total Assets:* £753,355
*Registered Office:* 248 Upper Newtownards Road, Belfast, BT4 3EU
*Shareholders:* Glen Tyrrell Simpson; Laura Anne Simpson
*Officers:* Glen Tyrrell Simpson, Secretary; Glen Tyrrell Simpson [1971] Director/Pharmacist; Laura-Anne Simpson [1970] Director/Pharmacist

**Sinduram Healthcare International Ltd**
*Incorporated:* 23 March 2018
*Registered Office:* 56 Weighton Road, Harrow, Middlesex, HA3 6HZ
*Major Shareholder:* Sindhupriya Chintalapudi
*Officers:* Sindhupriya Chintalapudi [1986] Director

**Sintal Impex Limited**
*Incorporated:* 20 January 2015
*Registered Office:* 91 Wellington Street, Luton, Beds, LU1 5AF
*Shareholders:* Muhammad Ramzan; Muhammad Ramzan
*Officers:* Muhammad Ramzan [1982] Director [Pakistani]

**Sintetica Limited**
Incorporated: 13 January 2016  Employees: 4
Net Worth Deficit: £633,481  Total Assets: £183,928
Registered Office: 30th Floor, 40 Bank Street, Canary Wharf, London, E14 5NR
Shareholders: Luca Bolzani; Mario Bonomi
Officers: Luca Giuseppe Ambrogio Bolzani [1958] Director/Business Executive [Swiss]; Darren Fergus [1970] Director; Augusto Mitidieri [1971] Director [Swiss]; Oliver Tweedie [1968] Director/Consultant Anaesthetist

**Sipco Nutrition (UK) Ltd**
Incorporated: 7 April 2018
Registered Office: 60 Longleat Walk, Ingleby Barwick, Stockton on Tees, Cleveland, TS17 5BW
Major Shareholder: Ashu Puri
Officers: Ashu Puri, Secretary; Ashu Puri [1977] Director

**Sipco Pharma UK Ltd**
Incorporated: 6 February 2013
Net Worth Deficit: £11,480  Total Assets: £9,937
Registered Office: 11 Enterprise Court, Queens Meadow Business Park, Hartlepool, Cleveland, TS25 2FE
Major Shareholder: Sonia Puri
Officers: Sonia Puri [1974] Director

**Sivanta Resourcing Limited**
Incorporated: 3 December 2014
Registered Office: 11 Ingleby Road, Ilford, Essex, IG1 4RX
Major Shareholder: Jayman Patel
Officers: Jayman Patel [1980] Director/IT Consultant

**Six Ways Birmingham Ltd**
Incorporated: 19 February 2010
Net Worth: £34,681  Total Assets: £215,951
Registered Office: 7 Birchfield Road, Birmingham, B19 1SU
Major Shareholder: Abbas Jaffer Roowala
Officers: Abbas Jaffer Roowala [1980] Director/Navy Officer; Batul Abbas Roowala [1980] Director/Pharmacist

**SJ Enterprises Limited**
Incorporated: 26 March 1990
Net Worth: £2,913  Total Assets: £5,047
Registered Office: 40 Taylor Drive, Bramley, Tadley, Hants, RG26 5XP
Officers: Nalin Mahinda Jayawardena, Secretary; Indira Maureen Jayawardena [1961] Director/Housewife; Nalin Mahinda Jayawardena [1949] Director/Accountant

**Skarby Gai Ltd**
Incorporated: 20 January 2017
Net Worth: £66,543  Total Assets: £115,441
Registered Office: Craven House, 40-44 Uxbridge Road, Ealing, London, W5 2BS
Major Shareholder: Rafal Slabik
Officers: Paulina Kopanko [1987] Director [Polish]; Rafal Slabik [1976] Director [Polish]

**Skindoc Formula Limited**
Incorporated: 26 September 2014
Net Worth Deficit: £106,030  Total Assets: £169,000
Registered Office: First Floor, 85 Great Portland Street, London, W1W 7LT
Major Shareholder: Dirk Kremer
Officers: Dirk Dr. Kremer [1970] Director/Medical Doctor [German]

**Skingen UK Ltd**
Incorporated: 3 November 2010
Previous: Silderm Limited
Net Worth Deficit: £399,528  Total Assets: £158,563
Registered Office: Dane Mill Business Centre, Broadhurst Lane, Congleton, Cheshire, CW12 1LA
Parent: Skingen International Inc
Officers: David John Bryant [1968] Director/Manager; Aileen Cameron [1964] Director; Fateme Kasravi Gheshlagh [1977] Medical Director [Iranian]

**Skinlab Medical Ltd**
Incorporated: 6 August 2018
Registered Office: 12 Mendoza Close, Hornchurch, Essex, RM11 2RP
Major Shareholder: Malgorzata Gouzd
Officers: Magdalena Gouzd [1981] Director/Beautician [Polish]; Malgorzata Gouzd [1960] Director/Beautician [Polish]

**SkInOne UK Ltd**
Incorporated: 6 November 2018
Registered Office: Crown House, North Circular Road, Park Royal, London, NW10 7PN
Major Shareholder: Sohail Amjed
Officers: Sohail Amjed [1961] Director/Pharmacist; Abdulshakur Abdulgafur Saiyed [1966] Director/Businessman

**Skinska Pharmaceutica Limited**
Incorporated: 24 December 2018
Registered Office: 34 Ingledew Court, Leeds, LS17 8TP
Major Shareholder: Sindhupriya Chintalapudi
Officers: Sindhupriya Chintalapudi [1986] Director

**Sky Hemp Ltd**
Incorporated: 22 August 2018
Registered Office: 227 Martindale Road, Hounslow, Middlesex, TW4 7HF
Shareholders: Juveer Padda; Harvir Ubhi
Officers: Juveer Padda [1995] Director/Engineer; Harvir Ubhi [1994] Director/Physiotherapist

**Skylark Services Limited**
Incorporated: 10 May 2018
Registered Office: 17 School Road, Hall Green, Birmingham, B28 8JG
Major Shareholder: Mohammed Munir Karim
Officers: Mark Cheetham [1978] Director; Mohammed Munir Karim [1966] Director

**Skymedic UK Limited**
Incorporated: 14 May 2018
Registered Office: 85 Mary Rose Square, London, SE16 7EL
Major Shareholder: Lorenzo Pomponi
Officers: Eric Casas Lloveras [1987] Marketing Director [Spanish]; Lorenzo Pomponi [1990] Director [Italian]

**SL Clinical Ltd**
Incorporated: 19 November 2018
Registered Office: 73 Willian Road, Hitchin, Herts, SG4 0LS
Major Shareholder: Sukfan Liu
Officers: Suk Fan Liu [1976] Director

**Smart Medical Limited**
Incorporated: 25 July 2002  Employees: 3
Net Worth: £114,506  Total Assets: £365,048
Registered Office: Kenton House, Oxford Street, Moreton in Marsh, Glos, GL56 0LA
Shareholders: Brian Collins; Phillip Michael Collins; Simon Dickinson
Officers: Jennifer Ruth Noble, Secretary; Brian Collins [1948] Director; Phillip Michael Collins [1969] Director; Simon Rodney Dickinson [1965] Director

**Smartway Pharmaceuticals Limited**
Incorporated: 9 April 2013  Employees: 62
Net Worth: £26,921,700  Total Assets: £36,737,676
Registered Office: The Old Mill, 9 Soar Lane, Leicester, LE3 5DE
Parent: Smartway PW Holdings Limited
Officers: Kirti Patel [1968] Director

**Robert Smith & Co, (Derry) Limited**
Incorporated: 18 October 1950
Registered Office: A & L Goodbody, 42-46 Fountain Street, Belfast, BT1 5EF
Parent: Alchem PLC
Officers: Damien Moynagh, Secretary; Grainne McAleese [1979] Director [Irish]; Louise Tallon [1979] Director [Irish]

**Smoketrees Ltd**
Incorporated: 22 January 2018
Registered Office: 41 The Rand, Eastriggs, Dumfries-shire, DG12 6NN
Major Shareholder: Timothy Rees
Officers: Timothy Rees [1986] Director

**So'dran Ltd**
Incorporated: 25 April 2013
Net Worth: £22,763  Total Assets: £36,000
Registered Office: 21 Tollgate Road, Dartford, Kent, DA2 6BS
Major Shareholder: Olusola Ogundiran
Officers: Olusola Ogundiran [1966] Director/Nurse Manager

**Soho Flordis UK Limited**
Incorporated: 22 June 2015  Employees: 46
Net Worth: £3,832,280  Total Assets: £9,538,450
Registered Office: Douglas Bank House, Wigan Lane, Wigan, Lancs, WN1 2TB
Parent: Ginsana SA
Officers: Annette Louise Dawson [1960] Director; Robert Charles Gerard Hendriks [1963] Director [Dutch]; Alessandro Modica Agnello [1977] Director [Italian]

**Solana Trade Ltd**
Incorporated: 11 April 2013
Net Worth Deficit: £7,955  Total Assets: £516,257
Registered Office: 3rd Floor, 207 Regent Street, London, W1B 3HH
Major Shareholder: Andrew Rodney Noel Dickson
Officers: Andrew Rodney Noel Dickson [1964] Director

**Solarius UK & Overseas Limited**
Incorporated: 15 January 2018
Registered Office: The Gate Business Centre, Keppoch Street, Cardiff, CF24 3JW
Shareholder: Tamer Mohamed Hassan Elzokrod
Officers: Tamer Aly Emam Aly Elkaramany [1975] Director [Egyptian]; Tamer Mohamed Hassan Elzokrod [1976] Director/Pharmacist [Egyptian]

**Soliphar Limited**
Incorporated: 13 July 1998
Net Worth Deficit: £60,776  Total Assets: £17,502
Registered Office: 4th Floor, 115 George Street, Edinburgh, EH2 4JN
Major Shareholder: Rodolfo Wehe
Officers: Marta Irene Diaz de Saavedra, Secretary; Marta Irene Diaz de Saavedra [1955] Director [Panamanian]; Dianeth Isabel Matos de Ospino [1960] Director [Panamanian]; Jose Eugenio Silva Ritter [1963] Director [Panamanian]

**Solo Nutrition Limited**
Incorporated: 30 December 1999
Net Worth Deficit: £770  Total Assets: £33,920
Registered Office: 37 Shiphay Lane, Torquay, Devon, TQ2 7DU
Major Shareholder: Nigel Anthony John Grosse
Officers: Nigel Anthony John Grosse [1966] Director/Sales

**Sonal Pharma (UK) Ltd**
Incorporated: 24 July 2018
Registered Office: Devonshire House, 582 Honeypot Lane, Stanmore, Middlesex, HA7 1JS
Major Shareholder: Pareshkumar Dodhia
Officers: Pareshkumar Dodhia [1977] Director/Business Owner [Kenyan]

**Sonchat Limited**
Incorporated: 30 May 2018
Registered Office: Kanta House, Victoria Road, Ruislip, Middlesex, HA4 0JQ
Major Shareholder: Sonya Rashmi Chatwani
Officers: Sonya Rashmi Chatwani [1989] Director

**Sonifar Pharma Expert Limited**
Incorporated: 23 November 2017
Registered Office: 2 Bartle Green, Burnley, Lancs, BB11 5BF
Shareholders: Songul Emritte; Nizam Mohamed Emritte
Officers: Zohra Allimah Shadoobuccus [1985] Director

**Sonik Products Limited**
Incorporated: 11 April 1996  Employees: 5
Net Worth: £1,162,354  Total Assets: £1,935,199
Registered Office: Block C, Woodside End, Wembley, Middlesex, HA0 1UR
Shareholders: Ramji Naran Kanbi; Ratan Ramji Kanbi
Officers: Ratan Ramji Kanbi, Secretary; Ramji Naran Kanbi [1959] Director/Wholesaler

**Sood-UK Ltd**
Incorporated: 9 December 2013  Employees: 2
Net Worth: £25,269  Total Assets: £270,736
Registered Office: 63 Roehampton Lane, London, SW15 5NE
Major Shareholder: Botan Awni Yousif
Officers: Sally Ibrahim Hasan Al-Suhail [1968] Director [Iraqi]; Botan Awni Yousif [1963] Director/Entrepreneur [Iraqi]

**Soothingproducts Ltd**
Incorporated: 21 November 2011
Net Worth: £42,368  Total Assets: £72,505
Registered Office: 19 Burton Row, Beeston, Leeds, LS11 5NX
Officers: Robert Anthony Deegan [1946] Director; Martin Stead [1980] Director; Chloe Stead Deegan [1994] Director; Hannah Stead Deegan [1998] Director

## Sophos Medical Limited
*Incorporated:* 25 January 2017
*Registered Office:* 39 The Generals Wood, Washington, Tyne & Wear, NE38 9BN
*Major Shareholder:* Paul William Allinson
*Officers:* Paul William Allinson [1980] Director

## Sotra Pharma Ltd.
*Incorporated:* 14 September 2004
*Net Worth Deficit:* £43,045  *Total Assets:* £1,980
*Registered Office:* 342 Regents Park Road, London, N3 2LJ
*Officers:* Michael Wijsmuller, Secretary/Director [Danish]; Dennis David Wijsmuller [1970] Director [Dutch]; Michael Peter Wijsmuller [1968] Director [Dutch]

## Source Healthcare Ltd
*Incorporated:* 13 January 2017  *Employees:* 1
*Net Worth:* £107  *Total Assets:* £19,872
*Registered Office:* Unit 1a Highway Point, 239 Torrington Avenue, Coventry, Warwicks, CV4 9AP
*Major Shareholder:* Andrew Richard Skene
*Officers:* Andrew Skene, Secretary; Andrew Richard Skene [1979] Director; Laura Frances Skene [1982] Director

## South China Bio-Pharma Co Ltd.
*Incorporated:* 9 January 2018
*Registered Office:* 7-11 Minerva Road, Park Royal, London, NW10 6HJ
*Major Shareholder:* Xiaofeng Zhang
*Officers:* Xiaofeng Zhang [1973] Director [Chinese]

## Southampton Medical Group Ltd
*Incorporated:* 17 August 2018
*Registered Office:* 9 Suttones Place, Southampton, SO15 2SJ
*Shareholders:* Siven Pillay Rungien; Vivek Kaul; Mayuragoban Balasubramaniam
*Officers:* Dr Mayuragoban Balasubramaniam [1981] Director/Doctor; Dr Vivek Kaul [1961] Director/Doctor; Dr Siven Pillay Rungien [1981] Director/Manager

## Sovereign House Properties Limited
*Incorporated:* 2 December 1998
*Previous:* Sovereign House Properties PLC
*Net Worth:* £3,550,000  *Total Assets:* £4,879,000
*Registered Office:* Suite 1, 3rd Floor, 11-12 St James's Square, London, SW1Y 4LB
*Parent:* Waymade PLC
*Officers:* Mark John Cotterill [1965] Director/Accountant; Bhikhu Chhotabhai Patel [1947] Managing Director; Vijay Kumar Chhotabhai Patel [1949] Director/Chairman

## SP Services (UK) Limited
*Incorporated:* 26 August 1997  *Employees:* 39
*Net Worth:* £3,440,052  *Total Assets:* £4,571,751
*Registered Office:* Bastion House, Hortonwood 30, Telford, Salop, TF1 7XT
*Major Shareholder:* Steven John Bray
*Officers:* Steven John Bray, Secretary; Steven John Bray [1964] Director; Simon Anthony Leggett [1967] Managing Director

## Spadeground Limited
*Incorporated:* 7 June 1979  *Employees:* 2
*Net Worth:* £1,085,231  *Total Assets:* £1,272,832
*Registered Office:* 8 Wicksteed Close, Bexley, Kent, DA5 2BZ
*Shareholders:* Indravadan Narayanbhai Patel; Charulata Indravadan Patel
*Officers:* Indravadan Narayanbhai Patel, Secretary; Charulata Indravadan Patel [1958] Director/Housewife; Dr Dev Indravadan Patel [1989] Director/Dentist; Indravadan Narayanbhai Patel [1950] Director/Chemist

## Spatone Limited
*Incorporated:* 10 October 1986  *Employees:* 13
*Net Worth:* £2,899,000  *Total Assets:* £7,425,000
*Registered Office:* Nelsons House, 83 Parkside, Wimbledon, London, SW19 5LP
*Shareholders:* Robert Nelson Wilson; Patrick Russell Wilson
*Officers:* Claire Ferguson [1977] Director; Patrick Russell Wilson [1965] Director/Deputy Chairman; Robert Nelson Wilson [1962] Director/Chairman

## Specialised Marketing Services Limited
*Incorporated:* 26 September 1989
*Net Worth Deficit:* £33,045  *Total Assets:* £661
*Registered Office:* 12-16 Lionel Road, Canvey Island, Essex, SS8 9DE
*Major Shareholder:* Peter John Holliman
*Officers:* Peter John Holliman [1950] Sales Director

## The Specials Laboratory Limited
*Incorporated:* 12 July 1999
*Previous:* Craig & Hayward Limited
*Registered Office:* Unit 2 Regents Drive, Low Prudhoe Industrial Estate, Prudhoe, Northumberland, NE42 6PX
*Parent:* PCCA (UK) Holdings Limited
*Officers:* Sharon Clift [1976] Managing Director; Jimmy Ray Smith [1960] Director/Company President [American]; Lester David Sparks [1943] Director [American]

## Specials Pharma Ltd
*Incorporated:* 11 December 2018
*Registered Office:* 29 Chigwell Park Drive, Chigwell, Essex, IG7 5BD
*Shareholder:* Umesh Gopal Chauhan
*Officers:* Umesh Gopal Chauhan [1964] Director/Pharmacist

## Specialty Diagnostix Limited
*Incorporated:* 26 September 2012  *Employees:* 2
*Net Worth:* £458  *Total Assets:* £92,403
*Registered Office:* Pendragon House, 65 London Road, St Albans, Herts, AL1 1LJ
*Shareholders:* Margaret Mary Price; David Philip Price
*Officers:* David Philip Price [1952] Director; Margaret Mary Price [1951] Director

## Specialty Pharma of London Ltd
*Incorporated:* 6 May 2016  *Employees:* 1
*Net Worth:* £400,085  *Total Assets:* £3,198,265
*Registered Office:* Suite 314, 33 Cavendish Square, London, W1G 0PW
*Shareholder:* Andre Luis Pereira
*Officers:* Andre Luis Pereira [1976] Director/Economist [Italian]

## The Top UK Pharmaceutical Wholesalers

**Spectrum Biomedical UK Limited**
*Incorporated:* 30 August 2018
*Registered Office:* The Pinnacle, 170 Midsummer Boulevard, Milton Keynes, Bucks, MK9 1FE
*Officers:* Dr Pierre Debs [1966] Managing Director [American]; Cosmo Feilding Mellen [1985] Managing Director, Beckley Canopy Therapeutics; Phillip Stephen Shaer [1973] Director/Chief Legal Officer [Canadian]; Marc Wayne [1966] Director/Business Executive [Canadian]

**Speedx Limited**
*Incorporated:* 20 May 2016  *Employees:* 2
*Net Worth Deficit:* £233,083  *Total Assets:* £161,624
*Registered Office:* Acre House, 11-15 William Road, London, NW1 3ER
*Officers:* Andrew Leslie Denver [1948] Director [American]

**Spey Limited**
*Incorporated:* 7 February 2017
*Registered Office:* Astra House, Arklow Road, London, SE14 6EB
*Parent:* Abstragan Limited
*Officers:* Sadullo Abdulloev [1980] Director/Pharmaceutical Business [Tajikistani]

**Spey Pharma Limited**
*Incorporated:* 8 February 2017
*Registered Office:* Astra House, Arklow Road, London, SE14 6EB
*Parent:* Abstragan Limited
*Officers:* Sadullo Abdulloev [1980] Director/Pharmaceutical Business [Tajikistani]

**Alan Spivack Limited**
*Incorporated:* 27 April 1973  *Employees:* 6
*Net Worth:* £1,961,463  *Total Assets:* £2,902,353
*Registered Office:* Acre House, 11-15 William Road, London, NW1 3ER
*Parent:* Vilcabamba Limited
*Officers:* Michael Andrew Gore [1973] Commercial Director; David Daniel Spivack [1974] Commercial Director

**SPL (2010) Limited**
*Incorporated:* 17 June 2010  *Employees:* 1
*Net Worth:* £11,813,111  *Total Assets:* £11,813,111
*Registered Office:* 3 Young Place, Kelvin Industrial Estate, East Kilbride, G75 0TD
*Parent:* Munro Healthcare Group Limited
*Officers:* John Cochrane [1957] Director

**Spodefell Pharma Chemicals Limited**
*Incorporated:* 11 December 2014
*Registered Office:* Unit 1 Olds Approach, Tolpits Lane, Watford, Herts, WD18 9TD
*Officers:* Deepak Anantrai Ghelani [1961] Director; Bhavesh Amratlal Radia [1965] Director

**Sports Star Distribution UK Limited**
*Incorporated:* 11 July 2018
*Registered Office:* 35 Wolseley Road, Preston, Lancs, PR1 8EU
*Major Shareholder:* Jaspreet Kaur
*Officers:* Jaspreet Kaur [1978] Director

**Springbourne Management and Trading Ltd**
*Incorporated:* 11 February 2013
*Net Worth Deficit:* £39,006  *Total Assets:* £1,122,176
*Registered Office:* 33 Alfred Place, Fitzrovia, London, WC1E 7DP
*Major Shareholder:* Sameer Shrivastava
*Officers:* Sameer Shrivastava [1971] Director/Businessman [Indian]

**Springs Healthcare Limited**
*Incorporated:* 17 March 2017
*Registered Office:* 7 Barley Mow View, Ashford, Kent, TN23 3FB
*Major Shareholder:* Elizabeth Oluseun Mofolasayo
*Officers:* Adenrele Temitope Mofolasayo [1972] Director [British/Nigerian]; Elizabeth Oluseun Mofolasayo [1972] Director; Ikeoluwapo Naomi Mofolasayo [2001] Director

**Springwell Transport and Logistics Ltd**
*Incorporated:* 24 December 2018
*Registered Office:* 7 Hazel Avenue, West Drayton, Middlesex, UB7 9EN
*Major Shareholder:* Sumaria Parvez
*Officers:* Sumaria Parvez [1986] Director/Transport and Logistics Professional

**Sprint Moto UK Ltd**
*Incorporated:* 4 September 2009
*Net Worth Deficit:* £58,288  *Total Assets:* £25,349
*Registered Office:* 86 Breamore Road, Ilford, Essex, IG3 9NJ
*Major Shareholder:* Sheraz Wahid Butt
*Officers:* Waqas Afsar Ali [1982] Director/Self Employed [Pakistani]

**Sprint Pharma Limited**
*Incorporated:* 1 July 2015
*Net Worth Deficit:* £1,375  *Total Assets:* £14,292
*Registered Office:* Suite 126, Higham Hill JSC, 313 Billet Road, London, E17 5PX
*Officers:* Karel Marik [1983] Director [Czech]

**SQR Pharma Consulting Ltd**
*Incorporated:* 19 February 2014  *Employees:* 1
*Net Worth:* £1,423,255  *Total Assets:* £3,556,039
*Registered Office:* Unit 502, 30 Great Guildford Street, London, SE1 0HS
*Major Shareholder:* Alfonso Sciotti
*Officers:* Angelo Priore [1978] Director [Italian]; Alfonso Sciotti [1958] Director/Businessman [Italian]; Ilya Zaltsman [1963] Director [Kazakh]

**Srigen Pharma Ltd**
*Incorporated:* 27 May 2016  *Employees:* 2
*Net Worth Deficit:* £29,520  *Total Assets:* £138,827
*Registered Office:* 269 Farnborough Road, Farnborough, Hants, GU14 7LY
*Major Shareholder:* Kurt Kloos
*Officers:* Srishti Jain [1989] Director [Indian]; Kurt Kloos [1956] Director [German]

**SRS Pharma Limited**
*Incorporated:* 2 November 2015  *Employees:* 1
*Net Worth:* £7,083  *Total Assets:* £70,310
*Registered Office:* 41 St Thomas's Road, Chorley, Lancs, PR7 1JE
*Shareholders:* Binita Shah; Siddharth Shah
*Officers:* Binita Shah [1963] Director; Siddharth Shah [1960] Director/Pharmaceutical Trader

**SSCP Blink Bidco Limited**
*Incorporated:* 19 April 2015  *Employees:* 31
*Net Worth Deficit:* £2,368,192  *Total Assets:* £10,881,720
*Registered Office:* Fernbank House, Springwood Way, Tytherington Business Park, Macclesfield, Cheshire, SK10 2XA
*Officers:* Ian Martin Snelson, Secretary; Roland Bruhin [1964] Director/Chief Executive [Swiss]; Ian Martin Snelson [1967] Director/Chartered Accountant

**SSPharma4You Limited**
Incorporated: 18 February 2019
Registered Office: Oak Farm, Broughton, Aylesbury, Bucks, HP22 5AW
Major Shareholder: Snehal Mahendrabhai Patel
Officers: Snehal Mahendrabhai Patel [1974] Director/Manager [Indian]

**St George's Medical Limited**
Incorporated: 18 May 2007
Net Worth Deficit: £1,640   Total Assets: £167,865
Registered Office: 55 St Georges Road, Elephant and Castle, London, SE1 6ER
Major Shareholder: Atul Sumantbhai Patel
Officers: Sukesha Patel, Secretary; Atul Sumantbhai Patel [1967] Director

**St Georges Pharmaceuticals Limited**
Incorporated: 31 January 2018
Registered Office: Victoria House, 18 Dalston Gardens, Stanmore, Middlesex, HA7 1BU
Major Shareholder: Atul Sumantbhai Patel
Officers: Atul Sumantbhai Patel [1967] Director

**St Marks Medical Ltd**
Incorporated: 25 May 2017
Registered Office: 8B Accommodation Road, Golders Green, London, NW11 8ED
Major Shareholder: Mohammad Hussein Dehabadi
Officers: Dr. Mohammad Hussein Dehabadi [1986] Director

**Stada UK Holdings Ltd.**
Incorporated: 5 August 2013   Employees: 1
Net Worth: £444,660,640   Total Assets: £861,665,920
Registered Office: 200 Longwater Avenue, Reading, Berks, RG2 6GP
Parent: Stada Arzneimittel Aktiengesellschaft
Officers: Edwin Charles Blythe [1968] Finance Director; Frank Seiler [1968] Director/Vice President Corporate Treasury [German]

**Stainweld Limited**
Incorporated: 20 February 1980
Net Worth: £170   Total Assets: £32,424
Registered Office: 15-17 Church Street, Stourbridge, W Midlands, DY8 1LU
Major Shareholder: David Ian Stubley
Officers: David Ian Stubley [1957] Director

**Stallergenes (UK) Ltd**
Incorporated: 14 March 2008
Net Worth Deficit: £757,100   Total Assets: £610,500
Registered Office: Tower Bridge House, St Katharine's Way, London, E1W 1DD
Parent: Stallergenes Greer PLC
Officers: Nunzio Antonelli [1960] Director [Italian]

**Stan-Pol Ltd**
Incorporated: 5 August 2008   Employees: 9
Net Worth: £46,471   Total Assets: £66,921
Registered Office: 48 Hinckley Road, Leicester, LE3 0RB
Major Shareholder: Stanislaw Pawelek
Officers: Stanislaw Pawelek [1977] Director [Polish]

**Standard Organics International (UK) Ltd**
Incorporated: 3 November 2006
Net Worth Deficit: £20,348   Total Assets: £57,042
Registered Office: Willows End, Hadleigh Heath, Hadleigh, Ipswich, Suffolk, IP7 5NY
Major Shareholder: Manjit Singh Kailey
Officers: Manjit Singh Kailey, Secretary; Manjit Singh Kailey [1967] Director

**Standford Ltd**
Incorporated: 24 October 2018
Registered Office: 17 Church Road, Waterloo, Liverpool, L22 5NA
Major Shareholder: James Alexander Mitton
Officers: James Alexander Mitton [1985] Director

**Stanex Limited**
Incorporated: 26 April 2006
Net Worth: £896,815   Total Assets: £1,992,370
Registered Office: Room 403, Intershore Suites, Dowgate Hill House, 14-16 Dowgate Hill, London, EC4R 2SU
Officers: Constantinos Koudellaris [1957] Director/Businessman [Cypriot]

**Stanningley Pharma Limited**
Incorporated: 28 June 2010
Net Worth: £178,469   Total Assets: £577,892
Registered Office: Biocity, Pennyfoot Street, Nottingham, NG1 1GF
Major Shareholder: Imran Khan
Officers: Razwana Kausar [1978] Director; Imran Khan [1977] Director/Pharmaceutical Consultant

**Stanton Ocean Services Limited**
Incorporated: 5 June 1882
Registered Office: 74 Victoria Parade, New Brighton, Wirral, Merseyside, CH45 2PH
Shareholders: Simon Richard Harrison; Trevor Paul Harrison
Officers: Trevor Paul Harrison, Secretary; Simon Richard Harrison [1969] Director; Trevor Paul Harrison [1966] Director

**Star Freight Forwarding Limited**
Incorporated: 7 August 2017
Net Worth: £1   Total Assets: £1
Registered Office: 23 Norfolk Road, Margate, Kent, CT9 2HU
Officers: Abrar Mohammed [1971] Director

**Star Pharmaceuticals Limited**
Incorporated: 16 February 2000
Net Worth: £786   Total Assets: £3,741,231
Registered Office: 39a Joel Street, Northwood Hills, Northwood, Middlesex, HA6 1NZ
Major Shareholder: Anuj Somchand Shah
Officers: Anuj Somchand Shah [1966] Director

**Star Powa Limited**
Incorporated: 15 March 2018
Registered Office: Haslers, Old Station Road, Loughton, Essex, IG10 4PL
Shareholders: Jonathan Gallagher; Narinder Singh Bassi
Officers: Narinder Singh Bassi [1970] Director; Jonathan Gallagher [1995] Director

**Stegram Pharmaceuticals Limited**
Incorporated: 20 October 1989
Net Worth: £243,572   Total Assets: £375,203
Registered Office: 72 High Beeches, Banstead, Surrey, SM7 1NW
Officers: Peter William Ellson, Secretary; Peter William Ellson [1935] Director/Accountant; Paul George Margetts [1974] Director/Doctor; Lyn Janet Pugh [1970] Director/Doctor

**Stellar Labs Ltd**
*Incorporated:* 2 January 2019
*Registered Office:* Suite 11, Stellar Labs, 2F Sefton Park Road, Liverpool, L8 0TH
*Shareholders:* Akhira Khan Sharif; Omar Sharif
*Officers:* Akhira Khan Sharif [1981] Director/Pharmacist [Swedish]; Omar Sharif [1977] Director/Marketing Consultant [Swedish]

**Stem Cellx Limited**
*Incorporated:* 7 November 2016
*Net Worth Deficit:* £44  *Total Assets:* £5,305
*Registered Office:* 3 Greystones Rise, Sheffield, S11 7JP
*Shareholders:* Endre Kiss-Toth; Visaron Tech Korlatolt Felelossegu Tarsasag
*Officers:* Paul Cooper [1957] Director/Veterinary Surgeon; Dr Lajos Haracska [1967] Director/Scientist [Hungarian]; Dr Endre Kiss-Toth [1967] Director/University Lecturer

**Stephar (U.K.) Limited**
*Incorporated:* 18 May 1983
*Net Worth Deficit:* £3,548,622  *Total Assets:* £6,978,415
*Registered Office:* Unit 4 Castell Close, Swansea Enterprise Park, Swansea, SA7 9FH
*Parent:* Christopher Racey
*Officers:* Christopher Stephen Racey, Secretary/Director; Christopher Stephen Racey [1958] Managing Director; Jacqueline Mary Racey [1954] Director

**Steripharm (UK) Limited**
*Incorporated:* 23 August 2005
*Net Worth Deficit:* £1,005,575  *Total Assets:* £22,748
*Registered Office:* Unit 14 Kernick Industrial Estate, Kernick Road, Penryn, Cornwall, TR10 9EP
*Shareholders:* Rajalakshmi Jayaprasad; Jayaprasad Kaippallil Raman Pillai
*Officers:* Jayaprasad Kaippallil Raman Pillai, Secretary; Rajalakshmi Jayaprasad [1967] Director [Indian]; Jayaprasad Kaippallil Raman Pillai [1955] Director [Indian]

**Steritech Limited**
*Incorporated:* 30 November 1987  *Employees:* 30
*Net Worth:* £1,043,273  *Total Assets:* £5,168,218
*Registered Office:* Unit 27 The IO Centre, Salbrook Road, Salfords, Redhill, Surrey, RH1 5GJ
*Officers:* Michael John Andrews [1967] Finance Director; Darren Beckett [1973] Director; Darren Lee Mulhall [1975] Managing Director; Gavin Williams [1977] Director

**Steritech UK Limited**
*Incorporated:* 7 May 1999
*Net Worth:* £17,840  *Total Assets:* £24,104
*Registered Office:* Steepleton House, Andoversford, Cheltenham, Glos, GL54 4JL
*Shareholders:* Eileen Teresa Buck; Primesafe Pty Ltd; Robert Stuart Buck
*Officers:* Robert James Kelly, Secretary/Businessman [Irish]; Eileen Teresa Buck [1957] Director/Businesswoman; Robert Stuart Buck [1960] Director/Businessman

**Sterling Bio-Pharma Ltd**
*Incorporated:* 10 September 2015  *Employees:* 1
*Net Worth Deficit:* £6,914  *Total Assets:* £862
*Registered Office:* Solar House, 282 Chase Road, London, N14 6NZ
*Officers:* Hassan Masood [1981] Director/Businessman

**Sterling London Ventures Limited**
*Incorporated:* 2 December 2015  *Employees:* 1
*Net Worth Deficit:* £20,931  *Total Assets:* £9,784
*Registered Office:* 23 The Mount, Wembley, Middlesex, HA9 9EE
*Major Shareholder:* Megha Prachanda Wijayatilake
*Officers:* Megha Prachanda Wijayatilake [1969] Director/Business Executive

**Stiefel Laboratories Limited**
*Incorporated:* 6 May 1982
*Registered Office:* Eurasia Headquarters, Concorde Road, Maidenhead, Berks, SL6 4BY
*Parent:* Stiefel Laboratories (U.K.) Ltd
*Officers:* Dr Sheryl Vikas Surve [1974] Director [Swedish]

**Stiltec Global (UK) Ltd**
*Incorporated:* 17 March 2017
*Net Worth Deficit:* £13,729  *Total Assets:* £7,941
*Registered Office:* 71-75 Shelton Street, Covent Garden, London, WC2H 9JQ
*Officers:* Paris Sophie Mann [1995] Director/Marketer

**Stockman (UK) Ltd**
*Incorporated:* 7 February 2005
*Net Worth:* £2  *Total Assets:* £2,132
*Registered Office:* Suite 211, Cornwall Buildings, 45 Newhall Street, Birmingham, B3 3QR
*Officers:* Androniki Christodoulou [1978] Director [Cypriot]

**Stockport Healthcare Limited**
*Incorporated:* 3 August 2017
*Registered Office:* Unit 18 Neills Road, Bold Industrial Park, Bold, St Helens, Merseyside, WA9 4TU
*Shareholder:* Mahmoud Muhiyye
*Officers:* Khalid Muhiyye [1983] Director; Mahmoud Muhiyye [1984] Director

**Stop Ltd**
*Incorporated:* 3 July 2018
*Registered Office:* 27 Old Gloucester Street, London, WC1N 3AX
*Major Shareholder:* Deram Saied
*Officers:* Dr Deram Saied [1971] Director/Doctor

**Storepharm UK Ltd**
*Incorporated:* 6 March 2017  *Employees:* 1
*Net Worth Deficit:* £4,087  *Total Assets:* £371,903
*Registered Office:* Unit 6 Vickers Close, Preston Farm Industrial Estate, Stockton on Tees, Cleveland, TS18 3TD
*Shareholders:* Mark Ashley Nicholls; Bemal Patel
*Officers:* Madaline Nicholls, Secretary; Mark Ashley Nicholls [1973] Director

**Stragen UK Limited**
*Incorporated:* 23 August 2004  *Employees:* 3
*Net Worth:* £344,460  *Total Assets:* £531,932
*Registered Office:* Springfield House, Springfield Road, Horsham, W Sussex, RH12 2RG
*Parent:* Stragen Investment BV
*Officers:* Leonard Cretney [1955] Managing Director; Jean-Luc Tetard [1944] Director [Swiss]

**Strandland Limited**
Incorporated: 7 November 1984  Employees: 2
Net Worth: £794,400  Total Assets: £799,819
Registered Office: 1st Floor, Cloister House Riverside, New Bailey Street, Manchester, M3 5FS
Shareholders: Joanna Levers; Jonathan Simon Charles Green
Officers: Joanna Levers, Secretary; Jonathan Simon Charles Green [1964] Director; Joanna Levers [1961] Director/School Principal

**Strathclyde Pharmaceuticals Limited**
Incorporated: 23 September 2004  Employees: 144
Net Worth: £15,588,454  Total Assets: £20,101,060
Registered Office: 3 Young Place, East Kilbride, G75 0TD
Parent: Munro Healthcare Group Limited
Officers: John Cochrane [1957] Director; Shirley Agnes Gorrell [1967] Commercial Director

**Stratlab Limited**
Incorporated: 18 January 2002  Employees: 7
Net Worth: £49,899  Total Assets: £317,747
Registered Office: Unit 1 Norwood Road, March, Cambs, PE15 8QD
Shareholders: John Fernall Bateson; Alison Jane Bateson
Officers: Alison Jane Bateson, Secretary/Administration Supervisor; Alison Jane Bateson [1959] Director; John Fernall Bateson [1959] Director

**Streamline Pharmaceuticals Ltd**
Incorporated: 27 March 2018
Registered Office: c/o Charterwells, Old Brewery House, Park Lane, 189 Stanmore Hill, Stanmore, Middlesex, HA7 3HA
Major Shareholder: Nimesh Suraj Dave
Officers: Nikita Nimesh Dave, Secretary; Nikita Nimesh Dave [1986] Director/Chartered Accountant; Nimesh Suraj Dave [1984] Director/Pharmacist

**Strides Pharma Global (UK) Ltd**
Incorporated: 29 July 2015  Employees: 2
Net Worth: £16,483,671  Total Assets: £20,348,244
Registered Office: Unit 4 Metro Centre, Tolpits Lane, Watford, Herts, WD18 9SS
Parent: Strides Arcolab International Limited
Officers: Vikesh Kumar [1984] Director/Service [Indian]; Krishnan Tirucherai Parthasarathy [1971] Director [Indian]; Mohana Kumar Pillai [1956] Director [Indian]

**Style Global Trading FZE Ltd**
Incorporated: 28 November 2018
Registered Office: 71-75 Shelton Street, London, WC2H 9JQ
Major Shareholder: Haytham Abu Goush
Officers: Haytham Abu Goush, Secretary; Haytham Abu Goush [1981] Director/General Manager [Jordanian]

**Suerte Pharma Limited**
Incorporated: 23 May 2016  Employees: 2
Net Worth: £100  Total Assets: £157,405
Registered Office: 5 Northolt Trading Estate, Belvue Road, Northolt, Middlesex, UB5 5QS
Shareholder: Nishali Mehta
Officers: Nishali Mehta, Secretary; Nishali Mehta [1987] Director/Lawyer; Tanisha Mehta [1989] Director/Consultant

**Sufi Enterprise Wholesalers Ltd**
Incorporated: 7 January 2019
Registered Office: 6 Whitehall Road, Uxbridge, Middlesex, UB8 2DF
Major Shareholder: Hassan Mohamoud Sufi
Officers: Hassan Mohamoud Sufi [1994] Director/Teacher

**Summit Pharmaceuticals Europe Limited**
Incorporated: 16 May 2001  Employees: 38
Net Worth: £3,933,118  Total Assets: £15,805,989
Registered Office: Vintners' Place, 68 Upper Thames Street, London, EC4V 3BJ
Shareholders: Sumitomo Corporation Europe Limited; Sumitomo Corporation
Officers: Toshiya Kitamura [1965] Director/Businessman [Japanese]; Yoshiaki Miyamoto [1977] Director/Businessman [Japanese]; Harumasa Morizumi [1967] Director [Japanese]; Takahiro Nishihara [1962] Director [Japanese]; Yoshiki Terawaki [1959] Director/Chief Executive Officer [Japanese]; Takashi Yamana [1963] Director [Japanese]

**Sun Exim Ltd**
Incorporated: 28 May 2013
Previous: Nevis Pharma Ltd
Net Worth: £118,064  Total Assets: £124,091
Registered Office: Conway House, Springfield Road, Hayes, Middlesex, UB4 0LG
Major Shareholder: Chintankumar Chunilal Vaghasiya
Officers: Prakash Shantilal Jyani [1977] Director; Chintankumar Chunilal Vaghasiya [1988] Director/Pharmacy [Indian]

**Sunmed Pharma Ltd**
Incorporated: 19 October 2018
Registered Office: Unit G4, Riverside Industrial Estate, Riverside Way, Dartford, Kent, DA1 5BS
Major Shareholder: Gurdev Singh Ruprai
Officers: Gurdev Singh Ruprai [1960] Director/Pharmacist

**Sunniside Healthcare Limited**
Incorporated: 6 April 2011  Employees: 10
Previous: M.R. Crowder Ltd
Net Worth: £559,768  Total Assets: £696,088
Registered Office: Lakeside House, Kingfisher Way, Stockton on Tees, Cleveland, TS18 3NB
Major Shareholder: David Graham Jarvis
Officers: Marisa Jane Arden [1977] Director/Pharmacist; David Graham Jarvis [1966] Director/Pharmacist; Kevin Alan Simpson [1958] Director/Pharmacist

**Sunovion Pharmaceuticals Europe Ltd.**
Incorporated: 1 May 1997  Employees: 50
Net Worth Deficit: £65,309  Total Assets: £14,098,638
Registered Office: First Floor, Southside, 97-105 Victoria Street, London, SW1E 6QT
Parent: Sumitomo Dainippon Pharma Co., Ltd.
Officers: Gregory M Bokar, Secretary; David Frawley [1968] Director/EVP and Chief Commercial Officer; Nobuhiko Tamura [1956] Director/Chairman and Chief Executive Officer [Japanese]

**Sunrize Trade Limited**
Incorporated: 19 September 2014
Registered Office: 22 Brondesbury Park, London, NW6 7DL
Officers: Lilia Kader [1967] Director

**Sunstik Ltd**
Incorporated: 6 May 2014
Net Worth Deficit: £40,916  Total Assets: £6,904
Registered Office: 9 Thorney Leys Park, Witney, Oxon, OX28 4GE
Shareholders: Fiona Christine Lunn; Paul Boodell
Officers: Paul Boodell [1967] Director

**Sunstore Limited**
Incorporated: 12 March 1998  Employees: 4
Net Worth: £571,361  Total Assets: £819,153
Registered Office: 7 Morgans Business Park, Bettys Lane, Norton Canes, Staffs, WS11 9UU
Shareholders: Garry Alfred Dyer; Stephen John Bramble; Paul Simon Richards
Officers: Paul Simon Richards, Secretary; Stephen John Bramble [1958] Director; Garry Alfred Dyer [1958] Managing Director

**Sup-Up Ltd**
Incorporated: 25 September 2018
Registered Office: 81 Juniper Crescent, London, NW1 8HQ
Major Shareholder: Anis Daou
Officers: Anis Daou [1992] Director/Student

**Suplan Ltd**
Incorporated: 22 June 2018
Registered Office: Station House, Midland Road, Luton, Beds, LU2 0HS
Major Shareholder: Asif Iqbal
Officers: Asif Iqbal [1979] Director/Export Specialist

**Supphero Ltd**
Incorporated: 11 October 2018
Registered Office: Unit 5c Wallyford Industrial Estate, Wallyford, Musselburgh, E Lothian, EH21 8QJ
Major Shareholder: Sean Rollo
Officers: Sean Rollo [1990] Director

**Supplemax Ltd**
Incorporated: 21 June 2018
Registered Office: 5 Windmill Meadow, Norton, Doncaster, S Yorks, DN6 9GG
Major Shareholder: Mark Rusling
Officers: Mark Rusling [1971] Managing Director

**Support To Perform Ltd**
Incorporated: 27 March 2018
Registered Office: Catalyst Inc, The Innovation Centre, Queens Road, Belfast, BT3 9DT
Major Shareholder: Jonathan Robert Bloomfield
Officers: Dr Jonathan Robert Bloomfield [1979] Director/Consultant

**Supra Enterprises Limited**
Incorporated: 24 June 1987  Employees: 6
Net Worth: £3,241,443  Total Assets: £3,588,197
Registered Office: Unit 2 Charnwood Edge Business Park, Syston Road, Cossington, Leics, LE7 4UZ
Major Shareholder: Sudhir Mansukhlal Ruparelia
Officers: Rekha Sudhir Ruparelia [1964] Director; Sudhir Mansukhlal Ruparelia [1961] Director/Pharmacist

**Sure Health & Beauty Limited**
Incorporated: 22 February 2005  Employees: 9
Net Worth: £899,633  Total Assets: £1,598,176
Registered Office: Unit 2 Eastleigh Works, Campbell Road, Eastleigh, Hants, SO50 5AD
Officers: Karen Elizabeth Moore, Secretary; Karen Elizabeth Moore [1970] Director; Andrew David Sault [1962] Director; James Henry Skelton [1960] Director; Peter David Vanstone [1962] Director

**Surgery Supplies (UK) Limited**
Incorporated: 22 March 2002
Registered Office: 12 Lammas Street, Carmarthen, Dyfed, SA31 3AD
Shareholders: Christopher John James; Terry Baugh Griffiths
Officers: Christopher John James, Secretary/Chemist; Terry Baugh Griffiths [1946] Director

**Surgicaide Medical Supplies UK Ltd**
Incorporated: 3 May 2018
Registered Office: Building 3, North London Business Park, Oakleigh Road South, London, N11 1GN
Major Shareholder: Shabbir Bhai Gulam Abbas Sunely
Officers: Shabbir Bhai Gulam Abbas Sunely [1960] Director [Indian]

**Surgical Devices Developers Ltd**
Incorporated: 19 October 2016
Net Worth: £50,184  Total Assets: £945,169
Registered Office: Kemp House, 160 City Road, London, EC1V 2NX
Major Shareholder: Marcelo Mercant Santa Cruz
Officers: Marcelo Mercant Santa Cruz [1976] Director/Businessman [Uruguayan]

**Surgidoc Limited**
Incorporated: 9 November 2007
Net Worth Deficit: £9,563
Registered Office: Kelvin House, Kelvin Way, Crawley, W Sussex, RH10 9WE
Shareholder: Muhammad Imran Ashraf
Officers: Muhammad Imran Ashraf [1974] Director/Certified Chartered Accountant

**Surgihoney Limited**
Incorporated: 17 July 2015
Registered Office: 2 Michaels Court, Hanney Road, Southmoor, Abingdon, Oxon, OX13 5HR
Parent: Matoke Holdings Limited
Officers: Ian David Pearson Jenkins, Secretary; Ian David Pearson Jenkins [1946] Director/Solicitor; Ian Lawrence Staples [1946] Director/Chief Executive

**Surgitrac Instruments UK Limited**
Incorporated: 4 January 1995
Previous: S D Healthcare Limited
Net Worth: £3,472,669  Total Assets: £5,181,813
Registered Office: 10 Wharfside Business Park, Irlam Wharf Road, Irlam, Salford, M44 5PN
Parent: Archrye Limited
Officers: Margaret Anne Lawson, Secretary; Steven Nigel Bourne [1959] Sales Director; Margaret Anne Lawson [1955] Director [Australian]

**Sustainable Ethical Enterprises Limited**
Incorporated: 2 November 2016  Employees: 2
Net Worth Deficit: £302  Total Assets: £287
Registered Office: 3 Warners Mill, Braintree, Essex, CM7 3GB
Shareholders: Tara Chandra; Susan Charlene Allen
Officers: Susan Charlene Allen [1985] Operations Director; Tara Chandra [1987] Managing Director [American]

**Sutherland Health Group Limited**
Incorporated: 11 October 2004
Previous: Sutherland Health Group PLC
Net Worth: £1,391  Total Assets: £4,935
Registered Office: Unit 1 Rivermead, Pipers Way, Thatcham, Berks, RG19 4EP
Officers: Stephen John Coke, Secretary/Chartered Accountant; Stephen John Coke [1961] Director/Chartered Accountant; Sheena Sukumaran [1971] Marketing Director

**SV Syon Med Ltd**
Incorporated: 30 June 2015
Previous: SV Synomed Ltd
Registered Office: Office Gold, Building 3, Chiswick Park, 566 Chiswick High Road, London, W4 5YA
Major Shareholder: Kshitij Singhvi
Officers: Kshitij Singhvi [1977] Director [Indian]

**SW Medical Solutions Limited**
Incorporated: 30 March 2011
Net Worth: £2,211  Total Assets: £9,452
Registered Office: 45 Mill Lane, Newbury, Berks, RG14 5RE
Major Shareholder: Simon Philip Ward
Officers: Simon Philip Ward [1973] Director/Sales Agent

**Swanson Trade Ltd**
Incorporated: 14 November 2014
Registered Office: 3rd Floor, 207 Regent Street, London, W1B 3HH
Major Shareholder: Martin John Wickens
Officers: Martin John Wickens [1958] Director

**Swerve Cycling Limited**
Incorporated: 13 May 2014
Net Worth Deficit: £355  Total Assets: £18,840
Registered Office: Kelso Place, Upper Bristol Road, Bath, BA1 3AU
Major Shareholder: Anjela Theresa Ubogu
Officers: Anjela Theresa Ubogu [1966] Director [Australian]

**Swiftpath Corporation Limited**
Incorporated: 25 October 2001
Net Worth Deficit: £443  Total Assets: £2,704
Registered Office: Regent House, 316 Beulah Hill, London, SE19 3HF
Major Shareholder: Yunus Vakhpiev
Officers: Ivan Antonio Molino Alvarez, Secretary; Manuel Carrera Lopez [1981] Director/Consultant [Panamanian]

**Swingward Limited**
Incorporated: 29 March 1976
Net Worth: £255,889  Total Assets: £2,808,811
Registered Office: Unit 29 Devonshire Road, Worsley, Manchester, M28 3PT
Parent: Medihealth International Limited
Officers: Craig Bernard Fishwick, Secretary; Craig Bernard Fishwick [1974] Director/Accountant

**Swiss Pharma UK Limited**
Incorporated: 13 July 2012
Registered Office: 8 Rowland Avenue, Kenton, Harrow, Middlesex, HA3 9AF
Officers: Anil Mansukhlal Pandya, Secretary; Anil Mansukhlal Pandya [1962] Financial Director

**Swiss-American CDMO International Limited**
Incorporated: 20 June 2016
Registered Office: Suite 414, Arthur House, Arthur Street, Belfast, BT1 4GB
Officers: Richard Cory Johnson, Secretary; Richard Cory Johnson [1981] Director [American]; Philip Joseph O'Neill Jr [1937] Director [American]

**Sword Medical UK Limited**
Incorporated: 21 August 2014  Employees: 4
Net Worth Deficit: £648,831  Total Assets: £181,773
Registered Office: Vienna House, International Square, Birmingham International Park, Solihull, W Midlands, B37 7GN
Major Shareholder: Colm Moynihan
Officers: Colm Moynihan, Secretary; Colm Moynihan [1957] Director [Irish]; Dermot Moynihan [1967] Director [Irish]

**Sylk Limited**
Incorporated: 8 July 1996  Employees: 3
Net Worth: £766,258  Total Assets: £930,472
Registered Office: Wellington House, Aylesbury Road, Princes Risborough, Bucks, HP27 0JP
Major Shareholder: Mark Iain Shelley
Officers: Nicola Gaylor [1974] Director; Mark Iain Shelley [1971] Director

**Symbio Europe Limited**
Incorporated: 15 March 2012
Net Worth Deficit: £240,885  Total Assets: £111,793
Registered Office: Suite 1, GPF Lewis House, Olds Approach, Tolpits Lane, Watford, Herts, WD18 9AB
Major Shareholder: Shamir Pravinchandra Budhdeo
Officers: Shamir Pravinchandra Budhdeo, Secretary; Shamir Pravinchandra Budhdeo [1967] Director; Joshy Mathew [1973] Director

**Symbiosis Biosciences Limited**
Incorporated: 13 December 2018
Registered Office: B307, The Biscuit Factory, 100 Drummond Road, London, SE16 4DG
Shareholder: Liangyin Liu
Officers: Liangyin Liu [1986] Director [Chinese]; Jon James Lundberg [1984] Director/Consultant [American]

**Symmetry Inc Ltd**
Incorporated: 26 January 2017
Registered Office: 20-22 Wenlock Road, London, N1 7GU
Major Shareholder: Edidiong Mathias Essien
Officers: Oguntuase Olugbenga Bankole [1974] Director; Edidiong Mathias Essien [1982] Director [Nigerian]

**Symom Limited**
Incorporated: 18 September 2017
Registered Office: 67 Walton Avenue, Harrow, Middlesex, HA2 8QY
Shareholders: Bhavna Chandarana; Ranjana Nathwani; Unnati Chandarana
Officers: Bhavna Chandarana [1969] Director/Nursery Teacher

**Syner-Medica Limited**
Incorporated: 22 February 2002
Net Worth: £1,558,453  Total Assets: £3,932,237
Registered Office: DS House, 306 High Street, Croydon, Surrey, CR0 1NG
Major Shareholder: Dipak Devji Bhatti
Officers: Pratima Dipak Bhatti, Secretary; Dipak Devji Bhatti [1956] Director; Pratima Dipak Bhatti [1960] Director; Viraj Bhatti [1990] Director

**Synergetic Global Limited**
Incorporated: 5 February 2019
Registered Office: 56 Moat View, Roslin, Midlothian, EH25 9NZ
Major Shareholder: Jaskarn Singh Nottay
Officers: Jaskarn Singh Nottay [1985] Director/Chief Executive

**System Deep Clinic Limited**
Incorporated: 13 December 2016
Registered Office: No 2 The Barns, Vine Cottage, Sarnau, Llanymynech, Powys, SY22 6QR
Major Shareholder: Philip Simon Joseph
Officers: John Arthur Worrall, Secretary; Philip Simon Joseph [1985] Director

**T-In Medical Limited**
*Incorporated:* 20 March 2017
*Registered Office:* 4th Floor, Park Gate, 161-163 Preston Road, Brighton, BN1 6AF
*Shareholders:* David Jonathan Redfern; Joel Didier Claude Vernois; Paul Jonathan Winsor
*Officers:* David Jonathan Redfern [1969] Director/Surgeon; Joel Didier Claude Vernois [1966] Director/Doctor [French]; Paul Jonathan Winsor [1974] Director

**T-Pharma Limited**
*Incorporated:* 4 March 2015  *Employees:* 3
*Net Worth:* £48,817  *Total Assets:* £201,141
*Registered Office:* 101 Walton Road, Stockton Heath, Warrington, Cheshire, WA4 6NR
*Shareholders:* Anthony Robert Mills; Jennifer Mills
*Officers:* Anthony Robert Mills [1958] Director/Medical Supply; Jennifer Mills [1954] Director

**T.K. Impex Limited**
*Incorporated:* 22 March 1982  *Employees:* 5
*Net Worth:* £249,437  *Total Assets:* £607,199
*Registered Office:* 81 Mill Lane, London, NW6 1ND
*Shareholders:* Kamruddin Fidahusein Khaki; Zeenatbanu Khaki
*Officers:* Zeenatbanu Khaki, Secretary; Kamruddin Fidahusein Khaki [1950] Director/Pharmacist

**TA-65 (UK) Wholesale Limited**
*Incorporated:* 24 May 2018
*Registered Office:* Old Rectory, North End Road, Little Yeldham, Halstead, Essex, CO9 4LE
*Major Shareholder:* David Christopher Heather
*Officers:* David Christopher Heather [1962] Director

**Tabtime Limited**
*Incorporated:* 28 August 2001  *Employees:* 4
*Net Worth:* £76,488  *Total Assets:* £93,733
*Registered Office:* Curtis House, 34 Third Avenue, Hove, E Sussex, BN3 2PD
*Major Shareholder:* Aziz Haque Tarafder
*Officers:* Aziz Haque Tarafder [1977] Director

**Tagma Pharma (UK) Ltd**
*Incorporated:* 26 April 2006
*Net Worth:* £2,779  *Total Assets:* £3,276
*Registered Office:* Morgan Reach House, 136 Hagley Road, Birmingham, B16 9NX
*Major Shareholder:* Muhammad Naeem Shami
*Officers:* Muhammad Naeem Shami [1969] Director

**Z Tahir Limited**
*Incorporated:* 18 October 2005
*Net Worth Deficit:* £36,424  *Total Assets:* £171,998
*Registered Office:* 48 Calgary Road, Lammack, Blackburn, Lancs, BB2 7DS
*Major Shareholder:* Zeshan Tahir
*Officers:* Iram Zaheer, Secretary; Zeshan Tahir [1980] Director/Locum Pharmacist

**Taineng Medicine Ltd**
*Incorporated:* 20 March 2018
*Registered Office:* Fifth Floor, 3 Gower Street, London, WC1E 6HA
*Major Shareholder:* Jianxin Tong
*Officers:* Jianxin Tong, Secretary; Jianxin Tong [1966] Director [Chinese]

**Takeda UK Limited**
*Incorporated:* 25 April 1997  *Employees:* 192
*Net Worth:* £33,735,072  *Total Assets:* £91,023,712
*Registered Office:* Building 3, Glory Park Avenue, Wooburn Green, High Wycombe, Bucks, HP10 0DF
*Parent:* Takeda Pharmaceuticals International AG
*Officers:* Jon Neal [1971] Director/General Manager; Andrius Varanavicius [1979] Director/Chief Financial Officer EuCAN [Lithuanian]; William Charles Walker [1953] Director/Business Operations Manager

**Tanberg Limited**
*Incorporated:* 25 August 2006
*Registered Office:* Ground Floor, Solar House, 282 Chase Road, Southgate, London, N14 6NZ
*Major Shareholder:* Rustem Imbragimov
*Officers:* Michalakis Koullouros, Secretary; Vasiliki Argyrou [1959] Director/Businesswoman [Cypriot]

**Tank Puffin (Wholesale) Limited**
*Incorporated:* 28 January 2014
*Previous:* Tank Puffin (Franchising) Limited
*Net Worth:* £43,400  *Total Assets:* £173,913
*Registered Office:* Unit 10 Peartree Business Centre, South Road, Harlow, Essex, CM20 2BD
*Officers:* Avril Clarice Hall [1988] Director; Sophie Louise Searle [1992] Director

**Tanner Pharma UK Limited**
*Incorporated:* 29 April 2015  *Employees:* 14
*Net Worth Deficit:* £1,522,755  *Total Assets:* £400,996
*Registered Office:* 2 Adelaide Street, St Albans, Herts, AL3 5BH
*Major Shareholder:* Raymond Fairbanks Bourne
*Officers:* Raymond Fairbanks Bourne [1971] Director/Executive [American]

**Tannerlac UK Limited**
*Incorporated:* 20 January 2016
*Net Worth Deficit:* £17,459  *Total Assets:* £7,149
*Registered Office:* 2 Adelaide Street, St Albans, Herts, AL3 5BH
*Parent:* Tanner Pharma UK Limited
*Officers:* Raymond Bourne [1971] Director [American]

**Target Healthcare Limited**
*Incorporated:* 4 September 2012  *Employees:* 12
*Net Worth:* £605,041  *Total Assets:* £2,610,823
*Registered Office:* 8 Redwood Crescent, East Kilbride, S Lanarks, G74 5PA
*Major Shareholder:* Lewis Campbell
*Officers:* Lewis Campbell [1993] Director

**Targeter (UK) Limited**
*Incorporated:* 5 October 1950  *Employees:* 5
*Net Worth:* £361,980  *Total Assets:* £872,668
*Registered Office:* Third Floor, 24 Chiswell Street, London, EC1Y 4YX
*Shareholder:* Nabil Idriss
*Officers:* Elton Shane, Secretary; Abdul Rahman Ibrahim Al Ghamdi [1955] Director [Saudi Arabian]; Abdul Mohsen Ibrahim Al Ghamdi [1965] Director [Saudi Arabian]; Nabil Idriss [1946] Director/Businessman [Lebanese]

**Tarus Group Limited**
*Incorporated:* 26 July 1999
*Registered Office:* Chemidex House, Unit 7 Egham Business Village, Crabtree Road, Egham, Surrey, TW20 8RB
*Shareholders:* Navinchandra Jamnadas; Varsha Navinchandra
*Officers:* Dr Nikesh Engineer, Secretary; Nikesh Engineer [1985] Director/Doctor

**Tarus Laboratories Limited**
Incorporated: 15 July 2011
Previous: Tarus Laboratories Limited Limited
Net Worth Deficit: £8,722  Total Assets: £78
Registered Office: 7 Egham Business Village, Crabtree Road, Egham, Surrey, TW20 8RB
Shareholders: Navinchandra Jamnadas; Varsha Navinchandra
Officers: Nikesh Engineer [1985] Director/Doctor


**Tauva Limited**
Incorporated: 11 June 2003
Net Worth: £122,257  Total Assets: £127,218
Registered Office: 54 South Park Road, Ilford, Essex, IG1 1SS
Major Shareholder: Trusha Patel
Officers: Sumitra Patel, Secretary; Trusha Patel [1967] Director/Managing


**TBD Wellness Limited**
Incorporated: 22 November 2018
Registered Office: 82 St John Street, London, EC1M 4JN
Major Shareholder: Adrian Hope
Officers: Clarice Neves Borges [1978] Director; Adrian Hope [1958] Director


**Tearfilm Therapeutics Ltd**
Incorporated: 17 August 2018
Registered Office: c/o Anderson Ross, 35 Beaufort Court, Admirals Way, London, E14 9XL
Shareholders: Max Baumann; Ali Reza Pashazadeh Monadjemi
Officers: Max Baumann [1983] Director/Chief Business Officer [German]; Dr Ali Reza Pashazadeh Monadjemi [1971] Director/Chief Executive Officer


**Tech Innovation Laser Limited**
Incorporated: 19 July 2017
Registered Office: Cary Chambers, 1 Palk Street, Torquay, Devon, TQ2 5EL
Major Shareholder: Frederic Noir
Officers: Elisa Noir, Secretary; Frederic Noir [1970] Director [French]


**Techdow Pharma England Limited**
Incorporated: 6 December 2016  Employees: 3
Net Worth Deficit: £1,074,637  Total Assets: £294,657
Registered Office: Surrey Technology Centre, Surrey Research Park, 40 Occam Road, Guildford, Surrey, GU2 7YG
Major Shareholder: Rafal Piotr Zieba
Officers: Stephen John Higgins [1958] Managing Director; Jianke Li [1962] Director [American]


**Technical & General Limited**
Incorporated: 4 March 1986  Employees: 8
Net Worth: £1,291,885  Total Assets: £1,756,937
Registered Office: 2 Albion Place, London, W6 0QT
Major Shareholder: Ahmad Youssef
Officers: Dr Abir Youssef, Secretary; Dr Ahmad Youssef [1946] Director/Engineer


**Technoglobal Ltd**
Incorporated: 29 April 2015
Registered Office: 141 Praed Street, London, W2 1RL
Shareholders: Vahid Abbassioun; Leyla Sedghi
Officers: Vahid Abbassioun [1971] Director [Iranian]; Mehrdad Daftari [1947] Director; Leyla Sedghi [1978] Director [Iranian]


**Ted Medical Ltd**
Incorporated: 20 October 2017
Net Worth: £3,951  Total Assets: £61,331
Registered Office: 9 Washburn Avenue, Ellesmere Port, Cheshire, CH65 8AN
Major Shareholder: Dilek Dag Obruklu
Officers: Dilek Dag Obruklu [1978] Director [Turkish]


**Telephone House Limited**
Incorporated: 2 August 2012  Employees: 8
Net Worth: £218,178  Total Assets: £1,144,091
Registered Office: c/o Telephone House, Pharmacy, 71 High Street, Southampton, SO14 2NW
Shareholders: Anil Nandlal Sheth; Himatbala Sheth
Officers: Anil Nandlal Sheth [1950] Director; Himatbala Sheth [1948] Director


**Teoxane UK Limited**
Incorporated: 27 October 2005  Employees: 19
Previous: Lifestyle Aesthetics Limited
Net Worth: £1,966,430  Total Assets: £3,792,919
Registered Office: 54-55 Shrivenham Hundred Business Park, Majors Road, Watchfield, Swindon, Wilts, SN6 8TY
Parent: Teoxane SA
Officers: Sandra Fishlock [1967] Director/Product Specialist


**Testerworld Limited**
Incorporated: 10 April 1986  Employees: 576
Net Worth: £21,248,000  Total Assets: £75,448,000
Registered Office: 7 Regents Drive, Prudhoe, Northumberland, NE42 6PX
Parent: Calmband Limited
Officers: Mark Gulliford [1969] Director; David Horry [1964] Director/Chairman; Leslie King [1958] Director/Sales Manager; Haydn Peter Smith [1966] Group IT Director; Derek Andrew Wilson [1964] Director/Chartered Accountant


**Tetra Hydro Cannabinoid Oils Global Ltd**
Incorporated: 17 October 2018
Registered Office: 66 Hindes Road, Harrow, Middlesex, HA1 1SL
Major Shareholder: Brian Francis McKay
Officers: Brian Francis McKay [1974] Director/Artist


**TFS Med UK Limited**
Incorporated: 18 January 2010  Employees: 2
Net Worth: £397  Total Assets: £35,945
Registered Office: 4 Ladywood Grange, Oakwood, Leeds, LS8 2LU
Shareholders: Gurpreet Singh Bhamra; Sarah Louise Bhamra
Officers: Sarah Louise Bhamra, Secretary; Gurpreet Singh Bhamra [1979] Director/IT Test Manager


**THD (UK) Limited**
Incorporated: 9 April 2008  Employees: 7
Net Worth Deficit: £1,539,227  Total Assets: £1,424,958
Registered Office: Unit 3 Great Western Business Park, McKenzie Way, Worcester, WR4 9PT
Parent: THD SpA
Officers: Matthew Brian Morris, Secretary; Filippo Bastia [1968] Director [Italian]; Matthew Brian Morris [1955] Director; Giuliano Spaggiari [1957] Director [Italian]

**Thea Pharmaceuticals Limited**
*Incorporated:* 15 February 2008 *Employees:* 50
*Previous:* Spectrum Thea Pharmaceuticals Limited
*Net Worth:* £2,334,542 *Total Assets:* £8,378,239
*Registered Office:* IC5 Building, Innovation Way, Keele, Newcastle-under-Lyme, Staffs, ST5 5NT
*Parent:* Laboratoires Thea SAS
*Officers:* Christopher Ainley, Secretary; Henri Chibret [1940] Director [French]; Jean-Frederic Chibret [1975] Director [French]; David Ponchon [1971] Director [French]; Philip Lewis Williams [1957] Commercial Director

**Theramex HQ UK Limited**
*Incorporated:* 4 September 2017
*Registered Office:* Sloane Square House, 1 Holbein Place, Belgravia, London, SW1W 8NS
*Parent:* IWH UK Midco Limited
*Officers:* Ciaran Joseph Barr [1964] Director [Irish]; Matthew Frankel [1968] Director/Solicitor; Anish Kirit Mehta [1973] Director [American]

**Thexo Pharma Limited**
*Incorporated:* 20 June 2017
*Registered Office:* Zaj Associates, 41a Mill Lane, West Hampstead, London, NW6 1NB
*Major Shareholder:* Ashrf Elhoush
*Officers:* Ashrf Elhoush [1973] Director/Trade [Libyan]

**Third Hand Healthcare Ltd**
*Incorporated:* 6 August 2014
*Net Worth Deficit:* £1,574 *Total Assets:* £11,671
*Registered Office:* 20-22 Wenlock Road, London, N1 7GU
*Major Shareholder:* Rodgers Phiri
*Officers:* Rodgers Phiri [1969] Director

**Thlala Kolo (UK) Ltd**
*Incorporated:* 1 March 2012
*Registered Office:* 4 Meadow Court, 1 Ivy Street, London, N1 5HR
*Major Shareholder:* Thlala Kolo
*Officers:* Thlala Kolo [1968] Director/Trading

**ThriveExtreme Health Limited**
*Incorporated:* 20 March 2015
*Net Worth Deficit:* £5,280 *Total Assets:* £517
*Registered Office:* Office 12, York Eco Business Centre, Amy Johnson Way, York, YO30 4AG
*Major Shareholder:* Robert Taylor Yates
*Officers:* Robert Taylor Yates [1976] Director

**THS Solutions Limited**
*Incorporated:* 27 July 2018
*Registered Office:* 22 Lindsay Court, Sherwood Park Road, Sutton, Surrey, SM1 2SN
*Major Shareholder:* Mustafa Ozcan
*Officers:* Mustafa Ozcan [1966] Director/Business Manager [Turkish]

**Thurgab Medicals Ltd**
*Incorporated:* 18 January 2011
*Registered Office:* 213 Eversholt Street, London, NW1 1DE
*Shareholder:* Henry Chukwudi Osadebe
*Officers:* Henry Chukwudi Osadebe, Secretary; Anita Ndidi-Amaka Okonkwo [1991] Director [Nigerian]; Arthur Nwabunike Okonkwo [1952] Director [Nigerian]; Hellen Nkiru Okonkwo [1966] Director [Nigerian]; Henry Chukwudi Osadebe [1971] Director [Nigerian]

**Tia Marie Ltd**
*Incorporated:* 11 December 2017
*Registered Office:* Gibson House, 800 High Road Tottenham, London, N17 0DH
*Officers:* Philip George, Secretary; Philip George [1985] Director/Consultant

**Tiamat Agriculture Ltd**
*Incorporated:* 16 January 2019
*Registered Office:* Ibex House, 61 Baker Street, Weybridge, Surrey, KT13 8AH
*Officers:* Charles Waite Morgan [1959] Director/Entrepreneur; Melissa Josephine Sturgess [1966] Director/Entrepreneur

**Tillomed Laboratories Limited**
*Incorporated:* 28 September 1990 *Employees:* 37
*Net Worth:* £8,127,429 *Total Assets:* £17,229,562
*Registered Office:* 220 Butterfield, Great Marlings, Luton, Beds, LU2 8DL
*Parent:* Emcure Pharma UK Ltd
*Officers:* Susan Gaynor Hide, Secretary; Zarir Jal Cama [1947] Director; Vineet Kumar Dixit [1979] Director/Accountant [Indian]; Samit Satish Mehta [1980] Director [Indian]; Tajuddin Shaikh [1974] Director/Accountant [Indian]; Ajit Chand Srimal [1958] Director/Chief Executive

**Timeocean Ltd**
*Incorporated:* 17 January 2017
*Net Worth Deficit:* £13,450 *Total Assets:* £707,131
*Registered Office:* 235 Knights Hill, West Norwood, London, SE27 0QT
*Major Shareholder:* Christopher Ekenemchukwu Arafiena
*Officers:* Austin Arafiena, Secretary; Christopher Arafiena, Secretary; Christopher Ekenemchukwu Arafiena [1981] Director/Pharmacist

**Timpext (Trading-Import-Export) Ltd**
*Incorporated:* 19 June 2018
*Registered Office:* 16 Wyatt Road, Oxford, OX2 7HZ
*Major Shareholder:* Kubu Mounguengui Basanti
*Officers:* Prince Ronald Basanti, Secretary; Christ Maryse Manomba [1986] Director/Secretary [Congolese]

**Timstar Laboratory Suppliers Limited**
*Incorporated:* 24 February 1988 *Employees:* 44
*Net Worth:* £1,512,000 *Total Assets:* £2,233,000
*Registered Office:* Phoenix House, Stafford Drive, Battlefield Enterprise Park, Shrewsbury, Salop, SY1 3FE
*Parent:* Wall Family Europe Limited
*Officers:* Muhammed Chaudry [1974] Director/Executive [American]; Lori Jo Cross [1960] Director [American]; Paul Michael Finnie [1961] UK Managing Director; James Victor James [1960] Director [American]; Louise Mary Claire MacDonald [1955] Director [American]; Jude David Rake [1958] Director [American]; Daniel Rashke [1964] Director/Owner-Operator [American]; Anne Marie Wall [1955] Director [American]; Brendan Wall [1961] Director/Owner-Operator [American]; Kevin Joseph Wall [1959] Director [American]

**Titan Med Limited**
*Incorporated:* 13 April 2016
*Net Worth:* £1,712 *Total Assets:* £68,571
*Registered Office:* Unit 8 Soverign Business Park, Barnsley Road, Shepley, Huddersfield, W Yorks, HD8 8FW
*Major Shareholder:* Nicholas Andrew Bone
*Officers:* Nicholas Andrew Bone [1974] Director

**TMZ Naturals Limited**
*Incorporated:* 21 September 2018
*Registered Office:* 565-567 Cheetham Hill Road, Manchester, M8 9JE
*Major Shareholder:* Waqar Munir Mohammad
*Officers:* Waqar Munir Mohammad [1973] Director [Italian]

**TNF (UK) Ltd**
*Incorporated:* 24 July 2012
*Net Worth:* £95,649  *Total Assets:* £139,927
*Registered Office:* 60 Wensleydale Road, Hampton, Surrey, TW12 2LX
*Major Shareholder:* Tasleem Abdulla
*Officers:* Jamila Dhala [1961] Director/Pharmacist

**Toiletry Sales Limited**
*Incorporated:* 4 May 1984  *Employees:* 63
*Net Worth:* £2,781,712  *Total Assets:* £12,016,796
*Registered Office:* Crigglestone Industrial Estate, High Street, Crigglestone, W Yorks, WF4 3HT
*Officers:* David James Milnes, Secretary; David Lyndon Barraclough [1950] Director; Geoff Carroll [1967] Sales Director; Christopher Stuart Patterson [1971] Director/Chief Executive; Keith Randall [1960] Technical Director; Ian Simons [1965] Operations Director; Richard John Walker [1961] Director

**Topcell Pharma Limited**
*Incorporated:* 26 October 2017
*Registered Office:* 23 Cottingham Way, Thrapston, Kettering, Northants, NN14 4PL
*Shareholder:* Charles Phizacklea
*Officers:* Joanne Phizacklea, Secretary; Charles Phizacklea [1967] Director

**Topnot Ltd**
*Incorporated:* 9 July 2018
*Registered Office:* 3 Ambrose Avenue, London, NW11 9AP
*Officers:* Sylvie Hoffman [1995] Director

**Tor Generics Limited**
*Incorporated:* 2 May 2002  *Employees:* 4
*Net Worth:* £1,826,859  *Total Assets:* £1,889,992
*Registered Office:* The Tudor House, Northgate, Northwood, Middlesex, HA6 2TH
*Major Shareholder:* Alison Stevenson
*Officers:* Alison Stevenson [1963] Director

**Torrent Pharma (UK) Ltd**
*Incorporated:* 11 May 2010  *Employees:* 16
*Net Worth Deficit:* £3,950,688  *Total Assets:* £12,814,323
*Registered Office:* 3rd Floor, 4 Gatwick Road, Crawley, W Sussex, RH10 9BG
*Officers:* Amul Kamal Kumar Agrawal [1977] Service Director [German]; Jamie Lee Durbidge [1978] Director; Sanjay Gupta [1965] Service Director [Indian]; Sudhir Menon [1972] Service Director [Indian]; Kaushal Singh Solanki [1967] Director [Indian]

**Total Body Care Limited**
*Incorporated:* 22 February 1999
*Registered Office:* Handel House, 95 High Street, Edgware, Middlesex, HA8 7DB
*Officers:* Sonia Walia, Secretary/Housewife; Vijay Kant Walia [1951] Director/Pharmacist

**Total Medcare Limited**
*Incorporated:* 1 May 2009  *Employees:* 23
*Net Worth:* £135,808  *Total Assets:* £1,265,759
*Registered Office:* Suite 213, 2nd Floor, Signal House, Lyon Road, Harrow, Middlesex, HA1 2AQ
*Parent:* Total Medcare UK Ltd
*Officers:* Phalvinder Singh Dhanjal [1956] Director/Pharmacist; Gurvinder Singh Sabharwal [1982] Director/Pharmacist

**Totally Pharmacy Ltd**
*Incorporated:* 24 February 2009  *Employees:* 9
*Net Worth:* £350,169  *Total Assets:* £627,885
*Registered Office:* Congress House, 14 Lyon Road, Harrow, Middlesex, HA1 2EN
*Shareholders:* Kamaljeet Singh Saundh; Rajpal Kaur Saundh
*Officers:* Kamaljeet Singh Saundh [1978] Director/Pharmacist; Rajpal Kaur Saundh [1977] Director/Pharmacist

**Tour N' Cure International Ltd.**
*Incorporated:* 10 January 2019
*Registered Office:* Suite 1, 3rd Floor, 11-12 St James's Square, London, SW1Y 4LB
*Major Shareholder:* Sherine Hassan Abbas Helmy
*Officers:* Athina Sideri, Secretary; Dr Sherine Hassan Abbas Helmy [1960] Director [Egyptian]; Athina Sideri [1973] Director [Greek]

**TPC Pharma Limited**
*Incorporated:* 19 June 2006
*Net Worth:* £409  *Total Assets:* £7,942
*Registered Office:* 3 Farrier Crescent, Chapelton, Strathaven, S Lanarks, ML10 6SR
*Shareholder:* Michael Cooper
*Officers:* Michael Thomas Cooper, Secretary; Michael Thomas Cooper [1956] Director; Nicholas Carel Cooper [1980] Director

**Tradebuffalo Ltd**
*Incorporated:* 3 February 2017
*Registered Office:* 47 Maxy House Road, Cottam, Preston, Lancs, PR4 0DR
*Major Shareholder:* Sufal Thakuri
*Officers:* Sufal Thakuri [1991] Director/Engineer

**Tradewings Worldwide Ltd**
*Incorporated:* 18 June 2008  *Employees:* 2
*Net Worth:* £229,756  *Total Assets:* £944,749
*Registered Office:* 506 Kingsbury Road, London, NW9 9HE
*Shareholders:* Globe International Limited; Aspire Trade Worldwide Limited
*Officers:* Nitinkumar Ramanlal Patel [1967] Director; Raxit Kirit Kumar Shah [1976] Director [Indian]

**Trafalgar Pharma Ltd**
*Incorporated:* 19 January 2017
*Net Worth Deficit:* £20,685  *Total Assets:* £17,242
*Registered Office:* Concorde House, Kirmington Business Centre, Limber Road, Kirmington, N Lincs, DN39 6YP
*Shareholders:* Weeliat Chong; Colin Dyer
*Officers:* Melinda Li Yen Chong [1975] Director; Dr Weeliat Chong [1975] Director/Chairman and Consultant Pharmacist; Colin Dyer [1965] Managing Director; Hui Dyer [1975] Director

**Trans Swiss Ltd**
*Incorporated:* 3 July 2015
*Net Worth:* £8,001  *Total Assets:* £8,001
*Registered Office:* 27 Old Gloucester Street, London, WC1N 3AX
*Major Shareholder:* Joginder Kaur
*Officers:* Joginder Kaur [1953] Director [Indian]

## TRB Chemedica (UK) Limited
*Incorporated:* 23 November 2001  *Employees:* 10
*Net Worth:* £739,099  *Total Assets:* £1,398,420
*Registered Office:* 9 Evolution, Hooters Hall Road, Lymedale Business Park, Newcastle, Staffs, ST5 9QF
*Major Shareholder:* Guido Dinapoli
*Officers:* Andrew John Vickerman, Secretary; Isaac Abad [1968] Director [Swiss]; Desmond Alexander Justin Flanagan [1959] Managing Director; Janet LEA [1968] Director

## Treas Biotechnology UK Ltd
*Incorporated:* 16 September 2016
*Registered Office:* International House, 24 Holborn Viaduct, London, EC1A 2BN
*Major Shareholder:* Dong Zhou
*Officers:* Dong Zhou [1975] Director [Chinese]

## Treatlines Limited
*Incorporated:* 28 September 2018
*Registered Office:* Flat 9, 3 Coltswood Court, Pickard Close, London, N14 6JE
*Major Shareholder:* Dilar Sahin
*Officers:* Dilar Sahin [1980] Director/Manager [Turkish]

## Treforest Pharmacy Limited
*Incorporated:* 26 August 2009  *Employees:* 6
*Net Worth:* £407,703  *Total Assets:* £727,592
*Registered Office:* Celtic House, Caxton Place, Pentwyn, Cardiff, CF23 8HA
*Parent:* Watts Reed Limited
*Officers:* Justin James Reed [1970] Director/Pharmacist; Victoria Jane Reed [1976] Director/Pharmacist; Niki Jay Watts [1979] Director/Pharmacist; Rebecca Tammy Suzanne Watts [1976] Director

## Trent Dent Products Limited
*Incorporated:* 26 January 2010  *Employees:* 2
*Net Worth:* £128,751  *Total Assets:* £658,927
*Registered Office:* 12 Woodford House, 4 Thurstan Street, Chelsea Creek, London, SW6 2GB
*Major Shareholder:* Kambiz Rahnama
*Officers:* Saloomeh Filsouf [1982] Director/Manager [Iranian]; Kambiz Rahnama [1974] Director/Businessman [Iranian]

## Triaton Ltd
*Incorporated:* 31 October 2018
*Registered Office:* Office 50044, 5 Percy Street, Fitzrovia, London, W1T 1DG
*Major Shareholder:* Dmitry Veligura
*Officers:* Dmitry Veligura [1968] Director [Russian]

## Trical Pharm Ltd
*Incorporated:* 4 July 2016
*Net Worth:* £210  *Total Assets:* £29,592
*Registered Office:* 315 Dalgin Place, Campbell Park, Milton Keynes, Bucks, MK9 4AS
*Major Shareholder:* Neha Pabari
*Officers:* Neha Pabari [1985] Director/Pharmacist

## Tricodent Limited
*Incorporated:* 3 December 1982  *Employees:* 2
*Net Worth:* £49,249  *Total Assets:* £486,320
*Registered Office:* 8a Teknol House, Victoria Road, Burgess Hill, W Sussex, RH15 9LH
*Shareholders:* Raymond Leslie Noakes; Christine Louise Noakes
*Officers:* Christine Louise Noakes, Secretary; Raymond Leslie Noakes [1952] Director

## Trilogy Medical Systems Limited
*Incorporated:* 20 October 2016
*Net Worth:* £10  *Total Assets:* £10
*Registered Office:* 14d Adelaide Park, Belfast, BT9 6FX
*Shareholders:* Prodigy Healthcare Limited; Trilogy Systems Limited
*Officers:* Michael Roumi [1954] Director [Canadian]; Frederick John Topping [1970] Director/Sales Manager

## Trimark International Limited
*Incorporated:* 24 March 1986
*Registered Office:* Suite 21, CP House, Otterspool Way, Watford, Herts, WD25 8HP
*Officers:* Norman Arnold Davis, Secretary; Mark Leonard Davis [1964] Managing Director

## Trinity Impex Limited
*Incorporated:* 19 September 2013
*Net Worth:* £21,908  *Total Assets:* £21,908
*Registered Office:* 13 Yew Tree Drive, Guildford, Surrey, GU1 1PD
*Major Shareholder:* Shajeel Saleem
*Officers:* Shajeel Saleem [1983] Director

## Trinity VN Limited
*Incorporated:* 28 January 2019
*Registered Office:* Nabwood Farm, Offerton, Stockport, Cheshire, SK2 5HG
*Major Shareholder:* Christopher Stephen Jubb
*Officers:* Christopher Stephen Jubb [1951] Director

## Trion Pharma Limited
*Incorporated:* 4 November 2014
*Net Worth:* £27,167  *Total Assets:* £199,601
*Registered Office:* Desai & Co Accountants, Desai House, 9-13 Holbrook Lane, Coventry, Warwicks, CV6 4AD
*Officers:* Vipulkumar Patel [1979] Director

## Trishool Pharma Ltd
*Incorporated:* 26 May 2018
*Registered Office:* Conway House, Springfield Road, Hayes, Middlesex, UB4 0LG
*Major Shareholder:* Amitkumar Kalubhai Avaiya
*Officers:* Amitkumar Kalubhai Avaiya [1986] Director [Indian]; Pankitkumar Barot [1987] Director [Indian]

## Trotwood Pharma Limited
*Incorporated:* 6 November 2012
*Net Worth:* £1,391,897  *Total Assets:* £1,855,266
*Registered Office:* Bampton Road, Harold Hill, Romford, Essex, RM3 8UG
*Parent:* Ethypharm Holdings UK Ltd
*Officers:* Roseline Georgette Joannesse [1959] Director/Vice President Legal Affairs [French]; Jean-Hugues Louis Marie Lecat [1956] Director [French]; Philip Edward Parry [1965] Director/Quality Assurance Professional

## TRT Global Ltd
*Incorporated:* 3 March 2016
*Registered Office:* 30 Carlton Road, Manchester, M16 8LN
*Major Shareholder:* Tarek Radwan Taher
*Officers:* Tarek Radwan Taher [1962] Director/Wholesales Manager [Libyan]

## Truscreen Limited
*Incorporated:* 11 July 2013
*Net Worth Deficit:* £6,533  *Total Assets:* £10,702
*Registered Office:* 1 Adam Street, London, WC2N 6LE
*Officers:* Martin James Albert Dillon [1961] Director/Chief Executive [Australian]; Christopher Lawrence Horn [1949] Director/Chartered Accountant [Australian]

**Trutek Europe Ltd**
*Incorporated:* 18 December 2009
*Net Worth Deficit:* £1,042,166  *Total Assets:* £52,304
*Registered Office:* 326 Church Road, Northolt, Middlesex, UB5 5AR
*Officers:* Ashok Wahi, Secretary; Hakimddin Saifuddin Adenwalla [1961] Director; Ashok Wahi [1950] Director/Businessman [American]

**TSI Health Sciences (Europe) Limited**
*Incorporated:* 14 June 2005  *Employees:* 3
*Net Worth:* £299,090  *Total Assets:* £3,352,161
*Registered Office:* Warth Business Centre, Warth Road, Bury, Lancs, BL9 9TB
*Parent:* TSI Group Ltd
*Officers:* Adrian Stewart Lindridge [1963] Director; Jingshi Joe Zhou [1962] Director/Chief Executive Officer [American]

**TTC Medical GTS Limited**
*Incorporated:* 3 April 2017
*Net Worth:* £5,279  *Total Assets:* £7,237
*Registered Office:* 15-16 Waverley Industrial Units, Waverley Street, Bathgate, W Lothian, EH48 4HY
*Parent:* Semtrad Limited
*Officers:* Steven Murray, Secretary; Steven Edward Murray [1969] Director

**TTO Ventures Ltd.**
*Incorporated:* 13 May 2013
*Net Worth:* £44  *Total Assets:* £273
*Registered Office:* 20 Sexton Road, Tilbury, Essex, RM18 7BA
*Major Shareholder:* Titus Olatunji Osunro
*Officers:* Titus Olatunji Osunro [1962] Director/Business Administrator/Registered Mental Nurse

**TTops Healthcare Limited**
*Incorporated:* 7 April 2011
*Registered Office:* 3 Uplands, Beckenham, Kent, BR3 3NB
*Major Shareholder:* Patricia Ojo
*Officers:* Patricia Asiah Ojo [1970] Director/Pharmacist

**TTS Pharma Limited**
*Incorporated:* 15 October 2012
*Net Worth:* £190,215  *Total Assets:* £1,032,797
*Registered Office:* Liverpool Science Park, 131 Mount Pleasant, Liverpool, L3 5TF
*Officers:* Mark Tucker, Secretary; Samuel Redcliffe Sneddon [1944] Director; Mark Rupert Tucker [1965] Director

**Tuba Ltd**
*Incorporated:* 4 May 2018
*Registered Office:* Healys LLP, Atrium Court, 15-17 Jockey's Fields, London, WC1R 4BW
*Major Shareholder:* Mona Elsayed Elbadawy Mohamed Shehata
*Officers:* Mona Elsayed Elbadawy Mohamed Shehata [1981] Director [Egyptian]

**Tudor Pharma Ltd**
*Incorporated:* 10 April 2018
*Registered Office:* 20-22 Wenlock Road, London, N1 7GU
*Major Shareholder:* Alan Kwok Wing Chung
*Officers:* Alan Kwok Wing Chung [1974] Director

**The Tulip Cup Limited**
*Incorporated:* 13 March 2018
*Registered Office:* Kemp House, 160 City Road, London, EC1V 2NX
*Major Shareholder:* Shaun Bennett-Roberts
*Officers:* Shaun Bennett - Roberts, Secretary; Shaun Bennett - Roberts [1980] Director

**Tuluh Solutions Ltd**
*Incorporated:* 16 January 2018
*Registered Office:* 35 Sunny Bank, Sheffield, S10 2DF
*Shareholders:* Farhan Ali Mahamud Jibril; Said Hussein Mohamoud
*Officers:* Farhan Ali Mahamud Jibril [1989] Director/Management Accountant

**Turtle Rouge Ltd**
*Incorporated:* 16 July 2003  *Employees:* 1
*Previous:* Tortue Rouge Limited
*Net Worth Deficit:* £288,309  *Total Assets:* £3,604
*Registered Office:* Clint Mill, Cornmarket, Penrith, Cumbria, CA11 7HW
*Major Shareholder:* Petre Sefton
*Officers:* Alan McViety, Secretary; Petre Sefton [1955] Director/Agriculture

**Twinklers Limited**
*Incorporated:* 23 February 1996  *Employees:* 6
*Net Worth:* £905,143  *Total Assets:* £1,128,086
*Registered Office:* Unit 4, 165 Granville Road, London, NW2 2AZ
*Major Shareholder:* Jeremy Ian Metter
*Officers:* Harjeet Singhrai, Secretary; Jeremy Ian Metter [1959] Director

**George Twist (Wholesale) Limited**
*Incorporated:* 3 April 1974  *Employees:* 22
*Net Worth:* £895,035  *Total Assets:* £1,770,391
*Registered Office:* Leopold Street, Lamberhead Industrial Estate, Pemberton, Wigan, Lancs, WN5 8DH
*Shareholders:* George Twist; Jonathan George Twist
*Officers:* George Twist, Secretary; George Twist [1947] Director/Manager - Wholesalers; Jonathan George Twist [1974] Director

**Tynatex Limited**
*Incorporated:* 13 August 2012
*Registered Office:* 25 Duxbury Road, Leicester, LE5 3LR
*Major Shareholder:* Rayyaz Hassim
*Officers:* Rayyaz Hassim [1978] Director

**Tytek UK Medical Co Ltd**
*Incorporated:* 22 February 2019
*Registered Office:* Units PD 011-012, The Science Centre, Glaisher Drive, Wolverhampton, W Midlands, WV10 9RU
*Major Shareholder:* Christopher Charles Tyler
*Officers:* Matthew John Eccles [1969] Director; Christopher Charles Tyler [1950] Director; James Tyler [1984] Director [American]

**U A Ali Ltd**
*Incorporated:* 24 September 2018
*Registered Office:* 2 Branklyn Place, Glasgow, G13 1GH
*Major Shareholder:* Ubayd Ali
*Officers:* Ubayd Ali [1996] Director/Chemist

**U L Medicines Limited**
*Incorporated:* 21 February 2007  *Employees:* 23
*Net Worth:* £9,471,765  *Total Assets:* £10,884,467
*Registered Office:* Quantum House, Hobson Industrial Estate, Burnopfield, Co Durham, NE16 6EA
*Officers:* Amanda Miller, Secretary; Graeme Petrie [1973] Managing Director Interim; David Alan Sanson [1959] Quality Director; Michael James Tagg [1982] Finance Director

**UK Beauty Cosmetics International Group Ltd**
Incorporated: 26 September 2017
Registered Office: Unit G25, Waterfront Studios, 1 Dock Road, London, E16 1AH
Major Shareholder: Weihong Liu
Officers: Weihong Liu [1974] Director [Chinese]

**UK Biopharma Ltd**
Incorporated: 18 July 2012
Net Worth Deficit: £25,005   Total Assets: £10,316
Registered Office: 22 Worcester Street, Wolverhampton, W Midlands, WV2 4LD
Major Shareholder: Gayane Chobanyan
Officers: Dr Gayane Chobanyan [1965] Director/Doctor

**UK Branded Medicines Ltd**
Incorporated: 19 November 2015   Employees: 2
Net Worth Deficit: £532,964   Total Assets: £107,808
Registered Office: 10 Philpot Lane, London, EC3M 8AA
Parent: Fomento de Gestion Farmaceutica SL
Officers: Francisco Lopez Garcia [1964] Director/General Manager [Spanish]

**UK Eagle Ltd**
Incorporated: 28 January 2016
Net Worth: £204,612   Total Assets: £208,555
Registered Office: 9 Mauldeth Road, Manchester, M20 4NE
Major Shareholder: Mohammed Shaban Mohammed
Officers: Mohammed Shaban Mohammed [1969] Director [Iraqi]

**UK Heluns Industry Co., Limited**
Incorporated: 29 April 2014
Registered Office: Unit G25, Waterfront Studios, 1 Dock Road, London, E16 1AH
Major Shareholder: Fangyu Cao
Officers: Fangyu Cao [1976] Director [Chinese]

**UK Lab Supplies Ltd**
Incorporated: 29 January 2018
Registered Office: 20-22 Wenlock Road, London, N1 7GU
Major Shareholder: Kiran Reddy Kadari
Officers: Kiran Reddy Kadari [1981] Director

**UK Lemenic International Medical Group Limited**
Incorporated: 1 August 2018
Registered Office: Suite 1, 3rd Floor, 11-12 St James's Square, London, SW1Y 4LB
Major Shareholder: Lei Zhang
Officers: Lei Zhang [1986] Director [Chinese]

**UK Lites Ltd**
Incorporated: 8 May 2014
Net Worth: £23,689   Total Assets: £69,561
Registered Office: Suite 2, First Floor, Ellerslie House, Ellerslie Court, Edgerton, Huddersfield, W Yorks, HD2 2AG
Major Shareholder: Mohammed Abid Ghaffar
Officers: Mohammed Abid Ghaffar [1982] Director

**UK Medical Centre Ltd**
Incorporated: 25 January 2006
Net Worth Deficit: £46,443   Total Assets: £2,904
Registered Office: 2 Rippingham Road, Manchester, M20 3EX
Major Shareholder: Ibraheem Abdulazize Al Bajari
Officers: Ibraheem Abdulazize Al Bajari [1958] Director/Businessman

**UK Pharma Direct Limited**
Incorporated: 23 November 2018
Registered Office: Westgate Park, Unit 5-7 Tintagel Way, Aldridge, Walsall, W Midlands, WS9 8ER
Shareholders: Dai Fuge; CST Holdings (UK) Limited
Officers: Alexander Clarke [1991] Director; Carl Falzon [1977] Commercial Director; Dai Fuge [1985] Director/Educationalist; Daniel Mark O'Connor [1981] Director

**UK Pharma Impex Limited**
Incorporated: 28 March 2013   Employees: 5
Net Worth: £123,748   Total Assets: £19,698,228
Registered Office: Office Suite 131, Hexagon Tower, Crumpsall Vale, Manchester, M9 8GQ
Major Shareholder: Michael Thomas Gordon
Officers: Mark Vivian Law [1965] Director/Accountant

**UK Pharmacies Ltd**
Incorporated: 10 April 2017
Net Worth: £100   Total Assets: £100
Registered Office: 27 Old Gloucester Street, London, WC1N 3AX
Shareholders: Martin James McGowan; Nicola Cardozo
Officers: Nicola Cardozo [1982] Director; Martin James McGowan [1980] Director

**UK Vimin Industry Co., Limited**
Incorporated: 4 April 2014
Registered Office: Unit G25, Waterfront Studios, 1 Dock Road, London, E16 1AH
Major Shareholder: Min Liu
Officers: Min Liu [1981] Director [Chinese]

**Ukcann Ltd**
Incorporated: 18 January 2019
Registered Office: 80 Hollyfield Road, Sutton Coldfield, W Midlands, B75 7SH
Parent: Cannvalate Pty Ltd
Officers: Darryl Davies [1985] Director

**Ultimate Health Products Limited**
Incorporated: 6 September 1995   Employees: 1
Net Worth Deficit: £86,829   Total Assets: £1,077
Registered Office: Accountancy House, 90 Walworth Road, London, SE1 6SW
Major Shareholder: Armand David Israel
Officers: Armand David Israel, Secretary; Armand David Israel [1971] Director

**Ultrascan Solutions Ltd**
Incorporated: 29 January 2018
Registered Office: 1st Floor, 6 St John's Court, Upper Fforest Way, Swansea Enterprise Park, Swansea, SA6 8QQ
Shareholders: Guy Peter Michael Noott; Michael Timothy Noott; Oscar Nyatanga
Officers: Guy Peter Michael Noott [1992] Director/Radiographer; Michael Timothy Noott [1958] Director; Oscar Nyatanga [1983] Director/Radiographer [Zimbabwean]

**Ultrasoundgel Ltd**
Incorporated: 22 June 2012
Registered Office: Pinnacle House Business Centre, Newark Road, Peterborough, Cambs, PE1 5YD
Major Shareholder: Alistair Martin Ashworth
Officers: Alistair Martin Ashworth [1963] Director

**Ultrasun (UK) Limited**
Incorporated: 24 January 1997  Employees: 10
Net Worth: £1,721,670  Total Assets: £2,030,502
Registered Office: 41 Holmethorpe Avenue, Redhill, Surrey, RH1 2NB
Officers: Abigail Claire Cleeve [1971] Director/Business Manager; Wendy Northover [1942] Director

**Una Health Limited**
Incorporated: 30 June 2009  Employees: 9
Net Worth Deficit: £191,119  Total Assets: £425,226
Registered Office: Unit 3 Scotia Road Business Park, Stoke on Trent, Staffs, ST3 4HN
Parent: Una Health Holdings Limited
Officers: Ashley Nicholas Jacobs [1961] Director; Fiona Jacobs [1962] Business Development Director

**Uni Supply Ltd**
Incorporated: 1 November 2016
Net Worth Deficit: £1,331  Total Assets: £28,408
Registered Office: 17 Ridware House, Hobs Road, Lichfield, Staffs, WS13 6SY
Officers: Min Sun [1973] Director/Secretary

**Unidus Limited**
Incorporated: 23 May 2018
Registered Office: 27 Old Gloucester Street, London, WC1N 3AX
Major Shareholder: Virendra K Chawla
Officers: Virendra K Chawla, Secretary; Virendra K Chawla [1942] Director [American]

**Unifarco Ltd**
Incorporated: 4 December 2017
Registered Office: 33 Darnley Road, Gravesend, Kent, DA11 0SD
Shareholders: Cristina Racca; Pispo Ltd
Officers: Cristina Racca [1978] Director [Italian]

**Unimed Global Limited**
Incorporated: 21 June 2018
Registered Office: The Old Mill, 9 Soar Lane, Leicester, LE3 5DE
Shareholders: Ronak Vijay Thakkar; Rahkesh Vijay Thakkar
Officers: Rahkesh Vijay Thakkar [1990] Director; Ronak Vijay Thakkar [1988] Director

**Unimed Healthcare Supplies Limited**
Incorporated: 21 August 2018
Registered Office: The Old Mill, 9 Soar Lane, Leicester, LE3 5DE
Major Shareholder: Dip Shameet Thakkar
Officers: Dip Shameet Thakkar [1987] Director

**Unipharm Limited**
Incorporated: 11 May 2009  Employees: 9
Net Worth: £527,148  Total Assets: £701,842
Registered Office: 290 Brixton Road, London, SW9 6AG
Major Shareholder: Ataur Rahman
Officers: Mujibun Rahman, Secretary; Ataur Rahman [1973] Director/Pharmacist; Sayedur Rahman [1980] Director

**Unique Health Company Limited**
Incorporated: 15 February 2019
Registered Office: Egerton House, 55 Hoole Road, Chester, CH2 3NJ
Major Shareholder: Benjamin Parry
Officers: Benjamin Parry [1988] Director/Builder

**Unison Pharmaceuticals Ltd**
Incorporated: 17 September 2018
Registered Office: 59 Isham Road, Norbury, London, SW16 4TG
Major Shareholder: Bhagyesh Nitinkumar Shah
Officers: Bhagyesh Nitinkumar Shah [1983] Director/Businessman [Indian]

**Unit 10 Distribution Limited**
Incorporated: 11 September 2008  Employees: 11
Net Worth: £315,670  Total Assets: £998,909
Registered Office: 175 High Street, Blackwood, Gwent, NP12 1AA
Shareholders: Paul Robert Mayberry; Jane Michelle Mayberry
Officers: Paul Robert Mayberry [1967] Director/Pharmacist

**Unit Medic-Aids Limited**
Incorporated: 7 February 1978  Employees: 2
Net Worth: £121,692  Total Assets: £315,570
Registered Office: 29 Blackberry Lane, Hasbury, Halesowen, W Midlands, B63 4NX
Shareholders: Mark Stanley Holloway; Michaela Jane Holloway
Officers: Michaela Jane Holloway, Secretary; Mark Stanley Holloway [1960] Director; Michaela Jane Holloway [1966] Director/Company Secretary

**United Kingdom Medica Ltd**
Incorporated: 14 September 2016
Net Worth: £216  Total Assets: £216
Registered Office: 71-75 Shelton Street, Covent Garden, London, WC2H 9JQ
Major Shareholder: Karen Holohan
Officers: Karen Holohan, Secretary; Karen Holohan [1985] Director

**United Med Ltd**
Incorporated: 28 May 2014
Net Worth: £4,447  Total Assets: £59,286
Registered Office: Office 3, Unit 1-3 Wayvern Estate, Beverley Way, New Malden, Surrey, KT3 4PH
Major Shareholder: Zaher Almahmoud
Officers: Zaher Almahmoud [1978] Director

**United Orphan Pharma Limited**
Incorporated: 15 May 2018
Registered Office: Arquen House, 4-6 Spicer Street, St Albans, Herts, AL3 4PQ
Major Shareholder: Aya Abd El Rahim Mohamed Abd El Rahim El Bakoury
Officers: Aya Abd El Rahim Mohamed Abd El Rahim El Bakoury [1983] Director

**United Pharma Group Limited**
Incorporated: 17 October 2017
Registered Office: Zaj Associates, 41A Mill Lane, West Hampstead, London, NW6 1NB
Major Shareholder: Ashrf Elhoush
Officers: Ashrf Elhoush [1973] Director [Libyan]

**United Pharma Ltd**
Incorporated: 28 June 2013  Employees: 6
Net Worth: £99,580  Total Assets: £665,115
Registered Office: Premier Business Center, 47-49 Park Royal Road, London, NW10 7LQ
Shareholder: Zeyad Almthqal
Officers: Zeyad Almthqal [1971] Director/Consultant [Syrian]; Monzer Moneer Shnaf [1975] Director/Consultant [Syrian]

**United Therapeutics Europe, Ltd.**
*Incorporated:* 3 March 2000  *Employees:* 15
*Net Worth:* £23,296,564  *Total Assets:* £26,513,814
*Registered Office:* The Officers' Mess, Royston Road, Duxford, Cambs, CB22 4QH
*Parent:* United Therapeutics Corporation
*Officers:* Marc Charles Dalby, Secretary; Michael Ian Benkowitz [1971] Director [American]; James Edgemond [1967] Director [American]; Doctor Edwin Robert Grover [1960] Director; Martine Rothblatt [1954] Director/Biotech Executive [American]

**Univape Global Ltd**
*Incorporated:* 29 June 2018
*Registered Office:* 8 Oaksway, Leicester, LE2 2HR
*Officers:* Rahkesh Vijay Thakkar [1990] Director/Businessman; Ronak Vijay Thakkar [1988] Director

**Universal Biologicals (Cambridge) Limited**
*Incorporated:* 19 May 1980  *Employees:* 3
*Net Worth:* £146,280  *Total Assets:* £227,948
*Registered Office:* Passhouse Farm House, Papworth St Agnes, Cambridge, CB23 3QU
*Major Shareholder:* Kenneth Stanley Liddle
*Officers:* Janice Elizabeth Liddle, Secretary; Elliot Spencer Liddle [1979] Director; Kenneth Stanley Liddle [1944] Director

**Universal Marine Medical Limited**
*Incorporated:* 20 June 2008  *Employees:* 25
*Net Worth:* £28,171  *Total Assets:* £1,724,482
*Registered Office:* Unit 24a Greatbridge Road, Romsey, Hants, SO51 0HR
*Parent:* Universal Marine Medical Supply International LLC
*Officers:* Drew Schaefer [1961] Director/Business Executive [American]; Paul David Slade [1967] Director

**Universal Procurement Services Ltd**
*Incorporated:* 14 August 2002  *Employees:* 2
*Net Worth:* £904,403  *Total Assets:* £2,109,599
*Registered Office:* Basepoint Business Centre, 1 Winnall Valley Road, Winchester, Hants, SO23 0LD
*Major Shareholder:* Benjamin John Funnell
*Officers:* Alison Margaret Funnell [1988] Director; Benjamin John Funnell [1976] Director/Salesperson

**Universal Supplies (International) Ltd**
*Incorporated:* 25 May 2005
*Net Worth:* £970  *Total Assets:* £1,697
*Registered Office:* 57 Kings Avenue, Chadwell Heath, Romford, Essex, RM6 6BD
*Major Shareholder:* Hakan Salih
*Officers:* Hakan Salih, Secretary; Hakan Salih [1964] Director

**Unmaan Healthcare Limited**
*Incorporated:* 3 April 2018
*Registered Office:* Kemp House, 160 City Road, London, EC1V 2NX
*Major Shareholder:* Avtar Singh Panesar
*Officers:* Avtar Panesar, Secretary; Avtar Singh Panesar [1949] Director/Salesman; Kultar Panesar [1991] Director/Salesman

**Uno Healthcare Limited**
*Incorporated:* 14 May 2013
*Net Worth:* £1,700,939  *Total Assets:* £8,004,642
*Registered Office:* Amelia House, Crescent Road, Worthing, W Sussex, BN11 1QR
*Major Shareholder:* Fabio Da Silva Lisboa
*Officers:* Fabio Da Silva Lisboa [1970] Director/Entrepreneur [Brazilian]

**Unomedical Limited**
*Incorporated:* 13 April 1970
*Net Worth:* £11,649,000  *Total Assets:* £13,679,000
*Registered Office:* GFC Building, First Avenue, Deeside Industrial Park, Deeside, Flintshire, CH5 2NU
*Parent:* Unomedical Holdings Limited
*Officers:* Clare Jane Bates [1976] Director/Solicitor; Christopher John Sedwell [1976] Director/Chartered Accountant; Simon James Whitfield [1966] Business Director

**Ursus UK Limited**
*Incorporated:* 10 March 2015  *Employees:* 1
*Net Worth:* £21,515  *Total Assets:* £28,138
*Registered Office:* 153 Mortimer Street, Herne Bay, Kent, CT6 5HA
*Major Shareholder:* Christopher Pierre Georges Caporali
*Officers:* Christopher Pierre Georges Caporali [1971] Director

**Usme Limited**
*Incorporated:* 19 July 2017
*Registered Office:* 1 Kendall Place, London, W1U 7JL
*Officers:* Hitesh Chandrakantbhai Patel [1975] Director

**Utech Products Limited**
*Incorporated:* 1 May 2014  *Employees:* 1
*Net Worth:* £480,334  *Total Assets:* £1,052,142
*Registered Office:* Dock 10, Exploration Drive, Leicester, LE4 5NU
*Officers:* Bart Van Der Meer, Secretary; Rakesh Madan [1960] Director [American]

**Uvita Health Limited**
*Incorporated:* 10 May 2018
*Registered Office:* 71-75 Shelton Street, Covent Garden, London, WC2H 9JQ
*Major Shareholder:* Gulbir Singh
*Officers:* Gulbir Singh, Secretary; Gulbir Singh [1971] Director

**V Sales and Marketing Limited**
*Incorporated:* 27 October 2004
*Net Worth Deficit:* £700  *Total Assets:* £12,861
*Registered Office:* Oliver House, 23 Windmill Hill, Enfield, Middlesex, EN2 7AB
*Shareholders:* Christiaan Andre Cardon; Maarten Julius Gerard Lejaeghere
*Officers:* Christiaan Andre Cardon, Secretary/Pharmacist [Belgian]; Jeroen Peter Annie Bastijns [1969] Director/Consultant [Belgian]; Christiaan Andre Cardon [1968] Director/Pharmacist [Belgian]; Maarten Julius Gerard Lejaeghere [1973] Director/Sales Manager [Belgian]

**V.S. Limited**
*Incorporated:* 15 June 1995
*Net Worth:* £155,761  *Total Assets:* £156,381
*Registered Office:* 2 Wyevale Business Park, Kings Acre, Hereford, HR4 7BS
*Shareholders:* Margaret Gardiner; Nina Elizabeth Leach
*Officers:* Robert Norman Gardiner [1934] Director/Pharmacist

**V2M Pharma Limited**
*Incorporated:* 30 July 2018
*Registered Office:* Central Pharma, Caxton Road, Elms Farm Industrial Estate, Bedford, MK41 0XZ
*Officers:* Navdeep Kainth [1971] Director; Stephen Leonard Kemp [1964] Director

**Vak Enterprise Limited**
*Incorporated:* 30 October 2017
*Registered Office:* 30 Westbury Close, Townsend Industrial Estate, Houghton Regis, Beds, LU5 5BL
*Major Shareholder:* Kv Puri
*Officers:* Viresh Patel [1979] Director/Businessman [Indian]

**Valentis Life Sciences Limited**
*Incorporated:* 30 November 2016  *Employees:* 2
*Previous:* Valentis Life Science Limited
*Net Worth Deficit:* £73,864  *Total Assets:* £131,490
*Registered Office:* 268 Bath Road, Slough, Berks, SL1 4DX
*Shareholder:* Rakesh Sharma
*Officers:* Rakesh Sharma [1981] Director [Indian]

**Valley Northern Limited**
*Incorporated:* 28 August 2014  *Employees:* 23
*Net Worth:* £404,343  *Total Assets:* £1,758,301
*Registered Office:* Valley Northern, Carver Road, Astonfields, Stafford, ST16 3BP
*Officers:* Adrian Pittock [1987] Director/Operations Manager; Dale Pittock [1985] Director/Sales Manager; Oliver John Pittock [1965] Managing Director; Priscilla Pittock [1966] Director/Accounts

**Value Generics Limited**
*Incorporated:* 5 September 1986
*Registered Office:* 7 Regents Drive, Prudhoe, Northumberland, NE42 6PX
*Parent:* Doncaster Pharmaceuticals Group Limited
*Officers:* Mark James Gulliford [1969] Director; Derek Andrew Wilson [1964] Director

**Value Medical Limited**
*Incorporated:* 12 February 2019
*Registered Office:* 13 The Courtyard, Timothy's Bridge Road, Stratford upon Avon, Warwicks, CV37 9NP
*Major Shareholder:* Stuart James Gray
*Officers:* Stuart James Gray [1969] Director; Dr Samer Taslaq [1980] Director

**Valugen Pharma Limited**
*Incorporated:* 23 November 2018
*Registered Office:* c/o KP & Co, Avanta House, 79 College Road, Harrow, Middlesex, HA1 1BD
*Major Shareholder:* Benno Ranjitkumar Sabapathy
*Officers:* Benno Ranjitkumar Sabapathy [1968] Director

**Valupharm UK Limited**
*Incorporated:* 5 February 2013
*Net Worth Deficit:* £470  *Total Assets:* £9,730
*Registered Office:* 9 Cator Lane, Chilwell, Nottingham, NG9 4AX
*Officers:* Dr Marie Amaning, Secretary; Clement Amaning [1963] Director/Project Manager; Dr Marie Amaning [1965] Director/Medical Practitioner

**Vascular Products Limited**
*Incorporated:* 4 October 1977
*Registered Office:* 2 Wyevale Business Park, Kings Acre, Hereford, HR4 7BS
*Shareholders:* Robert Norman Gardiner; Anthony John Leach
*Officers:* Robert Norman Gardiner [1934] Director/Pharmacist; Anthony John Leach [1927] Director/Chartered Accountant

**Vasmed Technologies Limited**
*Incorporated:* 7 May 2013
*Registered Office:* Unit 14 Kernick Industrial Estate, Kernick Road, Penryn, Cornwall, TR10 9EP
*Shareholders:* Jayaprasad Kaippallil Raman Pillai; Rajalakshmi Jayaprasad
*Officers:* Rajalakshmi Jayaprasad [1967] Director [Indian]; Jayaprasad Kaippallil Raman Pillai [1955] Director [Indian]

**Ved Healthcare Limited**
*Incorporated:* 5 September 2016
*Net Worth:* £39,140  *Total Assets:* £99,010
*Registered Office:* 69 Moore Court, Station Grove, Wembley, Middlesex, HA0 4AF
*Major Shareholder:* Kanjikumar Mandanka
*Officers:* Kanjikumar Mandanka [1984] Director

**Veda Biosciences Limited**
*Incorporated:* 15 January 2019
*Registered Office:* 85 Great Portland Street, London, W1W 7LT
*Shareholders:* Natasha Managarova; Exagenica Limited
*Officers:* Natasha Managarova [1979] Director [Macedonian]

**Vedic Medical Hall Limited**
*Incorporated:* 14 March 1990  *Employees:* 1
*Net Worth Deficit:* £56,763  *Total Assets:* £2,844
*Registered Office:* 6 Chiltern Street, London, W1U 7PT
*Major Shareholder:* Sandeep Kumar Garg
*Officers:* Charoo Garg, Secretary; Sandeep Kumar Garg [1964] Director

**Veenak International Limited**
*Incorporated:* 23 January 1991  *Employees:* 40
*Net Worth:* £1,309,932  *Total Assets:* £18,264,696
*Registered Office:* 1406 Coventry Road, South Yardley, Birmingham, B25 8AE
*Major Shareholder:* Mohamed Gulamali Kanani
*Officers:* Abbas Mohamed Kanani, Secretary; Shan Abbas Hassam [1985] Director; Abbas Mohamed Kanani [1984] Director/Pharmacist

**Veenak Sourcing Limited**
*Incorporated:* 11 April 2018
*Registered Office:* 1406 Coventry Road, South Yardley, Birmingham, B25 8AE
*Parent:* MSA Global Holdings Limited
*Officers:* Shan-E-Abbas Hassam, Secretary; Abbas Mohamed Kanani, Secretary; Shan-E-Abbas Hassam [1985] Director; Abbas Mohamed Kanani [1984] Director/Pharmacist

**Veepharm Limited**
*Incorporated:* 10 January 2019
*Registered Office:* Flat 14, Southwood Court, 97 Stafford Avenue, Hornchurch, Essex, RM11 2FA
*Major Shareholder:* Vaishali Ghai
*Officers:* Vaishali Ghai [1992] Director

**Vegamed UK Limited**
*Incorporated:* 27 October 2016
*Registered Office:* 117a Harley Street, London, W1G 6AT
*Major Shareholder:* Sabeel Shamsudeen
*Officers:* Dr Sabeel Shamsudeen [1988] Director [Indian]

**Venture Four Ltd.**
Incorporated: 24 April 2018
Registered Office: 71-75 Shelton Street, Covent Garden, London, WC2H 9JQ
Officers: John Psyllos, Secretary; John Psyllos [1976] Director/Electronic Engineer [Greek]; Troy Christopher Rahme [1975] Director [Italian]; Jaco Van Der Merwe [1971] Director/Dental Surgeon; Ilias Xanthoulis [1970] Director/Engineer

**Venture Pharma Ltd**
Incorporated: 21 December 2009
Net Worth: £125,145 Total Assets: £261,668
Registered Office: 30 Highfield Avenue, Kingsbury, London, NW9 0PY
Major Shareholder: Milesh Patel
Officers: Milesh Patel [1977] Director

**Veramic Limited**
Incorporated: 24 April 2012
Net Worth: £5,210 Total Assets: £57,765
Registered Office: Unit B2, Livingstone Court, 55 Peel Road, Harrow, Middlesex, HA3 7QT
Major Shareholder: Dimitris Kalogiannidis
Officers: Dr Dimitris Kalogiannidis [1981] Director/Doctor [Greek]; Irene Kalogiannidis [1984] Director/Interior Designer [Greek]

**Veriton Pharma Limited**
Incorporated: 21 January 1997 Employees: 36
Previous: Special Products Limited
Net Worth: £4,870,489 Total Assets: £6,863,314
Registered Office: Unit 16 Trade City, Avro Way, Brooklands Business Park, Weybridge, Surrey, KT13 0YF
Parent: March Medical Limited
Officers: Dr Hannah Mary Talbot Aiken [1979] Director; Chris James Grimes [1975] Director; Dr Stephen Philip Jones [1957] Director/Pharmacist; Carole Iris March [1949] Director; Dr Graham Alan March [1945] Director/Pharmacist; Jason Asnam Saiban [1972] Director/Solicitor; Theresa Anne Wallis [1957] Director; Roderick William Wild [1967] Director/Chartered Accountant

**Vertibax Limited**
Incorporated: 22 August 2006
Net Worth: £1,000 Total Assets: £1,000
Registered Office: Anvil House, Main Street, Long Preston, Skipton, N Yorks, BD23 4ND
Major Shareholder: Angus MacNab
Officers: Jenny Elisabeth MacNab, Secretary; Angus Bernard Rupert MacNab [1973] Director

**Vestex Trade Ltd**
Incorporated: 3 March 2009
Net Worth: £1,000 Total Assets: £1,000
Registered Office: 19 Kathleen Road, London, SW11 2JR
Officers: Izeth Del Carment Samudio Tapia [1972] Director/Manager [Panamanian]

**Vet Direct Services Limited**
Incorporated: 1 July 2004 Employees: 29
Net Worth: £2,158,769 Total Assets: £3,368,402
Registered Office: CVS House, Owen Road, Diss, Norfolk, IP22 4ER
Parent: Vet Direct Holdings Limited
Officers: Richard Fairman [1967] Director; Simon Campbell Innes [1960] Director/Chief Executive

**The Vet Store Trading Limited**
Incorporated: 24 February 2017
Registered Office: 17 Great Russell Court, Fieldhead Business Centre, Bradford, BD7 1JZ
Officers: Amran Riaz, Secretary; Amran Riaz [1977] Director

**Veterinary Surgeons Supply Company Limited**
Incorporated: 12 June 1956 Employees: 50
Net Worth: £5,887,605 Total Assets: £14,182,157
Registered Office: 29 Enterprise Crescent, Ballinderry Road, Lisburn, Co Antrim, BT28 2BP
Officers: Siobhan McKee, Secretary; John Henderson [1971] Director/Veterinary Surgeon; John James Paul Johnston [1968] Director/Veterinary Surgeon [Irish]; Neil Johnston [1968] Director/Veterinary Surgeon; Andrew Mayne [1965] Director/Veterinary Surgeon; James Norman McMordie [1955] Director; Shane Patrick Murray [1974] Director/Veterinary Surgeon

**Vetsonic (UK) Ltd**
Incorporated: 16 March 2011 Employees: 14
Net Worth: £1,554,029 Total Assets: £2,764,781
Registered Office: Vetsonic, Riccal Drive, York Road Business Park, Malton, N Yorks, YO17 6YE
Shareholders: Raymond Paul Rochester; Anthony Kimmo Atkinson
Officers: Anthony Kimmo Atkinson [1964] Director; Raymond Paul Rochester [1953] Director

**Veyda Pharma Ltd**
Incorporated: 16 October 2018
Registered Office: 20-22 Wenlock Road, London, N1 7GU
Major Shareholder: Ajay Kirpal
Officers: Ajay Kirpal [1983] Director

**Vicars Cross Healthcare Ltd**
Incorporated: 10 December 2018
Registered Office: St Johns Chambers, Love Street, Chester, CH1 1QN
Major Shareholder: Nicholas James Goodwin
Officers: Karon Goodwin [1990] Director; Nicholas James Goodwin [1991] Director

**Victoria Meds Mondial Ltd**
Incorporated: 2 August 2018
Registered Office: Victoria Chemist, 524 London Road Cheam, Sutton, Surrey, SM3 8HW
Shareholders: Bhushankumar Natubhai Amin; Rajeshkumar Natubhai Amin
Officers: Bhushankumar Natubhai Amin [1956] Director

**Victoria Pharma London Ltd**
Incorporated: 27 May 2005
Previous: Osom Limited
Net Worth: £2 Total Assets: £2
Registered Office: 407 Britannia House, 1-11 Glenthorne Road, London, W6 0LH
Major Shareholder: Peter Hajnal
Officers: Peter Hajnal [1953] Director [Hungarian]

**Viemeds Limited**
Incorporated: 22 January 2016
Net Worth Deficit: £16,959 Total Assets: £6,509
Registered Office: 18 Long Beech Drive, Farnborough, Hants, GU14 0PR
Major Shareholder: Vivian Alobwede Ewane
Officers: Vivian Alobwede Ewane [1970] Director/Pharmacist/Pharmacy Manager [Belgian]

**View Pharm Limited**
*Incorporated:* 25 July 2011
*Previous:* Crystal Pharma (UK) Limited
*Net Worth:* £4,670  *Total Assets:* £113,531
*Registered Office:* 37 Chestnut Drive, Harrow, Middlesex, HA3 7DL
*Major Shareholder:* Hitesh Kothari
*Officers:* Hitesh Kothari [1960] Director

**Vifor Pharma UK Limited**
*Incorporated:* 26 February 2008  *Employees:* 76
*Net Worth:* £11,983,526  *Total Assets:* £17,251,612
*Registered Office:* 5 New Street Square, London, EC4A 3TW
*Parent:* Galenica AG
*Officers:* Georg Martin Frey [1984] Director/Head of Corporate Legal [Swiss]; Siegfried Michel [1957] Director/Head of Commercial Affairs [German]; Alexandros Sigalas [1972] Director/Chief Financial Officer [Swiss]

**ViiV Healthcare Overseas Limited**
*Incorporated:* 23 September 2009
*Net Worth:* £131,093,000  *Total Assets:* £131,581,000
*Registered Office:* 980 Great West Road, Brentford, Middlesex, TW8 9GS
*Parent:* ViiV Healthcare Limited
*Officers:* Jill Dawn Anderson [1964] Director; Karen Marion Grainger [1978] Director/Pharmaceutical Regulatory Executive [Irish]; Deborah Jayne Waterhouse [1967] Director

**ViiV Healthcare Trading Services UK Limited**
*Incorporated:* 5 August 2009
*Net Worth:* £52,910,000  *Total Assets:* £3,306,328,064
*Registered Office:* 980 Great West Road, Brentford, Middlesex, TW8 9GS
*Parent:* ViiV Healthcare Limited
*Officers:* Jill Dawn Anderson [1964] Director; Karen Marion Grainger [1978] Director/Pharmaceutical Regulatory Executive [Irish]; Deborah Jayne Waterhouse [1967] Director

**ViiV Healthcare UK Limited**
*Incorporated:* 13 August 2009  *Employees:* 175
*Net Worth:* £4,456,565,248  *Total Assets:* £7,015,779,840
*Registered Office:* 980 Great West Road, Brentford, Middlesex, TW8 9GS
*Parent:* ViiV Healthcare Limited
*Officers:* Jill Dawn Anderson [1964] Director; Karen Marion Grainger [1978] Director/Pharmaceutical Regulatory Executive [Irish]; Deborah Jayne Waterhouse [1967] Director

**Viking Court Limited**
*Incorporated:* 28 October 1991  *Employees:* 2
*Net Worth:* £751,202  *Total Assets:* £759,275
*Registered Office:* Viking Court, 31 Princess Road, Dronfield, Derbys, S18 2LX
*Major Shareholder:* John Robert Clague
*Officers:* John Robert Clague [1946] Director

**Vine Pharmaceuticals Limited**
*Incorporated:* 11 July 2014  *Employees:* 2
*Net Worth:* £214  *Total Assets:* £326
*Registered Office:* 16 Wembury Park Road, Plymouth, PL3 4NG
*Major Shareholder:* Asemokhai Yakubu
*Officers:* Asemokhai Yakubu [1987] Director/Pharmacist [Nigerian]; Olivia Akunna Yakubu [1984] Director/Pharmacist

**Vipharm Limited**
*Incorporated:* 12 May 2016
*Registered Office:* 25 Bedford Square, London, WC1B 3HH
*Major Shareholder:* Vivien Christian Charles Nagdelaine
*Officers:* Hussain Al-Tahan [1992] Director/Pharma Analyst; Vivien Christian Charles Magdelaine [1972] Director [French]

**Virbac Limited**
*Incorporated:* 5 September 1972  *Employees:* 52
*Net Worth:* £3,488,437  *Total Assets:* £13,986,033
*Registered Office:* Woolpit Business Park, Windmill Avenue, Woolpit, Bury St Edmunds, Suffolk, IP30 9UP
*Parent:* Virbac SA
*Officers:* Kevin Michael Barton, Secretary; David Ellerton [1960] Managing Director; Sebastien Huron [1970] Director [French]; Christian Karst [1958] Director [French]; Hubert Trentesaux [1958] Director [French]

**Virudist Ltd**
*Incorporated:* 20 March 2018
*Registered Office:* 20-22 Wenlock Road, London, N1 7GU
*Major Shareholder:* Barry Dimes Young
*Officers:* Barry Dimes Young [1966] Director/Operations Manager

**Vise Services Ltd**
*Incorporated:* 24 May 2018
*Registered Office:* 20-22 Wenlock Road, London, N1 7GU
*Officers:* Chandana Gunna [1985] Director/Pharmacist [Indian]

**Vise Services PVT Ltd**
*Incorporated:* 5 September 2018
*Registered Office:* 20-22 Wenlock Road, London, N1 7GU
*Officers:* Sudarshan Reddy Arra, Secretary; Chandana Gunna [1985] Director/Pharmacist [Indian]

**Vision Matrix Limited**
*Incorporated:* 29 January 1996  *Employees:* 7
*Net Worth:* £361,176  *Total Assets:* £725,074
*Registered Office:* 31 East Parade, Harrogate, N Yorks, HG1 5LQ
*Shareholders:* Glynn Charles Allen; Elizabeth Ann Allen; Rosemary Ann Morphitis-Byrne
*Officers:* Rosemary Ann Morphitis-Byrne, Secretary; Elizabeth Ann Allen [1961] Director; Glynn Charles Allen [1960] Director/Medical Sales; Bryan John Byrne [1956] Director/Chartered Quantity Surveyor; Rosemary Ann Morphitis-Byrne [1958] Director/Medical Sales

**Vision Pharmaceuticals Ltd**
*Incorporated:* 9 October 1987  *Employees:* 31
*Net Worth:* £6,845,896  *Total Assets:* £8,731,841
*Registered Office:* Fernbank House, Tytherington Business Park, Macclesfield, Cheshire, SK10 2XA
*Parent:* SSCP Blink Bidco Limited
*Officers:* Ian Martin Snelson, Secretary; Roland Bruhin [1964] Director/Chief Executive [Swiss]; Ian Martin Snelson [1967] Director/Chartered Accountant

**Vision.Net Limited**
*Incorporated:* 19 November 1996  *Employees:* 2
*Net Worth:* £63,932  *Total Assets:* £66,272
*Registered Office:* 3 Castlegate, Grantham, Lincs, NG31 6SF
*Shareholders:* Palaniswamy Sunderraj; Kalpana Devi Sunderraj
*Officers:* Jane Elizabeth Whitton, Secretary; Kalpana Devi Sunderraj [1961] Director; Dr Palaniswamy Sunderraj [1959] Director/Medical Doctor

**Vita Nova International Ltd**
*Incorporated:* 4 July 2018
*Registered Office:* Nabwood Farm, Marple Road, Stockport, Cheshire, SK2 5HG
*Shareholders:* Omar Awad; Oliver Gareth Paul Jubb
*Officers:* Omar Awad [1982] Director; Oliver Gareth Paul Jubb [1981] Director

**Vitachem Limited**
*Incorporated:* 12 September 1991
*Net Worth:* £52,941  *Total Assets:* £133,598
*Registered Office:* 43 Southbrook Road, Norbury, London, SW16 5QU
*Shareholders:* Ila Vinod Shah; Vinod Thakorlal Shah
*Officers:* Ila Vinod Shah, Secretary; Vinod Thakorlal Shah [1948] Director

**Vitaempower Ltd**
*Incorporated:* 3 August 2018
*Registered Office:* 15 Grayling Grove, Hemel Hempstead, Herts, HP2 7DD
*Shareholders:* Snehalkumar Himmatlal Boghani; Shashikanth Varala
*Officers:* Snehalkumar Himmatlal Boghani [1985] Director; Shashikanth Varala [1981] Director

**Vitafree Health Limited**
*Incorporated:* 21 September 2010  *Employees:* 1
*Net Worth:* £16,365  *Total Assets:* £25,962
*Registered Office:* 4 Green Wall, Lewes, E Sussex, BN7 2NX
*Shareholders:* Janos Skare; Arpad Jozsef Kiraly
*Officers:* Tamas Butkovics [1980] Director [Hungarian/British]; Arpad Jozsef Kiraly [1958] Director [Hungarian]; Janos Skare [1972] Director [Hungarian]

**Vital Haven Ltd**
*Incorporated:* 5 February 2019
*Registered Office:* 20 Bracey Street, London, N4 3BJ
*Shareholders:* Bruno Muongkhot; Louis-Gregoire Victor Stanislas Jean Marie Jehl de la Goublaye de Menorval
*Officers:* Louis-Gregoire Victor Stanislas Jean Marie Jehl de La Goublaye de Menorval [1986] Director [French]; Bruno Muongkhot [1987] Director [French]

**Vital Life International Limited**
*Incorporated:* 29 May 2008
*Net Worth:* £4,274  *Total Assets:* £4,868
*Registered Office:* Unit 9F, Havelock Terrace, Hewlett House, Havelock Terrace, London, SW8 4AS
*Officers:* Gillian Ann Waddell [1960] Director

**Vital Pharma Limited**
*Incorporated:* 4 February 2015
*Net Worth Deficit:* £46,711  *Total Assets:* £185,697
*Registered Office:* 3rd Floor, Vyman House, 104 College Road, Harrow, Middlesex, HA1 1BQ
*Major Shareholder:* Abdul Rehman Khan
*Officers:* Abdul Rehman Khan [1974] Director

**Vital Supplies (UK) Limited**
*Incorporated:* 24 June 2005
*Net Worth:* £1,347  *Total Assets:* £328,273
*Registered Office:* 240 Uppingham Avenue, Stanmore, Middlesex, HA7 2JS
*Major Shareholder:* Mohamed Rahemani
*Officers:* Fatema Rahemani, Secretary; Dr Ramasamy Danapal [1946] Director/GP; Mohammed Jaffer Rahemani [1979] Director/Businessman

**Vitalit Trade Limited**
*Incorporated:* 6 July 2017
*Registered Office:* 30 City Road, London, EC1Y 2AB
*Officers:* Dr Senem Ertan Ahmed, Secretary; Hatice Oncel [1966] Director [Turkish]

**Vitamed Int Ltd**
*Incorporated:* 13 June 2016
*Registered Office:* 27 Old Gloucester Street, London, WC1N 3AX
*Officers:* Azar Guliyev [1979] Director/Doctor [Azerbaijani]

**Vitamineral Limited**
*Incorporated:* 28 April 1993
*Net Worth Deficit:* £5,953  *Total Assets:* £877
*Registered Office:* 37 High Street, East Grinstead, W Sussex, RH19 3AF
*Officers:* Gunilla Gerber, Secretary [Swedish]; Dr Karin Ziolko Lange [1952] Director/Medical Doctor [German]

**Vitaminka Ltd**
*Incorporated:* 20 December 2016
*Total Assets:* £1,000
*Registered Office:* Lower Ground Floor, 40 Bloomsbury Way, London, WC1A 2SE
*Major Shareholder:* Slawomir Kosinski
*Officers:* Slawomir Kosinski [1985] Director [Polish]

**Vitamins To Buy Ltd**
*Incorporated:* 15 February 2013
*Net Worth:* £13,620  *Total Assets:* £30,996
*Registered Office:* Lime Farm, Little Missenden, Amersham, Bucks, HA7 0RQ
*Officers:* Torgeir Fossum [1956] Director [Norwegian]

**Vitane Pharma Limited**
*Incorporated:* 5 August 2011
*Net Worth Deficit:* £12,061  *Total Assets:* £4,817
*Registered Office:* 49 Peregrine Close, Watford, Herts, WD25 9AP
*Parent:* Vitane Pharma GmbH
*Officers:* Mohammed Mohsin Reza Lilani [1969] Director

**Vitanutrition UK Ltd.**
*Incorporated:* 9 June 2010
*Registered Office:* Suite 1, The Studio, St Nicholas Close, Elstree, Herts, WD6 3EW
*Major Shareholder:* Deepak Sharma
*Officers:* Deepak Sharma, Secretary; Deepak Sharma [1977] Director [Irish]; Sagina Taneja [1978] Director [Indian]

**Vitapro Limited**
*Incorporated:* 9 January 2017
*Registered Office:* 46 Cardinals Walk, Leicester, LE5 1LF
*Major Shareholder:* Petrit Ukmata
*Officers:* Petrit Ukmata [1976] Director/Research Assistant

**Vitb12 Academy Ltd**
*Incorporated:* 11 May 2018
*Registered Office:* 2 Trust Court, Vision Park, Histon, Cambridge, CB24 9PW
*Shareholders:* Anita Jayne Earsdon Glenister; Denise Anne Hogan
*Officers:* Anita Jayne Earsdon Glenister [1963] Director; Denise Anne Hogan [1966] Director

**Vitgarden Ltd**
*Incorporated:* 22 January 2013  *Employees:* 1
*Net Worth:* £13,930  *Total Assets:* £36,478
*Registered Office:* 101 Joan Court, 57 Fortune Green Road, West Hampstead, London, NW6 1DW
*Officers:* Puja Kanel [1980] Director/Accountant

**Vitopia Ltd**
*Incorporated:* 13 September 2016
*Registered Office:* 18 Wimpole Street, London, W1G 8GD
*Officers:* AMR Abdelmonem Ibrahim Mosa [1986] Director/Wholesale

**Vitwell Limited**
*Incorporated:* 19 July 2018
*Registered Office:* 3rd Floor, Argyle House, Northside, Joel Street, Northwood Hills, Northwood, Middlesex, HA6 1NW
*Officers:* Satyam Dilipkumar Popat [1982] Director; Shivam Dilip Popat [1978] Director

**Vityz Nutrition Limited**
*Incorporated:* 13 September 2017
*Registered Office:* 88 Stafford Road, Ruislip, Middlesex, HA4 6PF
*Officers:* Nidhi Poddar [1980] Director/IT Consultant; Pravin Poddar [1978] Director/Scientist

**Vivacy Laboratoires Ltd**
*Incorporated:* 30 October 2018
*Registered Office:* 1st Floor, 14 Berkeley Street, London, W1J 8DX
*Major Shareholder:* Waldemar Stanislaw Kita
*Officers:* Gregory John Connor, Secretary; Gregory John Connor [1965] Director/Attorney at Law [Swiss]; Waldemar Stanislaw Kita [1954] Director/President of Vivacy [French]

**Vivaorganiclife Ltd**
*Incorporated:* 6 August 2018
*Registered Office:* 2nd Floor, College House, 17 King Edwards Road, Ruislip, Middlesex, HA4 7AE
*Major Shareholder:* Elise Herro
*Officers:* Elise Herro [1988] Director/Software Engineer [Lebanese]

**Vivus UK Limited**
*Incorporated:* 27 December 1995
*Registered Office:* 1st Floor, West Wing, Davidson House, Forbury Square, Reading, Berks, RG1 3EU
*Officers:* Mark Oki [1968] Director [American]; John L Slebir [1965] Director/SVP, General Counsel, Vivus, Inc [American]

**VLCare Limited**
*Incorporated:* 26 October 2018
*Registered Office:* Batchworth House, Batchworth Place, Church Street, Rickmansworth, Herts, WD3 1JE
*Shareholders:* Dimitrios Panaritis; Emmanouil Kakridas; Thomas Tsevis
*Officers:* Martin Jose Irisarri [1964] Director/Bank Manager

**Vog Limited**
*Incorporated:* 20 May 2009
*Net Worth:* £110,324  *Total Assets:* £128,361
*Registered Office:* Regent House, 316 Beulah Hill, London, SE19 3HF
*Officers:* Arthur Joseph Grice [1942] Director/Consultant

**A.Vogel Limited**
*Incorporated:* 28 September 2018
*Registered Office:* 2 Brewster Place, Riverside Business Park, Irvine, N Ayrshire, KA11 5DD
*Officers:* Bernhard Bartschi [1966] Director [Swiss]; Thomas Fehr [1962] Director [Swiss]; Peter Gmunder [1966] Director [Swiss]; Janyn Elizabeth Tan [1963] Director; Jen Wei Tan [1960] Director

**Vwin Lifestyle Limited**
*Incorporated:* 13 August 2018
*Registered Office:* Ground Floor, Avalon, 26-32 Oxford Road, Bournemouth, BH8 8EZ
*Officers:* Hemanth Battula [1982] Director

**Vygon (U.K.) Limited**
*Incorporated:* 28 August 1973  *Employees:* 165
*Net Worth:* £33,537,000  *Total Assets:* £38,871,000
*Registered Office:* The Pierre Simonet Building, V Park, Gateway North, Latham Road, Swindon, Wilts, SN25 4DL
*Parent:* Vygon SA
*Officers:* Dale Michael Keegan, Secretary; Bertrand Cuny [1936] Director [French]; Leslie Clive Robert Davies [1972] Managing Director; Stephane Regnault [1961] Director [French]

**Vyom International Ltd.**
*Incorporated:* 23 July 2018
*Registered Office:* 71-75 Shelton Street, Covent Garden, London, WC2H 9JQ
*Major Shareholder:* Vikram Sharma
*Officers:* Swati Sharma, Secretary; Swati Sharma [1979] Director [Indian]; Dr Vikram Sharma [1975] Director [Indian]

**W.B. Superdrug Ltd.**
*Incorporated:* 15 December 1997
*Registered Office:* 85 Ward Point, Hotspur Street, London, SE11 6UE
*Shareholder:* William Amegbor Boafor
*Officers:* William Amegbor Boafor, Secretary/Chemist [Ghanaian]; Paul Frederick Austin [1936] Director/Businessman; George Boafor [1970] Director/Mechanical Engineer; William Amegbor Boafor [1933] Director/Chemist [Ghanaian]

**Donald Wardle and Son Limited**
*Incorporated:* 31 March 1994
*Net Worth:* £19,920,000  *Total Assets:* £27,647,000
*Registered Office:* Merchants Warehouse, Castle Street, Manchester, M3 4LZ
*Parent:* Bestway Pharmacy NDC Limited
*Officers:* Lynette Gillian Krige [1966] Director/Chief Finance Officer [South African]; John Branson Nuttall [1963] Director/General Manager Health Care Group

**Water-Jel International Ltd**
*Incorporated:* 13 May 2016
*Net Worth:* £1,000  *Total Assets:* £1,000
*Registered Office:* Fiveways, 57-59 Hatfield Road, Potters Bar, Herts, EN6 1HS
*Officers:* Mark Edwin Lait, Secretary; III Harnett [1943] Director and Executive Officer [American]

**K. Waterhouse Limited**
*Incorporated:* 29 January 1970  *Employees:* 12
*Net Worth:* £9,445,797  *Total Assets:* £9,957,925
*Registered Office:* SDC (2012) Ltd P/A Shah Dodhia & Co, 173 Cleveland Street, London, W1T 6QR
*Officers:* Vinay Lalji Shah, Secretary; Amritlal Lalji Shah [1941] Director; Anil Lalji Shah [1949] Director; Nalin Lalji Shah [1957] Director; Vinay Lalji Shah [1947] Director

**Wave Pharma Limited**
*Incorporated:* 8 January 2013
*Net Worth:* £122,458  *Total Assets:* £562,583
*Registered Office:* 4th Floor, Cavendish House, 369 Burnt Oak Broadway, Edgware, Middlesex, HA8 5AW
*Shareholders:* Mohammed Arsalaan Khan; Romana Khan
*Officers:* Romana Khan, Secretary; Mohammad Arsalaan Khan [1967] Director/Industrial Pharmacist; Romana Khan [1971] Director/Pharmacist

**Waymade PLC**
*Incorporated:* 17 October 1984  *Employees:* 68
*Net Worth:* £39,851,000  *Total Assets:* £44,720,000
*Registered Office:* Suite 1, 3rd Floor, 11-12 St James's Square, London, SW1Y 4LB
*Major Shareholder:* Vijaykumar Chhotabhai Kalidas Patel
*Officers:* Mark John Cotterill [1965] Director/Accountant; Bhikhu Chhotabhai Patel [1947] Managing Director; Vijay Kumar Chhotabhai Patel [1949] Director

**WD Pharma (UK) Limited**
*Incorporated:* 10 September 2013
*Previous:* Estina Limited
*Net Worth Deficit:* £1,317  *Total Assets:* £12,651
*Registered Office:* Unit 16, 806 High Road Leyton, London, E10 6AE
*Major Shareholder:* Norma Williams
*Officers:* Norma Williams [1972] Director/Businesswomen [Jamaican]

**WE Pharma Ltd**
*Incorporated:* 17 November 2008  *Employees:* 14
*Net Worth:* £4,145,514  *Total Assets:* £4,998,185
*Registered Office:* 111 Power Road, London, W4 5PY
*Officers:* Marion Mary Anne Kane, Secretary; Marion Mary Anne Kane [1977] Director; Jaswant Singh Khera [1976] Director

**Webstar Dixon Limited**
*Incorporated:* 25 October 2011
*Net Worth:* £3,322  *Total Assets:* £33,091
*Registered Office:* 806 High Road Leyton, London, E10 6AE
*Major Shareholder:* Laurence Onwufuju
*Officers:* Laurence Onwufuju [1965] Director

**Steven F Webster Limited**
*Incorporated:* 28 August 1998
*Net Worth:* £1,730,000  *Total Assets:* £2,350,000
*Registered Office:* 7 Queen Street, Peterhead, Aberdeenshire, AB42 1TN
*Shareholders:* Steven Falconer Webster; Stephen Webster
*Officers:* Stephen Webster, Secretary/Teacher; Diane Webster [1972] Director/Teacher; Stephen Webster [1946] Director/Teacher/Retired; Steven Falconer Webster [1971] Director/Pharmacist; Suzanne Elaine Webster [1975] Director/Retail Manager

**Welcome Health Pharmacies Limited**
*Incorporated:* 11 May 2017
*Registered Office:* 26 Mappleton Drive, Seaham, Co Durham, SR7 7DY
*Parent:* Welcome Health Limited
*Officers:* Vaibhav Singh Chhatwal [1980] Director/Pharmacist

**Welcome Medical Group Ltd**
*Incorporated:* 17 November 2017
*Registered Office:* 38 Vince Street, Smethwick, W Midlands, B66 4JD
*Officers:* Liona Nosisa Ngwenya [1993] Director; Michelle Lethokuhle Ngwenya [1996] Director/Secretary; Sikhanyisiwe Moyo Ngwenya [1968] Director/Secretary; Welcome Ngwenya [1964] Director

**Welfar Healthcare Limited**
*Incorporated:* 16 April 2014
*Net Worth Deficit:* £44,012  *Total Assets:* £28,458
*Registered Office:* TMS House, Cray Avenue, Orpington, Kent, BR5 3QB
*Major Shareholder:* Elshad Safarov
*Officers:* Elshad Safarov [1982] Director/Business Person [Azerbaijani]

**Welfare Healthcare (UK) Ltd**
*Incorporated:* 25 July 2013  *Employees:* 9
*Net Worth:* £210,211  *Total Assets:* £573,287
*Registered Office:* 68 Friar Gate, Derby, DE1 1FP
*Officers:* Mustafa Hakimudin Bhaiji [1977] Director/Pharmacist; Hau Wee Lim [1987] Director/Pharmacist [Malaysian]; Yew Huey Thong [1989] Director/Pharmacist [Malaysian]

**Wellacy Limited**
*Incorporated:* 4 September 2018
*Registered Office:* 2nd Floor, College House, 17 King Edwards Road, Ruislip, Middlesex, HA4 7AE
*Major Shareholder:* Mark Cooper
*Officers:* Mark Cooper [1988] Director

**Wellbeing Products Limited**
*Incorporated:* 31 October 1989  *Employees:* 2
*Net Worth:* £343,372  *Total Assets:* £381,992
*Registered Office:* 13 Portland Road, Edgbaston, Birmingham, B16 9HN
*Shareholders:* Lynda Irene Jones; Richard Jones
*Officers:* Richard Jones, Secretary; Lynda Irene Jones [1960] Director/Office Supervisor; Richard Jones [1953] Director

**Wellness Clinical Supplies Limited**
*Incorporated:* 19 July 2016
*Registered Office:* 55c Ruskin Gardens, Harrow, Middlesex, HA3 9PY
*Major Shareholder:* Bhumika Sanjaykumar Zalawadiya
*Officers:* Bhumika Sanjaykumar Zalawadiya [1985] Director

**Wellspring Pharmaceutical Services Limited**
*Incorporated:* 12 December 2008
*Registered Office:* Number Three, South Langworthy Road, Salford, M50 2PW
*Parent:* Mawdsley-Brooks & Co Limited
*Officers:* Stephanie Joy Ellison, Secretary; Ian Colin Brownlee [1948] Director; Stephanie Joy Ellison [1958] Director

**Wellspring Pharmaceutical Services UK Limited**
*Incorporated:* 11 December 2008
*Registered Office:* Number Three, South Langworthy Road, Salford, M50 2PW
*Parent:* Mawdsley Brooks & Co Limited
*Officers:* Stephanie Joy Ellison, Secretary; Ian Colin Brownlee [1948] Director; Stephanie Joy Ellison [1958] Director

**Wenimed Ltd**
*Incorporated:* 22 February 2019
*Registered Office:* Pixel Building, 110 Brooker Road, Waltham Abbey, Essex, EN9 1JH
*Major Shareholder:* Ahmet Murat Cinar
*Officers:* Ahmet Murat Cinar [1975] Director/Businessman [Turkish]

**Wep Group Holdings Limited**
*Incorporated:* 19 December 2017
*Registered Office:* G.07 The Light Box, 111 Power Road, Chiswick, London, W4 5PY
*Shareholder:* Jaswinder Singh Khera
*Officers:* Marion Mary Anne Kane [1977] Director; Jaswant Singh Khera [1976] Director; Jaswinder Singh Khera [1963] Director

**Wesbee Ventures Limited**
*Incorporated:* 12 July 2002
*Net Worth Deficit:* £9,712  *Total Assets:* £1,828
*Registered Office:* Suite 61, Battersea Business Centre, 99-109 Lavender Hill, London, SW11 5QL
*Officers:* Isha Dumbuya, Secretary; Isha Dumbuya [1968] Director/Trader [Sierra Leonean]

**Wescroft Limited**
*Incorporated:* 4 April 2016
*Net Worth Deficit:* £35,881  *Total Assets:* £26,656
*Registered Office:* 4th Floor, Clerks Well House, 20 Britton Street, London, EC1M 5UA
*Officers:* Frances Ann Gordon [1954] Director

**L E West Ltd**
*Incorporated:* 22 August 1951  *Employees:* 72
*Net Worth:* £1,046,206  *Total Assets:* £10,622,399
*Registered Office:* Building 4, Chiswick Park , 566 Chiswick High Road, London, W4 5YE
*Shareholders:* Pascal Marie Georges Rey-Herme; Arnaud Paul Alain Vaissie
*Officers:* Greg Ronald Anderson Tanner, Secretary; Christo Jaco Von Elling [1971] Director [South African]; Michael Richardson Gardner [1966] Director [Australian]; Laurent Sabourin [1957] Group Managing Director [French]; Arnaud Paul Alain Vaissie [1954] Director/Chairman and CEO [French]

**Jon West Trading Limited**
*Incorporated:* 5 October 2011  *Employees:* 1
*Net Worth:* £434,766  *Total Assets:* £478,492
*Registered Office:* Brunswick House, 1 Weirfield Green, Taunton, Somerset, TA1 1AZ
*Major Shareholder:* Jonathan West
*Officers:* Jonathan West [1962] Director/Salesman

**Westbourne Medical Limited**
*Incorporated:* 25 June 2008  *Employees:* 3
*Net Worth Deficit:* £17,224  *Total Assets:* £91,216
*Registered Office:* 9 Westbourne Drive, Wilmslow, Cheshire, SK9 2GY
*Shareholders:* John Peter Stuart Birtwistle; Danielle Birtwistle
*Officers:* Danielle Birtwistle [1969] Director; John Peter Stuart Birtwistle [1967] Director

**Westland Pharmaceuticals Limited**
*Incorporated:* 20 June 1977  *Employees:* 4
*Net Worth:* £161,640  *Total Assets:* £364,994
*Registered Office:* Granite Building, 6 Stanley Street, Liverpool, L1 6AF
*Major Shareholder:* Raymond Leslie Squire
*Officers:* Alison Mountney, Secretary; Pauline Squire [1946] Director; Raymond Leslie Squire [1939] Director

**Westmead International Limited**
*Incorporated:* 13 February 1985  *Employees:* 2
*Net Worth:* £108,140  *Total Assets:* £142,662
*Registered Office:* Highfield, Blackpool Road, Clifton, Preston, Lancs, PR4 0XL
*Major Shareholder:* Alan Duncan Emery
*Officers:* Francesca Ellen Leathers, Secretary; Alan Duncan Emery [1948] Managing Director; Francesca Ellen Leathers [1989] Director

**Whiterose Supplements Limited**
*Incorporated:* 13 June 2018
*Registered Office:* 17 Godwin Place, Bradley, Huddersfield, W Yorks, HD2 1RE
*Officers:* Julie Towler [1958] Director

**WHL Contracts Ltd**
*Incorporated:* 1 February 2017
*Net Worth Deficit:* £1,098  *Total Assets:* £1,570
*Registered Office:* The Die Pat Centre, Broad March, Long March Industrial Estate, Daventry, Northants, NN11 4HE
*Parent:* Residual Barrier Technology Ltd
*Officers:* Christine Linda Brander [1957] Director; David Dennis McIntosh [1963] Director

**Wholesale 2 U Ltd**
*Incorporated:* 30 March 2017
*Registered Office:* 2 Bush Hill Road, Winchmore Hill, London, N21 2DS
*Major Shareholder:* Kunal Chotai
*Officers:* Panna Chotai, Secretary; Kunal Chotai [1985] Director/Pharmacist

**Whyte International Limited**
*Incorporated:* 9 March 1998
*Net Worth:* £932,639  *Total Assets:* £3,185,288
*Registered Office:* Berkhamsted House, 121 High Street, Berkhamsted, Herts, HP4 2DJ
*Major Shareholder:* Ashok Mittra
*Officers:* Ashok Mittra [1950] Director/Chief Executive Officer; Niharika Mittra [1981] Director [Indian]

**Wigmore Laboratories Limited**
*Incorporated:* 11 July 2014
*Registered Office:* 23 Wigmore Street, London, W1U 1PL
*Officers:* Jeffrey David Burr [1960] Director; Bedros Loutfig Eghiayan [1949] Director

**Wilkies International Ltd**
*Incorporated:* 28 June 2018
*Registered Office:* Suite 11, West Africa House, Ashbourne Road, London, W5 3QP
*Major Shareholder:* Gurmeet Kishore Singh
*Officers:* Gurmeet Kishore Singh [1965] Director [Singaporean]

**Wilkinson Healthcare Limited**
*Incorporated:* 19 November 2014  *Employees:* 28
*Net Worth:* £436,184  *Total Assets:* £5,712,483
*Registered Office:* Monkstone House, City Road, Peterborough, Cambs, PE1 1JE
*Shareholders:* Hugh Rees; Jacqueline Anne Hills
*Officers:* David Hugh Thomas Rees [1953] Director/Business Manager

**Willbay Limited**
*Incorporated:* 25 January 2007 *Employees:* 2
*Net Worth Deficit:* £879,292 *Total Assets:* £4,895
*Registered Office:* Lynton House, 7-12 Tavistock Square, London, WC1H 9LT
*Shareholders:* Carlos Iglesias Jimenez; Maria Rueda de Valenzuela
*Officers:* Maria Rueda de Valenzuela, Secretary/Lawyer [Spanish]; Carlos Iglesias Jimenez [1965] Director/Pharmacist [Spanish]; Maria Rueda de Valenzuela [1967] Director/Lawyer [Spanish]

**Willgen Consulting Limited**
*Incorporated:* 24 June 2011
*Net Worth:* £68,683 *Total Assets:* £125,873
*Registered Office:* Suite 6, First Floor, High Street, Sedgefield, Stockton on Tees, Cleveland, TS21 3AR
*Major Shareholder:* Richard Willis
*Officers:* Lynsey Willis [1977] Director/Human Resources; Richard Willis [1972] Director

**Winchpharma (Consumer Healthcare) Ltd**
*Incorporated:* 28 August 2012
*Net Worth Deficit:* £121 *Total Assets:* £2,538
*Registered Office:* c/o Byotrol PLC, Building 303, Thornton Science Park, Pool Lane, Chester, CH2 4NU
*Parent:* Byotrol PLC
*Officers:* Denise Yvonne Keenan, Secretary; Dr Thomas Trevor Francis [1950] Director; David Thomas Traynor [1965] Director

**Windzor Pharma Limited**
*Incorporated:* 23 August 2017
*Registered Office:* Unit 4 Wintonlea, Monument Way West, Woking, Surrey, GU21 5EN
*Shareholder:* Rory Walter O'Riordan
*Officers:* Parag Khiroya [1963] Director; Nilesh Nathwani [1961] Director/Pharmacist; Rory Walter O'Riordan [1961] Director/Pharmacist [Irish]

**Winelia Company Limited**
*Incorporated:* 30 May 2012
*Net Worth:* £2 *Total Assets:* £7,451
*Registered Office:* 11 Engine Lane, Broughton, Aylesbury, Bucks, HP22 7BB
*Shareholder:* Wellington Gotah
*Officers:* Benedicta Gotah, Secretary; Wellington Gotah [1976] Director/Assistant Quantity Surveyor [Ghanaian]

**Winsor Pharma UK Limited**
*Incorporated:* 11 February 2015
*Registered Office:* 111a Headstone Road, Harrow, Middlesex, HA1 1PG
*Major Shareholder:* Karunaratna Weddikkara Arachchilage
*Officers:* Karunaratna Weddikkara Arrachchilage [1973] Director [Sri Lankan]

**Wonder World Ltd**
*Incorporated:* 19 July 2012
*Net Worth:* £9,616 *Total Assets:* £3,084,576
*Registered Office:* 1a Crown Lane, London, SW16 3DJ
*Major Shareholder:* Elena Protsenko
*Officers:* Cristino Guevara Salazar [1964] Director/Consultant [Panamanian]

**Christopher Wood IXRS Consulting Ltd**
*Incorporated:* 12 October 2017
*Registered Office:* 4 Cross Street, Beeston, Nottingham, NG9 2NX
*Shareholders:* Christopher Wood; Louise Wood
*Officers:* Louise Wood, Secretary; Christopher Wood [1982] Director/Project Manager

**Peter John Wood Limited**
*Incorporated:* 2 March 1994
*Previous:* Southern Chemical Services Limited
*Registered Office:* 118 Old Milton Road, New Milton, Hants, BH25 6EB
*Shareholders:* Peter Dixon Clegg; Sharon Noble; Michael Stephen Lester
*Officers:* Peter Dixon Clegg [1956] Director/Chartered Accountant

**Carl Woolf Limited**
*Incorporated:* 6 May 2010
*Net Worth:* £386,123 *Total Assets:* £418,694
*Registered Office:* 1st Floor, 314 Regents Park Road, London, N3 2LT
*Major Shareholder:* Carl Daniel Woolf
*Officers:* Carl Daniel Woolf [1970] Director/Pharmacist

**World Medicine Limited**
*Incorporated:* 12 November 2004 *Employees:* 5
*Net Worth:* £1,218,859 *Total Assets:* £2,779,074
*Registered Office:* Ground Floor, Gadd House, Arcadia Avenue, Finchley, London, N3 2JU
*Major Shareholder:* Raushan Tahiyeu
*Officers:* Zafer Karaman, Secretary; Raushan Tahiyeu [1969] Sales and Marketing Director [Belarusian]

**World Trends Ltd**
*Incorporated:* 9 March 2018
*Registered Office:* 25 Wilding Drive, Crewe, Cheshire, CW1 4GP
*Major Shareholder:* Itthiphon Klaharn
*Officers:* Itthiphon Klaharn, Secretary; Itthiphon Klaharn [1998] Director/Owner [Thai]

**Worldtrition Ltd**
*Incorporated:* 31 December 2018
*Registered Office:* Unit F5, Phoenix Industrial Estate, Rosslyn Crescent, Harrow, Middlesex, HA1 2SP
*Major Shareholder:* Zohaib Shariff
*Officers:* Zohaib Shariff [1983] Director

**Wowwax Ltd.**
*Incorporated:* 23 July 2009
*Registered Office:* Pinnacle House Business Centre, Newark Road, Peterborough, Cambs, PE1 5YD
*Major Shareholder:* Alistair Martin Ashworth
*Officers:* Alistair Martin Ashworth [1963] Director/Engineer

**WPG Wholesale Trading Ltd**
*Incorporated:* 2 August 2011
*Previous:* Winchpharma Group Limited
*Net Worth:* £96,227 *Total Assets:* £105,437
*Registered Office:* 13 Bridge Street, Barnsley, S Yorks, S71 1PL
*Shareholder:* Nathan Joseph Winch
*Officers:* Nathan Joseph Winch [1990] Director

**WR Mediservices Limited**
*Incorporated:* 4 September 2015
*Registered Office:* 31 Wycombe End, Beaconsfield, Bucks, HP9 1LZ
*Major Shareholder:* Risha Story
*Officers:* Risha Story [1985] Director/Dentist; Dr William Peter Story [1986] Director/Dentist

**WTE Services Limited**
*Incorporated:* 30 March 2004  *Employees:* 4
*Net Worth:* £133,998  *Total Assets:* £269,420
*Registered Office:* The Surgery, Mill Road, Market Rasen, Lincs, LN8 3BP
*Shareholder:* Julia Weeks
*Officers:* Dr Robert Victor Weeks, Secretary/Medical Practitioner; Dr Therese Mary Nation [1964] Director/Medical Practitioner; Dr Robert Victor Weeks [1961] Director/Medical Practitioner

**Wycombe Locum Services Ltd**
*Incorporated:* 19 April 2017
*Net Worth:* £3,061  *Total Assets:* £30,558
*Registered Office:* 157 Spearing Road, High Wycombe, Bucks, HP12 3LB
*Officers:* Abid Yaqoob [1989] Director/Businessman

**Xanton Limited**
*Incorporated:* 1 November 2012  *Employees:* 8
*Net Worth Deficit:* £266,405  *Total Assets:* £755,494
*Registered Office:* Unit 2, Plot 2, Sketchley Meadows Industrial Estate, Hinckley, Leics, LE10 3EN
*Shareholders:* Glyn Ian Matthews; Rebekka Angela Matthews
*Officers:* Glyn Ian Matthews [1975] Director

**Xenium International Limited**
*Incorporated:* 30 July 2018
*Registered Office:* 19 Edinburgh Drive, Staines upon Thames, Surrey, TW18 1PJ
*Major Shareholder:* Varinder Kaur Kalsi
*Officers:* Simran Kaur Kalsi [1997] Director [Kenyan]; Varinder Kaur Kalsi [1969] Director [Kenyan]

**Y A Toner Limited**
*Incorporated:* 5 September 2002  *Employees:* 1
*Net Worth Deficit:* £8,058  *Total Assets:* £6,161
*Registered Office:* 424 Margate Road, Westwood, Ramsgate, Kent, CT12 6SR
*Major Shareholder:* Yvette Antoinette Toner
*Officers:* Donal Malachy Stephen Toner, Secretary/Bank Manager [Irish]; Yvette Antoinette Toner [1960] Director/Pharmacist [Irish]

**Yaubag Limited**
*Incorporated:* 18 February 2010  *Employees:* 1
*Net Worth:* £51,228  *Total Assets:* £76,606
*Registered Office:* 32a East Street, St Ives, Cambs, PE27 5PD
*Major Shareholder:* Jimmy Yau
*Officers:* Jimmy Yau [1972] Director

**Yawskin Limited**
*Incorporated:* 1 June 2012
*Net Worth Deficit:* £11,399  *Total Assets:* £6,267
*Registered Office:* 31 Swale Road, Brough, E Yorks, HU15 1GG
*Major Shareholder:* Victor Koku
*Officers:* Victor Olasubomi Koku [1970] Director/Pharmacist

**Yiling Ltd**
*Incorporated:* 22 October 2010  *Employees:* 4
*Net Worth:* £124,418  *Total Assets:* £152,348
*Registered Office:* Units 3 and 4 Quidhampton Business Units, Polhampton Lane, Overton, Basingstoke, Hants, RG25 3ED
*Officers:* Chenguang Li [1973] Director [Chinese]; Xiuqing Li [1978] Director and Company Secretary [Chinese]; Tianqiang Wang [1980] BD Director [Chinese]; Xiangjun Wu [1975] Director [Chinese]

**YJBPort Limited**
*Incorporated:* 19 April 2007  *Employees:* 1
*Net Worth:* £298,504  *Total Assets:* £1,868,543
*Registered Office:* 74 Briarwood Drive, Northwood, Middlesex, HA6 1PL
*Major Shareholder:* Yogendra Patel
*Officers:* Jitendrakumar Patel, Secretary; Yogendra Patel [1979] Director

**Youmed Limited**
*Incorporated:* 31 July 2015
*Net Worth:* £3,701  *Total Assets:* £61,520
*Registered Office:* 5 Bisham Court, Bisham, Marlow, Bucks, SL7 1SD
*Shareholders:* Christopher Robin Brain; Elizabeth Brain
*Officers:* Christopher Robin Brain [1980] Director; Elizabeth Brain [1981] Director

**Your Products Limited**
*Incorporated:* 20 November 2014
*Net Worth:* £120,422  *Total Assets:* £248,439
*Registered Office:* 118 Pall Mall, London, SW1Y 5ED
*Officers:* Andrew Davis [1965] Director; Adrian Patrick Giles [1962] Director; Ben Holdsworth [1984] Director/Pharmaceutical Professional; Adam Spencer Knights [1970] Director

**Ypsomed Limited**
*Incorporated:* 21 January 2010  *Employees:* 28
*Net Worth:* £3,422,275  *Total Assets:* £8,237,436
*Registered Office:* 1 Park Court, Riccall Road, Escrick, N Yorks, YO19 6ED
*Officers:* Simon Michel [1977] Director/Senior Vice President - Marketing and Sales [Swiss]; Niklaus Ramseier [1963] Director [Swiss]

**Z T Locums Ltd**
*Incorporated:* 18 October 2018
*Registered Office:* 322 Gibbet Street, Halifax, W Yorks, HX1 4JW
*Major Shareholder:* Zenib Jabeen Tariq
*Officers:* Zenib Jabeen Tariq [1995] Director

**Zaaz Limited**
*Incorporated:* 18 May 2018
*Registered Office:* 27 Old Gloucester Street, London, WC1N 3AX
*Major Shareholder:* Aamit Kapoor
*Officers:* Aamit Kapoor [1981] Director [Indian]

**Zaitun Limited**
*Incorporated:* 1 March 2007  *Employees:* 4
*Net Worth:* £45,432  *Total Assets:* £131,414
*Registered Office:* 5 Broomhill Drive, Leeds, LS17 6JW
*Major Shareholder:* Munavvar Hussain
*Officers:* Saiqa Hussain, Secretary; Munavvar Hussain [1982] Director

**Zanoprima Holdings Limited**
*Incorporated:* 9 July 2014  *Employees:* 2
*Net Worth:* £15,506  *Total Assets:* £148,557
*Registered Office:* 5th Floor, Charles House, 108-110 Finchley Road, London, NW3 5JJ
*Major Shareholder:* Ashok Narasimhan
*Officers:* Nicholas Peter Hyde [1959] Director; Ashok Narasimhan [1955] Director

**Zanoprima LifeSciences Limited**
Incorporated: 10 June 2014  Employees: 2
Net Worth Deficit: £135,260  Total Assets: £1,508
Registered Office: 5th Floor, Charles House, 108-110 Finchley Road, London, NW3 5JJ
Parent: Zanoprima Holdings Limited
Officers: Nicholas Peter Hyde [1959] Director; Ashok Narasimhan [1955] Director

**Zanza Specials International Limited**
Incorporated: 11 June 2012  Employees: 5
Net Worth: £60,894  Total Assets: £741,188
Registered Office: Unit 1, 76 Stephenson Way, Formby Business Park, Formby, Merseyside, L37 8EG
Parent: Apollo Generics Limited
Officers: Richard Alan Rawlinson [1968] Director

**Zarroug Limited**
Incorporated: 7 December 2018
Registered Office: 32 Roger Drive, Sandal, Wakefield, W Yorks, WF2 7NE
Major Shareholder: Osman Hamza Osman Zarroug
Officers: Osman Hamza Osman Zarroug [1988] Director/Pharmacist

**Zeal Products Limited**
Incorporated: 5 April 1989  Employees: 8
Net Worth: £157,402  Total Assets: £339,953
Registered Office: Zeal House, Ikon Industrial Estate, Droitwich Road, Hartlebury, Kidderminster, Worcs, DY10 4EU
Shareholders: Andrew Roger Apperly; William George Jakeman
Officers: Andrew Roger Apperly, Secretary; Andrew Roger Apperly [1946] Director/Pharmaceutical Chemist; William George Jakeman [1956] Director/Wholesaler

**Zecare Limited**
Incorporated: 29 March 2005  Employees: 25
Net Worth: £568,259  Total Assets: £4,738,532
Registered Office: 3 Howard Road, Eaton Socon, St Neots, Cambs, PE19 8ET
Major Shareholder: Nazma Tasneem Ginai
Officers: Ian Alan Walter, Secretary; Musharraf Mahmood Ginai [1954] Director; Nazma Tasneem Ginai [1957] Director

**Zefer Pharma Ltd.**
Incorporated: 29 June 2011
Net Worth: £8,239  Total Assets: £48,150
Registered Office: 1a Crown Lane, London, SW16 3DJ
Officers: Jan Harm Snyman [1968] Director/Consultant [South African]

**Zelens Limited**
Incorporated: 24 February 2011  Employees: 7
Net Worth: £1,177,970  Total Assets: £2,072,717
Registered Office: Flat 27, 152 Grosvenor Road, London, SW1V 3JL
Major Shareholder: Marko Bojan Lens
Officers: Dr Marko Bojan Lens [1969] Director/Surgeon [Italian]

**Zena Cosmetics (U.K.) Limited**
Incorporated: 19 January 1973  Employees: 1
Net Worth: £14,789  Total Assets: £36,536
Registered Office: c/o Pooleys, 45 Lemon Street, Truro, Cornwall, TR1 2NS
Major Shareholder: Moira Felicity Starr
Officers: Moira Felicity Starr, Secretary; Moira Felicity Starr [1950] Director; Oliver Henry Starr [1990] Director

**Zentiva Pharma UK Limited**
Incorporated: 28 August 1987
Previous: Winthrop Pharmaceuticals UK Limited
Registered Office: One Onslow Street, Guildford, Surrey, GU1 4YS
Parent: Al Sirona (Luxembourg) Acquisition S.A.R.L.
Officers: Jane Hill [1976] Director/General Manager; Manish Khandelwal [1973] Director/CFO-Zentiva Pharma UK Ltd [Indian]

**Zerocann Ltd**
Incorporated: 9 November 2016
Registered Office: 46 Nova Road, Croydon, Surrey, CR0 2TL
Major Shareholder: Michal Takac
Officers: Michal Takac [1979] Director [Czech]

**Zeroderma Limited**
Incorporated: 12 July 2000
Registered Office: Linthwaite Laboratories, Linthwaite, Huddersfield, W Yorks, HD7 5QH
Parent: Thornton & Ross Ltd
Officers: Edwin Charles Blythe, Secretary; Charles Ashley Brierley [1963] Director

**Zeymos Pharma Ltd**
Incorporated: 29 October 2018
Registered Office: 1 Sir Alexander Close, London, W3 7JQ
Major Shareholder: Zeyad Almthqal
Officers: Zeyad Almthqal [1971] Director [Syrian]

**Zhongfu (UK) Limited**
Incorporated: 24 January 2019
Registered Office: Office One, 10 New Era Square, Sheffield, S2 4BF
Officers: Hao Jiang [1988] Director [Chinese]

**Zhpharma Ltd**
Incorporated: 2 August 2013  Employees: 1
Net Worth Deficit: £4,001  Total Assets: £23,293
Registered Office: 67 Buxton Street, Leicester, LE2 0FL
Major Shareholder: Zubair Haveliwala
Officers: Zubair Haveliwala, Secretary; Zubair Haveliwala [1986] Director/Pharmacist

**Zimmer Biomet UK Limited**
Incorporated: 13 November 1962  Employees: 306
Previous: Zimmer Limited
Net Worth: £74,042,000  Total Assets: £127,072,000
Registered Office: The Courtyard, Lancaster Place, South Marston Park, Swindon, Wilts, SN3 4FP
Parent: Zimmer UK Ltd
Officers: Bo Vendelboe, Secretary; Urs Mueller [1960] Director/Senior Legal Counsel [German]; Steven Orange [1972] Director/VP North Region; Bo Vendelboe [1969] Finance Director [Danish]

**Zina Chemist Limited**
Incorporated: 3 April 1986  Employees: 9
Net Worth: £936,193  Total Assets: £1,747,159
Registered Office: 76-78 Godstone Road, Kenley, Surrey, CR8 5AA
Shareholders: Kalpana Vijay Ghedia; Vijay Ghedia
Officers: Kalpana Ghedia, Secretary; Vijay Ranchod Ghedia [1958] Director/Chemist

### Zista Pharma Limited
*Incorporated:* 11 December 2015  *Employees:* 1
*Previous:* EYWA Pharma Limited
*Net Worth:* £641,023  *Total Assets:* £655,031
*Registered Office:* Amba House, 4th Floor, Kings Suite, 15 College Road, Harrow, Middlesex, HA1 1BA
*Officers:* Brijesh Kumar [1975] Director Business Development; Senthil Kumar Pachaiyappan [1976] Director of Regulatory & Pharmacovigilance; Jayakumar Ramamoorthy [1971] Director/Businessman [Indian]; Srinivasan Seshan [1966] Director [Indian]

### ZMI Investments Limited
*Incorporated:* 16 February 2017
*Registered Office:* 2nd Floor, 9 Portland Street, Manchester, M1 3BE
*Major Shareholder:* Zubair Malik
*Officers:* Zubair Malik [1975] Director/Pharmacist

### Zoetis UK Limited
*Incorporated:* 22 June 2012  *Employees:* 162
*Net Worth:* £64,257,000  *Total Assets:* £106,904,000
*Registered Office:* 5th Floor, 6 St Andrew Street, London, EC4A 3AE
*Officers:* Dr Ben Backmann [1975] Director/Attorney [German]; Jamie Andrew Brannan [1972] Director/Vice President and Cluster Lead

### Zolex Global Limited
*Incorporated:* 19 December 2017
*Registered Office:* Flat 1, Wren Court, 29 Bounds Green Road, Wood Green, London, N22 8SD
*Shareholders:* Alexandra Georgopoulou; Zoltan Feher
*Officers:* Zoltan Feher [1985] Director [Hungarian]

### Zoono Holdings Limited
*Incorporated:* 23 October 2017
*Registered Office:* 59 Abbeygate Street, Bury St Edmunds, Suffolk, IP33 1LB
*Shareholders:* Paul Hyslop; Margaret Jane Morgan
*Officers:* Paul Russell Hyslop [1957] Director [New Zealander]; James Alexander John Milnes [1976] Director

### Zoop Pharma Ltd
*Incorporated:* 24 December 2018
*Registered Office:* 4 The Arches, Furmston Court, Icknield Way, Letchworth Garden City, Herts, SG6 1UJ
*Shareholders:* Anzal Qurbain; Claire Qurbain
*Officers:* Dr Anzal Qurbain [1972] Director/Doctor

### Zota Healthcare Limited
*Incorporated:* 28 March 2017
*Net Worth Deficit:* £213  *Total Assets:* £100
*Registered Office:* 29 Sunningdale Gardens, London, NW9 9NB
*Major Shareholder:* Moxesh Zota
*Officers:* Moxesh Zota [1990] Director/Businessman [Indian]

### ZS Pharma Limited
*Incorporated:* 23 June 2017
*Net Worth Deficit:* £14,444  *Total Assets:* £9,405
*Registered Office:* The Zak Partnership Ltd, 20 Ashfield Road, Leicester, LE2 1LA
*Officers:* Tarique Ali [1985] Director; Madhvi Bindah [1981] Director; Nawal Haddouch [1989] Director; Rahima Hoque [1971] Director; Shaheda Khanom [1988] Director; Sarfraz Patel [1983] Director; Zahid Patel [1992] Director; Amrit Kaur Roshan [1962] Director

### ZS Solutions Limited
*Incorporated:* 30 November 2012  *Employees:* 2
*Net Worth:* £4,685  *Total Assets:* £42,109
*Registered Office:* Suite 11, Penhurst House, 352-356 Battersea Park Road, London, SW11 3BY
*Shareholders:* Zahirbhai Abbasbhai Patel; Sumaiya Patel
*Officers:* Sumaiya Patel, Secretary; Sumaiya Patel [1984] Director; Zahirbhai Abbasbhai Patel [1984] Director [Indian]

### ZTK Business Services Limited
*Incorporated:* 4 December 1996
*Registered Office:* 41 The Woodlands, Linton, Cambs, CB21 4UG
*Shareholders:* Zafer Karaman; Turan Karaman
*Officers:* Turan Karaman, Secretary; Zafer Karaman [1958] Director

### Zululan Pharma Ltd
*Incorporated:* 27 March 2018
*Registered Office:* 272 Bath Street, Glasgow, G2 4JR
*Shareholders:* Farooq Mohammad; Akheel Mohammed
*Officers:* Mateenuddin Mohammed Khaja [1980] Director/Pharmacist [Indian]

### Zymix Limited
*Incorporated:* 6 November 2015
*Registered Office:* Bank Chambers, Brook Street, Bishops Waltham, Hants, SO32 1AX
*Major Shareholder:* Richard George Stead
*Officers:* Richard Stead, Secretary; Richard George Stead [1949] Director

# Index of Directorships

**Aabo, Gitte Pugholm**
Leo Laboratories Limited

**Aal-Oleiwi, Mohammed Dhaffer**
Chelsea Pharma Limited

**Abad, Isaac**
TRB Chemedica (UK) Limited

**Abbas, Awad Kazem**
Best-Bio Ltd

**Abbas, Mohaned Awad**
Bio Global Limited

**Abbassi, Hannah May**
House of Filler Limited

**Abbassioun, Vahid**
Technoglobal Ltd

**Abdel Latif, Ehab**
Bidaya UK Ltd.

**Abdelgalil, Ahmed Ibrahim Fadel**
IPS International Corporation Ltd

**Abdelhamid, Osama**
Layan Pharma Ltd

**Abdul Careem, Aroos**
Life Science Healthcare UK Ltd

**Abdul Rahman, Mohd Rodzi Bin**
RR Cosmeceuticals (UK) Ltd

**Abdul Razak, Norzaidah**
Pinklady International Ltd

**Abdullaev, Farkhod**
Medintek Holdings Ltd

**Abdulloev, Sadullo**
Spey Limited
Spey Pharma Limited

**Abdulrahman, Firdowsa**
Naskalmik Limited

**Abell, Martin James**
Clinigen CTS Limited
Clinigen Group PLC
Clinigen Healthcare Limited
Idis Group Holdings Limited
Idis Limited

**Abid, Mohammed**
Al-Ghani Limited

**Abley, Ben**
Orkal Ltd

**Abley, Gillian Lesley**
Orkal Ltd

**Abley, Kevan**
Orkal Ltd

**Aboobacker, Zuhail**
Comfylife Ltd

**Abora, Abigail Amma Afriyie**
Curist Health Limited

**Abou-El-Wafa, Moamen Moustafa**
Entrust & UK Ltd

**Abou-El-Wafa, Moamen**
Dr Kool Ltd

**Abraham, Zachariah**
Quramax Limited

**Abrar, Mohammed**
Bioavexia Ltd
HealthVillagePlus Limited

**Abu Goush, Haytham**
Style Global Trading FZE Ltd

**Abu Sheikha, Omar Mahmood**
B.R. Pharmaceuticals Limited

**Abu Sheikha, Ziad Mahmoud Mousa**
B.R. Pharmaceuticals Limited
Creative Brand Concepts Ltd

**Abu-Ammouneh, Said**
Pharmasky Ltd

**Abusheikha, Taisir**
B.R. Pharmaceuticals Limited

**Achite, Amine, Dr**
European Nutriceutical Products Ltd

**Ackerstaff, Klaus**
Simcro (UK) Limited

**Davies, Nicola Jane**
The Active Prescription Ltd

**Adam, Jeanie**
Omega Surgical Instruments Ltd

**Adamson, Ian Robert**
East Midlands Pharma Limited

**Adan, Ali Ismail Osman**
1st Class Medical Ltd

**Addo, David Frempong**
Curist Health Limited

**Adebisi, Adedoyin**
Adedoyin Adebisi Ltd

**Adebisi, Banjo Ayodeji Samuel**
Ba-Inspire Limited

**Adegbesan, Adeniyi Adesanmi, Dr**
Model Medics Limited

**Adegbesan, Akindayo Habeeb**
NSA Pharma Limited

**Aden, Abdulqafar Mohamed**
Medix Supply International Ltd

**Adenwalla, Hakimddin Saifuddin**
Trutek Europe Ltd

**Adewakun, Ademola Eniola**
Shieldasset Limited

**Adewakun, Anne Elvina Mausi**
Shieldasset Limited

**Adeyileka, Olumide Olumuyiwa**
Codix Pharma (UK) Limited

**Adigun, Ganiat Folakemi Bose**
Rifaray Limited

**Adjei, Felicia Gloria**
Akro Pharmaceutical Co Ltd

**Adjei, Karl**
Akro Pharmaceutical Co Ltd

**Adjei, Samuel Tetteh**
Akro Pharmaceutical Co Ltd

**Adkins, Nat G Jr**
Ocusoft UK Limited

**Adnan, Sobia**
Global Additives Ltd

**Samra, Ranjit Singh**
The Aesthetics Clinic Dot Ltd

**Agaba, Betrand Kachukwu**
Busky Limited

**Agbejule, Adewale Olanrewaju**
Maplewood Investments Limited

**Agbejule, Irenitemi Michael Oluwatobiloba**
Maplewood Investments Limited

**Agbejule, Tinuola Sarah Anike**
Maplewood Investments Limited

**Aggarwal, Raj Kumar**
NPA Services Limited

**Aggarwal, Rohini**
RSS Wholesaling Limited

**Aghadiuno, Andrew Nwachukwu**
Jules Pharma Limited

**Aghadiuno, Robert**
Ragit Services Ltd
Randa Pharma Ltd

**Agrawal, Amul Kamal Kumar**
Aptil Pharma Limited
Torrent Pharma (UK) Ltd

**Agyei, Eric Kwaku**
Ontyme Logistics and Healthcare Ltd

**Ahern, William**
Aneid UK Limited
Mycology Research Laboratories Ltd

**Ahmad, Adeel**
Focus Pharma Holdings Limited
Focus Pharmaceuticals Limited

**Ahmad, Arif Mushtaq, Dr**
I.T.T.I.D. (Trading) Ltd

**Ahmad, Attaul-Haleem**
Saving Life Technologies Ltd

**Ahmad, Sahar, Dr**
I.T.T.I.D. (Trading) Ltd

**Ahmad, Salman**
Health Source Limited

**Ahmadkhanbeigi, Raha**
Rak Pharma Ltd

**Ahmed Mostafa, Yasser Kamaleldin**
Modern Innovations Limited Ltd

**Ahmed, Abdel Rahman, Dr**
CoAcS Trading Limited

**Ahmed, Ahmed Yusuf**
Damum UK Limited

**Ahmed, Ahmed**
Medsupply Ltd

**Ahmed, Baseer**
Medicure Scientific Limited

**Ahmed, Hafiz**
Healtholozy UK Limited

**Ahmed, Hamzat Yusuf**
Damum UK Limited

**Ahmed, Ibrahim Yusuf**
Damum UK Limited

**Ahmed, Maqsood, Dr**
Pennine Pharmaceuticals Ltd

**Ahmed, Mian Naveed**
Comebro International Ltd

**Ahmed, Mohamed Ahmed Shafiek Mohamed**
Avanzcare Limited

**Ahmed, Mushtaq**
Farah Chemists Limited

**Ahmed, Nabeel**
Farah Chemists Limited

**Ahmed, Nuradeen Yusuf**
Damum UK Limited

**Ahmed, Riaz**
Isra Limited

**Ahmed, Shakeel**
Farah Chemists Limited

**Ahmed, Shakeela**
Farah Chemists Limited

**Ahmed, Syed Naseer**
Esthetica Pure Ltd
Microskin Cosmeceuticals UK Ltd

**Ahmed, Syed Salmaan**
Esthetica Pure Ltd
Microskin Cosmeceuticals UK Ltd

**Ahomaki, Satu Maarit**
Orion Pharma (UK) Limited

**Aiken, Hannah Mary Talbot, Dr**
Veriton Pharma Limited

**Aimar, Andrea**
Harmonium Investments Limited

**Ainsworth, Ian Howard**
Irls Yorkshire Limited

**Airhiavbere, Ewan Prince**
ABC Pharmaceuticals Ltd

**Aitchison, Iain Allan**
Apple Pharma Limited

**Aitchison, Julie Wilson Smith**
Apple Pharma Limited

**Ajaegbu, Osinachi Chinagozim**
Natchy Ltd

**Ajgaonkar, Atul Vijay**
Medicom Healthcare Limited

**Akenroye, Temidayo**
Phaximed Limited

**Akhavan Zanjani, Jahanshah**
Paraxmed Limited

**Akindele, Akintoye Adeoye**
Curist Health Limited

**Akindele, Olutobi Olusola**
Phaximed Limited

**Akinsanya, Abiola**
Codix Pharma (UK) Limited

**Akram, Zulfkar**
Resource Medical (UK) Ltd

**Akter, Roushanara**
Aariana Impex Limited

**Akudi, Habib Ebrahim Ullah**
Biogenix Ltd

**Al Azawi, Ali Hussein Mahmood**
Diaylaa Ltd

**Al Bajari, Ibraheem Abdulazize**
UK Medical Centre Ltd

**Al Bajari, Ibraheem**
Britannia Medical Limited

**Al Bajary, Samir**
Britannia Medical Limited

**Al Fadhli, Talal**
Medcare Life UK Ltd

**Al Ghamdi, Abdul Mohsen Ibrahim**
Targeter (UK) Limited

**Al Ghamdi, Abdul Rahman Ibrahim**
Targeter (UK) Limited

**Al Grou, Hamed Mohammed Ahmed**
Britannic Pharma Ltd

**Al Jabari, Abbas**
Rosefield Pharma Ltd

**Al Mulla, Authman**
Eton Pharma Ltd

**Al-Allaq, Taife**
Britannia Medical Limited

**Al-Ani, Salah, Dr**
Britannia Medical Limited

**Al-Doori, Mohammed**
Crescent Pharma Limited
Crescent Pharma OTC Limited

**Al-Dzhadir, Mukhaled, Dr**
Euro Capital Management (ECM) Ltd

**Al-Hadethee, Sanaa**
Pharmacare International Ltd

**Al-Hashimi, Ali**
Masa Pharma Ltd

**Al-Hemyari, Ahmed**
Centline Ltd

**Al-Janabi, Mazin Julien**
Biogenez Ltd

**Al-Kassar, Bader Wasim**
Appleby Pharmacy Limited

**Al-Maeedh, Abdulrazzaq**
Absolute Brands Ltd

**Al-Mashta, Sameer, Dr**
S M Locum Consultants Ltd

**Al-Naib, Kameran, Dr**
Kamo Dental Products Limited

**Al-Saadi, Ahmed**
Irasco Ltd

**Al-Shalechy, Mustafa**
Curelife Ltd

**Al-Shelby, Esam**
Britannia Medical Limited

**Al-Suhail, Sally Ibrahim Hasan**
Sood-UK Ltd

**Al-Tahan, Hussain**
Vipharm Limited

**Alallaq, Ahmed, Dr**
Medica Ltd

**Alallaq, Riyadh, Dr**
Medica Ltd

**Alam Bhuiyan, MD Saiful**
Rexcel Trading Ltd

**Alavi, Mehdi**
Dream Pharma Ltd

**Albahnasawy, Ahmed Hassan Ahmed**
Aventa International Corporation Ltd

**Albayati, Lina Taher**
Meds Global Limited

**Albrecht, Patrick**
Beiersdorf UK Ltd.

**Alcock, Fiona Elizabeth**
Oxford Biosystems Limited

**Alderwish, Samira**
Hemp Remedy Ltd

**Aldib, Talaat Abdelhamid Ahmed**
BDCP Ltd

**Alfayoumi, Suhad, Dr**
Healthcare Source Limited

**Ali Saleh, Abdul Kader**
Pharmex International Ltd

**Ali, Abdul Hamin**
Nasila Pharma Limited

**Ali, Abdulrahman**
Alixport Ltd

**Ali, Akhtar**
Hashmats Health Ltd

**Ali, Anwar**
Cubic Pharmaceuticals Limited

**Ali, Asad Mohsin**
Ipsen Limited

**Ali, Asad**
Dispensing Healthcare Ltd

**Ali, Dilshad**
Hashmats Health Ltd

**Ali, Fahid**
Hashmats Health Ltd

**Ali, Farida**
Seren Plus Limited

**Ali, Fayroz**
Fayroz Pharma Limited

**Ali, Mohammed Naveed**
London Health Suppliers Ltd

**Ali, Syed Mohammad**
G9UK Limited

**Ali, Syed Mustafa**
G9UK Limited

**Ali, Syed Noor Uz Zia, Dr**
G9UK Limited

**Ali, Tarique**
ZS Pharma Limited

**Ali, Ubayd**
U A Ali Ltd

**Ali, Waqas Afsar**
Sprint Moto UK Ltd

**Ali, Zehra Ambreen**
G9UK Limited

**Alidina, Husainali**
Kings Medical Supplies Limited

**Allen, Alfred David**
Adallen Pharma Limited

**Allen, Elizabeth Ann**
Vision Matrix Limited

**Allen, Evelyn**
LM3 Business Ltd

**Allen, Glynn Charles**
Vision Matrix Limited

**Allen, Jane Mary**
Mcall Consulting Ltd

**Allen, Patrick Thompson**
Optident Labline Limited

**Allen, Peter Vance**
Clinigen Group PLC

**Allen, Peter**
Appia Healthcare Limited
Cryotag Limited

**Allen, Richard Oliver**
Adallen Pharma Limited

**Allen, Samuel Adebambo**
LM3 Business Ltd

**Allen, Susan Charlene**
Here We Flo Ltd
Sustainable Ethical Enterprises Ltd

**Allinson, Paul William**
Sophos Medical Limited

**Allison, Andrew Laurence, Mr**
Randall Allison Limited

**Almahmoud, Zaher**
United Med Ltd

**Almeshal, Talal, Dr**
Al Razi Pharma UK Ltd

**Almthqal, Zeyad**
United Pharma Ltd
Zeymos Pharma Ltd

**Almustafa, Karam**
Medex Pharma Limited

**Aloum, Fatima**
Florence Health & Beauty Ltd

**Alrahow, Hassan**
Moogle Meds Ltd

**Alshamari, Mohammed Ali**
Curelife Ltd

**Altaie, Muthana**
MM Medical Equipment UK Ltd

**Altman, Jeffrey Allen**
Cardio Pro Limited

**Alwahebi, Abdullah Wahebi**
Alhaddag Phrma Ltd

**Alyanai, Dazan**
SAR Health Limited

**Alzahrani, Saeed Radad**
Al Razi Pharma UK Ltd

**Amaning, Clement**
Valupharm UK Limited

**Amaning, Marie, Dr**
Valupharm UK Limited

**Amano, Motoyuki**
Amano Enzyme Europe Limited

**Ambaw, Abebaw Biru**
Medpharm Global UK Limited

**Ambrose, Tim**
Nascot Health Ltd

**Amery, James David**
Max Healthcare Limited
Max Remedies Limited

**Amin, Anand Pankaj**
Elmstone Healthcare Limited

**Amin, Bhushankumar Natubhai**
Victoria Meds Mondial Ltd

**Amin, Ketan**
Multi Pharma Limited

**Amin, Naseem Sajjid**
GMP-Orphan United Kingdom Ltd

**Amin, Pallavi Bhupesh**
PB's Locum Services Limited

**Amin, Priyankaben**
Care Healthcare Ltd

**Amin, Shailesh**
Metropharm Limited

**Amjed, Sohail**
SkInOne UK Ltd

**Ammann, Catherine Susanne**
Santhera (UK) Limited

**Amozandeh, Babak, Dr**
Dr Ba Limited

**Amweg, Levin Kim**
Cannerald Group Ltd

**Ananthamohan, Thanaluxmy**
Micro Industries Limited

**Anastasiou, Ioannis**
Frezyderm UK Limited

**Anastasov, Boyan, Dr**
Rex Pharmaceuticals Ltd

**Anderson, Edward**
Cambridge Biotics Ltd

**Anderson, Jill Dawn**
ViiV Healthcare Overseas Ltd
ViiV Healthcare Trading Services UK
ViiV Healthcare UK Limited

**Anderson, Mark Leroy**
Rembrook Developments Limited

**Anderson, Robert**
Merlin Vet Export Ltd

**Anderson, Stephen William**
G Pharma Limited
Nucare Limited
Nupharm Limited
Phoenix Healthcare Distribution Ltd
Phoenix Medical Supplies Ltd

**Anderson, Toby Matthew**
AAH Pharmaceuticals Limited
Barclay Pharmaceuticals Ltd
Blackstaff Pharmaceuticals Ltd
Lloyds Pharmacy Clinical Homecare
Masta Limited
Prima Brands Limited
Sangers (Northern Ireland) Ltd

**Andrawes, Maged**
Bristol Consumer Health Ltd

**Andreano, Giuseppe**
Dompe UK Limited

**Andrell, Gregory James Robert**
Dermatonics Ltd
Dermatonics Trading Limited

**Andrews, Amanda Grace**
Excel Health Care Limited

**Andrews, Brian George**
CooperVision Lens Care Limited

**Andrews, Douglas Bruce**
Double Wing Health & Beauty Ltd
Double Wing Pharma Development Ltd

**Andrews, Douglas**
Double Wing Medical Ltd

**Andrews, Hilary Ann**
Beegood Enterprises Limited

**Andrews, Ian James**
Currentmyth Limited

**Andrews, John Mark**
N H Southeast Ltd

**Andrews, Lynn**
Currentmyth Limited

**Andrews, Magda**
Bristol Consumer Health Ltd

**Andrews, Michael John**
Steritech Limited

**Andrews, Paul Edward**
Excel Health Care Limited

**Andrich, Olaf**
Devicor Medical UK Limited

**Andriot, Pierre Jean Bernard**
Servier Laboratories Limited

**Angelopoulou, Anastasia**
A B Alliance Limited

**Anglim, Bryan Michael, Dr**
Mill Pharm Limited

**Anglin, Brendan**
BTA Pharm Limited

**Anglin, Melanie**
BTA Pharm Limited

**Anthony, Elisabeth Nest**
Eurostar Scientific Limited

**Antonelli, Nunzio**
Stallergenes (UK) Ltd

**Anwar, Muhammad Harun**
Kamm Trading Limited

**Apergi, Evangelia**
NC Trade UK Ltd

**Apperly, Andrew Roger**
Zeal Products Limited

**Arafiena, Christopher Ekenemchukwu**
Timeocean Ltd

**Arden, Marisa Jane**
Sunniside Healthcare Limited

**Argomandkhah, Dane**
RX Pharma (Europe) Limited

**Argomandkhah, Hassan**
RX Pharma (Europe) Limited

**Argyrou, Vasiliki**
Tanberg Limited

**Arh, Joze**
KRKA UK Ltd

**Arikawe, Olutayo**
Omark Plus Ltd

**Arikawe, Oluwagbemileke**
Omark Plus Ltd

**Aristeidou, Andreas**
Goldsmith Resources Limited

**Armstrong, Alan David**
Galen Limited
Intergal Pharma Limited

**Armstrong, Allan**
CIGA Healthcare Limited

**Armstrong, Elsie Maureen**
C.D. Medical Limited
M & A Pharmachem Limited

**Armstrong, George William Irwin**
CIGA Healthcare Limited

**Armstrong, Neill**
CIGA Healthcare Limited

**Arnold, Lynda**
RX Pharma (Europe) Limited

**Arnott, Stewart Craig**
Dene Healthcare Limited

**Arogbo, Ayodele Olubunmi**
Curist Health Limited

**Arogundade, Aaran Abdul-Razak Oladipo**
Better'er Limited

**Arowojolu, Olusola Olurotimi**
Phaximed Limited

**Artioli, Andrea**
Bioplax Limited

**Arumugam, Madhana Sundaram**
Druid Pharma Limited

**Asadi, Parisa**
Dermal Aesthetics Clinic Ltd

**Asba, Germaine**
Nigem International Limited

**Ashford, Avril Mary**
Colour Distributors Limited

**Ashraf, Amar**
ORAA Ltd

**Ashraf, Muhammad Imran**
Surgidoc Limited

**Ashworth, Alistair Martin**
Apretique Limited
Beauty Shopper Ltd.
Couch Rolls Limited
Couchrolls.Com Ltd
Couchrolls.co.uk Ltd
Econo-Supplies Ltd
Salon Professional Limited
Salon Professional.Com Limited
Ultrasoundgel Ltd
Wowwax Ltd.

**Ashworth, Alistair**
Econo-Beauty Ltd
Econo-Care Ltd
Econo-Group Ltd

**Asiedu, Emmanuel**
Emra Consult Limited

**Atac, Huseyin Murat**
M.E.D. Supplies Limited

**Atac, Isobel Cathryn**
M.E.D. Supplies Limited

**Atanasoff, Silvia Maria**
Pharm Med Ltd

**Atanasov, Nikolay Atanasov**
Nikopharm Ltd

**Atkinson, Anthony Kimmo**
Vetsonic (UK) Ltd

**Atkinson, Michael Stanley**
Blue Bean Medical Ltd

**Atkinson-Reed, Giorgina**
Dentitreat Co Ltd

**Attunuri, Venkata Narasa Reddy**
Amarox Limited

**Attwood, Frederick Lauder**
Apollo Medical Technologies Ltd

**Auld, Joyce**
Alp Trading Limited
Alpco Ltd

**Auld, Robert**
Alp Trading Limited
Alpco Ltd

**Auret, Rogan Luke**
Riebeeckstad Limited

**Austin, Paul Frederick**
W.B. Superdrug Ltd.

**Avaiya, Amitkumar Kalubhai**
Trishool Pharma Ltd

**Avcil, Dr Muhammet**
Imperial Bioscience Ltd

**Awad, Omar**
Vita Nova International Ltd

**Ayaz, Mohammed**
GP Meds Direct Limited

**Aylott, James Anthony**
Ardant Pharmaceuticals Ltd.
Ardent Pharmaceuticals Ltd

**Ayres, Richard**
Ascot Treatments Ltd

**Aysan, Umran**
Mast - Art Group Limited

**Ayton, Mark**
Pharmac Limited

**Azam, Sadaqat**
Bradley Stoke Bristol Limited

**Aziz, Khalid**
Bri Trade Solutions Limited

**Aziz, Rauhan Munir**
Medica Pharma UK Ltd

**Backmann, Ben, Dr**
Zoetis UK Limited

**Badawy, Ahmed Aboelenin Mohamad**
Rashedeen Pharma Group Ltd

**Badawy, Ahmed**
Layan Pharma Ltd

**Baden, Daniel**
Biomedica Nutraceuticals (UK) Ltd

**Baderin, Richard**
Attentive Pharma Limited

**Badgujar, Prakash**
Lifenza UK Limited

**Badiani, Hemang Chhotalal**
Medik Ostomy Supplies Limited

**Baeyens, Patrick**
Pro Teeth Whitening Co Limited

**Bagga, Shiv Kumar**
Patient Care Holdings Ltd

**Bagnall, Maxwell**
The Bagnall Group (Europe) Ltd

**Bagnall, William**
The Bagnall Group (Europe) Ltd

**Bagwan, Abdulmateen**
Concord Pharma Services (UK) Ltd

**Baharani, Sunder Premchand**
Kinetic Enterprises Limited

**Baig, Mirza Azkar Ahmed, Dr**
Nutrabizz Nutraceuticals Ltd

**Bailey, Gemma**
Bailey Instruments Ltd

**Bailey, Joseph**
Bailey Instruments Ltd

**Bailey, Nicholas James**
Novo Nordisk Limited

**Bailey, Sally Jane**
Bailey Instruments Ltd

**Bailey, Timothy Martin**
Bailey Instruments Ltd

**Bailly, Damien Rodolphe Edmond**
Baxalta UK Investments Ltd.
Shire Pharmaceuticals Limited

**Bains, Michael Binder**
Liberty Pacific Limited

**Bair, Teresa Brophy**
Athenex Euro Limited

**Baker, Ian James**
Arkad Healthcare Limited
Noru Pharma PVT Ltd.

**Baker, Jamal**
Dermocore Ltd.

**Baker, Stuart David**
Mundibiopharma Limited
Mundipharma Medical Co Ltd
Napp Laboratories Limited
Napp Pharmaceutical Group Ltd
Napp Pharmaceutical Holdings Ltd
Napp Pharmaceuticals Limited
Qdem Pharmaceuticals Limited

**Bakiler, Vasif Baha**
Deva Pharma Medical Ltd

**Balasubramaniam, Mayuragoban, Dr**
Pharmaethical Ltd
Southampton Medical Group Ltd

**Balasubramanian, Krishnamurthy**
Ria Generics Limited

**Ball, George**
Gainland (International) Ltd

**Balsiger, Alan David**
Salon Sales Limited

**Bambra, Vermeet Kaur**
Edi Beryl Ltd

**Bamford, Carl**
Exmed Worldwide Limited

**Bandy, Brian Edward**
Bio Nutrition Health Products Ltd

**Bandy, Janet Frances**
Bio Nutrition Health Products Ltd

**Banerjee, Amitabha**
Cadila Pharmaceuticals (Europe) Ltd

**Banfield, Sarah Marcelle, Dr**
Global Pharma Care Ltd

**Banga, Rajinder Singh**
Lionmark Limited

**Banham, Michael Harry Arthur**
Crosskills (P.E.) Limited

**Bankole, Oguntuase Olugbenga**
Symmetry Inc Ltd

**Bannor - Addae, Evelyn**
Chesdeg Limited

**Bapu, Tahera**
Rhodes Pharma Limited

**Barakat, Abdullah**
Global Medical Supply UK Ltd

**Hackman, Detmar Albert**
Paul Baratte International Ltd

**Hackman, Eunhee**
Paul Baratte International Ltd

**Barbara, Wadih Toni**
Galenus Biomedical Limited

**Bard, Brigette Anne**
Biosure (UK) Limited

**Bargit, Imran**
Newstar Healthcare Limited

**Barmaki, Mohammad Reza**
Capella Medical Device Ltd

**Barnes, Paul Martin**
Besins Healthcare (UK) Limited

**Barnes, Richard William**
Medbarn Limited

**Baron de Juan, Alfredo**
Almirall Limited

**Barons, Andrew Richard Paul**
Probar Services Limited

**Barot, Pankitkumar**
Trishool Pharma Ltd

**Barr, Ciaran Joseph**
Theramex HQ UK Limited

**Barraclough, David Lyndon**
Toiletry Sales Limited

**Barratt, Cynthia L**
Ocusoft UK Limited

**Barrett, Kevin Paul**
CooperVision Lens Care Limited

**Barroso, Arbelio Jose**
Greens Roads UK Ltd

**Bartenstein, Martin, Dr**
Gerot Lannach UK Limited

**Basharat, Mohammed Shabaz**
MSB Pharma Ltd

**Bashari, Mohammad**
Pharco Ltd

**Basheer, Fawad**
Health Remit Limited

**Bashir, Adal**
AAP Healthcare Ltd

**Bashir, Kharul**
Medbury Limited

**Bashir, Mohamed Naveed**
NSK Global Ltd

**Bashir, Shakeel Ahmed**
Dispensing Healthcare Ltd

**Basi, Navdeep**
Branded Healthcare Ltd

**Bassi, Narinder Singh**
Star Powa Limited

**Bastia, Filippo**
THD (UK) Limited

**Bastijns, Jeroen Peter Annie**
V Sales and Marketing Limited

**Bataillard, Thierry Stephane**
Incyte Biosciences UK Ltd

**Bates, Clare Jane**
Unomedical Limited

**Bateson, Alison Jane**
Stratlab Limited

**Bateson, John Fernall**
Stratlab Limited

**Bath, Christopher William**
Norgine Pharmaceuticals Ltd

**Bathala, Sudhakar**
Sanhak Ltd

**Batra, Pardeep**
GB Pharma Limited

**Battershill, David Frederick**
Espere Healthcare Limited

**Battula, Hemanth**
Vwin Lifestyle Limited

**Batty, Peter**
Fagron UK Ltd

**Baumann, Astrid Irmgard Elfriede**
Biomarin (U.K.) Ltd.

**Baumann, Max**
Tearfilm Therapeutics Ltd

**Bavetta, Adrian**
Intramed Limited

**Bavetta, Julian**
Intramed Limited

**Bavetta, Sebastiano**
Intramed Limited

**Baxter, Jamie Richard**
Home Health (U.K.) Limited

**Baxter, John Peter**
Home Health (U.K.) Limited

**Bayati, Aiden**
Acre Aesthetics Limited

**Bayer, Christoph Martin**
Raumedic U.K. Limited

**Beak, Alan**
Ruger Barber Limited

**Bebu, Ashwin**
Pharmex-UK Ltd

**Beckett, Darren**
Steritech Limited

**Bedarkar, Vijay**
Leafxtracts Ltd

**Beden, Ahmed**
Mesopotamia Surgical Ultima Vitality Ltd

**Beden, Anne Grace, Dr**
Mesopotamia Surgical Ultima Vitality Ltd

**Bedra, Mariusz**
MSP Pharm Ltd

**Beeching, Russell**
ACG Europe Limited

**Begovic, Asmir**
Gelu Life Limited

**Behl, Vivek**
JAO Enterprises Ltd

**Belcher, Darren Robert**
Mawdsley-Brooks & Co Ltd

**Belcher, Jim Alfred**
HMD Europe Ltd

**Belgotra, Devendra Kumar**
Quramax Limited

**Belousov, Nikolay**
Eurotech Medical Ltd

**Benati, Luca Stefano**
Gelu Life Limited

**Benes, Marian**
Flow Wealth Ltd

**Benfield, William James**
Hotteeze International Limited

**Benkowitz, Michael Ian**
United Therapeutics Europe, Ltd.

**Bennett, Daniel Patrick**
Ecomed UK Limited

**Bennett, Daniel Thomas, Dr**
Blackpool Medicines Limited

**Bennett, Nancy**
Medhub Limited
Sawa Trading & Shipping Ltd

**Bennett, Norman John**
Leptrex Ltd.

**Bennett, Roger John**
Docsinnovent Limited

**Benning, Dominic Michael**
Ever Pharma UK Limited

**Berdanis, Maria**
Active Export Ltd
Alexpharm GmbH Ltd

**Berger, Genevieve Bernadette, Professor**
Astrazeneca PLC

**Bertrand, Claude Philippe**
Servier IP UK Limited

**Bessant, Edwin Charles**
Halo GB Ltd

**Bettesworth, Hugh**
Mirada Medical Limited

**Beyls, Pieter-Jan**
Coriungo Limited

**Bhaidani, Aziz**
Astra Pharma (UK) Limited

**Bhaiji, Mustafa Hakimudin**
Welfare Healthcare (UK) Ltd

**Bhamra, Gurpreet Singh**
TFS Med UK Limited

**Bhandal, Charnjit Singh**
AMG Pharmaceuticals Limited
N & G Pharma Limited

**Bharaj, Harmeet Singh**
Arya House Pharma Ltd

**Bhargava, Sarvesh**
Despina Pharma Ltd

**Bhatia, Gurvinder Singh**
Mychem Limited

**Bhatia, Mohit**
Omnicell Limited

**Bhatt, Saumil Kiritkumar**
Cubic Pharmaceuticals Limited

**Bhatti, Dipak Devji**
Syner-Medica Limited

**Bhatti, Muhammad Sajjad**
Aston-Med Limited

**Bhatti, Pratima Dipak**
Syner-Medica Limited

**Bhatti, Viraj**
Syner-Medica Limited

**Bhatty, Mabroor Ahmed, Dr**
Esthetica Pure Ltd
Microskin Cosmeceuticals UK Ltd

**Bhatty, Nicola Susan**
Esthetica Pure Ltd
Microskin Cosmeceuticals UK Ltd

**Bhogal, Kamaldeep Singh**
PharmXC Ltd

**Bhola, Saira Murad**
AIG Unico Ltd

**Bhurawala, Mohammed Amin**
Amin Locum Limited

**Bhusan, Bharat**
Benatur Limited

**Bibi, Jonathan**
Raw Medicus Ltd

**Biggs, James Martin, Dr**
Nurse Prescribers Limited

**Billback, Emil Anders**
Bone Support UK Ltd

**Bilski, Tomasz Andrzej**
Pure Light Vision Ltd

**Bilton, David Kenneth**
IPG Pharma Limited
Intela Europa Ltd
Pharmadreams Limited

**Bilton, Eileen**
IPG Pharma Limited

**Bilton, Gregory David**
IPG Pharma Limited
Pharmadreams Limited

**Bindah, Madhvi**
ZS Pharma Limited

**Bingham, Dawn**
ABI Training Academy Limited

**Lindstrom, Tuija Maarit Anneli**
Mark Birch Hair Ltd

**Birch, Garry John**
GJB Pharma Limited

**Birken, Andrew Keith**
McKesson Global Sourcing UK Ltd

**Biro, Peter**
Merck Serono Limited

**Birtwistle, Danielle**
Westbourne Medical Limited

**Birtwistle, John Peter Stuart**
Westbourne Medical Limited

**Bjorklund, Hakan**
Neolife International Ltd

**Black, Kenneth John**
G Pharma Limited
Nupharm Limited
Phoenix Healthcare Distribution Ltd
Phoenix Medical Supplies Ltd

**Blackmore, Steven John**
Lifeshield Limited

**Bleasdale, Claire Chan, Dr**
21CEC PX Pharm Ltd

**Blickling, Patrik**
A & P Blickling Ltd

**Calero de Blickling, Ana Eugenia**
A & P Blickling Ltd

**Blinkovskaja, Ira**
Blink Street Limited

**Blom, Peter**
Karo Pharma UK Ltd

**Bloom, Claudine Nicola**
Collardam PLC

**Bloomfield, Jonathan Robert, Dr**
Support To Perform Ltd

**Blount, Mark Anthony Paul**
Fresh Cache Holdings Limited

**Blount, Tina Marie**
Diamond Pharma Limited

**Blythe, Edwin Charles**
Crosspharma Limited
Stada UK Holdings Ltd.

**Boadu, Rebecca Abena**
Fijez Ltd

**Boafor, George**
W.B. Superdrug Ltd.

**Boafor, William Amegbor**
W.B. Superdrug Ltd.

**Boakye Ansah, David**
Candover UK Ltd

**Bodevin, Jacques**
Galderma (U.K.) Limited

**Bodineau, Emeric Marc**
Servier Laboratories Limited

**Bodle, Linda**
Med Procure Ltd

**Bodle, Peter Martin**
Med Procure Ltd

**Boghani, Snehalkumar Himmatlal**
Vitaempower Ltd

**Bogsch, Erik Attila**
Medimpex UK Limited

**Bohloli, Hamid, Dr**
Biomedoc Limited
Biomedox International Ltd

**Bohner, Jochen Norbert**
Astellas Pharma Europe Ltd.

**Bold, Adrian**
J L J Healthcare Limited

**Armstrong, Elsie Maureen**
The Bolton Pharmaceutical Company 100

**Gatenby, Michael**
The Bolton Pharmaceutical Company 100

**Pessagno, Gerard Michael Dominic**
The Bolton Pharmaceutical Company 100

**Bolton, Charles Trevor John**
DMS Plus Limited

**Bolton, Penelope Anne**
DMS Plus Limited

**Bolzani, Luca Giuseppe Ambrogio**
Sintetica Limited

**Bonacker, Lutz Guenter, Dr**
CSL Behring Holdings Limited
CSL Behring UK Limited

**Bone, Nicholas Andrew**
Titan Med Limited

**Boodell, Paul**
Sunstik Ltd

**Boom, Evert Charles**
Green Guru Enterprices Ltd.

**Booth, John Michael**
Aura-Soma Limited

**Bora, Bhaskar Jyoti**
Elmstone Healthcare Limited

**Bordley, Kevin Paul**
KPB Healthcare Limited

**Borger, James**
Allen & Hanburys Limited
Glaxo Laboratories Limited
Glaxo Wellcome UK Limited

**Borges, Clarice Neves**
TBD Wellness Limited

**Borkowski, Andrew Thomas**
Bionical Limited
Ellis Pharma Limited

**Bornet, Edgar Gilbert**
Alcyon Corporation Ltd

**Borson, Marc**
Active Pharma Supplies Limited

**Botha, Stefan**
Botha Group Ltd

**Botros, John Adel Youssef Tabdros**
Avanzcare Limited

**Boudet, Jean-Pierre**
Kestrel Ophthalmics Limited

**Bouffard, Jennifer**
Knightsbridge Importers Ltd

**Boukouris, George Demetrios**
Flowonix Medical Ltd

**Boulton, Andrew Frederick**
Drilltex GB Ltd

**Boulton, Godfrey William Victor**
Advanced Medical Systems Ltd.

**Boulton, Imogen Ruth**
Drilltex GB Ltd

**Boulton, Marko**
Advanced Medical Systems Ltd.

**Bourne, Oliver Henry**
Glenmark Pharmaceuticals Europe Ltd

**Bourne, Raymond Fairbanks**
Tanner Pharma UK Limited

**Bourne, Raymond**
Tannerlac UK Limited

**Bourne, Steven Nigel**
Surgitrac Instruments UK Ltd

**Bouvet, Marie, Dr**
Genevet Ltd

**Bouyer, Jerome Stephane**
AbbVie Ltd

**Bowden, Adam**
AB Pharma Logistics Ltd

**Bowden, Diane**
Pharma Modus Limited

**Box, Jonathan**
GlaxoSmithKline US Trading Ltd

**Boyd, Alan Keith**
Clinigen Group PLC

**Boyne, Isobel Louise**
Ipsen Limited

**Brabetz, Michael Gregor**
Dark Atom Limited

**Bracey, Daniel**
M D M Healthcare Ltd

**Brad, Blake Baljit Singh**
BN Medical Ltd

**Meier, Nuala**
J. Bradbury (Surgical) Limited

**Anderson, Toby Matthew**
J. Bradbury (Surgical) Limited

**Hilger, Marcus**
J. Bradbury (Surgical) Limited

**McDermott, Catherine**
J. Bradbury (Surgical) Limited

**Swift, Nigel**
J. Bradbury (Surgical) Limited

**Bradford, Daryl**
Biosure (UK) Limited

**Bradley, Liam Martin**
Liam Bradley Ltd
Omapharm Limited

**Bradshaw, Charles James Anthony**
K588 Limited

**Bradshaw, Robert John**
RPG Medical Limited

**Brady, John Michael, Sir**
Mirada Medical Limited

**Brady, Paul Declan**
Crosscare Export Limited

**Brain, Christopher Robin**
IMI Ventures Limited
Imperial Medical Innovations Ltd
Youmed Limited

**Brain, Elizabeth**
Youmed Limited

**Bramble, Stephen John**
Sunstore Limited

**Brander, Christine Linda**
WHL Contracts Ltd

**Brandon, Graham**
Scandasystems Limited

**Brandon, Rosalyn Marsha**
Scandasystems Limited

**Brankov, Georgi**
Medaesthetics Limited

**Brannan, Jamie Andrew**
Zoetis UK Limited

**Bratica, Joseph**
Sarepta International UK Ltd.

**Bratt, Anthony Brian**
Nordic Pharma Limited

**Brault, Jean-Yves**
Meda Pharmaceuticals Limited
Mylan UK Healthcare Limited

**Bray, Steven John**
SP Services (UK) Limited

**Brazier, David Thomas**
Corpus Nostrum Limited

**Breakspear, Antonia Anne**
New Seasons Natural Products Ltd

**Breakspear, Bill Nicholas George**
New Seasons Natural Products Ltd

**Breakspear, Jonathan Richard**
New Seasons Natural Products Ltd

**Brennand, William Richard John**
Bigvits Limited

**Brenyah, Ama Serwah**
Chesdeg Limited

**Brenyah, Samuel Kwesi**
Chesdeg Limited

**Brewster, Christopher James**
Animalcare Ltd

**Bridge, Julie Louise**
Exeter Health Limited

**Bridger, Andrew David, Dr**
Aroschem Limited

**Brierley, Charles Ashley**
Genus Pharmaceuticals Holdings Ltd
Genus Pharmaceuticals Limited
Zeroderma Limited

**Bright, Lisa Jane**
Intercept Pharma Europe Ltd.

**Brilus, Ray John**
Pure Products London Limited

**Brinkmann, Stefan**
Merz Pharma UK Limited

**Bristow, Catherine Mary**
Bigvits Limited

**Sonpal, Pritesh Ramesh**
The British Association of European Pharmaceutical Distributors

**Sudera, Ashwani Kumar**
The British Association of European Pharmaceutical Distributors

**Freudenberg, Richard Emil**
The British Association of European Pharmaceutical Distributors

**Cochrane, John**
The British Association of European Pharmaceutical Distributors

**Jimenez, Julio Iglesias**
The British Association of European Pharmaceutical Distributors

**Brito, Aida**
Lad & Company Private Limited

**Britten, Ross Mark**
Poldark Limited

**Brixey, Richard, Dr**
DDWS Limited

**Broadley, Philip Arthur John**
Astrazeneca PLC

**Broderick, Dennise, Dr**
Galen Limited
Intergal Pharma Limited

**Broeer, Thomas**
Milpharm Limited

**Brookes, Anita**
DNB Pharma Limited

**Brookes, David Norris**
DNB Pharma Limited

**Brookman, Kevin Kwesi**
Brookmed Limited

**Brough, Miles Alan**
Lighthouse Mercury Limited

**Brouquet-Laclaire, Yves**
Kestrel Ophthalmics Limited

**Brown, David Justin**
N.I.P. Pharma Limited

**Brown, David Paul**
A B International Limited

**Brown, Ian David**
Boston Healthcare Limited

**Brown, Lynette Amanda**
Beiersdorf UK Ltd.

**Brown, Rebecca**
A B International Limited

**Brown, Vance Ronald**
Augmenix UK Limited

**Johns, Paul Robert Rees**
ET Browne (UK) Limited

**Neis, Arnold Hayward**
ET Browne (UK) Limited

**Neis, Robert Charles**
ET Browne (UK) Limited

**Browning, Kirsty Ann Louise**
Sentinel Laboratories Limited

**Brownlee, Ian Colin**
Mawdsley-Brooks & Co Ltd
Wellspring Pharmaceutical Services
Wellspring Pharmaceutical Services UK

**Bruening, Lars Friedrich**
Bayer PLC

**Brughera, Marco Maria**
Leadiant Biosciences Limited

**Bruhin, Roland**
SSCP Blink Bidco Limited
Vision Pharmaceuticals Ltd

**Brukner, Peter Damian**
Premax Europe Limited

**Brundan, Simon George**
Exeter Health Limited

**Bruni, Alessio**
Satio Pharma Ltd.

**Bruni, Riccardo**
Satio Pharma Ltd.

**Bryant, David John**
Skingen UK Ltd

**Bryce, James**
Carbosynth Limited

**Buchan, Mark**
MB Pharma Limited

**Buchanan, Ian Yule, Dr**
Aroschem Limited
Aroschem UK Limited

**Buchanan, Jennifer Mary**
Aroschem UK Limited

**Buchanan, William Andrew**
Phytoceutical Limited

**Buck, Eileen Teresa**
Biocare Supplies Limited
Steritech UK Limited

**Buck, Robert Stuart**
Biocare Supplies Limited
Steritech UK Limited

**Buckingham, Adrian**
Parasure Limited

**Buddhadev, Rinkle Rameshkumar**
Acme Pharma Ltd

**Budhdeo, Shamir Pravinchandra**
Symbio Europe Limited

**Burchkard, Alessia**
1LIFE Distribution Limited

**Burges, Johannes Franz**
Hermes Pharmaceutical Limited

**Burgess, Michael John**
Arkad Healthcare Limited

**Burgin, Chad William**
Bbeauty Lounge Limited
Bluesky Cosmetics Limited

**Burgin, Nicholas Conrad**
Eisai Limited
MGI Pharma Limited

**Burke, Donna Margaret**
Hotteeze International Limited

**Burke, Michael Hilary**
Chanelle Vet U.K. Limited

**Burke, Michael**
Chanelle Medical GB Limited

**Burling, Raymond Richard**
Pharma World Ltd

**Burnford, Richard Peter, Dr**
DDWS Limited

**Burniston, Christopher Robert**
Colgate-Palmolive (U.K.) Ltd

**Burns, Alan George**
Allen & Hanburys Limited
Glaxo Laboratories Limited
Glaxo Wellcome UK Limited

**Burns, Garry Gardner**
RPG Medical Limited

**Burr, Jeffrey David**
Wigmore Laboratories Limited

**Burrell, Jayne Katherine**
Acorus Therapeutics Limited

**Burt, James, Dr**
Accord Healthcare Limited

**Burton, Susan Mary, Dr**
Lab-Club Limited

**Bushra, Sabeen**
Beautons Ventures Ltd

**Butkovics, Tamas**
Vitafree Health Limited

**Butler, David Michael**
Astek Innovations Limited

**Butler, Timothy Jonathon Charles**
Biophage Therapeutics Ltd

**Butt, Abdul**
Pharma 313 Limited

**Butter, Satnam Singh**
In 2 Healthcare Limited

**Butterfield, Timothy Robert**
Optident Labline Limited

**Bux, Mohammed**
Positive Pharma Ltd

**Byrne, Bryan John**
Vision Matrix Limited

**Byrne, Patrick**
American Biochemical and Pharmaceuticals

**Bystrom, Eric Gustaf**
Iaso Ltd

**Caddick, Trevor**
HH Pharma Limited

**Cain, Damien**
EVC Compounding Ltd

**Calcraft, Robert Michael**
K588 Limited

**Caldwell, Jacqueline**
Northwise Services Limited

**Caldwell-Nichols, Matthew**
Precision Healthcare Limited

**Calleja Crespo, Elena**
Pharma Mar Limited

**Calvert, Gary**
Identimed Limited
Nex Pharma Limited

**Calvert, Natalie Jayne**
Nex Pharma Limited

**Calvin, Joshua**
Monarch Health Ltd

**Cama, Zarir Jal**
Emcure Pharma UK Ltd
Tillomed Laboratories Limited

**Cameron, Aileen**
Skingen UK Ltd

**Campbell, Nicola Veronica**
NV Campbell Limited

**Campbell, Clare**
Principle Healthcare Limited

**Campbell, Esther**
Campbell Medical Supplies Ltd

**Campbell, Gary**
Client-Pharma Ltd
Client-Pharmacy UK Ltd

**Campbell, Ian Patrick**
Leverton & Co Ltd

**Campbell, James Paul**
Campbell Medical Supplies Ltd

**Campbell, Lewis**
Leca Pharma Limited
Target Healthcare Limited

**Campbell, Sean-Robbie**
Advanced Formulations (Europe) Ltd

**Campbell, Stephen**
Galen Limited
Intergal Pharma Limited

**Cane, Claudio**
Applied Medical Technology Ltd

**Cane, Paolo**
Applied Medical Technology Ltd

**Cankiran, Burcu**
HB Sirius Ltd

**Cann, Michael Graham Andre**
Septodont Limited

**Canning, Paul Robin**
Pharmacy Supplies Limited

**Cantarell Rocamora, Luis**
CM & D Pharma Limited

**Cantello, Brett Leigh**
Pharma Modus Limited

The Top UK Pharmaceutical Wholesalers dellam

**Cao, Fangyu**
UK Heluns Industry Co., Ltd

**Caporali, Christopher Pierre Georges**
Ursus UK Limited

**Cardon, Christiaan Andre**
V Sales and Marketing Limited

**Cardozo, Nicola**
UK Pharmacies Ltd

**Carless, John Bradley**
London Supplements Distribution Ltd

**Carocci, Giancarlo**
Project & Communications Ltd

**Caron, Beau**
Pharma Trading Limited

**Carpenter, Gary Richard**
Biosure (UK) Limited

**Carr, Dominique Claire**
Eurocare Impex Services Ltd

**Carr, Robin**
Biotech International Limited

**Carrera Lopez, Manuel**
Swiftpath Corporation Limited

**Carrington, Helen**
John Carrington Limited

**Carrington, John**
John Carrington Limited

**Carroll, Geoff**
Toiletry Sales Limited

**Carroll, Ian**
Farmvet Limited

**Carroll, John**
Pembroke Healthcare Limited

**Carruthers, David, Dr**
Allergan Limited

**Carter, David James**
Hambleden Herbs Limited

**Carter, John James**
56 Flowers Ltd

**Carter, Pauline**
HH Pharma Limited

**Caso, Charles Robert**
Meridian Bioscience UK Limited

**Castell, Denise Claire**
Iophtha Limited

**Castellucci, Corrado**
Orphan Europe (UK) Limited

**Castle, Deborah Mary**
Casmed International Limited

**Catmull, Gregory James**
La Lune Noire Ltd

**Catt, James Peter**
Imphatec Ltd

**Tims, Geoffrey Alan**
P & A J Cattee (Wholesale) Ltd.

**Cattee, Angela Jane**
P & A J Cattee (Wholesale) Ltd.

**Cattee, Peter**
P & A J Cattee (Wholesale) Ltd.

**Cattee, Angela Jane**
Manor Drug Company (Nottingham) Ltd

**Cattee, Peter**
Euanet Limited
Manor Drug Company (Nottingham) Ltd

**Caunce, Andrew John**
Medihealth (Northern) Limited

**Cavaliere, Francesco**
Apotheke San Biagio SRL Ltd

**Cavanaugh, Stefanie LEA**
Apollo Endosurgery UK Ltd

**Cavill, Simon Rafe**
Beegood Enterprises Limited

**Cavin, Jean-Pierre**
E.U.K. Limited

**Chachan, Mamta**
Britpharma UK Limited

**Chachan, Prasanna**
Britpharma UK Limited

**Chachapura, Brijeshkumar Bhagvati Prasad**
Health Supplies Limited

**Chahal, Sarabjit Singh, Dr**
378 Co Ltd

**Chan, Albert Weng Wah, Dr**
Angulus Pharma Limited

**Chan, Barbara**
Aegerion Pharmaceuticals Ltd

**Chan, Gary Kai Wai**
Chronicles Medical Consulting Ltd

**Chan, Gary**
Medicstar (UK) Limited

**Chan, Kin Sum**
Beijing Tong Ren Tang (UK) Ltd

**Chandarana, Bhavna**
Symom Limited

**Chandarana, Rohit**
RB UK Hygiene Home Commercial Ltd

**Chandaria, Nemu**
Farmachem Limited

**Chandaria, Nyalchand**
Farmachem Limited

**Chandavarkar, Ameya Ashok**
F D C International Limited

**Chandavarkar, Ashok Anand**
F D C International Limited

**Chandavarkar, Nandan Mohan**
F D C International Limited

**Chandra, Tara**
Here We Flo Ltd
Sustainable Ethical Enterprises Ltd

**Chanengeta, Raymond**
Citux Medical Limited

**Chapman, Julie**
Juice Sauz Ltd

**Chapman, Liam Martin**
Juice Sauz Ltd

**Chapman, Robert Peter**
Dutscher Scientific UK Limited
Scientific Laboratory Supplies Group Ltd

**Chapper, Philip**
Philip Chapper & Co Ltd

**Chapper, Vera**
Philip Chapper & Co Ltd

**Chapper, Jonathan Simon**
Philip Chapper & Co Ltd

**Chapper, Paul Anthony**
Philip Chapper & Co Ltd

**Charlesworth, Simon Edwin**
Bailey Instruments Ltd

**Charlick, Rachel Elizabeth**
Opus Pharmacy Services Limited

**Chase, William Joseph**
AbbVie Ltd

**Chaston, Clay William Linley**
MCL Healthcare Limited
MedRx Distribution Limited

**Chatwani, Jawahar Jamnadas**
Davis and Dann Limited
Kanta Enterprises Limited

**Chatwani, Rashmi Jamnadas**
Davis and Dann Limited
Kanta Enterprises Limited

**Chatwani, Satish Jamnadas**
Davis and Dann Limited
Kanta Enterprises Limited

**Chatwani, Sonya Rashmi**
Sonchat Limited

**Chatwani, Sonya**
Easho Limited

**Chatzipavlis, Ioannis**
Chefarma Limited

**Chaudry, Faisal Ahmed**
F Chaudry Limited

**Chaudry, Muhammed**
Timstar Laboratory Suppliers Ltd

**Chauhan, Daksha**
Greens Pharmacy Limited

**Chauhan, Mahindra**
D & M Enterprises (UK) Limited

**Chauhan, Umesh Gopal**
Specials Pharma Ltd

**Chawla, Virendra K**
Unidus Limited

**Cheema, Jaipal Singh**
Allcures PLC
Allcures.Com (2006) Limited
Allgenpharma Limited
Allkare Limited

**Cheema, Kirandeep Singh**
Allcures PLC

**Cheetham, Mark**
Skylark Services Limited

**Chenery, Paul Nigel**
English Herbal Medicines Ltd

**Cherfi, Nour Eddine**
Impexport Services Limited

**Cherrett, Natasha Eugenie**
Josana Limited

**Cheshire, Richard Michael**
CooperVision Lens Care Limited

**Chesworth, Clare Maria**
Oswell Penda Pharmaceutical Ltd

**Chetia, Manav**
Buduscheye Techniqa Ltd

**Cheung, Daniel Chun Ying**
MDX Healthcare Ltd

**Cheung, Douglas Chi Shing**
Pavay Venture International Ltd

**Chhatwal, Vaibhav Singh**
Welcome Health Pharmacies Ltd

**Chibret, Henri**
Thea Pharmaceuticals Limited

**Chibret, Jean-Frederic**
Thea Pharmaceuticals Limited

**Chiesi, Alberto**
Chiesi Healthcare Limited
Chiesi Limited

**Chiesi, Alessandro**
Chiesi Healthcare Limited
Chiesi Limited

**Chiesi, Paolo**
Chiesi Healthcare Limited
Chiesi Limited

**Chigurupati, Krishna Prasad**
Granules Europe Limited

**Chika Onyechi, Chisom**
Chirock Trading Ltd

**Chilton, Shaun Edward**
Clinigen CTS Limited
Clinigen Group PLC
Clinigen Healthcare Limited
Idis Group Holdings Limited
Idis Limited

**Chintalapudi, Sindhupriya**
Sinduram Healthcare International Ltd
Skinska Pharmaceutica Limited

**Chipchase, Graham**
Astrazeneca PLC

**Chirackal, Peelipose**
Bioturm Limited

**Chitty, Mavis Irene**
ATI Atlas Ltd.

**Chitty, Nigel Bryan**
ATI Atlas Ltd.

**Chiu, Alice Woon Kuen**
Alice & Associates Limited

**Chiu, Fung Ha Sharan**
MDX Healthcare Ltd

**Chiu, Hiang Sim**
Riviere Groupe (Europe) Ltd

**Chobanyan, Gayane, Dr**
UK Biopharma Ltd

**Chokshi, Divyesh**
MDS Pharmaceuticals Ltd

**Cholakyan Wistuba, Margarita**
Guardian Pharmaceuticals Co Ltd

**Chong, Anthony Kwang Aun**
Indrugco (UK) Limited

**Chong, Elaine Frances**
Indrugco (UK) Limited

**Chong, Melinda Li Yen**
Trafalgar Pharma Ltd

**Chong, Weeliat, Dr**
Trafalgar Pharma Ltd

**Chotai, Kunal**
Wholesale 2 U Ltd

**Chou, John Gardner**
Animal Prescriptions Limited

**Choudhry, Junaid Nazir**
Mayomed Limited

**Choudhry, Mohammed Azeem Azram**
Kamm Trading Limited

**Choung, Jai Jun, Dr**
Oxbridge Pharma Limited

**Chow, Sheung Wah**
Sampsonstore.Com (UK) Ltd

**Chowdhury, Dewan Fazlul Hoque**
Black and White Health Care Ltd

**Chowdhury, Utpal**
Edmond Finance Ltd

**Christensen, Lars**
Pharmacosmos UK Limited

**Christodoulou, Androniki**
Labmedical System Limited
Stockman (UK) Ltd

**Chubb, Patrick Anthony Kingsford**
Genesis Pharmaceuticals Ltd

**Chudasama, Amitkumar**
London Health Suppliers Ltd

**Chudasama, Mehul**
London Health Suppliers Ltd

**Chudgar, Binish Hasmukhbhai**
Accord Healthcare Limited

**Chung, Alan Kwok Wing**
Tudor Pharma Ltd

**Chung, Ho Ching**
MDX Healthcare Ltd

**Chung, Wing Leung**
Morn View Chemicals (UK) Ltd

**Church, Helen Elizabeth**
Biovendor Ltd

**Cinar, Ahmet Murat**
Wenimed Ltd

**Ciocchini, Henrietta**
Medicern Export Ltd

**Ciocchini, Juan Cruz**
Medicern Export Ltd

**Ciuchcinski, Dominik**
Proup Ltd

**Clague, John Robert**
Viking Court Limited

**Clare, Victoria Gail Tamsin**
Sentinel Laboratories Limited

**Claremont, Melville Anthony**
Lillidale Ltd.

**Claremont, Michelle Anne**
Lillidale Ltd.

**Glynn, Marshall Anthony**
C G Clark Limited

**Golombeck, Anthony**
C G Clark Limited

**Clark, James Scott, Dr**
Expedite Therapeutics Limited

**Clark, Malcolm**
Mycology Research Laboratories Ltd

**Clarke, Alexander**
UK Pharma Direct Limited

**Clarke, Peter William**
Qualitech Healthcare Ltd

**Clarkson, Neil John**
Acre Aesthetics Limited

**Cleall-Harding, Geoffrey Stuart**
Pharma Medico Limited

**Cleary Jr, James Francis**
Animal Prescriptions Limited

**Cleary, Emma Jane**
Device Technologies UK Ltd.

**Cleeve, Abigail Claire**
Ultrasun (UK) Limited

**Clements, Katherine Rhiannon**
Mooncup Ltd

**Clemo, Brett Timothy**
Eco Animal Health Group PLC

**Close, Michael Stuart**
Shard Speciality Pharma Ltd

**Close, Michael**
Celloxess (Europe) Limited

**Clough, Patricia Anne**
Reliance Medical Ltd

**Clough, Simon Christopher, Dr**
Alturix Limited

**Cloutier, Laure-Anne**
Guest Medical Limited

**Cochrane, John**
Chanelle Medical U.K. Limited
Doctors Dispensing Services Ltd
Ecosse Hospital Products Ltd
Ecosse Pharmaceuticals Limited
Global Dispensing Limited
Healthcare Pharma Limited
Munro Healthcare (Caucasus & Middle Asia)
Munro Healthcare Group Limited
Munro Healthcare Pharma Ltd
Munro Medical Limited
Munro Wholesale Medical Supplies Ltd
Newco Pharma Limited
Pharmabuyer Limited
SPL (2010) Limited
Strathclyde Pharmaceuticals Ltd

**Cockcroft, Philip**
Mosaic Pharma Limited

**Cocoli, Amarildo**
Alverda Ltd

**Cohen, Delbert Alva**
Besins Healthcare (UK) Limited

**Coke, Stephen John**
Condomania (UK) Limited
Condomania PLC
Sutherland Health Group Ltd

**Coker, Alexander James**
Discount Healthcare Ltd

**Cole, Christopher Anthony**
Kavia Tooling Limited

**Collette, Terry**
DC Surgical Supplies Limited

**Collier, Andrew John**
Newbridge Pharma Ltd.

**Collier, Lynne**
Newbridge Pharma Ltd.

**Collins, Adam**
Medihealth (Northern) Limited

**Collins, Brian**
Protec Medical Limited
Scanmed (UK) Limited
Smart Medical Limited

**Collins, Nicholas John Heywood**
Optima Consumer Health Limited

**Collins, Phillip Michael**
Protec Medical Limited
Smart Medical Limited

**Collins, Sharon Mary**
Periproducts Limited

**Comb, Donald, Dr**
New England Biolabs (U.K.) Ltd

**Concannon, Paul Joseph**
Ethypharm UK Limited

**Connor, Christopher Sean Guthrie**
Alk-Abello Limited

**Connor, Gregory John**
Vivacy Laboratoires Ltd

**Conway, Michelle**
Elkay Laboratory Products (U.K.) Ltd

**Conway, Richard Gary**
Hemastem Ltd

**Conway, Robin**
Elkay Laboratory Products (U.K.) Ltd

**Cook, Anne Marie**
Sage Therapeutics Limited

**Cooke, Doreen Bennett**
Pharma Maiden Ltd

**Cooke, Jonathan**
Matoke Holdings Limited

**Cooke, Lisa Jane**
Mediport Limited
Mediwin Limited

**Cookson, Rachel Claire**
Chloraco Healthcare Limited

**Shah, Khilan Mahendra**
G. D. Cooper & Co Ltd

**Shah, Mahendra Meghji**
G. D. Cooper & Co Ltd

**Shah, Rahul Mahendra**
G. D. Cooper & Co Ltd

**Cooper, Nicholas**
DB & A Cooper (Suffolk) Ltd

**Cooper, Angela**
DB & A Cooper (Suffolk) Ltd

**Cooper, Catherine**
Galar Ireland Ltd

**Cooper, Dean Michael**
Ratiopharm (UK) Limited

**Cooper, Mark**
Wellacy Limited

**Cooper, Michael Thomas**
TPC Pharma Limited

**Cooper, Michael**
Galar Ireland Ltd

**Cooper, Nicholas Carel**
TPC Pharma Limited

**Cooper, Paul Dominic**
Galar Ireland Ltd

**Cooper, Paul**
Stem Cellx Limited

**Cooper, Randall Lyall**
Premax Europe Limited

**Cooper, Sarah** [2-1957]
Galar Ireland Ltd

**Cooper, Sarah** [11-1974]
Aeglos Ltd

**Cope, Colin John**
A.J. Cope & Son Limited

**Cope, Brian Lewis**
A.J. Cope & Son Limited

**Ackee, Ellen**
A.J. Cope & Son Limited

**Cope, Claire**
A.J. Cope & Son Limited

**Cope, Nigel Henry**
A.J. Cope & Son Limited

**Hodgson, John Robert**
A.J. Cope & Son Limited

**Williams, Jonathan Stephen Thomas**
A.J. Cope & Son Limited

**Cope, Elizabeth Mary, Dr**
Mill Pharm Limited

**Coppack, Richard**
EVC Compounding Ltd

**Cordrey, Anthony Leonard**
Accord Healthcare Limited

**Corker, Barry John**
Pricecheck Toiletries Limited

**Corneillo, Dominique Patricia**
Doksy Limited

**Cornes, Samuel**
Poseidon Pharmaceutical UK Ltd

**Cosentino, Ugo**
Harmonium Investments Limited

**Cottam, Sara Lisa Gresham, Dr**
Hughenden Valley Pharma Ltd

**Cotterill, Mark John**
Atnahs Pharma US Limited
Marlborough Pharmaceuticals Ltd
Sovereign House Properties Ltd
Waymade PLC

**Cotton, Richard John**
Dechra Veterinary Products Ltd

**Counsell, Rosemary Frances**
Boots International Limited

**Courtney, Alona**
Drugsdirect Limited

**Courtney, Matthew George**
Crest Medical Limited
First Aid Supplies Limited

**Cousin, James Douglas**
IQ Pharma Ltd

**Couzens, Richard George Armitt**
BBI Healthcare Limited

**Cox, Deborah Margaret**
Norsworthy Limited

**Cox, Peter Ross**
SDM Healthcare Limited

**Cradduck, Robert George**
Morgan Steer Developments Ltd

**Crauford Taylor, Gavin Charles**
Adelphi (Tubes) Limited

**Crawford, Warren Anthony**
Samax Pharma Ltd

**Crawford, Yasmin Jayne**
Aerona Clinical Limited

**Cretney, Leonard**
Stragen UK Limited

**Crichton, Andy**
Norgine Pharmaceuticals Ltd

**Cripps, Caroline Jane**
Cripps Medical Limited

**Cripps, Christopher Anthony**
Cripps Medical Limited

**Crispin, Iain Phillips**
Crispin Enterprises Limited

**Critchlow, Paul Douglas**
Distinctive Medical Products Ltd

**Croft, Andrew**
Pure Skincare Limited

**Croft, Darren**
Insight Biotechnology Limited

**Croot, Gillian Mary, Dr**
Mill Pharm Limited

**Cross, Hedley Edwin**
Econo-Supplies Ltd

**Cross, Lori Jo**
Timstar Laboratory Suppliers Ltd

**Crowe, Martin David**
Novus Medicare Ltd

**Crowne, Ashley**
Aviva Health Solutions Limited

**Cruickshank, Alexander Douglas Miller**
Panorama Healthcare Limited

**Cuffe, Jeremy John**
Norgine Pharmaceuticals Ltd

**Cuffe, Jonathan Charles Edmund Alexander**
Clever Connect Ltd

**Culita, Maria Cristina**
Maria-Cristina Culita Ltd

**Cullen, Christopher Patrick, Dr**
Mill Pharm Limited

**Cumming, David**
Medics Direct Pharmacy Limited

**Cunningham, Barry**
Crest Medical Limited

**Cunningham, Ciaran**
Agrihealth (N.I.) Limited

**Cuny, Bertrand**
Vygon (U.K.) Limited

**Curran, Christopher**
ANP Pharma Ltd

**Curran, Glen**
Lifecell EMEA Limited

**Currey, Hannah Gillian**
CG Pharma Ltd

**Currie, James Andrew**
Matoke Holdings Limited

**Currie, James Balfour**
Currie Marketing Limited

**Currimjee, Carol**
Mawdsley-Brooks & Co Ltd

**Curtin, Owen**
Healthcare 21 (UK) Limited

**Curtis, Derek Alfred**
Intermedical (UK) Ltd

**Curtis, Santina**
Intermedical (UK) Ltd

**Cutting, Robert Fletcher**
Ever Pharma UK Limited

**D'abreo, Annette Zita**
Halo GB Ltd

**D'ambrosio, Carmine**
Okle Systems Limited

**D'souza, Colin**
Design Masters (Sales) Limited

**Da Rocha, Russell Francis**
Rocha Products Limited

**Daftari, Mehrdad**
Technoglobal Ltd

**Dahir, Abdul Razak**
Bipsco Ltd

**Dahir, Mohamed Haji**
Roble Medical Ltd

**Dalton, Viktoriya**
My Premium Nutrition Limited

**Dalziel, James Thomson**
EVR Biosciences (UK) Ltd

**Danapal, Ramasamy, Dr**
Vital Supplies (UK) Limited

**Dang, Colin**
C T Dang Limited

**Dang, Fiona**
C T Dang Limited

**Dang, Tony**
C T Dang Limited

**Daniels, Anna**
Medivast Limited

**Daou, Anis**
Sup-Up Ltd

**Daou, Ismaila**
Pharmayas UK Limited

**Darlington, Karen Sandra**
Longevity Life Ltd

**Darroch, Colin Pollock**
Biobos Limited
Boston Healthcare Limited

**Darsot, Suleman Musa**
Nationwide Healthcare Solutions Ltd

**Daryanani, Sunil Mohan**
London United Exports Limited

**Daukantas, Andrius**
Elcon Pharma Limited
Innomedi Limited

**Dave, Hasmukhlal**
Ozone Medical Supplies Ltd

**Dave, Nikita Nimesh**
Streamline Pharmaceuticals Ltd

**Dave, Nimesh Suraj**
Streamline Pharmaceuticals Ltd

**Davidoff, Rahel**
Be and Are Sales Limited

**Davidson, Angus Murray**
11 Health & Technologies Ltd

**Davidson, Mark Wayne**
Pfizer Consumer Healthcare Ltd

**Doshi, Rajesh**
Gordon Davie Chemist Limited

**Davies Jones, Gwawr**
G & C Pharma Limited

**Davies, Andrew Michael**
Principle Healthcare Limited

**Davies, Darryl**
Ukcann Ltd

**Davies, Derek**
Aspen Pharmacare UK Limited

**Davies, Leslie Clive Robert**
Vygon (U.K.) Limited

**Davies, Michael John**
Principle Healthcare Limited

**Davies, Michael Paul**
Interpharm Limited

**Davies, Mollie**
Clinres UK Limited

**Davies, Philip Benjamin**
Principle Healthcare Limited

**Davies, Robin**
Alissa Healthcare Research Ltd

**Davies, Steven**
Auramedicann Ltd

**Davis, Andrew Simon**
Planehill Limited

**Davis, Andrew**
Your Products Limited

**Davis, Barry**
Angel & Lockhart (Pharma) Ltd

**Davis, George Eric**
Biomarin (U.K.) Ltd.

**Davis, Jacqeline**
Dental Warehouse Ltd

**Davis, Mark Leonard**
Trimark International Limited

**Davis, Martyn Douglas**
Davcaps Limited

**Davis, Sean Anthony**
Parapharm Development Limited

**Davis, Susan Joyce**
Davcaps Limited

**Davis, Tim John**
Dental Warehouse Ltd

**Davis de Riz, Michael James**
Euanet Limited

**Dawe, Barry Keith**
Coates Agencies Ltd

**Dawes, Philip Jonathan**
Carbosynth Limited

**Dawson, Annette Louise**
Soho Flordis UK Limited

**Day, Hywel Rhys**
Napp Pharmaceuticals Limited
Qdem Pharmaceuticals Limited

**De Beer, Willem Marthinus**
Izida Pharma Group Limited

**De Kloet, Hellen**
Ranbaxy (U.K.) Limited

**De Lambilly, Alain Humbert Marie Antoine Mathieu**
Devicor Medical UK Limited

**De Medeiros, Mathieu**
Pro Teeth Whitening Co Limited

**De Silvestri, Fabrizio**
New Health Global Solutions Ltd

**De Souza, Elicca Anne**
Biomed Limited
Neutradvance Limited

**De Souza, Everyll**
Biomed Limited

**De Souza, Keith Francis**
Biomed Limited

**De Souza, Remmie Anne**
Biomed Limited

**De Zulueta, Susan Elizabeth**
Halewood Health Limited

**Deakin, Charles David Seymour, Professor**
Prometheus Medical Ltd

**Dean, Andrew Simon Michael**
Saint-Germain Pharma Ltd

**Debs, Pierre, Dr**
Spectrum Biomedical UK Limited

**Deegan, Robert Anthony**
Soothingproducts Ltd

**Defourt, Xavier Anne Jean-Louis**
Curium Pharma UK Ltd.

**Degg, Richard Francis**
Longevity Life Ltd

**Dehabadi, Mohammad Hussein, Dr**
St Marks Medical Ltd

**Dehareng, Renaud Albert Gaston**
Curium Pharma UK Ltd.

**Deiro, Osman Farah**
Euromed Technologie Limited

**Deitsch, Ivor**
Lambsmead Limited

**Deitsch, Lancelot Piers Duncan**
Lambsmead Limited

**Deitsch, Sandra Estelle**
Lambsmead Limited

**Deitsch, Sebastian Richard Oliver**
Lambsmead Limited

**Dekou, Evangelia Vanessa, Dr**
Clinical Services International Ltd

**Delahoyde, Thomas Joseph**
Chiesi Healthcare Limited
Chiesi Limited

**Delie, Bruno**
Luye Pharma Ltd

**Demetroudi, Elias**
Novmedic Limited

**Dencher, Dennis**
Aspen Pharmacare UK Limited

**Dengler, Christoph**
Britannia Pharmaceuticals Ltd

**Denton, Janet**
Bioconnections Ltd

**Denton, Kenneth**
Bioconnections Ltd

**Denver, Andrew Leslie**
Speedx Limited

**Depau, Alexandro**
Alcura UK Limited
Alliance Healthcare (Distribution)
Beachcourse Limited
OTC Direct Limited

**Dermish, Mohamed Ali Mohamed**
Prime Medical Equipment Ltd

**Desai, Arjun Kumar Somabhai**
Medi Saha Limited

**Desforges, Charles Desmond, Dr**
DLG Partners Limited

**Desforges, Edouard-Henri Olivier**
DLG Partners Limited

**Desorh, Jagjeevan Lal**
ACI Group Ltd

**Devlukia, Meena Prabodhkumar**
Acle Medical Limited

**Devlukia, Meena**
Lime Pharmacy Limited

**Devlukia, Prabodh Nilkanth**
Acle Medical Limited
Lime Pharmacy Limited

**Devlukia, Prabodh**
Beechcroft Supplies Limited

**Devraj, Katarzyna Agata**
Beauty Boosters Ltd

**Deyoung, Peter Daniel**
Piramal Critical Care Limited

**Dhala, Jamila**
TNF (UK) Ltd

**Dhaliwal, Bhupinder Singh**
Euromed Pharmaceuticals Ltd

**Dhaliwal, Rashpal Singh**
PharmXC Ltd

**Dhanjal, Phalvinder Singh**
Total Medcare Limited

**Dhanraj, Harold Ian**
Pharma-X Consultancy Ltd

**Dharamshi, Shirazali Sharif**
In 2 Healthcare Limited

**Dhillon, Cheryl Charanjit**
Otsuka Pharmaceuticals (U.K.) Ltd.

**Di Francesco, Ugo**
Chiesi Healthcare Limited
Chiesi Limited

**Di Nola, Massimo**
Okle Systems Limited

**Di Palma, Luca**
Bracco UK Limited

**Diaconescu, Cristian Stefan**
Livewell Naturals Limited

**Diaz de Saavedra, Marta Irene**
Perrington & Co Limited
Soliphar Limited

**Dickens, James Norman**
Cambpharma Ltd

**Dickinson, Andrew Philip**
Chiesi Healthcare Limited
Chiesi Limited

**Dickinson, Jonathan Elliott**
Incyte Biosciences UK Ltd

**Dickinson, Simon Rodney**
Smart Medical Limited

**Dickson, Andrew Rodney Noel**
Advanced Laboratory Technologies Europe
Hartwood & Brooks Limited
Solana Trade Ltd

**Dickson, Klavdiia**
Genopharm Ltd

**Dill, Nicola Ann**
Qualitech Healthcare Ltd

**Dillon, Martin James Albert**
Truscreen Limited

**Dillon, Richard Anthony**
Infinite Percent Limited

**Dimetrios, Essam Halim, Dr**
B.P. Pharma Limited

**Dingemans, Simon Paul**
GlaxoSmithKline UK Limited

**Diston-Hunter, Kathryn Louise**
Lucis Pharma Ltd

**Diston-Hunter, Stuart**
Lucis Pharma Ltd

**Dixit, Vineet Kumar**
Tillomed Laboratories Limited

**Dixon, Carla Ann**
Apetamintko Limited

**Dixon, Caroline Rebecca Louise**
Meda Pharmaceuticals Limited
Mylan UK Healthcare Limited

**Dixon, John**
RB (China Trading) Limited
RB UK Commercial Limited

**Dixon, Michael Jonathon**
Chiesi Healthcare Limited
Chiesi Limited

**Dixon, Sheriden Dianne**
Mitochondrial Therapy Ltd

**Doades, Jane Elizabeth**
L & R Medical UK Ltd.

**Dobson, Danielle**
MD Salisbury Ltd

**Dobson, Mark**
MD Salisbury Ltd

**Docking, Christopher Paul**
Clinitech Medical Ltd

**Dodhia, Pareshkumar**
Sonal Pharma (UK) Ltd

**Dolfini, Enrico Maria**
Sarepta International UK Ltd.

**Donaghy, Louise Mary**
Pharmacy Supplies Limited

**Donegan, Scott**
Baymed Healthcare Ltd.

**Donkin, Angus Ewart**
Agri-Bio Limited

**Doran, Jon-Paul**
Nascot Health Ltd

**Dos Santos, Antonio**
Medisca UK Limited

**Douglas, Karl Andrew**
Emkado Ltd.

**Douglas, Tony Jack**
Rotapharm Limited

**Dover, Richard Martin**
Baymed Group Ltd.
Baymed Healthcare Ltd.

**Dow, Duncan William**
Bausch & Lomb U.K. Limited

**Dowling, Janis**
Fortis Egregius Limited

**Dowling, William John**
Fortis Egregius Limited

**Dr. Kremer, Dirk**
Skindoc Formula Limited

**Drakard, Michael**
Dene Healthcare Limited

**Dresdner, Marcus**
Eyepak Limited

**Drewnowska, Alicja**
Cambridge Diagnostics (UK) Ltd

**Dring, Charles William**
Merck Serono Limited

**Drury, Richard**
Ethicor Pharma Ltd

**Dryden, Matthew Scott**
Matoke Holdings Limited

**Drywa, Katarzyna**
Ivee Group Ltd

**Drywa, Michal**
Ivee Group Ltd

**Duckworth, Alexander James**
Brancaster Pharma Limited

**Duffy, Michael Philip**
Lantheus MI UK Limited

**Duggan, Alexander James Hanbury**
Appia Healthcare Limited

**Duggan, Marielle Virginie Isabelle**
Appia Healthcare Limited

**Duhalde, Francois-Xavier**
Aventis Pharma Limited
Genzyme Therapeutics Limited
Hoechst Marion Roussel Limited

**Duisenova, Zhanar**
Seltfar Ltd

**Duman, Kaya**
London Health Sciences Ltd

**Dumbuya, Isha**
Wesbee Ventures Limited

**Duncan, Graeme Neville**
Focus Pharma Holdings Limited
Focus Pharmaceuticals Limited

**Duncan, Rachel**
Duncan Inc Ltd

**Duncan, Stephen Peter**
Duncan Inc Ltd

**Dunkel, Matthias Peter Hermann**
Geistlich Sons Limited

**Dunne, Laurence Michael**
Scope Ophthalmics Limited

**Dunoyer, Marc Pierre Jean**
Astrazeneca PLC

**Durand, Benoit**
Sebbin UK Ltd

**Durbidge, Jamie Lee**
Aptil Pharma Limited
Torrent Pharma (UK) Ltd

**Durocher, Philip**
Colgate-Palmolive (U.K.) Ltd

**Duxbury, Matthew Philip**
Kisska International Limited

**Duxbury, Paul Thomas**
Kisska International Limited

**Duxbury, Stephen Matthew**
Kisska International Limited

**Dyer, Colin**
Trafalgar Pharma Ltd

**Dyer, Garry Alfred**
Sunstore Limited

**Dyer, Hui**
Trafalgar Pharma Ltd

**Dzhansyz, Hanna**
Mayfair Export London Limited

**Dzitko, Tomasz**
Farmedic (UK) Limited

**Eakin, Jeremy David**
Ostomart Limited
Respond Healthcare Limited
Respond Healthcare Scotland Ltd
Respond Plus Limited

**Eakin, Paul Andrew**
Ostomart Limited
Respond Healthcare Limited
Respond Healthcare Scotland Ltd
Respond Plus Limited

**Eakin, Thomas George**
Respond Healthcare Limited

**Earsdon Glenister, Anita Jayne**
Vitb12 Academy Ltd

**Eastman, Anthony Neville Chisholm**
MGC Pharma (UK) Ltd

**Eastwick-Field, Vanessa Mary, Dr**
Carbosynth Limited
Carbotang Limited
Czech, Moravian and Slovak Chemicals

**Ebrahim, Sharif Mohamed**
Evees (UK) Limited

**Ebrahimjee, Mustanseir**
Egroup (UK) Limited

**Ebubedike, Charles**
Clinova Limited

**Eccles, Matthew John**
Tytek UK Medical Co Ltd

**Echeverria, Natalie**
Asaya Cosmeceuticals Limited

**Edgemond, James**
United Therapeutics Europe, Ltd.

**Edlund, Carl Magnus**
Medical Need UK Ltd

**Edomobi, Kelechi Chizoma**
Ethicor Pharma Ltd

**Edwards, Richard James**
RJE Agencies Limited

**Eggleston, Richard Stuart**
Flamingo Pharma (UK) Ltd

**Eghiayan, Bedros Loutfig**
Cambridge Pharmaceuticals Ltd
Wigmore Laboratories Limited

**Egorov, Alexey**
Medison Pharma Limited

**Egstrand, Claus**
BBI Healthcare Limited

**Egwaikhide, Alli Moh**
Crossbridge Concepts Limited

**Ejiohuo, Morgan**
Gideotech Limited

**Ekeanyanwu, Gold Ifechikwadoro**
Goldpharma Ltd

**Ekpen, Immaculate Nwabuisi**
N-Pen Ltd.

**El Bakoury, Aya Abd El Rahim Mohamed Abd El Rahim**
United Orphan Pharma Limited

**El Sherbini, Yasser Mahmoud, Dr**
Nutrifast Ltd

**El Sheshtawy Ali Nasr, Nabeil Salah Al Dein**
Europharmacia Ltd

**El-Maksoud, Wesam**
A1 Natural Ltd

**El-Serafy, Ahmed Ibrahim**
Eye Guard Ltd

**El-Sherbini, Khaled Mahmoud, Dr**
Nutrifast Ltd

**Elbahy, Rafif**
Eastern Lighthouse Ltd

**Elbawab, Mohamed**
My Nutrition London Ltd

**Eldamarawy, Salma**
SHL Medical Limited

**Eldracher, Deborah Disanzo**
Astrazeneca PLC

**Elhoush, Ashrf**
Thexo Pharma Limited
United Pharma Group Limited

**Elkaramany, Tamer Aly Emam Aly**
Solarius UK & Overseas Limited

**Ellard, James**
New England Biolabs (U.K.) Ltd

**Ellerton, David**
Virbac Limited

**Elliot, Robert**
Biomedical Reproductive Research Ltd

**Elliott, Christopher**
P.I.C. International Ltd

**Ellis, Anthony**
Medicaleaf Limited

**Ellis, Benjamin James**
Lupin Healthcare (UK) Limited

**Ellison, Stephanie Joy**
Mawdsley-Brooks & Co Ltd
Wellspring Pharmaceutical Services
Wellspring Pharmaceutical Services UK

**Ellson, Peter William**
Stegram Pharmaceuticals Ltd

**Elman, Barry**
Barry Elman (Wholesale) Ltd

**Elmasry, Sherif Mohamed Aboelnaga Mohamed**
E.P.G Pharma Ltd

**Elzawi, Abdussalam**
PPQUK Ltd

**Elzokrod, Tamer Mohamed Hassan**
Solarius UK & Overseas Limited

**Emery, Alan Duncan**
Westmead International Limited

**Eneli, Nnaemeka Obumneke**
Hooben Distributors Limited

**Eneli, Obinna**
Hooben Distributors Limited

**Engineer, Nikesh**
Chemidex Generics Limited
Essential Pharma Limited
Firstchem Limited
Healthcare Generics Limited
NHS Generics Limited
Tarus Group Limited
Tarus Laboratories Limited

**Ennett, Noel Christopher**
Greiner Bio-One Limited

**Eom, Noella Soo**
Five Star International Consulting

**Epifanis, Alexandros**
Altin Medical Ltd

**Erdil, Yeliz**
Day Pharma Limited

**Erman, Barbara Lumini Jean**
Pharmacohub Limited

**Erman, Dillan Marion, Dr**
Pharmacohub Limited

**Ertl, Rudolf**
Gilead Sciences Ltd

**Esa, Adam**
Pharmacy Business Consultancy Ltd

**Esmail, Anisha Karim**
Excel Pharma Limited
Intellix (Holdings) Limited

**Esmail, Arif**
Excel Pharma Limited
Intellix (Holdings) Limited
Nasila Pharma Limited

**Esmail, Riazali**
Fairview Health Limited

**Caunce, Andrew John**
H.N. Espley & Sons Limited

**Essien, Edidiong Mathias**
Symmetry Inc Ltd

**Essuman, Francis Kwame**
Leap Pharma Ltd

**Estcourt, Simon**
Aposave Ltd

**Eutick, Malvin Leonard, Dr**
Ethicor Pharma Ltd

**Evans, David Richard**
Daleacre Wholesale Limited

**Evans, John Anthony**
Plurafores Pharma Limited

**Everitt, Caroline Rosalind, Dr**
Mill Pharm Limited

**Eversley-Robertson, Ryan Adrian Charles**
ATI Pharmaceuticals Limited

**Ewane, Vivian Alobwede**
Viemeds Limited

**Exner, Andree**
DCMP 8E Cepac Limited
Herbialis Limited
International Pharma Co Ltd

**Eze, Kingsley Chidi**
New Generation Business UK Ltd

**Fagan, Michael Earl, Dr**
Attends Limited

**Fagleman, Alexander**
Malcolm B. Fagleman Ltd

**Fagleman, Malcolm Bernard**
Malcolm B. Fagleman Ltd

**Fagleman, Vivien**
Malcolm B. Fagleman Ltd

**Fairfield, Alan David**
Phoenix Healthcare Distribution Ltd

**Fairman, Richard**
Vet Direct Services Limited

**Fakouri, Bahram**
Schulz Medical Supplies Ltd

**Fallouh, Adib**
Inventive Medical Solutions Ltd

**Falzon, Carl**
C. S. T. Pharma Limited
UK Pharma Direct Limited

**Famojuro, Kehinde Olufunke**
Detafinas Limited

**Famojuro, Samson Olufemi**
Detafinas Limited

**Farah, Amin**
Evolve Generics Limited
Evolve Healthcare Partners Ltd
Evolve Pharma Limited
Lamyra International Limited
RI Pharma Limited

**Farboud, Jahangir**
Pennine UK Procedure Packs Ltd

**Farbrother, Sean LEA**
Clinimed Limited

**Farley, Richard Andrew**
AF First Aid Ltd

**Farrant, Andrew David**
Charlwood Pharma Limited

**Farrant, Eleanor Margaret Craig**
Charlwood Pharma Limited
Odiham OH Products Limited

**Farshineh Adl, Sina**
Masir Ltd

**Faruq, Umar**
Essex Medical Supplies Ltd

**Faulkner, Wendy Jane**
Appia Healthcare Limited

**Fazal, Abbas Ali**
Celestial Pharma Ltd

**Fazal, Mohamed Gulamabbas**
Interchem (Chemist Wholesale) Ltd

**Fazal, Nassir**
Interchem (Chemist Wholesale) Ltd

**Fazal, Shaheed**
Interchem (Chemist Wholesale) Ltd

**Fazwani, Sinnan**
Royce Health Sciences Ltd

**Fearnley, Annette Catherine**
Epsilon Pharmaceuticals Ltd

**Fecsuova, Natalia**
CEU Pharm Ltd

**Fedyshyn, Denys**
Medicia Ltd

**Feher, Zoltan**
Zolex Global Limited

**Fenech, Alexander**
Mediva Pharma Limited

**Fennell, Thomas**
Fen Health Ltd

**Ferdowsian, Farshad**
Aria Vape Ltd
RF Vapes Limited

**Fergus, Darren**
Sintetica Limited

**Ferguson, Claire**
Spatone Limited

**Ferris, Julie**
Cis Pharmassist Limited

**Fielder, Andrew Michael**
Ascot Treatments Ltd

**Fielding, Alexander Lawrence**
ANXT Ltd

**Fielding, Richard Henry**
Max Healthcare Limited
Max Remedies Limited

**Filsouf, Saloomeh**
Trent Dent Products Limited

**Finnie, Paul Michael**
Timstar Laboratory Suppliers Ltd

**Fisher, Helmut Karl**
Phoenix Medical Supplies Ltd

**Fisher, Simon Andrew**
Alturix Limited

**Fishlock, Sandra**
Teoxane UK Limited

**Fishwick, Craig Bernard**
Swingward Limited

**Fitz-Gibbon, Keir**
Canconc Ltd

**Fladrich, Mark**
Grunenthal Limited

**Flanagan, Amanda**
Grunenthal Limited

**Flanagan, Desmond Alexander Justin**
TRB Chemedica (UK) Limited

**Flanagan, Sean Francis**
GBY (UK) Ltd

**Flanigan III, Patrick Eugene**
Celgene Limited

**Flannery, Chris**
1966 Health International Ltd

**Flather, John Nicholas, Doctor**
Mill Pharm Limited

**Fletcher, Anthony Keith**
A.K. Fletcher (Preston) Ltd

**Fletcher, Maureen Anne**
A.K. Fletcher (Preston) Ltd

**Fletcher, Joanna Ruth**
Espere Healthcare Limited

**Fletcher, Maureen Anne**
Greenheys - Weenytot Limited

**Fletcher, Michael Dean**
Greenheys - Weenytot Limited

**Florczyk, Waldemar**
Global 4 Care Ltd

**Flower, David**
Lyshaug Enterprises Limited

**Fong, Chan Kwai**
CKF Limited

**Ford, Michael**
Leadiant Biosciences Limited

**Ford, Paul Anthony**
Medicaleaf Limited

**Ford, Stephen Kelsey**
Optima Consumer Health Limited

**Forget, Sylvain Luc Alexandre**
Doksy Limited

**Fornoles, Adielmofranches**
Frontrow International UK Ltd

**Fossum, Torgeir**
Vitamins To Buy Ltd

**Foster, Harold Stacy**
Ocusoft UK Limited

**Foster, Monica**
CBD Platinum Ltd

**Fouad, Naser Michel, Dr**
Archangel's Pharmaceutical Services

**Fouda, Ibrahim Abdelrazik Albayoomi**
Evorin Pharma Limited

**Foulds, Timothy Weston**
Instantly White Ltd

**Fournier, Jean Claude**
Pharmeurope UK Limited

**Foxley, Michael**
Fox Group Global Ltd
Fox Group International Ltd
Fox Pharma Limited

**Francis, Thomas Trevor, Dr**
Winchpharma (Consumer Healthcare) Ltd

**Frank, Kajsa Lena Elisabet**
MMP Marketing Limited

**Frank, Per Stefan**
MMP Marketing Limited

**Frankel, Matthew**
Theramex HQ UK Limited

**Franklin, Ian Eric**
Hospira UK Limited
Meridian Medical Technologies Ltd
PF OFG UK 3 Ltd
Pfizer Consumer Healthcare Ltd
Pfizer Limited
Pfizer OFG UK Limited

**Franklin, Philip David**
Purple Surgical UK Limited

**Fraser-Pye, Graham Julian**
Aspire Pharma Holdings Limited
Aspire Pharma Limited
Attentive Pharma Limited

**Fraux, Claire**
Acupuncture Direct Ltd

**Fraux, Gerard**
Acupuncture Direct Ltd

**Frawley, David**
Sunovion Pharmaceuticals Europe Ltd.

**Frazier, Jessica Marie**
Jessica Inc Limited

**Frazzette, Michael**
Genesis Medical Limited

**Frederick, David Charles**
Healthcare 21 (UK) Limited

**Freedman, David**
Danel Trading Limited
Neutradvance Limited
Pharmethicals Limited

**Freedman, Neil Ailon**
Danel Trading Limited

**Freedman, Rachel**
Danel Trading Limited
Neutradvance Limited
Pharmethicals Limited

**Freeman, Elliot Jamie**
Profoot (UK) Ltd

**Freeman, Lewis Andrew**
Profoot (UK) Ltd

**Freeman, Simon**
Profoot (UK) Ltd

**Freimane, Julia**
J & G Equipment Limited

**Frellsen, John Morell**
Atrimusrx Ltd

**Frey, Alain**
Santhera (UK) Limited

**Frey, Georg Martin**
Vifor Pharma UK Limited

**Freyne, John**
Scope Ophthalmics Limited

**Freyne, Tom**
Scope Ophthalmics Limited

**Friday, Dean Leslie**
Astral Health Ltd

**Friedberg, Robert Michael**
Active Global Ltd

**Fritze, Marcus**
M D M Healthcare Ltd

**Frude, Michael**
Granules Europe Limited

**Fry, Hugo Rupert Alexander**
Aventis Pharma Limited
Hoechst Marion Roussel Limited

**Fuchs, Friedrich Josef**
APC Pharmaceuticals & Chemicals (Europe)

**Fugate, Ronald Lee**
Perricone MD Cosmeceuticals UK Ltd

**Fuge, Dai**
UK Pharma Direct Limited

**Fulton, David Hall**
Moreton Pharmacy Ltd.

**Funnell, Alison Margaret**
Universal Procurement Services Ltd

**Funnell, Benjamin John**
Universal Procurement Services Ltd

**Furstenberg, Holger Christian Wilhelm**
Genesis Medical Limited

**Gaag, Gijsbert Van Der**
Novalabb Limited

**Gabbitas, Lucy Victoria**
Prestige Dental Products Ltd

**Gadhia, Jitesh Kishorekumar, Lord**
Accord Healthcare Limited

**Gadhvi, Nickesh Ravindra**
NSA Pharma Limited

**Gagliardi, Livio**
Intermedical (UK) Ltd

**Gagnon, Beth**
Gagnon Direct Ltd

**Gaikwad, Sushil Waman**
Gos Pharma Limited

**Gall, Matthew Garrett**
Sarepta International UK Ltd.

**Gallacher, Matthew**
MRG Creations Ltd

**Gallagher, Anne**
Roe Pharmacy Ltd

**Gallagher, Jonathan**
Star Powa Limited

**Gallagher, Kevin**
Prometheus Medical Ltd

**Gallagher, Rodney**
Roe Pharmacy Ltd

**Gallifant, Deborah**
Kinesis Limited

**Gallifant, Jamie Ronald**
Kinesis Limited

**Gambrill, Donna Mary**
Oakways Healthcare Limited

**Games, Robert Harland**
Dosego Limited

**Gandhi, Anuj Singh**
Healthcaps Europe Ltd

**Gandhi, Sanyam**
Healthy Era Ltd

**Gandhi, Saumil Mahendra**
Aarkios Health PVT Limited

**Gardiner, Bruce Montgomery**
S.T.D. Pharmaceutical Products Ltd

**Gardiner, Karen Jane, Dr**
Purple Orchid Pharma Limited

**Gardiner, Margaret Florence**
S.T.D. Pharmaceutical Products Ltd

**Gardiner, Robert Norman**
S.T.D. Pharmaceutical Products Ltd
V.S. Limited
Vascular Products Limited

**Garella, Rahul**
Par Laboratories Europe, Ltd.

**Garg, Nitin Sham**
R. N. Europe Limited

**Garg, Rohit Sham**
R. N. Europe Limited

**Garg, Sandeep Kumar**
Vedic Medical Hall Limited

**Glenie, Robert**
Alston Garrard & Co Limited

**Glenie, Saul**
Alston Garrard & Co Limited

**Garton, David John**
Seagrave Pharma Consultancy Ltd.

**Garton, Karen Lynn**
Seagrave Pharma Consultancy Ltd.

**Garton, Thomas William, Dr**
Acer Agri Ltd

**Garvey, Richard Stephen**
MH (Newry) Ltd

**Gasser, Andreas**
Gerot Lannach UK Limited

**Gatenby, Michael**
C.D. Medical Limited
Linderma Limited
M & A Pharmachem Limited

**Gaughan, Katie**
Avail Group UK Limited

**Gavin, Rowland**
Leafxtracts Ltd

**Gavrielidou, Androula Orphanidou**
Rawmmed Trading Co Ltd

**Gaylor, Nicola**
Sylk Limited

**Gee, Hee Young**
Max Motivation Limited

**Gehlot, Ravi**
Harley Dentist Limited

**Gem, Joan Mary**
Bailey Instruments Ltd

**George, Alun Michael, Dr**
DDWS Limited

**George, Philip**
Tia Marie Ltd

**George, Sagitha**
Aadverv Sourcing Solutions Ltd

**Georgi, Sameh**
Alpha Pharma Ltd

**Gerdes, Klaus, Doctor**
Sanochemia Diagnostics UK Ltd

**Gertenbach, Jacobus Johannes**
Lil-Lets UK Ltd

**Ghaffar, Mohammed Abid**
UK Lites Ltd

**Ghai, Rajesh**
Raj Ghai Associates Limited

**Ghai, Vaishali**
Veepharm Limited

**Gharagozloo, Parviz**
Celloxess (Europe) Limited

**Ghare, Amit**
Ascend Laboratories (UK) Ltd

**Ghasemi Firoozabadi, Behrooz, Dr**
Hedigen Limited
Pharmagona Limited

**Ghatala, Ritaben Gordhanbhai**
Niv Ltd
Nivja Healthcare Ltd

**Ghattas, Nancy**
Allergan Limited

**Ghedia, Vijay Ranchod**
Zina Chemist Limited

**Ghelani, Deepak Anantrai**
Ascot Pharma Ltd
Spodefell Pharma Chemicals Ltd

**Gheshlagh, Fateme Kasravi**
Skingen UK Ltd

**Ghith, Hamada, Dr**
Eastern Lighthouse Ltd

**Gholamhosseini, Babak**
Haoma Pharma Ltd

**Ghosh, Soumendranath**
Cellchem UK Limited
Kosei Pharma UK Ltd.

**Giannelli, Alessandra**
Martini International Ltd

**Gibbons, Mark**
Baxalta UK Investments Ltd.
Shire Pharmaceuticals Limited

**Gibbons, Sally**
LB Pharma Limited

**Giblin, Mary Emma, Dr**
Glemsford Services Limited

**Gibson, Dale Mark**
DMG Trading Limited

**Gibson, Victoria, Dr**
Carbosynth Limited
Czech, Moravian and Slovak Chemicals

**Gietka, Rafal**
Karczek Ltd

**Gilani, Nayl Ghaus**
Odyssey Healthcare Limited

**Gilbert, Yosef Binyomin**
Jagmed Limited

**Gilbey, Bernhard David**
11 Health & Technologies Ltd

**Giles, Adrian Patrick**
Your Products Limited

**Gill, Amrik Singh**
ASG Pharma Ltd

**Gill, Arvinder Singh**
Kerita Ltd

**Gill, Hardeep Singh**
Prescribe International Ltd

**Gill, Lakhvir Singh**
Myly Pharma Limited

**Gill, Malcolm**
M.G. Dental Supplies Limited

**Gill, Manjit Singh**
Gilsun Healthcare Ltd
Gilsun Limited

**Gill, Margaret Elizabeth Davies**
M.G. Dental Supplies Limited

**Gillies, Louise Aanne**
First Choice Suppliments Ltd

**Gilliot, Eric**
RB UK Hygiene Home Commercial Ltd

**Gilson, Jeremy David**
Countrywide Healthcare Supplies Holdings

**Ginai, Musharraf Mahmood**
Zecare Limited

**Ginai, Nazma Tasneem**
Zecare Limited

**Girard, Wilfrid Pierre**
Medeuronet (UK) Limited

**Giunta, Leonard Charles, Dr**
Jackson Immunoresearch Europe Ltd

**Glanvill, Sheryl Anne**
BR Pharma International Ltd

**Glason, Matthew Sean Lawrence, Dr**
Mill Pharm Limited

**Gleen, Carmen**
Durbin PLC

**Gluck, Samuel Julian**
Honest Health Limited

**Glynn, Marshall Anthony**
Dakota Pharma Limited

**Glynne-Jones, Antonia**
Friends of Pyrethrum Ltd

**Gmunder, Peter**
Bioforce (U.K) Limited

**Goddard, John Geoffrey**
Accord Healthcare Limited

**Godvan, Mykola**
Din Commerce Ltd

**Goffart, Anthony**
Aromanature Limited

**Goga, Octavian**
Gama Group Services Ltd

**Gohil, Amit**
Purple Pharma Limited

**Gohil, Arjunsinh**
Accmede Pharmaceuticals Ltd

**Gold, Janet Vivienne**
NLR Exports Limited

**Goldberg, Daniel**
Molab Ltd

**Golden, Randal Louis**
CooperVision Lens Care Limited

**Goldman, Howard**
Rayburn Trading Co Ltd

**Goldman, Michael David**
Rayburn Trading Co Ltd

**Goldman, Russell Stuart**
Rayburn Trading Co Ltd

**Golombeck, Anthony**
Dakota Pharma Limited

**Gomez Cortes, Francisco Javier**
Fitness and Nutrition of Europe Ltd.

**Gomez Fernandez, Maria Angeles Silvia**
Dr Kool Ltd

**Gonzalez, German Augusto**
Hapa Medical UK Ltd

**Goodall, Jason**
Excelsior Scientific Limited

**Goode, Karl Graham**
IMI Ventures Limited

**Goodman, Alan Gilbert**
Aclardian Limited

**Goodwin, Karon**
Vicars Cross Healthcare Ltd

**Goodwin, Nicholas James**
Vicars Cross Healthcare Ltd

**Gordon, Benjamin James**
Medicines By Design Ltd

**Gordon, Frances Ann**
Wescroft Limited

**Gordon, Michael Thomas**
Anfarm Generics UK Limited

**Gordon, Natalie Carol**
JLS Pharma Limited

**Gordon, Robert**
Omapharm Limited

**Gordon, Steven**
Kadmon International Ltd

**Gorenskaja, Viktoria**
New Horizon Pharma (UK) Ltd.

**Gorrell, Shirley Agnes**
Ecosse Pharmaceuticals Limited
Munro Wholesale Medical Supplies Ltd
Newco Pharma Limited
Strathclyde Pharmaceuticals Ltd

**Gorton, Robert**
Gorton Trading Limited

**Goss, Helen Elizabeth**
Arena Pharmaceuticals Limited

**Goss, Peter**
Arena Pharmaceuticals Limited

**Gotah, Wellington**
Winelia Co Ltd

**Gotzev, Kristiyan Krassimirov**
KDC-UK Ltd.

**Gould, Caron Lynn, Dr**
Epsilon Pharmaceuticals Ltd

**Gould, William Michael**
Epsilon Pharmaceuticals Ltd

**Gourlay, Frederick Thomas**
MAF Pharma Limited

**Gouzd, Magdalena**
Skinlab Medical Ltd

**Gouzd, Malgorzata**
Skinlab Medical Ltd

**Gower, David Nicholas**
Cosmedic Pharmacy Limited

**Graham, Richard**
Azurite Health Ltd

**Graham, Thomas Kenneth**
Biosensors International UK Ltd

**Graieg, Patsy**
Go Medical UK Limited

**Grainger, Karen Marion**
ViiV Healthcare Overseas Ltd
ViiV Healthcare Trading Services UK
ViiV Healthcare UK Limited

**Granena Aracil, Ariadna**
RB UK Commercial Limited

**Grant, Christopher Keith Neil**
Crowncrest Services UK Limited

**Grant, Deborah Mary**
Crowncrest Services UK Limited

**Grant, Geoffrey**
Autono-Med Limited

**Grant, Ian Austen**
Medi UK Ltd

**Grant, Martin John**
Receptor Technologies Limited

**Gray, Ross**
GQC Solutions Ltd

**Gray, Samuel James Caiger**
Mirada Medical Limited

**Gray, Stuart James**
Value Medical Limited

**Gray, William Alasdair**
FTS Bio Limited
Fast Track Sourcing Limited

**Swift, Ben**
The Great British Bee Co Ltd

**Greatorex, Richard**
Libertas Medical Ltd

**Green, Jay Wade**
GlaxoSmithKline US Trading Ltd

**Green, John**
General Shop Ltd

**Green, Jonathan Simon Charles**
Strandland Limited

**Green, Richard**
GlaxoSmithKline Consumer Trading Services

**Greene, Eileen**
Mooncup Ltd

**Greenep, Ian James**
Oxford PCS Limited
P & D Pharmaceuticals Ltd.

**Greensmith, Richard Mark**
Pharmalab Limited
Reckitt Benckiser Asia Pacific Ltd

**Grekulov, Dmytro**
Biotus Ltd

**Grice, Arthur Joseph**
Vog Limited

**Griffin, Anthony Gerard**
Dechra Veterinary Products Ltd

**Griffiths, Terry Baugh**
Healthcare (Wales) Ltd.
Surgery Supplies (UK) Limited

**Grigg, Terry**
Dexcel-Pharma Limited
Discovery Pharmaceuticals Ltd

**Grigorescu-Popescu, Cristian**
OFC Molecular Ltd

**Grimes, Brian Owen**
Dene Healthcare Limited

**Grimes, Chris James**
Veriton Pharma Limited

**Grippon, Laurent**
Allergan Limited

**Groat, Malcolm**
NKCell Plus PLC

**Grobe-Natrop, Frank**
Phoenix Medical Supplies Ltd

**Grochowalska, Anna Krystyna**
Immortalis Distribution Ltd.

**Groombridge, Adrian**
Pioneer Veterinary Products Ltd

**Groombridge, Lucy**
Pioneer Veterinary Products Ltd

**Grosse, Nigel Anthony John**
Solo Nutrition Limited

**Grossman, Moses**
Pharma Products Limited

**Grotowska, Malgorzata**
Maximed Ltd

**Grove, Paul Allen**
Credenhill Limited

**Grover, Amanda**
A K Worldwide Trading Limited

**Grover, Edwin Robert, Doctor**
United Therapeutics Europe, Ltd.

**Grundy, Peter Robert Whitfield**
Durham Pharmaceuticals Limited

**Grunfeld, Leslie Eric Giles**
Besins Healthcare (UK) Limited

**Grzebellus, Martin**
American Biochemical and Pharmaceuticals

**Grzymala, Agnieszka**
Medica Finance UK Ltd

**Gualano, Mario Pietro**
BBI Healthcare Limited

**Guan, Mo**
Elim Springs Biotech Ltd

**Gudgin, David**
Mirada Medical Limited

**Gudipati, Srinivas**
Life on Healthcare Ltd

**Guerin, Michael Francis**
NPA Services Limited
Omapharm Limited

**Guevara Salazar, Cristino**
Gulfstream Equity & Development Ltd

**Guinan, Sean**
Agrihealth (N.I.) Limited

**Gujer, Remo**
Celgene Limited

**Gul, Mariam**
Better Earth Limited

**Gulaid, Leeban**
LGS Pharma Limited

**Gulielmetti, Robert**
Pharmacosmos UK Limited

**Guliyev, Azar**
Vitamed Int Ltd

**Gulliford, David James**
Islestone Limited

**Gulliford, Mark James**
Doncaster Pharmaceuticals Group Ltd
Doncaster Pharmaceuticals Ltd
Eclipse Generics Limited
Renfield Limited
Value Generics Limited

**Gulliford, Mark**
Testerworld Limited

**Gulliford, Peter, Dr**
Islestone Limited

**Gulzar, Kasim**
Rightdose Solutions Limited

**Gunabalsinkam, Thangarajah**
Herbal Food Life Limited

**Gunna, Chandana**
Vise Services Ltd
Vise Services PVT Ltd

**Gunning, Michael Joseph**
Moscow Flyer Limited

**Gunstone, Anthony Edward, Dr**
DDWS Limited

**Guo, Wei**
Ironbridge Medical Services Ltd

**Guo, Yijian**
HEC Pharm UK Limited

**Gupta, Achin**
Glenmark Pharmaceuticals Europe Ltd

**Gupta, Gaurav**
Dilmaherbals Limited

**Gupta, Jyoti**
Kganesha Pharma Ltd

**Gupta, Monika**
Elektro Genesis Limited

**Gupta, Sanjay**
Aptil Pharma Limited
Torrent Pharma (UK) Ltd

**Gupta, Tarun**
Elektro Genesis Limited

**Gurusamy, Kalyanakumar, Dr**
Innovius Life Drugs Ltd

**Guse, Kyle**
Atossa Genetics UK Ltd

**Gustafson, Arnold Leonard**
Quantum Biomed Ltd

**Ha, Jae-Young**
Oxbridge Pharma Limited

**Haagen, Tomas**
Novo Nordisk Limited

**Habib, Muhammad**
Limes Pharma Ltd

**Hackett, John Edward**
Max Healthcare Limited
Max Remedies Limited

**Hacking, Christopher Stewart**
Bailey Instruments Ltd

**Hackman, Detmar Albert**
Sabona Rheumatic Relief Co Ltd

**Hackman, Eunhee**
Sabona Rheumatic Relief Co Ltd

**Hackman, Robert Edward**
Sabona Rheumatic Relief Co Ltd

**Haddad, George Michel, Dr**
Gelu Life Limited

**Haddouch, Nawal**
ZS Pharma Limited

**Hagisufi, Ahmed**
Limes Pharma Ltd

**Hahn, Vera**
Bayer PLC

**Haidzir, Heidi Shafiq**
Pinklady International Ltd

**Hajnal, Peter**
Victoria Pharma London Ltd

**Halder, Kamalesh**
Adicam Pharmaceuticals Ltd

**Halko, Timea, Dr**
Medimpex UK Limited

**Hall, Avril Clarice**
Tank Puffin (Wholesale) Ltd

**Hall, Ian Michael**
Astellas Pharma Ltd.
Bripharm Limited

**Hallahan, Jamie**
Deise Pharm Ltd

**Hallay, Lothar Otto**
Medicalstore-24 Limited

**Hallett, Susan Caroline**
Jackson Immunoresearch Europe Ltd

**Halpin, Timothy John**
Neubria Limited

**Hamed, Aljali, Dr**
Balagrae Ltd

**Hamid, Madiha**
Mayfair Distributors Limited

**Hamid, Osman Naveed**
Arnolds Pharmacy Limited
Barton Pharmacy Limited

**Hamill, Helen Louise**
Purepharm Ltd

**Hamill, Michael**
Chameleon Planet Ltd

**Hamill, Turlough Malachy, Dr**
Paragen Pharma Ltd
Purepharm Ltd

**Hamilton, Alan James**
Blue Horizon Healthcare Consulting

**Hamilton, Helen Louise**
Blue Horizon Healthcare Consulting

**Hana, Zac**
Hana Healthcare Ltd

**Hanciles, Eva**
Morvigor (UK) Ltd

**Handel, Thomas**
Meridian Medical Technologies Ltd

**Haniff, Nigel**
Kohilam Limited

**Hanlon, James**
Crosspharma Limited

**Hanna, Jean**
Prominent Life Style Ltd

**Hannah, Richard Anthony**
Countrywide Healthcare Supplies Holdings

**Hanson, Emma Charlotte**
Home Health (U.K.) Limited

**Hanson, Mark Richard**
Home Health (U.K.) Limited

**Haq, Hassan**
Haq Pharm Ltd

**Hara, Kunio**
Amano Enzyme Europe Limited

**Haracska, Lajos, Dr**
Stem Cellx Limited

**Harania, Venichand Ranmal**
Chemys Limited
EMT Healthcare Limited

**Hardie, John**
Arctic Medical Limited

**Harding, Elisabeth Belly Suami**
Osteo-Ti UK Limited

**Hardy, Rachel**
Oxford Nutrition Limited

**Hardy, Robert**
Oxford Nutrition Limited

**Hargan, William John**
Piramal Critical Care Limited

**Haria, Premila**
Harley's (UK) Ltd
Medimax (UK) Ltd

**Hariharan, Rajesh**
Enjoy Marketing Limited

**Harki, Nihad Qader Bakr**
Elite Pharma UK Limited

**Harnett, Denise Jean**
Pfizer Consumer Healthcare Ltd
Pfizer Limited

**Harnett, Iii**
Water-Jel International Ltd

**Harris, Claire**
G & C Pharma Limited

**Harris, Mark Wayne**
H4 Medical Limited

**Harris, Neil**
Abbott Healthcare Products Ltd
Abbott Laboratories Limited

**Harris, Wendy**
Novochem Limited

**Harrison, Generald Richard**
Albert Harrison & Co.Limited

**Harrison, Graham Coupe**
Albert Harrison & Co.Limited

**McKenna, Cara**
Albert Harrison & Co.Limited

**Sanderson, Paul**
Albert Harrison & Co.Limited

**Harrison, Deborah**
Pricecheck Toiletries Limited

**Harrison, Jonathan Edward**
Pricecheck Toiletries Limited

**Harrison, June**
Showman's Surgical Ltd

**Harrison, Simon Richard**
Stanton Ocean Services Limited

**Harrison, Trevor Paul**
Stanton Ocean Services Limited

**Harshbarger, Benjamin Scott**
Aegerion Pharmaceuticals Ltd

**Hart, Janet Margaret**
McKinley Pharma Limited

**Hart, Luke Ingmire**
Creo Pharma Holdings Limited
Creo Pharma Limited

**Hart, Sharon Ingmire**
Creo Pharma Holdings Limited
Creo Pharma Limited

**Cornwell, Richard**
Paul Hartmann Limited

**Coupe, Trevor John**
Paul Hartmann Limited

**Perez, Marc**
Paul Hartmann Limited

**Hartup, John**
Clinigen Group PLC

**Harty, Mark Stephen**
CooperVision Lens Care Limited

**Harvey, Carol Ann**
Ongar Medical Limited

**Harvey, Christopher Michael**
Ongar Medical Limited

**Harvey, Matthew James Richard**
Optima Consumer Health Limited

**Hashi, Mohamed Abdiaziz**
Britpharm Limited

**Hassam, Shan Abbas**
Flintlow Limited
Veenak International Limited

**Hassam, Shan-E-Abbas**
Veenak Sourcing Limited

**Hassan Ghalyaie, Maryam**
Clinic Supply Ltd

**Hassan, Nazmul**
Beximco Pharma UK Limited

**Hassan, Sadia**
Daryeel Medicines International Ltd

**Hassanin Yousif, Doha Mohamed**
Ikatrad Ltd

**Hassim, Rayyaz**
Tynatex Limited

**Hatch, David Andrew**
Remote Pharma Solutions Ltd

**Hathi, Alpa**
Gowrie Laxmico Limited
Laxmi BNS Holdings Limited
Laxmico Limited

**Hathi, Govindji Thakershi**
Gowrie Laxmico Limited
Laxmi BNS Holdings Limited
Laxmico Limited

**Hathi, Samit Govindji**
Laxmi BNS Holdings Limited

**Hathi, Samit**
Gowrie Laxmico Limited
Laxmico Limited

**Haveliwala, Zubair**
Zhpharma Ltd

**Hawker, Heather**
R & H Trading Limited

**Hawker, Robert William**
R & H Trading Limited

**Hawksworth, Liz**
Healthmed Supplies (HMS) Ltd

**Hayburn, Colin**
Galen Limited
Intergal Pharma Limited

**Hayes, Jennifer**
Aqua Hydration Limited

**Hayward, Ann Margaret**
Cripps Medical Limited

**Hayward, Miles Timothy**
Cripps Medical Limited

**Hayward, Stephen Martin David**
Cyan Trading Ltd

**Hazlett, Shaun Kent**
Orion Medical Supplies Ltd

**Heathcote, Mark**
GlaxoSmithKline US Trading Ltd

**Heather, David Christopher**
TA-65 (UK) Wholesale Limited

**Binder, Lisa Simone**
The Heatpack Co Ltd

**Cohen, Ben David, Dr**
The Heatpack Co Ltd

**Cohen, Howard David**
The Heatpack Co Ltd

**Cohen, Valerie Ann**
The Heatpack Co Ltd

**Cohen, Jonathan Stuart**
The Heatpack Co Ltd

**Hedley, Mark Anthony**
MAF Pharma Limited

**Heer, Andre Reinhold**
Incline Therapeutics Europe Ltd.

**Heerema, Rob**
Orly Pharma Limited

**Heino, Mary Anne**
Lantheus MI UK Limited

**Helimi, Nor Faiz Bin Ahmad**
RR Cosmeceuticals (UK) Ltd

**Helmy, Sherine Hassan Abbas, Dr**
Tour N' Cure International Ltd.

**Helowicz, Karol**
Lab-PCR Limited

**Hemington, David**
EMT Healthcare Limited

**Henderson, John**
Veterinary Surgeons Supply Co Ltd

**Henderson, Mary Elizabeth**
Merck Serono Limited

**Hendler, Gary Bryan**
Eisai Limited
MGI Pharma Limited

**Hendriks, Bram**
Bhendriks Resale and Retale Ltd

**Hendriks, Robert Charles Gerard**
Soho Flordis UK Limited

**Henn, David Friedrich Wilhelm John**
Cannamedical Pharma UK Limited

**Hennah, Adrian Nevil**
RB (China Trading) Limited

**Henriquez-Ramirez, Antonio**
Canary Islands Marketing Board Ltd

**Herbert, Kevin Douglas**
Rothes Pharma Limited

**Herdem, Adem**
Menar UK Biotech Ltd

**Herfeld, Stefan**
Phoenix Medical Supplies Ltd

**Herman, Daniel Andrew Richard**
Bio-Synergy Limited

**Herman, Peter Ian**
PI Herman Trading as Peter's Ltd

**Hermida, Ines**
Macacha Health Limited

**Herold, Mark Wilfried**
Nema Pharma Trade Limited

**Herro, Elise**
Vivaorganiclife Ltd

**Herron, Brian Nigel**
Humn Pharmaceuticals (UK) Ltd

**Hersee, Keith**
Ashtons Healthcare Limited
Ashtons Medical Limited
Ashtons Medical Supplies Ltd

**Hersi, Adam**
Pharmedics Ltd

**Hestler, Tobias**
GlaxoSmithKline Consumer Trading Services

**Heywood, Anya, Dr**
378 Co Ltd

**Heywood, Peter, Dr**
378 Co Ltd

**Heywood, Shane Lebert**
Portland Ventures Inc Ltd

**Hibbert, Catherine**
Pioneer Veterinary Products Ltd

**Hickey, Liam**
Dragonstone Group Limited

**Hickson, Katherine Anne**
Restate Management Ltd

**Hickson, Stephen John Dudley**
Incimed Ltd

**Higgins, Stephen John**
Techdow Pharma England Limited

**Higson, Graham Charles**
Intercept Pharma Ltd

**Hilaire, Jean-Francois**
RPH Pharma Ltd

**Hilger, Marcus**
AAH Pharmaceuticals Limited
Barclay Pharmaceuticals Ltd
Blackstaff Pharmaceuticals Ltd
Lloyds Pharmacy Clinical Homecare
Masta Limited
Prima Brands Limited
Sangers (Northern Ireland) Ltd

**Hill, David Michael**
Arkad Healthcare Limited
H C Healthcare Ltd
Paragen Pharma Ltd

**Hill, Graham Alexander Fenton**
Fenton Pharmaceuticals Ltd

**Hill, Jane**
Zentiva Pharma UK Limited

**Hill, Judith**
Fenton Pharmaceuticals Ltd

**Hill, Luke Thomas**
Hemp Remedy Ltd

**Hill, Sarah Deirdre**
Advanced Eyecare Research Ltd

**Hill, Simon John**
Infinite Percent Limited

**Hill, Stephen Charles**
Advanced Eyecare Research Ltd

**Hillman, Florence Edith**
Insight Medical Products Ltd

**Hillman, Wayne Anthony**
Insight Medical Products Ltd

**Hills, Albert Edward**
Jorvik Pharma Ltd

**Hills, Albert**
Saxon Pharmaceuticals Limited

**Hindmarsh, James**
Cured CBD Ltd

**Hine, Stephen John**
PMS Korea Ltd

**Hinton, Kerry**
Medicines By Design Ltd

**Hirano, Masaaki**
Astellas Pharma Europe Ltd.

**Hirst, Christopher**
RPH Pharma Ltd

**Hiwaizi, Surud**
Pharmat Limited

**Hiyama, Yoshio**
Hisamitsu Pharmaceutical UK Ltd
Hisamitsu UK Limited
Salonpas UK Limited

**Hjelm, Hans**
Attends Limited

**Hoareau, Mary Jane**
AAR Pharma Ltd
Miltonia Health Science Ltd

**Hobbs, Jeffrey**
Parapharm Development Limited

**Hobby, Rowan Helen**
Mooncup Ltd

**Hobson, Tony**
Rayburn Trading Co Ltd

**Hocking, Adrian Niall**
Dosego Limited

**Hodgson, Andrew James**
Andrews Pharmacy Limited

**Hoffman, Sylvie**
Topnot Ltd

**Hogan, Denise Anne**
Vitb12 Academy Ltd

**Hohne, David**
Cannaid Ltd

**Holdcroft, Simon John**
Cytoplan Limited

**Holdsworth, Ben**
Your Products Limited

**Holliman, Peter John**
Specialised Marketing Services Ltd

**Holloway, Mark Stanley**
Unit Medic-Aids Limited

**Holloway, Marvin Scott**
Fittleworth Medical Limited

**Holloway, Michaela Jane**
Unit Medic-Aids Limited

**Holme, Richard**
HRA Pharma UK & Ireland Ltd

**Holmes, Jonathan Lindsay**
Pioneer Medical Europe Limited

**Holmes, Omama**
Aesthetic & Wellness Pharmacy Ltd

**Holohan, Karen**
United Kingdom Medica Ltd

**Holoran, Jamie Ian**
Heisenberg Technologie Ltd

**Holroyd, Angela Christine**
Adelphi (Tubes) Limited

**Holroyd, Stephen Barron**
Adelphi (Tubes) Limited

**Barker, Alan**
The Homeopathic Supply Co Ltd

**Barker, Anne**
The Homeopathic Supply Co Ltd

**Barker, Robert Edward**
The Homeopathic Supply Co Ltd

**Honnah, Ezinne Tochi**
Ezhonsi Ltd

**Honnah, Isioma Charles**
Ezhonsi Ltd

**Honnah, Ndubuisi Patrick**
Ezhonsi Ltd

**Honti, Judit**
A.J. Prime Ltd

**Hood Jr, Ralph C**
Jackson Immunoresearch Europe Ltd

**Hood, Daniel Carey Cazel**
Intercept Pharma Ltd

**Hope, Adrian**
Horopito Limited
TBD Wellness Limited

**Hope, Peter John**
Neon Diagnostics Ltd

**Hopkins, Angela**
AMH (N.I.) Ltd

**Hopkins, Kristy**
Derma Distribution Ltd

**Hopkins, Simeon Francis McKay**
Pan Globus Limited

**Hoque, Rahima**
ZS Pharma Limited

**Horikawa, Kazuhiko**
Amano Enzyme Europe Limited

**Horn, Christopher Lawrence**
Truscreen Limited

**Hornbuckle, Darroll**
Candover UK Ltd

**Horry, David**
Doncaster Pharmaceuticals Group Ltd
Eclipse Generics Limited
Testerworld Limited

**Hoskins, Michael Patrick**
Matoke Holdings Limited

**Hossain, Sakina Ferdous**
Sigmasis UK Limited

**Hosseini, Javad**
RX Pharma (Europe) Limited

**Hou, Guoqiang**
Flydonging Eletctronic Ltd

**Houtari, Olli Heikki**
Orion Pharma (UK) Limited

**Howard, James Edward, Dr**
DDWS Limited

**Howard, Philip**
Creative Supply Solutions Ltd

**Howard, Robin Michael**
CBD Labz Ltd

**Howden, Guy**
Hillcroft Surgery Supplies Ltd

**Howden, Roger Alan**
Hillcroft Surgery Supplies Ltd

**Howell, Paul Valentine**
Arquella Ltd

**Hristudor, Constantin Eduard**
Organic Iway Ltd

**Hsu, Elut**
Asymchem Limited

**Hubbard, Stephen Martin**
Incimed Ltd

**Hudson, Kevin Robert**
G Pharma Limited
Nucare Limited
Nupharm Limited
Phoenix Healthcare Distribution Ltd
Phoenix Medical Supplies Ltd

**Hudson, Nicholas Iain**
Lifecell EMEA Limited

**Huelsbeck, Marco Wolfgang**
M D M Healthcare Ltd

**Hughes, Russell**
Biosensors International UK Ltd

**Hulett, Peter Guy**
Afdos Pharmaceuticals Limited

**Hulson, Robb**
Melyd Medical Limited

**Humphris, James Marcus**
Anti Venom Ltd

**Humpish, Ian James**
Medilife Ltd

**Hundal, Solange Tammy**
Pharmazon Limited

**Hundle, Kavaljeet Singh**
Pura (UK) Ltd

**Hunjan, Kamaljit Singh**
Healthcare Product Services Ltd
Healthcare Services Group Ltd
Movianto UK Limited
Pharmacare Logistics Limited

**Hunt, Kristina Mary**
Elanco UK AH Limited

**Hunter, Ashley**
A & E Healthcare Limited

**Hunter, Gary Francis**
Hunter Urology Ltd

**Hunter, John Bryan**
Hunter International Associates Ltd

**Hurkmans, Jacobus Franciscus Gerard Marie**
Added Pharma Ltd

**Huron, Sebastien**
Virbac Limited

**Hussain, Akeel**
Medi-Arch Ltd

**Hussain, Amjad**
Health Nutrient Products Ltd

**Hussain, Ashfaq**
Best Value America (UK) Ltd

**Hussain, Haidar Mahmood Hussain**
Astra MCR Limited

**Hussain, Khalid**
I-Pharma Healthcare Ltd

**Hussain, Munavvar**
Zaitun Limited

**Hussain, Zulfiqar**
Diamate Biotechnologies Ltd
Global Medical Supplies Ltd

**Hutton, William Neil**
Belfast Drug Ltd

**Huynh, Trinh To**
Nativis Bio Ltd

**Huys, Luc**
McNeil Healthcare (UK) Limited

**Hyde, Nicholas Peter**
Zanoprima Holdings Limited
Zanoprima LifeSciences Limited

**Hyland, Anne Philomena**
Clinigen Group PLC

**Hyslop, Paul Russell**
Zoono Holdings Limited

**Ibish, Hassan**
AAP Healthcare Ltd

**Ibrahim, Mohamed Islam**
SHL Medical Limited

**Idriss, Nabil**
Targeter (UK) Limited

**Iglesias Fernandez, Luis Miguel**
Santen UK Limited

**Iglesias Jimenez, Carlos**
Willbay Limited

**Iguchi, Kimi Ellen**
Sage Therapeutics Limited

**Ihenagwa, David Nkemdilim**
Norlington Trading Ltd

**Ihenagwa, Rita Gold**
Norlington Trading Ltd

**Ijaz, Mohammed**
Newmeds Wholesale Limited

**Ikhlas, Amir Wahid**
KW Wholesale Ltd

**Ilkhomzhon, Mirzoev**
Abstragan Holding Limited

**Imam, Mohamed Said Moustafa Ahmed, Dr**
Imamcom Ltd

**Ingelfinger, Thomas**
Beiersdorf UK Ltd.

**Innes, Kim**
Ratiopharm (UK) Limited

**Innes, Simon Campbell**
Vet Direct Services Limited

**Insall, Nicholas Hugh Meryon**
Baxalta UK Investments Ltd.
Shire Pharmaceuticals Limited

**Inwang, Inwang Bassey, Dr**
Inbamay Resources (UK) Ltd.

**Inwang, Nse Bassey**
Inbamay Resources (UK) Ltd.

**Iqbal, Asif**
Suplan Ltd

**Irechukwu, Leon**
Pharmadynamics UK Limited

**Irechukwu, Tony**
Pharmadynamics UK Limited

**Iriajen, Collins**
Korlyns Therapeutics Limited

**Irisarri, Martin Jose**
VLCare Limited

**Irons, David John Burton**
Bugband Europe Ltd

**Irvine, Michael Hamilton**
CIGA Healthcare Limited

**Irwin, Peter Thomas John, Dr**
Mill Pharm Limited

**Isla Rodriguez, Miguel**
Recordati Pharmaceuticals Ltd

**Ismail, Mowafak**
Britannia Medical Limited

**Ismail, Mushtaq Jafferali**
Pharmaco Halesowen Limited

**Ismail, Tarek Elsayed Abdelaziz**
Sigmatec Limited

**Isobe, Yuichi**
Hisamitsu Pharmaceutical UK Ltd
Hisamitsu UK Limited
Salonpas UK Limited

**Israel, Armand David**
Ultimate Health Products Ltd

**Issat, Mohammed Adam**
Alpharma Limited

**Iyer, Nandita Ramachandran**
Prolife (UK) Limited

**Iyer, Ramachandran Venkataraman**
Prolife (UK) Limited

**Jaaniste, Jenna Catherine**
New Seasons Natural Products Ltd

**Jackson, Andrew Spencer**
Kingspeed Services Limited

**Jackson, David**
Prima Brands Limited
Sangers (Northern Ireland) Ltd

**Jackson, Dylan**
GlaxoSmithKline Export Limited

**Jackson, Lynn Diana**
Seedos Ltd.

**Jackson, Natasha**
House of Filler Limited

**Jackson, Robert Ward**
Ethicor Pharma Ltd

**Jackson, Robert**
Biophage Therapeutics Ltd

**Jacob, Dhanya**
Bioturm Limited

**Jacobs, Ashley Nicholas**
Una Health Limited

**Jacobs, Fiona**
Una Health Limited

**Jacobsen, Thomas**
Acure Pharma Limited

**Jacobson, Ian**
Aspire Pharma Holdings Limited
Aspire Pharma Limited

**Jadawji, Mehboob Abid**
Jay & Jay Limited

**Jadawji, Shaina Mehboob**
Jay & Jay Limited

**Jain, Dilipkumar Kishanlal**
Johnlee Pharmaceuticals (UK) Ltd

**Jain, Girish Kishanlal**
Johnlee Pharmaceuticals (UK) Ltd

**Jain, Kuldeep**
Orange Healthcare Limited

**Jain, Neha Vishal**
Nevik Limited

**Jain, Nitin**
Iberia Skin Brands Ltd

**Jain, Pradeep Kumar**
Ananta Medicare Ltd
Angelina SW Ltd

**Jain, Sanjeev**
Nicholas LifeSciences Ltd.

**Jain, Shashank**
Cellchem UK Limited

**Jain, Srishti**
Srigen Pharma Ltd

**Jaiswal, Vinay Kumar**
LV Global Limited

**Jakeman, William George**
Zeal Products Limited

**Jalota, Sanjay**
Sandyvale Limited

**Jalota, Usha Kumari**
Sandyvale Limited

**Jama, Saed Mohamed**
Luban & Murr Ltd

**Jamall, Fuzail Anis, Dr**
RDO Medical UK Limited

**James, Emily**
Cambpharma Ltd

**James, James Victor**
Timstar Laboratory Suppliers Ltd

**James, Karen**
Cambpharma Ltd

**James, Kevin**
Bray Pharma Limited

**James, Robert**
Imex International Group Ltd

**Jameson, Richard Major**
Camurus Ltd

**Jamieson, Christopher James John**
Advanced Eyecare Research Ltd

**Jamieson, Pamela Edith Angela**
Advanced Eyecare Research Ltd

**Janhohamed, Murtaza**
Euroworld Enterprises Limited

**Janke, Margaret Louise**
Newville Trading Limited

**Janke, Megan**
Cebrenex Limited

**Janke, Stephanus**
Human Reproduction Group Ltd

**Janmohamed, Feroze Issa Ismail**
Medipharma Limited

**Janmohamed, Mohsin**
Academy Hair and Beauty (UK) Ltd

**Jarvis, David Graham**
Sunniside Healthcare Limited

**Jarvis, Lesley Caroline**
IQ Pharma Ltd

**Jassal, Sima**
Pharmunity Limited

**Jaundrell Thompson, Gillian Margaret**
QED Scientific Ltd

**Jaundrell Thompson, Ian**
QED Scientific Ltd

**Javed, Omair**
EPE Global Limited

**Jayaprasad, Rajalakshmi**
Steripharm (UK) Limited
Vasmed Technologies Limited

**Jayawardena, Indira Maureen**
SJ Enterprises Limited

**Jayawardena, Nalin Mahinda**
SJ Enterprises Limited

**Jeffrey, Beverley Jane**
Hygamp Limited

**Jeffrey, Phillip, Dr**
Hygamp Limited

**Jeger, Rolf Franz**
Geistlich Sons Limited

**Jehl de La Goublaye de Menorval, Louis-Gregoire Victor Stanislas Jean Marie**
Vital Haven Ltd

**Jelert, Soren**
Alk-Abello Limited

**Jelley, Matthew James**
Morgan Steer Developments Ltd

**Jenkins, Ian David Pearson**
Matoke Holdings Limited
Surgihoney Limited

**Jenks, Stuart**
Dr Sproglet Ltd

**Jetha, Salim Kassamali Esmail**
Avicenna Ltd
Selsdon Healthcare Limited

**Jeyapragash, Sabanathan**
Abra Wholesales Ltd

**Jha, Pranav, Dr**
Edi Beryl Ltd

**Jhala, Janaksinh**
Accmede Pharmaceuticals Ltd

**Jhamat, Anil Kumar**
Pharmassist Locums Limited

**Jiang, Chengzhen**
Carbotang Limited

**Jiang, Hao**
Zhongfu (UK) Limited

**Jiang, Hua**
Luye Pharma Ltd

**Joannesse, Roseline Georgette**
Dallas Burston Ashbourne Holdings
Trotwood Pharma Limited

**Jobling, Suzanne**
Derma Distribution Ltd

**Jogia, Merisha Jade**
Diamond Pharma Limited

**Johansson, Lars Hakan**
Bone Support UK Ltd

**Johansson, Leif Valdemar**
Astrazeneca PLC

**Johansson, Patrik**
P.I.C. International Ltd

**John, Anthony Charles**
Iophtha Limited

**Johnson, Bryony Jane**
Modor & Bearn Limited

**Johnson, Emma Jane**
EUSA Pharma (UK) Limited

**Johnson, Nicholas James**
DCH Subco Ltd

**Johnson, Paul**
Allergan Limited
Lifecell EMEA Limited

**Johnson, Richard Cory**
Swiss-American CDMO International

**Johnston, John James Paul**
Veterinary Surgeons Supply Co Ltd

**Johnston, Neil**
Veterinary Surgeons Supply Co Ltd

**Jolley, John David Raby, Dr**
J & T World Trade (UK) Limited

**Jolly, David Alan, Dr**
Lifecare Limited

**Jones, David Leigh**
Leigh Jones & Associates Ltd

**Jones, Sonia Margaret**
Leigh Jones & Associates Ltd

**Jones, Rebecca Frances**
R M Jones Limited

**Jones, Suzannah**
R M Jones Limited

**Jones, Andrew Alfred, Dr**
Eco Animal Health Group PLC

**Jones, Christine**
Instant Test Ltd

**Jones, Daniel**
CBD Vape Ltd

**Jones, John Samuel**
Aqua Hydration Limited

**Jones, Lynda Irene**
Wellbeing Products Limited

**Jones, Mervyn Roderick**
Flairpath Limited

**Jones, Nicholas John**
Boston Healthcare Limited

**Jones, Richard**
Wellbeing Products Limited

**Jones, Stephen Philip, Dr**
Veriton Pharma Limited

**Joon, Preeti**
Corwhite Solutions Limited

**Joseph, Jason**
Biofex Limited
Fluidx Limited

**Joseph, John Gbolahan**
Shaz Logistics Limited

**Joseph, Philip Simon**
System Deep Clinic Limited

**Joseph, Tojin**
Allans Healthcare Limited

**Joseph-Ebare, Osenadia**
JE Medical Associates Ltd.

**Josephson, Jeremy Michael**
DGI Technologies Limited

**Joshi Aka Sharma, Atrey Satishkumar**
Nagarjun Healthcare Limited

**Joshi, Arun James Neel**
Patient Care Holdings Ltd

**Joubert, Evaline Sophie**
Novamed Pharma Ltd

**Joubert, Maria Francina**
Nova Pharmacare Ltd

**Joyce, Peter**
Global Pharma Direct Ltd

**Jubb, Christopher Stephen**
Trinity VN Limited

**Jubb, Oliver Gareth Paul**
Vita Nova International Ltd

**Judd, Marcus Lee**
Oswell Penda Pharmaceutical Ltd

**Juer, Caterina Musgrave**
Pharmed Health Care Organisation Ltd

**Julien, Gilbert Marius**
Bial Pharma UK Limited

**Jyani, Prakash Shantilal**
Sun Exim Ltd

**Kabba, Alimatu Fatim**
Falama Services Group Limited

**Kabir, Syed Kaiser**
Renata (UK) Limited

**Kadari, Kiran Reddy**
UK Lab Supplies Ltd

**Kadel, Sulochana Gautam**
Optimal Pharma Ltd

**Kader, Lilia**
Sunrize Trade Limited

**Kadri, Sunil, Dr**
Europharma Scotland Ltd

**Kahwati, Georges**
Ever Pharma UK Limited

**Kailey, Manjit Singh**
Standard Organics International (UK) Ltd

**Kailondo, Lansana**
LK Health Ltd

**Kain-Duncan, Colin**
HCP Limited
KD Pharmacon Ltd

**Kainth, Navdeep**
V2M Pharma Limited

**Kaippallil Raman Pillai, Jayaprasad**
Vasmed Technologies Limited

**Kalia, Mandeep**
MKK Consulting Ltd

**Kallat, Adel Taher, Dr**
Mena Pharma UK Limited

**Kallend, John**
Alloga UK Limited

**Kalogiannidis, Dimitris, Dr**
Veramic Limited

**Kalogiannidis, Irene**
Veramic Limited

**Kalsi, Simran Kaur**
Xenium International Limited

**Kalsi, Varinder Kaur**
Xenium International Limited

**Kamal, Haseeb**
Cotton Craft Limited

**Kamal, Ihab**
Dr Kool Ltd

**Kamara, Mohamed**
Falama Services Group Limited

**Kamath, Vikram Laxman**
Focus Pharma Holdings Limited
Focus Pharmaceuticals Limited

**Kambham, Raveendranatha Reddy**
Amarox Limited

**Kamran Saeed, Muhammad**
K N B Services Ltd

**Kanani, Abbas Mohamed**
Flintlow Limited
Globegen Laboratories Limited
Veenak International Limited
Veenak Sourcing Limited

**Kanani, Julie**
Accordia Investments Ltd

**Kanani, Mohamed Gulamali**
Globegen Laboratories Limited

**Kanani, Mohamed Rajabali**
Accordia Investments Ltd

**Kanaparthy, Sri Lakshmi Narasimha Vara Prasad**
Coward Pharmacy Limited

**Kanaparthy, Vijaya Chaitanya**
Coward Pharmacy Limited

**Kanbi, Ramji Naran**
Sonik Products Limited

**Kandasamy, Kumar**
Kohilam Limited

**Kane, Marion Mary Anne**
WE Pharma Ltd
Wep Group Holdings Limited

**Kanel, Puja**
Vitgarden Ltd

**Kang, Ying**
Rose Europe UK Ltd
Rose Gentec Ltd

**Kanji, Hasanain Giulamabbas Abdulla**
Ross London Limited

**Kanji, Mohamed Raza**
Beta Pharmaceuticals Limited

**Kanu, Denis**
Dizzo Consulting (UK) Limited

**Kapadia, Amir Tayebali**
Lam Cash and Carry Limited

**Kapadia, Rafique Amir**
Lam Cash and Carry Limited

**Kapadia, Sandip**
Intercept Pharma Europe Ltd.
Intercept Pharma UK & Ireland Ltd

**Kapoor, Aamit**
Zaaz Limited

**Kappou, Vasiliki**
Artmedica Ltd

**Karaman, Zafer**
Insuphar Laboratories Limited
ZTK Business Services Limited

**Karamat, Ghazanfar**
GK Locums Ltd

**Karavas, Vassilios**
Bpharm Group Limited

**Karelis, Harry**
HAPA Group Holdings Limited

**Karia, Jagdish Prabhudas**
Chemilines Group Holdings Ltd
Chemilines Limited

**Karia, Ravindra Prabhudas**
Chemilines Group Holdings Ltd
Chemilines Limited

**Karikari, Magdalene Rosamund**
Allipharm (UK) Limited

**Karikari, Patrick Kofi**
Allipharm (UK) Limited

**Karim, Arsalan**
Clinova Limited

**Karim, Mohammed Munir**
Gill Pharma Limited
Skylark Services Limited

**Karlson, Jari Ilmari**
Orion Pharma (UK) Limited

**Karst, Christian**
Virbac Limited

**Kassam, Nurdin**
Amalgamated Technology Corporation

**Kassam, Shabbir**
Astra Pharma (UK) Limited

**Katafuchi, Shinya**
Medreich PLC

**Kaul, Vivek, Dr**
Southampton Medical Group Ltd

**Kaur, Harjit**
GHC Medical Ltd

**Kaur, Jaspreet**
Sports Star Distribution UK Ltd

**Kaur, Joginder**
Trans Swiss Ltd

**Kaur, Rajvinder**
GHC (UK) Ltd
GHC Global Limited

**Kausar, Razwana**
Stanningley Pharma Limited

**Kearney, Tara**
Healthcare 21 (UK) Limited

**Keeble, Christopher John**
Pharma Medico Limited

**Keelan, Edward**
Countrywide Healthcare Supplies Holdings

**Keeley, Robert Coleman**
Fittleworth Medical Limited

**Keeling, David Mark William**
MWK Healthcare Limited

**Keeton, Paul James**
A V Pharma Limited

**Keller, Adam**
Dent.O.Care Distribution Ltd
Dent.O.Care Limited

**Keller, Elio, Dr**
Ceracoat Ltd

**Keller, Natalie Claire**
Dent.O.Care Distribution Ltd
Dent.O.Care Limited

**Kellett, Darren**
Kelisdar Enterprises Limited

**Kellett, Lisa**
Kelisdar Enterprises Limited

**Kelly, Ann Margaret**
AMK & Associates Ltd

**Kelly, Kevin**
Omapharm Limited

**Kelly, Nigel Joseph**
Ethigen Limited

**Kemp, Stephen Leonard**
V2M Pharma Limited

**Kemps, Serge**
Nipro Diagnostics (UK) Limited

**Kenawy, Walid**
Secret Line Ltd

**Kennedy, Steven**
Bracco UK Limited

**Kenny, John Patrick**
Meridian Bioscience UK Limited

**Keown, Nicholas Charles Lamson**
Ebbcourt Limited

**Kerhoas, Delphine**
Mediwin Limited

**Kerstein, Christoph**
Hameln Pharmaceuticals Ltd
Patient Ready Products Limited
Phoenix Pharma Ltd.

**Keshavarzi, Mehdi**
Hayat Gostar Ltd

**Keshmiri, Salma**
Global Pharma Direct Ltd

**Kettleborough, James Michael**
Alturix Limited

**Kettleborough, Sara Jane**
Alturix Limited

**Khajoo, Shaghayegh**
ACESO Global Ltd

**Khaki, Kamruddin Fidahusein**
T.K. Impex Limited

**Khalil, Mohamed**
MK Medicals (UK) Ltd

**Khaliq, Khalil Ahmed**
Lansdales Pharmacy Limited

**Khaliq, Saliya Halima**
Lansdales Pharmacy Limited

**Khan, Abdul Rehman**
Direct Pharma Limited
Vital Pharma Limited

**Khan, Amjad**
Al-Ghani Limited

**Khan, Amjid Malik**
Prescribe Direct Limited

**Khan, Azam**
Bradley Stoke Bristol Limited

**Khan, Ijaz**
Pharmaethics International Ltd

**Khan, Imran**
Stanningley Pharma Limited

**Khan, Jawad Ali**
Campmed Limited

**Khan, Kamran**
Aces Pharma Limited

**Khan, Mohammad Arsalaan**
Wave Pharma Limited

**Khan, Mohammad Usman**
Al-Ghani Limited

**Khan, Muhammad Haaroon**
Al-Ghani Limited

**Khan, Romana**
Wave Pharma Limited

**Khan, Shamim Fatima**
Marigold Footcare Ltd.

**Khan, Yousaf**
Better Earth Limited

**Khandelwal, Manish**
Zentiva Pharma UK Limited

**Khanna, Shivani Gore**
Pharmapoint UK Ltd

**Khanom, Shaheda**
ZS Pharma Limited

**Khara, Jaskirat**
Noru Pharma PVT Ltd.

**Kharileh, Ramina**
BB Lifestyle UK Limited

**Khattak, Mussarat Fawad, Dr**
Alizcare Limited

**Khatun, Mussarraf Hossain**
Pericia Ltd

**Khera, Jaswant Singh**
WE Pharma Ltd
Wep Group Holdings Limited

**Khera, Jaswinder Singh**
Wep Group Holdings Limited

**Khetyar, Maher**
Elias Med Limited

**Khevenheuller, Johannes**
Bowmed Ibisqus Limited

**Khiroya, Parag**
Disposable Medical Equipment Ltd
Windzor Pharma Limited

**Khiroya, Varsha**
Disposable Medical Equipment Ltd

**Kiani, Massi Joseph**
11 Health & Technologies Ltd

**Kieda, Agata**
Iberia Skin Brands Ltd

**Kiiru, Jeremiah Nguru**
Harvey Pharma Ltd

**Kilham, Jonathan Paul**
Client-Pharma Ltd
Client-Pharmacy UK Ltd

**Kim, Sung Eun**
Dong Hwa UK Ltd

**Kimura, Shigeki**
Amano Enzyme Europe Limited

**Kimura, Teiji**
Eisai Limited

**King, David Stephen**
Kingspeed Services Limited

**King, Leslie**
Testerworld Limited

**King, Martin Ian, Dr**
Cosmedic Pharmacy Limited

**King, Rebecca Anne**
DCH Subco Ltd

**King, Sharon Lesley**
Cosmedic Pharmacy Limited

**Kinghorn, Nicola Mary**
Merlin Vet Export Ltd

**Kingston, Katie Georgina**
Kingston Pharma Limited

**Kiraly, Arpad Jozsef**
Vitafree Health Limited

**Kirk, Adrian Christopher**
Neubria Limited

**Kirpal, Ajay**
Veyda Pharma Ltd

**Kiss-Toth, Endre, Dr**
Stem Cellx Limited

**Kita, Waldemar Stanislaw**
Vivacy Laboratoires Ltd

**Kitamura, Toshiya**
Summit Pharmaceuticals Europe Ltd

**Kitching, Alastair Richard**
Countrywide Healthcare Supplies Holdings

**Klados, Charalabos**
Colgate-Palmolive (U.K.) Ltd

**Klaharn, Itthiphon**
World Trends Ltd

**Klee, Thomas Bo Bjorn**
Lundbeck Limited

**Kloos, Kurt**
Srigen Pharma Ltd

**Klug, Gerard Darcy**
Ecogen Europe Ltd

**Knechtel, Thomas**
Raumedic U.K. Limited

**Knights, Adam Spencer**
Your Products Limited

**Knizek, Jorg**
Arex Pharma Ltd

**Knorr, Wolfgang**
Immortalis Distribution Ltd.

**Knowles, Nigel, Sir**
Biosure (UK) Limited

**Knox, Branden**
Knox Pharmaceuticals Limited

**Knox, Laura Ann**
Habberpharm Limited

**Knox, Laura**
Knox Pharmaceuticals Limited

**Knox, Paul Allan, Dr**
Reliance Medical Ltd

**Kobke, Casper Lykkegaard**
Curas Limited

**Kocfelda, Lukas**
Dollano Trading Limited

**Kochhar, Amit**
Cannabinoidmeds Limited

**Kodag, Ganesh**
AG Pharmahealth Ltd

**Kohli, Aditya**
Meditec International England Ltd

**Kohli, Akhil**
Meditec International England Ltd

**Kohli, Anita**
Meditec International England Ltd

**Kohli, Manjinder Kaur**
M & N Traders Limited

**Kohli, Vinod**
Meditec International England Ltd

**Koku, Victor Olasubomi**
Yawskin Limited

**Kolaczynski, Alex**
Apricot Forest Ltd

**Kolawole-Moradeyo, Adetunji**
Cofad Ventures Ltd

**Kolli, Anusha**
Frontier Lab Scientific Ltd

**Kolo, Thlala**
Thlala Kolo (UK) Ltd

**Konasagar Jayanna, Sathish Kumar**
Relonchem Limited

**Konopate, Angela**
Eyekonic Wellbeing Limited

**Konopate, Paul**
Eyekonic Wellbeing Limited

**Konstantinou, Anastasis**
Dexcel-Pharma Limited
Discovery Pharmaceuticals Ltd

**Kopanko, Paulina**
Skarby Gai Ltd

**Koppel, Elisha**
Behsarel Trading Ltd

**Korn, Leonard**
CM Healthcare Limited

**Korn, Philip Ashley**
CM Healthcare Limited

**Korosec, Bostjan**
KRKA UK Ltd

**Korsh, Leslie Brian**
National Veterinary Services Ltd

**Kosche, Dirk Armin, Dr**
Astellas Pharma Europe Ltd.

**Kosinski, Slawomir**
Vitaminka Ltd

**Koskie, Steven**
Infinite Percent Limited

**Kostka, Michal**
Oxford Biosystems Limited

**Kotecha, Monisha Nikesh**
Morningside Pharmaceuticals Ltd
Remedi Medical Holdings Ltd

**Kotecha, Nikesh Rasiklal, Dr**
Morningside Pharmaceuticals Ltd
Remedi Medical Holdings Ltd

**Kothari, Hitesh**
View Pharm Limited

**Kotra, Gowardhan**
SG Pharma UK Limited

**Koudellaris, Constantinos**
Stanex Limited

**Kouparanis, Niklas Alexander**
Farmako Limited

**Kousar, Aysha**
Orphic Limited

**Kowalski, John Joseph Alfons**
Pioneer Medical Europe Limited

**Kowalski, Susan Rosalyn**
Pioneer Medical Europe Limited

**Kowsor, Nelufa Yasmin**
Seren Plus Limited

**Kreddan, Ibrahim**
OT Masters Limited

**Krige, Lynette Gillian**
Bestway Pharmacy NDC Limited

**Krishna, Ganesh**
Life on Healthcare Ltd

**Krogh, Fillip**
Real Estate Alliance Ltd

**Kronborg, Anders**
Leo Laboratories Limited

**Kronohage, Kenneth**
10x Rational Ambulance Yield Ltd

# The Top UK Pharmaceutical Wholesalers

**Krotenko, Pavlo**
ANP Partners Ltd

**Kruger, Paal Christian**
Europharma Scotland Ltd

**Krupa, Viliam**
Remedy JV Limited

**Kseib, Anthony Adel**
Diana Royal Jelly Limited

**Kseib, Antoinette**
Diana Royal Jelly Limited

**Kubiak, David**
RDO Medical UK Limited

**Kucherenko, Serhii**
Dynamic Development Laboratories Co Ltd

**Kuehne, Eberhard Karl Heinz**
Bausch & Lomb U.K. Limited

**Kuiper, Peter Sjoerd**
Genzyme Therapeutics Limited

**Kujore, Olusola Olayinka**
Eddohealthcare Ltd

**Kukhaleishvili, George**
Geoorganics Limited

**Kular, Dilkiran Singh**
Nouveau Health Ltd

**Kulur, Emek Zubeyde**
Dentlaser Limited

**Kumar, Amit**
Ascend Laboratories (UK) Ltd

**Kumar, Ashok**
GP Laboratories Limited
LBC Solutions Limited

**Kumar, Brijesh**
Zista Pharma Limited

**Kumar, Debbie**
GP Laboratories Limited

**Kumar, Dev, Dr**
EUSA Pharma (UK) Limited

**Kumar, Vikesh**
Strides Pharma Global (UK) Ltd

**Kunnil Sulaiman, Sajid Sulaiman**
Comfylife Ltd

**Kuoni, Claudio**
CM & D Pharma Limited

**Kurasinski, Artur Piotr**
Hapharm Ltd

**Kurdikar, Sreeparna Arun**
Bayer PLC

**Kwan, Hon Kan**
Essentialink Limited

**Kyriacou, Antonis Loizou**
Beauty Hair Products Limited

**Kyriacou, Kyriacos Costas**
Alium Medical Limited

**Kyriacou, Michael**
Beauty Hair Products Limited

**Kyriakopoulos, Kyriakos**
Bacteflora Ltd
Macrobiotics Group Ltd

**La Barbera, Sergio**
Alzirr Ltd

**Labarre, Francois Paul Pierre**
Curium Pharma UK Ltd.

**Labutyte, Jolanta**
Apex Lab Scientific Ltd

**Cope, Colin John**
The Labwarehouse Limited

**Cope, Brian Lewis**
The Labwarehouse Limited

**Lacey, Angela Marie**
EVC Compounding Ltd

**Ladak, Rizwan**
Royce Health Sciences Ltd

**Ladi, Szabolcs Zoltan, Dr**
Biogenic Health Europe Ltd

**Ladva, Dhirajlal Mavji Daya**
DML Pharma Consultancy Limited

**Lafaix-Houser, Patricia**
Servier IP UK Limited

**Laghezza, Valerio**
Immortalis Distribution Ltd.

**Lait, Mark**
MDD Europe Limited

**Lakhani, Semina**
Astra Pharma (UK) Limited

**Lakhwani, Johnny Mohan**
Iam Finance Limited

**Lakhwani, Kishore Kumar Mohan**
Macks Ltd.

**Laklouk, Abdulmoez**
AZL Holdings Ltd

**Laklouk, Ahmed Abdulrraziq Ali**
Med-Link Limited

**Laklouk, Ziad**
AZL Holdings Ltd

**Tims, Geoffrey Alan**
Roy Lamb Limited

**Cattee, Peter**
Roy Lamb Limited

**Lamb, Andrew Richard**
Gemapharm Limited

**Lamb, Beverley Anne**
Lamb's Locum Services Ltd

**Lamb, Catherine**
Ipsen Limited

**Lamb, Roy**
Lamb's Locum Services Ltd

**Lambert, Darren**
PLA Medical Supplies Limited

**Lanham, Penelope Jane**
Adelphi (Tubes) Limited

**Lannen, David**
Acehides Limited

**Larke, Paul**
BritaniaMark Limited

**Larsson, Stefan**
Bosses Onlinestore Ltd

**Larwood, Andrew Paul**
Salutem Supplements Ltd

**Lassota, Karolina**
Medica Finance UK Ltd

**Lassota, Konrad**
Medica Finance UK Ltd

**Latif, Sura**
Aesthetic & Wellness Pharmacy Ltd

**Latz, Christian Guenter**
GCL Marketing Ltd

**Law, David**
Mycology Research Laboratories Ltd

**Law, Mark Vivian**
UK Pharma Impex Limited

**Law, Tony Kwok Fai**
Ananda Trading Limited

**Lawal, Bunmi**
De-Bulad & Co Ltd

**Lawal, Isiaka Oladimeji, Dr**
Birmingham Management Centre (UK)

**Lawal, Lanre**
De-Bulad & Co Ltd

**Lawal, Maryam Dupeola**
De-Bulad & Co Ltd

**Lawson, Margaret Anne**
Surgitrac Instruments UK Ltd

**Lawson, Sylvia Adjoa**
Curist Health Limited

**Lazarev, Dmitry**
Akvion Limited

**Lazarou, Nikolaos**
Decahedron Ltd

**Le Moli, Paolo**
Rafarm UK Limited

**Lea, Bryan George**
Mundibiopharma Limited
Mundipharma Medical Co Ltd
Napp Laboratories Limited
Napp Pharmaceuticals Limited
Qdem Pharmaceuticals Limited

**Lea, Janet**
TRB Chemedica (UK) Limited

**Leach, Anthony John**
S.T.D. Pharmaceutical Products Ltd
Vascular Products Limited

**Leach, Nina Elizabeth**
S.T.D. Pharmaceutical Products Ltd

**Leaning, Mark**
Clyde Valley Cannaceuticals Ltd

**Leathers, Francesca Ellen**
Westmead International Limited

**Leau, Florin-Benone**
Inmed Ltd

**Leaver, Andrew Derrick**
Bionical Limited

**Leaver, Darren**
Bionical Limited

**Lecat, Jean-Hugues Louis Marie**
Dallas Burston Ashbourne Holdings
Ethypharm UK Limited
Trotwood Pharma Limited

**Lee Scott, Harvey**
Guerbet Laboratories Limited

**Lee, Chen-Hsing**
Cellcosmo Suisse Limited

**Lee, Geon**
Pharmdex UK Ltd

**Lee, Hangi**
Celltrion Healthcare United Kingdom

**Leece, Colin Andrew**
Bakhu Limited

**Lees, Jennifer Dolores**
Dentanurse (U.K.) Limited

**Leese, Andrew Glyn**
Independence Products Ltd

**Legg, Karl**
PKA Healthcare Ltd

**Leggett, Simon Anthony**
SP Services (UK) Limited

**Leitner-Murphy, Ashley**
Modor & Bearn Limited

**Lejaeghere, Maarten Julius Gerard**
V Sales and Marketing Limited

**Lemon, Aaron Kris**
P C LDN Ltd

**Lemon, Peter George**
Sangers (Northern Ireland) Ltd

**Lenke, Markus**
Juvela Limited

**Lennon, Edward Ronald**
Ballymote Pharmacy Limited

**Gray, Adam Miles**
The Lens Factory (N.E) Ltd

**Hepple, Paul**
The Lens Factory (N.E) Ltd

**Lens, Marko Bojan, Dr**
Zelens Limited

**Leonida, Anthony Joseph**
Enfield Nutrition Club Ltd

**Leslie, Gavin Scott**
Cannapharm Limited

**Lestner, David Andrew**
Higherplateau Limited

**Leung, Kimberley**
Leung Healthcare Limited

**Leung, Wai Fong**
Medicstar (UK) Limited

**Lever, Timothy Matthew**
Tim Lever Distribution Ltd.

**Truman, Julie**
Tim Lever Distribution Ltd.

**Levermore, Martin Leslie**
MDTI Pharma Retail Division Ltd

**Levers, Joanna**
Strandland Limited

**Levin, Aaron**
Oscar & Louis Limited

**Levy, John Andrew Goodman**
CSL Behring Holdings Limited
CSL Behring UK Limited

**Balcombe, David**
B.R. Lewis Pharmaceuticals Ltd

**Wilson, Derek Andrew**
B.R. Lewis Pharmaceuticals Ltd

**Lewis, Brian Robert**
Impact Health Limited
Lewis Healthcare Limited

**Lewis, Carmen**
A1 Pharmaceuticals Holdings Ltd
A1 Pharmaceuticals PLC
Pharmacy4life Ltd

**Lewis, Christopher**
Elanco UK AH Limited

**Lewis, Gary Stephen**
A1 Pharmaceuticals Holdings Ltd
A1 Pharmaceuticals PLC
Pharmacy4life Ltd

**Lewis, Mark**
LSP Bio Limited

**Lewis, Matthew**
Matt L Consultancy Ltd

**Lewis, Patricia Olivia**
Lewis Healthcare Limited

**Lewis, Thomas Benjamin**
Dermapure Aesthetics Limited

**Lewis-Jagne, Warren**
Eureka Health Limited

**Ley, Anthony Manfred Thomas**
Hilotherapy UK Limited

**Li, Chenguang**
Yiling Ltd

**Li, Jianke**
Techdow Pharma England Limited

**Li, Jun**
Elim Springs Biotech Ltd

**Li, Kejiang**
Lorteben Trading Co., Ltd

**Li, Xiuqing**
Yiling Ltd

**Libera, Daniele Della**
Simcro (UK) Limited

**Liddell, Caroline**
Hunger Control Limited

**Liddle, Ailsa Claire**
Macratio Limited

**Liddle, Elliot Spencer**
Universal Biologicals (Cambridge)

**Liddle, Janice Elizabeth**
Precision Fluid Controls Ltd

**Liddle, Kenneth Stanley**
Precision Fluid Controls Ltd
Universal Biologicals (Cambridge)

**Lightowlers, Michael Henryk**
Optima Consumer Health Limited

**Lilani, Mohammed Mohsin Reza**
Vitane Pharma Limited

**Lim, Eng Teong**
IM High Tech Limited

**Lim, Hau Wee**
Welfare Healthcare (UK) Ltd

**Lim, Kareen Siau Yen**
Nativis Bio Ltd

**Limuaco, Lourdes Stephanie**
Got Heart UK Ltd

**Lin, Qing**
Pavay Venture International Ltd

**Lindridge, Adrian Stewart**
TSI Health Sciences (Europe) Ltd

**Link, Helmut-Detlef**
OL123 Limited

**Lipovaca, Maja**
Novelius Medical Limited

**Lipperts, George Joseph Hubertus**
Genrx UK Lipperts Ltd.

**Lisboa, Fabio Da Silva**
Uno Healthcare Limited

**Lister, Neil Thomas**
Galpharm International Limited
Omega Pharma Limited
Perrigo Pharma Limited

**Liu, Jianhua**
Legendbio Beauty Group Limited

**Liu, Liangyin**
Symbiosis Biosciences Limited

**Liu, Min**
UK Vimin Industry Co., Limited

**Liu, Suk Fan**
SL Clinical Ltd

**Liu, Weihong**
UK Beauty Cosmetics International Group

**Liu, Zhiwen**
Qingdao Polychem (U.K.) Ltd

**Livesey, James Edward**
Beiersdorf UK Ltd.

**Livingston, Natalie Laura**
Miller & Miller (Chemicals) Ltd

**Livingstone, Christopher Robert**
Ecco Healthcare Limited

**Livingstone, Joanne Elizabeth**
Ecco Healthcare Limited

**Lloveras, Eric Casas**
Skymedic UK Limited

**James, Christopher John**
Walter Lloyd & Son Limited

**Griffiths, Terry Baugh**
Walter Lloyd & Son Limited

**Griffiths, Megan Jayne**
Walter Lloyd & Son Limited

**Lloyd, John Llewellyn**
John Lloyd Dental Equipment Services

**Lloyd, Benjamin**
Mammoth Dental Supplies Ltd

**Lloyd, Sarah**
Mammoth Dental Supplies Ltd

**Lloyd-Jones, Jacqueline**
J L J Healthcare Limited

**Lo, Chin Yu**
Beijing Tong Ren Tang (UK) Ltd

**Loebenstein, Rivkah**
CHM Trading Limited

**Lomas, Sarah**
Reviv Pharma Ltd

**Lombardi, Ronald**
Clear Eyes Pharma Limited
Prestige Brands (UK) Limited

**Lomia, Merab, Dr**
Geopharma UK Ltd.

**Longmuir, Shona Gillian**
Condom Dot Com Ltd.

**LooSeniore, John Colin**
Beegood Enterprises Limited

**Loomes, Marc Denham**
Eco Animal Health Group PLC

**Loonat, Ismail**
I L Locum Ltd

**Lopes, Cleves Valdo**
My-Kaya Ltd

**Lopez Garcia, Francisco**
UK Branded Medicines Ltd

**Lopez-Belmonte Encina, Ivan**
Rovi Biotech Limited

**Lory, Nicholas Kasper**
Satio Pharma Ltd.

**Lotzof, Sarah Catherine Russell, Dr**
Josana Limited

**Lovy, Sebastien**
Inter Trade Pharma Limited

**Lowdon, Andrew William McLeod**
FTS Bio Limited
Fast Track Sourcing Limited

**Lowe, Michael Philip**
Autono-Med Limited

**Lozuk, Mariusz Andrzej**
Art Pharma Oxford Ltd

**Lucas, Stuart James**
Phoenix Healthcare Distribution Ltd

**Ludzker, Benjamin Mathew**
Kays Medical Limited

**Ludzker, David Henry**
Kays Medical Limited

**Ludzker, Joyce**
Kays Medical Limited

**Luitgaren, Marjolein Van De**
NBS Scientific Limited

**Lundberg, Jon James**
Symbiosis Biosciences Limited

**Lusby, Adam Millar**
Purple Surgical UK Limited

**Lycett-Green, John Peregrine**
DLG Partners Limited

**Lythe, Amanda Jane**
Pricecheck Toiletries Limited

**Lythe, Mark Andrew**
Pricecheck Toiletries Limited

**MacDonald, Louise Mary Claire**
Timstar Laboratory Suppliers Ltd

**MacKenzie, Christopher Jamie**
CBD -Tec Limited

**MacNab, Angus Bernard Rupert**
Vertibax Limited

**MacQuillan, Paul**
Ostomart Limited
Respond Healthcare Limited
Respond Healthcare Scotland Ltd
Respond Plus Limited

**Mack, Kimberley**
Perfect Vascular Natural Ltd

**Mack, Stephen Maurice**
Perfect Vascular Natural Ltd

**Mackie, Marc Alexander Rene, Dr**
Allied Warden Marketing Ltd

**Madan, Aman**
Neo Health UK Limited

**Madan, Pankaj, Dr**
Nostrum Life Sciences Ltd

**Madan, Rakesh**
Utech Products Limited

**Maddaford, Keith William**
Kemsource Limited

**Maddaford, Nicola**
Kemsource Limited

**Madhok, Anuj, Dr**
Novalio Pharma Limited

**Magdelaine, Vivien Christian Charles**
Vipharm Limited

**Maggs, Terence James**
Intro International (TRDG) Ltd

**Maguire, Ciaran**
Agrihealth (N.I.) Limited

**Maguire, Gareth Robert James**
Excip Limited

**Maguire, Paul Oliver**
Excip Limited

**Mahamud Jibril, Farhan Ali**
Tuluh Solutions Ltd

**Maherovskyi, Pavlo**
Honest Health Limited

**Mahmood, Shahid**
Ordinant Medical Solutions Ltd

**Mahmoud, Ahmed, Dr**
Bioxane Ltd

**Mahmoud, Medhat**
Marvellous Pharma Ltd

**Mahmud, Ali Ahmed**
Premium Pharma UK Limited

**Mahoney, Katie**
Clinitech Medical Ltd

**Maia Devesa Gama Da Silva, Antonio Manuel**
Leadiant Biosciences Limited

**Main, Steven Brian**
EVR Biosciences (UK) Ltd

**Majeed, Mahmood Qasim, Dr**
MQS Group London Limited

**Makadia, Arvind**
Kaam Pharma Limited

**Makharia, Sunil**
Lupin Healthcare (UK) Limited

**Makolli, Egzona**
Lyferoots Ltd

**Makore, Kumbirai**
KHM Global Ltd

**Malaeb, Khalil Fawwaz**
10x Rational Ambulance Yield Ltd

**Malcolm, James Paxton**
OL123 Limited

**Malde, Deepakkumar Shantilal**
C & N Medical Ltd
Medi-Gen Limited

**Malde, Nikunj Shantilal**
C & N Medical Ltd
Medi-Gen Limited

**Malekshahi, Amirsaeed**
Day International Limited
Dayonix Pharma Limited

**Malem, Hilal, Dr**
Malem Medical Limited

**Malem, Valerie Joy**
Malem Medical Limited

**Malhi, Ravinder**
Europa Health Limited

**Malik, Zeeshan**
Maze Healthcare Ltd.

**Malik, Zubair**
ZMI Investments Limited

**Malone, Peter Generald**
Crescent Pharma OTC Limited

**Malty, Mariam Ibrahim**
B.P. Pharma Limited

**Mamtora, Nilesh**
Kestrol International Limited

**Mamukashvili, Nino**
Nino and Blue Spruce Ltd

**Managarova, Natasha**
Veda Biosciences Limited

**Mancini, John-Michael**
Sasmar Limited

**Mandanka, Kanjikumar**
Ved Healthcare Limited

**Mangan, Simon**
L & R Medical UK Ltd.

**Mangaroliya, Kaushik Kumar Bhagvanbhai**
Molecule Healthcare Limited

**Mangayi Tsika, Elie Guy Hervais**
Lufuma B2b Services Ltd

**Mann, Paris Sophie**
Stiltec Global (UK) Ltd

**Mann, Tracey**
Perricone MD Cosmeceuticals UK Ltd

**Manners, Judith**
Opus Pharmacy Services Limited

**Mannino, Ronald**
Interchem Europe (UK) Limited

**Manolescue, George Victor**
Collardam PLC

**Manomba, Christ Maryse**
Timpext (Trading-Import-Export) Ltd

**Manoocheheri, Amir Ali**
Kaboodan Limited

**Mansukh, Vinay**
OM Medical Limited

**Mantzourani, Theodora, Dr**
Dermconcept Ltd

**March, Carole Iris**
Veriton Pharma Limited

**March, Graham Alan, Dr**
Veriton Pharma Limited

**Marchington, Geoffrey Philip**
Medikit Limited

**Maree, Don Wessel**
Alumier Medical UK Limited

**Margaret Myerscough, Susan**
Bowmed Ibisqus Limited

**Margetts, Paul George**
Stegram Pharmaceuticals Ltd

**Marik, Karel**
Sprint Pharma Limited

**Markaryan, Elena**
Enteromed Limited

**Markham, Rudolph Harold Peter**
Astrazeneca PLC

**Markovitch, Daniel Andrew**
Inov8 Medical Solutions Ltd

**Marks, Caroline Daphne**
Cytoplan Limited

**Marks, Nicolas John**
Cytoplan Limited

**Marquess of Downshire, Arthur Francis Nicholas Wills, Lord**
Animalcare Ltd

**Marquilles Escola, Roger**
Accord Healthcare Limited

**Marshall Jr, Robert J**
Lantheus MI UK Limited

**Marshall, Andrew Roy**
Par Laboratories Europe, Ltd.

**Marth, William Steven**
Emcure Pharma UK Ltd

**Martin, Adrian Spencer**
Optident Labline Limited

**Martin, Edward James**
SDM Healthcare Limited

**Martin, John**
Eyecon Vision Limited

**Martin, Paul Anthony**
Prestige Dental Products Ltd

**Martin, Peter**
Norgine Pharmaceuticals Ltd

**Martin, Simon Jonathan**
Medicom Healthcare Limited

**Martin, Stephen Jeremy**
Penlan Pharmaceuticals Limited

**Martinez, Alberto**
Mundibiopharma Limited
Mundipharma Medical Co Ltd

**Martini, Flavia**
Martini International Ltd

**Martini, Valerio**
Martini International Ltd

**Martiska, Ladislav**
Plurafores Pharma Limited

**Masano, Kazuhiko**
Eisai Limited

**Mashingaidze, Michael Haruwisi**
International Medical Supplies Ltd

**Mason, Joseph**
Hennessy Mason Ltd

**Mason, Peter John**
Crest Medical Limited
First Aid Supplies Limited

**Mason, Rupert Bernard Stuart, Dr**
Espere Healthcare Limited

**Masood, Almaan**
Equimed Medical Supplies Ltd

**Masood, Hassan**
Sterling Bio-Pharma Ltd

**Masoud, Jihad**
M2 Healthcare Ltd

**Masoud, Navid**
Go Go Chemist Limited

**Master, Hasan**
ATI Pharmaceuticals Limited

**Masters, Suzad**
Masters Pharmaceuticals Ltd

**Masters, Zulfikar**
Masters Pharmaceuticals Ltd

**Masurkar, Anjula**
Entod Research Cell (UK) Ltd

**Masurkar, Nikhil Kishore**
Entod Research Cell (UK) Ltd

**Matharu, Jasveer**
Elara Care Limited

**Matheson, Gordon John**
Medinox (London) Limited

**Mathew, Joshy**
Symbio Europe Limited

**Mathews, Cheryl**
P A M Medical Supplies Limited

**Mathews, Paul**
P A M Medical Supplies Limited

**Mathieson, Stephen**
CooperVision Lens Care Limited

**Matos de Ospino, Dianeth Isabel**
Perrington & Co Limited
Soliphar Limited

**Matsumiya, Toshihiro**
Charmant UK Co., Limited

**Matta, Youssef William**
Ayva Pharma Limited

**Matthews, Glyn Ian**
Xanton Limited

**Maukonen, Ville Kullervo**
GlaxoSmithKline UK Limited

**Mavani, Neeta Avinash**
Dil More Remedies UK Ltd

**Maw, Stephen Vernon Patrick**
P Y Imports Limited

**Mawdsley, John Howard, Dr**
Mawdsley-Brooks & Co Ltd

**Maxwell, Alastair Generald Lees**
Crest Medical Limited
First Aid Supplies Limited

**Mayberry, Paul Robert**
Unit 10 Distribution Limited

**Mayne, Andrew**
Veterinary Surgeons Supply Co Ltd

**Mazhandu, Daniel**
Decibel Biopharm Limited

**Mazumdar Shaw, Kiran**
Biocon Pharma UK Limited

**Mballa Nama, Joseph**
IPY Healthcare Ltd

**McAleer, Jerome Francis, Dr**
Lumiradx International Ltd

**McAleese, Grainne**
Alchem PLC
Mansett Limited

**McAllister, Michael Joseph**
Agrihealth (N.I.) Limited

**McAnsh, Antonia Jane**
Field House Pharma Limited

**McAnsh, Gordon Campbell, Dr**
Field House Pharma Limited

**McCallum, Charles Frederick Jones**
CBD -Tec Limited

**McCarron, Courtney Leigh**
Roberts McCarron Ltd

**McCarron, Donald Andrew**
Roberts McCarron Ltd

**McCartney, Matthew**
FPD Group Limited

**McComb, Stanton**
McKesson Global Procurement & Sourcing

**McConville, John Patrick**
Sangers (Maidstone) Limited

**McCormack, Trevor Ronald**
Ocusoft UK Limited

**McCoy, Anthony, Sir**
Chanelle McCoy CBD UK Ltd

**McCoy, Chanelle Lady**
Chanelle McCoy CBD UK Ltd

**McCoy, Anthony, Sir**
Chanelle McCoy Pharma UK Ltd

**McCoy, Chanelle Lady**
Chanelle McCoy Pharma UK Ltd

**McCoy, Chanelle**
Chanelle Vet U.K. Limited

**McCoy, Chanelle, Lady**
Chanelle Medical GB Limited

**McCoy, Sherilyn Dawn**
Astrazeneca PLC

**McCready, Jeremy William Jonathan**
Remedy JV Limited

**McCullough, John**
Medreich PLC

**McDermott, Andrew James**
Bessacarr Ltd

**McDermott, Catherine**
AAH Pharmaceuticals Limited
Barclay Pharmaceuticals Ltd
Blackstaff Pharmaceuticals Ltd
Lloyds Pharmacy Clinical Homecare
Masta Limited
Prima Brands Limited
Sangers (Northern Ireland) Ltd

**McEwan, Brian**
Iniaso Ltd
Iniaso Pharma Ltd

**McFadyen, Anthony James**
Dr. Falk Pharma UK Limited

**McGarvey, David Morris**
Pharmaxis Pharmaceuticals Ltd

**McGill, Jonathan Marcus**
Niche Pharma Limited

**McGill, Sarah-Jane**
Niche Pharma Limited

**McGlynn, Gabriel Thomas**
Neubourg Pharma (UK) Limited

**McGowan, Brian Dennis**
Matoke Holdings Limited

**McGowan, Martin James**
UK Pharmacies Ltd

**McGrath, John Paul**
Norbrook Laboratories (G.B.) Ltd

**McGread, Tom**
Omapharm Limited

**McGrory, James Gilbert**
Nascot Natural Health Limited

**McGrouther, Tod**
HAPA Group Holdings Limited

**McGuigan, John Paul**
Pharmacy Supplies Limited

**McInnes, Blair**
Humn Pharmaceuticals (UK) Ltd

**McIntosh, David Dennis**
WHL Contracts Ltd

**McKay, Brian Francis**
Tetra Hydro Cannabinoid Oils Global Ltd

**McKing, Priscilla Adwoa Asamaniwa**
Keziah Ltd

**McMordie, James Norman**
Veterinary Surgeons Supply Co Ltd

**McNally, Martin**
Nalchem Ltd

**McNish, Aran Douglas**
Opalbond Limited

**McNish, Dee Louise**
Opalbond Limited

**McParland, Corrin**
Berkshire Wholesale Supplies (2002) Ltd

**McParland, Heather Audrey**
Berkshire Wholesale Supplies (2002) Ltd

**McQuilkin, Lindsay Reid**
McQuilkin & Co Limited

**McQuilkin, Walter Gordon Campbell**
McQuilkin & Co Limited

**McQuilkin, Walter Scott Kelso**
McQuilkin & Co Limited

**McRobbie, Duncan Stuart Douglas**
Mcall Consulting Ltd

**McWilliams, Christopher Michael Francis**
Meta Innovation Nutrition Ltd

**Meader, Jeremy David**
Phoenix Healthcare Distribution Ltd

**Meads, Simon John Lewis**
Salutem Supplements Ltd

**Grantham, Robert Frederick**
The Medical Warehouse Limited

**Grantham, Susan Leona**
The Medical Warehouse Limited

**Lee, Susan Joan**
The Medical Warehouse Limited

**Giersiefen, Helmut Josef**
The Medicines Company UK Ltd

**Heer, Andre**
The Medicines Company UK Ltd

**Van Willigenburg, Arnout Sven**
The Medicines Company UK Ltd

**Medounitsyn, Andrei**
Oxford Laboratories Limited

**Meermans, Bart**
RB UK Commercial Limited

**Megas, Michalakis Nestor**
GP Mediplus Ltd

**Mehboob, Ishrat**
AI Medicines Limited

**Mehdi, Sayed Afzal**
A Wise World Limited

**Mehroof, Jawad**
Ihsan Pharma Ltd

**Mehta, Anish Kirit**
Theramex HQ UK Limited

**Mehta, Ashish**
Bradley Stoke Bristol Limited

**Mehta, Bharat Himatlal**
NSL (Holdings) Limited
NSL Group Limited
Necessity Supplies Limited
Primecrown Limited

**Mehta, Bharat Prataprai**
Genesis Pharmaceuticals Ltd

**Mehta, Jagdish Vanichand**
J.J. Worldhealth Limited
JJ Nutrihealth Ltd

**Mehta, Jagruti Jagdish**
J.J. Worldhealth Limited
JJ Nutrihealth Ltd

**Mehta, Ketan Chandrakant, Dr**
NeilMed Holding Co Ltd

**Mehta, Ketan Himatlal**
NSL (Holdings) Limited
NSL Group Limited
Necessity Supplies Limited
Primecrown Limited

**Mehta, Ketan, Dr**
Neilmed Limited

**Mehta, Manish Ramniklal**
Hamilton Pharmaceuticals Ltd

**Mehta, Nilesh Prataprai**
Athem Pharma Limited
Genesis Pharma Limited
Genesis Pharmaceuticals Ltd
Maps Healthcare Limited

**Mehta, Nina**
NeilMed Holding Co Ltd
Neilmed Limited

**Mehta, Nishali**
Suerte Pharma Limited

**Mehta, Rohit Babulal**
Medigroup Ltd

**Mehta, Samit Satish**
Emcure Pharma UK Ltd
Tillomed Laboratories Limited

**Mehta, Sidharth**
Maps Healthcare Limited

**Mehta, Tanisha**
Suerte Pharma Limited

**Mehta, Yati**
By Direct Limited

**Meier, Nuala**
Blackstaff Pharmaceuticals Ltd
Sangers (Northern Ireland) Ltd

**Melano, Massimiliano**
2M PH. Intl. Limited

**Melder, Patrick, Dr**
Chitorhino Ltd

**Mellen, Cosmo Feilding**
Spectrum Biomedical UK Limited

**Melville, Caron Jayne**
Ram Enterprises Bristol Ltd

**Melville, Robert Arthur**
Acre Aesthetics Limited
Acre Medical Limited
Acre Pharma Limited
Ram Enterprises Bristol Ltd

**Memari, Massoud**
Honilac Nutrition Limited

**Memon, Dr Mohammed Iqbal**
Biotek Diagnostics Limited

**Tolan, Paul**
A. Menarini Diagnostics Ltd

**Samaille, Nico Noel Andre**
A. Menarini Diagnostics Ltd

**Masselli, Gianni**
A. Menarini Diagnostics Ltd
A. Menarini Pharmaceuticals U.K. Ltd

**Mei, Pio**
A. Menarini Pharmaceuticals U.K. Ltd

**Menega, Evangelia**
ME Healthy Living H & L Ltd

**Menegas, George**
GPM Pharma Limited
Medicare Europe Ltd

**Menon, Ravindra Narayan**
APC Pharmaceuticals & Chemicals (Europe)

**Menon, Sudhir**
Aptil Pharma Limited
Torrent Pharma (UK) Ltd

**Menon, Tejus Ravindra**
APC Pharmaceuticals & Chemicals (Europe)

**Menon, Thiruthipalli Gopal**
APC Pharmaceuticals & Chemicals (Europe)

**Merabishvili, Levan**
Clifton Organic Limited

**Merali, Jawad Mohamed**
Fairview Health Limited

**Mercant Santa Cruz, Marcelo**
Surgical Devices Developers Ltd

**Merritt, Austen David**
Matter Drinks Trading Ltd

**Mertens, Alexis Hadelin Regis Ludovic Ghislain**
Bioloka Ltd

**Meszaros, Peter**
Chirock Trading Ltd

**Metter, Jeremy Ian**
Twinklers Limited

**Mevzos, Dimitri**
Dasapharm Limited

**Mew, Stephen Godfrey**
Guest Medical Limited

**Meyer, Uwe Helmut**
Medi UK Ltd

**Miah, Ali**
Pharmazon Limited

**Michel, Bertrand**
Mediport Limited
Mediwin Limited

**Michel, Jean-Hugues**
Mediport Limited
Mediwin Limited

**Michel, Siegfried**
Vifor Pharma UK Limited

**Michel, Simon**
Ypsomed Limited

**Mickler, Barry Joseph**
Jolinda Medical Supplies Ltd

**Micklethwaite, Amy, Dr**
378 Co Ltd

**Miesch, Willi**
Medartis Limited

**Mijbel, Mansur**
Safenet Direct Ltd

**Milata, Matej**
Oxford Biosystems Limited

**Miles, Caroline Margaret**
M.R.S. Scientific Limited

**Millard, Richard Cole**
Pan Globus Limited

**Miller, Allan Albert**
Core Environmental PLC

**Miller, David**
Miller & Miller (Chemicals) Ltd

**Miller, Jean Rosemary**
Athrodax Healthcare International

**Miller, John Simon**
Miller & Miller (Chemicals) Ltd

**Miller, Simon John**
Athrodax Healthcare International

**Millington, Darren Michael**
Rayner Pharmaceuticals Limited

**Mills, Anthony Robert**
T-Pharma Limited

**Mills, Jennifer**
T-Pharma Limited

**Milne, Ross**
Moogle Meds Ltd

**Milne, Stephanie Louise**
Blackpool Medicines Limited

**Milnes, James Alexander John**
Zoono Holdings Limited

**Minkov, Michael Mihaylov**
Delta Sales Ltd

**Minowitz, Robert Nathan**
Optident Labline Limited

**Mirov, Firuz**
Evolet Healthcare Limited

**Mirza, Jaffar Ali**
Medbase Systems Ltd

**Mirza, Shahbaz Baig**
Celestial Pharma Ltd

**Mirzoev, Ilkhomzhon**
Abstragan Limited
Evolet Healthcare Limited

**Mirzoev, Zafarkhon**
Abstragan Limited
Evolet Healthcare Limited

**Mistry, Rajesh**
Mistry Medical Supplies Ltd

**Mistry, Raman Ambaram**
Mistry Medical Supplies Ltd

**Mitchell, Brett Anthony**
MGC Pharma (UK) Ltd

**Mitchell, Mary Jane, Dr**
Hughenden Valley Pharma Ltd

**Mitidieri, Augusto**
Sintetica Limited

**Mitsopoulos, Aristeidis**
Rafarm UK Limited

**Mitton, James Alexander**
Standford Ltd

**Mittra, Ashok**
Whyte International Limited

**Mittra, Niharika**
Whyte International Limited

**Miyachi, Masao**
Charmant UK Co., Limited

**Miyamoto, Yoshiaki**
Summit Pharmaceuticals Europe Ltd

**Miyanishi, Kazuhito**
Kobayashi Healthcare Europe Ltd

**Mji, Nolitha, Dr**
Rabimed International Limited

**MoTlwala, Mohammed Hanif**
Bannersbridge Limited

**Mobara, Fariba**
Pharmartel Limited

**Moden, Matthew**
Eden CBD Limited

**Modi, Bipinchandra**
HMS Wholesale Ltd

**Modi, Rajiv Indravadan, Dr**
Cadila Pharmaceuticals (Europe) Ltd

**Modica Agnello, Alessandro**
Soho Flordis UK Limited

**Mofolasayo, Adenrele Temitope**
Springs Healthcare Limited

**Mofolasayo, Elizabeth Oluseun**
Springs Healthcare Limited

**Mofolasayo, Ikeoluwapo Naomi**
Springs Healthcare Limited

**Moghariya, Maya Jasrajbhai**
JSK PVT Limited

**Mohamed Rafaudeen, Husni Ahamed**
Life Science Healthcare UK Ltd

**Mohamed, Dadir Habib Mohamed**
Limes Pharma Ltd

**Mohamed, Khaled Haj**
Jana Healthcare Ltd

**Mohamedbhai, Tayabali**
Cradlecrest Limited
Day Lewis Medical Limited

**Mohammad, Waqar Munir**
TMZ Naturals Limited

**Mohammed Khaja, Mateenuddin**
Zululan Pharma Ltd

**Mohammed, Abrar**
Star Freight Forwarding Ltd

**Mohammed, Al-Ameen**
Simcare Global Premium Healthcare Ltd

**Mohammed, Assif**
Simcare Global Premium Healthcare Ltd

**Mohammed, Huda Ali**
Shkar Enterprise Limited

**Mohammed, Marwan**
MM Medical Equipment UK Ltd

**Mohammed, Mohammed Shaban**
UK Eagle Ltd

**Mohammed, Rashid Khalid**
Fayroz Ltd

**Mohley, Chhavi**
Mulberry Pharma Ltd

**Moin, Adnan**
Global Additives Ltd

**Mojikon, Germaine**
Bejaa Medical (UK) Limited

**Mok, Tony Shu Kam**
Astrazeneca PLC

**Molnar, Lorant**
Mensana Pharma Ltd.

**Molnar, Melinda**
M & M Taste of Harmony Export Ltd

**Moloney, Anthony Peter**
Melcare (Europe) Limited

**Molyneux, Allan John**
Medilink Limited

**Molyneux, Anne Heather, Dr**
DDWS Limited

**Monassebian, Bijan**
Prema Naturals Limited

**Monassebian, Dalia**
Prema Naturals Limited

**Monks, Claire**
Juvela Limited

**Montante, Augusto**
Heathrow.Net Limited
Noroc Concepts Ltd

**Monteith, Tanya**
Clarity Commercial Ltd
Clarity DTP Ltd
Clarity Markets Ltd
Clarity Pharma Holdings Ltd
Clarity Pharma Ltd
Clarity Woundcare Ltd
Clarity at Home Ltd

**Montoriol, Pierre**
Hemodia UK Ltd

**Mooney, Justin**
Labjoy Ltd

**Moor, Marlo**
Imex Ltd

**Moore, Brendan**
Omapharm Limited

**Moore, Karen Elizabeth**
Sure Health & Beauty Limited

**Moosa, Allison Jane**
Rhodes Pharma Limited

**Moosa, Iqbal**
Hambleton (UK) Limited

**Mora Capitan, Luis**
Pharma Mar Limited

**Morad, Hassan Oliver James**
Imphatec Ltd

**Moradi, Ali**
RND Pharma Limited

**Moradi, Homayoun**
Aryahakim Medical Equipment Co Ltd.

**More, Diliprao Pandurang, Dr**
Dil More Remedies UK Ltd

**More, Janice Kathleen Mary**
Bausch & Lomb U.K. Limited

**Morey, Patricia**
Biotest (U.K.) Limited

**Morgan, Bethan Rhian**
BR Scientific Limited

**Morgan, Charles Waite**
Tiamat Agriculture Ltd

**Morgan, Chay Bradwen**
Biomarin (U.K.) Ltd.

**Morgan, George Oliver**
Passion Dental Design Studio (Laboratory)

**Morgan, Leslie**
Durbin PLC

**Morgan, Stephen John**
LSP Bio Limited

**Morizumi, Harumasa**
Summit Pharmaceuticals Europe Ltd

**Morley, Lee Scot**
EUSA Pharma (UK) Limited

**Morphitis-Byrne, Rosemary Ann**
Vision Matrix Limited

**Morra, Sossio**
Serp Sales (UK) Limited

**Morrill, Kristine**
Medeuronet (UK) Limited

**Morris, Matthew Brian**
THD (UK) Limited

**Morris, Richard Gideon**
Biomarin (U.K.) Ltd.

**Morris, Stephen, Dr**
Contract QP Resource Limited

**Morrissey, Raymond Noel**
Infutech Limited

**Morse, Carolyn Elice**
Powerlung Ltd.

**Morton, Bryan Geoffrey**
EUSA Pharma (UK) Limited

**Mosa, AMR Abdelmonem Ibrahim**
Vitopia Ltd

**Mosa, Mohamed Abdelkader Abdelhamid**
GMP-Orphan United Kingdom Ltd

**Moss, Colin**
Med-Col Limited

**Moss, Michael Harvey**
Med-Col Limited

**Moss, Stephen Humphrey, Dr**
CoAcS Trading Limited

**Mostafa, Hani Mostafa Awadalla, Dr**
Gumsaver Limited

**Mostafavi, Seyed Mahmoud**
Sanzenica Limited

**Mottram, Jonathan Tony**
IQ Pharma Ltd

**Mount, Jacqueline Ann**
Meridian Medical Technologies Ltd
Pfizer Consumer Healthcare Ltd

**Mount, Julian David**
Alcura UK Limited
Alliance Healthcare (Distribution)
Alloga UK Limited

**Mountrichas, Georgios**
Abbott Healthcare Products Ltd
Abbott Laboratories Limited

**Moussavi, Sheida**
BFN Limited

**Moynihan, Colm**
Sword Medical UK Limited

**Moynihan, Dermot**
Sword Medical UK Limited

**Mruk, Grzegorz Michal**
GMM Sales Ltd

**Mueller, Urs**
Zimmer Biomet UK Limited

**Mughal, Ambreen Shahzad**
Orphic Limited

**Muhiyye, Khalid**
Stockport Healthcare Limited

**Muhiyye, Mahmoud**
Stockport Healthcare Limited

**Muir, Richard Gareth**
EMT Healthcare Limited

**Muir, Rodney David**
EMT Healthcare Limited

**Muir, Stephen Lindsay**
EMT Healthcare Limited

**Mukherjee, Abhijnan**
Leeds Industries (UK) Ltd

**Mukhtar, Faheem**
Pennine Pharmaceuticals Ltd

**Mukul, Rohan**
Bioleys Care Ltd

**Mukuruva, Nobantu**
Legacy Private Limited

**Mulhall, Darren Lee**
Steritech Limited

**Mullane, Noreen**
Medisca UK Limited

**Muller, Joost**
EAM Wholesale Ltd

**Mullinder, Darren Paul**
Poseidon Pharmaceutical UK Ltd

**Muma, Paul Scott**
Meridian Medical Technologies Ltd

**Mumtaz, Nasir**
Britannic Pharma Ltd

**Mundy, Tom**
Everhealth Ltd

**Mungwari, Faith**
Faith and Pharma Limited

**Munroop, Elliott-Jay Anthony**
Pure Solace Ltd

**Munzinger, Julia**
Healthcare Product Services Ltd
Healthcare Services Group Ltd
Movianto UK Limited
Pharmacare Logistics Limited

**Muongkhot, Bruno**
Vital Haven Ltd

**Muralidharan, Venugopalan**
Milpharm Limited

**Murdoch, Douglas Bruce**
Double Wing Medical Ltd

**Murdock, Martin Patrick**
Norbrook Laboratories (G.B.) Ltd

**Murphy, Anne Louise**
Boots International Limited

**Coatham, Susan Claire**
Paul Murray PLC

**Cox, Mark**
Paul Murray PLC

**Eastwood, Charlotte Ann**
Paul Murray PLC

**Eastwood, Thomas**
Paul Murray PLC

**Hadaway, Leigh**
Paul Murray PLC

**Hayton, Nicholas Brian**
Paul Murray PLC

**Murray, Karen Julia**
Paul Murray PLC

**Murray, Maxwell John**
Paul Murray PLC

**Murray, Paul Travis**
Paul Murray PLC

**Robertson, Gemma Louise**
Paul Murray PLC

**Murray, Darren Clarke**
Eurocare Impex Services Ltd

**Murray, John David**
Eurocare Impex Services Ltd

**Murray, Jonathan Conrad**
Eurocare Impex Services Ltd

**Murray, Linda**
Eurocare Impex Services Ltd

**Murray, Shane Patrick**
Veterinary Surgeons Supply Co Ltd

**Murray, Steven Edward**
Clinical Direct Ltd
TTC Medical GTS Limited

**Murtagh, Sarah**
Elm Healthcare Limited

**Musse, Ciise Sandhere**
Daryeel Medicines International Ltd

**Mustafa, Abdul**
IPSA Pharmacy Limited

**Muthir, Mohammed**
Appleby Pharmacy Limited

**Bhandal, Charnjit Singh**
Adam Myers Solutions Limited

**Bhandal, Ravinder Kaur**
Adam Myers Solutions Limited

**Nabarro, Ruth Mary Grace, Dr**
Mill Pharm Limited

**Nadarajah, Anju**
Inglasia Ltd

**Nadiadi, Abbas**
Instinct Health Ltd

**Nagle, Liam**
Norbrook Laboratories (G.B.) Ltd

**Naik, Ravindra Dineshchandra, Dr**
MMEU 20/20 Ltd

**Najeeb, Omar**
K Chem (North East) Ltd

**Nandiraju, Suresh Kumar**
Neo Farma Ltd

**Naqesh-Bandi, Mariam**
NMB Medical Limited

**Naqesh-Bandi, Nazik**
NMB Medical Limited

**Narang, Manish**
Ascend Laboratories (UK) Ltd

**Narasimhan, Ashok**
Zanoprima Holdings Limited
Zanoprima LifeSciences Limited

**Nasir, Muhammed Aslam, Dr**
Docsinnovent Limited

**Nasr, Bassim Subhi Farah Khoury**
RI Pharma Limited

**Nasrullah, Nadeem**
N N Pharma Ltd

**Nasser, Waziri**
Nasser Waziri Ltd

**Nassief, Nazmy**
Ayva Pharma Limited

**Nathan, Peter**
New England Biolabs (U.K.) Ltd

**Nathwani, Nilesh**
Disposable Medical Equipment Ltd
Windzor Pharma Limited

**Nathwani, Panna**
Disposable Medical Equipment Ltd

**Nation, Therese Mary, Dr**
WTE Services Limited

**Naude, Diederick Petrus**
Gester Invest Limited

**Navarre, Thierry**
Ontex Retail UK Limited

**Nazir, Ammar**
Ascent (Hartlepool) Limited

**Nazir, Qammar**
Ascent (Hartlepool) Limited

**Naziri, Sayed Arif**
Sanos Healthcare Ltd

**Ndawula, Richard, Dr**
Rind Pharma Limited

**Neal, Jon**
Takeda UK Limited

**Neal, Jonathan Clark**
Baxalta UK Investments Ltd.
Shire Pharmaceuticals Limited

**Nealon, Rory Peter**
Amryt Pharma (UK) Limited

**Nejad, Mohammad Reza Ashkan**
Pura Pharmaceuticals Ltd

**Nekooie, Saeed**
Advanced Medical Products Ltd

**Nemcokova, Andrea**
S & D Pharma Limited

**Neubourg, Thomas, Dr**
Neubourg Pharma (UK) Limited

**Neumann, Alexander Hans-Josef**
Livanova UK Limited

**Newman, Paul**
Orpharma Limited

**Newman, Timothy Paul**
Lexon (UK) Limited

**Newton, Andrew John, Professor**
10x Rational Ambulance Yield Ltd

**Newton, Angela Mary**
Arena (Eyewear) Limited
Mirage Eyewear (1993) Limited

**Newton, Colin Francis**
Newtons Medical Supplies Ltd

**Newton, Marjorie Diane**
Mirage Eyewear (1993) Limited

**Newton, Matthew Phillip**
Arena (Eyewear) Limited

**Newton, Patrick Jonathan**
PKA Healthcare Ltd

**Newton, Ronald**
Mirage Eyewear (1993) Limited

**Nguyen, Thoai**
Park Health Ltd

**Ngwenya, Liona Nosisa**
Welcome Medical Group Ltd

**Ngwenya, Michelle Lethokuhle**
Welcome Medical Group Ltd

**Ngwenya, Sikhanyisiwe Moyo**
Welcome Medical Group Ltd

**Ngwenya, Welcome**
Welcome Medical Group Ltd

**Nicholls, Ian James**
Jackson Immunoresearch Europe Ltd

**Nicholls, Mark Ashley**
Storepharm UK Ltd

**Nicholson, Ian James**
Clinigen Group PLC

**Nickson, Emma Louise**
Kelpharma Ltd

**Nickson, Keith**
Kelpharma Ltd

**Nicol, Alastair McPherson, Dr**
Prometheus Medical Ltd

**Nielsen, Kim**
Nordic Nutraceuticals UK Ltd

**Niemann, Oliver Herbert**
Devilbiss Healthcare Limited

**Nigam, Anil**
Euro Lifecare Ltd

**Nikodimou, Iordanis Christodoulou**
Birch & Beech Limited

**Nind, Nicholas Alan**
Eye2eye Contact Ltd

**Niranjan, Abhishek Singh**
Glector Limited

**Niranjan, Anurag Singh**
Glector Limited

**Nishihara, Takahiro**
Summit Pharmaceuticals Europe Ltd

**Nita, Adrian**
Lucky Herbalife24 Limited

**Noakes, Raymond Leslie**
Tricodent Limited

**Nocera, Carlos German**
Connexon Global Networks Ltd

**Noir, Frederic**
Tech Innovation Laser Limited

**Chukwumah, Ononuju Nkem**
The Noohra Limited

**Nooshabadi, Massoud**
Logichem Ltd

**Noott, Guy Peter Michael**
Ultrascan Solutions Ltd

**Noott, Michael Timothy**
Ultrascan Solutions Ltd

**Nordkamp, Hendrikus Hermannus**
PF OFG UK 3 Ltd
Pfizer Consumer Healthcare Ltd
Pfizer Limited
Pfizer OFG UK Limited

**Noronha, Selwyn Mariano Jonas**
ACG Europe Limited

**Norris, Michael John**
Rivertime Distribution Ltd

**North, Philip Michael, Dr**
Northwise Services Limited

**Northover, Wendy**
Ultrasun (UK) Limited

**Nosher, Safiullah**
Nosher Pharma Private Ltd

**Notarianni, Giancarlo**
Intercept Pharma UK & Ireland Ltd

**Note, Paul Druon Michael**
Geistlich Sons Limited

**Nottay, Jaskarn Singh**
Synergetic Global Limited

**Nowak, Artur**
Premium Pharm Ltd

**Nowakowska, Ewa**
Gemi Pharma Limited

**Nowakowska, Iwona**
Gemi Pharma Limited

**Nowakowska, Katarzyna**
Gemi Pharma Limited

**Nuttall, John Branson**
Bestway Pharmacy NDC Limited
Ideal Healthcare Limited

**Nwafornso, Sylvia Chinwendu**
Safe Pharma Consulting Ltd.

**Nyamapfene, Mary**
Construct4lyfe Ltd

**Nyatanga, Oscar**
Ultrascan Solutions Ltd

**O'Connell, Andrew**
Caragen (UK) Limited

**O'Connell, Catherine**
Pharmacy Supplies Limited

**O'Connor, Daniel Mark**
Acre Aesthetics Limited
Acre Medical Limited
Acre Pharma Limited
C. S. T. Pharma Limited
UK Pharma Direct Limited

**O'Connor, Stephen Clifford**
Kent Pharma UK Limited

**O'Daly, Conor James**
Kora Healthcare UK Ltd

**O'Daly, James Patrick**
Kora Healthcare UK Ltd

**Kinninmonth, Julia Sian**
John O'Donnell Limited

**O'Donnell, Philip James**
John O'Donnell Limited

**Odonnell, John Michael**
John O'Donnell Limited

**Odonnell, Margaret Betty**
John O'Donnell Limited

**O'Donnell, Lawrence Michael**
Jackson Immunoresearch Europe Ltd

**O'Donoghue, Daniel Fraser John**
Medilain Marketing Ltd

**O'Farrell, Kevin Francis**
Bright Polar Limited

**O'Hanlon, Paul John**
Omnicell Limited

**O'Hara, Neil**
GlaxoSmithKline Consumer Trading Services

**O'Kane, Laurence Gregory**
Pharmacy Supplies Limited

**O'Kane, Maura**
Pharmacy Supplies Limited

**O'Keefe, Amy**
Devilbiss Healthcare Limited

**O'Neal, Paige Devon**
Arquella Ltd

**O'Neill Jr, Philip Joseph**
Swiss-American CDMO International

**O'Reilly, Patrick Gerard**
Activated Smile Ltd

**O'Reilly, Thomas Joseph**
Semenalysis Limited

**O'Reilly, Vicrtoria Anne**
Semenalysis Limited

**O'Riordan, Rory Walter**
Windzor Pharma Limited

**Oakes, Nigel Philip**
Creative Supply Solutions Ltd

**Obeed, Muthana**
Florence Health & Beauty Ltd

**Obili, Ukah James**
Health Medbio Ltd

**Obruklu, Dilek Dag**
Ted Medical Ltd

**Odulate, Rotimi Koyejo**
Kuramo (UK) Limited

**Odunlami, Abiola Folayemi**
Dunamis Pharmaceutical Services Ltd

**Oduro, Godwin**
G Pharmaceuticals Ltd

**Ofege, Edith**
Ofege Pharm Ltd

**Ogundiran, Olusola**
So'dran Ltd

**Ogunjimi, Samson**
Codix Pharma (UK) Limited

**Ojo, Patricia Asiah**
TTops Healthcare Limited

**Oki, Mark**
Vivus UK Limited

**Okonkwo, Anita Ndidi-Amaka**
Thurgab Medicals Ltd

**Okonkwo, Arthur Nwabunike**
Thurgab Medicals Ltd

**Okonkwo, Hellen Nkiru**
Thurgab Medicals Ltd

**Okoro, Stanley Udoka**
Irving and Skinner Ltd

**Okupa, Brown**
Sharepool Limited

**Okuwoga, Adeyinka Adebayo, Dr**
Nissi Business Services Ltd

**Okuwoga, Mojisola Adewunmi**
Nissi Business Services Ltd

**Olaniyan, Gbadebo Sunday**
Medicines Extra Healthcare Ltd

**Olaniyan, Janice Oluwagbemisoye, Dr**
Medicines Extra Healthcare Ltd

**Olaniyi, Julie Adedayo**
Irismed Pharma Ltd

**Olby, Alan Musgrave**
Acorus Therapeutics Limited

**Oldroyd, Mark**
Purple Surgical UK Limited

**Olusanya, Bolajoko, Dr**
Bosville Limited

**Olusanya, Jacob Olusegun**
Bosville Limited

**Omar, Khaled Mohammed Ali**
Pharmasol London Ltd

**Omar, Zli Mohamed Ramdan**
New Medical World Ltd

**Omer, Irfan**
Pacific Pharma UK Limited

**Oncel, Hatice**
Vitalit Trade Limited

**Ondhia, Aruna Yashvantrai**
Cambridge Healthcare Supplies 2012
Cambridge Healthcare Supplies Ltd

**Ondhia, Harsh Kantilal**
Onpharma Limited

**Ondhia, Parveen Chandrakant**
Amdeepcha Limited

**Ondhia, Punam**
Cambridge Healthcare Supplies 2012
Cambridge Healthcare Supplies Ltd

**Ondhia, Shreeya**
Onpharma Limited

**Ondhia, Yashvantrai Vallabhji**
Cambridge Healthcare Supplies 2012
Cambridge Healthcare Supplies Ltd

**Ongen, Can Davut**
Galderma (U.K.) Limited

**Onwuachu, Nneka**
Nebel Healthcare Limited

**Onwubiko, Evarest, Dr**
Katvic Limited

**Onwufuju, Laurence**
Rich Almond (UK) Limited
Ripple Pharma Limited
Webstar Dixon Limited

**Oppenheim, Alan**
Ego Pharmaceuticals (UK) Ltd

**Oppenheim, Victoria Marie Jane**
Ego Pharmaceuticals (UK) Ltd

**Fox, Jayne Elizabeth**
The Orange Square Co Ltd.

**Hawksley, Christopher Michael**
The Orange Square Co Ltd.

**Orange, Steven**
Zimmer Biomet UK Limited

**Oren, Dan**
Dexcel-Pharma Limited

**Ortiz, William Patrick O'Neill**
Parallel Investments Limited

**Osadebe, Henry Chukwudi**
Thurgab Medicals Ltd

**Osborn, Ben John**
Hospira UK Limited

**Osborn, Ben**
Pfizer Limited

**Osorio Puentes, Juan Sebastian**
A.T. Medical Ltd

**Ostermayr, Andreas**
Beiersdorf UK Ltd.

**Osunro, Titus Olatunji**
TTO Ventures Ltd.

**Osunsanya, Samuel**
NSA Pharma Limited

**Othman, Fairouz, Dr**
Eastern Lighthouse Ltd

**Otsuki, Satoshi**
Charmant UK Co., Limited

**Overend, Stuart John**
Chanelle Medical U.K. Limited
Healthcare Pharma Limited
Munro Healthcare Group Limited
Munro Healthcare Pharma Ltd

**Owen, Nicholas David Sutherland**
Fast Track Sourcing Limited

**Owens, Edward**
CSL Behring Holdings Limited
CSL Behring UK Limited

**Ozcan, Mustafa**
THS Solutions Limited

**Ozgey, Ebru**
Novamedi Limited

**P'pool, William**
Clear Eyes Pharma Limited
Prestige Brands (UK) Limited

**Pabari, Hiten Shantilal, Dr**
Quatromed Limited

**Pabari, Neha**
Trical Pharm Ltd

**Pabari, Sarla Shantilal**
Shantys Limited

**Pabari, Shantilal Laxmidas**
Shantys Limited

**Pace, Christopher James**
Healthcare Procurement Services Ltd

**Pace, Nicholas Joseph**
Healthcare Product Services Ltd
Healthcare Services Group Ltd
Movianto UK Limited
Pharmacare Logistics Limited

**Pachaiyappan, Senthil Kumar**
Zista Pharma Limited

**Padda, Juveer**
Sky Hemp Ltd

**Padhani, Hassan Mehdi**
Medcare Life UK Ltd

**Padhani, Shabir Hassanali**
Medcare Life UK Ltd

**Padley, Robert George, Dr**
Lifecare Limited

**Page, Brian John, Dr**
Lab.Tv Limited

**Page, Ian David**
Dechra Veterinary Products Ltd

**Page, Lidell**
NKCell Plus PLC

**Pahal, Kuldip Kaur**
Medshires Limited

**Pakenham, Jeremy Edwin Montague**
Cytoplan Limited

**Palamoudian, Bared**
Pharmapal Limited

**Palamoudian, Raffi Kevork**
Pharmapal Limited

**Palmer, Graham Laurence**
Omron Healthcare UK Limited

**Palmer, Yanike**
Allpa Kallpa Ltd

**Palos, Mark**
Betpharma UK Limited

**Panagiotidis, Charalampos**
Glaxo Wellcome UK Limited
GlaxoSmithKline Caribbean Ltd

**Panchal, Abha Popatlal**
Novachem Limited

**Panchmatia, Hettal**
Bahati19 Limited

**Panchmatia, Hitesh Kantilal**
RSR Pharmacare Limited

**Panchmatia, Pritee Hitesh**
RSR Pharmacare Limited

**Panda, Chandramani**
Amarox Limited

**Pandey, Rajendra Kumar, Dr**
378 Co Ltd

**Pandya, Anil Mansukhlal**
Swiss Pharma UK Limited

**Panesar, Avtar Singh**
Unmaan Healthcare Limited

**Panesar, Kultar**
Unmaan Healthcare Limited

**Papageorgiou, Pantelis**
ACL Medical Limited
GPM Pharma Limited

**Papisetty, Krishnapriya**
Medspero Pharma Ltd

**Papp, Laszlo**
Megapharma Ltd

**Papp, Sandor**
Megapharma Ltd

**Paraskevas, Evangelos**
Berryfarm Ltd

**Parekh, Dipak Chandravaden**
Livewell Naturals Limited

**Parekh, Jignesh**
Exmed Worldwide Limited

**Parekh, Pritesh Chandravaden**
Livewell Naturals Limited

**Parikh, Samir Haresh**
Nexcape Pharmaceuticals Ltd

**Park, Jun-Young Anthony**
Max Motivation Limited

**Parker, Alan Michael**
Meridian Bioscience UK Limited

**Parker, Andy**
Parker Trading Ltd

**Parker, David John**
Beegood Enterprises Limited

**Parker, Steven David**
Kavia Tooling Limited

**Parkinson, Amanda**
Healthpoint Limited

**Parkinson, Graeme**
Cuttlefish Limited

**Parmar, Bhasker Dhirendrabhai**
East Midlands Infotech PVT Ltd

**Parmar, Nilesh**
Accord Healthcare Limited

**Parrish, Nicholas Bryan**
Medirite Limited

**Parry, Benjamin**
My Chu Limited
Unique Health Co Ltd

**Parry, Philip Edward**
Ethypharm UK Limited
Trotwood Pharma Limited

**Parthasarathy, Krishnan Tirucherai**
Generic Partners UK Ltd
Strides Pharma Global (UK) Ltd

**Parvez, Sumaria**
Springwell Transport and Logistics Ltd

**Pascoe, Craig John**
Mediclock Devices Limited

**Pascoe, Tanya Jane**
Mediclock Devices Limited

**Pashazadeh Monadjemi, Ali Reza, Dr**
Tearfilm Therapeutics Ltd

**Pashine, Sanjay Shrikishan**
Bristol Laboratories Limited

**Pass, Anne Elizabeth**
Pharma Insight Ltd

**Pass, Duncan Ian**
Pharma Insight Ltd

**Pass, Nicholas Stephen**
Derma UK Limited

**Patel Bsc Mrpharms, Umesh Babubhai**
NPA Services Limited

**Patel Junior, Jayanti Chimanbhai**
Budget Pharma UK Limited
East Midlands Pharma Limited

**Patel, Nisha**
Nisha Patel Ltd

**Patel, Ajay**
Mountrow Trading Limited

**Patel, Ajaybhai Dilipkumar**
Mirage Distribution Limited
Nutridrinks Limited

**Patel, Akeet Mukesh**
Niayara Global Limited

**Patel, Amish**
Infohealth Limited

**Patel, Amit Balubhai**
Glenhazel Limited

**Patel, Amit Vijaykumar**
Atnahs Pharma US Limited
Marlborough Pharmaceuticals Ltd

**Patel, Amit**
ANP Pharma Ltd

**Patel, Anish**
Nutravit Ltd.

**Patel, Anwer Ibrahim**
Medihealth (Northern) Limited
Prinwest Limited

**Patel, Ashokkumar Dahyabhai**
Elite Pharma (Surrey) Limited

**Patel, Ashokkumar Naranbhai**
Hanseco Ltd
Interpharm Limited

**Patel, Asif**
Pharmasif Direct Limited

**Patel, Atul Sumantbhai**
St George's Medical Limited
St Georges Pharmaceuticals Ltd

**Patel, Balubhai Khushalbhai**
Glenhazel Limited

**Patel, Belinda**
Sabel Pharmacy Ltd

**Patel, Bemal**
Coombe KP Limited
Direct Care Homes Limited
Directpharm Ltd
Interport Direct (Europe) Ltd
Interport Direct Limited
K P Pharma Limited
Pedalglass Limited
Pharmaceutical Direct Limited
Pharmaceuticals Direct Limited

**Patel, Bharatkumar Rajnikant**
Payal London Consolidated Ltd
Payal Pharma UK Ltd

**Patel, Bharti**
Pharma Concept UK Limited

**Patel, Bhikhu Chhotabhai**
Marlborough Pharmaceuticals Ltd
Sovereign House Properties Ltd

**Patel, Bhikhu Chhotabhai** [8-1947]
Waymade PLC

**Patel, Bhikhu Chhotabhai** [11-1949]
Atnahs Pharma US Limited

**Patel, Bina Hitesh**
Fair Pharm Limited

**Patel, Chaitanyakumar Jayantilal**
Dejure Limited

**Patel, Chandrakant**
Mayapharm Limited

**Patel, Charulata Indravadan**
Spadeground Limited

**Patel, Chintu** [11-1966]
Creo Pharma Limited

**Patel, Chintu** [10-1971]
Creo Pharma Holdings Limited

**Patel, Chirag**
Creo Pharma Limited
Creo Pharma Holdings Limited

**Patel, Chiragkumar Ranchhodbhai**
Rkonnect Limited
Silicon Pharma Limited

**Patel, Darshakkumar**
Assencion Pharmaceuticals Ltd

**Patel, Daxa Sailesh**
Maplespring Limited

**Patel, Deepa Rajendrakumar**
ANP Pharma Ltd

**Patel, Dev Indravadan, Dr**
Spadeground Limited

**Patel, Dilip**
Healthaid Holdings Limited
Healthaid Limited

**Patel, Dilipkumar Nathubhai**
Mirage Distribution Limited

**Patel, Dineshkumar Bhanubhai**
Aum Pharms Limited

**Patel, Dipak Kumar** [7-1971]
Impact Health Limited

**Patel, Dipak Kumar** [2-1973]
Prayosha Healthcare Limited

**Patel, Dipakkumar Kumar**
Prayosha Enterprises Limited

**Patel, Dipen Vijaykumar**
Atnahs Pharma US Limited
Marlborough Pharmaceuticals Ltd

**Patel, Divyesh Kumar**
Pharmadose Limited

**Patel, Ekta**
Kyo Ltd

**Patel, Enayat Iqbal**
Nationwide Healthcare Solutions Ltd

**Patel, Gautam** [8-1953]
Enlon Limited

**Patel, Gautam** [5-1972]
Creo Pharma Holdings Limited

**Patel, Gautam**
Creo Pharma Limited

**Patel, Hansa Jitendra**
Grandbydale Limited
HJ Wholesale Limited

**Patel, Harindra**
Hanseco Ltd

**Patel, Harshadrai Ishwarbhai Ashabhai**
Interport Limited

**Patel, Hasmukh Manibhai**
HNS Pharma Limited

**Patel, Heena**
Cradlecrest Limited
Day Lewis Medical Limited

**Patel, Hinal**
Prayosha Healthcare Limited

**Patel, Hital**
Coombe KP Limited
K P Pharma Limited
PS Dent Limited
Pharmaceuticals Direct Limited

**Patel, Hiten Mukesh**
Prayosha Enterprises Limited

**Patel, Hiten**
E-Pharm Limited

**Patel, Hitendra**
ATP Medical Limited
Chelmack Limited

**Patel, Hitesh Chandrakantbhai**
Usme Limited

**Patel, Hitesh Ramesh**
Silkgrange Limited

**Patel, Hitesh Vanmali**
Fair Pharm Limited

**Patel, Indravadan Narayanbhai**
Spadeground Limited

**Patel, Jay Prakash**
Janvit Ltd

**Patel, Jayanti Chimanbhai**
HQEM Pharma Limited

**Patel, Jayantibhai Chimanbhai**
Cradlecrest Limited
Day Lewis Medical Limited

**Patel, Jayesh Kumar Manilal**
Click Solutions Ltd

**Patel, Jayman**
Sivanta Resourcing Limited

**Patel, Jetunkumar Ravajibhai**
Niv Ltd
Nivja Healthcare Ltd

**Patel, Jignesh**
Actipharm Limited

**Patel, Jitendra Kantibhal**
Grandbydale Limited
HJ Wholesale Limited

**Patel, Kalpana Bharat**
Payal London Consolidated Ltd
Payal Pharma UK Ltd

**Patel, Kalpen**
Eico Ltd

**Patel, Kamlesh Kanubhai**
RIC Chemicals Limited

**Patel, Kanchanlal Naginbhai**
Ria Generics Limited

**Patel, Kevin**
8 Pharma Ltd
8 Trading Limited

**Patel, Khyati**
Prime Pharmacare Ltd

**Patel, Kirit Chimanbhai Tulsibhai**
Budget Pharma UK Limited
HQEM Pharma Limited

**Patel, Kirit Vaghjibhai**
Janvit Ltd

**Patel, Kirti**
ATP Medical Limited
Chelmack Limited
Smartway Pharmaceuticals Ltd

**Patel, Krishan Janak**
Pharmadose Limited

**Patel, Krishma Vikash**
Manichem Limited

**Patel, Lakhman**
Phonepimps Limited

**Patel, Mayank Harendra**
Pearl Chemist Group Limited
Pearl Services (Tooting) Ltd

**Patel, Mayur**
Richardson Healthcare Limited

**Patel, Meghna Chirag**
PS Dent Limited

**Patel, Mikesh**
Nutravit Ltd.

**Patel, Milesh**
Venture Pharma Ltd

**Patel, Mirag**
Rapid Pharma Limited

**Patel, Mukesh Chhotabhai**
Riteaim Limited

**Patel, Mukund Kacharalal**
Kaam Pharma Limited

**Patel, Naeem Aziz**
Nationwide Healthcare Solutions Ltd

**Patel, Nainesh Mahendra**
Arrowedge Limited

**Patel, Natasha Harshad, Dr**
Interport Limited

**Patel, Neel Bharat**
Payal London Consolidated Ltd

**Patel, Nilen**
HNS Pharma Limited

**Patel, Nileshkumar Indubhai**
Astriza UK Ltd
Connective Pharma Limited
Healthbiotics Ltd

**Patel, Nimeshkumar Somabhai**
Clinimarg Ltd

**Patel, Niral Narendra**
Manichem Limited

**Patel, Nitinkumar Ramanlal**
Pergamon Ltd
Tradewings Worldwide Ltd

**Patel, Paaras Shamir Kumar**
Perush Ltd

**Patel, Pankajkumar Vastaram**
Celtis Healthcare Ltd

**Patel, Parim Umakant**
Prayosha Enterprises Limited

**Patel, Piyushbhai Khushalbhai, Dr**
Glenhazel Limited

**Patel, Prakash**
P R Pharma Limited

**Patel, Pranav Hariprasad**
New Health Supplies Limited

**Patel, Prashant Hariprasad**
New Health Supplies Limited

**Patel, Pratikkumar**
Baron Medicare UK Limited

**Patel, Pravinkumar Vaghjibhai**
Janvit Ltd

**Patel, Priyan**
Rapid Pharma Limited

**Patel, Rachael Louise**
Sabel Pharmacy Ltd

**Patel, Rajendra Ambalal**
Healthaid Holdings Limited
Healthaid Limited

**Patel, Rajendra Chandrakant**
Mapaex Consumer Healthcare (UK) Private

**Patel, Rajendra Chhotabhai**
P R Pharma Limited

**Patel, Rajesh Ramniklal**
NPA Services Limited

**Patel, Rajiv**
Fire N Ice Ltd

**Patel, Rajive**
Infohealth Limited

**Patel, Rakesh Vinodrai**
Nordic Generics Ltd

**Patel, Rakhee**
RSR Pharmacare Limited

**Patel, Ramesh Chhaganbhai**
Silkgrange Limited

**Patel, Ramesh Vasudev**
Elite Pharma (Surrey) Limited

**Patel, Ravi Ashwin**
Aidwell Limited

**Patel, Rupeshkumar Dinubhai**
Medipro Pharma Limited

**Patel, Rushil Shamir Kumar**
Perush Ltd

**Patel, Sailesh Manubhai, Dr**
Maplespring Limited

**Patel, Salim Habib**
HBS Healthcare Limited

**Patel, Sameer**
Exmed Worldwide Limited
Mayapharm Limited

**Patel, Samir Madhusudan**
Sabel Pharmacy Ltd

**Patel, Sandeep Ashokbhai**
Ambe Limited

**Patel, Sandhya Virendra**
Numedex Limited

**Patel, Sarfraz**
HS Pharma Limited
ZS Pharma Limited

**Patel, Shailesh**
Pharma Concept UK Limited

**Patel, Shamir Kumar Sumantbhai**
Perush Ltd

**Patel, Sharan**
Cape Pharmaceuticals Ltd
Cygnus Pharma Ltd
Euro-Link Pharma Ltd

**Patel, Sharmistahbahen**
Baron Medicare UK Limited

**Patel, Smita Chaitanya**
Dejure Limited

**Patel, Snehal Mahendrabhai**
SSPharma4You Limited

**Patel, Subhash Kantibhai**
K & K Pharmaceuticals Limited

**Patel, Sumaiya**
ZS Solutions Limited

**Patel, Sunil Rameshchandra**
Propharma-UK Ltd

**Patel, Svikrut**
Pharmadose Limited

**Patel, Trusha**
Tauva Limited

**Patel, Ullas Mahendrakumar**
Arrowedge Limited

**Patel, Umakant Natubhai**
Prayosha Healthcare Limited

**Patel, Umesh**
Ruby Box Limited

**Patel, Vanitaben Pankajkumar**
Celtis Healthcare Ltd

**Patel, Venin Pankajkumar**
Celtis Healthcare Ltd

**Patel, Versha Kamlesh**
RIC Chemicals Limited

**Patel, Vijay Kumar Chhotabhai**
Marlborough Pharmaceuticals Ltd
Sovereign House Properties Ltd
Waymade PLC

**Patel, Vijaykumar Bhikhabhai**
Ozone Medical Supplies Ltd

**Patel, Vijaykumar Chhotabhai**
Atnahs Pharma US Limited

**Patel, Vijaykumar Harendra**
Pearl Chemist Group Limited
Pearl Services (Tooting) Ltd

**Patel, Vikash**
Manichem Limited

**Patel, Vilochna**
Ruby Box Limited

**Patel, Vipulkumar** [11-1979]
Trion Pharma Limited

**Patel, Vipulkumar** [12-1980]
B & B Wholesale Limited

**Patel, Viresh** [11-1979]
Vak Enterprise Limited

**Patel, Viresh** [7-1985]
Manichem Limited

**Patel, Yakub Ibrahim**
Prinwest Limited

**Patel, Yatin Mahendrakumar**
Arrowedge Limited

**Patel, Yogendra**
YJBPort Limited

**Patel, Yogendrabhai Natvarlal**
Coramandel Limited

**Patel, Zahid**
ZS Pharma Limited

**Patel, Zahirbhai Abbasbhai**
ZS Solutions Limited

**Patels, Keronn**
Emkkay of London Limited

**Paterson, Keiron David**
A D Healthcare Limited

**Paterson, Richard Graham, Dr**
Aroschem Limited

**Paterson, Roger**
A D Healthcare Limited

**Pathak, Hemant Kumar**
Overseas Merchandising Corporation Ltd

**Pathan, Muhammed Salman**
Globyz Pharma (UK) Ltd

**Patsi, Tuomo Tapani**
Celgene Limited

**Pattani, Pravin**
Blackbird Pharmacy Limited

**Patterson, Christopher Stuart**
Toiletry Sales Limited

**Pattni, Ajay**
Dilcare Health Limited

**Patton, Robert Henry**
Agrihealth (N.I.) Limited

**Paul, Harold John Christopher**
Latam HQ Health Ltd

**Paul, Simon John Christopher**
Latam HQ Health Ltd

**Pavel, Bogdan Nicolae**
Pharmnet Group Ltd

**Pawelek, Stanislaw**
Stan-Pol Ltd

**Pay, Alexander George**
Sangers (Maidstone) Limited

**Pay, Dennis Charles**
Sangers (Maidstone) Limited

**Payne, Craig**
56 Flowers Ltd

**Pazik, Karol**
Corpus Nostrum Limited

**Peake, Mark Anthony**
Curans Care Limited

**Peake, Michele**
Curans Care Limited

**Pear, Andrew Mark**
Pleskarn Limited
Reliance Medical Ltd

**Pear, Joshua Joseph Adam**
Pleskarn Limited
Reliance Medical Ltd

**Pear, Thomas Andrew**
Reliance Medical Ltd

**Pearce, Stewart Benjamin**
Otsuka Pharmaceuticals (U.K.) Ltd.

**Pearlman, David**
Mensana Pharma Ltd.

**Pearson, Edwin James**
Hospira UK Limited
Meridian Medical Technologies Ltd
PF OFG UK 3 Ltd
Pfizer Consumer Healthcare Ltd
Pfizer Limited
Pfizer OFG UK Limited

**Pearson, Islam**
Greenliving Pharma Ltd

**Pearson, Jonathan Frank Richard**
Greiner Bio-One Limited

**Pearson, Paul Davidson**
Nutresco Ltd

**Pelusi, Pietro**
Evideon Daily Ltd

**Pender, Alan**
IQ Pharma Ltd

**Penna, Ignatius Dominic**
Pennamed Limited

**Pennington, Ivan**
Gee Lawson Limited

**Penny, Peter George Worsley**
Morton Medical Limited

**Peplar, Anthony Graeme**
Citco Chemicals Ltd.

**Pereira, Andre Luis**
Specialty Pharma of London Ltd

**Pesen Okvur, Devrim Devrim**
Initio Cell Limited

**Pessagno, Gerard Michael Dominic**
C.D. Medical Limited
Linderma Limited
M & A Pharmachem Limited

**Peter, Richard**
Fortissa Ltd

**Peters, Brian**
CPX Solutions Limited

**Peterson, Alan Edward**
BBI Healthcare Limited

**Peterson, Karen**
Abbott Laboratories Limited

**Petersone, Angelika**
Petersone Group Ltd

**Petrie, Graeme**
U L Medicines Limited

**Petropoulakis, Georghios**
GP Mediplus Ltd

**Petrunin, Aleksandr**
CBS Trade Limited

**Pettigrew, Michel Lucien**
Ferring Pharmaceuticals Ltd

**Pettitt, Tracy**
Atrimusrx Ltd
Idea Medica Limited

**Peyami, Arash**
Pro Teeth Whitening Co Limited

**Peyami, Babak**
Pro Teeth Whitening Co Limited

**Phelps, Charlotte**
Parapharm Development Limited

**Philipose, Suphil**
Bioturm Limited

**Philipps, Matthew Frank**
LDC International Limited

**Phillips, Berkeley Simon, Dr**
Pfizer Limited

**Phillips, Gary Jonathan**
Pharmaxis Pharmaceuticals Ltd

**Phiri, Rodgers**
Third Hand Healthcare Ltd

**Phizacklea, Charles**
Topcell Pharma Limited

**Photay, Avtar Singh**
G.A.P. Research Co Ltd

**Photay, Gurnam Singh**
G.A.P. Research Co Ltd

**Piasta, Agnieszka Maria**
JP & A Pharma Ltd

**Piasta, Jacek Bartosz**
JP & A Pharma Ltd

**Piccaver, Matthew Thomas, Dr**
Glemsford Services Limited

**Picillo, Salvatore**
Orion Medical Supplies Ltd

**Pierantozzi, Mara**
Melo Labs UK Ltd

**Pietersen, Robert Ralph**
Pharma 777 Limited

**Pietrantoni, David Francis**
Biofex Limited
Fluidx Limited

**Pietrowski, Maik Marcel**
Cannerald Group Ltd

**Pignolet, David Walter**
Celgene Limited
Celgene UK Distribution Ltd

**Pillai, Jayaprasad Kaippallil Raman**
Steripharm (UK) Limited

**Pillai, Mohana Kumar**
Generic Partners UK Ltd
Strides Pharma Global (UK) Ltd

**Pindoria, Alpesh**
Pharmunity Limited

**Pinkus, Anthony Stuart**
Ainsworths (London) Limited

**Pinotti-Lindqvist, Eva**
Camurus Ltd

**Piroli, Danilo**
Chiesi Healthcare Limited
Chiesi Limited

**Pittock, Adrian**
Valley Northern Limited

**Pittock, Dale**
Valley Northern Limited

**Pittock, Oliver John**
Valley Northern Limited

**Pittock, Priscilla**
Valley Northern Limited

**Pizza, Joseph**
Interchem Europe (UK) Limited

**Pletcher, Brett**
Gilead Sciences Ltd

**Pluntz, Gilles**
Ferring Pharmaceuticals Ltd

**Poco, Maria**
Afdos Pharmaceuticals Limited

**Poddar, Nidhi**
Vityz Nutrition Limited

**Poddar, Pravin**
Vityz Nutrition Limited

**Poggio, Tracey Sarah**
Antwerp Brokering Enterprises (U.K.)

**Pohl, Martin Johannes Ortwin**
L & R Medical UK Ltd.

**Pohlman, Kevin Michael**
National Veterinary Services Ltd

**Pomfret, Lyndsay**
LZ Pharma Ltd

**Pomponi, Lorenzo**
Skymedic UK Limited

**Ponchon, David**
Thea Pharmaceuticals Limited

**Pongrac, Robert**
Perfect Vascular Natural Ltd

**Ponsford, Ian Arthur**
Kestrel Medical Limited

**Ponsford, Meryl Julie**
Kestrel Medical Limited

**Ponti, Battista Pietro**
Mintheath Developments Limited

**Pooley, Colin Edward**
B D S I Limited

**Pooley, Sharon Gail**
B D S I Limited

**Poon, Shuk Han**
MDX Healthcare Ltd

**Pop, Adrian Nicolae**
AP Import Export Ltd

**Popat, Satyam Dilipkumar**
Vitwell Limited

**Popat, Shivam Dilip**
Vitwell Limited

**Pope, Keiron Francis Geraint**
Pope Enterprises Ltd

**Popescu, Sorin-Mihai**
OFC Molecular Ltd

**Portela, Antonio Luis de Azevedo**
Bial Pharma UK Limited

**Portela, Miguel Luis de Azevedo**
Bial Pharma UK Limited

**Soteriou, Christopher**
The Portobello Pharmacy Ltd

**Scurr, Martin John, Dr**
The Portobello Pharmacy Ltd

**Jordan, Sarah Catherine Anne**
The Portobello Pharmacy Ltd

**Haughton, Neil Duncan, Dr**
The Portobello Pharmacy Ltd

**Rashid, Soran**
Sara Post Ltd

**Potlapadu, Bhavani**
Dr Pradeep Reddy's Laboratories (UK & EU)

**Potlapadu, Pradeep Kumar Reddy, Dr**
Dr Pradeep Reddy's Laboratories (UK & EU)

**Potter, Colin**
Natures Healthworks Limited

**Potter, Graeme**
Naturenetics UK Limited

**Potter, Lisa Jane**
Charlwood Pharma Limited

**Potter, William David**
Charlwood Pharma Limited
Odiham OH Products Limited

**Powar, Randeep Singh**
Pura (UK) Ltd

**Power, Mary Ellen**
Devonshire Healthcare Services Ltd

**Poynter, Caroline**
C. S. T. Pharma Limited

**Prajapati, Amrut**
Dixons Pharmaceuticals UK Ltd

**Prakash, Manoj**
Amarox Limited

**Prakash, Prafful**
Apex Lab Scientific Ltd

**Prasad, Gorla Phaneemdra**
Milpharm Limited

**Pratt, Dean**
Colgate-Palmolive (U.K.) Ltd

**Prendergast, Anne Elizabeth**
Ocusoft UK Limited

**Prendergast, Anthony Ailwyn**
PKA Healthcare Ltd

**Cooke, Patricia Ann**
John Preston & Co. (Belfast) Ltd

**Cooke, Nicholas James Shelton**
John Preston & Co. (Belfast) Ltd

**Cooke, Christopher Alexander**
John Preston & Co. (Belfast) Ltd

**Price, David Philip**
Semenalysis Limited
Specialty Diagnostix Limited

**Price, Margaret Mary**
Semenalysis Limited
Specialty Diagnostix Limited

**Price, Paul Bryan**
Beiersdorf UK Ltd.

**Price, Stephen Ronald**
Optima Consumer Health Limited

**Prichard, Jason**
Medicare Products Limited
PH Medicare Ltd

**Priest, Samantha**
Arena (Eyewear) Limited

**Prinz, Andreas**
Croma-Pharma Limited

**Prinz, Gerhard**
Croma-Pharma Limited

**Priore, Angelo**
SQR Pharma Consulting Ltd

**Bloom, Adam Simon**
The Private Pharma Health Co Ltd

**Gilbert, Daniel Anthony**
The Private Pharma Health Co Ltd

**Bloom, Adam Simon**
The Private Pharmacy Group Ltd

**Gilbert, Daniel Anthony**
The Private Pharmacy Group Ltd

**Prive, Gael Vanessa**
Goldshore (UK) Limited

**Prive, Philippe Henri**
Goldshore (UK) Limited

**Procida, Shaji Mary**
MGI Pharma Limited

**Proctor, Lee, Dr**
Bakhu Limited

**Prowse, Andrew Thomas**
DCH Subco Ltd

**Pruzanski, Mark, Dr**
Intercept Pharma Europe Ltd.

**Psathas, Nikolaos**
Dermconcept Ltd

**Psyllos, John**
Venture Four Ltd.

**Puaar, Charanjit Singh**
AC Intertrade Limited

**Pugh, Lyn Janet**
Stegram Pharmaceuticals Ltd

**Pullin, Nick**
Healthcare 4life Ltd

**Puri, Ashu**
Sipco Nutrition (UK) Ltd

**Puri, Sonia**
Sipco Pharma UK Ltd

**Purnell, Gareth John**
Cimex Lectularius Limited

**Purohit, Vishva Vijaychandra**
Kanish Ltd

**Puthenvilayil Mathaikutty, Raju**
Bristol Laboratories Limited

**Puthyia Purayil, Thanveer Ahammed**
Feel and Heal UK Limited

**Qaiyum, Muhammad Abdul**
Redlight Exchange Ltd

**Qamar, Mohammed**
Qamar Limited

**Qazi, Abdul**
Biotek Diagnostics Limited

**Quay, Steven Carl, Dr**
Atossa Genetics UK Ltd

**Quinn, Victoria**
Fox Group Global Ltd
Fox Group International Ltd
Fox Pharma Limited

**Quinot, Jean**
Linepharma International Ltd

**Qurbain, Anzal, Dr**
Zoop Pharma Ltd

**Qureshi, Khizer**
Dispensing Healthcare Ltd

**Rabin, Bennie**
Alium Medical Limited

**Rabin, Joel**
BR Pharma International Ltd

**Rabin, Ruth Moira**
Alium Medical Limited

**Racca, Cristina**
ECommedical Limited
Pispo Ltd
Unifarco Ltd

**Racey, Christopher Stephen**
R.A. Racey (Gt. Yarmouth) Ltd

**Racey, Jacqueline Mary**
R.A. Racey (Gt. Yarmouth) Ltd

**Racey, Christopher Stephen**
Stephar (U.K.) Limited

**Racey, Jacqueline Mary**
Stephar (U.K.) Limited

**Rach, Mitul**
Remedine Limited

**Racklin Asher, Nicole Deborah**
Pound International Ltd

**Racklin, David Vaughan**
Pound International Ltd

**Racklin, Toni Rochelle**
Pound International Ltd

**Rad, Mahmoud**
Rolling Stones Trading Ltd

**Rad-Niknam, Mohammed, Dr**
Pharmacina Ltd

**Radford, Robbie Colin**
Lucid Wholesale Ltd

**Radia, Bhavesh Amratlal**
Ascot Pharma Ltd
Spodefell Pharma Chemicals Ltd

**Radley, Iris Edith**
R.B. Radley & Co Ltd

**Radley, Russell Brian**
R.B. Radley & Co Ltd

**Radley, Mark David**
R.B. Radley & Co Ltd

**Rafiq, Muhammad Awais Masood**
Nationwide Healthcare Solutions Ltd

**Rafiq, Tamoor**
Parasure Limited

**Rahal, Rahal**
J & T World Trade (UK) Limited

**Raheja, Ritu**
Raman Pharma Limited

**Rahemani, Mohammed Jaffer**
Vital Supplies (UK) Limited

**Rahman, Ambia**
IPSA Pharmacy Limited

**Rahman, Ataur**
Unipharm Limited

**Rahman, Sabera Nazneen**
Astrazeneca PLC

**Rahman, Salman**
Beximco Pharma UK Limited

**Rahman, Sayedur**
Unipharm Limited

**Rahmani, Benyamin, Dr**
Infinity Biomedical Ltd

**Rahme, Troy Christopher**
Venture Four Ltd.

**Rahnama, Kambiz**
Trent Dent Products Limited

**Rai, Baldeesh Kaur**
One Pharm Limited

**Rai, Sukhwant Singh**
One Pharm Limited

**Raja, Harshad Kumar,**
Simba Pharmatech Limited

**Raja, Zahid**
Fitnatix International Ltd

**Rajani, Kulsum**
Medicine Optimisation Limited

**Rajani, Pramod Tulsidas**
Pramod Rajani Organisation Ltd

**Rajdev, Ravi**
Fortune Industries Limited

**Rajdev, Ronak Narottam**
Fortune Industries Limited

**Rake, Jude David**
Timstar Laboratory Suppliers Ltd

**Ramachandran, Priti**
Bristol Laboratories Limited

**Ramachandran, Thembalath**
Bristol Laboratories Limited

**Ramajayam, Shyamala**
Peart Med Ltd

**Ramamoorthy, Jayakumar**
Zista Pharma Limited

**Ramiro Ferreira Pires, Nelson**
Recordati Pharmaceuticals Ltd

**Ramroop, Rosemary Anita**
R & R Post Op Box Ltd.

**Ramsay, Malcolm Clive**
European Veterinary Supplies Ltd
Manx Healthcare Limited
Manx Pharma Ltd

**Ramseier, Niklaus**
Ypsomed Limited

**Ramsey, Edward, Dr**
Leptrex Ltd.

**Ramsey, Peter John**
Inov8 Medical Solutions Ltd
Meditech Endoscopy Ltd

**Ramzan, Muhammad**
Sintal Impex Limited

**Randall, Claire**
Randall Allison Limited

**Randall, Jeremy Anthony Phillip**
Periproducts Limited

**Randall, Keith**
Toiletry Sales Limited

**Ranjbar, Mahsa**
Masir Ltd

**Ranson, Paul**
Cenote Pharma Limited

**Rashke, Daniel**
Timstar Laboratory Suppliers Ltd

**Rasmussen, Eric Scott**
Meridian Bioscience UK Limited

**Rasu, Krishnajeyam**
Relyer Health Limited

**Rasul, Adelle Elizabeth**
R.F. Medical Supplies Limited

**Rathnam, Shivprakash, Dr**
Novelgenix Therapeutics Ltd

**Ravat, Rashid Ahmed**
RAR Pharmaceutics Ltd

**Rawle, Andrew Thomas**
Beiersdorf UK Ltd.

**Rawlinson, Alison**
Insight Biotechnology Limited
Insight Health Limited

**Rawlinson, Anthony Paul**
Eco Animal Health Group PLC

**Rawlinson, John**
Insight Biotechnology Limited
Insight Health Limited

**Rawlinson, Richard Alan**
Zanza Specials International Ltd

**Rayat, Satvinder Singh**
Pharmatec Ltd

**Raynor, Donna Marie**
Bionutricals UK Ltd

**Raynor, Simon Paul**
Penlan Pharmaceuticals Limited

**Razaq, Sajid**
Dispensing Healthcare Ltd

**Rea, Katy Alice**
Cannaid Ltd

**Rebours-Mory, Veronique Marie**
Nordic Pharma Limited

**Redding, Helen Louise**
Optident Labline Limited

**Redfern, David Jonathan**
T-In Medical Limited

**Redondo, Jose Augusto Fernandes**
Bial Pharma UK Limited

**Reed, Justin James**
Treforest Pharmacy Limited

**Reed, Victoria Jane**
Treforest Pharmacy Limited

**Rees, David Hugh Thomas**
Wilkinson Healthcare Limited

**Rees, Frazer James**
Future Pharmacare Limited

**Rees, John Anthony, Dr**
1st Health Products Ltd

**Rees, Timothy**
Smoketrees Ltd

**Reeves, Duncan James**
Lifecell EMEA Limited

**Regan, Matt Joseph**
Novo Nordisk Limited

**Regnault, Stephane**
Vygon (U.K.) Limited

**Reiberg, Manuel**
Daiichi Sankyo UK Limited

**Reid, Terry Neil**
Groves Marchant Limited

**Reindel, Christopher Paul**
Santen UK Limited

**Renaut, Hugues Constant Guillaume**
Servier Laboratories Limited

**Renney, David John**
Nimrod Veterinary Products Ltd

**Renney, Donna Theresa**
Nimrod Veterinary Products Ltd

**Rentsch, Christoph Andreas**
Santhera (UK) Limited

**Revell, Erica Wendy**
Infolight Limited

**Revell, Mark**
Infolight Limited

**Reynolds, Helen**
Amdega Brands Limited

**Reza, Rabbur**
Beximco Pharma UK Limited

**Riaz, Amir**
I-Dispense Limited

**Riaz, Amran**
My Dental Store Limited

**Rice, Graham**
McNeil Healthcare (UK) Limited

**Richardson, David Robert**
Meds Online 247 Limited

**Bogsch, Erik Attila**
Gedeon Richter (UK) Limited

**Halko, Timea, Dr**
Gedeon Richter (UK) Limited

**Zolnay, Kriszta, Dr**
Gedeon Richter (UK) Limited

**Ricupati, Agostino**
CooperVision Lens Care Limited

**Riebensahm, Frank Michael**
Evolve Generics Limited

**Riedner, Thomas**
Beiersdorf UK Ltd.

**Riley, Martin Holt**
National Veterinary Services Ltd

**Riley, Stephen William**
Medisante Limited

**Rimmer, Robert Paul**
1LIFE Distribution Limited

**Rishi, Raj Kumari**
Rising Sun Ventures Ltd

**Rishi, Varun Kumar**
JMD Enterprises UK Limited
Rising Sun Ventures Ltd

**Ritchie, Alison June**
Angus Medical Supplies Ltd

**Ritovs, Krisjanis**
Nex Pharma Limited

**Ritovs, Martins**
Nex Pharma Limited

**Ritter, Daniel Everett**
Bugband Europe Ltd

**Rivas Cortes, Pablo**
Alloga UK Limited

**Rivas, Pablo Cortes**
Alcura UK Limited
Alliance Healthcare (Distribution)
Beachcourse Limited
OTC Direct Limited

**Rivers, Dominic James**
Galpharm International Limited
Omega Pharma Limited
Perrigo Pharma Limited

**Roach, Daniel James William**
Aclardian Limited

**Roberts, Alexandra May Howard**
Dacre Skincare Limited

**Roberts, Allison Jane**
Roberts McCarron Ltd

**Roberts, Andrew**
Meadow Laboratories Limited

**Roberts, Christopher**
Morvigor (UK) Ltd

**Roberts, Debra Joy**
Aspire Pharma Holdings Limited
Aspire Pharma Limited
Attentive Pharma Limited

**Roberts, Mark Derek**
Aspire Pharma Holdings Limited
Aspire Pharma Limited

**Roberts, Mark**
Perennial Pharma Ltd

**Robertson, Lindon**
Biofex Limited
Fluidx Limited

**Robinson, Michelle Lesley**
Elleco Limited

**Robinson, Robert Edward**
Concord Extra Limited

**Robinson, Sarah Louise**
Countrywide Healthcare Supplies Holdings

**Rocha, Joao Carlos Nunes**
Lundbeck Limited

**Rochester, Raymond Paul**
Vetsonic (UK) Ltd

**Rodger, Christopher John**
Harben Medical Limited

**Rodgers, Trevor**
Healthcare 21 (UK) Limited

**Rodrigues, Elsa**
Anaiah Healthcare Ltd

**Rodrigues, Ryan**
Anaiah Healthcare Ltd

**Rohrbach, Raymond Gerard**
Nutresco Ltd

**Roig Zapatero, Gabriel**
Laboratoires Forte Pharma UK Ltd

**Rollo, Sean**
Supphero Ltd

**Rollocks, Godwyn Joseph Orlando Roy**
Green Guru Enterprices Ltd.

**Romberg, Val Gene**
CSL Behring Holdings Limited

**Nooraldin Moosa, Ramin**
Rogia Romini Limited

**Rones, Adam Jamie**
Midmeds Limited

**Rones, David Jason**
Midmeds Limited

**Rones, Rebecca Elisa**
Midmeds Limited

**Roowala, Abbas Jaffer**
Six Ways Birmingham Ltd

**Roowala, Batul Abbas**
Six Ways Birmingham Ltd

**Rose, Matthew George**
DCH Subco Ltd

**Rose, Paul**
Pfizer Consumer Healthcare Ltd
Pfizer Limited

**Rose, Stuart Matthew**
Merz Pharma UK Limited

**Rose, Susan Louise, Dr**
Aroschem Limited

**Roshan, Amrit Kaur**
ZS Pharma Limited

**Ross, Andrew**
Larmed Limited

**Rossbach, Gerhard Otto Friedrich**
Brightfield Associates Ltd

**Rossi, Michael**
Genesis Medical Limited

**Rothblatt, Martine**
United Therapeutics Europe, Ltd.

**Roumi, Michael**
Trilogy Medical Systems Ltd

**Rowe, Andrew**
Medisca UK Limited

**Rowe, Lucy**
Bristol Buttr Ltd

**Anderson, Stephen William**
L.Rowland & Co Ltd

**Hudson, Kevin Robert**
L.Rowland & Co Ltd

**Rowley, David Alan, Mr**
Attentive Pharma Limited

**Rubens, Adam Marc**
Modern Aesthetic Solutions Ltd

**Rudd, Christopher Allan**
Galpharm International Limited
Omega Pharma Limited
Perrigo Pharma Limited

**Rudge, David**
Pharmed Health Care Organisation Ltd

**Rueda de Valenzuela, Maria**
Willbay Limited

**Ruggieri, Dario**
Medi Test Pharma Ltd

**Rule, Joanne**
Eurostar Scientific Limited

**Rule, Paul James**
Eurostar Scientific Limited

**Rungien, Siven Pillay, Dr**
Pharmaethical Ltd
Southampton Medical Group Ltd

**Ruparelia, Rekha Sudhir**
Shardman Healthcare Limited
Supra Enterprises Limited

**Ruparelia, Sudhir Mansukhlal**
Shardman Healthcare Limited
Supra Enterprises Limited

**Ruprai, Gurdev Singh**
Ennogen Healthcare Ltd
Ennogen Pharma Ltd
Sunmed Pharma Ltd

**Ruprai, Kalvinder Singh**
Aver Healthcare Ltd
Garusa Solutions U.K. Limited
Medpro Healthcare Limited

**Rusling, Mark**
Supplemax Ltd

**Russell, Mahammed**
Connected Healthcare Ltd

**Russell, Malcolm Quentin, Dr**
Prometheus Medical Ltd

**Russell, Robert Lannigan**
Hydro Tan Limited

**Rustemi, Muso**
Ham+Med Co Ltd

**Rutt, Michael Logan**
Eptheca Global Limited

**Ruzicka, Viktor, Dr**
Biovendor Ltd
Oxford Biosystems Limited

**Ryan, Aidan Joseph**
Kora Healthcare UK Ltd

**Ryan, Michael**
Healthpoint Limited

**Ryan, Robert F, Dr**
Nunataq Limited

**Saad, Peter**
Archangel's Pharmaceutical Services

**Sabapathy, Benno Ranjitkumar**
Pharma-Export Ltd
Valugen Pharma Limited

**Sabharwal, Gurvinder Singh**
Total Medcare Limited

**Sacco, Christine**
Clear Eyes Pharma Limited
Prestige Brands (UK) Limited

**Sacranie, Bashir**
Global Pharmaceuticals (UK) Ltd
Global Pharmaceuticals Ltd

**Sacranie, Iqbal, Sir**
Global Pharmaceuticals (UK) Ltd

**Sadik, Tabarak**
Brex Medical Supplies Limited

**Sadler, Craig Stephen William**
Bio Pathica Limited
Cyto-Solutions Limited

**Safadi, Sami**
Biovate Limited

**Safarov, Elshad**
Welfar Healthcare Limited

**Safri, Riyaz**
Rhodes Pharma Limited

**Saghatchi, Vahid**
Rolling Stones Trading Ltd

**Saglani, Kalpesh Kumar Prabhudas**
E-Pharm Limited

**Sagoo, Amrik Singh**
EMT Healthcare Limited

**Sagoo, Avtar Singh**
Simply Meds Pro Ltd

**Sagoo, Parvinder Singh**
Simply Meds Pro Ltd

**Sahin, Dilar**
Treatlines Limited

**Sahota, Gurpreet Kaur**
Go-Kyo Science Limited

**Sahota, Lakhveer Singh** [11-1974]
Go-Kyo Science Limited

**Sahota, Lakhveer Singh** [12-1974]
Alturix Limited

**Sahota, Pinder**
Novo Nordisk Limited

**Sahu, Muhammad Shahid Ali**
Sahu & Co Limited

**Saiban, Jason Asnam**
Veriton Pharma Limited

**Saied, Deram, Dr**
Stop Ltd

**Sail, Ranjit Vishawambar**
Biophos Labs Ltd
Chemx Ltd

**Saiyed, Abdulshakur Abdulgafur**
SkInOne UK Ltd

**Salazar, Cristino Guevara**
Wonder World Ltd

**Saldanha, Mark Bosco**
Relonchem Limited

**Saldanha, Sandra**
Relonchem Limited

**Sale, Christopher James**
Conceio Consulting Ltd

**Saleem, Shajeel**
Trinity Impex Limited

**Saleh, Khalid**
Mera Pharma Limited

**Salem, Mohammed Jasim**
Pharmavit (UK) Limited

**Salerno, Gianfranco**
Cannamedical Pharma UK Limited

**Salih, Hakan**
Universal Supplies (International) Ltd

**Salkin, Jon**
Kinesis Limited

**Salko, Inna Vladimirovna**
Arctic Medical Limited

**Salman, Mootaz Mowfak, Dr**
London Spirit for Trading Ltd

**Salmond, Hamish George**
Biobos Limited
Boston Healthcare Limited

**Samborskiy, Igor**
I Like Limited

**Sampalli, Sridhar Rao**
Graviti Healthcare Limited

**Sampong, Ernest Bediako**
Exeter Health Limited

**Samson, David Michael**
Bioquote Limited

**Sanders, William John**
Mawdsley-Brooks & Co Ltd

**Sanderson-Watts, Gail**
Mawdsley-Brooks & Co Ltd

**Sandhu, Kamal**
Inspiragen Limited

**Sangha, Rajinder Singh**
All Med Care Limited

**Sanghvi, Nishma Amit**
Pharmed Health Care Organisation Ltd

**Sanson, David Alan**
U L Medicines Limited

**Sanz, Jose Maria, Dr**
Astellas Pharma Ltd.
Bripharm Limited

**Saragnese, Eugene**
Mirada Medical Limited

**Sarkaz, Ahmad**
Oxford Medpharma Ltd

**Sarkaz, Sara Jane**
Oxford Medpharma Ltd

**Sarna, Rajiv**
RJP Impex Ltd

**Sarner, Marcus**
Martal Cosmetics Limited

**Sarwar, Akeel**
Akysha Limited

**Sarwar, Asim**
Rightdose Solutions Limited

**Sarwar, Mohammad**
Pharma 313 Limited

**Sasaki, Yuji**
Medreich PLC

**Sault, Andrew David**
Sure Health & Beauty Limited

**Saundh, Harinder Singh**
Inspiragen Limited

**Saundh, Kamaljeet Singh**
Totally Pharmacy Ltd

**Saundh, Rajpal Kaur**
Totally Pharmacy Ltd

**Saurabh, Shashi Bhushan**
Arco Iris Limited

**Savage, Damian**
Mad Doctor Holdings Limited

**Savalia, Dharmesh Gordadhanbhai**
Clymed Healthcare Ltd

**Savdas, Jay Ranjit**
Hot Pharma Ltd

**Savdas, Kalpesh**
Hot Pharma Ltd

**Savitt, Jonathan Alan**
Ozonex Limited

**Savitt, Maria Luise**
Ozonex Limited

**Savla, Prashant**
Ranbaxy (U.K.) Limited

**Saxena, Kunal**
Pharmacare (London) Limited

**Saxena, Navin Satyapal, Dr**
Pharmacare (London) Limited

**Saymour, Jenna May**
Internal Luxe Heights Ltd

**Schack, Bernard Jacques**
Gemapharm Limited

**Schaefer, Drew**
Universal Marine Medical Ltd

**Schauder, Colin, Dr**
Global Medical Supplies Ltd

**Scheefers, Johannes**
Schebo Biotech UK Limited

**Scheefers-Borchel, Ursula, Dr**
Schebo Biotech UK Limited

**Schiele, Martin John**
Boost Hair Limited
Rosalique Skincare Limited
Salcura Limited

**Schiller, Olivier Nestor**
Septodont Limited

**Schmid, Robert Andrew**
Gammaservice Limited

**Schmidt, Emmanuel**
Dallas Burston Ashbourne Holdings
Ethypharm UK Limited

**Schoeller, Martin**
Croma-Pharma Limited

**Schofield, Julian Paul, Dr**
Napp Pharmaceuticals Limited
Qdem Pharmaceuticals Limited

**Scholten, Melchior Catharina Martinus Jozef**
Orly Pharma Limited

**Schram, Hans, Drs**
Nordic Pharma Limited

**Schroeder, Peter**
MDD Europe Limited

**Schulz, Klemens Walter, Doctor**
L & R Medical UK Ltd.

**Schulze, Daniel Benjamin Matthias**
Astellas Pharma Europe Ltd.

**Schwabl, Herbert**
Padma Healthcare Limited

**Sciotti, Alfonso**
SQR Pharma Consulting Ltd

**Scott, Christopher John**
Pharmahouse Limited

**Scott, David, Dr**
Lumiradx International Ltd

**Scott, Nicholas Peter**
Aspen Pharmacare UK Limited

**Scott, Paul Guthrie**
Norpan Hymbre Ltd

**Scott, Siobhan Marie**
Kids Medicare Limited

**Scott, Terence Richard**
Bejaa Medical (UK) Limited

**Scrimgeour, Kenneth Eric**
Norgine Pharmaceuticals Ltd

**Searle, Sophie Louise**
Tank Puffin (Wholesale) Ltd

**Sebjan, Zsolt**
Gate Pharma Ltd

**Seddon, Peter James**
Morgan Steer Developments Ltd

**Sedghi, Leyla**
Technoglobal Ltd

**Sedwell, Christopher John**
Unomedical Limited

**See, Fritz Hans**
American Biochemical and Pharmaceuticals

**Seehra, Gurdeep Singh**
G S Seehra Limited

**Sefton, Petre**
Turtle Rouge Ltd

**Segev, Nativ**
MGC Pharma (UK) Ltd

**Seifi, Marjaneh**
Aneid UK Limited

**Seiler, Frank**
Stada UK Holdings Ltd.

**Seller, Colin Malcolm**
Pfizer Limited

**Sellers, Frank**
Geistlich Sons Limited

**Semmens, Phillip**
Accord Healthcare Limited

**Sempere, Thierry**
Linepharma International Ltd

**Semple, John**
CBD Oil Direct Limited

**Seng, San Bing**
Peter & Guys Salon Professional Ltd

**Seng, Sin Mon**
Peter & Guys Salon Professional Ltd

**Senior, Katie, Dr**
378 Co Ltd

**Seow, Soonick**
Instachem Limited

**Seres, Michael Joseph**
11 Health & Technologies Ltd

**Serry, Nakisa**
Celgene Limited
Celgene UK Distribution Ltd

**Seshan, Srinivasan**
Zista Pharma Limited

**Sethupathy, Raja**
E-Pharma Chemical Int. Limited

**Seyan, Muhamed Ismail Muhamed**
Mera Pharma Limited

**Seymour, Ruth**
Matt 6:33 Ltd

**Shaban, Jinan Shakir**
Hana Supplies Limited

**Shabir, Asad**
Ihealthcare Genius Limited

**Shadibaeva, Aziza**
Medtech Trading Limited

**Shadoobuccus, Zohra Allimah**
Sonifar Pharma Expert Limited

**Shaer, Phillip Stephen**
Spectrum Biomedical UK Limited

**Shafiq, Mohammed Choudhary, Dr**
O'Connell Pharma Ltd

**Shafiq, Robina Naz**
Henley Laboratories Limited

**Shah, Aarsh**
Sakar Healthcare UK Ltd.

**Shah, Alpesh Bhanuchandra**
Chemi-Call Ltd
Mobility2you Ltd

**Shah, Amratlal Velji**
Per-Medic Limited

**Shah, Amritlal Lalji**
Pharm - Tex Limited

**Shah, Anil Lalji**
Pharm - Tex Limited

**Shah, Anoop Shashikant**
Medipro Pharma Limited

**Shah, Anuj Ramniklal Shamji**
Global 1st Ltd

**Shah, Anuj Somchand**
Drugsrus Limited
P.I.E. Pharma Limited
Star Pharmaceuticals Limited

**Shah, Bhagyesh Nitinkumar**
Unison Pharmaceuticals Ltd

**Shah, Bhanuchandra**
Chemi-Call Ltd
Mobility2you Ltd

**Shah, Bharat Gulabchand**
R & D Healthcare Ltd

**Shah, Bharat Kumar Hansraj Devraj**
OPD Laboratories Limited
RX Farma Limited
Sigma Pharmaceuticals PLC

**Shah, Bharti Sureshchand**
Parkview Leicester Limited

**Shah, Bhavin Manish**
Sigma Pharmaceuticals PLC

**Shah, Binita**
SRS Pharma Limited

**Shah, Chetna**
R & D Healthcare Ltd

**Shah, Dilip Raichand**
Dasco (Wholesale) Limited
Dasco Investment Corporation Ltd

**Shah, Dipti Rajesh**
Prominer Limited

**Shah, Harshil, Dr**
Benident Limited

**Shah, Hasmukh Lalji**
Icone International Limited

**Shah, Hasmukh Velji**
Per-Medic Limited

**Shah, Hasu Shamir**
Icone International Limited

**Shah, Hatul Bharat Kumar**
Sigma Pharmaceuticals PLC

**Shah, Jayoti Bharat**
Sigma Pharmaceuticals PLC

**Shah, Kalpana Manish**
Sigma Pharmaceuticals PLC

**Shah, Kamal Hansraj**
OPD Laboratories Limited
Sigma Pharmaceuticals PLC

**Shah, Kamalkumar**
G P Supplies Limited
Myriad Medical Supplies Ltd

**Shah, Kiritkumar Meghji**
Elite Pharma (Surrey) Limited

**Shah, Manish Hansraj**
OPD Laboratories Limited
RX Farma Limited
Sigma Pharmaceuticals PLC

**Shah, Manish Somchand**
Anuva International Limited

**Shah, Mayurkumar Velji**
Per-Medic Limited

**Shah, Milan Yogesh**
Naturelo Ltd

**Shah, Milankumar**
Jambo Supplies Limited

**Shah, Minal**
Chela Animal Health Limited

**Shah, Naishadh**
Healthbest Limited

**Shah, Nalin Lalji**
Pharm - Tex Limited

**Shah, Neel Rameshchandra**
Sanay Ltd

**Shah, Niketkumar Dipakkumar**
Essential-Healthcare Ltd

**Shah, Nishal Kamal**
Sigma Pharmaceuticals PLC

**Shah, Paras Kamal**
Sigma Pharmaceuticals PLC

**Shah, Rajendra**
Metro Pharmacy Limited

**Shah, Rajesh Ramanlal**
Prominer Limited

**Shah, Rajiv Bharat Kumar**
Chela Animal Health Limited
Sigma Pharmaceuticals PLC

**Shah, Raxit Kirit Kumar**
Pergamon Ltd
Tradewings Worldwide Ltd

**Shah, Sachin Manish**
Sigma Pharmaceuticals PLC

**Shah, Sandhya Shailendra**
Shoebury West Road Ltd

**Shah, Shailendra Chandulal**
Shoebury West Road Ltd

**Shah, Shaili Anuj**
Global 1st Ltd

**Shah, Shila**
G P Supplies Limited
Myriad Medical Supplies Ltd

**Shah, Siddharth**
SRS Pharma Limited

**Shah, Siddhit**
Chemys Limited

**Shah, Sureshchand Bharmal**
Parkview Leicester Limited

**Shah, Syeda Sofia**
Accendo Pharma Ltd

**Shah, Tushar Jayantilal**
Moores Pharmacy Limited

**Shah, Tushar Vinodchandra**
Medipro Pharma Limited

**Shah, Vinay Lalji**
Pharm - Tex Limited

**Shah, Vinod Thakorlal**
Vitachem Limited

**Shah, Vipul**
Servipharm Limited

**Shah, Viral**
Sakar Healthcare UK Ltd.

**Shaheen, Lubna**
LS Pharma UK Limited

**Shahid, Dur-E-Shahwar, Dr**
Sahu & Co Limited

**Shahid, Muhammad Usman**
Bin'auf Limited

**Shahzad, Mohammed Khuram**
KW Wholesale Ltd

**Shaikh, Tajuddin**
Emcure Pharma UK Ltd
Tillomed Laboratories Limited

**Shaker, Jahanzeb**
Saving Life Technologies Ltd

**Shakespeare, Paul Anthony**
Shakespeare Pharma Ltd

**Shakespeare, Simon Robert**
2 Shy 2 Buy Limited
A V Pharma Limited
Ayva Pharma Limited

**Shakespeare, Simon**
Shakespeare Pharma Ltd

**Shallal, Ousameh**
Sanos Healthcare Ltd

**Shalviri, Mehdi**
Rolling Stones Trading Ltd

**Shami, Muhammad Naeem**
Tagma Pharma (UK) Ltd

**Shamoon, Matthew**
Brent Medicare Limited

**Shamoon, Zain Manhal, Dr**
Brent Medicare Limited

**Shamot, Durgham Wasif**
IMS Euro Limited

**Shamroukh, Samer**
Healthcare Source Limited

**Shamshudin, Farhan Karim**
Cibus Animal Nutrition Ltd

**Shamsudeen, Sabeel, Dr**
Vegamed UK Limited

**Shamsudin, Farouk**
Alfavet Animal Healthcare Ltd

**Shanahan, John Joseph**
Biomarin (U.K.) Ltd.

**Shane, Michael Kenneth**
Infinite Percent Limited

**Sharbain, Shadi Jabra**
All1 Limited

**Sharief, Mohamed**
Allied Pharmacies Limited

**Sharief, Suhail**
Sharief Pharma Limited

**Sharif, Akhira Khan**
Stellar Labs Ltd

**Sharif, Ala Towfiq, Dr**
A.H.P. Medical Supplies Ltd

**Sharif, Dara Karim**
Ely Pharma Ltd

**Sharif, Omar**
Stellar Labs Ltd

**Shariff, Zohaib**
Accendo Pharma Ltd
Worldtrition Ltd

**Sharma, Ajay**
Manek Healthcare Ltd

**Sharma, Deepak**
Ros Nutrition UK Ltd.
Vitanutrition UK Ltd.

**Sharma, Jitendra Mahavirprasad**
Relonchem Limited

**Sharma, Neeraj**
Ranbaxy (U.K.) Limited

**Sharma, Pranav**
Authentic Ayurveda Limited

**Sharma, Rakesh**
Valentis Life Sciences Limited

**Sharma, Ridhima**
Iberia Skin Brands Ltd

**Sharma, Siddhesh**
Authentic Ayurveda Limited

**Sharma, Swati**
Vyom International Ltd.

**Sharma, Vikram, Dr**
Vyom International Ltd.

**Sharman, John Stewart**
Medical Developments UK Ltd

**Sharov, Dmitrii**
Pharm Recon Ltd

**Sharpe, Gary L**
Distinctive Medical Products Ltd

**Sharpe, Robert**
Purple Surgical International Ltd
Purple Surgical UK Limited

**Sharples, Jane Anne, Dr**
Bray Pharma Limited
Henley Laboratories Limited

**Shaw, Keith Derek**
E.S.Shaw & Sons Limited

**Shaw, Alan Norman Sidney**
E.S.Shaw & Sons Limited

**Fothergill, Elizabeth Jane**
Ivor Shaw Limited

**Fryer, Luke Richard**
Ivor Shaw Limited

**Shaw, David Nicholas**
Ivor Shaw Limited

**Shaw, Ian Martin**
Ivor Shaw Limited

**Shaw, Barry Michael Howard**
Bio-Synergy Limited

**Shaw, John McCallum Marshall**
Biocon Pharma UK Limited

**Shaw, Julia Lauren**
C & P Medical Trading Limited
Crystal Healthcare Limited

**Shaw, Mark Jeffrey**
Animal Prescriptions Limited

**Shaw, Peter John**
C & P Medical Trading Limited
Crystal Healthcare Limited

**Shawki El Morsy Yousef, Mohamed, Dr**
Bioceutics UK Ltd

**Shear, Dalya**
Danel Trading Limited

**Sheffner, Marc John**
Pan Globus Limited

**Shehata, Mona Elsayed Elbadawy Mohamed**
Tuba Ltd

**Sheikh, Abdirahman**
Irmaan Limited

**Sheikh-Ahmed, Mohamed**
Irmaan Limited

**Shekhawat, Satpal Singh, Dr**
Lifecare Limited

**Sheldon, Timothy John Austin**
Adelphi (Tubes) Limited

**Shelley, Mark Iain**
Sylk Limited

**Sherali, Janali**
J Sherlee Ltd

**Sheth, Anil Nandlal**
Telephone House Limited

**Sheth, Himatbala**
Telephone House Limited

**Sheth, Kamlesh, Dr**
Doksy Limited

**Sheth, Kaushal Pravinchandra**
East Midlands Infotech PVT Ltd

**Shetty, Bavaguthu Raghuram, Dr**
Neo Farma Ltd

**Shi, Jun**
Everypharma Co., Ltd.

**Shipwright, Robert Ernest**
Old Latchmerians Limited

**Shirali, Pourya**
Paria Medical Aesthetics Ltd

**Shiwach, Ashwini Kumar**
AAR Pharma Ltd

**Shnaf, Monzer Moneer**
United Pharma Ltd

**Shodunke, Olubukola Taofik**
Koasta Limited

**Shrikhande, Bharatbhushan Krishnakant**
Authentic Ayurveda Limited

**Shrimanker, Jawahar**
Panacea Health UK Limited

**Shrimanker, Urshula**
Panacea Health UK Limited

**Shrivastava, Salil**
Chewton Ventures Limited

**Shrivastava, Sameer**
Rowtech Limited
Springbourne Management and Trading Ltd

**Siadati, Rana**
Gate2pharma Ltd

**Sibley, Aaron**
Allergan Limited

**Sidaway, Peter Anthony**
N & G Pharma Limited

**Siddique, Shabana**
Medstore Limited

**Sideri, Athina**
Tour N' Cure International Ltd.

**Sidhu, Amandip**
Aspect Pharma Limited

**Sidhu, Mandip Kaur**
Pharmaceutical Health Limited

**Sidhu, Manjinder Singh**
Sidhupharm Limited

**Sigalas, Alexandros**
Vifor Pharma UK Limited

**Sihra, Saranjit Singh, Dr**
Simply Meds Pro Ltd

**Silcox, Cheryll-Anne Patricia**
Aayur Limited

**Silcox, Nigel Patrick**
Aayur Limited

**Silva Ritter, Jose Eugenio**
Perrington & Co Limited
Soliphar Limited

**Silver, David Alan**
Mundibiopharma Limited
Mundipharma Medical Co Ltd
Napp Pharmaceuticals Limited
Qdem Pharmaceuticals Limited

**Simon, Sanford Robert**
Ethicor Pharma Ltd

**Simons, Ian**
Toiletry Sales Limited

**Simpson, Glen Tyrrell**
G & L Simpson Limited

**Simpson, Laura-Anne**
G & L Simpson Limited

**Simpson, Kevin Alan**
Sunniside Healthcare Limited

**Simpson, Mark**
Baymed Healthcare Ltd.

**Sims, Mel**
Biosure (UK) Limited

**Singh Chohan, Balraj**
SF Pharma Limited

**Singh, Gulbir**
Uvita Health Limited

**Singh, Gurmeet Kishore**
Wilkies International Ltd

**Singh, Gurnam**
Clinicpharma Limited

**Singh, Jeet**
Five Pharm Ltd

**Singh, Onkar**
Glucozen Limited

**Singh, Ripudaman**
Pharma Oasis Ltd

**Singh, Sandeep**
Ascend Laboratories (UK) Ltd

**Singh, Sawern Singh**
GHC (UK) Ltd
GHC Global Limited

**Singh, Somendra**
KGP Laboratories (UK) Limited

**Singhvi, Kshitij**
SV Syon Med Ltd

**Siokas, Grigorios**
Decahedron Ltd

**Sipkovits, Lajos, Dr**
Hyaluron Health Ltd

**Sira, Gurcharan Singh**
Medicare Products Limited
PH Medicare Ltd

**Sira, James Anthony Hari Singh**
Medicare Products Limited
PH Medicare Ltd

**Sirpal, Rakesh Kumar**
RSS Wholesaling Limited

**Sirpal, Sonam**
RSS Wholesaling Limited

**Sirpal, Sudesh Bala**
RSS Wholesaling Limited

**Sissou, Panikos, Dr**
Rothschild Pharmacy Limited

**Sivasubramanian, Appuraj**
Crown Global Traders Limited

**Skare, Janos**
Vitafree Health Limited

**Skelton, James Henry**
Sure Health & Beauty Limited

**Skene, Andrew Richard**
Source Healthcare Ltd

**Skene, Laura Frances**
Source Healthcare Ltd

**Skiadopoulos Seimenis, Anastasios**
Holistic Med Ltd

**Skillman, Samuel Andrew**
Nanocor World Holdings Limited

**Slabik, Rafal**
Skarby Gai Ltd

**Slade, Paul David**
Fab Medical Limited
Universal Marine Medical Ltd

**Slebir, John L**
Vivus UK Limited

**Slepetys, Raimondas**
PB & T Project Ltd

**Slevin, Patrick Cyril Peter**
Omapharm Limited

**Slicer, Mark Robert**
Augmenix UK Limited

**Smart, Gary**
Pharma Procurement Services Ltd

**Smejkal, Christopher, Dr**
Medisante Limited

**Smet, Franz Willi Gustav**
International Ingredients and Chemicals (IIC)

**Smit, Andre Louis**
Omron Healthcare UK Limited

**McAleese, Grainne**
Robert Smith & Co, (Derry) Ltd

**Tallon, Louise**
Robert Smith & Co, (Derry) Ltd

**Smith, Adam Robert**
Fittleworth Medical Limited

**Smith, Alan Anthony**
Reliance Medical Ltd

**Smith, Anthony Craig**
M.R.S. Scientific Limited

**Smith, Brett Michael**
M.R.S. Scientific Limited

**Smith, Brian John**
Sentinel Laboratories Limited

**Smith, Clinton Luke**
Nanocor World Holdings Limited

**Smith, Haydn Peter**
Doncaster Pharmaceuticals Group Ltd
Eclipse Generics Limited
Testerworld Limited

**Smith, Ivor Randle**
Schebo Biotech UK Limited

**Smith, Lesley Ann**
M.R.S. Scientific Limited

**Smith, Luke Andrew**
M.R.S. Scientific Limited

**Smith, Mark Anthony**
Medi-Inn (UK) Ltd

**Smith, Martyn James**
Quirky Vapes Ltd

**Smith, Michael Robert**
M.R.S. Scientific Limited

**Smith, Nathan James**
Leverton & Co Ltd

**Smith, Penelope Jane**
Sentinel Laboratories Limited

**Smith, Peter Jeffrey**
Axis Medical Limited

**Smith, Philip John**
FreshBreathOnline Limited

**Smith, Simon Addison**
Harben Medical Limited

**Smith, Timothy Peter**
Devonshire Healthcare Services Ltd

**Smolen-Kenawy, Aneta**
Secret Line Ltd

**Sneddon, Samuel Redcliffe**
TTS Pharma Limited

**Snell, Richard Andrew**
Dermocore Ltd.

**Snelson, Ian Martin**
SSCP Blink Bidco Limited
Vision Pharmaceuticals Ltd

**Snyman, Jan Harm**
Bestlon Limited
Zefer Pharma Ltd.

**Sodha, Anup**
LTT Pharma Limited
Lexon (UK) Limited
Lexon UK Holdings Limited
Norchem Limited

**Sodha, Nitin Trembaklal**
LTT Pharma Limited
Lexon (UK) Limited
Lexon UK Holdings Limited
Norchem Limited

**Sodha, Pankaj**
LTT Pharma Limited
Lexon (UK) Limited
Lexon UK Holdings Limited
Norchem Limited

**Sofuoglu, Sinan Cengiz**
Pharmargus Healthcare Ltd

**Sohawon, Muhammad Taha**
Centurion Park Pharmaceuticals Ltd

**Sokolov, Dmitry**
PTGO Sever UK Limited

**Solanki, Kaushal Singh**
Torrent Pharma (UK) Ltd

**Sollie, Philippe**
Flen Health UK Ltd

**Solomon, Daniel Emeka**
Randa Pharma Ltd

**Solomon, David Louis Charles, Dr**
Genesis Pharma Limited
Genesis Pharmaceuticals Ltd

**Somaiya, Nikita**
Lax Pharma Limited

**Somji, Munir**
Priors Pharma Limited

**Soni, Ashok**
Hurley Assets Limited

**Sonn, Young Sun**
Oak Zone Biotech UK Ltd

**Sonpal, Pritesh Ramesh**
LTT Pharma Limited
Lexon (UK) Limited
Lexon UK Holdings Limited
Norchem Limited

**Sooch, Gursharen Singh**
Kingsley Specials Limited

**Sooch, Gursharen**
Mulberry Pharma Ltd

**Sooch, Gursheran**
MKS Pharma Ltd

**Sopolinski, Sobieslaw Arkadiusz**
MSP Pharm Ltd

**Soriot, Pascal Claude Roland**
Astrazeneca PLC

**Sos, Natasa**
Saxonia Medical Ltd.

**Sothimaheswaran, Sothinagaratnam**
Abra Wholesales Ltd

**Soumahoro, Souleymane**
Benatur Limited

**Spaggiari, Giuliano**
THD (UK) Limited

**Spain, Abraham**
Eden CBD Limited

**Spang, Angela Helen**
June Medical International Ltd

**Spang, Angela Helene, Lady**
June Medical Ltd

**Sparrow, Christopher William**
JLVET Ltd
Mossvet Limited

**Sparrow, Christopher**
Farmvet Limited

**Sparrow, Dermot S.H**
Mossvet Limited

**Sparrow, Juliet Rosalie**
Mossvet Limited

**Sparrow, Juliet**
JLVET Ltd

**Sparrow, Michael John Frederick**
Grey Traders Limited

**Sparrow, Olwyn Anne**
Grey Traders Limited

**Spearman, Kevin Michael Heath**
Ace First Aid Supplies Ltd

**Spears, Joseph Brian**
Omnicell Limited

**Clift, Sharon**
The Specials Laboratory Ltd

**Smith, Jimmy Ray**
The Specials Laboratory Ltd

**Sparks, Lester David**
The Specials Laboratory Ltd

**Spence, Alex**
Full Spectrum Pharma Limited

**Spence, Harvey Graeme**
Kavia Tooling Limited

**Spencer, Joanne**
Priory Pharma Ltd

**Spicer, Charles Alexander Evan**
11 Health & Technologies Ltd

**Spiller-Boulter, Lucy Catherine, Dr**
Instant Test Ltd

**Spindler, Thomas**
Grunenthal Limited

**Spiteri, Robert**
Mediva Pharma Limited

**Gore, Michael Andrew**
Alan Spivack Limited

**Spivack, David Daniel**
Alan Spivack Limited

**Spooner, Christopher Paul**
Acorus Therapeutics Limited

**Spotswood, Dean Cameron**
Acre Medical Limited

**Spotswood, Dean**
Acre Pharma Limited

**Sprey, Laurence Simon**
Ashtons Healthcare Limited
Ashtons Medical Limited
Ashtons Medical Supplies Ltd

**Sproat, Dave**
Astek Innovations Limited

**Squindo, Fritz**
Recordati Pharmaceuticals Ltd

**Squire, Pauline**
Westland Pharmaceuticals Ltd

**Squire, Raymond Leslie**
Westland Pharmaceuticals Ltd

**Sra, Amit Bir Singh, Dr**
JAO Enterprises Ltd

**Srimal, Ajit Chand**
Emcure Pharma UK Ltd
Pharmazz Europe Limited
Tillomed Laboratories Limited

**Srivastava, Raka, Dr**
Anrise Trading Limited

**Stamato, Carmelo**
Panorama Healthcare Limited

**Staples, Ian Lawrence**
Matoke Holdings Limited
Surgihoney Limited

**Staples, Stuart Michael**
Matoke Holdings Limited

**Starr, Moira Felicity**
Zena Cosmetics (U.K.) Limited

**Starr, Oliver Henry**
Zena Cosmetics (U.K.) Limited

**Stead Deegan, Chloe**
Soothingproducts Ltd

**Stead Deegan, Hannah**
Soothingproducts Ltd

**Stead, Martin**
Soothingproducts Ltd

**Stead, Richard George**
Zymix Limited

**Steckler, Paul Leopold**
AF Healthcare Ltd

**Steeples, Christopher Keith**
Espere Healthcare Limited

**Stefanov, Vasil**
Bulgarian Healthy Products Ltd

**Steffen, Robert Tobias**
Oxford Supramolecular Biotechnology

**Stegeman, William Jackson**
Jackson Immunoresearch Europe Ltd

**Stein, Alexandra Margaret Murray**
Hilotherm Ltd

**Stein, Callum Wallace Alexander**
Hilotherm Ltd

**Stein, Katharine Elisabeth Derdre**
Hilotherm Ltd

**Stein, Wallace George William**
Hilotherapy UK Limited
Hilotherm Ltd

**Stephens III, Jack Thomas**
McKesson Global Procurement & Sourcing
McKesson Global Sourcing UK Ltd

**Stephens, Kevin**
Galen Limited
Intergal Pharma Limited

**Stephenson, Deborah Anne**
MD-Reproductive Health Solutions Ltd

**Stephenson, Peter Murray**
MD-Reproductive Health Solutions Ltd

**Stevens, Angela Susan**
ABC Healthcare Limited

**Stevenson, Alison**
Tor Generics Limited

**Stevenson, Laraine**
Mercia Dental Equipment Ltd

**Stevenson, Neil**
Mercia Dental Equipment Ltd

**Stockdale, Kevin Anthony**
Eco Animal Health Group PLC

**Stockdale, Tracy Anne**
SDM Healthcare Limited

**Stockley, Peter Darran**
Independence Products Ltd

**Stocks, Steven**
Boston Healthcare Limited

**Stone, Jason Vincent**
Bial Pharma UK Limited

**Story, Risha**
WR Mediservices Limited

**Story, William Peter, Dr**
WR Mediservices Limited

**Strachan, Ian Cameron**
NPA Services Limited

**Straup, Kenneth Alan**
Fittleworth Medical Limited

**Straus, Daniel Reuben**
S & D Pharma Limited

**Straus, John**
Astek Innovations Limited

**Stringer, Dustin**
Probiotec (UK) Limited

**Stringer, Wesley**
Probiotec (UK) Limited

**Strub, Oliver**
Santhera (UK) Limited

**Stubbs, Michael Anthony**
Ash Medical Limited

**Stubley, David Ian**
Stainweld Limited

**Sturgess, Melissa Josephine**
Tiamat Agriculture Ltd

**Stylianou, Stylianos**
Ray Pharm Limited

**Styring, Leah Jane**
Leverton & Co Ltd

**Sudera, Ashwani**
Europlus Pharma Ltd
N.G. Limited

**Sudera, Sudha**
N.G. Limited

**Sudera, Vijay Kumar**
Europlus Pharma Ltd
N.G. Limited

**Suessle, Wolfgang**
L & R Medical UK Ltd.

**Sufi, Hassan Mohamoud**
Sufi Enterprise Wholesalers Ltd

**Sugumaran, Subbiah**
Einoxy Limited

**Sukumaran, Sheena**
Condomania PLC
Langdales Limited
Sutherland Health Group Ltd

**Sullivan, Christine Olga**
Pharmasure Limited

**Sullivan, Ronald Thomas**
Cosmestore Limited

**Sullivan, Terence**
Pharmasure Limited

**Sultana, Shahista**
Orphic Limited

**Sumaria-Shah, Surendra Kumar**
Docsinnovent Limited

**Summers, Janet Catherine**
Receptor Holdings Limited

**Summers, Steven William, Dr**
Receptor Holdings Limited

**Sun, Dandan**
H & S Beauty Care Limited

**Sun, Min**
Uni Supply Ltd

**Sunderraj, Kalpana Devi**
Vision.Net Limited

**Sunderraj, Palaniswamy, Dr**
Vision.Net Limited

**Sunely, Shabbir Bhai Gulam Abbas**
Surgicaide Medical Supplies UK Ltd

**Surve, Sheryl Vikas, Dr**
Stiefel Laboratories Limited

**Suthi, Amandeep Singh, Dr**
GHC Global Limited

**Suthi, Govinder Singh, Dr**
GHC Global Limited

**Suthi, Gurdeep Singh, Dr**
GHC Global Limited
GHC Medical Ltd

**Svoboda, Tomas**
Manta Medical Limited

**Sweeney, Kevin**
Castle Green (N.I.) Ltd

**Sweet, Andrew Timothy, Dr**
Indigo Diagnostics Limited

**Sweet, Ruth Margaret, Dr**
Indigo Diagnostics Limited

**Swift, Benjamin**
GBBC Ltd

**Swift, Nigel**
AAH Pharmaceuticals Limited
Barclay Pharmaceuticals Ltd
Blackstaff Pharmaceuticals Ltd
Lloyds Pharmacy Clinical Homecare
Masta Limited
Prima Brands Limited
Sangers (Northern Ireland) Ltd

**Syed, Mohammed Nayem**
Beximco Pharma UK Limited

**Sylla, Ali**
Millennium Global Limited

**Szymczak, Brian**
Apollo Endosurgery UK Ltd

**Tagg, Michael James**
U L Medicines Limited

**Taha, Mohammed Abdul Hameed**
London Healthcare Limited

**Taher, Tarek Radwan**
TRT Global Ltd

**Taher, Tarek**
RD & Med Co Ltd

**Tahir, Zeshan**
Z Tahir Limited

**Tahir, Sheroz**
Cynosure Group Ltd

**Tahiyeu, Raushan**
World Medicine Limited

**Tailor, Bhasker**
Euro Ceuticals Limited

**Takac, Michal**
Carun (UK) Limited
Zerocann Ltd

**Takasu, Kazuo Koshiji**
Santen UK Limited

**Takizawa, Hiromasa**
Medreich PLC

**Takrouri, Fadel**
SF Pharma Limited

**Takrouri, Sireen**
SF Pharma Limited

**Talbot, Richard Ian**
Leverton & Co Ltd

**Tallon, Louise**
Alchem PLC
Mansett Limited

**Talsma, Claudia**
Rosalique Skincare Limited
Salcura Limited

**Tammewar, Sachin**
SG Pharma UK Limited

**Tams, Dean**
Full Spectrum Pharma Limited

**Tamura, Nobuhiko**
Sunovion Pharmaceuticals Europe Ltd.

**Tan, Harriet Mei-Lin, Dr**
Bioforce (U.K) Limited

**Tan, Janyn Elizabeth**
Bioforce (U.K) Limited

**Tan, Jen Wei**
Bioforce (U.K) Limited

**Tan, Johannes**
Bioforce (U.K) Limited

**Tan, Li-Anna Elizabeth, Dr**
Bioforce (U.K) Limited

**Tan, Sow Poh**
IM High Tech Limited

**Taneja, Sagina**
Ros Nutrition UK Ltd.
Vitanutrition UK Ltd.

**Tang, Yilin**
Carbotang Limited

**Tang, Yuk-Ki**
Sante Primaire Limited

**Tanna, Nikin**
Primrose Hudson Limited

**Tannenbaum, Charles Mendel**
Euromed (U.K) Limited
Jenson Chemicals Limited

**Tannenbaum, Fiona**
Euromed (U.K) Limited
Jenson Chemicals Limited

**Tanner, Mark Edwin**
Incyte Biosciences UK Ltd

**Tapia, Izeth Del Carmen Samudio**
Dion Trade Ltd.

**Tapia, Izeth Del Carment Samudio**
Vestex Trade Ltd

**Tapia, Izeth Samudio**
SD Alliance Ltd.

**Tarafder, Aziz Haque**
Tabtime Limited

**Tariq, Zenib Jabeen**
Z T Locums Ltd

**Tasbihgou, Hamid Reza**
Koln Pharma Ltd
Logichem Ltd

**Taslaq, Samer, Dr**
Value Medical Limited

**Tatar, Alina Ligia**
Farmsvet Ltd

**Taunk, Manu Bhagwanlal**
Ria Sales Corporation Ltd

**Taylor, David Winston**
Merlin Vet Export Ltd

**Taylor, Michael James**
Manx Generics Limited

**Taylor, Paul Norman**
Rafarm UK Limited

**Taylor, Richard Jeffery**
Manx Generics Limited
Oakways Healthcare Limited

**Taylor, Richard William**
Accutest Solutions Limited

**Taylor, Simone Elizabeth**
European Veterinary Supplies Ltd
Manx Healthcare Limited
Manx Pharma Ltd

**Tedham, Martin John**
Qualiti (Burnley) Limited

**Tejani, Amirali Sharif**
In 2 Healthcare Limited

**Tejani, Karim Sharif Dharamshi**
In 2 Healthcare Limited

**Tejani, Nazirali Sharif Dharamshi**
In 2 Healthcare Limited

**Tejani, Salim Sharif Dharamshi**
In 2 Healthcare Limited

**Telica, Pavels**
RP Pharma International Ltd

**Telka, Lydia Alexandra**
Medisale Limited

**Tenda, Balambila Gloria**
Hasting Pharma Ltd

**Teodor, Elena Daniella**
Axe Pharma Ltd

**Terawaki, Yoshiki**
Summit Pharmaceuticals Europe Ltd

**Tesfai, Amaniel**
Moriah Healthcare Distribution Ltd

**Tetard, Jean-Luc**
Stragen UK Limited

**Teuliere, Remi**
Hemodia UK Ltd

**Thacker, Ashwin Jethalal**
Flamingo Pharma (UK) Ltd

**Thacker, Pranay Ashwin**
Flamingo Pharma (UK) Ltd

**Thakkar, Dip Shameet**
Unimed Healthcare Supplies Ltd

**Thakkar, Dip**
Global SCS Limited
Nutramax Ltd

**Thakkar, Rahkesh Vijay**
Unimed Global Limited
Univape Global Ltd

**Thakkar, Ronak Vijay**
Unimed Global Limited
Univape Global Ltd

**Thakuri, Sufal**
Tradebuffalo Ltd

**Thau, Edmund Johannes Heinrich**
Dentel Group Ltd

**Thayananthan, Bhavani**
Abra Wholesales Ltd

**Thayananthan, Thuraichamy**
Abra Wholesales Ltd

**Theobald, Nigel James**
N4 Biotech Limited

**Theofanous, Faidra**
Deltapharma Limited

**Thomas, Andrew David**
Evolve Generics Limited
Evolve Pharma Limited
Lamyra International Limited

**Thomas, Carolyn Maria**
Haydn Healthcare UK Limited

**Thomas, Eric**
Biotest (U.K.) Limited

**Thomas, Gareth Bryn**
McKesson Global Procurement & Sourcing
McKesson Global Sourcing UK Ltd

**Thomas, Janette Denise**
Selective Supplies Limited

**Thomas, Martin John**
Haydn Healthcare UK Limited

**Thomas, Phillip Huw**
Selective Supplies Limited

**Thompson, Charlotte Valentina**
Anti Venom Ltd

**Thompson, Julian Keith, Doctor**
Pfizer Limited

**Thompson, William Andrew**
Creative Supply Solutions Ltd

**Thong, Yew Huey**
Pharmhouse Ltd
Welfare Healthcare (UK) Ltd

**Thorne, Kathryn**
KM Consulting (Chesterfield) Ltd

**Thorne, Mark William**
KM Consulting (Chesterfield) Ltd

**Thorpe, Richard John**
KDC-UK Ltd.
RJT Pharma Services Ltd

**Thrower, Keith James, Dr**
Atlanta Biological Europe Ltd

**Tiberg, Sven Fredrik**
Camurus Ltd

**Tickle, Stephen**
Epsilon Pharmaceuticals Ltd

**Tickner, Timothy Martin**
Biophage Therapeutics Ltd
Ethicor Pharma Ltd

**Tierney, Daniel Peter Nicholas**
Crosscare Export Limited

**Tierney, Donal Thomas Martin**
Crosscare Export Limited

**Tierney, Jonathan James**
Crosscare Export Limited

**Tilley, Alan**
Atlantic Imaging Limited

**Timmis, Jonathan**
Pharmalab Limited
RB (China Trading) Limited
Reckitt Benckiser Asia Pacific Ltd

**Timoney, Emillio Reuben Javan**
Arquella Ltd

**Tims, Geoffrey Alan**
Manor Drug Company (Nottingham) Ltd

**Tinsley, David John**
Pharmacare Logistics Limited
Healthcare Product Services Ltd

**Tinsley, David John**
Healthcare Services Group Ltd
Movianto UK Limited

**Titley, Paul Charlton**
N4 Biotech Limited

**Tkachenko, Jane**
Amaxa Pharma Ltd

**Tkachenko, Vladimir**
Amaxa Pharma Ltd

**Toda, Kohei**
Kosei Pharma UK Ltd.

**Todd, Graeme**
Natures Merchant Ltd

**Todorov, Todor**
Cellexa Limited

**Todorova, Tsvetelina Yankova**
Cellexa Limited

**Tojin, Aswathy**
Allans Healthcare Limited

**Tokatly, Gloria**
General Pharmaceuticals Ltd

**Tokatly, Ziad**
General Pharmaceuticals Ltd

**Toma, Jurijs**
Sfera Trading Limited

**Toncheva, Maria**
Medaesthetics Limited

**Toner, Yvette Antoinette**
Y A Toner Limited

**Tong, Jianxin**
Taineng Medicine Ltd

**Tooby, David Charles**
Beachcourse Limited

**Toomey, Charles Edward**
Matrix Healthcare Limited
Matrix Healthcare Solutions Ltd

**Toon, Peter John**
Future Healthcare Ltd

**Toor, Inderpal Kaur**
Herbert and Herbert Pharmacy Ltd

**Toor, Sarvjit Singh**
Herbert and Herbert Pharmacy Ltd

**Topp, Adam**
Humn Pharmaceuticals (UK) Ltd

**Topper, Brian**
Animal Prescriptions Limited

**Topping, Frederick John**
Prodigy Healthcare Limited
Trilogy Medical Systems Ltd

**Topping, Linda Jane**
Meadow Laboratories Limited

**Torelli, Stefano**
Livanova UK Limited

**Tourette, John**
Quantum Biomed Ltd

**Towler, Julie**
Whiterose Supplements Limited

**Traboulssi Barake, Abdelrahman**
Herbaleva Ltd

**Traynor, David Thomas**
Winchpharma (Consumer Healthcare) Ltd

**Trentesaux, Hubert**
Virbac Limited

**Trepp, Gian Baptista**
Precision Healthcare Limited

**Tretyakova, Alexandra**
Galderma (U.K.) Limited

**Trevaskis, Michael Bernard**
Device Technologies UK Ltd.

**Tridon, Frederic**
Bracco UK Limited

**Trikam, Maek Sultan**
Pharmaxone Limited

**Trivedi, Sameer**
Medical Drug Supplies Limited

**Trouse, Julia**
Eco Animal Health Group PLC

**Troutt, Peter**
Elanco UK AH Limited

**Truss, Francesca**
20 20 Optical Services Ltd

**Truss, Mark Patrick**
20 20 Optical Services Ltd

**Tsanev, Krasimir**
Brenton Invest and Trade Ltd

**Tsang, Chi Wai, Dr**
Pharhealth Limited

**Tsang, Fey**
Laogong Laopo Limited

**Tsoi, Wa Wing**
Biomedi Technology Limited

**Tucker, Mark Rupert**
TTS Pharma Limited

**Tudor, Cameron John**
Premax Europe Limited

**Tugnet, Anu Bala**
AG Pharmahealth Ltd

**Bennett - Roberts, Shaun**
The Tulip Cup Limited

**Tung, Nguyen Thanh**
Newtexko Ltd.

**Turk, Ebru**
ETP (UK) Limited

**Turk, Hasan**
ETP (UK) Limited

**Turner, Terence Frederick**
Pennine UK Procedure Packs Ltd

**Tuvsjoen, Bjorn**
Bugband Europe Ltd

**Tweedie, Oliver**
Sintetica Limited

**Twist, George**
George Twist (Wholesale) Ltd

**Twist, Jonathan George**
George Twist (Wholesale) Ltd

**Twyford, Antony**
Double Wing Medical Ltd

**Tyler, Christopher Charles**
Tytek UK Medical Co Ltd

**Tyler, James**
Tytek UK Medical Co Ltd

**Ubhi, Harvir**
Sky Hemp Ltd

**Ubogu, Anjela Theresa**
Swerve Cycling Limited

**Uddin, Ashraf**
GM Biopharma Ltd

**Uddin, Mohammed Osman**
London Health Suppliers Ltd

**Ukmata, Petrit**
Vitapro Limited

**Ullah, Imdad**
Global Supply (U.K.) Ltd

**Ullah, Rehan**
Regent Pharmaceuticals Limited

**Ulmann, Marion Sophie**
Linepharma International Ltd

**Unal, Eylem**
Bioactive T Pharma Limited

**Underwood, Neil Martyn**
Old Latchmerians Limited

**Ungar, Leon Alan**
Pharmacierge Group Limited
Pharmacierge Limited
Pharmacierge Technology Ltd

**Ungar, Robert David Lewis**
Pharmacierge Group Limited
Pharmacierge Limited

**Ungar, Stuart Charles, Dr**
Pharmacierge Group Limited

**Unwin, Charles Stephen**
R.I.S. Products Limited
Ris Healthcare Limited

**Unwin, Iris Dorothy**
R.I.S. Products Limited

**Unwin, Stephen Ronald**
R.I.S. Products Limited
Ris Healthcare Limited

**Upadhyay, Kaushik**
Piramal Critical Care Limited

**Upton, Mark**
Oxford Biosystems Limited

**Urbain, Jeremie Alexandre**
SERB Ltd

**Urbano, Paolo, Dr**
Five Star International Consulting

**Uruakpa, Chikwendu Onyemachi, Dr**
Chikhurst Limited

**Utomo, Harry Irawanto**
Barustore Limited

**Uvarov, Valery**
Respro-M Limited

**Uvarova, Irina**
Respro-M Limited

**Vaczi, Janos**
Creo Pharma Limited

**Vaghasiya, Chintankumar Chunilal**
Sun Exim Ltd

**Valji, Naseen**
Beta Pharmaceuticals Limited
Neon Diagnostics Ltd

**Van Den Berg, Henry**
Brituswip Limited

**Van Den Schrieck, Rene Patrick**
Sarbec Cosmetics Limited

**Van Der Merwe, Jaco**
Venture Four Ltd.

**Van Rijn, Diederik**
Kernfarm UK Limited

**Van Rijn, Gijs**
Kernfarm UK Limited

**Van Rijn, Tim**
Kernfarm UK Limited

**Van Rompay, Stijn**
Acure Pharma Limited

**Van Wyk, Frank Nellis**
Maxilabs Limited

**Vanapariya, Hetasveeben Mahendrabhai**
Astute Healthcare Limited

**Vandegrift, Susan**
Perricone MD Cosmeceuticals UK Ltd

**Vandenbogaerde, Steven Paul Jules**
Ontex Retail UK Limited

**Vanderdussen, David Brian**
NOD Europe Ltd.

**Vanstone, Peter David**
Sure Health & Beauty Limited

**Varala, Shashikanth**
Vitaempower Ltd

**Varanavicius, Andrius**
Takeda UK Limited

**Varavipour, Ehsan**
Pharmartel Limited

**Varma, Amit**
Areessco Ltd
Arisio Ltd

**Varma, Baldev**
Areessco Ltd

**Varndell, Tessa Margaret**
Credenhill Limited

**Vas, Zsolt**
Engelpharma UK Limited

**Vasani, Priti**
Infinity Pharmaceuticals Ltd

**Vasani, Priyanka**
Infinity Pharmaceuticals Ltd

**Vasilaki, Ioanna**
Palatina Ltd

**Vasileva, Antoaneta**
Berryfarm Ltd

**Vazirani, Elicca Anne**
Pharmethicals Limited

**Vazirani, Tushar**
Pharmethicals Limited

**Vecchia, Marco**
Chiesi Healthcare Limited
Chiesi Limited

**Velastegui Suquillo, Edison Rodolfo**
Aptitud Pharma Ltd

**Veligura, Dmitry**
Triaton Ltd

**Vendelboe, Bo**
Zimmer Biomet UK Limited

**Venn, Kenneth Clifford**
Medinox (London) Limited

**Verma, Alok**
Ascend Laboratories (UK) Ltd

**Vernois, Joel Didier Claude**
T-In Medical Limited

**Riaz, Amran**
The Vet Store Trading Limited

**Viaris de Lesegno, Benjamin Marie, Dr**
Iaso Ltd

**Vickers, David**
Rand Rocket Limited

**Vickers, Karen Lesley**
Rand Rocket Limited

**Vidamour, Alison**
AEV Consulting Ltd

**Vidamour, Roger**
AEV Consulting Ltd

**Vidmar Berus, Mojca**
KRKA UK Ltd

**Vigna, Emiliano**
Bio-Sight Ltd

**Vigus, Gill**
Key Nutrients 4 Life Ltd
Natures Healthworks Limited

**Virdi, Harminder Singh**
RB UK Commercial Limited

**Vlahovic, Marijana**
Pro Orbit Limited

**Tan, Janyn Elizabeth**
A.Vogel Limited

**Tan, Jen Wei**
A.Vogel Limited

**Bartschi, Bernhard**
A.Vogel Limited

**Fehr, Thomas**
A.Vogel Limited

**Gmunder, Peter**
A.Vogel Limited

**Vohra, Samir**
Blackpool Medicines Limited

**Volk, Andrea**
Santhera (UK) Limited

**Voll, Gabriel**
Atra Corporation Ltd

**Volle, Thierry Robert Andre**
Lupin Healthcare (UK) Limited

**Vora, Aniruddhakumar**
Molecule Healthcare Limited

**Voysey, Georgina Louise**
La Lune Noire Ltd

**Vumbaca, Antonio Simon**
Green Sun Ltd

**Vuyala, Lakshmi**
LV Global Limited

**Vyas, Haradri**
Aadverv Sourcing Solutions Ltd

**Vyas, Mina**
Propharma Consultancy Ltd
Propharma-UK Ltd

**Waddell, Gillian Ann**
Vital Life International Ltd

**Wadding, Patrick Michael**
N.I.P. Pharma Limited

**Waeschle, Sascha Adrian**
Cannerald Group Ltd

**Wagner, Flemming**
Abacus Medicine Ltd
Aposave Ltd

**Wahi, Ashok**
Trutek Europe Ltd

**Wajs, Stanley Adam**
Cambridge Diagnostics (UK) Ltd

**Waka, Mohammed Arif**
IMI Ventures Limited
Imperial Medical Innovations Ltd

**Wakefield, Michelle**
Furn WW Lux Ltd

**Wakeling, Andrew**
IMS Ultrasound (UK) Ltd
Ideal Medical Holdings Ltd
Ideal Medical Solutions Ltd

**Walberg, Peder Sven**
Medical Need UK Ltd

**Walchirk, Mark Steven**
National Veterinary Services Ltd

**Walia, Vijay Kant**
Total Body Care Limited

**Waling, Robert William**
Healthpoint Limited

**Walkden, Carl Michael**
Blue Bean Medical Ltd

**Walker, Adam**
GlaxoSmithKline Caribbean Ltd

**Walker, Adam** [11-1967]
GlaxoSmithKline Export Limited

**Walker, Adam** [2-1978]
GlaxoSmithKline US Trading Ltd

**Walker, Ann**
EVC Compounding Ltd

**Walker, Lee Philip**
Pricecheck Toiletries Limited

**Walker, Richard John**
Toiletry Sales Limited

**Walker, Thomas George**
Norsworthy Limited

**Walker, William Charles**
Takeda UK Limited

**Walkiewicz, Pawel**
Medical-Mac Ltd

**Wall, Anne Marie**
Timstar Laboratory Suppliers Ltd

**Wall, Brendan**
Timstar Laboratory Suppliers Ltd

**Wall, Kevin Joseph**
Timstar Laboratory Suppliers Ltd

**Wallace, Peter Austin**
Cytoplan Limited

**Wallenberg, Marcus**
Astrazeneca PLC

**Wallis, Theresa Anne**
Veriton Pharma Limited

**Wallner, Edgar**
Qualitech Healthcare Ltd

**Walsh, Timothy FitzGenerald**
Devilbiss Healthcare Limited

**Walters, Colin Stewart**
Seedos Ltd.

**Walton-Green, Andrew John Scott**
Client-Pharma Ltd
Client-Pharmacy UK Ltd

**Wang, Fangqian**
Oxford Supramolecular Biotechnology

**Wang, Tao**
Hitop Pharmaceuticals Limited

**Wang, Tianqiang**
Yiling Ltd

**Wang, Xiaoli**
Double Wing Health & Beauty Ltd
Double Wing Medical Ltd
Double Wing Pharma Development Ltd

**Ward, Colin Jonathan**
Eptheca Global Limited

**Ward, Conor Brendan**
Raumedic U.K. Limited

**Ward, Simon Philip**
SW Medical Solutions Limited

**Krige, Lynette Gillian**
Donald Wardle and Son Limited

**Nuttall, John Branson**
Donald Wardle and Son Limited

**Waring-Hughes, Jonathan**
Bionical Limited

**Warren, Herbert Lee**
Brituswip Limited

**Waseem, Mohammed Khalid**
Sanarah Ltd

**Washington, Robin**
Gilead Sciences Ltd

**Shah, Amritlal Lalji**
K. Waterhouse Limited

**Shah, Anil Lalji**
K. Waterhouse Limited

**Shah, Nalin Lalji**
K. Waterhouse Limited

**Shah, Vinay Lalji**
K. Waterhouse Limited

**Waterhouse, Deborah Jayne**
ViiV Healthcare Overseas Ltd
ViiV Healthcare Trading Services UK
ViiV Healthcare UK Limited

**Watkin, John**
BM Alliance Limited

**Watkin, Stephen Allen**
Hameln Pharmaceuticals Ltd
Patient Ready Products Limited
Phoenix Pharma Ltd.

**Watson, David**
I-Crackedit Ltd

**Watt, David Robertson Maxwell**
Autono-Med Limited

**Watts, Niki Jay**
Treforest Pharmacy Limited

**Watts, Rebecca Tammy Suzanne**
Treforest Pharmacy Limited

**Wayne, Marc**
Spectrum Biomedical UK Limited

**Webber, Paul James Hatton**
Cellpath Limited

**Webber, Peter James**
Cellpath Limited

**Webber, Philip Leslie John**
Cellpath Limited

**Webster, Diane**
Steven F Webster Limited

**Webster, Stephen**
Steven F Webster Limited

**Webster, Steven Falconer**
Steven F Webster Limited

**Webster, Suzanne Elaine**
Steven F Webster Limited

**Webster, Simon Rodrick**
DWH Pharma Limited

**Weddikkara Arrachchilage, Karunaratna**
Winsor Pharma UK Limited

**Weeks, Robert Victor, Dr**
WTE Services Limited

**Wei, Xue Li**
Pavay Venture International Ltd

**Wei, Xueli**
Huayawei Biomedical Co Ltd

**Weinberg, John**
Plexiam Limited

**Weiner, Simon**
Rayburn Trading Co Ltd

**Weir, Robert James**
Hunger Control Limited

**Welzig, Stefan, Dr**
Sanochemia Diagnostics UK Ltd

**Wencker, Dominique Etienne**
Scientific Laboratory Supplies Group Ltd

**Wesley, Neal Robert**
Norpan Hymbre Ltd

**Gardner, Michael Richardson**
L E West Ltd

**Elling, Christo Jaco Von**
L E West Ltd

**Sabourin, Laurent**
L E West Ltd

**Vaissie, Arnaud Paul Alain**
L E West Ltd

**West, Jonathan**
Jon West Trading Limited

**West, Steve Mark**
Dark Atom Limited

**Westall, Susan Penelope**
Mawdsley-Brooks & Co Ltd

**Westwood, Alan**
Matoke Holdings Limited

**Wheatley, Clement Trevor**
Cellpath Limited

**Wheeldon, Robert**
Coastal Core Ltd

**Wheeler, David John**
Powerlung Ltd.

**Wheeler, Gabriella**
Amaxa Ltd

**White Inman, David George**
Devicor Medical UK Limited

**White, Christina**
BR Pharma International Ltd

**White, Gwenan Mair**
AbbVie Ltd

**White, Peter John Pitt, Dr**
Nova Laboratories Limited

**Whitehead, Helen Joy**
PF Consultancy Plus Ltd

**Whitehead, Michael Harry**
PF Consultancy Plus Ltd

**Whitfield, Simon James**
Unomedical Limited

**Whitley, Brian Donald**
Biostate Limited

**Whitmore, Jane Mary**
GlaxoSmithKline Export Limited

**Wickens, Martin John**
Swanson Trade Ltd

**Wickham, George Simon Robert**
Moreton Pharmacy Ltd.

**Wijayatilake, Megha Prachanda**
Sterling London Ventures Ltd

**Wijesena, Sujith Nayanapriya**
Hampton Brand Management Co Ltd
Hampton Brands Limited

**Wijsmuller, Dennis David**
Sotra Pharma Ltd.

**Wijsmuller, Michael Peter**
Sotra Pharma Ltd.

**Wikstrom, Ake Gunnar**
Mundibiopharma Limited
Mundipharma Medical Co Ltd
Napp Laboratories Limited
Napp Pharmaceutical Group Ltd
Napp Pharmaceutical Holdings Ltd
Napp Pharmaceuticals Limited
Qdem Pharmaceuticals Limited

**Wilby, Leonard**
Omega Surgical Instruments Ltd

**Wilcher, Charles David Andrew**
Medartis Limited

**Wild, Daniel**
Lil-Lets UK Ltd

**Wild, Roderick William**
Veriton Pharma Limited

**Wiley, Joseph**
Amryt Pharma (UK) Limited

**Wilkes, Peter Frederick**
New Roots Herbal Limited

**Wilkins, Ross Generald**
Bio Global Limited

**Wilkinson, John Frederick**
Medikit Limited

**Wilkinson, Lloyd Alexander James**
CBD4You Limited

**Wilkinson, Michael Francis**
CooperVision Lens Care Limited

**Wilkinson, Paul William**
Cosmestore Limited
Minmar (1008) Limited

**Willenborg, Peter Heinz**
OL123 Limited

**Williams, Amanda**
Cytoplan Limited

**Williams, David John**
Medical Developments UK Ltd

**Williams, Emrys**
Medilink Limited

**Williams, Gavin**
Steritech Limited

**Williams, Norma**
WD Pharma (UK) Limited

**Williams, Peter Alan**
RxPharma Limited

**Williams, Philip Lewis**
Thea Pharmaceuticals Limited

**Williams, Russell David**
Relonchem Limited

**Williamson, Jonathan Timothy, Dr**
Garstang Medical Services Ltd

**Willis, Lynsey**
Willgen Consulting Limited

**Willis, Richard**
Willgen Consulting Limited

**Willis, William David**
Invicta Pharma Limited

**Wilson, Christopher**
Etab Health Group Limited
Etab Health Limited
Etab Pharma Limited

**Wilson, Derek Andrew**
Doncaster Pharmaceuticals Group Ltd
Doncaster Pharmaceuticals Ltd
Eclipse Generics Limited
Pharmaceutical Identity Ltd
Renfield Limited
Testerworld Limited
Value Generics Limited

**Wilson, Ian**
Farmvet Limited

**Wilson, Juliet Macaraya**
Cyto-Solutions Limited
Guna Biotherapeutics Limited
Guna Limited

**Wilson, Neil Antony**
Medicare Products Limited
PH Medicare Ltd

**Wilson, Patrick Russell**
Nelson & Russell Limited
Spatone Limited

**Wilson, Robert Nelson**
Natural Science.Com Limited
Nelson & Russell Limited
Spatone Limited

**Wilson, Roger Keith**
Bio Pathica Limited
Cyto-Solutions Limited
Guna Biotherapeutics Limited
Guna Limited

**Wilson, William**
Acehides Limited

**Wilton Morgan, Timothy James**
Eurostar Scientific Limited

**Winch, Nathan Joseph**
WPG Wholesale Trading Ltd

**Windholz, Oliver Thomas**
Phoenix Medical Supplies Ltd

**Winsor, Paul Jonathan**
T-In Medical Limited

**Winspear, Philip Richard**
RPG Medical Limited

**Winter, Jennifer Ann Julia**
Animalcare Ltd

**Winterford, Mark Donald**
Fortissa Ltd

**Wobo, Gift Ogechi**
Fulbo Ltd

**Womersley, Robin Neil**
Healthpoint Limited

**Wong, Eric KH**
Pharhealth Limited

**Wong, Hing Yu**
Riviere Groupe (Europe) Ltd

**Wood, Christopher**
Christopher Wood IXRS Consulting Ltd

**Clegg, Peter Dixon**
Peter John Wood Limited

**Wood, Andrew Douglas**
Bioconnections Ltd

**Wood, Colin**
Client-Pharma Ltd
Client-Pharmacy UK Ltd

**Wood, Dawn Sandra**
Bioconnections Ltd

**Wood, Philip Neil**
Leverton & Co Ltd

**Wood, Richard Kenneth**
Eco Animal Health Group PLC

**Wood, Robert Kenneth**
Britannia Pharmaceuticals Ltd
Brituswip Limited

**Woodfield, William Norman**
Bausch & Lomb U.K. Limited

**Woodman, Thomas, Dr**
Maxlott Ltd

**Woods, Gareth Karl**
Pneumech Limited

**Woods, John Stephen**
Nuview Ltd

**Woods, Thomas Harwood**
Jessica Inc Limited

**Woods, Thomas Milligan**
Greiner Bio-One Limited

**Woolf, Carl Daniel**
Carl Woolf Limited
Dispensing Direct Services Ltd

**Wright, David John**
HRA Pharma UK & Ireland Ltd

**Wright, Jane**
Apollo Endosurgery UK Ltd

**Wright, Stephen**
Shakespeare Pharma Ltd

**Wright, Stuart Martin**
Core Environmental PLC

**Wu, Xiangjun**
Yiling Ltd

**Xanthoulis, Ilias**
Venture Four Ltd.

**Xavier, Austin**
Pamx Enterprise Limited

**Xu, Yanzhong**
Shizhen TCM (UK) Limited

**Yagi, Takaki**
Kobayashi Healthcare Europe Ltd

**Yakubu, Asemokhai**
Vine Pharmaceuticals Limited

**Yakubu, Olivia Akunna**
Vine Pharmaceuticals Limited

**Yalamareddy, Mrudula**
Leems Solutions Limited

**Yamana, Takashi**
Summit Pharmaceuticals Europe Ltd

**Yang, Zhiying**
Pharma Plus Supplies Ltd

**Yap, Melissa**
Got Heart UK Ltd

**Yaqoob, Abid**
Wycombe Locum Services Ltd

**Yates, Jason Derick**
Acer Pharma Limited
Acre Medical Limited
Acre Pharma Limited
C. S. T. Pharma Limited

**Yates, Robert Taylor**
ThriveExtreme Health Limited

**Yau, Jimmy**
Yaubag Limited

**Yedoh, Hermann, Dr**
Generic Physics Limited

**Yellop, Daniel Mark**
Discount Healthcare Ltd

**Yii, Tze Chuan**
Fivtique Limited

**Yildirim, Ali Huseyin**
HB Sirius Ltd

**Yin, Chan Wai**
Concept Pharma UK Limited

**Yoor, Brian**
Abbott Healthcare Products Ltd

**Yorachi, Ham Mukama**
Drugget Ltd

**Yoshimitsu, Toru**
Astellas Pharma Europe Ltd.

**You, Sibin**
Rose Europe UK Ltd

**Youming, Lu**
RB (China Trading) Limited

**Young, Barry Dimes**
Virudist Ltd

**Young, Jean Marie**
Rapid Sample Processing Ltd

**Young, Neil**
Izida Pharma Ltd

**Young, Philip**
Dragonstone Group Limited

**Younghusband, Suzanne**
Invitech Ltd

**Younie, David**
Day Med Limited

**Younis Butt, Zaheer**
Butt & Hobbs Limited

**Younis, Mohammad Saeed**
Butt & Hobbs Limited

**Younis, Naheed**
Butt & Hobbs Limited

**Yousif, Botan Awni**
Sood-UK Ltd

**Youssef, Ahmad, Dr**
Technical & General Limited

**Yu, Jiang**
Genmed UK Limited

**Yussouf, Falak**
Ideal Cleaning Systems Ltd

**Yusuf, Mohamed, Dr**
Gateway for Africa Ltd

**Zabier, Tabassum**
Ordinant Medical Solutions Ltd

**Zafar, Adam**
Blackstone Pharma Ltd
iMedix Limited

**Zafar, Ayisha**
Prescribe Direct Limited

**Zalawadiya, Bhumika Sanjaykumar**
Wellness Clinical Supplies Ltd

**Zalawadiya, Sanjaykumar Babubhai**
Molecule Healthcare Limited

**Zaltsman, Ilya**
SQR Pharma Consulting Ltd

**Zaman, Humayun Kabir**
Gumsaver Limited

**Zanini, Fabio**
Pamy International Ltd

**Zarroug, Osman Hamza Osman**
Zarroug Limited

**Zeederberg, Margaret Rene**
Kelpharma Ltd

**Zemmouri, Younes**
Scientific Laboratory Supplies Group Ltd

**Zhang, Lei**
UK Lemenic International Medical Group

**Zhang, Xiaofeng**
South China Bio-Pharma Co Ltd.

**Zhang, Yehong**
Luye Pharma Ltd

**Zhao, Dan**
Foreverbeyoung Ltd

**Zhou, Dong**
Treas Biotechnology UK Ltd

**Zhou, Jingshi Joe**
TSI Health Sciences (Europe) Ltd

**Zhu, Lihua**
Shanghai Neopharm Co., Ltd

**Ziolko Lange, Karin, Dr**
Vitamineral Limited

**Zisu, Ionut-Alexandru**
Andrei & Maria Ltd

**Zohidov, Akobir**
Belinda Limited

**Zolnay, Kriszta, Dr**
Medimpex UK Limited

**Zomer, Roby Reuven**
MGC Pharma (UK) Ltd

**Zota, Moxesh**
Zota Healthcare Limited

**Zou, Dewei**
Medis Medical (UK) Limited

**Zrilic, Nemanja**
Moka Pharmaceuticals Limited

**Zussman, Simon**
Modor & Bearn Limited

**Zutshi, Abhijit**
Biocon Pharma UK Limited

*This page is intentionally left blank*

## Standard Industrial Classification
*excluding*
*Wholesale of pharmaceutical goods*

**01250 Growing of other tree and bush fruits and nuts**
Masir Ltd

**01280 Growing of spices, aromatic, drug and pharmaceutical crops** [12]
Alhaddag Phrma Ltd
Angel & Lockhart (Pharma) Ltd
Aventa International Corporation Ltd
Biogenix Ltd
Cannerald Group Ltd
Green Sun Ltd
Medicaleaf Limited
My-Kaya Ltd
Nascot Health Ltd
Redlight Exchange Ltd
Spectrum Biomedical UK Limited
Tiamat Agriculture Ltd

**01629 Support activities for animal production (other than farm animal boarding)**
Acer Agri Ltd
Vetsonic (UK) Ltd

**03210 Marine aquaculture**
Europharma Scotland Ltd

**09100 Support activities for petroleum and natural gas mining**
Gideotech Limited

**10390 Other processing and preserving of fruit and vegetables**
Overseas Merchandising Corporation Ltd

**10860 Manufacture of homogenized food preparations and dietetic food**
Vitafree Health Limited

**10890 Manufacture of other food products n.e.c.**
Cannaid Ltd
E-Pharm Limited
Florence Health & Beauty Ltd
Langdales Limited
Vitane Pharma Limited

**12000 Manufacture of tobacco products**
CBD Vape Ltd

**14190 Manufacture of other wearing apparel and accessories n.e.c.**
Sigmasis UK Limited

**19209 Other treatment of petroleum products (excluding petrochemicals manufacture)**
Areessco Ltd

**20130 Manufacture of other inorganic basic chemicals**
Cellpath Limited

**20140 Manufacture of other organic basic chemicals**
Biocon Pharma UK Limited

**20200 Manufacture of pesticides and other agrochemical products**
Corpus Nostrum Limited

**20411 Manufacture of soap and detergents**
Academy Hair and Beauty (UK) Ltd

**20420 Manufacture of perfumes and toilet preparations**
Coriungo Limited
Mast - Art Group Limited

**20530 Manufacture of essential oils**
Keziah Ltd
Pure Solace Ltd

**20590 Manufacture of other chemical products n.e.c.**
Carbosynth Limited
Czech, Moravian and Slovak Chemicals

**21100 Manufacture of basic pharmaceutical products** [103]
21CEC PX Pharm Ltd
A1 Pharmaceuticals Holdings Ltd
AAH Pharmaceuticals Limited
Akvion Limited
Al Razi Pharma UK Ltd
Alhaddag Phrma Ltd
Aptitud Pharma Ltd
Astrazeneca PLC
Atnahs Pharma US Limited
Avanzcare Limited
Bioavexia Ltd
Bioceutics UK Ltd
Britpharma UK Limited
Bulgarian Healthy Products Ltd
Cambridge Healthcare Supplies 2012
Cambridge Healthcare Supplies Ltd
Cannerald Group Ltd
Chela Animal Health Limited
Crescent Pharma Limited
Cutman Ltd
Cuttlefish Limited
Dil More Remedies UK Ltd
Dong Hwa UK Ltd
Dr Pradeep Reddy's Laboratories (UK & EU)
Dynamic Development Laboratories Co Ltd
E.P.G Pharma Ltd
Elanco UK AH Limited
Engelpharma UK Limited
Ennogen Healthcare Ltd
Ennogen Pharma Ltd
Essential Pharma Limited
Florence Health & Beauty Ltd
Fluidx Limited
Geistlich Sons Limited
Gelu Life Limited
Geoorganics Limited
Go-Kyo Science Limited
Graviti Healthcare Limited
Great British Bee Co Ltd
Hashmats Health Ltd
Health Remit Limited
Healthbiotics Ltd
Herbal Food Life Limited
Hermes Pharmaceutical Limited
Hospira UK Limited

Hunger Control Limited
Imphatec Ltd
Incline Therapeutics Europe Ltd.
Insuphar Laboratories Limited
Juice Sauz Ltd
Keziah Ltd
Kohilam Limited
Laxmi BNS Holdings Limited
Leeds Industries (UK) Ltd
Leptrex Ltd.
Lifeshield Limited
M & A Pharmachem Limited
MDX Healthcare Ltd
Manx Healthcare Limited
Manx Pharma Ltd
Marlborough Pharmaceuticals Ltd
Martini International Ltd
Medicaleaf Limited
Medisante Limited
Medison Pharma Limited
A. Menarini Diagnostics Ltd
NKCell Plus PLC
Nova Laboratories Limited
Nutramax Ltd
Oxbridge Pharma Limited
Oxford Supramolecular Biotechnology
P.I.E. Pharma Limited
PTGO Sever UK Limited
Pharma Maiden Ltd
Pharmacare International Ltd
Pharmacy Business Consultancy Ltd
Pharmadynamics UK Limited
Phytoceutical Limited
Piramal Critical Care Limited
Premax Europe Limited
Principle Healthcare Limited
Redlight Exchange Ltd
Regent Pharmaceuticals Limited
Ria Generics Limited
Rotapharm Limited
Royce Health Sciences Ltd
Salutem Supplements Ltd
Sanhak Ltd
Shire Pharmaceuticals Limited
Solarius UK & Overseas Limited
Spectrum Biomedical UK Limited
Spey Limited
Spey Pharma Limited
Star Pharmaceuticals Limited
Stegram Pharmaceuticals Ltd
Synergetic Global Limited
T-In Medical Limited
UK Biopharma Ltd
Vitane Pharma Limited
Wenimed Ltd
Winchpharma (Consumer Healthcare) Ltd
World Medicine Limited
Zota Healthcare Limited

## 21200 Manufacture of pharmaceutical preparations [89]

21CEC PX Pharm Ltd
Accord Healthcare Limited
Alhaddag Phrma Ltd
Amarox Limited
Ambe Limited
Apotheke San Biagio SRL Ltd
Aptitud Pharma Ltd
Asaya Cosmeceuticals Limited
Astrazeneca PLC
Auramedicann Ltd
Avanzcare Limited
Aventa International Corporation Ltd
Beegood Enterprises Limited
Bioceutics UK Ltd
Biocon Pharma UK Limited
Blackpool Medicines Limited
Bolton Pharmaceutical Company 100 Ltd
Boost Hair Limited
CM & D Pharma Limited
Cannerald Group Ltd
Clinigen Group PLC
Clyde Valley Cannaceuticals Ltd
Corpus Nostrum Limited
Crescent Pharma Limited
Cutman Ltd
DCMP 8E Cepac Limited
Dil More Remedies UK Ltd
Dr Pradeep Reddy's Laboratories (UK & EU)
Dynamic Development Laboratories Co Ltd
E.P.G Pharma Ltd
EVC Compounding Ltd
Elanco UK AH Limited
Evorin Pharma Limited
Focus Pharma Holdings Limited
Focus Pharmaceuticals Limited
GBBC Ltd
GM Biopharma Ltd
Genus Pharmaceuticals Limited
Geoorganics Limited
Go-Kyo Science Limited
Health Remit Limited
Hospira UK Limited
Huayawei Biomedical Co Ltd
Humn Pharmaceuticals (UK) Ltd
IPS International Corporation Ltd
Imphatec Ltd
Incline Therapeutics Europe Ltd.
Indigo Diagnostics Limited
Infohealth Limited
Koasta Limited
Langdales Limited
Leap Pharma Ltd
Life on Healthcare Ltd
Lifeshield Limited
M & A Pharmachem Limited
M D M Healthcare Ltd
Manx Pharma Ltd
Masters Pharmaceuticals Ltd
Morningside Pharmaceuticals Ltd
NKCell Plus PLC
Napp Pharmaceutical Group Ltd
Napp Pharmaceutical Holdings Ltd
Noohra Limited
Nova Laboratories Limited
Nunataq Limited
Omega Pharma Limited
Pharm Recon Ltd
Pharma Maiden Ltd
Prime Medical Equipment Ltd
Redlight Exchange Ltd
Remedi Medical Holdings Ltd
Rosalique Skincare Limited
Sage Therapeutics Limited
Salcura Limited
Sanhak Ltd
Sarepta International UK Ltd.
Shanghai Neopharm Co., Ltd
Sinduram Healthcare International Ltd
Skindoc Formula Limited
Skinska Pharmaceutica Limited
Sonifar Pharma Expert Limited
Spectrum Biomedical UK Limited
Spey Limited
Spey Pharma Limited
Synergetic Global Limited
Technical & General Limited
United Pharma Group Limited
Vitane Pharma Limited
Wenimed Ltd

## 23120 Shaping and processing of flat glass

R.B. Radley & Co Ltd

## 26600 Manufacture of irradiation, electromedical and electrotherapeutic equipment

Lorteben Trading Co., Ltd
Prime Medical Equipment Ltd
Ivor Shaw Limited
Wenimed Ltd

## 28990 Manufacture of other special-purpose machinery n.e.c.

PMS Korea Ltd

## 32300 Manufacture of sports goods

Nutramax Ltd

## 32500 Manufacture of medical and dental instruments and supplies [21]

Avanzcare Limited
Bioceutics UK Ltd
Biogenix Ltd
Biosensors International UK Ltd
Cellpath Limited
Docsinnovent Limited
E.P.G Pharma Ltd
Eastern Lighthouse Ltd
Global Medical Supplies Ltd
Infinity Biomedical Ltd
Lorteben Trading Co., Ltd
Medics Direct Pharmacy Limited
Morningside Pharmaceuticals Ltd
Nuview Ltd
Oswell Penda Pharmaceutical Ltd
Solarius UK & Overseas Limited
Trinity Impex Limited
Truscreen Limited
Twinklers Limited
United Kingdom Medica Ltd
Wenimed Ltd

## 32990 Other manufacturing n.e.c.

Activated Smile Ltd
Asaya Cosmeceuticals Limited
Biomedox International Ltd
Cellpath Limited
A.J. Cope & Son Limited

## 33200 Installation of industrial machinery and equipment

Buduscheye Techniqa Ltd
Megapharma Ltd

## 36000 Water collection, treatment and supply

Spatone Limited

## 41100 Development of building projects

Euro Capital Management (ECM) Ltd
Gilsun Limited
Pharmac Limited

## 41202 Construction of domestic buildings

Gideotech Limited
Winelia Co Ltd

## 43330 Floor and wall covering

Per-Medic Limited

## 45112 Sale of used cars and light motor vehicles

Design Masters (Sales) Limited
Gama Group Services Ltd
Genrx UK Lipperts Ltd.
Matt 6:33 Ltd
Zolex Global Limited

## 45310 Wholesale trade of motor vehicle parts and accessories

Millennium Global Limited
Nino and Blue Spruce Ltd
Sunrize Trade Limited
Suplan Ltd

## 45320 Retail trade of motor vehicle parts and accessories

Euromed Technologie Limited

## 46110 Agents selling agricultural raw materials, livestock, textile raw materials and semi-finished goods

Katvic Limited
Overseas Merchandising Corporation Ltd
Veterinary Surgeons Supply Co Ltd

## 46120 Agents involved in the sale of fuels, ores, metals and industrial chemicals

Areessco Ltd
Heathrow.Net Limited
Kaboodan Limited

## 46140 Agents involved in the sale of machinery, industrial equipment, ships and aircraft

Branded Healthcare Ltd
Dutscher Scientific UK Limited
Sigmasis UK Limited

## 46150 Agents involved in the sale of furniture, household goods, hardware and ironmongery

SJ Enterprises Limited

### 46160 Agents involved in the sale of textiles, clothing, fur, footwear and leather goods
Aariana Impex Limited
Global Supply (U.K.) Ltd
Healtholozy UK Limited
Matt 6:33 Ltd
Pericia Ltd
Sunrize Trade Limited
Tuluh Solutions Ltd

### 46170 Agents involved in the sale of food, beverages and tobacco
Aariana Impex Limited
Anrise Trading Limited
CBD Labz Ltd
Honilac Nutrition Limited
Icone International Limited
International Pharma Co Ltd
Millennium Global Limited
Ros Nutrition UK Ltd.
Triaton Ltd

### 46180 Agents specialised in the sale of other particular products [38]
AAR Pharma Ltd
Aeglos Ltd
Alfavet Animal Healthcare Ltd
Aston-Med Limited
Biophos Labs Ltd
Biovate Limited
Bosses Onlinestore Ltd
CBS Trade Limited
Cadila Pharmaceuticals (Europe) Ltd
Chemx Ltd
DLG Partners Limited
Device Technologies UK Ltd.
Excip Limited
Feel and Heal UK Limited
First Choice Suppliments Ltd
Fivtique Limited
Fulbo Ltd
GP Mediplus Ltd
Gate Pharma Ltd
Hapa Medical UK Ltd
Indigo Diagnostics Limited
JP & A Pharma Ltd
Leigh Jones & Associates Ltd
Lab-Club Limited
Leafxtracts Ltd
London Health Sciences Ltd
MRG Creations Ltd
Medimpex UK Limited
Novamed Pharma Ltd
P.I.C. International Ltd
Pharmac Limited
Proup Ltd
R & R Post Op Box Ltd.
Gedeon Richter (UK) Limited
Sonifar Pharma Expert Limited
United Kingdom Medica Ltd
Veda Biosciences Limited
Vyom International Ltd.

### 46190 Agents involved in the sale of a variety of goods [44]
AP Import Export Ltd
Aariana Impex Limited
All1 Limited
Aston-Med Limited

BFN Limited
Bbeauty Lounge Limited
Biotus Ltd
Bluesky Cosmetics Limited
Branded Healthcare Ltd
Brightfield Associates Ltd
Bristol Consumer Health Ltd
Crown Global Traders Limited
DLG Partners Limited
Dark Atom Limited
Feel and Heal UK Limited
Fivtique Limited
Flow Wealth Ltd
Fox Group International Ltd
Gate Pharma Ltd
Got Heart UK Ltd
Honilac Nutrition Limited
Jana Healthcare Ltd
Leigh Jones & Associates Ltd
Kaboodan Limited
LM3 Business Ltd
Leafxtracts Ltd
Matt 6:33 Ltd
McQuilkin & Co Limited
Micro Industries Limited
New Generation Business UK Ltd
OFC Molecular Ltd
Parker Trading Ltd
Pericia Ltd
R & R Post Op Box Ltd.
Rabimed International Limited
Sanay Ltd
Santen UK Limited
Shaz Logistics Limited
Stem Cellx Limited
UK Lemenic International Medical Group
Vog Limited
Vyom International Ltd.
Wellacy Limited
Wesbee Ventures Limited

### 46210 Wholesale of grain, unmanufactured tobacco, seeds and animal feeds
Farmsvet Ltd
Vyom International Ltd.

### 46220 Wholesale of flowers and plants
Cannaid Ltd
Vivaorganiclife Ltd

### 46230 Wholesale of live animals
Katvic Limited

### 46310 Wholesale of fruit and vegetables
Canary Islands Marketing Board Ltd
Health Supplies Limited
Healtholozy UK Limited
Zaaz Limited

### 46320 Wholesale of meat and meat products
Bri Trade Solutions Limited
Unidus Limited
Zaaz Limited

### 46330 Wholesale of dairy products, eggs and edible oils and fats
BFN Limited
Herbaleva Ltd
Honilac Nutrition Limited
Overseas Merchandising Corporation Ltd
Ros Nutrition UK Ltd.
Sports Star Distribution UK Ltd
Tuluh Solutions Ltd
Vitanutrition UK Ltd.

### 46341 Wholesale of fruit and vegetable juices, mineral water and soft drinks
Bri Trade Solutions Limited
Herbaleva Ltd
Lam Cash and Carry Limited
Neubria Limited
Rexcel Trading Ltd
Zolex Global Limited

### 46342 Wholesale of wine, beer, spirits and other alcoholic beverages
Nino and Blue Spruce Ltd
Wilkies International Ltd

### 46350 Wholesale of tobacco products
Aria Vape Ltd
RF Vapes Limited

### 46360 Wholesale of sugar and chocolate and sugar confectionery
Birmingham Management Centre (UK)
Crown Global Traders Limited
Fitness and Nutrition of Europe Ltd.
Rexcel Trading Ltd
E.S.Shaw & Sons Limited
Sports Star Distribution UK Ltd

### 46370 Wholesale of coffee, tea, cocoa and spices
Buduscheye Techniqa Ltd
Canconc Ltd
Icone International Limited
Nasser Waziri Ltd
Natures Merchant Ltd
Skarby Gai Ltd

### 46380 Wholesale of other food, including fish, crustaceans and molluscs
Evolve Pharma Limited
Fitness and Nutrition of Europe Ltd.
Matoke Holdings Limited
Nordic Nutraceuticals UK Ltd

### 46390 Non-specialised wholesale of food, beverages and tobacco [14]
Abra Wholesales Ltd
CKF Limited
Herbialis Limited
International Pharma Co Ltd
Lam Cash and Carry Limited
Life on Healthcare Ltd
MQS Group London Limited
Natures Merchant Ltd
Oak Zone Biotech UK Ltd
E.S.Shaw & Sons Limited
Sonchat Limited
Targeter (UK) Limited
Uni Supply Ltd
Vitanutrition UK Ltd.

### 46410 Wholesale of textiles
Blink Street Limited
Falama Services Group Limited
Gester Invest Limited
Global Supply (U.K.) Ltd
Oscar & Louis Limited
Springwell Transport and Logistics Ltd
World Trends Ltd

### 46420 Wholesale of clothing and footwear
Alizcare Limited
Blink Street Limited
Cynosure Group Ltd
Fitnatix International Ltd
Global Supply (U.K.) Ltd
Oscar & Louis Limited
Pinklady International Ltd
World Trends Ltd
ZS Solutions Limited

### 46439 Wholesale of radio, television goods & electrical household appliances (other than records, tapes, CDs)
Chirock Trading Ltd
H & S Beauty Care Limited

### 46440 Wholesale of china and glassware and cleaning materials
AP Import Export Ltd
B & B Wholesale Limited
Cellcosmo Suisse Limited
Topnot Ltd
Zaaz Limited

### 46450 Wholesale of perfume and cosmetics [138]
2M PH. Intl. Limited
A B International Limited
Alizcare Limited
Allied Warden Marketing Ltd
Almirall Limited
Amaxa Ltd
Asaya Cosmeceuticals Limited
Aviva Health Solutions Limited
Bbeauty Lounge Limited
Beegood Enterprises Limited
Beiersdorf UK Ltd.
Bessacarr Ltd
Best-Bio Ltd
Bio Global Limited
Biovate Limited
Bioxane Ltd
Mark Birch Hair Ltd
A & P Blickling Ltd
Blink Street Limited
Bluesky Cosmetics Limited
Boots International Limited
Bristol Consumer Health Ltd
Chronicles Medical Consulting Ltd
Clinova Limited
Colgate-Palmolive (U.K.) Ltd
Coriungo Limited
Croma-Pharma Limited
DLG Partners Limited
Dacre Skincare Limited
Dilmaherbals Limited
Drugget Ltd
Esthetica Pure Ltd
Eurocare Impex Services Ltd
Evorin Pharma Limited

Fair Pharm Limited
Feel and Heal UK Limited
Five Star International Consulting
Florence Health & Beauty Ltd
Foreverbeyoung Ltd
Fox Group International Ltd
FreshBreathOnline Limited
Frontrow International UK Ltd
GBBC Ltd
GP Mediplus Ltd
General Shop Ltd
Generic Physics Limited
Goldshore (UK) Limited
Great British Bee Co Ltd
Green Guru Enterprices Ltd.
Hampton Brands Limited
Harvey Pharma Ltd
Healthcare Procurement Services Ltd
Healtholozy UK Limited
Healthpoint Limited
Herbaleva Ltd
Here We Flo Ltd
Hisamitsu Pharmaceutical UK Ltd
Hisamitsu UK Limited
Iam Finance Limited
Iberia Skin Brands Ltd
Imamcom Ltd
Imperial Bioscience Ltd
Ivee Group Ltd
Leigh Jones & Associates Ltd
K588 Limited
Lambsmead Limited
Laogong Laopo Limited
Larmed Limited
Latam HQ Health Ltd
Layan Pharma Ltd
Legendbio Beauty Group Limited
Lionmark Limited
London Health Sciences Ltd
Luban & Murr Ltd
M & N Traders Limited
MGC Pharma (UK) Ltd
MQS Group London Limited
Macks Ltd.
Mast - Art Group Limited
Mayfair Export London Limited
Medica Ltd
Medipro Pharma Limited
Microskin Cosmeceuticals UK Ltd
Minmar (1008) Limited
Modern Innovations Limited Ltd
Nasser Waziri Ltd
Natures Merchant Ltd
Neolife International Ltd
Novmedic Limited
Optima Consumer Health Limited
Orange Square Co Ltd.
Organic Iway Ltd
Oscar & Louis Limited
Perricone MD Cosmeceuticals UK Ltd
Pharma Medico Limited
Pharmacare International Ltd
Pharmadose Limited
Pharmdex UK Ltd
Pinklady International Ltd
Pispo Ltd
Sara Post Ltd
Prema Naturals Limited
Pricecheck Toiletries Limited
Pure Skincare Limited
RR Cosmeceuticals (UK) Ltd
Rabimed International Limited

Rexcel Trading Ltd
Ris Healthcare Limited
Riviere Groupe (Europe) Ltd
Rogia Romini Limited
Royce Health Sciences Ltd
SHL Medical Limited
Salonpas UK Limited
Sanay Ltd
Sawa Trading & Shipping Ltd
Secret Line Ltd
Skindoc Formula Limited
Skinlab Medical Ltd
Solarius UK & Overseas Limited
South China Bio-Pharma Co Ltd.
TA-65 (UK) Wholesale Limited
Teoxane UK Limited
Tetra Hydro Cannabinoid Oils Global Ltd
Treas Biotechnology UK Ltd
Triaton Ltd
UK Beauty Cosmetics International Group
UK Heluns Industry Co., Ltd
UK Lemenic International Medical Group
UK Vimin Industry Co., Limited
Uni Supply Ltd
Unidus Limited
Ved Healthcare Limited
Veramic Limited
Victoria Pharma London Ltd
Vivacy Laboratoires Ltd
Winchpharma (Consumer Healthcare) Ltd
Zarroug Limited
Zerocann Ltd

### 46470 Wholesale of furniture, carpets and lighting equipment
Active Export Ltd
Bioloka Ltd
Flydonging Eletctronic Ltd
Springwell Transport and Logistics Ltd
World Trends Ltd

### 46480 Wholesale of watches and jewellery
Flydonging Eletctronic Ltd
Modern Innovations Limited Ltd
Mountrow Trading Limited
Rogia Romini Limited

### 46499 Wholesale of household goods (other than musical instruments) n.e.c [23]
Beiersdorf UK Ltd.
CM Healthcare Limited
Colgate-Palmolive (U.K.) Ltd
Dentlaser Limited
Dollano Trading Limited
Easho Limited
General Shop Ltd
Gester Invest Limited
Hotteeze International Limited
Hunger Control Limited
Iam Finance Limited
Jay & Jay Limited
Luban & Murr Ltd
Macks Ltd.
Neolife International Ltd
Pan Globus Limited
Pricecheck Toiletries Limited
RB UK Commercial Limited
RB UK Hygiene Home Commercial Ltd
Sampsonstore.Com (UK) Ltd
Sonchat Limited
Topnot Ltd
UK Lemenic International Medical Group

**46510 Wholesale of computers, computer peripheral equipment and software**
Millennium Global Limited

**46520 Wholesale of electronic and telecommunications equipment and parts** [15]
A.T. Medical Ltd
ANP Partners Ltd
Bbeauty Lounge Limited
Best-Bio Ltd
Bio Global Limited
Bluesky Cosmetics Limited
Elm Healthcare Limited
Flydonging Eletctronic Ltd
Kohilam Limited
LM3 Business Ltd
London Spirit for Trading Ltd
Lyshaug Enterprises Limited
Quirky Vapes Ltd
Suplan Ltd
Tradebuffalo Ltd

**46610 Wholesale of agricultural machinery, equipment and supplies**
Damum UK Limited
Palatina Ltd

**46620 Wholesale of machine tools**
Kuramo (UK) Limited

**46630 Wholesale of mining, construction and civil engineering machinery**
Irving and Skinner Ltd
Timpext (Trading-Import-Export) Ltd

**46650 Wholesale of office furniture**
Falama Services Group Limited

**46660 Wholesale of other office machinery and equipment**
Pan Globus Limited
Tradebuffalo Ltd

**46690 Wholesale of other machinery and equipment** [27]
Active Export Ltd
Biogenez Ltd
Birmingham Management Centre (UK)
Dentel Group Ltd
Dentlaser Limited
Diamate Biotechnologies Ltd
Elektro Genesis Limited
Evolve Pharma Limited
Gester Invest Limited
Ham+Med Co Ltd
Hayat Gostar Ltd
Kuramo (UK) Limited
LM3 Business Ltd
Lorteben Trading Co., Ltd
New Medical World Ltd
Niayara Global Limited
Parasure Limited
John Preston & Co. (Belfast) Ltd
Prime Medical Equipment Ltd
SD Alliance Ltd.
Surgicaide Medical Supplies UK Ltd
Surgitrac Instruments UK Ltd
TTO Ventures Ltd.

Tradewings Worldwide Ltd
Triaton Ltd
UK Pharma Impex Limited
Welcome Medical Group Ltd

**46711 Wholesale of petroleum and petroleum products**
Chesdeg Limited
Chikhurst Limited
Crown Global Traders Limited
Edmond Finance Ltd
MQS Group London Limited

**46719 Wholesale of other fuels and related products**
Angelina SW Ltd

**46720 Wholesale of metals and metal ores**
Anrise Trading Limited
Micro Industries Limited

**46730 Wholesale of wood, construction materials and sanitary equipment**
Deise Pharm Ltd

**46740 Wholesale of hardware, plumbing and heating equipment and supplies**
Deise Pharm Ltd

**46750 Wholesale of chemical products** [46]
A.T. Medical Ltd
ACI Group Ltd
AP Import Export Ltd
Arisio Ltd
Best-Bio Ltd
Bhendriks Resale and Retale Ltd
Bio Global Limited
Biophos Labs Ltd
Carbosynth Limited
Chemx Ltd
Chikhurst Limited
Czech, Moravian and Slovak Chemicals
Decibel Biopharm Limited
Detafinas Limited
E.U.K. Limited
Euro Lifecare Ltd
Evolve Generics Limited
Evolve Pharma Limited
Evorin Pharma Limited
Excip Limited
FTS Bio Limited
Fast Track Sourcing Limited
Huayawei Biomedical Co Ltd
Iam Finance Limited
Interchem Europe (UK) Limited
International Ingredients and Chemicals (IIC)
Interpharm Limited
Kora Healthcare UK Ltd
Macks Ltd.
McQuilkin & Co Limited
Morn View Chemicals (UK) Ltd
Oak Zone Biotech UK Ltd
Palatina Ltd
Pericia Ltd
Pharmadynamics UK Limited
Probar Services Limited
Ros Nutrition UK Ltd.
Salon Sales Limited

Septodont Limited
Sigmasis UK Limited
Simba Pharmatech Limited
South China Bio-Pharma Co Ltd.
Stratlab Limited
UK Pharma Impex Limited
Vitanutrition UK Ltd.
Peter John Wood Limited

**46760 Wholesale of other intermediate products** [18]
AIG Unico Ltd
Aromanature Limited
Bakhu Limited
Bannersbridge Limited
Belinda Limited
Biophos Labs Ltd
Canary Islands Marketing Board Ltd
Chemx Ltd
Dentanurse (U.K.) Limited
Diamate Biotechnologies Ltd
Evolet Healthcare Limited
Excip Limited
Interchem Europe (UK) Limited
Micro Industries Limited
Salon Sales Limited
South China Bio-Pharma Co Ltd.
Suplan Ltd
Winchpharma (Consumer Healthcare) Ltd

**46770 Wholesale of waste and scrap**
Bin'auf Limited
Unidus Limited

**46900 Non-specialised wholesale trade** [81]
ANP Partners Ltd
All1 Limited
Allpa Kallpa Ltd
Alverda Ltd
Ambe Limited
Anrise Trading Limited
B D S I Limited
Be and Are Sales Limited
Beauty Boosters Ltd
Beiersdorf UK Ltd.
Bhendriks Resale and Retale Ltd
Biogenez Ltd
Bioquote Limited
Biotech International Limited
Bracco UK Limited
Bristol Consumer Health Ltd
BritaniaMark Limited
CBS Trade Limited
CKF Limited
Canary Islands Marketing Board Ltd
Chirock Trading Ltd
Construct4lyfe Ltd
Coramandel Limited
Damum UK Limited
Dollano Trading Limited
Dutscher Scientific UK Limited
Easho Limited
Eastern Lighthouse Ltd
Elm Healthcare Limited
Fulbo Ltd
GCL Marketing Ltd
GP Mediplus Ltd
Gama Group Services Ltd
Gee Lawson Limited
Genesis Medical Limited

# The Top UK Pharmaceutical Wholesalers

Global SCS Limited
Ham+Med Co Ltd
Hamilton Pharmaceuticals Ltd
Albert Harrison & Co.Limited
Hayat Gostar Ltd
Ikatrad Ltd
Intermedical (UK) Ltd
Interport Limited
Intro International (TRDG) Ltd
J.J. Worldhealth Limited
Juice Sauz Ltd
Kohilam Limited
Layan Pharma Ltd
London Health Sciences Ltd
London Spirit for Trading Ltd
Lufuma B2b Services Ltd
Lyshaug Enterprises Limited
Masters Pharmaceuticals Ltd
Medicalstore-24 Limited
Medinox (London) Limited
N-Pen Ltd.
Naturelo Ltd
Niayara Global Limited
Pricecheck Toiletries Limited
Reliance Medical Ltd
Ria Sales Corporation Ltd
Rogia Romini Limited
Ross London Limited
Salon Sales Limited
Sawa Trading & Shipping Ltd
Seltfar Ltd
Septodont Limited
E.S.Shaw & Sons Limited
Shkar Enterprise Limited
Skarby Gai Ltd
Sonchat Limited
Sotra Pharma Ltd.
Sports Star Distribution UK Ltd
Standard Organics International (UK) Ltd
Star Freight Forwarding Ltd
Stem Cellx Limited
Supphero Ltd
Tradewings Worldwide Ltd
Venture Four Ltd.
Zhongfu (UK) Limited
Zolex Global Limited

**47110 Retail sale in non-specialised stores with food, beverages or tobacco predominating**
Frontrow International UK Ltd
Neubria Limited
Stan-Pol Ltd

**47190 Other retail sale in non-specialised stores** [15]
Alizcare Limited
Alverda Ltd
Beauty Boosters Ltd
Bhendriks Resale and Retale Ltd
Biotus Ltd
Eden CBD Limited
Kelisdar Enterprises Limited
Lionmark Limited
Meta Innovation Nutrition Ltd
Nunataq Limited
Sara Post Ltd
Remedy JV Limited
Sampsonstore.Com (UK) Ltd
Skarby Gai Ltd
TTops Healthcare Limited

**47240 Retail sale of bread, cakes, flour confectionery and sugar confectionery in specialised stores**
W.B. Superdrug Ltd.

**47250 Retail sale of beverages in specialised stores**
Nino and Blue Spruce Ltd

**47260 Retail sale of tobacco products in specialised stores**
Aria Vape Ltd
CBD Vape Ltd
Quirky Vapes Ltd
RF Vapes Limited
W.B. Superdrug Ltd.

**47290 Other retail sale of food in specialised stores**
General Shop Ltd
Herbal Food Life Limited
Immortalis Distribution Ltd.
Livewell Naturals Limited

**47540 Retail sale of electrical household appliances in specialised stores**
Quirky Vapes Ltd

**47640 Retail sale of sports goods, fishing gear, camping goods, boats and bicycles**
London Supplements Distribution Ltd
Swerve Cycling Limited

**47650 Retail sale of games and toys in specialised stores**
Sara Post Ltd

**47710 Retail sale of clothing in specialised stores**
Steven F Webster Limited

**47730 Dispensing chemist in specialised stores** [92]
A D Healthcare Limited
ANP Pharma Ltd
Aesthetic & Wellness Pharmacy Ltd
Aidwell Limited
Allans Healthcare Limited
Andrews Pharmacy Limited
Aroschem Limited
Arrowedge Limited
B.P. Pharma Limited
Belinda Limited
Biogenix Ltd
Liam Bradley Ltd
Butt & Hobbs Limited
Chelmack Limited
Chemi-Call Ltd
Clyde Valley Cannaceuticals Ltd
Gordon Davie Chemist Limited
Dejure Limited
Detafinas Limited
Dispensing Healthcare Ltd
ETP (UK) Limited
Eico Ltd
Evolet Healthcare Limited
Eyepak Limited
Ezhonsi Ltd

Faith and Pharma Limited
Five Pharm Ltd
Flintlow Limited
Fulbo Ltd
Gate2pharma Ltd
Glenhazel Limited
Go-Kyo Science Limited
Grandbydale Limited
Greens Pharmacy Limited
Guardian Pharmaceuticals Co Ltd
HB Sirius Ltd
HCP Limited
Hana Healthcare Ltd
Hashmats Health Ltd
HealthVillagePlus Limited
Herbert and Herbert Pharmacy Ltd
Hot Pharma Ltd
Ideal Healthcare Limited
Infohealth Limited
Instachem Limited
Kelisdar Enterprises Limited
Kingston Pharma Limited
Koasta Limited
Roy Lamb Limited
Lansdales Pharmacy Limited
Lifecare Limited
Lifeshield Limited
Walter Lloyd & Son Limited
MDX Healthcare Ltd
MSB Pharma Ltd
Manichem Limited
Maplewood Investments Limited
Medbury Limited
Medicines Extra Healthcare Ltd
Medics Direct Pharmacy Limited
Medicstar (UK) Limited
Medipro Pharma Limited
Metro Pharmacy Limited
Moscow Flyer Limited
Mychem Limited
N N Pharma Ltd
N-Pen Ltd.
NMB Medical Limited
Nelson & Russell Limited
Omark Plus Ltd
Onpharma Limited
Park Health Ltd
Parkview Leicester Limited
Pharm - Tex Limited
Pharmadose Limited
Pharmartel Limited
Pharmasure Limited
Rabimed International Limited
Rifaray Limited
Rightdose Solutions Limited
Ross London Limited
Shieldasset Limited
Six Ways Birmingham Ltd
Springs Healthcare Limited
T.K. Impex Limited
Totally Pharmacy Ltd
UK Pharmacies Ltd
Unipharm Limited
Vitaminka Ltd
W.B. Superdrug Ltd.
K. Waterhouse Limited
Steven F Webster Limited

**47741 Retail sale of hearing aids**
THS Solutions Limited

**47749 Retail sale of medical and orthopaedic goods in specialised stores (not incl. hearing aids) n.e.c. [51]**
1966 Health International Ltd
Aesthetic & Wellness Pharmacy Ltd
Aromanature Limited
Arquella Ltd
Barustore Limited
Baymed Group Ltd.
Coastal Core Ltd
Comfylife Ltd
Credenhill Limited
Dentel Group Ltd
Dr Kool Ltd
ETP (UK) Limited
Equimed Medical Supplies Ltd
Eyecon Vision Limited
Fijez Ltd
Fittleworth Medical Limited
Five Pharm Ltd
Global Medical Supplies Ltd
HB Sirius Ltd
Health Source Limited
Hyaluron Health Ltd
Imamcom Ltd
Instant Test Ltd
Kinetic Enterprises Limited
Kingston Pharma Limited
MM Medical Equipment UK Ltd
Medica Ltd
Mediclock Devices Limited
Megapharma Ltd
Metropharm Limited
Model Medics Limited
My-Kaya Ltd
N N Pharma Ltd
Newtexko Ltd.
Onpharma Limited
Organic Iway Ltd
Oxbridge Pharma Limited
Pharmacare International Ltd
Prescribe Direct Limited
Raw Medicus Ltd
Rocha Products Limited
S.T.D. Pharmaceutical Products Ltd
Smart Medical Limited
Surgicaide Medical Supplies UK Ltd
THS Solutions Limited
TMZ Naturals Limited
Tearfilm Therapeutics Ltd
Victoria Pharma London Ltd
Vitafree Health Limited
Vivacy Laboratoires Ltd
Wholesale 2 U Ltd

**47750 Retail sale of cosmetic and toilet articles in specialised stores [38]**
1966 Health International Ltd
Apotheke San Biagio SRL Ltd
B.P. Pharma Limited
Barustore Limited
Belinda Limited
A & P Blickling Ltd
Cellcosmo Suisse Limited
Coriungo Limited
Dacre Skincare Limited
Dejure Limited
Dollano Trading Limited
ETP (UK) Limited
Elara Care Limited
Evideon Daily Ltd

Evolet Healthcare Limited
Fittleworth Medical Limited
Foreverbeyoung Ltd
Frontrow International UK Ltd
Got Heart UK Ltd
HB Sirius Ltd
Herbert and Herbert Pharmacy Ltd
IPS International Corporation Ltd
Imamcom Ltd
K588 Limited
Luban & Murr Ltd
Maplewood Investments Limited
Mast - Art Group Limited
OFC Molecular Ltd
Orange Square Co Ltd.
Organic Iway Ltd
Parkview Leicester Limited
Pharmartel Limited
Pure Skincare Limited
Stan-Pol Ltd
Surgicaide Medical Supplies UK Ltd
UK Heluns Industry Co., Ltd
UK Vimin Industry Co., Limited
Vivacy Laboratoires Ltd

**47760 Retail sale of flowers, plants, seeds, fertilizers, pet animals and pet food in specialised stores**
Menar UK Biotech Ltd

**47782 Retail sale by opticians**
East Midlands Infotech PVT Ltd
Eye Guard Ltd
Eyekonic Wellbeing Limited

**47789 Other retail sale of new goods in specialised stores (not commercial art galleries and opticians)**
Herbert and Herbert Pharmacy Ltd
Steven F Webster Limited
Zerocann Ltd

**47799 Retail sale of other second-hand goods in stores (not incl. antiques)**
Timpext (Trading-Import-Export) Ltd

**47810 Retail sale via stalls and markets of food, beverages and tobacco products**
Kinetic Enterprises Limited

**47890 Retail sale via stalls and markets of other goods**
Got Heart UK Ltd
Great British Bee Co Ltd

**47910 Retail sale via mail order houses or via Internet [57]**
1st Health Products Ltd
A1 Natural Ltd
Acre Aesthetics Limited
Barustore Limited
Beauty Boosters Ltd
Better'er Limited
Biomedox International Ltd
Biotus Ltd
Blackpool Medicines Limited
CKF Limited
Cannaid Ltd
Cellcosmo Suisse Limited

Chameleon Planet Ltd
Chronicles Medical Consulting Ltd
Comfylife Ltd
Dent.O.Care Limited
Easho Limited
Fire N Ice Ltd
Foreverbeyoung Ltd
Gelu Life Limited
Hapa Medical UK Ltd
Hotteeze International Limited
Hyaluron Health Ltd
JMD Enterprises UK Limited
Kinetic Enterprises Limited
Latam HQ Health Ltd
Livewell Naturals Limited
MRG Creations Ltd
Manta Medical Limited
Menar UK Biotech Ltd
My-Kaya Ltd
Naturelo Ltd
Neubria Limited
New Seasons Natural Products Ltd
Niayara Global Limited
OFC Molecular Ltd
Pharma Medico Limited
Pharmasif Direct Limited
Pharmdex UK Ltd
Phonepimps Limited
Pinklady International Ltd
Premax Europe Limited
Private Pharma Health Co Ltd
Private Pharmacy Group Limited
Pure Light Vision Ltd
Pure Skincare Limited
R & D Healthcare Ltd
Sampsonstore.Com (UK) Ltd
Specials Laboratory Limited
Swerve Cycling Limited
Sylk Limited
TTops Healthcare Limited
Tulip Cup Limited
UK Heluns Industry Co., Ltd
UK Vimin Industry Co., Limited
Uni Supply Ltd
Vitafree Health Limited

**47990 Other retail sale not in stores, stalls or markets [15]**
21CEC PX Pharm Ltd
Arctic Medical Limited
Aspen Pharmacare UK Limited
Fayroz Ltd
First Choice Suppliments Ltd
H & S Beauty Care Limited
JMD Enterprises UK Limited
Karczek Ltd
Lab.Tv Limited
London Spirit for Trading Ltd
MRG Creations Ltd
Masta Limited
Naturelo Ltd
Swerve Cycling Limited
TTC Medical GTS Limited

**49200 Freight rail transport**
Newville Trading Limited

**49390 Other passenger land transport**
Shaz Logistics Limited

**49410 Freight transport by road**
A & P Blickling Ltd
Gideotech Limited
Healthcare Services Group Ltd
Movianto UK Limited
SD Alliance Ltd.
Springwell Transport and Logistics Ltd

**52103 Operation of warehousing and storage facilities for land transport activities**
Healthcare Services Group Ltd

**52290 Other transportation support activities**
Global SCS Limited
Vestex Trade Ltd

**53100 Postal activities under universal service obligation**
Andrews Pharmacy Limited
Wholesale 2 U Ltd

**53202 Unlicensed carriers**
Ontyme Logistics and Healthcare Ltd

**55209 Other holiday and other collective accommodation**
Chameleon Planet Ltd

**56103 Take-away food shops and mobile food stands**
Prominer Limited

**56290 Other food services**
Allpa Kallpa Ltd
Bulgarian Healthy Products Ltd
Herbialis Limited
International Pharma Co Ltd
Masa Pharma Ltd

**58110 Book publishing**
All1 Limited

**58190 Other publishing activities**
Ambe Limited

**58290 Other software publishing**
Mirada Medical Limited

**59111 Motion picture production activities**
Nunataq Limited

**59112 Video production activities**
Sharepool Limited

**61200 Wireless telecommunications activities**
Eptheca Global Limited

**61900 Other telecommunications activities**
Ross London Limited

**62012 Business and domestic software development**
East Midlands Infotech PVT Ltd

**62020 Information technology consultancy activities**
Arisio Ltd
Avail Group UK Limited
Busky Limited
Crossbridge Concepts Limited
East Midlands Infotech PVT Ltd
JAO Enterprises Ltd
Leems Solutions Limited
Medicalstore-24 Limited
Vityz Nutrition Limited

**62090 Other information technology service activities**
Allied Warden Marketing Ltd
Hunter International Associates Ltd
Medicalstore-24 Limited
Pharmunity Limited

**63120 Web portals**
Corwhite Solutions Limited
Medics Direct Pharmacy Limited

**63990 Other information service activities n.e.c.**
New Generation Business UK Ltd
ZTK Business Services Limited

**64201 Activities of agricultural holding companies**
Nascot Health Ltd

**64204 Activities of distribution holding companies**
1966 Health International Ltd
LDC International Limited
Medintek Holdings Ltd
ViiV Healthcare Overseas Ltd

**64205 Activities of financial services holding companies**
Theramex HQ UK Limited

**64209 Activities of other holding companies n.e.c.**
Harmonium Investments Limited
Human Reproduction Group Ltd
Kanta Enterprises Limited
Medigroup Ltd

**64301 Activities of investment trusts**
Euro Capital Management (ECM) Ltd

**64306 Activities of real estate investment trusts**
Gulfstream Equity & Development Ltd
Iberia Skin Brands Ltd

**64910 Financial leasing**
Eastern Lighthouse Ltd

**64929 Other credit granting n.e.c.**
Garusa Solutions U.K. Limited
Resource Medical (UK) Ltd

**64999 Financial intermediation not elsewhere classified**
Cellexa Limited
Garusa Solutions U.K. Limited
Petersone Group Ltd
UK Pharma Impex Limited

**66110 Administration of financial markets**
Parallel Investments Limited

**66190 Activities auxiliary to financial intermediation n.e.c.**
Pamy International Ltd

**66300 Fund management activities**
Parallel Investments Limited

**68100 Buying and selling of own real estate**
Ezhonsi Ltd
N N Pharma Ltd
Omark Plus Ltd

**68202 Letting and operating of conference and exhibition centres**
Petersone Group Ltd

**68209 Other letting and operating of own or leased real estate**
Garusa Solutions U.K. Limited
Novochem Limited
Rising Sun Ventures Ltd

**68310 Real estate agencies**
Allied Warden Marketing Ltd
Heathrow.Net Limited
Rising Sun Ventures Ltd
Sharepool Limited
Wesbee Ventures Limited

**68320 Management of real estate on a fee or contract basis**
Real Estate Alliance Ltd

**69101 Barristers at law**
Design Masters (Sales) Limited

**69109 Activities of patent and copyright agents; other legal activities n.e.c.**
Bioplax Limited
Pharm Recon Ltd

**69201 Accounting and auditing activities**
Design Masters (Sales) Limited
SJ Enterprises Limited

**69202 Bookkeeping activities**
Nevik Limited

**70100 Activities of head offices**
ANP Partners Ltd
Durbin PLC
Natural Science.Com Limited
ViiV Healthcare UK Limited

**70221 Financial management**
Edmond Finance Ltd
Irving and Skinner Ltd
PF Consultancy Plus Ltd
Real Estate Alliance Ltd

**70229 Management consultancy activities other than financial management** [51]
10x Rational Ambulance Yield Ltd
A.J. Prime Ltd
Aeglos Ltd
Areessco Ltd
Arisio Ltd
Biovate Limited
Bpharm Group Limited
Britpharma UK Limited
Clever Connect Ltd
Clinimarg Ltd
Connexon Global Networks Ltd
Cuttlefish Limited
Cynosure Group Ltd
Damum UK Limited
De-Bulad & Co Ltd
Dizzo Consulting (UK) Limited
Edmond Finance Ltd
Emra Consult Limited
Euro Capital Management (ECM) Ltd
Faith and Pharma Limited
Fire N Ice Ltd
Flow Wealth Ltd
Genmed UK Limited
Hayat Gostar Ltd
Hemastem Ltd
JAO Enterprises Ltd
Latam HQ Health Ltd
MD Salisbury Ltd
Medica Finance UK Ltd
Medspero Pharma Ltd
Nevik Limited
PF Consultancy Plus Ltd
Petersone Group Ltd
Pharmacina Ltd
Pharmacy Business Consultancy Ltd
Pharmatec Ltd
Project & Communications Ltd
Prometheus Medical Ltd
RJT Pharma Services Ltd
RxPharma Limited
Sahu & Co Limited
Shieldasset Limited
Specials Pharma Ltd
Stop Ltd
Support To Perform Ltd
Treatlines Limited
United Orphan Pharma Limited
WPG Wholesale Trading Ltd
ZS Solutions Limited
Zanoprima Holdings Limited
Zanoprima LifeSciences Limited

**71121 Engineering design activities for industrial process and production**
Buduscheye Techniqa Ltd

**71122 Engineering related scientific and technical consulting activities**
Infinity Biomedical Ltd
Katvic Limited
M & M Taste of Harmony Export Ltd
Pamy International Ltd

**71129 Other engineering activities**
Pamy International Ltd

**71200 Technical testing and analysis**
HealthVillagePlus Limited
Initio Cell Limited
Newville Trading Limited
P.I.C. International Ltd

**72110 Research and experimental development on biotechnology** [35]
Astrazeneca PLC
Bakhu Limited
Balagrae Ltd
Bioavexia Ltd
Biocon Pharma UK Limited
Biogenic Health Europe Ltd
Cambridge Biotics Ltd
Clinical Services International Ltd
Clinova Limited
Dark Atom Limited
Dermconcept Ltd
Diamate Biotechnologies Ltd
EUSA Pharma (UK) Limited
Entod Research Cell (UK) Ltd
Expedite Therapeutics Limited
Genzyme Therapeutics Limited
Huayawei Biomedical Co Ltd
Imperial Bioscience Ltd
Imphatec Ltd
Indigo Diagnostics Limited
Infinity Biomedical Ltd
Initio Cell Limited
Insight Biotechnology Limited
Insuphar Laboratories Limited
MGC Pharma (UK) Ltd
Medicaleaf Limited
Neo Health UK Limited
Novalio Pharma Limited
Oak Zone Biotech UK Ltd
Paraxmed Limited
Rotapharm Limited
Santen UK Limited
Treas Biotechnology UK Ltd
World Medicine Limited
Zota Healthcare Limited

**72190 Other research and experimental development on natural sciences and engineering** [18]
Academy Hair and Beauty (UK) Ltd
Boost Hair Limited
CM & D Pharma Limited
Carbosynth Limited
Clinova Limited
Corpus Nostrum Limited
Docsinnovent Limited
Eisai Limited
Focus Pharma Holdings Limited
Focus Pharmaceuticals Limited
Galenus Biomedical Limited
HealthVillagePlus Limited
Imperial Bioscience Ltd
Pfizer Limited
Rosalique Skincare Limited
Salcura Limited
Sonifar Pharma Expert Limited
United Therapeutics Europe, Ltd.

**72200 Research and experimental development on social sciences and humanities**
Azurite Health Ltd

**73110 Advertising agencies**
Sharepool Limited
Skymedic UK Limited

**73120 Media representation services**
Active Global Ltd
Chameleon Planet Ltd
Mountrow Trading Limited

**73200 Market research and public opinion polling**
Azurite Health Ltd

**74100 Specialised design activities**
CBS Trade Limited

**74209 Photographic activities not elsewhere classified**
A.J. Prime Ltd
ABC Healthcare Limited

**74300 Translation and interpretation activities**
Trans Swiss Ltd

**74909 Other professional, scientific and technical activities n.e.c.** [34]
Aston-Med Limited
Bakhu Limited
Beautons Ventures Ltd
Bidaya UK Ltd.
Biomedox International Ltd
Biotek Diagnostics Limited
Bpharm Group Limited
Clinical Direct Ltd
Elias Med Limited
Emra Consult Limited
Entod Research Cell (UK) Ltd
Galenus Biomedical Limited
Generic Physics Limited
Gos Pharma Limited
Green Sun Ltd
Hunger Control Limited
Koasta Limited
Leems Solutions Limited
Leptrex Ltd.
Lighthouse Mercury Limited
Masa Pharma Ltd
National Veterinary Services Ltd
New Generation Business UK Ltd
Nissi Business Services Ltd
Novalio Pharma Limited
Okle Systems Limited
Symmetry Inc Ltd
Veda Biosciences Limited
ViiV Healthcare UK Limited
Vitaminka Ltd
Wave Pharma Limited
Wholesale 2 U Ltd
ZTK Business Services Limited
Zululan Pharma Ltd

**74990 Non-trading company**
Aspect Pharma Limited

**75000 Veterinary activities** [10]
Acer Agri Ltd
Animalcare Ltd
Cibus Animal Nutrition Ltd
Clever Connect Ltd
Europharma Scotland Ltd
Farmsvet Ltd
Inmed Ltd
R M Jones Limited
National Veterinary Services Ltd
Paraxmed Limited

**77330 Renting and leasing of office machinery and equipment (including computers)**
Martal Cosmetics Limited

**77390 Renting and leasing of other machinery, equipment and tangible goods n.e.c.**
Pharm Recon Ltd

**77400 Leasing of intellectual property and similar products, except copyright works**
Insuphar Laboratories Limited
Rotapharm Limited
Spey Limited
Spey Pharma Limited
World Medicine Limited

**78109 Other activities of employment placement agencies**
Falama Services Group Limited
Third Hand Healthcare Ltd

**78200 Temporary employment agency activities**
Pharmasif Direct Limited
TTO Ventures Ltd.

**78300 Human resources provision and management of human resources functions**
Bri Trade Solutions Limited
Cynosure Group Ltd

**79110 Travel agency activities**
Gama Group Services Ltd
JMD Enterprises UK Limited
Treatlines Limited

**79901 Activities of tourist guides**
A Wise World Limited

**81100 Combined facilities support activities**
A.J. Prime Ltd

**81210 General cleaning of buildings**
Construct4lyfe Ltd

**82110 Combined office administrative service activities**
Allied Pharmacies Limited

**82190 Photocopying, document preparation and other specialised office support activities**
A.T. Medical Ltd
Aeglos Ltd
Medspero Pharma Ltd

**82200 Activities of call centres**
Monarch Health Ltd

**82301 Activities of exhibition and fair organisers**
Secret Line Ltd

**82920 Packaging activities**
UK Beauty Cosmetics International Group

**82990 Other business support service activities n.e.c.** [30]
Active Export Ltd
Alexpharm GmbH Ltd
Allpa Kallpa Ltd
Bpharm Group Limited
Britpharma UK Limited
Chirock Trading Ltd
Colgate-Palmolive (U.K.) Ltd
Condomania PLC
Dent.O.Care Limited
Elara Care Limited
FTS Bio Limited
Fast Track Sourcing Limited
Lambsmead Limited
Medica Finance UK Ltd
Menar UK Biotech Ltd
Neo Health UK Limited
Palatina Ltd
Pennamed Limited
Pharmartel Limited
Pharmasure Limited
Pound International Ltd
Purple Surgical International Ltd
Purple Surgical UK Limited
Safenet Direct Ltd
Secret Line Ltd
Servipharm Limited
Symmetry Inc Ltd
ViiV Healthcare UK Limited
ZTK Business Services Limited
Zhongfu (UK) Limited

**84120 Regulation of health care, education, cultural and other social services, not incl. social security**
Eyekonic Wellbeing Limited
JE Medical Associates Ltd.
Medspero Pharma Ltd
Paria Medical Aesthetics Ltd
U A Ali Ltd

**85422 Post-graduate level higher education**
De-Bulad & Co Ltd

**85510 Sports and recreation education**
London Supplements Distribution Ltd

**85590 Other education n.e.c.**
10x Rational Ambulance Yield Ltd
Mark Birch Hair Ltd
Clinical Direct Ltd
Galenus Biomedical Limited
Priors Pharma Limited
Prometheus Medical Ltd
Roberts McCarron Ltd
Shieldasset Limited
TTC Medical GTS Limited

**86101 Hospital activities**
Cellexa Limited
Eyecon Vision Limited
Harley Dentist Limited
Model Medics Limited
PF Consultancy Plus Ltd
So'dran Ltd
Stop Ltd
TTO Ventures Ltd.

**86102 Medical nursing home activities**
B.P. Pharma Limited
Kestrel Ophthalmics Limited
Legacy Private Limited

**86210 General medical practice activities** [19]
Allipharm (UK) Limited
Coastal Core Ltd
Dr Kool Ltd
Dr Pradeep Reddy's Laboratories (UK & EU)
Honest Health Limited
Kestrel Ophthalmics Limited
Legacy Private Limited
Medical Need UK Ltd
Mesopotamia Surgical Ultima Vitality Ltd
Model Medics Limited
Nationwide Healthcare Solutions Ltd
Nebel Healthcare Limited
Noohra Limited
RJT Pharma Services Ltd
Sahu & Co Limited
Springs Healthcare Limited
UK Biopharma Ltd
United Med Ltd
Zarroug Limited

**86220 Specialists medical practice activities** [14]
Angel & Lockhart (Pharma) Ltd
Mark Birch Hair Ltd
Clinical Direct Ltd
Clyde Valley Cannaceuticals Ltd
Iaso Ltd
Instant Test Ltd
JE Medical Associates Ltd.
Jagmed Limited
Medical Need UK Ltd
Pharmacy Business Consultancy Ltd
Roberts McCarron Ltd
TTC Medical GTS Limited
Tour N' Cure International Ltd.
United Pharma Group Limited

**86230 Dental practice activities**
Dentel Group Ltd
Kamo Dental Products Limited

**86900 Other human health activities** [63]

Aayur Limited
Al-Ghani Limited
Allipharm (UK) Limited
Azurite Health Ltd
Blackpool Medicines Limited
Chikhurst Limited
Cimex Lectularius Limited
Concord Pharma Services (UK) Ltd
De-Bulad & Co Ltd
Dermal Aesthetics Clinic Ltd
Dispensing Healthcare Ltd
Dizzo Consulting (UK) Limited
E-Pharm Limited
Eddohealthcare Ltd
Engelpharma UK Limited
Eyekonic Wellbeing Limited
Fittleworth Medical Limited
Haoma Pharma Ltd
Healthcare 4life Ltd
Herbal Food Life Limited
Herbialis Limited
IQ Pharma Ltd
Imex International Group Ltd
Instant Test Ltd
International Medical Supplies Ltd
Iophtha Limited
Kamm Trading Limited
Kestrel Ophthalmics Limited
Lime Pharmacy Limited
Lloyds Pharmacy Clinical Homecare
MGC Pharma (UK) Ltd
Maplewood Investments Limited
Masta Limited
Medicine Optimisation Limited
Medilink Limited
Medipro Pharma Limited
N-Pen Ltd.
NKCell Plus PLC
New Medical World Ltd
Odyssey Healthcare Limited
Omark Plus Ltd
Paragen Pharma Ltd
Paraxmed Limited
Paria Medical Aesthetics Ltd
Park Health Ltd
Pharma-X Consultancy Ltd
Pharmadose Limited
Pharmadynamics UK Limited
RJT Pharma Services Ltd
Rah Pharma Ltd
Rifaray Limited
Sahu & Co Limited
Skymedic UK Limited
So'dran Ltd
Stop Ltd
TTS Pharma Limited
Z Tahir Limited
Target Healthcare Limited
Tour N' Cure International Ltd.
Treatlines Limited
UK Biopharma Ltd
Victoria Pharma London Ltd
Vivaorganiclife Ltd

**87100 Residential nursing care facilities**

Hana Healthcare Ltd
Legacy Private Limited

**87300 Residential care activities for the elderly and disabled**

Springs Healthcare Limited

**88100 Social work activities without accommodation for the elderly and disabled**

Third Hand Healthcare Ltd

**90020 Support activities to performing arts**

Health Supplies Limited

**90030 Artistic creation**

Pamx Enterprise Limited

**93199 Other sports activities**

Fitnatix International Ltd

**94120 Activities of professional membership organisations**

Noohra Limited

**94990 Activities of other membership organisations n.e.c.**

Pharmunity Limited

**96020 Hairdressing and other beauty treatment**

Beauty Hair Products Limited
Paria Medical Aesthetics Ltd
Roberts McCarron Ltd

**96040 Physical well-being activities**

Aayur Limited
Engelpharma UK Limited
London Supplements Distribution Ltd
Skymedic UK Limited
Support To Perform Ltd

**96090 Other service activities n.e.c.** [16]

Accordia Investments Ltd
Chanelle Medical U.K. Limited
Croma-Pharma Limited
Dacre Skincare Limited
Fox Group International Ltd
Gerot Lannach UK Limited
Kingston Pharma Limited
Newville Trading Limited
Old Latchmerians Limited
One Pharm Limited
Shizhen TCM (UK) Limited
Symmetry Inc Ltd
Tech Innovation Laser Limited
Timpext (Trading-Import-Export) Ltd
Vivaorganiclife Ltd
Wycombe Locum Services Ltd

**99999 Dormant company**

Hampton Brand Management Co Ltd
Jessica Inc Limited
New Health Global Solutions Ltd

Printed in 8pt Nimbus Sans L

Designed by URW++ Design and Development GmbH

Dellam Publishing Limited

2 Heath Drive, Sutton, Surrey, SM2 5RP

Fax: 020 8770 7478    email: enquiries@dellam.com

SAN: 0177881    EAN/GLN: 5030670177882

www.ingramcontent.com/pod-product-compliance
Lightning Source LLC
Chambersburg PA
CBHW081104080526
44587CB00021B/3449